The Best Damn Firewall Book Period, Second Editon

Thorsten Behrens
Brian Browne
Ralph Bonnell
Rob Cameron
Simon Desmeules
Adrian F. Dimcev
Eli Faskha
Stephen Horvath

Daniel Kligerman
Kevin Lynn
Steve Moffat
Thomas W. Shinder, MD
Debra Littlejohn Shinder
Michael Sweeney
Kenneth Tam
Stephen Watkins

KEY	SERIAL NUMBER
001	HJIRTCV764
002	PO9873D5FG
003	829KM8NJH2
004	BAL923457U
005	CVPLQ6WQ23
006	VBP965T5T5
007	HJJJ863WD3E
008	2987GVTWMK
009	629MP5SDJT
010	IMWQ295T6T

PUBLISHED BY
Syngress Publishing, Inc.
Elsevier, Inc.
30 Corporate Drive
Burlington, MA 01803

The Best Damn Firewall Book Period, Second Edition

Printed in the United States of America
1 2 3 4 5 6 7 8 9 0

ISBN 13: 978-1-59749-218-8

Publisher: Andrew Williams
Page Layout and Art: SPi
Copy Editor: Judy Eby

For information on rights, translations, and bulk sales, contact Matt Pedersen, Commercial Sales Director and Rights, at Syngress Publishing; email m.pedersen@elsevier.com.

Visit us at

www.syngress.com

Syngress is committed to publishing high-quality books for IT Professionals and delivering those books in media and formats that fit the demands of our customers. We are also committed to extending the utility of the book you purchase via-additional materials available from our Web site.

SOLUTIONS WEB SITE

To register your book, visit www.syngress.com/solutions. Once registered, you can access-our solutions@syngress.com Web pages. There you may find an assortment of valueadded features such as free e-books related to the topic of this book, URLs of related Web sites, FAQs from the book, corrections, and any updates from the author(s).

ULTIMATE CDs

Our Ultimate CD product line offers our readers budget-conscious compilations of some of our best-selling backlist titles in Adobe PDF form. These CDs are the perfect way to extend your reference library on key topics pertaining to your area of expertise, including Cisco Engineering, Microsoft Windows System Administration, CyberCrime Investigation, Open Source Security, and Firewall Configuration, to name a few.

DOWNLOADABLE E-BOOKS

For readers who can't wait for hard copy, we offer most of our titles in downloadable Adobe PDF form. These e-books are often available weeks before hard copies, and are priced affordably.

SYNGRESS OUTLET

Our outlet store at syngress.com features overstocked, out-of-print, or slightly hurt books at significant savings.

SITE LICENSING

Syngress has a well-established program for site licensing our e-books onto servers in corporations, educational institutions, and large organizations. Contact us at sales@syngress.com for more information.

CUSTOM PUBLISHING

Many organizations welcome the ability to combine parts of multiple Syngress books, as well as their own content, into a single volume for their own internal use. Contact us at sales@syngress.com for more information.

SYNGRESS®

Contributing Authors

Thorsten Behrens (CCMSE, CCSE+, CCNA, CNE) is a Senior Security Engineer with Integralis' Managed Security Services Team. Thorsten's specialties include Check Point FireWall-1, Cisco PIX, and ISS RealSecure. Thorsten is a German national who delights his neighbors in Springfield, MA with bagpipe practice sessions.

Brian Browne (CISSP) is the Principal Consultant with Edoxa, Inc., and provides both strategic and technical information security consulting. He has 14 years of experience in the field of information security and is skilled in all phases, from security management through hands–on implementation. His specific security experience includes Sarbanes-Oxley and HIPAA gap analysis and remediation, vulnerability assessments, network security, firewall architecture, virtual private networks (VPN), UNIX security, Windows Active Directory security, and public key infrastructure (PKI). He also conducts application performance assessments and network capacity planning using Opnet IT Guru. Brian resides in Willow Grove, PA with his wife Lisa and daughter Marisa.

Ralph Bonnell (CISSP, Linux LPIC-2, Check Point CCSI, Check Point CCSE+, Cisco CCNA, Microsoft MCSE: Security, RSA Security RSA/CSE, StoneSoft CSFE, Aladdin eSCE, CipherTrust PCIA, ArcSight ACIA, SurfControl STAR, McAfee MIPS-I, McAfee MIPS-E, Network Associates SCP, Blue Coat BSPE, Sygate SSEI, Sygate SSEP, Aventail ACP, Radware CRIE) is a Senior Information Security Consultant currently employed at SiegeWorks in Seattle, WA. Ralph has been working with Check Point products professionally since 1999. His primary responsibilities include the deployment of various network security products, network security product support, and product training. His specialties include Check Point and NetScreen deployments, Linux client and server deployments, Check Point training, firewall clustering, BASH scripting, and PHP Web programming. Ralph contributed to *Configuring Netscreen Firewalls* (Syngress Publishing, ISBN: 1-932266-39-9). Ralph also runs a Linux consulting firm called

Linux Friendly. Ralph is married to his beautiful wife, Candace. In memory of Vincent Sage Bonnell.

Rob Cameron (CCSA, CCSE, CCSE+, NSA, JNCIA-FWV, CCSP, CCNA, INFOSEC, RSA SecurID CSE) is an IT consultant who has worked with over 200 companies to provide network security planning and implementation services. He has spent the last five years focusing on network infrastructure and extranet security. His strengths include Juniper's NetScreen Firewall products, NetScreen SSL VPN Solutions, Check Point Firewalls, the Nokia IP appliance series, Linux, Cisco routers, Cisco switches, and Cisco PIX firewalls. Rob strongly appreciates his wife Kristen's constant support of his career endeavors. He wants to thank her for all of her support through this project.

Simon Desmeules (CCSI, ISS, RSA, CCNA, CNA) is the Technical Security Director of AVANCE Network Services, an Assystem company with more than 8,500 employees worldwide. AVANCE is located in Montreal, Canada. His responsibilities include architectural design, technical consulting, and tactical emergency support for perimeter security technologies for several Fortune 500 companies in Canada, France, and the United States. Simon has been delivering Check Point training for the past three years throughout Canada. His background includes positions as a firewall/intrusion security specialist for pioneer firms of Canadian Security, Maxon Services, and SINC. He is an active member of the FW-1, ISS, and Snort mailing lists where he discovers new problems and consults with fellow security specialists. Simon has worked with Syngress before while contributing to *Check Point Next Generation Security Administration* (Syngress, ISBN: 1-928994-74-1) and *Check Point Next Generation with Application Intelligence Security Administration* (Syngress, ISBN: 1-932266-89-5).

Adrian F. Dimcev is a consultant specializing in the design and implementation of VPNs. Adrian also has extensive experience in penetration testing.

Eli Faskha (CCSI, CCSA, CCSE, CCSE+, CCAE, MCP). Based in Panama City, Panama, Eli is Founder and President of Soluciones Seguras, a company that specializes in network security and is the only Check Point

Gold Partner in Central America and the only Nokia Internet Security partner in Panama. Eli is the most experienced Check Point Certified Security Instructor and Nokia Instructor in the region. He has taught participants from more than a dozen different countries. A 1993 graduate of the University of Pennsylvania's Wharton School and Moore School of Engineering, he also received an MBA from Georgetown University in 1995. He has more than seven years of Internet development and networking experience, starting with Web development of the largest Internet portal in Panama in 1999 and 2000, managing a Verisign affiliate in 2001, and running his own company since then. Eli has written several articles for the local media and has been recognized for his contributions to Internet development in Panama.

Stephen Horvath (CISSP) is an Information Assurance Engineer for Booz Allen Hamilton in Linthicum, MD. He has been working with Check Point Firewalls for the last seven years, including Check Point 3.0b, 4.1, NG with Application Intelligence, and NGX. Steve was also a beta tester for Check Point's Edge SOHO devices prior to their release in early 2004. Steve's technical background is with computer and network forensics, firewalls, enterprise management, network and host IDS/IPS, incident response, UNIX system administration, and DNS management. He has extensive experience in network design with emphasis on high availability, security, and enterprise resilience.

Daniel Kligerman (B.Sc, CCSE, CCIE #13999) is the Manager of the Data Diagnostic Centre at TELUS National Systems, responsible for the support and management of enterprise customers' data and VoIP networks. Daniel is the technical editor of *Check Point Next Generation with Application Intelligence Security Administration* (Syngress, ISBN: 1-932266-89-5), and the contributing author of *Building DMZs for Enterprise Networks* (Syngress, ISBN: 1-931836-88-4), *Check Point NG VPN-1/Firewall-1 Advanced Configuration and Troubleshooting* (Syngress, ISBN: 1-931836-97-3), *Nokia Network Security Solutions Handbook* (Syngress, ISBN: 1-931836-70-1), and *Check Point Next Generation Security Administration* (Syngress, ISBN: 1-928994-74-1). He resides in Toronto, Canada with his wife, Merita.

Kevin Lynn (CISSP) is a network systems engineer with International Network Services (INS). INS is a leading global provider of vendor-independent network consulting and security services. At INS, Kevin currently works within the Ethical Hacking Center of Excellence where he evaluates the security at many of the largest financial corporations. Kevin's more than 12 years of experience has seen him working a variety of roles for organizations including Cisco Systems, IBM, Sun Microsystems, Abovenet, and the Commonwealth of Virginia. In addition to his professional work experience, Kevin has been known to give talks at SANS and teach others on security topics in classroom settings. Kevin currently resides in Rockville, MD with his lovely wife Ashley.

Steve Moffat is an MCSA and has worked in IT support services for the last 25 years. Steve has been employed in the UK by Digital, Experian, Computacenter (to name but a few). He has also consulted with major companies and organizations such as Zurich Insurance, Seagram's, Texaco, Peugeot, PriceWaterhouseCoopers, and the Bermuda Government. He now lives and works in paradise. Since moving to Bermuda in 2001 to work for Gateway Ltd as a senior engineer/consultant, he has gained a wife, Hannah, has formed his own company and is currently CEO & Director of Operations for The TLA Group Ltd. He specializes in ISA Server deployments & server virtualization. He is also the owner & host of the well known ISA Server web site, www.isaserver.bm

Thomas W. Shinder, MD is an MCSE and has been awarded the Microsoft Most Valuable Professional (MVP) award for his work with ISA Server and is recognized in the firewall community as one of the foremost experts on ISA Server. Tom has consulted with major companies and organizations such as Microsoft Corp., Xerox, Lucent Technologies, FINA Oil, Hewlett-Packard, and the U.S. Department of Energy.

Tom practiced medicine in Oregon, Texas, and Arkansas before turning his growing fascination with computer technology into a new career shortly after marrying his wife, Debra Littlejohn Shinder, in the mid 90s. They co-own TACteam (Trainers, Authors, and Consultants), through which they teach technology topics and develop courseware, write books, articles, whitepapers and corporate product documentation and marketing materials, and assist small and large businesses in deploying technology solutions.

Tom co-authored, with Deb, the best selling *Configuring ISA Server 2000* (Syngress Publishing, ISBN: 1-928994-29-6), *Dr. Tom Shinder's ISA Server and Beyond* (Syngress, ISBN: 1-931836-66-3), and *Troubleshooting Windows 2000 TCP/IP* (Syngress, ISBN: 1-928994-11-3). He has contributed to several other books on subjects such as the Windows 2000 and Windows 2003 MCSE exams and has written hundreds of articles on Windows server products for a variety of electronic and print publications.

Tom is the "primary perpetrator" on ISAserver.org (www.isaserver.org), where he answers hundreds of questions per week on the discussion boards and is the leading content contributor.

Debra Littlejohn Shinder, MCSE, MVP is a technology consultant, trainer and writer who has authored a number of books on computer operating systems, networking, and security. These include *Scene of the Cybercrime: Computer Forensics Handbook,* published by Syngress, and *Computer Networking Essentials,* published by Cisco Press. She is co-author, with her husband, Dr. Thomas Shinder, of *Troubleshooting Windows 2000 TCP/IP,* the best-selling *Configuring ISA Server 2000, ISA Server and Beyond,* and *Configuring ISA Server 2004.* She also co-authored *Windows XP: Ask the Experts* with Jim Boyce.

Deb is a tech editor, developmental editor and contributor to over 20 additional books on subjects such as the Windows 2000 and Windows 2003 MCSE exams, CompTIA Security+ exam and TruSecure's ICSA certification. She formerly edited the Brainbuzz A+ Hardware News and currently edits Sunbelt Software's WinXP News and VistaNews, with over a million subscribers, and writes a weekly column on Voice over IP technologies for TechRepublic/CNET. Her articles on various technology issues are regularly published on the CNET Web sites and Windowsecurity.com, and have appeared in print magazines such as Windows IT Pro (formerly Windows & .NET) Magazine and Law & Order Magazine.

She has authored training material, corporate whitepapers, marketing material, and product documentation for Microsoft Corporation, Hewlett-Packard, GFI Software, Sunbelt Software, Sony and other technology companies and written courseware for Powered, Inc and DigitalThink.

Deb currently specializes in security issues and Microsoft products; she has been awarded Microsoft's Most Valuable Professional (MVP) status in

Windows Server Security for the last four years. A former police officer and police academy instructor, she lives and works with her husband, Tom, on a beautiful lake just outside Dallas, Texas and teaches computer networking and security and occasional criminal justice courses at Eastfield College (Mesquite, TX). You can read her tech blog at http://deb-tech.spaces.live.com

Michael Sweeney (CCNA, CCDA, CCNP, MCSE, SCP) is the owner of the Network Security consulting firm Packetattack.com. Packetattack.com specialties are network design and troubleshooting, wireless network design, security and analysis. The Packetattack team uses such industry standard tools such as NAI Sniffer, AiroPeekNX and Airmagnet. Packetattack.com also provides digital forensic analysis services.

Michael has been a contributing author for Syngress for the books *Cisco Security Specialist Guide to PIX Firewalls*, ISBN: 1-931836-63-9, *Cisco Security Specialist Guide to Secure Intrusion Detection Systems*, ISBN: 1-932266-69-0 and *Building DMZs For Enterprise Networks*, ISBN: 1-931836-88-4. Through PacketPress, Michael has also published Securing Your Network Using Linux, ISBN: 1411621778.

Michael graduated from the University of California, Irvine, extension program with a certificate in communications and network engineering. Michael currently resides in Orange, CA with his wife Jeanne and daughters, Amanda and Sara.

Kenneth Tam (JNCIS-FWV, NCSP) is Sr. Systems Engineer at Juniper Networks Security Product Group (formerly NetScreen Technologies). Kenneth worked in pre-sales for over 4 years at NetScreen since the startup days and has been one of many key contributors in building NetScreen as one of the most successful security company. As such, his primary role has been to provide pre-sale technical assistance in both design and implementation of NetScreen solutions. Kenneth is currently covering the upper Midwest U.S. region. His background includes positions as a Senior Network Engineer in the Carrier Group at 3com Corporation, and as an application engineer at U.S.Robotics. Kenneth holds a bachelor's degree in computer science from DePaul University. He lives in the suburbs of Chicago, Illinois with his wife Lorna and children, Jessica and Brandon.

Stephen Watkins (CISSP) is an Information Security Professional with more than 10 years of relevant technology experience, devoting eight of these years to the security field. He currently serves as Information Assurance Analyst at Regent University in southeastern Virginia. Before coming to Regent, he led a team of security professionals providing in-depth analysis for a global-scale government network. Over the last eight years, he has cultivated his expertise with regard to perimeter security and multilevel security architecture. His Check Point experience dates back to 1998 with FireWall-1 version 3.0b. He has earned his B.S. in Computer Science from Old Dominion University and M.S. in Computer Science, with Concentration in Infosec, from James Madison University. He is nearly a life-long resident of Virginia Beach, where he and his family remain active in their Church and the local Little League.

Contents

Chapter 1

Installing Check Point NGX

Solutions in this chapter:

- **Preparation**
- **Installing SecurePlatform**
- **Distributed Installation**
- **Gateway Installation**
- **SmartCenter Server Installation**
- **SmartConsole Installation**
- **SmartDashboard Configuration**

☑ **Summary**

Introduction

Check Point has worked hard to develop an easy-to-use interface for installing and configuring their product line. With the continuing development of SecurePlatform, installing FireWall-1/VPN-1 has become easier.

In this chapter we review what must be done prior to the actual installation and configuration of a Check Point environment. We then demonstrate how to install SecurePlatform and then install and configure the gateway and management server. Once communication between the different components is set up, we will install and configure the SmartConsole, which will be used to connect to the SmartCenter server to configure the security policy.

Preparing the Gateway

Prior to installation of the gateway, Check Point recommends following a simple check list to ensure that your gateway is fully functional after installation. One of the most important steps to do in preparation for your gateway is to harden the underlying operating system (OS). You must ensure that your OS is not running any unnecessary services that may leave your gateway vulnerable and take up valuable processing time. For example, if you plan to run FireWall-1/VPN-1 on a Windows 2000 server, there may be many unwanted services that were installed during the installation of the OS. Take the time to review the services and remove or disable those you will not be using. Typical services include NETBIOS Extended User Interface (NetBEUI), File Transfer Protocol (FTP), and Web servers. If you harden the system from isolated networks, no one can access it.

Your gateway's prime function after inspecting packets is to forward those packets to their proper destination. Take time to review your complete architecture and make note of any special routes that have to be manually added. Perform communication tests prior to installation (e.g., ping the remote devices from the OS that will host your Check Point installation).

Gateways often have several interface cards, which can become confusing if they are not properly identified. Properly identify the interface cards on the hardware itself and tag the cables that connect to them at either end. Proper identification will make connecting your gateway to the network easier and less time consuming.

Installation

This section walks you through an installation of Check Point NGX in a distributed environment, which is the recommended way to plan your installation of NGX. A distributed installation consists of separating the SmartCenter server from the FireWall-1/VPN-1 Pro gateway. The SmartCenter server, also known as the *management server*, contains all of the objects, security policies, user databases, time objects, logs, and so on that is required to push a security policy to a gateway. The gateway will contain an *inspect script* that it received from your SmartCenter server. The gateway will then determine whether or not to pass the traffic according to the security policy it received. The second type of installation is called a *stand-alone* configuration, which consists of installing the gateway and SmartCenter server on the same machine. The downside to a stand-alone configuration is that it requires a lot more time to rebuild in the case of disaster recovery.

SecurePlatform

SecurePlatform can be installed on Intel- or AMD-based systems with a CD-ROM, by using the Check Point-provided media kit. Simply insert the NGX CD1 and reboot the system. When the system reboots you will be prompted with the SecurePlatform Welcome Screen (assuming that your BIOS settings include the CD-ROM boot sequence). (See seen in Figure 1.1.)

Figure 1.1 SPLAT Welcome Screen

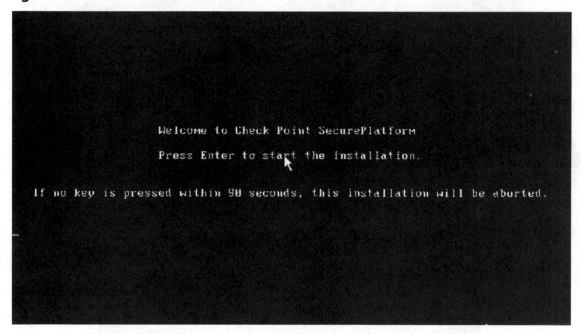

If a key is not pressed within 90 seconds, the SecurePlatform installation will abort and will not affect your system. Press any key on the keyboard to continue the installation. The Welcome Screen has several options. The Cancel option quits the installation process without affecting any data found on the OS. The Device List displays the devices that SecurePlatform has detected in terms of hardware. It is important that the operation of your gateway is compatible with all of your hardware, otherwise, it may cause problems later on. Check Point provides a Hardware Compatibility List (HCL) on their Web site, which should be consulted prior to purchasing a system to run SecurePlatform.

To add a hardware device to SecurePlatform, select **Add Drive**, which will prompt you for the path to the new driver. Selecting **OK** assumes that you are ready for installation.

Figure 1.2 Options Shown in the SecurePlatform Welcome Screen

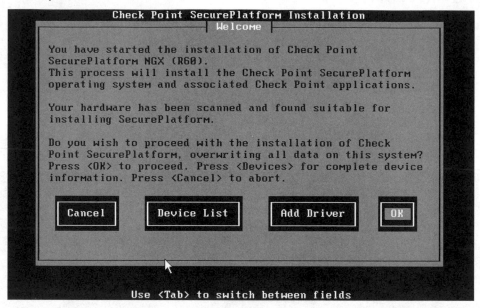

The next option provided is the "System Type." SecurePlatform Pro is a new addition to NGX, which also requires a license. If you do not plan to use the advanced routing capabilities in SecurePlatform Pro, simply select **SecurePlatform** and then press **OK** to continue. (See Figure 1.3.)

Figure 1.3 System Type

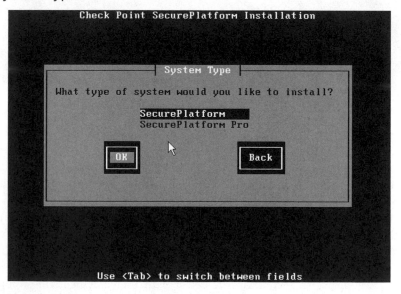

Depending on the region and the keyboard type that is attached to your gateway, you may have the ability to choose which keyboard type you want to use. For the purposes of this book, a U.S. keyboard is used and it is set at **default**. Click **OK** to continue.

Figure 1.4 Keyboard Selection

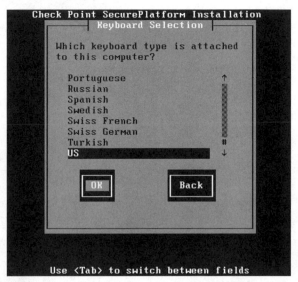

The next screen lists the Network Interface Cards (NIC) attached to the system. The screen also shows whether it detects a Link, No Link, or Unknown, if the interface doesn't support SecurePlatform's link detection protocol. (See Figure 1.5.)

When doing an initial installation of FireWall-1/VPN-1, it is recommended that it be installed on the interface that is facing the Internet. The installation process will determine that the installed interface is defined as external and will also be automatically listed in the OS' host's file. Select the external interface and then select **OK** to continue.

Figure 1.5 Network Device

Configure the external interface on the following screen. For installation instruction purposes, we have chosen private addressing space as the external interface. In most NGX installations, you will use routable Internet Protocol (IP) addressing provided by your Internet Service Provider (ISP). (See Figure 1.6.)

Figure 1.6 Network Interface Configuration

One of the best features of SecurePlatform is the ability to configure the OS from a Web-based browser such as Internet Explorer. Figure 1.7 displays the HTTPS Server Configuration screen, which prompts the user to decide whether or not to enable Web-based configuration and which port it should listen on. By default, it is enabled and most installations leave it enabled. However, it may be a good idea to change the default Hypertext Transfer Protocol Secure sockets (HTTPS) port 443 to another port. Once you have configured your options, select **OK** to continue.

Figure 1.7 HTTPS Server Configuration

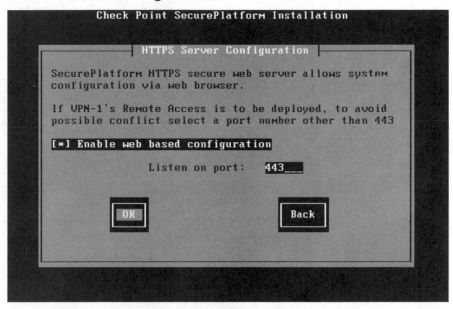

The next SecurePlatform installation screen is the confirmation screen. (See Figure 1.8.) This is the last step prior to the installation process, which will format and partition the disk. When you confirm your installation by selecting **OK**, the format process begins and Check Point SecurePlatform installs a pre-hardened OS within a couple of minutes.

Figure 1.8 Confirmation

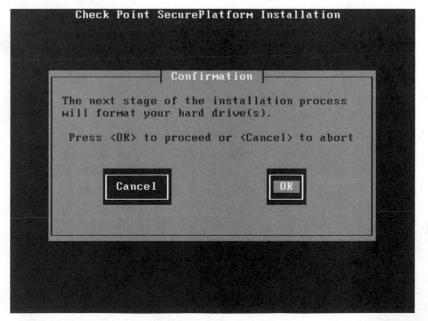

The installation process displays the progress of the installation. When you select **OK**, the system ejects the CD and reboots the OS. When the system is done rebooting, your login credentials by default are: username: admin and password: (See Figures 1.9 and 1.10.)

Figure 1.9 Complete Check Point SecurePlatform Installation

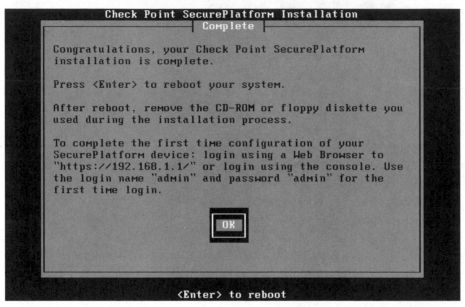

The login screen displays the current version of Check Point, and also indicates that you may connect to it with a Web browser in order to configure the OS and certain Check Point components via HTTPS.

Figure 1.10 Login Screen

Once you are successfully connected, you will automatically be prompted to enter a new password and then given the option to change the username, "admin." When selecting a new password, SecurePlatform has a password-checking library (*cracklib-2.7-23cp*), which checks to ensure that your password "montreal" is not easily guessed. If you try using a password such as "montreal," you will be prompted to choose a different one because it is based in a dictionary file. If you choose a password that is too short, you will be prompted to enter a longer password since it wasn't long enough. These are some of the nice features that are built into SecurePlatform.

To configure your OS and install Check Point products, you can either log into SecurePlatform by HTTPS or by using the *sysconfig* utility. (See Figure 1.11.)

Figure 1.11 Welcome Wizard

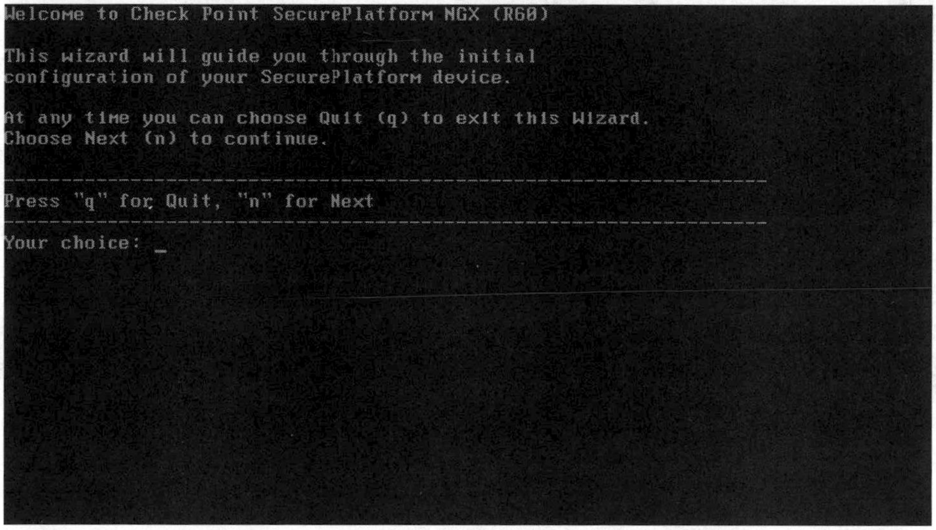

```
Welcome to Check Point SecurePlatform NGX (R60)

This wizard will guide you through the initial
configuration of your SecurePlatform device.

At any time you can choose Quit (q) to exit this Wizard.
Choose Next (n) to continue.
_____

Press "q" for Quit, "n" for Next
_____

Your choice: _
```

Selecting **n** for **Next** brings you to the various components that must be configured for your OS. Select all of the different components and go through the configuration screens. Ensure that you have properly configured all of the options; especially routing. With incorrect routing, your gateway will not be able to communicate with other devices on distant networks. (See Figure 1.12.)

Figure 1.12 Initial Configuration

```
Network Configuration
---------------------------------------------------------------
1) Host Name          3) Domain Name Servers  5) Routing
2) Domain Name        4) Network Connections
---------------------------------------------------------------
Press "q" for Quit, "p" for Previous, "n" for Next
---------------------------------------------------------------
Your choice: _
```

FireWall-1/VPN-1 Installation

We are now ready to install the initial FireWall-1/VPN-1 gateway. When going through the installation wizard, you are prompted with the Check Point Welcome Screen. There are several choices that can be made at this point, such as installing the products in Evaluation mode or Purchased Mode. Selecting **Next** will suffice because the Check Point license can be installed at any time and by default we can evaluate the product for 15 days. (See Figure 1.13.)

Figure 1.13 Check Point Welcome Screen

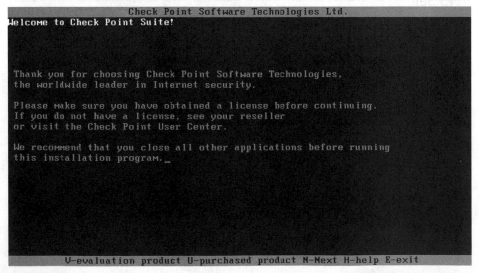

```
              Check Point Software Technologies Ltd.
Welcome to Check Point Suite!




   Thank you for choosing Check Point Software Technologies,
   the worldwide leader in Internet security.

   Please make sure you have obtained a license before continuing.
   If you do not have a license, see your reseller
   or visit the Check Point User Center.

   We recommend that you close all other applications before running
   this installation program._




          V-evaluation product U-purchased product N-Next H-help E-exit
```

Once you have read and accepted the license agreement, you must select either "Enterprise" or "Express." The main difference between these two options is the number of IP's that an Express gateway can protect. The Check Point Express product targets small- and medium-sized businesses with 500 IPs or less. This installation will use the Enterprise/Pro product by selecting **1** and then selecting **Next** to continue with the installation. (See Figure 1.14).

Figure 1.14 Enterprise/Express Selection

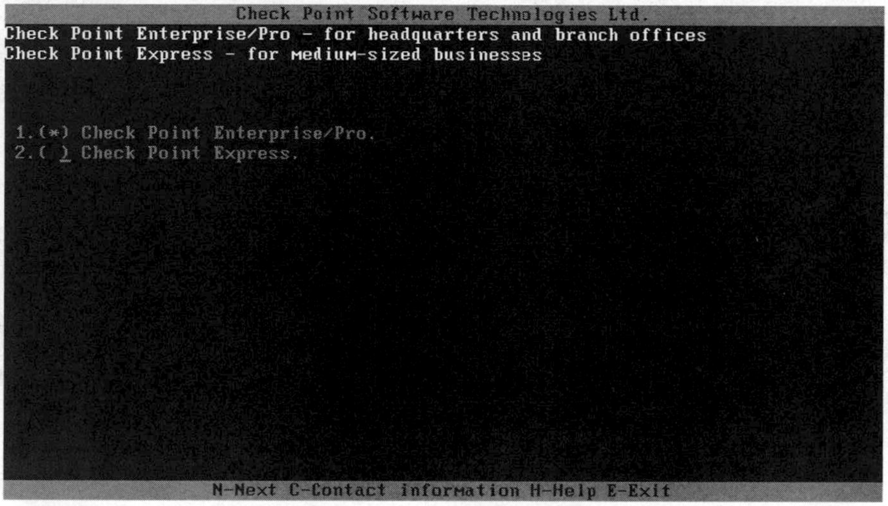

```
                    Check Point Software Technologies Ltd.
Check Point Enterprise/Pro - for headquarters and branch offices
Check Point Express - for medium-sized businesses




   1.(*) Check Point Enterprise/Pro.
   2.( ) Check Point Express.















            N-Next C-Contact information H-Help E-Exit
```

When selecting the Enterprise/Pro product feature, you are asked which products you want to install (See Figure 1.14). As mentioned earlier, you want to install a distributed architecture; therefore, select option 1 VPN-1 Pro. Keep in mind that by selecting VPN-1 Pro, you are also installing FireWall-1 and VPN-1. Both products are now merged into one. (See Figure 1.15.)

Figure 1.15 Select Products

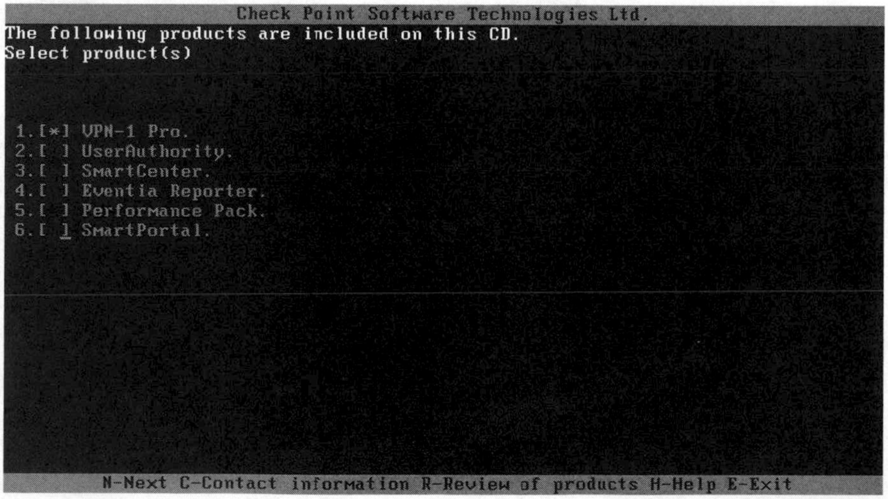

```
                    Check Point Software Technologies Ltd.
The following products are included on this CD.
Select product(s)



   1.[*] VPN-1 Pro.
   2.[ ] UserAuthority.
   3.[ ] SmartCenter.
   4.[ ] Eventia Reporter.
   5.[ ] Performance Pack.
   6.[ ] SmartPortal.







        N-Next C-Contact information R-Review of products H-Help E-Exit
```

The validation screen validates your choice of products. (See Figure 1.16.)

Figure 1.16 Validation

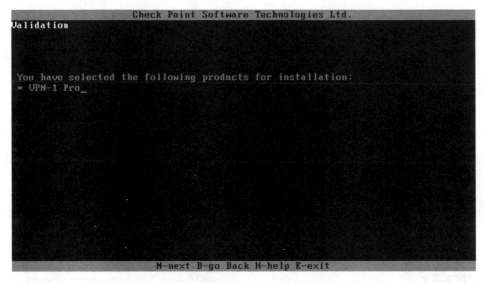

Once you have confirmed that you want to install VPN-1 Pro by selecting **Next**, Check Point will ask questions to help complete the installation. The series of questions asked at this point are configurable once the installation is complete and the machine has rebooted. (See Figure 1.17.)

The first question asks whether or not the gateway has a Dynamically Assigned IP (DAIP) address. Check Point supports the management of DAIP's and requires this information so that it can create a certificate to be sent to the SmartCenter server for management, logging, and VPN purposes.

The next question regards clustering. If you installed a clustering product such as ClusterXL, which would create a highly available system between two or more gateways, you would select **yes**; however, this installation demonstration does not use a clustering product. SecurePlatform will then disable IP forwarding, harden the OS security, and generate the default filter for the gateway. The default filter, which is a "drop all" rule except for some Check Point communication protocols, are applied when the system reboots.

Figure 1.17 OS configuration

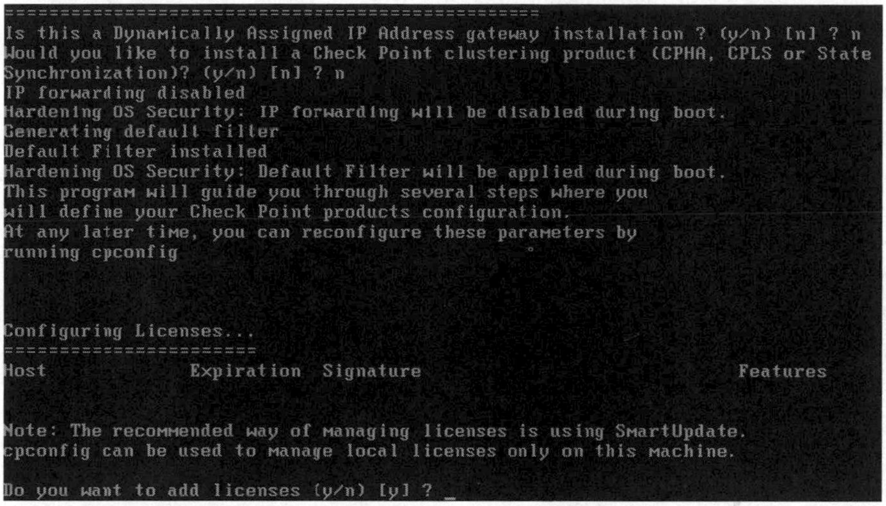

```
================================================
Is this a Dynamically Assigned IP Address gateway installation ? (y/n) [n] ? n
Would you like to install a Check Point clustering product (CPHA, CPLS or State
Synchronization)? (y/n) [n] ? n
IP forwarding disabled
Hardening OS Security: IP forwarding will be disabled during boot.
Generating default filter
Default Filter installed
Hardening OS Security: Default Filter will be applied during boot.
This program will guide you through several steps where you
will define your Check Point products configuration.
At any later time, you can reconfigure these parameters by
running cpconfig


Configuring Licenses...
==========================
Host            Expiration  Signature                        Features

Note: The recommended way of managing licenses is using SmartUpdate.
cpconfig can be used to manage local licenses only on this machine.

Do you want to add licenses (y/n) [y] ? _
```

Once the OS questions are done, you are prompted to configure the Check Point product that has been installed. Installing a license can be done at this time; however, it is easier to install through SmartUpdate.

One of the new features is the automatic collection of random data that is used for cryptographic operation. Prior to NGX, you would have to hit various keyboard values so that it could collect the random data. (See Figure 1.18.)

An important part to configure when doing a distributed installation is the SIC. The activation key is a one-time pass phrase that must be entered at any Check Point product that will be managed by a SmartCenter server. In this case, enter a pass phrase to establish SIC from the SmartCenter, install the policies, and then send.

Figure 1.18 Product Configuration

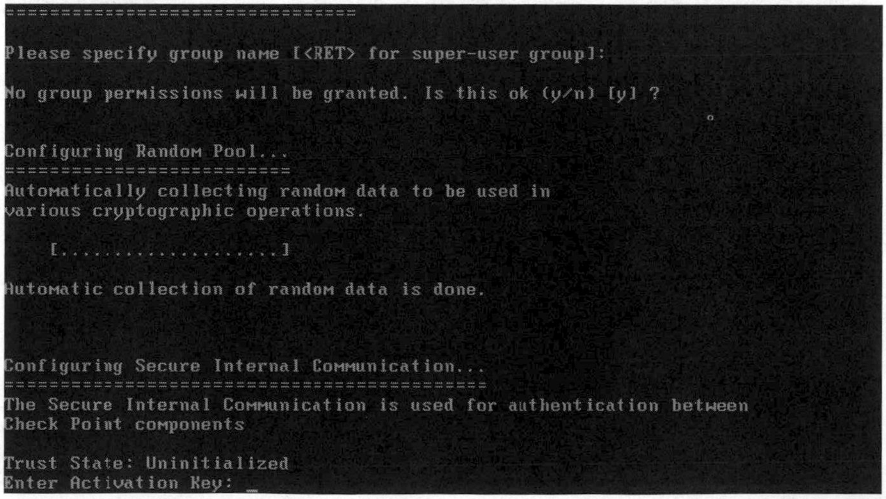

```
================================================
Please specify group name [<RET> for super-user group]:

No group permissions will be granted. Is this ok (y/n) [y] ?


Configuring Random Pool...
==========================
Automatically collecting random data to be used in
various cryptographic operations.

    [...................]

Automatic collection of random data is done.


Configuring Secure Internal Communication...
=============================================
The Secure Internal Communication is used for authentication between
Check Point components

Trust State: Uninitialized
Enter Activation Key: _
```

Once you have established the activation key you will be prompted to reboot the server. You are now ready to incorporate your gateway with the SmartCenter server.

SmartCenter Server Installation

Now that the installed the VPN-1 Pro server has been installed on a SecurePlatform OS, it is time to install the SmartCenter server. The SmartCenter server installation guide is done on a SecurePlatform OS, as seen earlier in the chapter. Start the demonstration with the SecurePlatform wizard after the OS has been installed.

Using the *sysconfig* (system configuration) command and going all the way through the wizard, prompts you to the Check Point product selection. Select option 3 to install the SmartCenter server. (See Figure 1.19.)

Figure 1.19 SmartCenter Server Product Selection

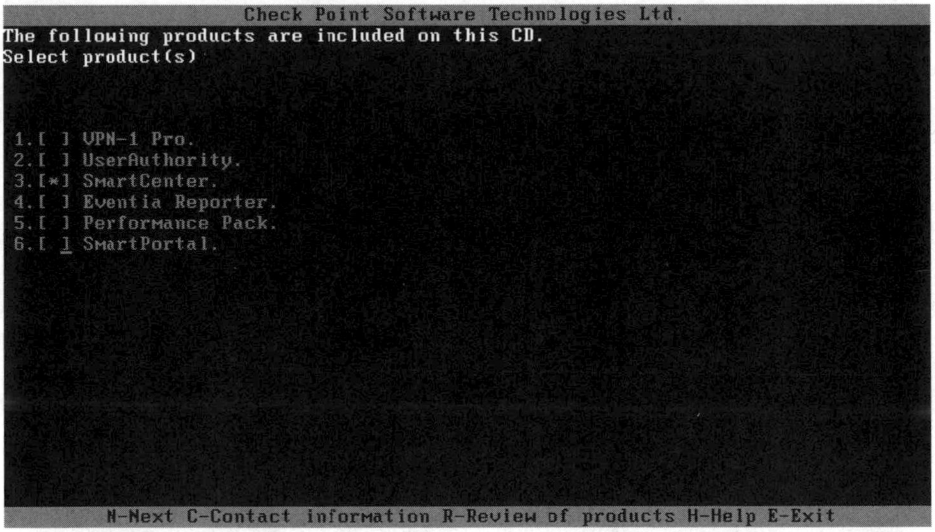

```
            Check Point Software Technologies Ltd.
The following products are included on this CD.
Select product(s)


   1.[ ] VPN-1 Pro.
   2.[ ] UserAuthority.
   3.[*] SmartCenter.
   4.[ ] Eventia Reporter.
   5.[ ] Performance Pack.
   6.[ ] SmartPortal.












        N-Next C-Contact information R-Review of products H-Help E-Exit
```

Once you have selected the SmartCenter server to be installed, the next option is to specify what type of SmartCenter server installation you are conducting. Check Point has the ability to perform Management High Availability (HA). Management HA gives the security administrator the choice to have a secondary SmartCenter server in case something happens to the first. This provides a robust solution for your SmartCenter server. For this installation demonstration, choose selection number 1, Primary SmartCenter. (See Figure 1.20.)

Figure 1.20 Primary SmartCenter

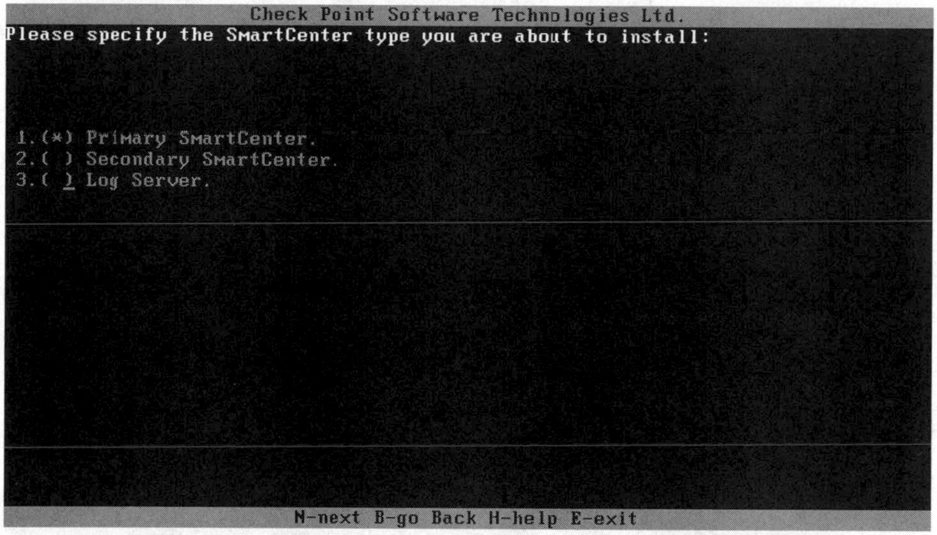

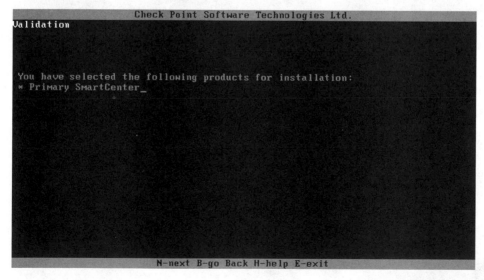

The validation screen shown in Figure 1.21 is standard prior to the installation process of the product. You can always go back a step and choose different options if you need to. Figure 1.22 shows the first SmartCenter Configuration screen. You may re-enter the Check Point configuration screen once the server reboots by typing the command **cpconfig** (Check Point Configuration).

Figure 1.21 SmartCenter Validation

The first question is whether or not you want to configure the SmartCenter server with a license. If you select **yes**, you can direct the configuration to the location of the license file (*.lic*) or you can enter the different sku's manually. The preferred method is to install it at a later time with the graphical user interface (GUI) SmartUpdate. SmartUpdate is the easiest way to configure and manage your licenses.

Figure 1.22 SmartCenter Configuration

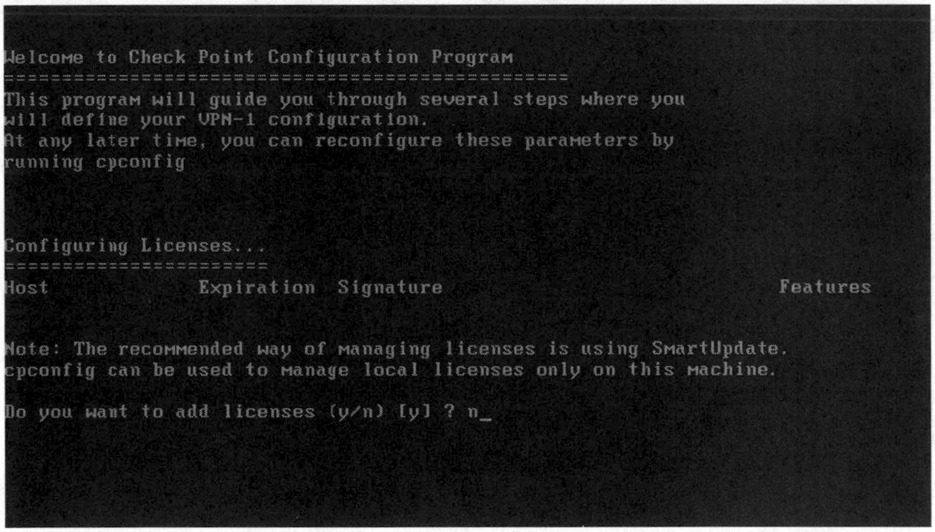

The next step is to define a SmartCenter server administrator that will be used when connecting with one of the SmartConsole GUIs. You can only define a single administrator, which will have full permissions over all Check Point products. Once the administrator is defined, you must configure a GUI client. (See Figure 1.23). A GUI client is the IP address of the machine from which the administrator will be connecting from. You may have several different GUI client IP's indicated here; however, they should be kept to a minimum. The administrators that will connect to the SmartCenter server should have fixed IP's, which will make maintaining this list easier. You are not limited to a number of IP's. We have entered the IP addresses 192.168.2.10 and 172.30.30.10 that will be allowed to connect to the SmartCenter server. You can always go back and configure more using the *cpconfig* command.

Figure 1.23 Configuring the SmartCenter Server

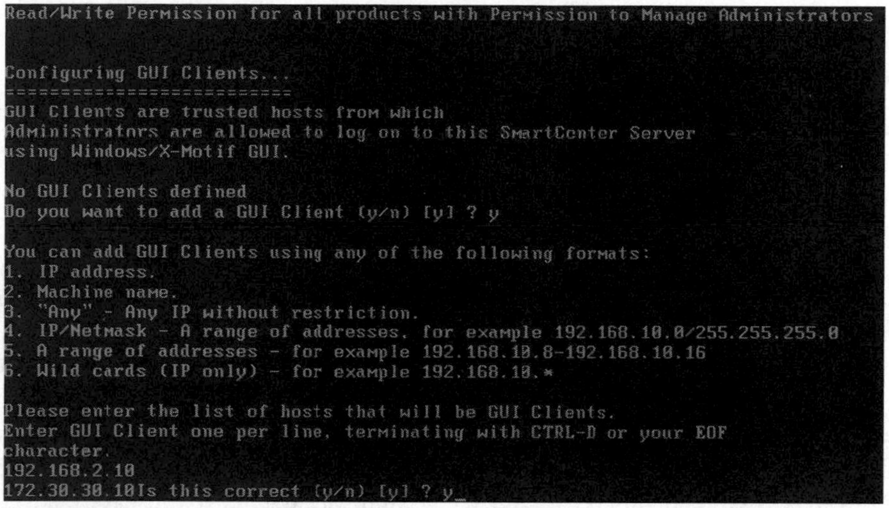

```
Read/Write Permission for all products with Permission to Manage Administrators

Configuring GUI Clients...
============================
GUI Clients are trusted hosts from which
Administrators are allowed to log on to this SmartCenter Server
using Windows/X-Motif GUI.

No GUI Clients defined
Do you want to add a GUI Client (y/n) [y] ? y

You can add GUI Clients using any of the following formats:
1. IP address.
2. Machine name.
3. "Any" - Any IP without restriction.
4. IP/Netmask - A range of addresses, for example 192.168.10.0/255.255.255.0
5. A range of addresses - for example 192.168.10.8-192.168.10.16
6. Wild cards (IP only) - for example 192.168.10.*

Please enter the list of hosts that will be GUI Clients.
Enter GUI Client one per line, terminating with CTRL-D or your EOF
character.
192.168.2.10
172.30.30.10Is this correct (y/n) [y] ? y_
```

The SmartCenter server is also a certificate authority, which was introduced in NG and has continued to be successful in NGX (version 6.0). The Internal Certificate Authority (ICA) is initialized during installation and generates a certificate with the hostname and domain name. (See Figure 1.24). It is important to have properly configured these options prior to configuring the ICA.

Once the ICA has been generated, you are prompted to save the certificate's fingerprint. The fingerprint can be used to validate that the ICA has not been tampered with. When first connecting with one of the SmartConsole GUI's, this same fingerprint will be displayed . It is good practice to validate the fingerprint with the one generated here. They should be identical; if they aren't, it means that somebody has tampered with your SmartCenter server configuration and it should be looked into immediately.

Figure 1.24 Configuring the ICA for SmartCenter Server

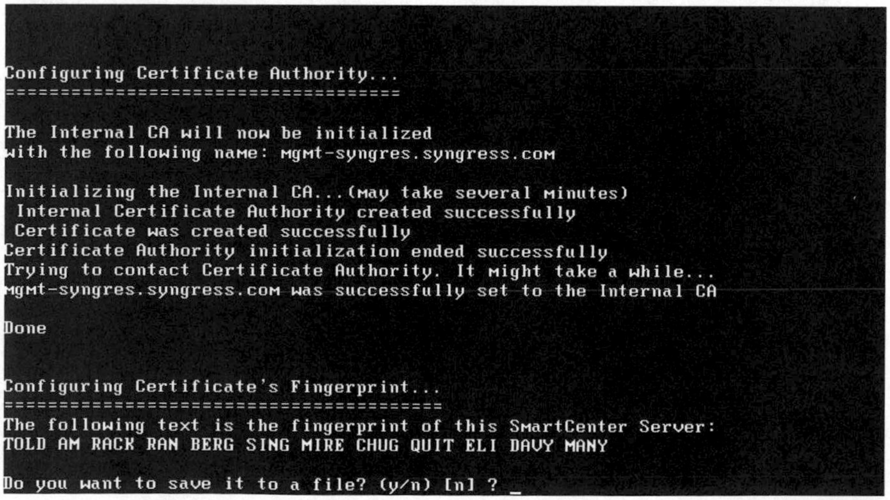

```
Configuring Certificate Authority...
=====================================

The Internal CA will now be initialized
with the following name: mgmt-syngres.syngress.com

Initializing the Internal CA...(may take several minutes)
 Internal Certificate Authority created successfully
 Certificate was created successfully
Certificate Authority initialization ended successfully
Trying to contact Certificate Authority. It might take a while...
mgmt-syngres.syngress.com was successfully set to the Internal CA

Done

Configuring Certificate's Fingerprint...
=====================================
The following text is the fingerprint of this SmartCenter Server:
TOLD AM RACK RAN BERG SING MIRE CHUG QUIT ELI DAVY MANY

Do you want to save it to a file? (y/n) [n] ? _
```

The certificate's fingerprint is the last option before being asked to reboot the system. Now that you have completed your installation of the Primary SmartCenter server, you must reboot with the reboot command. Once rebooted, you are ready to connect to the SmartCenter server with one of the SmartConsole GUI's.

SmartConsole Installation

This section walks you through the installation of installing your SmartConsole, which should be installed on one of the GUI clients defined during your SmartCenter server installation. If the SmartConsole will be installed on a new host that wasn't defined during the installation process, you can run **cpconfig** on the SmartCenter server, which will allow you to reconfigure different aspects of the Check Point products installed, including the GUI list.

The Check Point SmartConsole can be installed on a Windows platform (demonstrated later). Check Point also has the motif GUI, which is licensed for Solaris OS'.

To install the SmartConsole, either download the package from the Check Point Web site or download the package from the SecurePlatform HTTPS interface under **Product Configuration | Download SmartConsole**, or insert the NGX CD2 into the system. If you have enabled auto start on your CD-ROM, you will be prompted with Installation window. (See Figure 1.25). Click **Next → Accept the License agreement → Choose Enterprise Pro → New Installation** at which point you will select your SmartConsole options. (See Figure 1.26.)

Figure 1.25 NGX CD2 Auto Run

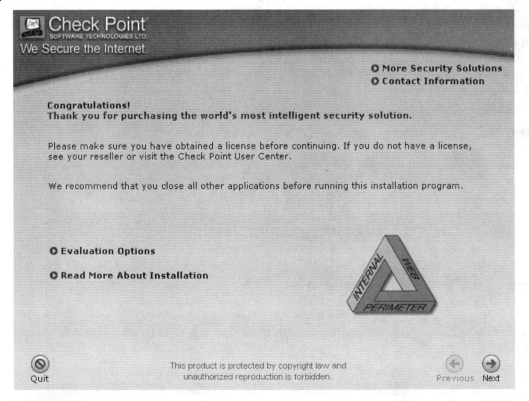

Figure 1.26 SmartConsole Options

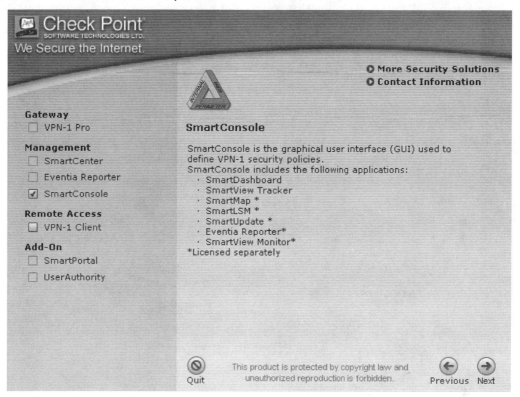

Select a SmartConsole product and leave your mouse over it to receive a brief description of what it consists of. Once you have selected the SmartConsole product to be installed, you will be prompted to select which products to install and what folder you want to install them to. By default, all options from SmartConsole are selected; however, if you did not purchase a particular product, you may want to remove them.

Putting It All Together

Now that you have installed your distributed configuration consisting of a VPN-1 Pro and a SmartCenter, you are ready to put it all together. Installing the SmartConsole consists of the Check Point framework called a *three-tier architecture*, which consists of the three different components communicating with each other. You will now see how to launch the SmartDashboard GUI and have it connect to the SmartCenter server. Once connected, you will create and ensure that all components are able to communicate with each other.

SmartDashboard

Now you will connect your SmartDashboard to the SmartCenter server to see if everything is working properly. First, you will launch the SmartDashboard GUI from GUI client 192.168.2.10, which was configured earlier in the SmartCenter server. If you connected from another IP address, an error message would appear indicating that you are not authorized to connect from that IP.

Start the SmartDashboard application from its default installation directory from within Windows; **Start → Programs → Check Point SmartConsole R60 → SmartDashboard**. When launching the SmartDashboard you will be prompted for the username, password, and SmartCenter server IP address. (See Figure 1.27.)

Figure 1.27 SmartDashboard Connect

A fingerprint is presented, which must be accepted in order to continue. As mentioned earlier, when installing the SmartCenter server, you have to verify the fingerprint shown against the one you exported. Accepting the certificate places a validation on the GUI client OS so that it doesn't have to check it every time. If for some reason the SmartCenter server has changed its certificate, a new certificate will be presented during the first connection. (See Figure 1.28.)

Figure 1.28 Fingerprint

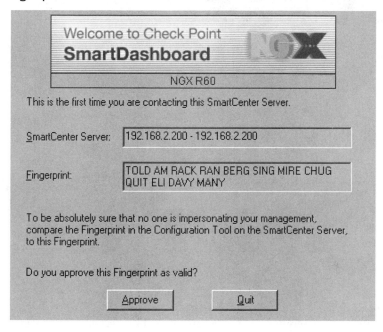

You must approve the certificate to continue, otherwise, the application will exit and you will have to double-check it to see why it has changed. When connected, the SmartCenter server object is created automatically. (See Figure 1.29). Because it is connecting to itself, it knows that there is a Check Point product installed and populates the objects database with itself.

Figure 1.29 Network Objects View

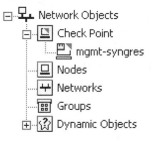

To complete the initial setup, you must define the VPN-1 Pro installed earlier. You can create new objects by expanding **Network Objects** and selecting **Check Point | New Check Point | VPN-1 Pro/Express Gateway**. If you have other Check Point objects to create, go to **Manage | Network Objects | New | Check Point | VPN-1 Pro/Express Gateway**. Both ways are valid. The latter method is the original way; however, the first method is the quickest.

There are two modes when creating a Check Point object. We demonstrate how to do it using the wizard (simple mode); however, you may opt to create a Check Point object using the classic mode. The result is the same, but the wizard mode has been greatly improved and very simple to use. (See Figure 1.30).

Figure 1.30 VPN-1 Pro Object Creation

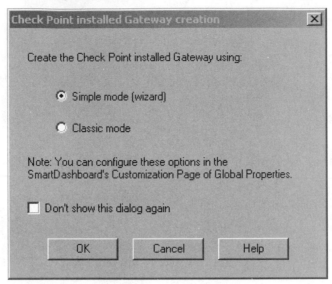

When choosing the wizard mode, it will prompt you to enter the gateway's name. (See Figure 1.31). Earlier in the chapter, you installed the VPN-1 module with IP address 192.168.1.1. You also saw the different options within the sysconfig utility that give the OS its identity. To create the VPN-1 Pro object with its host name to take advantage of the option "Get address," you must first populate the SmartCenter server hosts file.

Figure 1.31 Wizard Properties

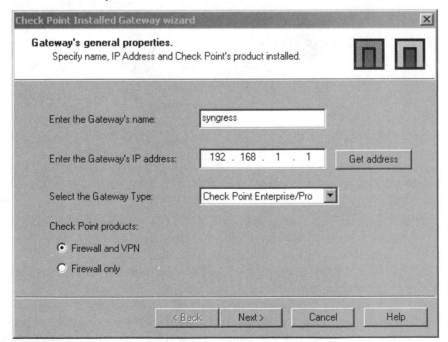

Once you have entered the gateway's name and fetched the IP address using **get address** you can choose the type of gateway that you want to install. The options are Enterprise/Pro or Express. Your installation of the gateway "syngress" was an Enterprise Pro. You must then select what products are licensed for the gateway. If you only have a FireWall-1 license, you can only select **Firewall only**; however, you can select "Firewall and VPN" if you are using the VPN functionalities. Once you have selected **next**, you are prompted to enter the Activation Key. (See Figure 1.32.)

Figure 1.32 SIC

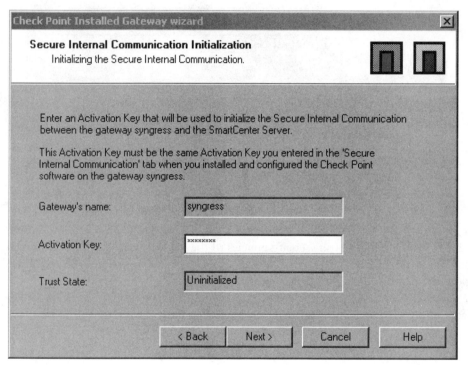

The activation key is the secure internal communication passphrase that you entered during the installation of the gateway. If you have forgotten the activation key, you can return to the module and enter **cpconfig** to re-activate a new passphrase. When you have entered the passphrase, select **Next** to test the communication status between the SmartCenter server and the VPN-1 Pro gateway. (See Figure 1.33).

Figure 1.33 Trust Established

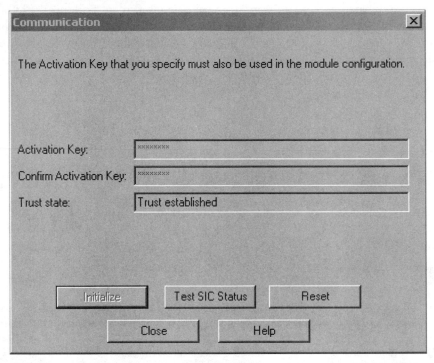

Once the trust has been established between the two Check Point products, the SmartCenter server is able to configure and push security policies to the gateway taking control over it. By default, the gateway sends the log files to the SmartCenter server when the trust has been established, assuming the correct routing and security rules are put in place.

After selecting **Close**, you can edit the newly created gateway's properties. The new object will be populated in the Objects tree under the Check Point heading. (See Figure 1.34.)

Figure 1.34 Objects List with Newly Create Gateway

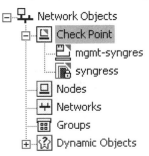

Now that you have successfully created your Check Point VPN-1 Pro gateway, you are on your way to creating your first security policy.

Summary

Check Point has put a lot of research and development into the creation of SecurePlatform and the new addition of SecurePlatform Pro with NGX. Providing a pre-hardened OS simplifies the task of preparing your host to run the Check Point suite.

With Check Point's extensive suite of Firewall products, ranging from the small, medium, and enterprise environments, there is a solution for every need.

The SmartCenter server provides a centralized location to control and push out your security policies to your different environments. The SmartDashboard utilizes a GUI to quickly comprehend and build your security policy. Interconnecting Check Point devices has become easier with NGX, which corresponds to everybody's needs.

Chapter 2

SmartDashboard and SmartPortal

Solutions in this chapter:

- **A Tour of the Dashboard**
- **New in SmartDashboard NGX**
- **Your First Security Policy**
- **Other Useful Controls on the Dashboard**
- **Managing Connectra and Interspect Gateways**
- **SmartPortal**

☑ **Summary**

Introduction

In this chapter, we will take a tour of the interface used to configure your NGX installation: the SmartDashboard. Once we are done with the tour, new users of Check Point should know where to return in order to configure more advanced features of NGX; those familiar with Check Point NG will see where things have changed and what new features they can use to make management of their systems easier. We will then run through setting up a simple security policy and applying it to your NGX firewall gateway. The new SmartPortal management interface will be visited; we will look at how to install it and how it will help administrate your organization's Check Point systems.

A Tour of the Dashboard

Those unfamiliar with the Check Point NG interface may find the SmartDashboard interface a little daunting at first sight, what with so many different panes, views, and toolbars on one screen! Indeed, a large screen is a good place to start Check Point—say, at least 800×600—but 1280×1024 over 19" is much more workable, and an excuse for the larger monitor you'd wanted for months.

The key to working with the interface is an understanding of what each area is for, and sticking to those you need. We will take a quick tour to help with this.

Logging In

First, we need to log in. Usually, you'd be connecting SmartDashboard to your SmartCenter, but there is also the option of Demo mode. This allows you to get familiar with the interface and take a look at some advanced configurations without risking doing any damage because the only configuration you are changing is the local Demo databases. You can choose a number of different Demo databases, varying in complexity from a firewall only, to advanced VPN scenarios. When you use Demo mode, SmartDashboard shows that it is connected to a SmartCenter named *local—that's really just some static files. You can run SmartDashboard in Demo mode without any SmartCenter installed—choose a Demo Installation from your NGX CD.

For our tour, we will log in using Demo mode with the Basic Firewall+VPN database, as shown in Figure 2.1.

Figure 2.1 Logging in Using Demo Mode

The SmartDashboard window includes a number of different panes. Our tour begins with the rulebases—those Check Point administrators who remember FireWall-1 v4 will recall when there was nothing more than the Security and Address Translation rulebases!

The Rulebase Pane

The tabs in Figure 2.2 are the default tabs we see in the Demo mode. Each tab configures a different product feature, the Security tab being the most commonly used—the firewall rulebase. Some of the tabs reflect a particular *policy*, where different policies can be loaded and applied to different gateways, whereas others apply *globally* across all the gateways managed by your SmartCenter. The combination of policies that you view at one time is called a *policy package*. Other tabs will appear if other product features are enabled.

Figure 2.2 Rulebase Pane Tabs

To get your first firewall policy up and running, you probably will make use of only the Security and perhaps Address Translation tabs, but here is the full list.

Security Tab

This tab is the policy-based definition of the firewall security policy. Rules here define what traffic is permitted through a firewall, whether to log the traffic, or does it require encryption or authentication. The Security rulebase is part of the Security and Address Translation policy.

Address Translation Tab

These policy-based rules define what Network Address Translation (NAT) should be performed on traffic through a firewall. They are part of the Security and Address Translation policy.

SmartDefense Tab

This tab is the global configuration of the firewall's attack detection and prevention features. This includes everything from low-level IP packet sanity checks up to application layer controls for Instant Messengers and Voice-over IP (VoIP). The functionality here has expanded greatly since the introduction of SmartDefense back in NG FP2.

Web Intelligence Tab

This tab is the global configuration of Web (HTTP) -related SmartDefense features, including new features that were introduced in the R55W (Web Intelligence) version of NG.

VPN Manager Tab

This is the global configuration of VPN gateways when using VPN Communities. This method of VPN configuration applies only when a *Simplified Mode* Security and Address Translation policy is enforced on the gateways, so this tab is not present if a *Traditional Mode* Security and Address Translation policy is part of the current policy package. The difference between Simplified and Traditional Mode will be explained in Chapter 8.

QoS Tab

This policy controls the behavior of the Quality of Service (QoS) (Floodgate-1) gateway module where it has been enabled. It allows granular control of bandwidth usage per protocol and source and destination IP. This tab is not available in the Basic demo database.

Desktop Security Tab

This tab is the policy defining the desktop firewall rulebase that will be downloaded to Secure Client remote users when they connect. Check Point's Secure Client secure remote access solution consists of client software (Secure Client) installed on each remote user machine; the VPN-1 gateway, which acts as the endpoint for the VPN tunnel to the client; and the Secure Client Policy Server, which runs on the gateway. The Policy Server will supply the latest Desktop Security policy to clients when they connect.

Web Access Tab

This tab is the global configuration of UserAuthority WebAccess modules. UA WebAccess software can be installed on Web servers to provide URL level access control and single sign-on integration with gateways. This tab is disabled by default—if you are installing a WebAccess module, enable it in the **Global Properties, UserAuthority** page (see Figure 2.3).

Figure 2.3 Enabling the Web Access Tab

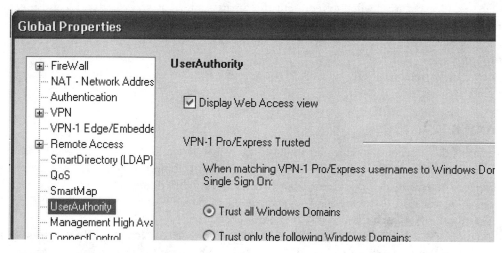

Consolidation Rules Tab

This policy controls the behavior of the Eventia Reporter Log Consolidator, if installed. To display this tab, use **View | Products | Reporter Log Consolidator**. Note that this removes all other tabs—to return to the previous view of tabs, use **View | Products | Standard**.

The Objects Tree Pane

To the left of the rulebases, you should see the Objects Tree, as shown in Figure 2.4.

Figure 2.4 The Objects Tree Pane

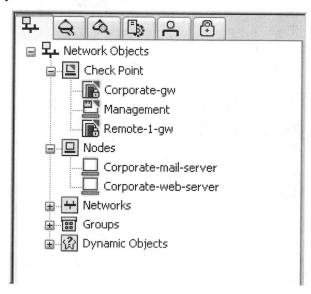

The tree is a convenient way to browse, edit, and create the objects that you need to define for your rulebases. Objects are needed to represent the SmartCenter, gateways, networks, and hosts you reference in policies, user accounts, and so on.

There are actually several trees of objects—use the tabs at the top of the pane to select the required tree.

To create new objects, simply right-click the top of the tree and choose **New**. To edit an object, double-click it.

Network Objects

This tree holds the objects that represent the hosts, gateways, networks, and address ranges that you reference in your policies. You can also create groups of network objects. There are a number of other special types of objects that can be defined here, representing DNS domains, external VPN peers, VoIP configuration, server load balancing controls, and routers managed by the Check Point OSE product.

By default, the Network Objects tree branches reflect each type of Network Object or can be sorted by color or name. Alternatively, a Group View will show each Network Object group as a branch, and its members within that branch—right-click the top of the tree to switch between **Arrange by Group** or **Classic View**.

Services

A wealth of objects resides here that define protocols that can be used in policies. The tree divides the objects by protocol type. The objects range from the obvious—like the telnet object that represents TCP port 23—to the obscure—such as SSL_v3, which represents an SSL connection, but enforces version 3 of the protocol.

Resources

Resource objects control the behavior of the firewall security servers—these are transparent proxy servers integrated into the firewall gateway. Security servers can be used for http, ftp, and smtp traffic. There is also a generic TCP proxy. A typical use of security servers is enabling redirection of web and mail traffic to third-party CVP or UFP servers that perform antivirus scanning or URL cataloging. An additional type of resource object is the CIFS resource that can be used to control and audit use of Microsoft networking—allowing restriction of what server shares can be accessed. This CIFS enforcement is performed without the use of a security server.

Servers and OPSEC Applications

Check Point can integrate with a wide range of other servers and applications. Objects are defined here to represent applications that will be integrated. These include certificate authorities, authentication servers, LDAP servers, and content checking servers. There is one predefined object: the *internal_ca* Certificate Authority (CA) object. This represents the internal CA that is integrated into the SmartCenter Server.

Users and Administrators

To connect to the SmartCenter for the first time, an administrator account is used that was created as part of the installation process using the *cpconfig* utility. This account is visible in SmartDashboard in the object *cpconfig_administrators*. Once connected using this account, additional administrator accounts should be created here in SmartDashboard for each user that will require access to the SmartCenter. Each account can then have different access permissions as required.

In addition, nonadministrative user accounts can be created to make use of the firewall and VPN authentication features. These accounts can be defined with a fixed password, certificate, or authentication backed off to an external authentication server.

To avoid the overhead of user account management in SmartDashboard, the provision of the user database can be passed to an external server in two ways: first, External User Profiles can be created that back off all authentication requests that do not match a locally defined user. Second, it is possible to fully integrate with a LDAP directory server. This includes using the server for authentication plus the ability to manage user accounts on the LDAP server directly through SmartDashboard—once configured, the directory will become accessible in this object tree. Integration with LDAP for user authentication is a licensed feature—Check Point calls it SmartDirectory. If you have a SmartCenter Pro license, SmartDirectory should be included.

VPN Communities

This provides a tree view of community objects—the same as those displayed in the VPN Manager rulebase tab.

The Objects List Pane

This pane shows objects in a list format. The contents of the list is controlled by what is currently selected in the Objects Tree. For example, select the **Network Objects – Nodes** branch to see a list of all nodes.

The SmartMap Pane

SmartMap provides a visual representation of the network topology that can be gleaned from the network objects that have been defined. SmartMap can be disabled in **Global Properties, SmartMap** page. If you are not using SmartMap, disable it—this avoids the overhead of SmartDashboard calculating the visual topology.

Menus and Toolbars

Although most of the policy and object management can be performed via the panes we've looked at, there is plenty more than can be achieved via the drop-down menus or, for some of the most common actions, the toolbars.

Working with Policy Packages

To save changes to objects and the current policy package, create new policy packages, or open a different policy package, use the File menu. Remember that a policy package is all the policies you can see on the rulebase pane. If you wish to take a copy of just one of the policies—say the Desktop Policy—and save it in a new package, use the Copy Policy to Package option and specify a name for your new policy package.

Installing the Policy

Saving the Policy Package does not actually change the policy running on your gateways—it's just updating the SmartCenter database. To update your gateways, use the Policy menu, Install Policy option—or find the toolbar icon for Install Policies.

There are plenty more menu options to explore in your own time. The final option we will look at is the big daddy of all: Global Properties, from the Policy menu.

Global Properties

The Global Properties window, as the name suggests, defines settings and fine-tuning of your Check Point systems that apply globally (rather than per policy or per gateway). To open the window, from the menus choose **Policy | Global Properties**, or from the toolbar, choose the icon that looks like a bulleted list (see Figure 2.5).

Figure 2.5 The Global Properties Window

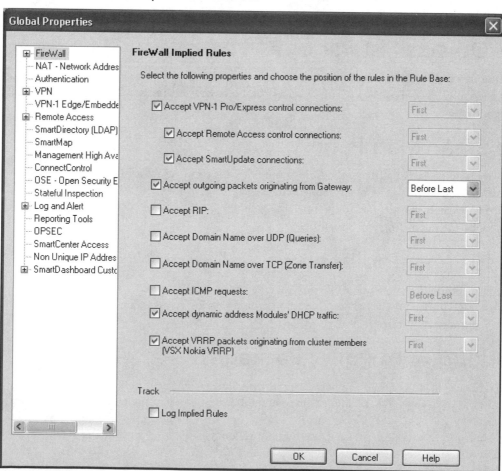

A detailed look at everything here easily could fill a whole book! We'll take a look at the more useful settings as well as new additions to NGX.

FireWall Page

The FireWall page shows Implied Rules settings. These "rules" are imposed over every security policy installed to your gateways. The idea is that they allow traffic that your gateways might need to function correctly—so you avoid pushing a policy that sends your gateway AWOL. There are obvious security implications here—to a degree, you are opening up "holes" in your security policy. Actually, as long as you are aware of what shape and size holes are involved, there is no need to panic. Fortunately, exactly this facility exists in SmartDashboard: with the Security rulebase displayed, use the View menu to choose View | Implied Rules. This will show the Implied Rules that are currently enabled by adding them to the view of your Security rulebase.

The tickbox for **VPN-1 Pro/Express Control Connections** enables a vast array of implied rules: the initial reaction may be to untick that box. However, on closer inspection, these rules are pretty specific—and in fact, if you disable these implied rules you will likely spend an awful lot of time recreating them as manual rules before you get back to a correctly functioning gateway. The decision is yours: the author's preference is to leave the option checked unless you are very confident you know what rules you will need to add manually. Are you sure you can avoid either a malfunctioning gateway or a bigger security hole than the implied rules may have left?

The option **Accept Outgoing packets originating from Gateway** is often left enabled, although we should consider whether we want to implicitly trust any and all connections from the gateway. Should the firewall gateway itself become in some way compromised, do we want to allow it unfettered access to the internal networks? It is preferable to investigate what outgoing traffic will be required from the gateway and accept only that in your rulebase. This is often just DNS queries to the configured DNS servers—remember that VPN-1 control connections (required to permit gateway to SmartCenter connections) are allowed elsewhere.

Of the other implied rules, most are undesirable. Consider the options for RIP and DNS: a sensible security policy would never allow these protocols without considering the source IP address. Those for Dynamic Address module DHCP traffic and Nokia VSX may be useful if relevant to your configurations, and are harmless enough. Note that the VSX VRRP setting does not apply for standard IPSO VRRP gateway clusters.

Finally, it is a good idea to enable **Log Implied Rules**. That way you can reassure yourself that you know exactly what connections are being allowed by the settings here, thanks to logging in SmartView Tracker. By default, Log Implied Rules is not enabled.

NAT—Network Address Translation Page

The default settings here are good for most configurations: be aware of the new option of **Merge manual proxy ARP configuration**. This allows the use of Automatic ARP when the old local.arp publishing method also is required on a Windows gateway. In gateway versions prior to NGX, if Automatic ARP configuration was enabled, the local.arp mechanism was disabled.

VPN Page

There are some global options here affecting site-to-site VPN gateways; however, most VPN configuration is performed in VPN community objects and VPN gateway objects.

VPN-1 Edge/Embedded Page

Where the SmartCenter is managing remote *VPN-1 Edge* or other similar Sofaware-based devices (e.g., *Nokia IP40*), this page controls some global behavior. This includes, new in NGX, the ability to inspect Web and mail content passing through these devices using central checking servers. Web traffic can be verified against a central UFP (URL filtering) server; SMTP and POP3 mail can be redirected via a central anti-virus scanning CVP server.

Remote Access Page

On the Remote Access page and its subpages, there is a wide range of configuration settings—usually best left at their defaults unless a specific configuration requires otherwise. New in NGX is the ability to configure here: SSL Network Extender, SecureClient Hotspot, Office Mode IP reuse across gateways and SCV connection exceptions.

SmartDirectory (LDAP) Page

If you wish to use LDAP integration, don't forget to enable it here first!

Stateful Inspection Page

Fundamental to the operation of the firewall gateway is stateful inspection: that is, tracking the progress of a TCP connection (or other protocol sessions) to ensure that all traffic that arrives is consistent with the connection state. This page allows this behavior to be fine-tuned, or to a degree, disabled.

Dropping out-of-state TCP packets is sometimes disabled in scenarios where TCP connections remain idle for long periods, so the gateway will timeout the connection and then drop packets in the future. If at all possible, avoid this; first try extending the *TCP Timeout* on the object for the service affected. Extending the timeout globally may significantly increase the amount of stale data in the gateway state tables.

New in SmartDashboard NGX

For readers familiar with previous versions of SmartDashboard, this chapter may have yet to uncover much that is new for them.

For those readers in particular, we will now have a look at the improvements in NGX.

Security Policy Rule Names and Unique IDs

In previous versions, every rule had a number. At a stretch, the administrator may have bothered to scroll over to the far left column of the rule to add a comment. Neither helped clearly identify the purpose of each rule when browsing through the rulebase.

NGX introduces *rule names*: now the first column in every rule. Describing each rule in one or two words should make the rulebase far more readable. Figure 2.6 shows an example of annotating a rulebase in this way.

Figure 2.6 Naming Rules

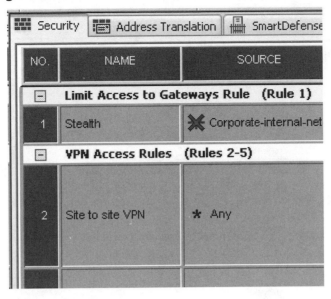

Also new are *Unique Rule IDs*. Every rule now has a hidden, unique ID that does not change throughout the rule's life span—unlike the visible rule number, which will change when rules above are added or removed. This feature comes into its own when viewing log entries in SmartView Tracker. Now it is possible to identify which rule triggered the log entry—whether or not the rule number has since changed. For good measure, the rule name is included in the log entry, too. An example of the logging you'll see is shown in Figure 2.7.

Figure 2.7 Logging with Rule IDs and Names

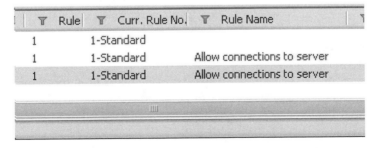

There is also an option in SmartDashboard to launch SmartView Tracker and view all logs relating to a rule. Right-click the rule to try this, as shown in Figure 2.8.

Figure 2.8 Launching SmartView Tracker for a Specific Rule

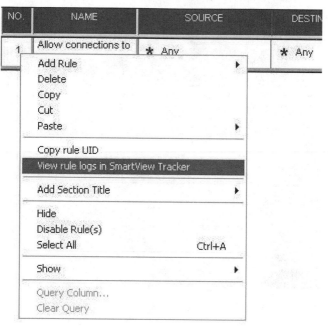

Group Object Convention

It is possible to specify a *convention* when defining a group. This consists of conditions based on object name, color, and IP, as shown in Figure 2.9.

This can be used to assist when adding members to a group: a list of existing objects that meet the convention is provided. In addition, in the future when a new object is defined, SmartDashboard will check whether it meets a group convention. If so, you will be prompted to add the object to the relevant group.

Group Hierarchy

The Network Objects view in the Object Tree pane has been enhanced for Group objects to allow "drilling down" into groups. Right-click the **Groups branch** and choose **Show Groups Hierarchy**, as shown in Figure 2.10.

Figure 2.9 Groups with Conventions

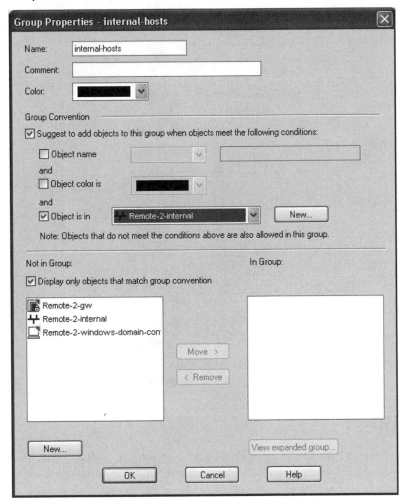

Figure 2.10 Enabling Group Hierarchy View

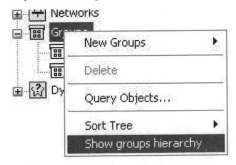

The tree will now show the members of groups, including subgroups. An example is shown in Figure 2.11.

Figure 2.11 Drilling into Groups

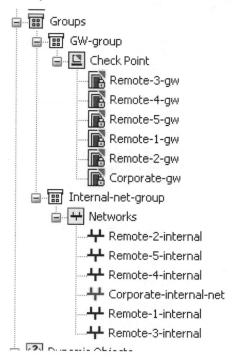

Clone Object

For those times when you need to create a large number of similar objects, **Clone Object** is here to help. Right-click any Node or Network object and you have the option to **Clone**. This creates a new object with the same properties. Just change the name and IP and you are done.

Session Description

In previous versions, it was possible to supply a Session Description when logging in to SmartDashboard, and this would be written to the Audit Log. This provided a rudimentary way of tracking the reason for which administrators had logged into SmartDashboard, should they choose to supply one.

SmartDashboard NGX provides the ability to require a Session Description in order to log in: enable this in **Global Properties, SmartCenter Access**. However, as yet there is no way of forcing the administrator to enter something helpful.

Tooltips

In the rulebase, tooltips are provided for host and network objects—hover your mouse pointer over an object for a summary for example, for a network, its IP, subnet mask, and object comment (see Figure 2.12). This is particularly useful when analyzing a rulebase, allowing you to understand what the objects used in rules are representing. Of course, to make the tooltip really useful, you do need to have provided a helpful Comment in the object definition. This should be considered standard practice in order to make the effect of your rulebase clear. Losing track of what objects represent can easily lead to your defined security policy not providing the protection that you expected, or perhaps (in practice, more often) blocking legitimate traffic.

Figure 2.12 Tooltips Are Your Friend

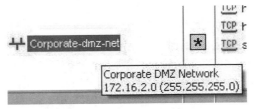

We've now completed our SmartDashboard tour and highlighted the new features in NGX. With some luck you are now familiar enough with the interface in order to create a simple security policy.

Your First Security Policy

We will now run through the steps of configuring and installing your first security policy. In our example, SmartCenter Express has been installed on a Windows 2003 Server named "sleigh." You have a dedicated firewall gateway host running Nokia IPSO that has VPN-1 Express gateway installed, named "vixen."

Having installed the SmartCenter software successfully, you should be able to connect your SmartDashboard for the first time. If you have installed SmartCenter on a Windows platform, you will be able to run the SmartDashboard locally. Otherwise, you will need to install the SmartConsole package on a Windows host and connect to the SmartCenter over the snetwork—make sure your *cpconfig* GUI clients settings allow the host to connect. Log in by specifying the administrator credentials that you configured in *cpconfig* and the hostname (or IP) of the SmartCenter, as shown in Figure 2.13.

Figure 2.13 Connecting to Your SmartCenter

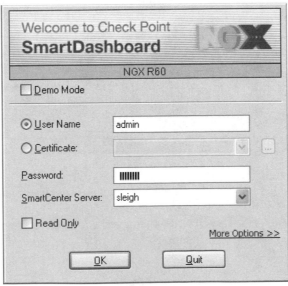

Once connected, you will notice in the Objects Tree that an object for the SmartCenter has been created automatically. Double-click the object to review the object settings: verify that the hostname, IP address, and OS are correct. If there are discrepancies, it might indicate a problem with the installation: double-check that the SmartCenter's host OS is configured correctly. The object for our SmartCenter *sleigh* is shown in Figure 2.14.

Figure 2.14 SmartCenter Object for *Sleigh*

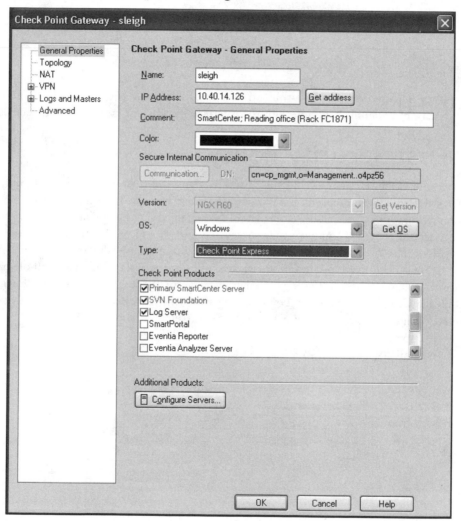

The Products Installed list indicates that *sleigh* is running a Primary SmartCenter, Log Server, and SVN Foundation (SVN is the base Check Point software module). In our example, no gateway is installed on *sleigh*, so Firewall, VPN, and QoS are all unchecked. We have provided a useful comment— here it identifies the location of the SmartCenter.

Creating Your Administrator Account

Your first job is to create an administrator's user account. Select the **Users** tab of the Objects Tree, right-click on **Administrators**, and choose **New Administrator**. Your user ID will be *clauss*. In order to configure your level of privileges, create a new **Permissions Profile** called *fulladmin*. You should select Read/Write Access, and the ability to Manage Administrators so that you can create further accounts for other admins, operators, and so on. Don't forget to choose an authentication method, too—in the object **Admin Auth** tab, you should select a Check Point password and set it. Note you can use stronger external mechanisms if you wish; for example, *RSA SecurID*. Additionally, you can create a certificate and use that to authenticate instead of a regular password.

Now, you have an administrator account; save your changes (**File | Save**) and then exit from SmartDashboard. Then, start SmartDashboard and log in again, this time using the new account.

Hooking Up to the Gateway

You are now ready to hook up the SmartCenter to your new VPN-1 gateway, *vixen*. As part of the installation of NGX on *vixen*, you were supplied a *SIC activation key*: you need that in order to define your object for the gateway.

To create your object, right-click on the **Network Objects** tree and choose **New | Check Point | VPN-1 Pro/Express Gateway**. You are prompted for the choice of a wizard or manual classic configuration. Unless you have a real aversion to wizards, the wizard is pretty reliable. We recommend that you use the wizard, supplying the following details:

- Gateway name: use the hostname of the gateway.

- IP Address: use the *external* IP of the gateway (also make sure that, on the gateway host itself, its own hostname resolves to this IP). Choosing the external IP is important for VPN configurations as clients or peers may use this IP for building the VPN tunnel, and the internal, private IPs are unlikely to be reachable. It is critical for the gateway's hostname to resolve correctly locally because the Check Point services on the gateway will use the resolved IP when locating the firewall object for that gateway. On UNIX platforms verify the hosts file is correct on the gateway. On Windows, it is not so straightforward: ping the gateways own hostname in order to determine which physical interface is considered the primary by Windows, then use that interface as the external interface.

- Gateway Type: Express or Pro (we are using Express). This depends on what license you have.

- Firewall or VPN: will you be using the VPN features of VPN-1? If not, only enable FireWall—this simplifies configuration. You can always switch on VPN later if needed. We'll have VPN from the start.

- SIC Activation Key: after supplying this key and clicking **Next**, the SmartCenter will attempt a connection to the gateway.

Hopefully the SIC connection is successful—if not, take a look at the sidebar, "Can't Communicate?" The wizard will now ask you whether to automatically retrieve interfaces and topology from the gateway. This will fetch a list of interfaces and inspect the routing tables on the gateway in order to identify what subnets are connected to each interface of the gateway, creating any necessary objects for you—on complex networks this can save you a lot of time. It is also important that the interface list is defined accurately, so automatically fetching the list is highly recommended.

When the wizard completes, you can check the box to **Edit the Gateways Properties** to review the configuration of the new object. The hostname, IP address, OS, and Products Installed should all be as required.

Reviewing the Gateway Object

It's worth reviewing all the objects settings: first, to make sure the wizard got it right (they aren't perfect, you know), and second, so that you are aware of the available options to be configured if you need to later. The object for *vixen* is shown in Figure 2.15.

Figure 2.15 Gateway Object for *Vixen*

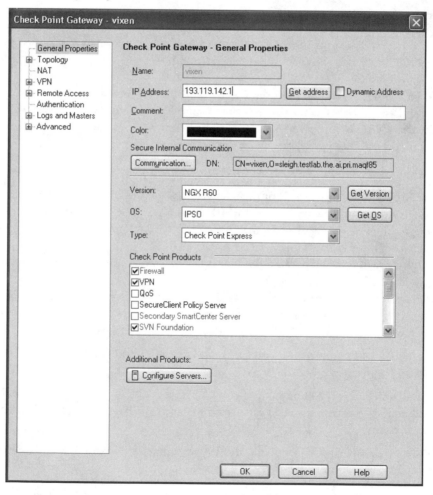

If you are satisfied that these general properties look good, move on to the Topology page for the object. Here you'll see a list of interfaces on the gateway and the IP addresses behind those interfaces, based on the routing tables. On your *vixen* gateway, the eth4c0 interface has an additional routed subnet behind that interface and SmartDashboard has created objects to reflect that. The topology is shown in Figure 2.16.

Figure 2.16 Gateway Topology

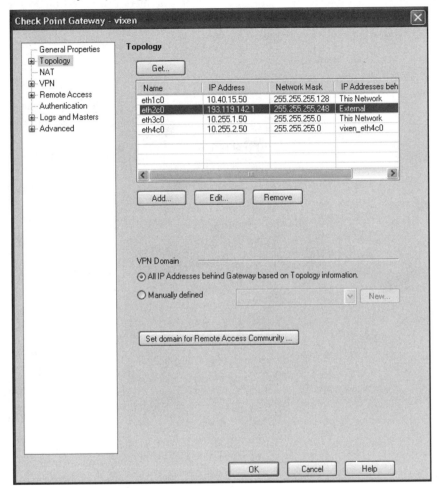

To edit the settings for each interface, just double-click the interface name. As well as the name and IP, the topology should be reviewed to ensure it correctly reflects what IP addresses lie behind that interface. Accurately configuring this allows Anti Spoofing protection to be enabled on the interface—essential in securing your networks against spoofed packets arriving at untrusted interfaces.

You may want to browse through the raft of other pages and settings available in the gateway object, but these are best left at their defaults for now.

Defining Your Security Policy

Before defining rules in your policy, you will likely need to define a few objects to represent internal hosts and networks. SmartDashboard automatically created objects for two of your internal networks when it fetched the gateway topology, so you can just change those object names to something more meaningful rather than creating new objects.

You will also create a group, *sleigh_internal*, which will include all your internal networks. To add the networks to the group, just drag and drop them into the group using the Objects Tree.

Figure 2.17 shows the Objects Tree with all our objects defined. You have objects for your networks plus an object for the Internet mail relay server on our DMZ. There is also a group that was automatically defined for use in the gateway topology.

Figure 2.17 The Objects Tree

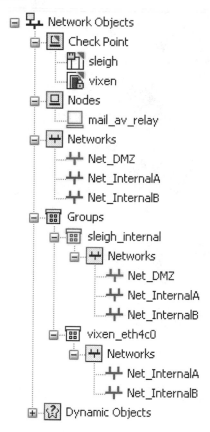

Policy Design

A firewall security policy should be designed with the principle of least privilege in mind: accept only the traffic that is required, drop anything else. When the firewall gateway implements the rulebase, each new connection is compared against the rulebase top down—when a rule is matched, that action is followed and no more rules are checked. Check Point helps you out with best practice by dropping any traffic that is not accepted by either implied rules or a rule you have added to the policy—in other words, there is an invisible rule at the bottom of rulebase: *drop anything*.

Two rules are usually explicitly added as part of every policy: the Stealth rule and the Clean Up rule.

A *Stealth rule* is placed near the top of the policy and explicitly blocks access to the firewall. It should be placed above other more general rules that would otherwise allow access (maybe a rule allowing internal users access to the Internet—i.e., any address—which would include the firewall itself). Don't forget to add a rule above the Stealth rule to allow access for administrators—for example ssh to the gateway.

A *Clean Up rule* is placed at the bottom of the policy and explicitly drops and logs all traffic that has not matched other rules. This traffic would have been dropped by the gateway anyway because of the invisible drop-anything rule, but the Clean Up rule ensures it gets logged.

In addition to the aforementioned rules, your security policy should be developed in order to reflect the formal network usage policies of your organization.

Creating Rules

Before we begin creating rules, it is a good idea to save the Policy Package using a descriptive name. You will notice that the current policy name is "Standard." It is good practice to use policy names that identify the date/time of the policy, or some versioning reference. There are two reasons for this—first, it is easy to check what revision of the policy package is installed on a gateway—SmartView Monitor will show the current installed package name. Second, it makes it easy to roll back changes to the policy (although be aware that saving the policy does not provide version control over changes to objects— we'll discuss Change Management later in this chapter). To save the policy under a new name, use **File | Save As**.

To add a rule to the rulebase, use the **Rules Toolbar**. This provides buttons for adding rules at the top or bottom of the policy, and above or below the current selected rule. Clicking one of these buttons adds a rule that by default, and will drop all traffic. First you should give the rule a **Name**; then we can modify the rule **Source**, **Destination**, and **Service** by dragging objects into the fields or right-clicking and adding objects from a list. Then choose the **Action** you wish to take if a connection matches this rule (right-click and choose from the list); to start with, choose between Accept or Drop. Other options can be used to perform authentication or require encryption. The Reject option drops traffic but informs the client by means of either a TCP Reset or ICMP destination unreachable message.

The full security rulebase for our example is shown in Figure 2.18.

Figure 2.18 A Full Example Rulebase

NO.	NAME	SOURCE	DESTINATION	VPN	SERVICE	ACTION	TRACK	IN
1	Manage vixen	admin_pc	vixen	*	TCP ssh_version_2 TCP https	accept	Alert	
2	Manage sleigh	admin_pc	sleigh	*	TCP ms-rdesktop CIFS	accept	Alert	
3	Stealth	* Any	vixen sleigh	*	* Any	drop	Log	
4	Mail in	* Any	mail_av_relay	*	TCP smtp	accept	Log	
5	Mail out	mail_av_relay	* Any	*	TCP smtp	accept	Log	
6	Web access	sleigh_internal	* Any	*	TCP http TCP https TCP ftp	accept	Log	
7	Clean Up	* Any	* Any	*	* Any	drop	Log	

Reviewing the rules, you have allowed our administrators PC access to the gateway and SmartCenter for the required protocols. You had to define a new Service object (right-click in the **Services** tab of Objects Tree) to represent the Microsoft Remote Desktop protocol (TCP port 3389). You ensure that ssh access to the gateway is using the more secure ssh version 2, not version 1, by using the special service *ssh_version_2*.

Once you have your policy defined, remember to review the implied rules that are enabled in Global Properties. The defaults in NGX are sensible, but make sure that you are aware what they are. In the example in this chapter, you have left Control Connections and Outgoing Packets from Gateway enabled. It is a good idea to enable Log Implied Rules so that it is clear what connections are being accepted and dropped.

Network Address Translation

To be allowed to access the Internet, and for your mail relay to receive incoming mail, you need to configure some address translation. Add Hide NAT to your internal networks (hiding behind the gateway itself) and Static NAT to your mail relay. The mail relay will be translated to an address supplied by our ISP, in the same range as our gateway external IP. This is simple to configure using Automatic NAT—edit the relevant objects and configure the NAT page. Figures 2.19 and 2.20 show the NAT configuration on an internal network object and the mail relay object.

Figure 2.19 Internal Network Hide NAT Configuration

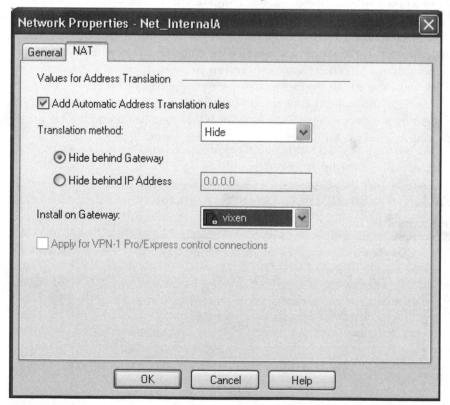

Figure 2.20 Host Object Static NAT Configuration

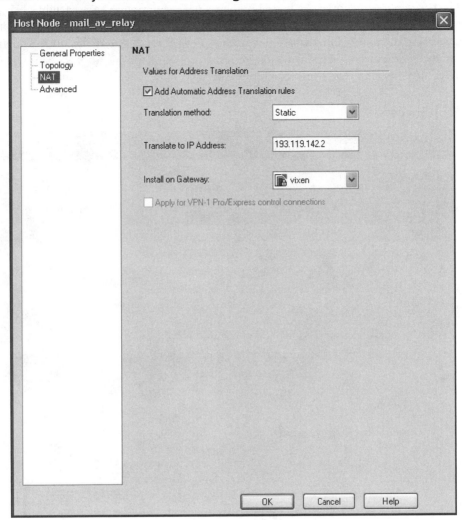

In the Network Address Translation rulebase tab, you can review the rules that have been created. You can add more rules to the rulebase manually if you need to—this is discussed further in the Network Address Translation chapter.

At last you are ready to test your policy!

Installing the Policy

To install the policy, use the Policy toolbar—the policy install button shows a rulebase with a downward arrow above it. SmartDashboard will prompt you to select which gateways the policy should be installed on—in this case, there is only one gateway to choose from, and it will be selected by default. If you later choose to enable the QoS or Policy Server modules on the gateway, you will also be able to select whether you wish to update the QoS and Desktop Security policies. Clicking OK to continue the process will show the Install Progress dialog box. This will indicate that the policy is first Verifying and then Installing. The Verify phase identifies any logical problems with your policy—for example, rules that "hide" later rules, making the later rule redundant. Installation is the process of connecting to the gateway, transferring the policy and database files to the gateway, instructing the gateway to update its policy, and waiting for a successful confirmation from the gateway. If all this succeeds, you will see a reassuring large green tick appear, as in Figure 2.21.

Figure 2.21 Success!

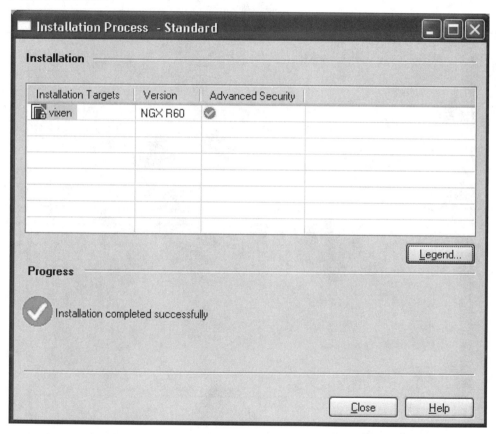

If you see anything else—red crosses, warnings, or the like—click the **Show Errors** button that will appear in order to view the reasons for this. This may not be critical in some cases—sometimes it is just a recommendation about your policy. Other times it will indicate the policy has not been installed, maybe due to connectivity to the gateway or some other serious error during the policy compilation process.

Before you make any further changes to the policy, you may want to save the current policy using a new name, indicating a new policy version.

Once you have your policy installed it is time to test whether connectivity is as expected: now is probably a good time to read the SmartView Tracker chapter so you can observe your connections being accepted, and the bad guys being dropped. Hopefully.

Other Useful Controls on the Dashboard

Once you are comfortable with the core features we've covered so far, you might want to explore some more SmartDashboard features. We'll quickly look at some of them now.

Working with Security Policy Rules

Rulebases tend to quickly become long and cumbersome—you might even end up with a few hundred rules. Keep in mind that the longer the rulebase, the more work the gateway needs to do per new connection. This can be reduced by making sure that the most common connections match rules early in the rulebase. The tools described in this section will help manage bigger rulebases.

Section Titles

As your rulebase gets larger you can use Section Titles to summarize the purpose of a group of rules, making the rulebase easier to read. To add a Section Title, right-click a rule number and choose **Add Section Title**. A section is the set of rules between two titles and it can be expanded or collapsed with a click.

Hiding Rules

Individual rules can be hidden (leaving a gray stripe instead) by right-clicking the rule number and choosing **Hide**. Once rules are hidden, you can store/restore the current list of hidden rules, unhide rules, and view hidden rules (without unhiding them!) using the menus—the **Rules | Hide** submenu.

Rule Queries

In order to locate rules that apply to a particular host or service (for example), use a *Rule Query*. These will hide all rules that don't match your query. To define queries, use the Search menu: **Search | Query Rules**.

Searching Rules

You can perform a simple text search through the Security Policy using the Search menu: **Search | Find in Rulebase**. This is useful as a quick way to locate an object in a rule, or, if you use the **Comments** field in a structured way, to locate some keyword or perhaps a change control reference.

Working with Objects

We'll take a look at a few useful tools we can use when we are working with Network Objects.

Object References

You can track all references to an object—right-click on any object and choose **Where Used?** This is very useful when you forgot why exactly you created that object all those months ago…

Who Broke That Object?

Curious who was the last person to edit an object? Right-click the object and choose **Last Modified**. You'll see when it was changed, by whom, and from where.

Object Queries

Under the Search menu, the **Query Network Objects** tool allows simple searching and filtering of Network Objects. You can also define a *Network Object group* based on your query.

Working with Policies

The policy you see in SmartDashboard is not automatically applied to the gateway—you have to install the policy (push it down to the gateway) first! If you are managing multiple gateways, this becomes more of an issue—are you sure you've installed the latest policy to all the gateways? Do you have different policies on each gateway? Which rules in your policy are relevant to a gateway?

What Would Be Installed?

If you are working with multiple gateways but a single policy, it is not always clear to see which rules would be applied to a particular gateway. You can use the Policy menu, **Policy | View Policy Of** tool in order to view selected gateway(s) rules. To return to the normal view, use the same tool and click **Clear**.

What's Really Installed?

You can check what Security policy is actually running on a gateway—rather than the one that you see in SmartDashboard, or the one that you think should be running. From the menus, choose **File | Installed Policies**.

No Security Please

It is possible to request that the Security Policy be unloaded from remote gateways: from the menu, **Policy | Uninstall**. This is a bad idea, as it leaves your firewall gateway with no protection (although it will no longer forward traffic, so connections cannot be made through the firewall). Ironically, the only time you would want to remove a policy from a gateway is when you've accidentally pushed a policy that blocks the connections from the SmartCenter to the gateway—in which case, the SmartDashboard will not be able to request the policy unload anyway! For those times, you will need to run the command **fw unloadlocal** from the command line of the gateway itself—disconnect untrusted network interfaces first to avoid leaving the gateway open to attack.

For the Anoraks

You can view the underlying script that is generated by your security policy, should that sort of thing interest you. Use the menus: **Policy | View**. The script displayed corresponds to the *<policyname>.pf* file on the SmartCenter. This tool is rarely required.

Change Management

It is possible to take a snapshot of the whole configuration database: rulebases, users, and objects. To do so, use the **Database Revision Control** feature from the File menu. To take a snapshot, **Create** a new version. It is possible to review that snapshot at a later date and, if you need to, restore it. You can even choose to create a new version on every policy install—if you do this, make sure you manage the number of database versions you have created: each snapshot increases the size of the SmartCenter configuration directories, and you risk the stability of the SmartCenter if you have hundreds of versions. Note that each version is tied to the SmartCenter software revision, so if you upgrade your

SmartCenter there is little point in maintaining the previous database revisions. Do not mistake Revision Control for a full system backup: if you badly corrupt your live database version, you may not be able to connect to SmartDashboard in order to restore an older database.

Managing Connectra and Interspect Gateways

Check Point SmartDashboard NGX allows the definition of **Check Point objects** for *Connectra* and *Interspect* gateways. Check Point *Connectra* is a SSL VPN gateway product; Check Point *Interspect* is an internal network security gateway. However, configuration management of these devices from SmartDashboard is limited to launching a dedicated management client for the device: Interspect SmartDashboard or a Web browser session to the management port of a Connectra gateway.

Configuring Interspect or Connectra Integration

Right-click on **Network Objects** in the Objects Tree and choose **New | Check Point | Connectra Gateway** or **Interspect Gateway**.

Define the object's name and IP, then use the **Communication** button to initialize SIC keys. Configured objects are shown in Figures 2.22 and 2.23.

Figure 2.22 Check Point Connectra Object

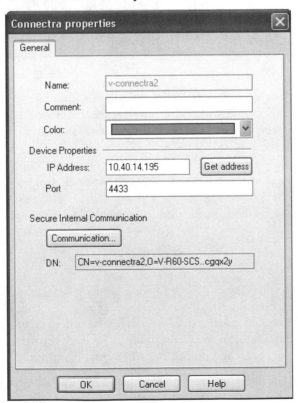

Figure 2.23 Check Point Interspect Object

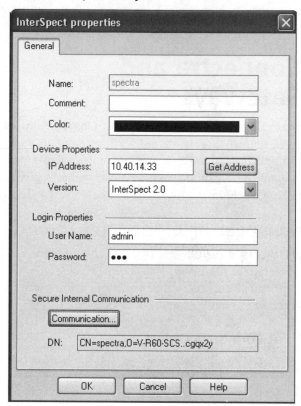

Once the object has been defined, you need to update the SmartCenter running configuration in order to allow connections from the device. To do this, use the SmartDashboard menus: **Policy | Install Database**. Then on the new object, you can right-click and choose **Manage Device** in order to launch the management client for the device.

In the Connectra or Interspect management interface, configure Central Management/Logging as per the device documentation. You will need to specify the SmartCenter name/IP and the object name that you have given to the new object.

After these changes have been made, the device logs should begin to appear in SmartView Tracker.

SmartDefense Updates

SmartDashboard also provides centralized SmartDefense Updates for Connectra and Interspect. If you have purchased a SmartDefense subscription for the device, you can update its SmartDefense features directly from the SmartDashboard rather than the management interface of the device: right-click on the object and choose **SmartDefense Service Update**. The latest SmartDefense database can then be downloaded to the SmartCenter and pushed out to internal Connectra and Interspect gateways, as shown in Figure 2.24.

Figure 2.24 Updating Connectra SmartDefense from SmartDashboard

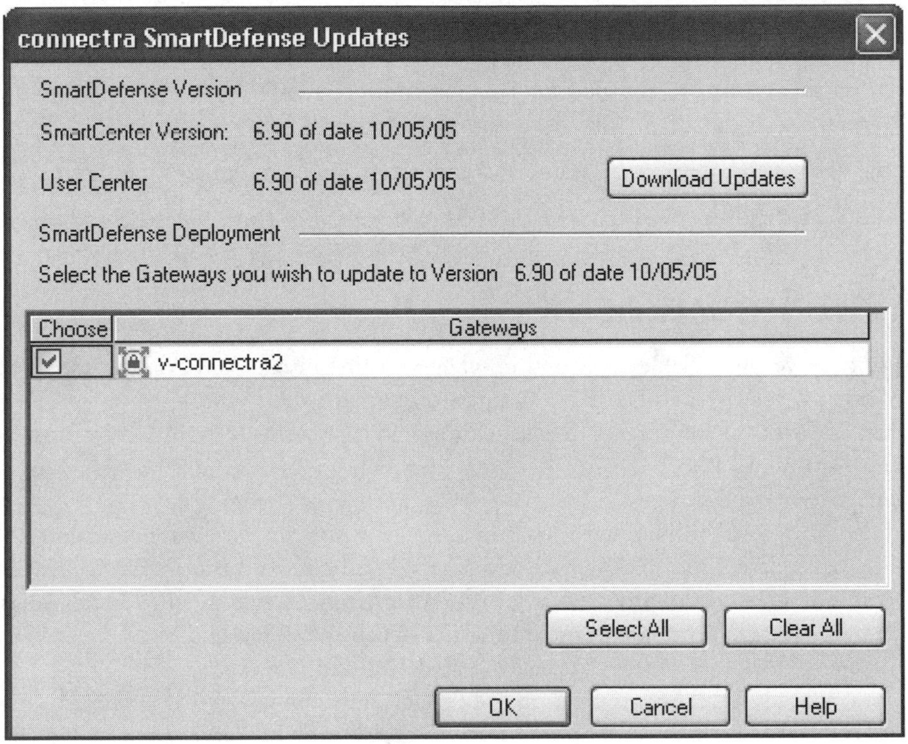

SmartPortal

The complexity and power of the Check Point management clients has a downside: the client software is a substantial suite of applications, not exactly lightweight. There are a number of situations when this is not ideal:

- There is often a requirement for operators to be able to view the logs or summary of status of the gateways, without any need for the full functionality of the SmartConsole suite.

- In a managed service environment, customers may want to view the logging from their sites' gateways, but not wish to install any software.

- Remote administrators may need to check on the status of the gateway, but are unable to install the software on the system they are using.

SmartPortal provides a browser-based alternative to the SmartConsole clients—ideal for these scenarios.

SmartPortal Functionality

The SmartPortal interface provides:

- **Status information** Similar information to the Gateway Status view of SmartView Monitor
- **Log viewer** Access to the traffic and audit logs, similar to SmartView Tracker
- **Policy and objects summary** A view of the *Security Policy* rulebase and object details

Installing SmartPortal

The SmartPortal server is available as an option when you first install NGX on the supported platforms: Windows, Solaris, Red Hat EL 3.0, and SecurePlatform.

Note that SmartPortal requires a license, although that license is included in most VPN-1 Pro and some extended VPN-1 Express licenses. To check yours, run *cplic check swp* on your SmartCenter.

If you didn't choose SmartPortal at install time, you can just run the wrapper again on Windows or Solaris—it should detect that NGX is already installed and give you the option to install additional products. Do this and choose SmartPortal. On SecurePlatform, you will need to install SmartPortal manually: enter Expert mode from a console session and run the command.

rpm –i /sysimg/CPwrapper/linux/CPportal/CPportal-R60-00.i386.rpm

Usually you would install SmartPortal on the SmartCenter; however, it is possible to install it on other Check Point hosts or its own dedicated server. The SmartPortal server then makes an onward connection to the SmartCenter. A dedicated server would be advisable if there are likely to be many concurrent SmartPortal users.

Once the product is installed, ensure that the relevant object has **SmartPortal** checked in the **Check Point Products** list. Having done so, perform a database install to the SmartCenter (**Policy | Install Database**).

To access the portal, point your browser to **https://smartcenter-host:4433**.

Tour of SmartPortal

At the welcome page (see Figure 2.25), supply your administrator credentials (this should be an account created in SmartDashboard) and the name (or IP) of the SmartCenter server.

Figure 2.25 Welcome to SmartPortal

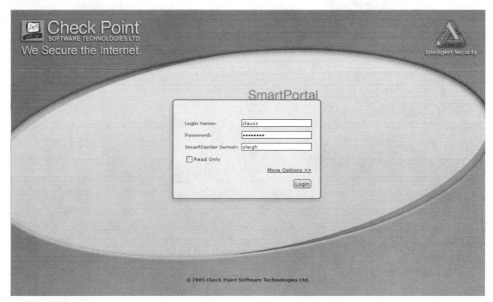

After a few seconds you should be connected to the SmartPortal front page, as shown in Figure 2.26. If the SmartPortal connection fails, check that you have correctly followed the installation steps and are using the correct SmartDashboard administrator credentials. Check that the SmartCenter Server name you supplied resolves successfully on the server running SmartPortal.

Figure 2.26 Logged In: SmartPortal Front Page

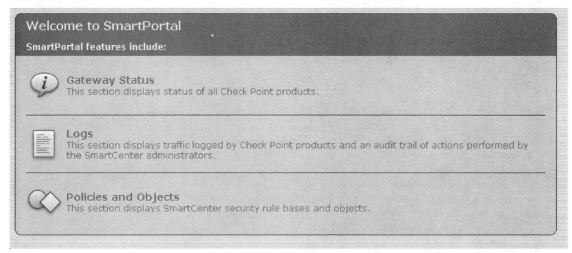

A sidebar allows selection of the different features.

The **Gateway Status** page will show a summary of status for each gateway and the SmartCenter itself (see Figure 2.27). To see more detailed status information, click the name of the gateway.

Figure 2.27 SmartPortal Gateway Status Page

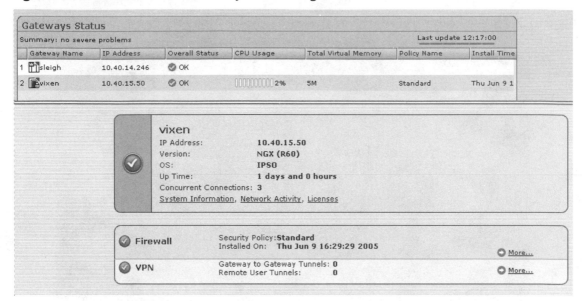

The **Logs** page can show either the **Traffic Log** or the **Audit Log**. The view is similar to SmartView Tracker but with a restricted set of columns shown. The Traffic Log is shown in Figure 2.28. Note the toolbar allowing navigation of the log, automatic scrolling, searching, filtering, and access to older log files. If the administrator has write access to the logs, it is possible to switch and purge logs. Clicking the record number will open a new window showing that log entry.

Figure 2.28 SmartPortal Traffic Log Page

...	Date	Time		Interface	...	.	.	..	Rule...	Service	Sou...	Destination	Info
27	9Jun2005	15:27:39		daemon	vixen								sys_message: ins
28	9Jun2005	15:27:44		eth1c0	vixen			udp	Clean Up	nbname	goliath.te	10.40.15.127	
29	9Jun2005	15:27:50			vixen								StormAgentName:
30	9Jun2005	15:27:50		eth1c0	vixen			tcp	Manage ...	http	admin_pc	vixen	service_id: http
31	9Jun2005	15:27:52		eth1c0	vixen			udp	Clean Up	nbname	bambi.te	10.40.15.127	
32	9Jun2005	15:27:53		eth1c0	vixen			udp	Clean Up	nbdatagram	goliath.te	10.40.15.127	
33	9Jun2005	15:27:54		eth1c0	vixen			udp	Clean Up	rip	contra.te:	10.40.15.127	
34	9Jun2005	15:28:19		eth1c0	vixen			tcp	Manage ...	ssh_version_:	admin_pc	vixen	service_id: ssh_v
35	9Jun2005	15:28:21		eth1c0	vixen			tcp		1932	vixen	admin_pc	TCP packet out of
36	9Jun2005	15:28:25		eth1c0	vixen			udp		domain-udp	vixen	10.40.14.2	session_id: 33920
37	9Jun2005	15:28:25		eth1c0	vixen			udp		domain-udp	vixen	10.40.14.2	session_id: 33921
38	9Jun2005	15:28:25		eth1c0	vixen			udp		domain-udp	vixen	10.40.14.2	
39	9Jun2005	15:28:25		eth1c0	vixen			udp		domain-udp	vixen	10.40.14.2	
40	9Jun2005	15:28:56		eth1c0	vixen			udp	Clean Up	rip	contra.te:	10.40.15.127	
41	9Jun2005	15:29:17		eth1c0	vixen			udp	Clean Up	nbname	goliath.te	10.40.15.127	
42	9Jun2005	15:29:25		eth1c0	vixen			tcp		1932	vixen	admin_pc	TCP packet out of
43	9Jun2005	15:29:26		eth1c0	vixen			tcp		FW1_ica_serv	vixen	sleigh	service_id: FW1_ic

The **Policy and Objects** page provides a view of the *Security* rulebase. Figure 2.29 shows the SmartPortal view of the policy that was created in SmartDashboard.

Figure 2.29 SmartPortal Policy View

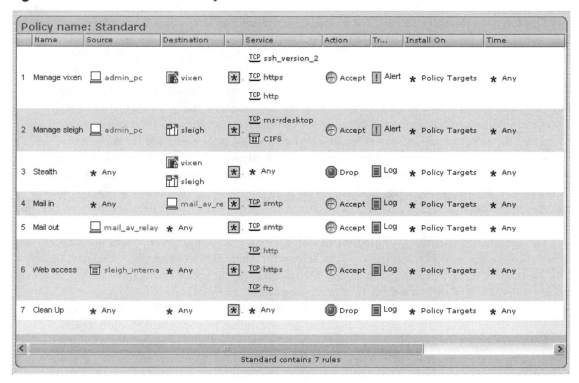

If you have multiple policy packages, you can view the security rulebase from these packages, too.

There are a number of pages for viewing objects: Network Objects, Services, Users, and Time objects. The views are equivalent to the Objects List view in SmartDashboard. A simple Filter on object name can be used to narrow down the list.

Summary

SmartDashboard provides an extremely powerful interface for configuring your Check Point installation—from the traditional firewall gateways, through VPN gateways, to the new Connectra and Interspect devices. It effectively provides a single management interface for your entire Check Point security infrastructure.

The interface, though complex, can be broken down into separate panes. Each provides different functionality and views of your configuration, and you can choose which panes are visible. This allows you to tailor the interface to suit the areas you need to work with and your preferred methods of accessing the settings.

The rulebase pane can be tailored to show just the policies and products you manage, again allowing simplification of the interface by hiding the functionality that you don't need to see. Conversely, when you have several different gateway products installed and therefore a number of different policies defined, these can be combined into a single policy package for the gateway.

The objects panes provide many different views onto your object database—with some experimentation you should be able to find a view ideal for your working style and requirements. Despite the ever-increasing range of object types available, these are broken down into different categories, and within each category, can be sorted and displayed so you see just the types that you are using.

The degree of fine-tuning allowed via the Global Properties windows increases in every software release, but the tree structure of the windows helps with navigation to the setting you need to adjust. The majority of the settings here can be left unchanged for most scenarios, so these pages can remain hidden away. We have outlined those that we do need to be aware of.

The NGX release introduces a range of new features to the interface that should be very helpful to administrators, making management and clear understanding of your configuration easier.

Your first security policy should be straightforward to define once you are familiar with the interface. Configuring a simple security rulebase and automatic NAT should have a typical Internet gateway up and running within minutes, or maybe an hour at the longest.

NGX begins to integrate management of Check Point Connectra and Interspect devices, continuing toward the goal of the SmartCenter being the single point of management for the whole network security infrastructure.

The new NGX SmartPortal Web interface provides a clientless management solution, enabling operator and managed customer access to view the status, logging, and configuration of a management server.

Chapter 3

Smart View Tracker

Solutions in this chapter:

- Tracker
- Log View
- Predefined Queries
- Custom Queries
- Active View
- Block Intruder
- Audit View
- Log Maintenance

☑ Summary

Introduction

Now that we have seen how to create our Check Point security infrastructure, it's time to see the traffic that is hitting our different components. SmartView Tracker enables the security administrator to visualize traffic that is passing by. What good is it to have a security policy if we are not able to see what is happening? The SmartView Tracker will be your daily friend—having the ability to parse through the logs is important to maintain and update your security policies.

Tracking users, connections, and administration through our logs is completely dependent on the gateway's configuration. To be able to audit rules, investigate misfeasors, or simply gather statistics, we need to enable logging for the items we care to examine. In some cases, we need minimal information about a particular connection. For example, if we are auditing a rule, we may need only to log it so that we can see the gateway's action for that connection. In other instances, we may desire more thorough data. If we need to audit HTTP requests, we need to not only log, but *Audit* the connections to receive more data.

In this chapter, we will discuss the need for tracking and walk through a few configuration examples. After reading this material, you should be able to parse through your firewall logs and easily find the data you are seeking.

Tracker

In our Check Point gateways, we, as administrators, have a very robust tool that allows us to customize our product so that we are running an optimal configuration. In this light, we can review our output (logs) and verify that it is running how we think it is. Also, it never hurts for an administrator to review changes to the security policy. Moreover, it is not considered a bad practice to take in and just watch traffic every once in a while. SmartView Tracker allows us to have all these tools and more. As a result, SmartView Tracker gives us the ability to do general oversight of our firewall, both over the administrative aspect as well as the security policy.

Depending on your configuration for SmartCenter or a Log Server, you can connect to one of them and have an immediate view of how your firewall is behaving. In larger networks, it may be helpful to use a distributed implementation that includes a separate log server. Also the quantity of traffic you are logging may have an impact on the configuration. You can also log locally to the firewall module. In any case, SmartView Tracker connects to either the Log Server or the SmartCenter Server in order to generate the views we use.

Once we open SmartView Tracker, we see that there are several frames to view and tabs from which to choose. The tabs let us choose between logged connection data, current connection data, and audit log data. The default view is the **Log** view. We will learn more about these views, how to navigate about SmartView Tracker, and how to generate custom views.

SmartView Tracker opens the current log file (*fw.log*) by default, but we can open an older saved log file if we want to parse through that to identify older connections. To do this, we click **File | Open** and choose the log file we want to examine. SmartView Tracker saves log files with a date/time format, so each file should be easily identifiable. Though this is the default naming convention, we can reconfigure this if so desired.

Log View

In the standard **Log** view, we see connection attempts that have reached our firewall. These attempts tell us many things about how the firewall is behaving. They may let us know that we are under attack if we see many similar attempts dropped or rejected. They may relay that we have routing problems or other networking issues if we see connection attempts that seem illogical. Also, these records may indicate a misconfiguration if we see traffic that either is passing but should not be permitted, or traffic that is not passing but should be allowed.

In the **Log** view, we have three panes. Right away, we can see that our connection details are viewable on the right-hand side, the *Records* pane. A second pane on the right side is the *Query Properties* pane. To display this pane, click **View | Query Properties** from the menu. When we do this, the *Query Properties* are viewable above the records in the top-right pane (which is now split between the *Records* and *Query Properties* panes). These properties define what appears in the *Records* pane by inserting filter data or checking/unchecking the **Show** box. Third, on the left side of the **Log** view window, is the *Query Tree* pane.

As we can see within the *Query Tree* pane on the left-hand side there is one root level *Log Queries* tree and two branches, the *Predefined* and *Custom* branches. The leaves from these branches identify saved queries. When we activate a particular query, these queries change the parameters for the *Records* pane. SmartView Tracker prepopulates many predefined queries for us. However, we do not see any custom queries because we must define them ourselves. A closer look at the prepopulated queries shows that many of them are labeled according to Check Point product names. Later, we will leverage this set of queries to create custom queries.

When in **Log** view, SmartView Tracker presents us with a special toolbar containing many swift tools. Looking at Figure 3.1, we can see the toolbar directly over the *Query Properties* pane.

Figure 3.1 SmartView Tracker Log Tab

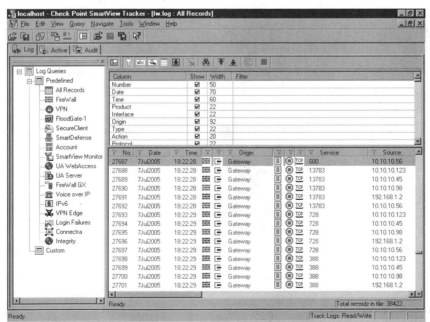

Here we briefly explain these buttons and their use. We will begin on the far left and make our way toward the right end.

- **Show or Hide Query Properties**   Toggling this button simply displays or removes the *Query Properties* pane from the current view. It is not necessary to have this showing, though it is greatly helpful when defining a customized view.

- **Apply Filter**   When enabled (default setting) a query is applied to the logs immediately. If we toggle this button, the query set is held in memory, but not applied to the current records. If this is off when we define a query, we simply click this button to apply the filter to the records.

- **Resolve IP**   By default, SmartView Tracker will display records with hostnames if possible. As this takes time, we can disable this setting so that we see only IP addresses of the source and destination involved in each record. On the other hand, if we employ a filter and want to see hostnames to simplify reading our log data, we can toggle this button to do so.

- **Resolve Services**   By default, SmartView Tracker will display records with any associated *Service* name such as *Telnet* for TCP port 23, *SMTP* for TCP port 25, and *Domain* for port UDP 53.

- **Show Null Matches**   This button tells the SmartView Tracker to display records that do not have the opportunity to match the current filter; in other words, records that are not necessarily included or excluded by the current filter. For example, if we define a query to include only records where the **Action** is equal to **Drop**, control records are **Null** matches since they do not have an **Action** entry.

- **AutoScroll**   Clicking this button tells the SmartView Tracker to continually update the view with the newest records. Essentially, it enables a pseudo-real-time view where you see the records as they reach the log server.

- **Clear All Filters**   If you have applied a filter, you can click on this button to clear all the filters and return to viewing all records.

- **Find in All Columns**   This button enables the standard string query against all the fields in each record.

- **Go to Top**   Clicking this button takes our view to the very first log entry. Again, be mindful that it takes us to the first record in the current view, not the first record in the log file.

- **Go to Bottom**   Clicking this button takes our view to the very last log entry. Not the very last record in the log file, but the last record in our current view.

- **Get Number of Filtered Records**   Clicking this button will tell us the total number of records returned out of the total number of log records. This button is available only if we define a filter against the current query (view).

- **Abort**   If there is a query or filter running and we want to end it prematurely, we can click this button to stop the action.

We can see that there are many other items in the **Log** tab view. We will cover these items more thoroughly in later sections of this chapter.

Active

The **Active** tab shows us the current open connections on the firewall. This allows us a bird's-eye view of all that is happening on a system. However, there is some performance cost, especially if you have a busy gateway. We will discuss some of the aspects of the **Active** windows and some of the operations we can execute from within this view.

Figure 3.2 displays the **Active** window with emphasis on some of the more important columns.

Figure 3.2 SmartView Tracker Active View

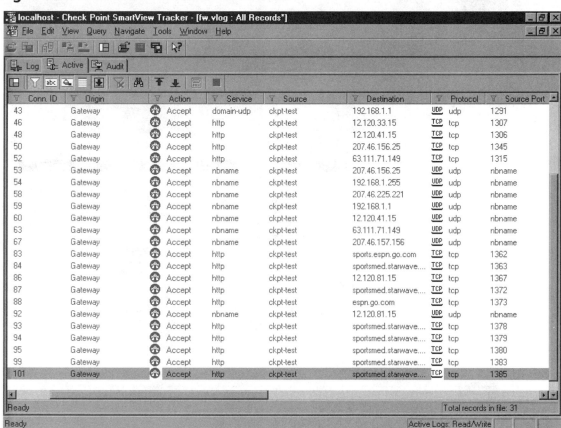

We see that this window adds a **Connection ID** column to the view we don't normally see in the **Log** view. As well, we see that the other fields are very similar to what we find in the **Log** tab of SmartView Tracker. Also, the **Active** tab has the *Query Properties* and *Query Tree* panes. They are not shown in Figure 3.2 to maximize the view of the records. SmartView Tracker displays the *Query Tree* by default, though the *Query Properties* pane is hidden by default. Just as with the **Log** tab, we have the ability to filter the records and save the results as custom queries.

Audit

The **Audit** tab view allows us to see what has been happening with respect to administration on the firewall and modifications to the firewall's security policy. We see in Figure 3.3 that the visual representation is very similar to that of the **Log** and **Active** tabs. Though the SmartView Tracker does not display the *Query Properties* pane by default, it is possible to view this pane by clicking the **Show or hide Query Properties** button on the toolbar.

Figure 3.3 SmartView Tracker Audit View

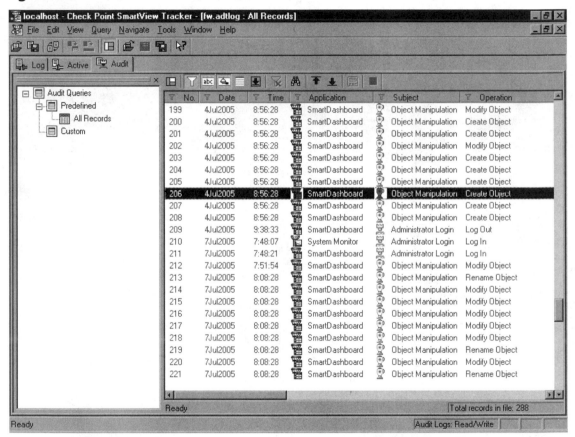

In the *Records* pane, we can see some of the entries that the system logs. In Figure 3.3, there are *Rename Object*, *Modify Object*, *Create Object*, *Log In*, and *Log Out* entries. These entries detail, to some degree, values administrators have changed in the security policy. And once more, we see that the toolbar is available for our use, but several of the buttons will not have an impact on some of the records.

Just as in the other tabs, we are able to create custom queries by modifying the predefined queries for our audit records. Consider if we wanted to know the last administrator to change the firewall policy and push it to the enforcement modules. This tab allows us the ability to filter the current records so that we can see only *Log In* operations. Also, we could filter to see the *Install Policy* records and correlate the two to identify who last pushed to policy. This activity allows us to collect details about a possible incident, or just clarify why certain changes have been made to the policy.

Predefined Queries

As we have seen in the different tabs, SmartView Tracker has numerous *Predefined Queries* for our use. These queries, primarily in the **Log** tab, filter the record entries based on product type. To view the different queries, we can double-click on the name and then view the properties in the *Query Properties* pane. Let's take a look at the **Firewall** predefined query shown in Figure 3.4.

Figure 3.4 Firewall Predefined Query

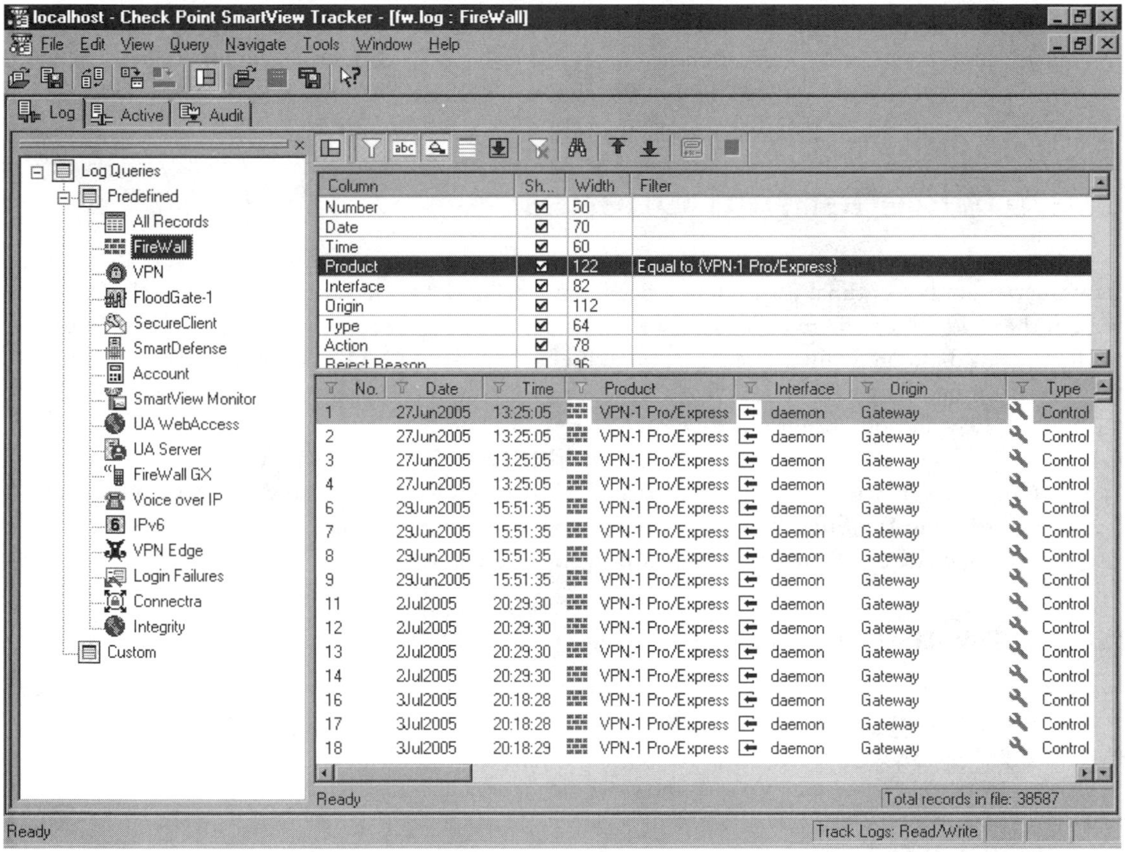

We need to take a careful look at the result of invoking the **Firewall** predefined query. For starters, we see in the *Query Properties* pane that the **Product** row has been automatically seeded with the **Filter** value *Equal to {VPN-1 Pro/Express}*. If desired, we are able to enter multiple values for each filter.

In addition, we see that several of the first columns have a check in the **Sh…** (Show) box. Each column with this setting enabled will appear in the *Records* pane. Further note that the **Column** column defines the layout of the *Records* pane (the order of the columns from left to right).

To adjust column width SmartView Tracker provides us a few options. First, as with many products, we may click-and-drag the edge of any column in the *Records* or *Query Properties* pane and adjust the width as appropriate. The *Query Properties* pane gives us another means to adjust a column's width within the *Records* pane. All we need to do is modify the value in the **Width** column for each heading we want to adjust in the *Records* pane. For instance, if we want to modify the number of characters we wish to see in the **Product** column of the *Records* pane (as highlighted in Figure 3.4), then we simply change the current value of **122** to a number that better suits our needs.

Now let's focus on the **Product** column in the *Records* pane. We see that SmartView Tracker has colored green the filter image on the left of the text. This particular imagery indicates that we have applied a filter to this column. We can enable multiple filters at the same time on numerous columns. Each column we apply a filter to will also have a green filter image.

In looking at this one query, we can see that it just separates the records by product as covered before. So these predefined queries are not the end all to our needs. We cannot invoke one or two predefined queries and become satisfied in the results. If we look to invoke a query at all, there must be a set of records we are looking for. For this reason, these predefined queries are, in essence, a launching pad for further detailed custom queries, as we will learn later.

Use for Predefined Queries

Now that we have seen what a predefined query looks like, let's talk about what we use it for. Though these queries are not optimal for finding a needle in a haystack, it will separate the haystacks from one another and tell us where to look. If we have a SmartCenter Server that manages many different products, then these predefined queries become useful in an immediate manner. We don't need to try to query millions of records for what we want to see when we can invoke a predefined query and immediately and significantly reduce our query scope.

Using the previous example, we could invoke the **Firewall** predefined query if we wish to begin finding traffic that may match a rule number. In this manner, we immediately weed out all records that do not relate to the firewall security policy. From this point, we can further define filters that sift through a smaller set of records, which in turn delivers faster results.

Adding Custom Queries

Since we have invoked a predefined query we are now able to define and save a custom query that better suits our needs. Although we do not necessarily need to invoke any predefined query to save a custom query, choosing one of these queries offers us a great start.

When we create these custom queries, we will see them populate the *Custom* branch of the *Query Tree* pane. SmartView Tracker automatically populates this particular branch with our saved custom queries. As well, Check Point writes the custom queries to a file on the local drive of the PC hosting the management console. SmartView Tracker saves these files with an *##.vd* filename where ## represents the next iteration in numerical order. For instance, if we already have a file named *19.vd*, then SmartView Tracker will save the next custom query as *20.vd*. We can find these files (in a default installation of SmartConsole) in the *\Program Files\CheckPoint\SmartConsole\R60\Program* directory.

It is important to note that these files exist only on the PC hosting the management console we use to view and save the queries. In order for us to use these queries on another machine, we must copy the *##.vd* files from one host to another. Another good bit of information is that SmartView Tracker automatically loads the file named *0.vd* when we first launch the application. So, if you want to change the default view in SmartView Tracker, all you need to do is save the current *0.vd* file to a backup copy and rename the desired default query to *0.vd*.

As we create and save our custom queries within SmartView Tracker, we will find this task both incredibly useful and less intimidating. Remember that a query is just a single filter or a set of compound filters. In this sense, all we need to do to define a custom query is apply different filters to the current *Records* pane, then save the query with a descriptive name.

Let's cover some simple steps that we can take to create a new custom query. First, open an existing query by following these steps:

- Double-click on a predefined (or existing custom query) query.

- Modify the filters as necessary.

- Save the new set of filters as a new custom query.

- Next, create a new query from the **All Records** (default) view. This query will enable you to do the following:

    - Modify the filters as desired.

    - Save the new set of filters as a new custom query.

Applying Filters

We've talked about filters and queries, but have yet to discuss how to implement a filter and save the settings as a query. Thanks to Check Point's easy-to-use GUI, we can effortlessly apply filters to the current records in SmartView Tracker. As usual, Check Point provides us with more than one way to easily implement such controls. As is always the case, both means deliver identical results.

The first way we are able to filter traffic is by utilizing the *Query Properties* pane. In this, we are able to right-click on the **Filter** column to bring up a menu. When we bring up the menu, the only option available (unless there are already filters applied to this attribute) is the **Edit Filter** option. Choose this and SmartView Tracker launches another window so that we can define the parameters for our filter. Figure 3.5 shows us what we see when we invoke a filter for the **Action** option.

Figure 3.5 Action Filter Options

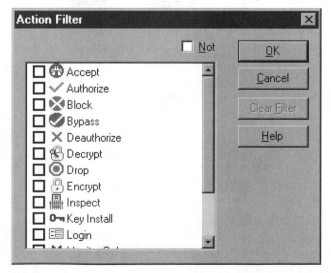

We can choose one or many filter options in this window and click **OK** to save the settings. This change will cause the settings we choose to show up in the *Query Properties* windows just as we saw with the **Firewall** predefined query.

The other method we use to implement filters is to right-click on any record (in the column you wish to filter) or the column header in the *Records* pane and choose **Edit Filter**. This action results in the same window as shown in Figure 3.5. From here, again we can choose which parameters to filter, and click **OK**.

Once more, we may add as many filters as we wish to as many columns (options) as necessary to achieve our desired result. Once we get to the point where our filters are optimal, we can save the set of filters as a custom query. To do so, all we need to do is click **Query | Save As...** from the File menu and type a name in the pop-up window. From there, we may need to expand the **Custom** queries tree to see our new entry, but we will be able to directly select this entry from this point forward to receive the current filtered view.

Custom Queries

Now that we have a better feel for what a custom query is and how to create one, let's dive deeper into the subject. We will look at some of the options we have to track records and how to implement these options. Also, we will cover some nuances with how SmartView Tracker keeps tabs on rules.

Matching Rule Filter

In SmartView Tracker, Check Point has given us the ability to investigate desired traffic by filtering log entries based on a certain rule. In some sense, this is a bit misleading because there are two ways that SmartView Tracker identifies a rule and then filters the records to show the matching log entries. These two methods are filtering by *Current Rule Number* or filtering by *Rule UID*.

The *Current Rule Number* ties the rule to the active security policy and associates it with its place within that policy. This value is dynamic in that it may change from one policy to another or even within the same policy. In this sense, when you add or delete a rule from the security policy, all the rule numbers below the removed rule change. This will track those changes and filter for the records that are associated with the rule number you submit as a filtering parameter.

On the other hand, the *Rule UID* is a great tool that overcomes rule number changes. Unlike the dynamic nature of the *Current Rule Number*, the *Rule UID* is static and does not change across policies. Each rule has a unique UID, and as such, tracking by this field will return the records no matter what the current rule number is for the desired rule. This filter proves beneficial after a change has been made to the policy. Since a rule may have a different rule number, filtering for *Current Rule Number* may return only records logged since the last policy push. If you truly want to see all the records for this rule, you can use the *Rule UID* filter so that SmartView Tracker will ignore any policy changes.

To invoke either of these filters, right-click any rule and choose the appropriate option. To filter based on the *Current Rule Number,* choose **Follow rule number: <number>**. Otherwise, choose **Follow rule: <rule name>** to filter for *Rule UID*.

Viewing the Matching Rule

Now that we've filtered for a rule in our security policy, SmartView Tracker allows us to actually view the rule in context with the remainder of the security policy. If we right-click a record, we can choose **View rule in SmartDashboard** from the menu and SmartView Tracker will launch a read-only window for SmartDashboard and highlight the current rule. SmartDashboard will even open with the last revision this rule is in if you have revision control enabled.

Viewing Log Records from SmartDashboard

Just as we can go from SmartView Tracker to SmartDashboard, we can also invoke the converse transition. If we are in SmartDashboard, we can simply right-click the **NO** (rule number) column for any give rule. The menu will allow us to choose **View rule logs in SmartView Tracker**. Upon doing so, the *Log* tab will open and apply an automatic filter for this *Current Rule Number*.

Also, we are able to copy the *Rule UID* from the SmartDashboard and paste it into a filter ourselves. In this manner we bypass any policy changes and pull all the records for this unique rule. We simply open SmartView Tracker and choose to edit the *Rule UID* **Filter** properties in the *Query Properties* pane.

Active View

With the **Active** view, SmartView Tracker gives us the ability to examine open connections just as we would examine log records of connections. Essentially, if we are auto scrolling through the log records we are just looking at these active records in a different manner. Each of these connections is also logging to the standard *fw.log* file.

Though there is a nice feature to **Active** mode **Block Intruder** (discussed later), there is also a performance penalty, as we mentioned earlier. Since the gateway must constantly update the table and forward the results to the SmartCenter Server, valuable resources are being used for this operation instead of being available for the firewall operations. However, utilizing the **Active** mode to catch or deter attackers may negate any penalty performance.

Live Connections

With this view, we see connections as they are formed and watch them disappear when they are torn down. The primary benefit here is that if we suspect an attack from a host or against an internal service, we can employ queries and filters to display only what we want to see. We can further examine these results to determine whether or not the attack is real.

If we conclude that an active attack is taking place, we can invoke a **Block Intruder** operation and block the source and destination or source, destination, and service triple. In essence, we want to block this connection and all identical subsequent requests. Although this command does not prevent the host/s from sending the message to the gateway, it does prevent the connection from being allowed and taking up extended resources on the gateway.

Custom Commands

SmartView Tracker allows us to use some utilities like *ping* and *nslookup* from within our views. We simply can right-click any of the records, and a list of commands appears at the bottom of the menu. We can choose any of these, and the gateway passes the appropriate parameters to complete the command.

To further make these tools usable, SmartView Tracker lets us define our own command line tools. These tools are all run from the local machine (the one SmartView Tracker is running on), so it is imperative you consider path variables and platforms when configuring these commands. In other words, if you are going to add a custom command, be sure that all the administrators for this SmartCenter Server have the same executable file in the same absolute path on the host they use to connect. Otherwise, some of the tools you create may not work as thought, or they may cause undesirable results.

To configure a custom tool, just click the **Tools | Custom Commands** option from the File menu. From here, it is a few easy steps to complete the configuration of the command. Enter the values as defined in the **Add New Command** window and then click **OK**. There are limited options as far as automated parameters are concerned, but you can enter manual parameters if necessary. Also, you can use the current commands as a model to correctly configure your own custom command.

Following a Source or Destination

SmartView Tracker has a convenient method to extend a source or destination filter so that we can quickly parse the logs for the desired data. If you are examining the logs and see a suspect source or destination, you can select the record, right-click, and choose either **Follow source: <source name/ip>** or **Follow destination: <destination name/ip>**. In this way, you do not have to make a note of the source or destination address (if it is foreign to you). Instead, you can take advantage of this shortcut method and quickly see the records without much clicking or typing. For obvious reasons, this filter is available only in the **Log** and **Active** views.

Block Intruder

SmartView Tracker gives us the ability to cease an active connection from a suspected intruder. We do so by identifying this suspect connection either in our **Log** *Records* pane or in the **Active** *Records* pane. To kill the connection we must utilize the **Active** tab. Once in the view, select the connection record and select **Tools | Block Intruder** from the File menu. This action causes the **Block Intruder** window to open (see Figure 3.6). From this point we need to configure some parameters that define our quarantine of the connection.

Figure 3.6 Block Intruder Window

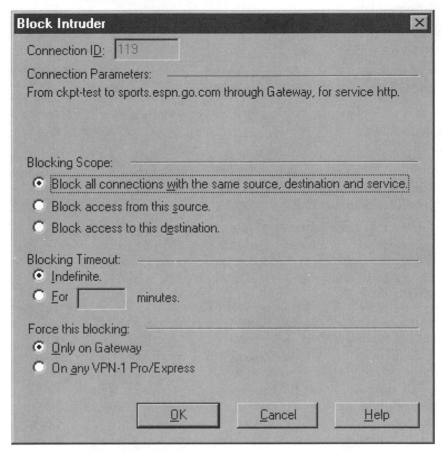

In the **Block Intruder** window shown in Figure 3.6, we see several fields. In the following list, we briefly describe each field and relate how each affects the gateway's behavior:

- **Blocking Scope** This field blocks all connections with the same source, destination, and service. This setting tells the gateway to block only connections that are exactly like the current connection. For instance, it will block an HTTP request from 192.168.1.50 to our server 10.10.1.10. However, it will not block an HTTP request from 192.168.1.50 to our other server 10.10.1.11.

- **Block access from this source** This option tells the firewall to deny any connection attempts from the source in this connection. In this way, any requests for any service to any destination inside our network coming from this one single source will not succeed.

- **Block access to this destination** Similar to the block source, but with the destination address. The gateway will drop any traffic requesting access to this destination, regardless of the source or service.

- **Blocking Timeout**   This setting defines the period of time that we would like to block such connections.

- **Indefinite**   This setting will block access until you manually remove the blocking settings.

- **For… minutes**   This setting sets a time limit for blocking. The gateway will allow these blocked connections when the time period expires.

- **Force this blocking**   This option defines on which gateways we wish to block the defined connection. We are able to limit the action to one gateway or enable the action across all our gateways.

- **Only on…**   This setting allows us to define which firewall module participates in the blocking action. In this way, we do not have to enforce the action on modules that will not see the connection attempts.

- **On any VPN-1 & Firewall-1 Module**   This setting enforces blocking on all modules in our architecture. One important concept is that they must be defined within the SmartCenter Server. In cases where your Log Server is not the same as your SmartCenter Server, the block will occur on all modules known to your Log Server.

Once we enable blocking, we can disable blocking manually by choosing **Tools | Clear Blocking** from the File menu. In some cases where items are questionable and we block the connection prematurely, this option comes in very handy in order to quickly restore someone's connectivity.

When we utilize SmartView Tracker to block a connection, there are several actions the gateway invokes to protect us from the potential attack. In addition, there are several ways for us to monitor our blocking rules and modify them if we so choose.

For starters, each time we manually block an intruder in SmartView Tracker, the gateway adds an entry to its *sam_blocked_ips* database. We can view these entries with the *fw tab* command line utility. As an example, let's say we have just blocked all connections from source 192.168.69.201 for an indefinite time period. Let's see what the Suspicious Activity Monitoring (SAM) database now looks like. We'll look at both the *sam_requests* table and the *sam_blocked_ips* table.

```
C:\>fw tab -t sam_requests
localhost:
-------- sam_requests --------
dynamic, id 8140, attributes: keep, expires never, limit 25000,
hashsize 512, kb
uf 6
<c0a845c9, 00000000, c0a84597, 00000050, 00000006; 00000008,
00010001, ffffffff,
  ffffffff, 0000001a, 00000000>
<c0a845c9, 00000000, 00000000, 00000000, 00000000; 00000008,
00010001, ffffffff,
  00000000, 0000001d, 00000000>
```

```
C:\>fw tab -t sam_blocked_ips
localhost:
-------- sam_blocked_ips --------
dynamic, id 8141, attributes: keep, limit 25000, hashsize 512
<c0a84597; 00000000, 00000000, 00000000, 00000000, 00000000,
00000000, 00000000,
  00000001, 00000000>
<c0a845c9; 00000001, 00000000, 00000000, 00000000, 00000000,
00000000, 00000000,
  00000001, 00000000>
```

As usual, our gateway dumps the output in hex format. Once we convert some of the values to decimal, we can match it with the address we enforced via SmartView Tracker (192.168.69.201). In the *sam_requests* table, we see two entries. The first field shows the blocked IP address. Since we only cared about blocking all connections from this host, some of the other fields are all zeros (all zeros in the first five fields indicate ANY). The rest of the fields are as follows: blocked source port #; blocked destination IP; blocked destination port #; IP protocol; log option; action option; source netmask; destination netmask; filtered packets counter; time left/total time. So, now we can verify that our settings (as we enforced via the GUI) are correctly blocking the connections we want to reject. When we translate the entries to decimal, they look like this.

```
<192.168.69.201; 0; 192.18.69.151; 80; 6; 8; inhibit or drop;

255.255.255.255; 255.255.255.255; 26; 0>
<192.168.69.201; 0; 0; 0; 0; 8; inhibit or drop; 255.255.255.255;

0.0.0.0; 29; 0>
```

After converting to decimal, we easily understand that the first entry specifically blocks access from the intruder source to our web server on port 80. The second rule follows blocking the source for all wildcard matches (ANY) for the destination/port pair. Now that we understand what our requests look like, we may be able to further understand what the *sam_blocked_ips* table shows us. Basically, this table tells us the number of requests for each block IP and its associated type of protocol filter. Knowing the hex conversion to decimal, we can now distinguish that the second entry says that there is one request to block the source IP 192.168.69.201.

To remove entries from the command line, all we need to do is invoke the *fw sam −D* command. This command removes all the current suspicious activity monitoring rules currently in the database. Of course, you may also remove single entries by applying additional parameters to the *fw sam* command (further discussion on this topic is not covered in this chapter).

Not only can these command line utilities help us understand more about our blocking actions, but we can also use GUI tools. Using SmartView Monitor, we can view the currently applied blocking rules, delete them individually or all together, and receive alerts when one of our blocked intruders attempts to make a connection. To do this, we need to open SmartView Monitor (from within SmartView Tracker, click **Window | SmartView Monitor**). Once we are in the monitor GUI, we open **Tools | Suspicious Activity Rules** to view the entries. When the window opens, we may need to select our firewall from the **Show on:** drop-down list or select **Show on all VPN-1 & Firewall-1** radio button. Figure 3.7 shows us what we should see when we activate a blocking rule.

Figure 3.7 Enforced Suspicious Activity Rules Window

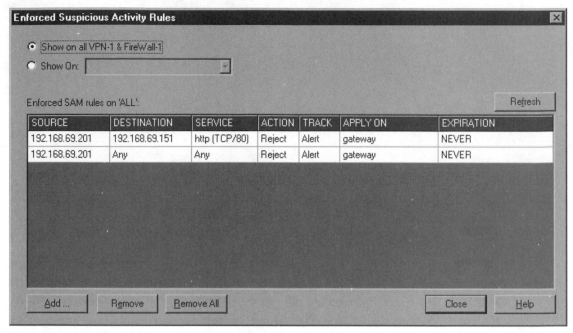

Right off the bat we notice that these rules resemble the output from the *fw tab –t sam_requests* command line utility. In order to remove any of the rules from the SAM database, all we need to do is highlight the rule and click the **Remove** button. As well, we may remove all the current rules by clicking **Remove All**. When we have SmartView Monitor open and an attacker attempts to bypass the firewall, the **Alerts** window pops up and notifies us about it and provides connection details. We see such a screen in Figure 3.8.

Figure 3.8 Alerts Window for Suspicious Activity Rule Violations

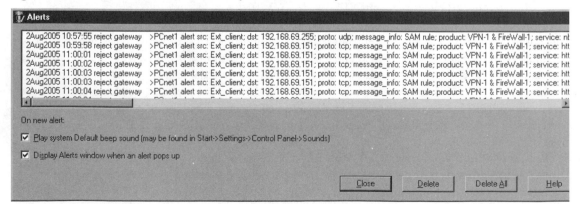

The entries in the **Alerts** windows look very similar to log messages. They provide information about the source, destination, protocol, services, and more. This window will appear only if you currently have the SmartView Monitor open and have not disabled the **Alerts** pop-ups. In this window, we are also able to remove individual messages or all the messages by clicking the appropriate button.

Audit View

What is most helpful in audit view is its accountability. We have all been in situations where we don't remember changing the policy and something is now being blocked. In this case, after we restore connectivity, we can review the **Audit** records to determine what happened and who did it.

Now let's take a peek in the **Audit** *Records* pane to see exactly what is there. When we double-click on an entry, we have a new window with the record's details. Figure 3.9 shows us these details after clicking on the **More Columns** option at the top right.

Figure 3.9 Install Policy Record Details

Record Details	
△ Previous ▽ Next ▣ Copy ▦ Less Columns	
Number	257
Date	7Jul2005
Time	14:28:19
Origin	Gateway (192.168.99.1)
Application	SmartDashboard
Subject	Policy Installation
Operation	Install Policy
Status	Success
Type	Log
Object Table	applications
Object Type	firewall_application
Performed On	Gateway
Changes	
Administrator	fwadmin
Client	ckpt-test
Uid	{A64D1947-6071-48FD-93B2-02A29E98B8DC}
Operation Number	7
General Information	Security Policy : Standard

We can see that this record contains a significant amount of information. First, it tells us exactly when the administrator installed the policy on the gateway. Also of importance is the identity of this administrator, in our case "fwadmin." Further, the details include the host from which our administrator installed the policy. In this case, the SmartView Tracker resolves the hostname to "ckpt-test." If the address did not resolve, we would see an IP address. Also we could disable name resolution and receive the same effect. Just as SmartDashboard assigns a UID to each rule when we create it, SmartDashboard does the same assignment for our users. Any user defined within SmartCenter Server possesses a unique ID. In short, these details provide valuable information for us to follow up on if we are investigating particular changes or policy installations.

As well as policy modifications and installations, the **Audit** tab records many other operations. These options then have other filtering options, so we are able to drill down and reveal only those actions we wish to display. Just as in the **Log** records, we are able to create custom queries and store them for later use. These records provide an excellent means to recreate suspicious management events.

Log Maintenance

The volume of traffic your firewall processes necessitates your needs for log maintenance. If your organization hosts many public services or you have a ton of outbound traffic, you may need to pay closer attention to your logs than if you have a small office or home office network.

Check Point provides an array of tools so that we can manage our logs responsibly. It is imperative that we have a comprehensive rotation and archive plan in place, especially if our organizational policy defines log retention parameters. SmartView Tracker contains several options that let us contribute to automated log maintenance. However, some of our automated log management settings are configured using SmartDashboard.

One key point is that if we are utilizing log servers and the firewall module cannot communicate with the log server, the firewall module stores the logs locally. When the module restores communications with the log server, all new records are sent to the log server. However, the records that were stored locally remain on the module, and we must utilize SmartView Tracker's **Tools | Remote Files Management** tool in order to retrieve the records from the module.

Check Point's Eventia Reporting Server can automatically import logs for advanced reporting capability. However, if we want to use our own reporting applications, we can export log files into ASCII text format or a format compatible with Oracle databases.

If your log server or firewall module (if logging locally) does not possess significant disk space, you can employ cyclical logging that removes old logs when disk space is low. In this way, the logging facility never ceases. However, you may lose unrecoverable connection records and audit data depending on the disk space available and how often log files are removed.

Daily Maintenance

Log rotation is a key aspect of log management. For one, we do not want our log files to grow to a size where they become unmanageable. Check Point automatically rotates log files when they reach 2GB (by default). We can configure this setting and the rotation schedule via the gateway's object properties page in SmartDashboard. To do this, we simply double-click our gateway object and select **Logs and Masters** from the left-hand pane. We can reveal additional settings by clicking on the + to expand the **Logs and Masters** subproperties.

There, we can define an automated log rotation schedule and a log file size limitation (other than the default 2GB). There are other options on this page as we see in Figure 3.10, but we reserve these details for another section in this book.

Figure 3.10 Gateway Log File Settings

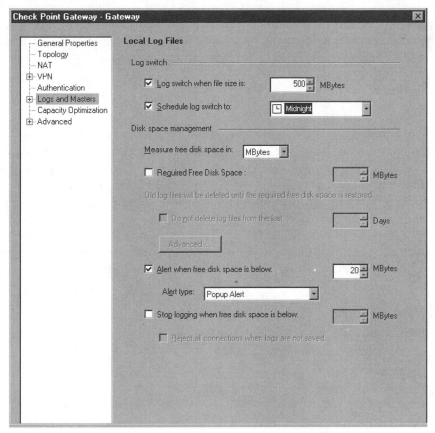

When we consider a rotation schedule, we need to mull over file size limitations as well. If we want to keep our log files under a specific size, we may incur this action prior to, say, a nightly log switch. This action results in having multiple log files for one single day of activity, as well as having multiple day entries within one single log file. However, if we want to keep only one day's log entries within one single log file we need to increase the log file size limitation so that the gateway does not truncate the log prematurely and start a new log file. This activity results in a separate log file for each day. In the event that our log file exceeds the prior maximum defined size and we have a scheduled nightly log rotation, SmartView tracker still executes the log switch at the predetermined time. The end result here is that we may have multiple log files for a single day, but we maintain our log day segregation since scheduled log rotations execute regardless of the current log file size (one file may be very larger while the other is significantly smaller).

To enable the rotation schedule and file size limitations, we need to place checks in the appropriate boxes under the gateway's object properties. For nightly rotation, place a check in the **Schedule log switch to:** and select **Midnight** from the drop-down box. To modify the file size, place a check in the **Log switch when file size is:** box and enter a value in MB for the file size. Remember that the default size is 2GB (2000MB).

After setting these options, we must audit our configuration following the first log rotation and possibly several subsequent log rotations. Getting the right setting may take a few days and include several configuration changes to the value of the log size. However, establishing a baseline for such procedures often requires a bit of tweaking. Once the process is defined and each of the values is set to our liking, there is really little to no further modification necessary.

Log Switch

In addition to an automated log rotation schedule, Firewall-1 gives us the ability to manually invoke a log change through SmartView Tracker. If we so desire, we simply click **File | Switch Active File**. This action saves the current log file (*fw.log*) with a default date/time filename format or a name you provide. After this, the gateway begins writing to a new *fw.log* file. You may invoke the manual log switch at any time and as often as you wish. For example, if you want to capture a defined timeframe within one log file, you can execute a manual log switch at the beginning of the time period, then again at the end of the time period. As long as your desired capture period either does not exceed your file size limitations or incur a nightly log rotation, all the traffic within the capture timeframe will exist in a single log file. In this sense, you may isolate suspect traffic into a single log file and perform further analysis without having to parse through a regular (dependent on your environment) size log file.

Summary

SmartView Tracker is a tool that helps us collect information about our traffic profiles, about our management changes, and shows us a glimpse of what is currently happening on our firewall. SmartView Tracker also lets us parse the log data by providing baseline queries, executing our custom queries, and applying our filter settings.

The most utilized tab in SmartView Tracker is the **Log** tab. Here we can invoke predefined queries or custom queries to quickly reveal records we are looking for. These records may be pseudo-real-time or latent records we are searching through for connection information.

The **Active** tab gives us insight into what connections currently exist on the firewall. One great aspect of this tool is that we can block intruders and deny the connections based on several options. The downside of this tab is that it carries a potential performance hit, but in the case of an active attack, it can prove invaluable.

The **Audit** tab reveals important accounting information regarding the management of our firewall. We can use this tool to investigate management incidents or audit our processes to verify we are meeting organizational policy guidelines and/or goals.

As firewall administrators, we need to realize the value of logs. In this sense, we need to learn how to configure our tools to produce meaningful data and then to massage these resultant logs to quickly divulge the information that we seek. We have now seen that SmartView Tracker is a comprehensive tool that not only displays our log files in an easily understood format, but provides to us sufficient tools to further manipulate the information into productive views.

Chapter 4

SmartDefense and Web Intelligence

Solutions in this chapter:

- **Network Security**
- **Application Intelligence**
- **Malicious Code**
- **Protocol Inspection**
- **DShield Storm Center**

☑ **Summary**

Introduction

Since the release of NG Feature Pack 2, Check Point has added a new component that can verify packet integrity up to and including layer 7 from the Open Systems Interconnection (OSI) model. To further concentrate on Web attacks, Check Point has separated Web Intelligence from SmartDefense and has made Web Intelligence a component of NG AI (R55W). SmartDefense and Web Intelligence are two distinct products, which are licensed separately. SmartDefense is licensed as an annual maintenance fee per number of VPN-1 Pro Gateways that your SmartCenter server manages. Having the proper SmartDefense license within the Check Point UserCenter enables you to download new SmartDefense and Web Intelligence signatures from the Check Point Web site.

SmartDefense and Web Intelligence combine to provide network, application, and Web server protection for your architecture. This chapter discusses both basic and advanced concepts for network security and reveal how Check Point's technologies supply relief for current threats. In addition, we walk through specific exercises to block particular threats.

Network Security

It is your job to provide administrative guidance over your network's perimeter, which means that you have control over your organization's gateway to the Internet. Let's begin by discussing some of the finer protections a NGX gateway offers and why it is recommended that you employ such protections.

In the most obvious sense, gateways (firewalls) are often the single device in your network path that handles every packet to and from the Internet. If the entire world were compliant and played by the rules, this would not be such a big deal. However, it has become commonplace for attackers to launch exploits remotely. In this sense, you now have become much more important in the grand scheme of protecting your information systems assets. After all, you manage the one device that handles all of the traffic. Congratulations, you have now graduated from firewall administrator to network security administrator. Check Point VPN-1 Pro Gateway (NGX) provides multiple technologies to protect your organization's assets in such a hostile environment.

Because most attackers seem to prefer to not be physically present while compromising your assets, you must consider how to introduce NGX's security controls to your network in such a manner that they will identify, prevent, notify, and possibly react to specific (or not) threats. We will refer to this group of actions as network security. In other words, exercising what it takes to reduce risk associated with permitting at least one host the ability to communicate with other hosts via some physical medium. Not to say that all communications through your gateway must interact with the Internet. There are certainly circumstances that do not call for Internet connectivity. Does the absence of the Internet make your network safer? Well, you could postulate that it certainly reduces risk in some sense. However, all risks are not associated with Internet hosts, so you cannot rest on the fact that your private network has no connectivity to the Internet. If you employ a VPN-1 Pro Gateway, there is obviously some reason you want to segregate one network (user population) from another. Your choosing to deploy this device is, in and of itself, risk mitigation for network security issues.

As we will cover later in this chapter, network security involves risk reduction for intercommunications between hosts (at several levels). This could be legitimate traffic between two good hosts, or legitimate traffic between a bad host and a good host, or any combination of good and bad hosts for that matter. The key here is that you either know what you are looking for or hope that something (bad) sticks out like a sore thumb. Network security may or may not be a legitimate science, but it is definitely an exercise in trial and error. The bad guys are turning out new threats faster than the good guys are protecting themselves against the known threats. Unfortunately, this fact implies that networks remain vulnerable to the unknown threats since most technologies rely on signature-based detection. The fact that worms and viruses continue to propagate through networks seems to adequately confirm this assertion.

To further define the scope of network security relevant to your VPN-1 Pro Gateway, you must consider the procedural aspect of sending information from one host to another over some type of network medium. This includes each host's network interfaces; hubs and/or switches, routers, firewalls, proxy servers, and any other device that helps packets get to their destination. Network security also encompasses devices that do not necessarily contribute to packet transfer (passive devices), but monitor the traffic on the network. A good example of this type of device is an Intrusion Detection System (IDS). Engaging security controls on any of theses devices will help reduce the possibility of a successful attack. IDS' is installed on your network to help you become aware of possible attacks. Moreover, your NGX gateway has the ability to intervene during an active attack. It can deny a connection, send reset packets to both hosts, or apply other means to halt the conversation. As you can see, network security comprises a broad spectrum of services, devices, and processes to provide protective measures.

In short, network security introduces solutions into your architecture that reduces the opportunity for successful attacks, notifies you of active attacks (successful or not), and diminishes the effects of a successful attack. A NGX solution aims to prevent or reduce the harm done by attacks against confidentiality, integrity, and availability associated with your hosts and the services they offer. With one product, Check Point can license many technologies to provide a wide range of network protections. Not only does your Check Point gateway possess access control capability, it can detect and prevent network attacks trying to traverse your gateway.

Threats

In today's technologically advanced society, there are many threats you must deal with when your duties include protecting your network. Although there may be more than one definition of a threat, we will use this term to convey the possibility that an attacker will successfully carry out an exploit against one of your assets. So how do you go about identifying threats and enacting measures to mitigate them, or in some cases accept them? The answer to this question is risk management; a simple term (though not the most simple process) that relates to procedures identifying risk, applying cost factors for these risks to your assets, and finally accepting the risk or introducing a solution to reduce the risk.

In recent history, attackers have predominantly shifted the focus of their attacks from network attacks to application layer exploits (more on the network model later). More to the point, miscreants often target a few application groups because of the global accessibility of these services. Two of these services—Hypertext Transfer Protocol (HTTP [default port 80]) and Structured Query Language (SQL) [default port 1521])—are widely deployed together to facilitate dynamic Web content. Because of the proliferation of servers available, and the lack of administration in some cases, attackers smell blood with regard to these services and attack when they discover a victim.

What kinds of threats exist? The answer to this question differs for each network. However, there are specific classes of threats that everyone must deal with. The following sections discuss some threat vectors and how you can configure your NGX gateway to prevent them. This will help you understand what to look for and how to utilize your Check Point technologies to locate it.

Structured Threats

Although the term may seem sophisticated, a *structured threat* is simply a threat an attacker targets to a certain asset because of a specific interest the attacker has in successfully exploiting that asset. In other words, some script-kiddie blindly launching a "sploit" to a range of addresses does not exactly embody the essence of this category. For example, professional criminal hackers carefully and meticulously plan and execute events so as to minimize the possibility of being caught, but maximize the probability of success. This is no suggestion that only professional criminal hackers are capable of posing a structured threat. What it does imply is that a deviant plans and targets an attack on an asset for a specific reason. For instance, say that an E-commerce Web site has an online database that houses credit card information for customer convenience. A miscreant may plan to attack the database in order to steal the credit card numbers so that he or she can sell them on the black market. The attacker in this case does reconnaissance to find out which database software is running, researches which vulnerabilities apply to this version of software, and carry out the exploit against the application. This chain of events demonstrates the backbone of a structured threat.

Sometimes it is the case that we often find out about these threats after an author/discoverer has already successfully exploited victims. For instance, earlier this year (2005) a Linux kernel exploit became public knowledge. The author of the exploit later recounted that he or she had already *owned* a significant amount of servers anyway, so it didn't bother him or her that it was then public. On the other hand, it is often the case that large public disclosures result from known vulnerabilities: ones in which vendors have already issued patches. If the vulnerability is significant and the result of the exploit is great gain, then it is likely that an attacker will try to launch the exploit against servers running the vulnerable application. Again, this is a structured threat; an attacker targets specific systems (possibly anything running application *X*) as intended victims of a specific exploit. Except in this case, an attacker does not have to be a professional criminal hacker, but just willing to perform reconnaissance and execution.

You can reduce the likelihood of these threats by understanding how to configure your NGX gateway to prevent them.

Denial of Service

A structured Denial of Service (DOS) attack usually involves the deliberate interruption of service by one individual to one victim. Sometimes, flooding a machine with requests is enough to deny service to legitimate customers. Some of these attacks may be unintentional, but most are usually the result of a deliberate attack. In some cases, attackers compromise other hosts and have them contribute to the DOS attack, which is called a Distributed Denial of Service (DDOS). These attacks cause resources to be unavailable to customers (users), which can result in lost productivity and lost sales, and cause you to have to spend large amounts of money in recovery.

Three such DOS attacks are the *Teardrop*, *Ping of Death*, and *LAND* attacks (described in later sections). Your NGX gateway has the ability to recognize and block such attempts against hosts within your protected zones. In addition, NGX can block non-Transmission Control Protocol (TCP)-based flooding attempts by limiting the percentage of the state table that non-TCP connections can occupy. (See Figure 4.1.)

Figure 4.1 Denial-of-Service Configuration Settings

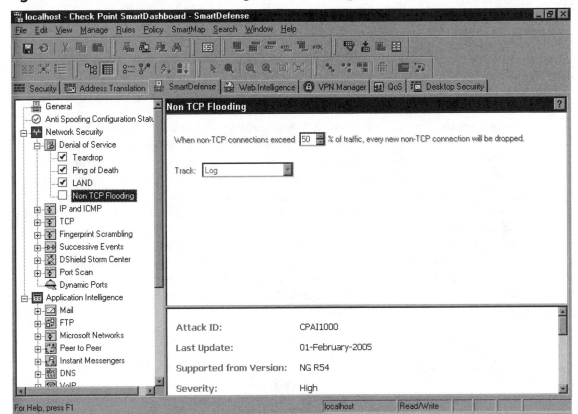

You can see in Figure 4.1 that all of the Non-TCP Flooding leaves are default-enabled. To disable any of these protections, delete the checkmark. For the first three leaves, the only options are to monitor or change the tracking method. For the Non-TCP Flooding settings, a percentage of the connections to trigger the action are defined. Be careful when enabling this prevention; NGX will drop all non-TCP connections if the threshold is met. This may be undesirable if you have legitimate non-TCP traffic traversing your gateway.

External Threats

Here is where we combine all threats that originate from outside of your network. In this case it could be anything or anyone perpetrating the act. What it boils down to is that you have vulnerable services or hosts; you permit external sources to initiate connections with these items, so now you have a threat on your hands. This, unfortunately, is a very commonplace for most administrators.

Consider a fairly standard network architecture consisting of a single VPN-1 Pro Gateway with a Demilitarized Zone (DMZ) interface, an external interface, and an internal protected interface. Also consider the loose rule base that allows the protected network to go anywhere; permits the DMZ hosts to talk back to private hosts for database or other lookup information; and then allows some HTTP, Hypertext Transfer Protocol Secure sockets (HTTPS), and File Transfer Protocol (FTP) to go from anywhere to a few DMZ hosts. This is where network administrators experience port scans, exploit attempts, and DOS attacks. A fair majority of the noise network administrators see on their networks comes from the outside. It could be college computer science students (or high school students) experimenting with scripts. The fact is it could be anyone doing a number of things to your network. Attackers on the outside are capable of defeating confidentiality, integrity, and availability even though they may not be inside your network.

Let's expand on that thought for a moment. External attacks are just that, external. They originate from a host on another network somewhere and attempt to compromise the security policy of one of your hosts. If the attack succeeds, what does that mean for your network now? Does this still pose an external threat? You must consider all possible scenarios when configuring your NGX gateway, securing your hosts, and protecting your network against attacks. Protecting your infrastructure from external threats is critical. What is even more critical is preventing a successful (external) attacker from being able to use your public hosts as stepping stones to reach your internal hosts. So ask yourself, "If I were an attacker, how could I use box *X* to get to the inside?" Remember, your VPN-1 Pro security policy allows outsiders into your DMZ. However, it does not permit them to initiate communications with your internal hosts. Since your devices are not smart enough to know who is initiating connections from which server (attacker or administrator), you must be more savvy than the attacker and consider the domino effect of a successful external attack.

Welchia Internet Control Message Protocol

During 2004, an attack known as the *Welchia* worm broke out across the Internet. This attack targeted systems running vulnerable versions of Microsoft's Distributed Component Object Model (DCOM) Remote Procedure Call (RPC) service. Once a system was compromised, the worm tried to spread itself using that service. One of the ways it did this was to scan the local network for other active hosts by sending out a specifically crafted Internet Control Message Protocol (ICMP) Echo Request message. Imagine that you have a large network and none of your workstations were patched against this vulnerability. The result was chaos. The reality for many organizations was unwanted down time. To prevent this from happening, all you need to do is configure your NGX gateway to block attacks from traversing the firewall. Go to **SmartDefense | Network Security | IP and ICMP** and place a check in the box next to **Block Welchia ICMP**. Again, there aren't many options as far as configuration goes. You can enable the "monitor only" option and change the tracking, but for the most part, it's on or off for this attack prevention mechanism.

Network Quota

In addition to the Welchia preventative measures, you can also configure your NGX gateway to limit the amount of connections that one (external or internal) host may have open to your protected hosts at any given time. A single Internet Protocol (IP) address could be passing a network-wide port scan or port sweep through your gateway. In this case, your NGX protections will block an offending machine from traversing the firewall if the gateway detects abuse. This setting applies to all source addresses. However, the advanced settings can be configured with a list of "exception" objects. In this case, you can allow your internal hosts to have as many connections open as necessary.

To enable this setting, go to **SmartDefense | Network Security | Network Quota**. When there, you will be able to set the number of connections and then click the **Advanced** button to change these settings. Other than the exclusion list, you can set a period of time to drop connections for the offending host. The Check Point default settings are 100 connections per host and a drop time of 60 seconds following an infraction.

Internal Threats

Internal threats are similar to external threats in that this category encompasses many attack vectors. However, internal threats now come with supplementary risk in that (some) attackers may possess privileged information. That is the key to internal threats. Whereas an external threat must overcome layers (you hope) of defense mechanisms, an internal threat may not be seen by any of your security devices.

It is often difficult to convince uninformed management folk that you need to protect your assets from internal threats. Time after time we see that statistics show most compromises come from employees of some kind. As mentioned before, what makes these threats so real is the inherent ease (in comparison to external attacks) with which the attacker executes an attack and the stealth-like manner in which he or she does it. For all you know, when your coworker exports the list of credit card numbers from the database, he or she could have disabled auditing, sanitized (removing suspicious events) the logs, or just plain removed the logs. When insiders launch attacks, it's not only the effects that arise from the breach that cause damage, but the fact that it may take a long time to realize there has been a breach. Further, there are times when an employee (commonly known as "disgruntled") is aware that the ax is coming down on him or her and he or she plants a time-delayed attack in the system. In this way, after the insider is gone, the attack shuts down some services, or worse, the entire network.

Not all internal threats stem from administrators gone bad. It could be as simple as an open campus-type network providing connectivity on an internal (private) network to any host that connects to the network—perhaps something similar to the way a university provides an open campus. When a student (or not) attaches to the network, he or she is not all of a sudden granted administrative privileges, but most often, internal connectivity implies less access control or other security controls. Sure, everyone has a network operating system (OS) that users must authenticate with in order to receive network services, but you aren't facing someone looking for service; rather, you are protecting your network against an attacker with malfeasance in mind.

As such, you should continue to deploy a defense-in-depth strategy to protect against internal threats. Further, you might concentrate on segregating your networks so that user populations must traverse access control devices, IDS/IPS devices, or other security control devices in order to reach your protected assets. In the case that you cannot provide such segregation, you should focus your security on the valued hosts. Enable sufficient auditing and logging so that events are discernable. Also, introduce separation of duty controls so that your organization doesn't have a one-man-show for any of your valuable assets. In this way, the admin who is about to be fired does not have sufficient privileges to disable all of the logging and auditing on the database server so he or she can implement an attack script.

Reconnaissance (Port Scans and Sweeps)

Though attackers may execute reconnaissance from external points on your network, an internal scan or sweep may result in a more telling result. Again, it is common for many organizations to allow any traffic originating from their internal networks to pass through their security rule base. For this reason, you should enable NGX's **Port Scan** configuration options. While it will not stop a port scan or port sweep against a resident network scan, it can be configured along with the *sam_alert* command to prevent scans against hosts that reside on different interfaces of your VPN-1 Pro Gateway.

To enable these protections, go to **SmartDefense | Network Security | Port Scan**. Figure 4.2 shows what you can expect to see when configuring a **Host Port Scan**. Note that when you make a change to a SmartDefense setting, or when a new protection is added when you make an online update, the setting turns to boldface and will have an asterisk after it until you install the policy.

Figure 4.2 Host Port Scan Configuration Options

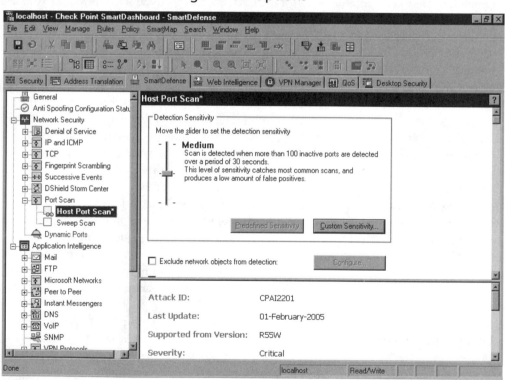

Note that the **Detections Sensitivity** can be changed to predetermined settings of High, Medium, or Low, to allow you to configure the detection of less obvious scans (high), or to only react to blatant port scanning attempts. Note that the descriptions mention that it will trigger on inactive ports. Since port scans are looking for any open ports on one or more hosts, you must consider these options. If you do not like the predefined levels, you can set your own **Custom**

Sensitivity… levels by clicking this button and entering values for the number of ports and the time period. Also note that you can configure an exception list using your defined objects. If you have some test servers or you have your settings set to detect even the most minute scan and one host keeps popping up (for legitimate traffic), you can set your protections to omit this particular server using the exclusion list.

It is also important to understand how a port sweep is different from a port scan. A port scan runs a range of ports over one host (too see which ones are open). A port sweep is when an attacker looks for a specific service running on multiple servers. Therefore, instead of hitting one or more hosts with a range of ports, he may scan many hosts for a single port to see which servers respond. The configuration settings for the **Sweep Scan** are similar to those in the port scan. Remember, you may find that what you think is okay will still set off an alarm when there isn't a true attack (false positive). In this case, you must tune your NGX protections so that it fits the characteristics of your network.

The OSI Model

All persons holding a (network) security-related job must be familiar with the OSI model. Not only does the model help you understand how packets go from one host to the other, it gives you perspective on how attackers exploit vulnerabilities in each layer in order to compromise your security policy. There are seven layers to the OSI model. (See Figure 4.3.)

Figure 4.3 The OSI Model

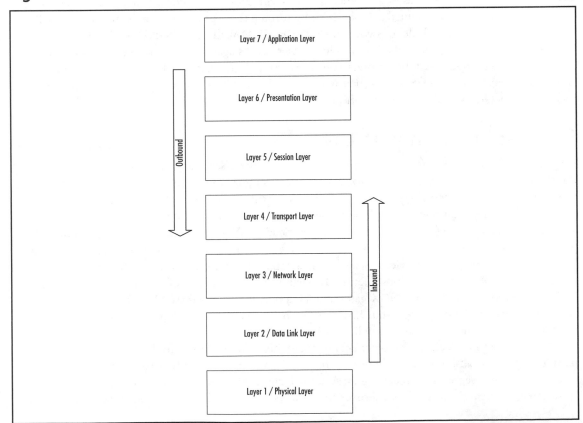

Notice in Figure 4.3 that layer 1 is on the bottom. This is because the diagram represents the flow of packets from one host to another (in a two-host communication). Consider that host A sends a packet to host B. The first thing that happens is the application layer creates the data. The flow then proceeds down the model to the physical layer where the packet travels to the other host. Once at the destination host, the packet travels up the model to layer 7 where the application processes the data.

To help you understand how your NGX gateway protections work, the following sections concentrate on three of these layers: the network layer, the transport layer, and the application layer, which represent the place where a majority of all remote attacks occur.

Layer 3: The Network Layer

IP and ICMP reside within this layer. As such, there are many attacks available against these protocols. For example, the *Ping of Death* attack targets ICMP (ping), and if it reaches a vulnerable host, it will crash, causing a DOS. Though other protocols exist within this layer (ARP, RARP, RIP, OSPF), SmartDefense only provides protections against IP and ICMP attacks. Protecting your network not only includes protection for applications, but also the protocols that carry application data. Check Point's SmartDefense technology provides sufficient coverage of these attacks and more.

To configure your VPN-1 Pro Gateway to detect and/or prevent these attacks, go to **SmartDefense | Network Security | IP and ICMP**, where you will find protections against such attacks as the aforementioned *Ping of Death* as well as other IP and ICMP protections. For instance, you can enable protections against an attack aimed at Cisco IOS. By turning these protections on, your gateway will block any attempts to attack devices with the **SWIPE**, **IP Mobility**, **SUN-ND**, or **PIM** protocols. Again, there are options that enable you to block other attacks against IP and ICMP; you should investigate which options will best protect your organization's network. Enabling these is straightforward. If you come across a setting or option that is unclear, Check Point's "help" files are an informative aid to help you determine how to set an option.

Layer 4: The Transport Layer

Devices process the Transport Control Protocol (TCP) and the User Datagram Protocol (UDP) in the transport layer. Recall that many of today's applications utilize one of these two transport layer protocols for data transfer. Again, there are vulnerabilities within implementations of these protocols, so that attackers can exploit them if you have vulnerable hosts. One such example is a synchronized (SYN) attack. In this attack, one (or more) hosts send an overload of SYN packets to the victim. As this single packet itself is not illegal, it does not complete the three-way handshake TCP connections are looking for. The attacker is hoping that the victim will allocate a connection for each of the SYN requests and wait for the handshake to complete. Subsequently, the victim host will run out of connections, resulting in a DOS for legitimate clients. Your NGX gateway, with a proper SmartDefense SYN Attack configuration, will detect this attack and protect your host from such a DOS. There are also numerous other attacks at the transport layer that your gateway will fend off.

To detect SYN attacks and protect against them, NGX offers a two-fold approach. First, it passively monitors all incomplete three-way-handshake attempts and only forwards the connections to the destination server after receiving an Acknowledgment (ACK) from the originating client. In doing so, the gateway enforces a shorter time-out period than the destination server. If a gateway considers a host to be under attack, it activates the second defense mechanism, "SYN Relay defense." This protection waits for the completion of the three-way-handshake prior to handing off the connection to the destination server. This prevents the destination server from receiving SYN packets that have no intention of being part of a valid connection. This counters the attack by not allowing the destination host to fill its connection buffer with bogus requests. Thus, the queue will not fill up with connection requests that have not completed the three-way-handshake (invalid attempts) and deny valid requests for new connections.

To enable this protection, go to **SmartDefense | Network Security | TCP | SYN Attack Configuration**. There is an option to set the timeout period that your gateways will enforce when deciding whether or not a SYN packet is part of an attack. You can also define whether or not to enforce this protection only on external interfaces (defined in your anti-spoofing settings), or on all interfaces. In addition, you can define how many packets will invoke SYN Relay defense. The last options to set are logging and tracking options.

Layer 7: The Application Layer

As mentioned before, all kinds of organizations are making their applications available via the Internet. As such, there are many attackers that seek to compromise these hosts and harvest data from them to sell to others. Moreover, a greater number of organizations have Web servers (HTTP/HTTPS), FTP servers, and remote access ability (Telnet, SSH, RDP) to servers available to hosts on the Internet. Although many of these organizations have installed an access control device for some of these services, the other services such as HTTP and FTP are meant to be available to anyone from anywhere. This is where NGX does more than just access control. NGX provides application-level protections in both SmartDefense and Web Intelligence.

What this means is that you must understand that thee are plenty of attacks for these services. Attackers have progressed from simple attempts against application configuration mistakes that lead to information disclosure (directory information, and so forth) to attacks that exploit the code-level vulnerabilities that lead to greater information disclosure (credit card data, trade secrets, intellectual property, and so forth). To protect your organization against such attacks, you must have a device that is capable of inspecting the data at the application layer. When you enable the associated options embedded within SmartDefense and Web Intelligence on your NGX VPN-1 Pro gateway, you gain protection from application layer attacks. Keep in mind that the technologies involved with Web Intelligence not only operate based on attack signatures, but also possess built-in logic to detect unknown attacks.

One such SmartDefense control within the application layer lets you manage how your organization handles instant messaging (IM) traffic. SmartDefense lets you configure your gateway for four IM products: MSN Messenger, Skype, Yahoo! Messenger, and ICQ. While the MSN settings allow you to get more granular, the other settings allow you to block proprietary protocols on all ports. Some of your staff may not realize that each message passes plaintext through an Internet-based server prior to reaching the other participant. For this reason, they may think that it is okay to discuss confidential dealings via IM applications. This NGX security control gives you the ability to reduce information disclosure.

NGX gets more specific for MSN Messenger. There are two settings for MSN, one for the Session Initiation Protocol (SIP) and one for the MSN Messenger Service (MSNMS). The controls for these two settings are similar. (See Figure 4.4.)

Figure 4.4 MSN Messenger over SIP Configuration Settings

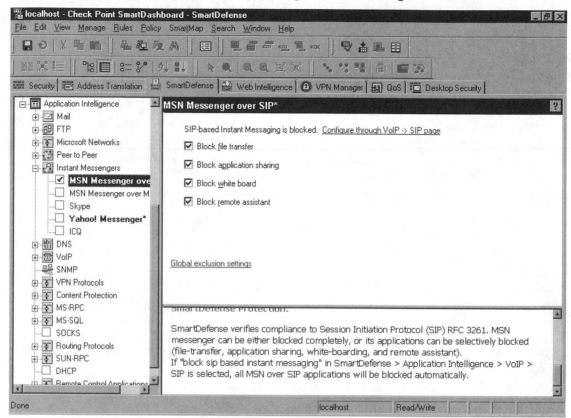

Note that you can configure SIP-based blocking through more than this option. If you have SIP blocking enabled on the VOIP settings, it will block MSN Messenger over SIP. Instead of blocking the whole application, you can configure NGX to block specific parts of the application. If you don't want anyone to invoke the remote assistant, you can place a check in this box. These settings can be changed to fit your network and the services you wish to offer your users. For the MSN Messenger over MSNMS settings, you have the additional ability to block multimedia (audio and video).

Though there are weaknesses in these applications, which may lead to attacks against your network, these NGX controls allow you to stop inadvertent information disclosure. This is not all that NGX offers the application layer. As mentioned previously, AI offers configuration options for many different services and protections against a variety of attacks.

The Need for Granular Inspection

Begin by considering what the term *granular* means in this context. You may understand it to communicate the idea that something is so dense with cohesive components that it must be broken down to fully evaluate the contents of the entity. That is precisely what you need to do in order to protect your applications and servers from attacks. You know that packets come across the wire in a standard format (headers, data, and so forth). Unfortunately, there are many ways in which attackers violate these standards in order to facilitate an attack. For this reason, it is necessary to employ solutions that sustain the ability to inspect each packet with respect to its individual components. In addition, these devices must assess the communication as a whole. To do this, your solutions must reassemble packets in order to restore the context of the request. In this manner, your device thoroughly examines each packet and also evaluates each request (as a whole).

In a previous section, you learned that attackers have migrated (for the most part) from localized attacks to network-based attacks. In this sense, remote attacks focus on violating internetworking standards and (application) protocol standards. Network packets have a structure that allows devices to determine the destination of the packet. The packet also contains the *data* portion of the communication between the hosts. If the request is small enough to fit into one packet, the *data* field inspection is both a granular examination and a contextual evaluation for this communication. However, some requests span multiple packets. In this manner, the originating host (or device in between) may fragment the request into *n* packets to conform to the network packet size limitations between hosts. Security devices are still able to inspect the *data* fields in each packet as they come across the wire. However, these devices must store and reassemble each *fragment* in order to evaluate the context of the request. These processes expose the network to vulnerability.

Attackers may tweak one of many bits within a transmission to alter the processing of a packet. There are several examples of attacks that violate the intended function of networking. For example, the *Teardrop* attack targets improper fragment reassembly. If two successive packets are sent with fragments, the second packet contains the first (within its offset). This attack exploits the lack of a proper fragment handling procedure; however, the NGX protections are intuitive enough to detect and block this attack. Other attacks exist that alter packet fields to induce chaos on devices. In some cases, creating a synchronization request (SYN) packet with the same source/destination (a LAND attack) and port pairings will crash the host. Again, this packet does not represent the intended use of networking, and exploits the fact that there is insufficient packet handling controls in place on a victim.

Besides network attacks, misfeasors often modify the data field of a packet in order to exploit an application vulnerability. If devices in the path of communication do not properly detect these attempts, the attack may succeed. For example, some post office protocol (POP) servers are vulnerable to long username or password parameters when authenticating users. To exploit this fault, an attacker may write a section of code that will populate the packet with a parameter that will violate the program and induce the desired result. As mentioned earlier in this chapter, this parameter can be included in one packet or spread across multiple packets. In either case, an undetected attack may result in server/service compromise. NGX has protections against this very weakness. The **Application Intelligence | Mail | POP3/IMAP Security** settings can be set to prevent binary data in the parameters, or place a limit on the number of characters for usernames and passwords. In addition, there are a couple of DOS settings that can be enabled for this application that increase protection.

Because of the proliferation of the Internet, there is widespread availability of scripts and programs that furnish semi-skilled users with the ability to craft packets containing invalid options, create corrupt data fields, or apply improperly attributed fragments. Because these programs make attacks easy to execute, you must defend your network, applications, and servers with robust security architecture. Check Point VPN-1 Pro NGX gateways provide such security.

Application Intelligence

To help you combat these types of threats (and more) and enable you to employ a more comprehensive perimeter defense, Check Point introduced its Application Intelligence (AI) technology a few versions ago. Since then, Check Point has split this advancement into two distinct technologies. The first is SmartDefense. This offering—the original product, which was all inclusive—concentrates on several layers of the Open Systems Interconnect (OSI) model. Although the concept is to protect and ensure data (and application) confidentiality, availability, and integrity, some of these attacks reside outside of the applications layer. The second offering is Web Intelligence, which focuses on protecting Web servers and Web-based applications. Both Web Intelligence and SmartDefense operate with the knowledge of known attacks, and also possess the capability to recognize potential risk even if it does not fit an established attack profile.

The following sections examine why these two technologies are pertinent to securing your network. Further discussion reveals the classes or protections for each of these technologies. In addition, these sections cover the options that SmartDefense and Web Intelligence offer. We also walk through examples of how to block *peer-to-peer* communications and how to prevent *SQL Injection* attacks.

The remainder of this chapter stands to dispense specific details about how you can utilize your NGX gateway to protect your network, standard applications (FTP, SMTP, etc.), and Web-based applications. As you have learned throughout the course of this text, Check Point demonstrates a keen understanding of ease-of-use by designing simple, logical GUIs. You will again experience this truth as we walk through these tasks, because the procedures remain quick and easy.

Configuring Hosts and Nodes for AI

To utilize some of the protections that NGX offers you must first properly configure your nodes. The Web-based protections only relate to defined Web servers and other protections only apply to certain servers. Let's walk through configuring a simple Web server and then enable some of the many protections that NGX offers.

To begin, go to **Security** in the SmartDashboard. Under **Objects Tree**, right-click **Network Objects | Nodes** and select **New Node | Host**. After entering the host name and IP address, click the **Configure Servers** button, which will give you the option of configuring your server for Web, Mail, or Domain Name Service (DNS). Choosing one of these options will generate a new branch in the left side or your host properties window. Place a check in the box next to **Web Server** and click **OK**. Now, if you expand the **Web Server** branch in the left pane, you see the protection options for this type of server (Web server). On the primary configuration page, you can define the OS and applications your web server uses. In addition, you can select which ports the server listens on. The **Protections** leaf lets you configure precise security controls that you want to enable or disable for this server. Once you are done configuring the options, click **OK** to save your new Web server. Not only does configuring a Web server object provide additional security, it also allows you to define further protections in Web Intelligence since it is a Web server object. Once you select any node as a Web server, you must have a Web Intelligence license in the SmartCenter or the policy will not install.

SmartDefense Technology

Check Point introduced SmartDefense technology as a means to protect your network and your applications from attackers. These protections not only span the three layers identified earlier in the OSI model (the Network Layer, the Transport Layer, and the Application Layer), but also protects layers 5 and 6 (Session Layer and Presentation Layer). SmartDefense accomplishes these protections by offering two separate means to detect attacks.

The first is via signature detection. As discussed earlier, your NGX gateway inspects packets as they come across the wire, and if one is found that matches a signature, your gateway invokes a predefined action, possibly blocking the connection. In addition, *SmartDefense* has the ability to detect anomalous network behavior. However, some anomaly detection actually occurs on the SmartCenter server instead of the enforcement module. This happens for several reasons. Consider an environment where you may have a clustered gateway architecture. Since connections may pass through all your active firewalls, one firewall may not see the connections profile as a whole. Further, each of the gateways sends log information to the SmartCenter server. For these reasons, it makes sense that the anomalous behavior detection happen on the SmartCenter server as opposed to each individual enforcement point. If the server detects an anomaly, it too can invoke several actions depending on the current configuration. In any case, SmartDefense offers you advanced protection for both your network and your hosts.

The following figure shows what the **SmartDefense** tab looks like in the Check Point GUI. (See Figure 4.5.)

Figure 4.5 The SmartDefense Tab

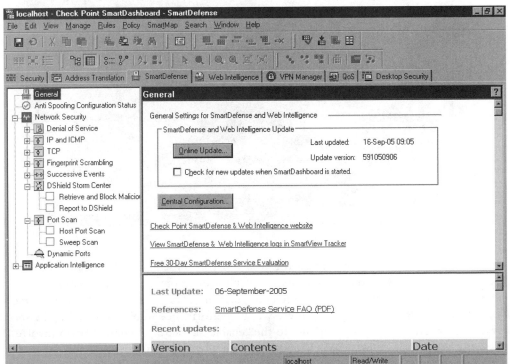

This view omits the Objects Tree in order to maximize the **SmartDefense** tab. You can see that the left-hand pane displays the different protections that SmartDefense offers. As you now know, there are both **Network Security** and **Application Intelligence** controls in this tab. You can expand each item with a + next to it to reveal further configuration capability. In later examples, you will see just how to utilize these controls to block peer-to-peer and SQL injection attack.

SmartDefense can be broken down into three class-like categories: defense against attacks, information disclosure protections, and abnormal behavior analysis. The following section discusses these particular classes as well as how to configure the central options for SmartDefense, what the SmartDefense Web site can do for you, and how to update SmartDefense.

Central Configuration and the SmartDefense Web Site

Figure 4.5 demonstrates that you can click the **Central Configuration** button to configure these options. When you do this, you will receive a simple window instead of a page full of checkboxes and drop-down menus. (See Figure 4.6.)

Figure 4.6 SmartDefense Central Configuration Settings

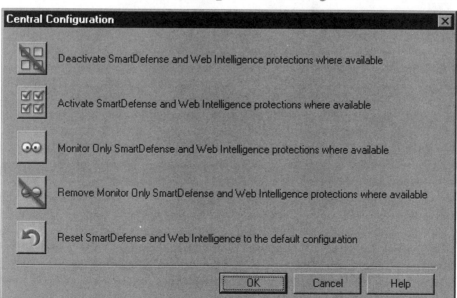

You now have five choices for configuring your SmartDefense and Web Intelligence options. The first option disables all settings except some default protections that are always on (FTP Bounce) and others that require more specific configuration. Next, you can enable everything so that your NGX gateway is a full IPS, but there will be performance implications. Also, the specific configuration protections exemption applies to the "enable all" settings. The next two involve "monitor only" settings. The first enables monitoring on all possible protections, and the second setting disables monitoring on the same protections. Keep in mind that not all protections have a "monitor only" option; therefore, these changes will not affect all of your configuration options. Lastly is the option to return to the default configuration of SmartDefense and Web Intelligence. Click this button and any changes you made to the protections are wiped out and the configuration returns to the install configuration. In any case, the changes do not occur until you select one option and click **OK**. In some cases, you will receive a window informing you about the side effects of your choice or seeking confirmation that you want to do what you have selected.

Check Point has also created a SmartDefense Web site to assist you with understanding threats and to receive pointers on how to combat these threats. If you already have a SmartDefense license, you can login using your UserCenter credentials. If you don't have a SmartDefense license, Check Point allows you to test drive the site for 30 days using your UserCenter credentials. Either way, you will find a lot of information on this site. Go to *http://www.checkpoint.com/defense* to see detailed explanations of current risks (vulnerabilities) and how to utilize your SmartDefense or Web Intelligence protections to defend the vulnerability.

Updating SmartDefense

Another **General** option is to update your protections for SmartDefense. When you click on the **Online Update** button, SmartDefense goes to the Check Point site to check for and download any updates to your SmartDefense and Web Intelligence protections. You must enter your UserCenter credentials in order to receive these updates. You can also configure automatic updates when you open SmartDashboard. If you save your credentials, you will only notice a slight delay in response when the update is occurring. Otherwise, you will be prompted every time a new update has to be downloaded to your SmartCenter server. Check Point offers frequent updates as new attacks become known or variants to current attacks pop up.

Defense Against Attacks

The first SmartDefense class teaches attack detection and prevention and covers known attacks as well as unknown attacks. SmartDefense has some capabilities that rely on the characteristics of an attack, not attack signatures. SmartDefense also has "always-on" protection from the FTP Bounce attack, which may allow an attacker to open a port on a non-originating client. In this case, your NGX gateway will not allow the attempt to compromise the host. Since NGX knows the true source of the connection, it has the ability to verify destination with respect to the open port command. If the destination does not fit the original client profile, NGX denies the connection before it arrives at your host.

Peer-to-Peer

Another example of non-signature based prevention is peer-to-peer protections. There are many peer-to-peer applications (protocols) that permit file sharing from one host to another. Doing this allows one host to download (or upload) files from another host's directory. An unsuspecting victim may accidentally download a file with malicious code meant to compromise the victim's host and/or extend the virus to other users. In any case, most organizations do not permit their protected hosts to run peer-to-peer applications (protocols).

Check Point NGX with SmartDefense enables you to block several popular file-sharing (peer-to-peer) protocols through a quick and easy process. Just like IM'g client options, NGX allows you to state whether or not to block these applications over proprietary protocols, block them if they tunnel over port 80 (HTTP), or both. Additionally, you can configure an exception list that allows one or more of your objects to bypass this protection.

To configure peer-to-peer blocking first, open SmartDashboard and click the **SmartDefense** tab. In the left-hand pane, expand the **Application Intelligence** tree by clicking the +. Next, expand the **Peer-to-Peer** branch by clicking the +. You will see six protocols listed including **Kazaa**, **Gnutella**, **eMule**, **Bit Torrent**, **Soulseek**, and **IRC**. Place a check in the box next to each protocol you wish to block. (See Figure 4.7). The last step is to save the configuration and install the policy on the enforcement module.

Figure 4.7 Peer-to-Peer Blocking

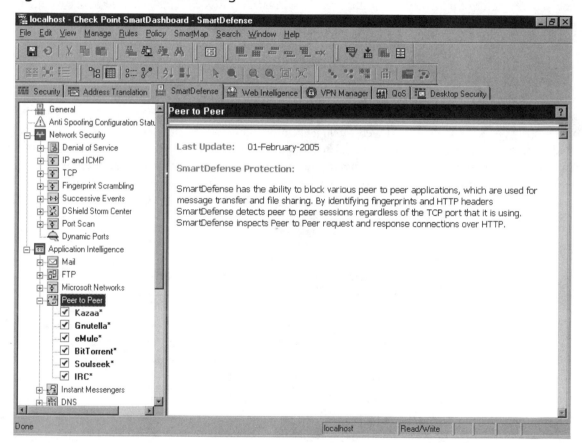

In Figure 4.7, you will see that each of the **peer-to-peer** protocol has a check in the box next to it. The result of this configuration is that the gateway will now block all of these protocols from passing either way (inbound/outbound) through the firewall.

Preventing Information Disclosure

The next class of protections is aimed to prevent information disclosure. You've already read about how NGX offers some information disclosure protections either directly or indirectly. Now consider the possibility that your hosts' behavior will reveal either its OS platform or which application software it is running. There are a few specific protections in SmartDefense that guard against information protection, such as **ISN Spoofing**, **IP Identifier (ID)**, and Time-to-Live (**TTL**). These protections reside under the **Network Security | Fingerprint Scrambling** branch of the SmartDefense settings. Be aware that activating these protections will disable any acceleration features like SecureXL or IPSO Flows.

Fingerprint Scrambling

In each of these scenarios, your host will probably respond to an attacker and inadvertently divulge some information regarding its OS or software. One such attack is against the Initial Sequence Number (ISN) of a host. For the most part, the ISN is supposed to be somewhat unique for each connection. However, the algorithm for selecting such number displays a weakness in that it has a degree of predictability. In this sense, attackers guess the ISN and if the victim responds, the attacker knows which OS the victim host is running. To further introduce uniqueness, some OS' introduced pseudo-random number generators (some people like to call them random number generators). However, these also have shown repeatability.

To further complicate matters, different OS platforms use different sequencing algorithms. Merely establishing connections with such hosts and studying the ISN for each connection may reveal an identifiable pattern for the ISN. Thus this reveals the OS to the attacker. To defend against this and the other attacks (TTL and IP ID) your NGX gateway will replace the value from the host with one from a more unique number producing algorithm (inherent to NGX). In the least, there are numerous connections passing through so if an attacker tried to establish connections and study the ISN relation, there would not be a discernable pattern. Turning on these protections is as easy as placing a check in the box next to the desired setting. There are minimal further configuration options for each attack, but it is not difficult to understand how each will affect the protection.

Abnormal Behavior Analysis

Similar to the way that we understand when a person is acting out of character by observing his or her behavior, network traces (logs) reveal abnormal connection profiles. Thus, NGX can identify questionable connections and actions based on these traces. In this chapter, you have seen an example with clustered enforcement modules and how the SmartCenter server carries out the anomalous behavior detection. This is apparent in port scan and port sweep attacks. To further expound on the cluster example and NGX's ability to detect port scans, consider that the attacker's packets are split among three enforcement points. If your configuration settings trigger at a higher level of packets than each of your members is receiving, the attack may go unnoticed. However, since your SmartCenter server receives the logs from each of these gateways, it will see all of the connection requests and can then detect the scan or sweep and invoke the proper response to alert an administrator or even to block the requests (with a user-defined alert and the **sam_alert** command).

A significant dependency for network anomaly detection exists in the fact that you must first know what "normal" is. In the same manner that you've come to understand normal human behavior, you must familiarize yourself with normal traffic patterns on your network. It will take time, but there are different NGX abilities to help you do this. However, Check Point's reporting server (Eventia Reporter), along with comprehensive logging, can provide you with a similar understanding of your traffic patterns. Once you have a basic understanding of what normal network traffic is, you can begin to identify suspect operations. Thus, you can provide even more specific configuration settings to your NGX protections to identify or drop anomalous connections you have identified. Check Point also offers Eventia Analyzer, which in real-time can correlate security events from different sources (firewalls, IPS', switches, routers, and so forth) and generate alerts immediately.

Abnormal behavior conveys one single implication: you must know what is normal to be able to label something abnormal. If you don't know what your connections profile resembles, then trying to find a single suspicious connection may take forever. However, if you have a general idea of what your network traffic looks like, you should be able to identify a connection that does not seem logical, or in the least, seems uncharacteristic.

Web Intelligence Technology

Check Point originally included Web Intelligence within the SmartDefense product, but the company broke Web Intelligence into its own entity to focus more energy on protecting your Web-based applications and your Web servers. This offering is what Check Point refers to as *Malicious Code Protector*, *Active Streaming*, and *Application Intelligence* technologies. These technologies work on signature recognition and anomaly. Since its primary focus is Web applications and Web servers, it has the ability to identify harmful code while it still resides in the data stream. It also has the capability to determine whether a user's submission (passed code) has ill-mannered intent. If so, your NGX gateway reacts with predetermined responses, either blocking the connection, or by alerting an administrator (or both). In any event, this technology applies what Check Point created in Application Intelligence and has cultivated a better product that focuses on a significant point of attack. Thus, Web Intelligence provides to you a security control that targets attacks aimed at your public applications and servers.

Malicious Code Protector

This patent-pending Check Point technology has the ability to recognize malicious code without having specific knowledge of the signature. This kernel-level function protects your Web servers and Web-based applications by inspecting all communications for their applications. If executable code is found within the data, it will then check to see if its intent is malicious. Should your NGX gateway determine yes, it will block the connection and execute the appropriate (defined) tracking option.

Active Streaming

This protection also resides at the kernel level of your gateway and protects your Web servers and Web-based applications by evaluating the context of the communication. There are several key aspects that active streaming applies to the connection in order to determine if there is harmful content. First, this is where fragment reassembly happens. As mentioned before, fragments don't embody the essence of the context, so diligent protection mechanisms must have the ability to reassemble the packets and evaluate the context. Next, if an attacker tries to encode worms or other harmful URLs, this technology will decode it so that it can be evaluated appropriately. Another function of active streaming is to initiate new sessions. If there is a protection in place that will send a new Hypertext Markup Language (HTML) page as the response to an identified attack, active streaming is where this response occurs. Lastly, active streaming possesses the ability to rewrite headers or strip out specific data. This response is useful in header spoofing attempts.

Application Intelligence

Application Intelligence technology aims to prevent attacks by knowing which communications have "bad" intentions. This collection of attack signatures and inappropriate command sequences lets you weed out some of the more harmful traffic from your network. Specifically, look at the Check Point-geared Application Intelligence to ensure compliance with protocols and application standards, to identify inappropriate usage of these protocols and standards, to block known attack signatures, and to prevent dangerous commands that some applications allow.

Looking at Figure 4.8, you see a similar screenshot as with the SmartDefense product. Again, this view omits the Objects Tree to increase recognition.

Figure 4.8 The Web Intelligence Tab

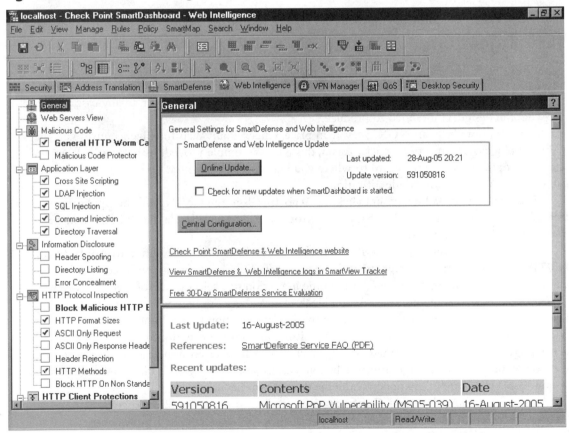

Again, in the left-hand pane you see an array of options to choose from regarding Web-based attacks. This time, in the right-hand pane, you see that there exists the ability to update the signatures and other settings associated with both SmartDefense and Web Intelligence. In the coming sections, you will dig deeper into these settings as you configure custom Web blocking for your firewall through a configuration example.

Web Application Layer

NGX offers specific protections for Web application layer detection. Specifically, it prevents an attacker from entering code into a Web page or other medium that will introduce harmful effects on the backend of the server. This acts in a similar manner to the malicious code detector. The biggest difference is that these protections are mostly based on known commands and other strings that may invoke harmful results.

As an example, you will learn how to configure your NGX gateway to block an SQL Injection attack. This attack embodies the essence of the protection in that an attacker tries to substitute commands or other strings in a data field to provoke the server into revealing alternative information. In the same sense, someone could try to place harmful tags or other malicious characters in a Web site that one of your users may visit. Let's look at how you can apply settings to your VPN-1 Pro Gateway in order to block such an attack.

SQL Injection

SQL injection attacks are meant to inject an SQL command into a place meant for data input only. An attacker visits a Web form, and instead of putting only his or her name into the "Last Name" field on the form, he or she puts in some code to execute on the back-end server. In any case, the result is not what the designers intended to produce.

Since you now have an NGX gateway in place, Check Point Web Intelligence gives you the ability to block SQL Injection attacks. Again, this is a very simple procedure, but you will see that additional options exist with regard to where you enforce the configuration and how you wish your gateway to react to a positive identification.

First, open SmartDashboard and click the **Web Intelligence** tab. Expand the Application Layer tree by clicking the +. Then select **SQL Injection** by clicking it. Place a check in the box next to the setting to enable the option.

In the top-right pane within the Protection Scope block, you have the option to **Apply to all HTTP traffic** or **Apply to selected web servers** (default). Choose an option based on whether you want to affect all traffic by this setting or limit the inspection to a select group of predefined Web servers.

In the top-right pane within the Action block, choose the action you want your gateway to enforce. Choosing no options in this box means you want the default action to block the connections. If you only wish to monitor the connections, choose the **Monitor only – no protection** option. Choose the **Send error page** option if you want to respond to the attacker with a custom Web page. You also need to define these properties by clicking the **Configure** button (enabled only when you check the box). Choose a Track option by selecting one of the options from the drop-down menu.

Lastly, under the **Advanced Configuration** heading, you can configure specific SQL commands to trigger the action for when the gateway detects them. When completed, your configuration may look similar to Figure 4.9.

Figure 4.9 SQL Injection Blocking

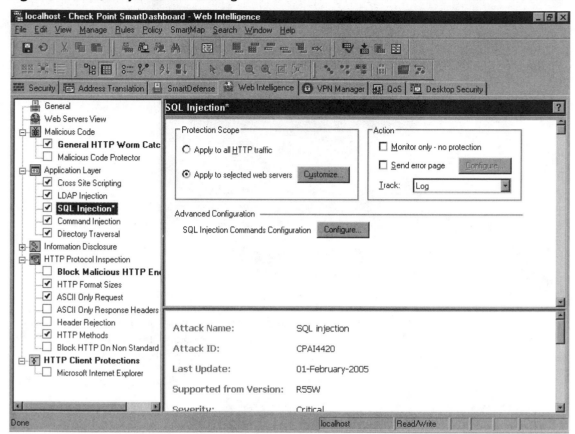

As seen in Figure 4.9, the Action block does not define one of the selections. For this reason, the gateway enforces the default action to block the connections. Again, when you experiment with these settings on your own network, you will identify what works best for you. In the beginning, with all of the options enabled, you may find that the gateway is blocking legitimate connections (false positives). If you do want to block this type of attack, you must approach this process as a learning opportunity: 1) to learn which settings will reduce the false positive rate, and 2), which commands your servers need to run to satisfy your business requirements.

Custom Web Blocking

As you have seen in the Web Intelligence interface, Check Point enables you to apply single settings to one, many, or all Web servers. Since you define your Web servers and applications, you should rest easy that security settings can be applied to whichever server you want; nothing less, nothing more. In this sense, you have a very customizable product that provides you with a security environment that best fits your organization. For instance, the SQL settings you saw during the configuration example. The selection of commands in Figure 4.10 shows you that if you had one specific command that was legitimate for your environment but all the rest indicated a possible attack, you could simply remove the check from this one box and carry on. It's that simple. (See Figure 4.10.)

Figure 4.10 Custom SQL Commands

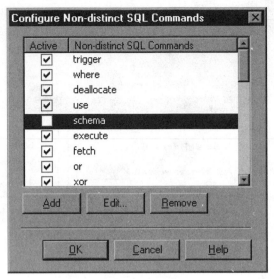

With this ease of use, Check Point has granted you the power to build a robust security perimeter with one device. Not only will your gateway perform advanced access control, but it will also deliver a high-performance security inspection technology implemented (by you) specifically for your organization's security concerns.

Preventing Information Disclosure

In previous sections, you learned that attackers sometimes perform reconnaissance to gain information to help them adapt an attack to a specific host's configuration. To do this, the attacker may send specific requests to the host in order to have it reveal information about the OS version, software application name and version, or other configuration information. When your server responds to these requests with information, it results in disclosure and gives the attacker information that will provide him leverage to further attack your host. To detect these requests and responses, NGX uses a set of regular expressions combined with known response codes and values. NGX lets you configure three specific attack detection profiles within the Web Intelligence tab: *Header Spoofing*, *Directory Listing*, and *Error Concealment*. The former embodies an attacker's attempt to gain information by deliberately sending the server a bad request. The response to the attacking client may reveal information about internal properties of the server and therefore lead to future structured attacks.

Header Spoofing

Though this is not a complicated attack, it can lead to a more direct attack. Specifically, reply headers usually contain the version of the Web server you are running. NGX allows you to configure this protection to identify these replies and substitute different text for the one you do not want the attacker to receive. (See Figure 4.11.)

Figure 4.11 Header Spoofing Configuration

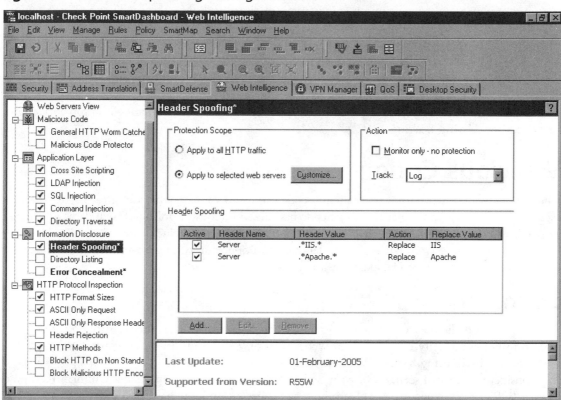

If the gateway sees that one of your Web servers is replying to a client with the text value ".*IIS.*", it will remove that value and substitute the value "IIS" in its place. This removes any versioning information from the header and reduces the attacker's information scope regarding your Web server. To add new strings in the detection, click **Add** and input the appropriate regular expressions; one for the header name and the other for the value you are looking for. In addition, if you want to replace the value with another one, you must input a text string for the replacement value. Once you've done that, click **OK** and you're done. Your new search string will show up in the window shown in Figure 4.11.

Directory Listing

Some Web servers list the contents of the current directory if there is no default page present (and the file permissions comply with the listing). In this case, one of your Web servers may give away too much information in script files or configuration files. When this happens, it usually means that there has been some kind of misconfiguration or mistake somewhere along the line. To configure this protection, you must identify your Web servers individually. In other words, once you enable the protection by placing a check in the box, you must click on the **Customize** button in the **Protection Scope** box to apply the settings for each server.

This prevention mechanism has three settings; low, medium, and high. The low setting only looks at suspicious responses and triggers on three indications of directory listing. The medium and high settings both look at suspicious and non-suspicious responses. However, the medium setting triggers on three indications, while the high setting only requires one indication of a directory listing to trigger the NGX action. When you click on the **Configure** button you receive a window where you must add the servers individually and where your defined Web Servers show up. To configure each server, highlight the one you wish to change and select **Edit**. You are now in the "host properties" window with the Web server properties displayed. To change the current setting, select the **Advanced** button adjacent to the **Directory Listing** heading.

Malicious Code

A hot topic over the past few years, malicious code can cause your organization great harm. In recent years, you are sure to know that malicious code has caused billions of dollars of total damage to small and large firms alike. Since your Check Point VPN-1 Pro Gateway includes the ability to reduce the risk of massive damage from harmful code, let's take this opportunity to go over the finer points of what constitutes malicious code and what it may look like.

Definition

NGX interprets malicious code as anything that, when executed, violates the security policy of or compromises the integrity of one of your Web servers or Web clients. In other words, anything that when executed will bring harm to your environment (server or client).

Consider the normal scenario of your typical Web session. When you open a Uniform Resource Locator (URL), you expect to download the text, images, or multimedia that you desire to see. What happens if there is code in the executable that will remove files from your hard drive or install a worm, virus, or other spyware utility on your computer? You did not intend for this to happen, you expected a completely different result from launching the site. You may not even know that your computer has been compromised. This is another reason to have an NGX gateway protect your network. Even though you may think that something is normal, there could be unexpected results. NGX protects your servers and clients from these undesirable results using its Malicious Code Protector technology.

Though this is a simple explanation for malicious code, it is clearly understandable. Now, translate that to one of your Web forms that accepts user input. What if a vulnerability exists in your form processing software, which allows an attacker to insert commands into the submission field. The result of this action will be that the system processes the command and returns a result (success, failure, list of data). In any case, the malicious code has compromised the system via information disclosure in that it produced an unintended result for the attacker.

Different Types of Malicious Code

It is incredible the number of worms, viruses, Trojans, or other exploits that magazine columnists write about these days. These different types of malicious code take advantage of poorly written application code or other weaknesses in hosts in order to compromise or wreak havoc on organizations. Malicious code can come through e-mail messages, IM clients, peer-to-peer file sharing, Web sites, and so forth.

The NGX gateway comes with signatures that identify harmful code as well as general detection capabilities that don't rely on a signature. When you enable the **Malicious Code | Malicious Code Protector** option in the Web Intelligence tab, you'll see that there really isn't much to configure. Other than the options to change the tracking and monitor settings, you only have an advanced configuration **Configure** button. When you click this button, you will see that there isn't much to this either. You actually only define two tradeoffs; one between memory consumption and speed and the other between a more secure search or a faster search. When you are done selecting these options, click **OK** and then install the policy on the enforcement points. Let's look at further protections that your NGX gateway provides in order to defend your hosts from malicious content.

General HTTP Worm Catcher

Because worms have the inherent ability to self-replicate, they are more dangerous than most attacks because they don't require human intervention. There is a significant amount of worms that use the Web to replicate to new hosts. To protect your organization from this, enable this setting. You'll see that there are 13 predefined worms that NGX checks for. This mechanism works solely on the regular expression patterns that you define within the configuration utility, and those added via an online update. In addition, you can configure this setting per server. Let's take a look at the configuration settings for the worm catcher. (See Figure 4.12.)

Figure 4.12 General HTTP Worm Catcher Configuration

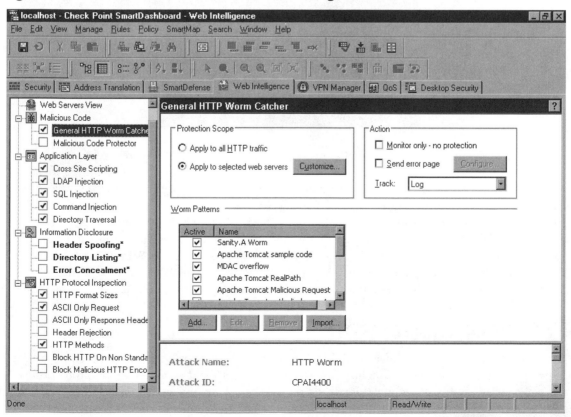

The setting mentioned earlier is in most of the Web Intelligence attack profiles. You can change the servers that receive the protection and how NGX enforces the protection (monitor only, send error page, or the default block). In addition, you can add regular expression patterns so that your gateway will detect specific threats. Let's look further into the patterns for the "Sanity.A" worm. Highlight the entry and click the **Edit** button. (See Figure 4.13.)

Figure 4.13 Worm Pattern Settings

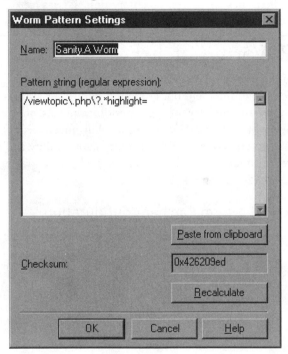

Notice that you must be fairly specific regarding the text string that you are looking for. Also notice that if you read about a new worm online (or anywhere else) and have copied the pattern to your clipboard, you can click the **Paste from clipboard** button to place that string into the pattern window. Sometimes it proves more accurate to copy a string rather than try to retype it yourself. You can also import individual worm patterns from the Check Point Web site. If you do this, you may want to calculate the checksum to make sure that the value is the same as the original value. If you don't want to do this, you can simply update all of the protections together. When SmartDefense or Web Intelligence updates are sought, they include new worm patterns. When you have entered the correct string and verified its checksum (if needed), click **OK** to save the new pattern to the profile.

Protocol Inspection

You may be asking what the difference is between all that you've learned to this point and Protocol Inspection. Well, in this section, you may discover some things about applications and protocols that don't necessarily jibe with the way things should be. As the name implies, a protocol, regardless of the context, is a set of rules or ways to do things. This layman's definition also applies to the protocols that you consider in terms of networking and applications. What you may not be aware of is the fact that often there are applications that do not conform to protocols as the designers intended. This nonconformity may be a mistake, or it could be an attempt to attack the protocol and produce undesirable results. Let's discuss more about protocol conformity and see how our Check Point gateway helps us enforce the intentions of the designers.

Conformity

As briefly mentioned earlier in this chapter, there are a considerable amount of applications whose aim is to comply with protocols. However, a subset of applications exists that, for whatever reason, simply do not conform to protocol X. Though this does not normally cause issues with the application, it does present problems for you if your firewall or other security device forces applications to conform to the protocol as the designer intended and as documented in the RFC. Because attackers know that some legitimate applications may not conform to protocol specifications, they may create malicious code with similar nonconformity that will violate your application or host. So this poses a threat to your network's security and the security of your applications and hosts.

Before you enable protocol standard enforcement on your firewall, you should be certain that you will not disable any critical applications. You may even learn of an application that is pertinent to the operation of your organization that does not fully comply with the RFC. In this case, you may or may not be able to continue enforcement, depending on the impact to your business. Let's review how NGX provides protocol enforcement for the DNS protocol.

DNS Enforcement

When an attacker wants to use DNS packets to exploit a host, he changes the payload in the packet and sends it on to the victim. NGX inspects these packets for both TCP and UDP queries (and other communications) to verify that they are in accordance with the DNS protocol. If they are not, the gateway blocks the packet from progressing. NGX allows you to enable this option for TCP only, UDP only, or both TCP and UDP packets. You also have the option to monitor illegal packets without blocking them. However, the most pressing issue here is volume. Since most applications want a fully qualified host name versus an IP address to identify the other party in the connection, they must query their local DNS server to translate the name into an IP address. This protection has the ability to severely reduce the performance of your gateway .

HTTP Inspection

Check Point's Web Intelligence provides enforcement of the HTTP protocol. When you view the settings in SmartDashboard, you will see that there are many different options from which to choose. Each of these settings either enforces strict adherence to the HTTP protocol, or enforces limitations with the intent to reduce risk associated with a threat model. In either case, these options permit you to define how granular you wish to lock down one, many, or all of your Web servers and applications.

In addition, this option provides you with the ability to block HTTP over nonstandard ports. Though not all servers running on ports other than 80 are mischievous in nature, servers do exist that provide no good purpose running on such ports. In practice, this may prove a difficult option to enable as many legitimate services run HTTP services over nonstandard ports. However, if you are certain that your organization does not need any such services, this option may come in very handy.

Being able to block access to servers running on these ports will unarguably reduce your organization's risk. Figure 4.14 shows the **HTTP Protocol Inspection** tree in the SmartDashboard interface.

Figure 4.14 HTTP Protocol Inspection

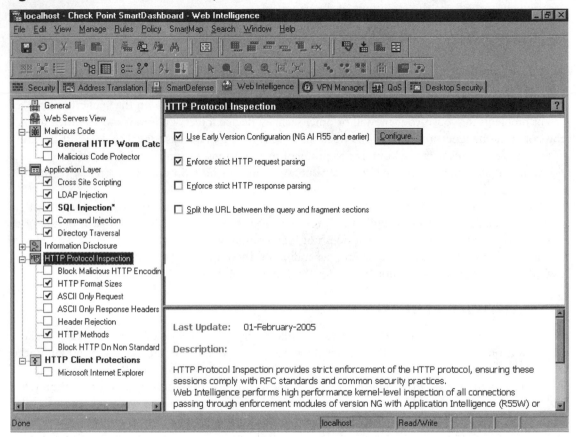

In any case, it is an easily configurable setting. If you sense an immediate or imminent threat, you can enable this setting for the duration and disable it to restore service to your organization. Just like many options within SmartDefense and Web Intelligence, this one is useful in either a short-term or a long-term role.

Default Configuration

When a Web server is defined, it inherits a set of default protections from NGX. With regard to protocol inspection, NGX performs three inspections: *HTTP Format Sizes*, *ASCII Only Request*, and *HTTP Methods*. These settings protect your server from buffer overflow attempts in the case of the format sizes. There isn't really a limit to the size of a URL; sometimes attackers try to submit an extremely long URL to attack a Web server. In addition, you can set limits on the length for headers and the number of headers. Further, NGX blocks all non- American Standard Code for Information Interchange (ASCII) HTTP requests, as well as non-ASCII values for form fields. This setting prevents an attacker from submitting a worm or other harmful values in binary formats.

NGX also offers protections against HTTP methods that most servers don't need (and most administrators don't disable). For example, the *trace* and *track* methods will probably always show up in a vulnerability scan if you do not disable them after turning on your Web server. NGX separates these methods into three categories: *standard safe*, *standard unsafe*, and *WebDAV*. As a baseline, NGX blocks all methods except for those in the standard safe group. To disable blocking for a specific method (or enable blocking) all you have to do is highlight the **HTTP Protocol Inspection | HTTP Methods** leaf in the left pane and click the **Configure** button. (See Figure 4.15.)

Figure 4.15 Select Blocked HTTP Methods Configuration

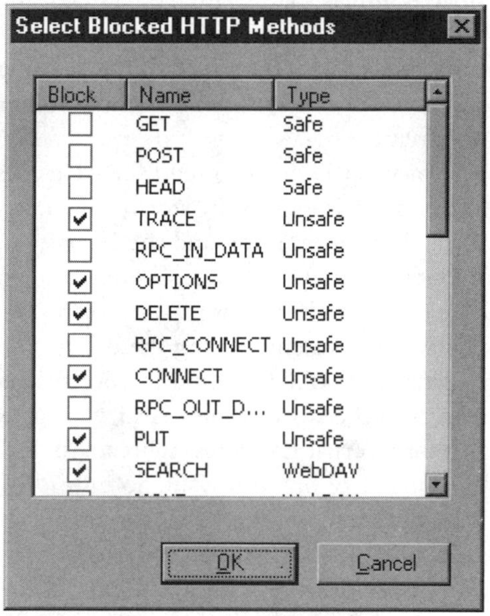

You can see the category that each method is in (far right column). To select or deselect a method, click in the box to place or remove the check mark. When you have modified the list to meet your needs, click **OK** and the SmartCenter server saves the changes to the profile. Don't forget that you must push the policy to the enforcement modules in order to apply the settings.

Remember, when you define a new host and configure it as a *Web Server*, the host inherits the default settings within the protection profiles. Some settings have the option to change the default level of protections, like we saw in the *Directory Listing* configuration options. Therefore, keep these protections in mind when you add a new server. You don't want to waste a lot of time trying to troubleshoot an issue when it could be an aggressive protection setting on your NGX gateway preventing the successful communication.

DShield Storm Center

As organizations become more security conscious, they begin to understand that they are not alone with regard to the threats they face. In addition, these organizations learn that the intrusion attempts they are seeing are not isolated to them. What you may discover is that organizations all over the world battle similar attacks. For this reason, Check Point integrated the ability to share your log information with the

DShield Storm Center (http://www.dshield.org). In addition, the storm center can send information about current threats and your firewall may invoke blocking lists based on this communication.

With the common threat model that everyone faces, professionals in all aspects of information security have begun to push for broad information sharing among organizations (corporate and government alike). In 2000, Euclidian consulting launched the DShield Storm Center to begin correlating worldwide traffic profiles to detect attacks. Soon thereafter, SANS (*http://www.sans.org*) joined the fray and began contributing to DShield Storm Center. As such, this engine is now the basis for the SANS Internet Storm Center. The aim of this effort is to combine network traffic organizations for the sake of consolidating these individual traffic models into one large model. From this point, automated systems discern similar traffic patterns and determine whether they are malicious in nature. In simplest terms, DShield Storm Center is a global correlation engine, which relies on you, other organizations, and its own population of collection engines for data. Everyone gains from sharing this type of information. The more information there is to evaluate, the more likely the system will find commonalities.

Some organizations may be somewhat hesitant to send their log files to a third party. After all, when you configure your firewall to submit logs to the storm center, it will include the source and destination IP addresses, source and destination ports, and the IP protocol of the connection. You may utilize private addresses within your protected networks, and disclosing that information, even to an organization that aims to help the cause, results in information disclosure. For this reason, Check Point has made certain that you have options concerning the data you select to send to DShield. The first option is that you can define a **TRACK** option in your security rule base and send only these (identified) specific log records to the storm center. Also, your gateway has the ability to sanitize your log files so as not to reveal your internal IP address scheme. You provide a bit mask that directs your gateway to change to 0 the number of bits you want. So instead of sending log entries to the storm center with 192.168.1.50 as the source of the connection, your 8-bit mask instead will cause the gateway to change the address to 0.0.0.50 (the number of mask bits tells how many bits to reveal; a zero mask reveals nothing and a 32-bit mask reveals all). In light of these configuration options, it makes sense that an organization should (properly) configure its firewall to share information with the storm center.

Essentially, DShield is an online correlation engine. Instead of having only one organization's logs to review and evaluate, the storm center accepts logs from any organization, inserts them into their database, and then looks for trends. In essence, the storm center provides free services to you if you so choose to utilize them. The service that you receive from DShield is invaluable. Consider that information sharing provides a platform for quick response in the face of a worldwide threat. For example, imagine that a new attack broke out and it was concentrated from a set of specific source IP addresses. Properly configured firewalls all over the world would experience this attack and as they submit their logs to the storm center, the correlation engine would recognize the threat. Automated evaluation of the logs ensues, and the system draws the attention of some administrators at the center who then publish reports on their Web site. In addition, the storm center updates their block list with the offending IP addresses. When your gateway downloads the block list again, you will have protected your network without really doing anything. Imagine this happening over a weekend, or while you are on vacation. Enabling this service is beneficial to you in many ways, especially with regard to convenience (convenience does not always result in the best policy, but you must determine this on your own). Not only that, but your information sharing efforts prove beneficial to other organizations as well.

Retrieving Blocklist

The configuration options you will work with are located in the SmartDefense tab. Let's walk through configuring the gateway to retrieve a blocklist from DShield Storm Center.

First, open SmartDashboard and choose the **SmartDefense** tab. Expand the **Network Security** tree by clicking the + and expand the **DShield Storm Center** branch by clicking the +. Place a check in the box next to **Retrieve and Block Malicious IPs**. In the upper right-hand pane, select whether you want to invoke this action for all of your gateways, or just a specific group of them. Your configuration should look similar to Figure 4.16.

Figure 4.16 Retrieving the Blocklist from DShield

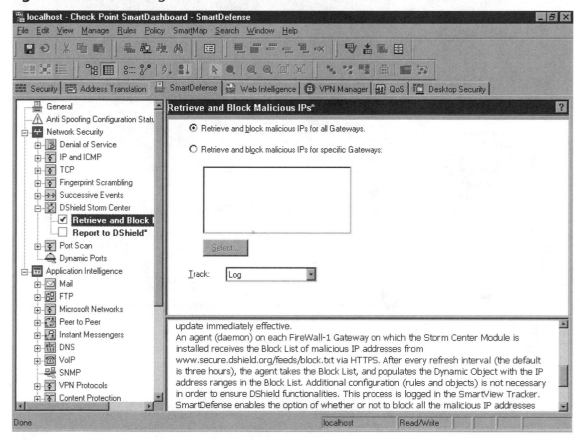

Submitting Logs

Now let's take a quick look at how to configure your gateway to send logs to DShield. Again, you have several options, as you will see, that you need to consider in order to safely and properly configure this setting. Note that you need to enter a password associated with an e-mail account in order to submit logs to DShield. You may create such an account by going to DShield's Web site and registering at *http://secure.dshield.org/cp/signup.php*. Enter the proper information and you will receive verification regarding your DShield account shortly.

Open SmartDashboard and choose the **SmartDefense** tab. Expand the **Network Security** tree by clicking +. Next, expand the **DShield Storm Center** branch by clicking +. Place a check in the box next to **Report to DShield***. In the upper-right pane's **Storm Center Login** block, enter *userid@domain.com* (your account's email address) for the **E-mail:** field. Then enter *xxxxxx* (your password) in the **Password:** field. Select the type of logs you want to submit and the frequency you want to send them to DShield. Now, select the mask you want to invoke to protect your internal addresses Remember that your mask tells the gateway how many bits to reveal. (See Figure 4.17.)

Figure 4.17 Submitting Logs to DShield

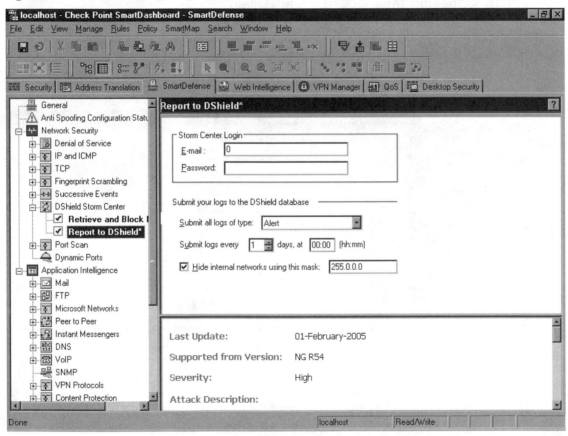

Summary

You should now have a good understanding of how a Check Point VPN-1 Pro Gateway (NGX) administrator has evolved into a network security administrator. The powerful options that Check Point NGX gateways offer help protect your network from internal and external threats. You will also appreciate the fact that some threats are arbitrary, but that some attackers target their exploits for specific applications or servers. Either way, NGX provides sufficient detection and prevention for such threats.

Throughout this chapter, you learned about specific examples of threats, peer-to-peer and SQL, and some ways to mitigate the risk associated with these threats. Deploying an NGX gateway properly takes more consideration than just implementing a typical security policy. You must consider where protections will provide you the most "bang for your buck." Check Point designed a comprehensive security product that you can leverage to protect your organization at the perimeter. NGX not only provides access control, but it allows you to employ solutions that detect, prevent, or block attacks targeting your protected hosts. You've seen some specific configuration examples and how easy it is to apply these protections. At this time, your understanding should be clearer about existing threats and ways to reduce the risk of successful compromise using your NGX gateway. While you apply these protections to your environment, keep in mind that securing your network is a continuous process. Strive to stay ahead of the curve by utilizing the tools that NGX provides to help you perform your duties. Check Point's NGX version of its VPN-1 Pro Gateway is an exceptional way to begin securing your network because it provides a multitude of protective and preventative tools to aid in the task of securing your environment.

Chapter 5

Network Address Translation

Solutions in this chapter:

- **Global Properties**

- **Configuring Dynamic Hide Mode NAT**

- **Configuring Static Mode NAT**

- **Configuring Automatic NAT**

- **Configuring Port Translation**

☑ **Summary**

Introduction

This chapter will allow you to enable or disable Network Address Translation (NAT) for a single host, for a range of addresses, or for an entire network. There are two different ways to employ NAT. In this chapter we will demonstrate and explain both methods in detail. In the first method, you configure a single address or a range of addresses to hide protected addresses; this is *Dynamic (Hide) mode NAT*. When you use the second method, *Static mode NAT*, you define a single address that allows a protected host to participate in two-way communications with hosts outside of the protected network.

To understand more about the impact NAT configuration changes have on the gateway, you first need to review a few fundamental concepts. As is easily conveyed by the term itself, Network Address Translation provides a means to convert the source address, destination address, source port, or destination port within a packet. The dominant use of NAT allows internal hosts with nonroutable IP addresses to successfully navigate to the Internet. Since many firewall administrators work with networks that have a limited number of public (routable) IP addresses, their internal private networks utilize private IP address ranges as defined in RFC 1918. For these hosts to be able to access public hosts and services on the Internet, they require a process that translates their private source address into a public, routable source address. NAT provides this very service. When the packet destined for the Internet reaches the gateway, NAT effectively changes the source address so that the destination host may reply to a routable address. When the gateway receives reply packets from the destination server, the NAT process executes a change from the public address to the private address. In doing so, the gateway may now forward the packet to the appropriate internal host. In this manner NAT provides the additional benefit of concealing the internal network topology from external entities.

There are two ways that you administer NAT behavior within the gateway. The easiest way is to define translation automatically within object properties. You will see that the gateway creates the necessary rules for translation in the Nat Rule Base (this topic is addressed later in this chapter). You have the option to automatically configure nodes, networks, and address ranges for automatic address translation. The other way you manage address translation is through manual configuration of the NAT Rule Base. In this way, you will possess greater manageability regarding how translation occurs. Manual NAT configuration also increases your ability to manipulate NAT rules for optimal benefit.

The NAT Rule Base is very similar to the Security Rule Base. Both rule bases process rules in sequential order and cease when a match is found. When you configure automatic NAT for objects, the rules are seamlessly created and placed into the rule base. Note that automatic NAT has a defined order for placing rules into the rule base. The gateway installs *Node* object rules first, then *Address Range* rules second, and finally, *Network* object rules constitute the last rules. On the contrary, you may create manual rules wherever you see fit. Again, this action is similar to adding a rule to the Security Rule Base where you create new NAT rules above or below an existing rule. Figure 5.1 shows the view you see when looking at the NAT Rule Base. The **Original Packet** and **Translated Packet** sections both have the same structure in that each contains a **Source**, **Destination**, and **Service**. We will later discuss how to configure NAT rules in order to satisfy your networking requirements.

Figure 5.1 Address Translation Tab

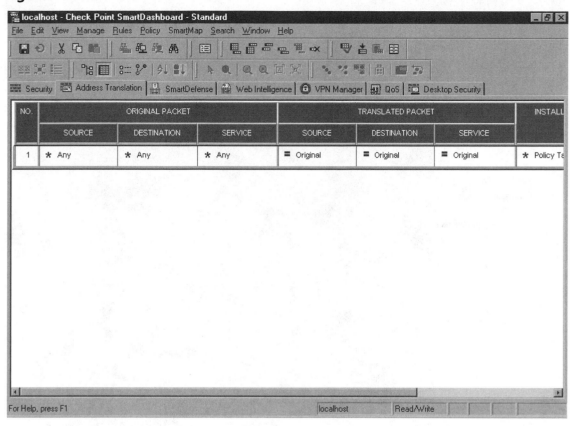

In the remainder of this chapter, we will cover what global settings exist and how each may affect the behavior of your gateway. Further, we will walk through configuring address translation in various ways. We will discuss manually configuring Static and Hide mode NAT, as well as using the automatic NAT features inherent to your Firewall-1 NGX gateway.

Global Properties

In Check Point NGX, you need to consider the **Global Properties** that affect NAT. You find these settings in SmartDashboard by clicking **Policy | Global Properties**, then choosing the **NAT – Network Address Translation** option in the left window. Figure 5.2 displays the settings we will review.

Figure 5.2 NAT Global Properties

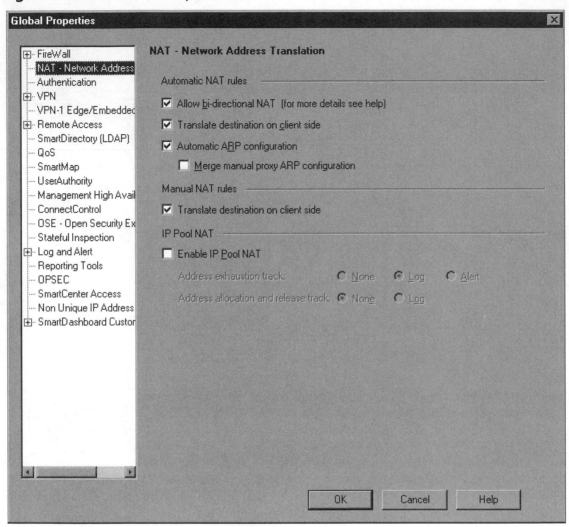

Network Address Translation

The **Allow bidirectional NAT** setting permits two hosts to communicate even though they are both hidden behind address translation. These subjects can be any single host, network address, or address range with an automatic NAT definition. When these two hosts communicate with one another, the gateway applies bidirectional NAT to successfully facilitate communication between the hosts. In essence, the bidirectional NAT lets a connection match two NAT rules. Normally the NAT Rule Base only permits one match and then subsequently exits the process. In the case of bidirectional NAT, if the source match is an automatic rule, the gateway continues to traverse the NAT rules to identify if there is a destination rule match. If the gateway finds a second match, it applies both NAT rules to the connection so that the packet is routed properly between source and destination. The gateway executes this translation in both ways, allowing either host to initiate communication with the other if the security policy permits.

The **Translate destination on client side** option, a gateway default setting, tells the gateway to translate destination addresses on the client side of the connection. This setting helps to remedy anti-spoofing and routing implications in previous versions of Check Point. In older versions of Check Point Firewall1, address translation occurred on the server side and static routes were necessary to forward packets to the correct destination. This setting allows backward compatibility within NGX if you have upgraded from a version without this functionality.

When enabled, **Automatic ARP configuration** instructs the gateway to automatically provide configuration changes to the ARP table in order to advertise for any automatically configured NAT addresses. Keep in mind that this is only for *Automatic* rules, not *Manually* created rules. In previous versions of Check Point, manual ARP entries were necessary for all NAT addresses. This enhancement removes the necessity to create a manual ARP entry for automatic NAT configurations.

The **Merge manual proxy ARP configuration** setting is new for Check Point NGX. What this option does is attempt to centralize ARP configuration to one single process. Since automatic NAT uses automatic ARP and manual NAT requires manual proxy-ARP entries, you can enable this setting to merge the two repositories into one single action. When Automatic ARP configuration is enabled, this setting (enabled) will merge the manual proxy-ARP configuration (in the local.arp) file with the automatic ARP entries (based on automatic NAT objects). In the case of address conflict, the gateway disregards the automatic ARP entry and instead publishes the manual proxy-ARP entry found in the local.arp file. If Automatic ARP configuration is enabled and this setting is not enabled, the gateway will disregard all manual ARP entries in the local.arp file.

In one manner, this setting could eliminate an unintentional duplication. Consider a case where you may accidentally configure automatic NAT for an address for which you have already defined a manual proxy-ARP entry in the local.arp file. Should this happen, you now know that the gateway will resolve the duplication issue by ignoring the automatic ARP entry and publishing the manual proxy-ARP entry. Although this inherent resolution may benefit you if the proxy-ARP entry is correct, it may induce undesirable results on your gateway, and possibly some undue stress on us, if the proxy-ARP entry is old and does not accurately reflect the desired configuration. So if you utilize this option, you must execute due diligence and audit your manual proxy-ARP entries to ensure that you do not have any duplicate entries, and that all your current entries are accurate.

Under the Manual NAT rules, the **Translate destination on client side** setting causes the same action as the same setting for automatic NAT rules. Again, older versions of the product translated the connection on the server side causing addition route configuration in order to facilitate a successful connection. Check Point recognized the growing need to resolve this and delivered this feature in their Check Point NG version.

Within the **IP Pool NAT** configuration settings, the **Enable IP NAT Pool** option primarily focuses on Secure Client/Secure Remote connections where there is an IP tunnel involved. Since the true address of the client may not be routable to hosts protected by the gateway, the IP NAT pool serves to create a range of addresses for such clients to utilize. In this manner, your gateway will translate a tunneled connection to a (internally) routable address for proper communications.

You may also configure the **Address exhaustion track:** and **Address allocation and release track:** options if you want to enable tracking for NAT pooling actions. If you have a need to troubleshoot an issue with routing to remote clients, then you can enable one or both of these options to the appropriate setting in order to populate your logs with usable information. In that way, you will see if you are running out of addresses to translate to, or you will simply be able to track which assignments are given to specific clients. In a sense, the tracking of allocation provides you with a small bit of an audit trail in that it accounts for the distribution of IP addresses to each requesting client.

Configuring Dynamic Hide Mode NAT

One of the most practical ways you employ address translation on your gateways is with *Dynamic Hide mode*. In this way, you protect internal hosts and preserve valuable routable IP addresses. In this chapter we will explore how to set up NAT rules so that an internal host, address range, or network is hidden behind a single public IP address.

Dynamic NAT Defined

When we speak of *Dynamic* NAT, we should simply consider this term the same as *Hide* NAT. Throughout this chapter, we will use the two expressions interchangeably. With that said, we will show you how to hide a single node, an address range, or an entire network behind a *Hide* NAT.

In the most simplistic configuration, you hide all the internal addresses behind the gateway's external interface address. If you want to use another routable address, you can define one, and then hide nodes behind it. Also, you may define a range of addresses to hide behind. In this case, an address range with a similar quantity of hosts would correlate almost one to one with a NAT range. For instance, if the address range is 10.1.1.100–110 and the NAT range is 192.168.1.10–20, then the address 10.1.1.102 would be hidden behind the address 192.168.1.12.

With *Hide* NAT you allow only outbound (one-way) communication from your internal hosts. This method does not permit external hosts to initiate connections with any of your protected hosts. Whereas most implementations of *Dynamic* NAT exhibit a many-to-one ratio, you are able to configure your gateway with a one-to-one *Static* relationship if you have such a need. In short, *Hide* NAT allows you either to translate private addresses so that your hosts can communicate with public addresses or to conceal the true addresses of your internal hosts so that you do not disclose confidential network topology.

Because *Hide* mode has the potential to conceal many connections behind a single address, the gateway has a unique way of handling connections. When your firewall receives a request for *Hide* NAT, it modifies not only the source address but also the source port. When the packet returns to the gateway, the firewall consults its tables to reveal which true client to send the packet to based primarily on the source port of the connection. If you think about the number of connections your gateway could potentially translate at any given time, up to 50,000 per server, you then understand why your gateway modifies the source port.

In most cases, the firewall uses high ephemeral ports when translating the source port. There are actually two port ranges from which your gateway chooses a translation source port. The first pool of ports ranges from 600 to 1023. In reality, your gateway only utilizes this range of ports for specific services matching more specific connection information. For instance, if you have an *rlogin*, *rshell*, or *rexec* connection request that is also using a source port less than 1024, the gateway will utilize this range of ports to choose the translated source port. On the other hand, the gateway assigns all other translation connections a port from the range of 10,000 to 60,000.

Although you are able to customize both ranges for translation ports, you must consider your environment prior to doing so. Keep in mind that the gateway is able to handle only up to 50,000 concurrent connections per server, hence the 10,000 to 60,000 port range. So, if you do modify the port ranges, you must ensure that your configuration satisfies this capability by providing no less than 50,000 source ports to choose from. For most environments, the default settings provide adequate coverage. For most of us, if you have more than 50,000 connections to one server, you are most likely experiencing a misconfiguration or some type of attack (possibly self induced).

To change these settings, you need to use the *dbedit* command-line utility. Essentially, you are changing the settings in the *objects_5_0.C* file on your firewall module. The valid range for the minimum high port is 1,025–60,000, and the valid range for the maximum high port is 10,003–60,000. When you execute the *dbedit* utility from the command line, you must supply administrative credentials in order to make changes to the database. Once you provide sufficient credentials, the firewall presents you with a *dbedit* command prompt. The following directives instruct the firewall to set the minimum high port to 15,000 and the maximum high port to 59,000.

```
C:\>dbedit -s localhost -u fwadmin -p password
Please enter a command, -h for help or -q to quit:
dbedit> modify properties firewall_properties hide_min_high_port 15000
dbedit> modify properties firewall_properties hide_max_high_port 59000
dbedit> update_all
properties::firewall_properties Updated Successfully
dbedit> quit
```

As you can see in the previous code snippet, there are several items you must know in order to actually execute the proper commands. In the *dbedit* command prompt, you can call the *−h* parameter to display usage guidelines. In this command, you want to *modify* from the *properties* table the *firewall_properties* object, and lastly the *hide_min_high_port* and *hide_max_high_port* fields. To save the changes you made, you must invoke the *update_all* directive. Then, you can quit the *dbedit* utility. To validate that your changes were made, you open the *objects_5_0.C* file on your enforcement module and search for the settings (*hide_min* should suffice as a search string). When you come upon the entry, you see both settings, one after another, with the modified values.

As previously mentioned, there isn't necessarily a need to modify these settings. Doing so without considerable reason and advanced understanding of the changes may invoke undesirable results on your firewall and may impede connectivity. As such, you may actually carry out a denial-of-service attack on yourself if you are not careful.

Advanced Understanding of NAT

Now that you somewhat understand how your firewall provides address translation, let's lift the hood and try to see what is really happening inside. In the firewall kernel, there are four distinct inspection points that move packets in one interface and out another. These four points are referred to as *i I o O*. They each provide a service so as to help the successful verification and routing of packets while they are being transferred through the firewall.

To begin, a packet must enter your firewall's external interface (use an inbound connection to a private server using NAT as an example). We refer to this action as the *inbound (i)* packet arriving at the kernel. Next the packet is submitted to the Security Rule Base. If the connection is permitted it subsequently is offered to the NAT Rule Base for translation of the destination address. The resultant packet is the (*I*) packet; accepted and translated for appropriate internal routing. Then the packet is sent through the TCP/IP stack and then to the appropriate firewall interface for *outbound* (*o*) processing. Again, the packet is matched against the NAT Rule Base, this time for source address translation. This is so that when your internal server receives the packet, it will have the correct address that the host can route a reply packet to. Lastly, the packet is sent out (*O*) the internal interface to your server to complete the connection.

On the return packet, you see a similar process as the packet enters the firewall's internal interface. This time the packet goes through the NAT Rule Base and translates the destination (original packet's source) to the true address. Next, the kernel passes the packet up the TCP/IP stack. Once more, the packet goes through the NAT Rule Base to translate the source (original destination) to its routable address. Finally, the packet moves through the firewall's external interface to the upstream router. It is important to note that this return packet does not pass through the firewall security policy. As the firewall accepts original request packets, it creates an entry in the connections table. When packets arrive at the firewall and are party to an existing connection (within the connections table) the firewall allows the packet to bypass the firewall's security policy inspection process. However, the packets continue to traverse the NAT Rule Base in order to satisfy any binding translation requirements.

As you may expect, Check Point provides you with a few tools to inspect translation tables and troubleshoot problems if necessary. One of these tools is the *fw monitor* command. If you are familiar with packet capture utilities, then you should not have any problems with this tool. Even if you are not familiar with such tools, the output from this command is understandable after some familiarization. When you use this tool with the *fw tab −t connections* command, you will see how the firewall maintains the connections with respect to both the Security Rule Base and the NAT Rule Base. The following example includes captures of these commands to illustrate the firewall's behavior.

```
1    C:\>fw tab -t connections
2    localhost:
3    -------- connections --------
4    dynamic, id 8158, attributes: keep, sync, expires 25,
     refresh, limit 25000, hash size 32768, kbuf 16 17 18 19 20 21 22 23
     24 25 26 27 28 29 30, free function f6c
5    2c210 0, post sync handler f6c2d6f0
6    <00000000, c0a845c9, 00000476, c0a86301, 00000050, 00000006> -> <00000000,
     c0a845c9, 00000476, c0a84597, 00000050, 00000006> (00000011)
7    <00000001, c0a86301, 00000050, c0a845c9, 00000476, 00000006> -> <00000000,
     c0a845c9, 00000476, c0a84597, 00000050, 00000006> (00000005)

1    C:\>fw monitor -m iIoO
2    monitor: getting filter (from command line)
3    monitor: compiling
4    Warning: COMPILER_DIR undefined, using FWDIR instead
5    : No error
6    monitorfilter:
7    Compiled OK.
```

```
8       monitor: loading
9       monitor: monitoring (control-C to stop)
10      PCnet1:i[48]: 192.168.69.201 -> 192.168.69.151 (TCP) len=48 id=6031
11      TCP: 1142 -> 80 .S.… seq=ca49b9f4 ack=00000000
12      PCnet1:I[48]: 192.168.69.201 -> 192.168.99.1 (TCP) len=48 id=6031
13      TCP: 1142 -> 80 .S.… seq=ca49b9f4 ack=00000000
14      PCnet1:o[48]: 192.168.99.1 -> 192.168.69.201 (TCP) len=48 id=28998
15      TCP: 80 -> 1142 .S..A. seq=4d96287f ack=ca49b9f5
16      PCnet1:O[48]: 192.168.69.151 -> 192.168.69.201 (TCP) len=48 id=28998
17      TCP: 80 -> 1142 .S..A. seq=4d96287f ack=ca49b9f5
18      PCnet1:i[40]: 192.168.69.201 -> 192.168.69.151 (TCP) len=40 id=6032
19      TCP: 1142 -> 80 ….A. seq=ca49b9f5 ack=4d962880
20      PCnet1:I[40]: 192.168.69.201 -> 192.168.99.1 (TCP) len=40 id=6032
21      TCP: 1142 -> 80 ….A. seq=ca49b9f5 ack=4d962880
```

As you see in the *fw tab −t connections* results, the firewall sends hex data to standard out. If you sift through the damage, you can identify the source and destination original and translated addresses. For instance, the original client in our example is 192.168.69.201. After translating the decimal to hex, you end up with *c0a845c9*. You can see in the results that this value exists in the sixth and seventh lines of the output. In addition, the NAT destination address, 192.168.69.151 (*c0a84597*) exists in the same connection. You then see the following connection entry in line 7 has a similar structure to the request connection in line 6.

To further simplify the hex output, let's take a look at the same lines compared with decimal format representation.

HEX <00000000, c0a845c9, 00000476, c0a86301, 00000050, 00000006> -> <00000000, c0a845c9, 00000476, c0a84597, 00000050, 00000006> (00000011)

DEC <0, 192.168.69.201, 1142, 192.168.99.1, 80, 6> -> <0, 192.168.69.201, 1142, 192.168.69.151, 80, 6> (17)

All right. Now you can see the resemblance of a connection. From left to right, you see the connection id, source, source port, destination, destination port, and protocol. The firewall associates this translated packet with the packet following the -> symbol. In this light you see that the firewall substitutes the NAT destination address (192.168.69.151) with the server's real address (192.168.99.1). Looking at line 7, you see the firewall executes a similar translation for the reply packet.

Now if you take a look at the *fw monitor* output, you can see that there are several connections going on, but that they meet what you expect to see after looking at the firewall's connections table. These captures show that the firewall is properly executing address translation. For instance, the first two captures beginning in lines 10 and 12 show that the source remains the same, but the destination address is different. Also, you can see reply packets in this output. You see that the gateway translates the reply packet in the manner you studied earlier. The packet comes into the interface (first capture line 14), then is translated if applicable (second capture line 16).

Several items to note in this particular set of output: First, the firewall left the source port for the connection unchanged during translation. Remember that only in *Dynamic* (Hide) mode does the firewall change the source port of the connection. Also, you see that you have a crude interpretation of the rule base. Recalling that there are four inspection points, you can combine that knowledge with this output and troubleshoot any problems with packets not being able to get through the firewall. Since you know that a packet first comes into an interface and then is sent to the Security Rule Base and NAT Rule Base, you may identify problems if the output does not reflect addresses translation (if applicable). In other words, if you see a packet come into the firewall, but do not see the translated packet bound for the destination host, you may safely presume that the connection did not satisfy your Security Rule Base. Lastly, if you have other packet capture utilities, you may use them in conjunction with any one or both of these tools to aid in troubleshooting issues or to just to learn more about your firewall's internal behavior.

When to Use It

Since Internet service providers (ISPs) and the Internet Assigned Numbers Authority (IANA) do not liberally allocate IP addresses to their customers, NAT allows you to preserve your limited allowance of public IP addresses. As such, the majority of your internal networks employ private address schemes. Creating this topology gives you the flexibility you need to populate your networks with all the appropriate servers, workstations, and other hosts you need without running into IP address limitations. Because of this, you need to employ NAT in order to route communication with hosts residing outside the scope of your network address space. The primary purpose in this sense is for packets bound for public address space; in essence, the Internet. However, you are also able to employ NAT when you simply do not want to expose your network topology to another party. In this manner, you may actually NAT from one private address to another or from a public address to a private address. This method is flexible in that it allows translation from any category address (public or private) to an identical range of addresses. Another way you configure NAT helps you to preserve address space.

Let's look at how you manually add a *Hide* NAT to your gateway so that your internal protected hosts are able to communicate with Internet hosts. For this example, consider that the internal network address is 192.168.90.0/24. Therefore, your gateway address (the default next hop for internal hosts) has an address of 192.168.90.1, and your internal hosts will use an address range from 192.168.90.2 to 254 (either using static or dynamic assignment via DHCP).

Now you need to open your NAT Rule Base by clicking the **Address Translation** tab in the SmartDashboard utility. You need to understand that there are going to be several objects that you will use to create this NAT rule. The first is the address range that you want to hide; the network object **Local_Net**. The other object, **Gateway**, will hide the internal addresses. As discussed earlier, you can hide behind other addresses, but you would need to create a separate object for such an address. Don't forget that routing and ARP issues may accompany this kind of NAT.

Begin by adding a rule to the rule base so that you can add your objects to it. From the menu, click **Rules | Add Rule | Bottom**. This action adds a rule to the rule base, as shown in Figure 5.1. Now, add your **Local_Net** object as the **Source** in the **Original Packet** section of the new rule. Since you want this rule to translate to any destination using any services, both the **Destination** and **Service** in the **Original Packet** section will remain **Any**.

Now determine how you want the translated packet to appear to outside hosts. In the **Source** section of the **Translated Packet** section, add your **Gateway** object selecting **Add (Hide)** from the pull-down menu when prompted. This tells your gateway to translate all packets from internal hosts using its external interface when going outbound. Since you are applying this to all packets, you do not change the value of **Destination** or **Service**. Both of these values should remain **Original**.

The **Install On** field defines which gateways will receive this policy. If you have defined policy targets, leave this value unchanged, reading **Policy Targets**. As for the **Comment** section, you just add a brief description of the rule "Hide NAT for Internal Network" to explain the rule's purpose. Figure 5.3 shows the completed NAT rule.

Figure 5.3 Completed NAT Rule

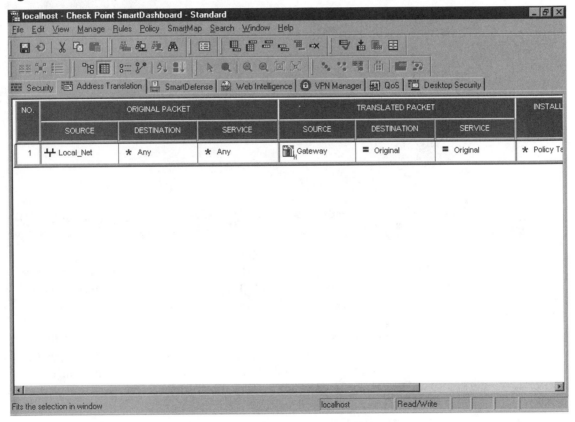

Again, your NAT rule does not permit your internal hosts to communicate; it just translates the packets in order to facilitate the connection. You need to be sure that there is a rule in your security policy that allows your internal hosts this communication. Figure 5.4 shows the characteristics of this rule.

Figure 5.4 Rule to Allow Outbound Traffic

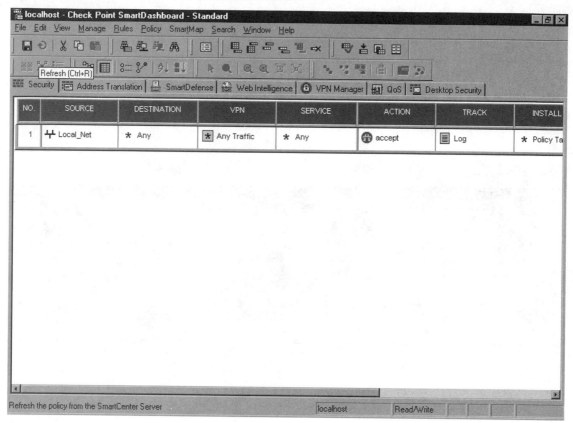

This rule has **Local_Net** as the source, destination and service remain **Any**, and the **Action** is **Accept**. This allows all traffic from your internal network, 192.168.90.0/24, to initiate connects to any destination. As desired, your NAT rule will translate outbound packets for proper routing and to conceal your private topology.

There are some instances where you may have a single host on your protected network that needs to communicate with an external server for one particular reason or another. Further, you may not desire any of your other protected hosts to share the ability to complete such connections. On the other end, your connection partner may also employ access control. For this reason, you need to inform them of the sole IP address that will request the connection. In this case, you can employ a one-to-one *Hide* NAT. This is where it may be easier for us to use the term *Hide* NAT. You are not configuring this rule for *Static* NAT, as discussed later in this chapter, but you must single out this one connection based on your requirements. In this way, the gateway will use one single NAT address for only this protected host.

Routing and ARP

Without delving too far into specifics, we shall consider basic routing with regard to NAT. To this end, let's agree that proper routing facilitates the successful transmission of a packet from source host to destination host. In simplest terms, a host forwards a packet to its appropriate next hop as defined in its local routing table. Each router or gateway in the communication path then sends the packet on to the next hop as determined in its own local routing table until the destination host's router receives the packet. Since this router belongs to the same local network as the intended destination, it delivers the packet to the destination host. In most cases, you don't NAT outside of your allocated public IP space. Since your upstream provider already routes this range to your perimeter router, you need not worry about making arrangements for new routes to your NAT address. However, if you utilize an address that your upstream provider does not currently route to your router, then you must request that your provider add the necessary routes to accommodate your NAT.

The Address Resolution Protocol (ARP) aids routing in that it translates an IP address to a physical hardware address (MAC address), and vice versa. Where routing tells a host which IP address to send the packet to next (next hop), ARP queries the current network to resolve which hardware address corresponds to that IP address. It is only following an ARP query and response that a router determines which host (router or gateway) is the next hop and transmits a packet to the host that owns the hardware address that the ARP query returned. Any device, including your Check Point gateway, that does NAT must have ARP entries for each address it translates. If it didn't, the gateway would not respond to an ARP query telling the originator it is the next recipient of the packet. As a consequence of the nature of ARP, your gateway's ARP behavior is no different for *Dynamic* or *Static* NAT.

Adding ARP Entries

Because Check Point is compatible with a host of operating systems, there are different ways to add ARP entries in order for them to survive a reboot. In this section, we touch on several platforms and how to achieve the desired result.

Secure Platform

To add ARP entries using Secure Platform, follow these steps:

1. Create the */etc/ethers* file.

2. Add a line to include your ARP entry:
     00:02:B1:C0:D7:78 192.168.1.100

3. Add the following line to the */etc/rc.local* file:
     arp –f /etc/ethers

Solaris

To add ARP entries using Solaris, follow these steps:

1. Create the file /etc/rc2.d/S99arp.

2. Add a line to include your ARP entry:
     arp –a 192.168.1.100 00:02:B1:C0:D7:78 pub

3. Change the file permissions to make it executable:
     chmod 744 S99arp

Windows

To add ARP entries using Windows, follow these steps:

1. Create a *local.arp* file in the $FWDIR\state directory.

2. Add a line to include your ARP entry:
    192.168.1.100 00:02:B1:C0:D7:78

3. Save the changes to the *local.arp* file.

IPSO

To add ARP entries using IPSO, follow these steps:

1. Log into the *Voyager* administrative interface.

2. Click the **Config** button.

3. Under the **System Configuration** heading, click **ARP**.

4. Scroll down to the **Proxy ARP Entries** section.

5. In the **Add a new Proxy ARP entry:,** add the appropriate address to the **IP address:** field.

6. Click **Apply**, then enter the appropriate MAC address in the field for this ARP entry.

7. Click **Save**.

Although these guidelines may provide you a successful persistent ARP entry, there are certainly other ways to negotiate ARP entries, especially with the flexibility of Linux and Solaris. You may be more comfortable doing things your way. The key point here is that your ARP entries survive a system restart. As the old saying goes; there is more than one way to skin a cat.

When you use *Hide* NAT, you may or may not run into routing and ARP issues. If you simply hide your internal objects behind the external gateway address, you shouldn't encounter any issues with either of these technologies. Because your upstream providers should be routing to the gateway's external address already, you are not required to modify any configuration settings to receive proper address translation. However, if you utilize a separate address for hiding your objects, one other than the gateway's external interface address, you must modify the ARP table to include this new address. In this way, the gateway responds to an ARP query for the NAT address with its external hardware address. As such, the upstream router forwards the packet to your gateway. Again, recall that your upstream provider must be made aware of any NAT address you use if it is not within the current network that they route to you. In this case, your provider may need to modify its routing tables accordingly. Later in this chapter, we will configure ARP manually and automatically.

Configuring Static Mode NAT

The single most obvious use for Static NAT is when you configure a protected host for public use. Again, if you have a limited IP address allocation, you may utilize private IP space within your DMZ network(s). In such cases, you must apply Static NAT to your servers that host your Web, mail, and other public services. In this chapter, we will examine configuring protected hosts with Static NAT.

Static NAT Defined

Similar to *Hide* NAT, *Static* NAT conceals a host's true address. The primary difference between the two modes is *Static* NAT's ability to allow an external host to initiate inbound connections. Instead of hiding your protected hosts, you are in some way announcing their address to the external networks. In contrast to *Hide* mode, *Static* rules must utilize the same object type for translation. Whereas you can create a hiding rule to hide a network behind a single address, *Static* NAT conveys a one-to-one relationship.

You have numerous options when it comes to configuring *Static* NAT. In this section we will further discuss these options, and later we describe how to configure a gateway for *Static* NAT.

When to Use It

To let servers and other service-oriented hosts communicate with the outside world, you need to uniquely identify them via NAT. Your DMZ hosts in this case utilize private addresses and must be converted to a public routable address when leaving your protected network. Similar to *Hide* NAT, you create a *Static Source* rule so that your server's real address is concealed during outbound connections when it reaches your gateway.

To configure this translation, add a rule to the NAT Rule Base above your hide rule. In addition, you will need to add an object that represents your **Web_Server** with internal address 192.168.90.10. Further, configure a **Web_Server_Valid** object that represents the routable address of your server, 198.53.145.2, as seen in Figure 5.5.

Figure 5.5 Web Server External Object

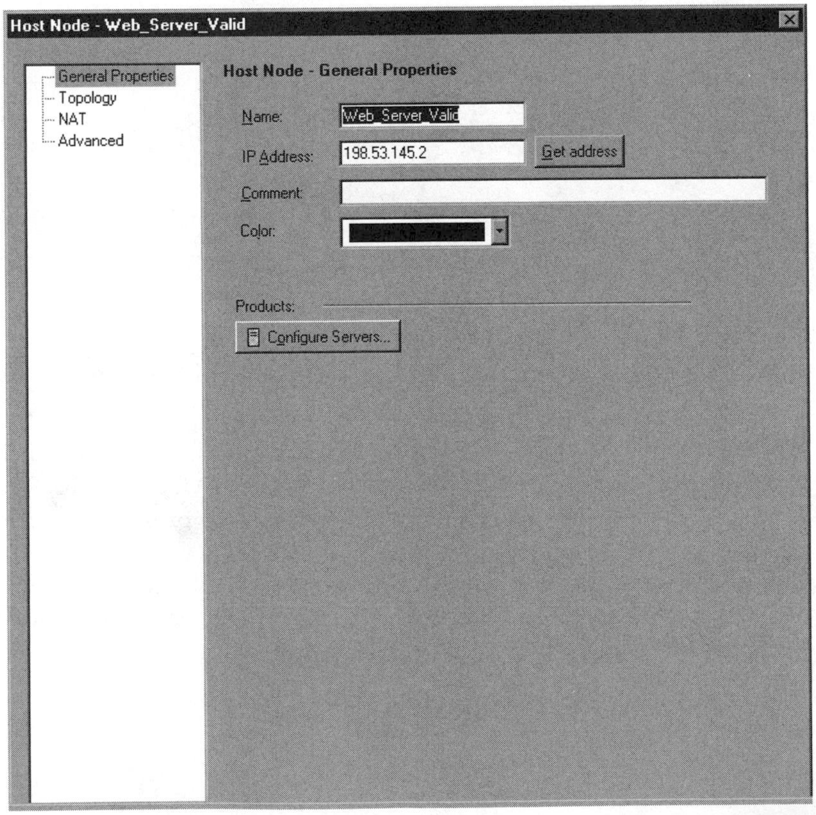

Now that you have your objects defined, move on to create the NAT rule. You need to **Add Rule | Above** your current *Hide* rule. You define the **Web_Server** object as the **Source** in the **Original Packet** section. The **Destination** and **Service** remain **Any**. On the **Translated Packet** side, set the **Source** to **Web_Server_Valid**. Again, the **Destination** and **Service** remain unchanged. Figure 5.6 shows the new rule base with the previous *Hide* rule and the new *Manual Static Source* rule.

Figure 5.6 Static Source NAT Rule

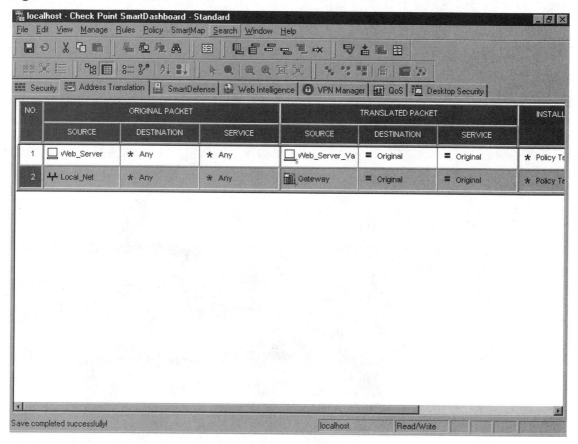

Once the gateway receives the packet, it translates the packet so that the external client can route the packet back to your gateway. This again is very similar to *Hide* NAT, except that you now see why *Static* NAT requires a one-to-one relationship for proper routing or packet forwarding to your public servers.

Lastly, verify that your security policy permits the **Web_Server** object to initiate connections outbound. If your Web server is in your internal network, the current rule would cover this traffic. However, if the server is in your DMZ, create rule 2, as seen in Figure 5.7.

Figure 5.7 Outbound Rule for Web Server

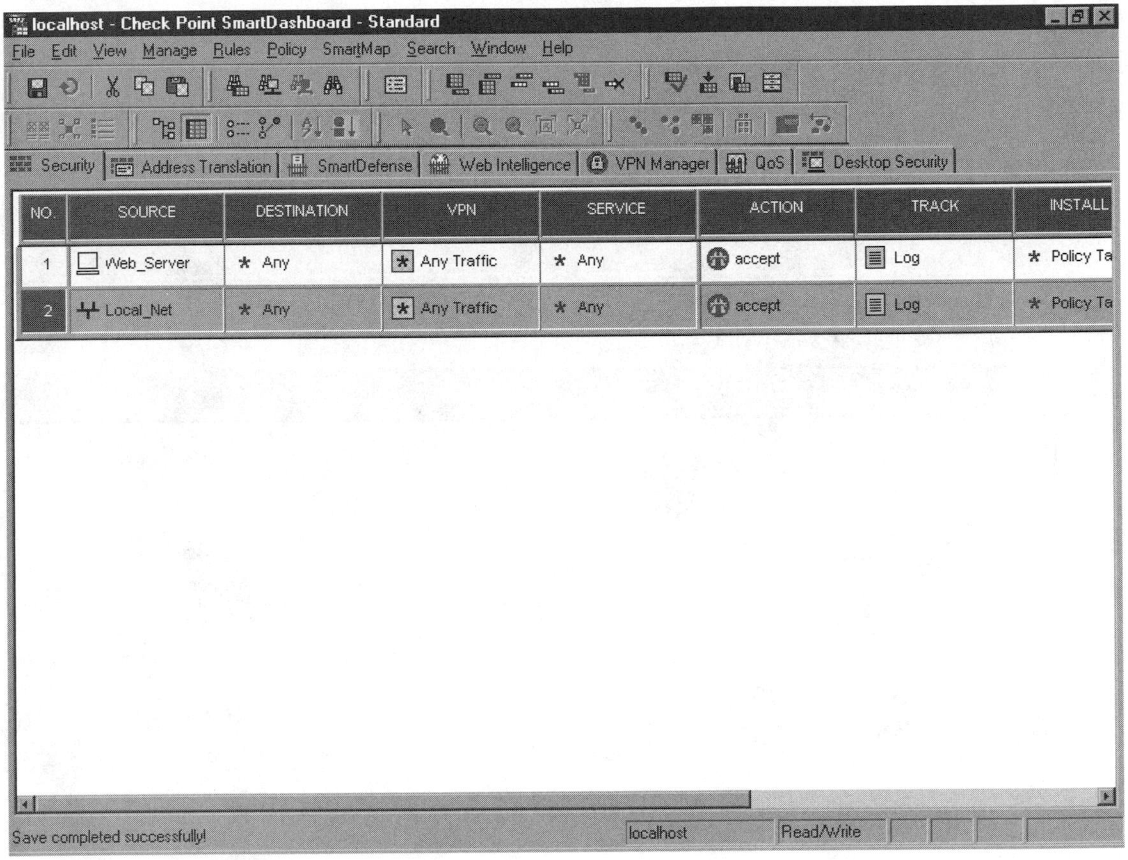

You also utilize *Static* NAT if you need to differentiate between your outgoing clients. Since *Hide* NAT converts many clients behind the same address, you need to use *Static* NAT to individually identify single clients. In this case, it is not necessary to add two NAT rules because inbound connectivity may not be necessary. Additionally, since *Hide* NAT modifies the source port, you must employ *Static* NAT if you use protocols that cannot survive such modifications.

Inbound Connections

We've already mentioned that you employ *Static* NAT when you want to let external hosts connect to your DMZ servers. In essence, you refer to this translation as *Static Destination*. In contrast to *Hide* NAT, this action doesn't translate the source of the packet, but translates the destination. So when an external host's connection request reaches your gateway (via a routable address), the destination address is converted to an internal protected address and then forwarded to the corresponding server.

To create this translation rule, choose **Add Rule | Below** from the menu to create it below your *Static Source* rule. In the **Original Packet** section, change the **Destination** to **Web_Server_Valid** and leave the **Source** and **Service** as **Any**. In the **Translated Packet** section, the **Destination** is **Web_Server** and the **Source** and **Service** remains **Original**. Figure 5.8 shows the completed NAT rule.

Figure 5.8 Static Destination Rule

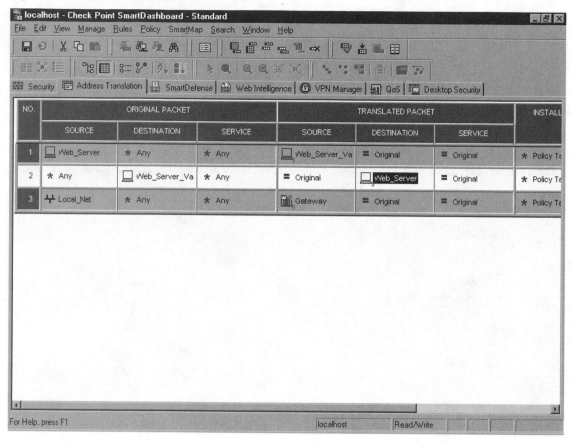

As is always the case, you need to verify that your security policy permits your desired traffic. In this case, you need to add a rule to allow any host to your **Web_Server_Valid** address. Since you want to allow only http to this host, set the **Source** to **Any**, the **Destination** to **Web_Server_Valid**, and the **Service** to **http**. Figure 5.9 displays the completed rule 2.

Figure 5.9 Rule for Incoming Traffic to Web Server

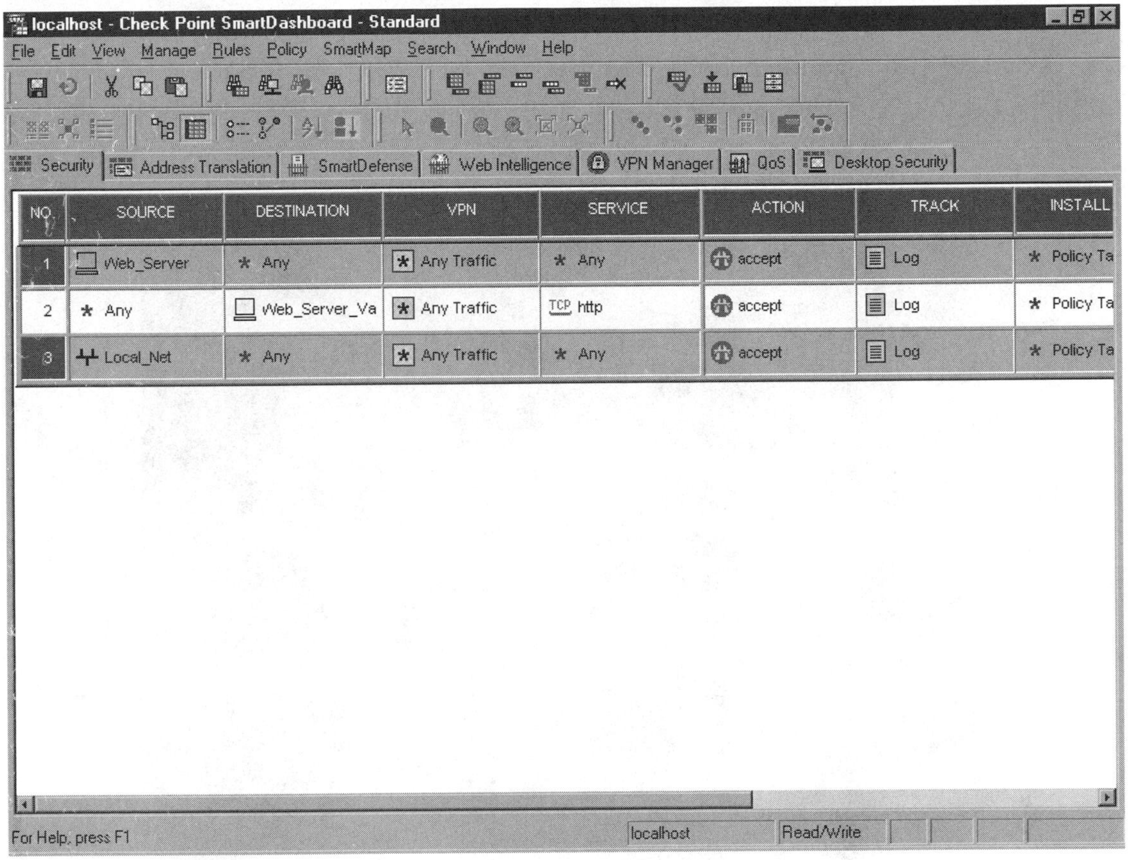

You must remember that your gateway not only performs NAT but also provides access control. When you want to employ *Static* NAT to let external clients initiate connections to your protected servers, you must configure Security rules as well. If you configure NAT without adding a Security rule, the gateway will not permit the client's request to communicate with the server. If you use Check Point's *Automatic* NAT feature, the Security rule's destination can be the internal host object. However, if you deploy a *Static* NAT rule manually, you need to define a second node object with the routable (translated) address. Then, you create the Security rule with your new public object as the destination.

Configuring Automatic NAT

Though you are able to create all the rules you need manually (as we have already discussed), Check Point's automatic NAT configuration ability also suits your needs. This method is generally easier to configure, decreases error rates, and also takes considerably less time.

When to Use It

Just as with manual configuration, you can configure *Hide* or *Static* NAT automatically. Under the same circumstances as your manual configuration, you can modify existing or new objects to do the translation automatically. Figure 5.10 shows the object with an automatic NAT configuration.

Figure 5.10 NAT Tab of Network Object

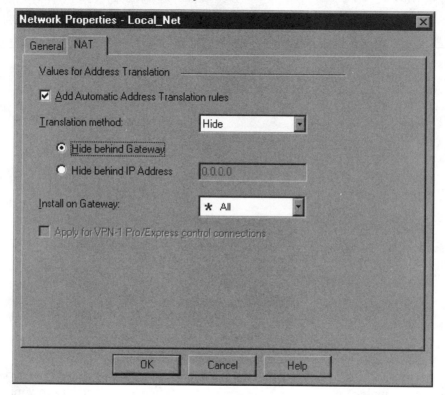

For *Hide* mode on your internal private network, all you need to do is modify the **Local_Net** object's properties. In SmartDashboard choose **Manage | Network Objects** from the File menu, then select **Local_Net** and click **Edit**. Select the **NAT** tab at the top and check the box for **Add Automatic Translation rules**. For **Translation Method** accept the default **Hide**. You also should not change the default setting of **Hide behind Gateway**. In the **Install on** box, select your gateway, or leave it the default setting **All**.

When you enable this setting, you essentially tell all the outside world that your connection source from all your internal clients is your firewall's external interface. Though you are able to easily configure this setting, there are some items you need to consider before making this decision.

Hiding all your internal addresses behind your gateway's address allows you to save IP address space. We've covered this topic before, so we won't expound on it again here. Another great benefit is that it minimizes your management of NAT within your firewall. Since all the internal IP space is hidden behind one IP address, you should introduce minimal configuration changes to your firewall. In addition, you need to provide only a single IP address to connection partners for access control on their end.

On the other hand, hiding all your internal clients behind your firewall's external address can attract undesirable attention. For instance, if you use an alternative IP address to hide all your internal clients behind, you are then able to shield your gateway address from the Internet (possibly adding an ACL to the upstream perimeter router). In this sense, your firewall maintains a low connection profile and provides a very limited footprint across the public wire. Though this configuration requires you to add an object to define the internal clients and configure NAT for this object, you still minimize the changes to a manageable level.

In the case where you require *Static* NAT (like our Web server example), you simply make a small adjustment to the same steps as *Hide* mode. Again, open SmartDashboard and choose **Manage | Network Objects** from the file menu, then select **Web_Server** and click **Edit**. Select the **NAT** tab from the left menu pane and check the box for **Add Automatic Translation rules**. For **Translation Method** choose **Static** from the pull-down menu. In the **Translate to IP Address** box, enter **198.52.145.2** (your routable address). Figure 5.11 shows the *Static* NAT configuration for the Web server.

Figure 5.11 NAT Tab of Web Server

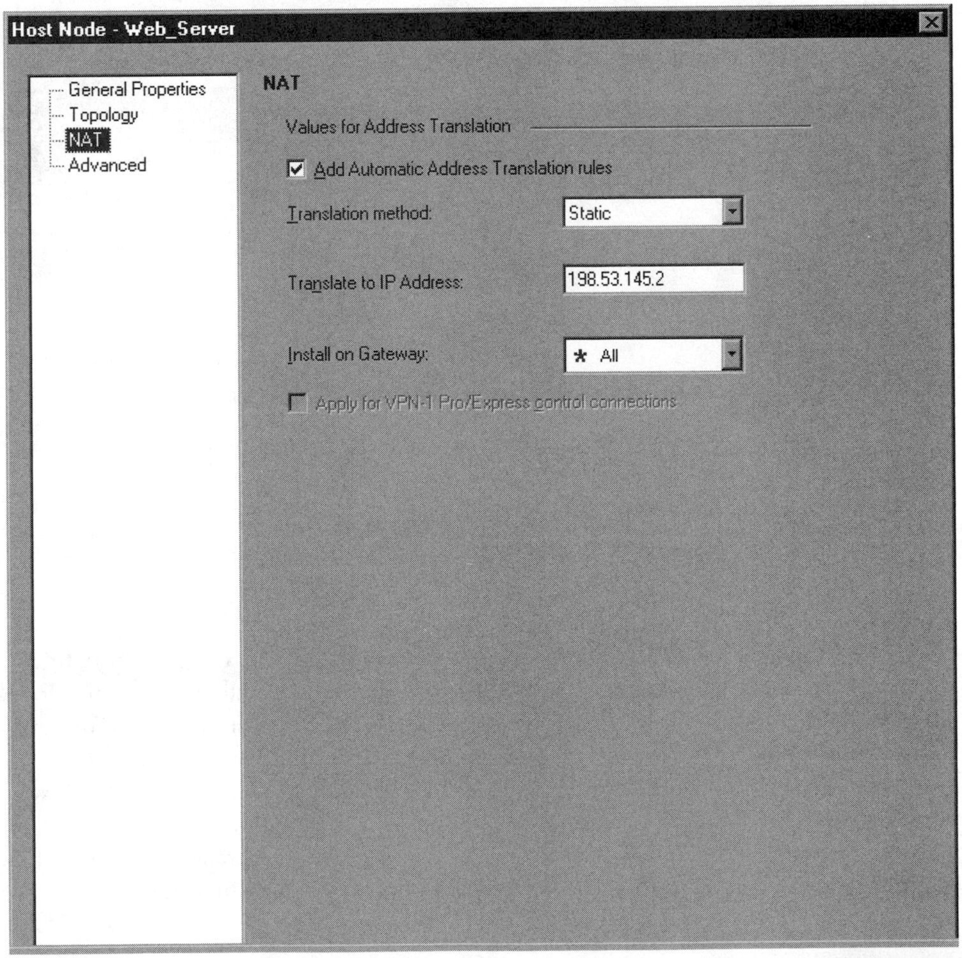

NAT Rule Base

Now let's take a look at the NAT Rule Base after you successfully configure your *Static* and *Hide* translations automatically. Figure 5.12 shows the new NAT Rule Base, and you can see that two automatic configurations have resulted in the gateway creating four rules.

Figure 5.12 Generated Address Translation Rules

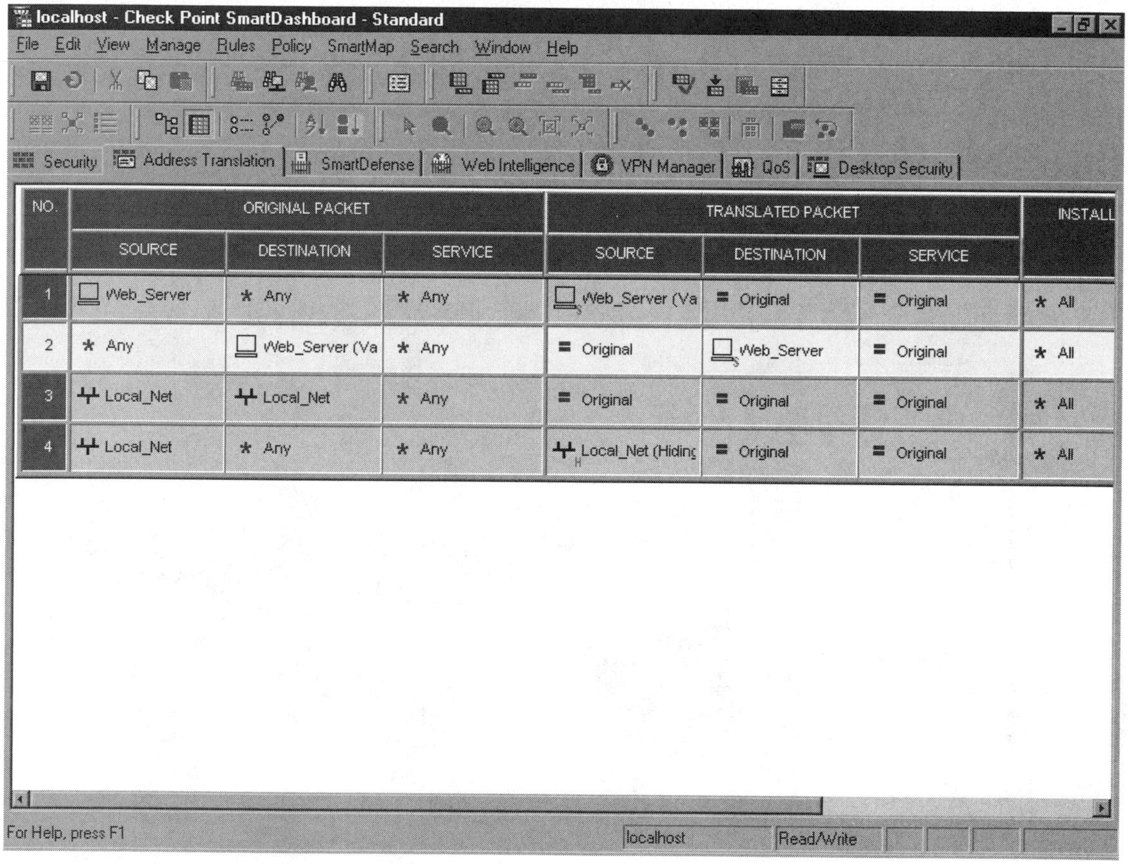

The first rule translates the **Web_Server** private address to the valid address you defined in the object's properties for outbound connections. The second rule translates the valid address for **Web_Server** into the private address for incoming connections. Both of these rules equate to your two *Static* rules you created manually: one for *Static Source* and another for *Static Destination*.

Likewise, rules 3 and 4 correspond to your *Hide* NAT rules you created manually. However, when you create *Hide* NAT automatically, the gateway generates a rule that does not translate packets from **Local_Net** hosts to other **Local_Net** hosts. This rule ensures that translation is not done internally and that routing from within **Local_Net** does not become complicated.

Figure 5.13 Gateway NAT Properties

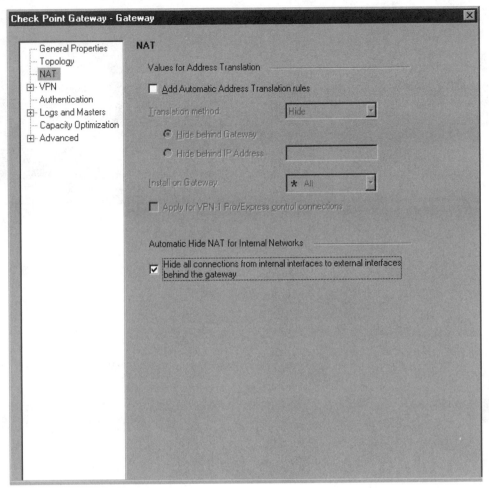

Access Control Settings

Just as with your other NAT rules, you need to configure proper access control via your security policy to ensure that you are permitting traffic as desired. One difference in the case of automatic configuration is that you are not required to define a separate object for the valid address of your Web server. The gateway intelligently handles all outside communications to your Web server with the valid address and any internal communications via the private protected address. Take a look at Figure 5.14 to see the difference between manual and automatic translations' effect on the security policy.

Figure 5.14 Security Policy for Automatic NAT

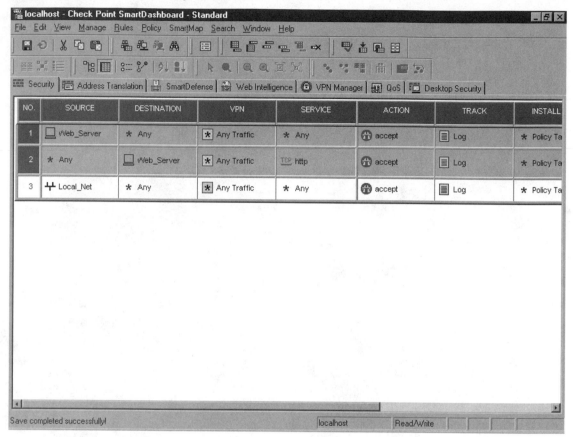

Configuring Port Translation

Essentially, you have already covered how to manually configure NAT, both in *Hide* mode and *Static* mode. In this section we discuss a different aspect of manual NAT, port translation. In this sense, you can further save IP address space if you have numerous servers that provide different services.

When to Use It

Consider three servers: an SMTP server, an HTTP server, and an FTP server. If you are considerably strained by having only a few public routable IP addresses, you may configure your gateway so that these requests could go to one single IP address. The gateway handles all the translation and, from the rules you create, will designate traffic to the appropriate internal application server.

You can even implement this technique when you have a service running on a nonstandard port and want to conceal the true port from external users. If you are running an HTTP server on port 8080, but want to respond to port 80 (standard HTTP port) requests from the outside, you can configure the gateway to translate the incoming request so that the client talks to the server on port 8080 without realizing it. In truth, the gateway translates destination port 80 to port 8080.

NAT Rule Base

As you configure manual NAT entries, your primary consideration concerning the NAT Rule Base is that you properly compose translation rules to intercept inbound and outbound packets. If you are using your gateway's address to advertise services homed on internal hosts (using port translation), then there must be a *Hide* NAT in place so that when the servers respond to external hosts, the packets will be routed appropriately (back to the gateway).

For instance, let's say thatyyour three servers are hiding behind the gateway's external address and that you are using port translation to redirect services. Figure 5.15 shows this configuration using the **DMZ_NET** and the corresponding NAT rules. In all, the gateway accepts connections to its external address for three separate internal servers, each one hosting a single application. When a client makes a connection request to the gateway for, say, FTP (rule 5 in Figure 5.15), the gateway translates the packet so that the destination is the **Ftp_Server** object's internal IP address. When the **Ftp_Server** replies to the client, the gateway then translates the packet's source to its own external IP address. In this manner, the requesting client and **Ftp_Server** continue a normal conversation as if both of them were talking directly to one another. The client in this case is unaware that the gateway is performing the translation.

Figure 5.15 Port Translation Rules

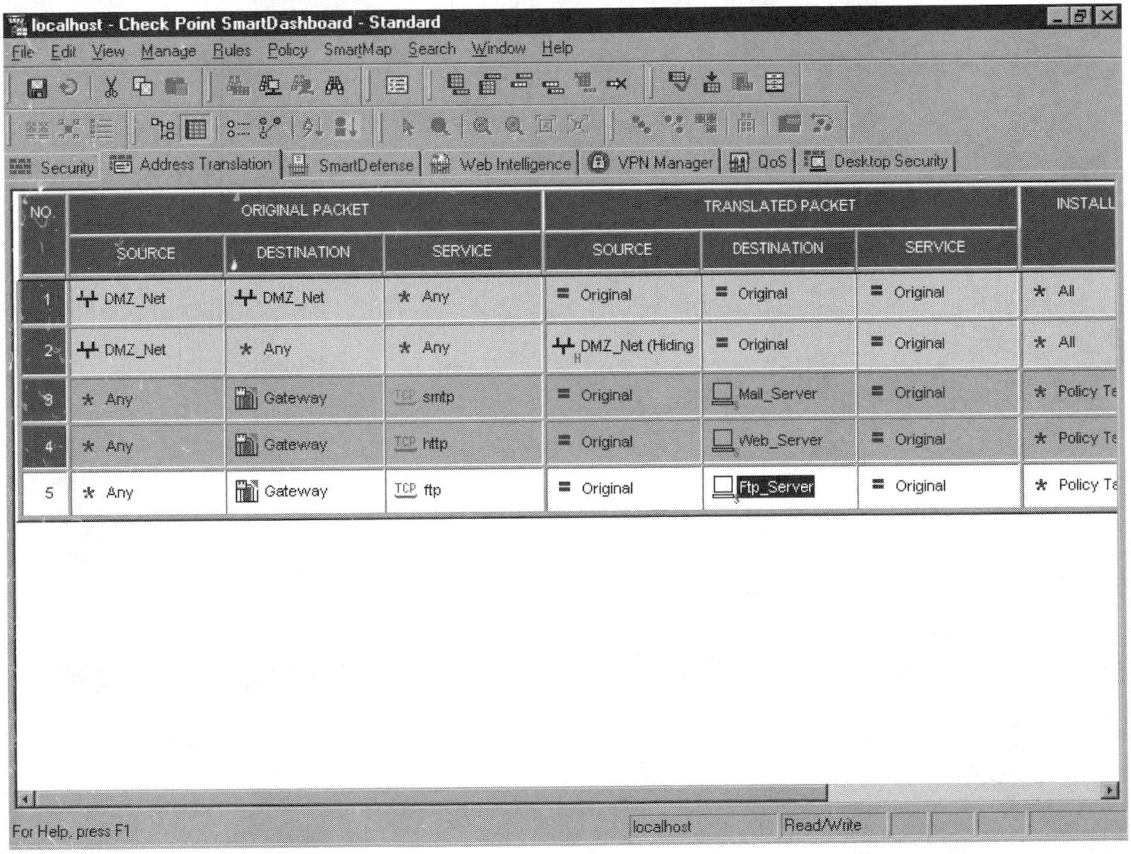

Security Policy Implications

Using port translation, you benefit from defining a set of NAT rules that makes one single IP address appear to host many services. To accompany these rules, you need access control rules that permit external hosts to talk to your servers. Since your server addresses are private and not routable from external sources, your rules must reflect a destination that matches the NAT rule. Similar to manual *Static* NAT from earlier, your security policy rule must use the routable object, not the true internal object as you used in automatic NAT. Figure 5.16 shows the security policy reflecting appropriate access control rules for port translation rules. Notice that you do not need to define rules explicitly permitting external clients access to your application servers. The gateway will accept the connections to its external address and apply the necessary NAT rules in order to facilitate a successful connection.

Figure 5.16 Security Policy for Port Translation

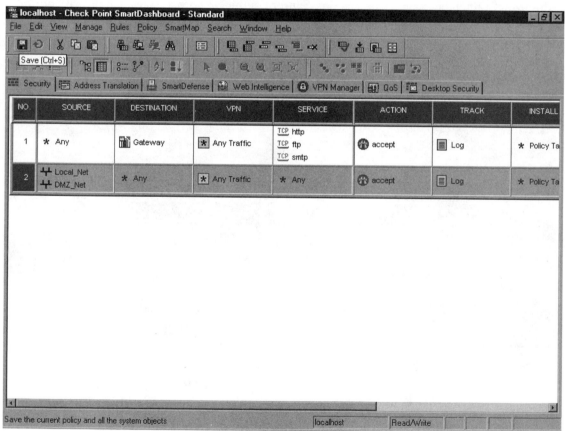

Summary

Network Address Translation gives you flexibility and protection within your architectures. It allows you to conserve valuable IP address space and prevents your production servers from being fully exposed to Internet threats.

Check Point provides two primary methods for deploying NAT: *Hide* mode and *Static* mode. Having said that, you are capable of manually configuring your rules or are able to take advantage of Check Point's intuitive automatic configuration utilities. Either method delivers the same end result.

Hide mode allows you to configure your gateway to translate outbound traffic so that your internal hosts may access the Internet (or other external hosts) without revealing your private topology. In addition, *Hide* NAT provides the necessary address change that is needed for proper routing on public networks.

Static mode provides similar address hiding, but permits you to offer services on your internal or DMZ servers. This option places a one-to-one relationship between two hosts and the gateway redirects all transactions bound for the public address to the coordinating internal address.

Not only does the gateway handle basic address translation needs, it also has the capacity to conduct advanced port translation so that you make optimal use of your minimal IP address allocation. Port translation provides the necessary means to utilize a single address for multiple services hosted on more than one server.

Now that you have learned to configure NAT with Firewall-1, you will be able to deliver advanced security for your networks. The tools you use for NAT help you to protect your networks from disclosure and minimize your hosts from exposure to the outside world. NAT is a key instrument in supplying a sound, optimal security policy.

Chapter 6

Authentication

Solutions in this chapter:

- **Authentication Overview**
- **Users and Administrators**
- **User Authentication**
- **Session Authentication**
- **Client Authentication**

☑ **Summary**

Introduction

Using Check Point NGX, you can control the traffic coming into or going out of your networks. A good definition of your networks, hosts, gateways, and services allows you to have granular control of traffic through the Security Gateway. However, there are times when you will need or want to authenticate specific users that are accessing your resources.

For example, an administrator might have to download privileged files using a restricted user's workstation, and would need to be granted special privileges for a specific amount of time. Networks that use DHCP with different classes of users in the same network would need to authenticate privileged users to grant them access to the resources they need. Enterprises might have a need for registering in the log the specific user accessing a specific Web site.

With authentication, Check Point NGX's features are greatly expanded and complement already strong security with the ability to implement security on a per user basis. Once you understand how NGX Authentication works, you will probably find many uses for it in your environment.

Authentication Overview

Check Point NGX works based on the information it has to permit or deny a connection. The firewall has no knowledge of which user is logged into a Microsoft Active Directory, or if a user is moving among different machines. To be able to authenticate a particular user that is crossing the firewall, it needs additional information to match the user and the connection. The main topic of this chapter addresses the best way to authenticate users so they can access privileged resources. There have not been many changes between how authentication works in NG with Application Intelligence and how it works in NGX, and we list the major changes in this chapter.

We will first address the issue of which users can authenticate. Check Point NGX is flexible enough to authenticate users created in various sources, databases, or external directory servers. We will then examine the different types of authentication that NGX allows, which are called User, Session, and Client Authentication. These authentication schemes are for unencrypted authentication.

Using Authentication in Your Environment

Using Authentication involves additional configuration of the firewall and planning an environment that allows users to access the resources they need. Some of the environments that can benefit from authentication include the following.

- You use DHCP without IP reservations in your network, but you need to give a few of your users access to special resources.

- Your CIO wants strict logging of the traffic habits of your users, and so you need your log to contain the username of every connection from your internal networks.

- A support technician needs to download drivers and antivirus programs from the Internet, on machines in a restricted segment that are not allowed to access the Internet.

- You have an extranet site and want to add an additional layer of password security via your firewall.

Users and Administrators

Think of a user as an entity: Bob, Peter, and so forth. To recognize (or authenticate) a user, the user either needs to know something (a password) or have something (a digital certificate). This chapter focuses on passwords, since Digital Certificates are for VPNs only. Most companies already have some sort of user database (MS Active Directory, a RADIUS server, etc.), and would like to integrate this database with their firewall, through the use of an Authentication Scheme.

Managing Users and Administrators

Before you can authenticate users, you need to define them and place them in groups. Check Point NGX is very flexible in this sense. You can use NGX's built-in user database, as well as external user directories. Let's first focus on the built-in database, which you'll probably use the most or at least have to interact with most often.

There are two ways you can access and edit the user database. You can access the *Manage Users and Administrators* dialog from the **Manage | Users and Administrators** menu (look at Figure 6.1). This dialog includes a listing of all user-related objects: users, groups, templates, administrators, external users groups, LDAP, and so on.

Figure 6.1 Manage Users and Administrators Dialog

You can also select the *Users* tab in the Object Tree, and then expand the different entity classes to edit their objects (as in Figure 6.2). You can right-click on any entity class to add new objects.

Figure 6.2 Object Tree Listing of User Entities and Their Icons

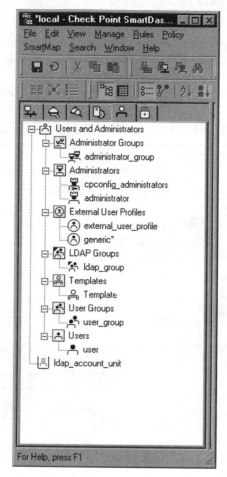

The first item you will see in the Manage Administrators dialog box will be a yellow icon named *cpconfig_administrators*. It represents the administrators configured by the *cpconfig* utility in the SmartCenter server. In NGX, you can define only one administrator via cpconfig (in the cpconfig menu, it now says Administrator instead of previous versions' Administrators). If you have upgraded from NG, you can migrate the existing cpconfig administrators to the SmartDashboard by using the **cp_admin_convert** command in the SmartCenter server (you need to use expert mode in SecurePlatform).

Each entity that you can create in the Users and Administrators dialog bog is represented by a different icon. Administrators have crowns over them, groups are represented by two users, templates are outlines, and external users have a circle around them. Look at Figure 6.2 to identify the different icons.

Permission Profiles

Before you create an administrator, you need to create a *Permissions Profiles*. Go to the **Manage | Permission Profiles** dialog, and select **New... | Permissions Profile...** (see Figure 6.3).

Figure 6.3 The Permissions Profiles Dialog

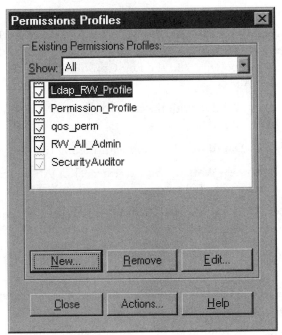

In the *General* tab, you can name the profile, select a color and enter a comment. In the *Permissions* tab, you allow access via two methods:

- **SmartPortal and Console Applications** Administrators can use SmartDashboard, and all the Smart management applications, as well as the SmartPortal web interface.

- **SmartPortal only** Administrators can access only the SmartPortal web interface, which is read-only and designed for auditors and restricted administrators.

In the *Permissions* tab, you also can choose the following profiles (see Figure 6.4):

- **None** Use this to disable an administrator's permissions.

- **Read/Write All** Allows full access to all NGX management applications. A Read/Write All profile can also select Manage Administrators, which will allow the administrator to create, modify, and delete other administrators from the SmartDashboard. It will also grant access to the Permission to Install setting for objects.

- **Read-Only All** Administrators will be able to read every configuration, but won't be able to change anything.

- **Customized** Here you can create a personalized profile for administrators with very specific functions. The permissions for each option can be None (disable the option with the Check Box next to the item), Read Only, and Read/Write.

You can select the following specific functions for a customized profile:

- **SmartUpdate**   Administrators can use SmartUpdate for managing product updates and assigning licenses. An administrator with Read/Write SmartUpdate access will automatically have Read/Write access to the Objects, LDAP and Users databases, the Security and QoS policies, and the Log Consolidator, Eventia Reporter, and UserAuthority Web Access.

- **Objects Database**   Working with the networks objects and services in the SmartDashboard interface.

- **Check Point Users Database**   Working with the internal user database.

- **LDAP Users Database**   Working with an external LDAP database using the SmartDirectory functionality (which requires a separate license).

- **Security Policy**   Working with the Security and Address Translation rules and installing a policy (with Read/Write access).

- **QoS Policy**   Working with the QoS rules and installing a policy (with Read/Write access).

- **Log Consolidator**   Working with the Consolidation Policy. Eventia Reporter uses that policy for compiling information from the logs.

- **Eventia Reporter**   Working with the Eventia Reporter tables.

- **Monitoring**   Access to the SmartView Monitor database for statuses.

- **UserAuthority Web Access**   Working with the UserAuthority Web Access product.

- **ROBO Gateways Database**   Working with Remote Office/Branch Office Gateways, using the SmartLSM (Large Scale Manager) application.

- **Events Database**   Working with the Eventia Analyzer database.

- **Event Correlation Policy**   Working with the Eventia Analyzer Events database.

- **Track Logs**   Accessing the Traffic Log and Active sessions in the SmartView Tracker. Users with Read/Write permissions can purge and switch the logs, and to Block Intruders from the Active Sessions page.

- **Audit Logs**   Accessing the Active sessions and Audit Logs in the SmartView Tracker. Users with Read/Write permissions can purge and switch the logs, and block intruders from the Active Sessions page.

Figure 6.4 The Permissions Tab of the Permissions Profile

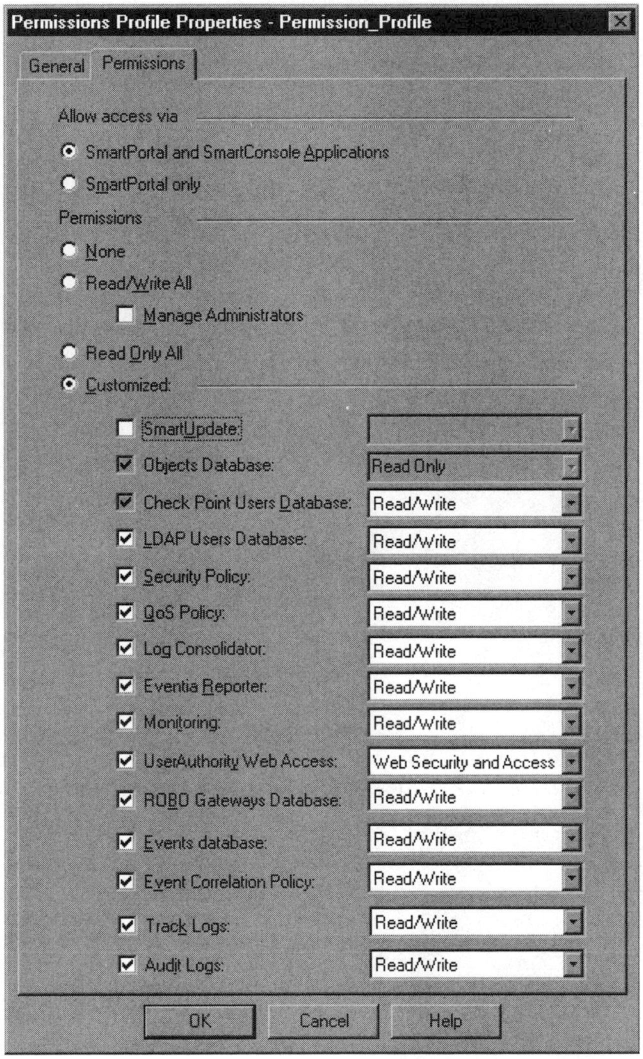

Administrators

The administrators are the users who have access to the configuration of the firewall. Depending on the Permissions Profile assigned to the administrators, they may or may not have permission to read and write to different parts of the security policy. Once you create or edit an administrator, you'll see the following tabs.

General Tab

In the **General** tab of the Administrator you can give a name to the administrator and select a previously created Permissions Profile. You can also click **New…** and directly create a new profile. **View Permissions Profile** allows you to view and edit existing profiles. Look at Figure 6.5.

Figure 6.5 Creating a New Administrator

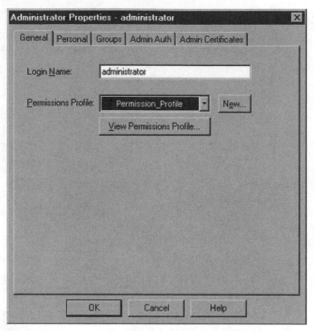

Personal Tab

You will find a **Personal** tab for both administrators and users. The **Expiration Date** field (in dd-mm-yyyy format) is used to set a valid time period for an administrator. For example, you can use an administrator with a set expiration date for an auditor that needs to review your policies during the next month. By default in NGX, the expiration date is December 31, 2008.

Enter a Comment for the Administrator and select a Color for the display of its icon. These fields are for informational use only.

Groups

You can select which Administrators Groups this administrator belongs to. You can **Add** and **Remove** from the **Available Groups** and the **Belongs to Groups** boxes.

Admin Auth

Here you can select what **Authentication Scheme** will be used for administrators, basically what you check the password against. The options are Undefined, SecurID, Check Point Password, OS Password, RADIUS, and TACACS. If you select Undefined, then the administrator will not be able to authenticate using a password, only a digital certificate.

Admin Certificates

One of the advantages of using SmartDashboard administrators is that you can implement authentication via digital certificates generated by the Internal Certificate Authority (ICA). In this tab, you will see the certificate **State** (there is no certificate for this object, or Object has a certificate), and the Distinguished Name if it has a certificate, as in Figure 6.6.

Figure 6.6 The Certificates Tab

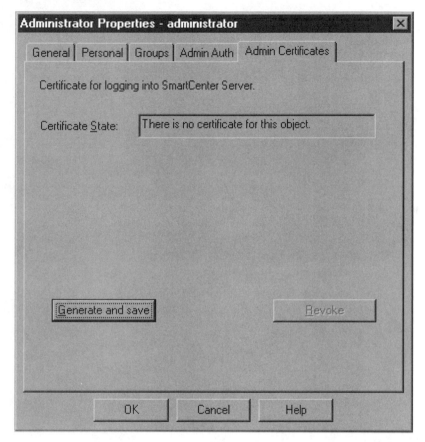

If there is no certificate for the administrator, you can click **Generate and Save**. You will see a prompt warning that the generation cannot be undone unless revoking the certificate, and then you can enter and verify the password for the certificate. Finally, you will select where to save the .P12 file in your hard drive. This file you can distribute to the appropriate administrators, save on a USB device, and so on. Once the administrator has a certificate, you use View… to see its details, or Revoke to eliminate the certificate.

Administrator Groups

You can create Administrator Groups and place administrators in them. You can use Administrator Groups by editing a Check Point Gateway, using the **Advanced | Permissions to Install** tab (see Figure 6.7). Here you can **Remove** the **Any** group from the selected groups and add the specific Administrator Groups you want to grant install access to. Only administrators with Manage Administrators permission can modify these properties.

Figure 6.7 The Permissions to Install Tab

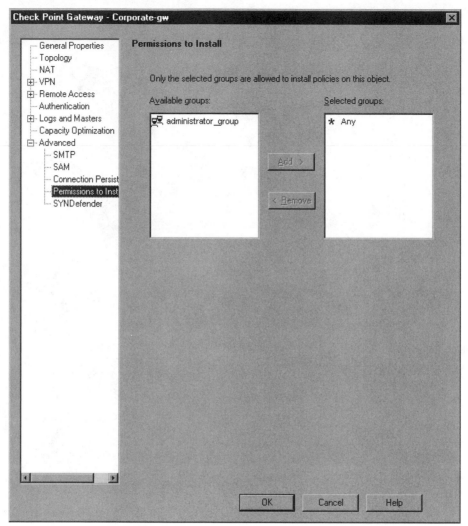

User Templates

Before you create users, you have to understand templates. Since there are many options to configure on users, templates save you time by preconfiguring options at the time of user creation. If you change an option on a template, it does not affect users already created from that template, only future users. The Standard template is preconfigured for quickly adding a user if you don't want to go into details. Let's look at the different Tabs you see once you select **New... | Template...**.

General

Select the **Name** the template will have. This is the name you will use when selecting **New... | User from Template...**.

Personal

The **Expiration Date** field (in dd-mm-yyyy format) is used to set a valid time period for users. For example, you can use a template for a group of temporary employees that will leave the company at a specific date. By default in NGX, the expiration date is December 31, 2008.

Enter a **Comment** for the Template and select a **Color** for the display of its icon. These fields are for informational use only.

Groups

You can select which User Groups the users will belong to. You can **Add** and **Remove** from the **Available Groups** and the **Belongs to Groups** boxes.

Authentication

Here you can select what form of **Authentication Scheme** will be used for these users. The options are Undefined, SecurID, Check Point Password, OS Password, RADIUS, and TACACS. If you select Undefined, then the user will not be able to authenticate using a password, only a digital certificate. You will only be able to select the Authentication Scheme, but won't be able to enter a Password for the Template, for security reasons.

Location

Location refers to the users' allowed sources and destinations. You will be able to select **Network Objects** and move them to either the **Source** or **Destination** boxes, or leave them as **Any**, as in Figure 6.8. The location then becomes a restriction as to where the users can connect from (i.e., IT_Users restricted to IT_Networks source location), and where the users can connect to (i.e., Extranet_Users restricted to Extranet_Servers destination). This field can give you flexibility in having few authentication rules that behave differently for specific users and groups. It's a bit complex to keep track of, but if you need it, it's very useful. When you configure an authentication rule, you can decide whether the rule has to intersect with the location of the users, or it can ignore it (we'll look at that later).

Figure 6.8 The Location Tab

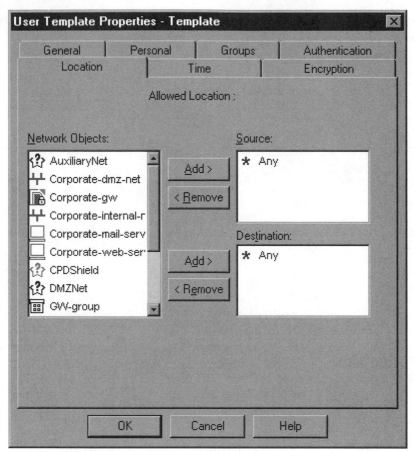

Time

You can select what day of the week and range of time **User may connect at**. Although you can select several **Day in week options**, you are limited to a single range for **Time of Day**.

Encryption

Encryption is used for VPN Remote Access, and will be covered in Chapter 9, "SecuRemote, SecureClient, and Integrity." If you select **IKE** for **Client Encryption**, the user will be able to participate in the Remote Access community.

User Groups

You can create User Groups and place users in them. You can select a **Name**, **Comment**, and **Color** for the group, and **Add** and **Remove** from the **Not in Group** to the **In Group** boxes, as in Figure 6.9.

Figure 6.9 Creating a User Group

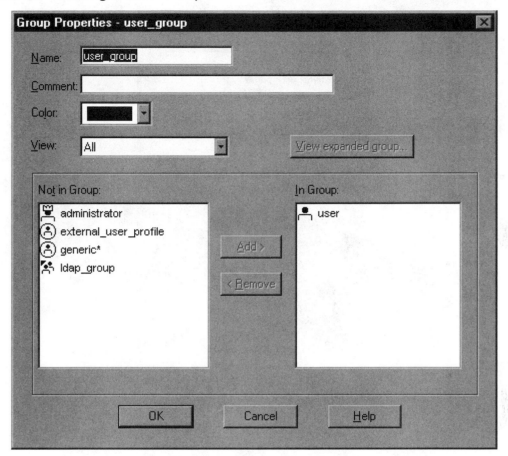

User Groups can also contain other groups in a nested fashion. When you add a group to another group, NGX will ask **Would you like to add each member of the group separately?** and each group would be expanded in the new group. With nested groups, if you change a group the change will be reflected in the parent group, but that will not happen if you expand the group.

Check Point NGX does not reference individual users directly in rules or object properties, so if you have a user, you will want to place them in the appropriate group. If they're not in any group, they're still part of the *All Users* group.

Users

When you want to create a user, you have to work based on an existing template. Once you select **New… | User from Template…** (see Figure 6.10), you can select the initial template you want and then you will see a dialog box with many tabs. Let's look at them.

Figure 6.10 Creating a User from a Template

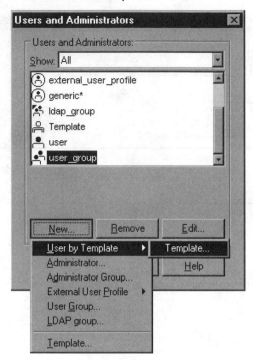

General

Select the **Login Name** for the users. It can have special characters in it, as well as spaces and periods, and long names.

Personal

The **Expiration Date** field (in dd-mm-yyyy format) is used to set a valid time period for a user. By default in NGX, the expiration date is December 31, 2008. Enter a **Comment** and select a **Color** for the display of its icon. These fields will be prepopulated with information from the Template.

Groups

You can select which User Groups the user belongs to. You can **Add** and **Remove** from the **Available Groups** and the **Belongs to Groups** boxes. The tab will be prepopulated according to the Template.

Authentication

Here you can select which **Authentication Scheme** the user will have. The options are Undefined, SecurID, Check Point Password, OS Password, RADIUS, and TACACS. If you select Undefined, then the user will not be able to authenticate using a password, only a digital certificate. If you select RADIUS or TACACS, you can select which server to use for verification.

  If you select Check Point Password, you can click **Enter Password** to assign and verify it. The passwords should be four to eight characters in length. Check Point stores a hash for these passwords in the internal database. A hash function is an irreversible, one-way, highly-sensitive-to-change function, specifically the UNIX *crypt* function, which can use only eight characters with DES-based encryption. There is virtually no probability that two strings will have the same hash value, even if they differ by only a letter. When a user inputs a password, the gateway compares the hash of the password with the hash stored in the user database to authenticate the user. For those technically inclined, when a user's password is modified, Check Point creates a random salt, which is then returned in the first two characters of the hashed result. You could programmatically create a file that uses the crypt function to create a large list of users and password that can then be imported with the *fwm dbimport* command.

Location

Here you can select specific **Source** and **Destination** locations for the users. The fields will be prepopulated from the template. Remember that when you configure an authentication rule, you can decide whether the rule has to intersect with the location of the users, or it can ignore it.

Time

You can select what day of the week and range of time **User may connect at**. Although you can select several **Day in week options**, you are limited to a single range for **Time of Day**. The fields will be prepopulated from the template.

Certificates

In this tab, you will see the **Certificate State** (the message can be *There is no certificate for this object*, *The certificate is pending for the* user, or *Object has a certificate*), and the **Distinguished Name** if a certificate exists. Digital Certificates for users apply only for Remote Access VPNs, and will be covered in the SecuRemote/SecureClient chapter.

Encryption

Encryption is used for VPN Remote Access, and will be covered in Chapter 9. If you select IKE, the user will be able to participate in the Remote Access community.

External User Profiles

If you're working with external directory servers (RADIUS, TACACS, OS Password, SecurID), you would still need to define each user that exists in the external directory server, and select the appropriate authentication method for the user. This can be a tedious and error-prone process. By creating *External User Profiles*, you can deal with users who are not defined in the Check Point user database. If users are recognized by an external directory server, they will be granted permissions based on the appropriate External User Profile.

Match by Domain

This profile allows you to selectively query an external user database base on the Domain that the user enters. The important properties are in the General Tab.

If you use Distinguished Name (DN) format, you can select a specific organizational unit, organization, or country to authorize. Or, you can use Free Format, where the domain will be separated from the username by a character like @ or \ (for Microsoft), either before or after the username. In Free Format you can choose Any Domain as Acceptable, or a specific Domain Name you select. Finally, select whether to omit the domain name when requesting authorization at the external directory server. See Figure 6.11 for details.

Figure 6.11 External User Profiles | Match by Domain

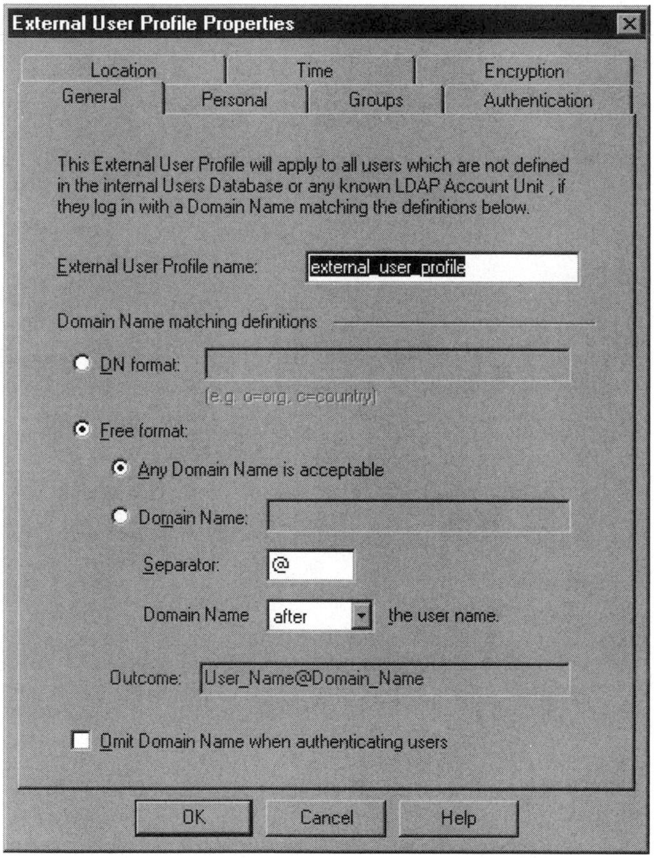

The other tabs in the External User Profile (Personal, Groups, Authentication, Location, Time, Encryption) function as they do in the normal user entity. Remember that in this scenario, you're leaving authentication and authorization decisions to an external entity.

Match All Users

If you don't need to be selective of a domain users have to log with, you can use the *Match All Users External Profile*. It is named *generic** and will match any user recognized by the external directory server. Remember that in this scenario, you're leaving authentication and authorization decisions to an external entity.

The other tabs in the External User Profile (Personal, Groups, Authentication, Location, Time, Encryption) function as they do in a normal user entity.

LDAP Group

If you are using SmartDirectory LDAP integration, you can create LDAP groups. You will give a name to the group, a comment and a color, and the Account Unit that the LDAP Group belongs to. You should have created the LDAP Account Unit from the Manage Servers and OPSEC Applications dialog box.

In the Group's Scope, you can select to recognize all the Account-Unit users, or only those in a certain subtree, branch, and prefix, or only a group in a branch, with a DN prefix. You can also apply a filter to create a dynamic group (for example, all users in ou=Access).

Understanding Authentication Schemes

Check Point NGX is flexible enough to work with several external directory servers, where a user entity can be defined in the Internal Check Point database, but the password is verified from different sources. Check Point refers to these as Authentication Schemes.

Undefined

The Undefined Authentication Scheme is used for disabling the user's ability to enter a password. This will force users to employ strong authentication with a digital certificate.

SecurID

Selecting SecurID as the Authentication Scheme will enable Check Point NGX to become an ACE/Agent for RSA's SecurID Tokens. This integration will require use of a special *sdconf.rec* generated by the ACE server, and will allow you to enter new PIN numbers and reauthenticate often to secure servers. However, it's a lot more difficult to configure than through SecurID's RADIUS interface.

Check Point Password

If you select Check Point Password (called VPN-1 & Firewall-1 Password previously), you will enter the user's password directly into NGX's internal database. Passwords are four to eight characters in length. Be aware that the only way to assign or change passwords is through the SmartDashboard interface.

RADIUS

The *Remote Authentication Dial-In User Service* (RADIUS) is a standard protocol that can authenticate users with a RADIUS server that holds a database. The RADIUS protocol is very flexible and relatively secure. It uses a specific secret key for securing the authentication and only authorized clients can request authentication from the server. You can also set up backup servers in case one of them is out of service.

To configure RADIUS Authentication, first create a RADIUS Server from the **Manage | Servers and OPSEC Applications...** dialog as in Figure 6.12. Select **New... | RADIUS...** to create the server. Input the appropriate data in the **Name**, **Comment**, and **Color.** For **Host**, select the physical server that is running the RADIUS server. If you don't have the server created, use the **New...** button to create a new node. Select the **Service** to use, either NEW-RADIUS (the official port number) or RADIUS (the most common port number used). The **Shared Secret** is a password used to secure the information sent between the Check Point Gateways and the RADIUS server(s). You can select the **Version** to use, either version 1.0 or 2.0. Also select a **Priority**, to know which server to use first if there is more than one available. You can also create **RADIUS groups** for high availability and load sharing. Figure 6.13 shows the dialog box for creating a RADIUS server.

Figure 6.12 The Manage Servers and OPSEC Applications Dialog

Figure 6.13 Creating a RADIUS Server

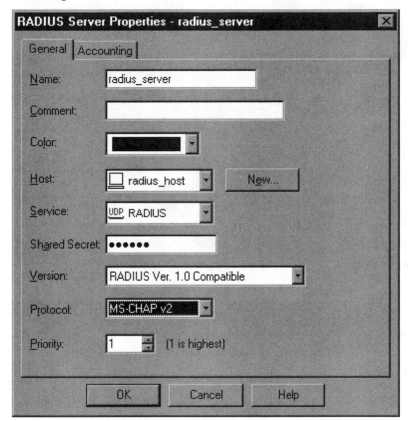

TACACS

The *Terminal Access Controller Access Control System* is a standard protocol that can authenticate users with an external user database. To configure TACACS Authentication, first create a TACACS Server from the **Manage | Servers and OPSEC Applications...** dialog. Select **New... | TACACS...** and input the appropriate data in the **Name**, **Comment** and **Color,** as in Figure 6.14. For **Host**, select the physical server that is running the TACACS server. If you don't have the server created, use the **New...** button to create a new Node. Select the **Type** of server used, either TACACS or TACACS+, which is more secure. If selecting TACACS+ you can also enter a **Secret Key** for encryption. Finally select the **Service** to use (UDP TACACS or TCP TACACSPLUS).

Figure 6.14 Creating a TACACS Server

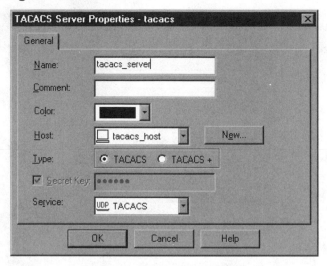

User Authentication

User Authentication allows privileged use of some common Internet protocols, with little change to the user experience. It works by intercepting connections that are passing through the firewall (Check Point calls this "folding" the connection), and modifying the traffic in such a way that the firewall asks the user to identify his- or herself before allowing the connection to pass through. Since the user requests a connection to his or her final destination, User Authentication is a type of *Transparent* authentication; in other words, the user doesn't need to go through an intermediate process. Also be aware that this type of authentication is very demanding on the firewall, if it needs to fold a large number of connections.

Because NGX needs to modify the traffic itself, it can do so only with four specific services that it can understand well: HTTP, FTP, Telnet, and RLOGIN. These services belong to the *Authenticated* group in the predefined Check Point services. When one of these services is used to access a restricted resource, and there's a rule configured to allow User Auth for that connection, the traffic is modified so the user can enter a password to enable the traffic. For Telnet, FTP, and RLOGIN, the user sees an intermediary prompt from the firewall, and once the user authenticates, a new connection to the final destination is made. In the case of HTTP traffic, the firewall instructs the user's browser to display an authentication dialog.

User Authentication is performed on each connection so that if a machine is being shared by different users (for example, in a client/server or thin client environment) each user will authenticate his or her connection only, which is safe. Because the firewall needs to examine the traffic of these authenticated services, it requires more processing power from the firewall than Session and Client authentication.

Configuring User Authentication in the Rulebase

To allow user authentication, create a new rule. In the source field, select **Add User Access**, and add the user groups that will be able to authenticate using that rule. You can also select a restriction for the origin of the user connections. Add the appropriate **Destination** to that rule (if you want to authenticate all traffic to the Internet, leave it as **Any**), select which **Services** you'll authenticate (remember, only HTTP, FTP, Telnet, or RLOGIN—if you enter any additional services, the policy will have compilation errors), select **User Auth** as the Action, and add appropriate **Track**, **Time**, and **Comment** configurations. See Figure 6.15 for a User Authentication Rule.

Figure 6.15 Create a User Authentication Rule

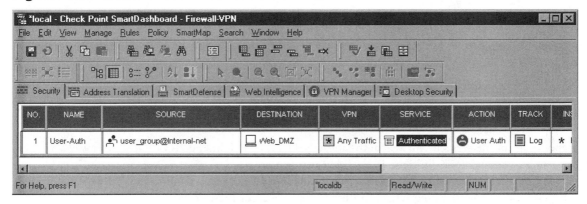

You should edit or verify the properties of the Action field in the User Authentication rule, as in Figure 6.16.

Figure 6.16 Properties of the User Authentication Action

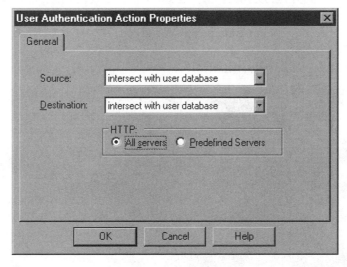

UserAuth | Edit Properties | General | Source

Source is used to control whether the Restrict To location in the source of the rule has to intersect the configured location of the user in the database, or if it can ignore the location. Select **Ignore** to override the user database.

UserAuth | Edit Properties | General | Destination

Destination is similar to Source, in which you can choose to ignore the user database so that if a user has a configured destination location, and that location does not intersect the destination of the rule, the authentication will still take place.

UserAuth | Edit Properties | General | HTTP

Here you can select whether you want to allow authentication to a restricted number of servers, or to any accessible machines. The default is **Predefined Server**. When Predefined Servers is selected, users will be able to access only the list of servers that can be defined in the **Policy | Global Properties | Firewall-1 | Security Servers** dialog. To be able to authenticate traffic to any destination on the Internet, you need to select **All Servers** in the properties of the User Auth action.

Interacting with User Authentication

Depending on the service you will authenticate (HTTP, FTP, Telnet, or RLOGIN), the way your users will authenticate is different. Remember that if users need to resolve Web addresses (e.g., www. checkpoint.com), they will need to have access for domain-udp requests through the firewall, or to an internal DNS server. Let's see what the user experience is for these services.

Telnet and RLOGIN

User Authentication for Telnet and RLOGIN is easy for the end user to understand. When a user tries a command like **telnet 172.29.109.1**, the firewall will intercept this command and present its own Telnet prompts, as in Figure 6.17. Once the user correctly authenticates, he or she will see the prompts from the original destination and can proceed accordingly.

Figure 6.17 Telnet User Authentication

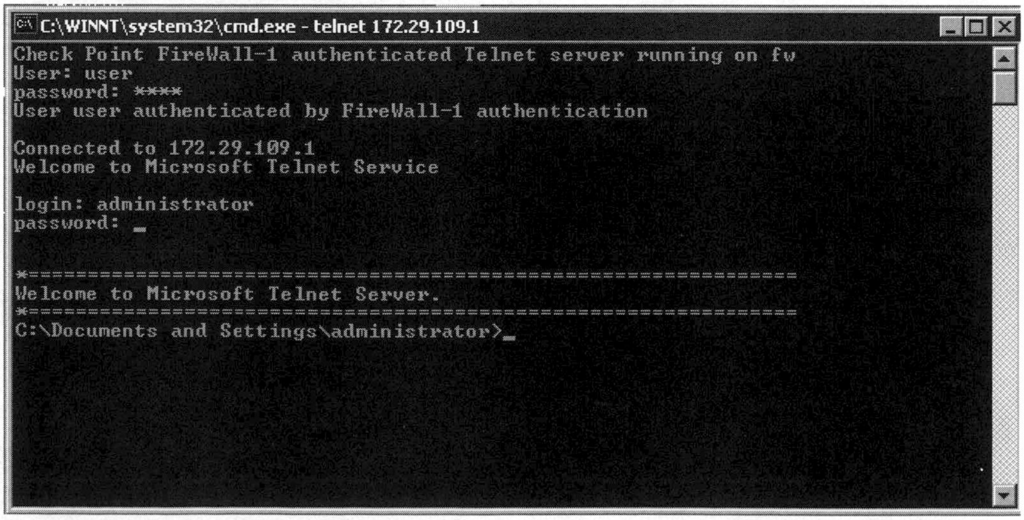

FTP

User Authentication for FTP is a bit more complex to understand. The user will still use the command **ftp 172.29.109.1**, which will be intercepted by the firewall's FTP security server, but the username will have to reflect the user that is authenticating at the FTP server (i.e., administrator), the user that is authenticating at the firewall (i.e., user), and the final destination of the FTP connection (even though it was used in the original ftp command). For example, in this case the username will be **administrator@user@172.29.109.1**, and the password will be the passwords of the FTP user separated by an @ sign from the password of the firewall user—**ftppassword@fwpassword**. Then a connection to the FTP server will be established. Look at Figure 6.18 for details.

Figure 6.18 FTP User Authentication

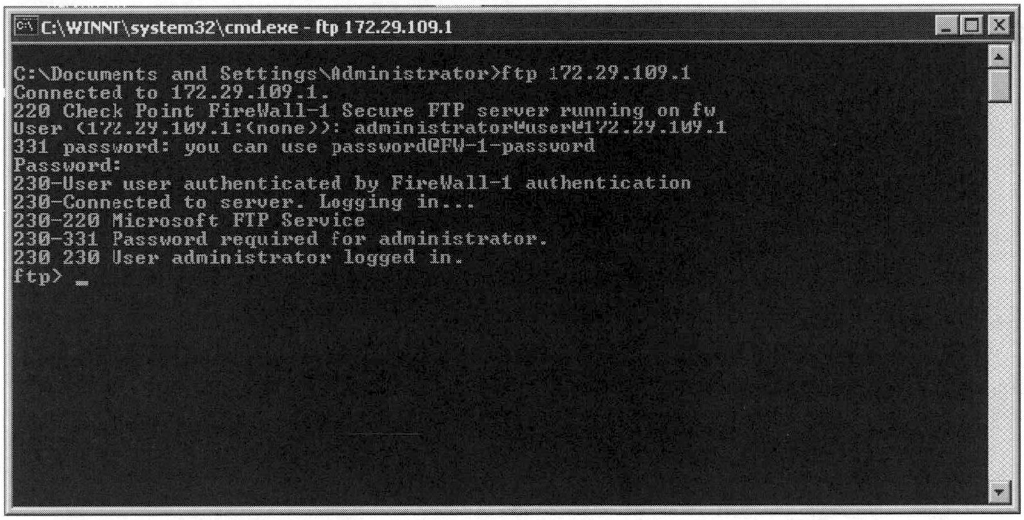

HTTP

User authentication for HTTP is simple for users to use. When activated, an HTTP connection that should be authenticated is modified by the firewall in such a way that the user's browser displays an authentication dialog box or prompt, using HTTP's authentication mechanism. The prompt says FW-1: No user. Once the user authenticates with this prompt, the requested site is displayed in the browser. Look at Figures 6.19 and 6.20 for examples using Microsoft Internet Explorer and Mozilla Firefox.

Figure 6.19 HTTP User Authentication with Microsoft Internet Explorer

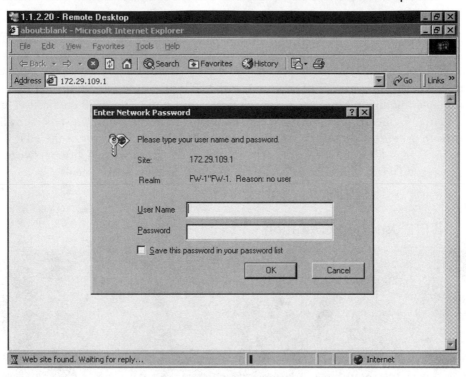

Figure 6.20 HTTP User Authentication with Mozilla Firefox

In Figure 6.21 you can look at the entry in the SmartView Tracker generated from the authenticated http access.

Figure 6.21 SmartView Tracker Entry for HTTP User Authentication

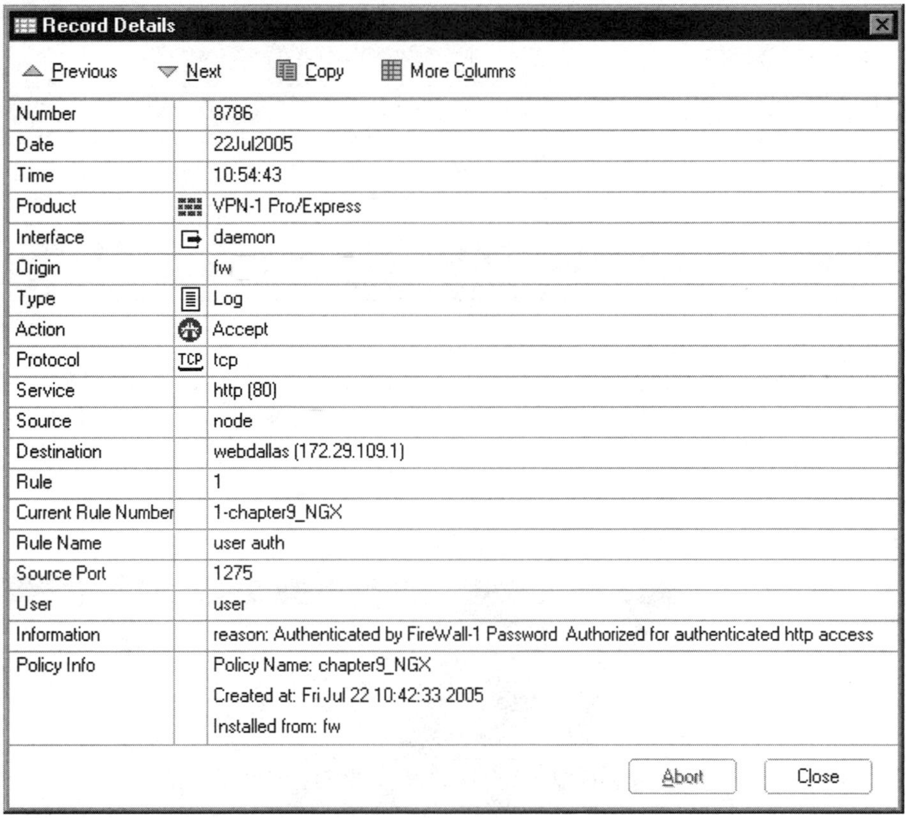

Record Details	
△ Previous ▽ Next 📋 Copy ▦ More Columns	
Number	8786
Date	22Jul2005
Time	10:54:43
Product	VPN-1 Pro/Express
Interface	daemon
Origin	fw
Type	Log
Action	Accept
Protocol	tcp
Service	http (80)
Source	node
Destination	webdallas (172.29.109.1)
Rule	1
Current Rule Number	1-chapter9_NGX
Rule Name	user auth
Source Port	1275
User	user
Information	reason: Authenticated by FireWall-1 Password Authorized for authenticated http access
Policy Info	Policy Name: chapter9_NGX
	Created at: Fri Jul 22 10:42:33 2005
	Installed from: fw
	Abort Close

Placing Authentication Rules

Check Point rules are sequential, which means that once a rule can be applied to traffic passing through the firewall, that rule is applied and the next packet is processed. However, there is one exception. If there is a rule that allows traffic to a destination, even if there is a rule that would require authentication before that rule, the traffic will pass through without the need for users to authenticate. The reason for this is that an authentication rule does not deny traffic that fails to authenticate.

For example, look at Figure 6.22. If a machine in Net_Internal tries to access Web_DMZ, you would think that NGX would require the user to authenticate. If the user successfully authenticates, the traffic will be allowed. However, if the user doesn't successfully authenticate, NGX would continue processing rules and would find the Any to Web_DMZ rule, and would allow the traffic nevertheless. Therefore, NGX will not ask for authentication.

Figure 6.22 Placing User Authentication in the Rulebase

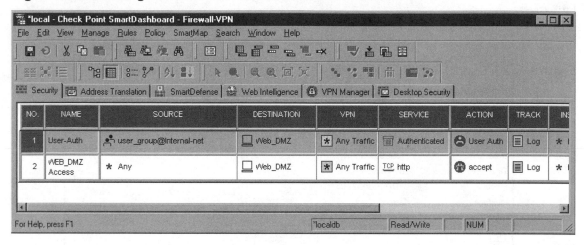

You could still require users in Net_Internal to authenticate before accessing Web_DMZ by creating a rule that will block the http traffic before it is allowed, as in Figure 6.23. This would force Check Point NGX to authenticate the users.

Figure 6.23 Forcing Users to Authenticate

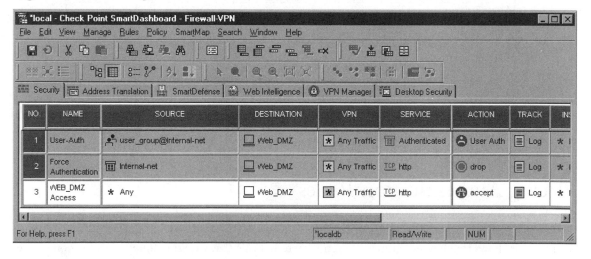

Advanced Topics

User Authentication is a useful and convenient way to add an extra layer of verification to your users' connections. However, many times you will find that the default configuration breaks some connections or isn't secure enough for your needs. There are a myriad of configurations that you can make to User Authentication, and here we cover some of the most frequently requested ones.

Eliminating the Default Authentication Banner

You should always try to avoid disclosing unnecessary information. Check Point's default banners (the initial identification) for the FTP, Telnet, and RLOGIN security servers identify your firewall as a Check Point Firewall. You can avoid this by setting the *undo_msg* property to *true* in the dbedit *firewall_properties*, using the *dbedit* utility. From a command prompt (or in SecurePlatform's expert mode), run **dbedit,** log in with a username and password, and type **modify properties firewall_properties undo_msg true** and then **update properties firewall_properties**. After installing a policy, you will no longer see the default prompt. Be aware that some FTP clients need a banner for them to connect. In the following topic you can set your own banner.

Changing the Banner

Traffic that is intercepted by the firewall, be it FTP, Telnet, RLOGIN, or HTTP, displays a message from Check Point NGX requesting authentication. It is advisable to change this default message to a generic one that doesn't broadcast the firewall's identity, and that can include additional information for users. You can select a file to be presented instead of the regular banner for FTP, Telnet, and RLOGIN (not for HTTP), in the SmartDashboard's **Global Properties | Firewall | Security Servers** dialog box, as in Figure 6.24.

Figure 6.24 Changing the Security Server Banners

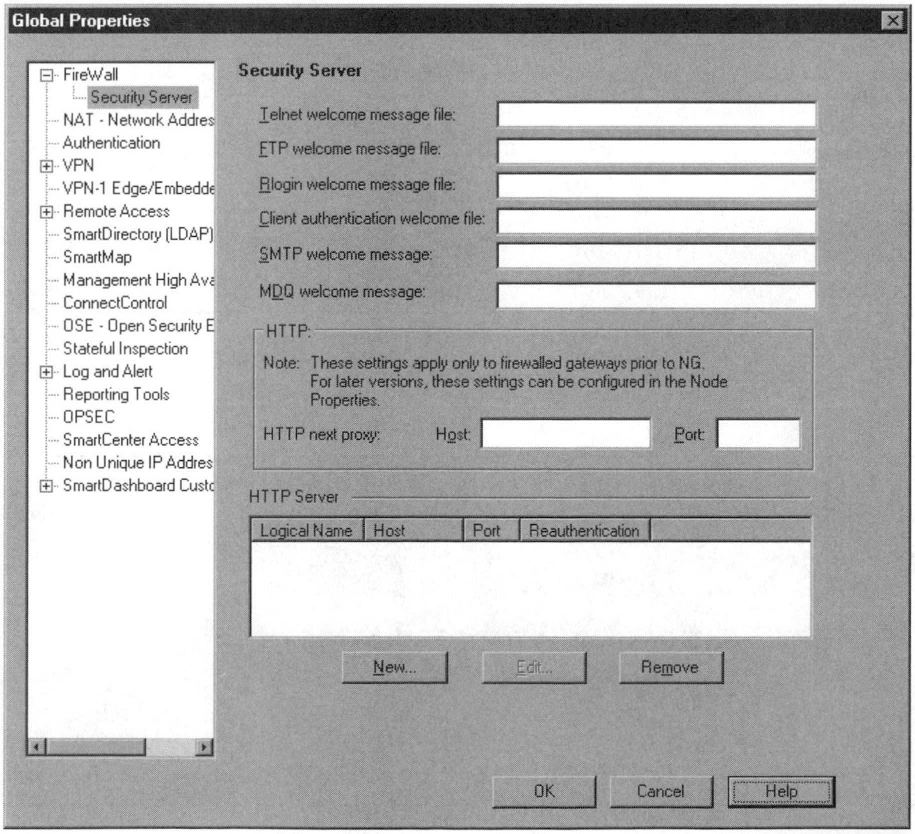

Use Host Header as Destination

If you are making HTTP connections, once the connection is authenticated, the firewall needs to redirect the original query to the intended destination. It does so by looking at the original URL's IP address and redirecting the user's browser to that IP. However, if the firewall resolves the destination URL to a nonroutable IP (i.e., the non-NAT'ed IP), or if the web server is configured to need the Host Header for access (i.e., a web hosting service that shares one IP with multiple web pages), then the connection will fail. To solve this, enable the setting *http_use_host_h_as_dst* using **Policy | Global Properties | SmartDashboard Customization | Configure | Firewall-1 | Web Security | HTTP Protocol**, as in Figure 6.25.

Figure 6.25 Changing Advanced Properties with SmartDashboard Customization

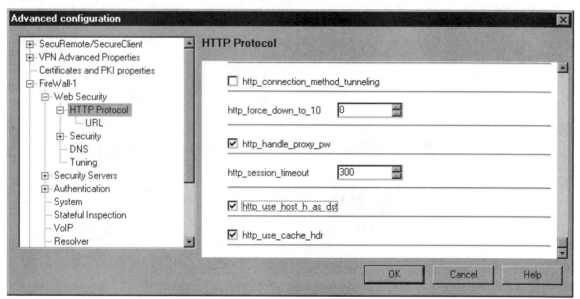

Tools & Traps...

User Authentication and Webmail Sites

When you activate user authentication, the firewall needs to process and modify the traffic going through it, using the Security Servers (which are better explained in the Content Security chapter). In HTTP's case in particular, having the traffic pass through the Security Server also means that the verifications that the firewall makes on HTTP traffic will be made on all authenticated traffic. These verifications might break some connections that your users regularly make. In particular, accessing sites like Hotmail and downloading attachments can be affected and should be thought of when activating this.

Two changes you will need to make to are enabling *http_allow_content_disposition* and *enable_propfind_method* setting in the **Policy | Global Properties | SmartDashboard Customization | Configure | Firewall-1 | Web Security | Security** section, as in Figure 6.26.

Figure 6.26 Allowing Webmail Sites through Security Servers

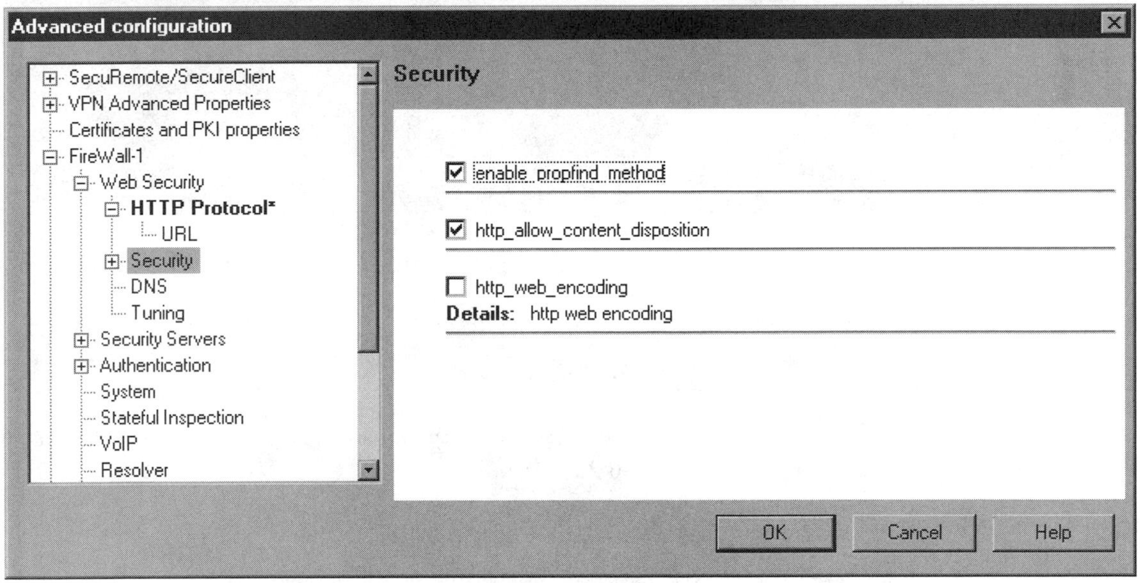

Session Authentication

Another method available for authentication in Check Point NGX is Session Authentication. This method uses a client program, called the Session Authentication Agent, which usually is installed on each machine that will be used for authentication. The Session Authentication Agent can be used for any service, and authenticates a particular session by the user. When the firewall encounters a rule with Session Authentication, it tries to query the appropriate machine using the FW1_snauth service on port 261. The Agent will then automatically present the user with an authentication dialog. Session Authentication combines User and Client Authentication, since it can authenticate per session for any service.

However, you need to consider that the Session Authentication Agent is a separate program that has to be installed in each user's machines, and that it is a Windows-Only program. Furthermore, the last available version is from NG Feature Pack 1 and there's no NGX version (yet).

Configuring Session Authentication in the Rulebase

To allow session authentication, create a new rule. In the source field, select **Add User Access**, and then add the user groups that will be able to authenticate, and optionally restrict the location from where those groups can connect. Then, add the appropriate destination to that rule (if you want to authenticate all traffic to the Internet, leave it as **Any**), select which services you'll authenticate (try not to use **Any**), select **SessionAuth** as the Action, and add the appropriate Track, Time, and Comment configurations, as in Figure 6.27.

Figure 6.27 Configuring Session Authentication in the Rulebase

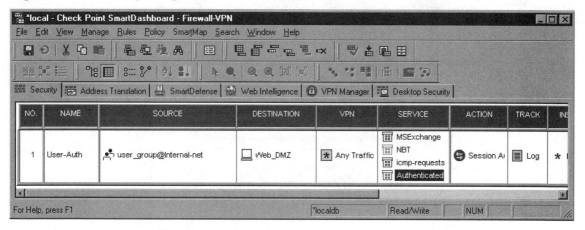

Let's take a look at the **Action** column of the Session Authentication Rule. Right-click on the field and select **Edit Properties**, as in Figure 6.28.

Figure 6.28 Properties of the Session Authentication Action

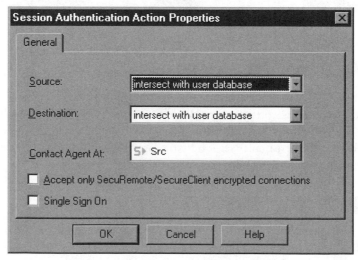

SessionAuth | Edit Properties | General | Source

Source is used to control whether the **Restrict To** location in the source of the rule has to intersect the configured location of the user in the database, or if it can ignore the location. Select **Ignore** to override the user database.

SessionAuth | Edit Properties | General | Destination

Destination is similar to Source, in which you can choose to ignore the user database so that if a user has a configured destination location, and that location does not intersect the destination of the rule, the authentication will still take place.

SessionAuth | Edit Properties | General | Contact Agent At

The Session Authentication Agent doesn't have to be installed in the machine that wants to access restricted resource (the source of the connection). You can define the location that Check Point NGX will query to authenticate a connection. The options are **Src** (the source of the connection), **Dst** (the destination of the connection), or you can select a specific host or gateway configured in the object tree. You would be able to configure this so that a supervisor grants access to specific resources, or for authenticating X Windows connections, or when a user wants to authenticate incoming connections.

SessionAuth | Edit Properties | General | Accept only SecuRemote/SecureClient Encrypted Connections

If you select this option, only users connecting via a remote access VPN will be able to authenticate.

SessionAuth | Edit Properties | General | Single Sign-On

Selecting this option will restrict authentication to UserAuthority and UserAuthority SecureAgent.

Configuring Session Authentication Encryption

One of the advantages of Session Authentication is that you can configure the Session Authentication Agent to communicate using SSL, to prevent password sniffing. You may change the **snauth_protocol** setting from the **Policy | Global Properties | SmartDashboard Customization | Configure | Firewall-1 | Authentication | Session Authentication** dialog box, as shown in Figure 6.29:

- **None**   (or blank) No encryption of the authentication will be performed.

- **SSL**   SSL will be active on all Session Authentication Agents. If you have an old agent you will not be able to authenticate.

- **SSL + None**   SSL will be active on all Session Authentication Agents, but if you have an old agent you will be able to authenticate without encryption.

Figure 6.29 Changing the Session Authentication Protocol

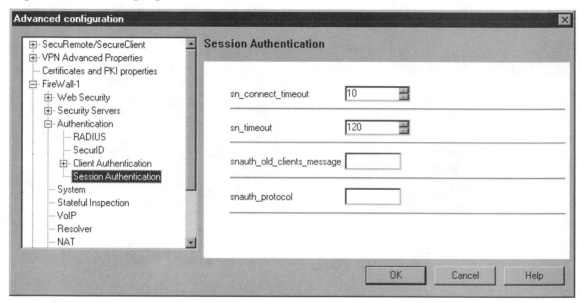

The Session Authentication Agent

The Agent is needed to use Session Authentication. It's a small 2MB program that installs without requiring a reboot. Since it is not included in the Check Point NGX CDs, you will have to download them from the Check Point User Center (usercenter.checkpoint.com) NG FP1 downloads section, as in Figure 6.30, or get them from a Check Point NG or Check Point NG with Application Intelligence CD.

Figure 6.30 Downloading the Session Authentication Agent from the Check Point User Center

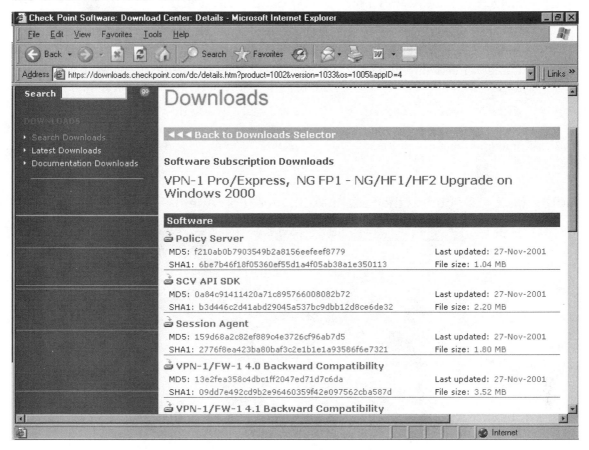

Once installed, the Session Authentication Agent will show up in the Windows Taskbar Notification Area as a blue circle with yellow and green arrows (see Figure 6.31), and open port 261 for listening to authentication requests from firewalls. If a request is received, the user automatically will see a Check Point prompt for username and password, making it easy for a novice user to understand what's going on.

Figure 6.31 The Session Authentication Agent Icon

If you double-click on the agent icon, you can modify its configuration via three sections.

Configuration | Passwords | Ask for Password

You can configure three behaviors for the Agent, as shown in Figure 6.32:

- **Every Request**   Passwords will not be cached, and every request will need to be authenticated. Very secure, but also very cumbersome.

- **Once per session**   Passwords will be cached the first time the user enters it. No reauthentication will be needed until the users logs out of the Windows session.

- **After X minutes of inactivity**   Passwords will be cached the first time the user enters it. Reauthentication will be needed after the agent doesn't authenticate connections for the amount of minutes entered.

Figure 6.32 Configuring the Session Authentication Agent Passwords

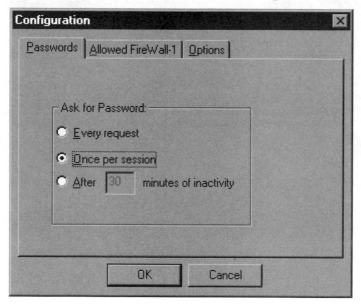

Configuration | Allowed Firewall-1 | Allow authentication request from

You can configure the Agent to accept requests from Any IP Address, or specify up to three IPs that the agent will respond to requests, as in Figure 6.33.

Figure 6.33 Configuring the Session Authentication Agent Allowed Firewall-1

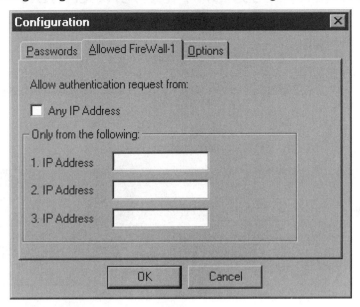

Configuration | Allowed Firewall-1 | Options

Here you can configure whether to Allow Clear Passwords or not. Uncheck Allow Clear Passwords to ensure SSL encryption is used, if you've configured the protocol for it. You can also configure whether the agent should resolve addresses with DNS (see Figure 6.34).

Figure 6.34 Configuring the Session Authentication Agent Options

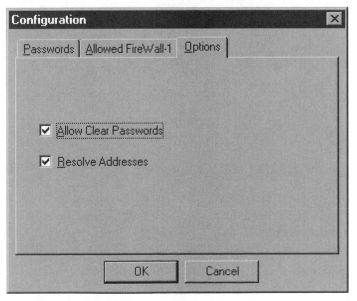

Interacting with Session Authentication

When you authenticate with Session Authentication, the user will be shown up to three prompts to authenticate a connection.

First, if it is the first time a particular firewall is requesting Session Authentication, the Session Authentication Agent will ask the user for permission to send authentication to that firewall, as in Figure 6.35. If accepted, it will also add the firewall's IP to the list of gateways from which it will accept requests.

Figure 6.35 Accepting Session Authentication Requests

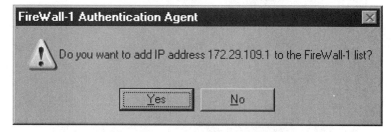

Second, the Agent will ask for the username. It will display the name of the firewall making the request, the destination of the connection, and the service requested, as in Figure 6.36.

Figure 6.36 Entering the Username for Session Authentication

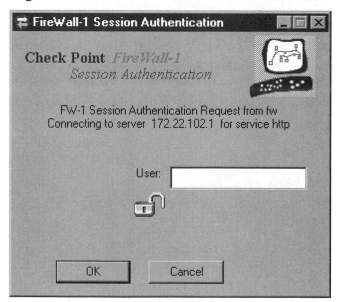

Finally, the user will enter the password and can then be granted access to the desired resource, as in Figure 6.37.

Figure 6.37 Entering the Password for Session Authentication

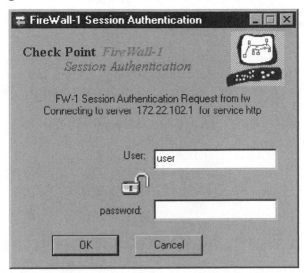

In the SmartView Tracker, you can see an authentication entry with the FW1_snauth protocol, and following that, the actual session. For every session, you will see an authentication entry above it, as in Figure 6.38.

Figure 6.38 Session Authentication in the SmartView Tracker

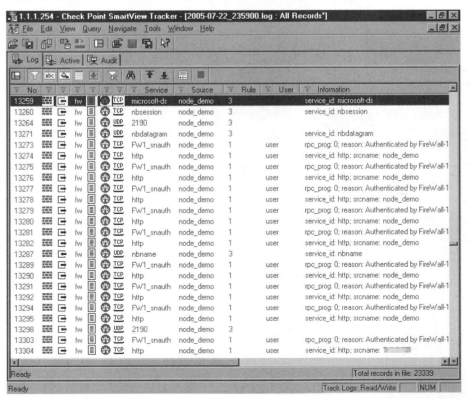

Client Authentication

Client Authentication is a versatile authentication method that can be used for most of your needs. Unlike User authentication, in which a connection is being authenticated, here you authenticate a machine or an IP (which the firewall considers the client). Client authentication is not transparent, which means that the connection has to be directed to the firewall so that it can ask for the specific authentication. Some of the benefits of client authentication are that any service can be authenticated, and that the authentication can last for a specific period of time or number of sessions (by default, five sessions in 30 minutes). Once a user achieves client authentication, traffic can flow freely with little intervention. Since the firewall doesn't have to interpret or modify the passing connections, is it faster than user or session authentication and doesn't intervene in the HTTP traffic passing through the gateway.

Configuring Client Authentication in the Rulebase

To allow client authentication, create a new rule above any rule that would block ports 900 and 259 to the firewall (usually the Stealth Rule). In the source field, select **Add User Access**, and then add the user group that will be able to authenticate, and optionally restrict to a location, where that group can connect from. Then, add the appropriate **Destination** to that rule (if you want to authenticate all traffic to the Internet, leave it as **Any)**, select which **Services** you'll authenticate (here you can use any service at all), select **Client Auth** as the Action, and add appropriate **Track**, **Time**, and **Comment** configurations, as in Figure 6.39.

Figure 6.39 Configuring Client Authentication in the Rulebase

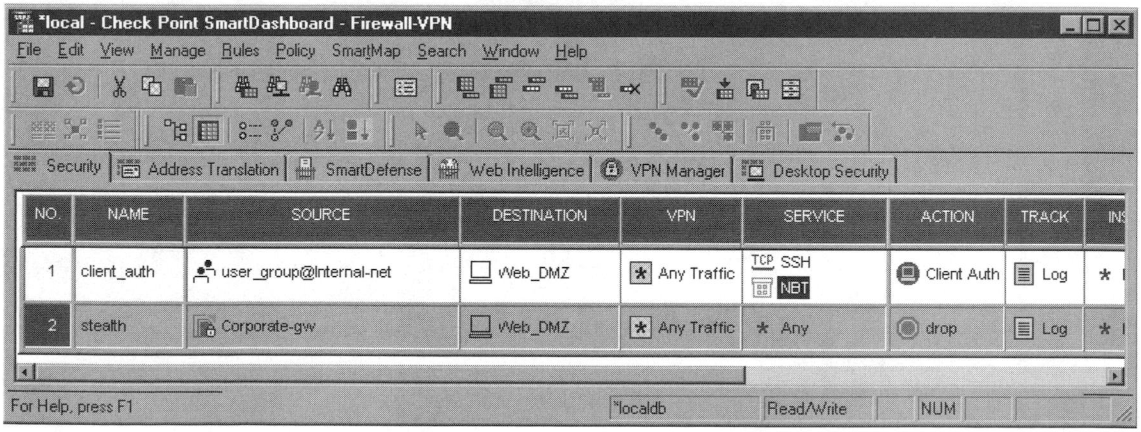

Let's take a look at the Action column of the Client Authentication Rule. There are many different behaviors that you have to select according to your desired policy. Once you select **Client Auth** as the Action, right-click on the field and select **Edit Properties**, and you will see the Client Authentication Action Properties window, as in Figure 6.40.

Figure 6.40 Configuring Client Authentication Action Properties

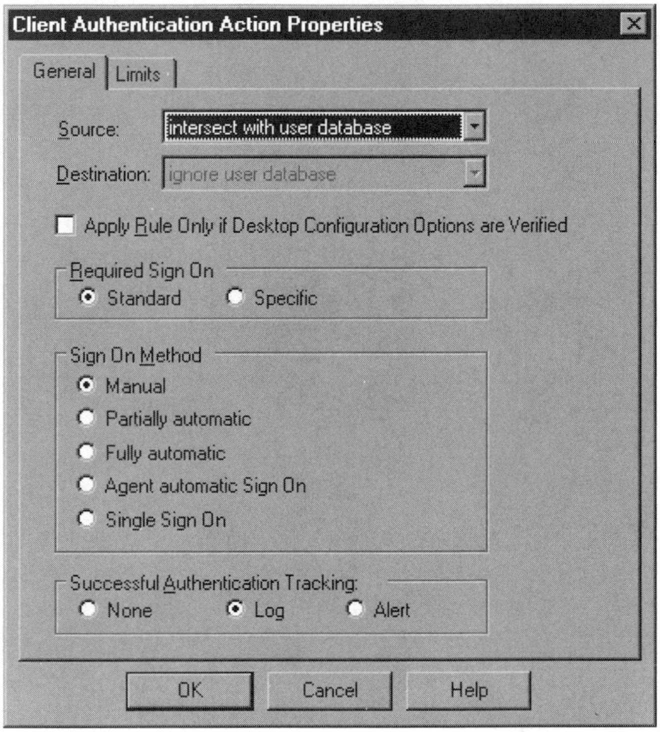

ClientAuth | Edit Properties | General | Source

As in other authentication actions, **Source** is used to control whether the source of the rule has to intersect the configured **Location** of the user, or if it takes precedence. Select **Ignore** if you want to override the location configured for the user.

ClientAuth | Edit Properties | General | Destination

Client Authentication cannot determine the final destination of a connection, since users are authenticating directly to the firewall. Therefore, the destination field is grayed out and cannot be selected.

ClientAuth | Edit Properties | General | Apply Rule Only if Desktop Configuration Options Are Verified

Checking this box will allow the client to access resources granted in the rule, once the user authenticates, only if they are using Check Point SecureClient and the Secure Configuration Verification (SCV) has succeeded.

ClientAuth | Edit Properties | General | Required Sign-In

If you select **Standard Sign-In**, users will be able to access all resources permitted in the rule at which they authenticated. If you select **Specific Sign-In**, users will have to explicitly specify, through a form or a sequence of prompts, the services and destinations allowed for the client. Specific Sign-In is useful for a kiosk machine, where an administrator can authorize access to certain sites or services only, without interacting with the firewall administrator.

ClientAuth | Edit Properties | General | Sign-On Method

The **Sign-on** method is one of the most important settings when using Client Authentication. Be sure to know how each method works to be able to select the most appropriate to your environment.

Manual Sign-On

Manual Sign-On method activates two ports on the Firewall Gateway for receipt of the authentication. They are port 900 using HTTP, and port 259 using Telnet (as in Figures 6.46, 6.47, and 6.48). Since users need to access these ports on the Firewall, the Client Authentication rule must be placed above the Stealth Rule (the one that drops all connections to the Firewall module).

This method is nontransparent, meaning that users will know they are first authenticating to a firewall, and then able to access the appropriate resources.

If you want to HTTP to port 900, you can look at Figure 6.41 where you enter the username, then in Figure 6.42 you enter the password, and in Figure 6.43, you select the sign-in method. If you select Specific Sign-In, you will see Figure 6.44, where you can enter a list of services and destinations to authorize, and in Figure 6.45 the successful authentication screen (both for Specific and Standard Sign-In methods).

Figure 6.41 HTTP Manual Client Authentication—Entering the Username

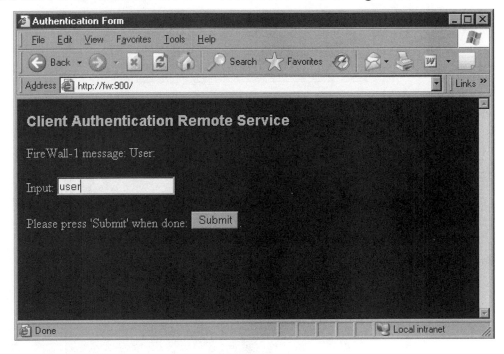

Figure 6.42 HTTP Manual Client Authentication—Entering the Password

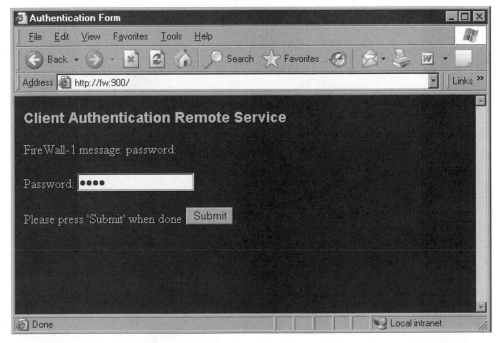

Figure 6.43 HTTP Manual Client Authentication—Selecting the Sign-In

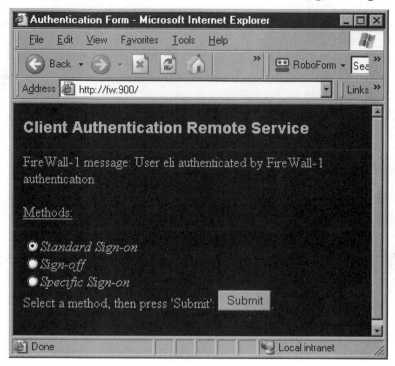

Figure 6.44 HTTP Manual Client Authentication—Specific Sign-In

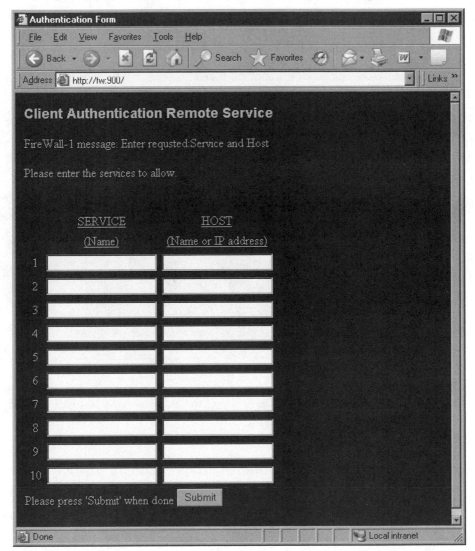

Figure 6.45 HTTP Manual Client Authentication—Successful Sign-In

If you want to Telnet to port 259, Figure 6.46 shows the Standard Sign-In method, and Figure 6.47 shows the Specific Sign-In method.

Figure 6.46 Telnet Manual Client Authentication—Standard Sign-In

Figure 6.47 Telnet Manual Client Authentication—Specific Sign-In

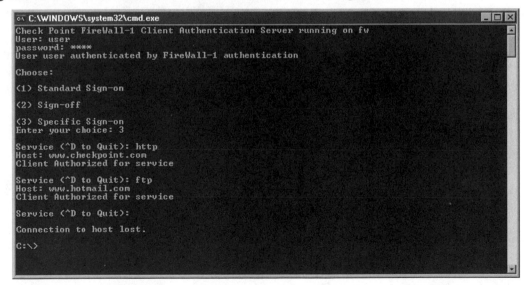

If you want to sign off, Figure 6.48 shows the Telnet client authentication Sign-Off method.

Figure 6.48 Telnet Manual Client Authentication—Sign-Off

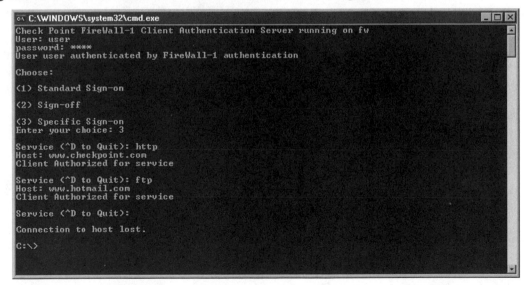

Partially Automatic Sign-On

With Partially Automatic Authentication, if a user tries to access a resource that he or she could authenticate for, using any of the Authenticated services (remember, HTTP, FTP, Telnet, or RLOGIN), then the firewall will intercept the connection and request authentication from the user, like it would do with User Authentication. Manual Authentication may still be used.

Once the user enters the username and password, the firewall interprets the authentication as it had been manually entered to the firewall as in client authentication. This is extremely useful, since now users will be required to authenticate only once and can use any resource that the rulebase allows them to. Partially Automatic Authentication is one of the most used methods of authentication. One thing to keep in mind is that as with User Authentication, it can be easy for an intruder sniffing the network to decipher usernames and passwords.

Fully Automatic Sign-On

With Fully Automatic Authentication, you further extend the ways the firewall can request authentication from the user. If an Authenticated service is used, the firewall intercepts the traffic and requests authentication as in User Authentication. For other services, it will try to invoke Session Authentication to authenticate the user at the connecting machine. Manual Authentication may still be used.

Agent Automatic Sign-On

With Agent Automatic Authentication, the firewall will try to authenticate connections using only the Session Authentication Agent at the connecting machine. Manual Authentication may still be used.

Single Sign-On

If you select Single-Sign On, the firewall will try to contact a User Authority server to query the identity of the user logged in at the station. You need to have a User Authority license, and the User Agent installed at the connecting machine.

General | Successful Authentication Tracking

Here you can select whether you want information or alerts sent to the log when a user successfully authenticates. If you select Alert it will also write the information to the log.

Once you configure the General properties for Client Authentication, you can configure the Limits for Client Authentication sessions. Figure 6.49 shows the tab for configuring these properties.

Figure 6.49 Configuring Client Authentication Limits Properties

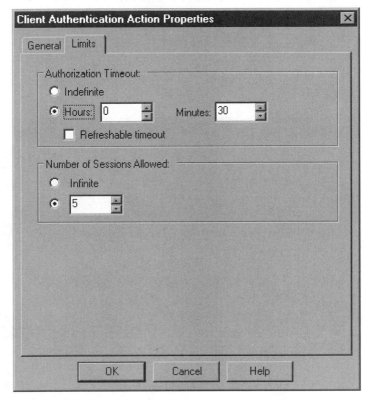

Limits | Authorization Timeout

Here you can select how long the user authorization lasts. Select indefinite to require an explicit sign-off from the user (via HTTP to port 900 or Telnet to port 259) to cancel the authorization (as in Figures 6.41 through 6.48). Select a specific time limit, in hours and minutes, if you want to require reauthentication after a time has lapsed. Select refreshable timeout if you want that as long as the connection is being used, the user will not be required to reauthenticate. This is similar to setting a time for a screen saver to come in—as long as there's activity in the machine, the screen saver doesn't come in. This is useful so that if a user leaves his machine, someone else can't sit down and use it.

Limits | Number of Sessions Allowed

This limits the amount of open connections an authenticated user can make through the firewall. If you're using FTP, Telnet, or RLOGIN connections, you could limit the number of sessions through this property. However, if you're using HTTP connections, you will need to select **Indefinite** sessions because a browser will normally open many sessions when browsing a single page.

Advanced Topics

Client Authentication opens up the functions of authentication to more services and more situations. These additional functions also have additional features to configure, and we look at some of them here.

Check Point Gateway | Authentication

There are some properties that you need to configure and verify per gateway, to fine-tune the authentication experience for your users, as in Figure 6.50.

Figure 6.50 Check Point Gateway | Authentication

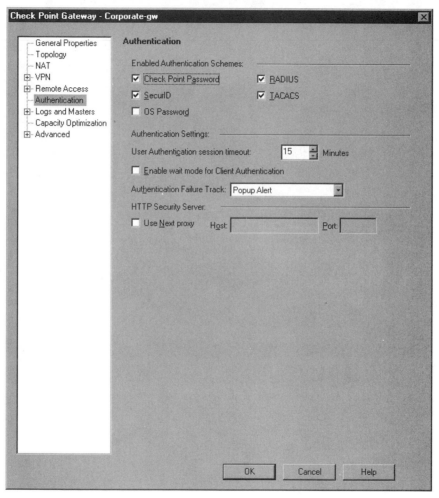

Enabled Authentication Schemes

It is very important to select which authentication schemes the gateway will allow for its users. If a user selects an authentication with a scheme that the gateway does not accept, the user will not be granted access to resources on the Gateway. You can select Check Point Password (previously VPN-1/Firewall-1 Password), SecurID, OS Password, RADIUS, and TACACS.

Authentication Settings

The user can select the following authentication settings:

- **User Authentication session timeout**   This setting (by default, 15 minutes) has two behaviors. For FTP and Telnet connections, connections with no activity are terminated after the timeout expires. For HTTP, it applies to the use of one-time passwords (i.e., SecurID tokens). Even though the timeout hasn't expired, the server will not request another one-time password for access to a previously authenticated server.

- **Enable Wait mode for Client Authentication**   This setting applies to Telnet Client Authentication, where the Telnet session remains open, and when the user closes the session (CTRL-C or some other manner), the authentication expires. If this option is not selected, the user will have to manually sign off or wait for the session timeout.

- **Authentication Failure Track**   Here, you can define if a failed authentication will generate an alert, a log, or no activity. We recommend at least logging all failed authentications.

HTTP Security Server

If you use an HTTP Security Server, you can configure an HTTP Proxy Server behind the Security Server. Enter the Host and Port for the proxy server to activate it.

Global Properties | Authentication

There are certain properties that are configured globally for all authentication performed by the Check Point gateways. Appropriately enough, you access them from the **Global Properties | Authentication** tab, as in Figure 6.51.

Figure 6.51 Global Properties | Authentication

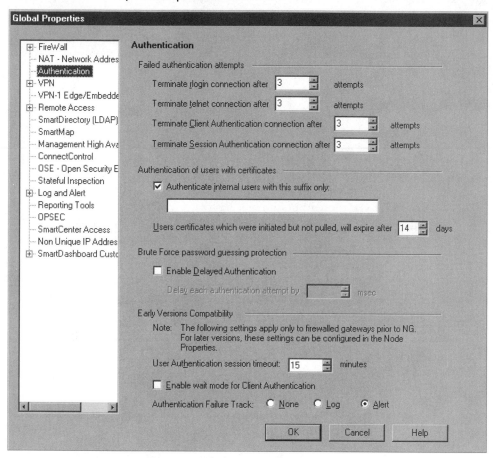

Failed Authentication Attempts

To prevent an intruder from brute-force guessing your passwords, the *Failed Authentication Attempts* setting can be used to terminate connections after a set number of failed attempts (i.e., wrong passwords). You can set a different amount of allowed tries for RLOGIN, Telnet, Client Authentication, and Session Authentication connections.

Authentication of Users with Certificates

For Remote Access VPNs, if you are using VPNs, you can restrict the gateway to accept only users who have a specific suffix in their certificates. Also, if an administrator *initializes* a certificate in the Certificate Authority, you can define how many days users have to pull that certificate before it expires.

Brute-Force Password Guessing Protection

To prevent an intruder from brute-force guessing your passwords, you can enable this protection, which is new for NGX. By setting a specific number of milliseconds to delay each authentication, you can dramatically affect any automatic password guessing system, while a user will barely notice a difference.

Early Version Compatibility

If you are managing gateways prior to NG, the following setting can be applied globally. For NG or later gateways, these settings are set per gateway. By the way, since there isn't the option to administer pre-NG gateways in NGX, you can probably ignore this section.

Registry Settings

Most of Check Point configuration is done from the SmartDashboard. However, some settings are not available through the SmartDashboard and have to be accessed directly in the Check Point internal registry. There are three ways you can access the registry:

- Some settings are available in the SmartDashboard through the **Policy Menu | Global Properties | SmartDashboard Customization**, which opens a tree of different settings you can change.

- You can use the GuiDBedit program, which is included in the installation folder of the Check Point SmartConsole clients. Its default location is **C:\Program Files\Check Point\SmartConsole\R60\PROGRAM\GuiDBedit.exe**. The program gives you complete access to the registry.

- You can use from the command line (or SecurePlatform's expert mode) the **dbedit** program, which is a text interface to the registry. You will need to know the exact setting you want to access, since it isn't very user-friendly.

Let's look at some of the settings you might need when dealing with Authentication.

New Interface

The default Client Authentication HTTP interface requires four pages for a successful login: the username page, password page, method page, and the optional specific sign-on page. If you enable the *hclient_enable_new_interface* setting using the **Policy Menu | Global Properties | SmartDashboard Customization | Firewall-1 | Authentication | Client Authentication | HTTP**, the HTTP interface will combine the username and password pages into one, thus streamlining the user experience, as in Figure 6.52.

Figure 6.52 Client Authentication HTTP New Interface

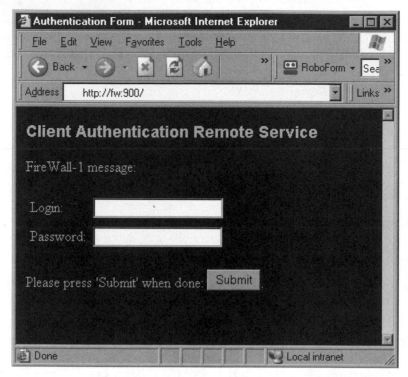

Use Host Header as Destination

If you are using Partially or Fully Automatic Sign-On with HTTP connections, once the connection is authenticated the firewall needs to redirect the original query to the intended destination. It does so by looking at the original URL's IP address, and redirecting the user's browser to that IP. However, if the firewall resolves the destination URL to a nonroutable IP (i.e., the non–NAT'ed IP), or if the web server is configured to need the Host Header for access (i.e., a web hosting service that shares one IP with multiple web pages), then the connection will fail. To avoid this, enable the *http_use_host_h_as_dst* setting using the **Policy Menu | Global Properties | SmartDashboard Customization | Firewall-1 | Web Security | HTTP Protocol**.

Opening All Client Authentication Rules

When you begin to create a complex policy with different rules for granting user access to different resources, you need to take into consideration that the default behavior for Client Authentication is to grant access for the rule only where you authenticated. If you need to authenticate once and be granted access by all rules that would permit the user, you have to enable the *automatically_open_ca_rules* setting using the **Policy Menu | Global Properties | SmartDashboard Customization | Firewall-1 | Authentication | Client Authentication** section.

Configuration Files

Besides the configuration of gateway properties, global properties, rules, and registry settings, some configuration files can change the authentication behavior, to include encryption or to present your own look and feel to the user.

Enabling Encrypted Authentication

Since Telnet and HTTP are not encrypted, Client Authentication is inherently less secure than Session Authentication. However, you can configure NGX to enable HTTPS Manual Authentication, which will give you the encryption you want when using the built-in HTTP server at port 900 for authentication. Look in the "Are You Owned?" sidebar for details.

Custom Pages

If you will use Client Authentication's HTTP interface, you will probably want to change its appearance and include your company's logo, an unauthorized use warning, and some nice graphics. You can do this by editing the HTML files in the directory *$FWDIR/conf/ahclientd*. Remember to leave the **%** commands intact, as they are used by NGX to insert the information it needs.

Installing the User Database

The Check Point User Database is independent of the SmartDashboard objects and rulebases. When you install a policy (from SmartDashboard, **Policy | Install…**), in fact the SmartDashboard saves the current policy, and installs the policy (containing the objects and rules) and the user database. If you have made changes only to the user database (password changes, created users, changed group membership), you might want to install only the user database, which is a lot faster.

To install the user database, from the SmartDashboard you can select **Policy | Install Database…**, or from the **Manage | Users and Administrators** dialog, click on **Actions…** and then select **Install…** as in Figure 6.53.

Figure 6.53 Using Actions in the Manage Users and Administrator Dialog

You will see the *Install Database* window, like in Figure 6.54. You can then select **OK** to install the database. If you have more than one gateway or SmartCenter, you will see different objects and select among them.

Figure 6.54 Installing the User Database

Summary

Many security rulebases do not have the need for individual user rights, and work with Hosts, Gateways, Networks, Groups, Ranges, and Servers. However, both for security and for tracking purposes you might need to integrate authentication with your security policy. You'll be able to identify users' navigation, and grant privileged users access to restricted resources or connections with specific services.

You have a choice of how to recognize a user, accessing external directory servers with RADIUS or TACACS, or using the internal user database. You can integrate with Microsoft Active Directory through the Microsoft Internet Authentication Service, or get the SmartDirectory license for LDAP integration.

You can choose between User, Client, and Session Authentication, depending on your needs and a balance of security, ease-of-use, and flexibility. User authentication is easy to use and transparent, but is not flexible, has no security, and can be cumbersome for accessing external web sites. Client Authentication is flexible and can be secure, but it is not transparent to the user and less secure than other methods. Session Authentication is flexible, secure, and easy to use, but installing the agent on each machine will be something you have to consider.

Check Point NGX gives you many options; you just have to choose which to implement.

Chapter 7

Content Security and OPSEC

Solutions in this chapter:

- **OPSEC**
- **Security Servers**
- **CVP**
- **UFP**
- **MDQ**
- **Secure Internal Communication**

☑ **Summary**

Introduction

In this chapter you will learn how Check Point FireWall-1 can integrate with third-party products. Check Point does Content Security by pushing traffic through built-in Application Layer Gateways. Also known as proxies, these engines allow you to actually scan and modify the data portion of TCP-based traffic.

Check Point FireWall-1 has the ability to redirect traffic to a third-party appliance for anti-virus scanning. Check Point also has a product that performs anti-virus scanning inside of the firewall product. Check Point certifies third-party solutions with the OPSEC (Open Platform for Security) Alliance. OPSEC compliant anti-virus scanners use the CVP (Content Vectoring Protocol) to communicate with FireWall-1. There are several interfaces available to OPSEC vendors to communicate with Check Point products.

We will cover all five proxies available to us in FireWall-1; each has unique options that allow you to further secure network environments. We will also cover internal Check Point communication and how certificates are used to secure the security products.

OPSEC

OPSEC (Open Platform for Security) represents Check Point's efforts to allow third-party companies to produce Check Point integrated solutions. The OPSEC Alliance is a collection of security vendors that have been OPSEC Certified by Check Point Software. There are hundreds of vendors that develop OPSEC-compliant software. A list of these products is available on the OPSEC Alliance Web site, www.opsec.com.

Check Point has made an API (Application Programming Interface) available for these companies to use to communicate with Check Point's product line. The SDK (Software Development Kit) requires knowledge of the C programming language. The SDK contains software to integrate with the following interfaces:

- **CVP** The Content Vectoring Protocol allows anti-virus solutions to talk to FireWall-1.

- **UFP** The URI Filtering Protocol allows Web filtering to integrate.

- **LEA** The Log Export API enables you to export log files to third-party log servers.

- **ELA** The Event Logging API allows Check Point to receive logs from third-party software.

- **SAM** The Suspicious Activity Monitor enables you to integrate intrusion detection systems.

- **CPMI** The Check Point Management Interface gives a third-party device access to the Check Point management utilities. For example, this would allow a device to read the object database.

- **AMON**   The Application Monitor allows a third-party device to tell Check Point its status. This will allow the product to show up in the SmartView Status monitoring application.

- **UAA**   The User Authority Agent allows Check Point to integrate into Microsoft environments.

- **SAA**   The Secure Authentication API allows for integration into authentication systems.

- **SCV**   The Secure Client Verification allows SecureClient to talk to third-party software on remote VPN clients to ensure end-user compliance.

Partnership

Any vendor of security-related products can sign up for the OPSEC Alliance at www.opsec.com. Access to OPSEC resources is free after you sign up. There is a small fee for certification for OPSEC compliance.

Anti-virus

Check Point FireWall-1 has the capability of doing anti-virus scanning using CVP (Content Vectoring Protocol). This protocol allows Check Point to redirect most TCP-based traffic to an anti-virus scanner and returns cleaned data. Check Point also has a product with built-in anti-virus functionality called Check Point Express CI. This virus scanner used the Computer Associate's anti-virus engine and is meant to add functionality to firewalls in organizations with 100 to 500 employees.

Web Filtering

Web filtering is performed using UFP (URI Filtering Protocol). There are several solutions available to curb excess Web site surfing. Check Point has the ability to take a text file of URLs and block access to them without using a UFP server, although it is not recommended to have over 50 entries in the list.

OPSEC Applications

When using an OPSEC-compliant solution on the firewall, an OPSEC Application object must be used. You can create one by clicking Manage → Servers and OPSEC Applications, then clicking New… → OPSEC Application… You can also click the fourth tab in the Objects Tree on the left, and right-click OPSEC Application and click New → OPSEC Application.

A Node object should be created beforehand so it can be selected in the Host box. There is a New… box you can click to create one while you are creating your OPSEC Application object (see Figure 7.1). There are predefined Vendors which select the Entities for you on the bottom. You can always leave the Vendor on User defined and select your own Server and Client Entities.

Figure 7.1 OPSEC Application Properties

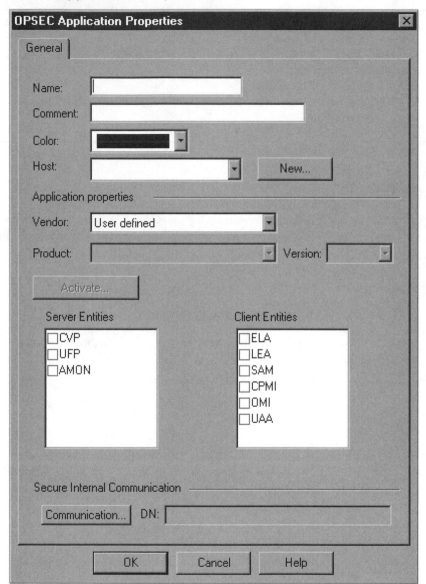

Security Servers

The Application Layer Gateways on Check Point FireWall-1 are referred to as Security Servers. These Security Servers run as separate processes on the firewall. Configuration is done through the SmartDashboard GUI. In order to use an antivirus scanning engine, or any product that scans layer 7 data, the data must first go through one of these Security Servers. Each Security Server has unique features based on functions in the protocol.

Figure 7.2 shows a resource used in the policy. To use a resource, right-click the service field and click Add With Resource.... When a resource is used in a rule, no other services can be in the same rule.

Figure 7.2 SmartDashboard Resources

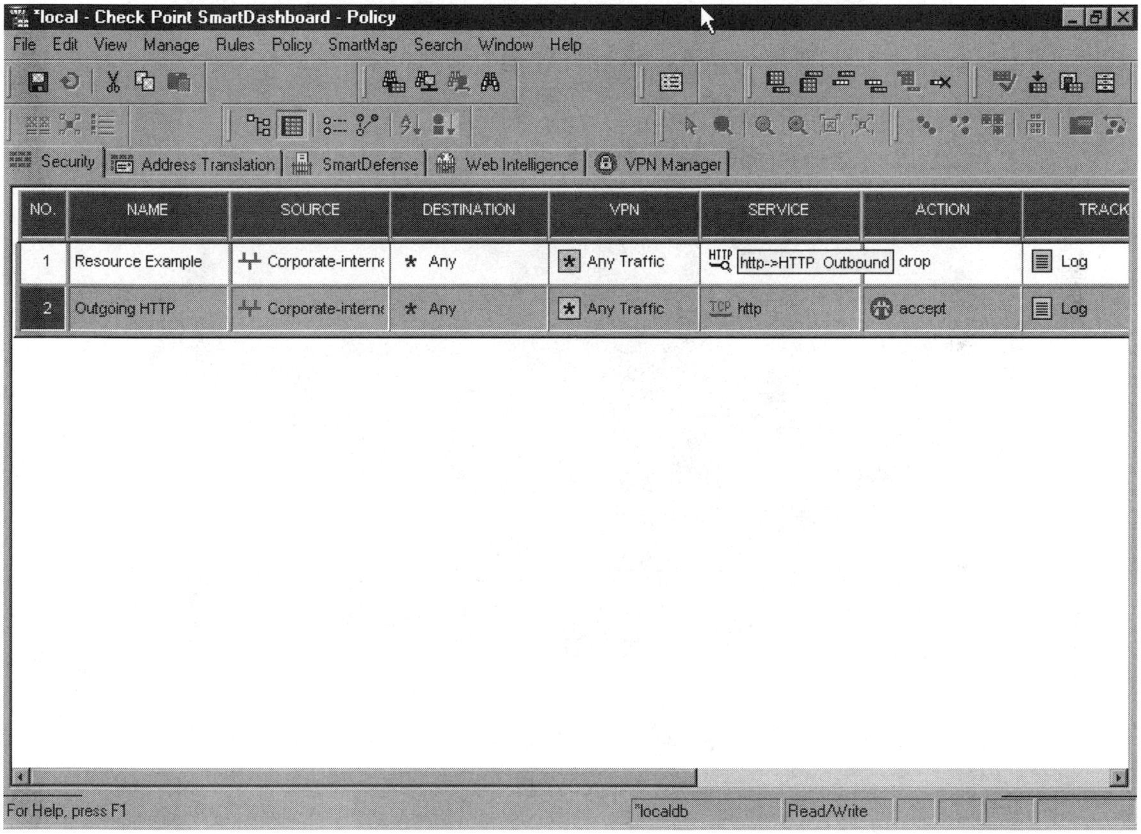

URI

The URI (Uniform Resource Identifier) Security Server is used for HTTP-based traffic. To create a URI Resource you can click Manage → Resources, then click New... → URI..., or click the third tab in the Objects Tree window on the left and right-click Resources and click New... → URI.

The default settings are shown in Figure 7.3. When Optimize URL logging is selected, all the other features of the resource are disabled. This is used to simply log the URL's (Uniform Resource Locator) your users are going to. Enforce URI capabilities gives you the most options. This allows you to do content inspection in the Security Server and send the traffic to a CVP or UFP server. Enhance UFP performance is used when all you want to do is send the URL to a server for Web filtering.

Figure 7.3 The URI Resource

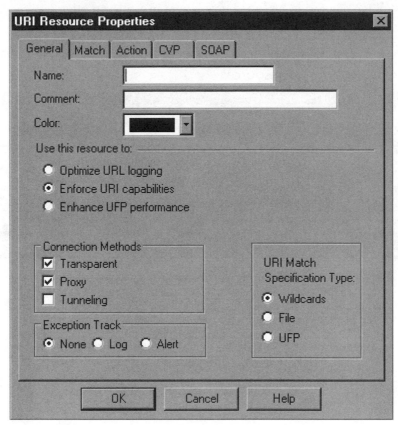

The URI Match Specification Type windows allow you to select the method you use in order to choose what URIs trigger this resource. Wildcards will allow you to type a string to look for. File allows you to import a file of strings to look for. We recommended that this file contain fewer than 50 strings. It can quickly become unmanageable! Selecting UFP allows you to send the URL to a UFP scanner for Web filtering.

The Match tab changes based on whether you pick Wildcard, File, or UFP in the first tab. Figure 7.4 is the result when Wildcard is chosen. By default it applies the resource to any URL.

Figure 7.4 Result from Selecting the URI Resource's Wildcard Option

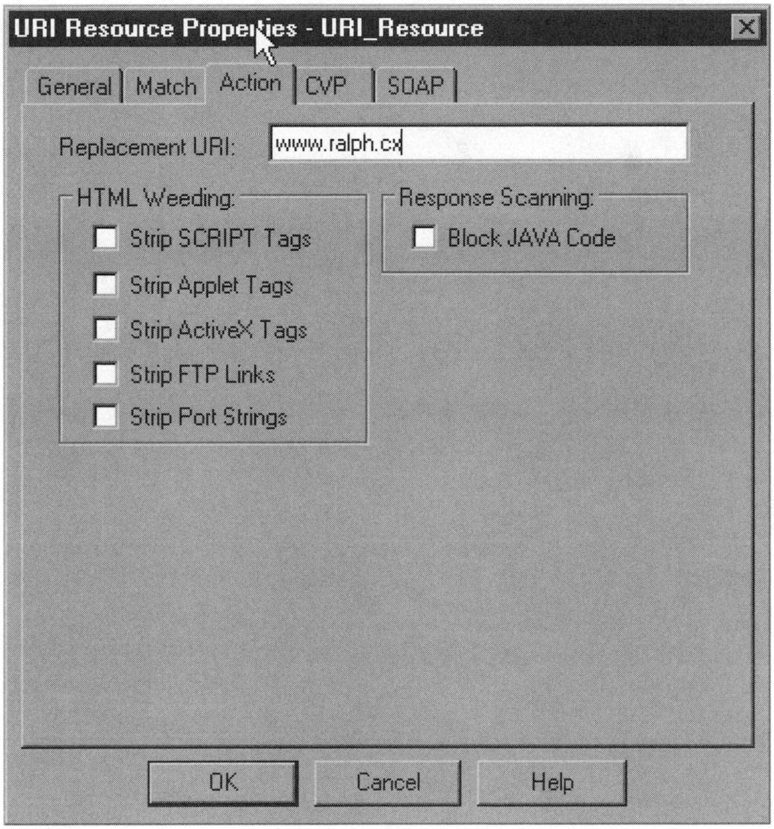

The Action tab allows you to perform HTML Weeding, which is striping selected data out of the content of the packets. A replacement URL can be chosen here to automatically send users to when they violate policies. You can also have the Security Server block JAVA code.

The CVP tab allows us to select an anti-virus server for scanning. We'll discuss CVP in more detail later in this chapter.

SOAP (Simple Object Access Protocol) is an XML-based Web protocol for transferring data. The last tab gives you the ability to block specific SOAP traffic (see Figure 7.5). Tracking options are available as well.

Figure 7.5 Blocking SOAP Traffic with the URI Resource

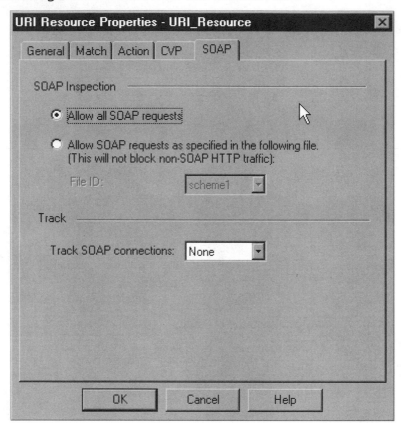

SMTP

The SMTP (Simple Mail Transfer Protocol) Resource is the most common proxy used on FireWall-1. When using this Resource you can modify and block e-mail.

As you can tell, the options in the SMTP Resource are quite a bit different from the URI Resource. The Mail Delivery Server setting is optional and allows you to enter a mail host to forward mail to (see Figure 7.6).

Figure 7.6 The SMTP Resource

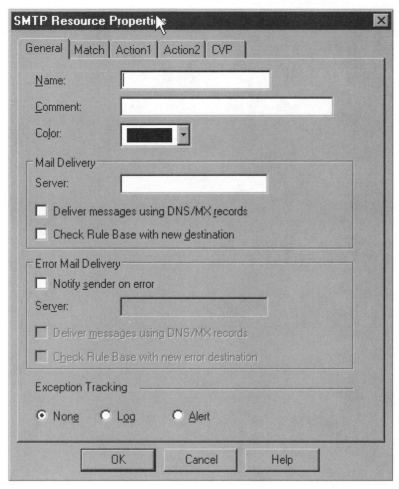

The Match tab allows you to specify which Senders and Recipients can be in the e-mail. Typically, two Resources are created, one for incoming e-mail and one for outgoing e-mail. You can specify a domain name in one of these boxes to make sure only e-mail with certain Senders or Recipients are passing in a certain direction (see Figure 7.7).

Figure 7.7 The SMTP Resource's Match Tab

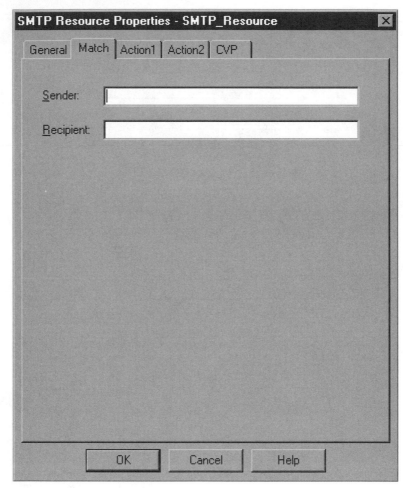

The Action1 tab allows for selective rewriting of SMTP headers. This is not used very often, but is a good way to hide to the outside world what type of e-mail clients are sending mail from the inside of your network (see Figure 7.8).

Figure 7.8 The SMTP Resource's Action1 Tab

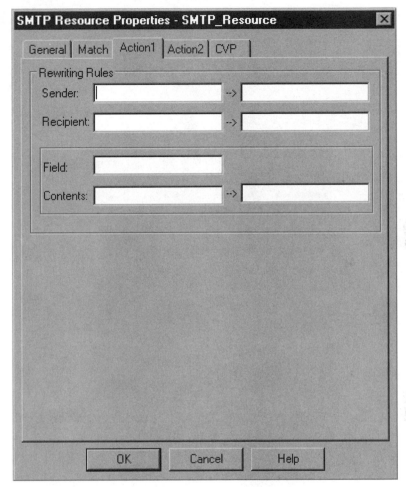

The Action2 tab allows for stripping of certain attachments and e-mail sizes. You can also strip out script content using the Weeding box at the bottom. The CVP tab allows for selection of the CVP server and associated options (see Figure 7.9).

Figure 7.9 The SMTP Resource's Action2 Tab

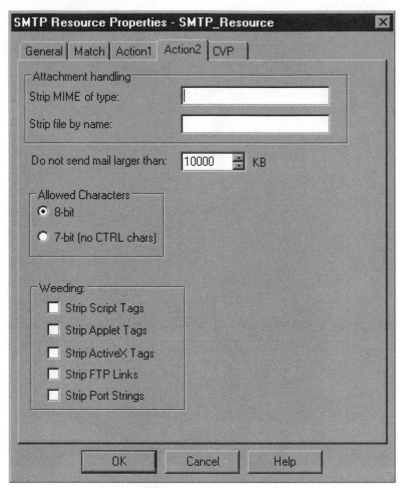

FTP

The FTP Security Server is not used very much, but has a few cool features. The one drawback to the FTP Security Server is that when you use it, downloads or uploads of files trickle down very slowly to the client while the firewall buffers the entire file, scans it, then pushes down the file in its entirety to the client. The users of the network should be informed of this behavior so they do not think the download is not working.

As you can see in Figure 7.10, the FTP Resource does not have too many options. Typically this resource is used only if you want to send FTP traffic to a CVP server for anti-virus scanning.

Figure 7.10 The FTP Resource

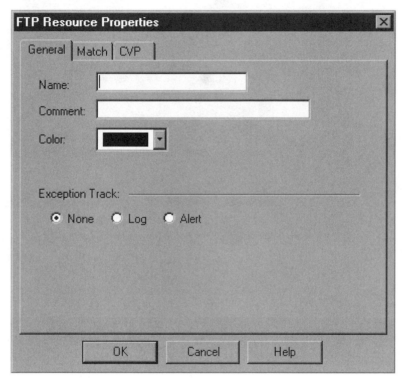

Using the screen shown in Figure 7.11, you can block GET or PUT FTP methods. This is an easy way to disallow uploading or downloading of files via FTP in a certain direction.

Figure 7.11 Blocking GET and PUT Methods with FTP Resource

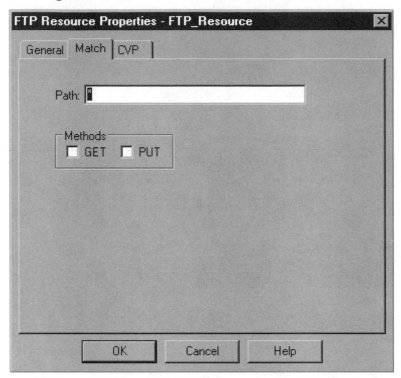

TCP

The TCP Resource is used only to send generic TCP traffic to a UFP or CVP server. This is useful if you want to apply content inspection to protocols other than the supported TCP protocols (see Figure 7.12).

Figure 7.12 The TCP Resource

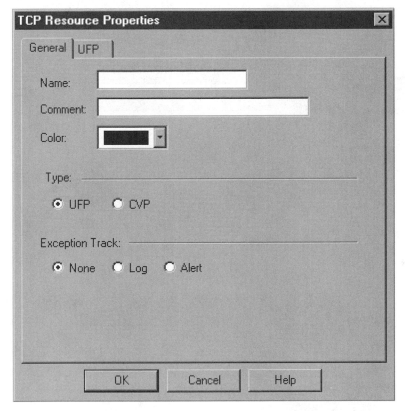

CIFS

The CIFS (Common Internet File System) Resource is used to proxy Microsoft networking traffic. Using this resource can ensure unwanted network paths and printer shares are allowed through the firewall.

This Resource also can block registry access. Keep in mind that your traffic has to go through the firewall for this Resource to take effect (see Figure 7.13).

Figure 7.13 The CIFS Resource

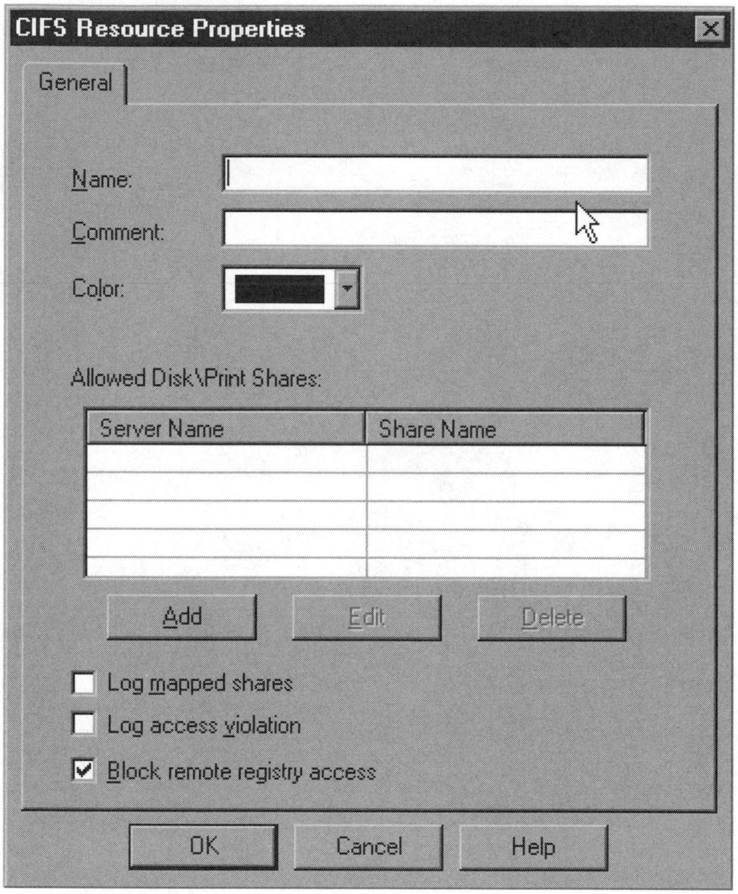

CVP

The Content Vectoring Protocol is how Check Point sends data to a third-party server for content inspection. Check Point uses TCP port 18181 to send data to the CVP server. The CVP server scans the data and sends the data back to the firewall on TCP port 18181. Check Point recommends that CVP servers be placed on a separate segment of the network directly connected to the firewall for best performance. If an extra interface is not available, then the CVP server should be placed in the DMZ.

Resource Creation

In order to use CVP for TCP traffic, a Resource of some type must be created. Every resource, with the exception of CIFS, has the ability to use the CVP protocol.

Figure 7.14 shows the CVP tab in the URI Resource object. An OPSEC application needs to be created first that has the CVP protocol box checked in it. When you select the drop-down menu next to CVP Server, it will list all the CVP server and CVP groups. When CVP servers are placed into a CVP group, they are load balanced.

Figure 7.14 The URI Resource's CVP Tab

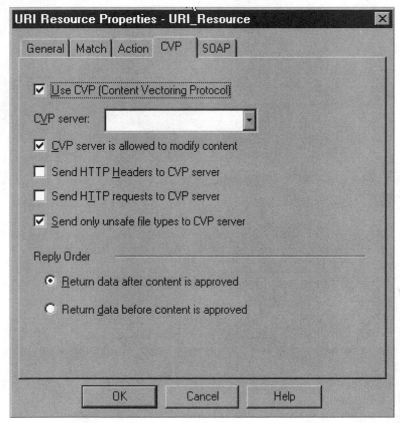

UFP

A UFP server allows you to send the URI of Web pages to a server that contains a list of several sites and tells FireWall-1 to allow or disallow access to that URI. Check Point uses TCP port 18182 to send data to the UFP server. There are products that contain lists of millions of Web sites, placed into categories. Categories can be blocked so users cannot access certain sites. Most filtering products also have the ability to block only at certain times of the day or limit how often a site is accessed. Configuring UFP is very similar to configuring CVP.

When an OPSEC Application object is created for a UFP server, the categories can be downloaded to the firewall by clicking Get Dictionary.... (see Figure 7.15).

Figure 7.15 A UFP Server

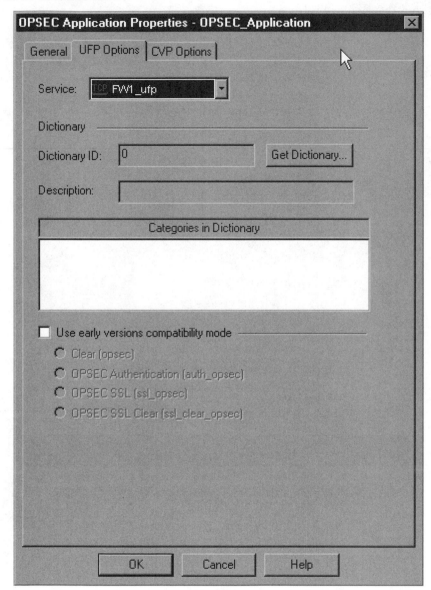

Resource Creation

To use UFP in a Resource, Enhance UFP performance can be checked or the URI Match Specification Type can be set to UFP. The UFP server can be selected on the Match tab along with the Categories that this Resource should match on. UFP Groups can also be created to load balance UFP traffic.

MDQ

The MDQ (Mail Dequeuer) runs as a process on FireWall-1. MDQ handles the spooling of e-mail for the SMTP Security Server. The process will show up as mdq on any FireWall-1 platform. MDQ Enqueuer accepts inbound e-mail and places it into the $FWDIR/spool directory. MDQ then sends a copy of that e-mail to a CVP server if the firewall policy calls for it. Then the MDQ Dequeuer sends the e-mail outbound. The terms inbound and outbound relate to the firewall and the policy, regardless of the direction of the e-mail.

How to Debug

At times the MDQ process can get overloaded. The command **fw mdq** will restart the MDQ process and start filtering e-mail again. A **cprestart** will also restart the MDQ process. It is possible a malformed e-mail may hang the process. If this happens, the e-mail should be tracked down in the $FWDIR/spool directory, moved out of that directory, and **fw mdq** should be run to restart the MDQ process. Every e-mail is in a separate file and this directory can be emptied while the firewall is stopped if MDQ is not working to make it work again.

Secure Internal Communication

SIC (Secure Internal Communication) refers to the technology that controls internal Check Point communication. When the Check Point Management Server is installed, Check Point creates a Certificate Authority. All internal Check Point traffic is encrypted with these certificates using PKI (public key infrastructure). The Check Point Management Server holds the master certificate and every Check Point product has one certificate cut from the master certificate.

When creating Check Point objects and OPSEC Application objects there is a SIC Communication box at the bottom of the object window. When the software is installed, a one-time password is required. When the object is created on the Check Point SmartDashboard, this one-time password is used to encrypt the certificate while it is being installed on the device. Once the certificate is downloaded, all future traffic is encrypted using this certificate.

Summary

In this chapter we learned about the ability of third-party products to communicate with Check Point products. Check Point has a vendor alliance called OPSEC. This program certifies third-party products for use with Check Point. There are several Application Programming Interfaces that Check Point has made available for communication with the Check Point product suite.

We learned about the Security Servers and the ability for Check Point to modify layer 7 traffic. Traffic can be send to an anti-virus server using the CVP protocol or a Web filtering server using the UFP protocol. We also learned about the MDQ process and how the SMTP Security Service works on FireWall-1.

Check Point NG introduced SIC (Secure Internal Communication), which encrypts internal Check Point communication with certificates.

Chapter 8

VPN

Solutions in this chapter:

- Encryption Overview
- Simplified vs. Traditional
- Route-Based VPN
- VPN Routing
- Site-to-Site VPN
- Multiple Entry Point (MEP)
- Tunnel Management and Debugging

☑ Summary

Introduction

The emergence of the Internet has allowed the increasing growth of companies that are using it as a backbone to connect remote offices, partners, and remote clients. The Internet is a public network, in that no single entity owns the Internet. When you send data through the Internet, you have no way of knowing who owns the devices that the traffic is passing through, or who may be able to view that data. Because of this, virtual private networks (VPN) were developed. A VPN provides a means of encrypting your data such that only other authorized systems can decrypt it. Because of this, VPNs allow you to maintain the confidentiality and integrity of your data across an inherently insecure medium.

This chapter will focus on configuring site-to-site VPNs and the different design considerations that are involved. Refer to Chapter 3 for more information on remote clients, and remote client VPNs. This chapter describes many new features that will be discussed and demonstrated so that you may easily set up a VPN between two Check Points or even another vendor's device, such as a Cisco PIX firewall. We will start by explaining some key VPN-related concepts and then explain and demonstrate the different methods for setting up a Check Point VPN and configuring your rulebase in order to complete your VPN solution. We will also explain troubleshooting steps you can take when working with VPNs.

Encryption Overview

Encryption is the process of turning something that is normally readable (plaintext) into something unreadable (ciphertext). The reverse process, decryption, will turn the ciphertext back into plaintext. In practice, encryption is done by applying a mathematical formula to the plaintext. There are many types of encryption formulas or algorithms, and some are more effective at keeping the plaintext secure than others. Some forms of encryption are intended to provide data confidentiality; others also have measures to provide data integrity as well. Before discussing Check Point's specific VPN implementation, we'll review some encryption basics.

One form of simple encryption is a substitution cipher, where one character of the plaintext is replaced with another character. The classic example of this is where a is 1, b is 2, c is 3, and so on. Thus the plaintext "checkpoint" becomes "03080503111615091420" as ciphertext. Although this may seem secure, it would take a typical computer less time to try every single letter, number, and punctuation mark substitution for each character of the ciphertext, than it would for you to type the ciphertext in the first place. Because of this, most modern forms of encryption rely on the use of a *key*. The encryption key is much like a physical key, in that you need it to encrypt or decrypt the ciphertext.

Symmetric and Asymmetric Encryption

A key is used to both encrypt (lock) and decrypt (unlock) the plaintext and ciphertext, respectively. When the two keys are the same, this is *symmetric* encryption. In this system, the security of the entire encryption process relies on keeping the key a secret. If anyone learns the key, they will be able to decrypt the ciphertext and read the original message. Because the recipient needs to have the key to decrypt the message, you must have a secure way of transferring the secret key to the recipient before he or she will be able to decrypt the ciphertext.

In addition to the logistics of getting your secret key to your intended recipient, if you have two different recipients you want to send encrypted messages to, but you don't want either of them to be able to read messages intended for the other, you would need to use two different keys. This doesn't sound too bad, but imagine if you were in a mid-sized company of 200 users. For each user to have a secret key for use with every other user would require 19,000 unique keys. In a company with more users the number would only get even more unmanageable.

With asymmetric encryption the sender and receiver don't need to have the same key. Instead they each have a different, but *mathematically related* key. This method greatly reduces the number of keys that are needed. Each person then needs only two keys, a *public* key and a *private* key. The public key is publicly known and can be distributed freely. When senders encrypt something with their private key, the public key can be used (by anybody) to decrypt it. This has the added benefit that you know the message was encrypted by the intended person or else the public key would fail to decrypt the message. When you send something to someone, you would use their public key to encrypt the message and only the intended recipient with the proper private key could decrypt the message.

Given the advantages of asymmetric encryption, you might wonder why anybody would ever use symmetric encryption. Primarily, it's a matter of speed. The additional computations needed to use asymmetric encryption generally make it far slower than using a symmetric algorithm. When you are sending large volumes of data, such as in a computer network, where encryption and decryption are done frequently, a hybrid approach typically is adopted. This usually involves the asymmetric encryption of a symmetric key. In this way the secret symmetric key can be encrypted and distributed securely. This symmetric key is then used for future bulk data transfers.

Certificate Authorities

Given the importance of exchanging keys securely, the questions arises of how you can be sure that the (public) key you are exchanging really belongs to the person or organization you think it does. A *certificate authority's* (CA) sole function is to provide a trusted way of obtaining public keys. When you are dealing with public keys outside your organization, typically you would need to rely on a trusted third party as your CA, such as VeriSign. For key distribution between internal devices and systems, you can act as your own CA, since you trust yourself to provide legitimate public keys. This enables you to use asymmetric encryption protocols internally without having to register and pay for each certificate to be used with each key.

Exchanging Keys

As you can see, reliable encryption depends on the secure distribution of encryption keys. Managing the distribution in a secure and reliable way is handled through a key exchange protocol. Although there are multiple key exchange protocols available, Internet Key Exchange (IKE), is one of the most widely deployed key exchange mechanisms. IKE is an industry standard (RFC 2409) that can be implemented on many different platforms to provide key management functionality. IKE functionality includes establishing a security association (SA), which is a set of parameters that are used to encrypt and decrypt information between two devices. The SA will include things such as what encryption algorithm to use, how to endure data integrity (a hash algorithm), and how to renew keys.

Tunnel Mode vs. Transport Mode

There are primarily two ways to encrypt IP-based traffic. One is *tunnel mode*, which takes the entire IP packet, and encrypts it, and then encapsulates this encrypted packet in a new header. The other is called *transport mode*, which encrypts only the data portion of the packet, and leaves the headers relatively intact. An advantage of tunnel mode is that it encrypts the entire original header, meaning that even the original IP addresses cannot be seen without decrypting the packet. This provides a higher degree of privacy than transport mode, which leaves the source and destination IP addresses and other header information unencrypted. On the other hand, because tunnel mode is encrypting the original packet in it's entirety, and adding a new header, it is increasing the packet size of every single packet.

Encryption Algorithms

Once you have decided that encryption is needed, and determined whether symmetric or asymmetric encryption would be more suitable, you need to choose an encryption algorithm to use. There are a large number of different encryption algorithms available. Check Point NGX supports the following encryption algorithms:

- Digital Encryption Standard (DES)
- Triple Digital Encryption Standard (3DES)
- Advanced Encryption Standard – 128 bit key (AES-128)
- Advanced Encryption Standard – 256 bit key (AES-256)

DES may be adequate for some encryption needs, but as processing power has increased, cracking DES by *brute forcing* the key (guessing every possible key combination) is becoming increasingly feasible. In July 1998 DES was cracked in three days by a specially built computer costing around $250,000. Only six months later in January of 1999, DES was again cracked by a distributed network of 100,000 Internet computers in 22 minutes. For this reason, DES is no longer considered adequate encryption for important data. 3DES is cryptographically stronger, and currently remains the minimum recommended encryption strength to be used.

Hashing Algorithms

Once you have encrypted a piece of data, you need some way to ensure that is had not been tampered with. A hash algorithm is a mathematical formula that takes a given string of input, and generates as output a unique string of a fixed size (a message digest). The computation is reproducible, meaning that the hash will be the same for the same input each time. If you change the input, the message digest will change as well. If you were to generate a message digest for the entire novel, *War and Peace*, and then changed a single character anywhere in it, the next message digest that you generate would be different from the first. The hash function is *not* reversible. This means that if you have the message digest, there should be no way to derive the original message that was used to produce it.

The practical use for a hash function (in a VPN) is to ensure data integrity. If you generate a hash of a given message before sending it, and the recipient then generates the same hash from the message they received, then you know that they received exactly what you sent. When you combine the message digest with an encryption algorithm, you can ensure both data integrity and confidentiality. Check Point NGX supports the following hash algorithms for VPNs:

- MD5
- Secure Hash Algorithm Version1 (SHA1)

A message digest also can be used to ensure the identity of the sender of the message. To do this, the sender encrypts the message digest using his or her private key. The recipient of the message can use the sender's public key to decrypt the message digest. The recipient then recalculates the message digest to ensure that it matches the one the sender provided. Assuming they match, the recipient knows that the message was unchanged, and that it was sent by right person. The process of encrypting the message digest to verify the identity of the sender and the integrity of the message is called a digital signature.

Public Key Infrastructure

As you can see there is a complicated interdependency between all these systems to make modern encryption work securely. If any one of these elements are compromised the entire communication stream is at risk for being intercepted. All these various systems and components work together to get the job done. The entire infrastructure that is used to provide secure public keys distribution and support digital signatures is referred to as a *public key infrastructure* (PKI).

Simplified vs. Traditional

In Check Point's VPN-1 there are two primary ways to configure your VPN between sites. One is the *traditional* way, which requires you to explicitly configure the access rules that specify what traffic should be encrypted. This method is more complex but allows for a high degree of control over exactly what gets encrypted. The other, *simplified* approach, allows you to simply specify what devices should have their communications encrypted, and the needed rules will be created automatically. This makes setting up a VPN between a branch office and the main office pretty painless. You can specify which method to use by going to **Policy | Global Properties | VPN** as shown in Figure 8.1.

Figure 8.1 VPN Configuration Method Selection

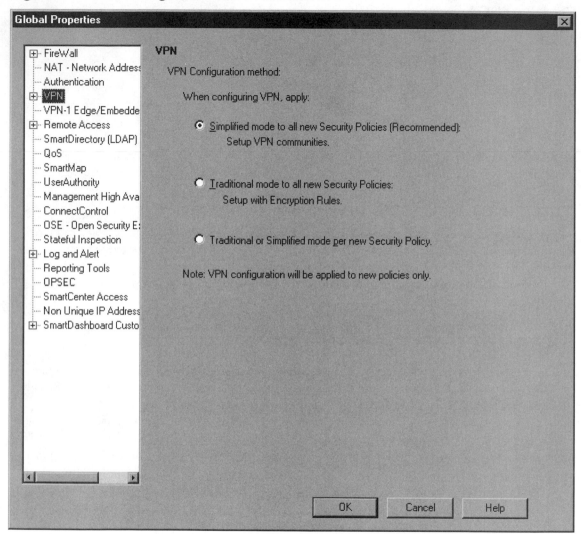

The following VPN examples will be configured between two Check Point Enterprise/Pro NGX devices. The devices should be able to communicate with each other and your secure internal communications (SIC) should be working properly.

Using the Simplified Configuration Method

Note that some of the features of Check Point's FW-1 and VPN-1 are available to you only if you use the simplified approach for VPN configuration. Generally, if you do not have a need for creating complicated and very granular encryption rules, the simplified method will be much easier to use. Because you can change methods only by creating and applying an entirely new policy, the decision of which method to use should be made with some caution. To configure a VPN using the simplified approach, follow these basic steps:

1. Enable the VPN product on the gateways.
2. Configure the VPN Domain.
3. Configure the VPN Community (Star of Mesh).
4. Install the policy.

VPN Communities

The first concept to understand when dealing with the simplified approach is the concept of VPN Communities. A VPN community is essentially a centralized object containing all the configuration settings needed for establishing an SA between devices. Members of a VPN community can be single machines, or entire sites. The community is merely a collection of objects who share the same encryption settings so that they can establish VPNs between them. By placing all these settings in a single community object, all the devices that need to use those setting in order to establish a VPN tunnel can be made members of the community. This method is not only simpler than manually configuring each of the individual gateways, but it reduces the chance of an error being made when entering the settings over and over.

There are two types of VPN communities you can create. One is the meshed, which simply stated, allows encrypted communication to occur between all gateways in the community. The meshed community usually will be the best one to use unless you have specific requirements to use the other type, the star community, which does not allow encrypted communication directly between the satellites in the star.

Meshed VPN Communities

A meshed VPN community is the simplest to configure and would be most appropriate in many cases. A meshed configuration would be adequate if you have multiple offices that all need to share data and communicate with each other across the public Internet. In this scenario, the communications are fairly distributed and all the offices need to communicate with each other to access various services that each site might hold.

The first step to establish a VPN tunnel is to go into the properties of both gateway devices and ensure that the **General Properties** sheet shows **VPN** as an enabled product. If it is not, you will need to select it and click **OK**. You may get an alert dialog box informing you that an internal CA certificate will be created and the IKE properties set. Click **OK** again. The property window for that device should close when the process is completed.

You must then configure each network object to ensure it has the proper VPN Domain configured. You can do this by viewing the object's properties and clicking **Topology** on the left side of the window. The default will be for all IP addresses behind the gateway to be a part of the same VPN domain. You can click the Show **VPN Domain button** and the objects will be highlighted in the SmartMap pane. This makes it easier to graphically see which devices are configured as part of the same VPN domain.

You must now define the VPN community itself. You can do this by going to the network objects tree and selecting the **VPN Communities** tab. Right-click **Site to Site**, and select **New Site to Site | Meshed** as seen in Figure 8.2. You can also do this without the network objects tree by right-clicking in an empty area in the **VPN Manager** tab and selecting **New Community | Meshed**.

Figure 8.2 Creating a New VPN Community

From the following window you will configure the properties of the VPN community, as shown in Figure 8.3. In the **General** section, choose a descriptive name for the community. Generally you will want to select **Accept all encrypted traffic**, which means that any traffic between the endpoints will be encrypted. This option also causes a rule to be added to the rulebase to *accept* the traffic. If you had some traffic between the two sites you did not want encrypted, you would leave this option unchecked. Then highlight **Participating Gateways** in the left pane. Click **Add** and select your two or more gateway end points and click **OK**. The **VPN Properties** section will allow you to specify the encryption and hashing algorithms to use for key exchange and the primary data encryption.

Figure 8.3 Meshed Community Properties

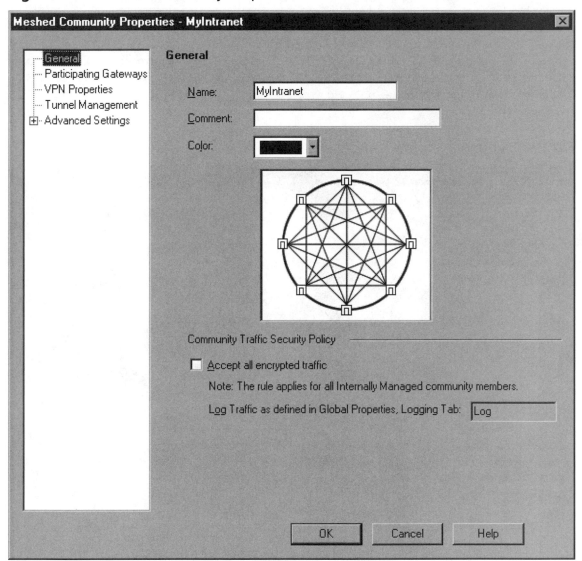

The next section is **Tunnel Management** (see Figure 8.4). When selected, these properties allow greater control over when a VPN tunnel is created. The **Set permanent tunnels** option will create the VPN tunnel and then leave it open even when there is no data to be sent across it. Because there is overhead in creating and tearing down tunnels, using permanent tunnels can improve performance, especially between sites with frequent need to send encrypted data. A remote office, who needs to get all their Internet access and file server access from the corporate office, would be a good candidate for configuring the tunnels to be permanent. If, on the other hand, the remote site only rarely had a need to send encrypted data back to the corporate office, leaving it unchecked would allow the tunnel to be created only when needed, freeing resources on the gateway the rest of the time.

Enabling route injection will cause the firewall to modify its routing table when the tunnels are unavailable. This option is only of value if the gateway device is using a dynamic routing protocol, so that it can propagate the routing changes to other devices. There are also options to log tunnel creation and tunnel failure. These options can be set for each community, or globally set for all communities under **Policy | Global Properties | Log and Alert | Community Default Rule**. The last option on this screen is for VPN Tunnel Sharing. This determines how many VPN tunnels to create between devices. Depending on the devices you have at either end, you may need any one of the three options.

Figure 8.4 Tunnel Management

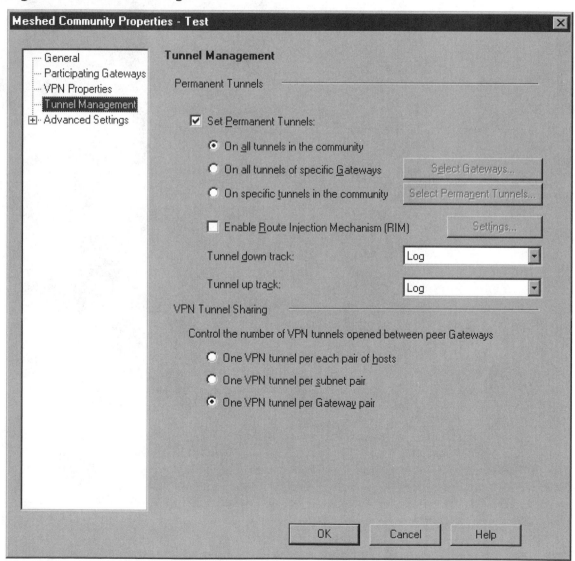

Once this is done, click **OK**. Using the simplified VPN configuration will cause the community to create a rule that encrypts the traffic. If you selected **Accept all encrypted traffic**, a new rule is also created to allow the encrypted traffic. If you didn't choose **Accept all encrypted traffic** you will need to create a rule in the rulebase to allow the traffic. The key here is that the simplified approach will create the rule to encrypt the traffic, but it still must be allowed on the gateway. To view the encryption rules select **View | VPN Rules**. If you selected **Accept all encrypted traffic**, you can view the rule that option creates by clicking **Created by community** at the top of the rulebase. You can also verify that there are no errors by checking the VPN section of the SmartView Tracker. A successful tunnel will have periodic encrypt and decrypt entries with a service of tunnel_test.

Star VPN Communities

Using the star-based communities is also referred to as *VPN Routing*, because the VPNs themselves can be made to route through a central hub gateway or group of gateways. In this way you can enforce a policy that requires all encrypted traffic to be inspected at a central office. For example you might want all the encrypted traffic for branch offices to be routed through the central office, where it is decrypted, inspected for malicious code, and then encrypted and sent to another branch office.

Configuring a star VPN community is similar to how you configured the meshed community, with only a couple of differences. You can create the new community by right-clicking in an empty area in the **VPN Manager** tab and selecting **New Community | Star**. You will see a window like the one shown in Figure 8.5. You will need to give the community a descriptive name, as before. If you want the access rule to allow the encrypted traffic to be created automatically, check **Accept all encrypted traffic**.

Figure 8.5 Star Community Properties

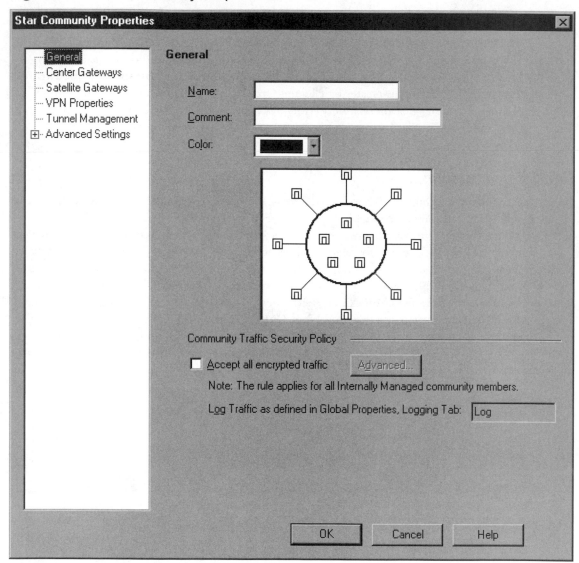

Now by clicking **Center Gateways** in the left-hand pane, you can add any gateway you wish to be at the center of the star here and click **OK**. If your organization is large enough to have several gateways at the central sight, you can check the box titled **Mesh Center Gateways**. If this box is not checked, the central gateways of the star will not be able to encrypt traffic between themselves. If you have only a single central gateway there is no impact for checking this box.

Next, click **Satellite Gateways** in the left pane. From this window, you will add any satellite gateways you wish. Remember, the satellite gateways will not be able to communicate via encrypted tunnels directly between themselves. The next step is to click **VPN Properties** in the left pane and set the parameters for encryption that all community members will use. After this is done, click **Tunnel Management** in the left-hand pane where you can specify how many tunnels to bring up in the same fashion as the meshed community.

If you click the **Advanced Setting** in the left pane, and then select **VPN Routing**, you will be presented with a properties screen as shown in Figure 8.6.

Figure 8.6 VPN Routing Settings

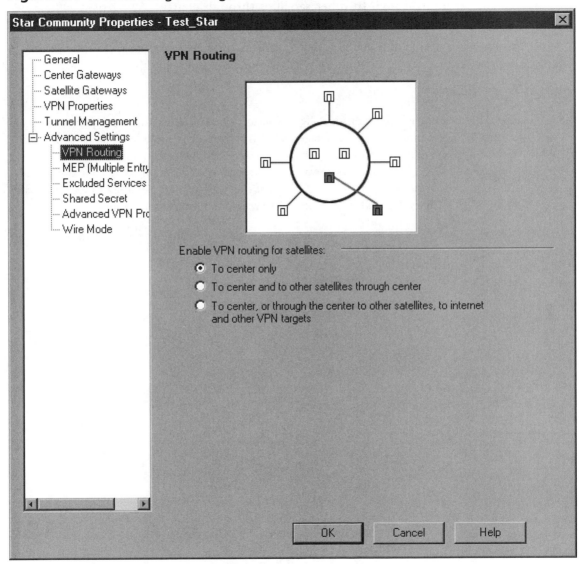

This is where the *VPN routing* aspect of a star VPN community comes into play. Although only three options are presented, they have a significant impact on how traffic is routed between the satellites and the hubs. The meaning of the options is summarized as follows:

- **To Center only** Strictly speaking, this option does not use any VPN Routing, since only encrypted traffic between the central hub and the satellites go through the VPN tunnel.

- **To Center and through to other satellites through center** All *encrypted* traffic passes through the hub(s), even traffic between satellites.

- To center, or through the center to other satellites, to Internet and other VPN targets *All traffic*, encrypted or unencrypted, must pass through the central hub(s).

Multiple Entry Point (MEP)

Multiple entry point (MEP) is a function that allows you to configure more than one gateway to act as the hub for a star VPN community. The advantage of this is that you can provide redundancy for your VPN termination from the satellite sites. In order to configure MEP, go into the properties for your star VPN community and click **Central Gateway** in the left pane. Add one or more central gateways that you wish to provide redundancy for each other. Then click **Advanced Settings** to expand it, and select **MEP (Multiple Entry Points)**. The MEP property screen is shown in Figure 8.7.

Figure 8.7 Configuring MEP

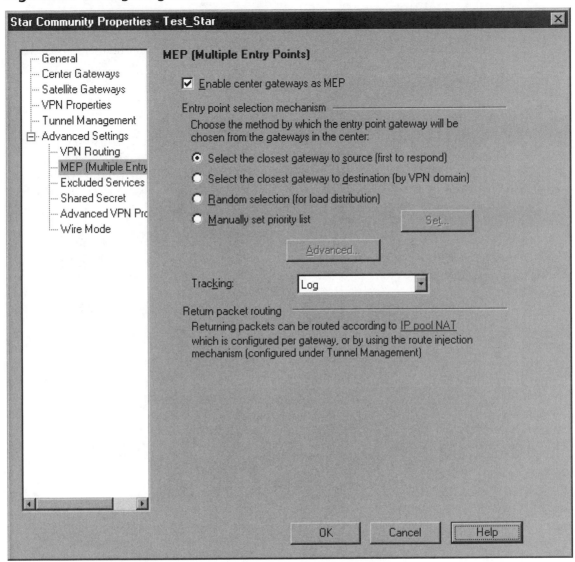

Once you have enabled MEP by checking the box **Enable center gateways as MEP**, you are given a few options as to how the entry point is chosen. The specifics on those options are as follows:

- **Select the closest gateway to source** With this option the first gateway to respond to a Check Point *proprietary* reliable data protocol (RDP) packet from the satellite in question becomes the gateway for that satellite.

- **Select the closest gateway to destination** With this option the gateway selected is the domain gateway whose IP belongs to the same VPN domain as the destination IP address for the VPN tunnel.

- **Random Selection** The terminating gateway will be chosen randomly. This serves to provide load balancing across the MEP group.

- **Manually set priority list** This option allows you to choose a first, second, and third priority gateway to be used and set any exceptions. This option might be useful if you had a high end firewall with another less robust machine acting as secondary, allowing you to configure the high end machine as the primary.

Installing the Policy

Once you have configured your policy in SmartDashboard you must install it. The first step is to verify the policy by clicking on **Policy | Verify**. You will be presented with a window allowing you to specify what elements you want to verify. The default will be for both **Security and Address Translation** and **QoS** to be checked. Unless you have a reason not to, it is recommended to leave both checked and click **OK**. The next window will list the results of the tests. Assuming the policy is verified successfully click **OK**.

Now click **Policy | Install**. You will be presented with a window that allows you to choose which devices to install the policy on, as shown in Figure 8.8. In this case you would select the hub gateway(s) and any satellite gateways and click **OK**.

Figure 8.8 Installing a Policy

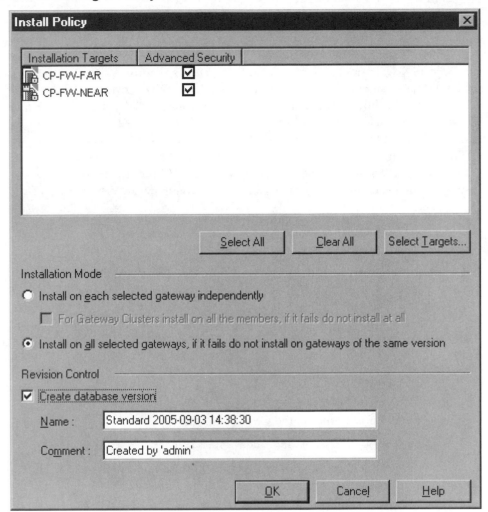

There are only a few options on this screen. One is the installation mode. Selecting **Install on all selected gateways, if it fails do not install on gateways of the same version** is recommended. This will ensure that if there is a problem, you don't end up with some gateways using a the new policy and others using the old policy, possibly resulting in an inoperable state. The revision control section also has an option to create a database version. Using this is recommended as well. This allows you to granularly track your policy changes and roll back easily if needed. After you click **OK** it will notify you that the database version was created successfully. It will also notify you if the policy name you are installing differs from the policy that is currently installed. When the install is completed you will see a window indicating that the install was successful. If there were any problems you will be able to view any errors or warnings associated with the installation process by clicking **Show Errors**.

Configuring a VPN with a Cisco PIX

At this point we have walked through configuring a simplified VPN with both a star and a mesh VPN community between two Check Point Enterprise/Pro NGX gateways. We will now show how to configure a mesh community with one endpoint of the VPN being a Cisco PIX 501 firewall. Even though the Cisco PIX will not be able to pull the VPN settings from the VPN Community, there could still be value in setting up the VPN with the simplified approach over the traditional approach. By using a community, additional Check Point gateways can still take advantage of the community settings, and the automatically generated rulebase will provide the needed connectivity to the PIX. You must still configure all the VPN settings on the PIX manually for the VPN tunnel to work.

The following example assumes you already have IP connectivity between the Cisco PIX firewall and the Check Point Enterprise/Pro NGX gateway. On the PIX enter the following commands while in privileged mode, followed by a carriage return, to configure the VPN tunnel.

```
configure terminal
access-list 101 permit ip 192.168.3.0 255.255.255.0 any
```

Access list 101 will be used to specify what traffic should be encrypted, in this case all traffic *from* 192.168.3.0.

```
access-list nonat permit ip 192.168.3.0 255.255.255.0 any
nat (inside) 0 access-list nonat
```

The named access list `nonat` is used to specify what traffic *not* to NAT, in this case any traffic from 192.168.3.0.

```
sysopt connection permit-ipsec
```

This tells the PIX to accept all IPSEC authenticated traffic. This setting is similar in function to the Accept all encrypted traffic setting on the Check Point device.

```
crypto ipsec transform-set rtptac esp-3des esp-md5-hmac
```

This configures the IPSEC encryption settings. The VPN community on the Check Point gateway will need to have identical settings for the VPN tunnel to work.

```
crypto map checkpointmap 10 ipsec-isakmp
crypto map checkpointmap 10 match address 101
crypto map checkpointmap 10 set peer 192.168.2.1
crypto map checkpointmap 10 set transform-set rtptac
```

This set of commands defines the cryptomap named `checkpointmap` to be used with peer 192.168.2.1.

```
crypto map checkpointmap interface outside
isakmp enable outside
```

These commands apply the cryptomap to the outside interface of the PIX.

```
isakmp key syngress address 192.168.2.1 netmask 255.255.255.255
```

This uses the shared secret key syngress for IKE authentication with peer 192.168.2.1.

```
isakmp policy 1 authentication pre-share
isakmp policy 1 encryption 3des
isakmp policy 1 hash md5
isakmp policy 1 group 2
isakmp policy 1 lifetime 86400
```

These settings define the ASAKMP policy for the PIX; again, these setting must match the VPN community settings. One this is done, you are ready to create the corresponding VPN community on the Check Point gateway. Right-click anywhere in the SmartMap area and select **New Network Object | Interoperable Devices**. On this screen, fill out a name, and the externally facing IP address. You will then need to click **Topology** on the left and manually enter the interface information for the PIX. Clicking **OK** at this point will save the interoperable device object and create a new *network* object to represent the private network behind the PIX.

You will need to create a VPN community as we did earlier, either a mesh or a star, with the appropriate encryption settings. While viewing the VPN community settings, click **Advanced Settings | Shared Secret** and click to enable **Use only shared secret for all external members**. Then, with the new PIX gateway, click **Edit** and enter the shared secret syngress and click **OK** twice to close the properties.

At this point encryption between the two gateways should be working. You will need to test by sending traffic to destinations behind the PIX gateway. If you try to generate test traffic with a destination IP of the PIX itself it might fail, while traffic destined to an IP behind the PIX is working properly.

You can access some PIX statistical information related to VPNs by using any of the following commands. The debug commands will show information on the console as the encryption process occurs. This allows you to see and troubleshoot the encryption process as it occurs. The **show** commands will display the current settings that are in working memory.

```
#debug crypto isakmp
#debug crypto ipsec
#show access-list
#show crypto ipsec security-association
#show crypto isakmp
```

Using the Traditional VPN Configuration Method

In some cases you might want more granularity over the encryption process. For example, to save on CPU cycles you might choose to encrypt only a particular traffic flow and leave the rest of the traffic unencrypted between locations. In this case, you can use the traditional method. Select the traditional method by going to **Policy | Global Properties | VPN**, as shown previously in Figure 8.1, and select **Traditional**. If you already have the policy defined as simplified, you must create a new policy (**File | New**) to use the traditional method. The basic steps of traditional VPN configuration are as follows:

1.   Enable the VPN product on the gateways.

2.   Configure the VPN Domain.

3. Configure the Traditional Mode Configuration properties on each gateway object.

4. Create the encrypt rule in the rulebase.

5. Install the policy.

The primary difference between the two approaches is that instead of the gateway deriving all of its encryption settings from the VPN community it belongs to, they are specified in the properties of each gateway object. View the gateway object's property pages as before, and ensure that **VPN** is an activated product. Now select **VPN** on the left pane, and click **Traditional Mode Configuration,** as shown in Figure 8.9.

Figure 8.9 Traditional Mode VPN Configuration

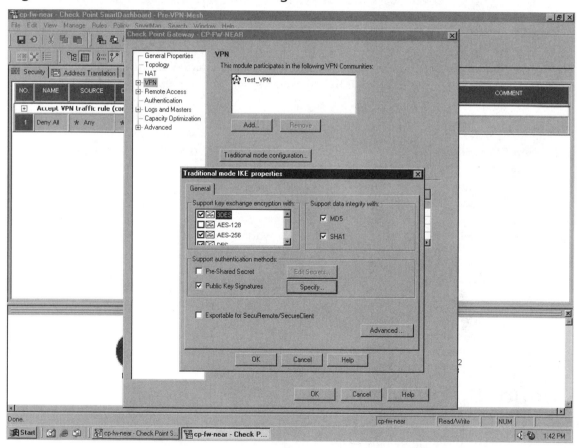

You must then manually configure the types of encryption to be used for key exchange and which hash algorithm to use for data integrity. You must also specify which authentication methods to use. Once this is completed, you must create a rule that specifies what traffic to encrypt. From within the **Security** tab, select **Add rule above current**. The rulebase gives you a high degree of control over what types of traffic you want to encrypt. If you want to encrypt all traffic between the two gateways, you create a group and add both gateway endpoints to the group. Once this is done modify the new rule and change both the source and destination to the new group you just created. Change the action to **encrypt**, and change the track to **Log**. Your rule should look like rule number 1 in Figure 8.10.

Figure 8.10 Traditional Mode Encrypt Rule

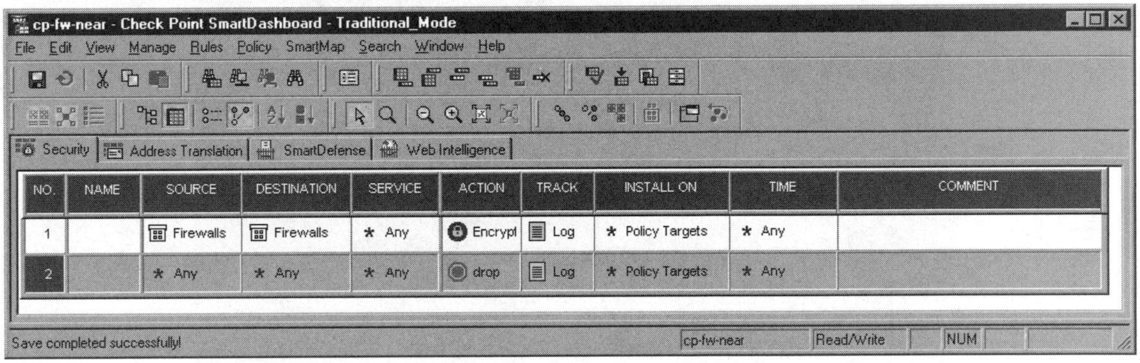

VPN Directional Matching

VPN Directional Match is an option you can enable that allows you to control when traffic should be encrypted, not only based on its source and destination within different VPN communities. This would allow you to specify that all traffic from a particular VPN community to any other community be encrypted, but traffic flowing from other communities into that community doesn't need to be. You can enable directional matching by going to **Policy | Global Properties | VPN | Advanced** and checking the box **Enable VPN directional match in VPN column**.

Once it is enabled, when you right-click on the VPN column and select Edit, you are provided a new window, with some additional options for encryption as seen in Figure 8.11. You can choose to encrypt traffic in both directions (the default behavior) or only in one direction. If you select **Match traffic in this direction only** and click **Add**, you are able to then select the source and destination community objects for the rule to match against.

Figure 8.11 VPN Directional Match

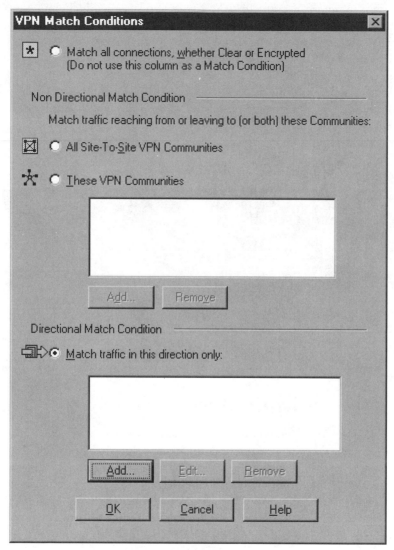

Route-Based VPN

Route-based VPNs are a mechanism whereby the VPN gateway can participate in and understand routing protocols and use that information to dynamically work around network failures. Before getting too deep into how this is done, it's worth discussing a little bit about what a *routing* protocol is.

Routing Protocols

When an IP packet is sent out across a network, routers have to make decisions about which interface to use to send the packet on its way. A router in this instance can be almost any network device, as long as it is connected to more than one network and it makes decisions as to which interface to send the traffic through. The router makes these decisions based on entries in a routing table. In a simple network this routing table is generally created by manually entering the routes or building automatically based on the network interface configuration. Once entered these manual routes don't change. If a link goes down, the router simply continues attempting to send the traffic out the interface indicated in its routing table. This means until the problem is fixed, traffic won't be able to reach its intended destination.

With a dynamic routing protocol, a router can learn about links to different networks and share that information with other routers. The learning process can be from a manually entered route, or because it heard about it from another router. In this way, if a link goes down, the router closest to the fault can inform the other routers and if there is an alternate path, they can adapt and route traffic through the alternate path so that it reaches its destination. Of course this is somewhat of a simplification as routing protocols can be very complex, with entire books dedicated to a single routing protocol and its use.

Routing protocols are not to be confused with *routable* protocols. A routing protocol is the specific protocol used by a router to learn and share information about routes. A routable protocol is a protocol that can be redirected based on the router's information. IP for example is a routable protocol, whereas BGP or OSPF are routing protocols.

Configuring VTIs

When using route-based VPNs you must configure a VPN tunnel interface (VTI) on the gateway. This *virtual* interface is configured and managed at the OS level. The decision to encrypt traffic is then made by the OS based on which interface the traffic is routed through, instead of being made based on parameters set within some other software running on the machine in question. For this to function, the gateway itself needs to participate in and understand a dynamic routing protocol. Thus, route-based VPNs allow the gateways to dynamically reroute the VPN traffic based on topology changes, much like a router would reroute IP traffic based on topology changes.

Both SecurePlatform and Nokia IPSO support route-based VPNs using open shortest path first (OSPF), but only SecurePlatform supports route-based VPNs using border gateway protocol (BGP4). The dynamic routing protocol is implemented via the GateD software. Also, when configuring the VTI, it can be configured as an unnumbered interface (Nokia IPSO 3.9 only) or a numbered interface. If the VTI is configured as an unnumbered interface, the source IP address of the encrypted traffic will be that of the physical interface.

Configuring VTI Example

We will now walk through an example where we configure VTI on a SecurePlatform Pro NGX machine. For the example, our two gateways can see each other and communicate, and SIC is working properly. We have already set up a meshed VPN community and encryption is working properly between the two gateways.

Start by configuring the virtual interface. You can access the commands to configure a virtual interface by going into the VPN shell by typing the following followed by a carriage return or pressing Enter:

```
vpn shell
```

The vpn shell is used to configure various setting related to VPNs. Once in the shell you can add a *numbered* VTI by entering the following command, filling in the appropriate IP addresses for your environment:

```
>/interface/add/numbered <local IP> <peer IP> <peer name> <interface name>
```

Specifying an interface name is optional; in my example I entered the following:

```
>/interface/add/numbered 192.168.2.90 192.168.2.1 CP-FW-NEAR
Interface 'vt-CP-FW-NEAR' was added successfully to the system
```

You can then use the ifconfig command to verify the interface configuration. The output should show the newly added interface in the list of interfaces. The next step is to enable the routing protocol. You enable a routing protocol, in this case OSPF by entering the following commands:

```
>router
>enable
#configure terminal
(config)#router ospf 1
(config-router-ospf)#router-id 192.168.2.90
(config-router-ospf)#redistribute kernal
(config-router-ospf)#network 192.168.2.1 0.0.0.0 area 0.0.0.0
(config-router-ospf)# network 192.168.2.90 0.0.0.0 area 0.0.0.0
(config-router-ospf)#exit
(config)#exit
#write memory
```

Then enter the following command to verify that the changes were saved and applied sucessfully.

```
#show ip ospf interface
```

You will then need to complete the configuration by enabling OSPF on all SecurePlatform or Nokia ISPO gateways in this VPN domain.

Tunnel Management and Debugging

Although Check Point makes setting up VPN tunnels relatively simple, there will be times when you need to troubleshoot a VPN tunnel that isn't working properly. In these cases you will need to use your understanding of the encryption process, and the tools available to you, to make some informed decisions about what the problem is. In the next section, we will discuss some of the most useful troubleshooting tools that are provided.

Using SmartView Tracker

The built in logging facility, SmartView Tracker, will be your primary source of information concerning the health and status of your gateways and VPNs. The SmartView Tracker comes with some preconfigured log queries. If you are consolidating and viewing a lot of logs from several different devices the logs can be a little overwhelming to sort through. The left-hand pane is where you can select some predefined queries. By going to **Log Queries | Predefined | VPN** you can restrict the view to only those entries related to tunnel creation and maintenance.

If you find you still have too many VPN entries to sort through effectively, you can filter the display even further. Do this by clicking a column at the top. For example if we wanted to see only VPN logs between two particular gateways, we would right-click the top of the **Origin** column and select **Edit Filter**. We are then presented with a list of objects in the left-hand pane of the window. Select the two you would like to view and click **Add**. This moves them to the right-hand pane as seen in Figure 8.12. When you are done click **OK**. The SmartView Tracker VPN query will now show only the VPN logs between the two devices you selected.

Figure 8.12 Filtering Logs in SmartView Tracker

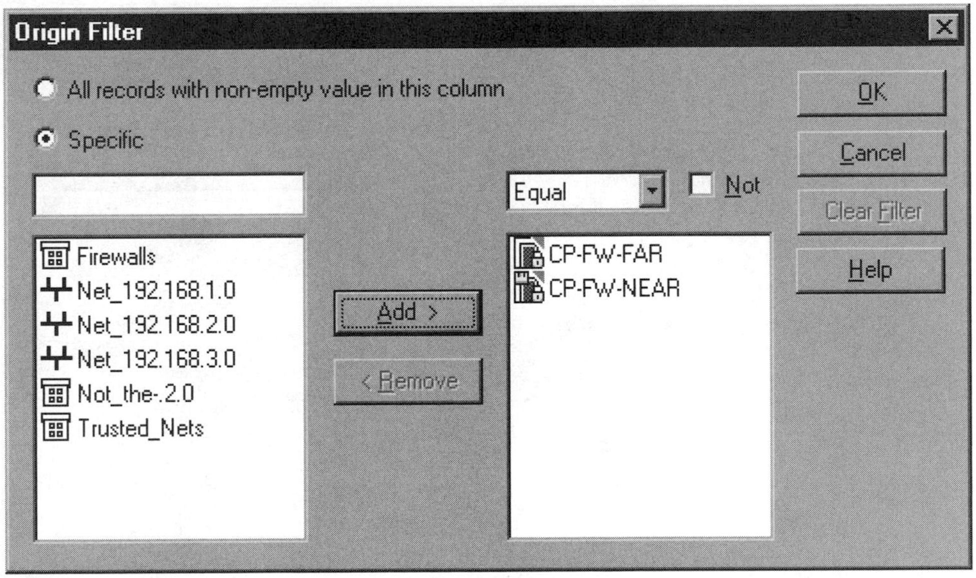

Check Point makes administration of the firewalls and VPNs easier by including some automatically generated rules in the security rulebase. If you go to **View | Implied Rules** you can see the rules that Check Point has created automatically. If you are using the simplified VPN configuration method, you can also enable the display of the automatically created VPN rules on the same menu. You'll notice all these automatic rules are set not to generate log entries. You cannot click on the **Track** column and edit these rules directly; instead, if you want to see log entries for the implied rules go to **Policy | Global Properties** and check the box at the bottom, **Log Implied Rules**. Depending on your configuration this may generate a lot of log entries so it is recommended to use this only if you are troubleshooting an issue or if the load on the gateways is minimal.

The Global Properties also has some additional settings you can enable by clicking **Log and Alert** in the left pane. This will display the screen shown in Figure 8.13. The first three settings relate specifically to VPN logging. They should be set to **Log** by default; however, you may want to make certain they are checked if you are not seeing all the log entries you should be.

Figure 8.13 Log and Alert Options in Global Properties

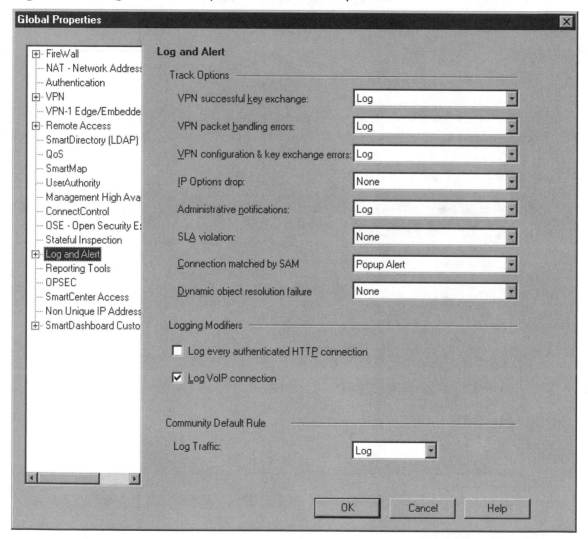

Using cpstat

Cpstat is another tool you can use to see the current status of the gateways. Cpstat is a command line tool without a GUI interface. To run it you can simply go to a command prompt and type **cpstat**. If you type it with no other parameters, you get the following help screen as output.

```
C:\WINNT>cpstat

Usage: cpstat [-p port][-f flavour][-o polling [-c count] [-e period]] [-d]
application_flag

-p Port number of the AMON server.
   Default is the standard AMON port (18192).

-f The flavour of the output (as appears in the configuration file).
   Default is to use the first flavour found in the configuration file.

-o Polling interval (seconds) specifies the pace of the results.
   Default is 0, meaning the results are shown only once.

-c Specifying how many times the results are shown.
   Default is 0, meaning the results are repeatedly shown.

-e Period interval (seconds) specifies the interval over which
   "statistical" oids are computed. Ignored for regular oids.

-d Debug mode
Available application_flags:
---------------------------------------------------------------
|Flag             |Flavours                                   |
---------------------------------------------------------------
|asm              |default, WS                                |
---------------------------------------------------------------
|fw               |default, interfaces, policy, perf, hmem, kmem, |
|                 |inspect, cookies, chains, fragments, totals,   |
|                 |ufp, http, ftp, telnet, rlogin, smtp, sync, all|
---------------------------------------------------------------
|fg               |all                                        |
---------------------------------------------------------------
|os               |default, ifconfig, routing, memory,        |
|                 |old_memory, cpu, disk, perf, multi_cpu,    |
|                 |multi_disk, all, average_cpu, average_memory, |
|                 |statistics                                 |
---------------------------------------------------------------
|persistency      |product, TableConfig, SourceConfig         |
---------------------------------------------------------------
|polsrv           |default, all                               |
---------------------------------------------------------------
|vpn              |default, product, IKE, ipsec, traffic,     |
|                 |compression, accelerator, nic, statistics, |
|                 |watermarks, all                            |
---------------------------------------------------------------
```

Although the cpstat can provide a wealth of information, for purposes of troubleshooting VPNs we are most concerned with the VPN application flag. By specifying the VPN application flag, you are telling cpstat that you want to see only VPN-related information. If you don't specify a "flavor" the default will be to output all the VPN-related information. The Flavor flag allows you to further specify what subset of information you want to see. The following example shows some of the output related to IKE negotiation:

```
cpstat -d vpn -f IKE <ENTER>
<content ommitted>
IKE current SAs:                                 1
IKE current SAs initiated by me:                 0
IKE current SAs initiated by peer:               1
IKE max concurrent SAs:                          2
IKE max concurrent SAs initiated by me:          1
IKE max concurrent SAs initiated by peer:        1
IKE total SAs:                                   4
IKE total SAs initiated by me:                   2
IKE total SAs initiated by peer:                 2
IKE total SA attempts:                           1
IKE total SA attempts initiated by me:           0
IKE total SA attempts initiated by peer:         1
IKE current ongoing SA negotiations:             0
IKE max concurrent SA negotiations:              1
IKE no response from peer (initiator errors):    0
IKE total failures (initiator errors):           0
IKE total failures (responder errors):           0
IKE total failures (initiator + responder):      0
<content ommitted>
```

Summary

At this point you should have a basic understanding of encryption principles and their application. Confidentiality of data is ensured through encryption, and the security of that encryption is dependent on the quality of the encryption algorithm used. Certificates issued by a trusted third-party certificate authority are attached to public encryption keys to validate who the owner of a given public key is. Message integrity and authentication are ensured through the use of digital signatures and certificate authorities. And the entire process of distributing keys securely is handled by key exchange protocols such as IKE.

All these things together are used to make secure communication across insecure media possible. If any one component is implemented improperly the entire process becomes vulnerable to compromise. The largest symmetric key won't be of any value if it's easily obtainable by unauthorized parties. The best encryption algorithm does no good if you can't validate to whom you are speaking. In short, the entire infrastructure and every component must be implemented with care and planning for it to provide the security that was intended.

Chapter 9

SecuRemote, SecureClient, and Integrity

Solutions in this chapter:

- **SecuRemote**
- **SecureClient**
- **Office Mode**
- **Secure Configuration Verification (SSV)**
- **Integrity**

☑ **Summary**

Introduction

The two most common cries of corporate management through the late 1990s and early 2000s were, "We must be secure" and "We must be flexible." In order to be flexible, a workforce must be mobile and adaptive to change. In essence, the workforce has to be fluid. The nature of security inherently places restrictions on the workforce. Either they can no longer access every file on a given share drive, or need to call a help desk because they can't remember the password for a particular server. Every one of these incidents creates a lag in time, where productivity seems to slow down or stop. Fluidity changes to solidity, and it's the fault of security… or at least that's how it's perceived.

This chapter is dedicated to the increasing number of employees that are either working comfortably at home or just simply away from the office, who need corporate access as if working locally. Since 1996, SecuRemote has been the primary VPN client from Check Point, made freely available, providing your firewall has proper VPN licensing. In 2001, Check Point released SecureClient, which provides additional and increased security over its little brother. SecureClient has the ability to receive a desktop policy from a VPN-1/Firewall-1 Policy Server. This increased security requires a SecureClient license, which is licensed by the number of users that can download a policy from your gateway.

In late 2003, Check Point focused the direction of their corporate strategy, increasing development on internal and web security. The new strategy boldly reflects their new approach to security: perimeter, internal and Web security. In early 2004, Check Point purchased Zone Labs, makers of the popular freeware desktop firewall ZoneAlarm, and brilliantly incorporated the enterprise version of ZoneAlarm, Integrity, with SecureClient to create Integrity SecureClient. Integrity is a desktop firewall that incorporates real-time protection against malicious code and is centrally manageable. In this chapter, we will discuss setup and configuration of these products to gain the highest level of client protection that Check Point offers its customers.

SecuRemote

SecuRemote is Check Point's VPN-1 Client product. It is an agent that sits on the client machine, providing encrypted secure access to a company's private network. It has been a mainstay of the security industry, as Check Point was one of the first companies to market an easy-to-use graphical user interface (GUI) VPN client. SecuRemote utilizes the IKE (ISAKMP) key exchange protocol to establish an encrypted tunnel between the desktop machine and the VPN-1 Firewall gateway. This allows the desktop to be connected to any Internet connection, and still allow the user to securely access a company's internal network resources, such as e-mail or internal web applications.

What's New with SecuRemote in NGX?

Some of the more interesting additions to SecuRemote in NGX are:

- **NAT-T Support.**   SecuRemote now supports the industry-standard Network Address Translation (NAT) Traversal. This is an improved way to handle NAT on VPN gateways.

- **Office Mode.**   The address assigned by office mode can now be utilized to access other gateways within the private network.

- **Multiple Entry Point (MEP)**.   With MEP configured, SecuRemote can now take advantage of a centrally managed connection profile providing a backup gateway, without needing to make a MEP decision.

- **General Connectivity**.   The encryption domain of the gateway can now be defined differently for site-to-site VPN, and for remote access VPN.

Standard Client

The standard SecuRemote client provides a GUI interface, allowing users to easily set up VPN connectivity to multiple sites residing in different encryption domains. An encryption domain is determined by the IP address of the destination you are attempting to access. For instance, if you are currently located at 10.10.10.10, and the resources you are attempting to reach are located at your company's private network, with an IP address of 192.168.100.120, the encryption domain for your company's private network might be 192.168.100.0/24 (given your company uses the entire subnet). This means any traffic destined for an IP address between 192.168.100.1 and 192.168.100.254 would be routed through your encrypted VPN tunnel to your company's private network. If you then added an additional site, giving it an encryption domain of 192.168.168.0/24, any resource you attempted to reach with an IP Address within the 192.168.168.0 subnet would be routed through a different encryption tunnel to reach that resource.

This flexibility allows users to connect to different locations to gain the specific access they require without having multiple remote access clients installed. Users should begin by installing the SecuRemote client after downloading it from Check Point's Web site, www.checkpoint.com, or obtaining a prepackaged version of the software that has already been configured using the SecureClient Packaging Tool, available with the Smart Center Management Suite.

Basic Remote Access

There are two main steps in setting up secure VPN connections to your private network. First, the Check Point VPN-1/Firewall-1 gateway must be configured to accept the incoming connection. The encryption domain must be defined, users must be created, and a Security Policy must be written to allow user connectivity to the gateway in order to access the private network. Depending on the size of your network, and the resources available to you, it may be a smart move to utilize an authentication mechanism such as RADIUS to authenticate your user community. Check Point supports multiple authentication methodologies, such as RADIUS, SecureID, TACACS, LDAP, Check Point Password, and Certificate Based Authentication via the internal Check Point CA, or a Check Point OPSEC partner CA product. This will save time defining hundreds or thousands of users in Check Point's Smart Console, and it is likely that even small to medium companies will have some type of user database available for authentication purposes. In large scale environments, it is necessary to explore user management and authentication outside of the Check Point Management Console. Check Point supports multiple authentication methodologies, such as RADIUS, SecureID, TACACS, LDAP, Check Point Password, and Certificate Based Authentication. Certificate Based Authentication is supported via the internal Check Point Certificate Authority (CA), or through a Check Point OPSEC Partner's CA product (such as Entrust). In this chapter, we will describe setting up authentication based on Check Point username and password authentication.

Next, the SecuRemote client must be installed and configured on the end user's machine with the correct site information for the VPN-1 gateway. The user then enters his or her credentials (username and password) and connects to the VPN-1 gateway. SecuRemote downloads the necessary information to build an encrypted tunnel to the VPN-1 gateway and the user can then access resources located within the company's private network.

Defining the Connection Policy

In this section, we will explain rule generation and policy definition of setting up SecuRemote/SecureClient Remote access. We will set up a simple policy that allows a predefined group of SecuRemote users access to the private corporate network. If you are not familiar with SmartDashboard, and how to create objects and users, refer to Chapter 2.

First, log in to SmartDashboard (see Figure 9.1).

Figure 9.1 Logging in to SmartDashboard

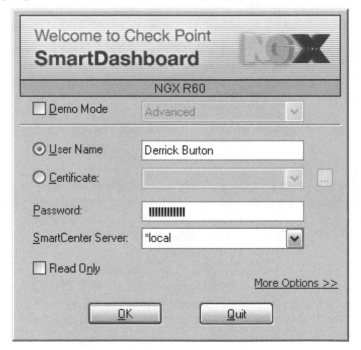

Identify where the new rule should belong in the security rule set and then right-click on the rule below where you want your new Remote access Rule. Select **Add Rule Above** (see Figure 9.2).

Figure 9.2 The Security Rule Set

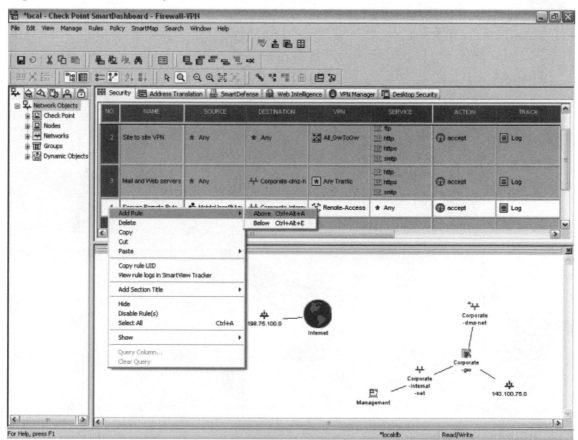

Double-click on the name field of the rule you just created, and type a brief descriptive name for this rule. For this example, the rule will be called new SecuRemote rule (see Figure 9.3).

Figure 9.3 Selecting the New SecuRemote Rule

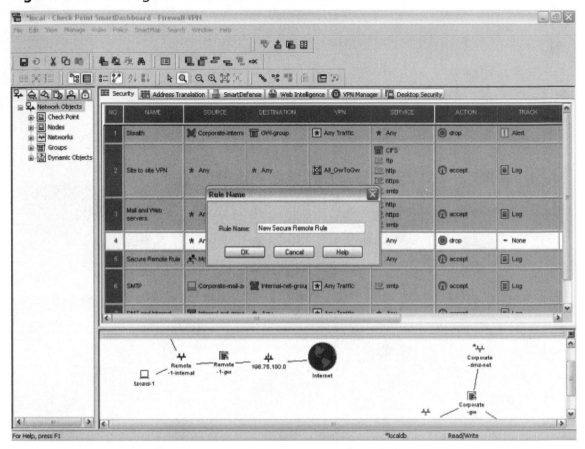

Next, right-click on the Source field of your "New SecuRemote Rule" and select **Add User Access...**.

This will bring up a new window that allows you to choose which groups can use this rule to connect to the VPN gateway. Select the MobileUser group and click **Edit** (see Figure 9.4).

Figure 9.4 Assigning User Access to the VPN Gateway

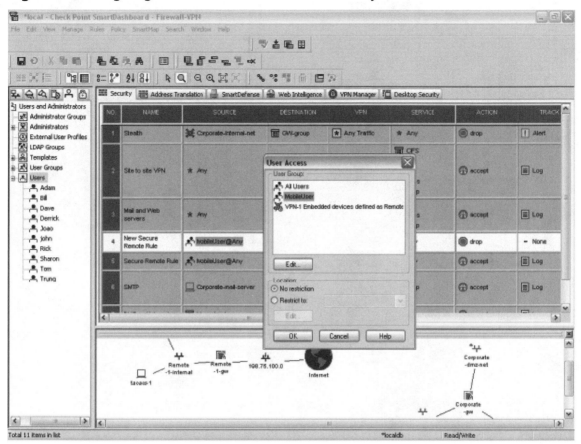

Another new window will open, giving you the ability to chose which users should be in the group MobileUser. Select the appropriate users and click **OK** (see Figure 9.5). At this point you can also define restrictions on from where this user group can access this rule. For example, this rule may be for internal users to access a protected network. You wouldn't want them to be able to access this network from anywhere, so you can restrict access based on the location from where they are attempting to connect. For the purpose of this example, we will allow this group of users to access the corporate network from any location. Leave the No restriction radio button selected, and click **OK**.

Figure 9.5 Choosing Users for the MobileUser Group

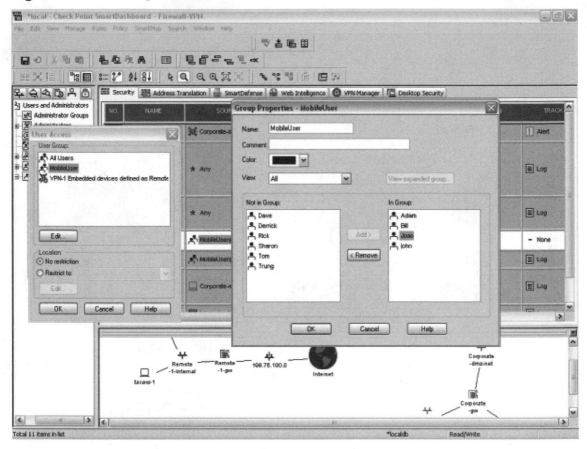

Next, right-click on the destination segment of your rule and select **Add....**(see Figure 9.6).

Figure 9.6 Selecting Add from the Destination Segment of a Rule

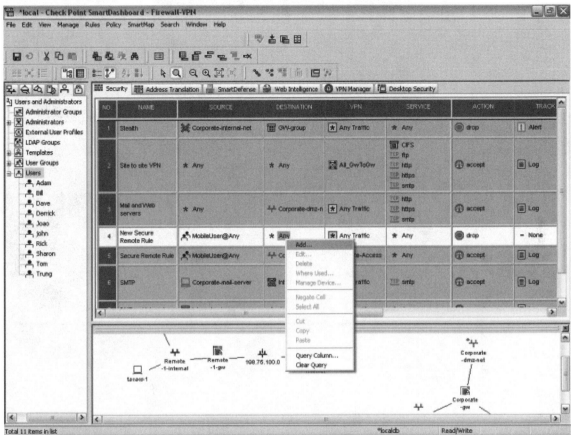

A new window will open and give you the ability to select the destination to which you want the user group to be allowed access. You can create a new network object, or select a previously created network object. Select the Corporate-internal-net and click **OK**. The point of this exercise is to allow a group of users to access the corporate private network from anywhere in the world (see Figure 9.7).

Figure 9.7 Selecting Destinations for MobileUser Group Users

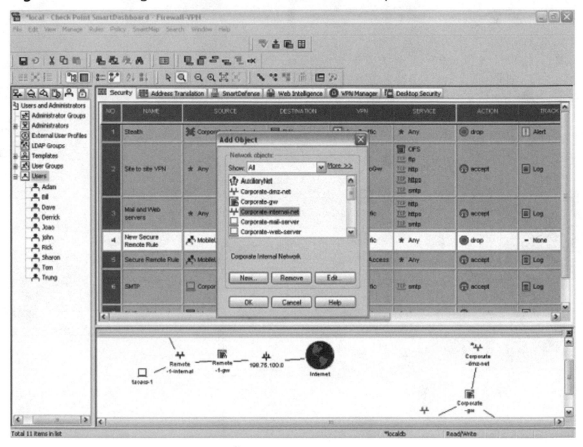

Next, select the VPN field in your current rule and right-click **Any Traffic** (see Figure 9.8). We are going to stipulate that this rule is a Remote Access VPN Rule.

Figure 9.8 Selecting the VPN Field

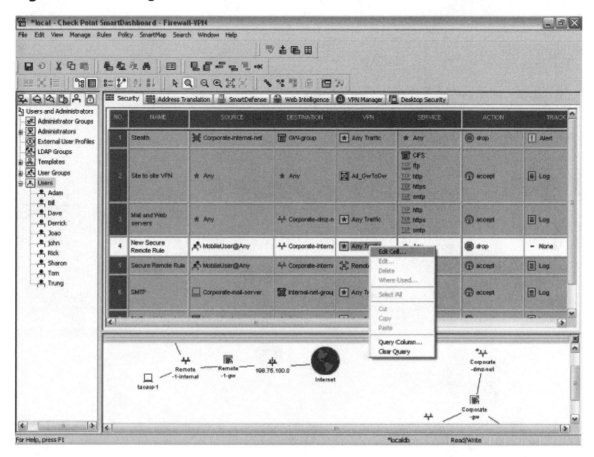

Once the new window opens, select the third option down, Only accept connections encrypted in specific VPN Communities (see Figure 9.9). This selection provides for connections from one of two options, either Site-to-Site connections between hosts in the VPN domain of Site-to-Site communities, or connections in specific VPN communities selected, in this case the Remote Access VPN community.

Figure 9.9 Selecting Connectivity Options

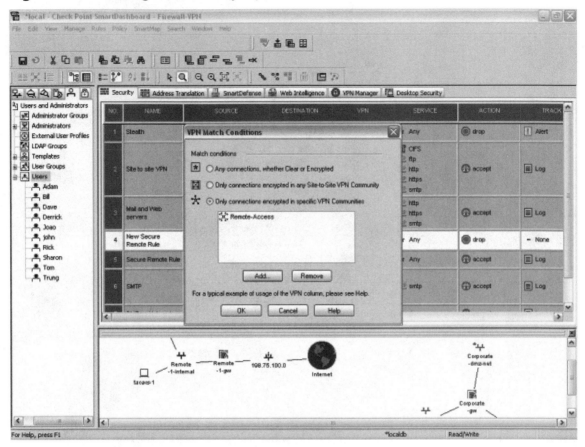

Click **Add** to add the VPN community to the rule, and select the Remote Access community. Click **OK** (see Figure 9.10).

Figure 9.10 Adding the VPN Community to a Rule

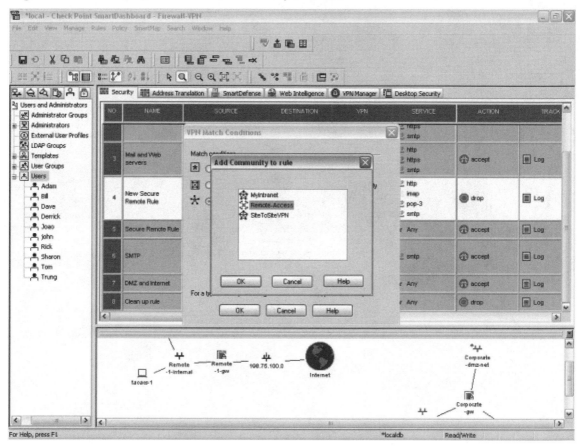

Now, click the VPN field, selecting the new Remote Access icon, and click **Edit** (see Figure 9.11).

Figure 9.11 Selecting Remote Access

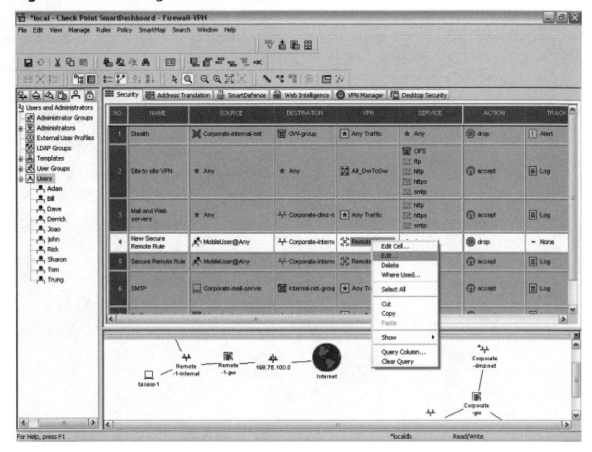

Now, select the second option down on the left, Participating Gateways(see Figure 9.12).

Figure 9.12 Selecting the Participating Gateways Option

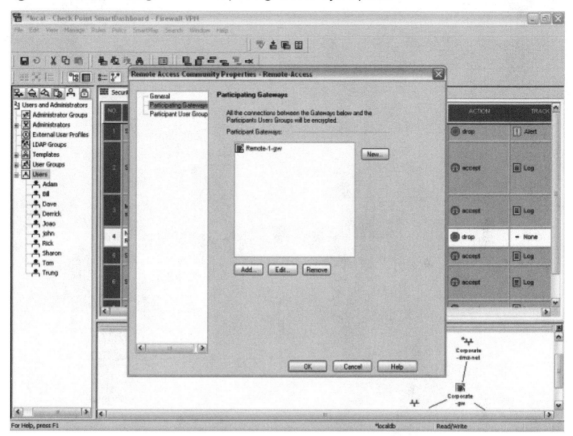

It may already have your VPN gateway listed, but if it doesn't, click **Add** and select the VPN gateway you want your users to connect to for access to the corporate network (see Figure 9.13). Click **OK** to select the participating gateway, and click **OK** again to close the edit community window.

Figure 9.13 Selecting the VPN Gateway

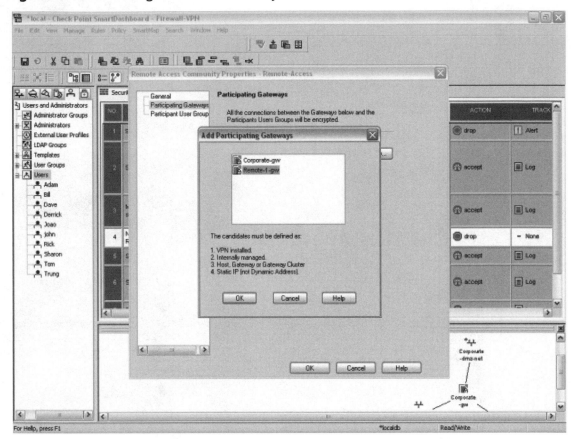

Next, right-click the **Any** icon under the services field of your rule and select **Add**. Here, you can select the services you want to allow your remote users the ability to use while connected to the corporate network via Remote Access (see Figure 9.14). For this example, we will use HTTP, SMTP, POP3, and IMAP4. This will allow users to browse Web pages on the internal network, as well as send and receive e-mail. Note: You can select as many services as you would like to let your Mobile

User group use when connected to the VPN gateway. You can also select multiple services at one time using the CTRL key.

Figure 9.14 Selecting Services for MobileUser Group Users

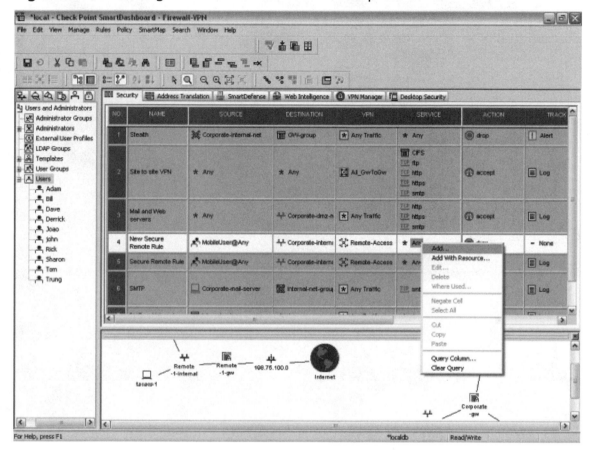

Once the Add Object window has popped up, select the HTTP, SMTP, POP3, and IMAP services, and click **OK** (see Figure 9.15).

Figure 9.15 Selecting Services

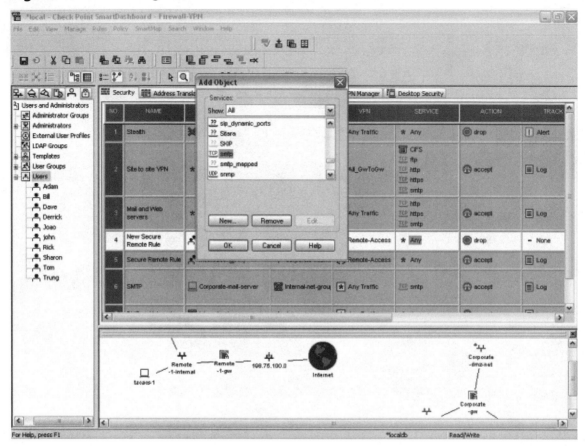

Now, we must provide an action when this rule is matched for access to the network. Right-click on the action field in the rule, and select Accept to allow SecuRemote Access (see Figure 9.16).

Figure 9.16 Allowing SecuRemote Access

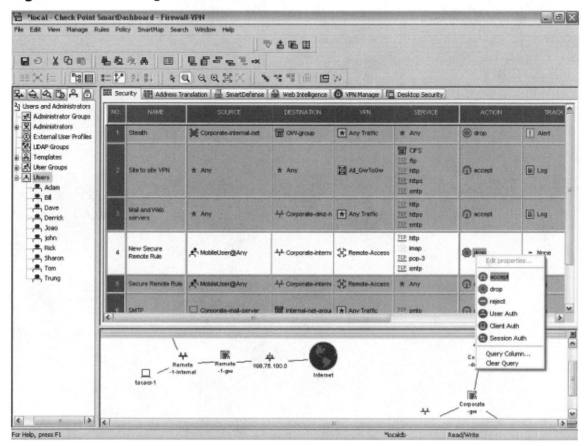

Another important field in each rule is the Track field (see Figure 9.17). The Track field provides a mechanism for maintaining information about the rule when it is matched. When a packet arrives that matches the rule we have created for Remote Access, the VPN gateway can alert, log, or begin another action defined by the VPN gateway administrator. Tracking provides the VPN gateway Administrators with the ability to troubleshoot connectivity issues, as well as obtain immediate notification information to be alerted when certain rules are matched, such as malicious traffic. In this example, we will log this rule, in order to be able to troubleshoot connectivity issues should they arise.

Figure 9.17 The Track Field

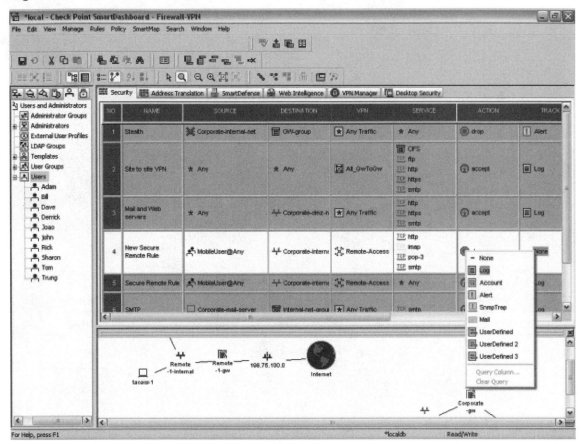

After selecting the appropriate tracking options, you must select the location to install this policy (see Figure 9.18). For this VPN example, the rule should be installed on the VPN gateways. Right-click on the **Install** field of your rule, select **Add**, and then select **Gateways**. In addition, you can also create a time object that can stipulate between what times your users can connect to your corporate network. We will be allowing our users access at all times, so you can leave this field unchanged.

Figure 9.18 Selecting the Location for Tracking Options

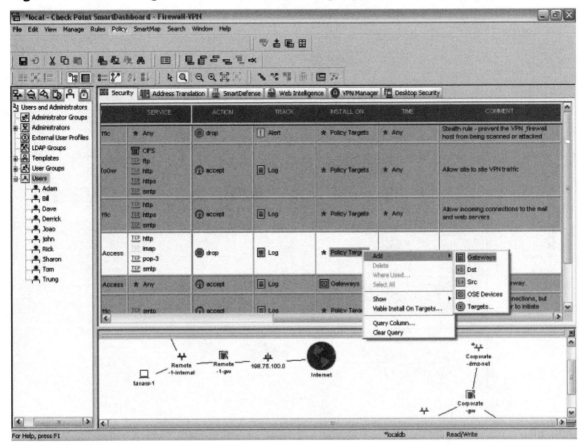

Finally, you can add a more descriptive comment to your rule, so you can quickly know exactly what it is doing (see Figure 9.19). This is especially valuable for other administrators, as it is easy to track who made what changes to the VPN gateway policy, if they are keeping good comments.

Figure 9.19 Adding Comments to a Rule

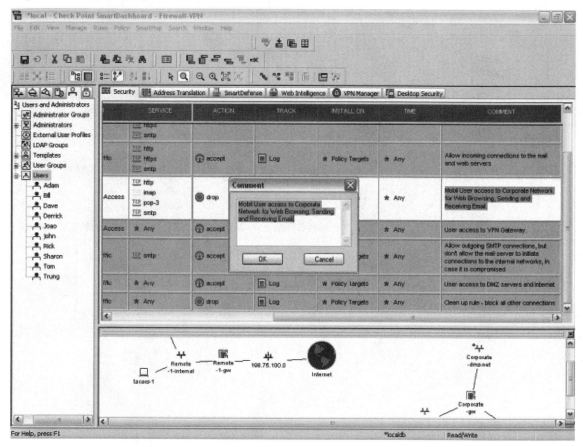

Once the final step has been completed, your rule is ready to be installed on the VPN gateway. Go to Policy | Install…. This will push your new policy out to the gateway, and the gateway should then be able to accept incoming SecuRemote connections from the users listed in the Mobile User group.

SecuRemote Installation and Configuration on Microsoft Windows

To begin the SecuRemote Installation, download the SecuRemote executable from www.checkpoint. com, or obtain a preconfigured package of the SecuRemote client from your Security Administrator. The advantage of the preconfigured version is exactly what it sounds like. Normally, the preconfigured version is already configured with the corporate site information and specific options direct from your security administrator. The standard SecuRemote client needs a small amount of manual configuration to connect to the VPN gateway. For the purpose of this chapter, we will assume a preconfigured SecuRemote package is not available, and we will walk through a manual installation of SecuRemote. From http://www.checkpoint.com/techsupport/eula_sr.html, you can download a configurable installation package (which you have to unzip), or an executable .exe or .msi file. You can also download files for Mac OS X, Red Hat Linux, or Pocket PC. After downloading, run the setup file to begin installation. You will be greeted with the SecuRemote installation welcome screen.

After the installation welcome screen, you will have to agree to Check Point's End User License Agreement (EULA). Click **Yes** to accept Check Point's EULA and proceed with the installation (see Figure 9.20).

Figure 9.20 Check Point's EULA

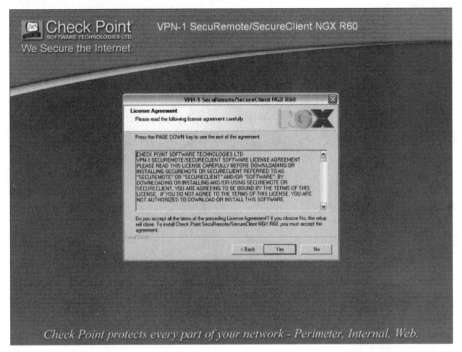

The SecuRemote/SecureClient installation wizard will prompt you for an installation location (see Figure 9.21). It is advisable to keep the default installation path, as it will decrease the time spent searching for configuration and log files during troubleshooting.

Figure 9.21 Choosing a Destination Location

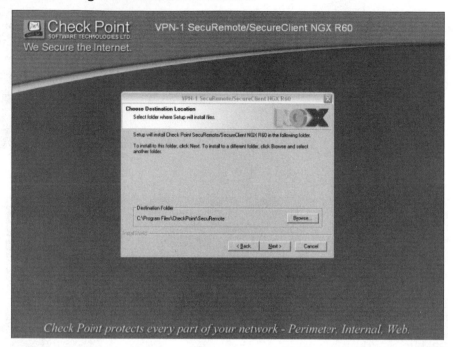

SecuRemote will then display an installation progress bar (see Figure 9.22). Once the progress bar reaches 100%, the installer will prompt you to install SecuRemote or SecureClient. Select **SecuRemote** and Click **Next** to continue the installation.

Figure 9.22 The Installation Progress Bar

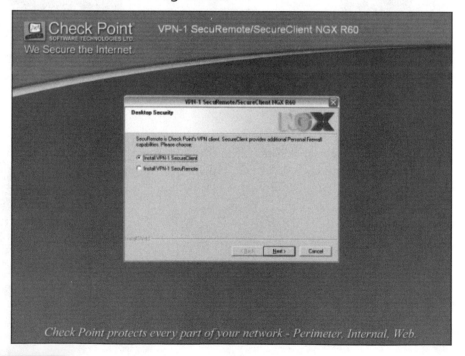

The SecuRemeote/SecureClient installer will then make some changes to the Windows Registry, and install the SecuRemote/SecureClient kernel (see Figure 9.23).

Figure 9.23 Installing the SecuRemote/SecureClient Kernel

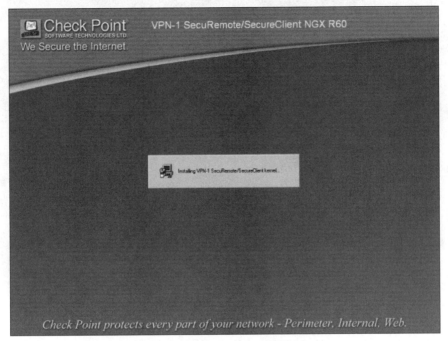

You will be prompted to reboot the machine when the install is completed. Select **Finish**, and the installer will reboot your machine for you (see Figure 9.24).

Figure 9.24 Rebooting the Machine

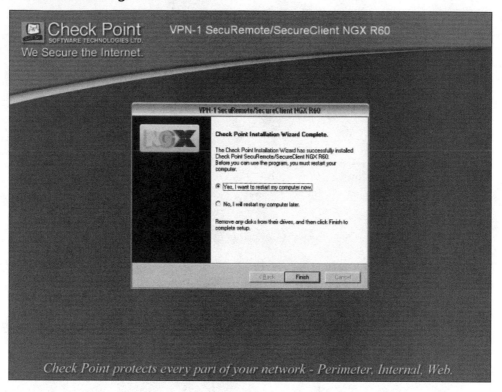

After the machine is rebooted, a new icon will be visible in the machine's system tray. The SecuRemote icon looks like a golden key with a red letter X above it (see Figure 9.25). In order to connect to the VPN gateway and build the encrypted tunnel necessary to access resources on the private corporate network, you need to first create a new site and configure it using the IP Address of the VPN gateway.

Figure 9.25 The SecuRemote Icon

Right-click on the SecuRemote icon to display the SecuRemote menu (see Figure 9.26). Click the **Settings** menu item.

Figure 9.26 Displaying the SecuRemote Menu

This opens the Settings dialog box. Click the button on the right labeled **New**. This will bring up the Site Wizard (see Figure 9.27).

Figure 9.27 The SecuRemote Settings Dialog Box

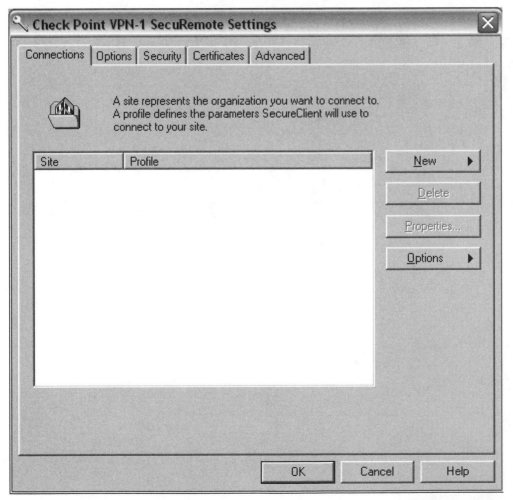

Type the IP Address/DNS name and a Display name of the VPN gateway you are trying to establish a VPN tunnel with and click **Next** (see Figure 9.28).

Figure 9.28 The Site Wizard

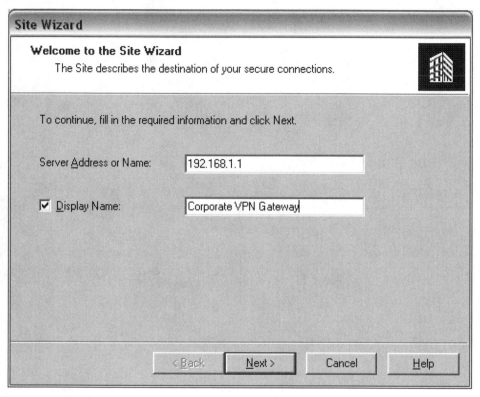

Select the Authentication method (see Figure 9.29). This must be configured correctly according to the settings on the VPN gateway. For this example, select **Username** and **Password** and click **Next**.

Figure 9.29 Selecting the Authentication Method

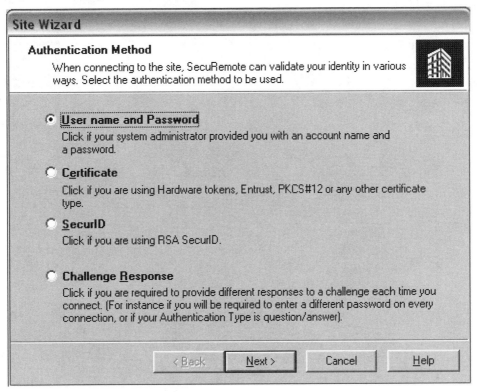

Type the username and password that was provided by your security administrator and click **Next** (see Figure 9.30).

Figure 9.30 Adding User Details to the Site Wizard

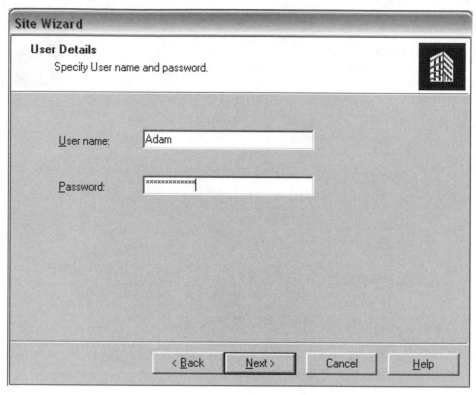

SecuRemote will then attempt to connect to the VPN gateway (see Figure 9.31). It will first check if you want to attempt a Standard or Advanced connection. Standard utilizes the normal method of IKE negotiation. If you experience issues when attempting a Standard connection with your VPN gateway, clicking **Advanced** will perform IKE over TCP. This solves most connectivity problems due to ISPs and other network administrators blocking the protocols and ports necessary for standard IKE.

Figure 9.31 Downloading Topology and Site Data from the VPN Gateway

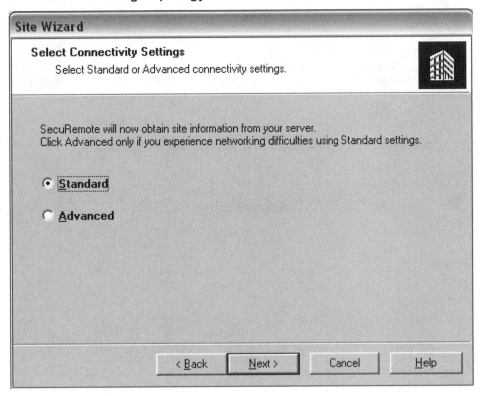

SecuRemote will attempt to validate the VPN gateway (see Figure 9.32). In some secure environments, the security administrator will provide the VPN gateway's internal Certificate Authority's certificate fingerprint. SecuRemote will present the certificate that it obtained from the VPN gateway and ask you to validate it against the information provided by your security administrator. Verify that the Common Name (CN) and Organization (O) are correct, and click **Next**.

Figure 9.32 Validating the VPN Gateway

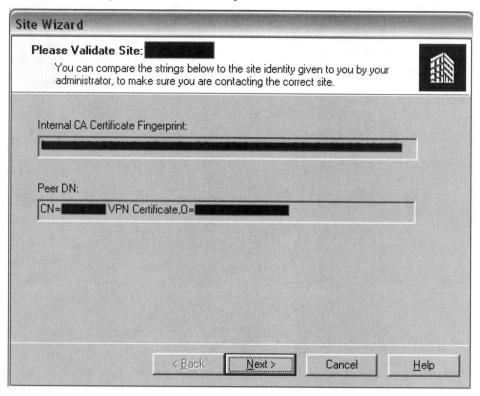

After clicking **Next**, SecuRemote will connect to the VPN gateway, download the necessary information to form encrypted connections, and display a Site Created Successfully dialog box (see Figure 9.33). Congratulations, your site has been created and you can now form a secure encrypted connection to your corporate VPN gateway.

Figure 9.33 Successful Creation of a Site

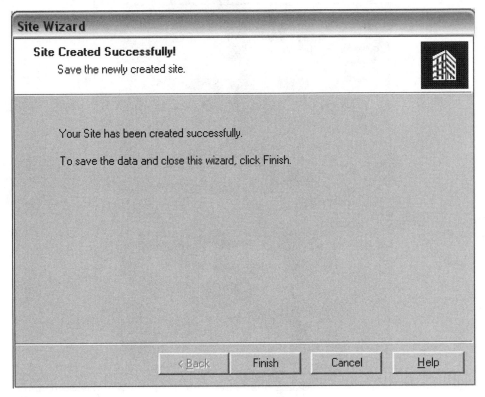

Connecting to the VPN-1 Gateway

To connect to the gateway, double-click the SecuRemote icon located on the task bar (see Figure 9.34).

Figure 9.34 Connecting to the Gateway

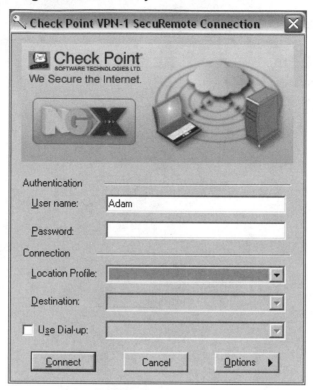

This will bring up the connection dialog box. Enter your username and password, and click **Connect** (see Figure 9.35).

Figure 9.35 The Connection Dialog Box

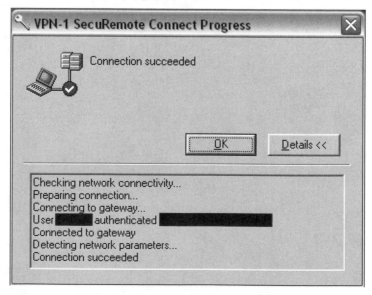

SecuRemote will open a new dialog box, and if you click the Details button, it will display the details of the connection that is being attempted. After the encrypted tunnel is built, SecuRemote will notify you that the connection has been established, and you can securely begin communicating with the private corporate network.

It is important to keep in mind that SecuRemote is able to provide only Remote Access connectivity. It contains no desktop security enhancements, and is not able to accept a Desktop Security policy to secure the desktop from attack. SecureClient, which is installed in the exact same manner, except you need to select Install SecureClient when prompted, provides the added benefits of enhanced desktop security and a centralized point to manage the Desktop Security policy.

SecureClient

Whereas SecuRemote provides the user with the ability to access the company's resources from remote locations, SecureClient allows for increased desktop security. As a corporation, it is important to ensure that your traveling workforce has the ability to access and transfer information to and from the company's private network. However, once information has been downloaded to a user's laptop or remote machine, the data is vulnerable to attack. Also, if a user's machine is compromised, the entire corporate private network could be vulnerable to malicious code such as worms, viruses, or even an attacker looking for proprietary information.

Check Point looks to solve this vulnerability with SecureClient, a centrally managed desktop firewall bundled with the SecuRemote VPN client. Upon connecting to the VPN-1 gateway, SecureClient downloads the most recent, applicable Desktop Security policy and enforces it on the end user's machine. SecureClient sits at the kernel level, inspecting all network traffic to and from the machine to protect the end user from malicious traffic and attacks.

The Desktop Security policy is similar to the FireWall-1 security policy. Rules are created for inbound and outbound access, and events can be logged or ignored. The Check Point administrator defines the Desktop Security policy from the SmartConsole administration center. The policy is then pushed out to all SecureClients once they update their site information.

SecureClient also adds some connectivity options to SecuRemote. SecureClient supports Office Mode, so that a virtual interface adapter on the remote machine can receive a virtual IP, Visitor Mode, so that the encrypted communication is tunneled over a single port, usually 443 (HTTPS), and Route All Traffic Through Gateway, so that when a VPN tunnel is active, all communications from the remote machine, include to the Internet, are routed first through the VPN gateway.

What's New in SC NGX?

SecureClient supports all new features incorporated in SecuRemote. Additionally, new features of NGX that apply to SecureClient are:

- **Policy Expiration**. When connected, SecureClient will now attempt to update the policy in exactly half the specified interval expire_time. If SecureClient is unable to download the most recent policy, it will not revert to the default policy.

- **RADIUS**. Policy enforcement on the desktop now allows for RADIUS groups.

Installing SecureClient on Microsoft Windows

In the previous section, we stepped through the process of installing SecuRemote. The installation process for SecureClient and even the installation package are identical to that of SecuRemote, provided earlier. The only difference is to select SecureClient instead of SecuRemote when you install the package. Because the Desktop Security policy is generated and maintained on the Policy Server, the configuration of SecureClient is also almost identical to that of SecuRemote. There are only two small differences that are obvious during configuration. First, upon the first successful connection to your newly created site, SecureClient will download the Desktop Security policy and begin enforcing it. Second, once the Desktop Security policy is loaded and enforced, a small blue lock becomes visible over the SecureClient icon on the taskbar to notify you that you are currently being protected.

Policy Server

The Policy Server for SecureClient is the overarching component that allows for centralized administration of the entire SecureClient deployment. It typically is incorporated with the VPN-1 gateway that SecureClient is configured to connect to. It provides SecureClient with network topology information as well as the Desktop Security policy. You can access the Desktop Security policy from the SmartDashboard Desktop Security tab.

Inherently, SecureClient seeks to obtain its Desktop Security policy from the Policy Server. In previous versions of Check Point's software, it was not possible to separate the Policy Server from the VPN-1 gateway SecureClient was connecting to. In NGX however, it is now possible to have a dedicated server supply the Desktop Security policy using a special parameter in the SecureClient Profile. In order to do so, perform the following: First, **Add** the separate Policy Server to the profile. Second, change the database entry use_profile_ps_configuration to **True** via the dbedit tool. When you attempt a connection to the VPN-1 gateway, it will direct SecureClient to the Policy Server to download the applicable Desktop Security policy.

Desktop Security Policies

One of the major arguments in paying for SecureClient licensing over utilizing SecuRemote is the ability to secure individual machines with Desktop Security policies. Desktop Security policies are similar to the policies that protect Check Point's perimeter suite of products, like Firewall-1/VPN-1. They provide security administrators with a familiar interface that can be used to create rules that protect their end user community. Desktop Security policies are essentially rules that can be defined by Source, Destination, Desktop, Service, and Action. They allow security administrators the ability to approve or deny traffic based on any combination of components: port, network, or service. For instance, if a new worm began spreading across the Internet, it would be possible for a security administrator to proactively update the Desktop Security policy and restrict access to the service or port that is vulnerable on every desktop in their environment that was currently utilizing SecureClient. Once the Desktop Security policy has been downloaded, it remains on the computer, protecting it from attacks when it is in both connected and disconnected states. Desktop Security policies are defined in two parts: an inbound policy, where connections originate from external sources attempting to reach the desktop; and an outbound policy, referring to connections originating from the desktop and attempting to reach external resources.

Configuring Desktop Security Policies

In this example, we will provide a step-by-step configuration of a Desktop Security policy that will allow users the rights to perform the following actions:

- Browse the Internet and access DNS information.

- Send and Receive e-mail from the corporate e-mail server through the VPN tunnel.

- Allow IT Personnel to access Corporate Network Resources via SSH and SFTP through the VPN tunnel.

- Utilize Instant Messaging Applications for Instant Messaging.

- Allow incoming SNMP traffic from corporate SNMP servers.

We will begin by launching the SmartDashboard (see Figure 9.36).

Figure 9.36 The SmartDashboard Welcome Screen

Once you have logged in, continue by clicking the **Desktop Security** tab in the right window. The Desktop Security policy should now be visible in the right window. Right-click the existing outbound rule and select **Add Rule | Below**. Repeat the last step to add four more rules to the outbound policy.

It's important to differentiate among user groups. When a Desktop policy contains the All Users group, the policy is applied both when the VPN tunnel is active and when it is not. The All Users rules are applied from the moment the machine receives a policy from the Policy Server. When a rule contains a specific group (IT_group, for example), then the rule is active only when a user in that group establishes a VPN tunnel to the gateway. This allows you to have a stricter set of rules when the VPN connection is active.

Create the rules shown in Table 9.1 in the outbound portion of the Desktop Security policy.

Table 9.1 Outbound Policy Rules

Rule Number	Desktop	Destination	Service	Action	Track	Comment
2	All Users @ Any	Any	HTTP HTTPS DNS	Accept	Log	Allow all users to browse Internet and corporate network.
3	All Users @ Any	Corporate-mail	SMTP IMAP POP-3	Encrypt	Log	Allow all users to connect to the corporate mail server to send/receive e-mail.
4	IT_Users @ Any	Corporate-Int.	SSH SSHv2	Encrypt	Log	Allow all users to access internal corporate resources via SSH and SSHv2 (including SFTP).
5	All Users @ Any	Any	Messenger_Apps	Accept	Log	Allow all users to access instant messenger applications for work collaboration.
6	All Users @ Any	Any	Any	Block	Log	Log all attempted activity from users attempting to establish connections outbound that is not expressly allowed above.

The Encrypt action allows only traffic that is encrypted through the VPN tunnel. This way you can be sure the traffic is not sent in the clear, which could be intercepted.

The **Outbound Rules** section should look like the screen in Figure 9.37 when you are finished.

Figure 9.37 Outbound Policy Rules

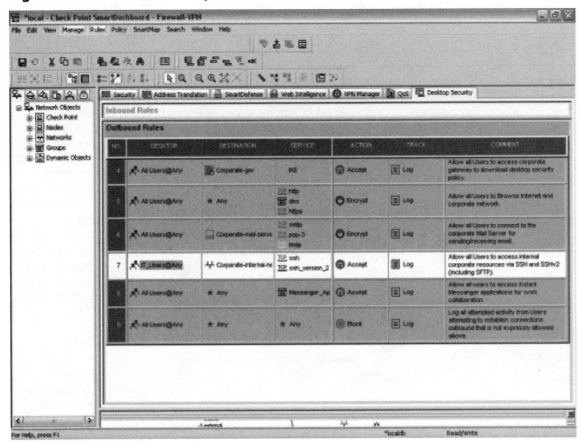

These rules grant permissions based on users, destination, and service. The comments in each rule are descriptive and explain the reason they appear in the policy. The outbound policy allows all users to accomplish specific tasks like Web browsing, sending e-mail, and utilizing Instant Messaging for collaboration. The final rule of the outbound policy stipulates that if a user attempts to access a resource other than those listed, the traffic will be blocked. This type of egress filtering typically is used for multiple reasons. First, it keeps the user community focused on their particular task or job duties by decreasing the actions that the user can perform. Second, it decreases the opportunity for an employee to access sensitive corporate information and transmit it to a third party without generating a noticeable amount of tracking information. Last, it decreases the likelihood of a worm or virus running wild on the corporate network, because the desktop machines that are secured with SecureClient will not accept incoming connections from other machines unless expressly allowed by the Desktop Security policy.

Once the outbound rules have been created, we will continue with securing the desktop by creating the inbound portion of our Desktop Security policy. Inbound rules will secure our users from outside attacks, but also allow important corporate services to initiate connections to them for monitoring and patch management.

Right-click on **rule number 1**, and select **Add Rule | Below**. Repeat this step so that three rules are visible under the inbound policy. Begin by creating the rules shown in Table 9.2.

Table 9.2 Inbound Policy Rules

Rule Number	Source	Desktop	Service	Action	Track	Comment
1	Corporate-AV-Mgmt Corporate-Patch-Mgmt	All Users @ Any	Patch-update AV-Def-update	Encrypt	Log	Allow AntiVirus and Patch management servers to connect to all user machines.
2	Corporate-Enterp-mgmt	All Users @ Any	SNMP SNMP-read SNMP-RO	Accept	Log	Allow corporate enterprise management servers to gather system information on all user machines.
3	Any	All Users @ Any	Any	Block	-	Deny all other connections originating from external sources.

The inbound policy should look like the screen shown in Figure 9.38.

Figure 9.38 Inbound Policy Rules

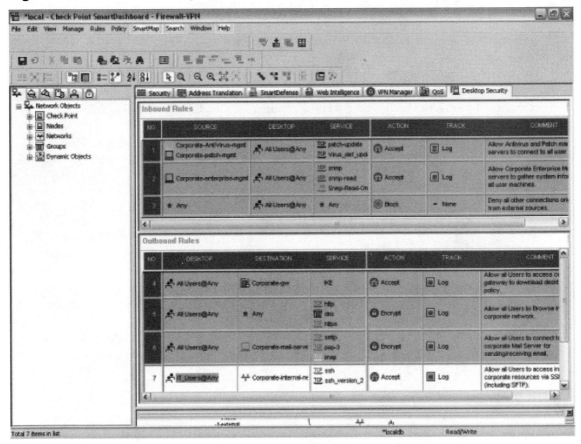

This Inbound policy will allow network administrators and information security engineers to force patch and anti-virus updates to all desktop machines. It is also going to allow auditors the ability to gather system specific information from each desktop via the Simple Network Management Protocol (SNMP). If traffic attempting initial connections to the desktop do not meet the previously mentioned requirements, it will not be accepted. Once the new inbound rules have been added, the rule numbers for the existing outbound rules will have been incremented (based upon the number of rules you added to the inbound policy. This is because SecureClient understands the policy as a rule set, and applies traffic to the policy in order. When the traffic reaches a rule that it applies to, SecureClient takes the action specified in the rule.

It is important to keep in mind that the connections we are discussing when creating policy rules are stateful. In essence, this means that while Check Point monitors each and every single bit of communication occurring between your computer and the remote system, it applies only the initial connection to the rules on the Desktop Security policy. When an incoming or outgoing connection is attempted, the SecureClient (sitting at the kernel level) determines which rule the attempted connection applies to and places the information about the traffic and the corresponding rule into a state table. When replies come from the desktop, or from a remote computer in response to that initial connection that had been accepted, SecureClient verifies that the traffic is related by checking it against the information in the state table, and allows it to pass into or out of the desktop.

For example, when you attempt to access a Web page on the Internet, a request is made by your computer to the computer that hosts the Web page. The computer hosting the Web page answers back with data, and your computer in turn responds, continuing a "conversation" with the computer hosting the Web page until the Web page is fully transferred to your computer. If it were necessary to have a rule for all individual traffic, it would be a configuration nightmare as well as infeasible to secure due to the sheer amounts of traffic and time required.

Once the Desktop Security policy has been Verified and Installed, the preceding rules will allow users who are currently running SecureClient, and have downloaded the Desktop Security policy, to perform the actions listed earlier (Internet browsing, e-mail, ssh). Traffic that is not accepted in the policy will match the last rule and be blocked.

Disabling the Security Policy

It may be necessary in special circumstances where SecureClient is enforcing a Desktop Security policy that is inhibiting the user community to disable the security policy. In any case where SecureClient is impeding users from a critical task, or important mission objective, the Desktop Security policy can be temporarily disabled. In order to disable the Desktop Security policy, locate the SecureClient icon on the system tray, and select it with a left mouse click.

This will open the SecureClient menu. Select **Tools | Disable Security Policy** (see Figure 9.39).

Figure 9.39 SecureClient Icon Menu

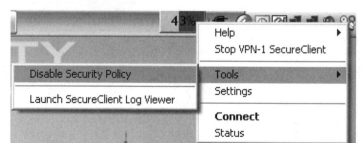

SecureClient will prompt the user to make sure they wish to disable the Desktop Security policy (see Figure 9.40). It also reminds the user that the computer is no longer protected by the SecureClient firewall. Click **Yes**, and the dialogue box will close. If you now move your mouse over the SecureClient icon in the system tray, a small notification box will open, letting you know if SecureClient is currently connected to a VPN-1 gateway, and that the Security Policy is currently disabled.

It is a best practice for users to complete whatever actions are necessary and quickly reenable the Desktop Security policy. The policy can be enabled by selecting the same menu items. This will bring the computer back into a protected mode.

Figure 9.40 SecureClient Verify Disable Policy Dialog

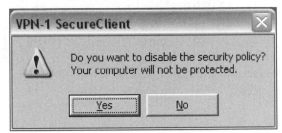

Secure Configuration Verification

Secure Configuration Verification (SCV) additionally provides the security administrator with the capability to verify if machines internal to the private network or attempting to remotely access the private network are compliant with the corporate security policy. SCV works by utilizing built-in checks to SecureClient to check for security updates, operating system versions, running processes, and even browser settings. If a machine is found to be out of compliance, their access to the private network can be revoked, and they are notified of their machine's discrepancies with the Corporate Security policy. Once the machine is brought back into a complaint state, they are again granted access to the private network. Secure Configuration Verification is discussed in greater depth later in this chapter.

Office Mode

After installing, configuring, and attempting to use SecuRemote or SecureClient, it is common for a specific concern to be quickly identified. For some unforeseen reason, the client is not able to communicate with any host inside the private network, and in some cases can't even establish a connection to the VPN-1 gateway. It doesn't take long for a security administrator to realize that an IP Address conflict has occurred between the user's home and the corporate networks, typically because both networks are using the same nonpublic address space. It is very common for an organization to utilize nonpublic address space behind a Network Address Translation (NAT) router or firewall in order to save money on purchasing publicly routable address space for all hosts on their network.

This is both fiscally responsible, as well as a security best practice. First, it is very difficult to obtain, and is expensive for small and medium sized businesses to use publicly routable IP address space for each and every computer that will open connections to the Internet. Second, using NAT can provide added security as it decreases the ability of an attacker to get into your network from a remote location. It also leaves less information about your network's topology out on the Internet for anyone to research. In essence, your company's network is less attractive to the average attacker because it takes an advanced skill set to gain remote access to a nonpublic address space. Using NAT, the vectors of attack have been greatly reduced. A good rule of thumb for securing your network is to keep anyone outside your organization from knowing too much about your network, its layout, or security controls. In fact, the less they know the better.

When a VPN user behind a NAT router or firewall with a nonpublic, reserved IP address (within networks such as 192.168.0.0/16, 172.16.0.0/12, or 10.0.0.0/8) attempts to connect to another network that already has a host with the same IP address, IP address conflicts occur, and traffic is not routed appropriately. This conflict is easily understood in today's world of broadband service providers. Most home users are behind broadband cable or DSL modems that obtain the IP address via Dynamic Host Configuration Protocol (DHCP). Most broadband users then connect some type of router to the broadband modem, and use NAT to connect multiple computers to a single connection with a single public IP address.

Another common problem that occurs with VPN users connecting into a private network is the network engineers or security administrators utilizing access control lists (ACLs) on the routers to help secure parts of the network. When ACLs are used, typically they are defined with only internal address space in mind. Obviously, with a mobile workforce, it would be technically infeasible to attempt to add new rules to the ACLs every time a user connected to the private network from a different IP address.

Why Office Mode?

Office Mode allows security administrators to overcome the ACL and IP address conflict problems by assigning every SecureClient an IP address for use while it is connected to the private network. Office mode works like this: Let's say, for example, a user attempts to connect to your corporate VPN gateway. The IP address of the remote user's computer is 192.168.1.10, which coincidently is the IP address of your company's internal e-mail server. Without office mode, all response traffic to the remote users requests would either be dropped, or misrouted to the e-mail server, which wouldn't recognize the traffic, and so would drop it. If, however, office mode is enabled, SecureClient enters a special configuration mode during the initial phase of IKE, and requests an IP address from the VPN gateway. This new IP address is then assigned to a virtual network adapter, which is then used to send traffic to the corporate internal network. Office Mode is available only on SecureClient.

Client IP Pool

Check Point's VPN-1 gateway provides many different options for assigning IP addresses for Office mode SecureClient configurations. Different conditions are better suited to different methods of assigning IP addresses. Check Point supports IP address assignment via a configuration file that resides on the VPN-1 gateway, and assigns IPs per individual user, RADIUS server, IP pools based on preassigned network blocks or DHCP server.

IP pools are defined as a range of addresses that are given to SecureClients requesting access to the private network while in Office mode. You can also assign domain names or WINS information along with IP addresses to make communication with remote users easier. Check Point VPN-1 can be configured to assign IP addresses to all SecureClient users or to a given group of users.

Configuring Office Mode with IP Pools

The simplest way to assign Office mode addresses is using a manual IP pool. The range of addresses assigned to SecureClient users has to be a range that is not used within your corporation. Moreover, there should be a static route on internal routers that directs the IP pools to the VPN gateway, especially if there is a chance that asymmetric routing could direct traffic to those addresses elsewhere. In a Cluster environment, each cluster member needs to have a different IP pool defined.

Configuring the VPN-1 Gateway for Office Mode

Configuring Office mode can be done quickly and easily with a simple configuration change to both the VPN-1 gateway and SecureClient. Start by launching the Smart Dashboard Policy Editor, and selecting the **Network Objects** tab in the left window. In order to configure Office mode with IP pools, we need to create a network object that will serve as the list of IP addresses reserved for SecureClient users. Right-click **Network Objects** and select **New | Network…**.

This will open a Network Properties window where you can enter the network information for the IP pool (see Figure 9.41). For this example, we are going to use one of the subnets in the reserved nonpublic class C address space 192.168.0.0. Be sure to enter **192.168.2.0** as the network address, and **255.255.255.0** as the net mask. This means when users connect to the VPN-1 gateway while in Office mode, they will obtain an address for use on the internal private network between **192.168.2.0** and **192.168.2.254**. Click **OK** to continue.

Figure 9.41 Creating an Office Mode IP Pool Network Object

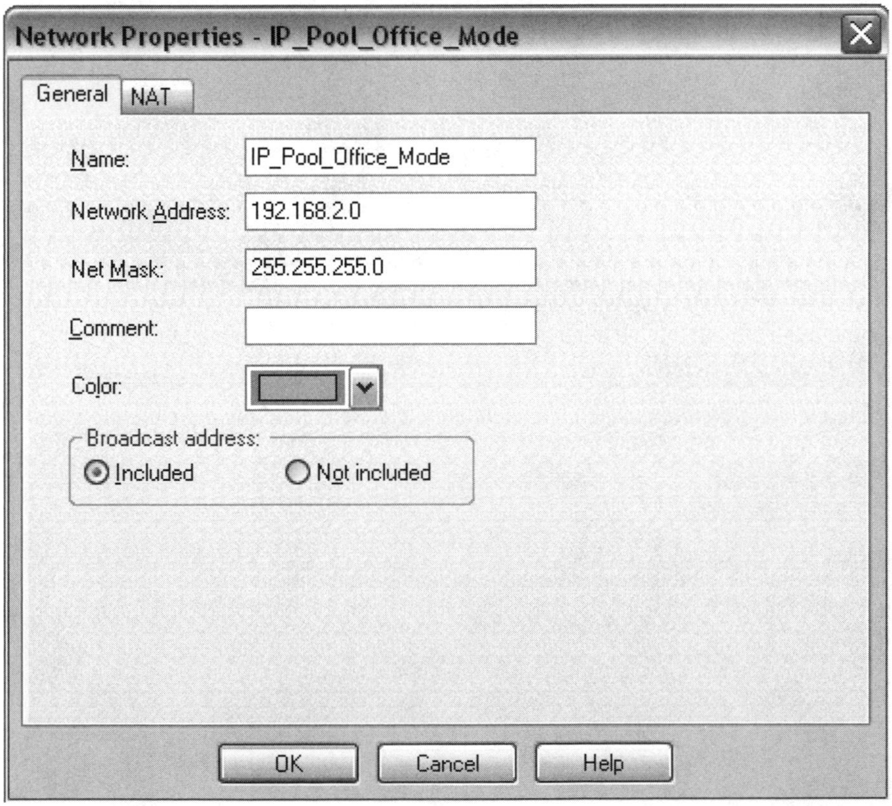

Once the IP pool network object has been created, right-click on the VPN-1 gateway on which you wish to enable Office mode, and select **Edit** (see Figure 9.42).

Figure 9.42 Office Mode Default Page

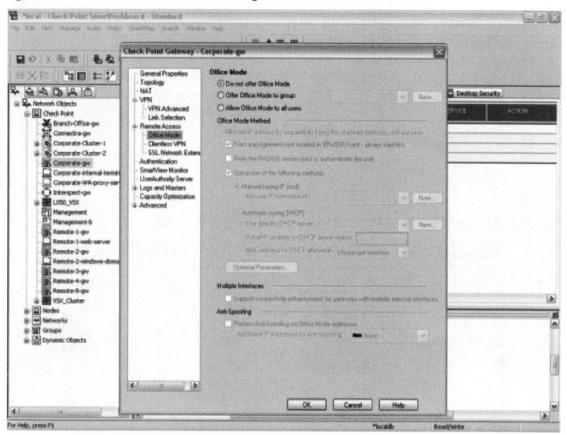

This will open the properties window for the VPN-1 gateway you selected. Expand the **Remote Access** selection and click **Office Mode**. Select the option **Allow Office Mode to all users** (see Figure 9.43).

Figure 9.43 Office Mode Gateway Configuration

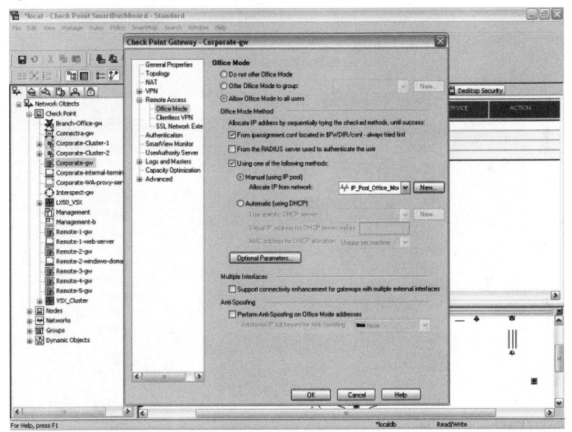

Click the radio button next to the Manual option, located just underneath the Office Mode Method heading. Click the drop-down box, and select the network that was created for IP pools. Click **OK** to continue. Verify and install the policy onto the VPN-1 gateway. The VPN-1 gateway is now read to provide users who are utilizing Office mode IP addresses that can be routed on the internal private network.

Configuring SecureClient for Office Mode

Begin by right-clicking the **SecureClient** icon in the system tray. Select **Settings** and the **Connections** tab and the Settings window will open (see Figure 9.44).

Figure 9.44 SecureClient Connection Settings

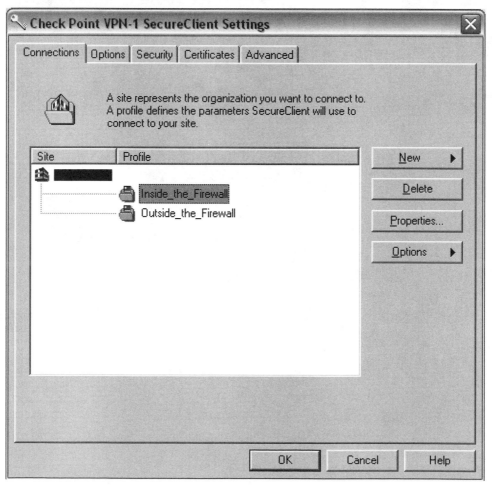

Select the profile for which you wish to enable Office mode and click **Properties**. When the Profile Properties dialog box appears, select the **Advanced** tab (see Figure 9.45).

Figure 9.45 SecureClient Profile Properties

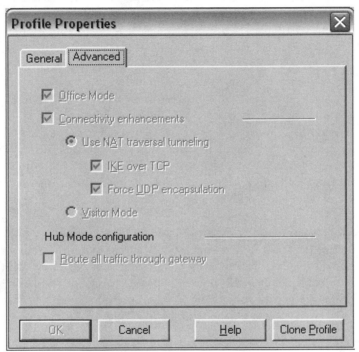

Under the **Advanced** tab, you can select **Office Mode** along with other useful options for SecureClient. Once you have checked the box for Office mode, continue by clicking **OK**.

SecureClient is now configured to connect to a VPN-1 gateway utilizing Office mode.

Secure Configuration Verification (SCV)

Even the least technically savvy know they need to be secure, and that it's important to the company to protect proprietary data. This, however, doesn't stop anyone from writing their password down on a sticky note and placing it under their keyboard. Security most commonly is met with fearsome apprehension; anyone who has attempted to restrict users to being less than administrators on their corporate machines knows exactly what I am talking about. Mostly, this is because security administrators sometimes lose sight of the purpose of the company in order to secure it. I know I have.

In the wake of more prolific worms and viruses, such as Code Red/Nimda, Blaster/Lovsan, and Nachi/Welchia, security administrators were pulling their hair out trying to fight mobile users from infecting the entire private network with these bandwidth crippling worms. Most security administrators knew to combat these viruses and worms by blocking the ports they utilized at the perimeter. In effect, the viruses or worms shouldn't be able to infect the private network because they couldn't get through the firewalls to the vulnerable machines. Unfortunately, it was then made painfully obvious how soft the underbelly of the private network was. In the end, it didn't take a critical firewall vulnerability to allow Distributed Denial of Service (DDoS) attacks to bring networks to their knees. It was as simple as an authorized user returning to work from telecommuting.

Worms like Blaster/Lovsan and Nachi/Welchia were blocked at the perimeter, however remote access (whether dial-in or VPN) and traveling users returning to the office introduced and spread the bulk of worm and virus infections. Some security administrators even denied all remote access initially in order to protect the network, and slowly allowed small pools of users connectivity to the private network in order to identify infected machines and have them cleaned and inoculated. This was an extremely expensive lesson for two reasons. First, many security professionals wasted hundreds, and in some cases, thousands of hours getting networks back up and machines secure. Second, the loss of employee productivity was incredible. Millions of dollars were lost because employees couldn't perform the simplest of business functions.

Check Point heard the screams of the security community and answered with Secure Configuration Verification (SCV). SCV gives the security administrator the ability to verify if a machine is compliant with the corporate security policy prior to granting access to the private network. SCV works on machines that exist inside the private network as well as machines attempting to form VPN tunnels into the private network from other locations. In order to take advantage of SCV, you must have a fully licensed copy of Check Point's SecureClient to enforce the corporate security policy.

What's New with Secure Configuration Verification (SCV) in NGX?

Some of the more interesting additions to Secure Configuration Verification in NGX are:

- Exceptions: It is now possible with the release of NGX to specify hosts or services that are allowed access to the private network even if the SCV check fails.

- OS Monitor is now able to recognize Windows 2003 server.

- SCV does not support SecuRemote, however it is now possible to allow SecuRemote clients access to the private network even if SCV checks are enabled. To enable this feature, find the parameter scv_allow_sr_clients in the userc.c file, and set the value to **true**.

- The following registry keys can now be checked with Registry Monitor: HKey_Local_Machine, HKey_Current_User, and HKey_User.

Configuring the Policy Server to Enable Secure Configuration Verification (SCV)

In order to enable Secure Configuration Verification (SCV), it is necessary to modify some minor settings in the Global Properties menu of your Firewall-1/VPN-1 gateway policy server. Specifically, login to SmartDashboard, and select **Policy | Global Properties...** from the menu bar. Once the Global Properties dialog box is open, expand the left menu for **Remote Access** and select **Secure Configuration Verification**. The window will look like the screen in Figure 9.46.

Figure 9.46 The Secure Configuration Verification Global Properties

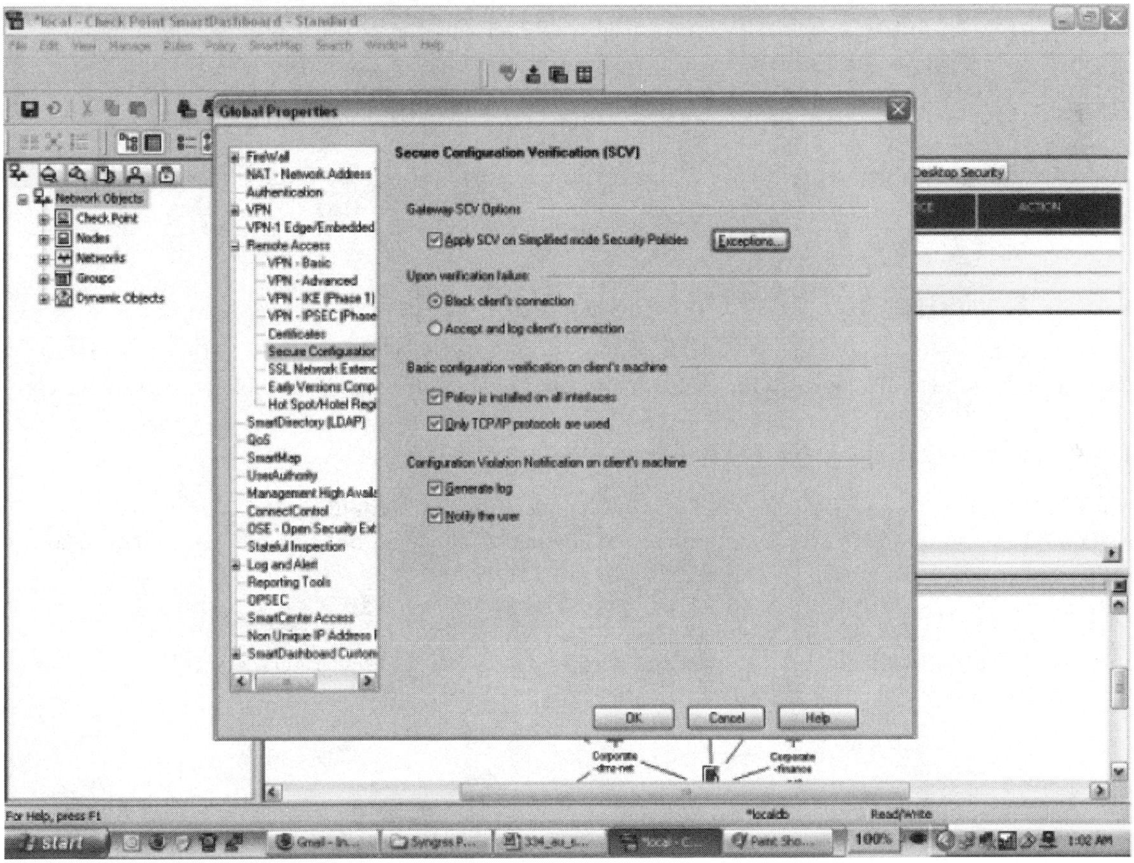

Ensure the first check box (Apply SCV for Simplified mode Security Policies) is selected and click **OK**.

In addition to making the aforementioned change, a policy file named local.scv, located in the Firewall Configuration Directory ($FWDIR/conf), must be configured to use the provided checks correctly to verify clients are within compliance.

Secure Configuration Verification (SCV) Checks Available

SecureClient NGX comes with SCV installed, and some SCV checks are predefined and ready for use:

- **Process Monitor.** Checks if a process is running or not.

- **Version Checker.** Checks the current version of SecureClient.

- **Group Monitor.** Checks if the user currently logged on to the machine running SecureClient is a member of a Domain User Group.

- **OS Monitor.** Verifies the version of the Operating System that is currently running, what service packs the OS is at, and the configuration of the screen saver.

- **HotFix Monitor.** Verifies that certain Microsoft Security patches are installed.

- **Browser Monitor.** Checks the current version of Internet Explorer, as well as its configuration and settings information.

Check Point OPSEC Vendor SCV Checks

Some Check Point OPSEC partners have developed their own SCV checks, such as Okena and PestPatrol. An updated list of OPSEC Partners and their service offerings is available at www.ospec.com.

Other Third-Party Checks

OPSWAT (www.opswat.com) has developed SCV checks for HfNetCheck and Norton AV. OPSWAT is also willing to write customized SCV checks. They can be contacted at their Web site.

Create Your Own Checks

In order to create SCV checks, you must utilize the SCV Software Developers Kit (SDK), available at www.opsec.com.

Integrity

Integrity is an interesting addition to the Check Point family of products. Originally, SecureClient was Check Point's desktop firewall, and aside from desktop security policies, was important from the perspective of centralized administration. Although SecureClient provides SecuRemote with the added connectivity options and the benefits of a rule-based desktop firewall policy and Secure Configuration Verification (SCV), Integrity goes further to secure the user's desktop. Integrity is a corporate desktop firewall, much like Zone Lab's ZoneAlarm. In fact, a common user would be hard pressed to find many differences between ZoneAlarm Pro and Check Point's initial offering of Integrity. In fact, many of the logos and icons that are used in the Integrity program still bear the label "Zone Labs." However, for security professionals, the differences between the two programs immediately stand out.

Integrity actually monitors the inbound/outbound traffic on multiple levels. It allows for rules similar to those found in the policy of the SecureClient desktop firewall, but also inspects each program that attempts to access the network, and prompts the user to ensure that this traffic should be allowed. It functions in the same way for incoming traffic to the desktop, prompting the user to ensure it is safe and should be granted access. This is important because the current state of information security does little to protect against malicious code and ad-ware that use typically open ports as vectors of attack. Newer attacks, and arguably the most dangerous ones, include DNS redirects, which send users that are browsing the Internet to phony Web sites that download malicious code to their computers. Most commonly, this includes ad-ware, Trojan horses, and key logging software. Since HTTP traffic typically is allowed outbound on both the perimeter and desktop firewalls, the traffic is never under too much scrutiny because it's compliant with the policy. Attackers have learned to use this type of attack in interesting new ways, and it causes the information security field to spend more and invest more time in defending against it.

Another major difference that will save security administrators time and effort will be the centralized administration via the Integrity Server. Check Point's Integrity Client is a complex program that allows for multiple configuration settings and centralized administration through an Integrity Advanced Server. Due to space limitations, it is not feasible to walk through and explain the server configuration or even all possible client configuration options that are available in this chapter. This chapter will then serve as an introduction to the Integrity Client, and some of the features it allows security administrators to use in securing the end user desktop environment.

The Integrity Server allows the security administrator the ability to centrally configure access policies, expert rules, program access defaults, privacy restrictions, predefined zone information and many other new functions. The security administrator even has the ability to determine the level of involvement that end users are able to have with the Integrity Client. For instance, upon deployment of the Integrity Client, a security department must decide whether to roll out the Integrity Agent, which is a silent version of the client that doesn't prompt the user for any actions; or the Integrity Flex Client, which gives the user privileges to allow or deny traffic, privacy controls, expert rules, or change other configuration options. Aside from different names, these two versions of the Integrity client provide completely different deployment solutions that can be tailored to the specific environment they will be used in. Depending on the deployment and resources of the corporate environment, it may behoove the security staff to roll out Integrity as a standalone product with no centralized administration. In that situation, Check Point makes available Integrity Desktop, which is the Flex version of the client without the centralized administration option.

History of Integrity

Following Check Point's acquisition of Zone Labs, they began to make additions and changes to ZoneAlarm that would allow for more flexibility in enterprise environments. Zone Labs was the original creator of ZoneAlarm, which was arguably one of the best personal desktop firewalls freely available for the Microsoft Windows environment. ZoneAlarm had a great reputation for being a robust, free, desktop firewall that was intuitive and easy to understand and use for most nontechnical end users. When any traffic was detected, the ZoneAlarm client provided the end user with allow/deny options, but also created MD5 checksum values for each program that requested Internet access. If the program's checksum value changed, ZoneAlarm knew that could mean the program could be a malicious Trojan, and again prompted the user on what action to take.

In essence, Check Point's new Integrity Client is ZoneAlarm with more advances in rule and policy governance of the desktop. It also incorporates centralized management, which allows easier integration with large-scale deployments for enterprise and government customers.

Integrity Client Installation

Installing Integrity is as simple as running a standard windows executable. The installation process is the same for the Integrity Flex, Integrity Agent, and Integrity Desktop clients. In this example, we will focus on the Installation and Configuration of Integrity Flex without configuring the integration with the Integrity Advanced Server.

Begin by downloading the Integrity Flex Client. Double-click the installer executable to begin installation (see Figure 9.47).

Figure 9.47 Integrity Flex License Agreement

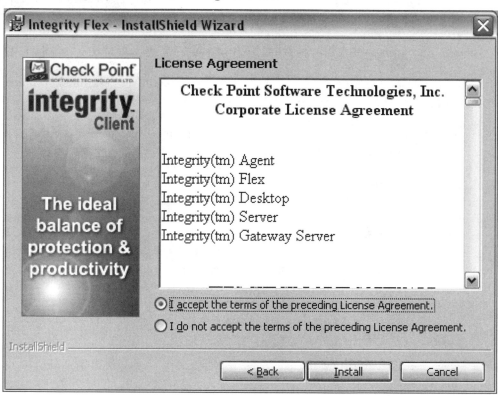

The Installer program will ask you to agree to Check Point's End User License Agreement. Select the radio button next to "I accept the terms of the preceding license agreement" and click **Install**.

The Integrity Flex installer will then prompt the user to approve the default installation location or enter a new location. Accept the default location and click **Next** (see Figure 9.48).

Figure 9.48 Integrity Flex Installation Location

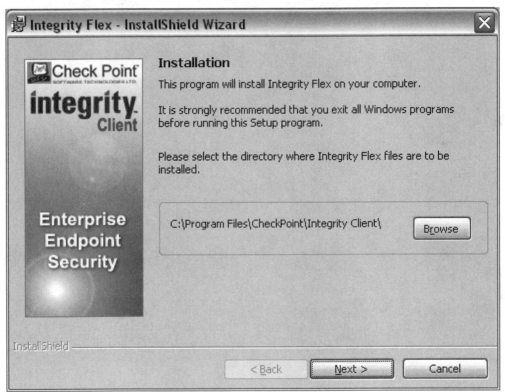

The Integrity Installer will now begin installing the client on the desktop machine (see Figure 9.49).

Figure 9.49 Integrity Flex Installation Progress

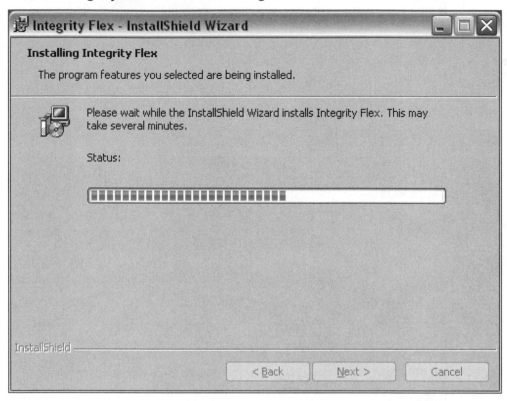

After the installation is completed, Integrity will prompt the user to reboot the system to fully complete the installation and begin using Integrity. Click **Yes** to restart the system.

After the system is rebooted, Integrity Flex will be available to protect the desktop (see Figure 9.50).

Figure 9.50 Integrity Flex Reboot Dialog

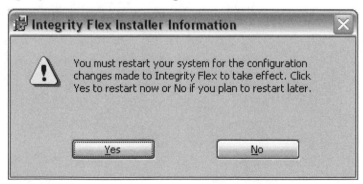

Integrity Client Configuration

After rebooting the system and attempting to launch Integrity, it will walk through a brief configuration wizard, and when it is completed, it is strongly recommended that anyone using Integrity use the tutorial for an in-depth explanation of how the Integrity Client works to secure the desktop.

Integrity Clientless Security

In some circumstances or environments, it may not be feasible or possible to install an Integrity client on every desktop machine to assist in securing end users from attacks. Check Point has provided a plug-in that creates a secure Integrity Browser, entering the user into a secure session during Web browsing. This browser is accessible when a user connects to the SSL Network Extender, both in a VPN-1 Pro gateway and in a Connectra gateway. It actively scans the desktop machine for malicious code, key loggers, spyware, and Trojan programs before it allows a user to provide information to a Web site. Integrity Clientless Security is configured and deployed without the hassle of touching each desktop computer. It also allows the administrator to easily select and search the desktop for malicious elements he is concerned with. Integrity Clientless Security incorporates privacy protection, ad-ware protection, and advanced protection from malicious code such as Trojan horses. It also protects any passwords, cookies, or attachments in e-mail messages that are used during the secure session. Integrity Clientless Security also provides a mechanism for administrators to deploy the Integrity Client automatically.

Summary

In this chapter, we explained the history and usefulness behind Check Point's SecuRemote, SecureClient, and Integrity products. One take-away that was presented consistently throughout the chapter is the interoperability of the products, and the security provided to the remote user and private network user community by proper configuration and maintenance of the clients and policies that secure the user community. Though there will always be obstacles to building a remote access infrastructure and securing it, we have tried to provide information that will assist in working around those issues, such as Office mode and Secure Configuration Verification.

It is also important to understand that although SecuRemote provides Remote Access security for mobile users, it protects only the information being sent through the encrypted tunnel. SecureClient and Integrity have the ability to protect the desktop and user community regardless of their physical location. They secure the desktop, ensuring data is secure while resting on the computer as well as in transit to the corporate private network. SecureClient also provides Secure Configuration Verification, which checks to ensure that users connecting to your private network meet certain configuration specifications to obtain access, such as being on a Windows XP machine with Service Pack 2, specific Hotfix patches installed, and browsers configured to disable javascript.

As SecureClient builds on SecuRemote, providing the functionality of a desktop firewall, it only allows the administrator to block entire services, sites, or networks. Most of the time, malicious code such as ad-ware and Trojan horses find their way onto end-user computers through seemingly normal traffic that is allowed by the SecureClient and even the perimeter firewall. Integrity builds on the functionality of SecureClient, proving additional security mechanisms to protect the user from attacks that utilize typically open ports or services as vectors. It creates a hash of any program that attempts to connect to the network, and if that hash value changes, it notifies the user that something is wrong.

All three clients serve an important role in enabling users to be secure and flexible. While utilizing Check Point's desktop clients, the end user can continue to travel, provide valuable productivity, and ensure that company proprietary or privacy information remains safe. It's a marriage of fluidity and security for the company on the move.

Chapter 10

Adaptive Security Device Manager

Solutions in this chapter:

- Features, Limitations, and Requirements

- Installing, Configuring, and Launching ASDM

- Configuring the PIX Firewall Using ASDM

- Configuring VPNs Using ASDM

☑ Summary

Introduction

In previous chapters in this section, our focus has been on the configuration and management of the PIX firewall using the command-line interface, or CLI. The PIX firewall also supports a graphical user interface (GUI), which used to be called the PIX Device Manager (PDM). PDM has been replaced in version 7.0 with the Adaptive Security Device Manager (ASDM), which allows an administrator to use a Web browser to install, configure, and maintain the PIX firewall.

ASDM is a Java-based GUI used to manage the Cisco PIX firewall. It consists of a software image that runs from flash memory on the PIX firewall, enabling administrative access via a Secure Sockets Layer (SSL) encrypted HTTPS session. ASDM completely replaces PDM, which was available for versions before 7.0. ASDM allows firewall administrators to work from a variety of authorized workstations configured with a compatible browser and includes nearly all PIX CLI functionality. For example, using ASDM, administrators can add, modify, and delete firewall rule sets, configure network address translation (NAT), or set up a virtual private network (VPN).

In addition to altering PIX configurations, ASDM facilitates administrative monitoring of the PIX firewall through powerful graph and table displays for near-real-time insight into PIX performance. This chapter introduces ASDM, and provides detailed information for using it to configure and monitor the PIX firewall.

Features, Limitations, and Requirements

ASDM provides nearly all functionality available in the PIX firewall CLI. This includes the ability to modify access, AAA, filter rules on the firewall, and implement and control NAT. ASDM also gives firewall administrators granular control of administrative functionality such as logging, IDS configuration, and user account maintenance while providing insight into current performance through the detailed ASDM graphical monitoring functionality. A wealth of performance metrics and real-time statistics can easily be generated and viewed using ASDM.

ASDM includes powerful wizards such as the Setup Wizard and the VPN Wizard. Both tools guide firewall administrators through the often-complex configuration of advanced features such as auto-update functionality and DHCP server setup or site-to-site and software client VPN configuration. ASDM also supports object grouping, NAT, LAN failover, several fixup configurations, and command authorization. For information regarding these and many other supported features in the ASDM interface, refer to the ASDM Version 5.0 Release Notes at www.cisco.com/en/US/customer/products/ps6121/prod_release_note_book09186a0080426ad1.html.

Cisco provides ASDM via Java applets embedded in the ASDM image stored on the PIX firewall. These signed applets are downloaded directly from PIX flash memory to facilitate PIX administration free of cumbersome client-side software. Therefore, no special client software other than a compliant Web browser is required for the ASDM client. However, there are several prerequisites for ASDM to run successfully. These hardware, software, and client-side requirements for ASDM are described in the following sections. In addition, Cisco has now made ASDM available as a downloadable application that can run locally.

Supported PIX Firewall Hardware and Software Versions

The ASDM replaces the PIX Device Manager (PDM) with PIX software v7.0. The following paragraphs discuss the hardware and software requirements for ASDM.

PIX Device Requirements

ASDM v5.0 software requires PIX software version 7.0(1), and runs on the following platforms:

- PIX 515/515E
- PIX 525
- PIX 535

ASDM cannot be used with earlier versions of the PIX software (v6.3 and earlier), nor can it be used for PIX 506/506E or PIX 501 platforms because they do not yet support version 7.0. Additionally, the PIX platform must have a Data Encryption Standard (DES) or 3DES activation key. The DES or 3DES activation key enables SSL-based communication between the remote Java management client and the PIX device. PIX devices shipped with software version 6.0 and higher already include a DES activation key and encryption capabilities. 3DES, which enables stronger encryption capabilities, is available from Cisco as an additional license.

Host Requirements for Running ASDM

Because Cisco created ASDM using Java technology, there are multiple client workstations capable of running the ASDM client software. Specifically, ASDM can be run from the operating systems shown in Table 10.1.

Table10.1 ASDM Client OS Requirements

Client Operating Systems	OS Version	Browser
Solaris	Solaris 8 or 9 running CDE window manager	Mozilla 1.7.3 with Java plug-in 1.4.2 or 1.5.0
Linux	Red Hat Linux 9.0 or Red Hat Linux WS, version 3 running GNOME or KDE	Mozilla 1.7.3 with Java plug-in 1.4.2
Windows	Windows 2000 (SP4), Windows XP	Internet Explorer 6.0 with Java plug-in 1.4.2 or 1.5.0

Adaptive Security Device Manager Limitations

You can use ASDM to configure almost every feature of the PIX; however, there are some limitations in terms of unsupported commands, unsupported character sets, and printing when compared with the traditional CLI.

Unsupported Commands

ASDM does not support the complete command set of the CLI. In most cases, ASDM ignores unsupported commands, leaving intact in the configuration. The following are effects of some of the unsupported commands:

- If ASDM loads an existing running configuration and finds IPv6-related commands, ASDM displays a dialog box informing you that it does not support IPv6. You cannot configure any IPv6 commands in ASDM, but all other configuration is available.

- If ASDM loads an existing running configuration and finds other unsupported commands, ASDM operation is unaffected. To view the unsupported commands, see **Options | Show Commands Ignored by ASDM on Device**.

- If ASDM loads an existing running configuration and finds the *alias* command, it enters Monitor-only mode. Monitor-only mode allows access to the following functions: the Monitoring area and the CLI tool (**Tools | Command Line Interface**), which lets you use the CLI commands.

To exit Monitor-only mode, use the CLI tool or access the security appliance console, and remove the *alias* command. You can use outside NAT instead of the *alias* command.

Unsupported Characters

ASDM does not support any non-English characters or any other special characters. If you enter non-English characters in any text entry field, they become unrecognizable when you submit the entry, and you cannot delete or edit them. If you are using a non-English keyboard or usually type in a language other than English, be careful not to enter non-English characters accidentally.

ASDM CLI Does Not Support Interactive Commands

The ASDM CLI feature does not support interactive user commands. If you enter a CLI command that requires interactive confirmation, ASDM prompts you to enter "[yes/no]" but does not recognize your input. ASDM then times out waiting for your response. For example, on the **ASDM Tools** menu, click **Command Line Interface**. Enter the command **crypto key generate rsa**. ASDM generates the default 1024-bit RSA key. Enter the command again: **crypto key generate rsa**.

Instead of regenerating the RSA keys by overwriting the previous one, ASDM displays the following error:

```
Do you really want to replace them? [yes/no]:WARNING: You already have RSA
ke0000000000000$A key

Input line must be less than 16 characters in length.
%Please answer 'yes' or 'no'.
Do you really want to replace them [yes/no]:
%ERROR: Timed out waiting for a response.
ERROR: Failed to create new RSA keys names <Default-RSA-key>
```

Printing from ASDM

ASDM supports printing for the following features:

- The Configuration | Features | Interfaces table
- All Configuration | Features | Security Policy tables
- All Configuration | NAT tables
- The Configuration | Features | VPN | IPsec | IPsec Rules table
- Monitoring | Features | Connection Graphs and its related table

Installing, Configuring, and Launching ASDM

This section of the chapter provides insight into the logical steps and procedures required to install, configure, and launch ASDM.

Preparing for Installation

Before attempting to use ASDM or configure a PIX device using ASDM, verify that the PIX firewall software version of the device is 7.0 or later. If it is not, the software version must be upgraded and DES must be activated before ASDM will function.

To verify the PIX firewall version, log in to the CLI and type **show version**. The first two lines of the response should display the current PIX firewall version and indicate whether ASDM is installed on the device. The following shows a PIX firewall with software version 7.0(1) and ASDM version 5.0(1) installed:

```
PIX1# show version
Cisco PIX Security Appliance Software Version 7.0(1)
Device Manager Version 5.0(1)
```

If the PIX firewall version is 7.0 or later and ASDM 5.0 is installed, proceed to the section "Configuring the PIX Firewall Using ASDM." If these are not installed, refer to the following steps to upgrade the PIX firewall, install the DES activation key, and install/upgrade ASDM.

Installing or Upgrading ASDM

As with all upgrade and installation procedures, begin by backing up all configuration data on the existing PIX firewall device that you plan to upgrade. If the PIX firewall is a production device, schedule the upgrade procedure during off-hours and notify the users of the potential service disruption. Doing so will help ensure a smooth upgrade process and will prevent complaints from the user community.

Verify that the PIX firewall meets all requirements listed previously in this chapter before starting with the upgrade and installation. Read all release notes carefully to determine whether any specific functionality has been removed or changed in the new release. Finally, be sure to have the software image of the PIX firewall version currently running on the PIX device backed up in the event the new version upgrade fails and you must roll back. The installation procedure is generally trouble free, but best practice always dictates preparation for version rollback in the event of a failure.

To install or upgrade ASDM:

1. Obtain a DES activation key.

2. Configure the PIX firewall for basic network connectivity.

3. Install a TFTP server and make it available to the PIX firewall.

4. Upgrade to the version of PIX firewall software and configure the DES activation key on the PIX device.

5. Install or upgrade ASDM on the PIX device.

Let's take a closer look at each of these steps.

Obtaining a DES Activation Key

The first step in configuring ASDM on a PIX firewall is obtaining a new activation key to enable DES encryption (if you do not already have one). A DES activation key is free from Cisco and is required for ASDM functionality. Because it could take some time for Cisco to issue the new key, it is best to start the request process before upgrading software on the PIX firewall. Use the *show version* command to obtain the PIX serial number. This number is required to request a new activation key. From a Web browser, go to www.cisco.com/go/license and fill out either the "DES (56-bit) Encryption License (Free)" or the "PIX Firewall 3DES/AES License Registration" request form. A Cisco representative will e-mail you the appropriate activation key shortly thereafter.

Configuring the PIX Firewall for Network Connectivity

To upgrade a PIX firewall and install ASDM, the PIX firewall must first be capable of basic network connectivity. If the PIX firewall device is already on the network and capable of connecting to other devices, proceed to the next section and install a TFTP server.

1. Establish a connection to the console port of the PIX device and log in to the CLI. Enter Enable mode by typing **enable** at the console prompt. Type **configure terminal** to enter Configuration mode on the PIX firewall. Enter the setup dialog box by typing **setup** after entering Configuration mode. Follow the setup dialog prompts and enter information for the following variables:

   - Enable password

   - Clock variables

   - IP address information

   - Hostname

   - Domain name

2. When prompted, save the information to write the configuration to memory.

When you're finished, physically attach the PIX firewall to the network and test for network connectivity using the *ping* command on the PIX firewall.

Installing a TFTP Server

After the PIX firewall is successfully configured on the network, a TFTP server must be installed to accommodate the new PIX firewall software and ASDM software upload. If a TFTP server already exists, proceed to the next section and upgrade the PIX firewall software.

Upgrading the PIX Firewall and Configuring the DES Activation Key

Because ASDM 5.0 only functions on PIX 7.0 and later, PIX devices with versions before 7.0 must be upgraded. Furthermore, the use of ASDM requires the activation of DES or 3DES to facilitate a secure, encrypted management session. To enable DES, the new key requested in previous steps must be activated either during a new PIX image load using the Monitor mode method on the PIX firewall or using the *activation-key* command. The key on the PIX firewall cannot be changed using the typical *copy tftp flash* command.

If the PIX device is already running software version 7.0 and you simply need to install the new DES or 3DES license key, use the *activation-key* command from the CLI. Type **activation-key** in Configuration mode, followed by the appropriate activation key hexadecimal code provided by Cisco. To verify the key, use the *show activation-key* command.

Installing or Upgrading ASDM on the PIX Device

After the PIX firewall software is successfully upgraded to 7.0 and the DES or 3DES key is installed, ASDM must be loaded into flash. As with the PIX firewall software upgrade, the installation of ASDM is a potentially difficult operation. Always make backups of configuration files and software images before proceeding with the installation. Always verify that the PIX firewall meets the requirements specified for ASDM.

To install or upgrade from PDM to ASDM:

1. Copy the ASDM binary file (asdm-501.bin) to a TFTP or FTP server on your network.

2. Log in to your security appliance using the console (or other appropriate method that you have configured).

3. Ensure that you have connectivity from your security appliance to your TFTP/FTP server. If you have an existing copy of the PIX Device Manager, delete it:

   ```
   delete flash:/pdm
   ```

4. Copy the ASDM binary onto your security appliance using the appropriate command:

   ```
   For TFTP: copy tftp://your-server-IP/pathtofile flash:/asdm-501.bin
   For FTP: copy ftp://your-server-IP/pathtofile flash:/asdm-501.bin
   ```

5. If you have more than one ASDM image, enter the following command to configure the location of the ASDM image:

   ```
   asdm image flash:/asdm501.bin
   ```

6. Enter the following command to enable the HTTPS server on the device:

   ```
   http server enable
   ```

7. Identify the systems or networks that are allowed to access ASDM. This is done by specifying one or more hosts/networks using the following command:

   ```
   http 10.1.1.1 255.255.255.255 inside
   ```

8. The IP address 10.1.1.1 is a host that may access ASDM and that is connected via the inside interface.

9. Verify that ASDM is installed correctly by connecting from the client system (10.1.1.1 in the preceding example) to the security appliance, using a supported browser. For example:

   ```
   https://10.1.1.1/admin/
   ```

Enabling and Disabling ASDM

To use ASDM, you need to enable the HTTPS server, and allow HTTPS connections to the security appliance. All of these tasks are completed if you use the *setup* command. This section describes how to manually configure ASDM access. The security appliance allows a maximum of five concurrent ASDM instances per context, if available, with a maximum of 32 ASDM instances between all contexts.

   To configure ASDM access:

1. To enable the HTTPS server, enter the following command:

   ```
   PIX1(config)# http server enable
   ```

2. To identify the IP addresses from which the security appliance accepts HTTPS connections, enter the following command for each address or subnet:

   ```
   PIX1(config)# http source_IP_address mask source_interface
   ```

3. For example, to enable the HTTPS server and let a host on the inside interface with an address of 192.168.1.2 access ASDM, enter the following commands:

   ```
   PIX1(config)# http server enable
   PIX1(config)# http 192.168.1.2 255.255.255.255 inside
   ```

4. To allow all users on the 192.168.3.0 network to access ASDM on the inside interface, enter the following command:

   ```
   PIX1(config)# http 192.168.3.0 255.255.255.0 inside
   ```

5. To disable ASDM, type **no http server enable** at the configure prompt. Doing so disables ASDM for all clients. To disable specific clients, type:

   ```
   no http <ip_address> <netmask> <interface>
   ```

Launching ASDM

ASDM management clients are only permitted from authorized IP addresses as specified previously by the *http* command. Before attempting to connect to the PIX via ASDM, verify that the management workstation meets all functional requirements previously detailed. In addition, verify that the ASDM management client is included in the *http* configuration statement on the PIX firewall. To verify that the client management station is configured for access to ASDM, use the *show http* command on the PIX device.

Now, complete this series of steps to connect to the PIX firewall with ASDM.

1. Launch a JDK 1.1.4 capable browser on an authorized ASDM management workstation and connect to the internal IP address of the PIX firewall using SSL.

2. A Security Alert window will appear upon connecting to ASDM the first time, as shown in Figure 10.1.

Figure 10.1 The Security Alert Window

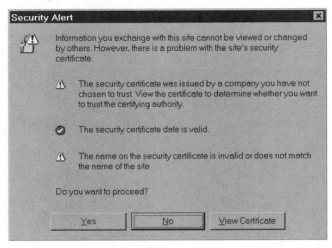

3. When you're prompted to proceed, choose to accept the SSL security certificate by clicking **Yes**.

4. After you accept the security certificate, an authentication prompt appears, as shown in Figure 10.2. When prompted for authentication credentials, do not enter a username unless you have already configured individual user accounts via the PIX CLI. Enter the enable password in the password field and click **OK**.

Figure 10.2 The ASDM Login Window

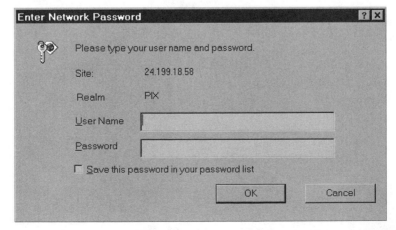

5. ASDM will display the window in Figure 10.3. This window permits you to either (1) download ASDM Launcher and Start ASDM, or (2) run ASDM as a Java Applet. The first option is a new feature of ASDM that allows you to run ASDM as an application from your desktop, while the second option is the traditional way of using the PIX Device Manager (PDM), ASDM's predecessor. Select the **download** option.

Figure 10.3 The Cisco ASDM Running Options

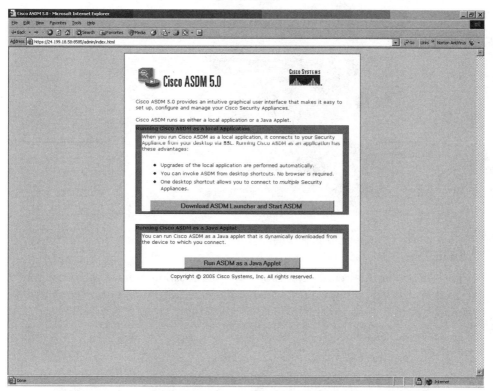

6. Select the **download** option and the ASDM download process will begin and the screen shown in Figure 10.4 will appear.

Figure 10.4 The ASDM Launcher

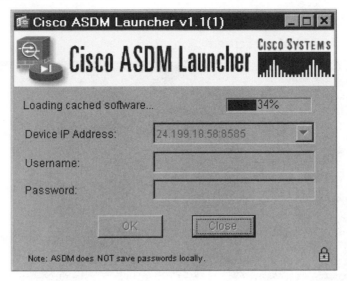

7. If you select the **Run ASDM as Java Applet option** from Figure 10.3, the Security Warning window will appear, as shown in Figure 10.5. Click **Yes**.

Figure 10.5 The Security Warning Window

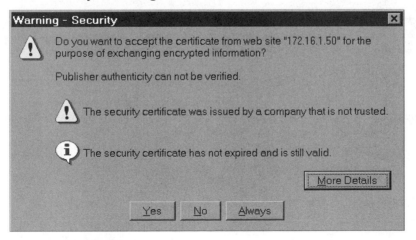

Both options result in the display of the ASDM main screen, as shown in Figure 10.6.

Figure 10.6 The ASDM Main Screen

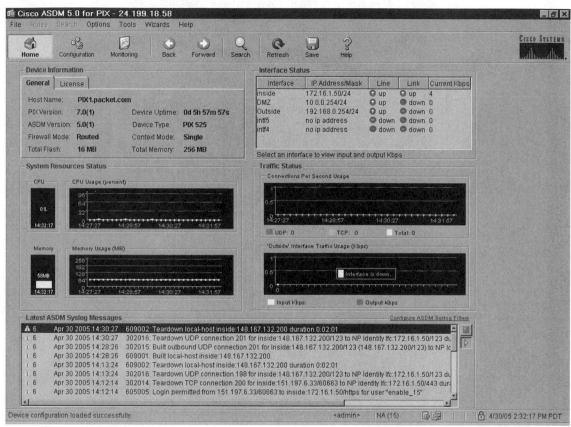

8. From the main ASDM screen, notice that there are pull-down menus, toolbar buttons, and some status panels. Click the pull-down menus and toolbar buttons to become familiar with the interface. The three main toolbar buttons are:

- **Home**   This screen is used to show a dashboard style status of the PIX.

- **Configuration**   This screen is used to configure the various aspects of the PIX.

- **Monitoring**   This screen is used to monitor the PIX firewall.

In addition to the main toolbar buttons available in ASDM, there are several useful pull-down menus. Figure 10.7 shows the options available from the File pull-down menu. You can write configuration changes to various locations such as a TFTP server or the PIX firewall, and view the running configuration, refresh the ASDM configuration, or reset the PIX to the factory default configuration. Resetting the PIX to the factory default configuration is a convenient way to erase any changes made to the configuration since it was installed and resort to an initial state of operation.

Figure 10.7 The File Pull-Down Menu Items

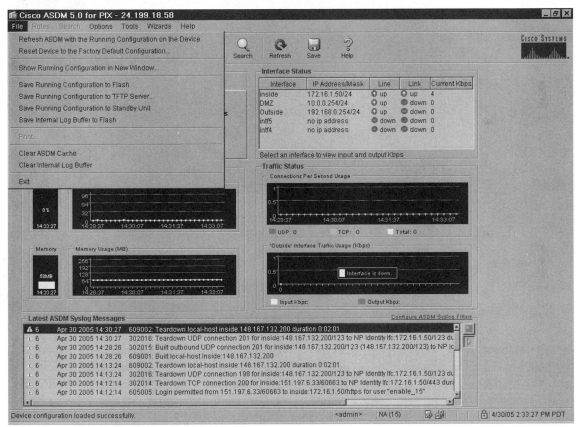

Figure 10.8 shows the options available from the Options pull-down menu.

Figure 10.8 The Options Pull-Down Menu Items

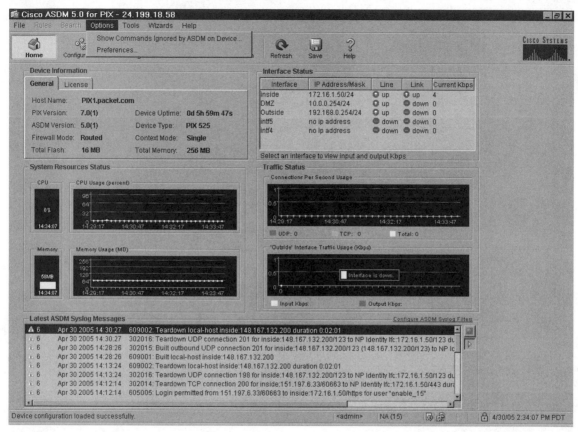

As discussed in the section titled "Adaptive Security Device Manager Limitations," ASDM does not support the complete command set of the CLI. In most cases, ASDM ignores unsupported commands, and they can remain in your configuration. Selecting the **Show Commands Ignored by ASDM on Device** item from the Options menu displays a list of commands that are ignored by ASDM in the current configuration, as shown in Figure 10.9.

Figure 10.9 The Commands Ignored by ASDM Window

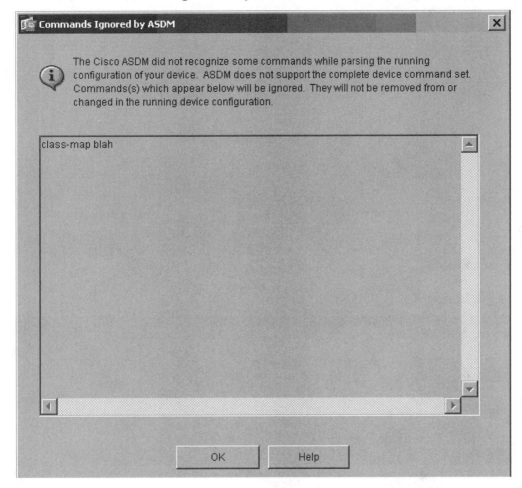

Selecting the Preferences menu item from the Options pull-down menu allows you to specify some options regarding your use of ASDM, as shown in Figure 10.10. For users who are unfamiliar with CLI commands, selecting the Preview commands before sending to the device option will show you the CLI commands that are generated when you configure various aspects of the PIX via ASDM. This preference can be used as a type of learning mode for CLI commands. The **Confirm before exiting from ASDM** option will ensure that you don't accidentally exit ASDM. The **Issue 'clear xlate' cmd when access-lists are deployed** option will implement a best practice regarding access-list modifications. Clearing the existing translations ensures that there are no stale translations. The **Alert about existence of the VPN Wizard when the VPN feature is accessed** will notify you that a VPN Wizard is available to help you configure VPNs on the PIX.

Figure 10.10 The ASDM Preferences Window

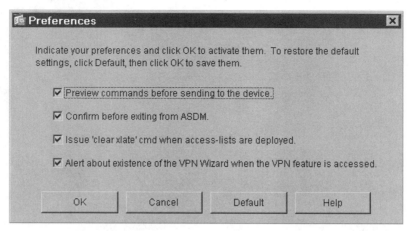

Figure 10.11 shows the options available from the Tools pull-down menu. The tools provide graphical windows from which you can configure aspects of the PIX.

Figure 10.11 The Tools Pull-Down Menu

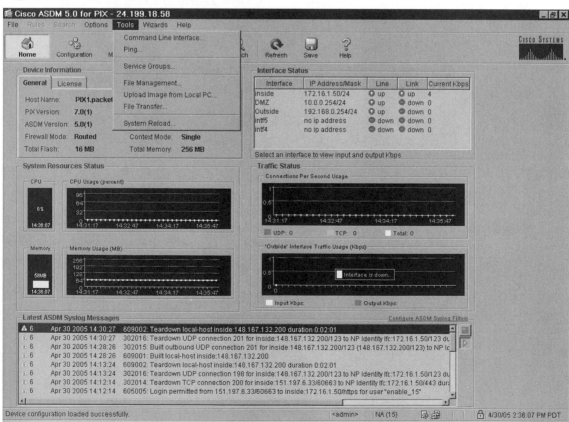

Selecting the **Command Line Interface** item from the **Tools** menu displays the window shown in Figure 10.12. This window allows you to enter a CLI command that will be sent to the PIX. The results are displayed in the **Response** panel within the window.

Figure 10.12 The ASDM Command Line Interface Window

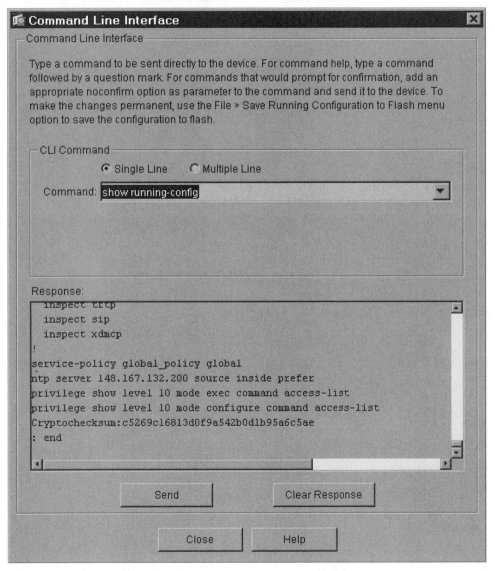

Selecting the **Ping** item from the **Tools** menu displays the window shown in Figure 10.13. This tool allows you to test basic network connectivity via the *ping* command.

Figure 10.13 The ASDM Ping Window

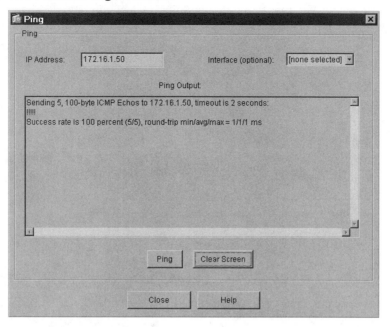

Selecting the **Manage Service Groups** item from the **Tools** menu provides the graphical interface to define TCP, UDP, and TCP–UDP services groups, as shown in Figure 10.14.

Figure 10.14 The ASDM Manage Service Groups Window

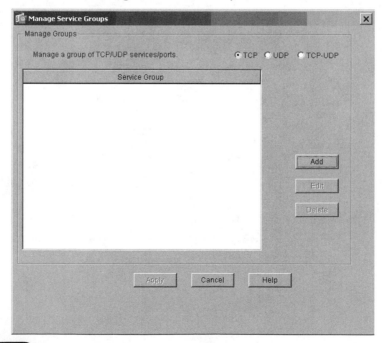

From the Manage Service Groups window, click **Add** to create a new service group. The Add Service Group window shown in Figure 10.15 appears. Create a new service group by specifying a name and description, selecting services or ports to include in the group, and click **OK**.

Figure 10.15 The ASDM Add Service Group Window

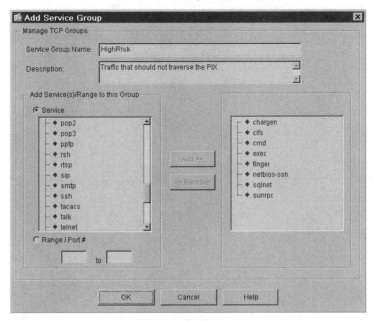

Selecting the **File Management** item from the **Tools** menu provides a Windows Explorer–like graphical interface to the PIX file system, as shown in Figure 10.16. You can manage the file system just as you would manage your local hard drive. You can create a new directory, and copy, cut, paste, delete, rename, and view files.

Figure 10.16 The ASDM File Management Window

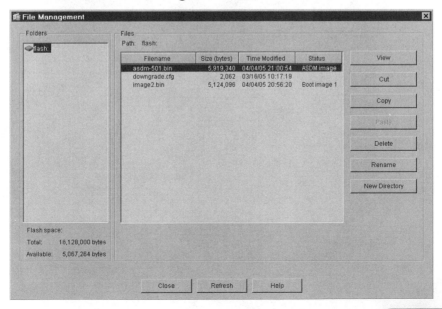

Selecting the **Upload Image from Local PC** item from the **Tools** menu provides a graphical interface for specifying a local ASDM or PIX image file to upload to the PIX, as shown in Figure 10.17.

Figure 10.17 The ASDM Upload Image from Local PC Window

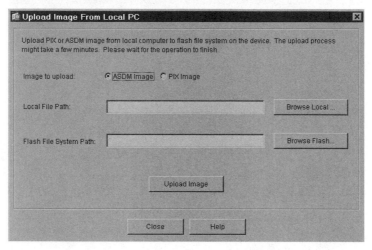

Selecting the **File Transfer** item from the **Tools** menu provides a graphical interface for specifying a file to transfer to or from the PIX, as shown in Figure 10.18. Within the window, you specify the source file, destination file, and the method of transfer (TFTP, FTP, HTTP, HTTPS).

Figure 10.18 The ASDM File Transfer Window

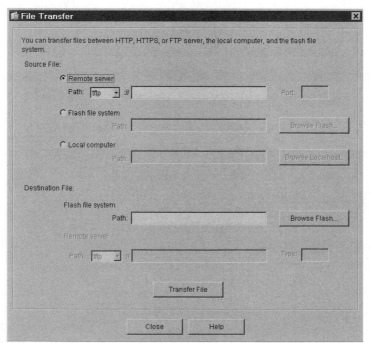

Selecting the System Reload item from the Tools menu provides a graphical interface for specifying an immediate or scheduled reload, as shown in Figure 10.19. You can also specify that the running configuration should be saved at the time of reload.

Figure 10.19 The ASDM System Reload Window

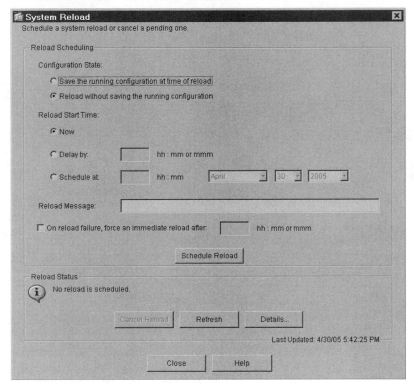

Figure 10.20 shows the options available from the Wizards pull-down menu. The Startup Wizard and VPN Wizard help you configure the PIX upon initial installation and configure VPN connections, respectively. Using the Startup Wizard is described in the section titled "Using the Startup Wizard." Using the VPN Wizard is described in Chapter 16.

Figure 10.20 The Wizards Pull-Down Menu

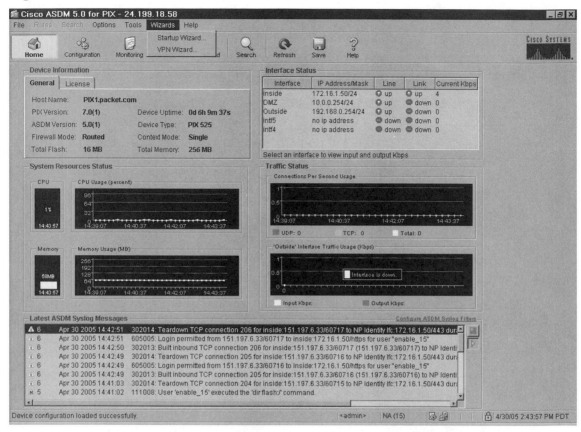

The final pull-down menu is Help. From Help, you will find links to detailed information regarding ASDM and the PIX firewall. Help features in ASDM are context sensitive.

Configuring the PIX Firewall Using ASDM

After successfully installing ASDM, connect to the PIX firewall via ASDM and begin configuring a specific security policy appropriate for your company. In this section, we discuss all the main toolbar buttons available in ASDM and work through several exercises typical of PIX firewall implementations, such as:

- Using the Startup Wizard
- Configuring firewall system properties
- Implementing NAT
- Allowing inbound traffic from external sources
- Configuring VPNs

Using the Startup Wizard

ASDM includes wizards to assist firewall administrators in the initial setup and ongoing maintenance of the PIX firewall. One of these wizards, the Startup Wizard, guides you through typical setup configuration prompts such as interface settings, passwords, auto-update information, and others. The Startup Wizard is an excellent tool to use initially and for regular configuration changes; it extracts the current configuration and provides these PIX attributes to the administrator automatically. Therefore, the Startup Wizard process will not overwrite the current PIX firewall configuration.

This section provides a step-by-step exercise through the Startup Wizard prompts.

1. To access the Startup Wizard, select **Startup Wizard** from the **Wizards** menu. The Startup Wizard Welcome window appears, as shown in Figure 10.21.

Figure 10.21 The ASDM Startup Wizard Welcome Screen

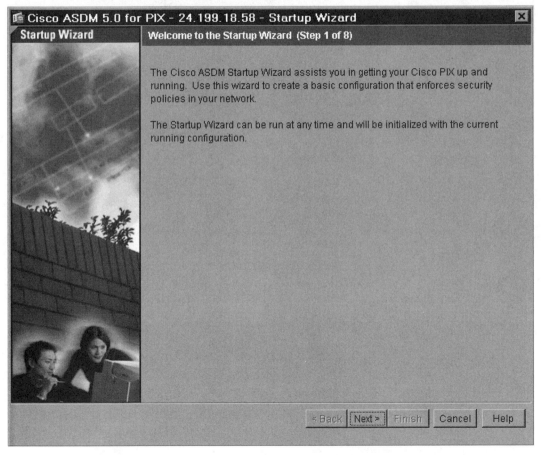

2. To proceed with the wizard, click **Next**. The Basic Configuration window appears, as shown in Figure 10.22. This window allows you to configure the PIX hostname and domain name, as well as the Enable password.

Figure 10.22 The ASDM Startup Wizard Basic Configuration Screen

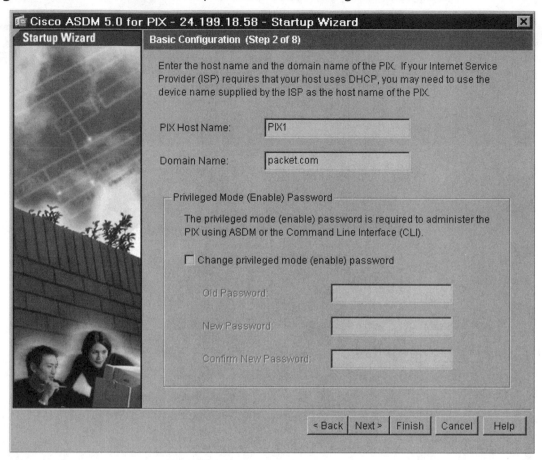

3. To change any of the settings, simply type a new hostname or domain name or click the
    Change Enable Password check box and enter new authentication credentials. To
    continue with the wizard, click **Next**. The Outside Interface Configuration window
    appears (see Figure 10.23).

Figure 10.23 The ASDM Startup Wizard Outside Interface Configuration Screen

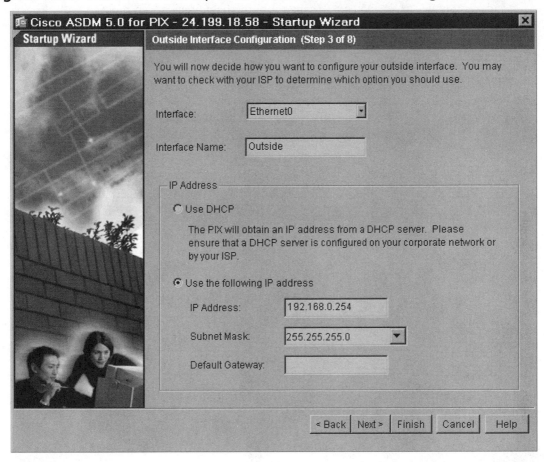

4. From the Outside Interface Configuration window, you can select the speed of the outside interface and determine how to address the outside interface. From the wizard, you can choose to automatically configure the interface via PPPoE. You can also select DHCP to automatically determine the address of the outside interface.

5. To statically configure the outside interface, select **Static IP Address** and provide the IP address, subnet mask, and default gateway in the field provided. To proceed with the wizard, click **Next** to set up auto-update functionality. The Other Interfaces Configuration window appears (see Figure 10.24).

Figure 10.24 The ASDM Startup Wizard Other Interfaces Configuration Screen

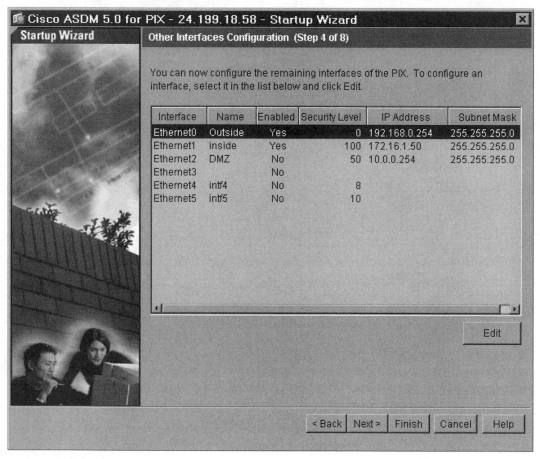

6. From the Other Interfaces Configuration window, you can configure the remaining PIX firewall interfaces. Select an interface from the list in the **Other Interfaces Configuration** window and click **Edit** to change interface parameters. Click **Next** to proceed to the DHCP Server Configuration window, as shown in Figure 10.25.

Figure 10.25 The ASDM Startup Wizard DHCP Server Screen

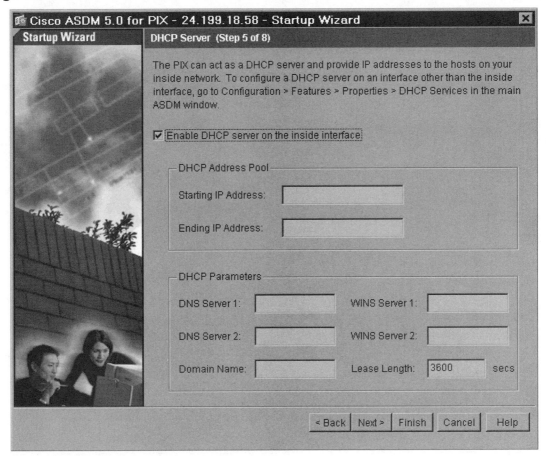

7. The PIX firewall can act as a DHCP server for internal clients, which is quite useful in small office/home office (SOHO) environments. From the DHCP Server Configuration window, you can establish a basic DHCP server configuration. To start DHCP server operations on the firewall, click **Enable DHCP server on the inside interface** and enter a DHCP address range in the space provided. You can also alter the DHCP lease length time from the wizard as well. When finished, click **Next**. The Address Translation (NAT/PAT) window is displayed, as shown in Figure 10.26.

Figure 10.26 The ASDM Startup Wizard Address Translation (NAT/PAT) Screen

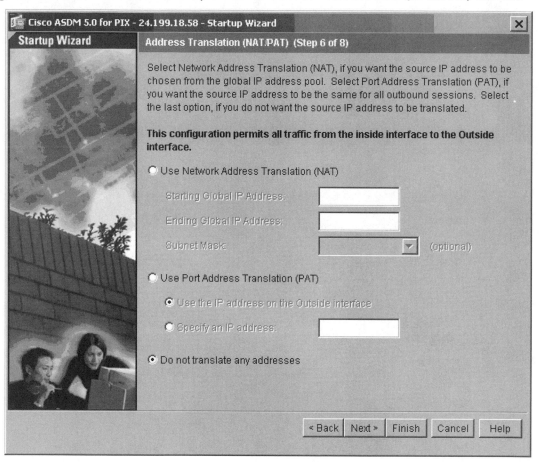

8. From this window, you can configure the different types of address translation available on the PIX firewall. To configure PAT, click **Use Port Address Translation (PAT)** and either use the outside interface as the PAT address or enter a specific IP address in the space provided. If you would like to configure NAT, click **Use Network Address Translation (NAT)** and enter the appropriate global address parameters. Finally, to turn NAT off, click **Do not translate any addresses**. When you're finished, click **Next**. The Administrative Access window appears, as shown in Figure 10.27.

Figure 10.27 The ASDM Startup Wizard Administrative Access Screen

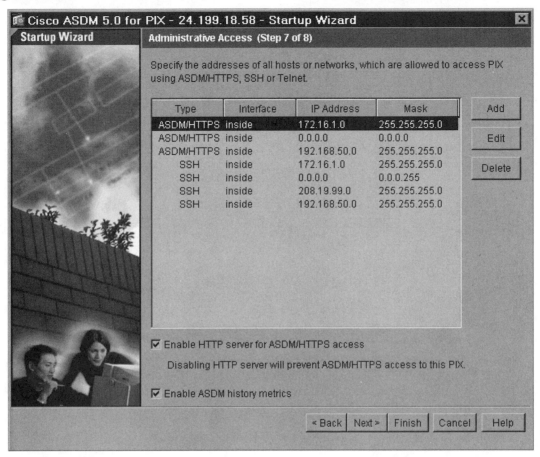

9. From this window, you can configure which addresses are allowed to access the PIX using the various access modes, including ASDM/HTTPS, SSH, or Telnet. This window also provides you the options of enabling the HTTP server for ASDM access and enabling ASDM history metrics. When finished, click **Next**. A screen appears to signify that the wizard is complete, as shown in Figure 10.28.

Figure 10.28 The ASDM Startup Wizard Administrative Access Screen

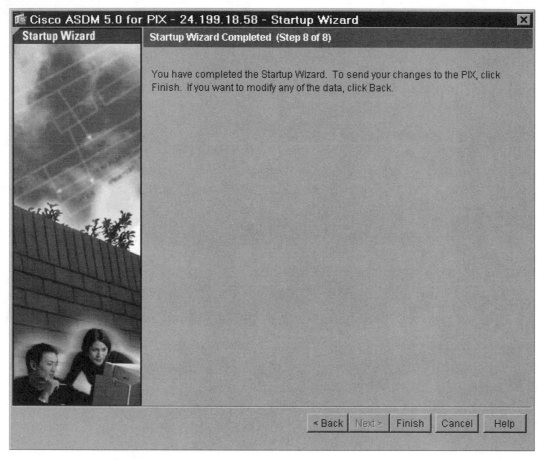

10. Click **Finish** to exit the wizard, save the changes made during the wizard process, and return to the ASDM window. After you complete the wizard, ASDM sends the updated configurations to the PIX firewall and refreshes the PIX configuration visible via the ASDM interface. After making changes to the PIX firewall, you must click **Save** to save updated configurations to the PIX flash memory. If you fail to do so, the new configurations will not be available after a reboot.

Configuring System Properties

Although the Startup Wizard is a convenient and helpful ASDM utility, configuring more granular and specific properties and rules on the PIX firewall requires the use of the toolbar buttons in the main ASDM window.

1. To configure the System Properties, click on the **Configure** toolbar button. This displays the window shown in Figure 10.29.

Figure 10.29 The ASDM Configuration Window

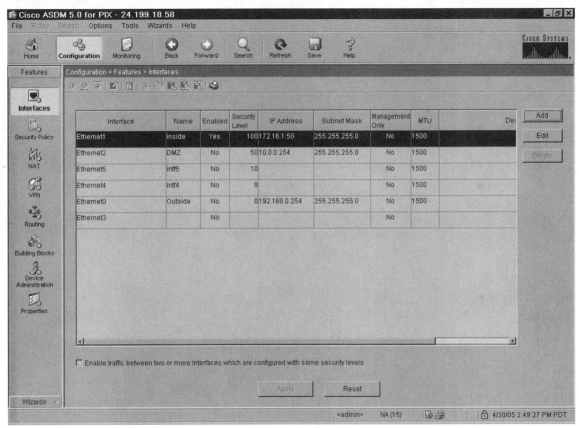

2. On the left side of the screen, click **Properties**. The window shown in Figure 10.30 appears.

Figure 10.30 The ASDM Configuration – Properties Window

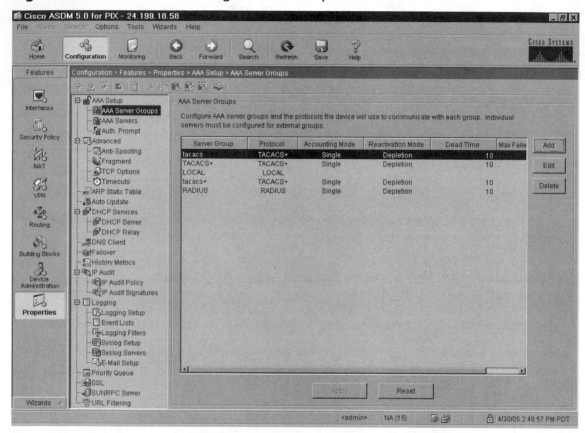

From this window, you can administer many important PIX system properties, as shown in the explorer panel on the left side of the window. The configurable properties include:

- AAA Setup
- Advanced
- ARP Static Table
- Auto Update
- DHCP Services
- DNS Client
- Failover
- History Metrics
- IP Audit
- Logging

- Priority Queue

- SSL

- SUNRPC Server

- URL Filtering

The AAA Menu

The AAA Setup menu item facilitates the configuration of Cisco authentication, authorization, and accounting variables through the AAA Server Groups, AAA Servers, and Auth. Prompt subcategories. Click each of these submenu items to view the options contained therein. The **AAA Server Groups Configuration** window is shown in Figure 10.31. Three AAA server groups are predefined and visible from the AAA Server Groups subcategory: TACACS+, RADIUS, and LOCAL. These default groups can be used in your configuration, or you can add new groups by clicking **Add**. New groups can be either RADIUS or TACACS+ based.

Figure 10.31 The ASDM AAA Server Groups Configuration Screen

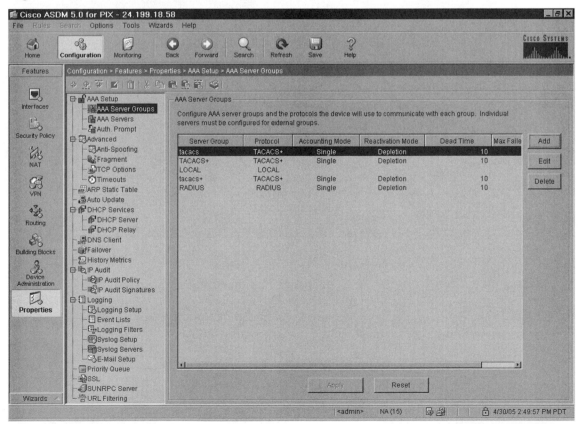

Clicking on the **AAA Servers** submenu item within the explorer pane displays the AAA Servers Configuration window shown in Figure 10.32. This window displays the AAA servers that have been defined on the PIX. To add a new AAA server, click **Add**, and specify the server group to which it should belong, the PIX interface where it resides, the IP address, the timeout (in seconds), and the appropriate AAA protocol (e.g., TACACS+, RADIUS) parameters.

Figure 10.32 The ASDM AAA Server Groups Configuration Screen

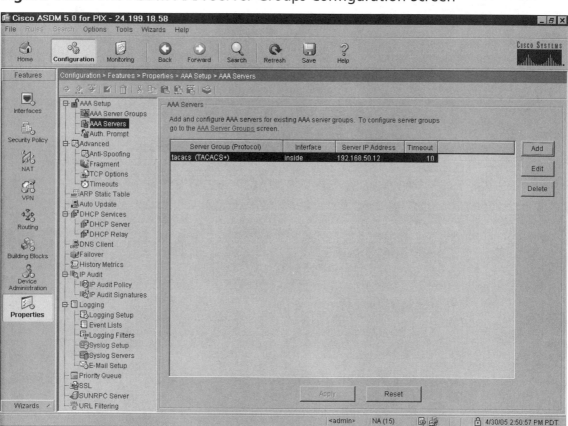

Clicking on the **Auth Prompt** submenu item within the explorer pane displays the Auth Prompt Configuration window shown in Figure 10.33. This window allows you to specify the messages that should be displayed when the user is prompted for the username and password, when the user authentication succeeds, and when the user authentication fails.

Figure 10.33 The ASDM Auth Prompt Configuration Screen

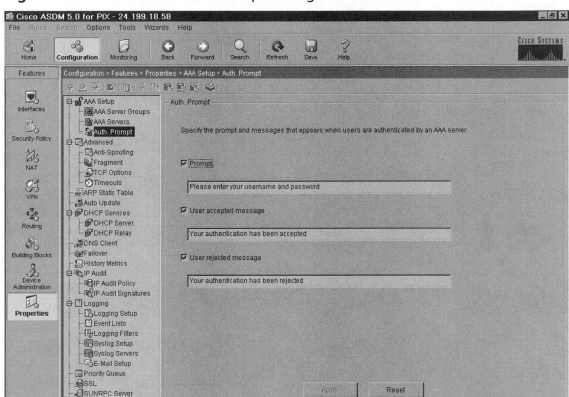

The Advanced Menu

The Advanced menu provides you with the ability to specify some advanced TCP/IP protocol security countermeasures, including anti-spoofing, fragment parameters, TCP option parameters, and timeout parameters.

Clicking on the **Anti-Spoofing** submenu item within the explorer pane displays the Anti-Spoofing Configuration window shown in Figure 10.34. This window allows you to enable Unicast Reverse Path Forwarding on the PIX interfaces, which guards against IP spoofing (a packet uses an incorrect source IP address to obscure its true source). The anti-spoofing protection is accomplished by ensuring that all packets have a source IP address that matches the correct source interface according to the PIX routing table. To enable Unicast RPF on an interface, simply highlight the interface and click **Enable**.

Figure 10.34 The ASDM Anti-Spoofing Configuration Screen

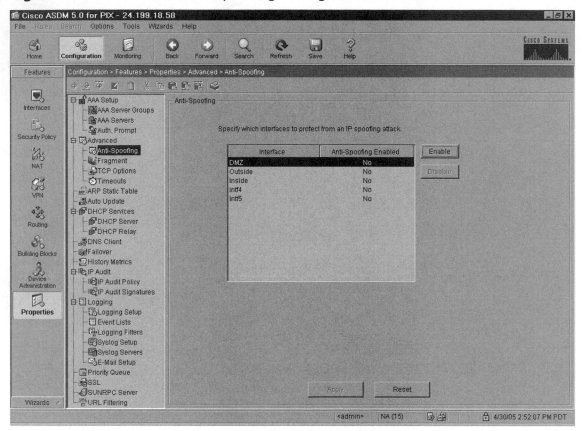

Clicking on the **Fragment** submenu item within the explorer pane displays the Fragment Configuration window shown in Figure 10.35. This window allows you to configure the IP fragment database on each PIX interface to improve compatibility with NFS. The fragment database consists of the following parameters for each interface:

- **Size**   The maximum number of fragments that can be awaiting reassembly (default 200).

- **Chain length**   The maximum number of fragments that a full packet can be fragmented into (default 24).

- **Timeout**   The maximum number of seconds to wait for an entire fragmented packet to arrive (default 5).

To change any of these settings for an interface, simply highlight the interface and click **Edit**.

Figure 10.35 The ASDM Fragment Configuration Screen

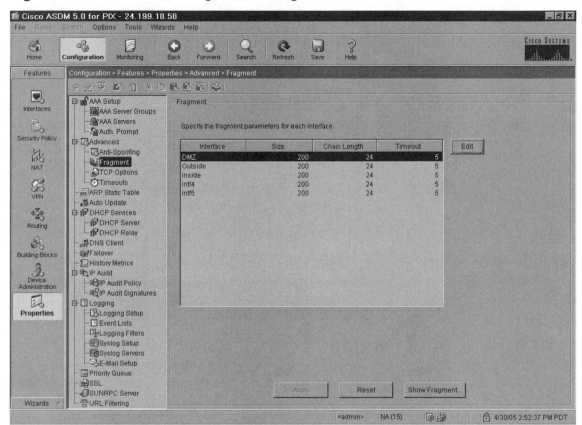

Clicking on the **TCP Options** submenu item within the explorer pane displays the TCP Options Configuration window shown in Figure 10.36. This window allows you to set options for TCP parameters, including:

- **Force Maximum Segment Size for TCP Proxy**   Sets the *maximum* value for maximum TCP segment size in bytes. If either the client or server attempts to set the maximum segment size to a value *greater* than the parameter, the PIX will override it and insert the value set here. To disable this feature, set the size to 0 bytes.

- **Force Minimum Segment Size for TCP Proxy**   Sets the minimum value for maximum TCP segment size in bytes. If either the client or server attempts to set the maximum segment size to a value *less* than the parameter, the PIX will override it and insert the value set here. This feature is disabled by default (i.e., set to 0 bytes).

- **Force TCP Connection to Linger in TIME_WAIT State for at Least 15 Seconds**   This feature enables you to configure the PIX to wait for an additional

15 seconds after the final normal TCP connection close. This can be useful for applications that do a quick release TCP connection close, because the PIX may release the connection before one of the communicating hosts has a chance to close its side of the connection. This could degrade the performance of the host.

- **Reset Inbound** Configures the PIX to send TCP resets for all TCP sessions that are attempting to traverse the security appliance and are denied based on access-lists. When this option is not selected, the PIX silently discards the packets of all such sessions.

- **Reset Outside** Configures the PIX to send TCP resets for all TCP sessions that arrive at the least secure interface or terminate at the least secure interface, and are denied based on access-lists. When this option is not selected, the PIX silently discards the packets of all such sessions.

Figure 10.36 The ASDM TCP Options Configuration Screen

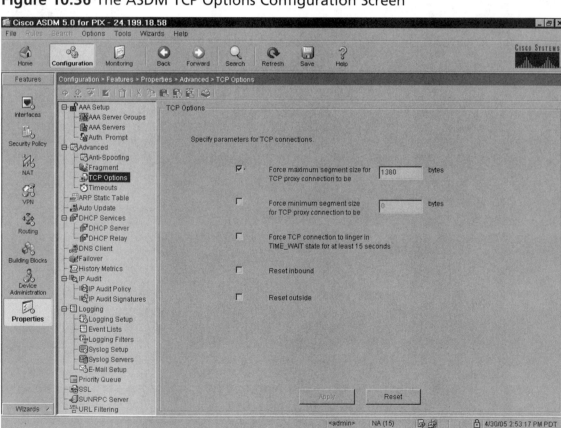

Clicking on the **Timeouts** submenu item within the explorer pane displays the Timeouts Configuration window shown in Figure 10.37. This window allows you set the timeout durations for use with the PIX. All durations are displayed in the format *hh:mm:ss*. You can set the idle time for the connection and translation slots of various protocols. If the slot has not been used for the idle time specified, the resource is returned to the free pool. TCP connection slots are freed approximately 60 seconds after a normal connection close sequence.

Figure 10.37 The ASDM Timeouts Configuration Screen

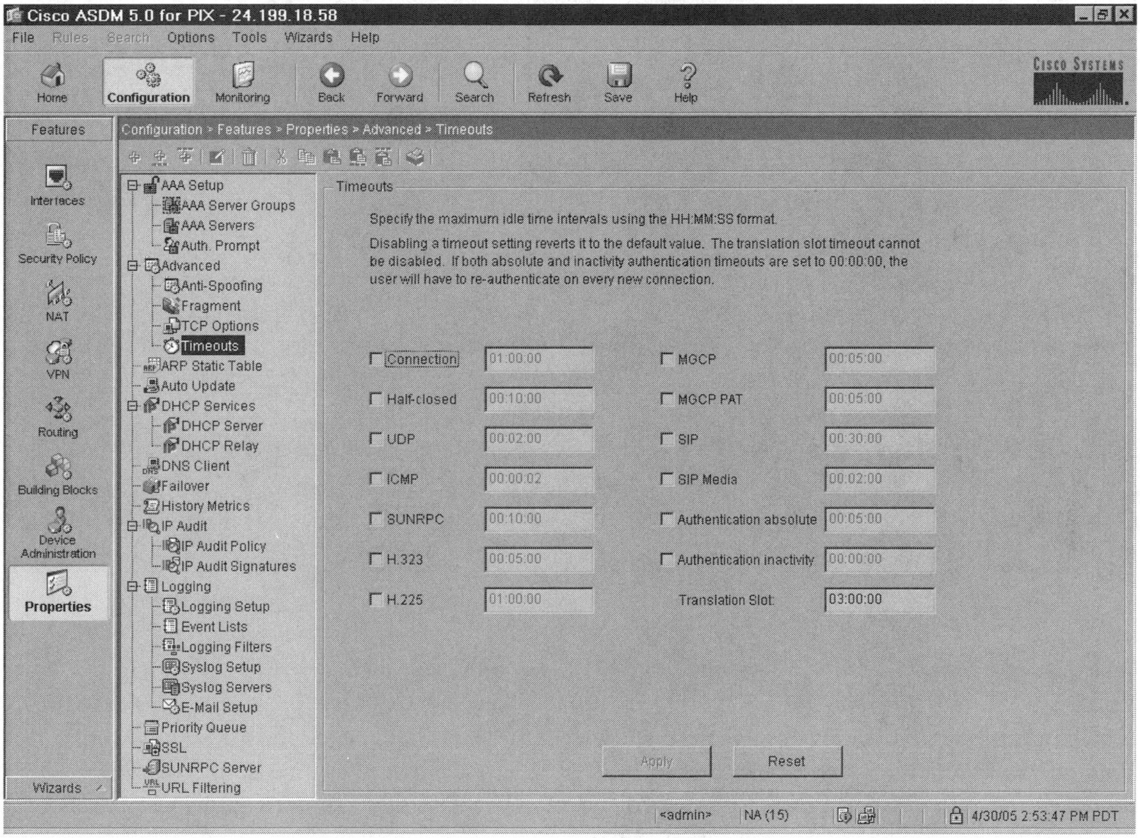

The ARP Static Table Menu

Clicking on the **ARP Static Table** menu item within the explorer pane displays the ARP Static Table Configuration window shown in Figure 10.38. This window allows you to add static ARP entries that map a MAC address to an IP address for a given interface.

Figure 10.38 The ASDM ARP Static Table Configuration Screen

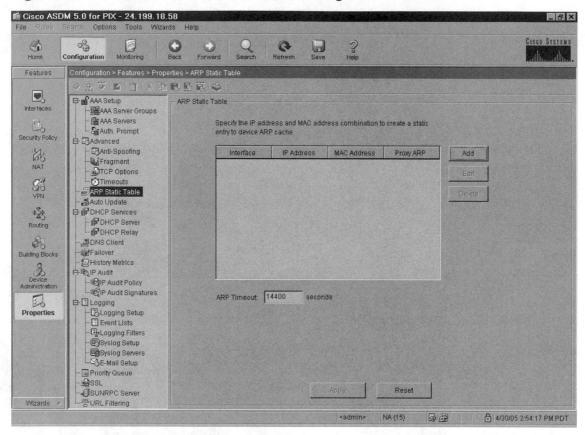

The Auto Update Menu

Clicking on the **Auto Update** submenu item within the explorer pane displays the Auto Update Configuration window shown in Figure 10.39. This window allows you to configure the PIX to be managed remotely from a server that supports Auto Update. This allows you to apply configuration changes to the PIX and receive software updates from a remote location. The automated update capability greatly simplifies firewall administration, especially in large corporate environments with multiple PIX firewalls.

Figure 10.39 The ASDM Auto Update Configuration Screen

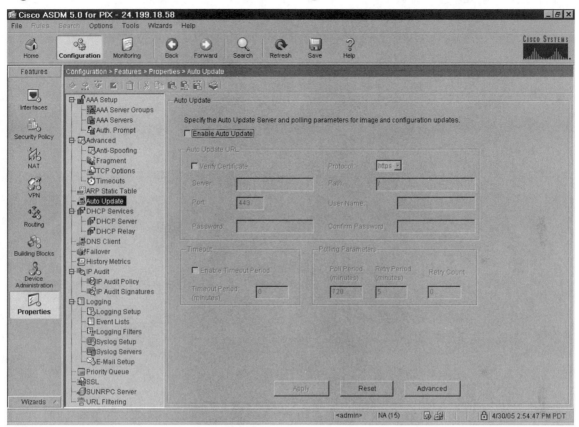

To use the automatic update feature, you must first configure a Web server to store the configuration files and provide update services. To enable automatic updates, click the **Enable Auto Update** check box. Several attributes must be configured before auto-update will function properly. From the Auto Update URL section of the screen, determine the server address, port, password, and protocol. Additionally, you must specify the path to the configuration file on the server. Other variables such as server timeout and polling parameters can also be configured from this screen.

The DHCP Services Menu

Clicking on the **DHCP Server** submenu item within the explorer pane displays the DHCP Server Configuration window shown in Figure 10.40. This window allows you to configure the PIX interfaces as DHCP servers. This is extremely beneficial in small office and home environments where access to additional server equipment could be limited. You can configure only one DHCP server per interface, and you cannot configure a DHCP server on an interface that has DHCP Relay configured on it.

Figure 10.40 The ASDM DHCP Server Configuration Screen

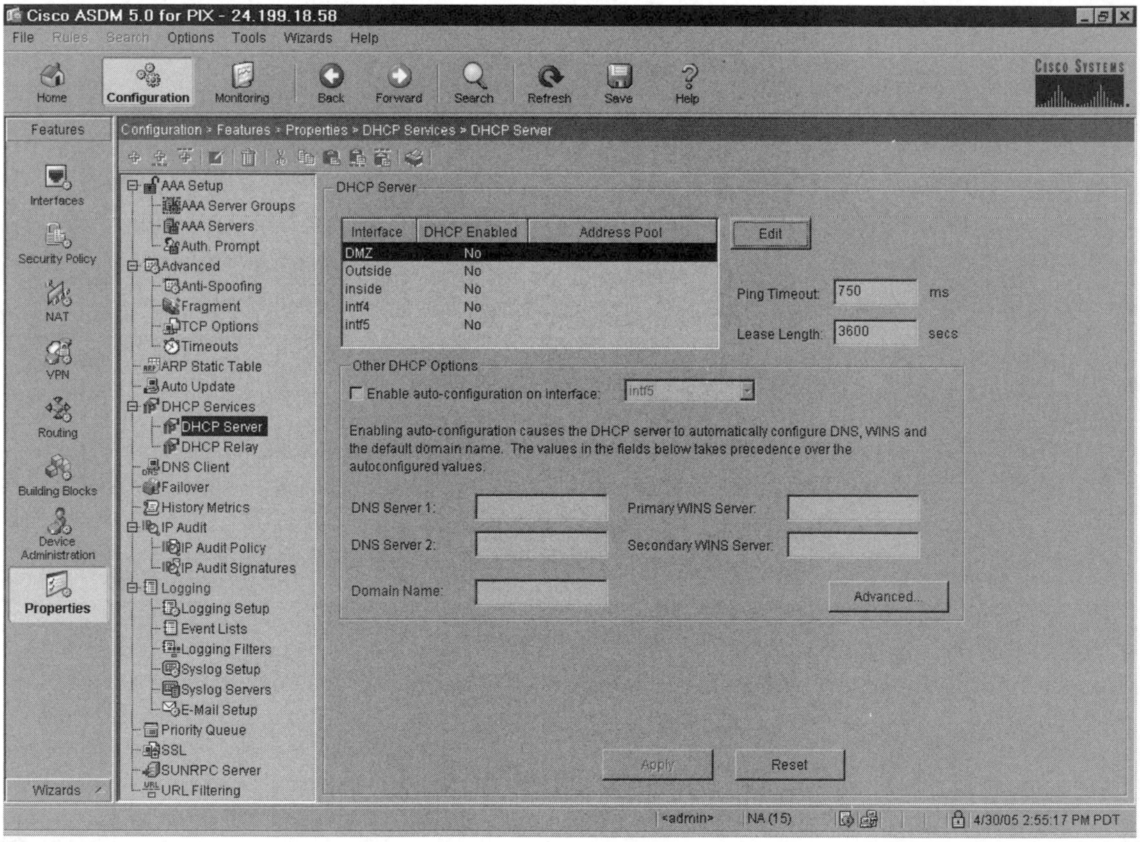

Enable DHCP services on the PIX firewall by highlighting the desired interface and clicking **Edit**. In the dialog box that appears, click the **Enable DHCP server** check box, specify the DHCP address pool, and click **OK**. From the main screen, you can specify **Other DHCP Options** such as DNS Servers, Domain Name, and WINS Servers. You can also specify the DHCP Lease Length and Ping Timeout values. Clicking **Advanced** lets you configure DHCP option parameters. You can use these to provide additional information to DHCP clients. For example, DHCP option 150 and DHCP option 66 provide TFTP server information to Cisco IP Phones and Cisco IOS routers.

Clicking on the **DHCP Relay** submenu item within the explorer pane displays the DHCP Relay Configuration window shown in Figure 10.41. This window allows you to configure DHCP relay services on the PIX. This passes DHCP requests received on one interface to a DHCP server located behind a different interface. To configure DHCP relay, you need to specify at least one DHCP relay server and then enable a DHCP relay agent on the interface receiving DHCP requests.

Figure 10.41 The ASDM DHCP Relay Configuration Screen

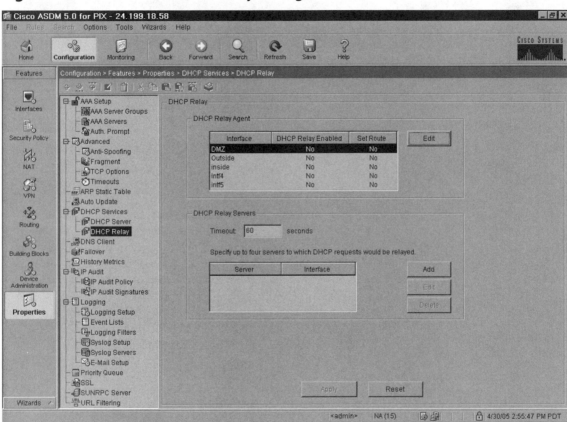

To configure DHCP relay, you first need to specify at least one DHCP relay server, and then enable a DHCP relay agent on the interface receiving DHCP requests. To specify a DHCP server, click **Add** in the **DHCP Relay Servers** panel. In the dialog box that appears, enter the IP address, specify the interface that should be used to reach the server, and then click **OK**. To enable DHCP relay on an interface, highlight the desired interface in the **DHCP Relay Agent** panel, and click **Edit**. In the dialog box that appears, check the **Enable DHCP Relay Agent** check box. From this box, you can also configure the PIX to modify the default router parameter being communicated by the DHCP server to be the PIX interface address. Click **OK**.

The DNS Client Menu

Clicking on the **DNS Client** submenu item within the explorer pane displays the DNS Client Configuration window shown in Figure 10.42. This window allows you to specify DNS servers for the PIX to use to resolve names to IP addresses.

Figure 10.42 The ASDM DNS Client Configuration Screen

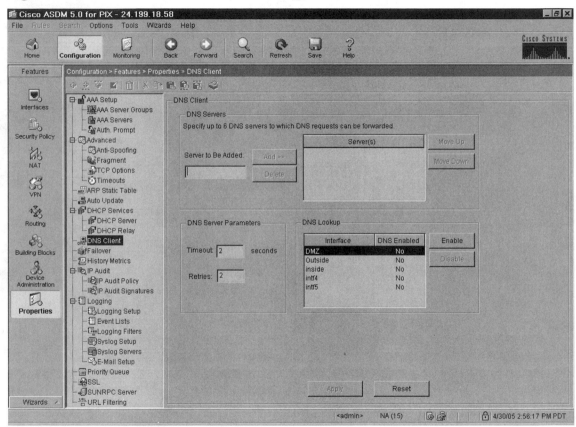

The Failover Menu

Clicking on the **Failover** submenu item within the explorer pane displays the Failover Configuration window shown in Figure 10.43. This window contains the tabs where you can configure Active/Standby failover in single context mode. For detailed information regarding failover, refer to Chapter 17, "Configuring Failover."

You can enable failover for the PIX from the **Setup** tab within the window, as shown in Figure 10.43. You also specify the failover link, the state link (if using stateful failover), and the LAN failover parameters (if using LAN failover instead of serial cable failover).

Figure 10.43 The ASDM Failover (Setup) Configuration Screen

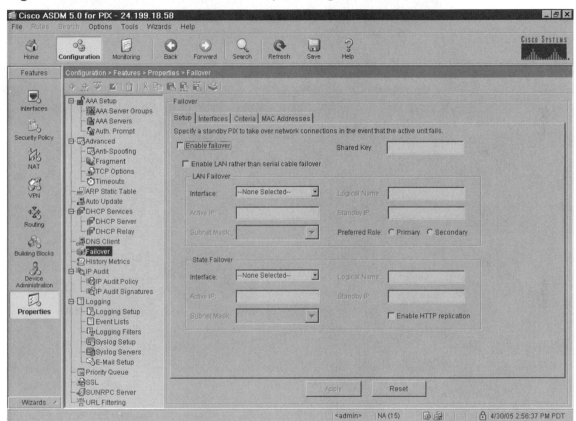

Clicking on the **Interfaces** tab brings up the window shown in Figure 10.44. Use this tab to define the standby IP address for each interface on the security appliance and to specify whether the status of the interface should be monitored. Simply highlight the desired interface, click **Edit**, and provide the standby IP address.

Figure 10.44 The ASDM Failover (Interfaces) Configuration Screen

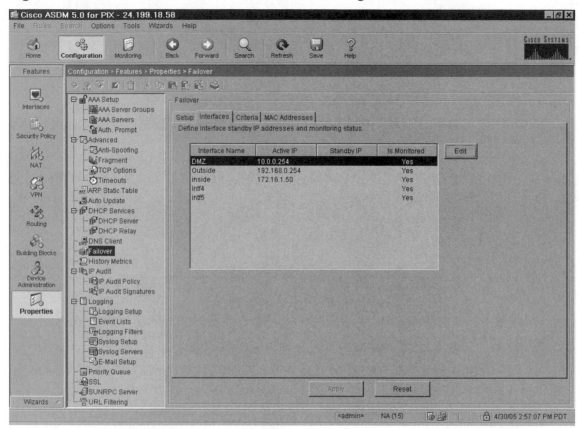

Clicking on the **Criteria** tab brings up the window shown in Figure 10.45. Use this tab to define criteria for failover, such as how many interfaces must fail and how long to wait between polls.

Figure 10.45 The ASDM Failover (Criteria) Configuration Screen

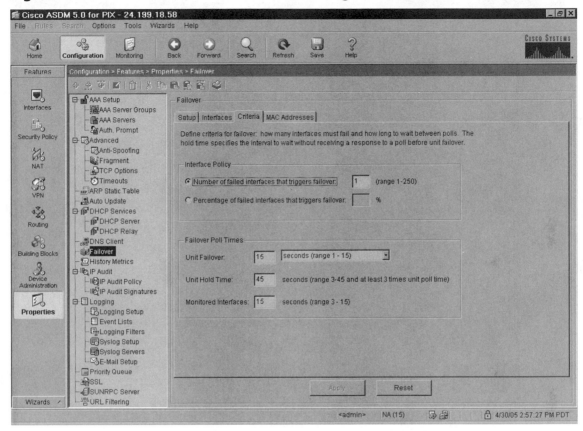

Clicking on the **MAC Addresses** tab brings up the window shown in Figure 10.46. Use this tab to configure the virtual MAC addresses for the interfaces in an Active/Standby failover pair.

Figure 10.46 The ASDM Failover (MAC Addresses) Configuration Screen

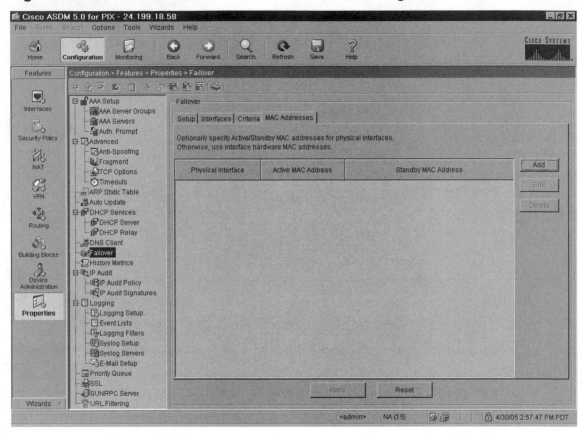

The History Metrics Category

Clicking on the **History Metrics** submenu item within the explorer pane displays the History Metrics window shown in Figure 10.47. This window allows you to configure the PIX to keep a history of various statistics that can be displayed by ASDM on any graph or table. If you do not enable history metrics, you can only monitor statistics in real time. Enabling history metrics lets you view statistics graphs from the last 10 minutes, 60 minutes, 12 hours, and 5 days.

Figure 10.47 The ASDM History Metrics Configuration Screen

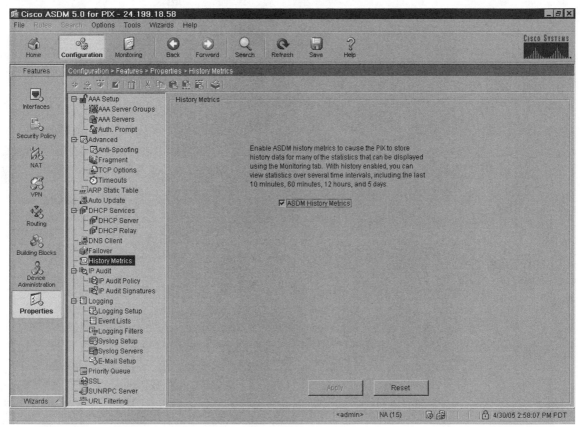

The IP Audit Menu

Clicking on the **IP Audit Policy** submenu item within the explorer pane displays the IP Audit Policy window shown in Figure 10.48. This window allows you to add attack and informational audit policies and assign them to interfaces. The attack policy determines the action to take with packets that match an attack signature, while the informational policy determines the action to take with packets that match an informational signature (e.g., port scan). For detailed information regarding the configuration of Intrusion Detection and Attack Management, refer to Chapter 12, "Filtering, Intrusion Detection, and Attack Management."

Figure 10.48 The ASDM IP Audit Policy Configuration Screen

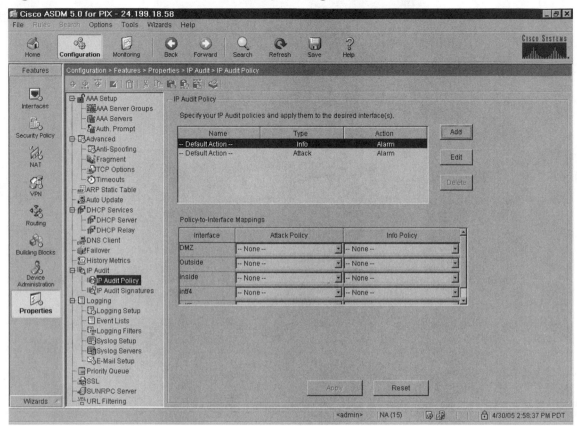

Clicking on the **IP Audit Signatures** submenu item within the explorer pane displays the IP Audit Signatures window shown in Figure 10.49. This window allows you to disable audit signatures. You might want to disable a signature if legitimate traffic continually matches a signature, and you are willing to risk disabling the signature to avoid large numbers of alarms. For detailed information regarding the configuration of Intrusion Detection and Attack Management, refer to Chapter 12.

Figure 10.49 The ASDM IP Audit Signatures Configuration Screen

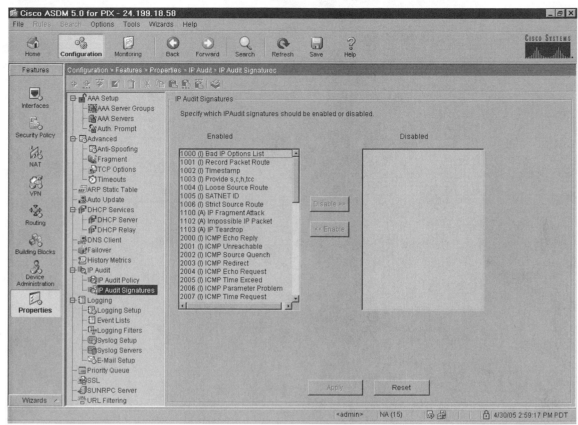

The Logging Menu

Clicking on the **Logging Setup** submenu item within the explorer pane displays the Logging Setup window shown in Figure 10.50. This window allows you enable system logging and configure logging parameters. For detailed information regarding the configuration of Logging, refer to Chapter 15.

Figure 10.50 The ASDM Logging Setup Configuration Screen

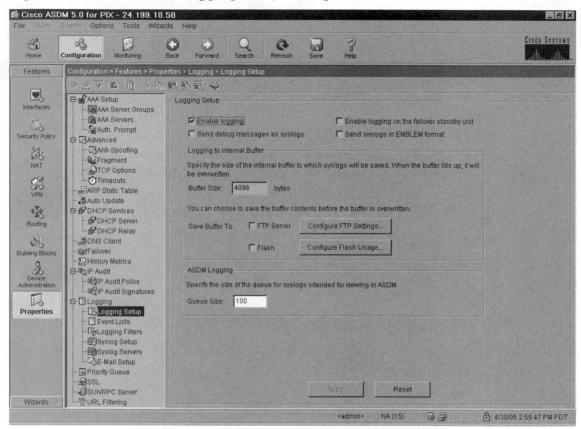

Clicking on the **Event Lists** submenu item within the explorer pane displays the Event Lists window shown in Figure 10.51. This window allows you to define a set of syslog messages to filter for transmission to a logging destination. To place each window in context, the previous window (Logging Setup) allows you to enable logging and set up logging parameters. This window (Event Lists) allows you to configure syslog filters that can be sent to a logging destination, and the next window (Logging Filters) allows you to specify a logging destination (e.g., buffer, console, syslog server) for event lists. For detailed information regarding the configuration of Logging, refer to Chapter 15.

Figure 10.51 The ASDM Event Lists Configuration Screen

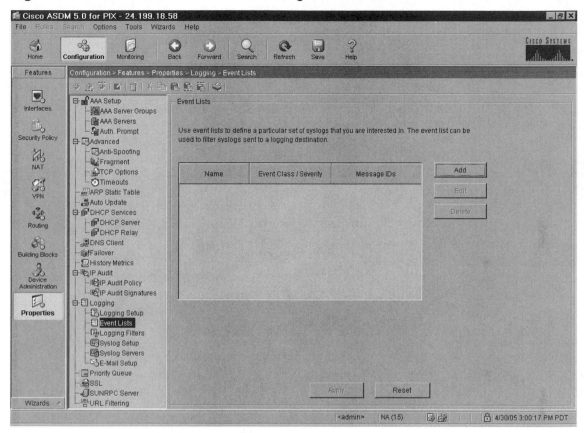

Clicking on the **Logging Filters** submenu item within the explorer pane displays the Logging Filters window shown in Figure 10.52. This window allows you to configure a logging destination for event lists (syslog filters) that have been configured using the previous window (Event Lists). The potential destinations include:

- Internal buffer
- Console
- Telnet sessions
- Syslog servers
- SNMP trap
- E-mail
- ASDM

For detailed information regarding the configuration of Logging, refer to Chapter 15.

Figure 10.52 The ASDM Logging Filters Configuration Screen

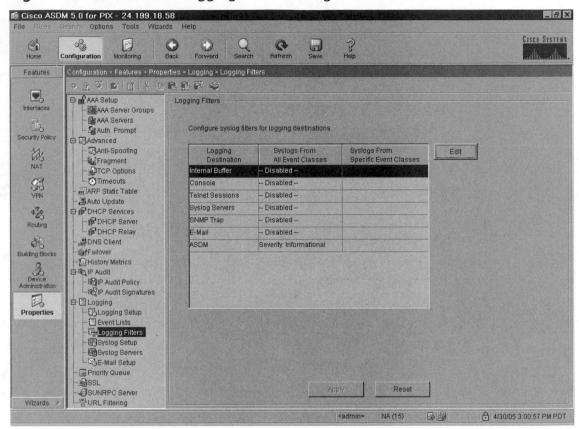

Clicking on the **Syslog Setup** submenu item within the explorer pane displays the Syslog Setup window shown in Figure 10.53. This window allows you to configure syslog parameters, including the facility code to include in syslogs, whether to include timestamps in syslogs, view syslog ID levels, modify syslog ID levels, and suppress syslog messages. For detailed information regarding the configuration of Logging, refer to Chapter 15.

Figure 10.53 The ASDM Syslog Setup Configuration Screen

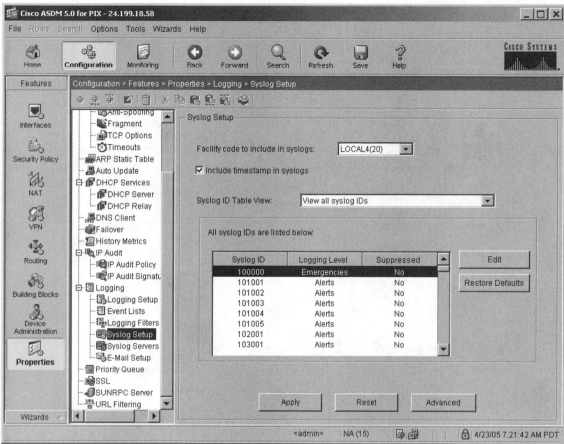

Clicking on the **Syslog Servers** submenu item within the explorer pane displays the Syslog Servers window shown in Figure 10.54. This window allows you to specify the syslog servers to which the security appliance will send syslog messages. To make use of the syslog server(s) you define, you must enable logging using the **Logging Setup** window (Figure 10.49) and set up the appropriate filters for destinations using the **Logging Filters** window (Figure 10.51). For detailed information regarding the configuration of Logging, refer to Chapter 15.

Figure 10.54 The ASDM Syslog Servers Configuration Screen

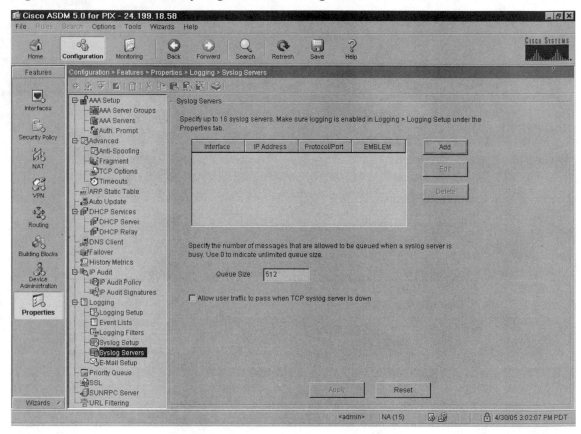

Clicking on the E-Mail Setup submenu item within the explorer pane displays the E-Mail Setup window shown in Figure 10.55. This window allows you to set up a source e-mail address and a list of recipients for specified syslogs to be sent as e-mails. For detailed information regarding the configuration of Logging, refer to Chapter 15.

Figure 10.55 The ASDM E-Mail Setup Configuration Screen

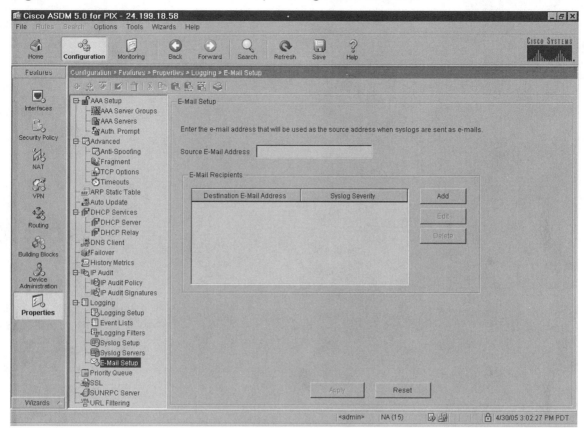

The Priority Queue Category

Clicking on the **Priority Queue** submenu item within the explorer pane displays the Priority Queue window shown in Figure 10.56. This window shows the priority queue parameters on each configured interface. It is disabled by default.

Figure 10.56 The ASDM Priority Queue Configuration Screen

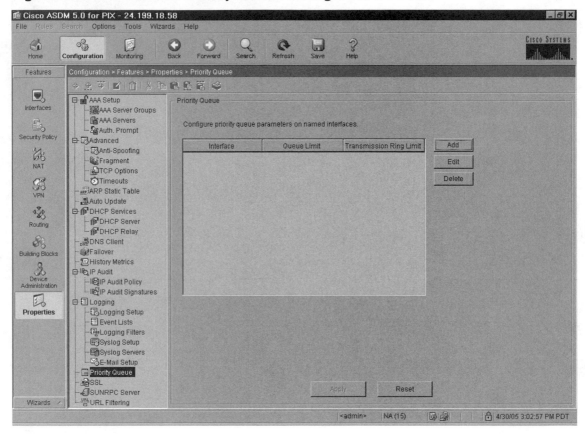

The SSL Category

Clicking on the **SSL** submenu item within the explorer pane displays the SSL window shown in Figure 10.57. This window allows you to configure SSL client versions, server versions, and encryption algorithms for use with ASDM and WebVPN sessions.

Figure 10.57 The ASDM SSL Configuration Screen

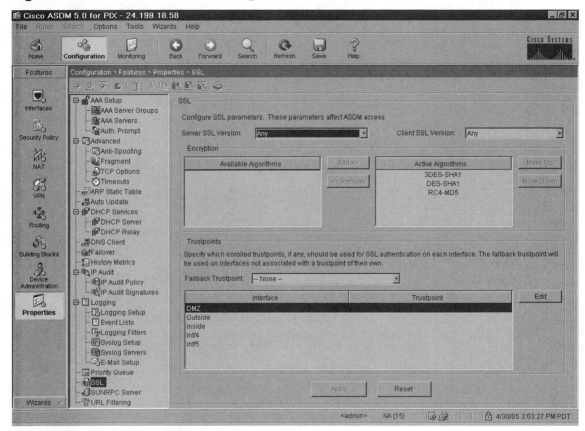

The SunRPC Server Category

Clicking on the **SunRPC Server** submenu item within the explorer pane displays the SunRPC Server window shown in Figure 10.58. This window shows what SunRPC services are allowed to traverse the security appliance and their specific timeout, on a per-server basis.

Figure 10.58 The ASDM SunRPC Server Configuration Screen

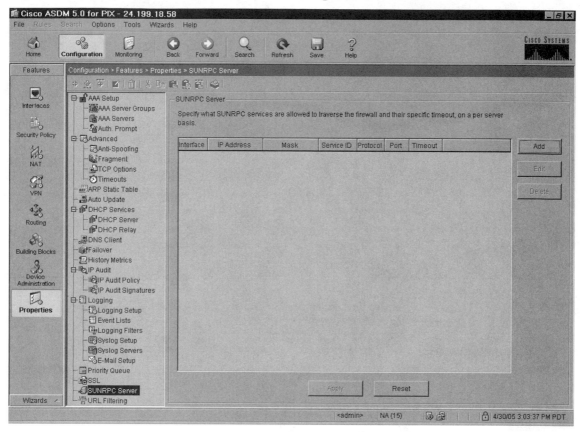

The URL Filtering Category

Clicking on the **URL Filtering** submenu item within the explorer pane displays the URL Filtering window shown in Figure 10.59. This window allows you to apply filtering to connection requests originating from a more secure network to a less secure network. Although you can use ACLs to prevent outbound access to specific content servers, managing usage this way is difficult because of the size and dynamic nature of the Internet. You can simplify configuration and improve security appliance performance by using a separate server running one of the following Internet filtering products:

- Websense Enterprise for filtering HTTP, HTTPS, and FTP.

- Sentian (by N2H2) for filtering HTTP only. (Although some versions of Sentian support HTTPS, the security appliance only supports filtering HTTP with Sentian.)

When filtering is enabled and a request for content is directed through the security appliance, the request is sent to the content server and to the filtering server at the same time. If the filtering server allows the connection, the security appliance forwards the response from the content server to the originating client. If the filtering server denies the connection, the security appliance drops the response and sends a message or return code indicating that the connection was not successful.

Figure 10.59 The ASDM URL Filtering Configuration Screen

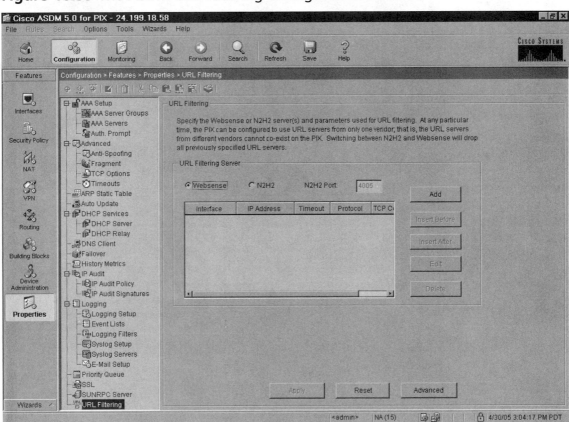

Configuring VPNs Using ASDM

The command-line configuration of VPNs is addressed in detail in Chapter 16. In this chapter, we show you how to configure both Site-to-Site and Remote Access VPNs using the ASDM VPN Wizard.

Configuring a Site-to-Site VPN Using ASDM

1. To launch the VPN Wizard, select the **VPN Wizard** from the **Wizards** drop-down menu, as shown in Figure 10.60.

Figure 10.60 Launching the ASDM VPN Wizard

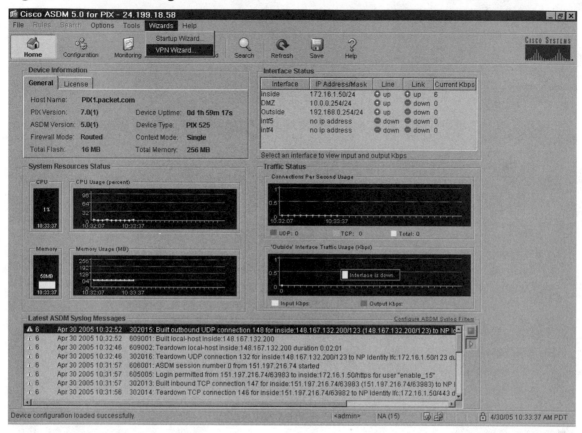

2. This brings up the ASDM VPN Wizard **Tunnel Type** screen shown in Figure 10.61. This screen prompts you to select the type of VPN that you want to configure:

    ■ **Site-to-Site**   A VPN tunnel between two devices that is bidirectional.

    ■ **Remote Access**   A VPN tunnel that is established from remote users such as telecommuters in order to access resources protected by the PIX.

    ■ **VPN Tunnel Interface**   The interface that establishes a secure tunnel with the remote VPN peer.

3. Select the **Site-to-Site** tunnel type and the **Outside** interface. Click **Next**.

Figure 10.61 ASDM VPN Wizard Tunnel Type Screen

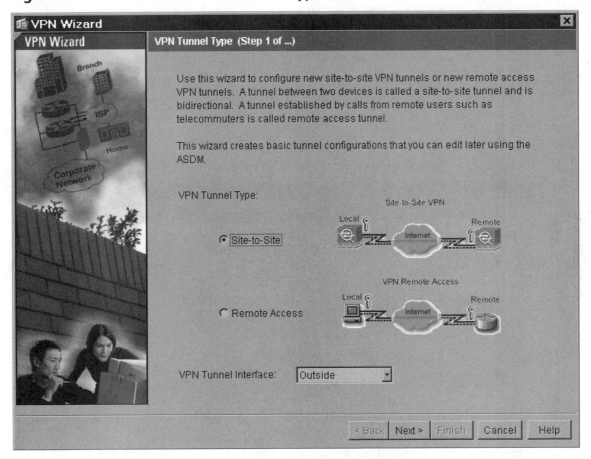

4. The **Remote Site Peer** screen appears, as shown in Figure 10.62, which prompts you for the following information:

- **Peer IP Address**   Enter the IP address of the remote VPN peer that terminates the tunnel. The peer could be another PIX, a VPN concentrator, or any other gateway device that supports IPsec.

- **Tunnel Group Name**   Enter a name to create a group that contains VPN connection policies for this connection. A group that you configure with this VPN wizard specifies an authentication method, and uses the PIX Default Group Policy.

- **Authentication**   Use this panel to specify how the remote site peer authenticates— with either a pre-shared key or a certificate.

- Pre-shared Key Click this button to use a pre-shared key for authentication between the PIX and the remote peer, and enter the pre-shared key value in the text box. Use a secure method to exchange the pre-shared key with the administrator of the remote site.

■ Certificate Click this button to use certificates for authentication between the PIX and the remote peer. To complete this section, you must have previously enrolled with a CA and downloaded one or more certificates to the PIX (refer to Chapter 16). Select the Certificate Signing Algorithm from the drop-down list (either rsa-sig for RSA or dsa-sig for DSA). Additionally, select the Trustpoint Name that identifies the certificate the PIX sends to the remote peer.

5. Enter the **Peer IP Address** and **Tunnel Group Name**, and select **Pre-shared Key** authentication with an appropriate value for the pre-shared key. Click **Next**.

Figure 10.62 ASDM VPN Wizard Remote Site Peer Screen

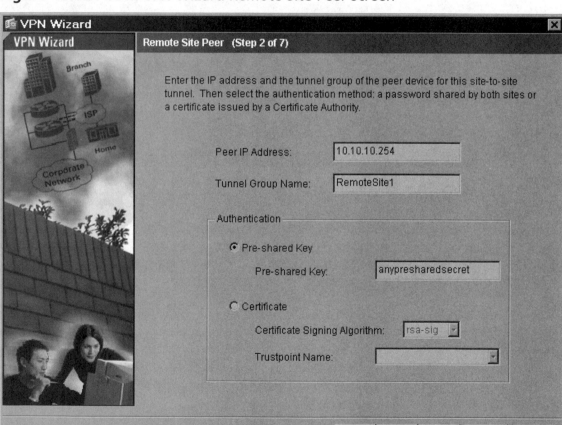

6. The **IKE Policy** screen appears, as shown in Figure 10.63. This screen prompts you for the **Encryption** algorithm, the **Authentication** algorithm, and the **Diffie–Hellman Group** that the two peers should use to negotiate an Internet Key Exchange (IKE) security association. Select the default values of **3DES**, **SHA**, and **2** for the **Encryption**, **Authentication**, and **DH Group** values, respectively. Click **Next**.

Figure 10.63 ASDM VPN Wizard IKE Policy Screen

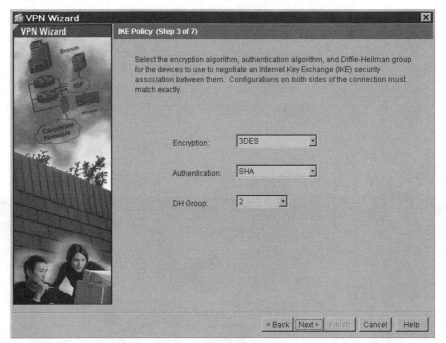

7. The **IPsec Encryption and Authentication** screen appears, as shown in Figure 10.64. This screen prompts you for the **Encryption** and **Authentication** algorithms to use for the actual VPN tunnel. Select the default values of 3DES and SHA for **Encryption** and **Authentication**, respectively. Click **Next**.

Figure 10.64 ASDM VPN Wizard IPsec Encryption and Authentication Screen

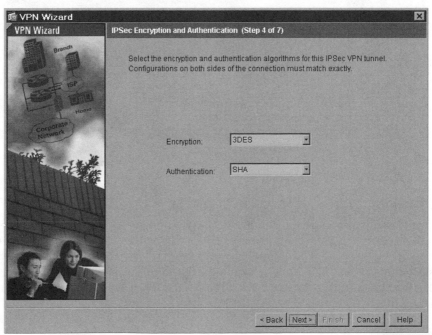

8. The **Local Hosts and Networks** screen appears, as shown in Figure 10.65. This screen prompts you to identify hosts and networks at the local site that can use this LAN-to-LAN IPsec tunnel to communicate with remote site devices. You can identify hosts and networks by IP address, DNS name or group policy. Depending on your choice, the remaining fields in this panel change. Make the desired selection(s) and click **Add**. Once all of the desired hosts and networks are listed in the **Selected Hosts/Networks** list, click **Next**.

Figure 10.65 ASDM VPN Wizard Local Hosts and Networks Screen

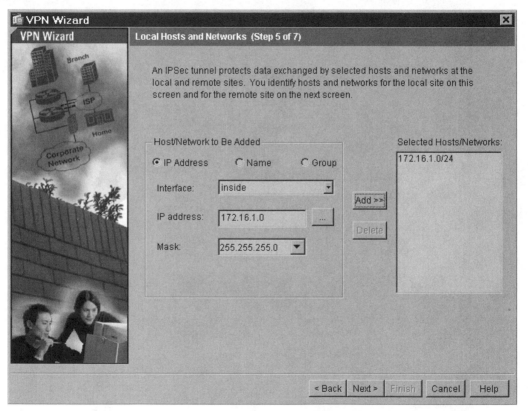

9. The **Remote Hosts and Networks** screen appears, as shown in Figure 10.66. This screen is similar to the previous one, but it prompts you to identify hosts and networks at the *remote* site that can use this LAN-to-LAN IPsec tunnel to communicate with *local* site devices. You can identify hosts and networks by IP address, DNS name, or group policy. Depending on your choice, the remaining fields in this panel change. Make the desired selection(s) and click **Add**. Once all of the desired hosts and networks are listed in the **Selected Hosts/Networks** list, click **Next**.

Figure 10.66 ASDM VPN Wizard Remote Hosts and Networks Screen

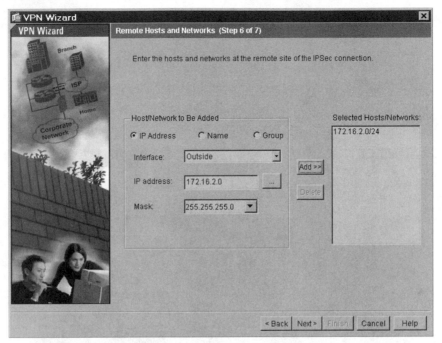

10. The **Summary** screen appears, as shown in Figure 10.66. This provides a summary of all of the VPN configuration information that you specified throughout the wizard process. Verify that the information is accurate, and click **Finish** to create the Site-to-Site VPN. If any of the information is inaccurate, use the **Back** button to go back to the appropriate screen and make changes.

Figure 10.67 ASDM VPN Wizard Summary Screen

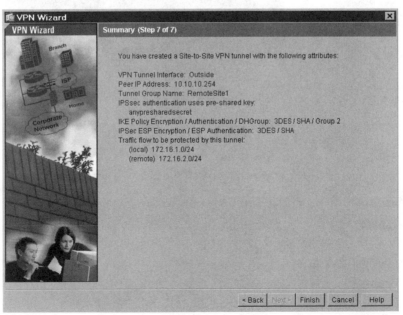

Configuring a Remote Access VPN Using ASDM

1. To launch the VPN Wizard, select the **VPN Wizard** from the **Wizards** drop-down menu, as shown in Figure 10.68.

Figure 10.68 Launching the ASDM VPN Wizard

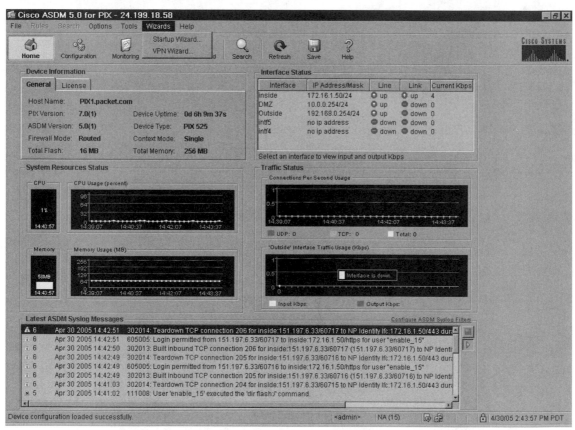

2. This brings up the ASDM VPN Wizard **Tunnel Type** screen shown in Figure 10.69. This screen prompts you to select the type of VPN that you want to configure:

   ■ **Site-to-Site** A VPN tunnel between two devices that is bidirectional.

   ■ **Remote Access** A VPN tunnel that is established from remote users such as telecommuters in order to access resources protected by the PIX.

   ■ **VPN Tunnel Interface** The interface that establishes a secure tunnel with the remote VPN peer.

3. Select the **Remote Access** tunnel type and the **Outside** interface. Click **Next**.

Figure 10.69 ASDM VPN Wizard Tunnel Type Screen

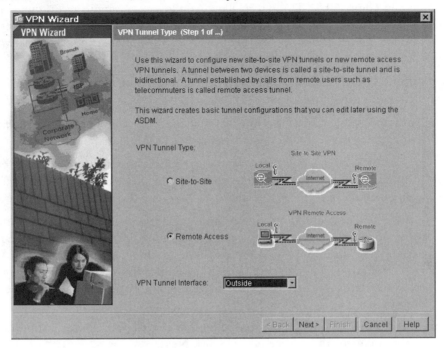

4. The **Remote Access Client** screen appears, as shown in Figure 10.70. Click the **Cisco VPN Client Release 3.x or higher, or other Easy VPN Remote product** button for IPsec connections, and click **Next**.

Figure 10.70 ASDM VPN Wizard Remote Access Client Screen

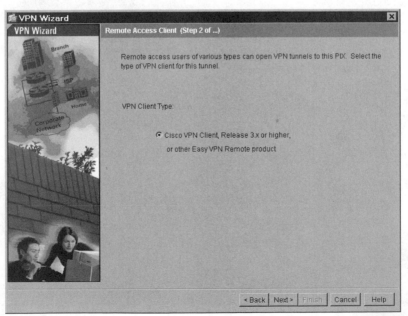

5. The **VPN Client Tunnel Group Name and Authentication Method** screen appears, as shown in Figure 10.71. This screen allows you to group remote access tunnel users based on common connection parameters and client attributes. You can create different remote access tunnel groups that have differing privileges when connecting to the network. It prompts you for the following information:

- **Tunnel Group Name**   Enter a name to create a group that contains VPN connection policies for this connection.

- **Authentication**   Use this panel to specify how the remote site peer authenticates— with either a pre-shared key or a certificate.

- Pre-shared Key Click this button to use a pre-shared key for authentication between the PIX and the remote peer, and enter the pre-shared key value in the text box. Use a secure method to exchange the pre-shared key with the administrator of the remote site.

- Certificate Click this button to use certificates for authentication between the PIX and the remote peer. To complete this section, you must have previously enrolled with a CA and downloaded one or more certificates to the PIX (refer to Chapter 16). Select the Certificate Signing Algorithm from the drop-down list (either rsa-sig for RSA or dsa-sig for DSA). Additionally, select the Trustpoint Name that identifies the certificate the PIX sends to the remote peer.

6. Enter the **Tunnel Group Name**, and select **Pre-shared Key** authentication with an appropriate value for the pre-shared key. Click **Next**.

Figure 10.71 ASDM VPN Wizard VPN Client Tunnel Group Name and Authentication Method Screen

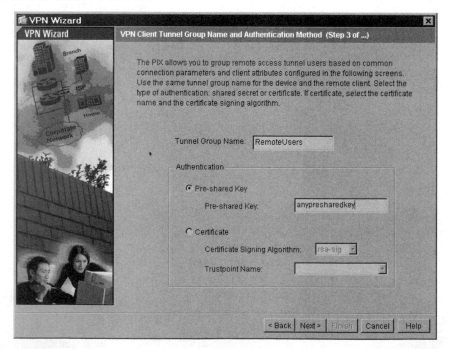

7. The **Client Authentication** screen appears, as shown in Figure 10.72. This screen allows you to specify the method used to authenticate remote access VPN users. You could authenticate them either using the local user database on the PIX, or using an external AAA server group via the RADIUS or TACACS+ protocols. Refer to Chapter 14, "Authentication, Authorization, and Accounting," for more detailed information on configuring AAA. Select the **Authenticate using an AAA server group** and select the appropriate group from the **AAA Server Group** drop-down list. Click **Next**.

Figure 10.72 ASDM VPN Wizard Client Authentication Screen

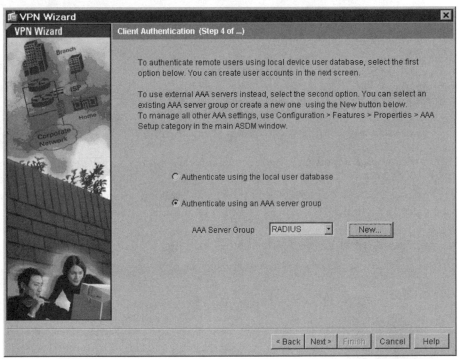

8. The **Address Pool** screen appears, as shown in Figure 10.73. This screen allows you to configure a pool of IP addresses for the PIX to allocate dynamically to Remote Access VPN users when they establish a connection. Specify the pool either by identifying a starting and ending value or by specifying a starting value and a subnet mask. Click **Next**.

Figure 10.73 ASDM VPN Wizard Address Pool Screen

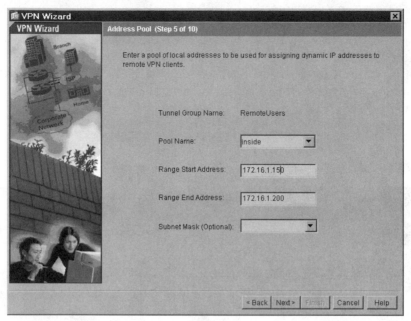

9. The **Attributes Pushed to Client** screen appears, as shown in Figure 10.74. This screen allows you to specify DNS, WINS, and domain name information for the PIX to communicate to Remote Access VPN users when they establish a connection. Enter the primary and secondary DNS and WINS servers and the default domain name. Click **Next**.

Figure 10.74 ASDM VPN Wizard Attributes Pushed to Client Screen

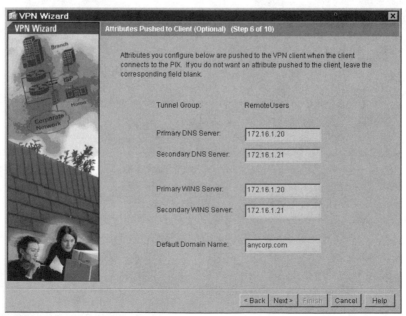

10. The **IKE Policy** screen appears, as shown in Figure 10.75. This screen prompts you for the **Encryption** algorithm, the **Authentication** algorithm, and the **Diffie-Hellman Group** that the two peers should use to negotiate an Internet Key Exchange (IKE) security association. Select the default values of **3DES**, **SHA**, and **2** for the **Encryption**, **Authentication**, and **DH Group** values, respectively. Click **Next**.

Figure 10.75 ASDM VPN Wizard IKE Policy Screen

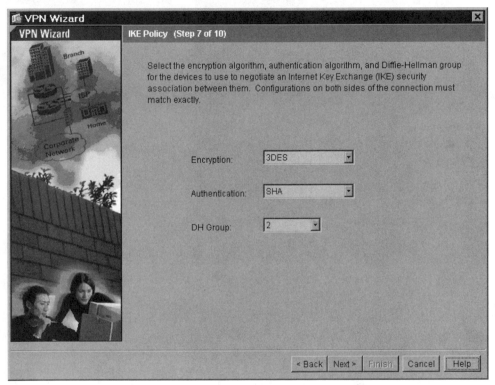

11. The **IPsec Encryption and Authentication** screen appears, as shown in Figure 10.76. This screen prompts you for the **Encryption** and **Authentication** algorithms to use for the actual VPN tunnel. Select the default values of **3DES** and **SHA** for **Encryption** and **Authentication**, respectively. Click **Next**.

Figure 10.76 ASDM VPN Wizard IPsec Encryption and Authentication Screen

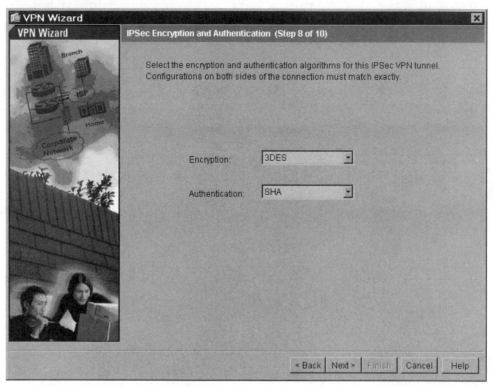

12. The **Address Translation and Split Tunneling** screen appears, as shown in Figure 10.77. This screen allows you to identify local hosts/networks that do not require address translation. By default, the PIX hides the real IP addresses of internal hosts and networks from outside hosts by using dynamic or static NAT. If you want all hosts and networks to be exempt from NAT, configure nothing on this panel. Otherwise, specify the hosts and/or networks and click **Add**.

This screen also allows you to configure split tunneling, which causes traffic for protected networks to be encrypted, while traffic to unprotected networks is unencrypted. When you enable split tunneling, the PIX pushes a list of IP addresses to the remote VPN client after authentication. The remote VPN client then encrypts traffic to the IP addresses that are behind the PIX, while sending all other traffic unencrypted directly to the Internet without involving the PIX.

Figure 10.77 ASDM VPN Wizard Address Translation and Split Tunneling Screen

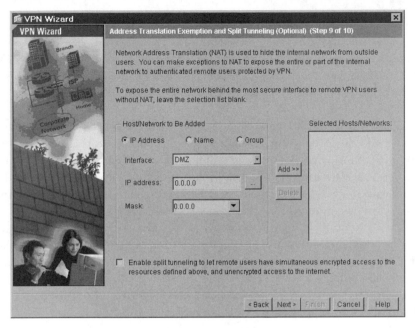

13. The **Summary** screen appears, as shown in Figure 10.78. This provides a summary of all of the VPN configuration information that you specified throughout the wizard process. Verify that the information is accurate, and click **Finish** to create the Remote Access VPN. If any of the information is inaccurate, use the **Back** button to go back to the appropriate screen and make changes.

Figure 10.78 ASDM VPN Wizard Summary Screen

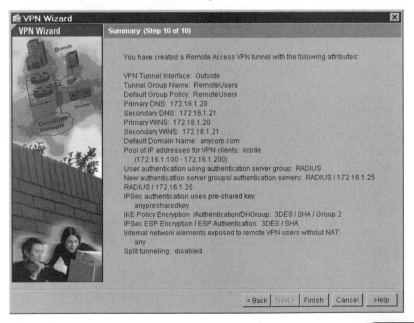

Summary

ASDM is a highly capable graphical interface for managing the PIX firewall. In addition to providing nearly all CLI functionality, ASDM includes several features to further simplify the ongoing maintenance and operations firewall administrators and security policymakers perform. Because ASDM is Java based and runs as a signed applet over an SSL-encrypted browser session, administrators can use it securely from any authorized client. This remote management capability can be highly valuable in large, distributed environments.

Of the vast ASDM functionality, perhaps most powerful are the ASDM wizards, which include the Startup Wizard and the VPN Wizard. Using these tools, administrators are guided using interactive prompts through the often-complex process of building PIX configurations and VPN tunnel services.

In addition to the wizard functionality, ASDM facilitates full configuration of PIX firewall access, AAA, filter, NAT rules, logging, user accounts, and IDS configurations. This functionality includes the ability to manage complex, grouped services and network objects.

The ASDM GUI is intuitive and well organized and helps prevent accidental syntax and configuration errors that could cause the firewall to fail. Moreover, ASDM can be used as a CLI learning tool for administrators who are not completely proficient with the PIX firewall command line by previewing all commands sent to the PIX.

Whether you are managing a single PIX firewall, five redundant PIX pairs, or 100 corporate firewalls, ASDM is a handy and powerful tool for firewall administrators.

Chapter 11

Application Inspection

Solutions in this chapter:

- New Features in PIX 7.0

- Supporting and Securing Protocols

- Application Layer Protocol Inspection

☑ Summary

New Features in PIX 7.0

The Cisco PIX firewall has been providing the ability to secure application protocols for many years now, and version 7.0 is no exception. The ability to correct or compensate for native insecurities in an application is a prime requirement for security. This feature is called application inspection in version 7.0. Prior to the release of version 7.0, the PIX firewall handled application inspection through the fixup feature. In version 7.0, this has been replaced by protocol inspection, which is configured and deployed as a subset of modular policy framework (MPF), which allows for flexible and easily reusable modular configuration of inspection features. Similar to the modular quality of service functionality in Cisco IOS software, MPF is configured in three steps—class-maps, policy-maps, and service-policies—which will be discussed in full detail later.

Although it is still possible to configure fixup in version 7.0, any such commands are automatically converted to the new protocol inspection commands. Therefore, it is desirable to use the new command set to avoid confusion between entered and displayed configuration, and to take advantage of the flexibility of the new protocol inspection methodology (see Figure 11.1). Using the MPF-based commands also reduces potential complexity in the way that fixup commands are translated; because of the added granularity and flexibility and MPF provides, conversion of fixup commands may not occur exactly as you might expect. As well, in future PIX releases the fixup commands will no longer be supported, and you will be required to use MPF-based configuration.

Prior to MPF, most of these actions were an all or nothing proposition: either all traffic transiting an interface was subject to the same policies or none of the traffic. With MPF, 7.0 provides granularity to allow you to pick subsets of traffic from the whole, and apply policies to it. MPF is new to PIX 7.0; there were no pre-7.0 equivalents. Arguably, you could have some of this functionality in pre-7.0 by cobbling together various parameters, but nothing as granular or flexible as MPF.

Figure 11.1 MPF Process

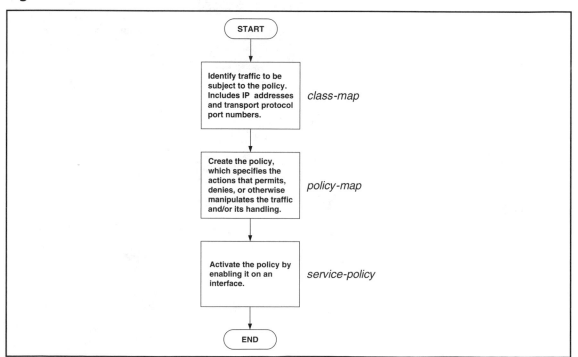

An important note: Despite their similar names, the PIX inspect command is not the same as the ip inspect command in Cisco IOS software. Their functionality or configuration syntax should not be confused.

Supporting and Securing Protocols

Controlling access to and from your network may be as simple as implementing access control lists that define what traffic may come and go, based on addresses and port numbers. But there is an additional level of complexity involved with securing your network while allowing certain protocols to function; protocols that open secondary channels on dynamically assigned ports, or those that embed IP addresses within data packets require application inspection to function securely.

One of earliest examples is File Transfer Protocol, or FTP (which we discuss in detail in the next section). The general problem these applications pose is that they use more than one connection to operate and only one of these connections occurs on a well-known port; the others use dynamically assigned port numbers, which are negotiated in the process of communication.

In this chapter, we will look at the protocols that fall into these categories, to understand their unique characteristics and the security concerns associated with them. We will then go into detail about how to configure the PIX firewall to effectively handle these protocols, so that required access is seamlessly provided, while the firewall handles the application-specific details behind the scenes. Our example network is shown in Figure 11.2.

Figure 11.2 Application Inspection

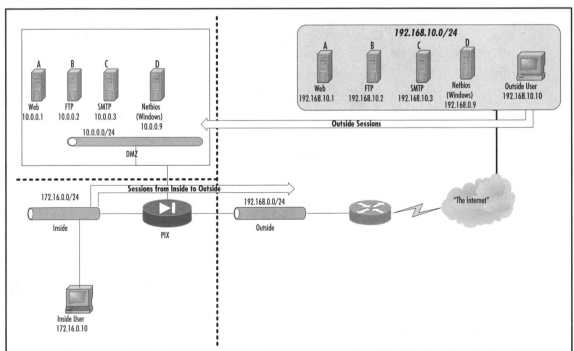

TCP, UDP, ICMP, and the PIX Firewall

Any firewall that wants to handle TCP, UDP, and ICMP negotiations well needs the ability to monitor them, understand them, and adjust its rules accordingly. This situation becomes even more complicated when NAT or PAT are involved; the firewall might need to change the data portion of a packet that carries embedded address information in order for the packet to be processed correctly by a client or server on the other side of PIX. There are many implementations of this feature for various firewalls—for example, Stateful Inspection in the Check Point product family. The PIX firewall makes use of the Adaptive Security Algorithm (ASA).

The ASA uses several sources of information during its operation:

- Access control lists (ACLs), which allow or deny traffic based on hosts, networks, and the TCP or UDP ports involved.

- Internal translation (xlate) and connection (xlate) tables, which store information about the state of the established connections and are used for fast processing of the traffic that belongs to these connections.

- Embedded rules for application inspection, which allow automatic processing of most of the complicated cases mentioned. Although some of these rules are configurable, others are fixed.

Here we look at the processing of a TCP packet by ASA, including application-level intelligence (not considering address translation):

1. If the packet is not the first one in a connection (with the SYN bit set), it is checked against internal tables to decide if it is a reply to an established connection. If it is not, the packet is denied.

2. If it is a SYN packet, it is checked against internal tables to decide if it is a part of another established connection. If it is, the packet is permitted and internal tables are adjusted in order to permit return traffic for this connection.

3. If this SYN packet is not a part of any established communication, it is checked against ACLs.

4. If the SYN packet is permitted, the PIX creates a new entry in internal tables (the XLAT and/or CONN table).

5. The firewall checks to see whether the packet needs additional processing by application-level inspection algorithms. During this phase, the firewall can create additional entries in internal tables. For example, it can open a temporary conduit for an incoming FTP connection based on the PORT command that it sees in the packet. "Temporary" means that this conduit will exist only until the FTP session terminates and will be deleted after the session is closed.

6. The inspected packet is forwarded to the destination.

The situation for UDP is similar, although simpler because there are no distinct initial packets in the UDP protocol, so the inspection simply goes through internal tables and ACLs and then through application inspection for each packet received.

The PIX uses source/destination port numbers to decide if application inspection is needed for a particular packet. Some of these ports are configurable and others are not. Table 11.1, courtesy of

Cisco (http://www.cisco.com/en/US/partner/products/sw/secursw/ps2120/products_configuration_
guide_chapter09186a00804231c0.html, table 21-1), summarizes the application inspection functions
provided by 7.0.

Table 11.1 Application Inspection Functions

Application	PAT?	NAT (1-1)?	Configure Port?	Default Port	Standards
CTIQBE	Yes	Yes	Yes	TCP/2748	—
DNS	Yes	Yes	No	UDP/53	RFC 1123
FTP	Yes	Yes	Yes	TCP/21	RFC 959
GTP	Yes	Yes	Yes	UDP/3386 UDP/2123	—
H.323	Yes	Yes	Yes	TCP/1720 UDP/1718 UDP (RAS) 1718–1719	ITU-T H.323, H.245, H225.0, Q.931, Q.932
HTTP	Yes	Yes	Yes	TCP/80	RFC 2616
ICMP	Yes	Yes	No	—	—
ICMP ERROR	Yes	Yes	No	—	—
ILS (LDAP)	Yes	Yes	Yes	—	—
MGCP	Yes	Yes	Yes	2427, 2727	RFC2705 bis-05
NBDS / UDP	Yes	Yes	No	UDP/138	—
NBNS / UDP	No	No	No	UDP/137	—
NetBIOS over IP	No	No	No	—	—
PPTP	Yes	Yes	Yes	1723	RFC2637
RSH	Yes	Yes	Yes	TCP/514	Berkeley UNIX
RTSP	No	No	Yes	TCP/554	RFC 2326, RFC 2327, RFC 1889
SIP	Yes	Yes	Yes	TCP/5060 UDP/5060	RFC 2543
SKINNY (SCCP)	Yes	Yes	Yes	TCP/2000	—
SMTP/ESMTP	Yes	Yes	Yes	TCP/25	RFC 821, 1123
SQL*Net	Yes	Yes	Yes	TCP/1521 (v.1)	—
Sun RPC	No	No	No	UDP/111 TCP/111	—
XDCMP	No	No	No	UDP/177	—

Depending on the protocol it is used with, application inspection provides the following functionality for complex protocols:

- Securely and dynamically open and close temporary conduits for legitimate traffic
- Network Address Translation
- Port Address Translation
- Inspect traffic for malicious behavior

Application Layer Protocol Inspection

Depending on the protocol, inspection may or may not be enabled by default. All protocol inspection in PIX version 7.0 is configured through the use of the Modular Policy Framework (MPF), which is a versatile and powerful way to apply protocol inspection to your firewall.

MPF has four main steps:

- Defining a traffic class
- Associating the traffic class with one or more actions
- Customizing the parameters of the application inspection for the protocol in question
- Applying the defined inspection to an interface

Defining a Traffic Class

Defining a traffic class is done through the use of the **class-map** command. The idea behind this command is that you want to identify a certain subset of the total traffic flowing through an interface. There are a number of possible methods of matching traffic, including:

- Using an access list
- Matching all traffic
- Using a list of predefined default IP protocols
- Matching traffic based on DSCP values
- Using a flow-based policy
- Matching specified TCP or UDP ports (without using an access list)
- Matching traffic based on IP precedence values
- Matching traffic based on RTP port numbers
- Matching a specified tunnel group

Prior to configuring any of these match conditions, the first step to configuring a traffic class is to define the traffic class and give it a name. To create a traffic class called "class1", enter:

```
PIX1(config)# class-map class1
PIX1(config-cmap)#
```

You will notice that following this command, your prompt changes to "config-cmap", indicating that you are now in class-map configuration mode, and may enter commands relating to the specific class map (in this case "class1") that you have defined. At this prompt, you have the option of entering a description for this traffic class:

```
PIX1(config-cmap)# description sample traffic class
```

You also have the ability to rename the traffic class without removing and recreating it. In this case, we will rename the traffic class from "class1" to "class2":

```
PIX1(config-cmap)# rename class2
```

The next step is to configure the traffic class to match certain traffic. To see all possible matching options:

```
PIX1(config-cmap)# match ?

mpf-class-map mode commands/options:
  access-list               Match an Access List
  any                       Match any packet
  default-inspection-traffic Match default inspection traffic:
                            ctiqbe----tcp--2748   dns-------udp--53
                            ftp-------tcp--21     gtp----udp--2123,3386
                            h323-h225-tcp-1720    h323-ras-udp-1718-1719
                            http------tcp--80     icmp------icmp
                            ils-------tcp--389    mgcp---udp--2427,2727
                            netbios---udp--137-138      rpc-------udp--111
                            rsh-------tcp--514    rtsp------tcp--554
                            sip-------tcp--5060   sip-------udp--5060
                            skinny----tcp--2000   smtp------tcp--25
                            sqlnet----tcp--1521   tftp------udp--69
                            xdmcp-----udp--177
  dscp                      Match IP DSCP (DiffServ CodePoints)
  flow                      Flow based Policy
  port                      Match TCP/UDP port(s)
  precedence                Match IP precedence
  rtp                       Match RTP port numbers
  tunnel-group              Match a Tunnel Group
```

To match traffic by access list, you must configure an access-list prior to configuring the traffic class. For example, to configure an access list called "acl1" that matches all traffic on TCP port 1111 and then apply it to the traffic class "class2":

```
PIX1(config)# access-list acl1 permit tcp any any eq 1111
PIX1(config)# class-map class2
PIX1(config
-cmap)# match access-list acl1
```

To match any traffic, simply enter:

```
PIX1(config-cmap)# match any
```

The PIX default inspection traffic ports are shown in Table 11.2 (table courtesy of Cisco; see http://www.cisco.com/en/US/partner/products/sw/secursw/ps2120/products_configuration_guide_chapter09186a00804231c0.html, Table 21-2).

To match the PIX default inspection traffic ports, simply enter:

Table 11.2 PIX Default Inspection Ports

Protocol Name	Protocol	Port
ctiqbe	tcp	2748
dns	udp	53
ftp	tcp	21
gtp	udp	2123,3386
h323 h225	tcp	1720
h323 ras	udp	1718–1719
http	tcp	80
icmp	icmp	N/A
ils	tcp	389
mgcp	udp	2427,2727
netbios	udp	N/A
rpc/sunrpc	udp	111
rsh	tcp	514
rtsp	tcp	554
sip	tcp, udp	5060
skinny	tcp	2000
smtp	tcp	25
sqlnet	tcp	1521
tftp	udp	69
xdmcp	udp	177

```
PIX1(config-cmap)# match default-inspection-traffic
```

To match traffic based on DSCP value, you may enter one or more of the following parameters, separated by a space:

```
PIX1(config-cmap)# match dscp ?

mpf-class-map mode commands/options:
  <0-63>      Differentiated services codepoint value
  af11        Match packets with AF11 dscp (001010)
```

```
af12        Match packets with AF12 dscp (001100)
af13        Match packets with AF13 dscp (001110)
af21        Match packets with AF21 dscp (010010)
af22        Match packets with AF22 dscp (010100)
af23        Match packets with AF23 dscp (010110)
af31        Match packets with AF31 dscp (011010)
af32        Match packets with AF32 dscp (011100)
af33        Match packets with AF33 dscp (011110)
af41        Match packets with AF41 dscp (100010)
af42        Match packets with AF42 dscp (100100)
af43        Match packets with AF43 dscp (100110)
cs1         Match packets with CS1(precedence 1) dscp (001000)
cs2         Match packets with CS2(precedence 2) dscp (010000)
cs3         Match packets with CS3(precedence 3) dscp (011000)
cs4         Match packets with CS4(precedence 4) dscp (100000)
cs5         Match packets with CS5(precedence 5) dscp (101000)
cs6         Match packets with CS6(precedence 6) dscp (110000)
cs7         Match packets with CS7(precedence 7) dscp (111000)
default     Match packets with default dscp (000000)
ef          Match packets with EF dscp (101110)
```

If you wish to match traffic based on a TCP or UDP port without using an access list, you may use the "match port" command. For example, to match the same TCP port 1111 as in the preceding example:

```
PIX1(config-cmap)# match port tcp eq 1111
```

Note that the "match port" command allows you to specify ranges of ports. To do so, substitute "eq" with "range", and then specify a lower and upper limit to the ports to match. For example, to match TCP ports 1111 through 1120:

```
PIX1(config-cmap)# match port tcp eq 1112
```

To match traffic based on its IP precedence, you may enter precedence values by name or number. For example, to match precedence values 2, 4, and 6:

```
PIX1(config-cmap)# match precedence 2 4 6
```

Associating a Traffic Class with an Action

Once you have identified traffic of interest, the next step is to associate that traffic with a particular action, in order to actually perform the protocol inspection. To do so, the first step is to define a policy map. For example, to create a policy map named "pol1":

```
PIX1(config)# policy-map pol1
PIX1(config-pmap)#
```

At this point, you will notice that the prompt is changed to "config-pmap", indicating all subsequent commands apply to the policy map. Just as with a class map, you have the option of adding a description to the policy map, or renaming it. The next step is to specify one or more traffic classes to the policy map. For example, to specify the traffic class we created earlier ("class2"):

```
PIX1(config-pmap)# class class2
PIX1(config-pmap-c)#
```

Notice that now the prompt has changed to "config-pmap-c", indicating that subsequent commands apply to the class map within the policy map. In order to enable protocol inspection, you may now use the inspect command. The following protocol inspection engines are available:

```
PIX1(config-pmap-c)# inspect ?

mpf-policy-map-class mode commands/options:
  ctiqbe
  dns
  esmtp
  ftp
  gtp
  h323
  http
  icmp
  ils
  mgcp
  netbios
  pptp
  rsh
  rtsp
  sip
  skinny
  snmp
  sqlnet
  sunrpc
  tftp
  xdmcp
```

For example, to enable FTP protocol inspection:

```
PIX1(config-pmap-c)# inspect ftp
```

Once you have completed the inspect configuration, you may wish to return to the policy map configuration mode in order to define additional traffic classes. To do so:

```
PIX1(config-pmap-c)# exit
PIX1(config-pmap)#
```

Notice that the prompt has now returned to "config-pmap". You may now enter additional configuration, or exit again to return to the main configuration mode.

Customizing Application Inspection Parameters

Although in general, protocol inspection will function without modifying the default parameters, there are times when you may wish to tune the various options associated with a protocol inspection engine. To do so, you must use application maps. Application maps are available for a number of protocols, and we will go into detail of how to configure these, when available, in each application-specific section of this chapter. An application map called httpmap1 is applied within the policy map configuration as follows:

```
PIX1(config-pmap-c)# inspect http httpmap1
```

Applying Inspection to an Interface

The final step to enabling protocol inspection is to apply the inspection you have configured to one interface, multiple interfaces, or all interfaces. To do so, use the service-policy command. For example, to apply the aforementioned policy map to the outside interface:

```
PIX1(config)# service-policy pol1 interface outside
```

Similarly, if you wish to apply this policy to all interfaces:

```
PIX1(config)# service-policy pol1 global
```

Domain Name Service

The main task of application inspection for DNS (known as *DNS Guard*) is to impose specific restrictions on DNS requests over UDP that pass through the firewall (compared with the generic processing of all UDP communications). Roughly speaking, the data part of each DNS request contains a serial number (ID) and the body of the request. For example, requests for A-records (address records) include the DNS name for which an IP address is sought. The reply to this request should contain the same ID and an IP address.

DNS Guard ensures the following:

- Only replies with the correct ID are accepted.

- Only one reply is accepted. In the case of multiple replies, all but the first one are ignored.

- The UDP connection associated with the DNS connection is destroyed as soon as a DNS reply is received, not after the UDP timeout has expired.

- IP addresses in A-record replies are translated if necessary. This process is controlled by the *alias* command. It also translates addresses to be consistent with NAT statements, including outside NAT, which was introduced in version 6.2. Generally, the *alias* command is not needed because of this outside NAT feature.

As an example for the last case, consider the configuration in which a client (192.168.0.1) and a Web server (web.company.com, IP address 192.168.0.5) are located on the inside interface of PIX and have nonroutable addresses. A DNS server is on the outside. The PIX is configured to translate both the client and the server addresses via PAT to a single IP of 1.2.3.4. This address is recorded on the DNS server as an address for web.company.com. When a client requests an IP address (an A-record) for the server, the PIX forwards the request to the DNS server, translating the source IP. When it receives the DNS server's reply, it not only translates the packet's destination IP address (changing 1.2.3.4 to 192.168.0.1), but it also changes the address of the Web server contained in the reply's data field (that is, 1.2.3.4 contained in the reply is changed to 192.168.0.5). As a result, the internal client will use the internal address 192.168.0.5 of the Web server to directly connect to it.

Not to be confused with DNS Guard, when the DNS server is on a more secure interface than the Web server and/or client, either outside NAT or *alias* commands are used. Outside NAT is very similar to the previous situation.

It is not possible to disable application inspection of DNS or change the DNS port from the default of 53.

Remote Procedure Call

Remote procedure call (RPC) is a very general mechanism for client-server applications developed by Sun Microsystems. Many applications are built on top of this system, the most important of which are Network File System (NFS) and Network Information System (NIS), which are used in many UNIX networks.

The RPC server is a collection of procedures, each of which can be called by a client sending an RPC request to the server, possibly passing some parameters. The server runs the required procedure and sends the results to the client. This data exchange is platform-independent and is encoded using External Data Representation (XDR) format. Each procedure is identified by an assigned program number, which the client indicates in the request. The default correspondence between program numbers and procedures is stored on UNIX hosts in the /etc/rpc file. To further complicate things, an RPC server can run various versions of each program at the same time. In this case, the version numbers are added to the request.

On TCP/IP networks, each version of a program running on the server is assigned a TCP and a UDP port (both ports have the same number). In order for this service to be generic (and because RPC programs do not use reserved port numbers), there is no fixed correspondence between program names (or numbers) and the ports they are running on. The ports are assigned dynamically by a separate daemon called *portmapper*, which functions as a multiplexing service. Each program has to register with portmapper in order to be available for RPC calls. Portmapper then reserves a TCP and a UDP port for it. When a client wants to make a call to a remote procedure, it first queries the portmapper daemon (which runs on port 111 by default), sending it a program number and receiving the number of a port it runs on. The client then connects to this port and interacts directly with the required program.

Here, the problem for a firewall arises when the RPC server is on a more secure interface; it is simple to permit incoming connections to the portmapper port 111, but it is not possible to know beforehand which extra ports need to be opened for incoming RPC requests to specific programs. The PIX does the following:

1. It inspects all outgoing packets that have a source port of 111.

2. When it notices a portmapper reply with some port number, the PIX opens embryonic TCP and UDP connections on this port.

3. The PIX does not inspect RPC packets for anything else. For example, it does not attempt to translate embedded IP addresses.

To enable RPC inspection, first create an access-list that matches RPC traffic:

```
PIX1(config)# access-list rpc permit udp any any eq 111
```

Next, create a traffic class that matches this access-list:

```
PIX1(config)# class-map rpc1
PIX1(config-cmap)# match access-list rpc
```

Next, create a policy map that specifies the traffic class created in the previous example and defines the inspection to perform:

```
PIX1(config)# policy-map rpcpol1
PIX1(config-pmap)# class rpc1
PIX1(config-pmap-c)# inspect rpc
```

Finally, apply this inspection configuration to the desired interface, in this case outside:

```
PIX1(config)# service-policy rpcpol1 interface outside
```

SQL*Net

SQL*Net, which is used to query SQL databases, is another firewall-unfriendly protocol. There are three versions of SQL*Net: SQL*Net v1 (an old version used in Oracle 7), SQL*Net v2, and Net8/Net9 (newer versions of Oracle, such as 8i). Versions 1 and 2 are incompatible, whereas Net8/Net9 is just a small improvement on version 2. All these protocols have common behavior: When a client wants to connect to an Oracle server, it first establishes a connection to the dedicated Oracle port (port 1525 by default in SQL*Net version 1, port 1521 in versions 2 and later) and then is redirected by this server to another instance of Oracle running on this machine or even another server. The client now has to establish a connection to the IP address and port it was told. In SQL*Net v2 and later, even after that the client can be redirected again.

The only case in which all communications happen only on one port without any redirection is when Oracle runs in Dedicated Server mode. This might need some extra configuration to function; refer to Oracle documentation if you are interested in this feature.

The problem with firewalls arises when the server is on a more secure interface than the client. Generally, the client will not be able to establish inbound connections to arbitrary ports and IP addresses. In order to process this correctly, the PIX needs to monitor the information exchange between the server and the client to notice which address/port number is negotiated and open a temporary conduit for inbound connections.

The default port is 1521. In case of SQL*Net v1, the PIX scans all messages from the server to the client, checks the address and port negotiation, performs NAT on the embedded address if necessary, and forwards the resulting packets to the client. The inbound connections from the client are also de-NATted correctly and permitted by a temporary conduit.

SQL*Net version 2 communications are much more complicated than version 1, so the inspection process is also more complex. Messages used in this protocol can be of the following types: Data, Redirect, Connect, Accept, Refuse, Resend, and Marker. When the PIX firewall notices a Redirect packet with zero data length, it sets an internal flag for this connection to expect the relevant address/port information. This information should arrive in the next message, which must be only of Data or Redirect type. The relevant part of the message looks like the following:

```
(ADDRESS=(PROTOCOL=tcp)(DEV=6)(HOST=a.b.c.d)(PORT=p))
```

The PIX then needs to NAT this a.b.c.d:p pair inside the message and permit inbound connections on the corresponding IP address/port pair. If anything other than a Redirect or Data packet arrives after the initial null Redirect packet, the internal flag is reset.

To enable SQL*Net inspection, first create an access-list that matches SQL*Net traffic:

```
PIX1(config)# access-list sqlnet permit tcp any any eq 1521
```

Next, create a traffic class that matches this access-list:

```
PIX1(config)# class-map sqlnet1
PIX1(config-cmap)# match access-list sqlnet
```

Next, create a policy map that specifies the traffic class created in the previous example and defines the inspection to perform:

```
PIX1(config)# policy-map sqlnetpol1
PIX1(config-pmap)# class sqlnet1
PIX1(config-pmap-c)# inspect sqlnet
```

Finally, apply this inspection configuration to the desired interface, in this case outside:

```
PIX1(config)# service-policy sqlnetpol1 interface outside
```

Internet Locator Service and Lightweight Directory Access Protocol

Microsoft developed the Internet Locator Service (ILS) protocol for use in products such as NetMeeting, SiteServer, and Active Directory services. It is based on Lightweight Directory Access Protocol (LDAP) version 2. The main purpose of ILS application inspection is to let internal users communicate locally, even while registered to outside LDAP servers. This is done by inspecting LDAP messages traversing the firewall and performing NAT when necessary. There is no PAT support, because only IP addresses are stored on the server. When attempting translation of an IP address, the PIX searches its internal XLATE table first, then DNAT tables. If neither contains the required address, it is left unchanged.

ILS/LDAP communications occur on a client/server model over TCP, so there is no need for any temporary conduits to be opened by the PIX. During client/server communications, the PIX monitors for ADD requests and SEARCH responses, decoding them with BER decode functions;

parses the message for IP addresses; translates them as necessary; encodes the message back, and sends the received packet to its destination.

To enable ILS inspection, first create an access-list that matches ILS traffic:

```
PIX1(config)# access-list ils permit tcp any any eq 389
```

Next, create a traffic class that matches this access-list:

```
PIX1(config)# class-map ils1
PIX1(config-cmap)# match access-list ils
```

Next, create a policy map that specifies the traffic class created in the previous example and defines the inspection to perform:

```
PIX1(config)# policy-map ilspol1
PIX1(config-pmap)# class ils1
PIX1(config-pmap-c)# inspect ils
```

Finally, apply this inspection configuration to the desired interface, in this case outside:

```
PIX1(config)# service-policy ilspol1 interface outside
```

HTTP Inspection

HTTP protocol inspection has the ability to check for the following items:

- Conforms to RFC 2616
- Message body, header, and URI length are no larger than a set limit
- Excludes methods on a set list
- Must include a specific transfer encoding method or application type
- The content of the body matches the content type specified in the header, and the content in the response matches the accept-type of the request
- The message includes a MIME type
- Defined keywords are present or missing from specific parts of the message

To enable HTTP inspection, first create a traffic class that matches port 80:

```
PIX1(config)# class-map http1
PIX1(config-cmap)# match port tcp eq 80
```

Next, create an HTTP map to configure the HTTP-specific parameters of the inspection engine. The various options are displayed:

```
PIX1(config)# http-map httpmap1
PIX1(config-http-map)# ?

Http-map configuration commands:
  content-length            Content length range inspection
  content-type-verification Content type inspection
```

```
max-header-length        Maximum header size inspection
max-uri-length           Maximum URI size inspection
no                       Negate a command or set its defaults
port-misuse              Application inspection
request-method           Request method inspection
strict-http              Strict HTTP inspection
transfer-encoding        Transfer encoding inspection
```

Next, create a policy map that specifies the traffic class created in the previous example and defines the inspection to perform, including the HTTP map:

```
PIX1(config)# policy-map httppol1
PIX1(config-pmap)# class http1
PIX1(config-pmap-c)# inspect http httpmap1
```

Finally, apply this inspection configuration to the desired interface, in this case outside:

```
PIX1(config)# service-policy httppol1 interface outside
```

FTP Inspection

One of the first application-level protocols that posed problems for simple packet-filtering devices was FTP, which is documented in RFC 959. FTP always uses two connections for operation. The *control connection* is a connection from the client FTP program to the server's FTP port (TCP port 21 by default). This connection is used for sending commands to the server and receiving informational replies. These commands and replies are a little different from what you enter on the keyboard. For example, when you log into an FTP server and enter your username, your FTP client sends the *USER username* command to the server and probably receives a reply *331 User name okay, need password*. It then asks you for your password, and the login process completes.

The second connection is opened for the actual file transfer operation and can behave differently depending on the mode in which the client is operating; it can be initiated either by the client or by the server. The main difference is whether the client tells the server to operate in *passive* or *active* mode.

Active versus Passive Mode

The first FTP servers and clients used *active* mode, where a file transfer happens as shown in Figure 4.3 and described here:

1. When the client (already connected to the server's FTP control port and logged in) needs to receive a file from the server, it sends a *PORT A1,A2,A3,A4,a1,a2* command, where A1, A2, A3, and A4 are the four octets of the client's IP address and *a1* and *a2* are the port numbers on which it will listen for connections. This port number is an arbitrary value and is calculated as a1*256+a2.

2. After receiving a *200 OK* reply from the server, the client sends the *RETR* command to start the transfer.

3. The server opens a connection to the port that the client specified and pipes the file's contents into this connection. After the file is transferred, this data connection is closed, while the control connection stays open until the client disconnects from the server. The source port of this connection is "ftp-data," TCP port 20.

Now, if the client is behind a firewall (or, in PIX terms, is on a higher security-level interface than the server), the connection from the server is likely to be refused unless the firewall permits inbound connections to all high ports on the client side, which, of course, is not good security practice. The PIX firewall can monitor FTP control connections, so when it discovers a *PORT* command issued by the client, it temporarily permits inbound connections to the port requested by the client in this command.

The other issue here is that when NAT or PAT are used, the PIX also translates the address and port number inside the command to the NATted IP and port. For example, consider a client with IP address 10.0.0.1 that will be translated to 192.168.0.1. In this case, the client will issue port command *PORT 10,0,0,1,4,10*, which says that the client is ready to receive connections to 10.0.0.1:1034. During its transit through the PIX it will be translated to *PORT 192,168,0,1,8,10*, and the server will then open the data connection to 192.168.0.1:2058. This destination will be properly translated by the PIX back to 10.0.0.1:1034.

The second mode of FTP operation is *passive* mode. In this mode, a file transfer happens as shown in Figure 4.4 and described here:

1. Soon after connecting to the server's FTP control port and logging in, the client sends the *PASV* command, requesting the server to enter the passive mode of operation.

2. The server responds with "227 Entering Passive Mode A1,A2,A3,A4,a1,a2." This response means that the server is now listening for data connections on the IP address and port it has specified in the reply.

3. The client connects to the specified port and sends the *RETR* command to start the transfer.

4. The server sends the file's contents over this second (data) connection.

This mode of operation does not cause a problem when the client is on a more secure interface, since by default the client is permitted to initiate any outbound connections. Unfortunately, there is a problem when the server is on a more secure interface than the client; the firewall will generally not allow the client to open an inbound connection on an arbitrary port. To overcome this problem, the PIX firewall monitors *PASV* commands and "227" replies, temporarily permits an inbound connection to the specified port, and modifies IP addresses and port numbers to correspond with NATted ones.

The full functionality of FTP application inspection consists of the following tasks:

1. Tracking of FTP command and response sequence (*PORT* and *PASV* commands and "227" replies).

2. Creating a temporary conduit for the data connections based on the result of this tracking (if necessary).

3. NATting of IP addresses inside the commands and replies.

4. Generating an audit trail.

An audit trail is generated in the following cases:

- An audit record 302002 is generated for each uploaded or downloaded file.

- Each download (*RETR*) or upload (*STOR*) command is logged.

- File operations are logged together with the FTP username, source and destination IP addresses, and NAT address.

- An audit record 201005 is generated if the firewall failed to allocate a secondary channel due to memory shortage.

If one of the following problems is encountered, the connection is denied or dropped:

- Clients are prevented from sending embedded commands. The connection that tries to use these commands is closed. This action is performed by checking how many characters are present in the *PORT* or *PASV* command after the IP address and port number. If there are more than eight characters, it is assumed that it is an attempt to add another command at the end of the line, and the connection is dropped.

- Before a new command is allowed, the server should send a reply to each command received.

- Only servers can generate "227" messages (protection against reply spoofing) and only clients can generate *PASV* and *PORT* commands (protection against command spoofing). The reason here is that without *strict*, a client can send any garbage to the server, including fake "227" messages—for example, *227 foobar A1, A2, A3, A4, a1, a2*, and although the server replies with an error message, the firewall could be fooled into permitting the connection with the parameters specified.

- Extra checking of "227" and *PORT* commands is performed to ensure that they are really commands/replies, not a part of some error message.

- Truncated commands; *PORT* and *PASV* commands are checked for the correct number of commas in them. Each should contain only five commas (see previous examples).

- Size of *RETR* and *STORE* commands; their length (including the filename for download/upload) should not be greater than an embedded constant. This is done to provide protection against possible buffer overflows.

- Invalid port negotiation; the port number used for the data connection must be a high port (that is, a port with number greater than 1024).

- Every FTP command sent by the client must end with *<cr><lf>* characters, as specified by RFC 959.

To enable FTP inspection, first create a traffic class that matches port 23:

```
PIX1(config)# class-map ftp1
PIX1(config-cmap)# match port tcp eq 23
```

Next, create an FTP map to configure the FTP-specific parameters of the inspection engine. The various options are displayed:

```
PIX1(config)# ftp-map ftpmap1
```

To deny specific FTP commands from being executed, for example, you have the following options with the FTP map configuration:

```
PIX1(config-ftp-map)# request-command deny ?
ftp-map mode commands/options:
  appe  Append to a file
  cdup  Change to parent of current directory
  dele  Delete a file at server site
  get   FTP client command for the retr command - retrieve a file
  help  Help information from server
  mkd   Create a directory
  put   FTP client command for the stor command - store a file
  rmd   Remove a directory
  rnfr  Rename from
  rnto  Rename to
  site  Specify server specific command
  stou  Store a file with a unique name
```

Next, create a policy map that specifies the traffic class created in the previous example and defines the inspection to perform, including the FTP map:

```
PIX1(config)# policy-map ftpppol1
PIX1(config-pmap)# class ftp1
PIX1(config-pmap-c)# inspect ftp ftpmap1
```

Finally, apply this inspection configuration to the desired interface, in this case outside:

```
PIX1(config)# service-policy ftppol1 interface outside
```

ESMTP Inspection

ESMTP is an enhanced version of SMTP that is very similar to SMTP, but offers features such as delivery status notification messages to improve performance and security.

ESMTP inspection works by limiting the commands that can be executed and by monitoring ESMTP connections. The commands that are permitted are *AUTH, DATA, EHLO, ETRN, HELO, HELP, MAIL, NOOP, QUIT, RCPT, RSET, SAML, SEND, SOML,* and *VRFY.*

All other commands are not permitted, since they are not required for ESMTP operation and therefore could be malicious.

To enable ESMTP inspection, first create a traffic class that matches port 25:

```
PIX1(config)# class-map esmtp1
PIX1(config-cmap)# match port tcp eq 25
```

Next, create a policy map that specifies the traffic class created in the previous example and defines the inspection to perform:

```
PIX1(config)# policy-map esmtppol1
PIX1(config-pmap)# class esmtp1
PIX1(config-pmap-c)# inspect esmtp
```

Finally, apply this inspection configuration to the desired interface, in this case outside:

```
PIX1(config)# service-policy esmtppol1 interface outside
```

ICMP Inspection

Although ICMP is a useful tool for determining device availability and network latency, it is possible for ICMP to be used maliciously. For example, a malicious user may attempt to flood your network with replies to ICMP requests that you never actually sent. Fortunately, the PIX includes an ICMP inspection engine that instructs the PIX to treat ICMP connections as stateful, matching outgoing queries to incoming responses.

To enable ICMP inspection, first create an access-list that matches ICMP traffic:

```
PIX1(config)# access-list icmp1 permit icmp any any
```

Next, create a traffic class that matches this access-list:

```
PIX1(config)# class-map icmp1
PIX1(config-cmap)# match access-list icmp1
```

Next, create a policy map that specifies the traffic class created in the previous example and defines the inspection to perform:

```
PIX1(config)# policy-map icmppol1
PIX1(config-pmap)# class icmp1
PIX1(config-pmap-c)# inspect icmp
```

Finally, apply this inspection configuration to the desired interface, in this case outside:

```
PIX1(config)# service-policy icmppol1 interface outside
```

H.323

H.323 is actually a suite of protocols rather than a single protocol. It was designed for establishing multimedia conferences, and is used by such application as Cisco CallManagers. This protocol embeds IP addresses within its packets, making it a challenge to NAT, and also uses dynamically allocated RTP connections to function. The PIX H.323 inspection engine allows H.323 to function securely, despite these factors.

To enable H.323 inspection, first create an access-list that matches H.323 traffic:

```
PIX1(config)# access-list h323 permit udp any any eq 1720
PIX1(config)# access-list h323 permit udp any any eq 1721
```

Next, create a traffic class that matches this access-list:

```
PIX1(config)# class-map h323-1
PIX1(config-cmap)# match access-list h323
```

Next, create a policy map that specifies the traffic class created in the preceding example and defines the inspection to perform:

```
PIX1(config)# policy-map h323poll
PIX1(config-pmap)# class h323-1
PIX1(config-pmap-c)# inspect h323 ras
PIX1(config-pmap-c)# inspect h323 h225
```

Finally, apply this inspection configuration to the desired interface, in this case outside:

```
PIX1(config)# service-policy h323poll interface outside
```

Simple Network Management Protocol (SNMP)

SNMP is used for managing and monitoring network nodes. Network management and monitoring tools may query devices via SNMP, and the device will return information about its current state.

There have been a number of iterations of SNMP, including versions 1, 2, 2c, and 3. Because older versions of SNMP are less secure, it is desirable to enable SNMP inspection and to deny all versions but the most recent, assuming all devices on your network are running that version.

To enable SNMP protocol inspection, first create a traffic class that matches this protocol:

```
PIX1(config)# class-map snmp1
PIX1(config-cmap)# match port tcp range 161-162
```

If you wish to deny certain versions of SNMP, create an SNMP map. The versions that you may deny are displayed:

```
PIX1(config)# snmp-map snmpmap1
PIX1(config-snmp-map)# deny version ?

snmp-map mode commands/options:
  1     SNMP version 1
  2     SNMP version 2 (party based)
  2c    SNMP version 2c (community based)
  3     SNMP version 3
```

Next, create a policy map that specifies the traffic class created in the preceding example and defines the inspection to perform:

```
PIX1(config)# policy-map snmppoll
PIX1(config-pmap)# class snmp1
PIX1(config-pmap-c)# inspect snmp snmpmap1
```

Finally, apply this inspection configuration to the desired interface, in this case outside:

```
PIX1(config)# service-policy snmppol1 interface outside
```

Voice and Video Protocols

The PIX supports the inspection of a number of voice and video protocols. Because networks are used more and more frequently for voice and video, rather than just data, it is important to be able to apply the same security measures to this traffic to maintain the integrity of your security policy.

SIP

The SIP protocol is used by voice-over-IP gateways to establish calls between parties. The PIX firewall is able to inspect SIP traffic, including the dynamically allocated ports used for streaming the media packets between hosts. Also, the inspection applies network address translation to the IP addresses embedded in the SIP packets.

To enable SIP protocol inspection, first create a traffic class that matches this protocol:

```
PIX1(config)# class-map sip1
PIX1(config-cmap)# match port tcp eq 5060
```

Next, create a policy map that specifies the traffic class created in the preceding example and defines the inspection to perform:

```
PIX1(config)# policy-map sippol1
PIX1(config-pmap)# class sip1
PIX1(config-pmap-c)# inspect sip
```

Finally, apply this inspection configuration to the desired interface, in this case outside:

```
PIX1(config)# service-policy sippol1 interface outside
```

CTIQBE

CTIQBE, which stands for Computer Telephony Interface Quick Buffer Encoding, is used to allow Cisco SoftPhones or other similar applications to communicate with a Cisco CallManager. Enabling application inspection of CTIQBE allows the PIX firewall to apply network address translation to the IP addresses embedded in the CTIQBE packets.

To enable CTIQBE protocol inspection, first create a traffic class that matches this protocol:

```
PIX1(config)# class-map ctiqbe1
PIX1(config-cmap)# match port tcp eq 2748
```

Next, create a policy map that specifies the traffic class created in the preceding example and defines the inspection to perform:

```
PIX1(config)# policy-map ctiqbepol1
PIX1(config-pmap)# class ctiqbe1
PIX1(config-pmap-c)# inspect ctiqbe
```

Finally, apply this inspection configuration to the desired interface, in this case outside:

```
PIX1(config)# service-policy ctiqbepoll interface outside
```

SCCP

SCCP, which stands for Skinny Client Control Protocol and runs on TCP port 2000, is an alternative Cisco proprietary protocol used for communication between Cisco IP phones and Cisco CallManagers. The PIX firewall supports all five versions of SCCP (through 3.3.2), and allows for network address translation and port address translation.

To enable SCCP protocol inspection, first create a traffic class that matches this protocol:

```
PIX1(config)# class-map sccp1
PIX1(config-cmap)# match port tcp eq 2000
```

Next, create a policy map that specifies the traffic class created in the preceding example and defines the inspection to perform:

```
PIX1(config)# policy-map sccppoll
PIX1(config-pmap)# class sccp1
PIX1(config-pmap-c)# inspect skinny
```

Finally, apply this inspection configuration to the desired interface, in this case outside:

```
PIX1(config)# service-policy sccppoll interface outside
```

Real-Time Streaming Protocol (RTSP), NetShow, and VDO Live

RTSP is a protocol used by applications such as RealAudio, QuickTime, RealPlayer, and Cisco IP/TV to transmit real-time, streaming media from server to client. The PIX firewalls support inspection of RTSP, although NAT and PAT of RTSP connections is not supported due to the nature of the embedded IP addresses within the RTSP packets. RTSP inspection involves parsing the setup response messages to apply normal stateful inspection, matching queries and responses to eliminate the possibility of malicious behavior.

To enable RTSP inspection, first create an access-list that matches RTSP traffic:

```
PIX1(config)# access-list rtsp permit tcp any any eq 554
PIX1(config)# access-list rtsp permit tcp any any eq 8554
```

Next, create a traffic class that matches this access-list:

```
PIX1(config)# class-map rtsp1
PIX1(config-cmap)# match access-list rtsp
```

Next, create a policy map that specifies the traffic class created in the preceding example and defines the inspection to perform:

```
PIX1(config)# policy-map rtsppol1
PIX1(config-pmap)# class rtsp1
PIX1(config-pmap-c)# inspect rtsp
```

Finally, apply this inspection configuration to the desired interface, in this case outside:

```
PIX1(config)# service-policy rtsppol1 interface outside
```

Summary

The Cisco PIX firewall is an advanced product and has many different options for supporting various application-layer protocols as well as protecting against network-layer attacks. It also supports content filtering for outbound Web access, intrusion detection, and various routing options such as RIP, OSPF, and multicast routing.

Many protocols embed extra IP address information inside the exchanged packets or negotiate additional connections on nonfixed ports in order to function properly. These functions are handled by the PIX application inspection feature. PIX supports FTP clients and servers in active and passive modes, DNS, RSH, RPC, SQL*Net, and LDAP protocols. It also supports various streaming protocols such as Real-Time Streaming Protocol. Another set of supported protocols includes all H.323, SCCP, and SIP—all used in VoIP applications. The PIX monitor passes packets for the embedded information and updates its tables or permits embryonic connections according to this information. It is also able to NAT these embedded addresses in several cases.

The PIX can also participate in RIP and OSPF dynamic routing. Although the PIX does not have all routing features present in a full-fledged router, in some cases its routing functionality will satisfy basic routing requirements. The same goes for multicast routing; although in many cases a true multicast router is required, having basic multicast routing support built-in to the PIX can allow your multicast network to function without additional devices adding complexity to your network.

Chapter 12

Filtering, Intrusion Detection, and Attack Management

Solutions in this chapter:

- **New Features in PIX 7.0**
- **Filtering Web and FTP Traffic**
- **TCP Attack Detection and Response**
- **Configuring Intrusion Detection/Auditing**
- **Attack Containment and Management**

☑ **Summary**

New Features in PIX 7.0

PIX 7.0 offers several enhancements for filtering, intrusion detection, and attack management that earlier versions did not.

Enhanced TCP Security Engine

The enhanced TCP security engine:

- Introduces new capabilities for detecting protocol and application layer attacks.
- Provides TCP stream reassembly and analysis services to detect attacks that are spread across a series of packets.
- Offers TCP traffic normalization services for detecting attacks, including advanced flag and option checking, TCP packet checksum verification, detection of data tampering in retransmitted packets, and more.

Improved Websense URL Filtering Performance

Improved Websense URL filtering offers:

- Improved scalability supports concurrent URL filtering lookups with Websense Enterprise Employee Internet Management (EIM) solutions.
- Supports FTP and HTTPS filtering.

Introduction

The PIX firewall can filter and block potentially harmful Web traffic, including Java and ActiveX applications. In this chapter, we look at how the PIX firewall can integrate with virus-filtering, spam-blocking, and adware mechanisms. The PIX firewall provides integrated intrusion detection for common information-gathering stacks and network attacks. We also look at how to use IDS signatures in the PIX firewall to detect common network attacks.

Filtering Web and FTP Traffic

Often, more resources are allocated to protecting internal networks from external malicious attempts, yet equal care and attention needs to be devoted to monitoring and filtering outbound connections initiated from internal networks. Such content inspection allows the firewall to enforce security policies such as an Acceptable Use Policy, which might be used to limit browsing to certain sets and types of Web sites. URL filtering is one such mechanism where the firewall is configured to pass each HTTP or HTTPS request to a filter server for a permit or deny decision. The firewall then acts accordingly: if the request is approved, it is forwarded to the outside server and the client receives the asked-for content. If the request is denied, it is silently dropped or the user is informed that the request violates policy.

Another reason for filtering is "active content" such as ActiveX or Java applets, which could be malicious. The PIX can protect your users from malicious sites that embed these executable applets (viruses or Trojan horses) in their pages. Content filtering can scan incoming applets and block or drop them if any harmful applets are found. The PIX firewall cannot provide content filtering by itself, but it can be configured to interoperate with content filtering servers that provide this protection.

Filtering URLs

It is possible to use access lists to filter certain Web sites, but management will become difficult and performance will suffer as the access control list (ACL) grows. Moreover, the use of Dynamic DNS enables attackers to rapidly change IP addresses, yet retain the same name. Access lists are also inflexible in that they cannot filter by specific pages, but must filter by the IP address associated with a Web site. Another limitation of ACLs is that they cannot handle multiple Web sites hosted on a single physical server, all of which have unique names, but use the same IP address. Denying or permitting access to a particular Web site hosted in such a fashion affects all Web sites on that server.

Enter dedicated filtering servers! The PIX firewall essentially hands the workload and authority for content filtering to a dedicated URL filtering server, which specializes in the task. This reduces the burden on the PIX firewall, and allows for fine-tuning of Web access controls. The filtering process is:

1. A client establishes a TCP connection to a Web server.
2. The client sends an HTTP request for a page on this server.
3. The PIX intercepts this request and hands it over to the filtering server.
4. The filtering server decides if the client should be allowed access to the requested page.
5. If the decision is positive, the PIX forwards the request to the server and the client receives the requested content.
6. If the decision is negative, the client's request is dropped.

There are several steps for setting up the filtering partnership between the PIX and the filtering server:

1. Identify the filtering server to the PIX.
2. (Optional) Buffer responses from the Web server.
3. (Optional) Cache addresses of Web servers to improve performance.
4. Configure HTTP filtering and the different options available.
5. Configure HTTPS filtering (Websense only).
6. Configure FTP filtering (Websense only).

Websense and Sentian by N2H2

The PIX can interact with two types of filtering servers: Websense (www.websense.com) and Sentian by N2H2 (www.n2h2.com). Websense has been supported since version 5.3 and later, and has been enhanced for greater speed in version 7.0. Sentian by N2H2 support was added in version 6.2. PIX URL filtering in version 7.0 can also be applied to FTP requests if a Websense server is being used. In version 7.0, the PIX supports inspecting HTTPS connections, but only with a Websense server.

To configure URL filtering:

1.   Specify the server to use for URL processing.

2.   Identify the traffic that the firewall is to inspect—ports and IP addresses.

3.   (Optional) Configure some server-specific parameters.

4.   Configure filtering rules on the filtering server.

To specify a filtering server for Websense:

```
url-server (<if_name>) host <local_ip> [timeout <seconds>] [protocol <tcp> | <udp>
[version 1|4]]
```

For example, the following example specifies that the PIX should use a server with IP address 10.0.0.1, located on the interface inside, and connect to it using UDP Websense protocol v4:

```
PIX1(config)# url-server (inside) host 10.0.0.1 protocol udp version 4
```

Particularly, *if_name* is an interface on which the server is located; the default here is the inside interface. *local_ip* is the IP address of the filtering server. The PIX uses *timeout* (default is five seconds) to decide how long it has to wait for a reply from the server until it gives up and switches to the next configured server or takes a default action if there are no more servers available.

Up to four servers may be configured, as long as they are all the same type. It is not possible to mix Websense and Sentian filtering servers in the same configuration. The first server configured is a primary filtering server and is attempted first. Protocol type and version parameters specify the Websense protocol that should be used for communication with the server. It can be either TCP protocol v1 (default) or 4, or UDP protocol v4. The version numbers refer to the version of the Websense communication protocol to be used by the PIX. As you will be deploying Websense 4 or later, v4 is the appropriate choice. UDP protocol v4 is the recommended choice if the Websense server is directly connected to a firewall interface and you want to achieve maximum throughput.

The Sentian by N2H2 server is specified by the command:

```
url-server (if_name) vendor n2h2 host <local_ip> [timeout <seconds>]
[port
<port_number>] [protocol tcp | udp]
```

The meaning of parameters is the same. The parameter *vendor n2h2* states that the server is a Sentian by N2H2 filtering server.

The default is *vendor websense*. Sentian by N2H2 servers have only one communication protocol version available, so it is not specified. You can change the port used for communicating with the N2H2 server via the *port_number* parameter.

Fine-Tuning and Monitoring the Filtering Process

When a user issues a request, the PIX firewall sends the request to the Web server and to the filtering server at the same time. If the filtering server does not respond before the Web server, the server response is dropped. This delays the response, which can cause the client to retry the request.

By enabling the HTTP response buffer, such replies are buffered and forwarded to the client if the filtering server allows it. This prevents the delay that might otherwise occur.

To enable buffering of responses to HTTP or FTP requests while awaiting a decision from the filtering server, enter the following command:

`url-block block` block-buffer-limit

The *block-buffer-limit* is the maximum number of 1550-byte blocks that will be buffered, from 0 to 128.

To configure the amount of memory available for buffering pending URLs (for Websense only—this command is not available for Sentian by N2H2 servers), enter the following command:

`url-block url-mempool` memory-pool-size

where *memory-pool-size* is a value from 2 to 10240 for a maximum memory allocation of 2 KB to 10 MB. Make sure to use a size that leaves your PIX firewall enough memory for all of its other functions.

The *url-block* command addresses the problem of long URLs, which can result from the practice of storing session and other information in the URL itself. A typical long URL could look like this:

```
http://www.somebettingcompany.com/?action=GoEv&class_id=1&type_id=2&ev_
id=4288&class_name=%7CFootball%7C&type_name=%7CChampions+League%7C+%7CQualifying+
Matches%7C&ev_name=%7CGenk%7C+v+%7CSparta+Prague%7C
```

In v7.0, the maximum URL length for Websense filtering is 4KB, and 1159 bytes for N2H2. To change the maximum URL length:

`url-block url-size` long_url_size

where *long_url_size* is the maximum allowed URL size for Websense filtering in KB—2, 3, or 4 KB.

The PIX supports options to the *filter url* command to adapt for URLs that exceed 1159 bytes when using a Websense server. We will look at the *filter url* command, which sets up the actual filtering of URLs, in detail in the next section "Configuring HTTP URL Filtering." The options we're concerned with here are those that pertain to handling long URLs:

`filter url` http | `<port>[-<port>] <local_ip> <local_mask> <foreign_ip>`
`<foreign_mask>` [`allow`] [`cgi-truncate`] [`longurl-truncate` | `longurl-deny`] [`proxy-`
`block`]

The *cgi-truncate* and *longurl-truncate / longurl-deny* parameters help us to deal with the problem of long URLs, which are common nowadays as session and other information is stored in the URL itself. A typical long URL could look like this:

```
http://www.somebettingcompany.com/?action=GoEv&class_id=1&type_id=2&ev_
id=4288&class_name=%7CFootball%7C&type_name=%7CChampions+League%7C+
%7CQualifying+Matches%7C&ev_name=%7CGenk%7C+v+%7CSparta+Prague%7C
```

In v7, the maximum URL length for Websense filtering is 4KB, and 1159 bytes for N2H2. The *longurl-truncate* parameter specifies that when the URL length exceeds the maximum, only the IP address or hostname from the request is sent to the filtering server. This truncation is prone to "false negatives" and "false positives" if a Web server hosts a number of sites that belong to different categories. The Web server IP is likely to be in a category that does not accurately reflect the sites hosted on it. The *longurl-deny* parameter specifies that all URL requests that exceed the buffer size should be dropped.

The *cgi-truncate* parameter specifies that only the CGI script name and its location (the part of the URL before the ? sign) should be passed as the URL to the Websense server. This skips the CGI parameter list, which can be quite long. Without this option enabled, the entire URL, including the parameter list, is passed.

For example, to strip CGI parameters from the URL being sent to Websense, we would use:

filter url http 0 0 0 0 **cgi-truncate**

The *url-cache* command can improve filtering performance. After a client initiates a request, the PIX can cache the Web server information for a certain amount of time, as long as every site hosted at the address is permitted by the filtering server. When a client accesses the Web site again, the PIX does not need to consult the filtering server again for a decision. The *url-cache* command looks like this:

url-cache dst | src_dst size

where *size* is a value for the cache size within the range of 1 to 128 (KB).

The *dst* parameter caches entries based on the URL destination address. Select this mode if all users share the same URL filtering policy on the Websense server.

The *src_dst* keyword caches entries based on both the source address initiating the URL request and the URL destination address. Select this mode if users do not share the same URL filtering policy on the Websense server.

You can view statistics of the caching process, including the hit ratio, by executing the *show url-cache stat* command. For example, the following command enables a cache of 32KB for all outgoing HTTP requests:

```
PIX1(config)# url-cache dst size 32
```

The following are cache statistics:

```
PIX1# show url-cache stat
URL Filter Cache Stats
----------------------
Size : 32KB
Entries : 360
In Use : 200
Lookups : 2000
Hits : 1000
```

Usage statistics for the memory pool can be viewed by using the *show url-block block stat* command. For example:

```
pix(config)# show url-block block stat
URL Pending Packet Buffer Stats with max block              128
-------------------------------------------------------
Cumulative number of packets held:                           0
Maximum number of packets held (per URL):                    0
Current number of packets held (global):                     0
Packets dropped due to exceeding url-block buffer limit:     0
Packet drop due to retransmission:                           0
```

Another command for viewing filtering statistics is *show url-server statistics*.

```
PIX1# show url-server stat
```

```
URL Server Statistics:
----------------------
Vendor                              websense
URLs total/allowed/denied           0/0/0
HTTPSs total/allowed/denied         0/0/0
FTPs total/allowed/denied           0/0/0
URL Server Status:
------------------
192.168.1.10                        DOWN
URL Packets Sent and Received Stats:
------------------------------------
Message             Sent        Received
STATUS_REQUEST      20          0
LOOKUP_REQUEST      0           0
LOG_REQUEST         0           NA
```

Commands such as *show perfmon, show memory*, and *show chunks* will also provide performance information of the URL filtering process.

Configuring HTTP URL Filtering

Now that the filtering servers have been defined, and we've tackled buffering, caching, and the handling of long URLS, the remaining task is to configure the filtering policy itself. It will determine the source and destination hosts and networks that are going to be subject to filtering, and allow us to enter exceptions. The relevant command for HTTP filtering is:

filter url http | <port>[-<port>] <local_ip> <local_mask> <foreign_ip> <foreign_mask> [**allow**] [**cgi-truncate**] [**longurl-truncate** | **longurl-deny**] [**proxy-block**]

This command specifies port numbers on which HTTP connections should be inspected. *local_ip* and *local_mask* specify which local clients are subject to monitoring (that is, the requests by the machines from this network will be checked with a URL filtering server). The *foreign_ip* and *foreign_mask* parameters specify that only requests to a specific set of servers are checked. The *allow* parameter defines that the PIX should permit traffic through if it is unable to contact the primary URL filtering server. Finally, the *proxy-block* parameter specifies that all requests from any clients to proxy servers will be denied. We discussed the *cgi-truncate* and *longurl* parameters previously.

For example, the following command defines that all HTTP requests to port 80 will be inspected:

```
PIX1(config)# filter url http 0 0 0 0
```

The following command configures inspection of all HTTP requests to port 8080 from clients on network 10.100.1.0/24 to any server, and allows the request to pass by default should the filtering server become unavailable:

```
PIX1(config)# filter url 8080 10.100.1.0 255.255.255.0 0 0 allow
```

Another variant of the *filter* command can specify that certain traffic be exempt from filtering.

```
filter url except <local_ip> <local_mask> <foreign_ip> <foreign_mask>
```

When entered after the *filter* command, this command exempts specified traffic from the policy. For example, the following sequence of commands means that all HTTP traffic to port 8080 will be inspected, but not traffic from network 10.100.1.0/24:

```
PIX1(config)# filter url 8080 0 0 0 0 allow
PIX1(config)# filter url except 10.100.1.0 255.255.255.0 0 0
```

Configuring HTTPS Filtering

Version 7.0 introduces the ability to filter HTTPS traffic, but only with Websense servers. Since HTTPS content is encrypted, the PIX sends the URL lookup without directory and filename information. When the filtering server approves an HTTPS request, the PIX allows the completion of SSL connection negotiation and reply to the client. If the filtering server denies the request, the PIX blocks the completion of SSL connection. The browser displays an error message such as "The Page or the content cannot be displayed."

The relevant command for HTTPS filtering is:

```
filter https https | <port>[-port] <local_ip> <local_mask> <foreign_ip>
<foreign_mask> [allow]
```

As with HTTP filtering, *allow* will allow the session if none of the filtering servers is available. There are no options to truncate long URLs. HTTPS URLs are encrypted and cannot be transmitted to the filtering server.

The following command defines that all HTTPS requests to port 443 will be inspected:

```
PIX1(config)# filter https https 0 0 0 0
```

The *filter https except* command works the same for HTTPS as it does for the *filter url except* command for HTTP.

Setting Up FTP Filtering

Version 7.0 provides the ability to filter FTP traffic, but only via Websense servers.

When the filtering server approves an FTP connection request, the PIX allows the successful FTP reply to the client, such as "250: CWD command successful." If the request is denied, the PIX alters the FTP response to show the connection was denied, such as "550 Requested file is prohibited by URL filtering policy."

The relevant command for FTP filtering is:

```
filter ftp ftp | port localIP local_mask foreign_IP foreign_mask
[allow] [interact-block]
```

The *interact-block* parameter can block interactive FTP sessions that do not provide the entire directory path. An interactive FTP client allows the user to change directories without typing the entire path. For example, the user might enter **cd ./files** instead of **cd /public/files**.

The following command defines that all FTP requests to port 21 will be inspected:

```
PIX1(config)# filter ftp ftp 0 0 0 0
```

Exceptions can be set up using *filter ftp except*, with the syntax otherwise being identical to the *filter url except* command.

Active Code Filtering

Active content in Web pages could contain harmful applets. The PIX firewall provides an effective way to prevent this content from reaching clients. In HTML, active content is denoted by two types of tags. The first is:

```
<object>
...
</object>
```

These tags are more common for ActiveX content, but can also be used by Java applets. In addition, they are used for multimedia content. There are Java-only tags:

```
<applet>
...
</applet>
```

When configured to look for active content, the PIX simply comments out both of these tags inside a TCP packet and the content between them. This commenting out causes the active content to be skipped by the client browser: the embedded code is not run. The PIX cannot perform this cleansing if the first tag is in one packet and the closing tag is in another packet; the Web page is passed to the client unmodified.

The following example shows the applet inactivation feature in action. The sample HTML code contains an applet reference.

```
<td width="185" height="68" valign="top">
  <applet codebase="/classes/" code="tscroll.class" align="absbottom" width="185"
height="68">
    <param name="bgcolor" value="8,51,128">
    <param name="enddelay" value="4000">
    <param name="scrolldelay" value="25">
    <param name="scrolljump" value="5">
    <param name="speed" value="2">
    <param name="size" value="11">
    <param name="hlcolor" value="255,0,0">
    <param name="centertext" value="false">
  </applet>
</td>
```

After being transformed by PIX, it becomes the code in the following output:

```
<td width="185" height="68" valign="top">
  <!-- <applet codebase="/classes/" code="tscroll.class"
align="absbottom" width="185" height="68">
    <param name="bgcolor" value="8,51,128">
```

```
    <param name="enddelay" value="4000">

    <param name="scrolldelay" value="25">

    <param name="scrolljump" value="5">

    <param name="speed" value="2">

    <param name="size" value="11">

    <param name="hlcolor" value="255,0,0">

    <param name="centertext" value="false">

  </applet> -->

</td>
```

After modification, the client browser will ignore everything between the *<td>* and *</td>* tags.

Filtering Java Applets

While Java has a more or less robust security model for its active code, "sandboxing" the code so it cannot do harm on the user's machine, it is as prone to security vulnerabilities as any other piece of networking code. You might want to filter Java applets and allow Java only on certain sites that you know are benign. Note, also, that this filtering is not perfect—it looks for applet HTML tags, which are not the only way to embed Java code into a Web site.

To configure filtering of Java applets, use the following command:

```
filter java <port>[-<port>] <local_ip> <mask> <foreign_ip> <mask>
```

Here are two examples:

```
PIX1(config)# filter java 80 0 0 0 0

PIX1(config)# filter java 80 192.168.2.17 255.255.255.255 0 0
```

The first command configures the PIX to drop all Java applets from incoming Web pages. The second is an alternative that prohibits only one host 192.168.2.17 from downloading Java applets. You would either use a "catch-all" command or be more specific—never both. The *port* parameter specifies the TCP port on which to perform the inspection.

Like the other filter commands, this command lets you specify exceptions. Use the following command to specify an exception:

filter java except `<local_ip> <mask> <foreign_ip> <mask>`

For example, these two commands would filter all Java applets with the exception of the applet on www.time.gov:

```
PIX1(config)# filter java 80 0 0 0 0
PIX1(config)# filter java except 0 0 129.6.13.35 255.255.255.255
PIX1(config)# filter java except 0 0 132.163.4.203 255.255.255.255
```

Filtering ActiveX Objects

By design, ActiveX objects have almost unrestricted access to the client's machine. The concern here is not just about security vulnerabilities, but also the inherent design risk of ActiveX. Keep in mind, however, that ActiveX is widely used, and that restricting your users from legitimate activity will only drive them to find ways around the firewall. Examples of Web applications that use ActiveX extensively are Windows Update and almost all SSL VPN appliances. Furthermore, because of the way ActiveX filtering works—it looks for an object HTML tag—this filter will also catch many Java applets and many forms of embedded multimedia.

The command to filter ActiveX code (and all active content that is embedded in "object" tags) is similar to Java filtering:

```
filter activex <port>[-<port>] <local_ip> <mask> <foreign_ip> <mask>
PIX1(config)# filter activex 80 0 0 0 0
```

This command configures the PIX to comment out all pairs of object tags from all incoming Web pages, disabling ActiveX, many embedded multimedia objects, and many Java applets.

Exemptions to blocking object tags work just like exemptions to blocking applet tags:

`filter activex except` `<local_ip> <mask> <foreign_ip> <mask>`

Virus Filtering; Spam, Adware, Malware, and Other-Ware Filtering

The PIX will not forward traffic transparently to content-inspection servers that scan e-mail, Web and FTP traffic for viruses and other malware, as it can for URL filtering. However, you can place content-inspection servers in a DMZ and configure clients (e.g. by using Active Directory group policies) to use these servers as proxy servers.

An example configuration might look something like Figure 12.1.

Figure 12.1 Content Inspection Server in a DMZ

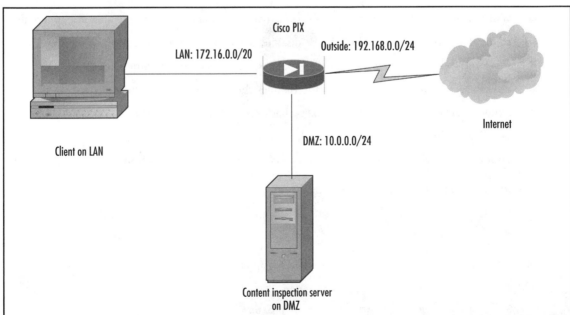

As with all DMZ servers, you will want to configure the PIX to allow traffic between the internal LAN and the DMZ server without address translation to avoid the overhead of NAT where it is not needed.

TCP Attack Detection and Response

TCP normalization will drop packets that do not appear normal; that is, packets that use options or flags that are not typically seen in everyday traffic. TCP normalization is used with the Modular Policy Framework to create a security policy applied. Once a policy for TCP has been created using the *policy-map* command, it is applied to an interface using the *service-policy* command.

For example, we can set a policy for TCP to allow the URG (URGent) pointer for certain applications, such as rsh, rlogin, FTP, and Telnet, but not for other traffic. Modular Policy Framework commands are used to set advanced TCP connection settings as follows:

1. Create a TCP map that allows urgent flag and urgent offset packets.

   - PIX1(config)# **tcp-map tmap**
   - PIX1(config-tmap)# **urgent-flag allow**

   TCP normalization includes the following settings, which are configurable in tcp-map configuration mode.

   - **queue-limit**   Maximum number of out-of-order packets that can be queued for a TCP connection.
   - **urgent-flag**   Allows or clears the URG pointer through the PIX.
   - **tcp-options {selective-ack | timestamp | window-scale}** Allows or clears the selective-ack, timestamps, or window-scale TCP options.
   - **window-variation**   Drops a connection that has changed its window size unexpectedly.
   - **ttl-evasion-protection**   Enables or disables the TTL evasion protection offered by PIX.
   - **reserved-bits**   Sets the reserved flags policy in the security appliance.
   - **check-retransmission**   Enables and disables the retransmit data checks.
   - **exceed-mss**   Allows or drops packets that exceed MSS set by peer.
   - **syn-data** Allows   or drops SYN packets with data.
   - **checksum-verification**   Enables and disables checksum verification.

2. Identify traffic by creating a class map using the *class-map command*.

   - PIX1(config)# class-map urg-class
   - PIX1(config-cmap)# match port tcp range ftp-data telnet

3. Add a policy map that references the class map and the TCP map.

   - PIX1(config)# **policy-map pmap**
   - PIX1 (config-pmap)# **class urg-class**

- `PIX1 (config-pmap-c)# set connection advanced-options tmap`

4. Activate the policy map globally, or apply it to a specific interface.

To activate the policy map globally, use this command:

- `PIX1(config)# service-policy pmap global`

To apply the policy map to a specific interface, use this command:

- `PIX1(config)# service-policy pmap interface <interface-name>`

Here is an example that would apply the policy map to the outside interface:

- `PIX1(config)# service-policy pmap interface outside`

5. To show the TCP map statistics, enter the following command:

- `PIX1# show service-policy set connection`

PIX Intrusion Detection

The PIX firewall offers a basic intrusion detection system (IDS) capability. Cisco has a specialized IDS product called Cisco Secure IDS (former NetRanger appliance), and a limited part of its functionality is implemented in both Cisco IOS and Cisco PIX. Because the PIX is basically an OSI Layer 3 and 4 filtering device, it supports detection of only simpler attacks that happen at these layers. It can detect attacks by inspecting a single packet in the traffic. IDS signatures (that is, descriptions of attacks) that the PIX supports are a subset of the Cisco Secure IDS signature set and are embedded in PIX software.

To upgrade this set of signatures, you need to upgrade the entire PIX firmware using a general upgrade procedure. These signatures describe very general and simple attacks, which may not occur very often. Intrusion detection can be configured on each interface in inbound and outbound directions. When the PIX detects each signature, the device produces an alert ("information" or "attack") depending on the severity of the attack, and records its occurrence to any configured syslog server.

Supported Signatures

The list of supported signatures has not changed since v6.2. If full intrusion detection and prevention (IDP) is desired, a separate IDP device should be deployed. The PIX will not be able to detect some of the new attacks that have been developed since PIX v6.2 was released. For version 7.0, syslog messages numbered from 400 000 to 400 050 are reserved for IDS messages. Their format is shown here:

```
%PIX-4-4000<nn>: : <sig_num> <sig_msg> from <IP_addr> to <IP_addr> on
    interface <int_name>
```

This syslog message means that PIX has detected an attack with number *sig_num* and name *sig_msg*. The two IP addresses show the origin and the destination of this attack. The interface on which the attack was detected is listed as well.

```
%PIX-4-400013 IDS:2003 ICMP redirect from 1.2.3.4 to 10.2.3.1 on
    interface dmz
```

Table 12.12 lists all signatures detected by PIX, with short descriptions.

Table 12.1 PIX IDS Signatures

Message Number	Signature ID	Signature Title	Signature Type
400000	1000	IP options-Bad Option List	Informational
400001	1001	IP options-Record Packet Route	Informational
400002	1002	IP options-Timestamp	Informational
400003	1003	IP options-Security	Informational
400004	1004	IP options-Loose Source Route	Informational
400005	1005	IP options-SATNET ID	Informational
400006	1006	IP options-Strict Source Route	Informational
400007	1100	IP Fragment Attack	Attack
400008	1102	IP Impossible Packet	Attack
400009	1103	IP Fragments Overlap	Attack
400010	2000	ICMP Echo Reply	Informational
400011	2001	ICMP Host Unreachable	Informational
400012	2002	ICMP Source Quench	Informational
400013	2003	ICMP Redirect	Informational
400014	2004	ICMP Echo Request	Informational
400015	2005	ICMP Time Exceeded for a Datagram	Informational
400016	2006	ICMP Parameter Problem on Datagram	Informational
400017	2007	ICMP Timestamp Request	Informational
400018	2008	ICMP Timestamp Reply	Informational
400019	2009	ICMP Information Request	Informational
400020	2010	ICMP Information Reply	Informational
400021	2011	ICMP Address Mask Request	Informational
400022	2012	ICMP Address Mask Reply	Informational
400023	2150	Fragmented ICMP Traffic	Attack
400024	2151	Large ICMP Traffic	Attack
400025	2154	Ping of Death Attack	Attack
400026	3040	TCP NULL flags	Attack
400027	3041	TCP SYN+FIN flags	Attack
400028	3042	TCP FIN only flags	Attack

Table 12.1 Continued

Message Number	Signature ID	Signature Title	Signature Type
400029	3153	FTP Improper Address Specified	Informational
400030	3154	FTP Improper Port Specified	Informational
400031	4050	UDP Bomb attack	Attack
400032	4051	UDP Snork attack	Attack
400033	4052	UDP Chargen DoS attack	Attack
400034	6050	DNS HINFO Request	Attack
400035	6051	DNS Zone Transfer	Attack
400036	6052	DNS Zone Transfer from High Port	Attack
400037	6053	DNS Request for All Records	Attack
400038	6100	RPC Port Registration	Informational
400039	6101	RPC Port Unregistration	Informational
400040	6102	RPC Dump	Informational
400041	6103	Proxied RPC Request	Attack
400042	6150	ypserv (YP server daemon) Portmap Request	Informational
400043	6151	ypbind (YP bind daemon) Portmap Request	Informational
400044	6152	yppasswdd (YP password daemon) Portmap Request	Informational
400045	6153	ypupdated (YP update daemon) Portmap Request	Informational
400046	6154	ypxfrd (YP transfer daemon) Portmap Request	Informational
400047	6155	mountd (mount daemon) Portmap Request	Informational
400048	6175	rexd (remote execution daemon) Portmap Request	Informational
400049	6180	rexd (remote execution daemon) Attempt	Informational
400050	6190	statd Buffer Overflow	Attack

The signature IDs listed in Table 12.1 correspond to signature numbers on the Cisco Secure IDS appliance. See www.cisco.com/univercd/cc/td/doc/product/iaabu/csids/csids1/csidsug/sigs.htm (*Cisco Secure Intrusion Detection System Version 2.2.1 User Guide*) for a complete reference.

All signatures are divided into two classes: informational and attack. The division is rather deliberate and cannot be changed, but it makes sense most of the time. For example, all DoS attacks are listed as attacks, and all information requests only have informational status. While you might feel that obtaining information on RPC services on one of your hosts is an attack, Cisco lists it as informational. Generalizing a little, it is possible to suggest the following reasoning on attack classification (from top to bottom in Table 12.1):

- Packets with IP options will not do any harm because they are always dropped by the PIX, so if these packets are detected, send only an informational message.

- Fragmented packets can pass through the firewall and are generally difficult to inspect, so they constitute an attack attempt.

- Legitimate ICMP traffic, although unwanted and maybe revealing some information about your network (e.g., ICMP Information Request), is not classified as an attack.

- Fragmented ICMP, Ping of Death, and so on are considered attacks.

- Invalid TCP flag combinations, such as SYN and FIN, or FIN only, are considered attacks because they are sometimes used for stealth scanning of networks.

- All floods/DoS attempts are classified as attacks.

- DNS transfers are classified as attacks; they reveal too much about the network.

- General RPC requests and all information requests for various RPC services are not considered that harmful and are classified as informational.

- Some specific one-packet attacks on RPC services are recognized separately.

Configuring Intrusion Detection/Auditing

Intrusion detection by the PIX is referred to as "auditing" by Cisco, and is configured via the *ip audit* command. Auditing can be disabled or enabled, different auditing policies can be created, the policies can be applied to specific interfaces, and specific signatures can be turned on or off. The easiest configuration requires you to assign a name for the auditing policy, specify actions (one for informational signatures and one for attack signatures) to be taken, and apply the policy to an interface. The actions that can be taken are:

- **Alarm** When PIX detects a signature in the packet, it reports with the message described previously to all configured syslog servers.

- **Drop** When this action is configured, PIX drops the offending packet.

- **Reset** This action means that PIX should drop the packet and close the connection if this packet was a part of an open connection.

The default action is alarm. Policy configuration usually takes no more than two commands:

```
ip audit name <audit_name> info action [drop | alarm | reset ]
ip audit name <audit_name> attack action [drop | alarm | reset ]
```

For example, the following commands create a policy with the name *myaudit* and specify that when an informational signature is matched, the PIX should send an alarm to syslog, and when an attack signature is matched, the PIX should drop the packet:

```
PIX1(config)# ip audit name myaudit info action alarm
PTX1(config)# ip audit name myaudit attack action drop
```

It is possible to omit the *action* in the configuration. In this case, the default action is applied. Default actions are configured via these commands:

```
ip audit info action [drop | alarm | reset ]
ip audit attack action [drop | alarm | reset ]
```

The default action is *alarm*. Note that if you issue only the following command but not the corresponding *attack* command, no attack signatures will be matched:

```
PIX1(config)# ip audit name myaudit info action alarm
```

However, if you configure the policy in the following manner, omitting the action for informational signatures, both informational and attack signatures will be matched, and the default action (alarm) will be applied when a packet is matched with an informational signature:

```
PIX1(config)# ip audit name myaudit info
PIX1(config)# ip audit name myaudit attack action drop
```

After creating a policy, you need to apply it to an interface to activate IDS on the interface. For example:

```
PIX1(config)# ip audit interface outside myaudit
```

This means that all signatures and actions configured should be matched on the outside interface. The general form of this command is:

```
ip audit interface <if_name> <audit_name>
```

- *if_name* is the name of an interface where the IDS has to check for packets.
- *audit_name* is the name of the policy that describes which actions to take.

The following configures an elementary IDS on the outside interface, which will send an alarm when an informational signature is matched and drop the connection when an attack signature is matched:

```
PIX1(config)# ip audit name myaudit info alarm
PIX1(config)# ip audit name myaudit attack action drop
PIX1(config)# ip audit interface outside myaudit
```

Each command has its *no* equivalent, which removes the command from the configuration. For example:

```
PIX1(config)# no ip audit interface outside myaudit
PIX1(config)# no ip audit name myaudit info
```

You can clear IDS configuration related to an interface, policy, or default action:

```
clear ip audit [name | signature| interface | audit | info | attack ]
```

The following set of commands displays the corresponding configuration of IDS related to the interface, audit, or default action. This code simply shows the commands you entered when configuring these parameters:

```
show ip audit interface <if_name>
show ip audit info
show ip audit attack
show ip audit name <audit_name>
```

Disabling Signatures

Imagine the following situation: You want to be alerted when the informational signature 6102, "RPC Dump" is matched. This means that you have to include all informational signatures in your policy with a command such as:

```
PIX1(config)# ip audit name myaudit info action alarm
```

Here comes the problem: Many other signatures are listed as informational, and some of them are very "noisy"—generating many alarms—for example, number 2000, "ICMP echo reply," which is simply a response to a ping. Chances are, you will be flooded with alarms on this latter signature and will not notice the former one, which is the one you are actually interested in. You can ignore the noisy signatures with the following command, which disables the detection of the signature with number *sig_number*:

```
ip audit signature <sig_number> disable
```

In our case, to disable the "ICMP echo reply" signature, use the following command:

```
PIX1(config)# ip audit signature 2000 disable
```

After this command is executed, signature number 2000 ("ICMP echo reply") will not be detected by the PIX. Note that disabling a signature means disabling it globally, not for a specific interface or audit.

It is possible to see the list of all disabled signatures with the command:

```
PIX1(config)# show ip audit signature
```

You can enable a disabled signature with a *no* command in Configuration mode:

```
no ip audit signature <sig_number> disable
```

Configuring Shunning

Shunning is a term used in the IDS context to describe blocking traffic from an attacking host; it is configured on the PIX using the following command:

```
shun <src_ip> [<dst_ip> <sport> <dport> [<protocol>]]
```

This technique temporarily blocks all traffic from the specified source IP address. To block all traffic from the source IP address of 10.0.1.1, use the following command:

```
PIX1(config)# shun 10.0.1.1
```

You can also deny specific traffic by specifying a source port, destination IP address, and destination port number. After the *shun* command is entered, the PIX deletes all matching connections from its internal connection table and drops all further packets that match the command's parameters. The action of this command takes priority over access list entries and even security levels on interfaces; all specified traffic is blocked, whether the offending host is on the inside or outside of the interface. To remove this blocking action, use the corresponding *no* command. For example:

```
PIX1(config)# no shun 10.0.1.1
```

This command is dynamic and is not displayed or stored in the configuration. If you want to view active shuns, use the *show shun* command. The *clear shun* command deletes all shun entries.

Attack Containment and Management

The Cisco PIX firewall has many other security features, some of which can be used to protect the network against various DoS attacks. Some of them are related to the processing of routing information—both unicast and multicast.

Placing Limits on Fragmentation

Fragmented packets are a challenge to firewalls. For example, nothing in the current Internet standards prevents a person from sending IP packets so fragmented that IP addresses of source and destination and TCP port information are located in different fragments or even in overlapping fragments. The firewall cannot determine what to do with the packet until it sees the entire TCP/IP header. Some firewalls simply pass the fragments without trying to reassemble the original packets, whereas others try to perform this reassembly. Reassembly can be a dangerous process; for example, it is very easy to send fragments that will cause the reassembled packet to be of illegal size, possibly crashing internal buffers of the IP stack implementation.

The *fragment* commands allow you to specify an interface by name, such as *outside*. If the interface parameter is left off a fragment command, it will apply globally to all interfaces.

The first command sets the maximum number of blocks that can be used for fragment reassembly. If an interface is not specified, the setting is global; otherwise, this setting is for the specific interface. The default number of blocks is 200 and should never be greater than the total number of available blocks of 1550 bytes' size. In general, a bigger database makes PIX more vulnerable to a DoS attack by flooding it with fragments and exhausting its memory.

The second command sets the maximum allowed number of fragments into which one IP packet is split. The default setting is 24 fragments; the maximum is 8200. Further fragments will be discarded and the packet will not be reassembled. The timeout setting specifies the timeframe in which all fragments of one IP packet should be received. The default timeout is 5 seconds and can be up to 30 seconds.

The last command, *clear fragment*, resets all three settings to their default values. The state of the fragments database can be displayed with the *show fragment* command:

```
pix(config)# show fragment outside
Interface:outside
Size:200, Chain:24, Timeout:5
Queue:150, Assemble:300, Fail:0, Overflow:0
```

This output shows that the database has default settings: the size of 200 blocks, 24 fragments in a chain, five-second timeout. There are 150 packets waiting to be reassembled, 300 were already successfully reassembled, and there were no failures or database overflows.

SYN FloodGuard

Another well-known DoS attack is SYN flooding, which occurs when an attacker sends large numbers of initial SYN packets to the host and neither closes nor confirms these half-open connections. This attack is a TCP attack. This causes some TCP/IP implementations to consume a great deal of resources while waiting for connection confirmation, preventing them from accepting any new connections until the backlog of these half-open connections is cleared. To curtail this attack, control the rate at which new connections are opened or the number of connections that are half-open (other names for this are *SYN Received* or *embryonic*) at any given time. This can be performed by specifying a limit on the number of embryonic connections in the *static* and *nat* configuration commands. The PIX uses the embryonic limit to trigger TCP Intercept, which protects inside systems from a DoS attack perpetrated by flooding an interface with TCP SYN packets. For example:

```
PIX1(config)# static (dmz, outside) 123.4.5.6 10.1.1.0 netmask
255.255.255.255 100 50
```

This creates a static NAT entry for the DMZ server 10.1.1.0 with an external IP address of 123.4.5.6. The number 100 means that only 100 connections to this server from the outside can be in an open state at any given time, and the number 50 is the number of half-open or embryonic connections to this server that can exist at any given time. The *nat* command is similar: Two numbers at the end specify the number of open and embryonic connections that can exist at any given time to each translated host:

```
nat (inside) 1 10.0.0.0 255.0.0.0 100 50
```

When any of these numbers is zero, the number of connections is not limited. Embryonic connections per host should be set to a small value for slow systems, and a bigger value for faster systems.

The TCP Intercept Feature

Since version 5.3, PIX uses a feature called *TCP Intercept* to contain SYN Flood attacks. If the number of embryonic connections for a host is reached, each new SYN packet to the affected host is intercepted, until the number of embryonic connections falls below threshold. Then, the PIX itself replies to the sender instead of the destination server with SYN/ACK. If the client finally replies with a legitimate ACK, the PIX firewall sends the original SYN to its destination (the server), performs a correct three-way handshake between the PIX and the server, and the connection is resumed between a client and a server.

Preventing IP Spoofing

To prevent IP spoofing, we will enable Unicast Reverse Path Forwarding (RPF) on an interface. Unicast RPF guards against IP spoofing (a packet uses an incorrect source IP address to obscure its true source) by ensuring that all packets have a source IP address that matches the correct source interface according to the routing table.

Normally, the PIX only looks at the destination address when determining where to forward the packet. Unicast RPF instructs the PIX to also look at the source address. For any traffic that we want to allow through the PIX, the PIX routing table must include a route back to the source address—which will be the case for all legitimate traffic. See RFC 2267 for more information.

For outside traffic, for example, the PIX can use the default route to satisfy the Unicast RPF protection. If traffic enters from an outside interface, and the source address is not known to the routing table, the PIX uses the default route to correctly identify the outside interface as the source interface.

If traffic enters the outside interface from an address that is known to the routing table, but is associated with the inside interface, the PIX drops the packet. Similarly, if traffic enters the inside interface from an unknown source address, the PIX drops the packet because the matching route (the default route) indicates the outside interface.

Unicast RPF is implemented as follows:

- ICMP packets have no session, so each packet is checked.

- UDP and TCP have sessions, although they are "virtual sessions" in the case of UDP, so the initial packet requires a reverse route lookup. Subsequent packets arriving during the session are checked using an existing state maintained as part of the session. Noninitial packets are checked to ensure they arrived on the same interface used by the initial packet.

To enable Unicast RPF, the following command is used:

```
PIX1(config)# ip verify reverse-path interface interface_name
```

Typically, we would want to enable Unicast RPF on all interfaces of the PIX.

To see statistics on anti-spoofing, this command can be used:

```
PIX1 # show ip verify statistics
interface outside: 0 unicast rpf drops
interface inside: 0 unicast rpf drops
```

Other Ways the PIX Can Prevent, Contain, or Manage Attacks

In PIX v7, new options have been added to protect inside hosts from attack. Most notable here is the class map feature, which allows you to specify "classes" of traffic and apply restrictions to that traffic. Some of these features overlap with features previously available, such as the SYN FloodGuard feature just discussed.

Configuring Connection Limits and Timeouts

Next, we look at how to set maximum TCP and UDP connections, maximum embryonic connections, connection timeouts, and how to disable TCP sequence randomization.

TCP sequence randomization should only be disabled if another in-line firewall is also randomizing sequence numbers and the result is scrambling the data. Each TCP connection has two Initial Sequence Numbers (ISNs): one generated by the client and one generated by the server. The PIX randomizes the ISN that is generated by the host/server. At least one of the ISNs must be randomly generated so attackers cannot predict the next ISN and potentially hijack the session.

To set connection limits:

1. Identify the traffic, and add a class map using the *class-map*. For our purposes here, we'll assume the matching criteria for the map is an access list:

```
PIX1(config)# class-map name
PIX1(config-cmap) match access-list
```

2. Add or edit a policy map that sets the actions to take with the *class map* traffic.

```
PIX1(config)# policy-map name
```

3. Identify the class map from step 1 to which you want to assign an action.

```
PIX1(config-pmap)# class class_map_name
```

4. Set the maximum connections (both TCP and UDP), maximum embryonic connections, or whether to disable TCP sequence randomization.

```
hostname(config-pmap-c)# set connection {[conn-max number] [embryonic-conn-max
number] [random-sequence-number {enable | disable}}
```

where *number* is an integer between 0 and 65535. The default is 0, which means no limit on connections. You can enter this command all on one line (in any order), or you can enter each attribute as a separate command. The command is combined onto one line in the running configuration.

5. Set the timeout for connections, embryonic connections (half-opened), and half-closed connections.

   - ```
     PIX1(config-pmap-c)# set connection {[embryonic hh[: mm[: ss]]]
     [half-closed hh[: mm[: ss]]] [tcp hh[: mm[: ss]]]}
     ```

   - Where **embryonic** *hh[:mm[:ss]* is a time between 0:0:5 and 1192:59:59. The default is 0:0:30. You can also set this value to 0, which means the connection never times out.

   - The half-closed hh[:mm[:ss] and tcp hh[:mm[:ss] values are a time between 0:5:0 and 1192:59:59. The default for half-closed is 0:10:0 and the default for tcp is 1:0:0. You can also set these values to 0, which means the connection never times out.

You can enter this command all on one line (in any order), or you can enter each attribute as a separate command. The command is combined onto one line in the running configuration.

6. Activate the policy map on one or more interfaces.

   - ```
     hostname(config)# service-policy policymap_name {global | interface
     interface_name}
     ```

Where **global** applies the policy map to all interfaces, and **interface** applies the policy to one interface. Only one global policy is allowed. You can override the global policy on an interface by applying a service policy to that interface. You can only apply one policy map to each interface.

Preventing MAC Address Spoofing

MAC address spoofing, also known as ARP spoofing, is an attack on the Layer-2 Ethernet addressing on the local segment. An attacker could spoof his MAC address and thus facilitate a man-in-the-middle attack, or fool a switch into sending packets to the attacker. For example, a host sends an ARP request to the gateway router; the gateway router responds with the gateway router MAC address. The attacker, however, sends another ARP response to the host with the attacker MAC address instead of the router MAC address. The attacker can now intercept all the host traffic before forwarding it on to the router.

ARP inspection prevents malicious users from impersonating other hosts or routers. ARP inspection ensures that an attacker cannot send an ARP response with the attacker MAC address, as long as the correct MAC address and the associated IP address are in the static ARP table.

ARP inspection relies on a static one-to-one relationship between IP address and MAC address. It is most applicable on security-critical and static network segments. A typical LAN interface containing PCs assigned IP addresses from a DHCP server would not be suitable for this configuration. A good match for ARP inspection is a mission-critical DMZ interface with a defined number of servers on static IPs.

To enable ARP inspection for transparent firewall mode, use the *arp-inspection* command in global configuration mode. To disable ARP inspection, use the *no* form of this command. ARP inspection checks all ARP packets against static ARP entries (see the *arp* command) and blocks mismatched packets. This feature prevents ARP spoofing.

```
arp-inspection interface_name enable [flood | no-flood]
no arp-inspection interface_name enable
```

- **enable** Enables ARP inspection.

- **flood**(default) Specifies that packets that do not match any element of a static ARP entry are flooded out all interfaces except the originating interface. If there is a mismatch between the MAC address, the IP address, or the interface, the PIX drops the packet.

- *interface_name* The interface on which we want to enable ARP inspection.

- **no-flood**(optional) Specifies that packets that do not exactly match a static ARP entry are dropped.

By default, ARP inspection is disabled on all interfaces; all ARP packets are allowed through the PIX. When you enable ARP inspection, the default is to flood nonmatching ARP packets.

Before enabling ARP inspection, we need to configure static ARP entries using the *arp* command. When we enable ARP inspection, the security appliance compares the MAC address, IP address, and source interface in all ARP packets to static entries in the ARP table, and takes the following actions:

- If the IP address, MAC address, and source interface match an ARP entry, the packet is passed through.

- If there is a mismatch between the MAC address, the IP address, or the interface, the PIX drops the packet.

- If the ARP packet does not match any entries in the static ARP table, we can set the PIX to either forward the packet out all interfaces (flood) or drop the packet.

The following example enables ARP inspection on the DMZ interface and sets the PIX to drop any ARP packets that do not match the static ARP entry:

```
PIX1(config)# arp dmz 192.168.1.10 000a.8cdf.3215
PIX1(config)# arp-inspection dmz enable no-flood
```

Summary

The Cisco PIX firewall is an advanced product and has many different options for protecting against network layer attacks. It also supports content filtering for outbound Web and FTP access and a limited form of intrusion detection.

Content filtering features on the PIX can be used to enforce a company's acceptable use policy. The PIX can interface with Websense (www.websense.com) or Sentian by N2H2 (www.n2h2.com) servers and deny or allow internal clients to access specific Web sites. The PIX is also able to filter out Java applets and ActiveX code from incoming Web pages to protect clients against malicious code.

Finally, the PIX has embedded protection against various DoS attacks, such as SYN floods, excessive fragmentation, and excessive connection establishment. IP address antispoofing is supported by the reverse-path forwarding feature.

Chapter 13

Services

Solutions in this chapter:

- DHCP Functionality
- PPPoE
- EasyVPN
- Routing and the PIX Firewall
- Queuing and Policing

☑ Summary

Introduction

In addition to performing its traditional firewall functions such as filtering traffic, the PIX firewall can also provide a variety of other services. These services are a convenient way to get added value from your firewall; rather than having to set up separate servers and applications to deliver these servers to your network, the firewall becomes an all-in-one appliance.

DHCP Functionality

DHCP is a convenient method of providing required configuration parameters to network nodes, such as IP address, default gateway, DNS servers, and WINS servers. Rather than configuring these parameters manually on every client, DHCP allows the configuration details to be set centrally, in this case on the PIX firewall, and then assigned to each node as required.

The PIX firewall is capable of acting as a DHCP server to a node connected to any of its interfaces. The firewall is also capable of acting as a DHCP relay server, where it forwards DHCP requests from clients to another DHCP server. Finally, the firewall has DHCP client functionality, allowing for the configuration of its own network parameters based on another DHCP server on the network.

DHCP Servers

You can configure the PIX firewall to issue IP addresses, as well as information such as DNS and WINS servers, the default gateway, and a DNS domain name. The process for configuring DHCP is relatively straightforward: define your parameters associated with an interface. *Do not forget to enable DHCPD on the appropriate interface!*

In Figure 13.1, we have four networks for which we want the PIX firewall to issue IP addresses.

Figure 13.1 PIX DHCP Services

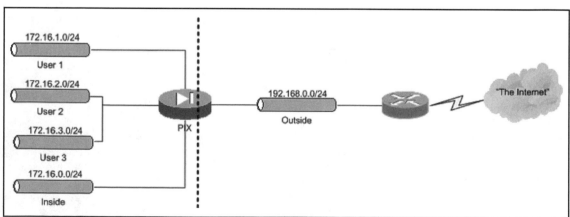

Notice how we have defined four separate pools and setups of parameters. These serve to illustrate that the PIX can uniquely provide this service to differing networks. The configuration for providing DHCP services to each of these networks is provided.

```
dhcpd address 172.16.0.100-172.16.0.200 inside
dhcpd dns 192.168.0.200
dhcpd wins 192.168.0.100
dhcpd lease 6000
dhcpd domain inside.syngress.com
dhcpd enable inside

dhcpd address 172.16.1.100-172.16.1.200 User1
dhcpd dns 192.168.0.200
dhcpd wins 192.168.0.100
dhcpd lease 6000
dhcpd domain user1.syngress.com
dhcpd enable user1

dhcpd address 172.16.2.100-172.16.2.200 User2
dhcpd dns 192.168.0.200
dhcpd wins 192.168.0.100
dhcpd lease 6000
dhcpd domain user2.syngress.com
dhcpd enable user2

dhcpd address 172.16.3.100-172.16.3.200 User3
dhcpd dns 192.168.0.200
dhcpd wins 192.168.0.100
dhcpd lease 6000
dhcpd domain user3.syngress.com
dhcpd enable user3
```

Commands are available for checking the state of the server. For example:

```
PIX1(config)# show dhcpd
dhcpd address 192.168.2.201-192.168.2.210 inside
dhcpd lease 3000
dhcpd ping_timeout 750
dhcpd dns 1.2.3.4 1.2.3.31
dhcpd enable inside
```

Other commands show the current state of IP bindings (which client has been assigned which IP address) and general server statistics:

```
PIX1(config)# show dhcpd binding
IP Address Hardware Address Lease Expiration Type
192.168.2.210 0100.a0c9.777e 84985 seconds automatic
```

Here, a client with MAC address 0100.a0c9.777e has obtained IP address 192.168.2.210, and this lease will expire in 84,985 seconds:

```
PIX1(config)# show dhcpd statistics
Address Pools 1
Automatic Bindings 1
Expired Bindings 1
Malformed messages 0
Message Received
BOOTREQUEST 0
DHCPDISCOVER 1
DHCPREQUEST 2
DHCPDECLINE 0
DHCPRELEASE 0
DHCPINFORM 0
Message Sent
BOOTREPLY 0
DHCPOFFER 1
DHCPACK 1
DHCPNAK 1
```

These statistics show the number of IP address pools configured, the number of active leases (bindings), expired bindings, messages received with errors, and a detailed breakdown on message type for correctly received and sent messages.

Cisco IP Phone-Related Options

In addition to the standard DHCP parameters such as IP address and default gateway, a Cisco IP phone makes use of DHCP to obtain the IP address of the TFTP server from which the phone can download its configuration. To configure the PIX firewall to respond to IP phone DHCP requests, enter the following commands:

```
PIX1(config)# dhcpd option 66 ascii 172.16.0.5
PIX1(config)# dhcpd option 3 ip 172.16.0.1
```

The first command will assign the IP phone a TFTP server of 172.16.0.5, and the second command will assign the phone a default gateway of 172.16.0.1. Note that you have the option of assigning more than one TFTP server. In this case, enter the following commands:

```
PIX1(config)# dhcpd option 150 ascii 172.16.0.5 172.16.0.6
```

This command assigns the phone 172.16.0.5 as the primary TFTP server and 172.16.0.6 as the secondary TFTP server.

DHCP Relay

If you want to use the PIX as a DHCP server, you can configure it to relay requests to a DHCP server located elsewhere. This is similar to the IP helper command in IOS. You simply specify the target DHCP server address and the interface to which it is associated. For example, the following command is used to relay DHCP requests to 192.168.0.250:

```
dhcprelay server 192.168.0.250 outside
```

DHCP Clients

When configured as a DHCP client, the PIX firewall can obtain the configuration of its outside interface from a designated DHCP server—for example, a server located at an ISP. This configuration includes the IP address, the subnet mask, and optionally, the default route.

This address can be used, for example, as a PAT address for all outgoing communications. This is configured in the following way (assuming that the DHCP client is already configured):

```
nat (inside) 1 0 0
global (outside) 1 interface
```

This configuration will work with any IP address assigned to the outside interface by DHCP. The configuration of the DHCP client is rather simple, and all you need to use is the following command:

```
ip address outside dhcp [setroute] [retry <retry_cnt>]
```

You do this instead of specifying a fixed IP address for an outside interface. The optional *setroute* keyword forces the PIX firewall to pick up the IP address, the subnet mask, and the default route. Do not configure a static default route on the firewall if you use the *setroute* option. The *retry* option tells the PIX firewall to try to contact a DHCP server a specified number of times before giving up. If this keyword is not specified, no retries are attempted. If this keyword is specified but no retry count is given, the default number of retries is four. For example, the following command configures a DHCP client on the outside interface to obtain an IP address, subnet mask, and default route from the DHCP server, and only one attempt will be made:

```
PIX1(config)# ip address outside dhcp setroute
```

The following command configures the DHCP client to obtain an IP address and subnet mask only and tries at least five times before giving up if no DHCP servers are available:

```
PIX1(config)# ip address outside dhcp retry 5
```

There are no special commands for renewing and releasing a DHCP lease; simply issue the same command again and the lease will be renewed. The address obtained can be viewed using:

```
PIX1# show ip address outside dhcp
```

This produces output similar to the following:

```
Temp IP Addr:123.1.2.3 for peer on interface:outside
Temp sub net mask:255.255.255.0
DHCP Lease server:123.1.2.31, state:3 Bound
DHCP Transaction id:0×4567
Lease:259200 secs, Renewal:129600 secs, Rebind:226800 secs
Temp default-gateway addr:123.1.2.1
Next timer fires after:100432 secs
Retry count:0, Client-ID:cisco-0000.0000.0000-outside
```

This output means that PIX has obtained an IP address of 123.1.2.3 and a subnet mask of 255.255.255.0 from the DHCP server 123.1.2.31. This DHCP lease is granted for 259200 seconds with renewal time of 129600 seconds. Time left until the next renewal is 100432 seconds, and there were no retries in contacting the server.

In case there are any issues with the DHCP client, you can troubleshoot using *debug* commands, including *debug dhcp packet*, *debug dhcpc detail*, and *debug dhcpc error*. The commands are self-explanatory. *debug dhcpc packet* displays all DHCP traffic between the PIX client and a remote server, the *detail* option shows details of negotiation, and the *error* option displays all errors in this communication.

PPPoE

Point-to-Point Protocol over Ethernet (PPPoE), documented in RFC 2516, is an encapsulation of Point-to-Point Protocol (PPP, RFC 1661) for Ethernet networks (which include DSL modems and cable connections). PPPoE is often used in SOHO environments because it allows ISPs to use their existing remote access infrastructure and, as its most important feature, allows authenticated IP address assignment. PPPoE links are established in two main phases:

- **Active discovery phase**   During this first phase, a PPPoE client attempts discovery of the PPPoE server, also called the *address concentrator* (AC). The PPPoE layer is established and a session ID is assigned.

- **PPP session phase**   A PPP link is established (encapsulated in Ethernet) by the usual means: options and link layer protocols are negotiated, etc. PPP authentication (PAP, CHAP, or MS-CHAP) is performed.

After the session is established, data travels between endpoints encapsulated in PPPoE headers.

The PIX firewall supports PPPoE since software v6.2. Most of the PPPoE configuration is performed using the *vpdn* command. PPPoE configuration starts with configuring the username and password to be used by the PIX in establishing a link to the server.

First, a VPDN group needs to be created:

```
vpdn group <group_name> request dialout pppoe
```

The *group_name* parameter can be anything you like. It is used to group all PPPoE settings together. For example:

```
PIX1(config)# vpdn group my-pppoe-group request dialout pppoe
```

Then, the authentication type needs to be selected (if required by an ISP):

```
vpdn group <group_name ppp> authentication pap | chap | mschap
```

PAP is Password Authentication Protocol, CHAP is Challenge-Handshake Authentication Protocol, and MS-CHAP is Microsoft's version of CHAP. With the same group name, this command selects an authentication protocol for this specific PPPoE group—for example, with CHAP authentication:

```
PIX1(config)# vpdn group my-pppoe-group ppp authentication chap
```

Your ISP assigns the username and password to your system, and they are configured on PIX with the following commands:

```
vpdn group <group_name> localname <username>
vpdn username <username> password <pass>
```

The second of these commands associates a username with the password, and the first command assigns the username to be used for a specific group; for example:

```
PIX1(config)# vpdn group my-ppoe-group localname witt
PIX1(config)# vpdn username witt password cruelmail
```

These commands assign the username *witt* and password *cruelmail* to be used for the PPPoE dial-out group *my-pppoe-group*. After configuring authentication, the next task is to enable the PPPoE client on the PIX. This is done in the configuration of the outside interface with the *ip address outside pppoe [setroute]* command. After this command is entered, the current PPPoE session is terminated and a new one is established. The *setroute* parameter allows automatically setting the default route for the outside interface. The MTU on the outside interface is automatically set to 1492, which is the correct setting to provide PPPoE encapsulation. It is also possible to designate a fixed IP address for the outside interface. The PIX still has to provide the ISP with the correct username and password to establish the session:

```
PIX1(config)# ip address outside 1.2.3.4 255.255.255.0 pppoe
```

It is possible to use the *dhcp auto_config* command if you run the DHCP server on PIX to pick up DNS and WINS settings from your provider via the PPPoE client:

```
PIX1(config)# dhcpd auto_config outside
```

To monitor and troubleshoot the PPPoE client, use the following commands:

```
show ip address outside pppoe
debug pppoe event | error | packet
show vpdn session pppoe [id <sess_id>|packets|state|window]
```

Examples of output are as follows:

```
PIX1(config)# show vpdn
Tunnel id 0, 1 active sessions
time since change 10240 secs
Remote Internet Address 10.0.1.1
Local Internet Address 192.168.2.254
```

```
1006 packets sent, 1236 received, 98761 bytes sent, 123765 received
Remote Internet Address is 10.0.1.1
Session state is SESSION_UP
Time since event change 10237 secs, interface outside
PPP interface id is 1
1006 packets sent, 1236 received, 98761 bytes sent, 123765 received
PIX1(config)# show vpdn tunnel
PPPoE Tunnel Information (Total tunnels=1 sessions=1)
Tunnel id 0, 1 active sessions
time since change 10240 secs
Remote Internet Address 10.0.1.1
Local Internet Address 192.168.2.254
1006 packets sent, 1236 received, 98761 bytes sent, 123765 received
PIX1(config)# show vpdn session
PPPoE Session Information (Total tunnels=1 sessions=1)
Remote Internet Address is 10.0.1.1
Session state is SESSION_UP
Time since event change 100238 secs, interface outside
PPP interface id is 1
1006 packets sent, 1236 received, 98761 bytes sent, 123765 received
```

EasyVPN

The purpose of EasyVPN is to simplify the management of VPN deployments. This is accomplished by centralizing the point of configuration for a VPN environment to the EasyVPN server, which then pushes the policies out to EasyVPN clients. EasyVPN is supported across a variety of Cisco platforms, including the PIX firewall, which supports both the EasyVPN client and server.

EasyVPN Server

To configure the PIX firewall as an EasyVPN server, first complete all the usual configuration necessary for the PIX to establish IP communication with its inside and outside networks. Next, add the standard VPN configuration elements, including IPsec transform sets and dynamic crypto maps, as well as applying the crypto map to the outside interface. Be sure to configure the phase 1 ISAKMP parameters as you would for any other VPN connection.

The configuration parameters specific to an EasyVPN server are specified with the *vpngroup* command. All configuration defined will automatically be pushed out and accepted by an EasyVPN client that connects to the PIX as an EasyVPN server. Here are some commonly used EasyVPN parameters:

```
PIX1(config)# vpngroup testgroup1 address-pool mypool1

PIX1(config)# vpngroup testgroup1 idle-time 1200
```

```
PIX1(config)# vpngroup testgroup1 password mypass1

PIX1(config)# vpngroup testgroup1 dns-server 192.168.1.1

PIX1(config)# vpngroup testgroup1 wins-server 192.168.2.1
PIX1(config)# vpngroup testgroup1 default-domain mydomain.com
```

Here, we are configuring the EasyVPN server to use the previously defined address pool mypool1, with an idle timeout of 1200 seconds, a password of mypass1, DNS and WINS servers of 192.168.1.1 and 192.168.2.1, respectively, and a default domain of mydomain.com. As you can see from this example, configuring such parameters centrally, rather than on each individual remote client, has great advantages in terms of efficiency. This is assuming that these parameters will be consistent across your network, including VPN remotely connected devices, but this is often the case.

Routing and the PIX Firewall

The PIX firewall can do a limited amount of routing. Let us not forget that it is a firewall, not a router. Its mission is to secure the network, not find the best path to a destination. Having said that, Cisco has incorporated a limited set of routing features into the PIX. As of this writing, the PIX can route via static routes, RIP, and OSPF, and, oddly enough, via network address translation.

In this discussion of routing, we will use the network architecture in Figure 13.2 to guide our efforts. Our goal with this architecture is to enable all three of the networks (and points behind them) to reach other.

Figure 13.2 Routing with the PIX

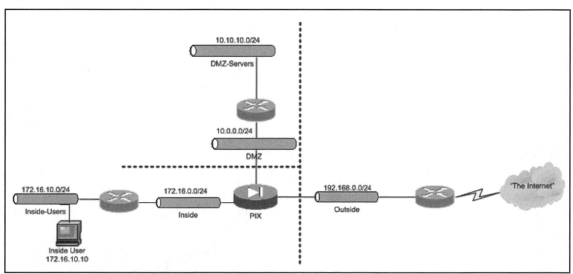

Unicast Routing

Unicast routing, as opposed to multicast routing, which we will cover later, includes static and dynamic routing, both of which are supported by the PIX. Static routing is most appropriate for cases where the PIX has only one or unchanging routes to its destinations. In these cases, it does not make sense to add the complexity and overhead of a dynamic routing protocol. In contrast, if there are multiple possible routes to a destination, such as two or more redundant paths to the same destination, and the PIX must evaluate which path to take, a dynamic routing protocol may be more appropriate.

Static Routes

The use of static routes has been a mainstay of PIX routing since its inception. It is the oldest and most static method of routing of the PIX firewall—make of that what you will. This command is largely unchanged from the previous versions. While similar to its IOS counterpart (specify the network and its next hop/interface), it is still obviously a PIX command.

The command is simple, with few options, as shown:

```
PIX1(config)# route ?
Current available interface(s):
  DMZ          Name of interface Ethernet2
  Outside      Name of interface Ethernet0
  inside       Name of interface Ethernet1

PIX1(config)# route DMZ ?

  Hostname or A.B.C.D The foreign network for this route, 0 means default

PIX1(config)# route DMZ 0.0.0.0 ?
  A.B.C.D The netmask for the destined foreign network

PIX1(config)# route DMZ 0.0.0.0 1.1.1.1 ?
  Hostname or A.B.C.D The address of the gateway by which the foreign network is
reached.

PIX1(config)# route DMZ 0.0.0.0 1.1.1.1 1.1.1.1 ?
  <1-255> Distance metric for this route, default is 1
  tunneled Enable the default tunnel gateway option, metric is set to 255
```

For our architecture in Figure 4.2, we need to enter the following commands to have full routing. Notice what interface each static route references.

```
route Outside 0.0.0.0 0.0.0.0 192.168.0.10 10
route inside 172.16.10.0 255.255.255.0 172.16.0.10 1
route DMZ 10.10.10.0 255.255.255.0 10.0.0.10 1
```

The first route in this example is a default route. A default route is simply a static route that includes all possible IP addresses, or 0.0.0.0 as the IP address and 0.0.0.0 as the netmask.

RIP

RIP takes the PIX firewall a few steps in the direction of automating routing on the PIX firewall. RIP is a distance vector routing protocol that suffers from a small routing diameter (anything over 15 hops is unreachable). Its use on the PIX firewall is mainly limited to immediate networks and immediate neighbors. Chances are, any neighbors of the PIX will have to run an additional routing protocol such as EIGRP or OSPF in order to expand the routing diameter.

The PIX supports both RIP versions 1 and 2; the latter fixes many problems of the former by adding support for variable length subnet masks (VLSM) and authentication for security.

Harkening back to our architecture in Figure 4.2., the following RIP configuration would enable routing between the networks.

```
PIX1(config)# rip DMZ default ?
  version RIP version, default is RIPv1
  <cr>

PIX1(config)# rip DMZ default version 2 ?
  authentication Authenticate using the specified mode
  <cr>

PIX1(config)# rip DMZ default version 2 authentication ?
  md5  Authenticate using md5 mode
  text Authenticate using text mode

PIX1(config)# rip DMZ default version 2 authentication md5 ?
  WORD < 17 char The shared key to be used for authentication

PIX1(config)# rip DMZ default version 2 authentication md5 syngress ?
  <0-255> The shared key id that matches the key

PIX1(config)# rip DMZ passive ?
  version RIP version, default is RIPv1
  <cr>

PIX1(config)# rip DMZ passive version ?
  1    RIP Version 1 (RIPv1)
  2    RIP Version 2 (RIPv2)

PIX1(config)# rip DMZ passive version 2 ?
  authentication Authenticate using the specified mode
  <cr>

PIX1(config)# rip DMZ passive version 2 authentication ?
  md5  Authenticate using md5 mode
  text Authenticate using text mode
```

```
PIX1(config)# rip DMZ passive version 2 authentication md5 ?
  WORD < 17 char The shared key to be used for authentication

PIX1(config)# rip DMZ passive version 2 authentication md5 syngress ?
  <0-255>     The shared key id that matches the key
```

PIX1(config)# **rip DMZ passive version 2 authentication md5 syngress 255**

```
rip outside passive version 2 authentication md5 thisisakey 2
rip outside default version 2 authentication md5 thisisakey 2
rip inside passive version 1
rip dmz passive version 2
```

We want our PIX firewall to transmit a route to its peers on out each of its interfaces, with the exception of the Outside interface where we just want it to learn RIP routers and populate its tables. Therefore, our configuration will be:

```
rip DMZ default version 2 authentication md5 syngress 255
rip inside default version 2 authentication md5 syngress 255
rip DMZ passive version 2 authentication md5 syngress 255
```

Notice that we are running version 2, as are our router neighbors, and that our router neighbors are injecting default routes, as well as routes from beyond. This will enable the PIX to reach these destinations.

OSPF

Support for the Open Shortest Path First (OSPF) on the PIX firewall has been around since version 6.3. With the introduction of 7.0, the configuration for OSPF remains largely unchanged. OSPF is a link state routing protocol that uses costs to determine the best (shortest) path to a network. OSPF operates by each router placing itself at the center of the network and hoarding and updating information about the links in the topology of the autonomous systems.

OSPF more than overcomes the limitations of RIP. It is a very robust, very fast routing protocol. It does require more planning and more attention to design, as it operates in a stricter hierarchy.

To accomplish our routing requirements for the network in Figure 13.2, we need to deploy the following configuration on our PIX firewall. If we assume that we are dealing with a single area at this time, we could have multiple areas.

```
router ospf 100
  network 10.0.0.0 255.255.255.0 area 0
  network 172.16.0.0 255.255.255.0 area 0
  network 192.168.0.0 255.255.255.0 area 1
  log-adj-changes
default-information originate always
```

Network Address Translation as a Routing Mechanism

With a creative design, you can use NAT to handle some of your routing needs. For the network in Figure 13.2, we have deployed NAT on each neighbor router, translating all source addresses heading to the PIX firewall to something on the subnet on each interface.

The PIX operates in blissful ignorance; it does not know about the networks behind each router. As far as it is concerned, there are only three networks. Because they are all connected, the PIX firewall can simply direct traffic to the appropriate interface, without using a static route, or dynamic routing protocol. The configuration required for this to work involves configuring NAT on the router attached to each PIX interface, which is beyond the scope of PIX configuration, and therefore this book. However, the key factor to keep in mind is that because the remote routers are translating all traffic to the IP addresses that are directly connected to the PIX, the PIX will therefore have connected routes to these networks by default. It is for this reason that the PIX does not require any static or dynamic routing in this case.

The only caveat or requirement for routing in this scenario is that you might want to or need to add a default route to handle traffic such as that that going to the Internet.

Multicast Routing

While unicast packets are sent from one source to one destination, multicast packets are sent from one source to multiple destinations. This is useful for applications that are designed to distribute information to two or more users, and especially to higher volumes of users, where sending individual copies of the data from the source to each destination can quickly create a congested network. Multicast, on the other hand, need not duplicate the same data along any one network segment; if two or more hosts on the same network segment are to receive a multicast stream of data, only one copy of the data needs to be sent by the source host.

A good example of an application that benefits from multicast is Microsoft Netmeeting. With Netmeeting, typically one presenter is transmitting information to multiple remote users. Rather than sending the data of the presentation individually to each user, multicast allows for a significant improvement in network efficiency.

Multicast traffic makes use of a defined set of IP addresses: 224.0.0.0 through 239.255.255.255. Many of these are reserved on the Internet (see www.iana.org/assignments/multicast-addresses).

Multicast routing is supported by the PIX firewall, in order to allow it to participate in a multicast network where routing is required for multicast traffic to reach its destination. The PIX supports stub multicast routing and PIM multicast routing. No matter which type of multicast routing you want to enable, the first step to enabling multicast routing support on the PIX is to enter this command:

```
PIX1(config)# multicast-routing
```

Once multicast routing is enabled globally, the PIX is ready to build a multicast routing table. This table's size is only restricted by the amount of memory installed in your PIX firewall. Table.13.1 describes the maximum number of routes the PIX can store based on its memory. This table is courtesy of Cisco (see www.cisco.com/en/US/partner/products/sw/secursw/ps2120/products_configuration_guide_chapter09186a00804231c6.html#wp1041648, Table 8.1).

Table 13.1 PIX Multicast Routing Table Size Limits

Table	16MB	128MB	128+MB
MFIB	1000	3000	5000
IGMP Groups	1000	3000	5000
PIM Routes	3000	7000	12000

Even though you have enabled multicast routing on the PIX, it is still possible to specify whether each interface should participate in multicast routing. This is done by enabling or disabling IGMP on a per-interface basis. Since IGMP is the protocol used by hosts to report group membership, disabling IGMP on an interface effectively disables multicast routing functionality on that interface. Note that by default, enabling multicast routing on the PIX enables IGMP on all interfaces. To disable IGMP on a specific interface, for example ethernet0, enter the following commands:

```
PIX1(config)# int ethernet0
PIX1(config-if)# no igmp
```

To re-enable IGMP on an interface where it was previously disabled, enter the following:

```
PIX1(config)# int ethernet0
PIX1(config-if)# igmp
```

Stub Multicast Routing

Stub multicast routing is a method of multicast routing that simply involves forwarding IGMP messages to another multicast-enabled router, rather than fully participating in the multicast routing protocol. This is an appropriate method to use in such cases where you want to centralize your multicast routing to your uplink router, and do not need to push full multicast functionality to other nodes, such as the PIX, but still want hosts behind the PIX to be able to function in a multicast environment.

Stub multicast routing is accomplished by configuring the PIX to act as a route proxy. To configure the PIX firewall to forward IGMP messages from one interface to another, for example from ethernet1 to ethernet0 (outside), enter the following commands:

```
PIX1(config-if)# int ethernet1
PIX1(config-if)# igmp forward interface outside
```

PIM Multicast Routing

An alternative to stub multicast routing is PIM (note that they cannot both be enabled concurrently). PIM stands for Protocol Independent Multicast, and is not dependent on a specific unicast routing protocol—it can function as long as IP connectivity is established through whatever static or dynamic unicast protocol is in use. By enabling PIM on the PIX, it is able to fully participate in multicast routing, which is appropriate in cases where there are hosts behind the PIX that make use of multicast applications, and there are multiple upstream multicast destinations for the PIX to route traffic to.

By default, when multicast routing is enabled on the PIX, PIM is also enabled on all interfaces. To disable PIM on an interface, for example ethernet0, enter the following commands:

```
PIX1(config-if)# int ethernet0
PIX1(config-if)# no pim
```

To re-enable PIM on an interface where it was previously disabled, enter the following:

```
PIX1(config-if)# int ethernet0
PIX1(config-if)# pim
```

Although there are three rendezvous-point (RP) modes—static RP, auto-RP, and BSR—the PIX firewall only supports static RP. To configure the PIX for a static RP, enter the following command:

```
PIX1(config)# pim rp-address 10.1.1.1
```

BGP through PIX Firewall

Allowing BGP through the PIX firewall is quite straightforward. Assuming you have configured the PIX to enable IP connectivity between the BGP routers, the only additional step is to allow the BGP traffic via an access-list. For example, to allow BGP traffic from a router with IP address 172.16.0.1 to another router with IP address 172.16.1.1, enter the following command:

```
PIX1(config)# access-list bgp1 permit tcp host 172.16.0.1 host 172.16.1.1 eq bgp
```

You will then need to apply this access-list to the appropriate interface. For example, to apply it to the outside interface, enter this command:

```
PIX1(config)# access-group bgp1 in interface outside
```

Queuing and Policing

Queuing and policing are part of the Quality of Service (QoS) functionality built in to the PIX. QoS, simply explained, is the prioritization of some traffic over other traffic, for the sake of providing the best service to the traffic that is most important or sensitive to network degradation.

The first step to enabling QoS on the PIX is to identify the traffic you would like to prioritize. Identifying traffic is done with class maps. Class maps can match traffic based on an access-list, a DSCP value, a TCP or UDP port, an IP destination, an IP precedence, an RTP port, or a tunnel group. Here is an example of a class map that matches all HTTP packets:

```
PIX1(config)# access-list allhttp permit tcp any any eq 80
PIX1(config)# class-map http-map
PIX1(config-cmap)# match access-list allhttp
```

Once the traffic you are interested in is identified by a class map, the next step is to use a policy map to apply an action to this traffic. Rate limiting, also known as policing, is applied this way.

For example, to limit HTTP traffic to 100,000 bits per second, with a 10,000 bytes per second burst size, enter the following commands:

```
PIX1(config)# policy-map httplimit
PIX1(config-pmap)# class http-map
PIX1(config-pmap-c)# policy outside 100000 10000
```

The final step is to enable the policy, either globally or on a specific interface. For example, to enable the previously defined HTTP policy on the outside interface of the PIX, enter the following command:

```
PIX1(config)# service-policy httplimit interface outside
```

To enable this policy on all interfaces rather than the outside interface:

```
PIX1(config)# service-policy httplimit global
```

Summary

The PIX supports a number of services that are designed to augment the value of the PIX beyond its core firewall functionality. DHCP allows the PIX to provide IP address and related assignment without the need for a separate server. The PIX's QoS functionality may be sufficient for your traffic prioritization needs, eliminating the need for another router that would otherwise be required. Furthermore, the routing functionality that is built in to the PIX provides a flexible set of unicast and multicast routing options that allow the PIX to establish full IP connectivity to the rest of the network.

Finally, with the PIX's EasyVPN functionality, it is capable of acting as an EasyVPN server, where it can be configured to propagate a variety of policy settings to any number of EasyVPN clients.

Chapter 14

Configuring Authentication, Authorization, and Accounting

Solutions in this chapter:

- Introducing AAA Concepts
- Using AAA Protocols+
- Configuring Console Authentication
- Configuring Local Authentication
- Configuring Command Authorization
- Configuring Local AAA Using the ASDM
- Configuring Authentication for Traffic through the Firewall
- Configuring Authorization for Traffic through the Firewall
- Configuring Accounting for Traffic through the Firewall

☑ Summary

Introduction

Managing one or two PIX firewalls is not very difficult. If the number of firewalls increases or configurations become more complex, management becomes more of a challenge. Authentication can become a huge challenge as you may end up spending much time setting new passwords because someone left a position, or a new person is hired, or you mistyped that password for the furthermost firewall on your network. Nobody needs headaches like this so Cisco has thoughtfully provided a method to simplify the management of passwords and permissions while allowing you to do the management securely. Welcome to the world of AAA, or authentication, authorization, and accounting. Many engineers and admins shudder when they read or hear AAA. There are justifiable horror stories floating around about wide scale lockouts due to misconfigurations. But, with planning and a solid understanding of AAA basics and its implementation steps, the task becomes management. This chapter will provide you with a solid ground in AAA on the Cisco PIX firewall.

New and Changed Commands in 7.0

Along with everything else that you have read about so far, Cisco PIX 7.0 has changed how AAA is configured. There are parameter changes for the following functions:

- VPN Remote Access users (IPSec, L2TP over IPsec)

- Cut-through authentication proxies for FTP, Telnet, HTTP, and HTTPS

- Device management

And these commands will be affected by the new changes in the 7.0 code when you upgrade from 6.3 to 7.0:

- aaa-server

- aaa-server radius-acctport

- aaa-server radius-authport

- auth-prompt

- floodguard

There are new commands along with the modified commands for AAA. A partial list of the new commands for the 7.0 code is:

- aaa local authentication attempts max-fail <number>

- aaa-server protocol

- clear aaa local user failed-attempts

- clear aaa local user lockout

- clear configure username <word>

- show running-config username

The good news is that when you upgrade from 6.x to 7.0, the AAA commands will automatically convert to the proper format so you will not have to make changes for your AAA configuration to work. We will cover these changes a bit later in this chapter.

Configuring authentication and authorization in order to give us more granular control of access to networks and tracking that access through Accounting is fundamental to overall network security. Developing user policies with AAA will help control access to different parts of a network. This chapter explains and demonstrates AAA on the Cisco PIX firewall, and how to utilize the RADIUS and TACACS+ security protocols.

The PIX firewall is capable of acting as an AAA client. The PIX can provide AAA functionality for administrative access to the firewall itself, as well as for traffic passing through the firewall.

Introducing AAA Concepts

AAA is an architectural framework for independent but related functions of authentication, authorization, and accounting, which are defined as follows:

- *Authentication* is the process of identifying and validating a user before allowing access to network devices and services. User identification is critical for authorization and accounting functions. The Cisco PIX can be configured to authenticate for the following list of connections and functions:

    - Telnet

    - SSH

    - Serial Console

    - ASDM

    - The **enable** command

    - VPN Access

    - Network Access to the PIX

- *Authorization* is the process of validating and controlling user privileges and access rights after they have been authenticated. The Cisco PIX can be configured to authorize the following:

    - Management commands

    - Network Access

    - VPN Access

- *Accounting* is the process of recording user activities for accountability, billing, auditing, or reporting purposes. It includes details such as the start and stop time, username, number of bytes for the session, the services used, and the duration of the session.

The AAA framework typically consists of a client and a server using a security protocol like TACACS+ or RADIUS to name a couple of the major protocols. The AAA client, which is typically a router, NAS, or firewall, will request authentication, authorization, and/or accounting services from an AAA server that either maintains a local database containing the relevant AAA information or communicates with an external database that contains the information. Some examples of external databases are a Windows NT domain, Active Directory, LDAP, a SQL Server database, and the UNIX password database. Here are some typical conditions under which using an AAA framework would be effective:

- **To provide centralized authentication for the administration of a large number of network devices such as switches, routers and firewalls**. An example is a small-to medium-sized business that has a relatively high ratio of devices to security administrators. Centralized authentication would ease the administrative burden, but because the number of administrators is low, centralized authorization and accounting might not be beneficial.

- **To provide flexible authorization capabilities**. An example is a global enterprise that has a large number of devices and many administrators. Administrative duties might be divided along operational and configuration lines such that the implementation of centralized authorization would be an effective addition to centralization authentication.

- **To provide relevant usage or billing information**. An example is a service provider that charges customers based on network usage statistics. In this case, the centralized authentication and authorization would be an effective means of supporting firewall administration, and centralized accounting would provide the business with network usage information for billing.

Examples of AAA happen in everyday life outside of computers and Cisco devices. For example, when you go to an automatic teller machine (ATM) to withdraw money, you must first insert your bankcard and enter your personal identification number (PIN). At this point, you are authenticating yourself as someone who has the authority to withdraw money from this account. If your card and PIN are both valid, you will successfully authenticate and can continue the task of withdrawing money. If you have entered an incorrect PIN or your card has been damaged (or stolen) and the criteria cannot be validated, you will not be able to continue. Once authenticated, you will be permitted to perform certain actions, such as withdraw, deposit, or check your balance on various accounts. Based on your identity (your bank card and your PIN), you have been preauthorized to perform certain functions. Finally, once you complete the tasks you are authorized to perform, you will be provided with a statement describing your transactions as well as the remaining balance in your account. The bank will also record your transactions (probably more verbosely than what is on your statement) for accounting purposes.

Now let's look at an example of the same principle applied to a Web site. In Figure 14.1, Client A is attempting to access the Web site www.syngress.com. In order to accomplish this goal, Client A must first connect to its local Internet service provider (ISP) to gain access to the Internet. When Client A connects to the ISP, it is prompted for a set of logon credentials (authentication) by the network access server, or NAS, before it can fully access the Internet.

Figure 14.1 Implementation of AAA at an ISP

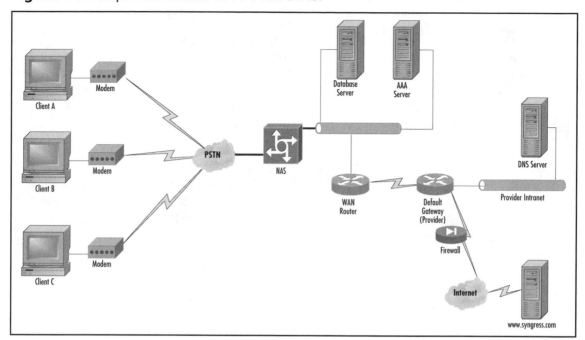

An NAS is a device that provides access to a target network (for example, an Internet, corporate network). A NAS has a connection to the target network, as well as one or more interfaces connected to an external network (such as the Internet or the public switched telephone network). It provides connectivity to clients on the external interface and provides access to the target network. A security server is typically a device such as a Windows NT or UNIX server providing TACACS+, RADIUS, or another service that enforces security. In Figure 14.1, the AAA server is an example of a security server. Once the client has entered its credentials and the AAA server has validated them, if the security policy permits it to use the Internet (authorization), it can now connect to the desired Web site (www.syngress. com). As a policy, the ISP has decided to log all customer connections to the AAA server (accounting). This example illustrates all three elements of AAA: authentication, authorization, and accounting.

Authentication

Authentication is the process of identifying and validating a user. This process typically relies on one or more of the following general methods:

- **Something the user knows**   The identity of the user is verified by something supposedly known only by the user. This is the most common and the weakest approach used for authentication today. Examples include both the UNIX and Windows NT/2000 login process, where the user typically authenticates with a password. The integrity of this process depends on the "something" being both a secret and also hard to guess—a dual goal that is not easily ensured. Some organizations have extended the UNIX and Windows NT/2000 login process to support tokens, smart cards, or biometrics, which are other authentication methods discussed in the points that follow.

- **Something the user possesses** The user's identity is verified by something possessed only by that particular user. This approach is becoming more common, usually in the form of keys and security badges. The integrity of this process depends on the "something" being unique and possessed only by the user, such as a smart card. If this object is lost or stolen, the authentication process is compromised.

- **Something the user is** Biometrics verifies the user identity with something that is unique *about* the user. This approach uses techniques such as fingerprint scans, retina scans, and voice analysis. ATMs are beginning to be deployed with biometric authentication. This is the strongest approach to authentication and avoids the common problems with the other approaches (such as a password being guessed or a card being lost or stolen). However, this approach is also the most difficult to implement.

Two-factor authentication uses a combination of two of the preceding approaches to authenticate user identities. Typically, two-factor authentication is a combination of something the user possesses and something the user knows. A common example is an ATM card (something possessed) and an associated PIN (something known) to access an account. In the information technology world, you can find two-factor authentication in the form of tokens, where a combination of a PIN plus a changing value on the token is used for authentication.

Within the AAA framework, authentication occurs when an AAA client passes appropriate user credentials to the AAA server and requests that the server authenticate the user. The AAA server attempts to validate the credentials, and responds with either an "accept" or a "deny" message. AAA authentication typically is used in the following scenarios:

- To control access to a network device such as a router, NAS, or firewall

- To control access to network resources through a network device such as a router, NAS, or firewall

Authorization

Authorization is the act of bestowing predefined rights or privileges to a user, a group of users, a system, or a process. A client will query the AAA server to determine the actions a user is authorized to perform. The AAA server will return a set of attribute-value (AV) pairs that defines the user's authorization. The client is then responsible for enforcing user access control based on those AV pairs. AAA authorization typically is used in the following scenarios:

- To provide authorization for actions attempted while logged into a network device

- To provide authorization for attempts to use network services through a network device

Accounting

Accounting records (or accounts) who, what, when, and where an action has taken place. Accounting enables you to track both the services that users are accessing and the amount of resources that they are consuming. This data can later be used for accountability, network management, billing, auditing, and reporting purposes. The client sends accounting records that consist of accounting AV pairs to the AAA server for centralized storage.

AAA Security Protocols

You can configure most Cisco devices, including routers, access servers, firewalls, and virtual private network (VPN) devices, to act as AAA clients. You can configure these network devices to request AAA services to protect the devices themselves from unauthorized access. You can also configure them to request AAA services to protect the network from unauthorized access by users attempting to use the devices as an access point.

RADIUS

The Remote Access Dial In User Service (RADIUS) protocol was developed by Livingston Enterprises, Inc., as an access server authentication and accounting protocol. Although many RFCs are available on RADIUS, the main specification can be found in RFC 2058, which was made obsolete by RFC 2865. The RADIUS accounting standard is documented in RFC 2059, which was made obsolete by RFC 2866.

RADIUS can be used as a security protocol for a network of any size, from large enterprise networks such as ISPs to small networks consisting of a few users requiring remote access. RADIUS is a client/server protocol. The RADIUS client is typically a NAS, firewall, router, VPN gateway, or even a wireless Access Point that requests a service such as authentication or authorization from the RADIUS server.

A RADIUS server is usually a daemon running on a UNIX machine or a service running on a Windows server. The daemon is software such as Cisco Secure ACS or another RADIUS server program that fulfills requests from RADIUS clients. Originally, RADIUS used UDP port 1645 for authentication traffic and 1646 for accounting traffic. However, due to an oversight in the standardization process, these ports were registered with the IANA to different services. To get around this issue, new port numbers were assigned to the RADIUS services (1812 for authentication and 1813 for accounting). Many RADIUS implementations still use the old port numbers.

Authentication Methods Used by RADIUS

RADIUS as used by the Cisco PIX firewall can use different methods of authentication. The methods available are:

- PAP

- CHAP

- MS-CHAPv1

- MS-CHAPv2 (IPsec users only)

RADIUS Functions Available on the Cisco PIX

There are certain functions available to the Cisco PIX from the RADIUS server. These functions can control access to the command line, commands, network access, VPN access and more. The available options are:

- User authentication for CLI access

- User authentication for the *enable* command

- Accounting for CLI access

- User authentication for network access

- User authorization for network access using dynamic ACLs per user

- User authorization for network access using a downloaded ACL name per user

- VPN authentication

- VPN authorization

- VPN accounting

- Accounting for network access per user or IP address

How RADIUS Works

When a client needs authorization information, the client passes the user credentials to the designated RADIUS server for checking. The server then acts on the configuration information necessary for the client to deliver services to the user. A RADIUS server can also act as a proxy client to other RADIUS servers. Figure 14.2 illustrates what happens when a user attempts to log in and authenticate to a NAS using RADIUS.

Figure 14.2 Authenticating with RADIUS

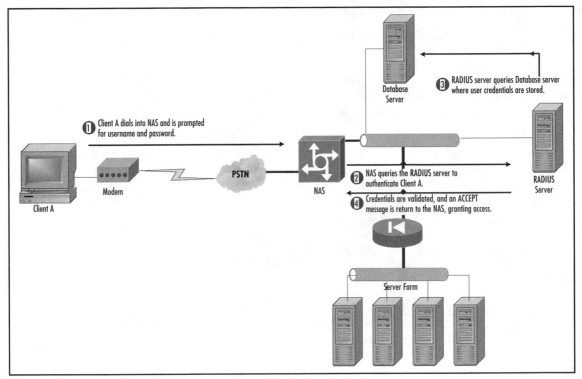

The sequence of events is as follows:

1. The remote user dials into a NAS and is prompted by the NAS for credentials such as a username and password.

2. The username and encrypted password are sent from the RADIUS client (NAS) to the RADIUS server via the network.

3. The RADIUS server queries the database in which user account definitions are stored.

4. The RADIUS server evaluates the credentials and replies with one of the following responses:

    ■ **REJECT**   The user is not authenticated; the user is prompted to reenter the username and password. Depending on the RADIUS configuration, the user is given a certain number of tries before user access is denied.

    ■ **ACCEPT**   The user is authenticated.

- **CHALLENGE** A challenge is issued by the RADIUS server, with a request for additional information from the user.

- **CHANGE PASSWORD** A request is sent from the RADIUS server specifying that the user must change his or her current password.

TACACS+

An older but still popular security protocol that is available is called Terminal Access Controller Access Control System Plus, or TACACS+. This should not be confused with TACACS and XTACACS, both of which are open standard protocols documented in RFC 1492 and no longer used. Despite the similar names, TACACS and XTACACS are not compatible with TACACS+. TACACS+ provides a method to validate users attempting to gain access to a service through a router or NAS. Similar to RADIUS, a centralized server running TACACS+ software responds to client requests in order to perform AAA.

Authentication Methods Used by TACACS+

TACACS+ on the Cisco PIX firewall can use different methods of authentication. The methods available are:

- TEXT

- PAP

- CHAP

- MS-CHAPv1

TACACS+ Functions Available to the Cisco PIX

There are certain functions available to the Cisco PIX from the TACACS+ server. These functions can control access to the command line, commands, network access, VPN access, and more:

- User authentication for CLI access

- User authentication for the *enable* command

- Accounting for CLI access

- User authentication for network access

- User authorization for network access

- VPN authentication

- VPN authorization

- VPN accounting

- User authorization for management command

- Accounting for network access per user or IP address

How TACACS+ Works

TACACS+ packets use TCP as the transport protocol and connect to TCP port 49 for communication. TACACS+ can encrypt the body of traffic travelling between the TACACS+ server and client. Only the packet header is left unencrypted. TACACS+ allows an administrator to separate the authentication, authorization, and accounting mechanisms, thereby providing the ability to implement each service independently. Each of the AAA mechanisms can be tied into separate databases.

Figure 14.3 illustrates the process that occurs when a user attempts to log in by authentication to a NAS using TACACS+:

Figure 14.3 Authenticating with TACACS+

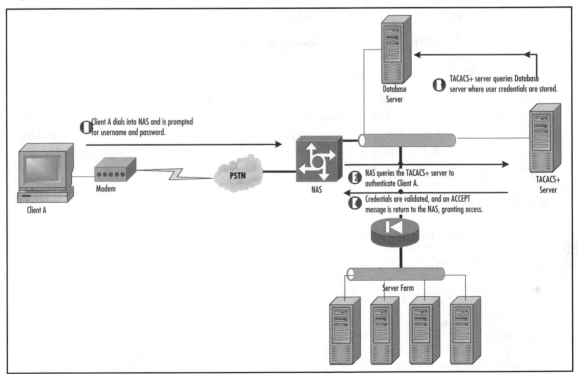

1. When the connection is established, the NAS contacts the TACACS+ server to obtain an authentication prompt, which is then displayed to the user. The user enters his or her username, and the NAS then contacts the TACACS+ server to obtain a password prompt. The NAS displays the password prompt to the user.

2. The user enters his or her password, and these credentials are then sent to the TACACS+ daemon running on a server.

3. The TACACS+ server queries the user database and compares Client A's credentials with those stored in the database server.

4. The NAS eventually will receive one of the following responses from the TACACS+ daemon:

   ■ **ACCEPT**   The user is authenticated and the service can begin.

   ■ **REJECT**   The user failed authentication. Depending on the TACACS+ daemon, the user may be denied further access or prompted to retry the login sequence.

   ■ **ERROR**   An error occurred at some point during the authentication process. This can be either at the daemon or in the network connection between the daemon and the NAS. If an ERROR response is received, the NAS typically will try to use an alternative method for authenticating the user.

   ■ **CONTINUE**   The user is prompted for additional authentication information.

Optional Security Protocols and Methods

A common method for authentication is the use of local usernames and a local database on the PIX itself. The use of local authentication can provide some features such as CLI authentication, VPN authorization/authentication, management command authorization, and one of the most important features, fallback support. Fallback is where the primary authentication/authorization method such as RADIUS has failed for some reason and you still need access to the device or function. With a local database configured as the fallback method, you can still have access even though the primary method failed. Fallback supports the following:

■ Console and enable password authentication

■ Command authorization

■ VPN authentication and authorization

This local database and authentication can be a lifesaver for the PIX administrator when the AAA server becomes unreachable, and the normal methods of authentication do not work.

The Cisco PIX can support the RSA SecureID or SDI servers for VPN authentication. The Cisco PIX can also support NT Server or NTLM version 1 for VPN authentication. The Cisco PIX can support Kerberos for VPN authentication and LDAP for VPN authentication.

AAA Servers

You now have a basic understanding of AAA functions and the most commonly implemented protocols (TACACS+ and RADIUS). To deploy AAA on the PIX firewall, you need to configure an AAA server. You can choose from many AAA server products; here is a short list of products that will work with the Cisco PIX firewall and many other devices:

- Cisco Secure ACS for Windows available as a 90-day demo at www.cisco.com/kobayashi/ sw-center/ciscosecure/cs-acs.shtml

- Cisco Secure ACS for UNIX available as a 90-day demo at www.cisco.com/kobayashi/ sw-center/ciscosecure/cs-acs.shtml

- TACACS+ available for Unix/Linux and FREE at www.gazi.edu.tr/tacacs/index.php

- FreeRADIUS available for FREE at www.freeradius.org

Configuring Console Authentication

AAA authentication either controls access *to* a network device (for example, a PIX firewall) or controls access *through* the network device (for example, Web services through a PIX firewall). This section discusses the use of the PIX firewall AAA mechanisms to control access to the PIX firewall itself via the console port, Telnet, HTTP, or SSH. The general steps necessary to configure AAA authentication for firewall access are:

1. Configure the AAA authentication database. This database can reside locally on the firewall, or on a RADIUS or TACACS+ server.
2. Specify the methods of firewall access (console, Telnet, SSH, HTTP) and the AAA authentication database that should be used.

When configuring console authentication, it helps to know exactly what Cisco means when referring to "console," and in what context. We mentioned briefly the console port, Telnet, and so on but let's take a closer look at what occurs when using different methods of console access and authentication.

- **Serial**   When connecting with a serial cable to the console port, you will be prompted to authenticate with the configured AAA server(s) before you can use the CLI.

- **Telnet**   You are prompted to authenticate before you can access the CLI.

- **SSH**   You will be prompted to authenticate, and are subject to a three-attempt limit. After three failed attempts, you will get the message "Rejected by Server." Don't take it personally!

- **HTTP** When you attempt to use the ASDM, a pop-up window appears to prompt you to login.

- **Enable** When you attempt to enter the privileged mode, you will be prompted for the password associated with your username. Much like SSH, there is a limit of three failed attempts before you get the "Access Denied" message.

Configuring Local Authentication

Though of limited value, nonetheless, a local database for authentication can be a useful failsafe. We will cover how to configure the Cisco PIX to use a local database, which can be a backdoor for recovery if we lose access to the external AAA server(s), normally, the primary source of authentication and authorization. If a mistake is made configuring the PIX to use a RADIUS or TACACS+ server, you still have access via the local database. Without this "back door" in place, your only option is to use password recovery on the PIX, which is fraught with disruptions. The mess from password recovery can be just the AAA configuration being whacked, to all the flash being erased if the *no service password-recovery* command had been used beforehand.

Defining a local database is as simple as specifying usernames and assigning passwords, per the command provided here.

```
username <username> {nopassword | password <password> [encrypted]} [privilege
<level>]
```

Specify the username that you want to assign to the user. Your usernames can be 4 to 127 characters long and passwords can be 3 to 63 characters long. You cannot use the @ symbol in the username or password. The ASDM limits you to 30 characters for the username and 15 characters for a password. Use the *nopassword* keyword to create a local account with no password. Use the *password* keyword to assign a password to a local account. If you already have the encrypted password (that is, the hash for the password), use the *encrypted* keyword to inform the PIX firewall so that it does not treat the hash as the actual password; otherwise, you'll be entering the hash as the password. Each username can be assigned a privilege level between 0 to 15 via the *privilege* keyword. These privilege levels determine what the user can do on the PIX firewall; the higher the level, the more privileges they have. For example, enable access is a level 15 privilege.

To configure a username with attributes for using a VPN connection, use the following command:

```
username <username> attributes
```

The attributes that you can choose are:

- group-lock

- password-storage

- vpn-access-hours

- vpn-filter

- vpn-framed-ip-address

- vpn-group-policy

- vpn-idle-timeout

- vpn-session-timeout

- vpn-simultaneous-logins

- vpn-tunnel-protocol

The following is an example of this command being used to specify attributes.

```
PIX1(config)# username johndoe password c1sc0t3st
PIX1(config)# username johndoe attributes
PIX1(config-username)# vpn-tunnel-protocol IPSec
PIX1(config-username)# vpn-simultaneous-logins 6
PIX1(config-username)# exit
```

The previous command produces a configuration as shown.

```
!
username johndoe password w7HxP2X.3V040EXo encrypted
username johndoe attributes
  vpn-simultaneous-logins 6
  vpn-tunnel-protocol IPSec
!
```

A new command in version 7.0 is *aaa local authentication attempts max-fail <number>*, which can set the number of failed attempts that local authentication can be queried before the account is locked out.

```
PIX1(config)# aaa local authentication attempts max-fail 5
```

The number five is the number of attempts that someone can try to authenticate before they are locked out. The range of numbers before lock out is between 1 and 16. Of course, if we can lock accounts, we have to give you a way to view the locked accounts. For that information, use a new command in version 7.0 called, *show aaa local user*, as shown:

```
PIX1# show aaa local user
Lock-time       Failed-attempts       Locked       User
-               0                     N            johndoe
```

You can unlock a user with the *clear aaa local user lockout* command or you can use *clear aaa local user failed-attempts* to clear the number of failed attempts counter, but keep the user locked out.

To remove a username from the PIX, version 7.0 gives us a new command, shown here:

```
clear configure username <word>
```

This command will clear all the usernames and their configurations unless you specify a specific username.

Once you have defined the local users, you need to specify that the local database should be used for the various access methods by executing the following command:

```
aaa authentication [serial | enable | telnet | ssh | http] console LOCAL
```

Use the *serial, enable, telnet, ssh,* or *http* keywords to specify the access method that requires authentication. For example, you can issue the following commands to establish a local user account and specify that the local database should be used when a user attempts to access the PIX firewall via Telnet, SSH, or HTTP (ASDM):

```
PIX1(config)# username pixadm password pixpassword
PIX1(config)# aaa authentication telnet console LOCAL
PIX1(config)# aaa authentication ssh console LOCAL
PIX1(config)# aaa authentication http console LOCAL
```

The enable and SSH access methods allow three tries before denying authentication. Serial and Telnet continue to prompt the user until a successful login takes place.

Configuring Local AAA Using the ASDM

The new ASDM for version 7.0 provides a rich set of point-and-click commands to configure AAA on the Cisco PIX. You can configure TACACS+, RADIUS, and Local databases for the various AAA components (authentication, authorization, and/or accounting). In the examples that follow, we will continue configuring the Cisco PIX to use local authentication and authorization. The first step in using the ASDM to configure the AAA parameters is to log into the Cisco PIX using a browser or the ASDM client for Windows. Once we are logged into ASDM, we can then create our local users as shown in Figure 14.4.

Figure 14.4 Choosing to Configure Local Users in the ASDM

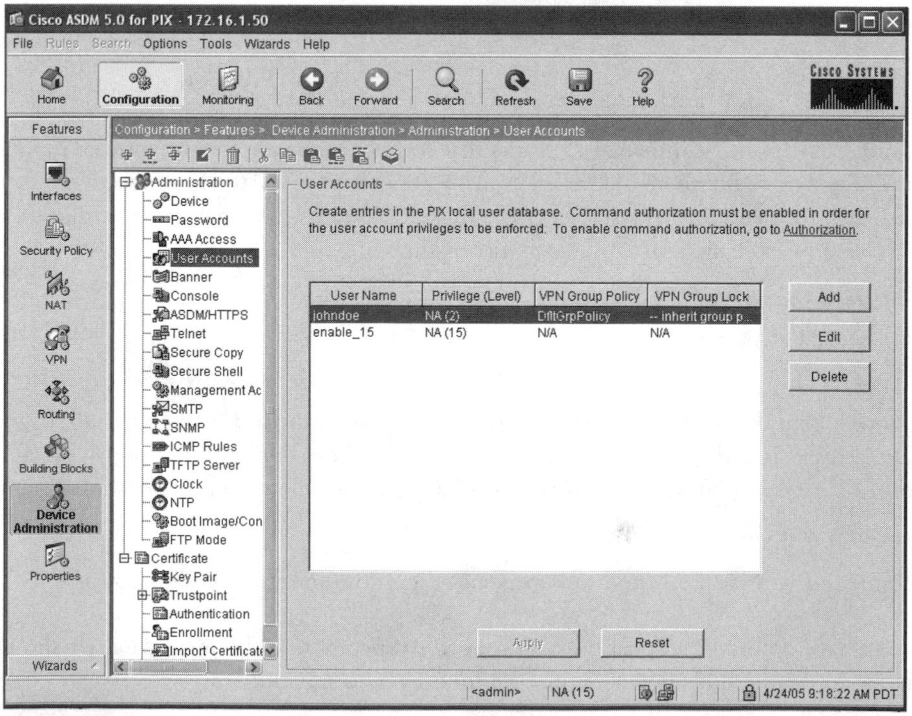

To create a new user, all you need to do is to click the Add button and complete the fields as shown in Figure 14.5. This will create the user and assign the Privilege Level. We can configure any VPN options as shown in Figure 14.6.

Figure 14.5 Creating New LOCAL Users

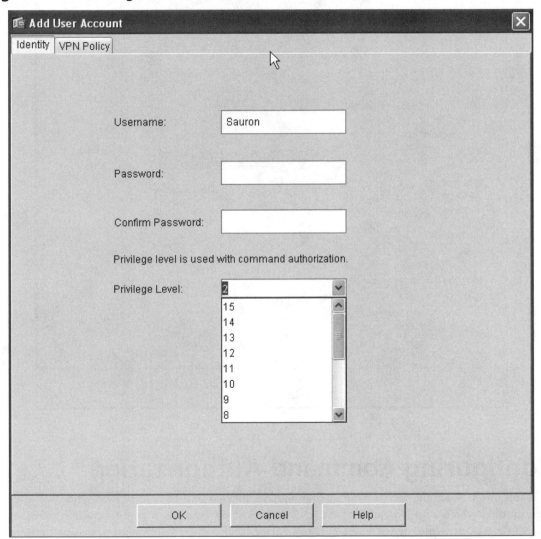

Figure 14.6 Adding VPN Settings to a LOCAL User

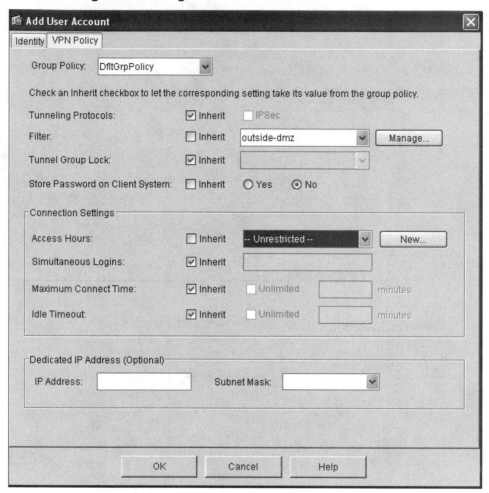

Configuring Command Authorization

This section discusses the use of the PIX firewall AAA mechanisms to control user actions on the firewall itself, which is called *authorization*. AAA authorization typically is used to control (allow or deny) user actions while logged into a network device (such as a PIX firewall) or attempts to use network services through the PIX firewall.

Beginning with version 6.2, the PIX has supported up to 16 privilege levels so that you can define and assign to users the privileges needed to accomplish their duties. This is similar to what has been available with Cisco IOS software. Sixteen privilege levels (0 through 15) are available: the higher the privilege level, the more access the level has. By default, most PIX firewall commands are assigned to Privilege Level 15 (commonly referred to as Enable or Privileged mode), with only a few assigned to Privilege Level 0.

By default, no commands are assigned to privilege levels between 1 through 14. You do not have to give a user full privileged access to the PIX firewall if the user needs to execute only a small subset of commands. This normally is accomplished by moving commands from Privilege Level 15 into lower privilege levels. You can also reassign commands from Privilege Level 0 to higher privilege levels. You can implement command authorization using either the PIX firewall local database or an AAA server.

The general steps you need to configure AAA authorization on the PIX firewall are as follows:

1. Assign commands to appropriate privilege levels. If you are enabling authorization using the PIX firewall local database, use the *privilege* command. If you are enabling AAA authorization using an AAA server, use the appropriate mechanism provided by the server.

2. Define user accounts assigned to appropriate privilege levels. If you are enabling AAA authorization using the PIX firewall local database, use the *username* command. If you are enabling AAA authorization using an AAA server, use the appropriate mechanism provided by the server.

3. Enable AAA authorization on the PIX firewall. Regardless of whether you are enabling AAA authorization using the PIX firewall local database or an AAA server, use the *aaa authorization* command.

Configuring Local Command Authorization

To implement command authorization using the PIX firewall local database, you must first assign the various commands to appropriate privilege levels using the following command:

```
privilege [show | clear | configure] level <level> [mode {enable |configure}]
command <command>
```

Select the appropriate command for which to set a privilege level (*show, clear,* or *configure,* or blank if it is not one of these). The *level* parameter specifies the privilege level to which to assign the command. The *mode* parameter specifies the mode (*enable* or *configure*) to which the specified level applies. Finally, *command* is the command you are adding to the privilege level.

Once you have assigned commands to the desired privilege levels, you need to assign users to the appropriate privilege levels based on their need for access. If you are using the local database, use the *username* command with the *privilege* keyword. The *username* command syntax was described previously in this chapter.

Now that you have assigned both commands and users to appropriate privilege levels, you are ready to enable AAA authorization on the PIX firewall using the following command:

```
aaa authorization command LOCAL
```

Here is an example of command authorization:

```
PIX1(config)# privilege show level 10 command access-list
PIX1(config)# privilege configure level 11 command access-list
PIX1(config)# privilege clear level 12 command access-list
PIX1(config)# username potter password apparate privilege 12
PIX1(config)# username sauron password ring privilege 11
```

```
PIX1(config)# username snape password potion privilege 10
PIX1(config)# aaa authorization command LOCAL
```

The *privilege* command sets the access-list command to different privilege levels. The *username* command defines users and assigns them privilege levels. The *aaa authorization* command enables *local* user authorization services. In our example, the user potter is authorized to configure, clear, and show access lists, the user sauron is authorized to configure and show access lists, and the user snape is authorized only to show access lists.

To determine the privilege level to which a particular command is assigned:

```
show privilege command <command>
```

To determine the commands assigned to a particular level:

```
show privilege level <level>
```

To show all the commands and the levels to which they are assigned:

```
show privilege all
```

Configuring TACACS+ and RADIUS Console Authentication

In this section, we will use TACACS+ in our examples; since the configuration is the same for TACACS+ and RADIUS, you can opt for RADIUS by simply specifying it instead of TACACS+. If you are configuring the PIX firewall to use RADIUS or TACACS+ to authenticate user access to the firewall itself, first use the following command to define a *group* for the AAA servers that the firewall will use:

```
aaa-server <group_tag> protocol <auth_protocol>
```

You need to specify a name for the server group (group_tag) and either tacacs+ or radius as the authentication protocol (auth_protocol).

Use the following command to define which specific AAA servers will be associated with the group:

```
aaa-server <group_tag> [(interface)] host <server_ip> [<key>] [timeout <seconds>]
```

Specify the name of the group (group_tag) to which the server will belong and the name of the interface (interface) on which the server will reside. If the interface is not specified, it is assumed to be the inside interface. Use the *host* keyword to specify the IP address of the AAA server. You can specify a secret key that will be used between the AAA client and the server. If the key is not specified, the PIX will use Unencrypted mode to communicate with the AAA server. Use the *timeout* keyword to specify the duration that the PIX firewall waits to retry access. The PIX will retry four times before choosing the next server to attempt authentication. The default value for the timeout is five seconds, and the maximum allowed is 30 seconds. You can specify a maximum of 16 AAA servers in a group. To remove a server from the configuration, use the *no aaa-server* command.

Once you have designated AAA authentication servers using the *aaa-server* command, you can verify your configuration using the *show aaa-server* command. Next, specify the AAA authentication database that should be used for the various access methods:

```
aaa authentication [serial | enable | telnet | ssh | http] console <group_tag>
```

The syntax is very similar for configuring local authentication. The *group_tag* parameter identifies the AAA server group to use for authentication. For example, you can issue the following commands to create the TACACS+ server group, assign a TACACS+ server to it, and specify that the group should used for authenticating access to the PIX firewall via Telnet, SSH, and HTTP:

```
PIX1(config)# aaa-server tacacs protocol tacacs+
PIX1(config)# aaa authentication telnet console
PIX1(config)# aaa authentication ssh console
PIX1(config)# aaa authentication ssh console tacacs
```

In the following example, I used a Red Hat 9 server running TACACS+ version tac_plus-F4.0.3.alpha-9a. The configuration for tac_plus is very basic, just enough to show how these commands work. We see the contents of the tac_plus.cfg file here:

```
[root@RedRum TAC]# less tac_plus.cfg
# superuser can execute any command on the pix
user = msweeney      {
                     default service = permit
                     login = cleartext "superuser"
                     }
#
```

The configuration will give the user msweeney as a default, with all privileges. On the Cisco PIX, our configuration will be as follows.
Configure our aaa-server group called "tacacs" and define the protocol to be used as TACACS+:

```
aaa-server tacacs protocol tacacs+
```

Next, configure the aaa-server group tacacs to use host 192.168.50.12 as the TACACS+ server:

```
aaa-server tacacs host 192.168.50.12
```

Setup the SSH authentication to the console to use the tacacs group:

```
aaa authentication ssh console tacacs
```

Finally, configure HTTP/ASDM authentication to the console to also use the tacacs group:.

```
aaa authentication http console tacacs
```

This resulting configuration configures both SSH and the ASDM to prompt you for the TACACS+ username and password defined in the tac_plus.cfg file as we see here in Figure 14.7, where we are trying to use the ASDM.

Figure 14.7 Logging into the Cisco PIX ASDM Using TACACS+ for Authentication

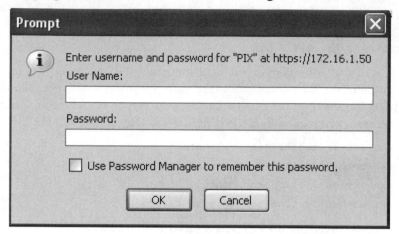

Debug traces of the AAA authentication occurring provides some useful information as shown:

```
PIX1(config)# uap allocated. remote address: 192.168.50.14, Session_id: 2147483716
Processing challenge for user msweeney, session id: 2147483716, challenge:
Password:
Processing challenge for user msweeney, session id: 2147483716, challenge:
Password:
Resetting 192.168.50.12's numtries
uap freed for user msweeney. remote address: 192.168.50.14, session id: 2147483716
uap allocated. remote address: 192.168.50.14, Session_id: 2147483717
::: trimmed for clarity::::
```

We can also see the status of the aaa-server by using the command *show aaa-server*.

```
PIX1# show aaa-server
Server Group:        LOCAL
Server Protocol:     Local database
Server Address:      None
Server port:         None
Server status:       ACTIVE, Last transaction at 06:47:21 PDT Thu Apr 28 2005
Number of pending requests  0
```

```
Average round trip time              0ms
Number of authentication requests    0
Number of authorization requests     3
Number of accounting requests        0
Number of retransmissions            0
Number of accepts                    3
Number of rejects                    0
Number of challenges                 0
Number of malformed responses        0
Number of bad authenticators         0
Number of timeouts                   0
Number of unrecognized responses     0


Server Group:                   tacacs
Server Protocol:                tacacs+
Server Address:                 192.168.50.12
Server port:                    49
Server status:                  ACTIVE, Last transaction at 06:47:25 PDT Thu
Apr 28 2005
Number of pending requests      0
Average round trip time         66ms
Number of authentication requests 96
Number of authorization requests  0
Number of accounting requests     0
Number of retransmissions         0
Number of accepts                 50
Number of rejects                 1
Number of challenges              51
Number of malformed responses     0
Number of bad authenticators      0
Number of timeouts                45
Number of unrecognized responses  0

PIX1#
```

If we look at the Sever Group tacacs, we can see the protocol, the server address, the port, whether it is active, the last time it was used, and other details. The same configuration on the Cisco PIX can be configured from the ASDM as shown in Figure 14.8.

Figure 14.8 Using the ASDM to Configure Authentication for HTTP/ASDM

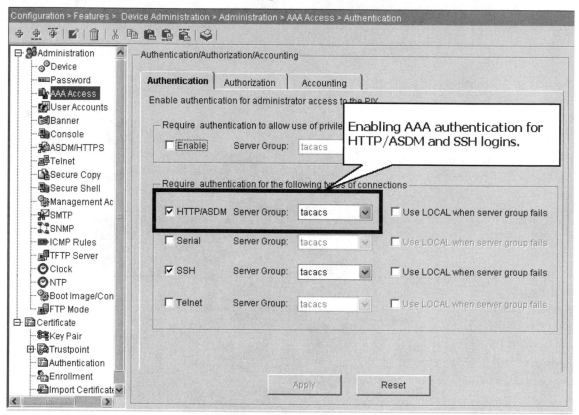

Configuring TACACS+ Command Authorization

The PIX firewall can be configured to use TACACS+ for AAA authorization. The primary advantage of using TACACS+ authorization rather than local authorization is that you can leverage the central TACACS+ database for multiple PIX firewalls without having to recreate a potentially complex configuration on each firewall.

When you implement TACACS+ command authorization on the PIX firewall, it sends the username, command, and command modifier (for example, *show, clear, no*) to the TACACS+ server for authorization. This occurs for each command that a user enters on the PIX firewall. Note that the information sent to the TACACS+ server does not include all the arguments that the user entered as part of the command.

The default for the Cisco PIX running 7.0 is that the following commands are assigned to privilege level 0. All the other commands are at set to level 15.

- show checksum

- show curpriv

- enable (enable mode)

- help

- show history

- login

- logout

- pager

- show pager

- clear pager

- quit

- show version

To set commands to a certain privilege level, use the following command:

```
# privilege [show | clear | cmd] level level [mode {enable | cmd}] command command
```

The commands *show, clear*, and *cmd* are optional, the *level* is the privilege level of between 0 and 15, and the *mode* is the context (enable or configure) in which the command is used.

For example, if you wanted to limit access to who could view your access lists on the PIX, set your privileges accordingly as shown.

PIX1(config)# **privilege show level 10 command access-list**

This configures the PIX to require that the privilege level required to use the command "show access-list" must be set to 10 or higher. Users with privileges below level 10 are denied use of this command. This is a good time to tell you how to check your current privilege level using the *show curpriv* command.

```
PIX1(config)# show curpriv
Username : enable_15
Current privilege level : 15
Current Mode/s : P_PRIV P_CONF
PIX1(config)#
```

You can also use the ASDM to set up the command authorization. In Figure 14.9 we see the opening ASDM screen of configuring command authorization.

Figure 14.9 Using the ASDM to Configure Command Authorization

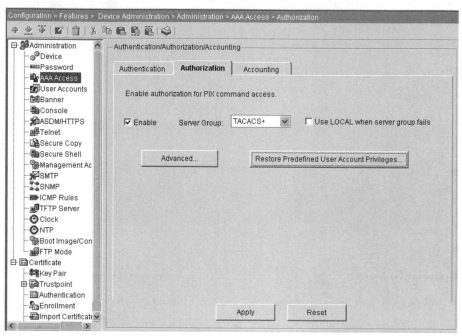

We can enable command authorization by clicking the check box next to the server group to identify which server group and protocol will be used. To choose our commands, click the Advanced… button as we see in Figure 14.10.

Figure 14.10 Choosing Commands and Setting Privilege Levels

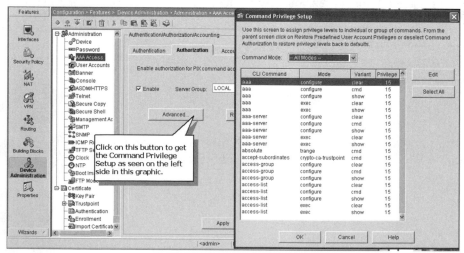

We can see in the command privilege setup window that each command is listed with the CLI, the mode, variant, and privilege level. Choose the command and then click Edit to reassign the levels.

Configuring Authentication for Traffic through the Firewall

The PIX firewall can authenticate and authorize access *through* the PIX firewall. Specifically, the PIX firewall allows you to implement authentication and authorization for inbound or outbound HTTP, FTP, and Telnet sessions. This functionality is provided by the cut-through proxy. The PIX supports other types of services using virtual Telnet.

Configuring Cut-through Proxy

Cut-through proxy controls services available through the firewall by user rather than by IP address, providing a finer granularity of control. User connection requests can be authenticated or authorized against either a TACACS+ or a RADIUS server. One of the most impressive features of cut-through proxy is its performance. In traditional proxy-based firewalls, every data packet in a session needs to be processed at the application layer, resulting in tremendous overhead and degraded performance. With its cut-through proxy function, the PIX transparently authenticates and authorizes the initial connection at the application layer. Once authentication and/or authorization have been performed, the session is shifted and traffic flows directly between the two hosts while state information is maintained, providing a significant performance advantage over proxy firewalls.

To implement AAA authentication to control user access to services *through* the PIX firewall, you need to complete the following high-level tasks:

1. Define the PIX firewall as an AAA client to your AAA server.

2. Define the users within the AAA server.

3. Define the AAA server group and AAA servers on the PIX firewall using the *aaa-server* command, as discussed previously.

4. Enable and configure AAA authentication on the PIX firewall using the *aaa authentication* command syntax to control user access to services *through* the PIX firewall. The syntax of this command is as follows:

```
aaa authentication {include | exclude} <authen_service> {inbound | outbound |
<interface>} <local_ip> <local_mask> <foreign_ip> <foreign_mask> <group_tag>
```

- *include*: Creates a new rule.

- *exclude*: Creates an exception to a previous rule.

- *authen_service:* Needs to be *any, ftp, http,* or *telnet*.

- *inbound* or *outbound:* Specifies inbound or outbound services, respectively.

- *Interface:* The interface from which to authenticate connections.

- *local_ip* and *local_mask:* Specifies the host or network that you want authenticated. To specify all hosts, use 0 for both.

- *foreign_ip* and *foreign_mask:* Specifies the host or network that you want to access *local_ip.* To specify all hosts, use 0 for both.

- *group_tag:* Specifies the AAA server group to use for authentication.

In the following configuration example, cut-through proxy is enabled for Telnet from any host to any host. Any outbound Telnet session to a device through the PIX firewall results in an authentication challenge from the PIX firewall. The user will be permitted access to the device to which the user initiated the session. The following example shows a Telnet connection through the PIX firewall to a Cisco router. After the user successfully authenticates to the PIX firewall, the Telnet session to the router is established.

```
PIX1(config)# aaa-server tacacs protocol tacacs+
PIX1(config)# aaa-server tacacs (inside) host 192.168.1.20 Ciscokey
PIX1(config)# aaa authentication include telnet outbound 0 0 0 0 tacacs
```

In the next example, any outbound FTP session to a host through the PIX firewall results first in an authentication challenge from the PIX firewall, then an authentication challenge from the device to which the user is connecting.

```
PIX1(config)# aaa-server tacacs protocol tacacs+
PIX1(config)# aaa-server tacacs (inside) host 192.168.50.20 Ciscokey
PIX1(config)# aaa authentication include ftp outbound 0 0 0 0 tacacs
```

In the following example, any outbound HTTP session to a host through the PIX firewall results first in an authentication challenge from the PIX firewall, then a session is established to the device to which the user is connecting. The HTTP host the user is connecting to may reprompt for authentication.

```
PIX1(config)# aaa-server tacacs protocol tacacs+
PIX1(config)# aaa-server tacacs (inside) host 192.168.50.20 Ciscokey
PIX1(config)# aaa authentication include http outbound 0 0 0 0 tacacs
```

Virtual HTTP

When cut-through proxy authentication is enabled for Web traffic (HTTP), users may experience problems connecting to Web sites based on Microsoft IIS with Basic Authentication or NT Challenge enabled. The Web server requires different login credentials from the PIX firewall's AAA server. When using HTTP authentication on a Microsoft IIS Web site with Basic Authentication or NT Challenge enabled, the browser appends the string "Authorization:Basic=Uuhjksdkfhk==" to the HTTP GET commands. Since this string contains the PIX authentication credentials and not the IIS authentication credentials, the user is denied access unless their AAA username and password match those defined on the Web server.

To work around this issue, the PIX firewall provides a virtual HTTP feature. The Web browser's initial connection is redirected to the virtual HTTP IP address on the PIX firewall. The user is then authenticated, and the browser is redirected to the actual URL that the user requested. Virtual HTTP is transparent to users. To define a virtual HTTP server, use the following command:

```
virtual http <ip_address> [warn]
```

The *ip_address* parameter specifies an unused IP address that is routed to the PIX firewall. The *warn* keyword lets users know that their requests were redirected and are applicable only for browsers that cannot redirect automatically.

For example, to enable virtual HTTP using the IP address 10.5.1.15:

```
PIX1(config)# virtual http 10.5.1.15 warn
```

Illustrated in Figure 14.11 is the sequence of events that occur when virtual HTTP is enabled.

Figure 14.11 Virtual HTTP Operation

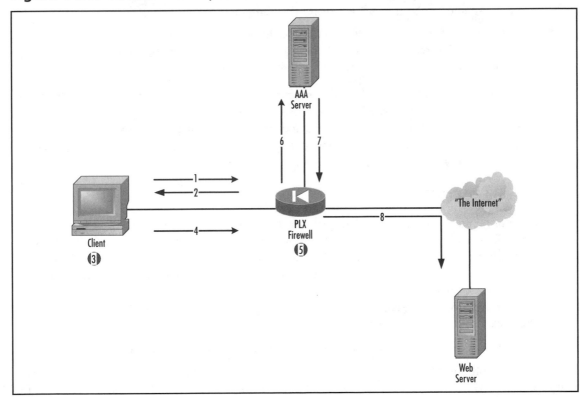

The steps identified in Figure 14.11 are described here:

1. The client sends an HTTP request to the Web server.

2. The PIX firewall intercepts the connection attempt and replies with an HTTP 401 Authorization Required response.

3. The client receives the response from the firewall and pops up a dialog box for the user to enter his or her username and password.

4. The client browser resends the original HTTP request with the username and password embedded as a base64 encoding of *username:password*. The actual field looks similar to the following:

   - ```
     Authorization: Basic ZnJlZDp0aGF0cyBtZQ==
     ```

   - where ZnJlZDp0aGF0cyBtZQ== is the base64 encoded *username:password* pair.

5. The PIX firewall receives the HTTP request and splits it into two requests: the AAA authentication request that contains the username and password and the original HTTP request without the username and password.

6. The PIX firewall sends the AAA authentication request to the AAA server.

7. The AAA server attempts to authenticate the user with the provided username and password and sends an ACCEPT or REJECT message.

8. Assuming that the user authenticated successfully, the PIX firewall will then forward the original HTTP request (without the username and password) to the Web server. If the Web server requires its own authentication, it will send its challenge back to the user.

With virtual HTTP enabled, once the user has authenticated, he or she will never have to authenticate again as long as there is a Web browser instance active. The *uauth* timer will not expire, because every subsequent Web request will include the encoded and embedded username and password.

Use the *show virtual http* command to show the configuration and the *no virtual http* command to disable the use of virtual HTTP.

Virtual Telnet

The *virtual telnet* command has syntax that is similar to the *virtual http* command, but it solves a completely different problem. This feature is useful if you want to preauthenticate users for services that do not support authentication (i.e., services other than HTTP, FTP, or Telnet). Virtual Telnet would have the user Telnet to the PIX and supply his or her username and password. Once the username and password are accepted, the PIX will close the Telnet session and allow the user to establish the connection. For example, if you enabled authentication for all protocols using the *any* keyword as follows:

PIX1(config)# **aaa authentication include any outbound 0 0 0 0 tacacs**

If the first outbound connection attempt is anything other than HTTP, FTP, or Telnet, the user will not be able to authenticate and gain access. However, we can configure a virtual Telnet server to preauthenticate the user so he or she can gain access:

virtual telnet <ip_address>

The *ip_address* parameter specifies an unused IP address that is routed to the PIX firewall. For example, to enable virtual Telnet on the PIX firewall using IP address 10.5.1.15, use the following command:

PIX1(config)# **virtual telnet 10.5.1.15**
     ```

The user can now Telnet to the virtual IP address to authenticate before using a service that does not support authentication such as TFTP. The user Telnets to the IP address of the virtual server and enters his or her AAA username and password. The PIX will then authenticate them, and close the Telnet connection. The PIX firewall will cache the authentication information for the duration of the *uauth* timer.

You can use virtual Telnet not just for logging in but for logging out as well. After successfully authenticating via virtual Telnet, you will not have to reauthenticate until the *uauth* timer expires. If you are finished and want to prevent any further traffic from using your authentication information, you can Telnet to the virtual IP address again. This effectively ends the session and logs you out.

Use the *show virtual telnet* command to show the configuration and the *no virtual telnet* command to disable the use of virtual Telnet.

Configuring Authorization for Traffic through the Firewall

Once authentication for traffic through the firewall using the cut-through proxy is configured, you can also configure *authorization* for the same. Authentication is a requirement for authorization. To implement authorization for traffic through the firewall, first configure the TACACS+ server for authorization.

The configuration process for services through the firewall is very similar. However, the commands that you enter should be the names of the services that you want to allow (for example, HTTP, Telnet, FTP). If you want to control the destinations that the user can access using the named service, simply enter the desired keyword (*permit* or *deny*) and the IP address in the argument text box.

After configuring the TACACS+ server for authorization, configure AAA authorization on the PIX firewall:

```
aaa authorization {include | exclude} <author_service> {inbound | outbound}
[<interface>] <local_ip> <local_mask> <foreign_ip> <foreign_mask> <group_tag>
```

The syntax for this command is very similar to the *aaa authentication* command. All parameters are the same except for *author_service*. Some possible values for *author_service* are *any, ftp, http, telnet,* or *<protocol/port>*. These can be 6 (TCP), 17 (UDP), 1 (ICMP), and so on. The port value can range from 1 to 65535 and is valid only for the TCP and UDP protocols. Setting the port value to 0 indicates all ports.

The following commands require authorization for all hosts for outbound Telnet, HTTP, and FTP service requests:

```
PIX1(config)# aaa authorization include telnet outbound 0 0 0 0 tacacs
PIX1(config)# aaa authorization include http outbound 0 0 0 0 tacacs
PIX1(config)# aaa authorization include ftp outbound 0 0 0 0 tacacs
```

Configuring Accounting for Traffic through the Firewall

Accounting is not always counting beans or dollars. In the case of our PIX firewall, accounting provides a way to log user network activity. Accounting can log successful authentications, services being accessed, or commands executed during the session.

Accounting can be configured for traffic through the firewall using either RADIUS or TACACS+:

```
aaa accounting {include | exclude} acct_service {inbound | outbound |
  <interface>} <local_ip> <local_mask> <foreign_ip> <foreign_mask>
    <group_tag>
```

Track commands used with the *aaa accounting command privilege <level> server-tag* command. This command logs commands of a certain privilege level or higher to a certain server group.

```
PIX1(config)# aaa accounting command privilege 10 tacacs
```

We are accounting for any command at level 10 or higher and sending that information to the tacacs server group. This particular command applies only to TACACS+ servers, not RADIUS servers.

The syntax for this command is very similar to the *aaa authentication* command. All parameters are the same except for *acct_service*. Possible values for the *acct_service* parameter are *any, ftp, http, telnet,* or *<protocol/port>*. The possible values for the IP protocol are 6 (TCP) and 17 (UDP), and the port value can range from 1 to 65535. Setting the port value to 0 indicates all ports.

For example, the following command generates accounting data for all hosts that generate any outbound service requests and sends the data to the AAA server in the tacacs group:

```
PIX1(config)# aaa accounting include any outbound 0 0 0 0 tacacs
```

You can configure accounting using the Cisco ASDM; ASDM might be the preferred (easier) way. Figure 14.12 shows the screen for configuring AAA accounting by setting the server group (tacacs) and the type of connection you want to enable AAA accounting on. In this case, it is HTTP/ASDM that we want to account for.

Figure 14.12 Configuring AAA Accounting Using the Cisco ASDM.

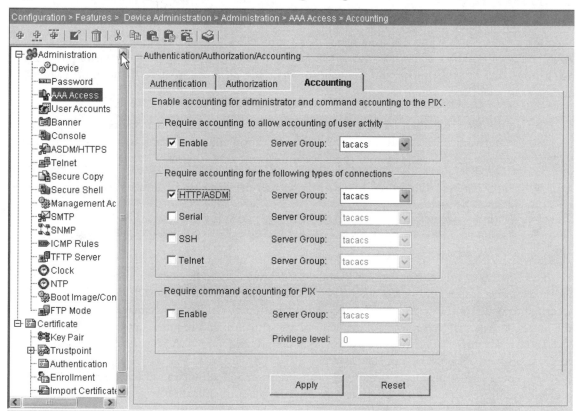

This is the same screen where we would enable accounting for commands by clicking the Enable button, then selecting the server group and setting the privilege level for which we want to account.

Summary

This chapter provided an overview of AAA and its benefits for Cisco PIX firewall administrators. We took a quick look at the new commands that 7.0 provides. Version 7.0 is just an enhancement to AAA and not a forklift upgrade. We learned about the RADIUS and TACACS+ security protocols. We learned that AAA comprises the three independent, but related, functions of authentication, authorization, and accounting:

- *Authentication* is the process of identifying and authenticating a user before allowing access to network devices and services. User identification and authentication are critical for the accuracy of the authorization and accounting functions.

- *Authorization* is the process of determining user privileges and access rights after users have been authenticated.

- *Accounting* is the process of recording user activities for accountability, billing, auditing, or reporting purposes.

The benefits of implementing AAA include scalability, increased flexibility and control, standardized protocols and methods, and redundancy. Cisco PIX firewalls support the RADIUS and TACACS+ security protocols for use within an AAA mechanism. Each protocol has its advantages and disadvantages; the protocol that is right for you will depend on your situation and requirements.

To take advantage of AAA, you must implement and configure an AAA server or use a local database on the PIX but give up a few features.

On the PIX firewall, you can configure authentication and authorization to control both user actions *on* the firewall and user actions *through* the firewall. Authentication of users attempting to access the PIX firewall itself is called *console authentication*. Authorization of user actions *on* the PIX firewall is called *command authorization*. For both console authentication and command authorization, you can use the local database, RADIUS, or TACACS+.

For user actions *through* the PIX firewall, Cisco provides a feature called *cut-through proxy* to support user authentication and authorization. Cut-through proxy allows you to implement authentication and authorization for inbound or outbound HTTP, FTP, and Telnet connections. This functionality allows you to control services available through the firewall by user identity rather than IP address, giving you a finer granularity of control. Because cut-through proxy only authenticates and authorizes the initial connection attempt, it provides performance advantages over traditional proxy firewalls because subsequent communication occurs directly between the two endpoints while being inspected by the firewall.

Virtual HTTP and virtual Telnet are features related to cut-through proxy. Virtual HTTP solves an authentication issue that exists for some Microsoft IIS servers that have Basic Authentication or NT Challenge enabled. Virtual Telnet provides a mechanism for users to preauthenticate to the PIX firewall before using services that do not support authentication.

Chapter 15

PIX Firewall Management

Solutions in this chapter:

- **Configuring Logging**
- **Configuring Remote Access**
- **Configuring Simple Network Management Protocol**
- **Configuring System Date and Time**

☑ **Summary**

Introduction

System management is an important part of configuring and maintaining your firewall. Without proper management, security policies cannot be enforced or monitored and a device might be compromised. In this chapter, we focus on managing Cisco PIX firewalls.

Logging is important, but not just for monitoring or troubleshooting; the data is invaluable for measuring system performance, identifying potential network bottlenecks, and in today's brave new security-conscious world, detecting potential security violations. In this chapter, you will learn how to enable and customize local and remote logging or syslog. Remote administration is another important component of system management. You will learn how to configure a variety of in-band management protocols, such as SSH, SNMP, Telnet, and HTTP, to remotely configure and monitor the PIX firewall. We will discuss the security implications of each protocol and situations in which one protocol might be more appropriate than another. We will discuss configuring the system date and time and why it plays a vital role in system management. Along with system date and time, you will learn how to use NTP to make easier the job of managing your time and data on the Cisco PIX accurate and consistent across multiple devices.

Configuring Logging

Logging is one of the most important functions for system management, yet is often neglected or treated as an afterthought. Logging offers a wealth of information about what is happening on the firewall, who is doing what, who is going where, and possible attacks or probes. The popular rumor is that logging is very complicated and cumbersome to do, but in reality, it is not that hard at all.

The Cisco PIX firewall provides a significant amount of logging functionality. However, all logging is disabled by default. It is up to you to decide how much or how little logging to enable, configure, and use. On the Cisco PIX, there are two ways to log information: local and remote.

Local logging is of limited archival value, so it is highly recommended that remote logging be used to gather information. Remote logging stores the syslog messages and uses scripts or third party applications, such as Sawmill, to examine the messages in detail, manipulate the data, and generate detailed reports. Remote message logging also lets you archive events and keep a historical record. For remote logging, the PIX firewall uses syslog, which is a traditional UNIX method of logging and is described in RFC 3164. The remote logging server (known as the *syslog server*) can be based on the Windows, Linux/UNIX, or Macintosh platform. In this chapter, we focus on Windows and Linux/UNIX syslog servers.

Logging on the PIX firewall can be performed at one of several levels of detail. Level 3 (error) is the default for the PIX. Level 7 (debug) is the most verbose and is recommended only when you are troubleshooting the PIX. In normal network operations, Cisco recommends using Level 4 (warning) or Level 3 (error).

In the course of normal logging (Level 3), the PIX firewall logs alerts (such as a failover link going down), error conditions (such as ICMP being blocked), and informational messages (such as a memory allocation error). If configured for a higher logging level, the PIX firewall logs connection setup and teardown, as well as the amount of traffic transferred in each session. This can be useful if you are trying to gather statistics on how much traffic is being exchanged per protocol or per session.

It is possible to view logging messages in real time, either through a Telnet or SSH session or on the console port. Both methods carry a risk of being overwhelmed by messages, depending on the logging level. A Telnet or SSH session can time out and drop the session, and the console port can lock up to the point where you cannot disable logging to recover your session. You must use caution when viewing log messages using these methods.

Logging Levels

Although the *logging* command has eight different severity levels that are used on the PIX (Levels 0 through 7), logging Level 0 (emergency) is not used. It is represented only for compatibility with UNIX syslog. When you configure logging, you must specify a severity level by number or keyword. When you specify a level, the PIX firewall logs all events equal to the specified level and all levels below it. For example, the default severity level for the PIX is 3 (error), which also logs Level 2 (critical), Level 1 (alert), and Level 0 (emergency) events. A complete list of the keywords and equivalent levels is shown in Table 15.1.

Table 15.1 Logging Levels and Messages

Keyword	Level	Message
emergency	0	System unusable
alert	1	Immediate action needed
critical	2	Critical condition
error	3	Error condition
warning	4	Warning condition
notification	5	Normal but significant condition
informational	6	Informational message only
debugging	7	Only used during debugging

A system log message that the syslog server will receive is structured like this:

```
%PIX-Level-message_number: Message_text
```

The syslog messages will be prefaced with a time and date stamp and the source IP address. This will be followed by the *Level*, which represents the logging level of the message. For example, the message snippet *%PIX-2-106016:* shows us that the logging level for this message is 2 (critical). The *message_number* is a numeric code that is unique for the type of message. This example of *106016* is for the message "Deny IP spoof from (*IP_addr*) to *IP_addr* on interface *int_name.*" When you configure the PIX to disable certain messages, you will use the numeric code to identify which message to disable.

Here are some sample messages at the various logging levels:

- **Level 1**

  ```
  %PIX-1-101002: (Primary) Bad fail over cable.
  %PIX-1-101003: (Primary) Fail over cable not connected (this unit)
  ```

- **Level 2**

  ```
  %PIX-2-106016: Deny IP spoof from (IP_addr) to IP_addr on interface
  int_name.
  %PIX-2-106017: Deny IP due to Land Attack from IP_addr to IP_addr.
  ```

- **Level 3**

  ```
  %PIX-3-201005: FTP data connection failed for IP_addr
  %PIX-3-201008: The PIX is disallowing new connections.
  %PIX-3-713132: Cannot obtain an IP address for remote peer
  ```

- **Level 4**

  ```
  %PIX-4-403110: PPP virtual interface int_name, user: user missing MPPE
  %PIX-4-313003: Invalid destination for ICMP error
  %PIX-4-412001: MAC mac-address moved from interface-1 to interface-2
  ```

- **Level 5**

  ```
  %PIX-5-199001: Reload command executed from telnet (remote IP_address)
  %PIX-5-718076: Fail to create tunnel group for peer IP_address.
  ```

- **Level 6**

  ```
  %PIX-6-110001: No route to dest_address from source_address
  %PIX-6-611310: VNPClient: XAUTH Succeeded: Peer: IP_address
  %PIX-6-611311: VNPClient: XAUTH Failed: Peer: IP_address
  ```

- **Level 7**

  ```
  %PIX-7-111009: User user executed cmd:string
  %PIX-7-718049: Created secure tunnel to peer IP_address
  ```

Dropped and Changed Syslog Messages from 6.x

In version 7.0, quite a few syslog messages were dropped due to the extensive changes to commands. The following example lists syslog messages from Cisco's release notes for messages no longer supported in 7.0 code. Many of these messages relate to failover, VPN connections, ACLs, and ISAKMP. There are a few others but biggest changes in the command line would obviously be reflected in the largest number of changed or dropped syslog messages.

```
103002
Old Syslog Message: %PIX-1-103002: (Primary) Other firewall network interface
interface_number OK
```

Deletion Reason: This syslog was not produced by PIX Version 6.3, nor will it be produced by PIX Version 7.0.

- 105031

Old Syslog Message: %PIX-1-105031: Failover LAN interface is up

Deletion Reason: Replaced by 105042.

- 105032

Old Syslog Message: %PIX-1-105032: LAN Failover interface is down

Deletion Reason: Replaced by 105043.

- 105034

Old Syslog Message: %PIX-1-105032: LAN Failover interface is down

Deletion Reason: Obsolete due to different implementation.

- 105035

Old Syslog Message: %PIX-1-105035: Receive a LAN failover interface down msg from peer.

Deletion Reason: Obsolete due to different implementation.

- 105036

Old Syslog Message: %PIX-1-105036: PIX dropped a LAN Failover command message.

Deletion Reason: Obsolete due to different implementation.

- 105037

Old Syslog Message: %PIX-1-105037: The primary and standby units are switching back and forth as the active unit.

Deletion Reason: Obsolete due to different implementation.

-

109013

Old Syslog Message: %PIX-3-109013: User must authenticate before using this service.

Deletion Reason: This syslog not produced by PIX Version 6.3, nor will it be produced by PIX Version 7.0.

- 109021

Old Syslog Message: %PIX-7-109021: Uauth null proxy error

Deletion Reason: No longer relevant in this release.

- 111006

Old Syslog Message: %PIX-6-309002: Permitted manager connection from IP_address.

Deletion Reason: Replaced by 605005 as per ICSA requirement.

- 210003

Old Syslog Message: %PIX-2-201003: Embryonic limit exceeded nconns/elimit for outside_address/outside_port (global_address) inside_address/inside_port on interface interface_name

Deletion Reason: Obsolete due to different implementation.

- 210010

Old Syslog Message: %PIX-3-210010: LU make UDP connection for outside_address: outside_port inside_address:inside_port failed

Deletion Reason: Obsolete due to different implementation.

•210020

Old Syslog Message: %PIX-3-210020: LU PAT port port reserve failed

Deletion Reason: Obsolete due to different implementation.

•210021

Old Syslog Message: %PIX-3-210021: LU create static xlate global_address ifc interface_name failed

Deletion Reason: Obsolete due to different implementation.

•211003

Old Syslog Message: %PIX-3-211003: CPU utilization for number seconds = percent

Deletion Reason: This is an error condition in the code; it is no longer relevant.

•215001

Old Syslog Message: %PIX-2-215001:Bad route_compress() call, sdb= number

Deletion Reason: The syslog number has changed to 216001.

•302302

Old Syslog Message: %PIX-3-302302: ACL = deny; no sa created

Deletion Reason: The code containing this syslog changed dramatically; it is no longer relevant.

•309002

Old Syslog Message: %PIX-6-309002: Permitted manager connection from IP_address

Deletion Reason: This is for PIX Firewall Management, which is no longer supported.

•316001

Old Syslog Message: %PIX-2-316001: Denied new tunnel to IP_address. VPN peer limit (platform_vpn_peer_limit) exceeded

Deletion Reason: This is not applicable in the current release, as SOHO devices are not supported by this release.

•320001

Old Syslog Message: %PIX-3-320001: The subject name of the peer certificate is not allowed for connection

Deletion Reason: This has been replaced by more granular syslogs (from 713001 to 713224).

•402101

Old Syslog Message: %PIX-4-402101: decaps: rec'd IPSEC packet has invalid spi for destaddr=dest_address, prot=protocol, spi=number

Deletion Reason: The code containing this syslog changed dramatically; it is no longer relevant.

•402102

Old Syslog Message: %PIX-4-402102: decapsulate: packet missing {AH|ESP}, destadr=dest_address, actual prot=protocol

Deletion Reason: The code containing this syslog changed dramatically; it is no longer relevant.

•402103

Old Syslog Message: %PIX-4-402103: identity doesn't match negotiated identity (ip) dest_address= dest_address, src_addr= source_address, prot= protocol, (ident) local=inside_address, remote=remote_address, local_proxy=IP_address/IP_address/port/port, remote_proxy=IP_address/IP_address/port/port

Deletion Reason: The code containing this syslog changed dramatically; it is no longer relevant.

•403500

Old Syslog Message: %PIX-6-403500: PPPoE - Service name 'any' not received in PADO. Intf:interface_name AC:ac_name

Deletion Reason: PPPoE is not supported in the current release, customer would not see this syslog.

•403501

Old Syslog Message: %PIX-3-403501: PPPoE - Bad host-unique in PADO - packet dropped Intf:interface_name AC:ac_name

Deletion Reason: PPPoE is not supported in the current release, hence customers would not see this syslog.

•403502

Old Syslog Message: %PIX-3-403502: PPPoE - Bad host-unique in PADS - dropping packet. Intf:interface_name AC:ac_name

Deletion Reason: PPPoE is not supported in the current release, hence customers would not see this syslog.

•404101

Old Syslog Message: %PIX-4-404101: ISAKMP: Failed to allocate address for client from pool string

Deletion Reason: This has been replaced by 713132.

•407001

Old Syslog Message: %PIX-4-407001: Deny traffic for local-host interface_name: inside_address, license limit of number exceeded

Deletion Reason: This is not applicable in the current release.

•501101

Old Syslog Message: %PIX-5-501101: User transitioning priv level

Deletion Reason: The code containing this syslog changed dramatically; it is no longer relevant.

•602102

Old Syslog Message: %PIX-6-602102: Adjusting IPSec tunnel mtu…

Deletion Reason: The code containing this syslog changed dramatically; it is no longer relevant.

•602201

Old Syslog Message: %PIX-6-602201: ISAKMP Phase 1 SA created (local <ip>/<port> (initiator|responder), remote <ip>/<port>, authentication=<auth_type>, encryption=<encr_alg>, hash=<hash_alg>, group=<DH_grp>, lifetime=<seconds>) Change Reason: Replaced by more granular syslog, look at 713xxx

Deletion Reason: This has been replaced by more granular syslogs (from 713001 to 713224).

•602203

Old Syslog Message: PIX-6-602203: ISAKMP session disconnected (local <ip> (initiator|responder), remote <ip>)

Deletion Reason: This has been replaced by more granular syslogs (from 713001 to 713224).

• 602301

Old Syslog Message: %PIX-6-602301: sa created...

Deletion Reason: This has been replaced by syslogs 713119 and 713120.

• 602302

Old Syslog Message: %PIX-6-602302: deleting sa

Deletion Reason: This has been being replaced by 713113, 713169, 713170, 713194, 715009, 715052, 715067 and 715068.

• 603108

Old Syslog Message: %PIX-6-603108: Built PPTP Tunnel at interface_name, tunnel-id = number, remote-peer = IP_address, virtual-interface = number, client-dynamic-ip = IP_address, username = user, MPPE-key-strength = number

Deletion Reason: PPPoE is not supported in the current release, hence customers would not see this syslog.

• 702201

Old Syslog Message: %PIX-7-702201: ISAKMP Phase 1 delete received (local <ip> (initiator|responder), remote <ip>)

Deletion Reason: This has been replaced by more granular syslogs (from 713001 to 713224).

• 702202

Old Syslog Message: %PIX-7-702202: ISAKMP Phase 1 delete sent (local <ip> (initiator|responder), remote <ip>)

Deletion Reason: This has been replaced by more granular syslogs (from 713001 to 713224).

• 702203

Old Syslog Message: %PIX-7-702203: ISAKMP DPD timed out (local <ip> (initiator|responder), remote <ip>)

Deletion Reason: This has been replaced by more granular syslogs (from 713001 to 713224).

• 702204

Old Syslog Message: %PIX-7-702204: ISAKMP Phase 1 retransmission (local <ip> (initiator|responder), remote <ip>)

Deletion Reason: This has been replaced by more granular syslogs (from 713001 to 713224).

• 702205

Old Syslog Message: %PIX-7-702205: ISAKMP Phase 2 retransmission (local <ip> (initiator|responder), remote <ip>)

Deletion Reason: This has been replaced by more granular syslogs (from 713001 to 713224).

• 702206

Old Syslog Message: %PIX-7-702206: ISAKMP malformed payload received (local <ip> (initiator|responder), remote <ip>)

Deletion Reason: This has been replaced by more granular syslogs (from 713001 to 713224).

•702207

Old Syslog Message: %PIX-7-702207: ISAKMP duplicate packet detected (local <ip> (initiator|responder), remote <ip>)

Deletion Reason: This has been replaced by more granular syslogs (from 713001 to 713224).

•702208

Old Syslog Message: %PIX-7-702208: ISAKMP Phase 1 exchange started (local <ip> (initiator|responder), remote <ip>)

Deletion Reason: This has been replaced by more granular syslogs (from 713001 to 713224).

•702209

Old Syslog Message: %PIX-7-702209: ISAKMP Phase 2 exchange started (local <ip> (initiator|responder), remote <ip>)

Deletion Reason: This has been replaced by more granular syslogs (from 713001 to 713224).

•702210

Old Syslog Message: %PIX-7-702210: ISAKMP Phase 1 exchange completed(local <ip> (initiator|responder), remote <ip>)

Deletion Reason: This has been replaced by more granular syslogs (from 713001 to 713224).

•702211

Old Syslog Message: %PIX-7-702211: ISAKMP Phase 2 exchange completed(local <ip> (initiator|responder), remote <ip>)

Deletion Reason: This has been replaced by more granular syslogs (from 713001 to 713224).

•702212

Old Syslog Message: %PIX-7-702212: ISAKMP Phase 1 initiating rekey (local <ip> (initiator|responder), remote <ip>)

Deletion Reason: This has been replaced by more granular syslogs (from 713001 to 713224).

•702301

Old Syslog Message: %PIX-7-702301: lifetime expiring...

Deletion Reason: Security associations do not expire in PIX Version 7.0; this syslog is no longer relevant.

•702302

Old Syslog Message: %PIX-3-702302: replay rollover detected...

Deletion Reason: The code containing this syslog changed dramatically; it is no longer relevant.

•702303

Old Syslog Message: %PIX-7-702303: sa_request...

Deletion Reason: This syslog has been replaced by 713041, 713042, 713043, and 713176.

•709002

Old Syslog Message: %PIX-7-709002: FO unreplicable: cmd=command

Deletion Reason: This syslog was intended to catch programming errors and is no longer needed because of code changes.

Along with the dropped messages, there were changes made to other syslog messages. The following example shows various changed messages:

•112001

Old Syslog Message: %PIX-2-112001: (string:dec) PIX Clear complete

New Syslog Message: %PIX-2-112001: Clear finished

Change Reason: The filename and line number (string:dec) are undesirable in a syslog message. The PIX keyword is removed to make the syslog platform independent.

•199002

Old Syslog Message: %PIX-6-199002: PIX startup completed. Beginning operation

New Syslog Message: %PIX-6-199002: Startup completed. Beginning operation

Change Reason: The PIX keyword is removed from the body of the syslog message to make the syslog platform independent.

•199005

Old Syslog Message: %PIX-6-199005: PIX Startup begin

New Syslog Message: %PIX-6-199005: Startup begin

Change Reason: The PIX keyword is removed from the body of the syslog message to make the syslog platform independent.

•201002

Old Syslog Message: %PIX-3-201002: Too many connections on {static|xlate} global_ address! econns nconns

New Syslog Message: %PIX-3-201002: Too many tcp connections on {static|xlate} global_address! econns nconns

Change Reason: This syslog is only applicable to TCP connection, hence the change.

•208005

Old Syslog Message: %PIX-3-208005: (function:line_num) pix clear command return code

New Syslog Message: %PIX-3-208005: Clear command return

Change Reason: The filename and line number are undesirable in a syslog message. The PIX keyword is removed to make the syslog platform independent.

•308001

Old Syslog Message: %PIX-6-308001: PIX console enable password incorrect for number tries (from IP_address)

New Syslog Message: %PIX-6-308001: Console enable password incorrect for number tries (from_IP address)

Change Reason: The PIX keyword is removed from the body of the syslog message to make the syslog platform independent.

- 315004

Old Syslog Message: %PIX-3-315004: Fail to establish SSH session because PIX RSA host key retrieval failed.

New Syslog Message: %PIX-3-315004: Fail to establish SSH session because RSA host key retrieval failed.

Change Reason: The PIX keyword is removed from the body of the syslog message to make the syslog platform independent.

- 606001

Old Syslog Message: %PIX-6-606001: ASDM session number number from IP_address started

New Syslog Message: %PIX-6-606001: ASDM session number number from IP_address started

Change Reason: The ASDM keyword is changed to ASDM to update the syslog platform for ASDM.

- 606002

Old Syslog Message: %PIX-6-606002: ASDM session number number from IP_address ended

New Syslog Message: %PIX-6-606002: ASDM session number number from IP_address ended

Change Reason: The ASDM keyword is changed to ASDM to update the syslog platform for ASDM.

- 611314

Old Syslog Message: %PIX-6-611314: VPNClient: Load Balancing Cluster with Virtual IP: IP_address has redirected the PIX to server IP_address

New Syslog Message: %PIX-6-611314: VPNClient: Load Balancing Cluster with Virtual IP:%I has redirected firewall to server

Change Reason: The PIX keyword is removed to make the syslog platform independent.

The complete listing of all syslog messages for the Cisco PIX and 7.0 code can be found at http://tinyurl.com/bu7e2.

Logging Facility

Each syslog message has a facility number, which can be thought of as *where* the message should be logged. Twenty-four different facilities are available (refer to RFC 3164 for more information), with numerical codes ranging from 0 to 23. The eight facilities commonly used for syslog are local0 through local7. You can think of facilities as pipes leading to the syslogd process. The syslogd process files or places the messages into the correct log file based on the facility or inbound pipe. On the PIX firewall, facility configuration is optional. If used, the facility must be specified using its numerical code:

```
logging facility <facility_code>
```

Table 15.2 shows the facility names associated with each of the numerical codes.

Table 15.2 Facility Numerical Codes and Names

Numerical Code	Name
16	local0
17	local1
18	local2
19	local3
20	local4
21	local5
22	local6
23	local7

The default setting for facility configuration on a Cisco PIX is local4 (20). By changing the facility number, you can direct the syslog messages from different Cisco PIX firewalls (or even different types and models of devices) to different files. For example, on a Linux/UNIX machine, the /etc/syslog.conf file is configured with this:

```
# PIX Firewall syslog messages
local7.*      /var/log/pix/pix1
```

You can configure the PIX firewall to send syslog messages to the local7 log file (/var/log/pix/pix1) using the following command:

```
PIX1(config)# logging facility 23
```

Now the PIX will send syslog messages to facility local7 on the Linux server. Any syslog message arriving at the Linux syslogd process for facility local7 will be stored in the /var/log/pix/pix1 log file; whereas any syslog message for local4 (20) will continue to be stored in the default message log file.

Local Logging

The PIX offers both local and remote message logging. Normally, remote logging is preferred over local logging, but when you're troubleshooting or configuring the Cisco PIX firewall, it can be useful to have local logging enabled. Three types of logging are available locally: buffered logging, console logging, and terminal logging. Since logging on the PIX is disabled by default, you need to enable it using the following command:

```
PIX1(config)# logging on
```

This command is required to start logging to all output locations such as the buffer, console, terminal, or syslog server. However, after entering this command, you still must specify the individual logging methods. To disable logging, use the *no* form of the command:

```
PIX1(config)# no logging on
```

Buffered Logging

The first method of local logging we discuss is *buffered logging*. When you use this method, all log messages are sent to an internal buffer on the PIX firewall. To enable buffered logging, use the following command:

```
PIX1(config)# logging buffered <level>
```

The *level* parameter specifies the level of detail you want to see in your logs. (Logging levels are discussed later in this chapter.) To view the messages held in the buffer, use the following command:

```
show logging
```

This command shows the logging configuration as well as the messages that are held in the log buffer. The PIX firewall can only log up to 100 messages to the log buffer, so it usually is not necessary to clear this buffer. However, if you choose, you can use the *clear logging* command in enable mode to clear out the buffer and start fresh. In order to disable buffered logging, use the *no logging buffered* command in configuration mode. Here is an example of the *show logging* command:

```
PIX1# show logging
Syslog logging: enabled
  Facility: 20
  Timestamp logging: disabled
  Standby logging: disabled
  Console logging: level debugging, 37 messages logged
  Monitor logging: disabled
  Buffer logging: level debugging, 9 messages logged
  Trap logging: disabled
  History logging: disabled
111008: User 'enable_15' executed the 'logging buffered 7' command.
111009: User 'enable_15' executed cmd: show logging
```

This command clearly shows the logging configuration in detail as well as the contents of the log buffer. We can see the types of logging that are enabled and the number of messages logged. In this example, console and buffered logging are enabled (both at level debugging). There are also two messages in the logging buffer in this example. We discuss console logging next.

Console Logging

When enabled, *console logging* sends log messages to the console (serial port) of the PIX firewall. To enable console logging, use the following command:

```
PIX1(config)# logging console <level>
```

The *level* parameter has the same meaning as discussed previously. Once entered, logging messages are printed to the console. If there are too many messages, it can be very distracting to type commands while messages are being displayed. Console logging also degrades the performance of the PIX firewall. To stop the printing of messages to the console, use the following command:

```
PIX1(config)# no logging console
```

Terminal Logging

Terminal logging sends log messages to a Telnet or SSH session. To enable terminal logging, use the following command:

```
PIX1(config)# logging monitor <level>
```

In addition to enabling this function at a global level, logging output must be enabled on a per-session basis. To enable the display of syslog messages in the current Telnet or SSH session, use the following command:

```
PIX1# terminal monitor
```

When you no longer want to view log messages in your Telnet or SSH session, you can disable monitoring using the *terminal no monitor* command in enable mode. It is possible to lose control of your Telnet or SSH session when too much data is being printed to the screen.

Remote Logging via Syslog

Syslog is one of the most common methods for capturing and saving log messages. In order for syslog to work, you need to configure the host that will send the syslog messages as well as the syslog server, which will receive the syslog messages. In our case, the PIX firewall will be the host sending the log messages to a syslog server, which can be Linux/UNIX, Windows, or even Macintosh based. Syslog by default will use UDP port 514 but the Cisco PIX can also use TCP port 514.

The syslog server determines where to place the log messages. Depending on which syslog server software is being used and how it is configured, the syslog server may write the messages to a file or send an alert to an engineer by e-mail or pager.

On a typical enterprise network, depending on the configured logging level, a busy PIX firewall can log messages to use up several gigabytes of space a day on the syslog server. A prudent engineer will configure a disk quota or some type of disk watcher to make sure that the syslog messages do not overrun available storage space.

As described previously, since logging on the PIX is disabled by default, you need to enable it:

```
PIX1(config)# logging on
```

To configure syslog on the PIX, you first need to tell the firewall which host to send the syslog messages to. To do this, use the following command:

```
logging host [<interface>] <ip_address>
```

The *interface* parameter specifies the interface you want to send the messages out on, and the *ip_address* parameter specifies the IP address of the syslog server on that interface. If not specified, the interface is assumed to be the inside interface. No log messages will be sent to syslog until you configure the logging level using the following command:

```
logging trap <level>
```

The *level* parameter specifies the severity level, as discussed later in this chapter.

Here is an example of configuring syslog on the PIX firewall:

```
PIX1(config)# logging host inside 192.168.50.8
PIX1(config)# logging trap debugging
PIX1(config)# logging on
PIX1(config)#
PIX1# show logging
Syslog logging: enabled
  Facility: 20
  Timestamp logging: disabled
  Standby logging: disabled
  Console logging: disabled
  Monitor logging: disabled
  Buffer logging: disabled
  Trap logging: level debugging, 38 messages logged
    Logging to inside 192.168.50.8
  History logging: disabled
```

In this example, logging is configured to send messages to the syslog server 192.168.50.8 on the inside interface with a severity level of debugging.

When configured to use syslog, the PIX firewall will send the log messages to the syslog server using UDP port 514 by default. You can change this default behavior by entering the longer form of the *logging host* command:

```
logging host [<interface>] <ip address> [tcp|udp/<port_number>]
```

You can configure either UDP or TCP for syslog, and the *port_number* parameter can be any value from 1025 to 65535. TCP is not a standard method for handling syslog, and most servers do not support it, but it can provide reliable logging. If you will be using a TCP connection to the syslog server, remember this caveat: if the syslog server goes down when you're using TCP, the default behavior for the PIX firewall is that all network traffic through the PIX will be *blocked*. The syslog connection will be slower than UDP since TCP relies on the three-way handshake to start a connection and each packet must be acknowledged. This will add to the overhead of the connection and slow the sending of syslog messages to the server.

In the following example, we configure syslog using TCP. The *port_number* parameter has been set to 1468, which is the default TCP port used by syslog servers that accept TCP syslog from PIX firewalls. Do not forget to configure the syslog server to listen on TCP port 1468 for syslog messages.

```
PIX1(config)# logging host inside 192.168.50.9 tcp/1468
PIX1(config)# logging trap debugging
PIX1(config)# logging on
PIX1(config)#
```

```
PIX1# show logging
Syslog logging: enabled
  Facility: 20
  Timestamp logging: disabled
  Standby logging: disabled
  Console logging: disabled
  Monitor logging: disabled
  Buffer logging: disabled
  Trap logging: level debugging, 31 messages logged
    Logging to inside 192.168.50.9 tcp/1468
  History logging: disabled
```

Although the PIX firewall can have multiple logging hosts configured, it can use only a single protocol with each logging host. In the event that your syslog server is offline, the PIX will start to queue the syslog messages in memory and then start to overwrite the held messages, starting with the oldest first. The following command is used to configure the size of the syslog message queue in memory:

```
logging queue <msg_count>
```

The default is 512 messages. The *msg_count* parameter specifies the size of the syslog message queue. If *msg_count* is set to 0, the queue size is unlimited and based on the available block memory.

To see the queue statistics and any discarded message statistics, use the following command:

```
PIX1# show logging queue
```

```
  Logging Queue length limit : 512 msg(s)
  Current 3 msg on queue, 5 msgs most on queue
```

One of the Cisco PIX firewall's features is the ability to have a failover PIX. One logging command allows the failover PIX to send syslog messages in order for the log files to be synchronized in the case of failover taking place. This command, *logging standby*, is disabled by default since it will double the amount of syslog traffic on the network. Once it is enabled, you can turn off this command using the *no logging standby* command.

To ensure that the syslog messages are sent to the syslog server with a timestamp, configure the *logging timestamp* command in configuration mode. This command requires that the *clock* command be set on the PIX. To turn off timestamps, use the *no logging timestamp* command in configuration mode.

The syslog messages are sent across the network in plain text as we see in the Ethereal packet trace file shown in Figure 15.1. The packet gives us all the information that the syslog server gets. This plain text is why many security experts recommend that the syslog information is sent via a SSH tunnel or to use a utility such as STUNNEL to prevent exposure of logging data.

Figure 15.1 Ethereal Syslog Trace

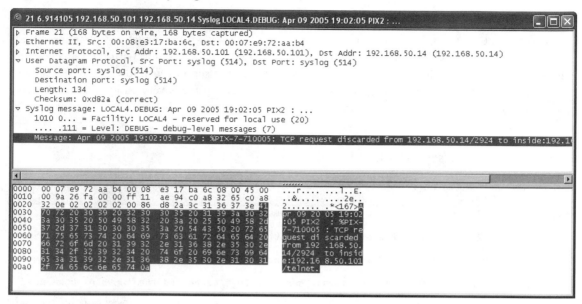

Many syslog server applications are available for both Microsoft Windows and Linux/UNIX. Virtually all Linux/UNIX systems have syslog enabled for logging local messages, and it only takes some minor adjustments to enable remote logging. Microsoft Windows requires that a syslog server be installed since syslog services are not a part of the operating system. One popular choice for a Microsoft Windows syslog server is the Kiwi Syslog Daemon, available at www.kiwisyslog.com, which runs on all versions of Windows, from Windows 98 to Windows XP. With Windows NT and Windows 2000, the Kiwi Syslog Daemon can be installed as a service. The Kiwi Syslog Server can be configured to use either UDP or TCP to accept syslog messages from the Cisco PIX firewall. Figure 15.2 shows the Kiwi Syslog Daemon default log screen.

Figure 15.2 The Kiwi Syslog Server Default Log Screen

Date	Time	Priority	Hostname	Message
04-09-2005	19:06:28	Local4.Debug	192.168.50.101	Apr 09 2005 19:06:55 PIX2 : %PIX-7-710005: UDP request discarded from 192.168.50.12/123 to inside:192.168.50.255/ntp
04-09-2005	19:06:17	Local4.Debug	192.168.50.101	Apr 09 2005 19:06:44 PIX2 : %PIX-7-710005: UDP request discarded from 192.168.50.235/138 to inside:192.168.50.255/netbios-dgm
04-09-2005	19:05:30	Local4.Debug	192.168.50.101	Apr 09 2005 19:05:57 PIX2 : %PIX-7-710005: UDP request discarded from 192.168.50.65/137 to inside:192.168.50.255/netbios-ns
04-09-2005	19:05:29	Local4.Debug	192.168.50.101	Apr 09 2005 19:05:56 PIX2 : %PIX-7-710005: UDP request discarded from 192.168.50.65/137 to inside:192.168.50.255/netbios-ns
04-09-2005	19:05:28	Local4.Debug	192.168.50.101	Apr 09 2005 19:05:55 PIX2 : %PIX-7-710005: UDP request discarded from 192.168.50.65/137 to inside:192.168.50.255/netbios-ns
04-09-2005	19:05:23	Local4.Debug	192.168.50.101	Apr 09 2005 19:05:50 PIX2 : %PIX-7-710005: UDP request discarded from 192.168.50.12/123 to inside:192.168.50.255/ntp
04-09-2005	19:04:20	Local4.Debug	192.168.50.101	Apr 09 2005 19:04:47 PIX2 : %PIX-7-710005: UDP request discarded from 192.168.50.12/123 to inside:192.168.50.255/ntp
04-09-2005	19:03:14	Local4.Debug	192.168.50.101	Apr 09 2005 19:03:41 PIX2 : %PIX-7-710005: UDP request discarded from 192.168.50.12/123 to inside:192.168.50.255/ntp

Another choice is the free PIX Firewall Syslog Server (PFSS) available from Cisco. If you have access to Cisco CCO, you can download PFSS at www.cisco.com/cgi-bin/tablebuild.pl/pix. PFSS is a very basic syslog server for Windows that can use either UDP or TCP syslog with the Cisco PIX firewall. PFSS runs under Windows NT as a service and does not support Windows 95, Windows 98, or Windows ME. Unlike Kiwi Syslog Server, the PFSS message log file is very basic in presentation, as shown in Figure 15.3.

Figure 15.3 The Cisco PFSS Log File

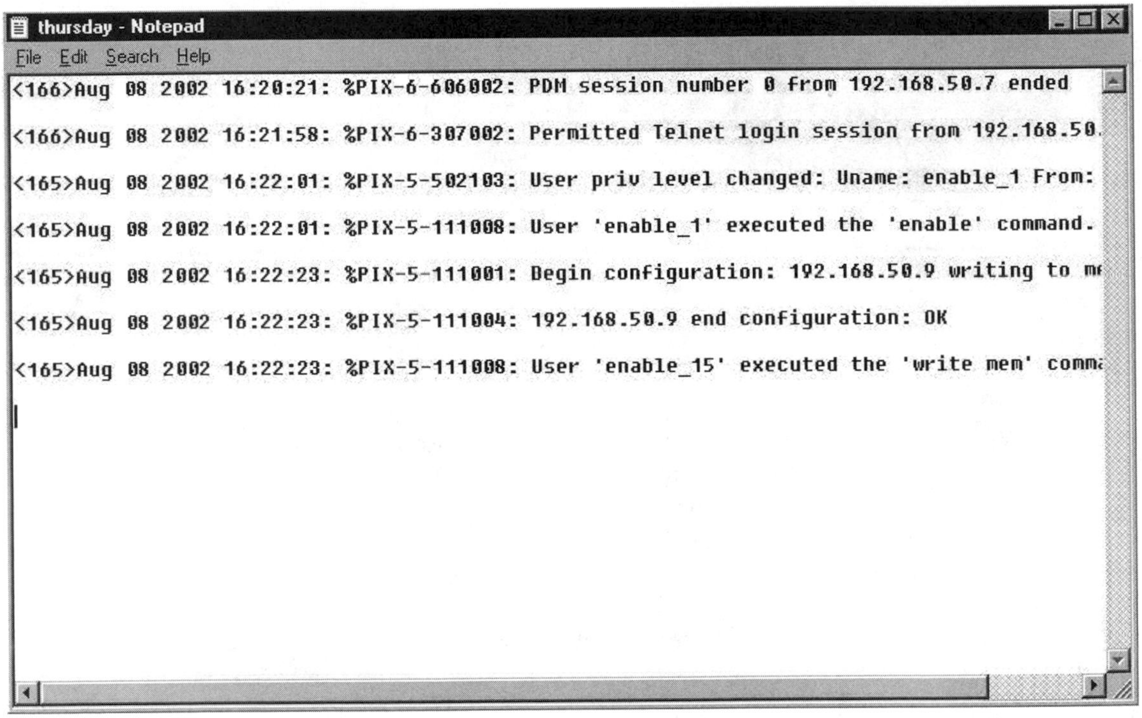

```
🗐 thursday - Notepad                                                    _ □ ×
File  Edit  Search  Help
<166>Aug 08 2002 16:20:21: %PIX-6-606002: PDM session number 0 from 192.168.50.7 ended   ▲

<166>Aug 08 2002 16:21:58: %PIX-6-307002: Permitted Telnet login session from 192.168.50.

<165>Aug 08 2002 16:22:01: %PIX-5-502103: User priv level changed: Uname: enable_1 From:

<165>Aug 08 2002 16:22:01: %PIX-5-111008: User 'enable_1' executed the 'enable' command.

<165>Aug 08 2002 16:22:23: %PIX-5-111001: Begin configuration: 192.168.50.9 writing to me

<165>Aug 08 2002 16:22:23: %PIX-5-111004: 192.168.50.9 end configuration: OK

<165>Aug 08 2002 16:22:23: %PIX-5-111008: User 'enable_15' executed the 'write mem' comma

◄ |                                                                              ► |
```

In the world of Linux/UNIX, syslog is normally a service or daemon that has been installed by default to provide local message logging. Some minor configuration changes might need to be made to enable remote syslog functions. The daemon that controls syslog on Linux/UNIX is called *syslogd*. This daemon is part of the normal startup of a Linux box. In the figures that follow, we use RedHat 7.1 as the Linux server.

The first requirement is to reconfigure syslogd to accept remote syslog messages. Log into the Linux machine with proper permissions and then use the *ps* command to verify that syslogd is running:

```
linux1# ps -ef | grep syslogd
root    2000    1 0 22:03 ?    00:00:00 syslogd -m 0
```

As you can see from the output of this command, on this particular machine the syslog daemon is running and has a process ID of 2000. In order for the Linux syslog daemon to accept messages from remote hosts, the syslog configuration needs to be changed by adding *-r* to the startup configuration. This is accomplished by editing the /etc/sysconfig/syslog file and adding -r to the SYSLOGD_OPTIONS so that it looks like this:

```
SYSLOGD_OPTIONS="-m 0 -r"
```

We will now restart the syslog daemon by using the following command:

```
linux1# /etc/rc.d/init.d/syslog restart
```

When syslogd has restarted, you should verify that it is running by issuing the *ps* command again:

```
linux1# ps -ef | grep syslogd
root     2160    1 0 22:05 ?   00:00:00 syslogd -m 0 -r
```

The system should now be ready to accept syslog messages from remote hosts.

Disabling Specific Syslog Messages

At times, you'll want to disable certain syslog messages, such as logging all information while troubleshooting a connection and being flooded with PING packets. You might want to disable any syslog message referencing ICMP to help diminish the flood of ICMP messages. Or an attack is ongoing against your PIX firewall, flooding your server with messages, consuming limited disk space. Cisco provides a very useful document with a complete list of all syslog messages and their ID numbers. You can find it at http://www.cisco.com/en/US/products/sw/secursw/ps2120/ products_system_message_guide_chapter09186a008041ad91.html. This document can be used to create lists of messages to be disabled, and can also serve as a troubleshooting aid. Along with each syslog message are suggestions for what to do if the message is an error. For example, here is a complete syslog message explanation and a recommendation:

```
%PIX-1-103001: (Primary) No response from other firewall (reason
code =

 code).
```

- **Explanation**   This is a failover message. This message is logged if the primary unit is unable to communicate with the secondary unit over the failover cable. *(Primary)* can also be listed as *(Secondary)* for the secondary unit.
- **Action**   Verify that the secondary unit has the exact same hardware, software version level, and configuration as the primary unit.

You can see that the document is very detailed. This document covers messages 100001 to 709007. There is one syslog message that you cannot disable:

```
%PIX-6-199002: PIX startup completed. Beginning operation.
```

In order to disable any other syslog message, use the following command:

```
no logging message <message_number>
```

The *message_number* parameter specifies the unique numeric message ID of each syslog message. For example:

```
PIX1(config)# no logging message 303002
```

In order to see which messages are disabled, use the *show logging disabled* command. For example:

```
PIX1# show logging disabled
no logging message 303002
```

In order to clear the disabled message so that it will be logged again, use the following command:

```
logging message <message_number>
```

The *message_number* parameter specifies the unique numeric ID of the disabled message. To re-enable all disabled messages, use the following command:

```
PIX1(config)# clear logging disabled
```

Configuring Remote Access

The ability to manage a Cisco PIX remotely is one of the blessings of remote management. You can always manage the PIX using the console port, but this requires you to be physically present at the PIX with a console connection. This solution is not very practical in most enterprise architectures. Fortunately, we have the option of using some type of remote access to manage the PIX. The tools we can use to remotely manage the PIX are Telnet, SSH, SNMP, or Cisco ASDM. Each remote management method has certain value and applicability in system management, but some fit better in certain situations than others. Knowing the various methods of remote management and their differences will enable you to make an informed decision about which method to use in your specific situation.

Two styles of remote access are available. The first and most commonly used is the *command-line interface,* or *CLI.* The CLI provides a very fast and low-overhead method of management. It also provides the ability to "cut and paste" configurations. The downside is that you need to know the commands and their structures. Cisco ASDM provides a more friendly method of managing the PIX remotely by providing a Windows-like GUI interface. You just point and click your way to configuring and monitoring the PIX firewall. The tradeoff is that ASDM has a higher overhead requirement than the basic CLI. If you have a fat network pipe, such as a LAN connection, ASDM makes good sense. Over a slower and bandwidth-constricted WAN connection, the lower overhead of the CLI makes it the preferred method of management. The CLI is remotely accessible through Secure Shell and Telnet.

Secure Shell

Secure Shell (SSH) secures TCP/IP communication sessions by encrypting the data. With encryption, neither the passwords nor the data are sent in clear text. SSH is not limited to the PIX firewall, but is used in a variety of ways, such as encrypting or forwarding X.11 connections, providing a secure copy (SCP) and a secure ftp (scftp). SSH is not just a Telnet replacement but a suite of secure applications. SSH is intended to be a replacement for rlogin, rsh, and rcp, which are insecure protocols. For this discussion, we use SSH as the preferred method to connect to a Cisco PIX firewall instead of using the traditional Telnet method.

Whether you use Windows, UNIX, Linux, or Mac OS as your operating system, many SSH clients are available. For Windows, one of the most popular free clients is Tera Term with SSH extensions. An alternative to Tera Term is PuTTY available at www.chiark.greenend.org.uk/~ sgtatham/putty/.

For UNIX and Linux there is OpenSSH, and for the Mac there is NiftyTelnet. The examples that follow use SSH Secure Shell from www.ssh.com on a Windows platform. The company SSH offers two version of the SSH client, one commercial and one free version (not for commercial use). Tera Term will support SSHv1 ONLY with the SSH extension. When you configure SSH on the Cisco PIX, you have a limit of 100 characters for the username and 50 characters for the password.

Enabling SSH Access

In order for the PIX to accept SSH connections, you must first enable SSH.

Before you can use SSH, you need to generate an RSA key set. This RSA key is sent to the SSH server by the client to encrypt the session key. Do the following:

1. To generate the RSA key, the first step is to assign a hostname and a domain name to the PIX:

    ```
    PIX1(config)# hostname PIX1
    PIX1(config)# domain-name packet.com
    ```

2. Once you have completed assigning the hostname and the domain name, you need to generate the RSA key pair (one public key, and one private key) and save them to flash memory. The command to generate the pair of keys is:

    ```
    crypto key generate rsa modulus <modulus-size>
    ```

    Cisco recommends 1024 bits for the **modulus**. This reflects RSA Security's own recommendations of using a key of 1024 bits for corporate use and 2048 bits for valuable keys. The larger the key, the longer it will take to generate the key and the longer it will take to crack it. The actual command for this example is as follows:

    ```
    PIX525(config)# crypto key generate rsa modulus 2048
    INFO: The name for the keys will be: <Default-RSA-Key>
    Keypair generation process begin. Please wait....
    ```

The default modulus size is 1024.

3. Once the generation process has completed, you can view the new RSA public key by entering the following command:

    ```
    PIX525# show crypto key mypubkey rsa
    Key pair was generated at: 20:44:05 UTC Mar 17 2005
    Key name: <Default-RSA-Key>
      Usage: General Purpose Key
      Modulus Size (bits): 2048
      Key Data:

       30820121 300d0609 2a864886 f70d0101 01050003 82010e00 30820109 02820100
       77cbf246 e512d6e7 60a03f63 4af21793 96a97614 478ed7ea 39f92892 6cd878bd
       be8973dc e0050462 289a7892 2a89ba87 29096f17 8506f22e 7f843f08 43804cb9
       02030100 01
    ```

```
Key pair was generated at: 23:05:44 UTC Mar 17 2005
Key name: <Default-RSA-Key>.server
  Usage: Encryption Key
  Modulus Size (bits): 768
  Key Data:

    307c300d 06092a86 4886f70d 01010105 00036b00 30680261 0098a1e2 7dc9b7eb
    ac6b5af0 0ee687a0 231c3353 7a689b14 94ef2f21 70c5498f 2a41b110 901ff066
    5a4e681c b17f5941 0c4b1662 9ec43055 6ec7feef f2f30c64 fdfa46b3 b02cabd1
    b43376b6 ab385cb5 c4967b25 c495f880 1bcf348d cd234938 e7020301 0001
PIX525# Note
```

4. With the RSA key pair generated, you need to save it to flash using the following command:

    ```
    PIX5251(config)# write terminal
    ```

5. Configure the PIX for the allowed hosts or subnets that can be SSH clients to the firewall. You also can set the SSH inactivity timeout at this point. The format to allow SSH connections is:

    ```
    ssh <ip_address> [<netmask>] [<interface>]
    ```

    If *netmask* is not specified, it is assumed to be 255.255.255.255; if *interface* is not specified, it is assumed to be the inside interface. In the following example, *ip_address* is 192.168.50.0 and *netmask* is 255.255.255.0. This allows the entire 192.168.50.0/24 subnet range SSH access to the PIX. The *interface* parameter specifies the name of the interface on which this subnet resides. In this case, it is the inside interface.

    ```
    PIX1(config)# ssh 192.168.50.0 255.255.255.0 inside
    ```

6. By default, the PIX will disconnect an SSH session after five minutes of inactivity. We can set the inactivity timeout between 1 and 60 minutes. To set the inactivity timeout to 10 minutes, use the following command:

    ```
    PIX1(config)# ssh timeout 10
    ```

7. Save the configuration changes to flash:

    ```
    PIX1# write memory
    ```

To verify the SSH configuration, use the *show ssh* command in enable mode.

To access the PIX firewall, you need to configure an SSH client. With SSHv2 introduced in version 7.0, certain version 1 only clients such as Tera Term no longer make sense. A replacement SSH client that supports both SSHv1 and SSHv2 is PuTTY. A second client that has proven to be very reliable is SSH Secure Shell. We will show screen shots using both client in the following section. PuTTY does not need to be installed as it will run from wherever you place the executable In Figure 15.4 we see the start-up screen of PuTTY. SSH Secure Shell is a Windows application that requires it to be installed, unlike PuTTY.

Figure 15.4 Starting the SSH Client PuTTY

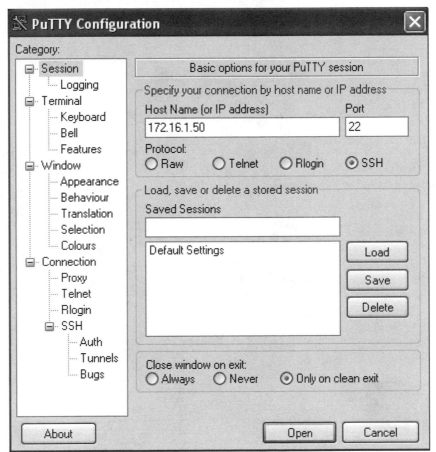

PuTTY offers a wealth of configuration options to adjust virtually any aspect of the program to better match how you want to do business. To establish a session to your PIX firewall using PuTTY, simply enter its IP address or hostname if registered in DNS, and then click Open.

SSH Secure Shell uses a different layout for their option screen, which is tied to profiles (see Figure 15.5).

Figure 15.5 Setting Options in SSH Secure Shell

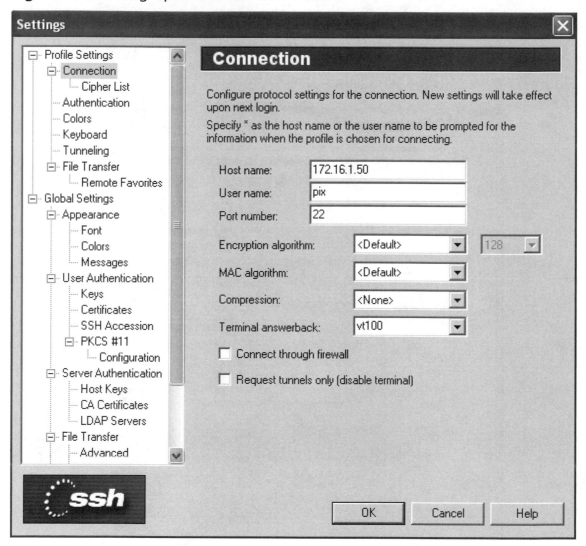

One of the more important configuration settings is to enable logging which we see in Figure 15.6 for PuTTY. Enabling logging using SSH Secure Shell is done from the menu item File | Log Session. PuTTY offers more choices for logging if that is important to you.

Figure 15.6 Enabling Logging in PuTTY

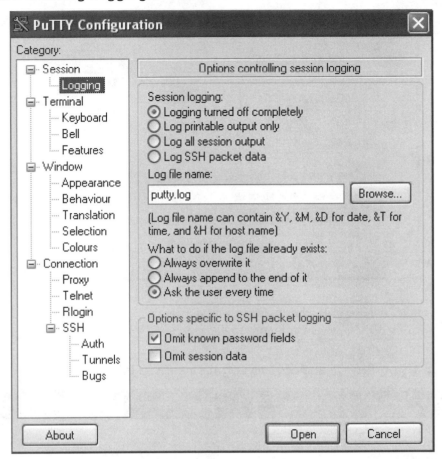

The default username for a Cisco PIX SSH connection that is *not* using AAA for authentication is *pix*. The passphrase is the password that is used for Telnet. Once the username and passphrase are authenticated, your SSH Secure Shell session will start. This authentication can take a few seconds due to the encryption process being settled at the onset. Figure 15.7 shows the dialog box where we will type the IP address and the user name of pix. The port defaults to 22 and the authentication method for SSH Secure Shell is password.

Figure 15.7 SSH Secure Shell Authentication Dialog Box

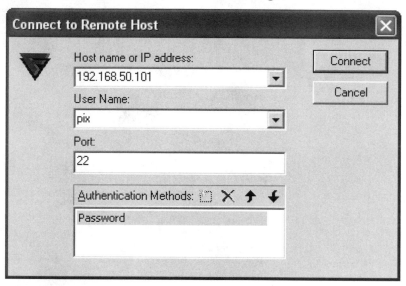

PuTTY handles the username and password a bit differently: you type both once the connection has been made to the PIX as we see in Figure 15.8.

Figure 15.8 Using PuTYY and SSH to Login to a Cisco PIX

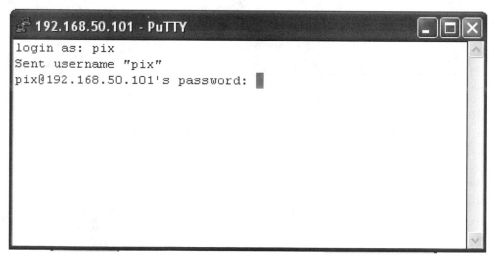

Troubleshooting SSH

At times you will need to troubleshoot the reason that the SSH connection is failing. In this case, use the *debug ssh* command on the PIX. The debug output on PIX is relatively easy to understand. The following example shows the output of the *debug ssh* command for a successful SSH connection.

```
152: SSH: Device opened successfully.
153: SSH: host key initialized
154: SSH0: SSH client: IP = '192.168.50.7' interface # = 1
155: SSH0: starting SSH control process
156: SSH0: Exchanging versions - SSH-1.5-Cisco-1.25
157: SSH0: send SSH message: outdata is NULL
158: SSH0: receive SSH message: 83 (83)
159: SSH0: client version is - SSH-1.5-TTSSH/1.5.4 Win32
160: SSH0: begin server key generation
161: SSH0: complete server key generation, elapsed time = 4170 ms
162: SSH0: declare what cipher(s) we support: 0x00 0x00 0x00 0x04
163: SSH0: send SSH message: SSH_SMSG_PUBLIC_KEY (2)
164: SSH0: SSH_SMSG_PUBLIC_KEY message sent
165: SSH0: receive SSH message: SSH_CMSG_SESSION_KEY (3)
166: SSH0: SSH_CMSG_SESSION_KEY message received - msg type 0x03, length
      272
167: SSH0: client requests DES cipher: 2
168: SSH0: send SSH message: SSH_SMSG_SUCCESS (14)
169: SSH0: keys exchanged and encryption on
170: SSH0: receive SSH message: SSH_CMSG_USER (4)
171: SSH0: authentication request for userid PIX
172: SSH(PIX): user authen method is 'no AAA', aaa server group ID = 0
173: SSH0: send SSH message: SSH_SMSG_FAILURE (15)
174: SSH0: receive SSH message: SSH_CMSG_AUTH_PASSWORD (9)
175: SSH0: send SSH message: SSH_SMSG_SUCCESS (14)
176: SSH0: authentication successful for PIX
177: SSH0: receive SSH message: SSH_CMSG_REQUEST_PTY (10)
178: SSH0: send SSH message: SSH_SMSG_SUCCESS (14)
179: SSH0: receive SSH message: SSH_CMSG_EXEC_SHELL (12)
180: SSH0: starting exec shell
```

The following example shows an example of an incorrect username. The Cisco PIX firewall will reject the login even if the password is correct.

```
184: SSH: Device opened successfully.
185: SSH: host key initialised
186: SSH0: SSH client: IP = '192.168.50.7' interface # = 1
187: SSH0: starting SSH control process
188: SSH0: Exchanging versions - SSH-1.5-Cisco-1.25
189: SSH0: send SSH message: outdata is NULL
190: SSH0: receive SSH message: 83 (83)
```

```
191: SSH0: client version is - SSH-1.5-TTSSH/1.5.4 Win32
192: SSH0: begin server key generation
193: SSH0: complete server key generation, elapsed time = 7090 ms
194: SSH0: declare what cipher(s) we support: 0x00 0x00 0x00 0x04
195: SSH0: send SSH message: SSH_SMSG_PUBLIC_KEY (2)
196: SSH0: SSH_SMSG_PUBLIC_KEY message sent
197: SSH0: receive SSH message: SSH_CMSG_SESSION_KEY (3)
198: SSH0: SSH_CMSG_SESSION_KEY message received - msg type 0x03, length
        272
199: SSH0: client requests DES cipher: 2
200: SSH0: send SSH message: SSH_SMSG_SUCCESS (14)
201: SSH0: keys exchanged and encryption on
202: SSH0: receive SSH message: SSH_CMSG_USER (4)
203: SSH0: authentication request for userid badname
204: SSH(badname): user authen method is 'no AAA', aaa server group ID = 0
205: SSH0: invalid userid badname
206: SSH0: send SSH message: SSH_SMSG_FAILURE (15)
207: SSH0: receive SSH message: SSH_CMSG_AUTH_PASSWORD (9)
208: SSH0: send SSH message: SSH_SMSG_FAILURE (15)
209: SSH0: receive SSH message: SSH_MSG_DISCONNECT (1)
210: SSH0: authentication failed for badname
211: SSH0: Session disconnected by SSH server - error 0x36 "Reset by client"
```

To see how many SSH sessions are on the PIX, use the following command:

```
show ssh sessions [<ip_address>]
```

The optional *ip_address* parameter allows you to check for SSH sessions from a particular IP address. An example of the results of using this command follows:

```
PIX525# show ssh sessions
SID   Client IP      Version    Mode   Encryption   Hmac    State Username
0     192.168.50.14  1.99       IN     3des-cbc     sha1    SessionStarted pix
                                OUT    3des-cbc     sha1    SessionStarted pix
PIX525#
```

In the last example, we saw a field called SID or session ID. To disconnect a specific SSH session, use the SID number, which is this case is 0, and then use the *ssh disconnect* command:

```
ssh disconnect <session_id>
```

For example:

```
PIX1(config)# ssh disconnect 0
```

To remove all SSH configuration statements from the Cisco PIX, use this command:

```
PIX1(config)# clear configure ssh
```

Telnet

Telnet is one of the simplest and most insecure ways to connect to a network device. Telnet is character-based, sending each character in clear text across the network. This means that any username and password are available to anyone who can capture packets. This vulnerability leads to a very large security risk in managing the PIX across a WAN link, the Internet, or even on a LAN. This is an excellent reason to configure and use SSH instead of Telnet.

To configure Telnet on the PIX firewall, use the following command.

```
telnet <ip_address> [<netmask>] [<interface>]
```

The *ip_address* parameter can be a single IP host or an entire range. The *netmask* parameter is a subnet mask associated with the IP address or range. The *interface* parameter specifies the interface name you want to enable Telnet on. In the following example, we have configured the entire 192.168.50.0/24 network on the inside interface to be allowed to Telnet to the PIX:

```
PIX1(config)# telnet 192.168.50.0 255.255.255.0 inside
```

There are some restrictions on Telnet depending on the interface you use. The inside interface allows Telnet without encryption, whereas encryption (through VPN) is required to use Telnet for the outside interface. You can set the idle timeout value for the Telnet session. The timeout value is specified in minutes and must be a value from 1 to 60. The default timeout is five minutes. In this example, we configure the timeout to 15 minutes:

```
PIX1(config)# telnet timeout 15
```

The *show telnet* command shows the current list of IP addresses and their interfaces that are authorized to access the PIX via Telnet. For example:

```
PIX1# show telnet
192.168.50.0 255.255.255.0 inside
```

The *no telnet* command will remove the Telnet privilege from an authorized IP address. The format for this command is:

```
no telnet [<ip_address> [<netmask>] [<interface>]
```

The *ip_address* parameter is the subnet or host IP that you want to clear. The *netmask* parameter is a subnet mask associated with the IP address or range. The *interface* parameter is the name of the interface that had this Telnet host or subnet IP enabled. For example:

```
PIX1(config)# no telnet 192.168.50.0 255.255.255.0 inside
```

To clear all of the Telnet configurations, use the *clear configure telnet* command.

The *who* command shows you which IP addresses currently have Telnet sessions open to the PIX. This example shows two Telnet sessions, one from 192.168.50.3 and the other from 192.168.50.8:

```
PIX1# who
     0: 192.168.50.3
     1: 192.168.50.8
```

The *kill <telnet_id>* command terminates an active Telnet session. No warning is given the user when the session is dropped. The *telnet_id* parameter specifies the session number that is shown when you use the *who* command. For example:

```
PIX1# kill 0
```

Restrictions

Before PIX software version 5.0, you could only Telnet to the PIX from the inside interface. With PIX OS 5.0 and later versions, you can Telnet to any interface, but the PIX firewall requires all Telnet traffic to the outside interface be encrypted with a protocol like IPsec. It is possible to use access lists and a static route to pass a Telnet session through the Cisco PIX from the outside interface to a Telnet server on the inside and then use the Telnet server to Telnet back to the inside interface. However, it is much easier and more secure to use SSH to open a CLI session to the outside interface. This meets the Cisco PIX requirement of using an encrypted connection for the Telnet session. You can use Telnet to an outside interface over an encrypted VPN session.

Configuring Simple Network Management Protocol

Simple Network Management Protocol (SNMP) is one of the easiest ways to manage a network device and to retrieve information from it. Many readers will be familiar with SNMP on Cisco routers, but on the Cisco PIX, things are a bit different. **SNMP on the Cisco PIX is read only.**

One key requirement: do not use a weak SNMP community string. You should never use the default string of *public* as your production SNMP string. Everyone knows this one and it defeats the purpose of trying to secure your PIX firewall. The string you choose should not be a dictionary-based word. For example, *UcanN0tGuEe$$ME* would be a very difficult community string to guess, and most dictionary attacks would fail against it.

There are three versions of SNMP. The Cisco PIX up to version 6.3 code will support SNMPv1, and the version 7.0 supports SNMPv2c. Various SNMP managers are available to manage the PIX firewall using SNMP, as partially listed here.

- HP OpenView
- SolarWinds
- CiscoWorks
- Castle Rock SNMPc
- The Multi Router Traffic Grapher (MRTG)

When we work with SNMP and the Cisco PIX, we need to understand that the SNMP community strings used are always Read Only (RO). This is unlike Cisco routers where we can use Read/Write SNMP strings to alter the configuration or to read the configuration using SNMP. The SNMP protocol by default uses UDP and port 161. As we discuss later in this section, this port number can be changed to suit your needs.

The one SNMP application that deserves special mention is the Multi Router Traffic Grapher (MRTG). Strictly speaking, MRTG is not an SNMP manager application but a graphing application that uses SNMP to gather data and generate graphs. MRTG generates graphs based on polled SNMP values. These graphs then can be inserted into documents, Web pages, or e-mail. MRTG is free for download and is available at www.mrtg.org. MRTG works well with the PIX firewall. An example of using MRTG with the PIX firewall can be found at www.somix.com/software/mrtg/. This Web site provides a script for monitoring the number of connections on a PIX firewall.

In order to make good use of SNMP to monitor the PIX firewall, you need to download the Cisco PIX Management Information Bases (MIBs). These MIBs can be found at http://www.cisco.com/public/sw-center/netmgmt/cmtk/mibs.shtml. Once you have downloaded the MIBs, you need to compile them in your SNMP manager before you can use them to manage the Cisco PIX beyond some simple OIDs.

There are two ways to get SNMP information from the PIX firewall. The first is to query the PIX using SNMP. The host will send a query to the PIX (also known as *polling* it for information) and receive a response. The second way is to have the PIX send "traps" to the SNMP management station. The traps sent are not the same as polled OIDs. A *trap* is a message that the PIX sends based on an event that has occurred, such as a link going up or down or a syslog event. Polling can be used to retrieve information or values that can be displayed by the SNMP management station in the form of gauges, bar charts, or another format. Polling can also retrieve system information about the PIX, such as the software version, interface statistics, and CPU utilization.

Configuring System Identification

Basic SNMP identification is accomplished using the following configuration mode commands:

```
snmp-server location <word>
snmp-server contact <word>
```

Both of these commands are optional. The *word* parameter in both commands can be any string up to 127 characters. The location can describe a building, closet, rack location, or any other standard that you use on your network. The contact can be a contact person or company that is responsible for administering the PIX. Verify SNMP configuration using the *show snmp* enable mode command. A point to remember is that location and contact information can easily be misused for a social engineering "attack" or reconnaissance probe. You have just given the hacker a real name to throw around as "Jim Bob" from IT and a location or office name. All the more reason to use strong SNMP strings and to restrict polling to authorized management workstations.

Configuring Polling

SNMP polling allows a SNMP management station to retrieve data using PIX SNMP OIDs. To configure polling, ensure that an SNMP community is set using the following configuration mode command:

```
snmp-server community <word>
```

The *word* parameter specifies the SNMP community (the password). You should not use easily guessed words or the commonly used PUBLIC string. There are many free dictionary-based SNMP community string crackers, so do not use a plain dictionary-based string. This parameter is required for SNMP to function correctly, is case sensitive, and limited to 32 characters. The PIX firewall must be configured with the IP address of the polling station. This is accomplished using the following command:

```
snmp-server host <interface> <ip_address> [trap | poll] [community text][version 1 |
version 2c [udp-port port]
```

The *ip_address* parameter is the IP address of the SNMP management station. The *interface* parameter specifies the interface where the management station is located. The *trap* parameter specifies that the management station will receive SNMP traps. The *poll* parameter specifies that the management station can query the PIX using SNMP. You may specify multiple polling station IP addresses by typing multiple *snmp-server host* commands. You can select which version of SNMP the Cisco PIX will use by specifying version 1 or version 2c. The default port for SNMP traps is UDP 162 and can be changed using the *udp-port* parameter.

In Figure 15.9, Castle Rock SNMPc is being used to poll the Cisco PIX firewall for system information.

Figure 15.9 Castle Rock SNMPc Manager Polling a PIX Firewall

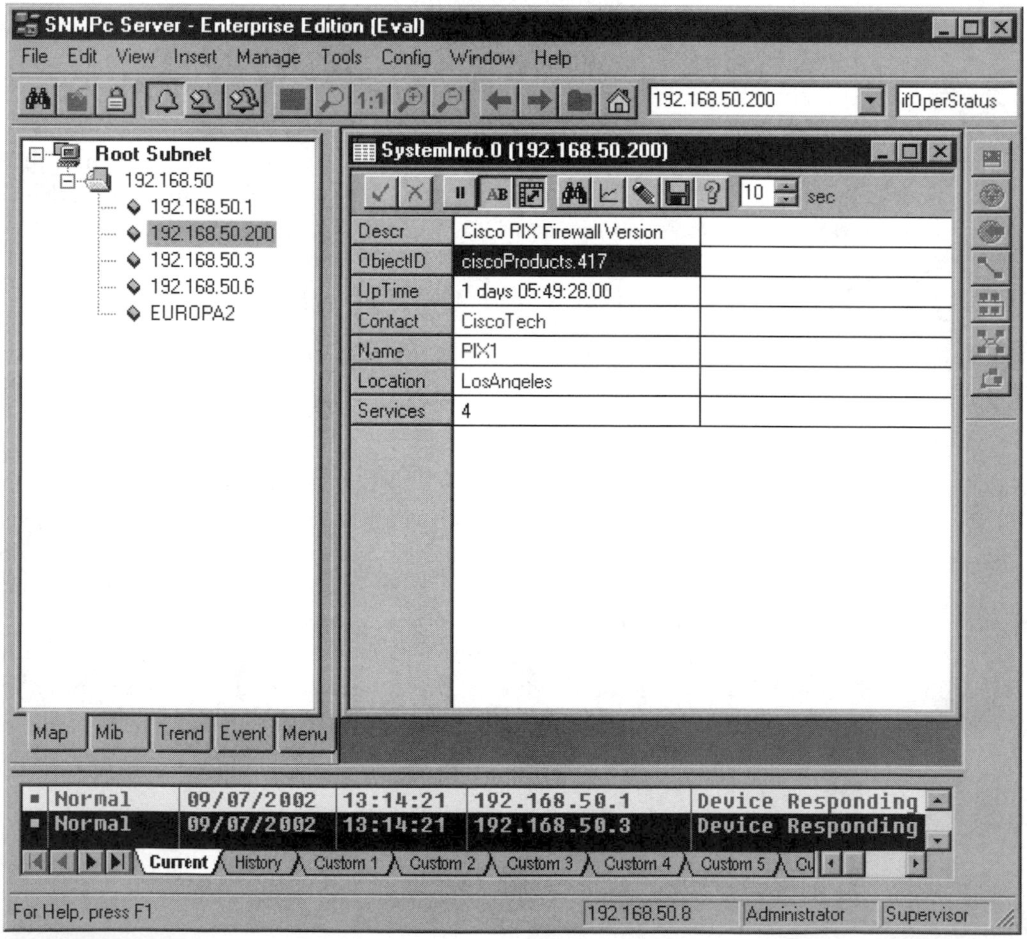

In Figure 15.10, we are using the Solarwinds MIB Walker to drill down into the Cisco PIX MIBs to look at the system OIDs. We can see several MIB names and their OIDs listed such as system name, interface description, and more.

Figure 15.10 Walking the PIX MIB

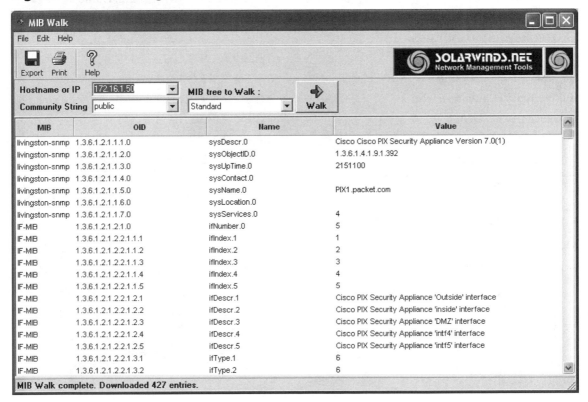

Some other favorite OIDs are shown in Table 15.3. To find all the OIDs for the PIX firewall, go to ftp://ftp.cisco.com/pub/mibs/oid/ and download the appropriate MIB.

Table 15.3 Useful Cisco PIX OIDs

Description	OID
System description	1.3.6.1.2.1.1.1.0
System uptime	1.3.6.1.2.1.1.3.0
Memory used	1.3.6.1.4.1.9.9.48.1.1.1.5.1
Memory free	1.3.6.1.4.1.9.9.48.1.1.1.6.1
Failover status	1.3.6.1.4.1.9.9.147.1.2.1.1.1.4.7

Continued

Table 15.3 Continued

Description	OID
Current connections in use	1.3.6.1.4.1.9.9.147.1.2.2.2.1.5.40.6
Most connections in use	1.3.6.1.4.1.9.9.147.1.2.2.2.1.5.40.7
CPU utilization (5 second)	1.3.6.1.4.1.9.9.109.1.1.1.1.3.1
CPU utilization (1 minute)	1.3.6.1.4.1.9.9.109.1.1.1.1.4.1
CPU utilization (5 minute)	1.3.6.1.4.1.9.9.109.1.1.1.1.5.1
IF Description (outside)	1.3.6.1.2.1.2.2.1.2.1
IF Description (inside)	1.3.6.1.2.1.2.2.1.2.2
IF Description (DMZ)	1.3.6.1.2.1.2.2.1.2.3
IF Description (interface 3)	1.3.6.1.2.1.2.2.1.2.4
IF Description (interface 4)	1.3.6.1.2.1.2.2.1.2.5

Configuring Traps

SNMP traps are messages that are triggered by an event such as an interface going down. SNMP traps are transmitted on UDP port 162 and are not encrypted. To configure and use SNMP traps, follow these steps:

1. Configure the SNMP community

   ```
   PIX1(config)# snmp-server community Il0v3CiSCo
   ```

2. Configure the SNMP host that will receive the traps. The syntax is similar to configuring a host for polling, except the *trap* keyword is used instead of *poll*:

   ```
   PIX1(config)# snmp-server host inside 192.168.50.8 trap
   ```

3. Enable SNMP traps:

   ```
   PIX1(config)# snmp-server enable traps
   ```

4. Set the logging level for SNMP traps using the *logging history* command. For example:

   ```
   PIX1(config)# logging history errors
   ```

5. Start sending traps to the SNMP management station using the *logging on* command:

   ```
   PIX1(config)# logging on
   ```

To stop SNMP traps, use the *no snmp-server enable traps* command.

Managing SNMP on the PIX

You can check and see how much SNMP traffic has been sent and what type it was by using the *snmp-server statistics* command as we see here:

```
PIX1# show snmp-server statistics
1165 SNMP packets input
  0 Bad SNMP version errors
  0 Unknown community name
  0 Illegal operation for community name supplied
  0 Encoding errors
  1162 Number of requested variables
  0 Number of altered variables
  11 Get-request PDUs
  1154 Get-next PDUs
  0 Get-bulk PDUs
  0 Set-request PDUs (Not supported)
1165 SNMP packets output
  0 Too big errors (Maximum packet size 512)
  3 No such name errors
  0 Bad values errors
  0 General errors
  1165 Response PDUs
  0 Trap PDUs
PIX1#
```

To view the existing SNMP configuration of the Cisco PIX firewall, use the show command as we see in this example:

```
PIX1# show running snmp-server
snmp-server host inside 172.16.1.1 community public
snmp-server host inside 192.168.50.12 community public
snmp-server host inside 192.168.50.14 community public
snmp-server host inside 192.168.50.9 community public
no snmp-server location
no snmp-server contact
snmp-server community public
snmp-server enable traps snmp
PIX1#
```

To clear an existing SNMP statistics or the configuration on a Cisco PIX, you will use the clear command as shown here:

```
PIX1# clear snmp-server statistics
PIX1# clear configure snmp-server
```

Configuring System Date and Time

An accurate system clock is one of the most vital system management requirements, yet it is often overlooked or not implemented. Many pieces of system management and security depend on an accurate time and date mechanism to be effective.

Why is clock and time zone accuracy and correctness so important? For starters, the clock and time zone information allow you to build an accurate timeline of what has happened, based on records in the log files. For example, if you need to build a legal case and use the log files from the PIX, the courts will expect the logs to be in the Coordinated Universal Time (UTC) format and they must be consistent across all the devices. Log file timestamp consistency provides the one constant reference point across the network. Without this consistency across all the log files, it becomes difficult, if not impossible, to rebuild an incident's timeline.

When we speak of UTC, we are referring to what used to be called Greenwich Mean Time (GMT). Cisco's implementation of Public Key Infrastructure (PKI) also uses the clock to verify that the certificate revocation list (CRL) has not expired. If the clock is not correct, the certificate authority (CA) may reject or allow a digital certificate based on the incorrect clock timestamp.

As vital as an accurate clock is, many times it is overlooked or viewed as "too much trouble" to configure. The good news is that the PIX firewall is easily configured for an accurate system time and date and can maintain consistency and accuracy via the Network Time Protocol (NTP).

In this section, you will learn how easy it is to configure the PIX firewall for an accurate clock and how NTP can be used for ease of managing the clock. The PIX firewall can be configured to adjust for daylight savings time. Multiple PIX firewalls can synchronize their time via a central time server. NTP can be configured to synchronize securely.

Setting and Verifying the Clock and Time Zone

You can adjust both the viewed time zone information and account for daylight savings time. These enhancements allow you to view the clock information in a readily understandable time format without having to convert the internal UTC into your local time.

There are three suggestions for configuring the PIX clocks across an enterprise network:

- Always display the "local" time zone for each device, based on where the device is located. This practice is useful when you have regional administrators for the firewalls and they frequently administer and monitor their local PIX firewalls.

- Set all devices internally to the UTC format for a standard clock across multiple time zones. We already discussed the benefits of using this method.

- Set all devices to display the local "headquarters" time zone. This is useful when you have a centralized IT staff that manages firewalls across the globe.

In Table 15.4, we have a handy chart that has all the UTC offsets already calculated for you.

Table 15.4 Conversion from UTC to Local Time Zones

Local Time Zone	From UTC	UTC 12:00
ADT - Atlantic Daylight	–3 hours	9 AM
AST - Atlantic Standard	–4 hours	8 AM
EDT - Eastern Daylight		
EST - Eastern Standard	–5 hours	7 AM
CDT - Central Daylight		
CST - Central Standard	–6 hours	6 AM
MDT - Mountain Daylight		
MST - Mountain Standard	–7 hours	5 AM
PDT - Pacific Daylight		
PST - Pacific Standard	–8 hours	4 AM
ADT - Alaskan Daylight		
ALA - Alaskan Standard	–9 hours	3 AM
HAW - Hawaiian Standard	–10 hours	2 AM
Nome, Alaska	–11 hours	1 AM
CET - Central European		
FWT - French Winter		
MET - Middle European	+1 hour	1 PM
MEWT - Middle European Winter		
SWT - Swedish Winter		
EET - Eastern European, USSR Zone 1	+2 hours	2 PM
BT - Baghdad, USSR Zone 2	+3 hours	3 PM
ZP4 - USSR Zone 3	+4 hours	4 PM
ZP5 - USSR Zone 4	+5 hours	5 PM
ZP6 - USSR Zone 5	+6 hours	6 PM
WAST - West Australian Standard	+7 hours	7 PM
CCT - China Coast, USSR Zone 7	+8 hours	8 PM
JST - Japan Standard, USSR Zone 8	+9 hours	9 PM
EAST - East Australian Standard GST		
Guam Standard, USSR Zone 9	+10 hours	10 PM
IDLE - International Date Line		
NZST - New Zealand Standard	+12 hours	Midnight
NZT - New Zealand		

To check the time on a PIX firewall, type *show clock*. If you decide to use the local clock on the PIX, use this command to set the clock:

```
clock set <hh:mm:ss month day year>
```

The *hh:mm:ss* parameter is the normal hours:minutes:seconds in the 24-hour format. The month should be the first three characters of the month, then the day using numerals 1 to 31, and lastly the year, from 1993 to 2035. PIX version 6.2 and later support daylight savings time (*summer-time*) and time zones.

The command format to set the *summer-time zone* parameter is as follows:

```
clock summer-time <zone> date <week weekday month hh:mm week weekday month hh:mm
[offset]>
```

The *zone* parameter is the name of the time zone, such as PST. The other parameters are used to set the start and the end of summer time. If you want to make this a recurring event, change the command slightly:

```
clock summer-time <zone> recurring <week weekday month hh:mm week weekday month
hh:mm [offset]>
```

The parameter *recurring* will start and stop the *summer-time* adjustment each year at the same point. Here is an example:

```
PIX1# show clock
04:22:19.659 UTC Mon Oct 7 2002
PIX1# configure terminal
PIX1(config)# clock summer-time pst date 7 april 2002 00:00 27 october
 2002 00:00
PIX1(config)#
PIX1# show clock
05:23:02.890 pst Mon Oct 7 2002
PIX1# show clock detail
05:23:05.751 pst Mon Oct 7 2002
Time source is user configuration
Summer time starts 00:00:00 UTC Sun Apr 7 2002
Summer time ends 00:00:00 pst Sun Oct 27 2002
```

To set the time zone for the display only, use the following configuration mode command:

```
clock timezone <zone> <hours> [<minutes>]
```

Keep in mind that *clock timezone* will set only the displayed time; the internal time is still kept in UTC format. The *zone* parameter is the name of the time zone. The *hours* parameter is the time offset from UTC. To disable the time zone, type **no clock timezone**.

In order to clear the clock settings, you can use the *clear clock* command. You can see in the following example that the command cleared the *summer-time* settings:

```
PIX1# show clock detail
17:01:43.480 pst Fri Sep 20 2002
```

```
Time source is user configuration
Summer time starts 00:00:00 UTC Sun Apr 7 2002
Summer time ends 00:00:00 pst Sun Oct 27 2002
PIX1# configure terminal
PIX1(config)# clear clock
PIX1# show clock detail
16:02:36.301 UTC Fri Sep 20 2002
Time source is user configuration
```

To clear the clock settings on the Cisco PIX, you would use the command:

```
PIX1(config)# clear configure clock
```

Configuring and Verifying the Network Time Protocol

It is possible to set the clock and time on just a single PIX firewall, but maintaining accurate time and date on multiple Cisco PIX firewalls could be a management problem were it not for the Network Time Protocol (NTP). NTP uses servers as the master reference point, and the NTP client, in this case the PIX firewall, will use the NTP server to get accurate time. The NTP server gets its own time from a radio source or atomic clock. The NTP servers listen on UDP port 123 for requests. The Cisco PIX firewall queries an NTP server and updates its clock. Once NTP is configured on the all the PIX firewalls, all the log files will have consistent and accurate timestamps.

There are two strata, or classes, of NTP servers. Stratum 1 NTP servers are directly connected to the time source. Stratum 2 servers are the second level and consider Stratum 1 servers to be authoritative. Cisco supports only Stratum 2 servers.

You can get the time from public Stratum 2 servers on the Internet or you configure your own NTP server on the LAN or WAN. A quick search for public NTP servers on the Internet reveals many public NTP Stratum 2 servers that you can use. To enable the Cisco PIX Firewall NTP client, use the following command:

```
ntp server <ip_address> source <interface>
```

The *ip_address* parameter specifies the IP address of the NTP server from which you want the Cisco PIX to get its time. The *interface* parameter specifies the source interface on which the PIX firewall will find the NTP server. To remove an NTP server, use the following command:

```
no ntp server <ip_address>
```

The following example shows this command and how to check the configuration to make sure the PIX is talking with the timeserver correctly using the *show ntp status* and *show ntp association* commands:

```
PIX1(config)# ntp server 192.168.50.3 source inside
PIX1(config)# show ntp status

Clock is unsynchronized, stratum 16, no reference clock
nominal freq is 99.9967Hz, actual freq is 99.9967Hz, precision is 2**6
```

```
reference time is 00000000.00000000 (06:28:16.000 UTC Thu Feb 7 2036)
clock offset is -4.0684 msec, root delay is 0.00 msec
root dispersion is 0.00msec, peer dispersion is 15875.02 msec
PIX1(config)# show ntp associations
  address      ref clock     st when poll reach delay offset
  disp
~192.168.50.3      0.0.0.0      16     -     64    0    0.0    0.00
  16000.
master (synced), # master (unsynced), + selected, - candidate, Ð
  configured
```

In the example we see the ~ mark in front of our NTP server. The ~ tells us that this server is statically configured. Other symbols we may see are a ★, which says that the Cisco PIX is synchronized to this peer. We may see a # sign, which says that the Cisco PIX is almost synchronized to this peer. The + sign says that the Cisco PIX could synchronize to this peer.

You can view the NTP configuration using the *show ntp* command in enable mode. To delete the NTP configuration, all you need to do is enter the *clear ntp* command in configuration mode. That's it; the NTP configuration will be completely cleared.

NTP Authentication

Given that we are dealing with a security device, we should always enable NTP authentication. One of the dangers of not using NTP authentication is that a clever hacker could reset the clock, which in turn would change the log file timestamps and possibly help cover up the signs of the security breach. Another hack would be to get around time-based security by resetting system clocks, and sending packets to the Cisco PIX with forged information.

Setting up NTP authentication on the PIX is simple. The authentication uses trusted keys to provide the authentication between the NTP server and the client. The authentication key on the PIX must match the authentication key on the server, which is a string that can be up to 32 characters, including spaces.

NTP authentication is disabled by default on the PIX. To configure NTP authentication, first start with enabling NTP authentication using the following command:

```
ntp authenticate
```

Now you need to define the authentication key. The only choice of encryption is MD5:

```
ntp authentication-key <number> md5 <value>
```

The *number* parameter is a value from 1 to 4294967295 that uniquely identifies the key. The *value* parameter is an arbitrary string of 32 characters, including all printable characters and spaces.

Now we define the trusted key that will be sent in the NTP packets:

```
ntp trusted-key <key_number>
```

The *key_number* parameter must be a number from 1 to 4294967295. The last step is to configure the server association, which lets the Cisco PIX firewall synchronize to the other server. Use the following command:

```
ntp server <ip_address> key <number> source <if_name> [prefer]
```

The *ip_address* specifies the IP address of the server to which you want the Cisco PIX to authenticate. The next piece, *key*, is the number of the shared key that you used when you configured the trusted-key command. The last part, *interface*, is the interface that will send the NTP packets to the server. The optional *prefer* keyword will have the Cisco PIX go to this server first to set the time.

Here is an example of configuring NTP authentication:

```
PIX1(config)# ntp authenticate
PIX1(config)# ntp authentication-key 1 md5 mG<!c>NSM@7i=AwF
PIX1(config)# ntp trusted-key 10
PIX1(config)# ntp server 192.168.50.3 key 1 source inside
PIX1(config)# show ntp
ntp authentication-key 10 md5 ********
ntp authenticate
ntp trusted-key 10
ntp server 192.168.50.3 key 10 source inside
```

To verify that we actually connected to the NTP server and authenticated, we will use the *show ntp associations detail* command as we see here:

```
PIX1# show ntp associations detail
  192.168.50.3 configured, authenticated, our_master, sane, valid, stratum 3
ref ID 148.167.132.200, time c5c3f251.f44ae85b (21:38:25.954 PST Sun Feb 20 2005)
our mode client, peer mode server, our poll intvl 64, peer poll intvl 64
root delay 98.04msec, root disp 32.33, reach 177, sync dist 207.016
delay 0.40msec, offset -0.1149msec, dispersion 125.47
precision 2**16, version 3
org time c5c3f288.a5b39e28 (21:39:20.647 PST Sun Feb 20 2005)
rcv time c5c3f288.a5c89997 (21:39:20.647 PST Sun Feb 20 2005)
xmt time c5c3f288.a5a84205 (21:39:20.647 PST Sun Feb 20 2005)
filtdelay =    0.40    0.41    0.37    0.38    0.35    0.37    0.55    0.00
filtoffset =  -0.11    0.16   -0.55   -0.76   -0.89   -1.33   -3.73    0.00
filterror =    0.02    0.99    1.97    2.94    3.92    4.90    5.87   16000.0
PIX1#
```

We see with the highlighted word "authenticated," that our PIX has in fact authenticated itself to our NTP server at 192.168.50.3. A second command that we use to verify that NTP is working correctly is the *ntp status* command that we see here:

```
PIX1# show ntp status
Clock is synchronized, stratum 4, reference is 192.168.50.3
nominal freq is 99.9967Hz, actual freq is 99.9946Hz, precision is 2**6
reference time is c5c3f2c8.a6a42196 (21:40:24.650 PST Sun Feb 20 2005)
```

```
clock offset is -0.2697 msec, root delay is 97.84 msec
root dispersion is 33.89 msec, peer dispersion is 0.32 msec
```

These results show that the PIX firewall has synchronized its clock to the NTP server at 192.168.50.3. It is a stratum level 4. It also gives information on the frequency used to calculate the clock and the actual time.

Now that we have our Cisco PIX on the right time, we can look at an improved command for the 7.0 code called *reload*. This command has been around on the PIX for a while, but in 7.0 we were given the ability to schedule a reload of the PIX based on time and date. The format of the reload command is:

```
reload [at hh:mm [month day | day month]] [cancel] [in [hh:]mm] [max-hold-time
[hh:]mm] [noconfirm] [quick] [reason text] [save-config]
```

We can set the hour, month, and day we want the Cisco PIX to reload, and we can also tell the PIX to not be interactive by using the *nocomfirm* parameter. When you use this parameter, the PIX will not be "nice" and ask if you want to save the configuration, it just reloads. To stop or cancel a scheduled reload, you will use the command *reload cancel*. You should understand that this cancels a scheduled reload, not a reload in progress for which there is no stopping of the process.

Management Using the Cisco PIX Adaptive Security Device Manager (ASDM)

Cisco PIX Adaptive Security Device Manager (ASDM) can be used as either a Web-based Java applet or a Windows application. ASDM allows you to manage the Cisco PIX with a GUI interface rather than a command line. We will just give you a very quick look at the possibilities of what ADSM can offer for management of your Cisco PIX; greater detail about ASDM is provided in Chapter 10. ASDM provides a GUI configuring various aspects of the PIX firewall, such as NTP, syslog, and basic device configuration. The Cisco ASDM makes use of tabs, drop-down menus, and other GUI tools to provide an easy administration interface. ASDM also offers graphs of firewall and traffic activity for viewing and printing as we see in Figure 15.11.

Figure 15.11 Opening Screen of ASDM

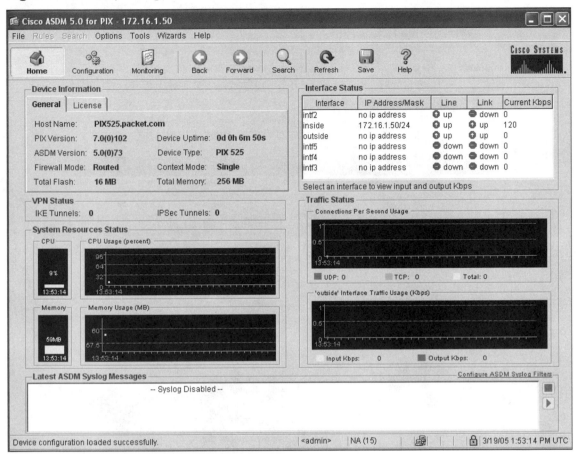

What we are most interested in for managing our Cisco PIX can be seen in Figure 15.12. System Properties and the Administration in ASDM provide a wealth of options for us to configure PIX firewalls.

Figure 15.12 Cisco PIX ASDM Management Menus

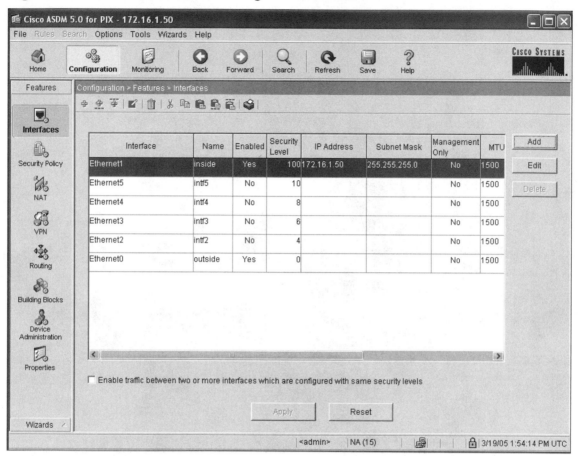

This is where we configure SNMP, Telnet access, set the passwords, configure the clock, configure NTP, and more. We will provide a quick overview to give you an idea how ASDM can be used to ease administrative burdens. Figure 15.13 provides an example involving NTP configuration, including authentication for NTP.

Figure 15.13 Enabling NTP Using the Cisco PIX ASDM

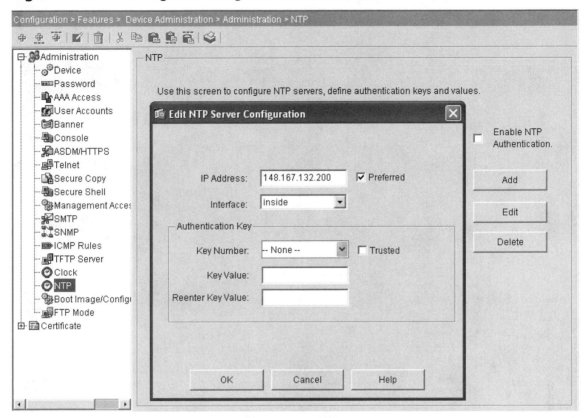

In Figure 15.14 we see the Cisco PIX ASDM screen for configuring the PIX to use SNMP. The ASDM interface does make some of these tasks much easier than trying to remember the command line method.

Figure 15.14 Using Cisco ASDM to Configure SNMP

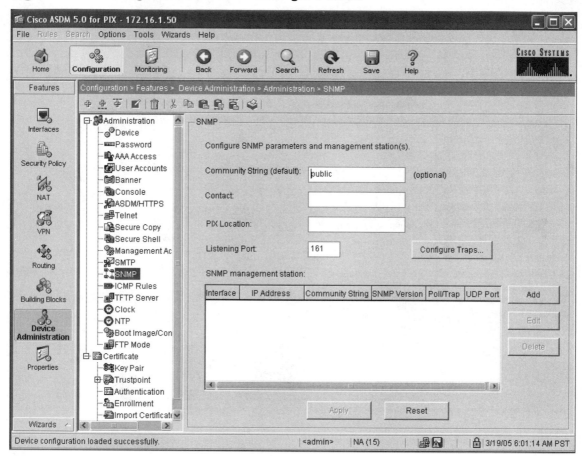

You can see that we can add our community string; system administrator name, location, and which interface should be used. We can also set our syslog messages to be sent as traps to the management station.

Summary

Network management, although appearing simple on the surface, can be quite complex. To effectively manage the Cisco PIX, you need to be aware of not just the PIX but also network-wide issues.

When configuring the PIX for logging, you can choose from a variety of logging options, such as buffered logging, console, Telnet/SSH sessions, syslog servers, or SNMP. You can select message severity levels ranging from Level 1 (alert) to Level 7 (debug) based on your needs. Aside from selecting the severity level, you can choose from several facility levels to direct the flow of the syslog messaging. The default facility level is local4 (20), but you can use other facility levels to redirect syslog messages from different sources to a syslog server destination of your choice. This system provides a method to store various sources of syslog messages in their own files on the syslog server.

You can specify that all syslog messages should be logged or you can filter out certain messages so they will not be sent. This functionality is very useful in troubleshooting a network issue where you might be in debug mode and the normal message flow would be overwhelming to work with.

The Cisco PIX firewall can be managed using a console port, though usually, the PIX will be managed by remote access. Two popular choices of protocol for remote access are Telnet and SSH. Telnet has been around for a long time and is used on a variety of network devices, but it is an insecure protocol and sends the information in clear text across the network. SSH, on the other hand, encrypts the session so that information such as passwords is not sent in clear text. SSH also provides a way to be able to log into the outside interface of the Cisco PIX, unlike Telnet, which is not permitted to directly log into the outside interface without an encrypted connection. The Cisco PIX firewall can act only as a server for SSH and Telnet services, not a client. An important point to remember about the Cisco PIX and SSH is to make sure you use a client that supports SSHv2 such as PuTTY or SSH Secure Shell.

An alternative method of accessing the PIX firewall remotely for system management is the Cisco ASDM utility. ASDM is either a Java application that allows the management of the Cisco PIX using a Web browser or a native Microsoft Windows application. The Cisco ASDM has good reporting functionality to build graphs showing various performance statistics, attack reports, and traffic activity.

The Cisco PIX supports read-only SNMP reporting or **Read-Only** and can either send traps to a host or be polled for information.

The Cisco PIX firewall has a wealth of system time and date functionality. This functionality goes from the basic time and date stamp to automatically adjusting for daylight savings time. The Cisco PIX clock can be set locally or NTP can be used to set the time from a central timeserver. The PIX uses the UTC time format but can be configured to display the time in a time-zone format such as PST. The PIX can use NTP authentication to keep the link to the timeserver secure from unauthorized adjustment of the system time. This provides a level of security for using digital certificates.

Configuring Virtual Private Networking

Solutions in this chapter:

- **What's New in PIX 7.0**

- **IPsec Concepts**

- **Configuring a Site-to-Site VPN**

- **Remote Access—Configuring Support for the Cisco Software VPN Clients**

☑ **Summary**

Introduction

Virtual private networks (VPNs) provide secure communications between internal networks over a public network (such as the Internet, for example). Connecting private networks or hosts by securely tunneling through a public network infrastructure has both commercial and practical applications. VPNs can connect branch offices, mobile users, and business partners.

VPNs ensure confidentiality and authentication. VPNs provide a number of solutions, including economical connectivity between offices (using site-to-site VPNs) and the ability to provision connections quickly (simply by installing VPN hardware on an existing Internet connection instead of having to wait for a dedicated leased line or Frame Relay PVC to be installed). Remote access VPNs provide connectivity for mobile workers or telecommuters, allowing them to securely gain access to their home network, regardless of where they are or how they connect.

The PIX firewall supports both site-to-site and remote access VPNs using IPsec. VPNs can be very complicated, and a single connection might be implemented using a combination of many protocols that work together to provide tunneling, encryption, authentication, access control, and auditing.

This chapter shows how to configure VPNs on the PIX firewall. We will configure site-to-site VPNs using IPsec and IKE with preshared keys and digital certificates. The PIX firewall can act as a concentrator for terminating Cisco software VPN clients for remote-access VPNs.

Figure 16.1 shows the two types of VPN tunnel: site-to-site and remote access.

Figure 16.1 VPNs in General

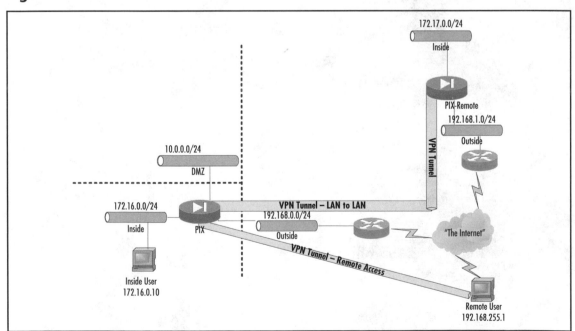

What's New in PIX 7.0

Version 7.0 is a comprehensive enhancement of previous versions of the PIX firewall operating system. This is particularly true for virtual private networking (VPN), as configuration is more consistent and manageable. There are several new features and enhancements for VPN. The following list is an excerpt from Cisco's PIX v7.0 documentation at www.cisco.com:

- **Automatic VPN Client Software Updates:** Cisco VPN clients and Cisco VPN 3002 hardware clients. Can specify updates based on client operating system and client version.

- **Improved Support for Non-Split Tunneling Remote-Access VPN Environments:** Can terminate remote-access VPN connections on the outside interface of a Cisco PIX, allowing Internet-destined traffic from remote-access user VPN tunnels to exit through the same interface it arrived (after firewall rules, URL filtering policies, and other security checks have been optionally applied).

- **Native Integration with Popular User Authentication Services:** Can authenticate VPN users via Microsoft Active Directory, Microsoft Windows Domains, Kerberos, Lightweight Directory Access Protocol (LDAP), and RSA SecurID (without requiring a separate RADIUS/TACACS+ server to act as an intermediary).

- **Cisco IOS Software Certificate Authority Support:** Online enrollment via lightweight X.509 certificate authority that simplifies the rollout of public key infrastructure (PKI)-enabled site-to-site VPNs.

PIX v7.0 also removes certain VPN functionality and streamlines the setup of site-to-site and remote access VPN tunnels. In particular, the following configurations are deprecated:

- Manual IPsec; that is, IPsec without using Internet Key Exchange

- L2TP/IPSEC tunnels with a Windows 2000 client

- PPTP VPN tunnels

IPsec Concepts

IPsec was developed by the Internet Engineering Task Force (IETF) as an IPv6 component, but can be implemented in IPv4. IPsec is based on open Layer 3 standards. IPsec standards documents (of which there are many) can be found at www.ietf.org/html.charters/ipsec-charter.html. For more information about the organization and collection of IPsec standards, start with RFC 2411 ("IP Security Document Road Map").

IPsec

IPsec's main design goals are to provide:

- **Data confidentiality** Encrypt data before transmission.

- **Data integrity** Each peer can determine if a received packet was changed during transit.

- **Data origin authentication**   Receiver can validate the identity of a packet's sender.

- **Anti-replay**   The receiver can detect and reject replayed packets, protecting it from spoofing and man-in-the-middle attacks.

IPsec Core Layer 3 Protocols: ESP and AH

IPsec provides confidentiality and integrity protection for transmitted information, authentication source and destinations, and anti-replay protection. Two main network protocols, Encapsulating Security Payload (ESP) and Authentication Header (AH), are used to achieve this goal. All other parts of the IPsec standard merely implement these protocols and configure the required technical parameters. Applying AH or ESP to an IP packet may modify the data payload (not always) and may insert an AH or ESP header between the IP header and the packet contents. See Figures 16.2 and 16.3 for illustrations of how these transformations are performed.

Figure 16.2 AH Encapsulation

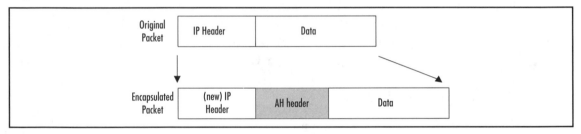

Figure 16.3 ESP Encapsulation

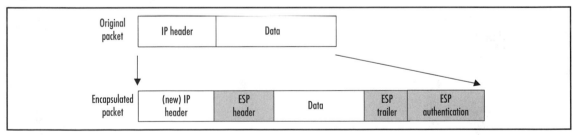

Authentication Header

The AH, which is defined as IP protocol 51, ensures:

- **Data integrity**   Calculates a hash of the entire IP packet, including the original IP header (but not variable fields such as the TTL), data payload, and the authentication header (excluding the field that will contain the calculated hash value). This hash, an integrity check value (ICV), can be either Message Authentication Code (MAC) or a digital signature. MAC hashes are more common than digital signatures. Hashing algorithms include MD5 and SHA-1. Both are known as *keyed hashes*, meaning that they use an extra value to calculate the hash, which is known only to the participating parties. When the packet is received, its content, excluding some fields, is hashed by the receiver and the result is compared with the ICV. If they are the same, the packet is declared authentic.

- **Data origin authentication**   AH provides source IP authentication. Since the source IP is included in the data used to calculate the hash, its integrity is guaranteed.

- **Replay protection**   AH also includes an IPsec sequence number, which provides protection against replay attacks because this number is also included in authenticated data and can be checked by the receiving party.

AH provides no confidentiality because no encryption is used.

Encapsulating Security Payload

ESP, which is defined as IP protocol 50, provides:

- Packet padding to prevent traffic analysis, and encrypts the results using ciphers such as DES, 3DES, AES, or Blowfish.

- Optional authentication using the same algorithms as the AH protocol. IP header information is not included in the authenticated data, which allows ESP-protected packets to pass through NAT devices. When a packet is created, authentication data is calculated after encryption. This allows the receiver to check the packet's authenticity before starting the computationally intensive task of decryption.

- Optional anti-replay features.

The original ESP definition did not include authentication or anti-replay, as it was assumed that the sender and receiver would use ESP and AH together to get confidentiality *and* authentication. Since ESP can also perform most of the AH functions, there is no reason to use AH. Because ESP works on encapsulation principles, it has a different format: All data is encrypted and then placed between a header and a trailer. This differentiates it from AH, where only a header is created.

IPsec Communication Modes: Tunnel and Transport

Both AH and ESP can operate in either transport mode or tunnel mode. In transport mode, only the data portion of an IP packet is affected; the original IP header is not changed. Transport mode is used when both the receiver and the sender are endpoints of the communication—for example, two hosts communicating directly to each other. Tunnel mode encapsulates the entire original packet as the data portion of a new packet and creates a new external IP header. (AH and/or ESP headers are created in both modes). Tunnel mode is more convenient for site-to-site VPNs because it allows tunneling of traffic through the channel established between two gateways.

In transport mode, the IP packet contains an AH or ESP header right after the original IP header and before upper layer data such as a TCP header and application data. If ESP is applied to the packet, only this upper layer data is encrypted. If optional ESP authentication is used, only upper layer data, not the IP header, is authenticated. If AH is applied to the packet, both the original IP header and upper layer data are authenticated. Figure 16.4 shows what happens to the packet when IPsec is applied in transport mode.

Figure 16.4 Packet Structure in Transport Mode

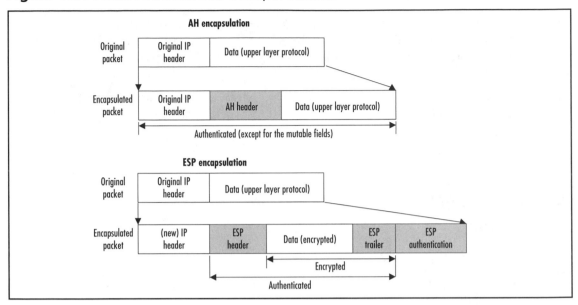

Tunnel mode is the only mode supported by PIX v7.0. Tunnel mode is typically used to establish an encrypted and authenticated IP tunnel between two sites. The original packet is encrypted and/or authenticated and encapsulated by a sending gateway into the data part of a new IP packet, and then the new IP header is added to it with the destination address of the receiving gateway. The ESP and/or AH header is inserted between this new header and the data portion. The receiving gateway performs decryption and authentication of the packet, extracts the original IP packet (including the original source/destination IPs), and forwards it to the destination network. Figure 16.5 demonstrates the encapsulation performed in tunnel mode.

Figure 16.5 Packet Structure in Tunnel Mode

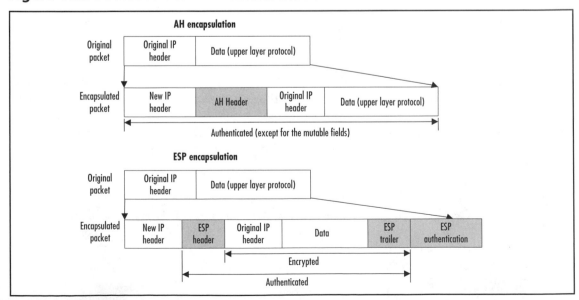

If AH is used, both the original IP header and the new IP header are protected (authenticated), but if ESP is used, even with the authentication option, only the original IP address, not the sending gateway's IP address, is protected. ESP is more than adequate since it is very difficult to spoof an IPsec packet without knowing many technical details. The exclusion of the new IP header from authenticated data also allows tunnels to pass through devices that perform NAT. When the new header is created, most of the options from the original IP header are mapped onto the new one—for example, the Type of Service (ToS) field.

Internet Key Exchange

IPsec protocols use cryptographic algorithms to encrypt and authenticate, and this requires encryption/ authentication keys. It is possible to configure these keys manually, but there are disadvantages to this approach. First, it is very difficult to scale; second, it is not possible to renegotiate Security Associations (SAs) because they are fixed until manually changed. Thus, there is a strong need for tools for managing keys and SAs. Key management includes generation, distribution, storage, and deletion of the keys. The initial authentication of the systems to each other and protecting the key exchange is critical. After keys are exchanged, the channel is protected with these keys and is used to set up other parameters, including SAs.

The protocol the IETF adopted for performing these functions is called Internet Security Association and Key Management Protocol (ISAKMP), defined in RFC 2408. RFC 2408 describes authenticated key exchange methods. ISAKMP has an IANA-assigned UDP port number of 500. ISAKMP is a generic protocol and is not tied to IPsec or any other key-using protocol.

ISAKMP can be implemented directly over IP or any transport layer protocol. When used with other key management protocols such as Oakley (RFC 2412) and Secure Key Exchange Mechanism (SKEME), we end up with a protocol called the Internet Key Exchange (IKE), which is defined in RFC 2409. Although not strictly correct, the abbreviations IKE and ISAKMP are often used interchangeably, even in Cisco configuration commands. In fact, on the PIX firewall, all IKE configuration is performed using the *isakmp* command.

IKE has two exchange phases, and each phase can operate in one or two modes. IKE Phase 1 starts when two peers need to establish a secure channel—that is, they do not have IPsec SAs needed for communication over IPsec. This phase includes authentication of systems by each other, agreement on encryption and authentication algorithms used from then on to protect IKE traffic, performing a Diffie-Hellman (DH) key exchange, and finally, establishing an IKE Security Association (IKE SA). IKE SAs are bidirectional; each IKE connection between peers has only one IKE SA associated with it.

IKE Phase 2 negotiates one or more IPsec SAs, which will be used for the IPsec tunnel between these peers. It uses key material from IKE Phase 1 to derive keys for IPsec. One peer tells the other which traffic it wants to protect and which encryption/authentication algorithms are supported. The second peer then agrees on a single protection set for this traffic and establishes the keys.

While implementing different phases adds processing overhead, there are advantages to this approach:

- Trust between peers is established in the first phase and used in the second phase.

- Key material established in the first phase can be used in the second phase.

- Renegotiations of the first phase can be assisted by the second-phase data.

Phase 1 has two modes: main mode and aggressive mode. Main mode uses three exchanges between peers; each exchange consists of two messages, a request, and a reply:

- The first exchange in main mode negotiates parameters to protect the IKE connection. The initiating side sends a proposal to its counterpart, and includes parameters it supports. These parameters include one encryption algorithm (DES, 3DES, etc.) and one of four authentication algorithms: preshared secret, RSA public key encryption with Diffie-Hellman exchange group 1 and 2, or public key RSA signature (this includes use of certificates). The other peer then selects and accepts a single pair from the offered set. If there is no match or agreement, the IKE tunnel cannot be established.

- The second exchange in main mode performs DH key establishment between peers. It exchanges two values called *nonces*, which are hashes that only the other party can decrypt. This confirms that the message is sent by the same hosts as the previous exchange.

- The third and last exchange authenticates the peers using the agreed-on methods: public keys signatures, public key encryption, or a preshared secret. This exchange is protected by an encryption method that was selected in the first exchange.

RFC 2408 provides more details on the packet format and algorithms used. At the end of the first phase, each host has an IKE SA, which specifies all parameters for this IKE tunnel: the authentication method, the encryption and hashing algorithm, the Diffie-Hellman group used, the lifetime for this IKE SA, and the key values.

Aggressive mode exchanges only three packets instead of six, so it is faster but not as secure. Fewer packets are sent because the first two packets in this exchange include almost everything in one message; each host sends a proposed protection set, Diffie-Hellman values, and authentication values. The third packet is sent only for confirmation and after the IKE SA is already established. The weakness in aggressive mode is that everything is sent in clear text and can be captured. However, the only thing the attacker can achieve is to DoS one of the peers, because it is not possible to discover the keys that are established by the Diffie-Hellman protocol. There have been recent attacks against VPN endpoints that relied on the properties of aggressive mode. It is recommended to turn aggressive mode off on the PIX using *isakmp am-disable*.

The most important mode of Phase 2 is quick mode. It can be repeated several times using the same IKE SA established in Phase 1. Each exchange in this mode establishes two IPsec SAs by each peer. One of these SAs is used for inbound protection, and the other is used for outbound protection. During the exchange, peers agree on the IPsec SA parameters and send each other a new nonce, which is used for deriving Diffie-Hellman keys from the ones established in Phase 1. When the IPsec SA lifetime expires, a new SA is negotiated in the same manner. Figure 16.6 summarizes the flow of the IKE protocol.

Figure 16.6 IKE Phases and Modes

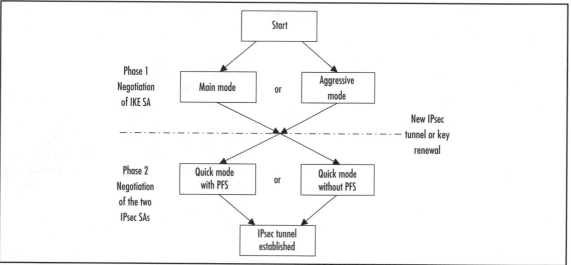

Security Associations

Previous sections assumed that an IPsec connection was already established and all parameters such as authentication and encryption keys were known to both parties. The data flow in each direction is associated with an entity called a *security association* (SA). Each party has at least two IPsec SAs: the sender has one for outgoing packets and another for incoming packets from the receiver, and the receiver has one SA for incoming packets from the sender and a second SA for outgoing packets to the sender. See Figure 16.7 for an illustration.

Figure 16.7 IPsec Security Associations and Their Use in Two-Way Communication

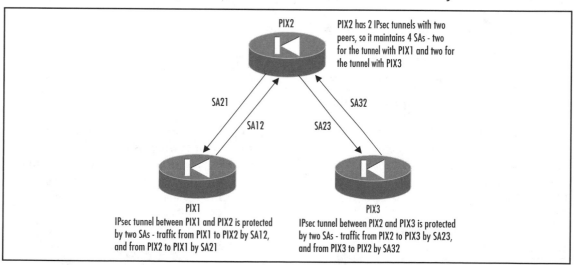

Each SA has three parameters:

- The Security Parameter Index (SPI), which is always present in AH and ESP headers
- The destination IP address
- The IPsec protocol, AH or ESP (so if both protocols are used in communication, each has to have its own SA, resulting in a total of four SAs for two-way communication)

Each peer maintains a separate database of active SAs for each direction (inbound and outbound) on each of its interfaces. This database is known as the Security Association Database (SAD). SAs from these databases decide which encryption and authentication parameters are applied to the sent or received packet. SAs may be fixed for the time of traffic flow (called *manual IPsec* in some documents), but when a key management protocol is used, they are renegotiated many times during the connection. For each SA, the SAD entry contains the following data:

- The destination address
- The SPI
- The IPsec transform (protocol and algorithm used—for example, AH, HMAC-MD5)
- The key used in the algorithm
- The IPsec mode (tunnel or transport)
- The SA lifetime (in kilobytes or in seconds); when this lifetime expires, the SA must be terminated, and a new SA established
- The anti-reply sequence counters
- Some extra parameters such as Path MTU

The selection of encryption parameters and corresponding SAs is governed by the Security Policy Database (SPD). An SPD is maintained for each interface and is used to decide on the following:

- Selection of outgoing traffic to be protected
- Checking if incoming traffic was properly protected
- The SAs to use for protecting this traffic
- What to do if the SA for this traffic does not exist

The SPD consists of a numbered list of policies. Each policy is associated with one or more selectors, which Cisco implements as an access-list. A *permit* statement means that IPsec should be applied to the matching traffic; a *deny* statement means that the packet should be forwarded without applying IPsec. SPD policies are configured on the PIX firewall with the *crypto map* command. The resulting map and a crypto access-list are applied to the interface, creating an SPD for this interface.

For outgoing traffic, when IPsec receives data to be sent, it consults the SPD to determine if the traffic has to be protected. If it does, the SPD uses an SA that corresponds to this traffic. If the SA exists, its characteristics are taken from the SAD and applied to the packet. If the SA does not exist yet, IKE establishes a new SA to protect the packet.

For incoming IPsec traffic, the SPI is culled from the AH or ESP header to find a corresponding SA in the SAD. If it does not exist, the packet is dropped. If an SA exists, the packet is checked/ decrypted using the parameters provided by this SA. Finally, the SPD is checked to ensure that this packet was correctly protected—for example, that it should have been encrypted using 3DES and authenticated with MD5 and nothing else. Figure 16.8 shows both sequences of events.

Figure 16.8 Processing of Outbound and Inbound Traffic by IPsec

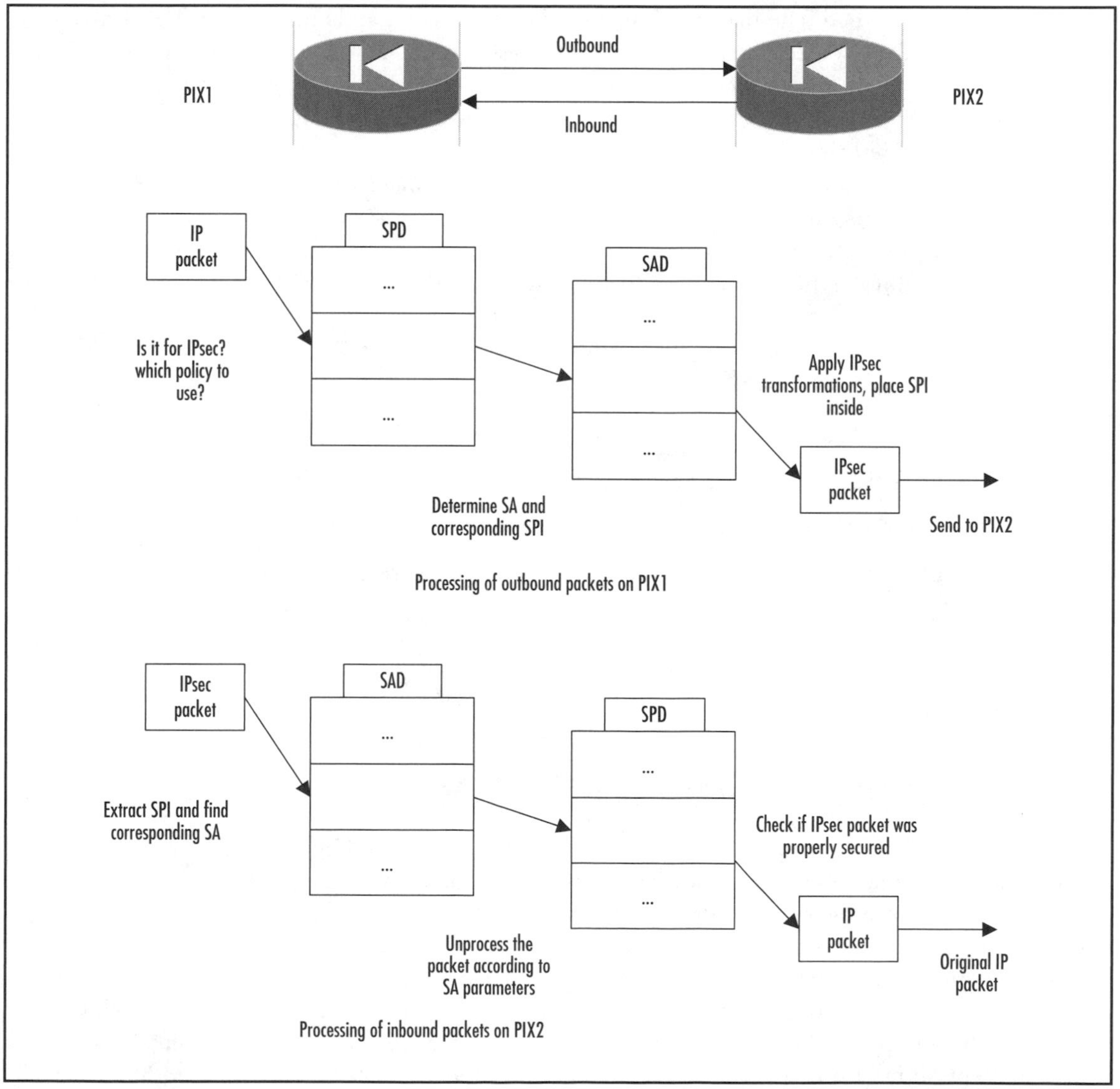

Certificate Authority Support

IKE authentication on the PIX firewall can be performed in two different ways:

- Using preshared keys, where the parties simply send each other a value—their own names, for example, which are encrypted using the shared key and a hash of some parameters

- Using RSA or DSA signature authentication (digital certificates)

With the second method, each party identifies itself by sending its name, its public certificate issued by a certificate authority (CA), and its RSA or DSA signature. A public key certificate contains a public key. The receiving party queries the CA and confirms the certificate belongs to the sender. If it does, the RSA or DSA signature is verified using the public key from the certificate, and the system's identity is verified. The biggest advantage of using CAs for authentication in IKE is that this scheme is easily scalable, especially in partial- or full-mesh environments. When a new peer is added to the IPsec network, the administrator only needs to enroll it with the CA and obtain a certificate from the CA. After that, each participant that recognizes this CA will be able to verify the identity of the new peer by its certificate.

To receive a certificate, a system must establish a trusted channel with the CA, generate a public/private key pair, and request a certificate. The CA then verifies the system's credentials (usually offline) and issues a certificate. A certificate can include the bearer's IP address, its name, the serial number of the certificate, the expiry date of the certificate, and a copy of the bearer's public key. The standard for the certificate format is X.509, of which Cisco supports version 3. The PIX firewall requires that the CA support the Simple Certificate Enrollment Protocol (SCEP). Currently, the following CAs are supported:

- Cisco IOS CS, a simple CA for quick deployment of PKI-enabled VPNs

- VeriSign Private Certificate Services (PCS) and On-Site service (www.verisign.com)

- Entrust VPN Connector version 4.1 or later (www.entrust.com)

- Baltimore Technologies UniCERT Certificate Management System, version 3.1.2 or later

- Microsoft Certificate Services, a part of Microsoft Windows 2000 Advanced server

- Netscape CMS

- RSA Keon

Configuring a Site-to-Site VPN

Site-to-site VPNs link two dispersed networks as they might be linked by a leased line or WAN circuit. The actual underlying infrastructure is immaterial as long as the two sites can reach each other via IP. The two sites can use either preshared keys or certificates to authenticate each other. With preshared keys, a key is shared between the sites for the purposes of mutual authentication and to establish the initial encryption over which can be exchanged IPsec parameters for the tunnel. Alternatively, the VPN may use digital certificates that belong to each site, which have been issued by a central CA to facilitate authentication and encryption of the initial key exchange between the two sites. IPsec tunnel encryption itself is identical for preshared key and certificate VPNs.

At a high level, the VPN configuration process on the Cisco PIX firewall consists of three major steps:

1. **Planning**   Decide the details of IPsec policies used, such as IKE parameters, including the peer authentication methods (using preshared keys or digital certificates), and the encryption algorithms. Ensure that the peers can communicate without IPsec. All IPsec packets must be permitted.

2. **Configuring IKE** Enable IKE on the firewall, configure policy parameters for Phases 1 and 2, and define the authentication method (preshared keys or CA).

3. **Configuring IPsec parameters**   Define interesting traffic, configure transform sets, create a crypto map, and apply to an interface.

The following example configures a site-to-site IPsec VPN using IKE.

Planning

Your first step is planning, including deciding key parameters. Figure 16.10 shows the networks and IP addresses that are used in the example.

Figure 16.9 Network Setup for a Site-to-Site VPN

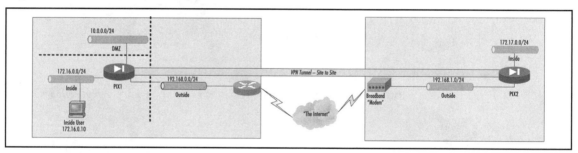

First, determine IKE Phase 1 parameters such as authentication method (preshared keys or digital certificates), encryption algorithm (DES, 3DES or AES), data authentication algorithm (MD5 or SHA-1), DH group identifier (Group 1, Group 2, Group 5, or Group 7), and IKE SA lifetime. These parameters together constitute an IKE policy. It is possible to configure different policies for each remote peer, but each firewall must have at least one common policy between them to establish the tunnel. The example configurations in this chapter use AES-128 encryption, SHA-1 authentication, DH Group 2, and a default IKE SA lifetime of 86,400 seconds.

Certificates require greater planning than preshared keys do. Good planning will make the difference between an easy CA rollout and one that presents challenges at every turn.

Selecting a CA server is a matter of determining which best meets your needs and budget. Our example in "Configuring Certificate Authority Support" uses Cisco IOS Certificate Server (Cisco IOS CS)—a "CA lite" that can be configured on Cisco routers since release 12.3(4)T. A data sheet can be found at www.cisco.com/en/US/tech/tk583/tk372/tech_brief09186a00801e05dc.html. Cisco IOS CS can be used by organizations that need a CA only establishing Cisco VPNs.

If possible, for maximum security, configure certificate revocation lists (CRLs), which are maintained by CAs identify revoked certificates. If you turn on CRL support, each certificate will be checked against this list during IKE negotiation before it is accepted. This requires a connection between the firewall and the CA at the time of authentication, which is not always possible. If you do not use CRLs, you only need connectivity with CA during enrollment, and all authentication of certificates afterward is done using the CA's public certificate, which the firewall obtains during enrollment.

Choose either RSA or DSA keys. Unless you have a specific reason to use DSA keys, RSA is generally considered the better choice. DSA keys cannot be used for SSH or SSL, and cannot be used for automatic enrollment (SCEP). DSA keys are limited to 1024 bits in size.

With RSA, you can use separate keys for signing and encryption, or a single key for both functions. Separate keys minimize exposure: SSL uses a key for encryption, but not for signing, while IKE uses a key for signing, but not for encryption. We will be using a single general-purpose key in this example.

Automatic enrollment using Simple Certificate Enrollment Protocol (SCEP) over HTTP, or manual enrollment? Manual enrollment is an administratively heavy process, but has the advantage that no initial VPN tunnel is needed if the CA is not reachable from a public network. In this example, we will use SCEP for easy rollout of keys. SCEP can reduce the time and overhead it takes to roll out VPN clients.

Choose your IPsec parameters. Configure peer IP addresses and names, and transform sets for each. At least one transform set must match between both firewalls to establish an IPsec SA and an IPsec tunnel. In this example, we configure a transform set using ESP protection with AES-128, and ESP authentication with SHA-1.

Now we are ready for configuration. Let's go through it step by step.

Allowing IPsec Traffic

In PIX v7.0, IPsec traffic is allowed by default. It is no longer necessary to specify *sysopt connection permit-ipsec*.

Enabling IKE

Enable IKE on the interface connected to the remote peer (usually the outside interface). This must be done on each peer using the following command:

isakmp enable `<interface_name>`

In our example, this command needs to be on the outside interface of each firewall:

```
PIX1(config)# isakmp enable outside
PIX2(config)# isakmp enable outside
```

IKE is enabled on all interfaces by default. It can be turned off on a specific interface (to prevent IKE denial-of-service (DoS) attacks on the interface) using the *no* form of the command:

no isakmp enable `<interface_name>`

The PIX can identify itself by IP address or a hostname; the default is IP address. Use hostnames if peers are authenticated by RSA signatures. The peer must either be defined on the firewall using the *name* command, or registered in DNS. Configure the identity mode on both peers (must be the same on both):

isakmp identity `{address | hostname | auto}`

If the identity method does not match, the peers will not negotiate an IKE SA and no IPsec SA will be established. *isakmp identity auto* configures ISAKMP negotiation by connection type: negotiation will automatically choose either IP address identity for preshared key or certificate Distinguished Name (DN) for certificate authentication.

Disable aggressive mode, for security reasons:

```
isakmp am-disable
```

Creating an ISAKMP Protection Suite

The PIX can have many IKE policies (also known as *ISAKMP protection suites*), which are distinguished by their priority (an integer from 1 to 65,534). The smaller this number, the higher the policy's priority. The IKE policy between peers must match. A policy with the highest priority is attempted first, and if not accepted by the remote peer, the next highest priority is attempted. This continues until a policy is accepted by the other peer or the list is exhausted. No match means that IKE establishment fails. To create a policy, use the following commands:

```
isakmp policy <priority> authentication {pre-share | dsa-sig | rsa-sig}
isakmp policy <priority> encryption {des | 3des | aes | aes-192 | aes-256 }
isakmp policy <priority> hash {md5 | sha}
isakmp policy <priority> group {1 | 2 | 5 | 7}
isakmp policy <priority> lifetime <lifetime>
```

These commands specify (in order) the encryption algorithm to be used, the data authentication algorithm, the peer authentication method, the Diffie-Hellman group identifier, and the IKE SA lifetime in seconds. The lifetime can be any number of seconds between 120 and 2147483647. Use 0 to specify an infinite lifetime. The default is 86,400 seconds (one day).

For our example, we will configure the following on both firewalls using a priority of 10:

```
isakmp policy 10 encryption aes
isakmp policy 10 hash sha
isakmp policy 10 group 2
```

If a value is not specified, default values are used: 3*des* for encryption, *sha* for data authentication, *2* for DH group, and *86,400* for IKE SA lifetime. Specify the peer authentication method. If you are using preshared keys, use the following command:

```
isakmp policy 10 authentication pre-share
```

If you are using digital certificates, use the following command:

```
isakmp policy 10 authentication rsa-sig
```

To verify the configuration of IKE policies, use the *show running-config crypto isakmp* command as shown (this output is for preshared keys):

```
PIX1# show running-config crypto isakmp
isakmp identity address
isakmp enable outside
isakmp policy 10 authentication pre-share
```

```
isakmp policy 10 encryption aes
isakmp policy 10 hash sha
isakmp policy 10 group 2
isakmp policy 10 lifetime 86400
isakmp policy 65535 authentication pre-share
isakmp policy 65535 encryption des
isakmp policy 65535 hash sha
isakmp policy 65535 group 2
isakmp policy 65535 lifetime 86400
```

There is also a default IKE policy with a priority of 65,535. If the configured ISAKMP policies do not match, the firewall tries this default policy as a last resort. If the default policy also does not match, ISAKMP negotiation fails.

Defining an ISAKMP Preshared Key

Please note that the steps defining an ISAKMP preshared key and configuring CA support are exclusive, and only one of them needs to be performed.

The most common site-to-site VPN is an IPsec tunnel with IKE using preshared keys. When establishing VPNs with multiple peers, the preshared keys should be unique for each pair. The key for establishing an IKE tunnel with a particular peer is based on the peer's IP address. The key itself is an alphanumeric string of up to 128 characters and must be configured the same on both gateways using the *tunnel-group* command:

```
PIX1(config)# tunnel-group 192.168.1.1 type IPSec-L2L
PIX1(config)# tunnel-group 192.168.1.1 ipsec-attributes
PIX1(config-ipsec)# pre-shared-key mykey1
PIX2(config)# tunnel-group 192.168.0.1 type IPSec-L2L
PIX2(config)# tunnel-group 192.168.0.1 ipsec-attributes
PIX2(config-ipsec)# pre-shared-key mykey1
```

This creates a tunnel group using the IP address of the VPN peer as its name of type *IPSEC-L2L*—meaning this will be a site-to-site VPN. A tunnel group of type *IPSec-RA* is used for remote access VPNs. We will look at remote access VPNs in the section "Remote Access—Configuring Support for the Cisco Software VPN Client."

We will also need to instruct the appliance to use the peer IP address to select a tunnel group name:

```
PIX1(config)# tunnel-group-map enable peer-ip
PIX2(config)# tunnel-group-map enable peer-ip
```

Configuring Certificate Authority Support

CAs can reduce the work and maintenance for large numbers of peers who can be added or removed at any time. Using preshared keys in such a scenario would require changing the configuration of several firewalls each time a new peer is added or removed. Using a CA can make this process easier, as each peer is configured separately and independently. Each peer has a certificate of its own and presents it to its counterpart during the IKE authentication phase. The other peer verifies the authenticity and validity of this certificate by consulting a CA. Once the certificate is validated, IKE authentication is successful. Figure 16.10 shows a small but complex network, with multiple remote sites. Each site needs to be fully meshed for redundancy. There is no central site (no hub). If we used preshared keys, we'd either have to use the same key at each site (very insecure and risky) or define unique keys for each site-to-site combination, which can become unmanageable, even with this small number of sites.

Figure 16.10 Multiple Site-to-Site VPNs

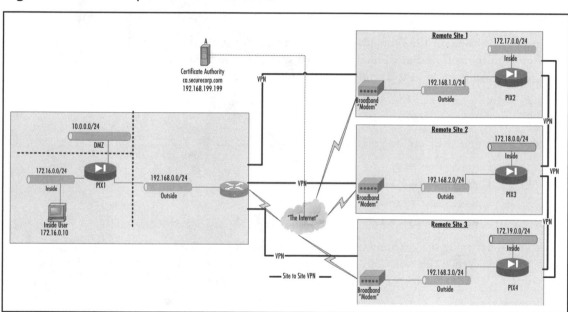

We can register and obtain a certificate for each site using VeriSign, Entrust, or even roll our own with a device such as Cisco IOS Certificate Server or Microsoft Certificate Server. Certificates are much more complex to deploy and require greater planning, but are more secure. In our example, we have opted to go with an in-house solution for economical and technical reasons.

The use of a CA and certificates for VPN authentication is also referred to as implementing PKI—Public Key Infrastructure. PKI can be used for more than just VPNs,

Enrollment is a complex process and includes the following steps:

1. Prepare the PIX for the use of CA infrastructure: verify that hostname, domain, time, and time zone are set correctly.

2. The PIX generates its own RSA or DSA public/private key pair.

3. The CA and its settings are configured on the PIX as a so-called trustpoint.

4   The PIX requests the CA's public key and certificate. This must either be done over a secure channel or be checked by some offline means—for example, by comparing certificate fingerprints. SCEP can be used for automatic enrollment.

5. The PIX submits a request for a new certificate. This request includes the public key generated at step 1 and is encrypted with the CA's public key obtained in step 2.

6. In the case of manual enrollment instead of using SCEP, the CA's administrator verifies the requester's identity and sends out a new certificate. In the case of using SCEP, the certificate is sent automatically as a response to the request in step 6. This certificate is signed by the CA, so its authenticity can be verified by anybody who has a copy of the CA's certificate.

Preparing the PIX to Use Certificates

Certificates are based on the fully qualified domain name (FQDN) of a peer. Certificates on both sides agree on the correct time. Enrollment starts with defining the firewall hostname and domain name, which will be used in its certificate later. The commands to configure these are:

```
hostname <hostname>
domain-name <domain-name>
```

In our example, we need to enter the following commands:

```
PIX1(config)# hostname PIX1
PIX1(config)# domain-name securecorp.com
PIX2(config)# hostname PIX2
PIX2(config)# domain-name securecorp.com
```

You can either set the date and time manually, or use NTP servers. NTP is a better choice to avoid time drift. While the time and time zone must be correct, not all devices need to be set to the same time zone. To manually set time on your PIX, use these commands:

```
clock timezone zone [-]hours [minutes]
clock summer-time zone recurring
clock set hh:mm:ss {month day | day month) year
```

The *clock timezone* command accepts a string for the zone name, such as PST or EST, and an offset in hours—and optionally minutes—from UTC. The *clock summer-time* command has many more options than are shown here, to accommodate global summertime (daylight savings time) rules. By default, the U.S. summertime rules will be assumed. Clocks used the 24-hour format, while month is specified by name.

In our example, let's assume the two PIX firewalls are on the east and west coast of the United States, respectively:

```
PIX1(config)# clock timezone EST -5
PIX1(config)# clock summer-time EST recurring
PIX1(config)# clock set 13:14:00 May 2 2005
PIX2(config)# clock timezone PST -8
```

```
PIX2(config)# clock summer-time PST recurring
PIX2(config)# clock set 10:14:00 May 2 2005
```

To use an NTP server, configure the time zone and summertime as before, and then use the *ntp server* command to specify one or more NTP servers. Use a trusted NTP server, ideally inside your network: manipulation of the time on your PIX could be used by an attacker to obfuscate a network attack.

ntp server ip-address **[prefer]**

Multiple NTP servers can be specified. The *prefer* keyword tells the PIX to prefer one server to another, if they are of similar accuracy.

You can view your settings using the *show clock* command:

```
PIX1(config)# show clock
13:14:06.090 EST Mon May 2 2005
```

Generating a Key Pair

To generate an RSA or DSA key pair to be used for digital certificate creation:

crypto key generate rsa [**usage-keys**|**general-keys**] [**modulus** <key_modulus_size>]
[**label** <key-label>]

crypto key generate dsa [**modulus** <key_modulus_size>] **label** <key-label>

Specifying a modulus size is optional; the default is 1024 bits. Specifying a key label is optional for RSA keys; the default label is *<Default-RSA-Key>* . Labels are required for DSA keys. RSA allows us to generate a general key pair or two separate key pairs. Use RSA and accept the defaults, unless you have other specific requirements:

```
PIX1(config)# crypto key generate rsa
PIX2(config)# crypto key generate rsa
```

You can view the key pair you just created using the *show crypto key mypubkey rsa* command:

```
PIX1(config)# show crypto key mypubkey rsa
Key pair was generated at: 06:37:47 EST May 2 2005
Key name: <Default-RSA-Key>
  Usage: General Purpose Key
  Modulus Size (bits): 1024
  Key Data:
  30819f30 0d06092a 864886f7 0d010101 05000381 8d003081 89028181 00cd5810
  f067de75 60c2cf4d 7b9b430b 78e5048e 91f330b5 5e018be5 2eb8ac33 105befc7
  fcff234c ef19d580 538c4208 f446dc52 dca48083 6ea79a94 6a213194 a933a01e
  304fb743 8e6c9b86 4714b0ac 5f737eda c9e815ee 15bcc583 a6a79919 600f2cc3
  683e20c5 d162254f f143f1b1 f1d75c31 7e13d171 b9dea42d e217e7f5 b7020301 0001
```

You can remove all configured key pairs from the PIX using the following command:

crypto key zeroize {rsa | dsa}

Configure a CA as a Trustpoint

After the key pair is generated, specify the CA to use for certificate verification. This is done by creating and configuring a trustpoint:

crypto ca trustpoint <trustpoint-name>

This command will place you in trustpoint configuration mode, where you may specify further settings:

```
PIX1(config)# crypto ca trustpoint main
PIX1(config-ca-trustpoint)#
PIX2(config)# crypto ca trustpoint main
```

Specify whether CRLs are required, optional, or will not be checked. Use the *optional* keyword to ensure your VPNs continue to operate even if the CA is not available:

```
crl required | optional | nocheck
```

Enter CRL configuration mode:

crl configure

Enable SCEP automatic enrollment and specify the URL for enrollment:

enrollment url <url>

Enable cut-and-paste manual enrollment (alternative to SCEP):

enrollment terminal

Specify the key pair to be named. This is the label given during key creation; in our case, <Default-RSA-Key>.

keypair <name>

Configure the peer to accept certificates issued by the CA associated with this trustpoint. This command is already set by default, and needed for our VPN PKI to function.

id-cert-issuer

Allow the peer to accept subordinate certificates during Phase 1 of IKE negotiation. This command is already enabled by default. It allows the peer to authenticate a certificate chain without having to install the entire chain locally.

accept-subordinates

Enable the trustpoint to validate remote user certificates. By default, this command is enabled.

support-user-cert-validation

Configuration of CRLs is done in crl configuration mode. Specify whether to retrieve CRLs from the distribution point specified in the certificate, from manually configured URLs, or both. The default is *cdp*. The main commands are:

policy cdp | static | both

Set URL(s) for statically configured CRL retrieval.

url <url>

Set the protocol for CRL retrieval. The default is *http. scep*. CRL retrieval cannot be used with *cdp*.

```
protocol http | ldap | scep
```

Set the time in minutes from 1 to 1440. The default is 60 minutes.

```
cache-time <minutes>
```

Most of the CRL configuration options are set to sensible defaults. All we really need to do to enable CRLs is issue the **crl optional** command. Once you are enrolled with a CA, you can use the **crypto ca crl request** command to test CRL retrieval. Let's look at our example configuration:

```
PIX1(config)# crypto ca trustpoint main
PIX1(config-ca-trustpoint)# crl optional
PIX1(config-ca-trustpoint)# enrollment url http://192.168.199.199:80
PIX1(config-ca-trustpoint)# keypair <Default-RSA-Key>
PIX2(config)# crypto ca trustpoint main
PIX2(config-ca-trustpoint)# crl optional
PIX2(config-ca-trustpoint)# enrollment url http://192.168.199.199:80
PIX2(config-ca-trustpoint)# keypair <Default-RSA-Key>
```

Should you need to "start over," clear your trustpoint configuration using the **clear configure crypto ca trustpoint** command. You can view your current configuration using the **show running crypto ca** command:

```
PIX1(config)# show running-config crypto ca
crypto ca trustpoint main
  crl optional
  enrollment url http://192.168.199.199:80/scep/
  keypair <Default-RSA-Key>
  crl configure
```

This concludes the configuration of the CA inside the PIX. We are now ready to enroll.

Authenticating and Enrolling with the CA

During enrollment, the firewall sends a request to the CA for a new certificate. The CA replies by signing the public key certificate, which it receives from the firewall as a part of the request and returns the results. After the CA signs it, it becomes a valid certificate and its authenticity can be validated by usual public key signature verification. Technically, the CA does not have to reply (issue a certificate) immediately; the certificate can be sent long after the request was received. However, the PIX expects these two events to happen during one transaction.

Authentication of and enrollment with the CA is started by the following commands:

```
crypto ca authenticate <trustpoint>
crypto ca enroll <trustpoint>
```

In our example, it would look like this:

```
PIX1(config)# crypto ca authenticate Main
INFO: Certificate has the following attributes:
Fingerprint: 3736ffc2 243ecf05 0c40f2fa 26820675
Do you accept this certificate? [yes/no]: y
Trustpoint 'Main' is a subordinate CA and holds a non self signed cert.
Trustpoint CA certificate accepted.

PIX1(config)# crypto ca enroll Main
%
% Start certificate enrollment ..
% Create a challenge password. You will need to verbally provide this
% password to the CA Administrator in order to revoke your certificate.
% For security reasons your password will not be saved in the configuration.
% Please make a note of it.
Password: Titp4CRa
Re-enter password: Titp4CRa
% The subject name in the certificate will be: PIX1.securecorp.com
% The fully-qualified domain name in the certificate will be:
PIX1.securecorp.com
% Include the device serial number in the subject name? [yes/no]: no
Request certificate from CA [yes/no]: yes
% Certificate request sent to Certificate authority.

isakmp identity auto
```

Lastly, the isakmp policy to be used with certificate authentication needs to be set to *rsa-sig* authentication instead of *pre-shared*:

```
PIX1(config)# isakmp policy 10 authentication rsa-sig
```

This finishes the configuration of IKE parameters, which determine how to establish the initial tunnel used to exchange keys for IPsec encryption. We move on to IPsec parameters.

Configuring Crypto Access-Lists

Start the IPsec configuration process by identifying what traffic needs IPsec protection. Traffic selectors will define the scope of SAs when they are created by IKE Phase 2. These selectors are defined using the *access-list* command. Crypto access-lists are applied to the interface using a *crypto map* command. It is possible to apply multiple crypto access-lists to a single interface to specify different parameters for different types of traffic. Actions in access-list entries have the following meaning:

- **Permit**   IPsec should be applied to the matching traffic.
- **Deny**   Packet should be forwarded and IPsec not applied.

The following access-list entry on PIX1 will match all IP traffic from the inside network (172.16.0.0/24), leaving the outside interface to be tunneled to PIX2 (172.17.0.0/24) and the]return tunneled IP traffic from 172.17.0.0/24 to 172.16.0.0/24:

```
PIX1(config)# access-list crypto1 extended permit ip 172.16.0.0
255.255.255.0 172.17.0.0 255.255.255.0
```

A packet from 172.16.0.3 to 172.17.0.4 will be matched by access-list *crypto1* and submitted to the IPsec engine. A packet from 172.16.0.3 to www.cisco.com will not be matched and thus transmitted in the clear. If an IPsec packet arrives from 172.17.0.4 to 172.16.0.3, it will be matched by the same access-list and forwarded to 172.16.0.3. If the IPsec packet originates from www.cisco.com, it will not be matched and will be dropped instead of being decrypted. Any clear-text packets from www.cisco.com will pass through and be permitted unmatched by this access-list.

When the first *permit* entry in an access-list is matched, it determines the SA that will be created for its protection. For example, in our case, all traffic from network 172.16.0.0/24 to network 172.17.0.0/24 will be protected by the same SA. Let's assume that you create an access-list on PIX1 using the following:

```
PIX1(config)# access-list crypto2 extended permit ip 172.16.0.0 255.255.255.128
172.17.0.0 255.255.255.0
PIX1(config)# access-list crypto2 extended permit ip 172.16.0.128 255.255.255.128
172.17.0.0 255.255.255.0
```

In this case, the traffic originating from 172.16.0.0/25 and the traffic from 172.16.0.128/25 will be protected by two different IPsec SAs.

Let's now return to our earlier example and configure the firewalls with access-lists:

```
PIX1(config)# access-list crypto1 extended permit ip 172.16.0.0 255.255.255.0
172.17.0.0 255.255.255.0
PIX2(config)# access-list crypto2 extended permit ip 172.17.0.0 255.255.255.0
172.17.0.0 255.255.255.0
```

At this point, we have not applied these lists yet. This will be done later using a *crypto map* command.

Defining a Transform Set

A *transform set* defines the protection values for a specific IPsec connection (an IPsec SA, to be precise). It specifies the algorithms used for encryption and authentication of traffic. PIX v7.0 has discontinued support for deprecated IPSEC options such as AH. ESP is the only protocol that was widely used in practice, and is the only protocol available in 7.0. While possible to configure multiple transform sets, at least one set must be common to both peers for each crypto map entry. Transform sets are configured using the following command:

```
crypto ipsec transform-set <transform-set-name> <transform1> <transform2>
```

We are going to configure two transforms: one to define the encryption algorithm, and the other to define the hash algorithm. The available transforms are:

- **esp-aes**   The AES encryption algorithm (128-bit key) is chosen for ESP encryption.
- **esp-aes-192**   The AES encryption algorithm (192-bit key) is chosen for ESP encryption.

- **esp-aes-256**   The AES encryption algorithm (256-bit key) is chosen for ESP encryption.

- **esp-des**   The DES encryption algorithm (56-bit key) is chosen for ESP encryption.

- **esp-3des**   The Triple DES encryption algorithm (168-bit key) is chosen for ESP encryption.

- **esp-md5-hmac**   The MD5-HMAC authentication algorithm is chosen for ESP.

- **esp-sha-hmac**   The SHA-1-HMAC authentication algorithm is chosen for ESP.

In our example, we use ESP encryption with AES-128 and authentication with SHA-1-HMAC:

```
PIX1(config)# crypto ipsec transform-set myset esp-aes esp-sha-hmac
PIX2(config)# crypto ipsec transform-set myset esp-aes esp-sha-hmac
```

Configured transform sets can be checked using the **show running-config crypto ipsec** command:

```
PIX1# show running-config crypto ipsec
crypto ipsec transform-set ESP-DES-MD5 esp-des esp-md5-hmac
```

Bypassing Network Address Translation

If we use NAT on all outbound traffic from inside networks to the Internet, we must exclude IPsec traffic from being translated. In other words, if we have configured our crypto access-lists to match the untranslated addresses of this traffic, we must ensure that it does not get translated. To bypass NAT, we can use the **nat 0** command with the same access-list that defines our IPsec traffic:

```
PIX1(config)# nat 0 access-list crypto1
PIX1(config)# nat (inside) 1 0 0
PIX1(config)# global (outside) 1 192.168.0.1
PIX2(config)# nat 0 access-list crypto2
PIX2(config)# nat (inside) 1 0 0
PIX2(config)# global (outside) 1 192.168.1.1
```

Configuring a Crypto Map

A *crypto map* ties all other IPsec-related bits together and creates an SPD for a specific interface, through which IPsec traffic is tunneled. A crypto map is identified by its name. An interface can have only one crypto map assigned to it, although this map may have many different entries, identified by their sequence numbers. Entries in a crypto map are evaluated in ascending order. Various entries are equivalent to the policies in SPD. The first entry that matches the traffic will define methods of its protection. Create a crypto map entry for IPsec with IKE and specify traffic selectors:

```
crypto map <map-name> <seq-num> match address <access-list-name>
```

In our case, these would look like:

```
PIX1(config)# crypto map pix1map 10 match address crypto1
PIX2(config)# crypto map pix2map 10 match address crypto2
```

Now we need to specify the IPsec peers with which the traffic protected by this entry can be exchanged:

```
crypto map <map-name> <seq-num> set peer {<hostname> | <ip-address>}
```

IPsec peers are identified either by their IP addresses (used with preshared keys) or by their hostnames (used with certificates). It is possible to specify multiple peers by repeating this command for one crypto map entry. For our example, we use the following configuration:

```
PIX1(config)# crypto map pix1map 10 set peer 192.168.1.1
PIX2(config)# crypto map pix2map 10 set peer 192.168.0.1
```

Specify which transform sets can be negotiated for the traffic matching this entry. Multiple (up to six) previously defined transform sets can be specified here:

```
crypto map <map-name> <seq-num> set transform-set <transform-set-name1>
  [<transform-set-name2> [<transform-set-name3> [<transform-set-name4>
    [<transform-set-name5> [<transform-set-name6>]]]]]
```

At least one transform set in each firewall's corresponding crypto map entry must have the same protocols and encryption/data authentication algorithms. For our simple example, we simply use one transform set on each firewall (*pix1map* on PIX1 and *pix2map* on PIX2):

```
PIX1(config)# crypto map pix1map 10 set transform-set myset
PIX2(config)# crypto map pix2map 10 set transform-set myset
```

In each case, *myset* is the transform set defined previously. It does not need to have the same name on each firewall, but the parameters must match.

The next two steps are optional: requesting that Perfect Forward Secrecy (PFS) should be used, and selecting the SA lifetime. PFS ensures that new encryption keys are not derived from previous ones, thereby limiting exposure if one key is compromised. PFS is requested for a crypto map entry using the following command:

```
crypto map <map-name> <seq-num> set pfs [group1 | group2 | group 5 | group 7]
```

The *group1* and *group2* keywords denote the DH group and are used for key exchange each time new keys are generated. To be effective, PFS has to be configured on both sides of the tunnel; otherwise, if only one peer supports PFS, the IPsec SA will not be established. We will not use this feature in our example.

It is possible to configure a nondefault IPsec SA lifetime for the specific crypto map entry using the following:

```
crypto map <map-name> <seq-num> set security-association lifetime {seconds
  <seconds> | kilobytes <kilobytes>}
```

This command limits the time an IPsec SA can be used or the maximum amount of traffic that can be transferred by this SA. Right before a timeout or the maximum amount of traffic is reached, the IPsec SA for this crypto map entry is renegotiated. The renegotiations start 30 seconds before a timeout expires or when the volume of traffic is 256 KB less than the specified volume lifetime.

During this renegotiation, one peer sends a proposal to the other, with one of its parameters being an SA lifetime. The second peer selects the lesser of the proposed values and its own lifetime value, and sets this as a common SA lifetime.

It is possible to change the default global IPsec SA lifetime using the following command, which has the same parameters:

```
crypto ipsec security-association lifetime {seconds <seconds> | kilobytes
  <kilobytes>}
```

If not specified, the defaults are 28,800 seconds and 4,608,000 KB.

The last configuration step is to apply the crypto map to an interface:

```
crypto map <map-name> interface <interface-name>
```

In our case, this will be:

```
PIX1(config)# crypto map pix1map interface outside
PIX2(config)# crypto map pix2map interface outside
```

You can check crypto map configuration using the following command:

```
PIX1(config)# show running-config crypto map
crypto map pix1map match address crypto1
crypto map pix1map set peer 192.168.1.1
crypto map pix1map set transform-set ESP-AES-SHA
crypto map pix1map interface outside
```

The state of established IPsec SAs can be checked with the *show crypto ipsec sa* command:

```
PIX1(config)# show crypto ipsec sa
interface: outside
  Crypto map tag: pix1map, local addr. 192.168.0.1
local ident (addr/mask/prot/port): (172.16.0.0/255.255.255.0/0/0)
  remote ident (addr/mask/prot/port): (172.17.0.0/255.255.255.0/0/0)
  current_peer: 192.168.1.1
    PERMIT, flags={origin_is_acl,}
    #pkts encaps: 10, #pkts encrypt: 10, #pkts digest 0
    #pkts decaps: 12, #pkts decrypt: 17, #pkts verify 0
    #pkts compressed: 0, #pkts decompressed: 0
    #pkts not compressed: 0, #pkts compr. failed: 0, #pkts decompress
      failed: 0
    #send errors 2, #recv errors 0
```

Troubleshooting

You can troubleshoot IKE SA or IPsec SA establishment using the *debug crypto isakmp* and *debug crypto ipsec* commands. These commands can produce a lot of output, but they are easy to understand if you know how IPsec works. For example, the following part of a log tells us that IKE negotiations were completed successfully:

```
ISAKMP (0): Checking ISAKMP transform 1 against priority 9 policy
ISAKMP:        encryption AES-CBC
ISAKMP:        hash SHA
ISAKMP:        default group 2
ISAKMP:        auth pre-share
ISAKMP:        life type in seconds
ISAKMP:        life duration (VPI) of 0x0 0x1 0x51 0x80
ISAKMP (0): atts are acceptable. Next payload is 0
ISAKMP (0): SA is doing pre-shared key authentication using id type ID_IPV4_ADDR
return status is IKMP_NO_ERROR
```

Conversely, something similar to the following output will tell you that the IKE main mode exchange failed (IKMP_NO_ERROR_NO_TRANS) because a common proposal (transform set) was not found:

```
VPN Peer: ISAKMP: Added new peer: ip:PIX2 Total VPN Peers:3
VPN Peer: ISAKMP: Peer ip:PIX2 Ref cnt incremented to:1 Total VPN
Peers:3
ISAKMP (0): beginning Main Mode exchange
crypto_isakmp_process_block: src PIX2, dest PIX1
return status is IKMP_NO_ERR_NO_TRANS
ISAKMP (0): retransmitting phase 1…
```

The most common configuration mistakes that prevent a tunnel from being established are:

- The parameters for IKE Phase 1 (the *isakmp policy*) do not match. Watch out for differing default values in different versions of PIX, such as DH group and lifetime. An error *no proposal chosen* during Phase 1 points to this kind of issue.

- The parameters for IKE Phase 2 (the *transform-set* and/or crypto access list) do not match. *No valid SA* or *Identity doesn't match negotiated identity* point to errors in the crypto access-list. In addition to the *Transform-set* parameters, watch out for enabled PFS and nonstandard IPsec SA lifetimes.

- Pre-shared keys do not match.

- Certificates are being used and time is not configured correctly on both sites. In addition, if CRLs are required, test whether the CRL server can be reached by both sides and is delivering CRLs.

Remote Access—Configuring Support for the Cisco Software VPN Client

Remote access VPNs focus on connecting individual users to organizational networks. The VPN choices for remote access are more varied and adaptable than are the choices for site-to-site VPNs. Typically, a user is at some remote location, not necessarily owned or controlled by his or her organization (such as hotspots at an airport), and needs to securely access the organization network. The purpose of a remote access VPN is twofold: provide remote access to the organization network, and provide security for that connection.

Remote access VPNs are indifferent of the underlying infrastructure. As long as the remote endpoint is reachable in some way, the VPN can be established. In this section, we provide examples of how to configure the PIX firewall to support remote access VPNs. Keep in mind that this is not a primary task of the Cisco PIX firewall. Normally, an organization of any meaningful size will have a dedicated solution (VPN concentrator, for example, or a special server [Microsoft]) solely for the purpose of establishing remote access VPNs.

Figure 16.11 shows an architecture where the user will connect to the PIX firewall to establish an IPsec tunnel using a Cisco VPN client on a Windows workstation.

Figure 16.11 Remote Access VPN via IPsec

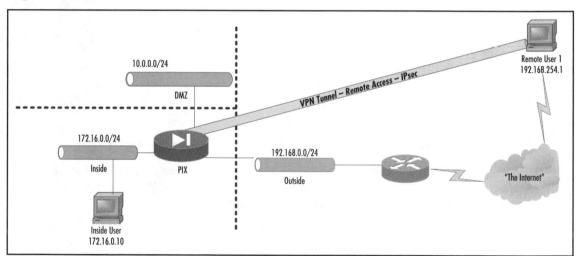

The Cisco software VPN client is client software for use with Cisco-based IPsec gateways. It supports Cisco VPN concentrators, PIX, and IOS-based devices. The VPN client is installed on a client computer and takes preference over the internal Windows IPsec client.

The latest version of the Cisco VPN client can be downloaded from Cisco's Web site. (You might be required to log in first.) Installation of the Cisco VPN client is straightforward. All you have to do is answer a few questions; for example, if you want to remove Internet connection sharing and disable the Windows internal IPsec policy service because the VPN client is not compatible with these two features.

Enabling IKE and Creating an ISAKMP Protection Suite

This step is identical to setting up a site-to-site VPN. To recap, these are the commands to enable IKE and create an ISAKMP policy using AES, SHA-1, and preshared keys:

```
PIX1(config)# isakmp enable outside
PIX1(config)# isakmp identity auto
PIX1(config)# isakmp am-disable
PIX1(config)# isakmp policy 10 encryption aes
PIX1(config)# isakmp policy 10 hash sha
PIX1(config)# isakmp policy 10 authentication pre-share
```

Defining a Transform Set

This step is also identical to setting up a site-to-site VPN. To recap, we are going to select an encryption algorithm and a hash algorithm using the following command:

```
crypto ipsec transform-set <transform-set-name> <transform1> <transform2>
```

The main available transforms we are concerned with for VPN clients are **esp-aes**, **esp-3des**, **esp-md5-hmac**, and **esp-sha-hmac**.

In our example, we use ESP encryption with AES-128 and authentication with SHA-1-HMAC:

```
PIX1(config)# crypto ipsec transform-set ra-set esp-aes esp-sha-hmac
```

Crypto Maps

We need to define a dynamic crypto map for this remote access VPN, and add the dynamic map to a crypto map. Generally, a PIX will support both site-to-site and remote access VPNs, so we will use the same crypto map name *pix1map* we used previously. Only one crypto map can be applied per interface, but it can contain multiple entries.

To define the dynamic crypto map, use this command:

```
crypto dynamic-map <dynamic-map-name> <seq-num> set transform-set
<transform-set-name>
```

In our example:

```
PIX1(config)# crypto dynamic-map pix1-ra-map 10 set transform-set ra-set
```

With the dynamic map created, we can now apply it to the crypto map, using a sequence number of 99. A high sequence number makes it easier to keep the site-to-site crypto map entries above the dynamic entry, which is the configuration ASDM requires. If the crypto *may pix1map* does not already exist, it will be created:

```
PIX1(config)# crypto map pix1map 99 ipsec-isakmp dynamic pix1-ra-map
```

Finally, apply the crypto map to the outside interface:

```
PIX1(config)# crypto map pix1map interface outside
```

Tunnel Groups and Group Policies

Tunnel groups of type *IPSec-RA* in v7.0 are used to set VPN parameters specific to client VPNs, such as client address pool, client DNS and WINS servers, split-tunnel configuration, and more. They replace VPN groups in PIX 6.3.4 and earlier. The tunnel group name is going to be the Group Authentication name entered in the Cisco VPN client. We are going to use the *tunnel-group* command to set preshared key authentication:

```
PIX1(config)# tunnel-group PIX-remote type ipsec-ra
PIX1(config)# tunnel-group PIX-remote ipsec-attributes
PIX1(config-ipsec)# pre-shared-key mykey1
```

Group policies in PIX v7.0 allow you to specify DNS and WINS servers for your clients to use, configure idle timeouts, and more. We are going to touch on the most commonly used group policy options.

```
PIX1(config)# group-policy RemotePolicy
PIX1(config)# group-policy RemotePolicy attributes
```

Specify that WINS servers at 172.16.0.33 and 172.16.0.34 are to be used:

```
PIX1(config-group-policy)# wins-server value 172.16.0.33 172.16.0.34
```

Specify the same servers for DNS:

```
PIX1(config-group-policy)# dns-server value 172.16.0.33 172.16.0.34
```

Set the default domain to be used by VPN clients in DNS queries:

```
PIX1(config-group-policy)# default-domain securecorp.com
```

Change the idle timeout from the default of 30 minutes to 2 hours:

```
PIX1(config-group-policy)# vpn-idle-timeout 120
```

To match a group policy to a tunnel policy, use the **default-group-policy** command:

```
PIX1(config)# tunnel-group PIX-remote general-attributes
PIX1(config-general)# default-group-policy RemotePolicy
```

Address Pool Configuration

Address pool configuration is an extension of the IKE protocol that allows you to assign IP addresses to the VPN client during the IKE negotiation process. The client uses this address later as an "internal" IP address in its communications over the IPsec tunnel. Because this address is already known to the firewall, it can easily be matched against the security policy (SPD). Address pool configuration allows for easy scalability of VPN networks, which have many clients with conflicting IP addresses behind SOHO routers.

Address pool configuration occurs between Phases 1 and 2 of IKE negotiation. During this process, it is possible to download an IP address and other IP-related settings such as DNS servers to the client.

There are two steps to configure address pool configuration on an PIX firewall:

1. Define an IP address pool. The command is as follows:

   ip local pool <pool-name> <pool-start-address>[-<pool-end-address>]

2. Reference the IP address pool in the tunnel group using the command:

   tunnel-group groupname> **general-attributes**

   address-pool <pool-name>

For example:

PIX1(config)# **ip local pool mypool 172.16.1.1–172.16.1.126**

PIX1(config)# **tunnel-group PIX-remote general-attributes**

PIX1(config-general)# **address-pool mypool**

These settings (if all the rest of IKE and IPsec are configured) will force PIX to initiate address pool configuration with each client who matches crypto map *mymap*. Clients will be assigned IP addresses from the 172.16.1.1–172.16.1.126 address range.

Split Tunneling

Prior to PIX v7.0, it was necessary to configure split tunneling if you wanted a VPN client to access the Internet while using a company VPN. With v7.0, you can allow clients to access the Internet securely through your PIX while connected to the company VPN by using this command:

PIX1(config)# **same-security-traffic permit intra-interface**

If you still prefer split tunneling, you would set it up as part of your group policy using the following commands:

PIX1(config)# **access-list ra-tunnel permit 172.16.0.0 255.255.255.0**

PIX1(config)# **group-policy RemotePolicy attributes**

PIX1(config-group-policy)# **split-tunnel-policy tunnel-specified**

PIX1(config-group-policy)# **split-tunnel-network-list value ra-tunnel**

This creates an access-list called *ra-tunnel* containing the inside network, and specifies that only traffic destined to networks in the access-list should be tunneled.

If your DNS servers are not set up to serve Internet addresses to remote access users, you would configure split DNS as well. Specify the domains that are to be resolved by requests to the configured VPN DNS server(s) using these commands:

PIX1(config)# **group-policy RemotePolicy attributes**

PIX1(config-group-policy)# **split-dns value securecorp.com securecorp.pri**

This will send all DNS requests for the domains *securecorp.com* and *securecorp.pri* through the tunnel. All other DNS requests will be handled by the client's configured local LAN or Internet DNS servers.

NAT Issues

Increasingly, VPN clients will be behind some type of NAT device, such as a SOHO router. The issue of two or more clients sharing the same IP address on their inside interface is resolved by the use of address pools. Pools ensure that each client is assigned a unique address. The issue of the VPN traffic not being able to travel through the NAT device because ESP does not provide a port number and thus "breaks" most all PAT (port address translation) implementations such as used by SOHO (Small-Office-Home-Office) Internet routers and firewalls can be tackled by turning on NAT-T (NAT Traversal).

NAT-T detects whether a NAT device is in use, and if so, will send all IPsec traffic over UDP port 4500. The command to globally enable NAT-T is:

isakmp nat-traversal [natkeepalive]

natkeepalive is a value in seconds, from 10 to 3600. The default is 20 seconds.

Authentication against Radius, TACACS+, SecurID, or Active Directory

IKE can be configured to authenticate a remote VPN user against an AAA server group. This is also called *xauth* (IXE Extended Authentication). *xauth* is useful when configuring the Cisco software VPN client to access the PIX firewall because it allows authentication to be performed after IKE Phase 1 and before Phase 2.

Without *xauth*, IKE can only authenticate a device, not a user. With *xauth*, IKE is enhanced to support user authentication as well by allowing the server to request a username and password from the client. On the PIX firewall, the user is verified against an external RADIUS' TACACS+, SecurID, or Active Directory server. (Local authentication cannot be used.) If verification fails, the IKE SA for this connection is deleted and the IPsec SAs will not be established. *Xauth* negotiation is performed before IKE mode configuration.

Before you enable *xauth*, you must define an AAA server group with AAA servers using the following commands:

aaa-server <server-tag> **host** <server-ip> [<key>] [**timeout** <seconds>]
aaa-server server-tag> **protocol** <auth-protocol>

For example:

```
PIX1(config)# aaa-server vpnauthgroup host 172.16.0.33 secretkey
  timeout 60
PIX1(config)# aaa-server vpnauthgroup protocol kerberos
```

This command specifies that the Kerberos, here Active Directory, server 172.16.0.33 is in the group *vpnauthgroup*, has key *secretkey*, and has a timeout of 60 seconds.

Xauth negotiation is enabled in the tunnel group. This is done using the following command:

tunnel-group <group-name> **general-attributes**
authentication-server-group <server-tag>

group-name is the name of the tunnel group for which *xauth* is enabled; *server-tag* is the name of a previously defined AAA group. For example, the following command forces IKE negotiations under tunnel group *PIX-remote* to use *xauth*, and authentication will be performed using the previously defined server 172.16.0.33:

```
PIX1(config)# tunnel-group PIX-remote general-attributes
PIX1(config-general)# authentication-server-group vpnauthgroup
```

Once *xauth* is configured, a VPN client will still connect using the tunnel group name and a preshared secret. A separate pop-up window will then allow the users to log in using their own usernames and passwords.

Automatic Client Update

PIX version 7.0 can notify clients when a new client version is available, which can reduce management headaches when you have a large number of clients. Use the following command in tunnel group configuration mode to configure client updates:

```
client-update type type {url url-string} {rev-nums rev-nums}
```

type specifies which clients to notify and can be one of *Windows* (all Windows platforms), *WIN9X* (Windows 95, 98, and Me), *WinNT* (Windows NT, 2000, XP) or *vpn3002* (VPN 3002 hardware client). *url-string* is the URL from which to download the new client version, and *rev-nums* specify the required revisions. You can specify up to four revisions, separated by commas.

Here is an example:

```
PIX1(config)# tunnel-group PIX-remote ipsec-attributes
PIX1(config-ipsec)# client-update type Windows
url http://www.securecorp.com/cupdate/cupdate.exe rev-nums 4.0,4.6
```

Configuring Client Firewall Requirements

In PIX v7.0, you can require a client to have a firewall configured and operational before allowing that client access to your network. The command to achieve this is entered in group policy mode. It can be applied for many different vendors, such as ZoneLabs, BlackICE, and Sygate. In this example, we'll look at using the firewall built in to the Cisco VPN client:

```
PIX1(config)# group-policy FirstGroup internal
PIX1(config)# group-policy FirstGroup attributes
PIX1(config-group-policy)# client-firewall req cisco-integrated acl-in
client-acl-in acl-out client-acl-out
```

FirstGroup is the name of the group policy being created. *client-acl-in* and *client-acl-out* are previously created ACLs that will be pushed to the client and will restrict incoming and outgoing traffic on the client.

Sample Configurations of PIX and VPN Clients

In this section, we consider a full configuration example of the PIX and a VPN client. Our example uses IKE with preshared keys, address pool configuration, and no split tunneling. The network setup is shown in Figure 16.12.

Figure 16.12 Network Setup for Cisco VPN Client Configuration

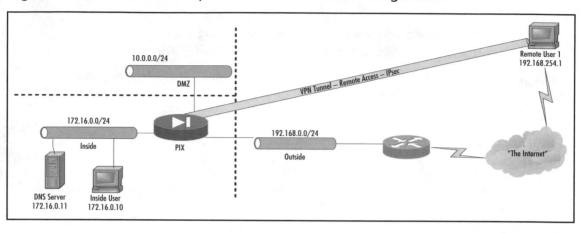

Clients will be assigned IP addresses from the pool 172.16.1.1–172.16.1.254, and IKE authentication will use a preshared key.

First, an IKE policy is configured (AES encryption and SHA-1 hashing):

```
PIX1(config)# isakmp enable outside
PIX1(config)# isakmp identity auto
PIX1(config)# isakmp am-disable
PIX1(config)# isakmp policy 10 encryption aes
PIX1(config)# isakmp policy 10 hash sha
PIX1(config)# isakmp policy 10 authentication pre-share
```

Transform sets and crypto maps are configured and applied. This is a simple crypto map with only a dynamic map as a subentry:

```
PIX1(config)# crypto ipsec transform-set ra-set esp-aes esp-sha-hmac
PIX1(config)# crypto dynamic-map pix1-ra-map set transform-set ra-set
PIX1(config)# crypto map pix1map 1 ipsec-isakmp dynamic pix1-ra-map
PIX1(config)# crypto map pix1map interface outside
```

A tunnel group is created and a preshared key assigned to it:

```
PIX1(config)# tunnel-group PIX-remote type ipsec-ra
PIX1(config)# tunnel-group PIX-remote ipsec-attributes
PIX1(config-ipsec)# pre-shared-key verysecret
```

Address pool configuration is enabled and an IP pool is created:

```
PIX1(config)# ip local pool mypool 172.16.1.1-172.16.1.254
```

```
PIX1(config)# tunnel-group PIX-remote general-attributes
PIX1(config-general)# address-pool mypool
```

Policy group settings are configured:

```
PIX1(config)# group-policy RemotePolicy
PIX1(config)# group-policy RemotePolicy attributes
PIX1(config-group-policy)# wins-server value 172.16.0.11
PIX1(config-group-policy)# dns-server value 172.16.0.11
PIX1(config-group-policy)# default-domain securecorp.com
PIX1(config-group-policy)# vpn-idle-timeout 60
PIX1(config)# tunnel-group PIX-remote general-attributes
PIX1(config-general)# default-group-policy RemotePolicy
```

The Cisco VPN client is configured as follows. Select **Start | All Programs | Cisco Systems VPN Client | VPN Client** and select **New** to create a new connection entry (see Figure 16.13).

Figure 16.13 Creating a New Connection Entry

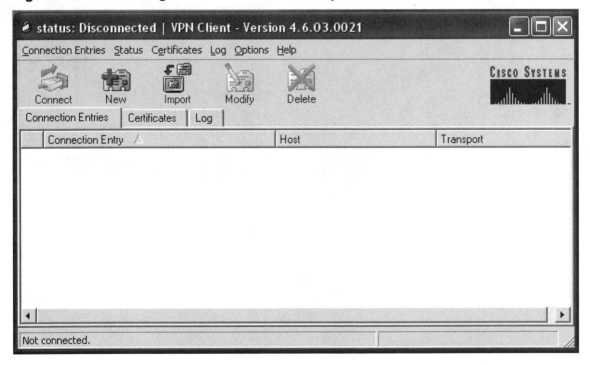

The New Connection Entry wizard starts. After asking you to name this connection (enter whatever you want here), it asks for the IP address of the server. In our case, this is the IP address of the outside interface of PIX1, where the tunnel will be terminated (see Figure 16.14). Enter the IP address.

Figure 16.14 Entering the Server IP Address

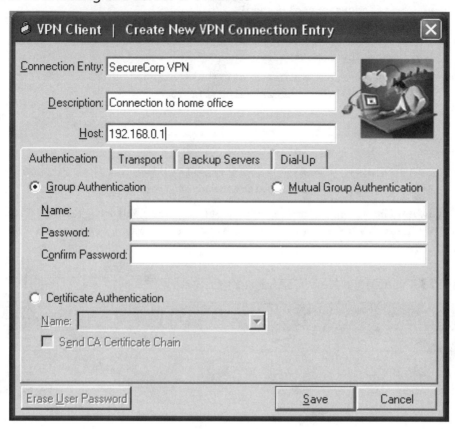

Next, you need to enter the name of the group and the shared IKE secret. In our case, this is the name of our tunnel group *PIX-remote*. The password is the shared key *verysecret* (see Figure 16.15).

Figure 16.15 Specifying the VPN Group and the IKE Shared Secret

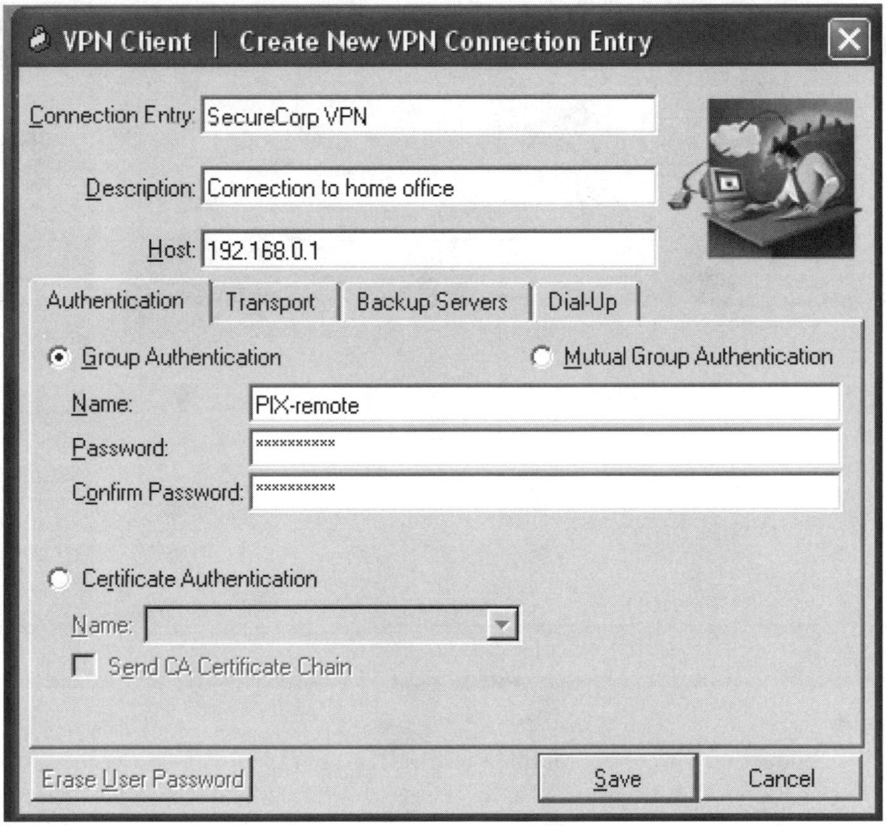

After clicking **Save**, we are done. It is possible to modify this entry's properties by clicking **Modify** in the main window of VPN Client. Among other properties, it is possible to change group name and password, set timeouts, and select the dial-up connection that must be dialed before establishing the tunnel.

Now you need to select the connection you just created and click the **Connect** button (see Figure 16.16).

Figure 16.16 Connecting to the Server

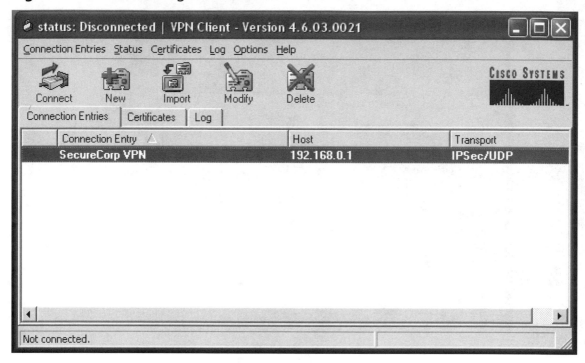

If network connectivity is correct (nothing blocks IKE port UDP/500 between your host and the firewall, for example), IKE negotiation starts. It checks for a shared secret, and if everything is correct, the tunnel is established and the PIX downloads settings such as an internal IP address, DNS, and WINS settings to the VPN client.

You can check that the connection works by pinging some internal PIX hosts from the client computer. It is also possible to monitor established tunnels by the usual PIX *debug* commands such as *debug vpdn event*, *debug vpdn error*, and *debug vpdn packet*. You can also use all IPsec and IKE-related *debug* commands.

Summary

Virtual private networks (VPNs) securely tunnel traffic between two sites over a public network such as the Internet. VPNs are commonly used to connect branch offices, mobile users, and business partners. The two common types of VPNs are site-to-site and remote access. The PIX firewall supports VPNs using IPsec.

The most robust tunneling solution for IP networks is the IPsec suite of protocols. It was developed by IETF as part of IPv6. IPsec operates at Layer 3 of the OSI model, which means that it can protect communications from the network layer (IP) and up. IPsec specifies encryption and authentication algorithms, AH and ESP protocols used for tunneling itself, and the IKE/ISAKMP key management protocol. IPsec's main goals are data confidentiality, data integrity, data origin authentication, and anti-replay service.

When a site-to-site IPsec tunnel is configured on a PIX firewall, one of two main methods of IKE authentication are used: preshared keys or digital certificates. The former is simpler to set up, but lacks scalability offered by the digital certificate solution.

In the second type of VPN, remote clients connect to a gateway. The PIX supports IPsec, which works with Layer 3 tunnels.

Cisco has its own software VPN client that provides full IPsec features when working with the PIX firewall. It can perform IKE authentication with both preshared keys and digital certificates. The PIX uses two extensions to IKE to provide VPN clients with an internal IP address (address pool configuration) and perform extra authentication of clients during IKE negotiation using Extended Authentication (*xauth*).

ISA Server 2006 Client Types and Automating Client Provisioning

Solutions in this chapter:

- **Understanding ISA Server 2006 Client Types**

- **Automating ISA Server 2006 Client Provisioning**

- **Automating Installation of the Firewall Client**

☑ **Summary**

Introduction

One of the most misunderstood, but most critical, issues relating to the installation and management of ISA Server 2006 firewalls is that of ISA Server 2006 client types. Some of these client types have a classic client/server relationship with the ISA Server. That is, the client makes a request for data from the server; the server subsequently performs the work of retrieving the data, and returning the data to the client. The client/server relationship is dependent on client software installed on the client computer that makes it possible to communicate with the particular services running on the server.

In the case of ISA Server, the client might request data in the form of a Web page on the Internet; the ISA Server would perform the work of retrieving the Web page and delivering it to the client. However, not all ISA Server 2006 clients have a classic client/server relationship with the firewall, and each client type accesses networks outside its own in a different fashion. Furthermore, some applications work with one ISA Server 2006 client type but not with another. It is critical to determine the ISA Server 2006 client type *before* you install and configure ISA Server 2006. Failure to implement the correct ISA Server 2006 client type can lead to the misconception that the firewall is not working correctly.

All machines connecting to resources by going through the ISA Server 2006 firewall are considered clients of the ISA Server 2006 firewall machine. This does not imply that all machines need to have client software installed or need their applications configured to connect directly with the ISA Server 2006 firewall computer. In the context of ISA Server 2006, the "client" does not always participate in the classic "client/server" relationship with the ISA Server 2006 firewall.

Understanding ISA Server 2006 Client Types

Computers that go through the ISA server to access resources outside their networks fall into one or more ISA Server 2006 client type categories. These are:

- The SecureNAT client
- The Firewall client
- The Web Proxy client

A single machine can be configured to act in multiple ISA Server 2006 client-type roles. For example, a Windows XP computer can be configured as a SecureNAT, Firewall and Web Proxy client. Another Windows XP computer can be configured as only a Firewall and Web Proxy client. A Linux machine can be configured as a SecureNAT client and Web Proxy client.

Table 17.1 provides an overview of the ISA Server 2006 client types, how each is installed or configured, which operating systems each supports, protocols supported by each, type of user-level authentication each supports, and special deployment considerations for each type.

Table 17.1 Overview of ISA Server 2006 Client Types

Feature	SecureNAT Client	Firewall Client	Web Proxy Client
Installation of client software required?	No. SecureNAT clients require only a default gateway address that can route Internet-bound requests through the ISA Server 2006 firewall. The default gateway is set in the TCP/IP properties for the computer's network adapter.	Yes. The Firewall client software must be installed from an installation share on the network. The Firewall client installation share can be on the ISA Server 2006 firewall itself, or (preferably) on a File Server located some where on the network.	No. However, Web browsers on client computers must be configured to use the ISA Server 2006 firewall as their Web Proxy. The proxy is set in the Web browser's connection settings.
Operating system support	SecureNAT supports all operating systems. The SecureNAT client type can be used with Windows, MacOS, Unix, Linux, and any other operating system that supports TCP/IP networking.	The Firewall client supports all post-Windows 95 platforms, from Windows 98 to Windows Server 2003	The Web Proxy client supports all platforms, but does so by way of a Web application. All Web browsers that can be configured to use a proxy server can function as Web Proxy clients.
Protocol support	All simple protocols are supported by SecureNAT. Complex protocols (those that require multiple connections) require that an application filter be installed on the ISA Server 2006 firewall machine.	The Firewall client supports all Winsock applications that use the TCP and UDP protocols; the Firewall client does not mediate non-TCP/UDP connections	The Web Proxy client supports HTTP, HTTPS (SSL/TLS), and HTTP tunneled FTP (proxied FTP)
User-level authentication supported?	No. SecureNAT clients cannot authenticate with the ISA Server 2006 firewall unless the client applications support SOCKS 5 and a SOCKS 5 application filter is installed on the firewall.	Yes. The Firewall client enables strong user/group-based access control by transparently forwarding client credentials to the ISA Server 2006 firewall.	Yes. Web Proxy clients will authenticate with the ISA Server 2006 firewall if the firewall requests credentials. No credentials are sent if an anonymous access rule enabling the connection is available to the Web Proxy client.

Continued

Table 17.1 Continued

Feature	SecureNAT Client	Firewall Client	Web Proxy Client
Deployment Considerations	All non-Windows operating systems can be configured as SecureNAT client if they require protocol access outside of HTTP/HTTPS and FTP. All post-Windows 95 Windows operating systems should be configured as Firewall clients if at all possible. All servers published via Server Publishing Rules should be configured as SecureNAT clients. Use SecureNAT on Windows clients only when outbound ICMP or PPTP is required.	All Windows operating systems that support Firewall client installation (post-Windows 95) should have the Firewall client installed unless there are technical or management barriers that prevent this. The Firewall client increases the overall level of security and accessibility for all machines with the Firewall client software installed.	All browsers should be configured as Web Proxy clients when authentication is required for Web (HTTP/HTTPS/FTP) access. If user authentication is not required, Web Proxy configuration is not required because the ISA Server 2006 firewall will provide transparent Web Proxy functionality for Firewall and SecureNAT clients.

Understanding the ISA Server 2006 SecureNAT Client

A SecureNAT client is any device configured with a default gateway address that can route Internet-bound connections through the ISA Server 2006 firewall. That is, the ISA Server role is closely related to the role of a router for outbound access. The SecureNAT client does not have a traditional client/server relationship with the ISA Server. There are three network scenarios in which the SecureNAT client is most commonly found:

- Simple
- Complex
- VPN client

A "simple network scenario" is one that has only a single subnet located behind the ISA Server 2006 firewall computer. For example, you have an ISA Server 2006 firewall sitting at the edge of the network with an interface directly connected to the Internet and a second interface connected to the Internal network. All the machines behind the ISA Server 2006 firewall are on a single subnet (for example, 10.0.0.0/8). There are no routers on the Internal network. Figure 17.1 depicts a typical simple network scenario.

Figure 17.1 SecureNAT Simple Network Scenario

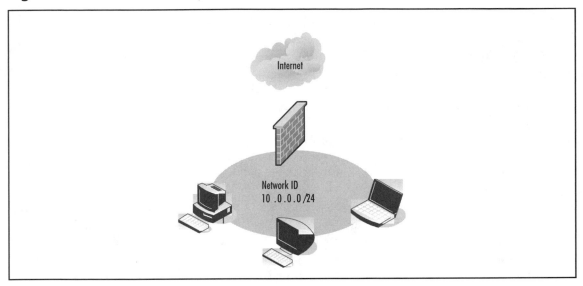

In the simple network scenario, the default gateway of the SecureNAT clients is configured as the IP address of the Internal interface of the ISA Server 2006 firewall. You can manually configure the default gateway address, or you can use DHCP to automatically assign addresses to the SecureNAT clients. The DHCP server can be on the ISA Server 2006 firewall itself, or it can be located on a separate machine on the Internal network.

In the "complex network scenario," the Internal network consists of multiple network IDs that are managed by a router or series of routers or layer 3 switch(s). In the case of the complex network, the default gateway address assigned to each SecureNAT client depends on the location of the SecureNAT client computer. The gateway address for the SecureNAT client will be a router that allows the SecureNAT client access to other networks within the organization, as well as the Internet. The routing infrastructure must be configured to support the SecureNAT client so that Internet-bound requests are forwarded to the Internal interface of the ISA Server 2006 firewall. Figure 17.2 depicts the SecureNAT complex network scenario.

Figure 17.2 SecureNAT Complex Network Scenario

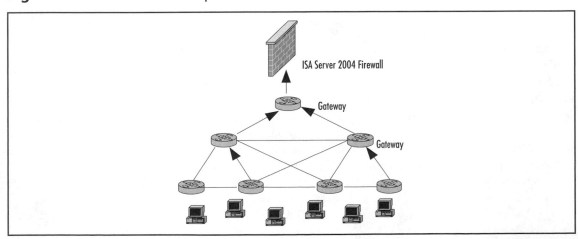

The "VPN client scenario" applies to machines that have created a VPN connection with the ISA Server 2006 firewall.

With ISA Server 2000, when a VPN client computer makes a connection with the VPN server, the client's routing table is changed so that the default gateway is an address on the VPN server. Unless changes are made to the default client configuration, the client will not be able to connect to resources on the Internet while connected to the ISA Server 2000 VPN server. It was possible to configure the ISA Server 2000 VPN client as a Firewall or Web Proxy client and allow the VPN client to access the Internet through the ISA Server 2000 firewall. Alternatively, the ISA Server 2000 VPN client could be configured to allow split tunneling. Either of these methods makes it possible for the client to be connected to internal resources through the VPN server and the Internet at the same time.

In contrast to ISA Server 2000, the ISA Server 2006 VPN server does not require you to configure the VPN clients to be Firewall or Web Proxy clients to access the Internet through the same ISA Server 2006 VPN server to which they connect. Because the VPN clients are not configured as Web Proxy or Firewall clients, they are de facto SecureNAT clients. This allows VPN users to access the corporate network via the VPN connection, while at the same time allowing them to access the Internet via their connection to the ISA firewall, and removes the risks inherent in split tunneling.

Note that you do not need to have a deep understanding of VPN client routing table configuration or how different versions of the Windows VPN client handle default route assignments. Just remember that when a VPN client creates a VPN connection with the ISA Server 2006 firewall/VPN server, that client will be able to connect to the Internet via the ISA Server 2006 firewall based on access rules that you configure.

SecureNAT Client Limitations

While SecureNAT clients are the simplest ISA Server 2006 client types to configure, they are also the least capable and the least secure of the three ISA Server 2006 client types. Limitations of the SecureNAT client include:

- Inability to authenticate with the firewall for strong user/group-based access control
- Inability to take advantage of complex protocols without the aid of an application filter
- Dependency on the routing infrastructure to access the Internet
- Requirement for a Protocol Definition to be configured on the ISA Server 2006 firewall to support the connection

SecureNAT clients do not send credentials to the ISA Server 2006 firewall because, in order for credentials to be sent to the firewall, there must be a client software component to send them. The basic TCP/IP protocol stack does not provide for user authentication and requires an application component to send user credentials. Thus, Firewall and Web Proxy clients can send user credentials, but the SecureNAT client cannot. The Firewall client uses the Firewall client software to send user credentials, and Web browsers configured to use the ISA Server 2006 firewall as a Web Proxy have the built-in capability to send user credentials. This means you cannot use strong user/group-based outbound access controls for machines configured *only* as SecureNAT clients.

SecureNAT clients cannot connect to the Internet (or any other location through the ISA Server 2006 firewall) using complex protocols without the aid of an application filter installed on the ISA Server. A complex protocol is one that requires multiple primary or secondary connections. A classic case of a complex protocol would be FTP standard (Port) mode connections.

When the standard mode FTP client establishes a connection to the FTP server, the initial connection (the "control channel") is established on TCP port 20. The FTP client and server then negotiate a port number on which the FTP client can receive the data (the file to download), and the FTP server returns the data from its own TCP port 21 to the negotiated port. This inbound connection is a *new* primary connection request and not a response to a primary outbound connection made by the FTP client.

The firewall must be aware of the communications going on between the FTP standard mode client and the FTP server so that the correct ports are available for the new inbound connection request to the ISA Server 2006 firewall. This is accomplished on ISA Server 2006 via its intelligent FTP Access Application Filter. Figure 17.3 depicts the FTP standard mode client and server communications.

Figure 17.3 FTP Standard Mode Client/Server Communciations

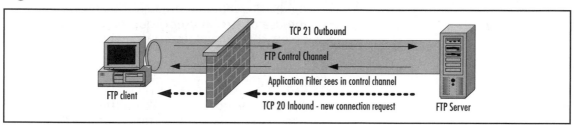

This limitation regarding complex protocols is especially problematic when it comes to Internet games and voice/video applications. These applications typically require multiple inbound and outbound primary connections. The SecureNAT client will not be able to use these applications unless there are specific application filters on the firewall to support them. In contrast, the Firewall client is easily able to handle applications that require multiple inbound and outbound primary connections without installing anything extra on the firewall.

Of course, there's an exception to every rule, and here's the exception to the statement above: Complex protocol support for SecureNAT clients is possible *if* the application installed on the SecureNAT client is designed to work with a SOCKS 4 proxy. In this case, the application is explicitly configured to communicate with the ISA Server 2006 firewall's SOCKS 4 service. The SOCKS 4 service can manage the connections on behalf of the SecureNAT client machine's application.

The SecureNAT client is dependent on the organization's routing infrastructure. Unlike the Firewall and Web Proxy clients, which send their Internet connection requests directly to the ISA Server 2006 firewall (and thus, only need to know the route to the Internal interface of the ISA Server 2006 firewall machine), the SecureNAT client depends on the routing infrastructure to forward Internet-bound requests to the Internal interface of the ISA Server 2006 firewall. If the connection encounters a router in the path that does not route Internet-bound connections through the ISA Server 2006 firewall, the connection attempt will fail.

- Because of the limitations of SecureNAT, a computer should only be configured as a SecureNAT client when at least one of the following conditions exists:

- The machine does not support Firewall client software (non-Windows clients) and requires protocol support outside of what the Web Proxy client can provide (protocols other than HTTP/HTTPS and FTP upload).

- The machine requires outbound access to the ICMP and PPTP.

- For administrative or political reasons, you cannot install the Firewall client on machines that require protocol access outside of that provided by the Web Proxy client configuration.

Disadvantages of the SecureNAT configuration are summarized in Table 17.2.

Table 17.2 Disadvantages of the SecureNAT Client Configuration

Disadvantage	Implication
Inability to authenticate with the ISA Server 2006 firewall	The SecureNAT client is unable to send user credentials (user name and password) to the ISA Server 2006 firewall. This prevents the use of strong user/group-based outbound access control over Internet access. The only outbound access control available for SecureNAT clients is based on a client source IP address.
Inability to use complex protocols	Complex protocols require multiple primary and/or secondary connections. Internet games, voice/video applications, and instant messaging applications often require complex protocol support. The SecureNAT client cannot access Internet applications using complex protocols without the assistance of an application filter installed on the ISA Server 2006 firewall machine. The only exception to this is when the application installed on the SecureNAT client is configured to support SOCKS 4.
Dependency on the existing network routing infrastructure	The SecureNAT client does not forward connections directly to the ISA Server 2006 firewall. Instead, it depends on the organization's routing infrastructure. Each router along the path from the SecureNAT client to the ISA Server 2006 firewall must be aware that the path to the Internet is through the ISA Server 2006 firewall. This may require reconfiguring network routers with new gateways of last resort (default gateways).
User information is not included in the Firewall and Web Proxy logs	The user name is only included in Firewall and Web Proxy logs when a client sends that information to the ISA firewall. A client piece is *always* required to send user information to the firewall since there are no provisions in the layer 1 through 6 headers to provide this

Table 17.2 Continued

Disadvantage	Implication
	information. Only the Firewall client and Web Proxy client configurations can send user information to the ISA firewall and have this information included in the log files. SecureNAT client connections allow for logging of the source IP address, but user information is never recorded.

SecureNAT Client Advantages

Despite the limitations discussed in the foregoing section, you should not conclude that the SecureNAT client is all bad. In fact, some of the SecureNAT client's weaknesses also represent the SecureNAT client's strengths. Advantages of the SecureNAT client configuration include:

- Support for non-Windows client operating systems

- Support for non-TCP/UDP (PPTP and ICMP)

- No requirement for client software installation or configuration

The primary purpose of the SecureNAT client configuration is to enable non-Microsoft operating systems to access a broader range of protocols than is supported by the Web Proxy client configuration. The Firewall client works only with Windows operating systems. Thus, without the SecureNAT client configuration, the only protocols that would be available to non-Microsoft operating systems are those provided by the Web Proxy client configuration (HTTP/HTTPS and FTP upload).

The SecureNAT client has an important use for Microsoft operating systems, as well. The Firewall client software intercepts outbound TCP and UDP connections established by Winsock applications and forwards them to the ISA Server 2006 firewall. However, the Firewall client software does not evaluate non-TCP/UDP communications. Networking protocols such as ICMP and GRE (used for the PPTP VPN protocols) do not use UDP or TCP as a transport protocol, and thus, are not evaluated by the Firewall client. You must configure client computers as SecureNAT clients to support outbound access through the ISA Server 2006 firewall using these protocols.

One significant downside of this situation is that you cannot use user/group-based access controls over which hosts can create outbound connections using non-TCP/UDP protocols. For example, you might want to allow outbound PPTP VPN connections for a specific group of users. This is not possible because PPTP requires GRE; this bypasses the Firewall client software, and therefore, no user information is passed to the ISA Server 2006 firewall. If you create an outbound PPTP Access Rule that requires user authentication, the connection attempt will fail. The only method available to control an outbound PPTP connection is by source IP address.

Probably the most common reason for implementing the SecureNAT client configuration is to avoid having to install or configure client software. Firewall and network administrators are loath to install software on client computers that imposes itself on the network stack. In addition, there is a perception that significant administrative overhead is involved with installing the ISA Server 2006 Firewall client and configuring the Web Proxy client, although in reality, there is not.

In fact, there is an extremely low likelihood that the Firewall client software will interfere with the networking components of any client software, and the administrative overhead is very small when you automate the Firewall client and Web Proxy client installation and configuration.

We will discuss how to automate client installation and configuration later in this chapter. Table 17.3 details the advantages of the SecureNAT client configuration.

Table 17.3 Advantages of the SecureNAT Client Configuration

Advantage	Implication
Provides additional protocol support for non-Windows operating systems	Non-Windows operating systems do not support the Firewall client software. If you wish to provide support for protocols other than those allowed via the Web Proxy client configuration (that is, HTTP/HTTPS/FTP upload), the SecureNAT configuration is your only option for non-Windows operating system clients such as Linux, UNIX, and Macintosh.
Support for non-TCP/UDP Protocols	The SecureNAT client is the only ISA Server 2006 client configuration that supports non-TCP/UDP protocols. Ping, tracert, and PPTP are some of the non-TCP/UDP protocols that require the SecureNAT client configuration. Note that you cannot exert strong user/group-based access controls for non-TCP/UDP protocols because the SecureNAT client configuration does not support user authentication.
Does not require client software installation or configuration	The SecureNAT client does not require that any software be installed or configured on the client computers. The only requirement is that the default gateway address on the client machine be configured so that Internet-bound requests are forwarded through the ISA Server 2006 firewall.
Best general configuration for published servers	When publishing a server to the Internet, the server often needs to not only accept connections from Internet-based hosts, but also needs to initiate new connections. The best example is an SMTP relay configured for both inbound and outbound relay. The SMTP relay does not need to be configured as a SecureNAT client to receive inbound connections from remote SMTP servers

Table 17.3 Continued

Advantage	Implication
	(because you have the option to replace the original source IP address of the Internet host with the IP address of the ISA Server 2006 firewall). However, the SMTP relay *does* need to be configured as a SecureNAT client to send outbound mail to Internet SMTP servers. We will cover this issue in more detail in Chapter 21.

Name Resolution for SecureNAT Clients

As we discussed earlier in the context of network services support, name resolution is a critical issue not only when installing the ISA Server 2006 firewall software on the server, but for all types of ISA Server 2006 clients. Each ISA Server 2006 client resolves names in its own way. The SecureNAT client resolves names for hosts on the Internal and External networks using the DNS server address configured on the SecureNAT client's own network interfaces.

The fact that the SecureNAT client must be able to resolve names based on its own TCP/IP configuration can pose challenges for Internet-connected organizations that require access to resources both while connected to the corporate network and when those same hosts must leave the Internal network and connect to corporate resources from remote locations. In addition, there are significant challenges when SecureNAT clients attempt to "loop back" through the ISA Server 2006 firewall to access resources on the Internal or other protected networks.

SecureNAT clients must be configured to use a DNS server that can resolve both Internal network names and Internet host names. Most organizations host their own DNS servers within the confines of the corporate network. In this case, the SecureNAT client should be configured to use the Internal DNS server that can resolve Internal network names, and then either perform recursion to resolve Internet host names, or use a DNS forwarder to resolve the Internet host names.

Name Resolution and "Looping Back" Through the ISA Server 2006 Firewall

Consider the example of an organization that uses the domain name *internal.net* for resources located on the Internal network behind the ISA Server 2006 firewall. The organization uses the same domain name to host resources for remote users and publishes those resources on the Internal network. For example, the company hosts its own Web server on the Internal network, and the IP address of that Web server on the Internal network is **192.168.1.10**.

The organization also hosts its own DNS resources and has entered the IP address **222.222.222.1** into the DNS database for the host name www.internal.net. External users use this name, www.internal.net, to access the company's Web server. The Web server is published using ISA Server 2006 Web Publishing Rules and external users have no problem accessing the published Web server.

The problem is that when SecureNAT clients on the Internal network try to reach the same Web server, the connection attempts always fail. The reason for this is that the SecureNAT clients are configured to use the same DNS server that is used by the external clients to resolve the name www. internal.net. This name resolves to the public address on the external interface of the ISA Server 2006 firewall that is used in the Web Publishing Rule. The SecureNAT client resolves the name www. internal.net to this address and forwards the connection to the external interface of the ISA Server 2006 firewall. The ISA Server 2006 firewall then forwards the request to the Web server on the Internal network.

The Web server then responds *directly to the SecureNAT client computer*. The reason for this is that the source IP address in the request forwarded by the ISA Server 2006 firewall to the Web Server on the Internal network is the IP address of the SecureNAT client. This causes the Web server on the Internal network to recognize the IP address as one on its local network and respond directly to the SecureNAT client. The SecureNAT client computer drops the response from the Web server because it sent the request to the public IP address of the ISA Server 2006 firewall, not to the IP address of the Web server on the Internal network. The response is dropped because the SecureNAT client sees this as an unsolicited communication. Figure 17.4 depicts the SecureNAT client looping back through the ISA Server 2006 firewall.

Figure 17.4 SecureNAT "Loop Back"

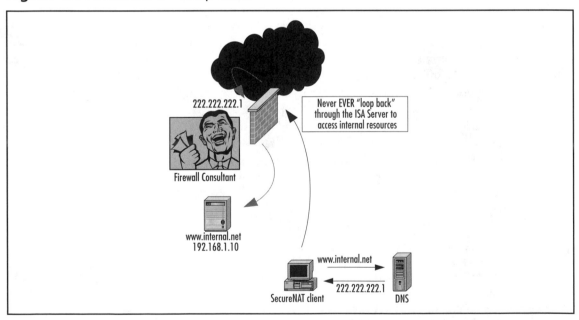

The solution to this problem is the split DNS infrastructure. In almost all cases in which the organization requires remote access to resources located on the Internal network, the split DNS infrastructure provides the solution to name resolution problems for SecureNAT and roaming clients (hosts that move between the Internal network and locations outside the corporate network).

In a split DNS infrastructure, the SecureNAT client is configured to use an Internal DNS server that resolves names for resources based on the resource's Internal network address. Remote hosts can resolve the same names, but the external hosts resolve the same names to the IP address on the external interface of the ISA Server 2006 firewall that publishes the resource. This prevents the SecureNAT client from looping back through the ISA Server 2006 firewall, and connection attempts to published servers succeed for the SecureNAT clients. Figure 17.5 demonstrates how the split DNS infrastructure solves the "looping back" issue for SecureNAT clients. Table 17.4 summarizes important DNS considerations for SecureNAT clients.

Figure 17.5 A Split DNS Solves the SecureNAT Paradox

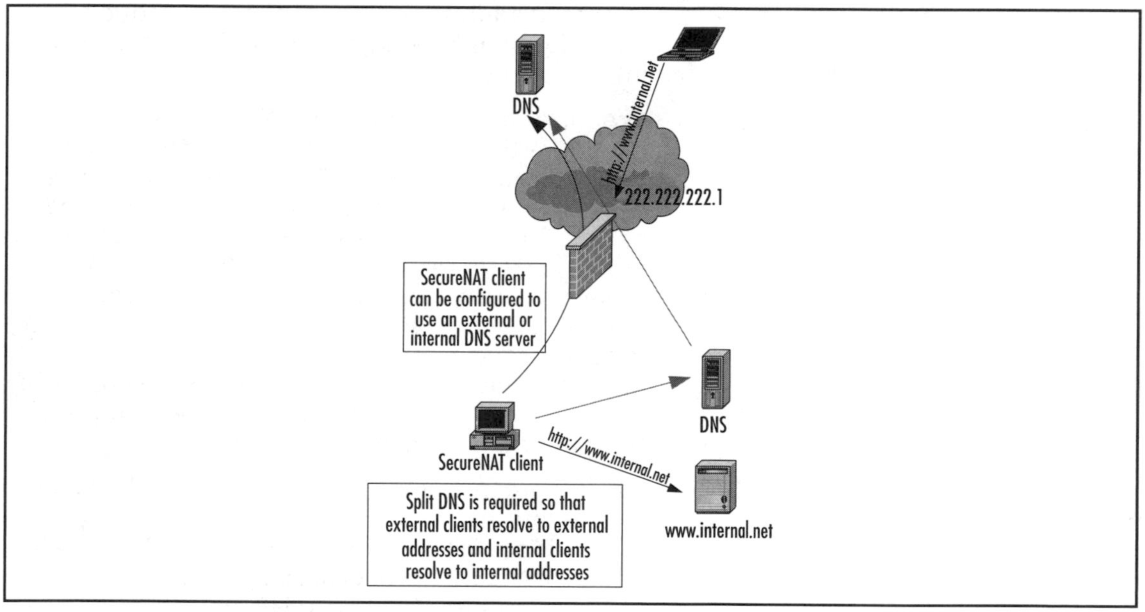

Table 17.4 DNS Considerations for SecureNAT Clients

SecureNAT DNS Consideration	Implications
Internal and external host name resolution	The SecureNAT client must be able to resolve all host names via its locally-configured DNS server address. The DNS server must be able to resolve Internal network names, as well as external Internet host names. If the DNS server that the SecureNAT client is configured to use is not able to resolve local names or Internet names, the name resolution request will fail and the connection attempt will be aborted.

Continued

Table 17.4 Continued

SecureNAT DNS Consideration	Implications
Looping back through the ISA Server 2006 firewall	SecureNAT clients must not loop back through the ISA Server 2006 firewall to access Internal network resources. The most common situation where this occurs is when a server on the Internal network has been published to the Internet. The SecureNAT client is configured with a DNS server that resolves the name of the server to the IP address on the external interface of the ISA Server 2006 firewall. The SecureNAT client sends a connection request to that IP address and the connection request fails. The solution is to design and configure a split DNS infrastructure.
Organizations with Internal DNS servers	Organizations with Internal DNS servers should configure those servers to resolve both internal and external host names. The Internal DNS servers are authoritative for the Internal network domain names. The DNS servers should be configured to either perform recursion against Internet DNS servers or use a forwarder to resolve Internet host names. Note that an organization may elect to use different servers for local and external name resolution, but the SecureNAT clients DNS point of contact must have a mechanism in place to resolve both internal and external names.
Organizations without Internal DNS servers	Smaller organizations may not have a DNS server on the Internal network. In this case, alternate methods are used for local name resolution, such as WINS, NetBIOS broadcast name resolution, or local HOSTS files. The SecureNAT clients should be configured to use a DNS located on the Internet (such as their ISP's DNS server) or configure a caching-only DNS server on the ISA Server 2006 firewall computer.
SecureNAT client cannot connect to the Internet	The most common reason for SecureNAT clients failing to connect to Internet resources is a name resolution failure. Check that the SecureNAT client is configured to use a DNS server that can resolve Internet host names. You can also use the **nslookup** utility to test name resolution on the SecureNAT client computer.
SecureNAT client cannot connect to servers on the Internal network	The most common reason for SecureNAT clients failing to connect to local resources using DNS host names is name resolution failure. Check that the DNS server configured on the SecureNAT client

Table 17.4 Continued

SecureNAT DNS Consideration	Implications
	is able to resolve names on the Internal network. Note that if the SecureNAT client is configured to use an Internet-based DNS server (such as your ISP's DNS server), the SecureNAT client will not be able to resolve local DNS host names. This can be solved by configuring the SecureNAT client to use an Internal DNS server that can resolve local and Internet host names, or by using an alternate method of Internal network host name resolution.
SecureNAT clients should be configured to use an Internal network DNS Server	Although small organizations may not have a DNS server responsible for name resolution on the Internal network, you should avoid using public DNS servers for your SecureNAT clients. Instead, configure the ISA Server 2006 firewall as a caching-only DNS server, and configure the SecureNAT clients to use the caching-only DNS server on the ISA Server 2006 firewall. Configure the caching-only DNS server on the ISA Server 2006 firewall to use a trusted DNS server, such as your ISP's DNS server, as a forwarder. This reduces the risks inherent from allowing SecureNAT clients to communicate directly with Internet DNS servers. The caching-only DNS server on the ISA Server 2006 firewall can be configured to prevent common DNS exploits, such as cache poisoning.

Understanding the ISA Server 2006 Firewall Client

The Firewall client software is an optional piece of software that can be installed on any supported Windows operating system to provide enhanced security and accessibility. The Firewall client software provides the following enhancements to Windows clients:

- Allows strong user/group–based authentication for all Winsock applications using TCP and UDP protocols

- Allows user and application information to be recorded in the ISA Server 2006 firewall's log files

- Provides enhanced support for network applications, including complex protocols that require secondary connections

- Provides "proxy" DNS support for Firewall client machines

- Allows you to publish servers that require complex protocols without the aid of an application filter

- The network routing infrastructure is transparent to the Firewall client

Allows Strong User/Group-Based Authentication for All Winsock Applications Using TCP and UDP Protocols

The Firewall client software transparently sends user information to the ISA Server 2006 firewall. This allows you to create Access Rules that apply to users and groups and allow or deny access to any protocol, site, or content, based on a user account or group membership. This strong user/group-based outbound access control is extremely important. Not all users require the same level of access, and users should only be allowed access to protocols, sites, and content they require to do their jobs.

The Firewall client automatically sends user credentials (user name and password) to the ISA Server 2006 firewall. The user must be logged on with a user account that is either in the Windows Active Directory or NT domain, or the user account must be mirrored on the ISA Server 2006 firewall. For example, if you have an Active Directory domain, users should log on to the domain, and the ISA Server 2006 firewall must be a member of the domain. The ISA Server 2006 firewall is able to authenticate the user and allows or denies access based on the user's domain credentials.

If you do not have a Windows domain, you can still use the Firewall client software to control outbound access based on user/group. In this case, you must mirror the accounts that users log on to on their workstations to user accounts stored in the local Security Account Manager (SAM) on the ISA Server 2006 firewall computer.

For example, a small business does not use an Active Directory, but they do want strong outbound access control based on user/group membership. Users log on to their machine with local user accounts. You can enter the same user names and passwords on the ISA Server 2006 firewall, and the ISA Server 2006 firewall will be able to authenticate the users based on the same account information they use when they log on to their local machines.

Allows User and Application Information to be Recorded in the ISA Server 2006 Firewall's Log Files

A major benefit of using the Firewall client is that when the user name is sent to the ISA Server 2006 firewall, that user name is included in the ISA Server 2006 firewall's log files. This allows you to easily query the log files based on username and obtain precise information on that user's Internet activity.

In this context, the Firewall client provides not only a high level of security by allowing you to control outbound access based on user/group accounts, but also provides a high level of accountability. Users will be less enthusiastic about sharing their account information with other users when they know that their Internet activity is being tracked based on their account name, and they are held responsible for that activity.

Provides Enhanced Support for Network Applications, Including Complex Protocols That Require Secondary Connections

Unlike the SecureNAT client, which requires an application filter to support complex protocols requiring secondary connections, the Firewall client can support virtually any Winsock application using TCP or UDP protocols, regardless of the number of primary or secondary connections, without requiring an application filter.

The ISA Server 2006 firewall makes it easy for you to configure Protocol Definitions reflecting multiple primary or secondary connections and then create Access Rules based on these Protocol Definitions. This provides a significant advantage in terms of Total Cost of Ownership (TCO) because you do not need to purchase applications that are SOCKS proxy aware, and you do not need to incur the time and cost overhead involved with creating customer application filters to support "off-label" Internet applications.

Provides "Proxy" DNS Support for Firewall Client Machines

In contrast to the SecureNAT client, the Firewall client does not need to be configured with a DNS server that can resolve Internet host names. The ISA Server 2006 firewall can perform a "proxy" DNS function for Firewall clients.

For example, when a Firewall client sends a connection request for ftp://ftp.microsoft.com, the request is sent directly to the ISA Server 2006 firewall. The ISA Server 2006 firewall resolves the name for the Firewall client based on the DNS settings on the ISA Server 2006 firewall's network interface cards. The ISA Server 2006 firewall returns the IP address to the Firewall client machine, and the Firewall client machine sends the FTP request to the IP address for the ftp.microsoft.com FTP site. The ISA Server 2006 firewall also caches the results of the DNS queries it makes for Firewall clients. This speeds up name resolution for subsequent Firewall client connections to the same sites. Figure 17.6 shows the name resolution sequence for the Firewall client.

Figure 17.6 Firewall Name Resolution Sequence

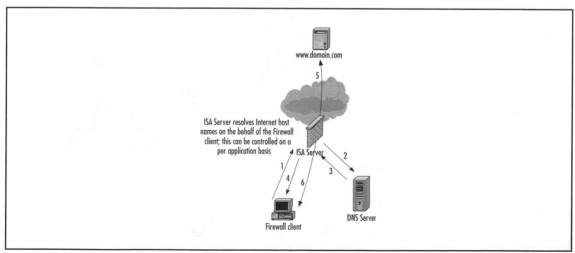

1. The Firewall client sends a request for ftp.microsoft.com.

2. The ISA Server 2006 firewall sends a DNS query to an Internal DNS server.

3. The DNS server resolves the name ftp.microsoft.com to its IP address and returns the result to the ISA Server 2006 firewall.

4. The ISA Server 2006 firewall returns the IP address of ftp.microsoft.com to the Firewall client that made the request.

5. The Firewall client sends a request to the IP address for ftp.microsoft.com and the connection is complete.

6. The Internet server returns requested information to the Firewall client via the Firewall client connection made to the ISA Server 2006 firewall.

The Network Routing Infrastructure Is Transparent to the Firewall Client

The final major benefit conferred by the Firewall client is that the routing infrastructure is virtually transparent to the Firewall client machine. In contrast to the SecureNAT client, which depends on its default gateway and the default gateway settings on routers throughout the corporate network, the Firewall client machine only needs to know the route to the IP address on the Internal interface of the ISA Server 2006 firewall. The Firewall client machine "remotes" or sends requests directly to the IP address of the ISA Server 2006 firewall. Since corporate routers are typically aware of all routes on the corporate network, there is no need to make changes to the routing infrastructure to support Firewall client connections to the Internet. Figure 17.7 depicts the "remoting" of these connections directly to the ISA Server 2006 firewall computer. Table 17.5 summarizes the advantages of the Firewall client application.

Figure 17.7 Firewall Client Connections to the ISA 2004 Firewall are Independent of the Default Gateway Configurations on Interposed Routers

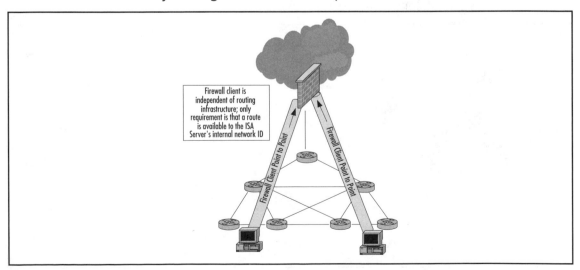

Table 17.5 Advantages of the Firewall Client Configuration

Firewall Client Advantage	Implication
Strong user/based authentication for Winsock TCP and UDP protocols	Strong user/based authentication for Winsock applications using TCP and UDP allows you fine-tuned granular control over outbound access and makes it possible for you to implement the principle of least privilege, which protocols not only your own network, but other corporations networks as well.
User name and application information is saved in the ISA Server 2006 firewall's logs	While strong user/group-based access controls increase the security the firewall provides for your network, user name and application name information saved in the ISA Server 2006 firewall's log increases the accountability and enables you to easily research what sites, protocols, and applications any user running the Firewall client software has accessed.
Enhanced support for network applications and protocols	The Firewall client can access virtually any TCP or UDP-based protocol, even those used by complex protocols that require multiple primary and/or secondary connections. In contrast, the SecureNAT client requires an application filter on the ISA Server 2006 firewall to be in place to support complex protocols. The overall effect is that the Firewall client reduces the TCO of the ISA Server 2006 firewall solution.
Proxy DNS support for Firewall clients	The ISA Server 2006 firewall can resolve names on behalf of Firewall clients. This offloads the Internet host name resolution responsibility from the Firewall client and allows the ISA Server 2006 firewall to keep a DNS cache of recent name resolution requests. This DNS proxy feature also enhances the security configuration for irewall clients because it eliminates the requirement that the Firewall client be configured to use a public DNS server to resolve Internet host names.
Enables publishing servers that require a complex networking protocol	Web and Server Publishing Rules support simple protocols, with the exception of those that have an application installed on the ISA Server 2006 firewall, such as the FTP Access application filter. You can install Firewall client software on a published server to support complex protocols, such as those that might be required if you wished to run a game server on your network.

Continued

www.syngress.com

Table 17.5 Continued

Firewall Client Advantage	Implication
The network routing infrastructure is virtually transparent to the firewall client	Unlike the SecureNAT client, which relies on the routing infrastructure through the organization to use the ISA Server 2006 firewall as its Internet access firewall, the Firewall client only needs to know the route to the IP address on the Internal interface of the ISA Server 2006 firewall. This significantly reduces the administrative overhead of supporting the Firewall client versus the SecureNAT client.

How the Firewall Client Works

The details of how the Firewall client software actually works are not fully documented in the Microsoft literature. What we do know is that the ISA Server 2006 Firewall client, unlike previous versions, uses only TCP 1745 for the Firewall client *Control Channel*. Over this control channel, the Firewall client communicates directly with the ISA Server 2006 firewall service to perform name resolution and network application-specific commands (such as those used by FTP and Telnet). The firewall service uses the information gained through the control channel and sets up a connection between the Firewall client and the destination server on the Internet.

Note that the Firewall client only establishes a control channel connection when connecting to resources not located on the Internal network. In ISA Server 2000, the Internal network was defined by the Local Address Table (LAT). The ISA Server 2006 firewall does not use a LAT because of its enhanced multinetworking capabilities. Nevertheless, the Firewall client must have some mechanism in place to determine which communications should be sent to the firewall service on the ISA Server 2006 firewall and which should be sent directly to the destination host with which the Firewall client wants to communicate.

The Firewall client solves this problem using addresses defined by the **Internal Network**. The Internal network for any specific Firewall client consists of all the addresses reachable from the network interface that is connected to the Firewall client's own network. This situation gets interesting on a multihomed ISA Server 2006 firewall that has multiple Internal networks associated with different network adapters. In general, all hosts located behind the same network adapter (regardless of network ID) are considered part of the same **Internal** network and all communications between hosts on the same Internal network should bypass the Firewall client.

Addresses for the Internal network are defined during installation of the ISA Server 2006 firewall software, but you can create other "Internal" networks as required.

The most significant improvement the ISA Server 2006 Firewall client has over previous versions of the Firewall client (Winsock Proxy Client 2.0 and ISA Server 2006 Firewall Client) is that you now have the option to use an encrypted channel between the Firewall client and the ISA Server 2006 firewall. Remember that the Firewall client sends user credentials transparently to the ISA Server 2006 firewall. The ISA Server 2006 Firewall client encrypts the channel so that user credentials will not be intercepted by someone who may be "sniffing" the network with a network analyzer (such as Microsoft Network Monitor or Ethereal). Note that you do have the option of configuring the ISA Server 2006 firewall to allow both secure encrypted and non-encrypted control channel communications.

For a very thorough empirical study on how the Firewall client application works with the firewall service in ISA Server 2000, check out Stefaan Pouseele's article **Understanding the Firewall Client Control Channel** at www.isaserver.org/articles/Understanding_the_Firewall_Client_Control_Channel.html.

Installing the Firewall Client Share

The Firewall client share contains the installation files for the Firewall client. Regardless of the method you use to distribute the Firewall client, you must install the Firewall client share on either the ISA Server 2006 firewall or a file server on the Internal network. We recommend that you do not install the Firewall client software on the ISA Server 2006 firewall.

When the Firewall client share is installed on the ISA Server 2006 firewall, a Firewall System Policy Rule (a type of Access Rule that is processed before using defined Access Rules) is created that allows a number of potentially dangerous protocols access to the firewall machine. These protocols include:

- Microsoft Common Internet File System (CIFS) (TCP)
- Microsoft CIFS (UDP)
- NetBIOS Datagram
- NetBIOS Name Service
- NetBIOS Session

In addition, File and Printer Sharing must be enabled on the Internal interface. These Microsoft File and Printer sharing services and protocols, as well as the Client for Microsoft Networks service, can pose a significant risk to the ISA Server 2006 firewall and should be disabled, if at all possible, on all ISA Server 2006 network interfaces. You can disable these services and still make the Firewall client share available to network users by installing the Firewall client share on another machine on the corporate network.

Do the following to install the Firewall client share on a file server on the Internal network:

1. Place the ISA Server 2006 CD into the CD tray on the file server.
2. Close the Autorun window when it appears.
3. Using windows explorer, browse the cd and copy the client folder to a network location of your choice and create the mspclnt share.
4. The default **Share Permissions** on the folder should be set to **Everyone Read**. The default NTFS permissions on the share should be:

- Administrators – Full Control
- Authenticated Users – Read & Execute, List Folder Contents and Read
- System – Full Control

Installing the Firewall Client

There are a number of methods you can use to install the Firewall client software. These include:

- Using an SMB/CIFS connection to a share on a file server
- Active Directory Group Policy Software Management
- Silent Installation Script
- Systems Management Server (SMS)

In this section, we will cover the manual installation of the Firewall client. Users who choose this method of installing the Firewall client software must be local administrators on the machine on which they install the software. For example, if the machine is a laptop computer that is also a member of the corporate domain, make sure the user has a local account on the laptop that is a member of the Administrators group. Have the user log off the domain and log on to the local computer. The user can then connect to the Firewall client share on the network file server. The user may need to enter network credentials when connecting to the File server if the laptop's local account the user is currently logged into is not mirrored on the file server or in the Active Directory (if the file server and the user are members of the same Active Directory domain).

All users of the computer have access to the Firewall client software after it is installed. That means the user can log off from the local account and log back in with domain credentials and still use the Firewall client software.

If you do not allow your users to be members of the Administrators group on their local machines, you must use one of the automated approaches that installs the Firewall client software *before* user log on. You can use Active Directory Group Policy Software Assignment or Systems Management Server (SMS) to accomplish this task.

Some things to take note of regarding installation of the Firewall client software:

- Do **not** install the Firewall client software on the ISA Server 2006 firewall machine.
- Do **not** install the Firewall client software on a domain controller or other network servers. The only exception to this rule is when you must publish a server that requires complex protocol support. For example, many game servers require multiple primary and secondary connections. In this case, the Firewall client must be installed on the published server
- The Firewall client software begins working immediately after installation is complete.
- You can install the Firewall client on any version of Windows (except Windows 95) as long as Internet Explorer 5.0 is installed.

Perform the following steps to install the Firewall client software from a file share on the Internal network:

The latest version can also be downloaded from Microsoft at https://www.microsoft.com/downloads/details.aspx?familyid=05C2C932-B15A-4990-B525-66380743DA89&displaylang=en

1. Click **Start** and then click **Run**.
2. In the **Run** dialog box, enter **\\FILESERVER\mspclnt\setup** (where FILESERVER is the name of the server having the mspclnt share) and click **OK**.

3. Click **Next** on the **Welcome to the Install Wizard for Microsoft Firewall Client** page.

4. Click **Next** on the **Destination Folder** page.

5. On the **ISA Server Computer Selection** page, select **Connect to this ISA Server computer**, and enter **remoteisa.msfirewall.org** in the text box below it. Click **Next**.

6. Click **Install** on the **Ready to Install the Program** page.

7. Click **Finish** on the **Install the Wizard Completed** page.

8. You will see the Firewall client icon in the system tray (see Figure 17.8). If there is an active TCP or UDP connection to a network that is not the Internal network, the icon will have a GREEN up-pointing arrow.

Figure 17.8 Firewall Client Icon

Firewall Client Configuration

There are two places where you can configure the Firewall client software: at the **Microsoft Internet Security and Acceleration Server 2006** management console and at the Firewall client computer itself. Configuration changes made in the **Microsoft Internet Security and Acceleration Server 2006** management console apply to all Firewall client computers, and those made at the client apply only to that individual client.

Centralized Configuration Options at the ISA Server 2006 Firewall Computer

Centralized Firewall client configuration options are carried out in the **Microsoft Internet Security and Acceleration Server 2004** management console. Firewall client configuration is done for each network configured to support Firewall client connections. Firewall client connections can be made from:

- Perimeter Networks
- Internal Networks

All other network types do not support Firewall client connections. When Firewall client connections are enabled for a network, incoming connections to TCP and UDP ports 1745 are enabled to the interface connected to that network.

You can reach the Firewall client configuration interface by opening the **Microsoft Internet Security and Acceleration Server 2004** management console, expanding the server name and then expanding the **Configuration** node. In the **Configuration** node, click the **Networks** node, and then click the **Networks** tab in the **Details** pane. Right click on the **Internal** network and click **Properties**.

On the **Firewall Client** tab, put a checkmark in the **Enable Firewall client support for this network** check box, as shown in Figure 17.9. In the **Firewall client configuration** frame, enter the name of the ISA Server 2006 firewall computer in the **ISA Server name or IP address** text box.

Figure 17.9 The Internal Network Properties Dialog Box

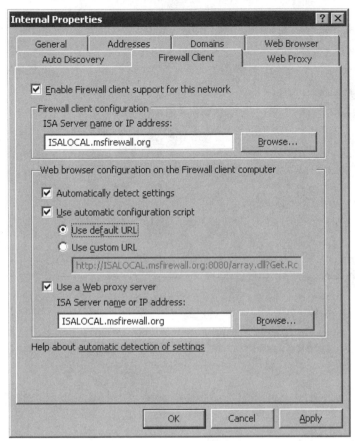

The default setting is to use the computer name (also known as the "NetBIOS" name). However, you should replace the NetBIOS name with the fully-qualified domain name (FQDN) of the ISA Server 2006 firewall. When you replace the computer name with the FQDN, the Firewall client machines can use the DNS to correctly resolve the name of the ISA Server 2006 firewall. This will avoid one of the most common troubleshooting issues with Firewall client connectivity. Make sure there is an entry for this name in your Internal network's DNS server. By default, all the interfaces on the ISA Server 2006 firewall will automatically register their names in the DNS, but if your DNS server does not support dynamic updates, you'll need to manually enter a Host (A) record for the ISA Server 2006 firewall.

The Web Proxy client configuration settings are available in the **Web browser configuration on the Firewall client computer** frame. These settings will automatically configure the Web browser as a Web Proxy client *when the Firewall client is installed*. Note that you can change the settings later and the Web browsers will automatically update themselves with the new settings.

The **Automatically detect settings** option allows the Web browser to automatically detect the Web Proxy service and configure itself based on the settings you configure on the **Web Browser** tab of the **Internal Properties** dialog box. Note that autodetection relies on Web Proxy AutoDiscovery (WPAD) entries being placed in DNS and/or DHCP.

The **Use automatic configuration script** option allows you to assign a proxy autoconfiguration file (PAC) address to the Web browser. The Web browser will then connect to the location you specify or use the default location; the default location is on the ISA Server 2006 firewall machine itself. Note that when you use the default location, you obtain the same information you would receive if you had configured the Web browser to use the **Automatically detect settings** option.

The **Use default URL** option automatically configures the browser to connect to the ISA Server 2006 firewall for autoconfiguration information. You can use the **Use custom URL** option if you want to create your own PAC file that overrides the settings on the automatically-generated file at the ISA Server 2006 firewall. You can find more information on PAC files and proxy client autoconfiguration files in **Using Automatic Configuration and Automatic Proxy** at http://www.microsoft.com/technet/prodtechnol/ie/reskit/5/part5/ch21auto.mspx?mfr=true

The **Use a Web Proxy server** option allows you to configure the Web browser to use the ISA Server 2006 as its Web Proxy, but without the benefits of the autoconfiguration script. This setting provides higher Web browsing performance than the SecureNAT client configuration, but you do not benefit from the settings contained in the autoconfiguration script. The most important configuration settings in the autoconfiguration script include site names and addresses that should be used for *Direct Access*. For this reason, you should avoid this option unless you do not wish to use Direct Access to bypass the Web Proxy to access selected Web sites.

Click the **Domains** tab, as shown in Figure 17.10.

Figure 17.10 The Domains Tab

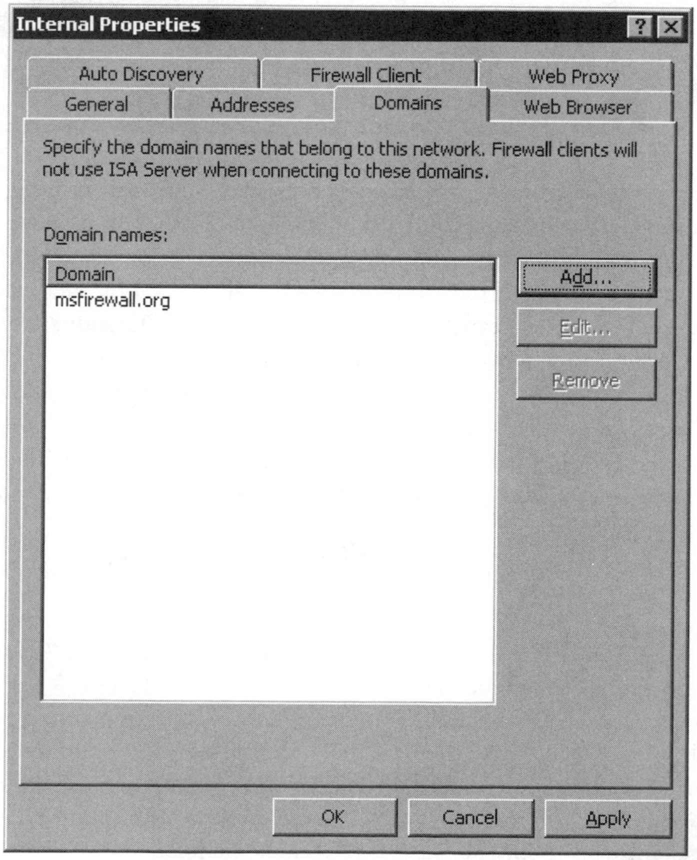

The **Domains** tab contains domains for which the Firewall client computer will not use the Firewall client software to establish a connection. The entries on the **Domains** tab have the same effect as adding machines in these domains to the Internal network (or whatever the network is named for which you are configuring Firewall client Properties). When a Firewall client makes a connection to a host that is located in one of the domains contained in the **Domains** tab, the Firewall client software is not used and the Firewall client machine attempts to connect directly to the destination host.

You can add domains by clicking the **Add** button, and choosing from the **Domain Properties** dialog box, as shown in Figure 17.11.

Figure 17.11 The Domain Properties Dialog Box

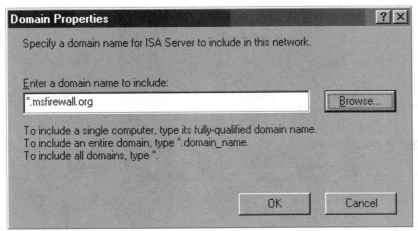

Note that you can use wildcards when specifying a domain. If you want to specify a single computer, just enter the fully-qualified domain name (FQDN) of that host. If you want to include all hosts in a single domain, then use an asterisk (*) just to the left of the leftmost period in the FQDN. If you want to avoid using the Firewall client for all domains, then just enter an asterisk. Click **OK** after making your entry.

You should always include all Internal network domains in the **Domains** tab, as you usually want to allow direct connections to hosts located in the same domain.

For example, if domain members are located on multiple subnets behind a single network interface representing a single network on the ISA Server 2006 firewall, you do *not* want hosts on the network to go through the ISA Server 2006 firewall to connect to hosts on the same network. This puts unneeded stress on the firewall, and the function of a network firewall is not to control these communications.

Enabling Support for Legacy Firewall Client/Winsock Proxy Clients

The ISA Server 2006 Firewall client uses a new and improved *Remote Winsock Proxy Protocol* that encrypts the communication channel between the Firewall client and the ISA Server 2006 firewall's Firewall service. This improves security because user credentials are transparently passed to the ISA Server 2006 firewall when the Firewall client makes an outbound connection request.

However, you have the option to allow non-encrypted Firewall client communications with the ISA Server 2006 firewall. This can provide you time to upgrade your existing Firewall client or Winsock Proxy 2.0 clients to the ISA Server 2006 Firewall client software.

Do the following to enable support for non-encrypted Firewall client connections from legacy Firewall/Winsock Proxy clients:

1. In the **Microsoft Internet Security and Acceleration Server 2006** management console, expand the server name, and then expand the **Configuration** node. Click on the **General** node.

2. On the **General** node, click the **Define Firewall Client Settings** link in the **Details** pane.

3. In the **Firewall Client Settings** dialog box, click the **Connection** node. Put a checkmark in the **Allow non-encrypted Firewall client connections** check box.

4. Click **Apply,** and then click **OK**.

5. Click **Apply** to save the changes and update the firewall policy.

6. Click **OK** in the **Apply New Configuration** dialog box.

Client Side Firewall Client Settings

There are some configuration options available to users who have the Firewall client software installed. These options can be accessed by right-clicking on the Firewall client icon in the system tray and clicking the **Configure** command.

On the **General** tab (see Figure 17.12) of the **Microsoft Firewall Client for ISA Server 2006**, confirm that there is a checkmark in the **Enable Microsoft Firewall Client for ISA Server 2006** check box.

Figure 17.12 The Firewall Client Configuration Dialog box

The **Automatically detect ISA Server** option takes advantage of a WPAD entry in a DHCP or DNS server to automatically detect the location of the ISA Server 2006 firewall, and then automatically obtain Firewall client configuration information.

Figure 17.13 illustrates the effect of clicking **Detect Now** button.

Figure 17.13 The Detecting ISA Server Dialog Box

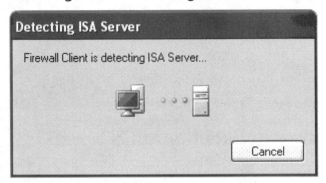

After the Firewall client finds the ISA Server 2006 firewall, you will see the dialog box shown in Figure 17.14.

Figure 17.14 The Detecting ISA Server Dialog Box

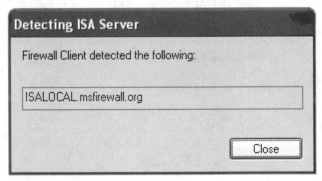

It's important to remember that autodetection will only work if you have configured a WPAD entry in a DHCP or DNS server. We will go through detailed procedures on how to configure the WPAD entries later in this chapter.

You also have the option to **Manually select ISA Server**. This option allows you to enter the IP address or DNS name of the ISA Server 2006 firewall and then click the **Test Server** button to find the firewall. When you enter an IP address, the client sends a request to TCP port 1745 and obtains the autoconfiguration information directly from the ISA Server 2006 firewall. Included in the autoconfiguration information is the name of the ISA Server 2006 firewall, which is listed in the **Detecting ISA Server** dialog box.

The Network Monitor trace shown in Figure 17.15 shows that a connection is made by the Firewall client and some of the information return to the Firewall client is shown in the Hex decode pane.

Figure 17.15 Firewall Client Packet Traces

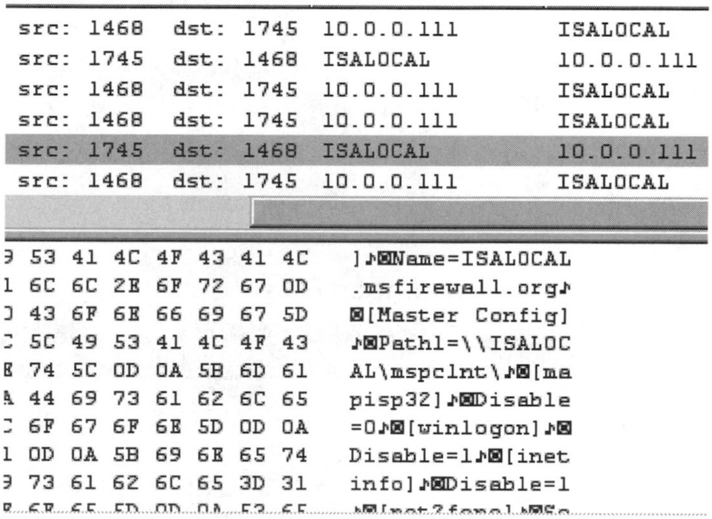

```
src: 1468   dst: 1745   10.0.0.111         ISALOCAL
src: 1745   dst: 1468   ISALOCAL           10.0.0.111
src: 1468   dst: 1745   10.0.0.111         ISALOCAL
src: 1468   dst: 1745   10.0.0.111         ISALOCAL
src: 1745   dst: 1468   ISALOCAL           10.0.0.111
src: 1468   dst: 1745   10.0.0.111         ISALOCAL
```

```
9 53 41 4C 4F 43 41 4C      ].Name=ISALOCAL
1 6C 6C 2E 6F 72 67 0D      .msfirewall.org.
] 43 6F 6E 66 69 67 5D      [Master Config]
: 5C 49 53 41 4C 4F 43      .Path1=\\ISALOC
8 74 5C 0D 0A 5B 6D 61      AL\mspclnt\.[ma
A 44 69 73 61 62 6C 65      pisp32].Disable
: 6F 67 6F 6E 5D 0D 0A      =0.[winlogon].
1 0D 0A 5B 69 6E 65 74      Disable=1.[inet
9 73 61 62 6C 65 3D 31      info].Disable=1
8 6E 65 5D 0D 0A 53 65      .[net2fone].So
```

Click on the **Web Browser** tab. Here you have the option to **Enable Web browser automatic configuration**. This option pulls information from the Web browser configuration you set earlier in the **Microsoft Internet Security and Acceleration Server 2006** management console. Users can click the **Configure Now** button, which makes it easy for users who inadvertently change the browser settings to get back to the ideal configuration with a click of a button. For this reason, you should not disable the Firewall client icon in the system tray.

Firewall Client Configuration Files

The Firewall Client software adopts the centralized settings you configured by the ISA Server 2006 computer. These settings determine things such as automatic Web Proxy client configuration, the ISA Server name, and ISA Server automatic detection. After the Firewall Client software is installed, ISA Server updates these client settings each time a client computer is restarted and every six hours after an initial refresh is made. The settings are also updated each time the user presses the **Test Server** button.

In addition to these settings, ISA Server automatically updates the Firewall client with information about IP addresses that the client should consider local (the "Internal" network for that particular Firewall client).

For almost all Winsock applications, the default Firewall client configuration works without any further configuration. However, there may be times when you want to modify the default settings. The Firewall client can be configured for each user and for each computer on the Firewall client computer.

The configuration is done by making changes to .ini files, which are installed on the Firewall client computer.

You can change the default settings for all components after installation. The new configuration settings take effect only when the client configuration is refreshed.

.ini Files

The configuration information is stored in a set of files, which are installed on the Firewall client computer. When the Firewall client is installed, the following files (also seen in Figure 17.16) are created on the Firewall client computer:

- **common.ini**, which specifies the common configuration for all applications
- **management.ini**, which specifies Firewall client management configuration settings

Figure 17.16 Firewall Client Configuration Files

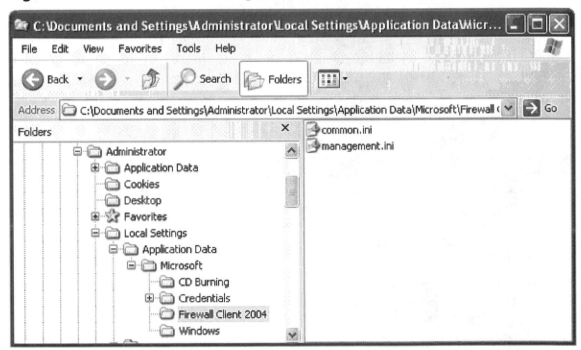

These files are created for all users logged on to the computer and may be created for each specific user on the computer. Per-user settings override the general configuration settings that apply to all users of the same Firewall client computer. These files are created in different locations, depending on the operating system. Unfortunately, we only have information on where these files are located on a Windows XP computer. You can use the **Search** function for your version of Windows to determine the location of the configuration files.

On Windows XP computers the files are located at:

- **\Documents and Settings\All Users\Application Data\Microsoft\ Firewall Client 2004**

- **\Documents and Settings\user_name\Local Settings\Application Data\ Microsoft\Firewall Client 2004 folder**

In addition to these files, the user may create another file called **Application.ini**, which specifies configuration information for specific applications.

There is an order of precedence regarding how the configuration .ini files are evaluated by the Firewall client. The order of evaluation is:

1. .ini files in the user's folder are evaluated first. Any configuration settings here are used by the Firewall client to determine how the Firewall client and applications that depend on the Firewall client will behave.

2. The Firewall client looks next in the **Documents and Settings\All Users** folder. Any *additional* configuration settings are applied. If a configuration setting specified contradicts the user-specific settings, it is ignored. The settings in the user's folder always take precedence.

3. The Firewall client detects the ISA Server computer to which it should connect and retrieves settings from the ISA Server 2006 firewall machine.

4. After retrieving the settings from the ISA Server 2006 firewall, the Firewall client examines the server-level settings. Any configuration settings specified on ISA Server are applied. If a configuration setting specified contradicts the user-specific or computer-specific settings, it is ignored.

Advanced Firewall Client Settings

The user on the Firewall client computer can create and modify the Firewall client configuration files and fine-tune the Firewall client behavior. The *common.ini* file, which is created when the Firewall client is installed, specifies the common configuration for all applications. The *application.ini* file controls configuration settings for applications on the client machine.

These files can be created for all users logged on to the computer and may be created for individual users on the computer. Individual user settings override settings that apply to all users of the computer. You can also use the **Microsoft Internet Security and Acceleration Server 2006** management console to modify the Firewall client configuration settings.

Table 17.6 lists entries you can include when configuring the Firewall client application settings. The first column lists the keys that can be included in the configuration files. The second column describes the values to which the keys can be set.

Be aware that some settings can be configured *only on the Firewall client* computer and not via the **Microsoft Internet Security and Acceleration Server 2004** management console.

Table 17.6 Firewall Client Configuration File Settings

Entry	Description
ServerName	Specifies the name of the ISA Server computer to which the Firewall client should connect.
Disable	Possible values: 0 or 1. When the value is set to 1, the Firewall client application is disabled for the specific client application.
DisableEx	Possible values: 0 or 1. When the value is set to 1, the Firewall client application is disabled for the specific client application. Applies only to the Firewall client for ISA Server 2006. When set, overrides the Disable setting.
Autodetection	(Can be set only on the Firewall client computer.) Possible values: 0 or 1. When the value is set to 1, the Firewall client application automatically finds the ISA Server computer to which it should connect.
NameResolution	Possible values: L or R. By default, dotted decimal notation or Internet domain names are redirected to the ISA Server computer for name resolution and all other names are resolved on the local computer. When the value is set to R, all names are redirected to the ISA Server computer for resolution. When the value is set to L, all names are resolved on the local computer.
LocalBindTcpPorts	Specifies a Transmission Control Protocol (TCP) port, list, or range that is bound locally.
LocalBindUdpPorts	Specifies a User Datagram Protocol (UDP) port, list, or range that is bound locally.
RemoteBindTcpPorts	Specifies a TCP port, list, or range that is bound remotely.
RemoteBindUdpPorts	Specifies a UDP port, list, or range that is bound remotely.
ServerBindTcpPorts	Specifies a TCP port, list, or range for all ports that should accept more than one connection.
Persistent	Possible values: 0 or 1. When the value is set to 1, a specific server state can be maintained on the ISA Server computer if a service is stopped and restarted and if the server is not responding. The client sends a keep-alive message to the server periodically during an active session. If the server is not responding, the client tries to restore the state of the bound and listening sockets upon server restart.
ForceCredentials	(Can be set only on the Firewall client computer.) Used when running a Windows service or server application as a Firewall client application. When the value is set to 1, it forces the use of alternate user authentication credentials that are stored locally on the computer running the service. The user credentials are stored on the client computer using the Credtool.exe application

Continued

Table 17.6 Continued

Entry	Description
	that is provided with the Firewall client software. User credentials must reference a user account that can be authenticated by ISA Server, either local-to-ISA Server, or in a domain trusted by ISA Server. The user account is normally set not to expire. Otherwise, user credentials need to be renewed each time the account expires.
NameResolution ForLocalHost	Possible values are L (default), P, or E. Used to specify how the local (client) computer name is resolved, when the gethostby-name API is called. The LocalHost computer name isresolved by calling the Winsock API function gethostbyname()using the LocalHost string, an empty string, or a NULL string pointer. Winsock applications call gethostbyname(LocalHost) to find their local IP address and send it to an Internet server. When this option is set to L, gethostbyname() returns the IP addresses of the local host computer. When this option is set to P, gethostbyname() returns the IP addresses of the ISA Server computer. When this option is set to E, gethostbyname() returns only the external IP addresses of the ISA Server computer—those IP addresses that are not in the local address table.
ControlChannel	Possible values: Wsp.udp or Wsp.tcp (default). Specifies the type of control channel used.

Firewall Client Configuration at the ISA Server 2006 Firewall

While the configuration files stored at the local Firewall client machine remain a bit of a mystery at the time we write this book, the centralized configuration of the Firewall client done at the **Microsoft Internet Security and Acceleration Server 2006** management console remains as useful as it was in ISA Server 2000 & 2004. You can access the centralized Firewall client configuration interface by opening the **Microsoft Internet Security and Acceleration Server 2006** management console, then expanding the server name and the **Configuration** node. Click on the **General** node, and then click the **Define Firewall Client Settings** link.

Figure 17.17 The Define Firewall Client Settings link

Click the **Application Settings** tab. A list of the built-in Firewall client application settings is shown in Figure 17.18.

Figure 17.18 The Firewall Client Settings Dialog Box

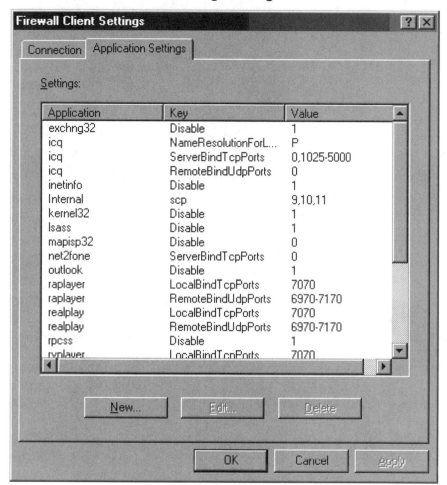

These settings are applied to all Firewall clients who obtain their settings from the ISA Server 2006 firewall. For example, you can see a setting **outlook Disable 0.** This setting tells the Firewall client software to bypass the Firewall client settings for the Microsoft Outlook application. This is an important setting, which allows the Outlook client to receive the proper new mail notification messages.

One especially useful function of the Firewall client settings feature is to block applications. For example, you may want to block users from using the **kazaa.exe** application. You can use the **Disable** key to block the application. Do the following to block the **kazaa.exe** application:

1. In the **Firewall Client Settings** dialog box, on the **Application Settings** tab, click **New**.

2. In the **Application Entry Settings** dialog box, enter **Kazaa** (without the file extension) in the **Application** text box. Select **Disable** from the **Key** drop-down list. Select the value **1** from the **Value** list.

3. Click **OK**.

4. The new entry for **kazaa** appears in the **Settings** list. Click **Apply**, and then **OK**.

5. Click **Apply** (Figure 17.19) to save the changes and update the firewall policy.

Figure 17.19 Apply Changes to Firewall Configuration

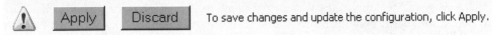

6. Click **OK** in the **Apply New Configuration** dialog box

At this point, any user that has the Firewall client software installed will not be able to use the **kazaa.exe** application.

ISA Server 2006 Web Proxy Client

The Web Proxy client is any computer that has its browser configured to use the ISA Server 2006 firewall as its Web Proxy server. You do not need to add any new software to make a machine a Web Proxy client. The only requirement is that you configure the browser on the client machine to use the ISA Server 2006 firewall as its Web Proxy. The Web browser isn't the only application that can be configured as a Web Proxy client. Other applications, such as instant messengers and e-mail clients can also be configured as Web Proxy clients.

Advantages of the Web Proxy client configuration include:

■ Improved performance for the Firewall client and SecureNAT client configuration for Web access

■ Ability to use the autoconfiguration script to bypass sites using Direct Access

■ Allows you to provide Web access (HTTP/HTTPS/FTP download) without enabling users access to other protocols

■ Allows you to enforce user/group-based access controls over Web access

■ Supports RADIUS authentication for outbound Web Proxy client requests

■ Allows you to limit the number of outbound Web Proxy client connections

■ Supports Web Proxy chaining, which can further speed up Internet access

Improved Performance for the Firewall Client and SecureNAT Client Configuration for Web Access

Web Proxy client machines communicate directly with the ISA Server 2006 firewall via the firewall's Web Proxy filter. The Web Proxy client connects directly to TCP port 8080 on the ISA Server 2006 firewall. TCP port 8080 is used by the ISA Server 2006 firewall's *Web Proxy listener*. The listener listens for outgoing Web requests and then exposes those communications to the firewall's Access Policies. This improves performance because connections from Firewall and SecureNAT clients must be passed to the Web Proxy filter instead of being received directly by the filter. You will find during your own testing that Web Proxy client computers access Web content noticeably faster.

Ability to Use the Autoconfiguration Script to Bypass Sites Using Direct Access

One of the most useful features of the Web Proxy client configuration is the ability to use Direct Access to bypass the Web Proxy filter for selected Web sites. This requires that the Web Proxy client computer be configured to use the autoconfiguration script. There are two ways you can configure the Web Proxy client to use the autoconfiguration script:

- Manually configure the client to use the autoconfiguration script

- Configure WPAD entries in DNS and /or DHCP and configure the Web Proxy client to use autodetection to access configuration information

You can manually configure the Web Proxy client browser to use the autoconfiguration script. Any application that pulls its own configuration from the Web browser settings can typically take advantage of the autoconfiguration script settings as well. Applications that do not pull their configuration from the Web browser are unlikely to be able to benefit from the autoconfiguration script settings.

A more efficient method of assigning the autoconfiguration script to the Web Proxy clients is to use WPAD entries in DNS and/or DHCP. The WPAD information will point the Web Proxy client to the IP address of the ISA Server 2006 firewall, from which the Web Proxy client will obtain autoconfiguration settings.

Support for the autoconfiguration script is critical for Web Proxy clients who want to access certain Java sites and also Hotmail e-mail. The autoconfiguration provides a centralized list of Web sites that should be accessed via Direct Access. When these sites are configured for Direct Access, the Web Proxy client computer will bypass the Web Proxy filter and allow other methods, such as the machine's SecureNAT and/or Firewall client configuration, to connect to the Web site.

Allows You to Provide Web Access (HTTP/HTTPS/FTP Download) without Enabling Users Access to Other Protocols

The Web Proxy client configuration allows you to provide Internet access to users who do not require the full range of Internet protocols to connect to the Internet. The Web Proxy client handles only the HTTP, HTTPS (SSL/TLS-over-HTTP) and HTTP-tunnel FTP download. If a user's computer is configured as *only* a Web Proxy client, that user will have access to those protocols and no others.

Web Proxy clients use a tunneled connection when they send their Internet requests to the ISA Server 2006 firewall. For example, when a user sends a request to **www.microsoft.com**, the Web Proxy client wraps this request in another HTTP header with the destination address being the ISA Server 2006 firewall computer's Internal interface and the destination port TCP 8080. When the ISA Server 2006 firewall receives the request, it removes the Web Proxy client's header and forwards the request to the Internet server at **www.microsoft.com**.

In the same way, when a Web Proxy client sends an FTP request to a site, such as **ftp://ftp. microsoft.com**, the Web Proxy client wraps the FTP request in the same HTTP header with the destination address of the Internal interface of the ISA Server 2006 firewall and the destination port TCP 8080. When the ISA Server 2006 firewall receives this request, it removes the HTTP header and forwards the request to the FTP server at **ftp.microsoft.com** as an actual FTP request, not an HTTP request. This is why we refer to the Web Proxy client's FTP support as HTTP-tunneled FTP.

Allows You to Enforce User/Group-based Access Controls Over Web Access

The Web Proxy client is able to send user credentials to the ISA Server 2006 firewall computer when required. In contrast to the Firewall client, which always sends user credentials to the ISA Server 2006 firewall, the Web Proxy client only sends credentials when asked to provide them. This improves performance, as authentication is only performed when required. If the Web Proxy client has access to an Access Rule that allows access to the site and content in the request, and if the Access Rule allows for anonymous access (allows "All Users" access to the rule), then the Web Proxy client does not send credentials and the connection is allowed (assuming that the Access Rule is an "allow" rule)

This feature explains many of the anonymous entries you have in your firewall log files. When the Web Proxy client sends a request to the ISA Server 2006 firewall, the first connection attempt does not include the Web Proxy client user credentials. This is logged as an anonymous request. If access to the site requires user credentials, then the ISA Server 2006 firewall will send an "access denied" message to the Web Proxy client machine and request the user to authenticate. Figure 17.20 illustrates that, at this point, the Web Proxy client has the option to authenticate using a number of different authentication protocols.

You can use the following authentication protocols for Web Proxy sessions:

- Windows-Integrated authentication
- Basic authentication
- Digest authentication
- Client Certificate authentication
- RADIUS authentication

Figure 17.20 The Authentication Dialog Box

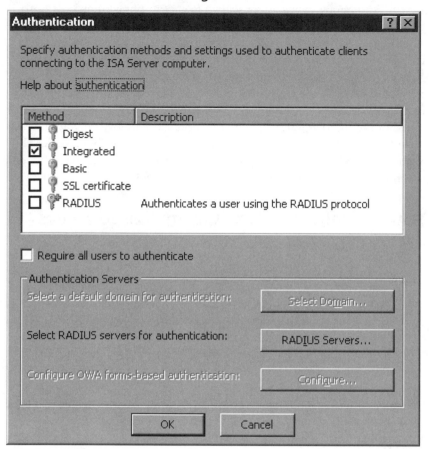

Credentials are passed to the ISA Server 2006 firewall transparently when Integrated authentication is enabled. However, both the ISA Server 2006 firewall and the Web Proxy client must be members of the same domain, or the ISA Server 2006 firewall must use RADIUS authentication to connect to the Active Directory or Windows NT 4.0 user account database. You can also get transparent authentication if you mirror user accounts in the local Security Account Manager (SAM) on the ISA Server 2006 firewall computer. However, for any but the smallest of organizations, the administrative overhead and the security risks of mirroring user accounts can be unacceptably high.

SSL certificate authentication is currently not available for browser to Web Proxy server connections. You can use SSL certificate authentication when configuring Web Proxy chaining. In this setup, a downstream Web Proxy server forwards Web requests to an upstream Web Proxy server. The downstream ISA Server 2006 Web Proxy server can authenticate with the upstream server by presenting a client certificate to the upstream ISA Server 2006 Web Proxy server. This provides a very secure Web Proxy chaining configuration that is not easily attainable with other Web Proxy solutions.

Users are prompted for user name and password when only **Basic** authentication is used. If the Web Proxy client and the ISA Server 2006 firewall are not members of the same domain, or if RADIUS authentication is not used, then Basic authentication is the best solution.

A new feature included with ISA Server 2006 is the ability to use RADIUS for Web Proxy authentication. When RADIUS is enabled as an authentication protocol for Web Proxy clients, the ISA Server 2006 firewall does not need to be a member of the user domain. This provides a slightly higher level of security because an attacker who may take control of the ISA Server 2006 firewall will not be able to leverage domain credentials to attack users on the protected network behind the ISA Server 2006 firewall. When a domain user tries to authenticate for a Web connection, the ISA Server 2006 firewall that is not a member of the user domain forwards the authentication request to a RADIUS server on the Internal network. The RADIUS server forwards the request to an authentication server and then returns the response to the ISA Server 2006 firewall.

Note that when you configure the ISA Server 2006 firewall to support RADIUS authentication, the ISA Server 2006 firewall becomes a RADIUS client. You can use any RADIUS server, including Microsoft's RADIUS implementation, the Internet Authentication Server (IAS).

RADIUS authentication does require that you create a RADIUS server on the Internal network and configure the Web Proxy listener for the Web Proxy client's network to use the RADIUS server. In addition, there must be an Access Rule that allows the ISA Server 2006 firewall to communicate with the RADIUS server using the RADIUS protocol. There is a default firewall System Policy that allows RADIUS messages to the Internal network. If your RADIUS server is not located on the Internal network, you will need to configure the firewall System Policy to allow the RADIUS protocol to the RADIUS server at its alternate location.

We will go through the procedures required to create the RADIUS server and configure the RADIUS client later in this chapter. However, in order to support Web Proxy clients, you will need to perform the following:

- Configure the Outgoing Web Requests listener to use RADIUS authentication

- Configure the user account for Remote Access Permission or configure Remote Access Policy to enable access

- Configure the Remote Access Policy to support PAP authentication

Do the following to configure the Web Proxy listener on the Web Proxy client's Network to use RADIUS:

1. In the **Microsoft Internet Security and Acceleration Server 2006** management console, expand the server name and then expand the **Configuration** node. Click on the **Networks** node and right-click on the **Internal** network (assuming that the Web Proxy clients are located on the Internal network, you would choose the appropriate network in your own configuration). Click **Properties**.

2. In the **Internal Properties** dialog box, click the **Web Proxy** tab.

3. On the **Web Proxy** tab, click the **Authentication** button.

4. In the **Authentication** dialog box, remove the checkmarks from the all the other check boxes. You will see dialog boxes informing you that there are no authentication methods available. Confirm that you have only the **RADIUS** option selected (see Figure 17.21).

Figure 17.21 The Authentication Dialog Box

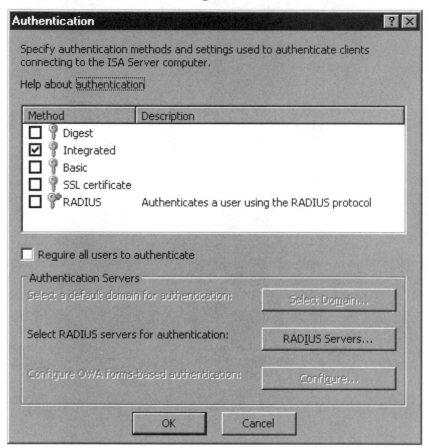

5. Click **RADIUS Servers**.

6. In the **Add RADIUS Server** dialog box, shown in Figure 17.22, enter a name or IP address for the RADIUS server in the **Server name** text box. If you enter a name, make sure that it's a fully-qualified domain name and that the ISA Server 2006 firewall can resolve that name to the correct IP address. Enter a description for the server in the **Server description** text box. Leave the **Port** and **Time-out (seconds)** values at their defaults unless you have a reason to change them. Confirm that there is a checkmark in the **Always use message authenticator** check box.

Figure 17.22 The Add RADIUS Server Dialog Box

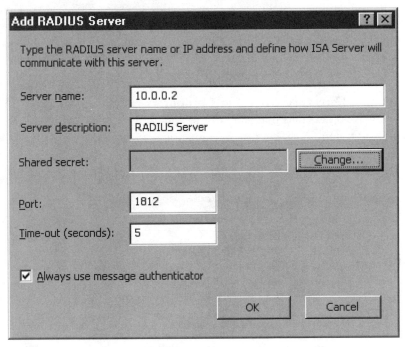

7. Click **Change**.

8. In the **Shared Secret** dialog box, enter and confirm a password in the **New secret** and **Confirm new secret** text boxes. This password is used to authenticate the RADIUS server and RADIUS client. Make sure that this is the same password you used when you configured the RADIUS client on the RADIUS server for the Internal network. Click **OK**. (NOTE: The RADIUS password should be long and complex; an ideal RADIUS password is one that is 24 characters and is created with a password generator application.)

9. Click **OK** in the **Add RADIUS Server** dialog box.

10. The RADIUS server entry now appears on the list. Note that you can create multipleRADIUS servers and they will be queried in the order listed.

11. Click **OK** in the **Authentication** dialog box.

12. Click **Apply** and **OK** in the **Internal Properties** dialog box.

13. Click **Apply** to save the changes and update the firewall policy.

14. Click **OK** in the **Apply New Configuration** dialog box.

The next step is to configure the user account to enable dial-in access. Note that this procedure is *not* required if the domain is in Windows 2000 or Windows Server 2003 Native Mode. The reason for this is that you can control access policy via Remote Access Policy, and the default setting for accounts controls access via Remote Access Policy when the domain is in Native Mode. For this reason, we highly recommend that you configure your Windows domains in Native Mode so that you do not need to enable each individual user account for dial-in access.

1. In the **Active Directory Users and Computers** console on a domain controller that contains the user accounts that you want to authenticate with Web Proxy RADIUS authentication, double-click on the account you want to allow to use RADIUS authentication.

2. In the user's **Properties** dialog box, click the **Dial-in** tab.

3. On the **Dial-in** tab, select the **Allow access** option.

4. Click **Apply**, and then click **OK**.

The user account is now able to use RADIUS for Web Proxy authentication.

The last step is to configure the Remote Access Policy so that PAP authentication is supported for Web Proxy client RADIUS authentication. It's important to note that PAP authentication is not secure, and you should use some method to protect the credentials as they as pass between the ISA Server 2006 firewall and the RADIUS server. The preferred method of protecting credentials is to use an IPSec transport mode connection.

Do the following to configure the Remote Access Policy:

1. At the IAS server on the Internal network, click **Start**, and point to **Administrative Tools**. Click **Internet Authentication Services**.

2. In the **Internet Authentication Services** console, click the **Remote Access Policies** node in the left pane of the console.

3. On the **Remote Access Policies** node, note that there are two Remote Access Policies in the right pane of the console. The first policy applies only to RAS connections from dial-up and VPN clients. The second policy, **Connections to other access servers** is the one used by the Web Proxy clients. Double-click **Connection to other access servers**.

4. In the **Connections to other access servers Properties** dialog box, click **Edit Profile**.

5. In the **Edit Dial-in Profile** dialog box, click the **Authentication** tab.

6. On the **Authentication** tab, put a checkmark in the **Unencrypted authentication (PAP, SPAP)** check box.

7. Click **Apply** and **OK**.

8. In the **Connections to other access servers Properties** dialog box (see Figure 17.23), confirm that the condition **Windows-Groups matches...** entry is included. This includes the groups of users who you want to have access to the Web Proxy service via RADIUS authentication. Use the **Add** button to add the group you want to have access. Also, confirm that the **Grant remote access permission** option is selected.

Figure 17.23 The Connections to other Access Servers Properties Dialog Box

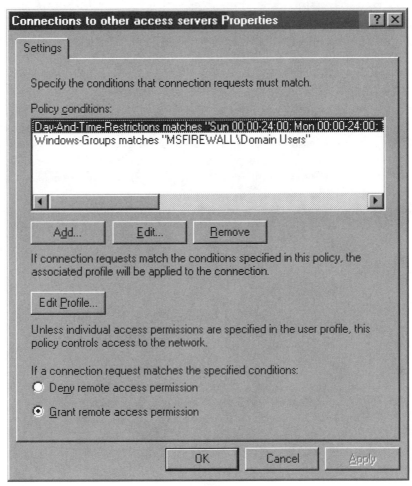

9. Click **Apply** and **OK** in the **Connections to other access server Properties** dialog box.

The policy will take effect immediately; you do not need to restart any equipment.

Allows you to Limit the Number of Outbound Web Proxy Client Connections

The number of Web Proxy client connections can be limited to a number that you specify. This can be helpful when you have limited bandwidth or you want to make sure that only a certain percentage of your users have access to the Internet at any single point in time.

You can access the configuration interface for the number of simultaneous Web Proxy client connections in the **Properties** dialog box of the network from which the Web Proxy clients access the Web. In the **Microsoft Internet Security and Acceleration Server 2004** management console, expand the server name, and then expand the **Configuration** node. Click the **Networks** node in the left pane of the console, and right-click the network in the **Details** pane. Click the **Properties** command.

In the network's **Properties** dialog box, click the **Web Proxy** tab. On the **Web Proxy** tab, click **Advanced**. In the **Advanced Settings** dialog box depicted in Figure 17.24, you can chose from the **Unlimited** and the **Maximum** options. When you select the **Maximum** option, you can enter a value for the maximum number of simultaneous connections. This also a **Connection timeout (seconds)** value that you can customize. The default value is **120** seconds. You can shorten or extend this value depending on your requirements. If you find that idle connections are using up the number of allowed simultaneous connections, you can shorten the timeout value. If you find that users complain about Web sessions being disconnected prematurely, you can extend the timeout value.

Figure 17.24 Advanced Settings

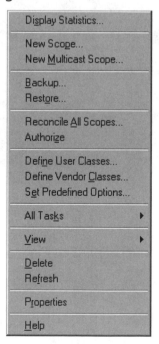

Supports Web Proxy Chaining, Which Can Further Speed Up Internet Access

Web Proxy chaining allows you to connect ISA Server 2006 and ISA Server 2000 firewall and Web Proxy servers to each other. The ISA Server firewall Web Proxy servers represent a chain, where the Web Proxy server farthest away from the centralized Internet access point represents the most "downstream" ISA Server Web Proxy and firewall server, and the ISA Server firewall and Web Proxy server closest to the centralized Internet connection is the most "upstream" ISA Server firewall Web Proxy server.

There are a number of scenarios where Web Proxy chaining can be configured. These scenarios include:

- Branch offices connecting to a main office ISA Server 2006 Web Proxy firewall server

- Campus networks with multiple workgroup/departmental LANs that connect to upstream ISA Server 2006 firewall Web Proxy servers upstream on a campus backbone or services network

- Back-to-back ISA Server 2006 firewall configurations where the downstream ISA Server 2006 firewall uses Web Proxy chaining to forward corporate network Web Proxy requests to the front-end ISA Server 2006 firewall. This configuration adds to the already-strong security of the back-to-back ISA Server 2006 firewall configuration.

ISA Server 2006 Multiple Client Type Configuration

A common point of confusion among ISA Server 2006 firewall administrators is whether or not a machine can be configured as multiple ISA Server 2006 client types. Many ISA firewall administrators are under the impression that a single machine cannot be configured as a Web Proxy, Firewall, and SecureNAT client. This is a misconception. It is possible and sometimes preferred that a single computer be configured as all three types of ISA client.

The truth is that a single machine cannot be configured to *act* as both a Firewall client and a SecureNAT client. The reason for this is when a machine is configured as a Firewall client, all Winsock TCP and UDP communications are intercepted by the Firewall client software. Therefore, the SecureNAT client configuration does *not* have access to these communications. For non-Winsock TCP and UDP communications, and for all other non-TCP/UDP communications, the SecureNAT client handles the requests. For example, if the machine is configured as both a SecureNAT and Firewall client, the SecureNAT client configuration handles all ping, tracert and PPTP connections. Ping and tracert use ICMP, and PPTP uses GRE. Neither ICMP nor GRE uses TCP or UDP as a transport.

Table 17.7 describes the behavior of machines that are configured as multiple client types.

Table 17.7 Application Behavior on Multiple Client Configuration Machines

ISA Server 2006 Client Configuration	Application Behavior
SecureNAT and Firewall Client	Firewall client handles all TCP and UDP communications from Winsock applications. SecureNAT client handles all TCP/UDP communications from non-Winsock applications and all non-TCP/UDP communications
SecureNAT and Web Proxy Client	Web Proxy client handles all HTTP/HTTPS/FTP download communications from the Web Proxy client application. From non-Web Proxy client applications, the SecureNAT client handles the HTTP/HTTP/FTP connections (both download and upload). If the Web Proxy client-configured browser is not able to use the Web Proxy service to access FTP resources, the client will "fall back" on the SecureNAT client configuration. All other protocols are handled by the SecureNAT client configuration.
Firewall and Web Proxy Client	The Web Proxy client configuration handles all HTTP/HTTPS/FTP download from Web Proxy client configured applications. The Firewall client handles all other Winsock TCP and UDP communications, including HTTP/HTTPS/FTP download and upload from applications not configured as Web Proxy clients. FTP download from Web Proxy clients can fall back on Firewall client configuration. No access to non-TCP/UDP protocols and no access to TCP and UDP protocols for non-Winsock applications.
SecureNAT, Firewall, and Web Proxy Client	Access to HTTP/HTTPS/FTP download via Web Proxy client configuration for applications configured as Web Proxy clients. Fall back to Firewall client configuration for FTP download if Web Proxy client configuration does not support connection. All TCP/UDP communications from Winsock applications handled by Firewall client. All other communications handled by SecureNAT client configuration.

Deciding on an ISA Server 2006 Client Type

The ISA Server 2006 client type you roll out depends on the level of functionality and level of security you require. Table 17.8 rates the various ISA Server 2006 clients, based on level of functionality, level of security, ease of deployment and management, and operating system compatibility.

Table 17.8 Grading Security, Functionality, Ease and Compatibility of ISA Server 2006 Client Types

Level of Functionality	Level of Security	Ease of Deployment and Management	Operating System Compatibility
Firewall client	Firewall client	SecureNAT client	SecureNAT client
SecureNAT client	Web Proxy client	Web Proxy client	Web Proxy client
Web Proxy	SecureNAT client	Firewall Client	Firewall client

Table 17.9 describes a number of parameters you should consider when selecting the ISA Server 2006 client type to use in your environment.

Table 17.9 Choosing the Appropriate ISA Server 2006 Client Type

You Require:	Suggested ISA Server 2006 Client type:
No software deployment to network clients.	The SecureNAT and Web Proxy client. TheSecureNAT client does not require software installation and only requires that you set the appropriate default gateway address. The Web Proxy client does not require client software installation; you only need to configure the Web Proxy applications to use the firewall as their Web Proxy server.
Only Web protocols: HTTP, HTTPS and FTP download through a Web browser and other Web Proxy-aware applications and Web caching.	Web Proxy client or SecureNAT client. Both of these clients will be able to benefit from the Web Proxy cache on the ISA Server 2006 firewall. The advantage to using the Web Proxy client over the SecureNAT client in this scenario is that the Web Proxy client will send user information to the ISA Server 2006 firewall and allow you to enforce strong user/group-based access control over what sites and content users access via the Web.
Authentication before allowing access. User name included in logs.	Firewall or Web Proxy client. The Web Proxy client enables you to enforce user/group-based strong access control over HTTP/HTTPS/FTP download connections via Web Proxy client applications. The Firewall client allows strong user/group-based access controls over all Winsock applications using TCP and UDP protocols. Whenever a user authenticates with the ISA Server 2006 firewall, that user's name is included in the logs.
Servers published to the Internet using Web or Server Publishing Rules	SecureNAT or "non-ISA Server 2006 client". The published server must be configured as a SecureNAT client if the original Internet client IP address is retained in the communication reaching the published server. This is the default configuration for Server Publishing Rules. For Web Publishing Rules, the default is to replace the original

Continued

Table 17.9 Continued

You Require:	Suggested ISA Server 2006 Client type:
	client IP address with the IP address of the ISA Server 2006 firewall's Internal interface (the interface that lies on the same Network as the published server). When the original source IP address is replaced with the ISA Server 2006 firewall's IP address, the published server only needs to know the route to the Internal IP address of the ISA Server 2006 firewall that forwarded the request. Note that for both Web and Server Publishing Rules you have the option to preserve the original client IP address.
Support for non-Windows operating systems	SecureNAT and Web Proxy clients. All operating systems support the SecureNAT client configuration because the SecureNAT client only requires the appropriate default gateway address configuration. All operating systems running applications that support Web Proxy client configuration can connect to the ISA Server 2006 firewall via the Web Proxy client configuration.
Support for Internet games	Firewall client. Most Internet games require multiple primary and secondary connections. Only the Firewall client supports complex protocols that require secondary connections (unless there is an application filter installed on the ISA Server 2006 firewall to support that specific application).
Support for Voice/Video applications	Voice and video applications that do not require Session Initiation Protocol (SIP) generally require secondary connections (ISA Server 2006 does not support SIP signaling). Only the Firewall client supports secondary connections without the aid of an application filter.

Automating ISA Server 2006 Client Provisioning

There are several methods available for automating the Web Proxy and Firewall client configurations. These include:

- Configuring DHCP Servers to Support Web Proxy and Firewall Client Autodiscovery

- Configuring DNS Servers to Support Web Proxy and Firewall Client Autodiscovery

- Automating Web Proxy Client Configuration with Group Policy

- Automating Web Proxy Client Configuration with Internet Explorer Administration Kit (IEAK)

The following sections discuss how to automate the configuration of Web Proxy and Firewall clients using the Web Proxy AutoDiscovery (WPAD) protocol and Active Directory Group Policy. We will not go into the details of how to use the Internet Explorer Administration Kit to automate Web proxy client configuration.

Note that there are two primary methods for supporting Autodiscovery for Web Proxy and Firewall clients: DNS and DHCP. Table 17.10 provides information that will help you decide which method best fits your needs.

Table 17.10 DNS and DHCP Support for Web Proxy and Firewall Client Autodiscovery

DHCP	DNS
Client must be DHCP client	Client must be able to resolve DNS names on the Internal network
Internet Explorer 5.0 and required	Internet Explorer 5.0 and above required
Must be able to send DHCPINFORM queries (Windows 2000, Windows XP, Windows Vista and Windows Server 2003 only)	Must be able to correctly qualify the unqualified name "WPAD" with a domain name to yield a FQDN that resolves to the ISA Server 2006 firewall's Internal IP address
User must be logged on as local administrator	Each domain must be configured with its own WPAD entry
ISA Server 2006 firewall can publish autodiscovery information on any available port	ISA Server 2006 firewall must publish autodiscovery information on TCP port 80
Each DHCP Server must be configured with a WPAD entry	Each DNS server must be configured with a WPAD entry. Branch offices may require a custom configuration to prevent Branch office clients from using the WPAD entry pointing to ISA Server 2006 firewalls at the Main office.

Configuring DHCP Servers to Support Web Proxy and Firewall Client Autodiscovery

DHCP clients can obtain autoconfiguration information from the ISA Server 2006 firewall computer by using DHCP Inform messages. The Firewall client and Web browser software can issue DHCP Inform messages to query a DHCP server for the address of a machine containing the autoconfiguration information. The DHCP server returns the address of the machine containing the autoconfiguration information, and the Firewall client or Web browser software requests autoconfiguration from the addresses returned by the DHCP server.

The DHCP server uses a special DHCP option to provide this information. In this section on configuring Web Proxy and Firewall clients to use DHCP to obtain autoconfiguration information via WPAD, we will discuss the following steps:

■ Installing the DHCP server

■ Creating the DHCP scope

■ Creating the DHCP 252 scope option

■ Configuring the client as a DHCP client

■ Configuring the client browser to use autodiscovery

■ Configuring the ISA Server 2006 firewall to publish autodiscovery information

■ Making the connection

Install the DHCP Server

The first step is to install the DHCP server. Use the **Add/Remove Programs** applet in the **Control Panel** to install the DHCP Server service.

Create the DHCP scope

A DHCP scope is a collection of IP addresses that the DHCP server can use to assign to DHCP clients on the network. In addition, a DHCP scope can include additional TCP/IP settings to be assigned to clients, which are referred to as *DHCP options*. DHCP options can assign various TCP/IP settings such as a DNS server address, WINS server address, and primary domain name to DHCP clients.

Do the following on the DHCP server to enable the DHCP server and create the DHCP scope:

1. Click **Start**, and then select **Administrative Tools**. Click **DHCP**.

2. In the **DHCP** console, right click on your server name in the left pane of the console. Click on the **Authorize** command.

3. Click **Refresh** in the button bar of the console. You will notice that the icon to the left of the server name changes from a red, down-pointing arrow to a green, up-pointing arrow.

4. Right-click the server name in the left pane of the console again, and click the **New Scope** command.

5. Click **Next** on the **Welcome to the New Scope Wizard** page.

6. Enter a name for the scope on the **Scope Name** page. This name is descriptive only and does not affect the functionality of the scope. You can also enter a **Description** in the description box, if you wish. Click **Next**.

7. Enter a range of IP addresses that can be assigned to DHCP clients on the **IP Address Range** page. Enter the first address in the range into the **Start IP address** range text box and the last IP address in the range in the **End IP address** text box. Enter the subnet mask for your IP address range in the **Subnet mask** text box.

8. In the example in Figure 17.25, the Internal network is on network ID 10.0.2/24. We do not want to assign all the IP addresses on the network ID to the DHCP scope, just a selection of them. So in this example, we enter **10.0.2.100** as the **Start IP address** and **10.0.2.150** as the end IP address and use a **24**-bit subnet mask. Note that on production networks, it is often better to assign the entire network ID to the IP address range used in the scope. You can then create *exceptions* for hosts on the network that have statically-assigned IP addresses that are contained in the scope. This allows you to centrally manage IP address assignment and configuration using DHCP. Click **Next**.

Figure 17.25 Configuring the DHCP Scope IP Address Range

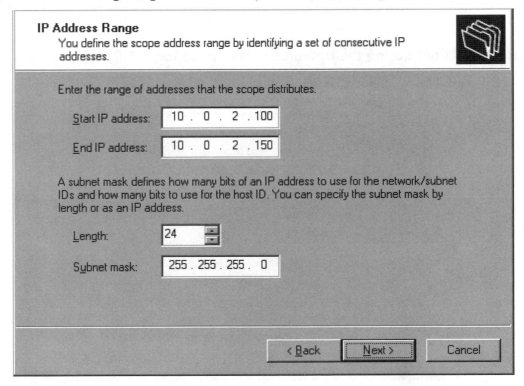

9. Do not enter any exclusions in the **Add Exclusions** dialog box. Click **Next**.

10. Accept the default settings on the **Lease Duration** page (8 days, 0 hours and 0 minutes), and click **Next**.

11. On the **Configure DHCP Options** page, select **Yes, I want to configure these options now,** and click **Next**.

12. Do not enter anything on the **Router (Default Gateway)** page. Note that if we were using SecureNAT clients on the network, we would enter the IP address of the Internal interface for the ISA Server 2006 firewall on this page. However, with the current scenario, we want to test *only* the Web Proxy and Firewall client configurations. Click **Next**.

13. On the **Domain Name and DNS Servers** page, enter the **primary domain name** you want to assign to DHCP clients, and the **DNS server address** you want the DHCP clients to use.

14. The **primary domain name** is a critical setting for your Firewall and Web Proxy clients. In order for autodiscovery to work correctly for Firewall and Web Proxy clients, these clients must be able to correctly fully qualify the unqualified name WPAD. We will discuss this issue in more detail later. In this example, enter **msfirewall.org** in the **Parent domain** text box (see Figure 17.26). This will assign the DHCP clients the primary domain name msfirewall.org, which will be appended to unqualified names. Enter the IP address of the DNS server in the **IP address** text box. In this example, the IP address of the DNS server is **10.0.2.2**. Click **Add** after entering the IP address. Click **Next**.

Figure 17.26 Configuring the Default Domain Name for DHCP Clients

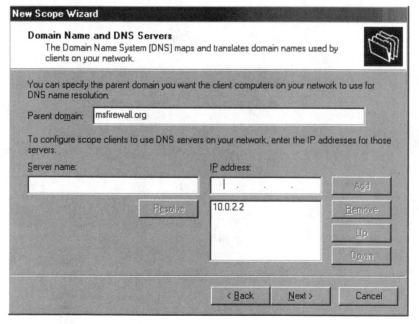

15. Do not enter a WINS server address on the **WINS Servers** page. In this example, we do not use a WINS server. However, WINS servers are very useful in VPN server environments if you wish your VPN clients to be able to browse the campus network using **My Network Places** or **Network Neighborhood** application. Click **Next**.

16. On the **Activate Scope** page, select **Yes, I want to activate this scope now**, and click **Next**.

17. Click **Finish** on the **Completing the New Scope Wizard** page.

18. In the right pane of the **DHCP** console, you see the two DHCP options you created in the Wizard, as seen in Figure 17.27.

Figure 17.27 Viewing the Scope Options

Scope Options		
Option Name	Vendor	Value
006 DNS Servers	Standard	10.0.2.2
015 DNS Domain Name	Standard	msfirewall.org

The next step is to create a custom DHCP option that will allow DHCP clients to autodiscover Web Proxy and Firewall client settings.

Create the DHCP 252 Scope Option and Add It to the Scope

The DHCP scope option number 252 can be used to automatically configure Web Proxy and Firewall clients. The Web Proxy or Firewall client must be configured as a DHCP client, and the logged-on user must be a member of the local administrators group or Power users group (for Windows 2000). On Windows XP systems, the Network Configuration Operators group also has permission to issue DHCP queries (DHCPINFORM messages).

Do the following at the DHCP server to create the custom DHCP option:

1. Open the **DHCP** console from the **Administrative Tools** menu and right-click your server name in the left pane of the console. Click the **Set Predefined Options** command, shown in Figure 17.28.

Figure 17.28 Selecting the Set Predefined Options Command

Display Statistics...

New Scope...
New Multicast Scope...

Backup...
Restore...

Reconcile All Scopes...
Authorize

Define User Classes...
Define Vendor Classes...
Set Predefined Options...

All Tasks ▶

View ▶

Delete
Refresh

Properties

Help

2. In the **Predefined Options and Values** dialog box (Figure 17.29), click **Add**.

Figure 17.29 The Predefined Options and Values Dialog Box

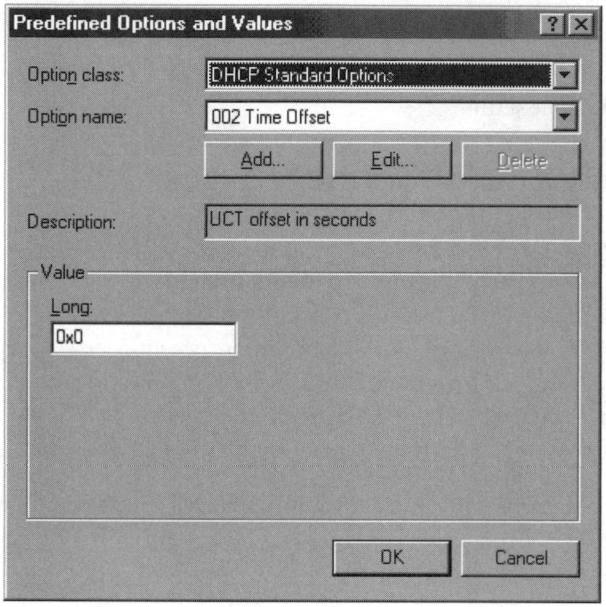

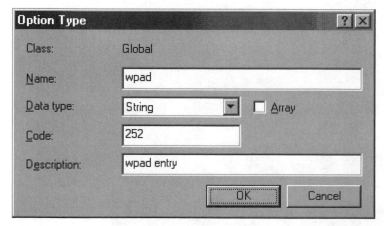

3. In the **Option Type** dialog box (Figure 17.30), enter the following information:
    Name: wpad
    Data type: String
    Code: 252
    Description: wpad entry
    Click **OK**.

Figure 17.30 The Option Type Dialog Box

4. In the **Value** frame, enter the URL to the ISA Server 2006 firewall in the **String** text box. The format for this value is:

    http://ISAServername:Autodiscovery Port Number/wpad.dat

    The default autodiscovery port number is TCP 80. You can customize this value in the **ISA Management** console. We will cover this subject in more detail later.

    As shown in Figure 17.31, enter the following into the **String** text box:

    http://isa2.msfirewall.org:80/wpad.dat

    Make sure to enter wpad.dat in all *lower case* letters. For more information on this problem, please refer to KB article **"Automatically Detect Settings" Does Not Work if You Configure DHCP Option 252** at http://support.microsoft.com/default. aspx?scid=kb;en-us;307502

    Click **OK**.

Figure 17.31 Predefined Options and Values Dialog Box

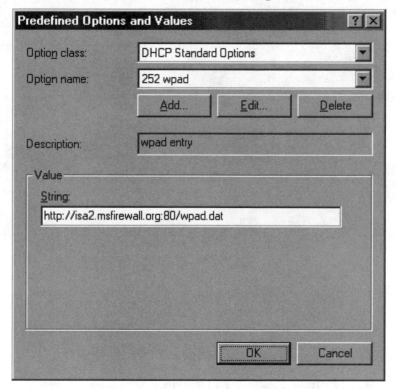

5. Right click the **Scope Options** node in the left pane of the console, and click the **Configure Options** command.

6. In the **Scope Options** dialog box (Figure 17.32), scroll through the list of **Available Options** and put a checkmark in the **252 wpad** check box. Click **Apply** and **OK**.

Figure 17.32 The Scope Options Dialog Box

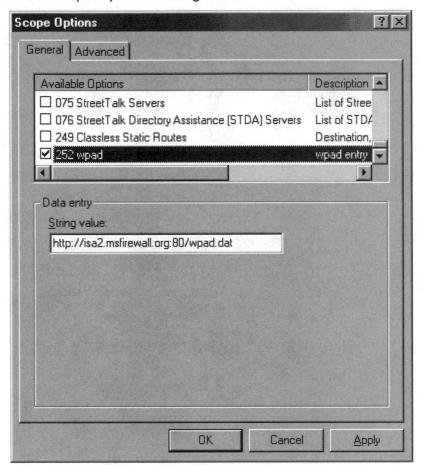

7. The **252 wpad** entry now appears in the right pane of the console under the list of **Scope Options**.

8 Close the **DHCP** console.

The next step is to configure the client computer as a DHCP client.

Configure the Client as a DHCP Client

In order to use DHCP to obtain autodiscovery information for Web Proxy and Firewall clients, the client computer must be configured as a DHCP client.

Do the following on the client machine to configure it as a DHCP client:

1. Right click **My Network Places** on the desktop, and click the **Properties** command.

2. Right click the **Local Area Connection** entry in the **Network and Dial-up Connections** window and click the **Properties** command.

3. In the **Local Area Connection Properties** dialog box, click the **Internet Protocol (TCP/IP)** entry and click **Properties**.

4. In the **Internet Protocol (TCP/IP) Properties** dialog box, select **Obtain an IP address automatically** and **Obtain DNS server address automatically**. Click **OK**.

5. Click **OK** in the **Local Area Connection Properties** dialog box.

6. Close the **Network and Dial-up Connections** window.

Now you're ready to configure the browser to use autodiscovery for automatically discovering its Web Proxy client settings.

Configure the Client Browser to Use DCHP for Autodiscovery

The browser must be configured to use autodiscovery before it can use the DHCP server option 252 to automatically configure itself. This is the default setting for Internet Explorer 6.0, but the default setting may have been changed at some time during the life of the browser on a particular machine. In the following example, we manually configure the browser to use autodiscovery to autoconfigure itself. We will discuss methods you can use to automatically set this option later.

Do the following on the Web Proxy client computer:

1. Right click on the **Internet Explorer** icon on the desktop and click **Properties**.

2. In the **Internet Properties** dialog box, click the **Connections** tab. Click the **LAN Settings** button.

3. In the **Local Area Network (LAN) Settings** dialog box, put a checkmark in the **Automatically detect settings** check box. Click **OK**.

4. Click **OK** in the **Internet Properties** dialog box.

ISA Server 2006 firewall must be configured to publish autodiscovery information before the Web Proxy client can obtain configuration information. That's the next step.

Configure the ISA Server 2006 Firewall to Publish Autodiscovery Information

All the settings required for the Web browser to configure itself are contained on the ISA Server 2006 firewall computer. By default, this option is disabled. You can enable publishing of autodiscovery information on the ISA Server 2006 firewall computer so that the Web Proxy client can obtain autoconfiguration settings.

Do the following on the ISA Server 2006 firewall computer to enable it to provide autoconfiguration information to Web Proxy and Firewall autodiscovery clients:

1. At this ISA Server 2006 firewall computer, open the **Microsoft Internet Security and Acceleration Server 2004** management console. Expand the server name in the left pane of the console, and then expand the **Configuration** node. Click the **Networks** node.

2. On the **Networks** node, click the **Networks** tab in the **Details** pane.

3. Right-click the **Internal** network on the **Networks** tab, and click **Properties** (see Figure 17.33).

Figure 17.33 Accessing the Internal Network Properties Dialog Box

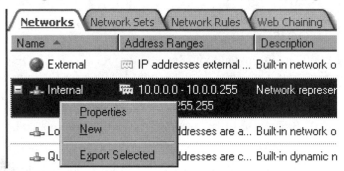

4. In the **Internal Properties** dialog box, put a checkmark in the **Publish automatic discovery information** check box. In the **Use this port for automatic discovery request** text box, leave the default **port 80** as it is.

5. Click **Apply** and **OK**.

6. Click **Apply** to save the changes and update the firewall policy.

7. Click **OK** in the **Apply New Configuration** dialog box.

Making the Connection

All the components are now in place for the Web browser to automatically connect to the ISA Server 2006 firewall's Web Proxy service using autodiscovery.

Do the following on the Web Proxy client computer:

1. Open **Internet Explorer** and enter the URL for the Microsoft ISA Server site at **www.microsoft.com/isaserver**

2. A Network Monitor trace shows the DHCP Inform messages sent by the Web Proxy client. The Web Proxy client uses the DHCP Inform messages, such as the one shown in Figure 17.34 to obtain the autodiscovery address contained in the DHCP option 252 entry.

Figure 17.34 Viewing the DHCPINFORM Request

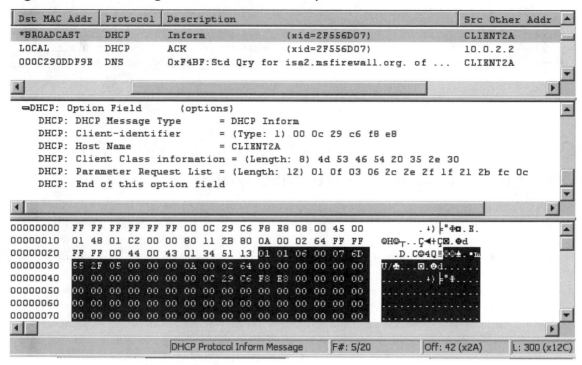

3. In Figure 17.35, you can see the ACK response to the Web Proxy client's DHCP inform message. In the bottom pane of the Network Monitor console, you can see that the DHCP server has returned the address you configured in the DHCP option 252 entry.

Figure 17.35 Viewing the contents of the DHCPINFORM request

```
000000F0  00 00 00 00 00 00 00 00 00 00 00 00 00 00 00 00   ................
00000100  00 00 00 00 00 00 00 00 00 00 00 00 00 00 00 00   ................
00000110  00 00 00 00 00 00 63 82 53 63 35 01 05 36 04 0A   ......céSc5◘6+▧
00000120  00 02 02 01 04 FF FF FF 00 0F 0F 6D 73 66 69 72   .◙◙◙+   .◘◘msfir
00000130  65 77 61 6C 6C 2E 6F 72 67 00 06 04 0A 00 02 02   ewall.org.♦+▧.◘◘
00000140  FC 27 68 74 74 70 3A 2F 2F 69 73 61 32 2E 6D 73   ∩'http://isa2.ms
00000150  66 69 72 65 77 61 6C 6C 2E 6F 72 67 3A 38 30 2F   firewall.org:80/
00000160  77 70 61 64 2E 64 61 74 00 FF                     wpad.dat.
```

4. After the Web Proxy client receives the address of the ISA Server 2006 containing the autodiscovery settings, the next step is for it to resolve the name of the ISA Server 2006 firewall to its Internal IP address. Name resolution is critical for multiple aspects of ISA Server 2006 functioning, and this is another example of this fact. You can see in the Network Monitor (Figure 17.36) that the Web Proxy client has issued a query for isa2.msfirewall.org, which was the URL contained in the DHCP 252 option.

Figure 17.36 Viewing the WPAD DNS Query

Dst MAC Addr	Protocol	Description		Src Other Addr
*BROADCAST	DHCP	Inform	(xid=2F556D07)	CLIENT2A
LOCAL	DHCP	ACK	(xid=2F556D07)	10.0.2.2
000C290DDF9E	DNS	0xF4BF:Std Qry for isa2.msfirewall.org. of ...		CLIENT2A

Configuring DNS Servers to Support Web Proxy and Firewall Client Autodiscovery

Another method that can be used to deliver autodiscovery information to Web Proxy and Firewall clients is DNS. You can create a wpad alias entry in DNS and allow browser clients to use this information to automatically configure themselves. This is in contrast to the situation we saw with the DHCP method, where the logged-on user needed to be a member of a specific group in the Windows operating system.

Name resolution is a pivotal component to making this method of Web Proxy and Firewall client autodiscovery work correctly. In this case, the client operating system must be able to correctly fully qualify the name *wpad*. The reason for this is that the Web Proxy and Firewall client only knows that it needs to resolve the name wpad; it does not know what specific domain name it should append to the query to resolve the name wpad. We will cover this issue in detail later.

We will detail the following steps to enable DNS to provide autodiscovery information to Web Proxy and Firewall clients:

- Creating the wpad entry in DNS
- Configuring the client to use the fully-qualified wpad alias
- Configuring the client browser to use autodiscovery
- Making the connection

Creating the wpad Entry in DNS

The first step is to create a wpad alias entry in DNS. This alias points to a Host (A) record for the ISA Server 2006 firewall, which resolves the name of the ISA Server 2006 firewall to the Internal IP address of the firewall. This Host (A) record must be created before you create the CNAME alias entry. If you enable automatic registration in DNS, the ISA Server 2006 firewall's entry will already be entered into DNS. If you have not enabled automatic registration, you will need to create the Host (A) record for the ISA Server 2006 firewall manually. In the following example, the ISA Server 2006 firewall has automatically registered itself with DNS.

Do the following on the DNS server of the domain controller on the Internal network:

1. Click **Start** and select **Administrative Tools**. Click the **DNS** entry. In the **DNS** management console shown in Figure 17.37, right-click on the forward lookup zone for your domain, and click the **New Alias (CNAME)** command.

Figure 17.37 Selecting the New Alias (CNAME) Command

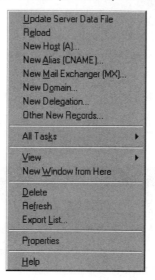

2. In the **New Resource Record** dialog box (Figure 17.38), enter **wpad** in the **Alias name** (uses parent domain if left blank) text box. Click the **Browse** button.

Figure 17.38 The New Resource Record Dialog Box

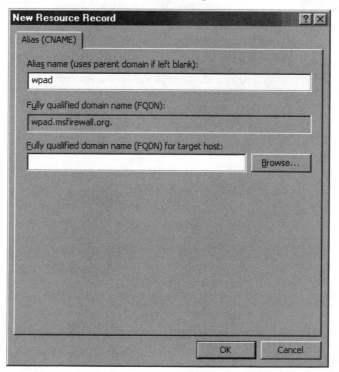

3. In the **Browse** dialog box, double-click on your server name in the **Records** list.

4. In the **Browse** dialog box, double-click on the **Forward Lookup Zone** entry in the **Records** frame.

5. In the **Browse** dialog box, double-click on the name of your forward lookup zone in the **Records** frame.

6. In the **Browse** dialog box, select the name of the ISA Server 2006 firewall in the **Records** frame. Click **OK**.

Figure 17.39 New Resource Dialog Box

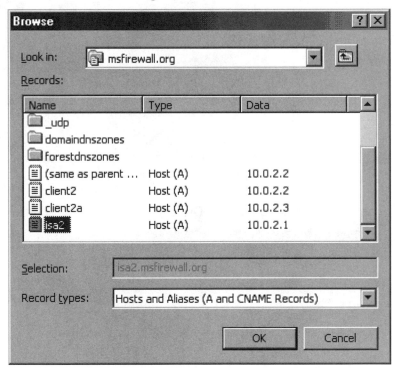

7. Click **OK** in the **New Resource Record** dialog box.

8. The **CNAME (alias)** entry appears in the right pane of the **DNS** management console.

Figure 17.40 Viewing the DNS WPAD Alias

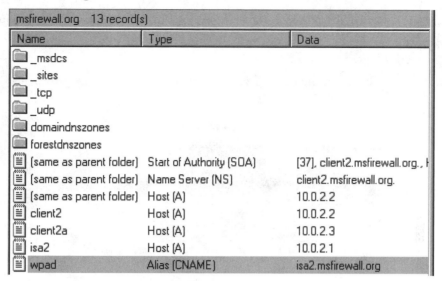

9. Close the **DNS Management** console.

Configure the Client to Use the Fully-Qualified wpad Alias

The Web Proxy and Firewall client needs to be able to correctly resolve the name *wpad*. The Web Proxy and Firewall client configurations are *not aware of the domain containing the wpad alias*. The Web Proxy and Firewall client operating system must be able to provide this information to the Web Proxy and Firewall client.

DNS queries must be *fully qualified* before the query is sent to the DNS server. A fully-qualified request contains a host name and a domain name. The Web Proxy and Firewall client only know the *host name* portion. The Web Proxy and Firewall client operating system must be able to provide the correct domain name, which it appends to the *wpad* host name, before it can send a DNS query to the DNS server.

There are a number of methods you can use to provide a domain name that is appended to the *wpad* name before the query is sent to the client operating system's DNS server. Two popular methods for doing this are:

- Using DHCP to assign a primary domain name
- Configuring a primary domain name in the client operating system's network identification dialog box.

We will detail these two methods in the following steps:

1. Right-click **My Computer** on the desktop, and click the **Properties** command.

2. In the **System Properties** dialog box, click the **Network Identification** tab. Click the **Properties** button.

3. In the **Identification Changes** dialog box (see Figure 17.41), click **More**.

Figure 17.41 The Identification Changes Dialog Box

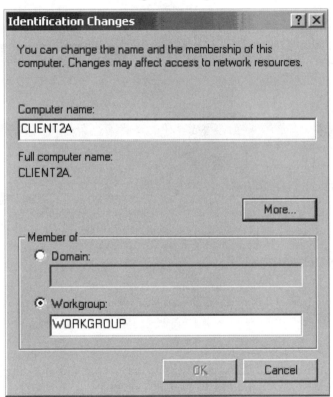

4. In the **DNS Suffix and NetBIOS Computer Name** dialog box shown in Figure 17.42, enter the domain name that contains your wpad entry in the **Primary DNS suffix of this computer** text box. This is the domain name that the operating system will append to the wpad name before sending the DNS query to the DNS server. By default, the primary domain name is the same as the domain name to which the machine belongs. If the machine is not a member of a domain, this text box will be empty. Note **Change primary DNS suffix when domain membership changes** is enabled by default. In the current example, the machine is not a member of a domain. Cancel out of each of the dialog boxes so that you do not configure a primary domain name at this time.

Figure 17.42 The DNS Suffix and NetBIOS Computer Name Dialog Box

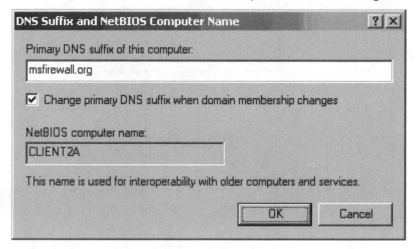

5.   Another way to assign a machine a primary domain name is to use DHCP. A DHCP server can be configured to supply DHCP clients a primary domain name by configuring a DHCP scope option. We did this earlier when we created a scope on the DHCP server using the DHCP scope wizard. In the current example, the **DNS Domain Name** scope option was set to deliver the domain name *msfirewall.org* to DHCP clients. This option (shown in Figure 17.43) has the same effect as manually setting the primary domain name. DHCP clients will append this name to unqualified DNS queries (such as those for wpad) before sending the DNS query to a DNS server.

Figure 17.43 Viewing Scope Options

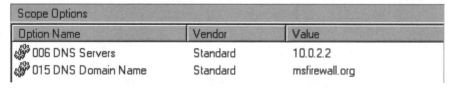

6.   Go to the DHCP client system and open a command prompt. At the command prompt, enter **ipconfig /all** and press **ENTER**. Notice that the machine has been assigned a **Connection-specific DNS Suffix** of **msfirewall.org**.

DHCP is the most efficient way to assign a primary DNS suffix to clients on your network, as seen in Figure 17.44. This feature allows you to automatically configure a DNS suffix on DHCP clients that connect to your network, which are not members of your Active Directory domain.

These clients can still correctly resolve the wpad name based on your current DNS infrastructure without requiring them to join the domain or manually configuring them.

Figure 17.44 DHCP client configuration

```
C:\>ipconfig /all

Windows 2000 IP Configuration

        Host Name . . . . . . . . . . . : CLIENT2A
        Primary DNS Suffix  . . . . . . :
        Node Type . . . . . . . . . . . : Hybrid
        IP Routing Enabled. . . . . . . : No
        WINS Proxy Enabled. . . . . . . : No
        DNS Suffix Search List. . . . . : msfirewall.org

Ethernet adapter Local Area Connection:

        Connection-specific DNS Suffix  . : msfirewall.org
        Description . . . . . . . . . . : AMD PCNET Family PCI Ethernet Ada
r #2
        Physical Address. . . . . . . . : 00-0C-29-C6-F8-E8
        DHCP Enabled. . . . . . . . . . : Yes
        Autoconfiguration Enabled . . . : Yes
        IP Address. . . . . . . . . . . : 10.0.2.100
        Subnet Mask . . . . . . . . . . : 255.255.255.0
        Default Gateway . . . . . . . . :
        DHCP Server . . . . . . . . . . : 10.0.2.2
        DNS Servers . . . . . . . . . . : 10.0.2.2
        Lease Obtained. . . . . . . . . : Sunday, January 11, 2004 4:17:20 I
        Lease Expires . . . . . . . . . : Monday, January 19, 2004 4:17:20 I

C:\>
```

Note that if you have multiple domains and clients on your Internal network that belong to multiple domains, you will need to create wpad CNAME alias entries for each of the domains. In addition, DNS support for WPAD entries can be a bit problematic when you have a single Internal network domain that spans WAN links. You can only enter a single WPAD entry per domain, and all hosts that fully qualify the WPAD entry with that domain name will receive the same server address. This can lead to Branch office hosts attempting to access the Internet via an ISA Server 2006 located at the Main office. The best solution to this problem is to create subdomains in the DNS that support Branch office clients.

Configure the client browser to use autodiscovery

The next step is to configure the browser to use autodiscovery. If you have not already done so, configure the Web browser to use autodiscovery to automatically configure itself to use the ISA Server 2006 firewall's Web Proxy service:

1. Right-click on the **Internet Explorer** icon on the desktop, and click **Properties**.

2. In the **Internet Properties** dialog box, click the **Connections** tab. Click the **LAN Settings** button.

3. In the **Local Area Network (LAN) Settings** dialog box, put a checkmark in the **Automatically detect settings** check box. Click **OK**.

4. Click **Apply**, and then click **OK** in the **Internet Properties** dialog box.

The next step is to configure the ISA Server 2006 firewall **Publish Autodiscovery Information** for autodiscovery Web Proxy and Firewall clients.

Configure the ISA Server 2006 Firewall to Publish Autodiscovery Information

Do the following on the ISA Server 2006 firewall computer to enable it to provide autoconfiguration information to Web Proxy and Firewall autodiscovery clients:

1. At the ISA Server 2006 firewall computer, open the **Microsoft Internet Security and Acceleration Server 2004** management console. Expand the server name in the left pane of the console, and then expand the **Configuration** node. Click the **Networks** node.

2. On the **Networks** node, click the **Networks** tab in the **Details** pane.

3. Right click the **Internal** network on the **Networks** tab, and click **Properties** (see Figure 17.45).

Figure 17.45 Accessing the Internal Network Properties Dialog Box

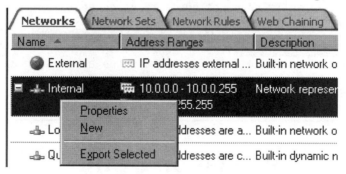

4. In the **Internal Properties** dialog box, put a checkmark in the **Publish automatic discovery information** check box. In the **Use this port for automatic discovery request** text box, leave the default port 80, as it is.

5. Click **Apply** and **OK**.

6. Click **Apply** to save the changes and update the firewall policy.

7. Click **OK** in the **Apply New Configuration** dialog box.

Making the Connection Using DNS for Autodiscovery

All the parts are now in place to allow the Web Proxy and Firewall client machine to use DNS to obtain autoconfiguration information. Perform the following steps on the Web Proxy client computer:

1. Open **Internet Explorer** and go to the **www.microsoft.com/isaserver/** home page.

2. A **Network Monitor** trace shows the Web Proxy client makes a DNS query for *wpad. msfirewall.org*. The DNS server responds to the query with the IP address (shown in Figure 17.46) of the ISA Server 2006 firewall computers.

Figure 17.46 Viewing DNS wpad Query Requests

Protocol	Description
DNS	0x406A:Std Qry for wpad.msfirewall.org. of type Host Addr on class INET addr.
DNS	0x406A:Std Qry Resp. for wpad.msfirewall.org. of type Host Addr on class INET
TCP	....S., len: 0, seq: 773548798-773548798, ack: 0, win:16384, src:

3. After it obtains the IP address of the ISA Server 2006 firewall computer and the port from which it can obtain autoconfiguration information, the Web Proxy client sends a request (see Figure 17.47) for wpad autoconfiguration information. You can see this request in the bottom pane of the Network Monitor Window, **GET /wpad.dat HTTP/1.1**.

Figure 17.47 Viewing the Details of a DNS wpad Query Request

```
00000000   00 0C 29 30 5B 64 00 0C 29 C6 F8 E8 08 00 45 00    . +)0[d. +) ⊢°‡▫. E.
00000010   00 96 00 61 40 00 80 06 E1 FD 0A 00 02 03 0A 00    .û. a@.Ç±ß²▫.◆♥▫.
00000020   02 01 04 23 00 50 2E 1E 6A FF 16 22 EE 43 50 18    ◆◘‡#.P.←j −"=CP↑
00000030   44 70 6C 3D 00 00 47 45 54 20 2F 77 70 61 64 2E    Dpl=..GET /wpad.
00000040   64 61 74 20 48 54 54 50 2F 31 2E 31 0D 0A 41 63    dat HTTP/1.1♪▣Ac
00000050   63 65 70 74 3A 20 2A 2F 2A 0D 0A 55 73 65 72 2D    cept: */*♪▣User-
00000060   41 67 65 6E 74 3A 20 4D 6F 7A 69 6C 6C 61 2F 34    Agent: Mozilla/4
00000070   2E 30 20 28 63 6F 6D 70 61 74 69 62 6C 65 3B 20    .0 (compatible;
```

Automating Installation of the Firewall Client

The Firewall client software can be installed on virtually any 32-bit version of Windows except Windows 95. There are a number of compelling reasons for installing the Firewall client software on all machines that it supports:

- The Firewall client allows you to create user/group-based access controls for *all* TCP and UDP protocols. This is in contrast to the Web Proxy client configuration, which only suppots HTTP, HTTPS and FTP.

- The Firewall client has access to all TCP and UDP-based protocols, including those requiring secondary connections. In contrast, the SecureNAT client does not support application protocols that require secondary connections *unless* there is an application filter to support it.

■ The Firewall client provides much better performance than the SecureNAT client.

■ The Firewall client sends application information to the ISA Server 2006 firewall service; this allows the Firewall service logs to collect application usage information and helps you determine which applications users are using to access Internet sites and services.

■ The Firewall client sends user information to the Firewall service; this enables the ISA Server 2006 firewall to control access based on user account *and* record user information in the Firewall service's access logs. This information can be extracted and put into report form.

With these features, the Firewall client provides a level of functionality and access control that no other firewall in its class can match. For this reason, we always recommend that you install the Firewall client on any machine that supports the Firewall client software.

However, because the Firewall client configuration requires the Firewall client software to be installed, many firewall administrators are hesitant to avail themselves of the full feature set provided by the Firewall client. Many ISA Server 2006 firewall administrators don't have the time or the resources to "touch" (visit) each authorized computer on the corporate network in order to install the Firewall client software.

The solution to this problem is to automate the installation of the Firewall client. There are two methods that you can use. These methods require no additional software purchase and can greatly simplify the installation of the Firewall client software on large numbers of computers on the corporate network. These methods are:

■ Group Policy-based software installation and management

■ Silent installation script

In the following section, we will discuss these methods, as well as some key ISA Server client configuration settings that you should make in the **ISA Management** console.

Configuring Firewall Client and Web Proxy Client Configuration in the ISA Management Console

There are a few configuration options you should set for the Firewall client installation *before* you configure a Group Policy or a silent installation script to install the Firewall client software. These settings, made at the **Microsoft Internet Security and Acceleration Server 2006** management console, determine issues such as Firewall client autodiscovery behavior and whether (and how) the Web browser is configured during installation of the Firewall client.

Perform the following steps on the ISA Server 2006 firewall computer to configure these settings:

1. In the **Microsoft Internet Security and Acceleration Server 2006 management console**, expand the server name, and then expand the **Configuration** node.

2. Click the **Networks** node, and then click **Networks** on the **Details** tab. Right-click the Internal network, and click **Properties**.

3. In the **Internal Properties** dialog box, click the **Firewall Client** tab.

4. On the **Firewall Client** tab, put a checkmark in the **Enable Firewall client support for this network** check box. In the **Firewall client configuration** frame, enter the name of the ISA Server 2006 firewall computer in the **ISA Server name or IP address** text box. The default setting is the computer name. However, you should replace the computer (NetBIOS) name with the fully-qualified domain name of the ISA Server 2006 firewall. When you replace the computer name with the FQDN, the Firewall client machines can use DNS to correctly resolve the name of the ISA Server 2006 firewall. This will avoid one of the most common troubleshooting issues with Firewall client connectivity. Make sure there is an entry for this name in your Internal network's DNS server.

The Web Proxy client configuration settings are available in the **Web browser configuration on the Firewall client computer** frame. These settings will automatically configure the Web browser as a Web Proxy client. Note that you can change the settings later, and the Web browsers will automatically update themselves with the new settings.

The **Automatically detect settings** option allows the Web browser to detect the Web Proxy service and configure itself based on the settings you configure on the **Web Browser** tab of the **Internal Properties** dialog box, shown in Figure 17.48.

Figure 17.48 Internal Properties Dialog Box

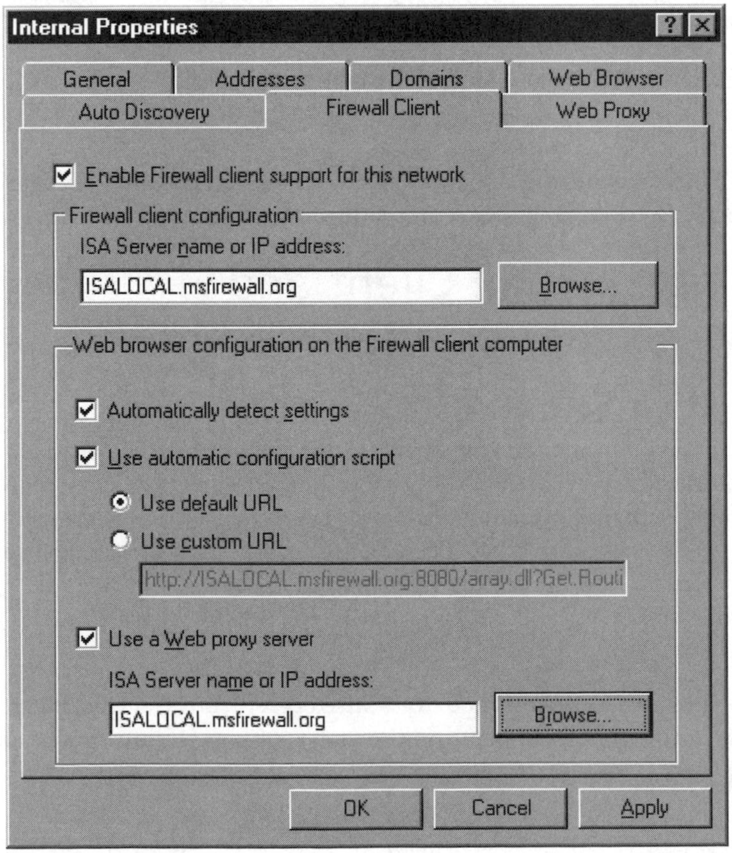

The **Use automatic configuration script** option allows you to assign a proxy autoconfiguration file (PAC) address to the Web browser. The Web browser will then query the location you specify or use the default location; the default location is on the ISA Server 2006 firewall machine. Note that when you use the default location, you obtain the same information you would receive if you had configured the Web browser to use the **Automatically detect settings** option. The **Use default URL** option automatically configures the browser to connect to the ISA Server 2006 firewall for autoconfiguration information. You can use the **Use custom URL** if you want to create your own PAC file that overrides the settings on the automatically-generated file at the ISA Server 2006 firewall. You can find more information on PAC files and proxy client autoconfiguration files in **Using Automatic Configuration and Automatic Proxy** at **http://www.microsoft.com/technet/prodtechnol/ie/reskit/5/part5/ ch21auto.mspx?mfr=true**

The **Use a Web Proxy server** option allows you to configure the Web browser to use the ISA Server 2006 as its Web Proxy, but without the benefits of the autoconfiguration script information. This setting provides higher performance than the SecureNAT client configuration, but you do not benefit from the settings contained in the autoconfiguration script. The most important configuration settings in the autoconfiguration script include site names and addresses that should be used for *Direct Access*. For this reason, you should avoid this option unless you do not wish to use Direct Access to bypass the Web Proxy service to access selected Web sites.

5. Click the **Web Browser** tab, as shown in Figure 17.49. There are several settings in this dialog box that configure the Web Proxy clients via the autoconfiguration script. Note that in order for these options to take effect, you must configure the Web Proxy clients to use the autoconfiguration script either via autodiscovery and autoconfiguration or via a manual setting for the location of the autoconfiguration script.

    The **Bypass proxy for Web server in this network** option allows the Web browser to use Direct Access to directly connect to servers that are accessible via a *single label name*. For example, if the user accesses a Web server on the Internal network using the URL **http://SERVER1**, the Web Proxy client browser will *not* send the request to the ISA Server 2006 firewall. Instead, the Web browser will directly connect to the SERVER1 machine. This reduces the load on the ISA Server 2006 firewall and prevents users from *looping back* through the ISA Server 2006 firewall to access Internal network resources.

    The **Directly access computers specified in the Domains tab** option allows you to configure Direct Access to machines contained in the **Domains** tab. The **Domains** tab contains a collection of domain names that are used by the Firewall client to determine which hosts are part of the Internal network and bypass the ISA Server 2006 firewall when contacting hosts that are part of the same domain. The Web Proxy client can also use the domain on this list for Direct Access. We recommend that you always select this option as it will reduce the load on the ISA Server 2006 firewall by preventing Web Proxy clients from looping back through the firewall to access Internal network resources.

    The **Directly access these servers or domains** list is a list of computer addresses or domain names that you can configure for Direct Access. Click the **Add** button.

Figure 17.49 Web Browser Tab on the Internal Properties Dialog Box

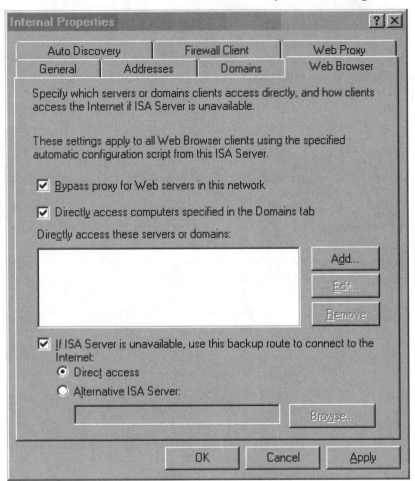

6. In the **Add Server** dialog box shown in Figure 17.50, you can select the **IP address within this range** option, and then enter an IP address or IP address range of machines that you want to Directly Access. You also have the option to select the **Domain or computer** option and enter the computer name or the FQDN of the machine that you want to access via Direct Access. A common domain name to enter for Direct Access is the **msn.com** domain, because this domain, along with the **passport.com** and the **hotmail. com** domains must be configured for Direct Access to simplify Web Proxy client connections to the Microsoft Hotmail site.

Figure 17.50 The Add Server Dialog Box

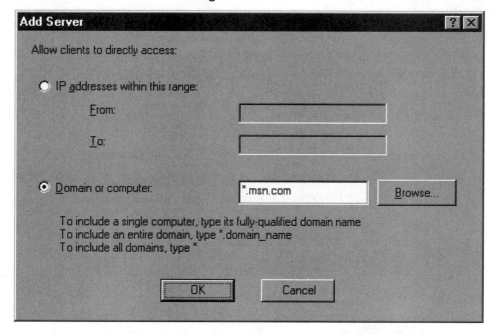

7. If the ISA Server is unavailable, **use this backup route to connect to the Internet** option allows machines configured as Web Proxy clients to use other means to connect to the Internet. Typically, this means that the Web Proxy client will leverage their SecureNAT or Firewall client configuration to connect to the Internet. If the machine is not configured as a SecureNAT and/or Firewall client, then no access will be allowed if the Web Proxy service becomes unavailable.

8. Click **Apply**, and then click **OK**, after making the changes to the configuration in the **Internal Properties** dialog box.

9. Click **Apply** to save the changes and update the firewall policy.

At this point the Firewall and Web Proxy client configuration is ready, and you can install the Firewall client on the client machines behind the ISA Server 2006 firewall and have these settings automatically configured on the clients.

Group Policy Software Installation

You might not wish to install the Firewall client on all machines. For example, domain controllers and published servers should not be configured as Firewall clients. You can gain granular control over Group Policy-based software installation by creating an organizational unit for Firewall clients and then configuring an Organization Unit (OU) group policy object to install the Firewall client only on computers belonging to that OU.

Perform the following steps on the domain controller to create the OU, and then configure software installation and management to install the Firewall client on machines belonging to the OU:

1. Click **Start**, and select the **Administrative Tools** menu. Click **Active Directory Users and Computers**. Right-click on your domain name, and click **Organizational Unit**.

2. In the **New Object – Organizational Unit** dialog box, enter a name for the OU in the **Name** text box. In this example, we will call the OU **FWCLIENTS**. Click **OK**.

3. Click on the **Computers** node in the left pane of the console. Right-click your client computer, and click the **Move** command.

4. In the **Move** dialog box, click the **FWCLIENTS** OU, and click **OK**.

5. Click on the **FWCLIENTS** OU. You should see the computer you moved into this OU.

6. Right-click the **FWCLIENTS** OU, and click the **Properties** command.

7. Click the **Group Policy** tab in the **FWCLIENTS** dialog box. Click the **New** button to create a **New Group Policy Object**. Select the **New Group Policy Object** and click **Edit**.

8. Expand the **Computer Configuration** node, and then expand the **Software Settings** node. Right-click on **Software** installation, point to **New** and click **Package**.

9. In the **Open** text box, type the path to the Firewall client's Microsoft installer package (.msi file) in the **File name** text box. In this example, the path is:

    \\isa2\mspclnt\MS_FWC.MSI

    Where **isa2** is the NetBIOS name of the ISA Server 2006 firewall computer or the name of the file server hosting the Firewall client installation files; **mspclnt** is the name of the share on the ISA Server 2006 firewall computer that contains the Firewall client installation files, and **MS_FWC.MSI** is the name of the Firewall client Microsoft installer package. Click **Open** after entering the path.

Figure 17.51 Entering the Installer Path

10. In the **Deploy Software** dialog box, select the **Assigned** option (see Figure 17.52) and click **OK**. Notice that you do not have the **Published** option when installing software using the **Computer Configuration** node. The software is installed before the user logs on. This is critical because only local administrators can install the Firewall client software *if* there is a logged-on user. In contrast, you can assign software to machines without a logged-on user. Click **OK**.

Figure 17.52 Choosing the Assigned Option

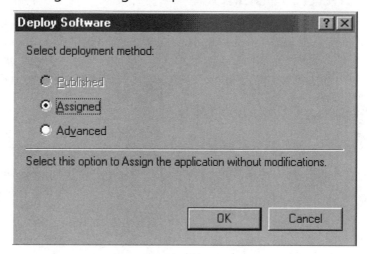

11.   The new managed software package appears in the right pane of the console. All machines in the OU will have the Firewall client software installed when they are restarted. You can also manage the Firewall client software from here, as shown in Figure 17.53.

Figure 17.53 Managed Software

12.   Close the **Group Policy Object Editor** and the **Active Directory Users and Computers** console.

13.   When you restart the machines in the **FWCLIENTS** OU, you will see the log-on dialog box (Figure 17.54) provide information about how managed software is being installed on the Windows client operating system.

Figure 17.54 Logging On

Silent Installation Script

Another useful method you can use to install the Firewall client software on those machines that are not members of the domain is to use a silent installation script. This method is useful when the logged-on user is a member of the local administrator's group. The silent installation script does not expose the user to any dialog boxes, and the user does not need to make decisions during the installation process.

Open notepad; copy the following line into the new text document, and save the file as "fwcinstall.cmd":

> **msiexec /i \\ISA2\mspclnt\MS_FWC.msi /qn /l*v c:\mspclnt_i.log**

The **\\ISA2** entry is the computer name of the ISA Server 2006 firewall computer and will vary for each installation location. The rest of the line can be used exactly as listed above. Users can then go to a Web page, or click a link in an email message pointing them to this batch file. The process is very simple and only requires the user to click the link to run the script. The installation is completely transparent, and the only thing the user will see is a momentary command prompt window and the Firewall client icon in the system tray when the procedure is completed.

Systems Management Server (SMS)

Organizations using Systems Management Server (SMS) 2003 can use the software distribution feature of SMS to deploy the Firewall client software. The Software distribution routine in SMS 2003 provides the ability to deploy Windows Installer (.msi) files to any computer that is assigned to the SMS environment in a manner similar to the Active Directory Group Policy software management feature. Do the following to deploy the Firewall client using SMS 2003:

1. Create a collection that includes all the machines on which you want the Firewall client installed. An SMS collection is a group of network objects, such as computers or users, which are treated as an SMS management group. You can configure requirements such as IP address, hardware configuration, or add clients directly by name to group all computers that require the Firewall client software.

2. Create a package by importing the Firewall client Windows file (**MS_FWC.msi**). The Windows Installer file automatically includes a variety of attended and unattended installation options that can be used on a per-system or per-user basis. Programs are also created to uninstall the client. The per-system programs are configured to install the client with administrative rights whether or not the user is logged on. The per-user programs install the client using the credentials of the logged-on user. This provides an advantage over the Group Policy method, which does not allow you to temporarily elevate privileges to install the Firewall client application.

3. Create an SMS advertisement, which specifies the target collection and program to install. In order to control deployment, you can schedule a time for the program to be advertised to collection members.

Summary

A server is of little use without clients, but the ISA server is unusual in that there are a number of different ways that a computer can be configured to act as an ISA client. In fact, there are three distinct ISA client types: the SecureNAT client, the Firewall client and the Web Proxy client. Determining which is most appropriate in a given situation depends on a number of factors, including the client operating system, the protocols that need to be supported, and whether it is desirable or feasible to install client software on the client computers.

The SecureNAT client requires no software installation and no changes to the client computer's Web browser. By simply setting the client computer's TCP/IP settings so that the default gateway is that of the ISA server, any computer, running any popular operating system, can benefit from ISA Server 2006's firewall protections. This includes non-Microsoft operating systems such as Linux/UNIX and Macintosh, as well as older Microsoft operating systems, such as Windows 95, Windows 3.x and MS-DOS, which are not supported by the Firewall client software. All simple protocols are supported by SecureNAT, and even complex protocols can be supported by installing application filters on the ISA Server computer. SecureNAT is the logical choice when you have a variety of different client operating systems that need ISA's protection, and the client systems need to access protocols other than HTTP/HTTPS or FTP.

The Web Proxy client will also work with all operating system platforms, so long as a compatible Web browser (one that can be configured to use a proxy server) is installed. However, the Web Proxy client is much more limited in the protocols it supports; only HTTP/HTTPS and HTTP-tunneled FTP are supported. In many cases, this will be all that is needed, and indeed, this limitation acts as an extra security measure by preventing access to other applications. One advantage of the Web Proxy client over SecureNAT is its ability to authenticate with the ISA firewall (if the firewall requests credentials). SecureNAT clients are able to authenticate only with client applications that support SOCKS 5 and only if a SOCKS 5 application filter is installed on the ISA Server machine.

The Firewall client is the "client of choice" for modern Windows client machines – or at least, it should be. It can be installed on Windows 98 and all subsequent Windows operating systems, and it supports all Winsock applications that use TCP/UDP, including those that require complex protocols. No application filters are needed, reducing administrative overhead on the server side. Best of all, the Firewall client allows you to take advantage of strong user/group-based access controls, as credentials are sent to the ISA Server for authentication without any special configuration or action required on the part of the client. The Firewall client also gives administrators more control via logging of user and application information.

Client configuration problems are a common cause of access and security problems. However, configuring the Web Proxy client and installing the Firewall client don't have to be difficult or time-consuming. Both processes can be easily automated, and administrators have several automation methods from which to choose. DHCP servers can be configured to support Web Proxy and Firewall client autodiscovery, as can DNS servers. Installation can be automated via Group Policy or a silent installation script, or you can use the Internet Explorer Administration Kit (IEAK) to configure the Web Proxy client. If you have Systems Management Server (SMS) on your network, you can use it to deploy the Firewall client.

Selecting the correct client configuration and properly configuring the client computers is an essential ingredient in a successful deployment of ISA Server 2006, so it's important to understand the three client types and the step-by-step process for configuring each *before* you install your ISA Server.

Installing and Configuring the ISA Firewall Software

Solutions in this chapter:

- **Pre-installation Tasks and Considerations**

- **Performing a Clean Installation on a Multihomed Machine**

- **Default Post-installation ISA Firewall Configuration**

- **The Post-installation System Policy**

- **Quick Start Configuration for ISA Firewalls**

- **Hardening the Base ISA Firewall Configuration and Operating System**

☑ Summary

Pre-installation Tasks and Considerations

There are several key pre-installation and tasks and considerations you need to address before installing the ISA firewall software. These include:

- System Requirements
- Configuring the Routing Table
- DNS Server Placement
- Configuring the ISA Firewall's Network Interfaces
- Unattended Installation
- Installation via a Terminal Services Administration Mode Session

System Requirements

The following are requirements for installing the ISA firewall software:

- Intel or AMD system with a 773 megahertz (MHz) or higher processor
- Microsoft Windows Server 2003 32-bit operating system with Service Pack 1 (SP1) or Microsoft Windows Server 2003 R2 32-bit.
- A practical minimum of 512 MB of memory for non-Web caching systems, and 1000 MB for Web-caching ISA firewalls
- At least one network adapter; two or more network adapters are required to obtain stateful filtering and stateful application-layer inspection firewall functionality
- An additional network adapter for each network connected to the ISA Server computer
- One local hard-disk partition that is formatted with the NTFS file system, and at least 150 MB of available hard disk space (this is exclusive of hard-disk space you want to use for caching)
- Additional disk space, which ideally is on a separate spindle, if you plan on using the ISA firewall's Web-caching feature

Another important consideration is capacity planning. While the above reflects minimal system requirements for installing and running the ISA firewall software, the ideal configuration is obtained when you size the hardware to optimize the ISA firewall software performance for your site. Table 18.1 provides basic guidelines regarding processor, memory, disk space and network adapter requirements based on Internet link speed.

Table 18.1 Basic Processor, Memory, Disk Space and Network Adapter
Requirements Based on Link Speed

Internet Link Bandwidth	Up to 5 T1	Up to 25 Mbps	Up to T3	90 Mbps	Notes
Processors	1	1	2	2/2	
Processor type	Pentium III750 megahertz (MHz) or higher	Pentium 4 3.0–4.0 gigahertz(GHz)	Xeon 3.0–4.0 GHz	Xeon Dual Core AMD Dual Core 2.0–3.0 GHz	You can use other processors with comparable power that emulate the IA-32 instruction set.
					In deployments requiring only stateful filtering ("stateful packet inspection" – that is, when there is no need for higher security stateful application-layer inspection), the Pentium 4 and Xeon processor recommendations reach LAN wire speeds.
Memory	512 MB	512 MB	1 GB	2 GB	With Web caching enabled, these requirements may be increased by approximately 256–512 MB.
Disk space	150 MB	2.5 GB	5 GB	10 GB	This is exclusive of hard-disk space you need to use for caching and logging.
Network adapter	10/100 Mbps	10/100 Mbps	100/1000 Mbps	100/1000 Mbps	These are the requirements for the network adapters not connected to the Internet.

Continued

www.syngress.com

Table 18.1 Continued

Internet Link Bandwidth	Up to 5 T1	Up to 25 Mbps	Up to T3	90 Mbps	Notes
Concurrent Remote-access VPN connections	150	700	850	2000	The Standard Edition of the ISA firewall supports a hard-coded maximum of 1000 concurrent VPN connections. The Enterprise Edition supports as many connections as are supported by the underlying operating system and has no ISA-based hard coded limitation.

For an exceptionally thorough and comprehensive discussion on ISA firewall performance optimization and sizing, please refer to the Microsoft document **ISA Server 2006 Performance Best Practices** at http://www.microsoft.com/technet/isa/2006/perf_bp.mspx

Configuring the Routing Table

The routing table on the ISA firewall machine should be configured before you install the ISA firewall software. The routing table should include routes to all networks that are not local to the ISA firewall's network interfaces. These routing table entries are required because the ISA firewall can have only a single default gateway. Normally, the default gateway is configured on the network interface that is used for the External Network. Therefore, if you have an internal or other Network that contains multiple subnets, you should configure routing table entries that ensure the ISA firewall can communicate with the computers and other IP devices on the appropriate subnets. The network interface with the default gateway is the one used to connect to the Internet, either direction or via upstream routers.

The routing table entries are critical to support the ISA firewall's "network-within-a-Network" scenarios. A network within a Network is a network ID located behind a NIC on the ISA firewall that is a non-local network.

For example, Figure 18.1 is an example of a simple network-within-a-Network scenario.

Figure 18.1 Network within a Network

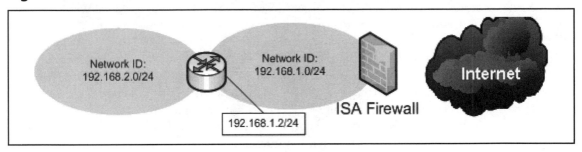

This small organization's IP addressing scheme uses two network IDs for the corporate network: 192.168.1.0/24 and 192.168.2.0/24. The network local to the ISA firewall's internal interface is 192.168.1.0/24. The network remote from the ISA firewall's internal interface is 192.168.2.0/24. A corporate network router separates the network and routes packets between these two network IDs.

The ISA firewall's networking model includes both of these networks as part of the same Network (Note: A capital "N" indicates an ISA firewall-defined network). You would naturally assume that the 192.168.1.0/24 would be an ISA-defined Network since it includes an entire network ID, but you might also assume that network ID 192.168.2.0/24 would be defined as a second ISA firewall-defined Network. That would be incorrect because the ISA firewall's Network model includes *all networks (all IP addresses)* reachable from a specific interface on the ISA firewall as being part of the same network.

The rationale behind this is that hosts on the same ISA-defined Network do not use the ISA firewall to mediate communications between themselves. It makes no sense for the ISA firewall to mediate communications between hosts on networks IDs 192.168.1.0/24 and 192.168.2.0/24, as this would require hosts to loop back through the firewall to reach hosts to which they should directly communicate.

In this example, there should be a routing table entry on the ISA firewall indicating that in order to reach network ID 192.168.2.0/24, the connection must be forwarded to IP address 192.168.2.1 on the corporate router. You can use either the RRAS console or the command line **ROUTE** and **netsh** commands to add the routing table entry.

The ISA firewall must know the route to *each* internal network ID. If you find that connections are not being correctly forwarded by the ISA firewall to hosts on the corporate network, confirm that there are routing table entries on the ISA firewall indicating the correct gateway for each of those network IDs.

DNS Server Placement

DNS server and host name resolution issues represent the most common ISA firewall connectivity problems. Name resolution for both corporate network and Internet hosts must be performed correctly. If the company's name resolution infrastructure isn't properly configured, one of the first victims of the flawed name resolution design will be the ISA firewall.

The ISA firewall must be able to correctly resolve both corporate and Internet DNS names. The ISA firewall performs name resolution for both Web Proxy and Firewall clients. If the firewall cannot perform name resolution correctly, Internet connectivity for both Web Proxy and Firewall clients will fail.

Correct name resolution for corporate network resources is also critical because the ISA firewall must be able to correctly resolve names for corporate network resources published via Web Publishing rules. For example, when you create a secure-SSL Web Publishing Rule, the ISA firewall must be able to correctly forward incoming connection requests to the FQDN used for the common name on the Web site certificate bound to the published Web server on the corporate network.

The ideal name resolution infrastructure is the split DNS. The split-DNS infrastructure allows external hosts to resolve names to publicly-accessible addresses and corporate network hosts to resolve names to privately-accessible addresses. Figure 18.2 depicts how a split-DNS infrastructure works to enhance name resolution for hosts inside your corporate network, as well as those that roam between the corporate network and remote locations on the Internet.

Figure 18.2 The Miracle of the Split-DNS Infrastructure

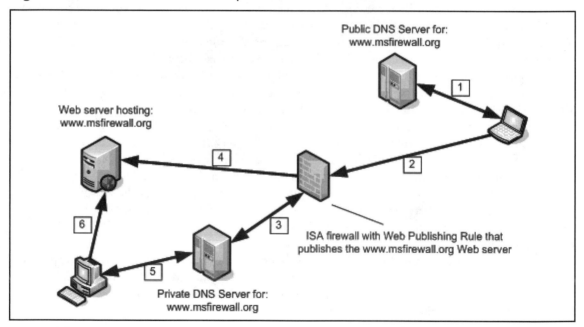

1. A user at a remote location needs to access resources on the corporate Web server, www.msfirewall.org. The www.msfirewall.org Web server is hosted on an ISA firewall–Protected Network and published using an ISA firewall Web Publishing Rule. The remote user sends a request to www.msfirewall.org, and the name is resolved by the public DNS server authoritative for the msfirewall.org domain. The name is resolved to an IP address on the external interface of the ISA firewall used by the Web listener designated in the Web Publishing Rule.

2. The remote Web client sends the request to the IP address on the external interface used by the Web Publishing Rules Web listener.

3. The ISA firewall resolves the name www.msfirewall.org to the actual IP address bound to the www.msfirewall.org Web site on the corporate network by querying the Internal network DNS server authoritative for the msfirewall.org domain.

4.   The ISA firewall forwards the connection to the actual IP address bound to the www.msfirewall.org Web site on the corporate network.

5.   A host on the corporate network needs to access resources on the www.msfirewall.org Web site. The corporate user sends a request to the corporate DNS server that is authoritative for the msfirewall.org domain. The corporate DNS server resolves the name www.msfirewall.org to the actual IP address bound to the www.msfirewall.org Web site on the corporate network.

6.   The Web client on the corporate network connects directly to the www.msfirewall.org Web server. The Web client doesn't loop back to reach the www.msfirewall.org Web site on the corporate network because Web Proxy clients are configured for direct access to resources on the msfirewall.org domain.

The split-DNS infrastructure provides transparent access to resources for users regardless of their location. Users can move between the corporate network and remote locations and use the same name to reach the same corporate resources. They don't need to reconfigure their mail clients, news clients, and other applications because *the same name* is used to access the resources regardless of location. Any organization needing to support users that roam between the corporate network and remote locations should implement a split DNS infrastructure.

Requirements for the split-DNS infrastructure include:

■   A DNS server authoritative for the domain that resolves names for resources for that domain to the internal addresses used to access those resources

■   A DNS server authoritative for the domain that resolves names for resources in that domain to the publicly-accessible addresses used to access those resources

■   Remote users must be assigned DNS server addresses that forward requests for the domain to a public DNS server. This is easily accomplished using DHCP.

■   Corporate users must be assigned DNS server addresses that forward requests for the domain to the private DNS server. This is easily accomplished using DHCP.

■   The ISA firewall must be able to resolve names of published resources and all other resources hosted on a ISA firewall-Protected Network to the private address used to access that resource.

Most organizations that use the ISA firewall will have one or more internal DNS servers. At least one of those DNS servers should be configured to resolve both internal and Internet host names, and the ISA firewall should be configured to use that DNS server. If you have an internal network DNS server, you should never configure the ISA firewall's interfaces to use an external DNS server. This is a common mistake and can lead to slow or failed name resolution attempts.

Configuring the ISA Firewall's Network Interfaces

Perhaps one of the least understood ISA firewall configuration issues is how to correctly configure the IP addressing information on the ISA firewall's network interfaces. The reason for this is that name resolution issues have the potential for being complex, and fledging firewall administrators are often too busy to get lost in the details of DNS host name and NetBIOS name resolution.

There are two main networks interface configuration scenarios:

■   An established name-resolution infrastructure on the corporate network protected by the ISA firewall

■   *No* established name-resolution infrastructure on the corporate network protected by the ISA firewall

Tables 18.2 and 18.3 show the correct IP addressing information for both these scenarios in dual-homed ISA firewalls.

Table 18.2 Established Corporate Network Name-Resolution Infrastructure

Parameters	Internal Interface	External Interface
Client for Microsoft Networks	Enabled	Disabled
File and Print Sharing for Microsoft Networks	Enabled only if the ISA firewall hosts the Firewall client share	Disabled
Network Monitor Driver	Enabled when Network Monitor is installed on the ISA firewall (recommended)	Enabled when Network Monitor is installed on the ISA firewall (recommended)
Internet Protocol (TCP/IP)	Enabled	Enabled
IP address	Valid IP address on the network the internal interface is connected to	Valid IP address on the network the external interface is connected to. Public or private depending on your network infrastructure
Subnet mask	Valid subnet mask on the network the internal interface is connected to	Valid subnet mask on the network the external interface is connected to
Default gateway	NONE. Never configure a default gateway on any internal or DMZ interface on the ISA firewall.	IP address of upstream router (either corporate or ISP depending on next hop) allowing access to the Internet
Preferred DNS server	Internal DNS server that can resolve both internal and Internet host names	NONE. Do not enter a DNS server address on the external interface of the ISA firewall
Alternate DNS server	A second internal DNS server that can resolve both internal and Internet host names	NONE. Do not enter a DNS server address on the external interface of the ISA firewall.

Table 18.2 Continued

Parameters	Internal Interface	External Interface
Register this connection's addresses in DNS	Disabled. You should manually create entries on the Internal network DNS server to allow clients to resolve the name of the ISA firewall's internal interface.	Disabled
WINS	Enter an IP address for one more Internal network DNS server. Especially helpful for VPN clients who want to browse Internal network servers using NetBIOS name/browser service	NONE
WINS NetBIOS setting	Default	Disable NetBIOS over TCP/IP
Interface order	Top of interface list	Under internal interface

Table 18.3 *No* Established Corporate Network Name-Resolution Infrastructure

Parameters	Internal Interface	External Interface
Client for Microsoft Networks	Enabled	Disabled
File and Print Sharing for Microsoft Networks	Enabled only if the ISA firewall hosts the Firewall client share	Disabled
Network Monitor Driver	Enabled when Network Monitor is installed on the ISA firewall (recommended)	Enabled when Network Monitor is installed on the ISA firewall (recommended)
Internet Protocol (TCP/IP)	Enabled	Enabled
IP address	Valid IP address on the network the internal interface is connected to	Valid IP address on the network the external interface is connected to. Public or private depending on your network infrastructure. Alternatively, DHCP if required by ISP
Subnet mask	Valid subnet mask on the network the internal interface is connected to	Valid subnet mask on the network the external interface is connected to. May be assigned by ISP via DHCP

Continued

Table 18.3 Continued

Parameters	Internal Interface	External Interface
Default gateway	NONE. Never configure a default gateway on any internal or DMZ interface on the ISA firewall.	IP address of upstream router (either corporate or ISP depending on next hop) allowing access to the Internet. May be assigned by ISP via DHCP
Preferred DNS server	External DNS server that can resolve Internet host names. Typically your ISP's DNS Server. **Note:** If the external interface uses DHCP to obtain IP addressing information, do not enter a DNS server on the ISA firewall's internal interface.	None, unless assigned by ISP via DHCP.
Alternate DNS server	A second external DNS server that can resolve Internet host names **Note:** If the external interface uses DHCP to obtain IP addressing information from your ISP, do not enter a DNS server on the ISA firewall's internal interface.	NONE. Do not enter a DNS server address on the external interface of the ISA firewall unless assigned via DHCP by ISP.
Register this connection's addresses in DNS	Disabled	Disabled
WINS	NONE	NONE
WINS NetBIOS setting	Default	Disable NetBIOS over TCP/IP
Interface order	Top of interface list **Note:** If the external interface of the ISA firewall uses DHCP to obtain IP addressing information from your ISP, then do not move the internal interface to the top of the list.	Top of interface list if using ISP DHCP server to assign DNS server addresses

You should already be familiar with configuring IP addressing information for Windows Server interfaces. However, you may not be aware of how to change the interface order. The interface order is used to determine what name server addresses should be used preferentially.

Perform the following steps to change the interface order:

1. Right-click **My Network Places** on the desktop, and click **Properties**.

2. In the **Network and Dial-up Connections** window, click the **Advanced** menu, then click **Advanced Settings**.

3. In the **Advanced Settings** dialog box (Figure 18.3), click the internal interface in the list of **Connections** on the **Adapters and Bindings** tab. After selecting the internal interface, click the up-arrow to move the internal interface to the top of the list of interfaces.

Figure 18.3 The Advanced Settings Dialog Box

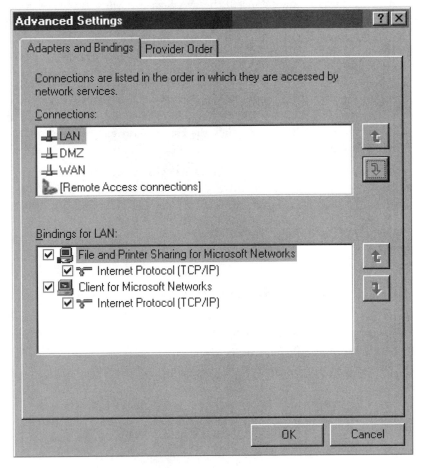

4. Click **OK** in the **Advanced Settings** dialog box.

Installation via a Terminal Services Administration Mode Session

You can install the ISA firewall via an Admin mode Terminal services connection. After installing is complete, a System Policy rule is configured to allow RDP connections only from the IP address of the machine that was connected during the ISA firewall software installation. This is in contrast to the default System Policy setting when installing the ISA firewall software at the console, where any host on the Internal Network can initiate an RDP connection to the ISA firewalls Internal interface.

Performing a Clean Installation on a Multihomed Machine

The following steps demonstrate how to install the ISA Server 2006 software on a dual-homed (two Ethernet cards) Windows Server 2003 machine. This is a "clean machine" that has only the Windows Server 2003 software installed and the IP addressing information configured on each of the machine's interfaces. The routing table has also been properly configured on this machine.

Perform the following steps to install the ISA firewall software on the multihomed machine:

1. Insert the ISA Server 2006 installation CD into the CD-ROM drive or connect to a network share point hosting the ISA Server 2006 installation files. If the installation routine does not start automatically, double-click the **isaautorun.exe** file in the root of the installation files folder tree.

2. On the **Microsoft Internet Security and Acceleration Server 2006** page, click the link for **Review Release Notes** and read the release notes. The release notes contain very important and topical information regarding changes in basic firewall software functionality. This information may not be included in the Help file or elsewhere, so we highly recommend that you read this information. After reviewing the release notes, click the **Read Setup and Feature Guide** link. You may want to read the guide now, just review the major topics covered in the guide, or print it out. Click the **Install ISA Server 2006** link.

3. Click **Next** on the **Welcome to the Installation Wizard for Microsoft ISA Server 2006** page.

4. Select **I accept the terms in the license agreement option** on the **License Agreement** page. Click **Next**.

5. On the **Customer Information** page, enter your name and the name of your organization in the **User Name** and **Organization** text boxes. Enter your serial number in the **Product Serial Number** text box. If you installed an evaluation copy of the ISA firewall software and now are installing a licensed version, then backup your configuration using the ISA firewall's integrated backup tool and uninstall the evaluation version. Restart the installation of the licensed version of the software. Click **Next**.

6. On the **Setup Type** page (Figure 18.4), select **Custom**. If you do not want to install the ISA Server 2006 software on the C: drive, click **Change** to change the location of the program files on the hard disk. Click **Next**.

Figure 18.4 The Setup Type Page

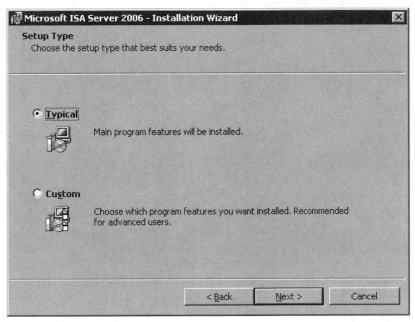

7. On the **Custom Setup** page (Figure 18.5), choose which components to install. By default, when you select **Custom**, the **Firewall Services**, **ISA Server Management**, and **Advanced Logging** features are installed. The **Advanced Logging** feature is MSDE logging, which provides superior log search and filtering features. Use the default settings, and click **Next**.

Figure 18.5 The Custom Setup Page

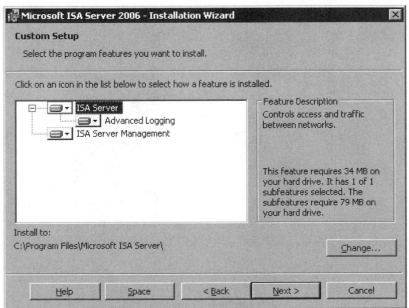

8. On the **Internal Network** page in Figure 18.6, click **Add**. The Internal Network is different from the internal network that was implied by the Local Address Table (LAT) was used by ISA Server 2000. In the case of ISA Server 2006, the Internal Network contains trusted network services with which the ISA firewall must communicate. Examples of such services include Active Directory domain controllers, DNS servers, DHCP servers, terminal servers, and management workstations. The firewall System Policy uses the Internal Network for a number of System Policy rules. We will look at the System Policy later | in this chapter.

9. Define the addresses included on the default Internal Network on the Internal Network setup page. You can manually enter the addresses to be included in the Internal Network by entering the first and last addresses in the Internal Network range in the **From** and **To** text boxes and then clicking the **Add** button. A better way to configure the default Internal Network is to use **Select Network Adapter**. This allows the ISA firewall setup routine to use the routing table to determine addresses used for the default Internal Network. This is one reason why it is important to make sure that you have correctly configured your routing table entries before installing ISA. Click **Select Network Adapter**. (See Figure 18.6.)

Figure 18.6 The Internal Network Address Page

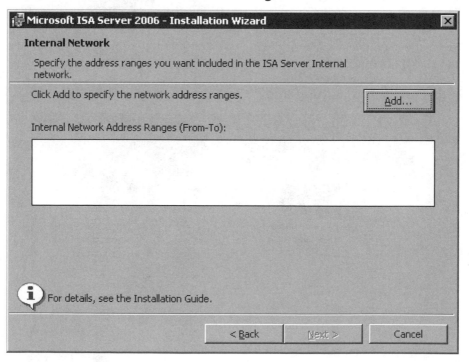

10. In the **Addresses** dialog box, Select the internal network adapter. . Add the address ranges based on your own internal range. In this example, we have renamed the network interfaces so that the interface name reflects its location. Click **OK**.

Figure 18.7 The Select Network Adapter Page

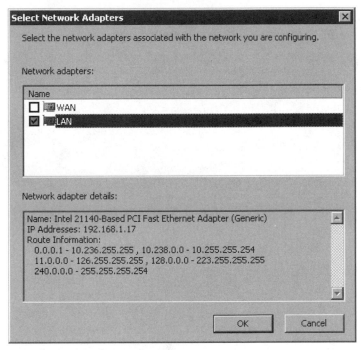

11.   If applicable, choose one of the predefines private subnets. (Figure 18.8, **Addresses**)

Figure 18.8 Automatic entry of various private subnets

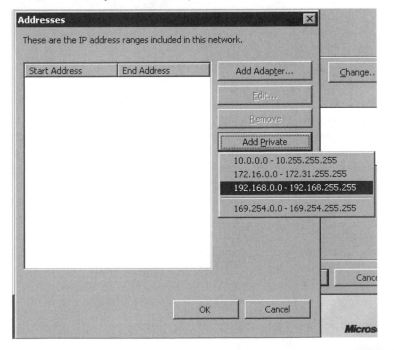

12.   Click **OK** on the **Addresses** dialog box, as shown in Figure 18.9.

Figure 18.9 Internal Network Address Ranges

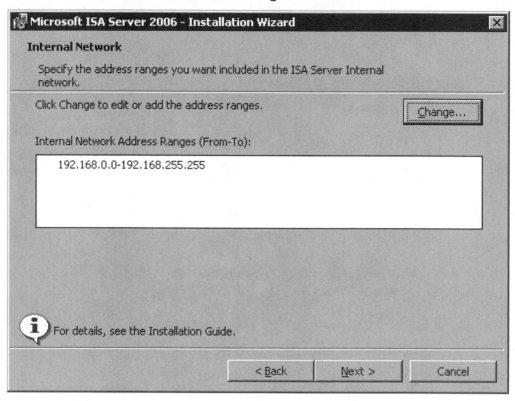

13.   Click **Next** on the **Internal Network** page.

14.   Put a checkmark by **Allow non-encrypted Firewall client connections** (Figure 18.10) if you want to support Firewall clients running previous versions of the Winsock Proxy (Proxy Server 2.0) or the ISA Server 2000 Firewall client software. This will allow you to continue using the ISA Server 2000 Firewall client software as you migrate to ISA Server 2006. When you migrate your Firewall clients to the ISA 2006 version of the Firewall client, the channel between the Firewall clients and the ISA firewall will be encrypted. The ISA 2006 Firewall client software encrypts the user credentials that are transparently sent from the Firewall client machine to the ISA firewall. For best security practice, it is recommended that you deploy the latest version of the Firewall Client software. This can be downloaded from http://www.microsoft.com/downloads/details. aspx?displaylang=en&FamilyID=05c2c932-b15a-4990-b525-66380743da89

Click **Next**.

Figure 18.10 The Firewall Client Connection Settings Page

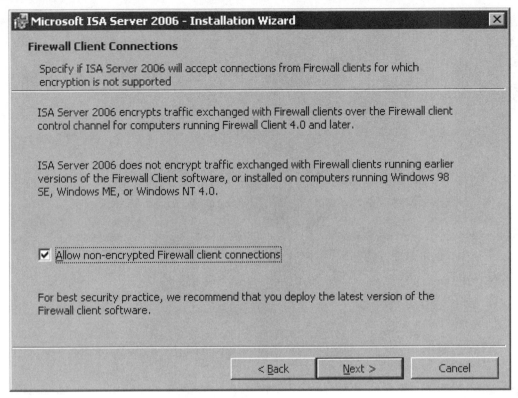

15. On the **Services** page, note that the **SNMP** and **IIS Admin Service** will be stopped during installation. If the **Internet Connection Firewall (ICF) / Internet Connection Sharing (ICF)**, and/or **IP Network Address Translation** (RRAS NAT service) services are installed on the ISA firewall machine, they will be disabled, as they conflict with the ISA firewall software.

16. Click **Install** on the **Ready to Install the Program** page.

17. On the **Installation Wizard Completed** page, click **Finish**.

18. Click **Yes** on the **Microsoft ISA Server** dialog box informing that you must restart the server (see Figure 18.11). Note that you will not need to restart the machine if you have installed the ISA firewall software on this machine before. The reason for the restart is that the TCP/IP stack is changed so that the dynamic port range of the TCP/IP driver is extended to 65535. If the installation routine recognizes that this range has already been extended, then the restart will not be required.

Figure 18.11 Warning Dialog Box regarding a Potential System Restart

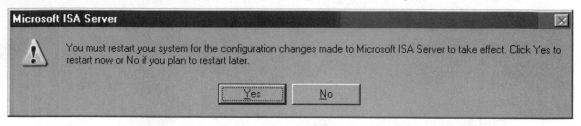

19. Log on as an **Administrator** after the machine restarts.

20. Click **Start**, and point to **All Programs**. Point to **Microsoft ISA Server**, and click **ISA Server Management**. The **Microsoft Internet Security and Acceleration Server 2006** management console opens and displays the **Welcome to Microsoft Internet Security and Acceleration Server 2006** page.

Three setup logs are created on the ISA firewall machine. These are:

- **ISAWRAP_*.log** Provides information about installation success and failure and MSDE log files setup

- **ISAMSDE_*.log** Provides detailed information about MSDE setup, if the Advanced Logging feature was selected

- **ISAFWSV_*.log** Provides detailed information about the entire ISA firewall installation process

If you choose to not install certain components, such as Advanced Logging (MSDE logging), you can use the Control Panel's **Add/Remove Programs** applet to re-run the installation routine and install these additional components at a later time.

Default Post-installation ISA Firewall Configuration

The ISA firewall installation routine incorporates the settings you entered during the setup Wizard process. The install routine also sets up some default settings for User Permissions, Network Settings, Firewall Policy, and others. Table 18.4 lists the settings that you did not explicitly define during the installation process.

We can quickly summarize the default post-installation configuration with the following:

- System Policies allow selected traffic to and from the ISA firewall itself.

- No traffic is allowed through the ISA firewall because there is only a single Deny-access rule.

- A route relationship is set between the VPN/VPN-Q Networks to the Internal Network.

- A NAT relationship is set between the Internal Network and the default External Network.

- Only Administrators can alter ISA firewall policy.

Table 18.4 Post-Installation ISA Firewall Settings

Feature	Post-installation Settings
User permissions	Members of the Administrators group on the local computer can configure firewall policy. If the ISA firewall is a member of the domain, domain admins are automatically added to the local administrators group.
Network settings	The following Network Rules are created by the installation wizard: **Local Host Access** Local Host Access defines a Route relationship between the Local Host network and all networks. Allow communications from the ISA firewall to all other hosts to be routed (does not use NAT; there would be no point to using NAT from Local Host to any Network). **Internet Access** Internet Access defines a Network Address Translation (NAT) relationship from the Internal network, Quarantined VPN Clients network, and the VPN Clients network to the External network. NAT is used from these three Networks for any communications sourcing from them to the External Network. Access is allowed only if you configure the appropriate access policy. **VPN Clients to Internal Network** VPN Clients to Internal Network defines a Route relationship between the VPN Clients Network and the Internal Network. Access is allowed only if you enable virtual private network (VPN) client access.
Firewall policy	A default Access Rule (named **Default Rule**) denies traffic between all networks.
System policy	The ISA firewall is secure by default. Some system policy rules are enabled to allow necessary services. You should review the system policy configuration and customize it so that only services critical to your specific deployment are enabled.

Continued

Table 18.4 Continued

Feature	Post-installation Settings
Web chaining	A default rule (named **Default Rule**) specifies that all Web Proxy client requests are retrieved directly from the Internet. That is to say, there is no Web chaining configured by default. Web chaining rules were called Web routing rules in ISA Server 2000.
Caching	The cache size is set to 0. All caching is therefore disabled. You will need to define a cache drive to enable Web caching.
Alerts	Most alerts are enabled. You should review and configure alerts in accordance with your specific networking needs.
Client configuration	Firewall and Web Proxy clients have automatic discovery enabled by default. Web browser applications on Firewall clients are configured when the Firewall client is installed.
Autodiscovery for Firewall and Web Proxy Clients	Publication of autodiscovery information is disabled by default. You will need to enable publication of autodiscovery information and confirm a port on which autodiscovery information is published.

The Post-installation System Policy

ISA Firewall Policy is a collection of Access Rules controlling access to and from the Local Host network. System Policy controls access to and from the *system*. You do **not** configure System Policy for network access between any other hosts. One of the most common errors made by new ISA firewall administrators is to use System Policy to control access from Protected Network hosts to non-Protected Network hosts.

Table 18.5 shows the list of System Policy rules and their status after installing the ISA firewall software. The **Order/Comments** column includes our advice regarding configuration of the specific System Policy Rule.

Table 18.5 Default Post-installation System Policy

Order/Comments	Name	Action	Protocols	From/Listener	To	Condition
1 Is the ISA firewall a member of the domain? If not, disable this rule.	Allow access to directory services for authentication purposes	Allow	LDAP LDAP (UDP) LDAP GC (global catalog) LDAPS LDAPS GC (Global Catalog)	Local Host	Internal	All Users
2 If no one is going to use the remote MMC to manage the ISA firewall, disable this rule.	Allow remote management from selected computers using MMC	Allow	Microsoft Firewall Control NetBIOS datagram NetBIOS Name Service NetBIOS Session RPC (all interfaces)	Remote Management Computers	Local Host	All Users
3 Confirm that the Remote Management Computers Computer Set has the addresses of the hosts that will manage the ISA firewall; if you don't want to allow RDP management of the ISA firewall, disable this rule.	Allow remote management from selected computers using Terminal Server	Allow	RDP (Terminal Services)	Remote Management Computers	Local Host	All Users

Continued

Table 18.5 Continued

Order/Comments	Name	Action	Protocols	From/Listener	To	Condition
4 (Disabled by default) ■ Enable this rule if you want to log to SQL servers.	Allow remote logging to trusted servers using NetBIOS	Allow	NetBIOS Datagram NetBIOS Name Service NetBIOS Session	Local Host	Internal	All Users
5 Will you be using RADIUS authentication? If not, disable this rule.	Allow RADIUS authentication from ISA Server to trusted RADIUS servers	Allow	RADIUS RADIUS Accounting	Local Host	Internal	All Users
6 Will the ISA firewall be authenticating users? If not, disable this rule.	Allow Kerberos authentication from ISA Server to trusted servers	Allow	Kerberos-Sec (TCP) Kerberos-Sec (UDP)	Local Host	Internal	All Users
7 This rule must be enabled so that the ISA firewall can initiate DNS queries.	Allow DNS from ISA Server to selected servers	Allow	DNS	Local Host	All Networks (and Local Host)	All Users
8 If the ISA firewall isn't going to act as a DHCP client, disable this rule.	Allow DHCP requests from ISA Server to all networks	Allow	DHCP (request)	Local Host	Anywhere	All Users
9 If the ISA firewall isn't going to act as a DHCP client, disable this rule.	Allow DHCP replies from DHCP servers to ISA Server	Allow	DHCP (reply)	Internal	Local Host	All Users

10 Confirm that you have configured the proper IP addresses for the Remote Management Computers Computer Set.	Allow ICMP (PING) requests from selected computers to ISA Server	Allow	Ping	Remote Management Computers	Local Host	All Users
11 This rule must be enabled so that the ISA firewall can carry out network management tasks via ICMP.	Allow ICMP requests from ISA Server to selected servers	Allow	ICMP Information Request ICMP Timestamp Ping	Local Host	All Networks (and Local Host Network)	All Users
12 (disabled by default) This rule is automatically enabled when you enable the ISA firewall's VPN server component.	All VPN client traffic to ISA Server	Allow	PPTP	External	Local Host	All Users
13 (disabled by default) This rule is automatically enabled when you enable a site-to-site VPN connection to this ISA firewall.	Allow VPN site-to-site traffic to ISA Server	Allow	NONE	External IPSec Remote Gateways	Local Host	All Users

Continued

Table 18.5 Continued

Order/Comments	Name	Action	Protocols	From/Listener	To	Condition
14 (disabled by default) This rule is automatically enabled when you enable a site-to-site VPN connection to this ISA firewall.	Allow VPN site-to-site traffic from ISA Server	Allow	NONE	Local Host	External IPSec Remote Gateways	All Users
15 Will you be trying to access file shares from the ISA firewall? If not, disable this rule	Allow Microsoft CIFS from ISA Server to trusted servers	Allow	Microsoft CIFS (TCP) Microsoft CIFS (UDP)	Local Host	Internal	All Users
16 (disabled by default) ■ Enable this rule when you choose SQL logging.	Allow remote SQL logging from ISA Server to selected servers	Allow	Microsoft SQL (TCP) Microsoft SQL (UDP)	Local Host	Internal	All Users
17 Unless you want to allow the ISA firewall to contact the Windows Update site itself, disable this rule. I prefer to down load updates to a management machine, scan them, and then copy them out of band to the ISA firewall and install them from that.	Allow HTTP/HTTPS requests from ISA Server to specified sites	Allow	HTTP HTTPS	Local Host	System Policy Allowed Sites	All Users

18 (disabled by default) This rule is enabled when you create an HTTP/HTTPS connectivity verifier.	Allow HTTP/HTTPS requests from ISA Server to selected servers for connectivity verifiers	Allow	HTTP HTTPS	Local Host	All Networks (and Local Host Network)	All Users
19 (disabled by default) This rule is enabled if the Firewall client share is installed on the ISA firewall.	Allow access from trusted computers to the Firewall Client installation share on ISA Server	Allow	Microsoft CIFS (TCP) Microsoft CIFS (UDP) NetBIOS Datagram NetBIOS Name Service NetBIOS Session	Internal	Local Host	All Users
20 (disabled by default) Enable this rule if you want to perform remote performance monitoring of ISA firewall.	Allow remote performance monitoring of ISA Server from trusted servers	Allow	NetBIOS Datagram NetBIOS Name Service NetBIOS Session	Remote Management Computers	Local Host	All Users
21 Unless you plan to access file shares from the ISA firewall, disable this rule.	Allow NetBIOS from ISA Server to trusted servers	Allow	NetBIOS datagram NetBIOS Name Service NetBIOS Sessions	Local Host	Internal	All Users
22 ■ Unless you plan to use RPC to connect to other servers, disable this rule.	Allow RPC from ISA Server to trusted servers	Allow	RPC (all interfaces)	Local Host	Internal	All Users
23 This rule allows the ISA firewall to send error reports to Microsoft.	Allow HTTP/HTTPS from ISA Server to specified Microsoft error reporting sites	Allow	HTTP HTTPS	Local Host	Microsoft Error Reporting sites	All Users

Continued

Table 18.5 Continued

Order/Comments	Name	Action	Protocols	From/Listener	To	Condition
24 (disabled by default) This rule should be enabled if SecurID authentication is enabled.	Allow SecurID authentication from ISA Server to trusted servers	Allow	SecurID	Local Host	Internal	All Users
25 (disabled by default) ■ Enable this rule if you use MOM to monitor the ISA firewall.	Allow remote monitoring from ISA Server to trusted servers, using Microsoft Operations Manager (MOM) Agent	Allow	Microsoft Operations Manager Agent	Local Host	Internal	All Users
26 (disabled by default) Enable this rule if you want the ISA firewall to access CRLs – required if the ISA terminates any SSL connections.	Allow all HTTP traffic from ISA Server to all networks (for CRL downloads)	Allow	HTTP	Local Host	All Networks (and Local Host)	All Users
27 You should change this rule by allowing contact with a The Internal entry allows it to contact all servers anywhere in the world.	Allow NTP from ISA Server to trusted NTP servers	Allow	NTP (UDP)	Local Host	Internal	All Users

#	Notes	Name	Action	Protocol	From	To	Users
28	If you don't plan on using SMTP to send alerts, you should disable this rule. If you do plan on sending SMTP alerts, you should replace the Internal Destination with a specific computer that will accept SMTP messages from the ISA firewall.	Allow SMTP from ISA Server to trusted servers	Allow	SMTP	Local Host	Internal	All Users
29 (disabled by default)	This rule is automatically enabled when Content Download Jobs are enabled.	Allow HTTP from ISA Server to selected computers for Content Download Jobs	Allow	HTTP	Local Host	All Networks (and Local Host)	System and Network Service
30	Unless you plan on using the remote MMC, disable this rule	Allow Microsoft Firewall Control communication to selected computers	Allow	All Outbound traffic	Local Host	Remote Management Computers	All Users

The ISA firewall's System Policy Rules are evaluated before any user-defined Access Rules in the order listed in the **Firewall Policy** first column. View the ISA firewall's System Policy by clicking **Firewall Policy** in the left pane of the console and then clicking the **Tasks** tab. In the **Tasks** tab, click **Show System Policy Rules**. Click **Hide System Policy Rules** when you're finished viewing the firewall's system policy.

You can edit the ISA firewall's System Policy by clicking **Edit System Policy** on the **Tasks** tab. This opens the **System Policy Editor,** as shown in Figure 18.12. For each System Policy Rule there is a **General** tab and a **From** or **To** tab. The **General** tab for each **Configuration Group** contains an explanation of the rule(s), and the **From** or **To** tab allows you to control protocol access to or from the ISA firewall machine itself.

Figure 18.12 The ISA Firewall's System Policy Editor

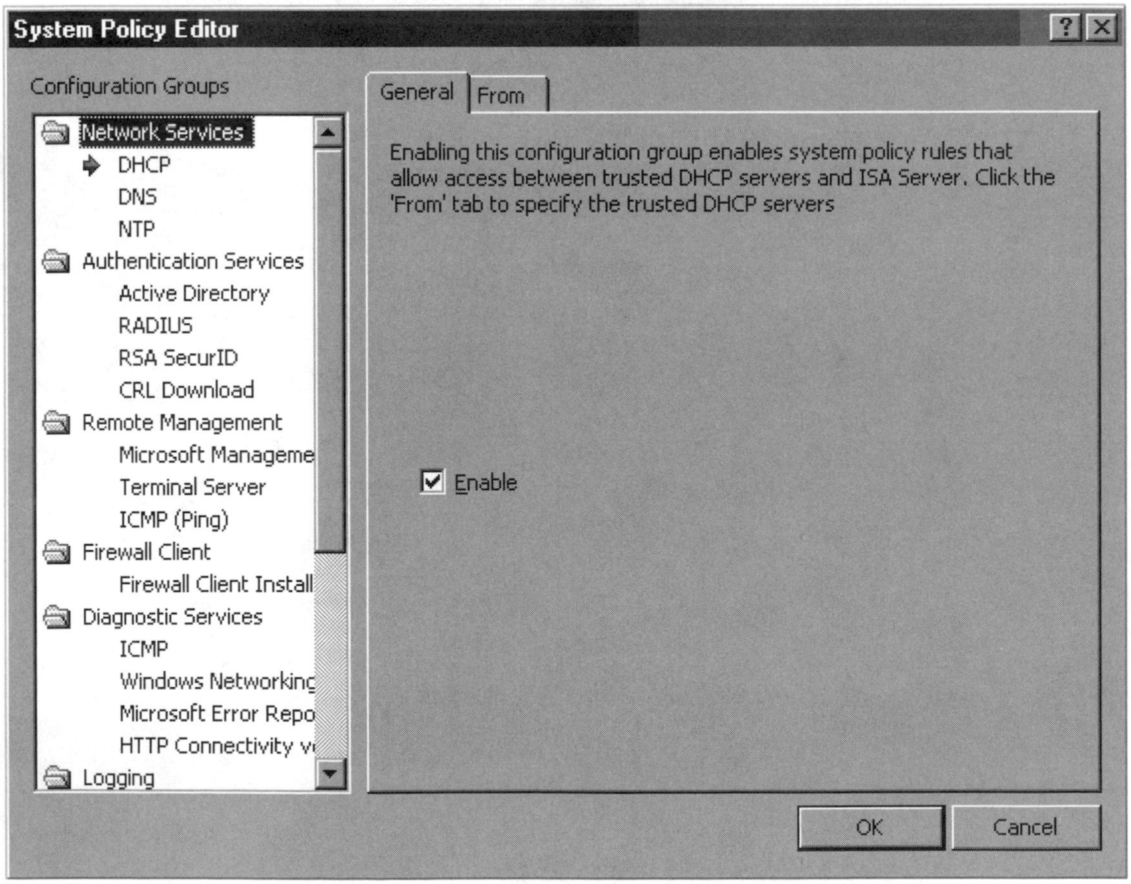

See Table 18.6 for post-installation ISA Firewall System Configuration default settings.

Table 18.6 Default Post-installation ISA Firewall System Configuration

Feature	Default Setting
User permissions	Members of the Administrators group on the local computer can configure firewall policy. If the ISA firewall is a member of the domain, then the Domain Admins global group is automatically included in the local machine's Administrators group.
Definition of Internal network	The Internal network contains IP addresses you specified during setup of the ISA firewall software.
Network Rules	**Local Host Access** Defines a route relationship between the Local Host network and all networks. All connections between the Local Host network (that is, the ISA firewall machine itself) are routed instead of NATed. **Internet Access** Defines a NAT (Network Address Translation) relationship between the Internal Network, Quarantined VPN Clients Network, and the VPN Clients Network – to the External network. From each of these three Networks to the Internet, the connection is NATed. Access is allowed only if you configure the appropriate Access Rules. **VPN Clients to Internal Network** Defines a route relationship between the VPN Clients Network and the Internal Network. Access is allowed only if you enable virtual private network (VPN) client access.
Firewall policy	A default rule (named **Default Rule**) denies traffic between all networks.
System policy	ISA Server is secure by default, while allowing certain critical services to function. Upon installation, some system policy rules are enabled to allow necessary services. We recommend that you review the system policy configuration and customize it so that only services critical to your specific deployment are enabled.
Web chaining	A default rule (named **Default Rule**) specifies that all Web Proxy client requests are retrieved directly from the Internet.
Caching	The cache size is set to 0. All caching is, therefore, disabled.
Alerts	Most alerts are active. We recommend that you review and configure the alerts in accordance with your specific networking needs.
Client configuration	When installed or configured, Firewall and Web Proxy clients have automatic discovery enabled. Web browser applications on Firewall clients are configured when the Firewall client is installed.

Performing a Single NIC Installation (Unihomed ISA Firewall)

This ISA firewall software can be installed on a machine with a single network interface card. This is done to simulate the Proxy Server 2.0 configuration or the ISA Server 2000 caching-only mode. This 2006 ISA firewall does not have a caching-only mode, but you can strip away a significant level of firewall functionality from the ISA firewall when you install it in single-NIC mode.

When the ISA firewall is installed in single-NIC mode, you lose:

- Support for Firewall clients

- Support for full SecureNAT client security and functionality

- Server Publishing Rules

- All protocols except HTTP, HTTPS and HTTP-tunneled (Web proxied) FTP

- Remote Access VPN

- Site-to-Site VPN

- Multi-networking functionality (the entire IPv4 address space is the same network)

- Application-layer inspection except for HTTP

While this stripped version of the ISA firewall retains only a fraction of its ability to act as a network firewall protecting hosts on your corporate network, it does keep full firewall functionality when it comes to protecting itself. The ISA firewall will not be directly accessible to any host, external or internal, unless you enable system policy rules to allow access.

The NIC configuration on the unihomed ISA firewall should set the default gateway as the IP address of any current gateway on the network that allows the unihomed ISA firewall access to the Internet. All other non-local routes need to be configured in the unihomed ISA firewall's routing table.

If you only require a Web Proxy service to perform both forward and reverse proxy, then you can install the ISA firewall on a single NIC machine. The installation process differs a bit from what you find when the ISA firewall is installed on a multi-NIC machine.

Perform the following steps to install the ISA firewall software on a single-NIC machine:

1. Insert the ISA Server 2006 installation CD into the CD-ROM drive or connect to a network share point hosting the ISA Server 2006 installation files. If the installation routine does not start automatically, double-click the **isaautorun.exe** file in the root of the installation files folder tree.

2. On the **Microsoft Internet Security and Acceleration Server 2004** page, click **Review Release Notes**, and read the release notes. The release notes contain very important and topical information regarding changes in basic firewall software functionality. This information may not be included in the Help file or elsewhere, so we highly

recommend that you read it here. After reviewing the release notes, click **Read Setup and Feature Guide**. You may want to read the guide now, just review the major topics covered in the guide, or print it out. Click **Install ISA Server 2006**.

3. Click **Next** on the **Welcome to the Installation Wizard for Microsoft ISA Server 2006** page.

4. Select **I accept the terms in the license agreement option on the License Agreement** page. Click **Next**.

5. On the **Customer Information** page, enter your name and the name of your organization in the **User Name** and **Organization** text boxes. Enter your serial number in the **Product Serial Number** text box. If you installed an evaluation copy of the ISA firewall software and now are installing a licensed version, backup your configuration using the ISA firewall's integrated backup tool, and uninstall the evaluation version. Restart the installation of the licensed version of the ISA firewall software. Click **Next**.

6. On the **Setup Type** page, click the **Custom** option.

7. On the **Custom Setup** page you'll notice that the **Firewall Services**, **Advanced Logging**, and **ISA Server Management** options are selected by default. While you can install the **Firewall Client** share, keep in mind that the unihomed ISA firewall does not support Firewall or SecureNAT clients. The only client type supported is the Web Proxy client. However, if you have full service ISA firewalls on your network, you can install the Firewall client share on this machine and allow network clients to download the Firewall client software from the unihomed ISA firewall. There is no point to installing the SMTP message screener on the unihomed ISA firewall since this mode does not support Server Publishing Rules. Click **Next**.

8. On the **Internal Network** page click **Add**. On the **address ranges for internal network** page, click **Select Network Adapter**, as shown in Figure 18.13.

9. On the **Select Network Adapter** page, **Add the following private ranges** and **Add address ranges based on the Windows Routing Table** are selected. While you don't have to do anything is this checkbox, we recommend that you remove the checkmark from the **Add the following private ranges** option and put a checkmark in the box next to the single NIC installed on the unihomed ISA firewall. Click **OK**.

10. Click **OK** in the **Setup Message** dialog box informing you that the Internal Network was defined based on the routing table. This dialog box really doesn't apply to the unihomed ISA firewall, since all IP addresses in the IPv4 address range (except for the local host network ID) are included in the definition of the Internal Network. The reason why the local host network ID is not included is that this address is included in the Local Host Network definition.

11. In the Internal network address range dialog box (Figure 18.13), you'll see that all IP addresses are included in the definition of the Internal network. Click **OK**.

Figure 18.13 The Internal Network Definition on the Unihomed ISA Firewall

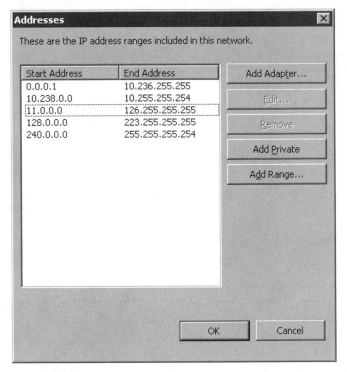

12. Click **Next** on the **Internal Network** page.

13. Click **Next** on the **Firewall Client Connection Settings** page. These settings don't mean anything because Firewall clients are not supported by the unihomed ISA firewall.

14. Click **Next** on the **Services** page.

15. Click **Install** on the **Ready to Install the Program** page.

16. Put a checkmark in the **Invoke ISA Server Management when the wizard closes** checkbox, and click **Finish**.

There are some significant limitations to the single NIC ISA firewall because there is no External network, there is lack of Firewall client support, and other factors. We discuss some of the implications of the unihomed ISA firewall and Access Policy related to this configuration in Chapter 21.

Quick Start Configuration for ISA Firewalls

Many of you will want to install and configure the ISA firewall as quickly as possible and then wait until later to get into the details of ISA firewall configuration. What you want to do is connect the ISA firewall to your network and your Internet connection, install the software, and create a rule that allows all hosts on your private network access to all protocols on the Internet as quickly as possible. Once you're up and running and connected to the Internet, you can then read the rest of this section at your leisure and get into the interesting and powerful configuration options available to you.

To help you, we have included a quick installation and configuration section. In order to make this a quick installation and configuration guide, we're making the following basic assumptions about your network:

- You don't have any other Windows servers on your network. While you can have other Windows services running Windows network services, this guide will include instructions on how to install DNS and DHCP services on the ISA firewall. If you already have a DNS server on your network, you do not need to install a DNS server on the ISA firewall. If you already have a DHCP server on your network, you do not need to install a DHCP server on the ISA firewall.

- We assume that you are installing ISA Server 2006 on Windows Server 2003.

- We assume you have installed Windows Server 2003 on a computer using the default installation settings and have not added any software to the Windows Server 2003 machine.

- We assume your Windows Server 2003 computer already has two Ethernet cards. One NIC is connected to the Internal Network and the other is directly connected to the Internet via a network router, or there is a DSL or cable NAT "router" in front of it.

- We assume that machines on the Internal network are configured as DHCP clients and will use the ISA Server 2006 firewall machine as their DHCP server.

- We assume the Windows Server 2003 machine that you're installing the ISA Server 2006 firewall software on is not a member of a Windows domain. While we recommend that you make the ISA firewall a member of the domain later, the computer running the ISA firewall software does not need to be a domain member. We make this assumption in this quick installation and setup guide because we assume that you have no other Windows servers on your network (you may have Linux, Netware, or other vendors servers, though).

Figure 18.14 shows the ISA firewall and its relationship to the internal and external networks. The internal interface is connected to a hub or switch on the internal network, and the external interface is connected to a hub or switch that also connects to the router.

Figure 18.14 The Physical Relationships between the ISA Server 2006 Firewall and the Internal and External Networks

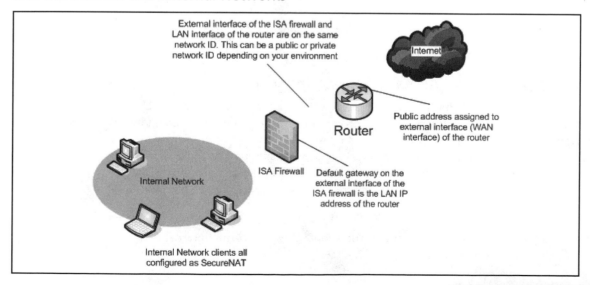

We will perform the following procedures to get the ISA firewall quickly set up and configured:

- Configure ISA firewall's network interfaces.

- Install and configure a DNS server on the ISA Server 2006 firewall computer.

- Install and configure a DHCP server on the ISA Server 2006 firewall computer.

- Install and configure the ISA Server 2006 software.

- Configure the internal network computers as DHCP clients.

Configuring the ISA Firewall's Network Interfaces

The ISA firewall must have at least one *internal* network interface and one *external* network interface. To correctly configure the network interfaces on the ISA firewall:

- Assign IP addresses to the internal and external network interfaces.

- Assign a DNS server address to the internal interface of the ISA firewall.

- Place the internal interface on top of the network interface order.

IP Address and DNS Server Assignment

First, we will assign static IP addresses to the internal and external interfaces of the ISA firewall. The ISA firewall also requires a DNS server address bound to its internal interface. We will *not* need to use DHCP on any of the ISA firewall's network interfaces because the internal interface should always have a static IP address, and the external interface doesn't need to support a dynamic address because it's behind a router.

If your Internet account uses DHCP to assign your public address, your DSL or cable router can handle the task of obtaining and renewing the public address. In addition, if you use PPPoE or VPN to connect to your ISP, your router can also handle these tasks.

In this section, we discuss:

- Configuring the internal network interface, and

- Configuring the external network interface

Configuring the Internal Network Interface

The internal interface must have an IP address that is on the same network ID as other computers on the directly-attached network. This address must be in the private network address range, and the address must not already be in use on the network.

We will configure the ISA firewall to use its internal interface address as its DNS server address.

The ISA firewall must have a *static* IP address bound to its internal interface. Perform the following steps on the Windows Server 2003 machine that will become the ISA firewall:

1. Right-click **My Network Places** on the desktop, and click **Properties**.

2. In the **Network Connections** window, right-click the internal network interface, and click **Properties**.

3. In the network interface's **Properties** dialog box, click **Internet Protocol (TCP/IP)**, and then click **Properties**.

4. In the **Internet Protocol (TCP/IP) Properties** dialog box, select **Use the following IP address**. Enter the IP address for the internal interface in the **IP address** text box. Enter the subnet mask for the internal interface in the **Subnet mask** text box. Do *not* enter a default gateway for the internal interface.

5. Select **Use the following DNS server addresses**. Enter the IP address of the *internal* interface for the ISA firewall in the **Preferred DNS server** text box. This is the same number you entered in step 4 in the **IP address** text box. Click **OK** in the **Internet Protocol (TCP/IP) Properties** dialog box.

6. Click **OK** in the internal interface's **Properties** dialog box.

Configuring the External Network Interface

Perform the following procedures to configure the IP addressing information on the external interface of the ISA firewall:

1. Right-click **My Network Places** on the desktop, and click **Properties**.

2. In the **Network Connections** window, right-click the external network interface, and click **Properties**.

3. In the network interface's **Properties** dialog box, click the **Internet Protocol (TCP/IP)** entry, and then click **Properties**.

4. In the **Internet Properties (TCP/IP) Properties** dialog box, select **Use the following IP address**. Enter the IP address for the external interface in the **IP address** text box. Enter the subnet mask for the external interface in the **Subnet mask** text box. Enter a **Default gateway** for the external interface in its text box. The default gateway is the LAN address of your router.

5. Click **OK** in the internal interface's **Properties** dialog box.

Network Interface Order

The internal interface of the ISA Server 2006 computer is placed on top of the network interface list to ensure the best performance for name resolution. Perform the following steps to configure the network interface on the Windows Server 2003 machine:

Perform the following steps to change the network interface order:

1. Right-click **My Network Places** on the desktop, and click **Properties**.

2. In the **Network and Dial-up Connections** window, click the **Advanced** menu, then click **Advanced Settings**.

3. In the **Advanced Settings** dialog box (Figure 18.15), click the internal interface in the list of **Connections** on the **Adapters and Bindings** tab. After selecting the internal interface, click the up-arrow to move it to the top of the list of interfaces.

Figure 18.15 The Advanced Settings Dialog Box

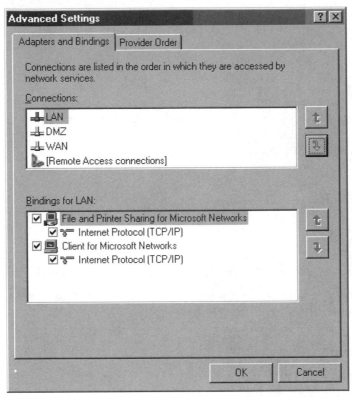

4. Click **OK** in the **Advanced Settings** dialog box.

Installing and Configuring a DNS Server on the ISA Server Firewall

We will install a caching-only DNS server on the ISA firewall. This will allow machines on the Internal Network and the ISA firewall to resolve Internet host names. Note that you *do not* need to perform this step if you already have a DNS server on your internal network. Even if you already have a DNS server located on the internal network, you might consider configuring the ISA firewall computer as a caching-only DNS server and then configure computers on the internal network to use the ISA Server 2006 machine as their DNS server or configure the internal network computers to use your Internal Network DNS server and configure the Internal Network DNS server to use the ISA firewall as a DNS forwarder.

Installing the DNS Service

The DNS Server service is not installed by default on Windows server operating systems. The first step is to install the DNS Server service on the Windows Server 2003 machine that will be the ISA firewall.

Installing the DNS Server Service on Windows Server 2003

Perform the following steps to install the DNS Server service on a Windows Server 2003 computer:

1. Click **Start**, point to **Control Panel**, and click **Add or Remove Programs**.

2. In the **Add or Remove Programs** window, click **Add/Remove Windows Components**.

3. In the **Windows Components Wizard** dialog box, select **Networking Services** from the list of **Components**. *Do not put a checkmark in the checkbox!* After highlighting the **Networking Services** entry, click the **Details** button.

4. In the **Networking Services** dialog box, put a checkmark in the **Domain Name System (DNS)** checkbox, and click **OK**.

5. Click **Next** in the **Windows Components** dialog box.

6. Click **OK** in the **Insert Disk** dialog box. In the **Files Needed** dialog box, provide a path to the i386 folder from the Windows Server 2003 installation CD in the **Copy files from** text box, then click **OK**.

7. Click **Finish** on the **Completing the Windows Components Wizard** page.

8. **Close** the **Add or Remove Programs** window.

Configuring the DNS Service on the ISA Firewall

The DNS Server on the ISA firewall machine performs DNS queries for Internet host names on behalf of computers on the internal network. The DNS Server on the ISA firewall is configured as a *caching-only* DNS server. A caching-only DNS Server does not contain information about your public or private DNS names and domains. The caching-only DNS Server resolves Internet host names and caches the results; it does not answer DNS queries for names on your private internal network DNS zone or your public DNS zone.

If you have an internal network DNS server supporting an Active Directory domain, you can configure the caching-only DNS server located on the ISA firewall to refer client requests to your internal network domain to the DNS server on your internal network. The end result is that the caching-only DNS server on the ISA Server 2006 firewall computer will not interfere with your current DNS server setup.

Configuring the DNS Service in Windows Server 2003

Perform the following steps to configure the DNS service on the Windows Server 2003 computer:

1. Click **Start** and point to **Administrative Tools**. Click the **DNS** entry.

2. Right-click the server name in the left pane of the console, point to **View**, and click **Advanced**.

3. Expand all nodes in the left pane of the DNS console.

4. Right-click the server name in the left pane of the DNS console, and click the **Properties** option.

5. In the server's **Properties** dialog box, click **Interfaces**. Select **Only the following IP addresses**. Click any IP address that *is not* an IP address bound to the internal

interface of the computer. After highlighting the non-internal IP address, click **Remove**. Click **Apply**.

6. Click the **Forwarders** tab, as shown in Figure 18.16. Enter the IP address of your ISP's DNS server in the **Selected domain's forwarder IP address list** text box, and then click **Add**. Put a checkmark in the **Do not use recursion for this domain** checkbox. This **Do not use recursion** option prevents the DNS server on the ISA firewall from trying to perform name resolution itself. The end result is if the forwarder is unable to resolve the name, the name resolution request stops. Click **Apply**.

Figure 18.16 The Forwarders Tab

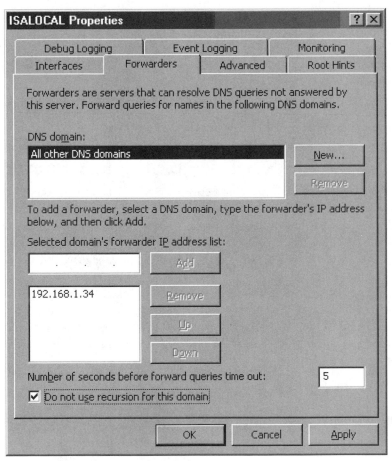

7. Click **OK** in the server's **Properties** dialog box.

8. Right-click the server name; point to **All Tasks**, and click **Restart**.

Perform the following steps *only if* you have an internal network DNS server that you are using to support an Active Directory domain. If you do not have an internal network DNS server and you do not need to resolve internal network DNS names, then bypass the following section on configuring a stub zone.

1. The first step is to create the reverse lookup zone for the Internal Network where the Internal DNS server ID is located. Right-click the **Reverse Lookup Zones** node in the left pane of the console, and click **New Zone**.

2. Click **Next** on the **Welcome to the New Zone Wizard** page.

3. On the **Zone Type** page, select **Stub zone**, and click **Next**.

4. Select **Network ID**. On the **Reverse Lookup Zone Name** page, enter into the **Network ID** text box the ID for the network where the internal network DNS server is located, as shown in Figure 18.17. Click **Next**.

Figure 18.17 The Reverse Lookup Zone Name Page

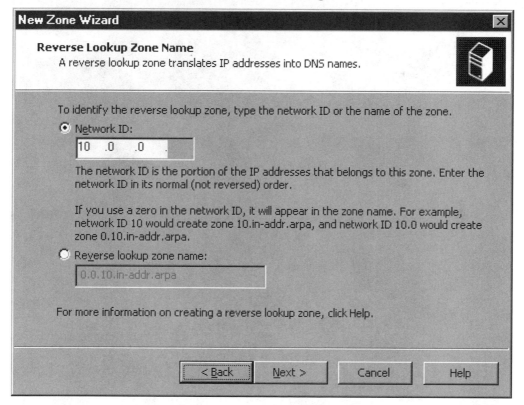

5. Accept the default file name on the **Zone File** page, and click **Next**.

6. On the **Master DNS Servers** page, enter the IP address of your internal network DNS server, and click **Add**. Click **Next**.

7. Click **Finish** on the **Completing the New Zone Wizard** page.

8. The next step is to create the forward lookup zone for the stub zone. Right-click the **Forward Lookup Zones** node in the left pane of the console, and click the **New Zone** command.

9. Click **Next** on the **Welcome to the New Zone Wizard** page.

10. On the **Zone Type** page, select **Stub zone**, and click **Next**.

11. On the **Zone name** page, type the name of your internal network domain in the **Zone name** text box. Click **Next**.

12. On the **Zone File** page (Figure 18.18), accept the default name for the zone file, and click **Next**.

Figure 18.18 The Zone File Page

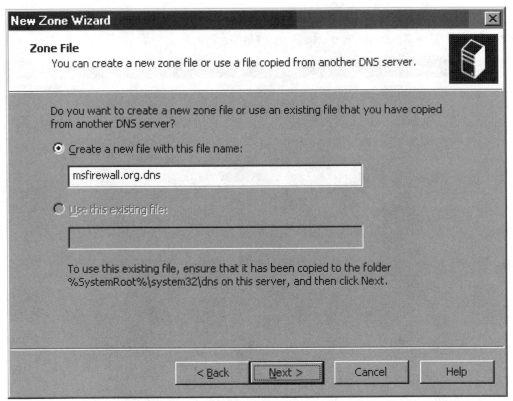

13. On the **Master DNS Servers** page, enter the IP address of your internal network's DNS server, and click **Add**. Click **Next**.

14. Click **Finish** on the **Completing the New Zone Wizard** page.

15. Right-click the server name in the left pane of the console; point to **All Tasks**, and click **Restart**.

Configuring the DNS Service on the Internal Network DNS Server

If your organization has an existing DNS infrastructure, you should configure your Internal network's DNS server to use the DNS server on the ISA Server 2006 firewall as its DNS forwarder.

This provides a more secure DNS configuration because your Internal network DNS server never communicates directly with an untrusted DNS server on the Internet.

The Internal network DNS server forwards DNS queries to the DNS server on the ISA Server 2006 firewall, and the DNS server on the ISA Server 2006 resolves the name, places the result in its own DNS cache, and then returns the IP address to the DNS server on the Internal network.

Perform the following steps on the *Internal network DNS server* to configure it to use the DNS server on the ISA firewall as its forwarder:

1. Click **Start** and point to **Administrative** tools, then click **DNS**.

2. In the **DNS Management** console, right-click the server name in the left pane of the console, and click **Properties**.

3. In the server's **Properties** dialog box, click the **Forwarders** tab, as shown in Figure 18.19.

4. On the **Forwarders** tab, enter the IP address on the Internal interface of the ISA Server 2006 firewall in the **Selected domain's forwarder IP address list** text box. Click **Add**.

5. The IP address for the internal interface of the ISA Server 2006 firewall appears in the list of forwarder addresses (Figure 18.19).

Figure 18.19 The Forwarders Tab

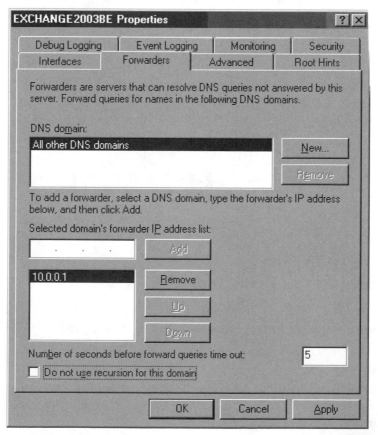

6. Put a checkmark in the **Do not use recursion for this domain** checkbox (Figure 18.20). This option prevents the Internal network DNS server from trying to resolve the name itself in the event that the forwarder on the ISA firewall is unable to resolve the name.

Figure 18.20 Disabling Recursion

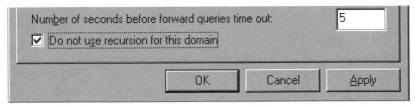

7. Click **Apply**, and then click **OK**.

Note that the DNS server on the Internal Network will not be able to resolve Internet host names yet. We still need to create an Access Rule allowing the DNS server access to the DNS server on the ISA firewall. We will create this Access Rule later in this section.

Installing and Configuring a DHCP Server on the ISA Server Firewall

Each of your computers needs an IP address and other information that allows them to communicate with each other and with computers on the Internet. The DHCP Server service can be installed on the ISA firewall and provide IP addressing information to Internal Network computers. We will assume that you need to use the ISA firewall as your DHCP server. If you already have a DHCP server on your network, you can bypass the following steps.

Installing the DHCP Service

The DHCP Server service can be installed on Windows 2000 Server and Windows Server 2003 computers. The procedure varies slightly between the two operating systems. In this section, we discuss procedures for installing the DHCP Server service on Windows 2000 Server and Windows Server 2003 computers.

Installing the DHCP Server Service on a Windows Server 2003 Computer

Perform the following steps to install the DNS Server service on a Windows Server 2003 computer:

1. Click **Start**; point to **Control Panel**, and click **Add or Remove Programs**.

2. In the **Add or Remove Programs** window, click **Add/Remove Windows Components**.

3. In the **Windows Components Wizard** dialog box, select **Networking Services** from the list of **Components**. *Do not put a checkmark in the checkbox!* After highlighting the **Networking Services** entry, click the **Details** button.

4. In the **Networking Services** dialog box (Figure 18.21), put a checkmark in the **Dynamic Host Configuration Protocol (DHCP)** checkbox, and click **OK**.

Figure 18.21 The Networking Services Dialog Box

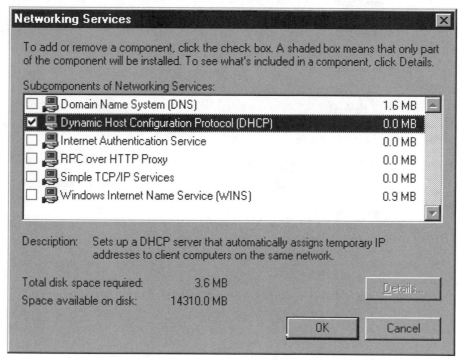

5. Click **Next** in the **Windows Components** dialog box.
6. Click **Finish** on the **Completing the Windows Components Wizard** page.
7. **Close** the **Add or Remove Programs** window.

Configuring the DHCP Service

The DHCP Server must be configured with a collection of IP addresses it can assign to machines on your private network. The DHCP Server also provides information in addition to an IP address, such as a DNS server address, default gateway, and primary domain name.

The DNS server and default gateway addresses assigned to your computers will be the IP address on the internal interface of the ISA firewall. The DHCP server uses a *DHCP scope* to provide this information to the internal network clients. You must create a DHCP scope that provides the correct IP addressing information to your internal network clients.

Perform the following steps to configure the Windows Server 2003 DHCP Server with a scope that will assign the proper IP addressing information to the internal network clients:

1. Click **Start** and point to **Administrative Tools**. Click **DHCP**.
2. Expand all nodes in the left pane of the **DHCP** console. Right-click the server name in the left pane of the console, and click **New Scope**.

3. Click **Next** on the **Welcome to the New Scope Wizard** page.

4. Type **SecureNAT Client Scope** in the **Name** text box on the **Scope Name** page. Click **Next**.

5. On the **IP Address Range** page, enter the first IP address and the last IP address for the range in the **Start IP address** and **End IP address** text boxes. For example, if you are using the network ID 192.168.1.0 with a subnet mask of 255.255.255.0, then enter the start IP address as **192.168.1.1** and the end IP address as **192.168.1.254**. Click **Next**.

6. On the **Add Exclusions** page, enter the IP address of the internal interface for the ISA firewall in the **Start IP address** text box, and click **Add**. If you have servers or workstations on the network that have statically-assigned IP addresses that you do not want to change, add those addresses to the exclusions list. Click **Next** after adding all addresses you want to exclude from the DHCP scope.

7. Accept the default value on the **Lease Duration** page, and click **Next**.

8. On the **Configuring DHCP Options** page, select **Yes, I want to configure these options now,** and click **Next**.

9. On the **Router** page, enter the IP address of the internal interface for the ISA firewall, and click **Add**. Click **Next**.

10. On the **Domain Name and DNS Servers** page, enter the IP address of the internal interface for the ISA firewall in the **IP address** text box, and click **Add**. *If you have an Active Directory domain on the Internal network*, enter the name of your Internal network domain in the **Parent domain** text box. Do *not* enter a domain name in the **Parent domain** text box *unless* you have an existing Active Directory domain on the internal network. Click **Next**.

11. Do not enter any information on the **WINS Servers** page unless you already have a WINS server on the internal network. If you already have a WINS server, enter that IP address in the **IP address** text box. Click **Next**.

12. Select **Yes, I want to activate this scope now** on the **Activate Scope** page, and click **Yes**.

13. Click **Finish** on the **Completing the New Scope Wizard** page.

Installing and Configuring the ISA Server 2006 Software

We're now ready to install the ISA firewall software.

The following steps demonstrate how to install the ISA firewall software on a dual-homed Windows Server 2003 machine:

1. Insert the ISA Server 2006 installation media into the CD-ROM drive or connect to a network share hosting the ISA Server 2006 installation files. If the installation routine does not start automatically, double-click the **isaautorun.exe** file in the root of the installation files tree.

2. On the **Microsoft Internet Security and Acceleration Server 2004** page, click **Review Release Notes** and read the notes. The release notes contain useful information

about important issues and configuration options. After reading the release notes, click **Read Setup and Feature Guide**. You don't need to read the entire guide right now, but you may want to print it to read later. Click **Install ISA Server 2004**.

3.   Click **Next** on the **Welcome to the Installation Wizard for Microsoft ISA Server 2006** page.

4.   Select **I accept the terms in the license agreement** on the **License Agreement** page. Click **Next**.

5.   On the **Customer Information** page, enter your name and the name of your organization in the **User Name** and **Organization** text boxes. Enter your serial number in the **Product Serial Number** text box. Click **Next**.

6.   On the **Setup Type** page, select the **Custom** option. If you do not want to install the ISA firewall software on the C: drive, click the **Change** button to change the location of the program files on the hard disk. Click **Next**.

7.   On the **Custom Setup** page, choose the components to install. By default, the **Firewall Services**, **ISA Server Management**, and Advanced Logging are installed. To install the **Firewall Client Installation Share** so that we have the option later to install the Firewall client on Internal Network client machines, we will have to copy the client share directory from the ISAServer 2006 cd to a location of your choice and share it manually.. The Firewall client adds a significant level of security to your network, and you should install the Firewall client on Internal network clients whenever possible. Click **Next**.

Figure 18.22 The Custom Setup Page

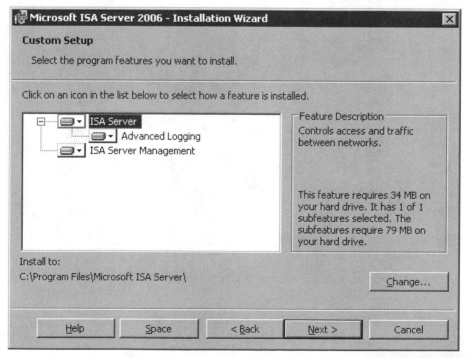

8. On the **Internal Network** page, click **Change**. The Internal network is different from the Local Address Table (LAT) used by ISA Server 2000. The Internal network contains trusted network services with which the ISA firewall must communicate. Examples of such services include Active Directory domain controllers, DNS, DHCP, terminal services client management workstations, and others. The firewall System Policy uses the Internal network definition in many of its System Policy Rules.

9. On the **Addresses** setup page, click the **Add Adapter** button.

10. Put a checkmark next to the adapter connected to the Internal network. In this example we have renamed the network interfaces so that the interface name reflects its location. Click **OK**.

Figure 18.23 The Select Network Adapter Page

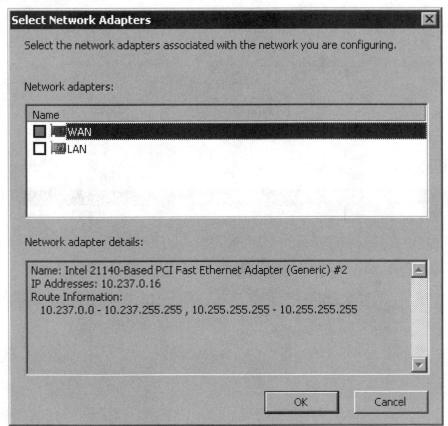

11. Click **OK** in the **Internal network address ranges** dialog box.

12. Click **Next** on the **Internal Network** page.

13. Put a checkmark by **Allow non-encrypted Firewall client connections** (Figure 18.10) if you want to support Firewall clients running previous versions of the Winsock Proxy

(Proxy Server 2.0) or the ISA Server 2000 Firewall client software. This will allow you to continue using the ISA Server 2000 Firewall client software as you migrate to ISA Server 2006. When you migrate your Firewall clients to the ISA 2006 version of the Firewall client, the channel between the Firewall clients and the ISA firewall will be encrypted. The ISA 2006 Firewall client software encrypts the user credentials that are transparently sent from the Firewall client machine to the ISA firewall. For best security practice, it is recommended that you deploy the latest version of the Firewall Client software. This can be downloaded from http://www.microsoft.com/downloads/details. aspx?displaylang=en&FamilyID=05c2c932-b15a-4990-b525-66380743da89

14. On the **Services** page, note that the **SNMP** and **IIS Admin Service** will be stopped during installation. If the **Internet Connection Firewall (ICF)/Internet Connection Sharing (ICF)** and/or **IP Network Address Translation** services are installed on the ISA Server 2006 machine, they will be disabled, as they conflict with the ISA Server 2006 firewall software.

15. Click **Install** on the **Ready to Install the Program** page.

16. On the **Installation Wizard Completed** page, click **Finish**.

17. Click **Yes** on the **Microsoft ISA Server** dialog box informing that you must restart the server.

18. Log on as an **Administrator** after the machine restarts.

19. Click **Start** and point to **All Programs**. Point to **Microsoft ISA Server**, and click **ISA Server Management**. The **Microsoft Internet Security and Acceleration Server 2006** management console opens and displays the **Welcome to Microsoft Internet Security and Acceleration Server 2006** page.

Configuring the ISA Firewall

Now we're ready to configure Access Policy on the ISA firewall. We need to create the following five Access Rules:

- A rule that allows Internal Network clients access to the DHCP server on the ISA firewall

- A rule that allows the ISA firewall to send DHCP messages to the hosts on the Internal network

- A rule that allows the Internal Network DNS server to use the ISA firewall as its DNS server. Create this rule only if you have an Internal Network DNS server.

- A rule that allows Internal Network clients access to the caching-only DNS server on the ISA firewall. Use this rule if you do not have a DNS server on the Internal Network, or if you have a DNS server on the Internal Network and you want to use the ISA firewall as a caching-only DNS server with a stub zone pointing to your Internal Network domain.

- An "All Open" rule allowing Internal Network clients access to all protocols and sites on the Internet

Tables 18.7 through 18.11 show the details of each of these rules.

Table 18.7 DHCP Request to Server

Name	DHCP Request to Server
Action	Allow
Protocols	DHCP (request)
From	Anywhere
To	Local Host
Users	All Users
Schedule	Always
Content Types	All content types
Purpose	This rule allows DHCP clients to send DHCP requests to the DHCP server installed on the ISA firewall.

Table 18.8 DHCP Reply from Server

Name	DHCP Reply from Server
Action	Allow
Protocols	DHCP (reply)
From	Local Host
To	Internal
Users	All Users
Schedule	Always
Content Types	All content types
Purpose	This rule allows the DHCP server on the ISA firewall to reply to DHCP requests made by Internal network DHCP clients.

Table 18.9 Internal DNS Server to Forwarder

Name	Internal DNS Server to DNS forwarder
Action	Allow
Protocols	DNS
From	DNS Server*
To	Local Host
Users	All Users
Schedule	Always
Content Types	All content types
Purpose	This rule allows the Internal network DNS server to forward queries to the DNS forwarder on the ISA Server 2006 firewall machine. **Create this rule only if you have an Internal Network DNS server.**

*User defined

Table 18.10 Internal Network to DNS Server

Name	Internal Network to DNS Server
Action	Allow
Protocols	DNS
From	Internal
To	Local Host
Users	All Users
Schedule	Always
Content Types	All content types
Purpose	This rule allows Internal network clients access to the caching-only DNS server on the ISA firewall. Create this rule if you do not have an Internal Network DNS server, or if you have decided that you want to use the caching-only DNS server as your caching-only forwarder for all Internal Network clients, even when you have an Internal Network DNS server.

Table 18.11 All Open

Name	All Open
Action	Allow
Protocols	All Outbound Traffic
From	Internal
To	External
Users	All Users
Schedule	Always
Content Types	All content types
Purpose	This rule allows Internal network clients access to all protocols and sites on the Internet.

In addition to these Access Rules, you should configure the firewall System Policy to allow DHCP replies from External network DHCP servers.

DHCP Request to Server Rule

Perform the following steps to create the **DHCP Request to Server** rule:

1. In the **Microsoft Internet Security and Acceleration Server 2004** management console, expand the server name, and click **Firewall Policy**.

2. In the **Firewall Policy** node, click the **Tasks** tab in the Task pane. On the Task pane, click **Create a New Access Rule**.

3. On the **Welcome to the New Access Rule Wizard** page, enter **DHCP Request to Server** in the **Access Rule name** text box. Click **Next**.

4. On the **Rule Action** page, select **Allow**, and click **Next**.

5. On the **Protocols** page, select the **Selected protocols** option from the **This rule applies to** list, and click **Add**.

6. In the **Add Protocols** dialog box (Figure 18.24), click the **Infrastructure** folder. Double-click the **DHCP (request)** entry, and click **Close**.

Figure 18.24 The Add Protocols Dialog Box

7. Click **Next** on the **Protocols** page.

8. On the **Access Rule Sources** page, click **Add**.

9. In the **Add Network Entities** dialog box, click the **Computer Sets** folder. Double-click the **Anywhere** entry, and click **Close**.

10. Click **Next** on the **Access Rule Sources** page.

11. On the **Access Rule Destinations** page, click **Add**.

12. In the **Add Network Entities** dialog box, click the **Networks** folder, and double-click **Local Host**. Click **Close**.

13. Click **Next** on the **Access Rule Destinations** page.

14. On the **User Sets** page, accept the default entry, **All Users**, and click **Next**.

15. On the **Completing the New Access Rule Wizard** page, review the settings, and click **Finish**.

DHCP Reply from Server Rule

Perform the following steps to create the **DHCP Reply from Server** rule:

1. In the **Microsoft Internet Security and Acceleration Server 2004** management console, expand the server name, and click **Firewall Policy**.

2. In the **Firewall Policy** node, click the **Tasks** tab in the Task pane. On the Task pane, click **Create a New Access Rule**.

3. On the **Welcome to the New Access Rule Wizard** page, enter **DHCP Reply from Server** in the **Access Rule name** text box. Click **Next**.

4. On the **Rule Action** page, select **Allow**, and click **Next**.

5. On the **Protocols** page, select the **Selected protocols** option from the **This rule applies to** list, and click **Add**.

6. In the **Add Protocols** dialog box, click the **Infrastructure** folder. Double-click **DHCP (reply)**, and click **Close**.

7. Click **Next** on the **Protocols** page.

Figure 18.25 The Protocols Page

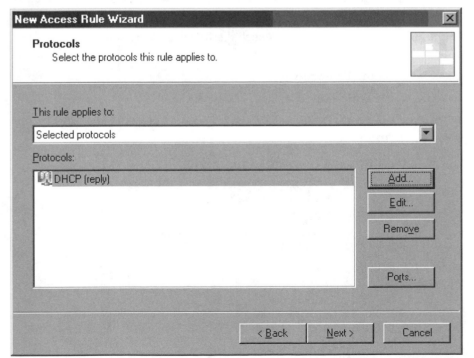

8. On the **Access Rule Sources** page, click **Add**.

9. In the **Add Network Entities** dialog box, click the **Networks** folder. Double-click the **Local Host** entry, and click **Close**.

10. Click **Next** on the **Access Rule Sources** page.

11. On the **Access Rule Destinations** page, click **Add**.

12. In the **Add Network Entities** dialog box, click the **Networks** folder, and then double-click the **Internal** entry. Click **Close**.

13. Click **Next** on the **Access Rule Destinations** page.

14. On the **User Sets** page, accept the default entry, **All Users**, and click **Next**.

15. On the **Completing the New Access Rule Wizard** page, review the settings, and click **Finish**.

Internal DNS Server to DNS Forwarder Rule

Perform the following steps to create the **Internal DNS Server to DNS Forwarder** rule:

1. In the **Microsoft Internet Security and Acceleration Server 2004** management console, expand the server name, and click **Firewall Policy**.

2. In the **Firewall Policy** node, click the **Tasks** tab in the Task pane. On the Task pane, click **Create a New Access Rule**.

3. On the **Welcome to the New Access Rule Wizard** page, enter **Internal DNS Server to DNS Forwarder** in the **Access Rule name** text box. Click **Next**.

4. On the **Rule Action** page, select **Allow**, and click **Next**.

5. On the **Protocols** page, select the **Selected protocols** option from the **This rule applies to** list, and click **Add**.

6. In the **Add Protocols** dialog box, click the **Infrastructure** folder. Double-click the **DNS** entry, and click **Close**.

7. Click **Next** on the **Protocols** page.

8. On the **Access Rule Sources** page, click **Add**.

9. In the **Add Network Entities** dialog box (Figure 18.26), click the **New** menu, then click **Computer**.

Figure 18.26 Selecting the Computer Command

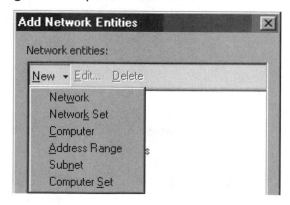

10. In the **New Computer Rule Element** dialog box, enter **Internal DNS Server** in the **Name** text box. Enter **10.0.0.2** in the **Computer IP Address** text box. Click **OK**.

11. In the **Add Network Entities** dialog box (Figure 18.27), click the **Computers** folder, and double-click **Internal DNS Server**. Click **Close**.

Figure 18.27 Selecting the New Computer Object

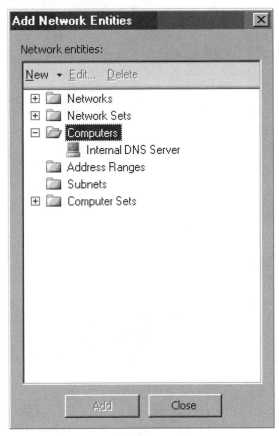

12. Click **Next** on the **Access Rule Sources** page.

13. On the **Access Rule Destinations** page, click **Add**.

14. In the **Add Network Entities** dialog box, click the **Networks** folder, and double-click **Local Host**. Click **Close**.

15. Click **Next** on the **Access Rule Destinations** page.

16. On the **User Sets** page, accept the default entry, **All Users**, and click **Next**.

17. On the **Completing the New Access Rule Wizard** page, review the settings, and click **Finish**.

Internal Network to DNS Server

Perform the following steps to create the **Internal Network to DNS Server** rule:

1. In the **Microsoft Internet Security and Acceleration Server 2006** management console, expand the server name, and click **Firewall Policy**.

2. In the **Firewall Policy** node, click the **Tasks** tab in the Task pane. On the Task pane, click **Create a New Access Rule**.

3. On the **Welcome to the New Access Rule Wizard** page, enter **Internal Network to DNS Server** in the **Access Rule name** text box. Click **Next**.

4. On the **Rule Action** page, select **Allow**, and click **Next**.

5. On the **Protocols** page, select the **Selected protocols** option from the **This rule applies to** list, and click **Add**.

6. In the **Add Protocols** dialog box, click the **Common Protocols** folder. Double-click the **DNS** entry, and click **Close**.

7. Click **Next** on the **Protocols** page.

8. On the **Access Rule Sources** page, click **Add**.

9. In the **Add Network Entities** dialog box, click the **Networks** folder. Double-click **Internal**, and click **Close**.

10. Click **Next** on the **Access Rule Sources** page.

11. On the **Access Rule Destinations** page, click **Add**.

12. In the **Add Network Entities** dialog box, click the **Networks** folder, and double-click **Local Host**. Click **Close**.

13. Click **Next** on the **Access Rule Destinations** page.

14. On the **User Sets** page, accept the default entry, **All Users**, and click **Next**.

15. On the **Completing the New Access Rule Wizard** page, review the settings, and click **Finish**.

The All Open Rule

Perform the following steps to create the **All Open** rule:

1. In the **Microsoft Internet Security and Acceleration Server 2006** management console, expand the server name, and click **Firewall Policy**.

2. In the **Firewall Policy** node, click the **Tasks** tab in the Task pane. On the Task pane, click **Create a New Access Rule**.

3. On the **Welcome to the New Access Rule Wizard** page, enter **All Open** in the **Access Rule name** text box. Click **Next**.

4. On the **Rule Action** page, select **Allow**, and click **Next**.

5. On the **Protocols** page, select **All outbound traffic** from the **This rule applies to** list, and click **Next**.

6. On the **Access Rule Sources** page, click **Add**.

7. In the **Add Network Entities** dialog box, click the **Networks** folder. Double-click **Internal**, and click **Close**.

8. Click **Next** on the **Access Rule Sources** page.

9. On the **Access Rule Destinations** page, click **Add**.

10. In the **Add Network Entities** dialog box, click the **Networks** folder, and double-click **External**. Click **Close**.

11. Click **Next** on the **Access Rule Destinations** page.

12. On the **User Sets** page, accept the default entry, **All Users**, and click **Next**.

13. On the **Completing the New Access Rule Wizard** page, review the settings, and click **Finish**.

Your Access Rule should look like those in Figure 18.28. Note that in this example, you do not need to reorder the rules. When you start creating advanced Access Rules to control inbound and outbound access, you may need to reorder rules to obtain the desired results.

Figure 18.28 The Resulting Firewall Policy

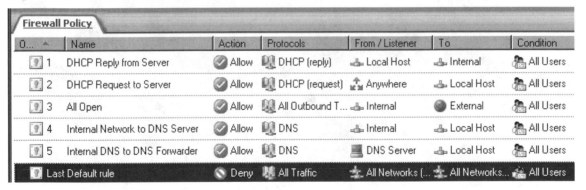

Configuring the Internal Network Computers

Internal Network computers are set up as ISA Server *SecureNAT* clients. A SecureNAT client is a machine with a default gateway address set to an IP address of a network device that routes Internet-bound requests to the internal IP address of the 2006 ISA Server 2006 firewall.

When Internal network computers are on the same network ID as the internal interface of the ISA firewall, the default gateway of the internal network computers is set as the internal IP address on the ISA firewall machine. This is how the DHCP scope on the DHCP server located on the ISA firewall is configured.

We will configure internal network computers that are on the same network ID as the internal interface of the 2006 ISA Server 2006 firewall and clients that may be located on network IDs that are not on the same network ID. This latter configuration is more common on larger networks that have more than one network ID on the internal network.

Configuring Internal Clients as DHCP Clients

DHCP clients request IP addressing information from a DHCP server. In this section, you will find out how to configure the Windows (Server or Professional) client as a DHCP client. The procedure is similar for all Windows-based clients. Perform the following steps to configure the internal network client and a DHCP client:

1. Right-click **My Network Places** on the desktop, and click **Properties**.

2. In the **Network Connections** window, right-click the external network interface, and click **Properties**.

3. In the network interface's **Properties** dialog box, click the **Internet Protocol (TCP/IP)** entry, and click **Properties**.

4. In the **Internet Protocol (TCP/IP) Properties** dialog box (Figure 18.29), select **Obtain an IP address automatically**.

Figure 18.29 The Internet Protocol (TCP/IP) Properties Dialog Box

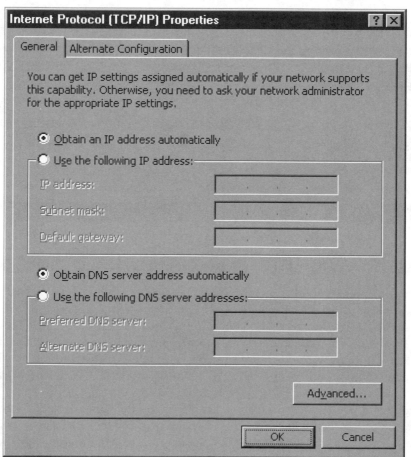

5. Select **Use the following DNS server addresses**. Enter the IP address of the internal interface in the **Preferred DNS server** text box. Click **OK** in the **Internet Protocol (TCP/IP) Properties** dialog box.

6. Click **OK** in the internal interface's **Properties** dialog box.

In Figure 18.30, you can see a Network Monitor trace of a Windows XP client sending a request to the caching-only DNS server on the ISA firewall for an Internal Network domain for which we created a stub zone. The following eight frames are in the trace:

1. The client sends a reverse lookup query to the DNS server for the IP address of the DNS server itself. This allows the client to ascertain the name of the DNS server.

2. The caching-only DNS server on the ISA firewall responds to the Windows XP client with the answer to the query made in frame #1.

3. The Windows XP client sends a query to the caching-only DNS server on the ISA firewall for www.msfirewall.org. The msfireall.org domain is the name of the Internal Network domain.

4. An ARP broadcast is made by the ISA firewall to discover the IP address of the DNS server authoritative for the Internal Network domain.

5. The DNS server returns its IP address to the ISA firewall in an ARP broadcast.

6. The ISA firewall sends a query to the Internal DNS server to resolve the name of the Internal domain host.

7. The Internal DNS server returns the answer to the query to the ISA firewall.

8. The ISA firewall returns the response to the Windows XP client that made the original request.

Figure 18.30 DNS Queries in Network Monitor Trace

```
DNS        0x1:Std Qry for 1.0.0.10.in-addr.arpa. of type Dom. na...    10.0.0.5        10.0.0.1
DNS        0x1:Std Qry Resp. for 1.0.0.10.in-addr.arpa. of type D...    10.0.0.1        10.0.0.5
DNS        0x2:Std Qry for www.msfirewall.org. of type Host Addr ...    10.0.0.5        10.0.0.1
ARP_RARP   ARP: Request, Target IP: 10.0.0.2
ARP_RARP   ARP: Reply, Target IP: 10.0.0.1 Target Hdwr Addr: 000C...
DNS        0x30F8:Std Qry for www.msfirewall.org. of type Host Ad...    10.0.0.1        10.0.0.2
DNS        0x30F8:Std Qry Resp. Auth. NS is msfirewall.org. of ty...    10.0.0.2        10.0.0.1
DNS        0x2:Std Qry Resp. Auth. NS is msfirewall.org. of type ...    10.0.0.1        10.0.0.5
```

Figure 18.31 shows the domains cached on the caching-only DNS server located on the ISA firewall. You can enable the Advanced View in the DNS console and see the **Cached Lookups** node. After expanding the **.(root)** folder, you can see the domains for which the DNS server has cached DNS query information. If you double-click on any of the domains, you will see the actual resource records that the DNS server has cached.

Figure 18.31 DNS Domains Cached by the Caching-only DNS Server on the ISA Firewall

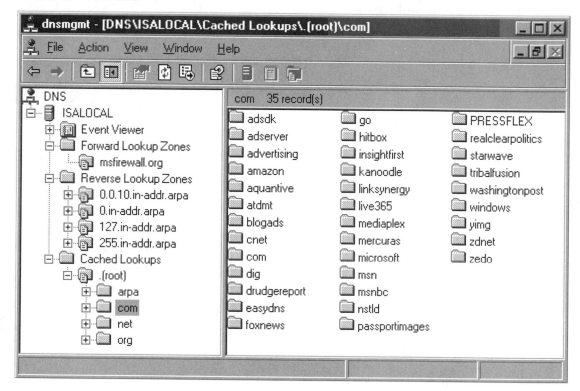

Hardening the Base ISA Firewall Configuration and Operating System

While the ISA firewall software does an exceptional job of protecting the firewall from attack, there are things you can do to further harden the ISA firewall configuration and the underlying operating system. In this section, we'll discuss the following hardening and local security issues:

- **ISA firewall service dependencies** You need to know what services the ISA firewall depends on before disabling services on the firewall. In this section, we'll present the list of ISA firewall software dependencies.

- **Service requirements for common tasks performed on the ISA firewall** There are several maintenance tasks that you can run on the ISA firewall that depend on features provided by the underlying operating system. In this section, we'll examine some of these features and the services they depend upon.

- **Client roles for the ISA firewall client rules** This ISA firewall may need to act as a network client to a variety of network services. In this section, we'll review some of the network client roles and operating system services required for the ISA firewall to fulfill those roles.

- **ISA firewall administrative roles and permissions** Not all ISA firewall administrators are created equal. In this section, we'll discuss the ISA firewall administrative roles and how to provide users more granular control over the ISA firewall configuration and management.

- **ISA firewall lockdown mode** The ISA firewall needs to protect itself and the networks dependent on it in the event that an attack shuts down the ISA firewalls Firewall Service. In this section, we'll discuss the ISA firewall's Lockdown Mode.

ISA Firewall Service Dependencies

One of the more frustrating aspects of the ISA Server 2000 firewall was that there was never any definitive guidance regarding what services were required for full firewall functionality. Many ISA fans attempted to divine the service dependencies, but no hard and fast guidance was ever developed. To make life even more difficult for the ISA Server 2000 firewall administrator, the ISA Server 2000 System Hardening Templates invariably broke key features of the firewall and the underlying operating system.

These problems are corrected with the new ISA firewall. Now we know the exact services required by the ISA firewall software. Table 18.12 lists the core services that must be enabled for ISA Server and the ISA Server computer to function properly.

Table 18.12 Services on which the ISA Firewall Software Depends

Service Name	Rationale	Startup Mode
COM+ Event System	Core operating system	Manual
Cryptographic Services	Core operating system (security)	Automatic
Event Log	Core operating system	Automatic
IPSec Services	Core operating system (security)	Automatic
Logical Disk Manager	Core operating system (disk management)	Automatic
Logical Disk Manager Administrative Service	Core operating system (disk management)	Manual
Microsoft Firewall	Required for normal functioning of ISA Server	Automatic
Microsoft ISA Server Control	Required for normal functioning of ISA Server	Automatic
Microsoft ISA Server Job Scheduler	Required for normal functioning of ISA Server	Automatic
Microsoft ISA Server Storage	Required for normal functioning of ISA Server	Automatic
MSSQL$MSFW	Required when MSDE logging is used for ISA Server	Automatic
Network Connections	Core operating system (network infrastructure)	Manual
NTLM Security Support Provider	Core operating system (security)	Manual

Continued

Table 18.12 Continued

Service Name	Rationale	Startup Mode
Plug and Play	Core operating system	Automatic
Protected Storage	Core operating system (security)	Automatic
Remote Access Connection Manager	Required for normal functioning of ISA Server	Manual
Remote Procedure Call (RPC)	Core operating system	Automatic
Secondary Logon	Core operating system (security)	Automatic
Security Accounts Manager	Core operating system	Automatic
Server*	Required for ISA Server Firewall Client Share (and others depending on your requirements)*	Automatic*
Smart Card	Core operating system (security)	Manual
SQLAgent$MSFW	Required when MSDE logging is used for ISA Server (not installed when Advanced Logging is not selected during installation)	Manual
System Event Notification	Core operating system	Automatic
Telephony	Required for normal functioning of ISA Server	Manual
Virtual Disk Service (VDS)	Core operating system (disk management)	Manual
Windows Management Instrumentation (WMI)	Core operating system (WMI)	Automatic
WMI Performance Adapter	Core operating system (WMI)	Manual

*The startup mode for the Server service should be set as **Automatic** in the following circumstances:

- You install Firewall client installation share on the ISA firewall

- You use Routing and Remote Access Management, rather than ISA Server Management, to configure a virtual private network (VPN). Required if you want to use EAP user certificate authentication for demand-dial VPN connections and troubleshooting of demand-dial VPN connections

- IF other tasks or roles table require the Server service

■   The startup mode for the Routing and Remote Access service is Manual. ISA Server starts the service only if a VPN is enabled. Note that the Server service is required only if you need access to Routing and Remote Access console (rather than **Microsoft Internet Security and Acceleration Server 2006** management console) to configure a remote-access VPN or site-to-site.

Service Requirements for Common Tasks Performed on the ISA Firewall

Specific services must be enabled in order for the ISA firewall to perform necessary tasks. All services that are not used should be disabled. Table 18.13 lists a number of tasks the ISA firewall's underlying operating system may need to perform. Enable those services required to perform the tasks you want to perform on the ISA firewall and disable services responsible for tasks you will not be using.

Table 18.13 Services Required for Common Tasks Performed on the ISA Firewall

Task	Usage Scenario	Services Required	Startup Mode
Application Installation locally using Windows Installer	Required to install, uninstall, or repair applications using the Microsoft Installer Service. Often required to install ISA firewall add-ins to enhance firewall functionality and protection	Windows Installer	Manual
Backup	Required if using NTBackup or other backup programs on the ISA firewall	Microsoft Software Shadow Copy Provider	Manual
Backup	Required if using NTBackup or other backup programs on the ISA firewall	Volume Shadow Copy	Manual
Backup	Required if using NTBackup or other backup program on the ISA firewall	Removable Storage Service	Manual
Error Reporting	Required for error reporting, which helps improve Windows reliability by reporting critical faults to Microsoft for analysis	Error Reporting Service	Automatic

Continued

Table 18.13 Continued

Task	Usage Scenario	Services Required	Startup Mode
Help and Support	Allows collection of historical computer data for Microsoft Product Support Services incident escalation	Help and Support	Automatic
Host the Firewall client installation share	Required to allow computers SMB/ CIFS connections to the ISA firewall to install the Firewall client software	Server	Automatic
MSDE logging	Required to allow logging using MSDE databases. If you do not enable the applicable service, you can log to SQL databases or to files. However, you will not be able to use the Log Viewer in off-line mode. Required only when ISA Advanced logging is installed	SQLAgent$MSFW	Manual
MSDE logging	Required to allow logging using MSDE databases. If you do not enable the applicable service, you can log to SQL databases or to files. However, you will not be able to use the Log Viewer in off-line mode. Required only when Advanced logging is installed	MSSQL$MSFW	Automatic
Performance Monitor – Background Collect	Allows background collecting of performance data on the ISA firewall	Performance Logs and Alerts	Automatic

Table 18.13 Continued

Task	Usage Scenario	Services Required	Startup Mode
Print to a remote computer	Allows printing from the ISA Server computer (not recommended)	Print Spooler	Automatic
Print to a remote computer	Allows printing from the ISA Server computer (not recommended that you send print jobs from the ISA firewall)	TCP/IP NetBIOS Helper	Automatic
Print to a remote computer	Allows printing from the ISA Server computer (not recommended that you send print jobs from the ISA firewall)	Workstation	Automatic
Remote Windows administration	Allows remote management of the Windows server (not required for remote management of the ISA firewall software)	Server	Automatic
Remote Windows administration	Allows remote management of the Windows server (not required for remote management of the ISA firewall software)	Remote Registry	Automatic
Time Synchronization	Allows the ISA firewall to contact an NTP server to synchronize its clock. An accurate clock is important for event auditing and other security protocols.	Windows Time	Automatic
Remote Assistant	Allows the Remote Assistance feature to be used on this computer (not recommended that you run remote assistance sessions from the ISA firewall)	Help and Support	Automatic

Continued

Table 18.13 Continued

Task	Usage Scenario	Services Required	Startup Mode
Remote Assistant	Allows the Remote Assistance feature to be used on this computer (not recommended that you run remote assistance sessions from the ISA firewall)	Remote Desktop Help Session Manager	Manual
Remote Assistant	Allows the Remote Assistance feature to be used on this computer	Terminal Services	Manual

Client Roles for the ISA Firewall

The ISA firewall may need to act in the role of client to network services located on protected and non-protected Networks. Network client services are required for the ISA firewall to act in its role of network client. Table 18.14 lists possible network client roles the ISA firewall may act as, describes when they may be required, and lists the services that should be enabled when you enable the role.

Table 18.14 Service Requirements Based on the ISA Firewall's Client Roles

Client Role	Usage Scenario	Services Required	Startup Mode
Automatic Update client	Select this role to allow automatic detection and update from Microsoft Windows Update.	Automatic Updates	Automatic
Automatic Update client	Select this role to allow automatic detection and update from Microsoft Windows Update.	Background Intelligent Transfer Service	Manual
DHCP client	Select this role if the ISA Server computer receives its IP address automatically from a DHCP server.	DHCP Client	Automatic
DNS client	Select this role if the ISA Server computer needs to receive name resolution information from other servers.	DNS Client	Automatic

Table 18.14 Continued

Client Role	Usage Scenario	Services Required	Startup Mode
Domain member	Select this role if the ISA Server computer belongs to a domain.	Network location awareness (NLA)	Manual
Domain member	Select this role if the ISA Server computer belongs to a domain.	Net logon	Automatic
Domain member	Select this role if the ISA Server computer belongs to a domain.	Windows Time	Automatic
Dynamic DNS registration	Select this role to allow the ISA Server computer to automatically register its name and address information with a DNS Server.	DHCP Client	Automatic
Microsoft Networking client	Select this role if the ISA Server computer has to connect to other Windows clients. If you do not select this role, the ISA Server computer will not be able to access shares on remote computers; for example, to publish reports.	TCP/IP NetBIOS Helper	Automatic
Microsoft Networking client	Select this role if the ISA Server computer has to connect to other Windows clients. If you do not select this role, the ISA Server computer will not be able to access shares on remote computers; for example, to publish reports.	Workstation	Automatic
WINS client	Select this role if the ISA Server computer uses WINS-based name resolution.	TCP/IP NetBIOS Helper	Automatic

After determining the appropriate service configuration for your ISA firewall, you can save the configuration in a Windows security template (.inf) file. Check www.isaserver.org for sample ISA security templates covering several common scenarios.

ISA Firewall Administrative Roles and Permissions

Not all firewall administrators should have the same level of control over the ISA firewall's configuration and management. The ISA firewall allows you to provide three levels of control over the firewall software based on the role assigned to the user.

The ISA firewall's Administrative Roles are:

- ISA Server Basic Monitoring
- ISA Server Extended Monitoring
- ISA Server Full Administrator

Table 18.15 describes the functions of each of these roles.

Table 18.15 ISA Firewall Administrative Roles

Role	Description
ISA Server Basic Monitoring	Users and groups assigned this role can monitor the ISA Server computer and network activity, but cannot configure specific monitoring functionality.
ISA Server Extended Monitoring	Users and groups assigned this role can perform all monitoring tasks, including log configuration, alert definition configuration, and all monitoring functions available to the ISA Server Basic Monitoring role.
ISA Server Full Administrator	Users and groups assigned this role can perform any ISA Server task, including rule configuration, applying of network templates, and monitoring.

Users assigned to these roles can be created in the ISA firewall's local SAM, or they can be domain users if the ISA firewall is a member of the Internal network Active Directory domain. Any users can be assigned to one of the ISA firewall's Administrative roles, and no special privileges or Windows permissions are required. The only exception to this is when a user needs to monitor the ISA Server performance counters using Perfmon or the ISA Server Dashboard; the user must be a member of the Windows Server 2003 Performance Monitors User group.

Each ISA Server role has a specific list of firewall administrator and configuration tasks associated with it. Table 18.16 lists some firewall tasks and the Administrative roles that are allowed to perform each task.

Table 18.16 ISA Firewall Tasks Assigned to ISA Firewall Administrative Roles

Activity	Basic Monitoring Permissions	Extended Monitoring Permissions	Full Administrator Permissions
View Dashboard, alerts, connectivity, sessions, services	X	X	X
Acknowledge alerts	X	X	X
View log information		X	X
Create alert definitions		X	X
Create reports		X	X
Stop and start sessions and services		X	X
View firewall policy		X	X
Configure firewall policy			X
Configure cache			X
Configure VPN			X

To assign administrative roles, perform the following steps:

1. Click **Start**, point to **All Programs**, point to **Microsoft ISA Server**, and click **ISA Server Management**.

2. Click the server name in the left pane of the **Microsoft Internet Security and Acceleration Server 2006** management console. Click **Define Administrative Roles** on the **Tasks** tab.

3. On the **Welcome to the ISA Server Administration Delegation Wizard** page, click **Next**.

4. On the **Delegate Control** page, click **Add**.

5. In **Group (recommended) or User** dialog box, enter the name of the group or user to which the specific administrative permissions will be assigned. Click the down arrow in the **Role** drop-down list and select the applicable administrative role. Click **OK**.

6. Click **Next** on the **Delegate Control** page.

7. Click **Finish** on the **Completing the Administration Delegation Wizard** page.

8. Click **Apply** to save the changes and update the firewall policy

9. Click **OK** in the **Apply New Configuration** dialog box.

Lockdown Mode

The ISA firewall sports a new feature that combines the need to isolate the firewall and all Protected Networks from harm in the event that the ISA firewall is attacked, to the extent that the Firewall services are shut down. The ISA firewall accomplishes a combination of protection and protective accessibility by entering *lockdown mode*.

Lockdown mode occurs when:

1. An attack or some other network or local host event causes the Firewall service to shut down. This can happen from a fault, or you can do it explicitly by configuring Alerts and then configuring an Alert Action that shuts down the Firewall service in response to the issue that triggered the Alert.

2. Lockdown mode occurs when the Firewall service is manually shut down. You can shut down the Firewall service if you become aware of an ongoing attack while configuring the ISA firewall and the network to effectively respond to the attack.

Lockdown Mode Functionality

When in lockdown mode, the following functionality applies:

1. The ISA Firewall's Packet Filter Engine (fweng) applies the lockdown firewall policy.

2. Firewall policy rules permits outgoing traffic from the Local Host network to all networks, if allowed. If an outgoing connection is established, that connection can be used to respond to incoming traffic. For example, a DNS query can receive a DNS response on the same connection. This does not imply that lockdown mode allows an extension of existing firewall policy for outbound access from the local host network. Only existing rules allowing outbound access from the local host network are allowed.

3. No new primary connections to the ISA firewall itself are allowed, unless a System Policy Rule that specifically allows the traffic is enabled. An exception is DHCP traffic, which is always allowed. DHCP requests (on UDP port 67) are allowed from the Local Host Network to all Networks, and DHCP replies (on UDP port 68) are allowed back in.

4. Remote-access VPN clients will not be able to connect to the ISA firewall. Site-to-site VPN connections will also be denied.

5. Any changes to the network configuration while in lockdown mode are applied only after the Firewall service restarts and the ISA firewall exits lockdown mode.

6. The ISA Server will not trigger any Alerts.

Connection Limits

The ISA firewall puts a limit on the number of connections made to or through it at any point in time. Connection limits allow the ISA firewall to block connections through the firewall for clients that may be infected with worms that attempt to establish large numbers of connections through the ISA firewall. Examples of such worms are mass mailing worms and the Blaster worm.

For Web Publishing Rules, you can customize a total number of connections limit by specifying a maximum number of concurrent connections in the Properties of the Web listener. Any new client requests will be denied when the maximum number of connections configured to the Web listener is reached.

You can limit the total number of UDP, ICMP, and other Raw IP sessions allowed by a Server Publishing Rule or Access Rule on a per-second basis. These limitations do not apply to TCP connections. When the specified number of connections is surpassed, new connections will not be created. Existing connections will not be disconnected.

You should begin by configuring low connection-limit thresholds. This enables the ISA firewall to limit malicious hosts from consuming resources on the ISA Server computer.

By default, connection limits for *non-TCP connections* are configured to 1000 connections *per second per rule* and to 160 connections *per client*.

Connection limits for TCP connections begin at 160 connections per client. You should not change these limits unless you notice that legitimate hosts are being blocked because the limiting is too low. You can determine if a host is being blocked because it has exceeded its connection limit by an associated Alert. The Alert will provide the IP address of the host exceeding its allowed number of connections.

Perform the following steps to configure connection limits:

1. Click **Start**, point to **All Programs**, point to **Microsoft ISA Server**, and click **ISA Server Management**.

2. Expand the server name in the left pane of the **Microsoft Internet Security and Acceleration Server 2006** management console, and expand the **Configuration** node. Click the **General** node.

3. Click **Configure Flood Mitigation Settings** in the details pane.

4. On the **Flood Mitigation** tab (Figure 18.32), click on each Edit button. You can then configure the number of **Connections created per second, per rule (non-TCP)** and **Connection limit per client (TCP and non-TCP)**. Some machines may need access in excess of these numbers, such as busy published servers. In that case, you can click **Add** and select a **Computer Set** to apply the **Customer connection limit** value.

Figure 18.32 The Connection Limits Dialog Box

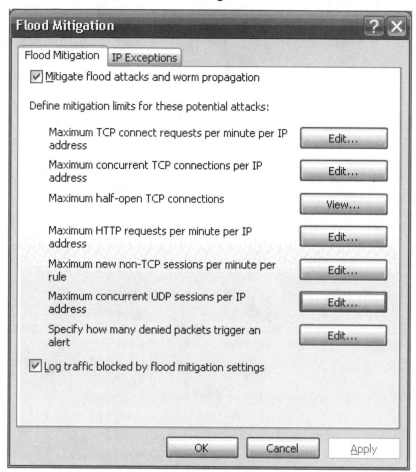

New connections will not be created after the specified number of connections is exceeded. However, existing connections will not be disconnected. Up to 1000 new connections are allowed per rule, per second by default. When this default limit is exceeded, an alert is triggered.

A log entry is recorded when the limit is exceeded:

- Action is Connection Denied
- Result code is FWX_E_RULE_QUOTA_EXCEEDED_DROPPED

You should limit the number of connections hosts can make to prevent flood attacks. Many requests are sent from spoofed source addresses when a UDP or IP flood attack occurs, and this can result in a denial of service.

Try the following when the limit is exceeded:

- If the malicious traffic appears to originate from an ISA firewall Protected Network, this may indicate a host on the Protected Network has a virus or worm infection. Immediately disconnect the computer from the network.

- Create a rule denying access to a computer set that includes the source IP addresses if the malicious traffic appears to originate from a small range of IP addresses on an external network.

- Evaluate the overall status of your network if the traffic appears to originate from a large range of IP addresses. Consider setting a smaller connection limit so that ISA Server can better protect your network.

If the limit has been exceeded due to a heavy load, consider setting a higher per-rule connection limit based on your analysis of your network's requirements.

In firewall chaining, and in some back-to-back ISA firewall scenarios, make sure to configure customized connection limits for the IP addresses of the chained server or back-end ISA firewall. Also, if your system publishes more than one UDP-based or raw IP-based service to the External network, you should configure smaller limits to help keep your network secure from flood attacks.

You can limit the total number of UDP, ICMP, and other Raw IP connections allowed per client. You can specify custom limits to apply to specific IP addresses. This is useful when you want to allow specific servers to establish more connections than allowed to other clients.

For TCP connections, no new connections are allowed after the connection limit is exceeded. Make sure you set connection limits high enough for TCP-based services, such as SMTP, so that SMTP servers can send outbound mail and receive inbound mail. For other connections (Raw IP and UDP), older connections are terminated when the connection limit is exceeded so that new connections can be created.

DHCP Spoof Attack Prevention

Some of you may want to use DHCP on the external interface of the ISA firewall so that it can obtain IP addressing information from your cable or DSL company's DHCP server. You might encounter problems with obtaining an IP address on the external interface when that interface is configured to use DHCP to obtain IP addressing information. A common reason for this problem is the DHCP Spoof Attack prevention mechanism.

It's important to understand the DHCP attack prevention mechanism to solve this problem. For each adapter on which DHCP is enabled, the ISA firewall maintains the list of allowed addresses. There is an entry in the registry for each DHCP enabled adapter:

The registry key name is

```
HKLM\SYSTEM\CurrentControlSet\Services\Fweng\Parameters\DhcpAdapters\<Adapter's
MAC>/<Adapter's hardware type>
```

The values under the key are:

1. The adapter's name

2. The ISA network name of the adapter

3. The adapter's MAC address

4. ISA network addresses

5. The adapter's hardware type

Figure 18.33 shows an example of the registry key.

Figure 18.33 Registry Key for DHCP Attack Prevention

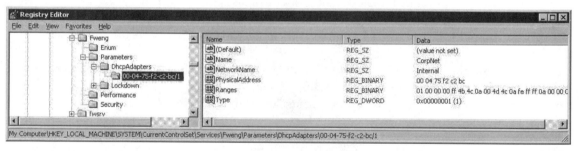

When the ISA firewall's driver sees a DHCP Offer message, it validates the offer using the following logic:

1. Using the DHCP "Client Ethernet Address" field and the "Hardware Type" field, the driver finds the corresponding registry key of the adapter.

2. If there is no registry key, the packet is allowed (this will be the case during initial setup of the ISA firewall software).

3. The driver verifies that "Your IP Address" field in the DHCP Offer contains an IP address within the addresses of the adapter's network element (as written in the registry).

4. If the verification fails, the packet is dropped, and an ISA alert is raised.

Figure 18.34 shows an example of a DHCP offer packet (the relevant fields are marked).

Figure 18.34 Network Monitor Capture of a DHCP Offer Packet

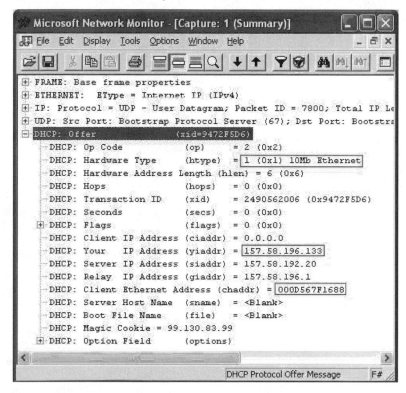

The invalid alert contains the following information (Figure 18.35).

Figure 18.35 An Invalid DHCP Offer Alert

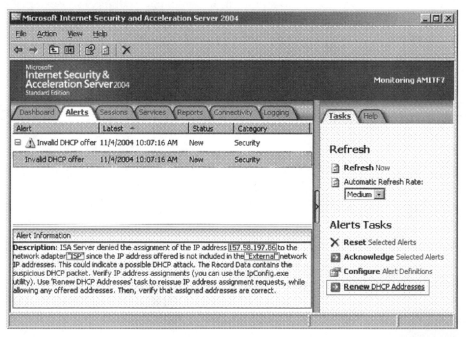

In case the network adapter should receive the offered address, the administrator should use the "Renew DHCP addresses" task that appears in the Task pane of the ISA firewall console. Figure 18.36 shows the warning dialog box you'll see when you click **Renew DHCP Addresses** in the Task pane.

Figure 18.36 The Renew DHCP Addresses Warning

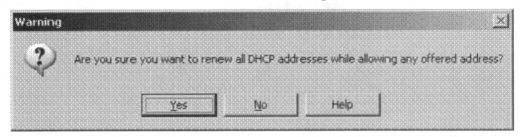

After clicking **Yes**, all registry keys related to DHCP attack prevention are deleted, and an "ipconfig /renew" is performed. This means that during this period, no offered address will be dropped by the driver (because there are no registry keys). Once the adapters receive their addresses, new registry keys are written with the new values, and the mechanism will be activated once again.

Dropped DHCP offers due to DHCP Attack Prevention may happen in the following scenarios:

1. If you have two DHCP adapters and you switched them. For example, the one that was connected to the internal network is now connected to the external network, and vice versa.

2. A DHCP adapter was moved to a different network. For example, ISA's external NIC was connected to a home network where another router made the connectivity to the ISP (and the Internet), and now you try replacing this router to use ISA's external NIC for connecting the ISP.

In such cases you need to use the **Renew DHCP Addresses** task, in order to allow the DHCP assignment. Note that once it's allowed, you will not need to allow it anymore. This procedure is needed only after changing the DHCP adapter in such a way that it becomes a member of a different ISA network element.

Summary

In this chapter, we discussed many issues related to planning and installing an ISA firewall. We also discussed default System Policy and Firewall configuration after installation is complete. A quick start configuration was discussed and described which will allow you to get up and running quickly.

Creating and Using ISA 2006 Firewall Access Policy

Solutions in this chapter

- ISA Firewall Access Rule Elements

- Configuring Access Rules for Outbound Access through the ISA Firewall

- Using Scripts to Populate Domain Name Sets

- Allowing Intradomain Communications through the ISA Firewall

☑ Summary

The ISA firewall's Access Policy (also known as firewall policy) includes Web Publishing Rules, Server Publishing Rules and Access Rules. Web Publishing Rules and Server Publishing Rules are used to allow inbound access and Access Rules are used to control outbound access.

The concepts of inbound and outbound access are somewhat more confusing with the new ISA firewall, when compared to their interpretations in ISA Server 2000. The reason for this is that ISA Server 2000 was Local Address Table (LAT) based. The definitions of inbound and outbound access were relative to the LAT. Inbound access was defined as incoming connections from non-LAT hosts to LAT hosts (external to internal). In contrast, the new ISA firewall does not have a LAT and there is not a comparable concept of an "internal" network in the same way that there was an internal network defined by the LAT in ISA Server 2000.

In general, you should use Web Publishing Rules and Server Publishing Rules when you want to allow connections from hosts that are not located on an ISA firewall Protected Network to a host on an ISA firewall Protected Network. Access Rules are used to control access between any two networks. The only limitation is that you cannot create Access Rules to control access between networks that have a Network Address Translation (NAT) relationship when the initiating host is on the non-NAT'd site of the relationship.

For example, suppose you have a NAT relationship between the default Internal Network and the Internet. You can create Access Rules that control connections between the Internal Network and the Internet because the initiating hosts are on the NAT'd side of the network relationship. However, you cannot create an Access Rule between a host on the Internet and the Internal Network because the Internet hosts are on the non-NAT'd side of the network relationship.

In contrast, you can create Access Rules in *both* directions when there is a route relationship between the source and destination Networks. For example, suppose you have a route relationship between a DMZ segment and the Internet. In this case, you can create Access Rules controlling traffic between the DMZ and the Internet and you can also create Access Rules that control traffic between the Internet and the DMZ segment.

The main job of the ISA firewall is to control traffic between source and destination networks. The ISA firewall's Access Policy permits clients on the source network to access hosts on a destination network and Access Rules also can be configured to block hosts on a source network from connecting to hosts on a destination network. Access Policy determines how hosts access hosts on other networks.

This is a key concept. The source and destination hosts must be on different networks. The ISA firewall should never mediate communications between hosts on the same ISA network. We refer to this type of configuration as "looping back through the ISA firewall". You should never loop back through the ISA firewall to access resources on the same network.

When the ISA firewall intercepts an outbound connection request, it checks both network rules and firewall policy rules to determine if access is allowed. Network Rules are checked first. If there is no Network Rule defining a NAT or Route relationship between the source and destination networks, then the connection attempt will fail. This is a common reason for failed connections and it is something you should check for when Access Policy does not behave the way you expect it to.

Access Rules can be configured to apply to specific source and/or destination hosts. Clients can be specified either by IP address (for example, by using Computer or Computer Set Network Objects) or by user name. The ISA firewall processes the requests differently depending on which type of client is requesting the object and how the Access Rules are configured.

When a connection request is received by the ISA firewall, the first thing the ISA firewall does is check to see if there is a Network Rule defining the route relationship between the source and destination networks. If there is no Network Rule, the ISA firewall assumes that the source and destination networks are *not connected*. If there is a Network Rule defining a route relationship between the source and destination network, then the ISA firewall processes the Access Policy rules.

After the ISA firewall has confirmed that the source and destination networks are connected, Access Policy is processed. The ISA firewall processes the Access Rules in the Access Policy from the top down (System Policy is processed before user-defined Access Policy).

If an Allow rule is associated with the outbound connection request, the ISA firewall will allow the request. In order for the Allow rule to be applied, the characteristics of the connection request must match the characteristics defined by the Access Rule. The Access Rule will match the connection request if the connection request matches the following Access Rule parameters:

- Protocol

- From (source location, which can include a source port number)

- Schedule

- To (destination location, which can include addresses, names, URLs and other Network Objects)

- Users

- Content groups

If the settings for each of these parameters match those in the connection request, then the Access Rule will be applied to the connection. If the connection request doesn't match the parameters in the Access Rule, then the ISA firewall moves to the next rule in the firewall's Access Policy.

If the Access Rule matches the parameters in the connection request, then the next step is for the ISA firewall to check the Network Rules once again to determine if there is a NAT or Route relationship between the source and destination Networks. The ISA firewall also checks for any Web chaining rules (if a Web Proxy client requested the object) or for a possible firewall chaining configuration (if a SecureNAT or firewall client requested the object) to determine how the request will be serviced.

For example, suppose you have an ISA firewall with two NICs: one NIC is connected to the Internet and the other connected to the Internal Network. You have created a single "All Open" rule which allows all users access to all protocol to connect to all sites on the Internet.

This "All Open" policy would include the following rules on the ISA firewall:

- A Network Rule defining the route relationship between the source network (the Internal Network) and the destination Network (the Internet).

- An Access Rule allowing all internal clients access to all sites at all times, using any protocol.

The default configuration is to NAT between the default Internal Network and the Internet. However, you can Route between the Internal network (and any other network) and the Internet if you like (as long as you have public addresses on the network).

ISA Firewall Access Rule Elements

You construct Access Rules using Policy Elements. One of the major improvements in the new ISA firewall over ISA Server 2000 is the ability to create all Policy Elements "on the fly". That is, you can create all Policy Elements from within the New Access Rule Wizard. This greatly improves on ISA Server 2000, where you have to plan out your Policy Elements in advance and then create Protocol Rules and Publishing Rules *after* you configure your Policy Elements.

The ISA firewall includes the following Policy Elements:

- Protocols
- User Sets
- Content Types
- Schedules
- Network Objects

Protocols

The ISA firewall includes a number of built-in protocols that you can use right out of the box to create Access Rules, Web Publishing Rules and Server Publishing Rules.

In addition to the built-in protocols, you can create your own protocols by using the ISA firewall's New Protocol Wizard. The pre-built protocols cannot be modified or deleted. However, you can edit or delete protocols you create yourself. There are some protocols that are installed with application filters that cannot be modified, but they can be deleted. You do have the option to unbind application filters from protocols. For example, if you don't want Web requests for SecureNAT and Firewall clients to be forwarded to the Web Proxy filter, you can unbind the Web Proxy filter from the HTTP protocol. We'll examine this issue in more detail later in this chapter.

When you create a new Protocol Definition, you'll need to specify the following information:

- **Protocol Type.**   TCP, UDP, ICMP, or IP-level protocol. If you specify an ICMP protocol, then you'll need to include the ICMP type and code. Note that you cannot publish IP-level or ICMP protocols.

- **Direction.**   For UDP, this includes Send, Receive, Send Receive, or Receive Send. For TCP, this includes Inbound and Outbound. For ICMP and IP-level, this includes Send and Receive.

- **Port range.**   (for TCP and UDP protocols) This is a range of ports between 1 and 65535 that is used for the initial connection. IP-level and ICMP protocols do not use ports, as ports are part of the transport layer header.

  Protocol number.   (for IP-level protocols). This is the protocol number. For example, GRE uses IP protocol number 47.

- **ICMP properties.**   (for ICMP protocol). This is the ICMP code and type.

- (Optional) **Secondary connections.**   This is the range of ports, protocol types, and direction used for additional connections or packets that follow the initial connection.

You can configure one or more secondary connections. Secondary connections can be inbound, outbound or both inbound and outbound.

User Sets

In order to enable outbound access control, you can create Access Rules and apply them to specific Internet Protocol (IP) addresses or to specific users or groups of users. When Access Rules are applied to a user or group, the users will have to authenticate using the appropriate authentication protocol. The Firewall client always uses integrated authentication and always sends the user credentials transparently. The Web Proxy client can use a number of different authentication methods.

The ISA firewall allows you to group users and user groups together in User Sets or what we like to call "firewall groups". User sets include one or more users or groups from any authentication scheme supported by the ISA firewall. For example, a user set might include a Windows user, a user from a RADIUS namespace, and another user from the SecurID namespace. The Windows, RADIUS and SecurID namespaces all use different authentication schemes, but users from each of these can be included in a single User Set.

The ISA firewall comes preconfigured with the following user sets:

- **All Authenticated Users.**   This predefined user set represents all authenticated users, regardless of the method used to authenticate. An Access Rule using this set applies to authenticated users. When a rule applies to authenticated users, connections from SecureNAT clients will fail. An exception to this is when the SecureNAT client is also a VPN client. When a user creates a VPN connection to the ISA firewall, the VPN client automatically becomes a SecureNAT client. Although normally a SecureNAT client cannot send user credentials to the ISA firewall, when the SecureNAT client is also a VPN client, the VPN log on credentials can be used to authenticate the user.

- **All Users.**   This predefined User Set represents all users. A rule defined using this set will apply to all users, both authenticated and unauthenticated, and no credentials are required to access a rule configured to use this User Set. However, the Firewall client will always send credentials to the ISA firewall, even when authentication is not required. You'll see this in effect in the **Microsoft Internet Security and Acceleration Server 2006** management console, in the **Sessions** tab when a user name has a question mark next to it.

- **System and Network Service.**   This pre-built User Set represents the Local System service and the Network service on the ISA firewall machine itself. This User Set is used in some System Policy Rules.

Content Types

Content types specify Multipurpose Internet Mail Extensions (MIME) types and file extensions. When you create an access rule that applies to the HTTP protocol, you can limit what Content Types the Access Rule applies to. Content Type control allows you to be very granular when configuring Access Policy because you can control access not only on a protocol and destination basis, but also by specific content.

Content Type control only works with HTTP and tunneled FTP traffic. Content Type control will not work with FTP traffic that isn't handled by the ISA firewall's Web Proxy filter.

When an FTP request is made by a host on an ISA firewall Protected Network, the ISA firewall will check the file extension in the request. The ISA firewall then determines if the rule applies to a Content Type that includes the requested file extension and processes the rule accordingly. If the Content Type doesn't match, then the rule is ignored and the next rule in the Access Policy is checked.

When a host on an ISA firewall Protected Network makes an outbound HTTP request, the ISA firewall sends the request to the Web server via the Web Proxy filter (by default). When the Web server returns the requested Web object, the ISA firewall checks the object's MIME type (which is found in the HTTP header information) or its file extension (depending on the header information returned by the Web server.) The ISA firewall determines if the rule applies to the specified Content Type including the requested file extension, and processes the rule accordingly.

The ISA firewall comes with a pre-built list of Content Types that you can use right out of the box. You can also create your own Content Types. When you create your own Content Types, you should specify both MIME type and file extension.

For example, to include all Director files in a content type, select the following file name extensions and MIME types:

- .dir

- .dxr

- .dcr

- application/x-director

You can use an asterisk (*) as a wildcard character when configuring a MIME type. For example, to include all application types, enter **application/***.

The ISA firewall comes with the following pre-built Content Types:

- Application

- Application data files

- Audio

- Compressed files

- Documents

- HTML documents

- Images

- Macro documents

- Text

- Video

- VRML.

Controlling access via MIME type can be challenging because different MIME types are associated with different file name extensions. The reason for this is that the Web server controls the MIME type associated with the Web object returned to the user. While there is general agreement on how MIME types are defined, a Web site administrator has complete control over the MIME type associated with any content hosted by his Web server. Because of this, you will sometimes see that content that you had thought you had blocked using Content Types is not blocked. You can determine the MIME type used by the Web server returning the response by doing a Network Monitor trace. The HTTP header will show the MIME type returned by the Web server for the Web content requested by the requesting client.

Schedules

You can apply a Schedule to an Access Rule to control when the rule should be applied. There are three built-in schedules:

- **Work Hours**   Permits access between 09:00 (9:00 A.M.) and 17:00 (5:00 P.M.) on Monday through Friday (to this rule)

- **Weekends**   Permits access at all times on Saturday and Sunday (to this rule)

- **Always**   Permits access at all times (to this rule)

Note that rules can be allow or deny rules. The Schedules apply to all Access Rules, not just allow rules.

Network Objects

Network Objects are used to control the source and destination of connections moving through the ISA firewall.

Configuring Access Rules for Outbound Access through the ISA Firewall

Access Rules always apply to outbound connections. Only protocols with a primary connection in either the outbound or send direction can be used in Access Rules. In contrast, Web Publishing Rules and Server Publishing Rules always use protocols with a primary connection with the inbound or receive direction. Access Rules control access from source to destination using outbound protocols.

In this section we'll go over in detail how to create an Access Rule and each of the options available to you when using the **New Access Rule Wizard,** along with additional options available to you in the **Properties** of the Access Rule.

To begin, open the **Microsoft Internet Security and Acceleration Server 2006** management console and expand the server name and click **Firewall Policy** node. Click the **Tasks** tab in the Task Pane and click the **Create New Access Rule** link. This brings up the **Welcome to the New Access Rule Wizard** page. Enter a name for the rule in the **Access Rule name** text box. In this example we'll create an "All Open" Access Rule that allows all traffic from all hosts outbound from the default Internal Network to the default External Network. Click **Next**.

The Rule Action Page

On the **Rule Action** page you have two options: **Allow** or **Deny**. In contrast to ISA Server 2000, the new ISA firewall has the **Deny** option set as the default. In this example, we'll select the **Allow** option and click **Next, as shown in Figure 19.1**.

Figure 19.1 The Rule Action page

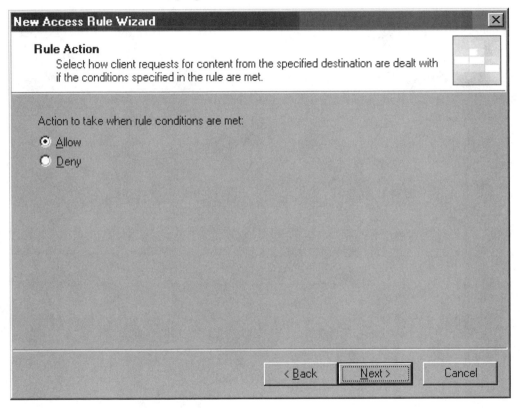

The Protocols Page

On the **Protocols** page, you decide what protocols should be allowed outbound from the source to destination location. You have three options in the **This rule applies to** list:

■ **All outbound traffic**   This option allows all protocols outbound. The effect of this option differs depending on the client type used to access this rule. For Firewall clients, this option allows all protocols outbound, including secondary protocols that are defined on the ISA firewall and some that are not defined. However, if a SecureNAT client attempts to connect via a rule that employs this option, outbound access will only be allowed for protocols that are included in the ISA firewall's **Protocols** list. If the SecureNAT client cannot connect to a resource when you use this protocol, try creating a new Protocol

Definition on the ISA firewall to support the SecureNAT client's connection. However, if secondary connections are required, such as is the case with FTP, you must employ the Firewall client or create an application filter to support that protocol for SecureNAT clients.

- **Selected protocols** This option allows you to select the specific protocols to which you want this rule to apply. You can select from the default list of protocols included with the ISA firewall right out of the box, or you can create a new Protocol Definition "on the fly". You can select one protocol or multiple protocols for a single rule.

- **All outbound traffic except selected** This option allows you to enable all protocols outbound (dependent only the client type) *except* for specific protocols outbound. For example, you might want to allow Firewall clients outbound access to all protocols except those you explicitly want to deny because of corporate security policy, such as AOL Instant Messenger, MSN Messenger and IRC. See Figure 19.2.

Figure 19.2 The Protocols page

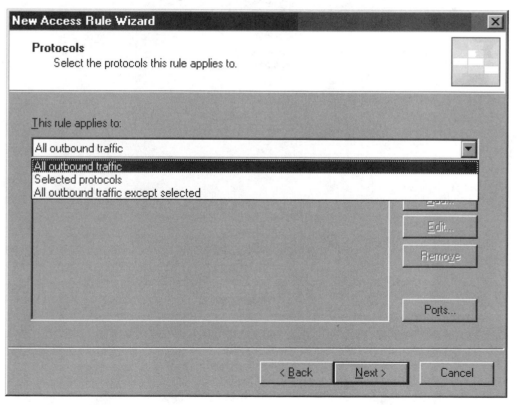

Highlight the **Selected Protocols** option and click the **Add** button. This brings up the **Add Protocols** dialog box. In the **Add Protocols** dialog box, you see a list of folders that group protocols based on their general use. For example, the **Common Protocols** folder contains protocols most commonly used when connecting to the Internet and the **Mail Protocols** folder is used to group protocols most commonly used when accessing mail services through the ISA firewall. The **User-Defined** folder contains all your custom protocols that you manually create on the ISA firewall. The **All Protocols** folder contains all protocols, both built-in and User-defined, configured on the ISA firewall.

Click the **All Protocols** folder and you'll see a list of all protocols configured on the ISA firewall. The ISA firewall comes with over 100 built-in Protocol Definitions you can use in your Access Rules, as shown in Figure 19.3.

Figure 19.3 The Add Protocols dialog box

If you need to use a protocol for which there isn't already a Protocol Definition, you can create a new one now but clicking the **New** menu. Clicking the **New** menu will allow you the option to create a new **Protocol** or new **RPC Protocol**. See the section earlier in this chapter on how to create new Protocol Definitions.

Once you identify the protocol you want to include in the rule, double click on it. Double click on any other protocol you want to include in the rule and then click **Close** in the **Add Protocols** dialog box. In this example, we want to allow access to all protocols, so click close in the **Add Protocols** dialog box.

On the **Protocols** page, select the **All outbound traffic** option from the **This rule applies to** list and click **Next**.

The Access Rule Sources Page

On the **Access Rule Sources** page, select the source location to which this Access Rule should apply. Click the **Add** button to add the source of the communication for which this rule will apply.

In the **Add Network Entities** dialog box you can choose the source location of the communication to which this Access Rule applies. If none of the source locations listed in the **Add Network Entities** dialog box works for you, you can create a new Network Object by clicking the **New** menu. Double click the location to which you want the rule to apply. Note that you can choose more than one source location by double clicking on multiple Network Objects.

In this example, click on the **Networks** folder to expand the folder and then double click on the **Internal** Network entry. Click **Close** to close the **Add Network Entities** dialog box as shown in Figure 19.4.

Figure 19.4 The Add Network Entities dialog box

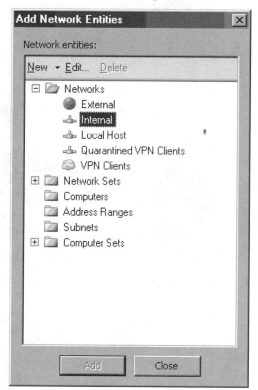

Click **Next** on the **Access Rule Sources** page.

The Access Rule Destinations Page

On the **Access Rule Destinations** page, select the destination for which you want this rule to apply. Click the **Add** button to add a destination location. The **Add Network Entities** dialog box appears and you can select a Network Object for the destination for which this Access Rule applies.

As in the previous page of the Access Rule Wizard, you can create a new destination location by clicking the **New** menu and creating the new location.

In this example, we'll click on the **Networks** folder and then double click on the **External** entry. Click **Close** to close the **Add Network Entities** dialog box. Click **Next** on the **Access Rule Destinations** page.

The User Sets Page

On the **User Sets** page, you can set the users to which this Access Rule applies. The default setting is **All Users**. If you want to remove this User Set or any other one from the list of users to which this rule applies, select the User Set and click the **Remove** button. You can also edit a user set in the list by clicking the **Edit** button.

You can add a User Set to the list by clicking the **Add** button. In the **Add Users** dialog box, you can double click on a Firewall Group to which you want the rule to apply. You can also create new firewall groups by clicking the **New** menu and you can edit existing firewall groups by clicking the **Edit** menu.

In this example, we'll use the default setting, **All Users**. Click **Close** in the **Add Users** dialog box and click **Next** on the **User Sets** page as shown in Figure 19.5.

Figure 19.5 The User Sets page

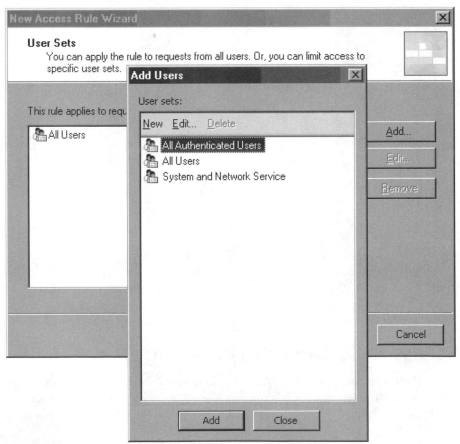

The **Completing the New Access Rule Wizard** page appears next. Review your settings and click **Finish**.

Access Rule Properties

There are several options you can configure in an Access Rule that aren't exposed in the New Access Rule Wizard. You can select these options by going into the **Properties** dialog box of the Access Rule.

The **Properties** dialog box of an Access Rule contains the following tabs:

- The General tab
- The Action tab
- The Protocols tab
- The From tab
- The Users tab
- The Schedule tab
- The Content Types tab

Right click the Access Rule and click the **Properties** command.

The General Tab

The first tab you see is the **General** tab. You can change the name of the Access Rule by entering the new name in the **Name** text box. The rule can be enabled or disabled by placing or removing the checkmark in the **Enable** checkbox.

The Action Tab

The Action tab provides several options that were not exposed in the New Access Rule Wizard. The options available on the Action tab include:

- **Allow**   Choose this option if you want connections matching the characteristics of this rule to be allowed through the ISA firewall

- **Deny**   Choose this option if you want to connections matching the characteristics of this rule to be denied access through the ISA firewall

- **Redirect HTTP requests to this Web page**   Choose this option if you want HTTP requests matching the characteristics of this rule to be redirected to another Web page. This option is only available if the rule is a Deny rule. When the user attempts to access a denied site, the request is automatically redirected to a Web page you configure in the text box below this option. Make sure that you enter the complete URL to which you want the user to be redirected, such as http://corp.domain.com/accesspolicy.htm.

- **Log requests matching this rule**   Connection attempts matching the Access Rule are automatically logged after you create the rule. There may be times when you don't want to log all connections matching a particular rule. One example of when you would not want to log connections matching a rule is when you create a rule matching protocols you have little interest in investigating, such as NetBIOS broadcasts. Later in this chapter, we will describe a procedure you can use to reduce the size of your log files by creating an Access Rule that does not log connections matching NetBIOS broadcast protocols.

Figure 19.6 shows the contents of the Action tab.

Figure 19.6 The Action tab

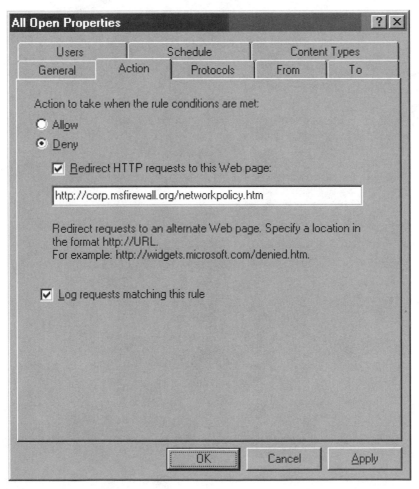

The Protocols Tab

The **Protocols** tab provides you many of the same options available in the New Access Rule Wizard. You have the same options in the **This rule applies to** list, which are: **Allow all outbound traffic**, **Selected protocols** and **All outbound traffic except selected**. You can use the **Add** button to add more protocols to the list. Use the **Remove** button to remove protocols that you select in the **Protocols** list and click the **Edit** button to edit protocols you select in the **Protocols** list.

There are application filters that you can configure for any of the protocols you've included in the **Protocols** list on the **Protocols** tab. The filters available depend on the protocols you've included in the list. Click the **Filters** button to view the configurable filters for the list of protocols included in the Access Rule as shown in Figure 19.7.

Figure 19.7 The Protocols tab

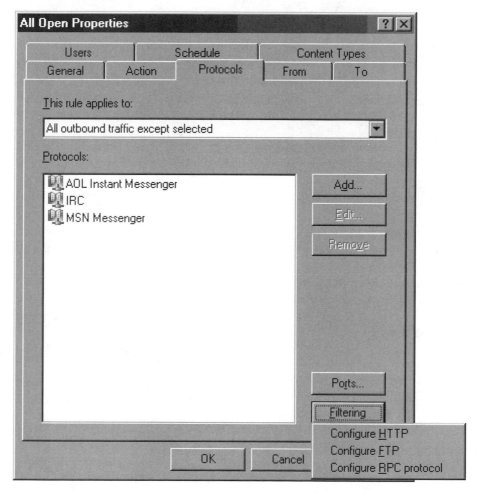

You also have control over the source ports allowed to access resources through the ISA firewall via each Access Rule. Click the **Ports** button and you'll see the **Source Ports** dialog box. The default setting is **Allow traffic from any allowed source port**. However, if you have applications for which you can control the source port, or those that use default source ports (such as SMTP), then you can limit the source ports allowed to access the rule by selecting the **Limit access to traffic from this range of source ports** option and enter the **From** and **To** source ports that represent the first and last ports in a range of source ports you want to allow. See Figure 19.8.

Figure 19.8 The Source Ports dialog box

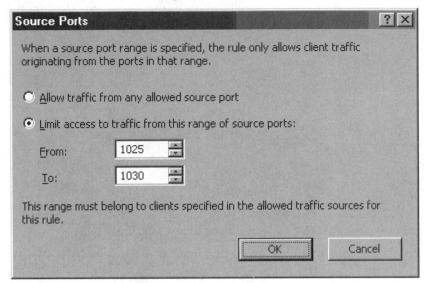

The From Tab

On the **From** tab you have options similar to those seen in the New Access Rule Wizard. However, an option not available in the Wizard is the ability to create an exception. If you want to add additional source locations for which this Access Rule should apply, click the **Add** button next to the **This rule applies to traffic from these sources** list. If you want to remove a source location, click the location and then click the **Remove** button. If you want to edit the characteristics of a location, click the **Edit** button.

You can apply this rule to all source locations in the **This rule applied to traffic from these sources** list *except* for certain source locations you specify in the **Exceptions** list. For example, suppose the Access Rule is configured to deny outbound access to the PPTP VPN protocol for all machines on the Internal Network. However, you want to allow machines that belong to the **Remote Management Computers** Computer Set access to this protocol. You can add the **Remote Management Computers** Computer Set to the list of **Exceptions** by clicking the **Add** button. Use the **Remove** and **Edit** button in the **Exceptions** list to remove and edit the locations in that list, as shown in Figure 19.9.

Figure 19.9 The From tab

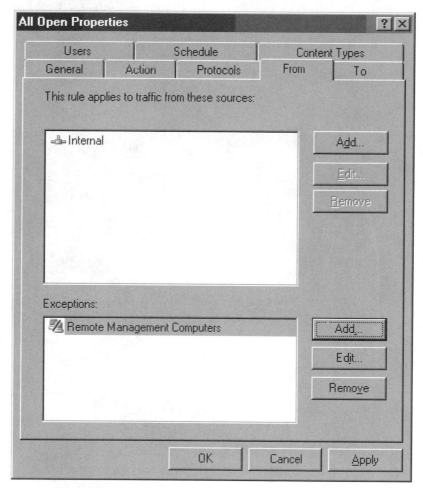

The To Tab

The **To** tab provides similar functionality as that on the **Access Rule Destination** page of the New Access Rule Wizard. However, you have the additional option to set an Exception to the destinations included in the **This rule applies to traffic sent to these destinations** list.

For example, suppose you create an Access Rule that allows outbound access to the HTTP protocol for all External sites. However, you do not want to allow users access to the Hotmail Web mail site. You can create a Domain Name Set for the domains required for Hotmail access and then use the **Add** button in the **Exceptions** section to add the Hotmail Domain Name Set. The rule will then will allow HTTP access to all sites *except* the Hotmail site. See Figure 19.10.

Figure 19.10 The To Tab

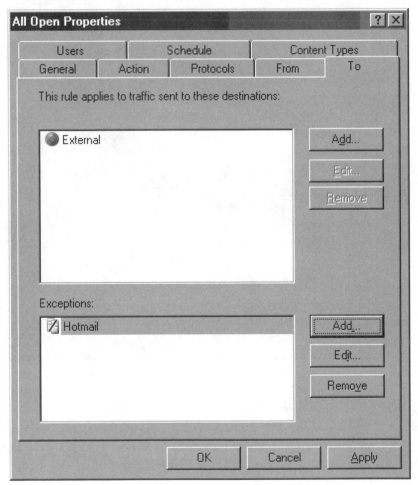

The Users Tab

The Users tab allows you to add firewall groups to which you want the Access Rule to apply, as shown in Figure 19.11. In addition, you have the option to add exceptions to the group to which the rule applies. For example, you could configure the rule to apply to **All Authenticated Users** but exclude other firewall groups, such as the built-in **System and Network Service** group.

Figure 19.11 The Users tab

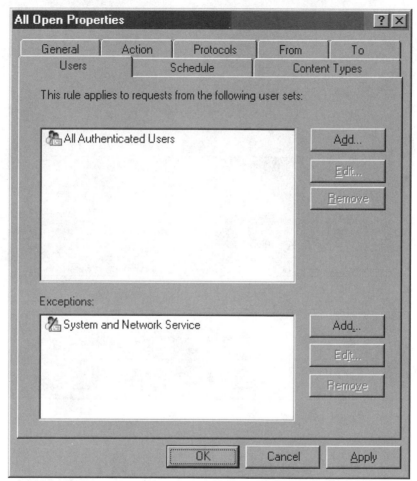

The Schedule Tab

On the **Schedule** tab, you set the times you want the rule to apply. The scheduling option isn't exposed in the New Access Rule Wizard interface. You can use one of the three default schedules: **Always**, **Weekends** or **Work hours,** or you can create a new custom schedule by clicking the **New** button, as illustrated by Figure 19.12.

Figure 19.12 The Schedule tab

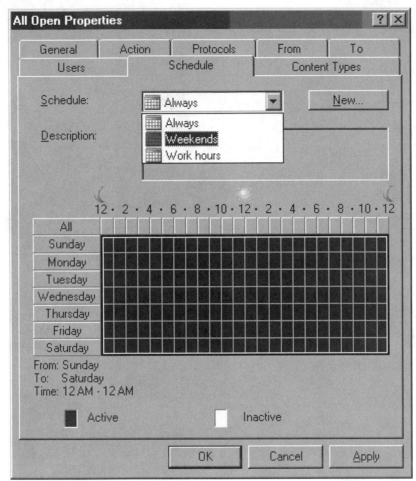

The Content Types Tab

Another option not exposed in the New Access Rule Wizard is the ability to apply content type control over the connection. On the **Content Types** tab, you can specify what content types will apply to the rule. Content Type constraints are only applied to HTTP connections; all other protocols ignore the settings on the Content Types tab.

The default setting is to have the rule apply to **All content types**. You can limit the content types the rule applies to by selecting the **Selected content types (with this option selected, the rule is applicable only HTTP traffic)** option and putting a checkmark in the checkboxes next to the content types to which you want the rule to apply. See Figure 19.13.

Figure 19.13 The Content Types tab

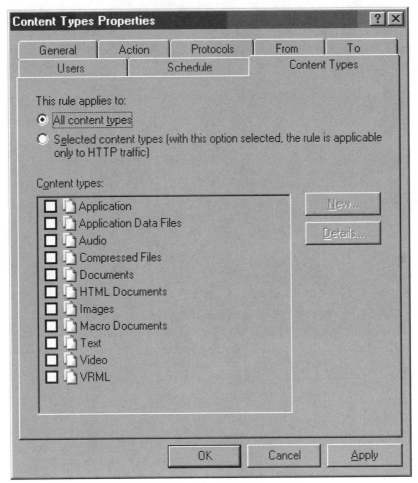

The Access Rule Context Menu Options

There are several options to choose from when you right click an Access Rule. These options include the following:

- **Properties**   This option brings up the Access Rule's **Properties** dialog box.
- **Delete**   This option deletes the Access Rule.
- **Copy**   This option allows you to copy an Access Rule and then paste a copy of the rule to the Firewall policy.
- **Paste**   This option allows you to paste an Access Rule that you've copied

- **Export Selected**   This option allows you to export the Access Rule to an .xml file. You can then import this file to another ISA firewall to replicate the rule to another machine.

- **Import to Selected**   This option allow you to import an Access Rule from an .xml file to the position selected in the Access Policy.

- **Move Up**   This option allows you to move the rule up on the list of Access Rules.

- **Move Down**   This option allows you to move the rule down on the list of Access Rules.

- **Disable**   This option allows you disable the Access Rule while keeping it on the list of Access Rules and allows you to re-enable it later if you require it again.

- **Enable**   This option allows you to enable an Access Rule that you've disabled.

- **Configure HTTP**   This option appears when the Access Rule includes the HTTP protocol. The Configure HTTP option allows you to configure the HTTP Security Filter to exert access control over HTTP connections using the ISA firewall's advanced application layer inspection mechanisms.

- **Configure FTP**   This option appears when the Access Rule includes the FTP protocol. When it is selected, you are presented with a dialog box that allows you to enable or disable FTP uploads.

- **Configure RPC Protocol**   This option appears when the Access Rule includes an RPC protocol. When it is selected, you are presented with a dialog box that allows you to enable or disable strict RPC compliance (which has the effect of enabling or disabling DCOM connections).

Configuring RPC Policy

When you create an Access Rule that allows outbound RPC, you have the option to configure RPC protocol policy. Access Rules that allow **All IP Traffic** also include RPC protocols. Right click the Access Rule and click **Configure RPC protocol** to configure RPC policy.

In the **Configure RPC protocol policy** dialog box, shown in Figure 19.14, you have a single option: **Enforce strict RPC compliance**. The default setting is enabled. When this setting is not enabled, the RPC filter will allow additional RPC type protocols, such as DCOM. If you find that some RPC-based protocols do not work correctly through the ISA firewall, consider disabling this option.

RPC policy is configured on a per-protocol basis. For example, you can enforce strict RPC compliance for one Access Rule and disable strict RPC compliance for another Access Rule in the ISA firewall's firewall policy.

Figure 19.14 The Configure RPC protocol policy dialog box

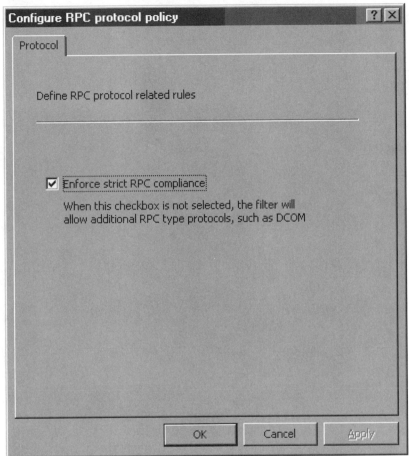

Configuring FTP Policy

When you created an Access Rule that allows the FTP protocol, you have the option to configure FTP policy. Right click the Access Rule and click the **Configure FTP** command. This brings up the **Configure FTP protocol policy** dialog box, shown in Figure 19.15. By default, the **Read Only** checkbox is enabled. When this checkbox is enabled, FTP uploads will be blocked. If you want to allow users to upload files using FTP, remove the checkmark from the checkbox.

FTP policy is configured on a per-rule basis.

Figure 19.15 The Configures FTP protocol policy dialog box

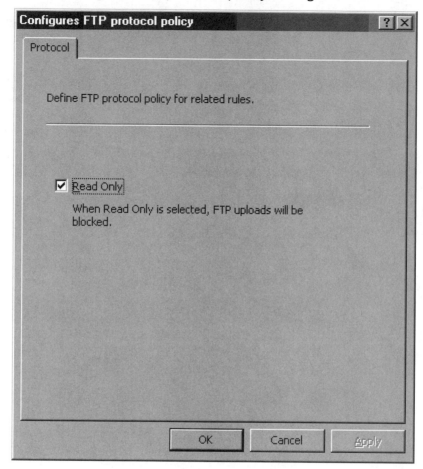

Configuring HTTP Policy

Whenever you create an Access Rule that allows HTTP connections, you have the option to configure HTTP policy. HTTP policy settings control the HTTP Security Filter. We discuss the configuration options available in the HTTP Security Filter in full detail in Chapter 21.

Ordering and Organizing Access Rules

The ordering of Access Rules is important to ensure that your Access Policy works the way you expect it to work. We recommend the follow ordering of Access Rules:

- Put Web Publishing Rules and Server Publishing Rules on the top of the list
- Place anonymous Deny Access Rules under the Web Publishing Rules and Server Publishing Rules. These rules do not require user authentication and do not require the client to be from a specific location (such as part of a Computer Set)

- Place anonymous Allow Access Rules under the Anonymous Deny Access Rules. These rules do not require user authentication and do not require the client to be from a specific location (such as part of a Computer Set)

- Place Deny Access Rules requiring authentication below the anonymous Allow Access Rules

- Place Allow Access Rules requiring authentication below the Deny Access Rules requiring authentication.

It is important that anonymous rules that apply to the same protocol as an authenticated access rule be applied first if it is your intent to allow anonymous access for that protocol. If you do not put the anonymous access rule before the authenticated Access Rule, then the connection request will be denied to the anonymous user (typically a SecureNAT client) for that protocol.

For example, suppose you have two Access Rules: one rule allows all users access to the HTTP protocol and the second rule allows members of the EXECS firewall group access to the HTTP, HTTPS, FTP, IRC and MSN Messenger protocols. If you place the rule allowing the EXECS group access before the anonymous access rule, then all HTTP connections outbound will require authentication and the anonymous access rule located under the authentication required rule will be ignored. However, if you had an anonymous access rule for the NNTP protocol under the rule allowing the EXECS outbound access to the HTTP, HTTPS, FTP, IRC and MSN Messenger protocols, then the anonymous NNTP connection would be allowed because the NNTP protocol doesn't match the characteristics of the rule allowing the EXECS users outbound access.

We found this model a bit confusing at first. When we first starting working with the ISA firewall, we assumed that when a rule applies to a particular firewall group, a connection request from a user that does not supply credentials to the ISA firewall would be ignored and the firewall would then continue down the list of rules until an anonymous Access Rule matching the connection parameters was found. However, this is *not* the case. Anonymous users might be considered members of the "Anonymous Users" group and that group does not match any group for which you might require authentication. Since the "Anonymous Users" group never matches an actual group, any rule for which authentication is required matching the connection request will be denied.

How to Block Logging for Selected Protocols

You may want to prevent the ISA firewall from logging information about certain protocols that reach the firewall. Common examples are the NetBIOS broadcast protocols: NetBIOS Name Service and NetBIOS Datagram. Both of these protocols regularly broadcast to the local subnet broadcast address and can fill the ISA firewall's Firewall Service log with information that isn't very useful to the ISA firewall administrator.

You can create an Access Rule that includes these protocols and then configure the Access Rule to not log information about connections associated with the rule. For example, you can perform the following procedure to block logging of these NetBIOS protocols:

1. In the **Microsoft Internet Security and Acceleration Server 2006** management console, expand the server name and click the **Firewall Policy** node.

2. In the Task Pane, click the **Tasks** tab and click the **Create New Access Rule** link.

3. On the **Welcome to the New Access Rule Wizard** page, enter a name for the rule in the **Access Rule name** text box. In this example, we'll name the rule **Block NetBIOS logging**. Click **Next**.

4. Select the **Deny** option on the **Rule Action** page and click **Next**.

5. On the **Protocols** page, select the **Selected protocols** option from the **This rule applies to** list. Click the **Add** button.

6. In the **Add Protocols** dialog box, click the **Infrastructure** folder. Double click the **NetBIOS Datagram** and **NetBIOS Name Service** entries. Click **Close**.

7. Click **Next** on the **Protocols** page.

8. On the **Access Rule Sources** page, click the **Add** button.

9. In the **Add Network Entities** dialog box, click the **Computer Sets** folder and then double click the **Anywhere** entry. Click **Close**.

10. Click **Next** on the **Access Rule Sources** page.

11. On the **Access Rule Destinations** page, click the **Add** button.

12. In the **Add Network Entities** dialog box, click the **Computer Sets** folder. Double click the **Anywhere** entry and click **Close**.

13. Click **Next** on the **Access Rule Destinations** page.

14. Click **Next** on the **User Sets** page.

15. Click **Finish** on the **Completing the New Access Rule Wizard** page.

16. Right click the **Block NetBIOS Logging** rule and click **Properties**.

17. In the **Block NetBIOS Logging Properties** dialog box, remove the checkmark from the **Log requests matching this rule** checkbox.

18. Click **Apply** and then click **OK**.

19. Click **Apply** to save the changes and update the firewall policy.

20. Click **OK** in the **Apply New Configuration** dialog box.

The rule you created in this example not only prevents logging of NetBIOS broadcasts, but prevents these protocols to and from the ISA firewall. Thus, you get two benefits from one rule!

Disabling Automatic Web Proxy Connections for SecureNAT Clients

There may be times when you want Firewall and SecureNAT client to bypass the Web Proxy service. By default, HTTP connections from SecureNAT and Firewall clients are automatically forwarded to the Web Proxy filter. The advantage of this configuration is that both SecureNAT and Firewall clients are able to benefit from the ISA firewall's Web Proxy cache (when caching is enabled on the ISA firewall).

The problem is that some Web sites are poorly written and are not compliant with CERN compliant Web proxies. You can solve this problem by configuring these sites for Direct Access and then unbinding the Web Proxy filter from the HTTP protocol.

Perform the following steps to disable automatic Web Proxy connections for Firewall and SecureNAT clients:

1. In the **Microsoft Internet Security and Acceleration Server 2006** management console, expand the server name and click the **Firewall Policy** node in the left pane of the console.

2. In the Task Pane, click the **Toolbox** tab. On the **Toolbox** tab, click the **Command Protocols** folder and double click the **HTTP** protocol.

3. In the **HTTP Properties** dialog box, click the **Parameters** tab.

4. On the **Parameters** tab, remove the checkmark from the **Web Proxy Filter** checkbox. Click **Apply** and then click **OK**.

5. Click **Apply** to save the changes and update the firewall policy.

6. Click **OK** in the **Apply New Configuration** dialog box.

One side effect of bypassing the Web Proxy filter is that HTTP Policy is not applied to the SecureNAT and Firewall clients. However, HTTP Policy is applied to machines that are explicitly configured as Web Proxy clients, even when the Firewall, SecureNAT and Web Proxy clients access the site using the same Access Rule.

For example, suppose you create a rule named **HTTP Access**. The **HTTP Access** Access Rule allows all users on the Internal network access to all sites on the External Network using the HTTP protocol. Let's say you configure HTTP Policy for this rule to block connections to the www. spyware.com domain. When Web Proxy clients attempt to connect to www.spyware.com, the connection will be blocked by the **HTTP Access** Access Rule. However, when the SecureNAT and Firewall clients attempt to access www.spyware.com via the **HTTP Access** rule (when the Web Proxy Filter is unbound from the HTTP protocol), that Access Rule will allow the SecureNAT and Firewall clients through.

Another side effect of unbinding the Web Proxy Filter from the HTTP Protocol Definition is that the configuration interface (**Configure HTTP policy for rule** dialog box) for the HTTP filter is removed from the **Microsoft Internet Security and Acceleration Server 2006** management console. For all rules that have an HTTP policy already configured, that policy is still enforced on Web Proxy clients. However, to change HTTP Policy on existing rule, or to configure HTTP policy on new Access Rules, you will need to re-bind the HTTP Filter to the HTTP Protocol Definition. You can then unbind the Web Proxy Filter again after configuring the HTTP policy.

Of course, you could just configure all clients as Web Proxy clients (which is our recommendation) and avoid the administrative overhead.

Using Scripts to Populate Domain Name Sets

One of the ISA firewall's strong suits is its exceptional stateful application layer inspection. In addition to performing the basic task of stateful filtering (which even a simple 'hardware' firewall can do), the ISA firewall's strong application layer inspection feature set allows the ISA firewall to actually understand the protocols passing though the firewall. In contrast to traditional second generation hardware firewalls, the ISA firewall represents a third-generation firewall that is not only network aware, but application protocol aware.

The ISA firewall's stateful application inspection mechanism allows you to control access not just to "ports", but to the actual protocols moving through those ports. While the conventional "hardware" firewall is adept at passing packets using simple stateful filtering mechanisms that have been available since the mid 1990's, the ISA firewall's stateful application layer inspection mechanisms bring the ISA firewall into the 21st century and actually control application layer protocol access. This allows strong inbound and outbound access control based on the firewall's application layer awareness, rather than through simple "opening and closing" of ports.

One powerful example is the ability to control what sites users can access through the ISA firewall. You can combine this ability to control the sites users can access by adding strong user/ group based access control as well as protocol control.

For example, you might have a group of users called "Web Users," and you might want to block access to a list of 1500 URLs or domains for those users. You can create an Access Rule that blocks only those 1500 sites and allows access to all other sites when members of that group authenticate with the ISA firewall.

Another example might be this: you want to create a block list of 5000 domains that you want to prevent all users except for domain admins from reaching via any protocol. You can create a Domain Name Set and then apply this Domain Name Set to an Access Rule blocking these sites.

The trick is to find a way to get those thousands of domains or URLs into Domain Name Sets and URL Sets. You can, of course, enter these URLs and domains manually using the built-in tools included in the ISA Management console. The problem with this approach is that you'll need to get your clicking thumb ready for a long weekend as you click your way through the user interface to add all of these domains and URLs.

A better way is to import the sites you want to include in your URL Sets and Domain Name Sets from a text file. There are a number of places on the Internet where you can find such files (I won't mention any here because I don't want to create an implicit endorsement of any of them). Once you have a text file, you'll want use a script to import the entries in the text file into a URL Set or a Domain Name Set.

First, let's start with the scripts. The first script below is used to import the entries in a text file into a URL Set. Copy the information into a text file and then save it as **ImportURLs.vbs**.

```
< -----Start with the line below this one--->
Set Isa = CreateObject("FPC.Root")
Set CurArray = Isa.GetContainingArray
Set RuleElements = CurArray.RuleElements
Set URLSets = RuleElements.URLSets
Set URLSet = URLSets.Item("Urls")
Set FileSys = CreateObject("Scripting.FileSystemObject")
Set UrlsFile = FileSys.OpenTextFile("urls.txt", 1)
For i = 1 to URLSet.Count
  URLSet.Remove 1
Next
Do While UrlsFile.AtEndOfStream <> True
  URLSet.Add UrlsFile.ReadLine
Loop
```

```
WScript.Echo "Saving..."
CurArray.Save
WScript.Echo "Done"
< ------End with the line above this one--->
```

The two entries in this file you need to change for your own setup are highlighted in yellow. In the line:

```
Set URLSet = URLSets.Item("Urls")
```

Change the **Urls** entry to the name of the URL Set you want to create on the ISA firewall. In the line:

```
Set UrlsFile = FileSys.OpenTextFile("urls.txt", 1)
```

Change the **urls.txt** entry to the name of the text file that contains the URLs you want to import into the ISA firewall's configuration.

The next script is used to import a collections of domains contained in a text file. Save the following information in a text file and name it **ImportDomains.vbs**.

```
< ------Start with the line below this one--->
Set Isa = CreateObject("FPC.Root")
Set CurArray = Isa.GetContainingArray
Set RuleElements = CurArray.RuleElements
Set DomainNameSets = RuleElements.DomainNameSets
Set DomainNameSet = DomainNameSets.Item("Domains")
Set FileSys = CreateObject("Scripting.FileSystemObject")
Set DomainsFile = FileSys.OpenTextFile("domains.txt", 1)
For i = 1 to DomainNameSet.Count
  DomainNameSet.Remove 1
Next
Do While DomainsFile.AtEndOfStream <> True
  DomainNameSet.Add DomainsFile.ReadLine
Loop
WScript.Echo "Saving..."
CurArray.Save
WScript.Echo "Done"
< ------End with the line above this one--->
```

The two entries in this file you need to change for your own setup are shown below. In the line:

```
Set DomainNameSet = DomainNameSets.Item("Domains")
```

Change the **Domains** entry to the name of the Domain Name Set you want to create on the ISA firewall. In the line:

```
Set DomainsFile = FileSys.OpenTextFile("domains.txt", 1)
```

Change the **domains.txt** entry to the name of the text file that contains the domains you want to import into the ISA firewall's configuration.

Using the Import Scripts

Now let's see how the scripts work. The first thing you need to do is create the URL Set and the Domain Name Set in the **Microsoft Internet Security and Acceleration Server 2006** management console. This is easy and involves only a few steps.

First, we'll create a URL Set named **URLs**, since that's the default name in our script. Remember, you can change the URL Set name in the script if you like; just make sure you first create a URL Set in the **Microsoft Internet Security and Acceleration Server 2006** management console with the same name.

Perform the following steps to create a URL Set with the name **URLs**:

- In the **Microsoft Internet Security and Acceleration Server 2006** management console, expand the server name and then click on the **Firewall Policy** node.

- In the **Firewall Policy** node, click the **Toolbox** tab in the Task Pane. In the **Toolbox**, click the **Network Objects** tab.

- In the **Network Objects** tab, click the **New** menu and click **URL Set**.

- In the **New URL Set Rule Element** dialog box, shown in Figure 19.16, enter **URLs** in the **Name** text box. Click **OK**.

Figure 19.16 The New URL Set Rule Element dialog box

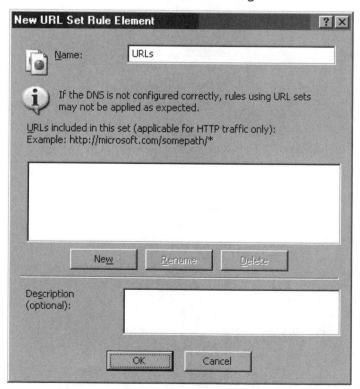

The URL Set now appears in the list of URL Sets, shown in Figure 19.17.

Figure 19.17 The URL Sets list

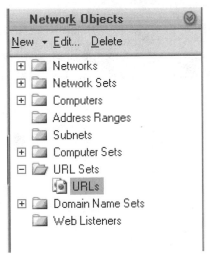

The next step is to create a Domain Name Set with the name **Domains**, which is the default name of the Set used in the ImportDomains script. Remember, you can use a different name for the Domain Name Set; just make sure the name is the same as the one you set in the script.

Perform the following steps to create the Domain Name Set with the name Domains:

1. In the **Microsoft Internet Security and Acceleration Server 2006** management console, expand the server name and then click on the **Firewall Policy** node.

2. In the **Firewall Policy** node, click the **Toolbox** tab in the Task Pane. In the **Toolbox**, click the **Network Objects** tab.

3. In the **Network Objects** tab, click the **New** menu and click **Domain Name Set**.

4. In the **New Domain Name Set Policy Element** dialog box, shown in Figure 19.18, enter **Domains** in the **Name** text box. Click **OK**.

Figure 19.18 The New Domain Set Policy Element dialog box

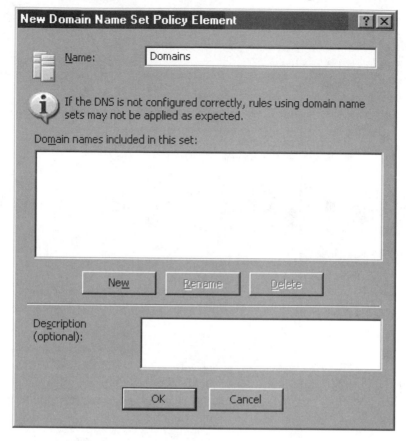

The new entry appears in the list of **Domain Name Sets,** shown in Figure 19.19.

Figure 19.19 The Domain Name Sets list

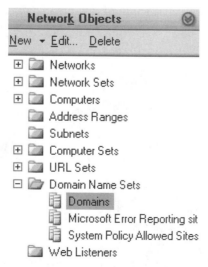

5. Click **Apply** to save the changes and update the firewall policy.

6. Click **OK** in the **Apply New Configuration** dialog box.

Now we need to create two text files: **urls.txt** and **domains.txt**. Those are the default names used in the scripts. You can change the names of the files, but make sure they match the names you configure in the scripts.

The **domains.txt** file will contain the following entries:

- stuff.com

- blah.com

- scumware.com

The **urls.txt** file will contain the following entries:

```
http://www.cisco.com
http://www.checkpoint.com
http://www.sonicwall.com
```

Next, copy the script files and the text files into the same directory. In this example, we'll copy the script files and text files into the root of the C: drive. Double click on the **ImportURLs.vbs** file. You'll first see a dialog box that says **Saving,** as shown in Figure 19.20. Click **OK**.

Figure 19.20 Saving the information

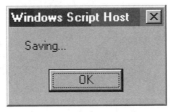

Depending on how many URLs you're importing, it will be a few moments or a few minutes until you see the next dialog box, shown in Figure 19.21, which informs you that the import was completed. Click **OK**.

Figure 19.21 Finishing the procedure

Now we'll import the Domains. Double click the **ImportDomains.vbs** file. You'll see the **Saving** dialog box again. Click **OK**. A few moments to a few minutes later, you'll see the **Done** dialog box. Click **OK**.

Close the **Microsoft Internet Security and Acceleration Server 2006** management console if it is open. Now open the **Microsoft Internet Security and Acceleration Server 2006** management console and go to the **Firewall Policy** node in the left pane of the console.

Click the **Toolbox** tab in the Task Pane and click the **Network Objects** bar. Click the **URL Sets** folder. Double click the **URLs** URL Set. You'll see that the URL Set was populated with the entries in your text file as shown in Figure 19.22. Cool!

Figure 19.22 URL Set entries

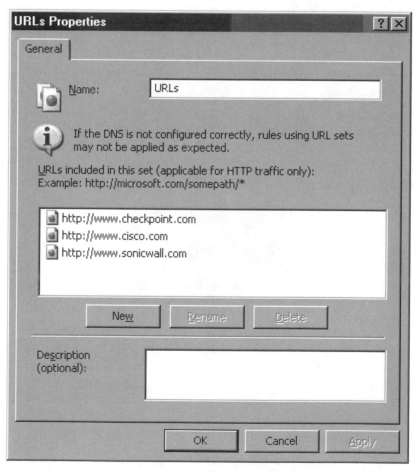

Click on the **Domain Name Sets** folder. Double click on the **Domains** entry. You'll see that the Domain Name Set is populated with domains you want to block, or allow, depending on your need. In this example we included a set of domains we'd like to block, shown in Figure 19.23.

Figure 19.23 Domain Name Set Properties

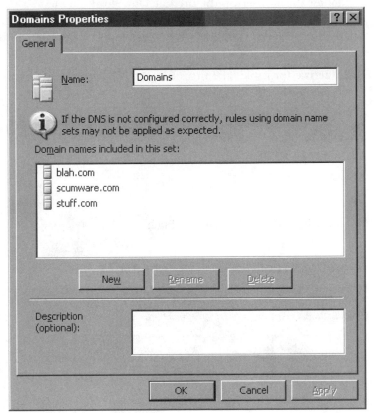

As you obtain more URLs, you can add them to the same text files and run the script again. The new entries will be added without creating duplicates of the domains or URLs that are already included in the Domain Name Set or URL Set.

Extending the SSL Tunnel Port Range for Web Access to Alternate SSL Ports

There will be times when your Web Proxy clients need to connect to SSL Web sites using an alternate port for the SSL link. For example, your users might try to access a banking Web site that requires an SSL connection on TCP port 4433 instead of the default port 443. This can also be problematic for SecureNAT and Firewall clients, since the default setting on the ISA firewall is to forward SecureNAT and Firewall client HTTP connections to the Web Proxy filter. Clients will see either a blank page or an error page indicating that the page cannot be displayed.

The problem here is that the Web Proxy filter only forwards SSL connections to TCP port 443. If clients try to connect to an SSL site over a port other than TCP 443, the connection attempt will fail. You can solve this problem by extending the SSL tunnel port range. However, to do so, you will need to download Jim Harrison's script at http://www.isatools.org, and enter the tunnel port range(s) you want the ISA firewall's Web Proxy component to use.

Perform the following steps to extend the ISA firewall's SSL tunnel port range:

1. Go to www.isatools.org and download the **isa_tpr.js** file and copy that file to your ISA firewall. *Do not use* the browser on the firewall. Download the file to a management workstation, scan the file, and then copy the file to removable media and then take it to the ISA firewall. Remember, you should *never* use client applications, such as browsers, e-mail clients, etc. on the firewall itself.

2. Double click the **isa_tpr.js** file. The first dialog box you see states **This is your current Tunnel Port Range list**. Click **OK**.

3. The NNTP port is displayed. Click **OK**.

4. The SSL port is displayed. Click **OK**.

5. Now copy the **isa_tpr.js** file to the root of the C: drive. Open a command prompt and enter the following:

```
isa_tpr.js /?
```

You will see the following dialog box, shown in Figure 19.24.

Figure 19.24 Help information for the isa_tpr.js script

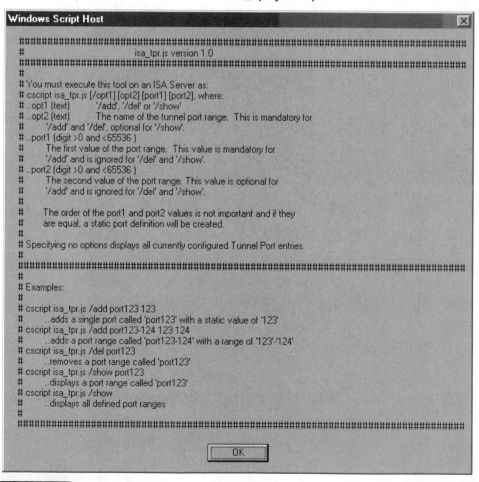

6. To add a new tunnel port, such as **8848,** enter the following command and press ENTER:

```
Cscript isa_tpr.js /add Ext8848 8848
```

You will see something like what appears in Figure 19.25 after the command runs successfully.

Figure 19.25 Running the isa_tpr.js script to add a port to the SSL tunnel port range

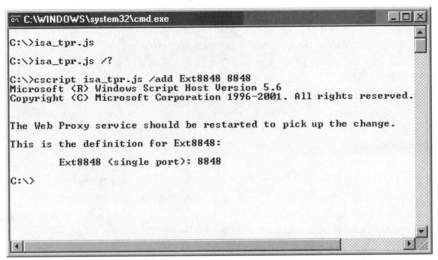

Alternatively, you can download the .NET application, **ISATpre.zip** file (written by Steven Soekrasno) from the www.isatools.org site and install the application on the ISA firewall. This application provides an easy to use graphical interface that allows you to extend the SSL tunnel port range. Figure 19.26 shows what the GUI for this application looks like.

Figure 19.26 Using Steven Soekrasno's .NET Tunnel Port Range extension application

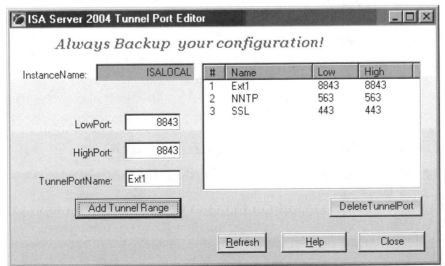

Avoiding Looping Back through the ISA Firewall for Internal Resources

A common error made by ISA firewall administrators involves allowing hosts on an ISA firewall Protected Network to loop back through the firewall to access resources on the same network where the client is located.

For example, suppose you have a simple ISA firewall configuration with a single external interface and a single internal interface. On the Internal network located behind the internal interface, you have a SecureNAT client and a Web server. You have published the Web server to the Internet using a Web Publishing Rule. The Web server is accessible to internal clients using the URL http://web1 and to external clients using the URL http://www.msfirewall.org.

What happens when users on the Internal Network attempt to connect to the Web server using the URL www.msfirewall.org? If you don't have a split DNS in place, the clients on the Internal Network will resolve the name www.msfirewall.org to the IP address on the external interface of the ISA firewall that is listening for incoming connections to www.msfirewall.org. The host then will try to connect to the Internal resource by looping back through the ISA firewall via the Web Publishing Rule. If the client is a SecureNAT client, the connection attempt may fail (depending on how the ISA firewall is configured) or the overall performance of the ISA firewall is severely degraded because the firewall is handling connections for local resources.

You should always avoid looping back through the ISA firewall for resources located on the same network as the requesting host. The solution to this problem is to configure SecureNAT, Firewall and Web Proxy clients to use Direct Access for local resources (local resources are those contained on the same ISA firewall Network as the host requesting those resources). A Direct Access solution depends on the following components:

■ Create a split DNS so that the clients can use the same domain name to reach the same resources both internally and externally. This requires two zones on two DNS servers. One zone is used by external clients and one zone is used by internal clients. The external client zone resolves names to the externally accessible address and the internal zone resolves names to internally accessible addresses. The key is that the zones are authoritative for the same domain name.

■ Configure the properties of the network on which the Protected Network Web Proxy client is located to use Direct Access to reach both the IP addresses on the Internal network and the internal network domain names. This is done on the Web Proxy tab.

■ Configure the properties of the network on which the Protected Network Firewall client is located to use Direct Access for internal domains.

Anonymous Requests Appear in Log File Even When Authentication is Enforced For Web (HTTP Connections)

A common question we encounter from ISA firewall admins relates to the appearance of anonymous connections from Web Proxy clients in the ISA firewall's Web proxy logs. These connections appear in spite of the fact that all rules are configured to require authentication. The short answer to this question is that this is normal and expected.

The long answer to this question involves how Web proxy clients normally communicate with authenticating Web proxy servers. For performance reasons, the initial request from the Web Proxy client is send *without* user credentials. If there is a rule that allows the connection anonymously, then the connection is allowed. If the client must authenticate first, then the Web proxy server sends back to the Web proxy client an access denied message (error 407) with a request for credentials. The Web proxy client then sends credentials to the ISA firewall and the user name appears in the log files.

Figure 19.27 shows the HTTP 407 response returned to the Web proxy client. On the right side of the figure, you'll see the ASCII decode of a frame taken from a Network Monitor trace. On the fifth line from the top, you'll see **HTTP/1.1 407 Proxy Authentication Required...** This is the 407 response the Web Proxy clients receive when an Access Rule requires authentication in order to connect to a Web site through the ISA firewall.

Figure 19.27 A 407 response is returned to the Web proxy client

```
00000000  00 0C 29 EE 9B C0 00 0C 29 5A 67 DB 08 00 45 00   ..)ε¢└..)Zg..E.
00000010  05 DC 9E D0 00 00 80 06 82 46 0A 00 00 01 0A 00   ..R╨..Ç.éF....
00000020  00 05 1F 90 04 3A CF 99 3C 69 5A 18 D7 CE 50 10   ...É.:╧Ö<iZ.╫╬P.
00000030  F9 83 E8 2F 00 00 48 54 54 50 2F 31 2E 31 20 34   ·âΦ/..HTTP/1.1 4
00000040  30 37 20 50 72 6F 78 79 20 41 75 74 68 65 6E 74   07 Proxy Authent
00000050  69 63 61 74 69 6F 6E 20 52 65 71 75 69 72 65 64   ication Required
00000060  20 28 20 54 68 65 20 49 53 41 20 53 65 72 76 65    ( The ISA Serve
00000070  72 20 72 65 71 75 69 72 65 73 20 61 75 74 68 6F   r requires autho
00000080  72 69 7A 61 74 69 6F 6E 20 74 6F 20 66 75 6C 66   rization to fulf
00000090  69 6C 6C 20 74 68 65 20 72 65 71 75 65 73 74 2E   ill the request.
000000A0  20 41 63 63 65 73 73 20 74 6F 20 74 68 65 20 57    Access to the W
```

Blocking MSN Messenger using an Access Rule

Blocking dangerous applications is a common task for the ISA firewall. There are a number of methods you can use to block dangerous applications:

- Use the HTTP Security Filter to block the application if the application uses a Web (HTTP) connection to reach the site
- Use Domain Name Sets or URL Sets to block the sites the dangerous application needs to access to establish a connection
- Block the protocol, or do not allow access to the protocol, required by the dangerous application if the application uses a custom protocol
- If the application can use both a custom protocol and Web connection to access the Internet, then block the custom protocol and then use Domain Name Sets or URL Sets to block its ability to access the Internet using a Web connection
- Simplify your life by using the Principle of Least Privilege. When you use Least Privilege, you create rules to allow access. Anything not explicitly allowed is blocked. In this way, you'll almost never need to create a Deny rule of any kind

To demonstrate one method you can use to block dangerous applications, we'll create an Access Policy that blocks the MSN Messenger 6.2 application. The elements of the solution include the following:

Create a Deny Rule that blocks the MSN Messenger Protocol

Create an Access Rule that blocks the MSN Messenger HTTP header.

In this example, we will create an "all open" rule that allows all protocols outbound, but include a signature in the HTTP Security Filter that blocks the MSN Messenger. The second rule blocks the MSN Messenger protocol. Tables 19.1 and 19.2 show the properties of each Access Rule.

Table 19.1 All Open Rule with MSN Messenger 6.2 HTTP Security Filter signature

Setting	Value
Name	All Open -1
Action	Allow
Protocols	HTTP and HTTPS
From/Listener	Internal
To	External
Condition	All Users
Purpose	This rule allows all traffic through the ISA firewall to all users and all sites. An HTTP signature is created to block the MSN Messenger 6.2 HTTP header

Table 19.2 Access Rule that denies the MSN Messenger protocol

Setting	Value
Name	Deny Messenger Protocol
Action	Deny
Protocols	MSN Messenger
From/Listener	Internal
To	External
Condition	All Users
Purpose	Blocks the MSN Messenger Protocol TCP 1863

You can use the information given earlier in this chapter on how to create the Access Rules listed in Tables 19.1 and 19.2. The **Deny Messenger Protocol** Access Rule must be placed above the **All Open** rule. Deny rules should always be placed above allow rules. Your firewall policy should look something like that in Figure 19.28.

Figure 19.28 Firewall Policy to block MSN Messenger

O... ▲	Name	Action	Protocols	From / Listener	To	Condition
🔲 1	Deny Messenger Protocol	🚫 Deny	🔳 MSN Messenger	⊥ Internal	🌐 External	👥 All Users
🔲 2	All Open -1	✅ Allow	🔳 All Outbound Traffic	⊥ Internal	🌐 External	👥 All Users
⊟ 🔲 3	Block NetBIOS Logging	🚫 Deny	🔳 NetBios Datagram 🔳 NetBios Name Service	⚡ Anywhere	⚡ Anywhere	👥 All Users
🖥 4	Web Publishing Rule	✅ Allow	🔳 HTTP	📠 HTTP	🖥 10.0.0.2	👥 All Users

After creating the Access Rules, right click on the **All Open -1** Access Rule and click the **Configure HTTP** command. In the **Configure HTTP policy for rule** dialog box, click the **Add** button. In the **Signature** dialog box, shown in Figure 19.29, enter the following information:

- **Name:** Enter a name for the MSN Messenger blocking signature
- **Description (optional):** Enter a description for the rule
- **Search in:** Select the **Request headers** option from the drop down list
- **HTTP Header:** Enter **User-Agent:** in the text box
- **Signature:** enter **MSN Messenger** in the text box

Click **OK** to save the signature and click **OK** in the **Properties** dialog box. Click **Apply** to save the changes and update the firewall policy and Click **OK** in the **Apply New Configuration** dialog box.

Figure 19.29 The Signature dialog box

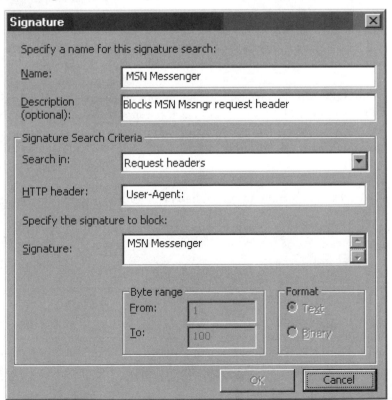

Figure 19.30 shows log file entries for the blocked connection from MSN Messenger. This first entry shows the connection using the MSN Messenger protocol being blocked and the third entry shows that the MSN Messenger connection was blocked by the HTTP Security Filter signature in the All Open rule.

Figure 19.30 Log file entries showing the HTTP Security Filter blocking the MSN Messenger connection

Destination Port	Protocol	HTTP Method	Action	URL	Rule	Filter Information
1863	MSN Messenger	-	Denied Connection	-	Deny Messenger Protocol	-
8080	http	GET	Allowed Connection	http://ISALOCAL/array.dll?Get.Routing.Script		
8080	http	POST	Denied Connection	http://gateway.messenger.hotmail.com/gatewa...	All Open -1	Blocked by the HTTP Security filter...

Allowing Outbound Access to MSN Messenger via Web Proxy

The MSN Messenger can access the Internet using its own protocol, or it can tunnel its communications in an HTTP header. However, you will run into problems if you want Web Proxy clients to access the MSN Messenger site because of an authentication issue that hounds both the MSN Messenger and Hotmail applications.

When the MSN Messenger sends credentials to the MSN Messenger site, those credentials are also sent to the ISA firewall. If the user name and password the user uses to access the MSN Messenger site aren't the same as the credentials the user uses on the corporate network, then the connection will fail. If you allow anonymous access to the MSN Messenger site, then you won't have problems because no credentials are sent to the ISA firewall because the firewall won't challenge the user for credentials.

You can get around this issue by enabling an anonymous access rule for Web Proxy clients so that they can use the HTTP and HTTPS protocols to reach the sites required by the MSN messenger. This limits your exposure because you're not allowing anonymous access to all sites, just MSN Messenger. However, you do lose out on user/group based access control. You can easily solve this problem by using the Firewall client on your hosts and enforcing authentication via the Firewall client and configuring the MSN sites for Direct Access.

You will need to allow anonymous access to the HTTP protocol to the following sites:

```
Config.messenger.msn.com
Gateway.messenger.hotmail.com
Loginnet.passport.net
Loginnet.passport.com
207.46.110.0/24 (this is a Subnet Network Object)
```

We obtained this information by viewing the log file entries in the ISA firewall console's real time log viewer. The subnet and domains may change over time, so if you find that the rule no longer works, you'll need to check your log files and see what sites are required by the Messenger.

Table 19.3 shows the settings in the Access Rule allowing Web Proxy clients access to the MSN Messenger site.

Table 19.3 Settings for a MSN Messenger Web Proxy Access rule

Setting	Value
Name	MSN Messenger Web Proxy Access
Action	Allow
Protocols	HTTP and HTTPS
From/Listener	Internal
To	Messenger Subnet
	Messenger Sites
Condition	All Users
Purpose	This rule allows Web Proxy clients access to the MSN Messenger Sites without requiring authentication. This rule must be above all other rules that require authentication for the HTTP and HTTPS protocols.

Changes to ISA Firewall Policy Only Affects New Connections

After a client initiates a request, the ISA firewall maintains an active state in the firewall state table for the session which permits the response to return to the client. The active state permits the client to send new requests. The ISA firewall removes the active state from the state table after the session is idle for an unspecified period of time (usually a minute or two).

For example, try the following:

- Open a command prompt on a host on a Protected Network and ping a host through the ISA firewall using the "ping –n IP address" command. The –n allows the ping to continue unabated during your test. When you're finished with your test, you can use the CTRL+C command to stop the ping. Make sure there is a rule that allows the host to ping the host through the ISA firewall.

- On the ISA firewall, apply a Deny rule for the Ping protocol and place it above any rule that currently allows the ping through the ISA firewall.

- The ping continues unabated even after the rule is applied. This is because there is an active state table entry for the ping from that client and the destination address being pinged.

- Open a second command prompt on the client that is pinging the remote host. Start a ping to a second host through the ISA firewall. The ping requests are denied because there is no state table entry for the ping protocol from that host to that destination host.

If you try to ping from a different client, the ping is denied.

Access Rules are applied immediately for *new* connections when you click **Apply** to save the changes and update firewall policy. To make changes apply to all existing connections, you can do either of the following:

- Disconnect existing sessions in the **Sessions** tab of the **Monitoring** node. To disconnect a session, open the **Microsoft Internet Security and Acceleration Server 2006** management console, click the **Monitoring** node, click the **Sessions** tab in the middle pane, click the session that you want to disconnect, and then click **Disconnect Session** on the **Tasks** tab.

- Another option is to restart the Microsoft Firewall service. In the **Microsoft Internet Security and Acceleration Server 2006** management console, click the **Monitoring** node, click the **Services** tab, click **Microsoft Firewall**, click **Stop Selected Service** on the **Tasks** tab, and then click **Start Selected Service** on the **Tasks** tab.

Allowing Intradomain Communications through the ISA Firewall

The new ISA firewall's enhanced support for directly attached DMZs has led to a lot of questions on how to allow intradomain communications through the ISA firewall from one network to another. You can now create multiple directly attached perimeter networks and allow controlled access to and from those perimeter networks. You can also safely put domain member machines on these DMZ segments to support a variety of new scenarios, such as dedicated network services segments that enforce domain segmentation.

For example, you might want to put an Internet facing Exchange Server or an inbound authenticating SMTP relay on a network services segment. In order to take advantage of the user database in the Active Directory, you need to join these machines to the Active Directory domain on the Internal network. Since the Internal network domain controllers are located on a network controlled by the ISA firewall, you need to configure the ISA firewall to allow the protocols required for intradomain communications.

The basic network configuration used in this example is seen in Figure 19.31.

Figure 19.31 Basic network configuration for trihomed DMZ

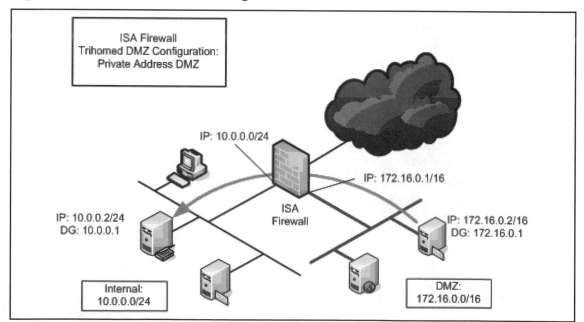

Table 19.4 shows the protocols required for intradomain communications, as well as other details included in an Access Rule we will create to support these communications.

Table 19.4 Protocols Required for Intradomain Communications

Name	Intradomain Communications
Action	Allow
Protocols	ADLogon/DirRep*
	Direct Host (TCP 445)**
	DNS
	Kerberos-Adm(UDP)
	Kerberos-Sec(TCP)
	Kerberos-Sec(UDP)
	LDAP (TCP)
	LDAP (UDP)
	LDAP GC (Global Catalog)
	RPC Endpoint Mapper (TCP 135)***
	NTP
	Ping
From	DMZ Member Server
	Internal Network DC
To	Internal Network DC
	DMZ Member Server
Users	All
Schedule	Always
Content Types	All content types

*ADLogon/DirRep:

Primary Connection: 50000 TCP Outbound (requires RPC key set on the back-end Exchange Server)

**Direct Host:

Primary Connection: 445 TCP Outbound (required to demonstrate an issue discussed in this section

***RPC Endpoint Mapper

Primary Connection: 135 TCP Outbound (required to demonstrate an issue discussed in this section)

RPC services configure themselves in the Registry with a universally unique identifier (UUID), which is similar in function to a globally unique identifier (GUID). RPC UUIDs are well-known identifiers (at least to RPC services), and are unique for each service.

When an RPC service starts, it obtains an unused high or ephemeral port, and registers that port with the RPC service's UUID. Some services choose a random high port while others try to always use the same high port if that port is not already in use. The high port assignment is static for the lifetime of the service and changes only after the machine or service is restarted.

When a client communicates with an RPC service, it doesn't know in advance which high port the service is using. Instead, the RPC client application establishes a connection to the server's RPC portmapper (endpoint mapper) service (on TCP 135) and requests the service it wants by using the service's specific UUID. The RPC endpoint mapper returns the corresponding high port number to the client and closes the connection endpoint mapper connection.

Finally, the client makes a new connection to the server, using the high port number it received from the endpoint mapper.

Because it's impossible to know in advance which port an RPC service will use, the firewall needs to permit all high ports through.

We want to limit the ports required for RPC to a single port. This allows us to know in advance what port to use and configure on the firewall. Otherwise, we would need to allow all high ports from the DMZ to the Internal network. We can limit the ports to a single port by making a Registry change on each domain controller. The Registry Key is:

```
HKEY_LOCAL_MACHINE SYSTEM CurrentControlSet Services NTDS Parameters
```

You need to add a DWORD value named **TCP/IP Port** and set the value to the port you want to use. You'll need to carry out this procedure on each of the domain controllers in your domain.

Perform the following steps on each of the domain controllers in your domain to limit the RPC replication port to **50000**:

1. Click **Start** and click **Run**. In the **Open** text box enter **Regedit** and click **OK**.

2. Go to the following Registry key:

3. HKEY_LOCAL_MACHINE SYSTEM CurrentControlSet Services NTDS Parameters

4. Click the **Edit** menu and point to **New**. Click **DWORD Value**.

5. Rename the entry from **New Value #1** to **TCP/IP Port**, then double click the entry.

6. In the **Edit DWORD Value** dialog box, select the **Decimal** option. Enter **50000** in the **Value data** text box. Click **OK**.

7. Restart the domain controller.

The ISA firewall allows you to control the route relationship between any two Networks. In this example, we will use a ROUTE relationship between the DMZ and the Internal network. Note that when you apply a Network Template to create a DMZ segment, the default route relationship is set as NAT. While there are some minimal advantages to using a NAT relationship, those advantages are outweighed by the limitations they impose in this scenario. If you used a Network Template, make sure to change the Network Rule that controls communications between the DMZ and Internal network to ROUTE as shown in Figure 19.32.

Figure 19.32 Configuring the Network Relationship

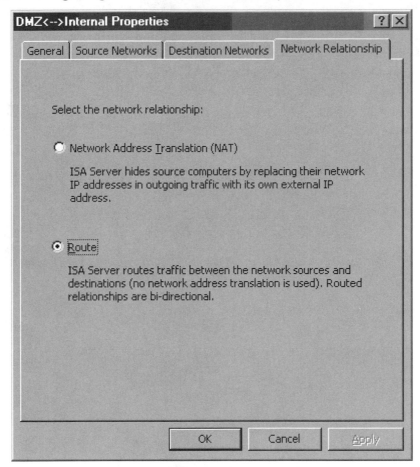

In the following example, we create a rule allowing intradomain communications between a single member server in the DMZ and a single domain controller on the Internal Network. We are using this scenario for simplicity's sake, but you are by no means limited to allowing communications between single servers.

For example, you might have several member server machines on the DMZ and multiple domain controllers on the Internal network. In this case, instead of creating computer objects representing single machines, you would create a Computer Set for the DMZ member servers and another Computer Set for the Internal Network domain controllers. You can then use the Computer Sets to control the Source and Destination locations for the intradomain communications rule.

Perform the following steps to create the intradomain communications rule that will allow machines in the DMZ segment to communicate with domain controllers on the Internal network:

1. In the **Microsoft Internet Security and Acceleration Server 2006** management console, expand the server name and then click the **Firewall Policy** node.

2. In the **Firewall Policy** node, click the **Tasks** tab on the Task Pane. Click the **Create a New Access Rule** link.

3. On the **Welcome to the New Access Rule Wizard** page, enter a name for the rule in the **Access Rule name** text box. In this example, we will call the rule **Member Server Internal DC**. Click **Next**.

4. On the **Rule Action** page, select the **Allow** option and click **Next**.

5. In the **This rule applies to** list, select the **Selected protocols** option. Click the **Add** button.

6. In the **Add Protocols** dialog box, click the **All Protocols** folder. Double click the following protocols:

   DNS

   Kerberos-Adm (UDP)

   Kerberos-Sec (TCP)

   Kerberos-Sec (UDP)

   LDAP

   LDAP (UDP)

   LDAP GC (Global Catalog)

   NTP (UDP)

   Ping

7. Click the **New** menu and click **Protocol**.

8. On the **Welcome to the New Protocol Definition Wizard** page, enter **ADLogon/ DirRep** in the **Protocol Definition name** text box. Click **Next**.

9. On the **Primary Connection Information** page, click **New**.

10. On the **New/Edit Protocol Connection** page, select **TCP** in the **Protocol type** list. Select **Outbound** in the **Direction** list. In the **Port Range** frame, enter **50000** in the **From** and **To** text boxes as shown in Figure 19.33. Click **OK**.

Figure 19.33 Creating a new Protocol Definitions

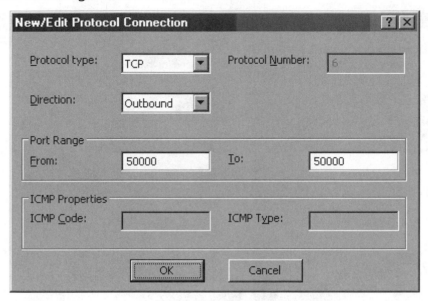

11.   Click **Next** on the **Primary Connection Information** page.

12.   Select the **No** option on the **Secondary Connections** page.

13.   Click **Finish** on the **Completing the New Protocol Definition Wizard** page.

14.   Click the **New** menu and click **Protocol**.

15.   On the **Welcome to the New Protocol Definition Wizard** page, enter **Direct Host** in the **Protocol Definition** name text box. Click **Next**.

16.   On the **Primary Connection Information** page, click **New**.

17.   On the **New/Edit Protocol Connection page**, select **TCP** in the **Protocol type** list. Select **Outbound** in the **Direction** list. In the **Port Range** frame, enter **445** in the **From** and **To** text boxes. Click **OK**.

18.   Click **Next** on the **Primary Connection Information** page as shown in Figure 19.34.

Figure 19.34 Configure the Primary Connection for the Protocol Definition

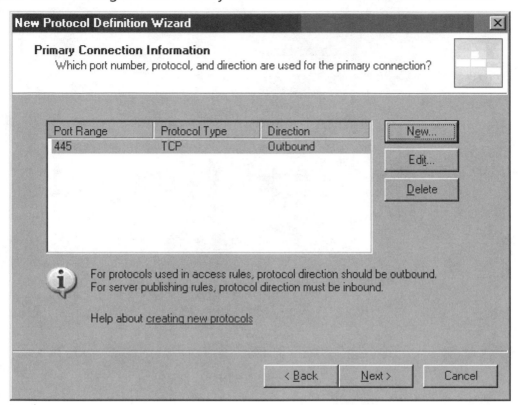

19. Select the **No** option on the **Secondary Connections** page.

20. Click **Finish** on the **Completing the New Protocol Definition Wizard** page.

21. Click the **New** menu and click **Protocol**.

22. On the **Welcome to the New Protocol Definition Wizard** page, enter **RPC Endpoint Mapper (TCP 135)** in the **Protocol Definition name** text box. Click **Next**.

23. On the **Primary Connection Information** page, click **New**.

24. On the **New/Edit Protocol Connection** page, select **TCP** in the **Protocol type** list. Select **Outbound** in the **Direction** list. In the **Port Range** frame, enter **135** in the **From** and **To** text boxes. Click **OK**.

25. Click **Next** on the **Primary Connection Information** page.

26. Select the **No** option on the **Secondary Connections** page.

27. Click **Finish** on the **Completing the New Protocol Definition Wizard** page.

28. In the **Add Protocols** dialog box, click the **User–Defined** folder. Double click the **ADLogon/DirRep, Direct Access** and **RPC Endpoint Mapper (TCP 135)** protocols. Click **Close**.

29. Click **Next** on the **Protocols** page.

30. On the **Access Rule Sources** page, click **Add**.

31. In the **Add Network Entities** dialog box, click the **New** menu. Click **Computer**.

32. In the **New Computer Rule Element** dialog box, enter **DMZ Member Server** in the **Name** text box. Enter **172.16.0.2** in the **Computer IP Address** text box. Click **OK**.

33. In the **Add Network Entities** dialog box, click the **New** menu. Click **Computer**.

34. In the **New Computer Rule Element** dialog box, enter **Internal DC** in the **Name** text box. Enter **10.0.0.2** in the **Computer IP Address** text box. Click **OK**.

35. In the **Add Network Entities** dialog box, click the **Computers** folder. Double click the **DMZ Member Server** entry. Click **Close**.

36. Click **Next** on the **Access Rule Sources** page.

37. On the **Access Rule Destinations** page, click **Add**.

38. In the **Add Network Entities** dialog box, click the **Computers** folder. Double click the **Internal DC** entry. Click **Close**.

39. Click **Next** on the **Access Rule Destinations** page.

40. On the **User Sets** page, accept the default entry, **All Users**, and click **Next**.

41. Review the settings on the **Completing the New Access Rule Wizard** page and click **Finish**.

42. Click **Apply** to save the changes and update the firewall policy.

43. Click **OK** in the **Apply New Configuration** dialog box, then you'll see what's shown in Figure 19.35 in the Firewall Policy tab.

Figure 19.35 Firewall Policy

You can test the rule by joining a machine in the DMZ to the Active Directory domain on the Internal network and then logging into the domain after joining the domain. Note that this rule doesn't allow all protocols through from the member servers to the domain controllers. You will need to create other Access Rules for other protocols, and additional Access Rules for communications to other machines on other networks.

Figure 19.36 below shows some log file entries for communications between the member server and the domain controller on the Internal network. There are some entries in the log file that highlight some undocumented issues with the ISA firewall and its configuration.

Figure 19.36 Log file entries showing communications between member server and domain controller

Client IP	Destinat... ▲	Destination Port	Protocol	Action	Rule	Source Network	Destination Net.
172.16.0.2	10.0.0.2	445	Microsoft CIFS (TCP)	Closed ...	Member Server <--> DMZ	DMZ	Internal
172.16.0.2	10.0.0.2	389	LDAP	Closed ...	Member Server <--> DMZ	DMZ	Internal
172.16.0.2	10.0.0.2	88	Kerberos-Sec (UDP)	Initiated...	Member Server <--> DMZ	DMZ	Internal
172.16.0.2	10.0.0.2	50000	AdLogon/DirRep	Initiated...	Member Server <--> DMZ	DMZ	Internal
172.16.0.2	10.0.0.2	135	RPC (all interfaces)	Initiated...	Member Server <--> DMZ	DMZ	Internal
172.16.0.2	10.0.0.2	88	Kerberos-Sec (UDP)	Initiated...	Member Server <--> DMZ	DMZ	Internal
172.16.0.2	10.0.0.2	88	Kerberos-Sec (UDP)	Initiated...	Member Server <--> DMZ	DMZ	Internal
172.16.0.2	10.0.0.2	389	LDAP	Initiated...	Member Server <--> DMZ	DMZ	Internal
172.16.0.2	10.0.0.2	88	Kerberos-Sec (UDP)	Initiated...	Member Server <--> DMZ	DMZ	Internal
172.16.0.2	10.0.0.2	88	Kerberos-Sec (UDP)	Initiated...	Member Server <--> DMZ	DMZ	Internal
172.16.0.2	10.0.0.2	445	Microsoft CIFS (TCP)	Initiated...	Member Server <--> DMZ	DMZ	Internal
172.16.0.2	10.0.0.2	389	LDAP (UDP)	Initiated...	Member Server <--> DMZ	DMZ	Internal
172.16.0.2	10.0.0.2	389	LDAP (UDP)	Initiated...	Member Server <--> DMZ	DMZ	Internal
172.16.0.2	10.0.0.2	389	LDAP (UDP)	Initiated...	Member Server <--> DMZ	DMZ	Internal
172.16.0.2	10.0.0.2	445	Microsoft CIFS (TCP)	Closed ...	Member Server <--> DMZ	DMZ	Internal

Notice on the first line the connection to TCP port 445. In the protocol column, the name of the protocol is **Microsoft CIFS (TCP)** and not **Direct Host**, which is the name of the Protocol Definition we created for that protocol. The reason for this is that the built-in protocols will be used preferentially in the event that you create a Protocol Definition that has the same settings as a built-in Protocol Definition.

In the fifth line from the top, you'll see a connection made to TCP port 135. The **Protocol** column lists this as the **RCP (all interfaces)** protocol, instead of the **RCP Endpoint Mapper** protocol that we created. Again, the reason for this is that there is a built-in **RPC (all interfaces)** protocol and it is used preferentially over the one we created. In addition, this built-in Protocol Definition automatically binds the ISA firewall's RPC filter, which adds a significant amount of protection for the RPC communications.

We do see one of our custom Protocol Definitions being used in the fourth line from the top. The **ADLogon/DirRep** Protocol Definition is used to communicate on the custom RPC port we configured in the Registry of the domain controller.

Summary

In this chapter we discussed how the ISA firewall processes Access Policy and how to configure Access Rules to control outbound access through the ISA firewall. We also discussed a number of special topics in ISA firewall Access Policy that you can use to further lockdown your network.

You learned about the elements that make up the ISA firewall access rules, including protocols, user sets, content types, schedules and network objects. We discussed how you can create your own protocols or use those built into the ISA Server firewall. We also discussed the user sets (firewall groups) that come preconfigured in ISA Server: all authenticated users, all users, and system and network service. We talked about how content type control works with HTTP and tunneled FTP traffic, and you learned about the pre-built content types, as well as how to create your own content types. We also discussed how to apply schedules to access rules.

Next, we provided step by step details on how to create access rules and all the options that are available when creating or configuring a rule. You also learned how to bypass the Wizard and create new rules by copying and pasting, then making changes to an existing rule. We showed you how to configure RPC, FTP and HTTP policies, and how to order and organize your access rules.

We discussed using scripts to populate domain name sets, and provided a sample script that will allow you to import entries into a Domain Name set or URL set from a text file.

You learned about some specific examples of tasks you might want to perform, such as how to block MSN Messenger using an access rule and how to allow outbound access to MSN Messenger via Web Proxy.

In the next section, we discussed the details of creating and configuring a public address trihomed DMZ (perimeter) network. We discussed reasons for using access rules instead of publishing rules to allow access to DMZ hosts, and described how to publish a public address DMZ host using access rules and how to test the rules.

Finally, we covered how to allow intradomain communications through an ISA Server Firewall. We discussed protocols required for intradomain communications and showed you how to edit the registry on your domain controllers to limit ports required for RPC to a single port, in order to make it easier to analyze the logs.

Creating Remote Access and Site-to-Site VPNs with ISA Firewalls

Solutions in this chapter:

- Overview of ISA Firewall VPN Networking
- Creating a Remote Access PPTP VPN Server
- Creating a Remote Access L2TP/IPSec Server
- Creating a PPTP Site-to-Site VPN
- Creating a L2TP/IPSec Site-to-Site VPN
- IPSec Tunnel Mode Site-to-Site VPNs with Downlevel VPN Gateways
- Using RADIUS for VPN Authentication and Remote Access Policy
- Using EAP User Certificate Authentication for Remote Access VPNs
- Supporting Outbound VPN connections through the ISA Firewall
- Installing and Configuring the DHCP Server and DHCP Relay Agent on the ISA Firewall

☑ Summary

Overview of ISA Firewall VPN Networking

Virtual private networking (VPN) has grown in popularity until it has become a standard for companies that have telecommuters, executives, and salespeople who need network access when on the road, and/or partners and customers who need access to resources on the corporate network. The purpose of VPN networking is to allow remote access to resources on the corporate network that would otherwise only be available if the user were directly connected to the corporate LAN. With a VPN connection, the user has a "virtual" point-to-point link between the remote VPN user and the corporate network. The user can work as if he/she were on site; applications and services running on the users' computers treat the VPN link as if it were a typical Ethernet connection. The Internet over which the client is connected to the corporate network is completely transparent to the users and applications.

One of the major advantages of using a VPN connection instead of a client/server Web application is that VPN users at remote locations can potentially access all of the protocols and servers on the corporate network. This means your users can access the full range of services on Microsoft Exchange Servers, Microsoft SharePoint Servers, Microsoft SQL Servers, and Microsoft Office Communication Servers just as they do when they are directly connected to the network at the corporate location. VPN client software is built into all modern Windows operating systems. A VPN user does not need any special software to connect to each of these services, and it's not necessary to create special proxy applications to allow your users to connect to these resources.

ISA Server 2000 was the first Microsoft firewall to provide tightly integrated VPN configuration and management. ISA 2000 firewall included easy-to-use wizards that made it simple to create remote access and site-to-site (gateway-to-gateway) VPN connections to the ISA 2000 firewall/VPN server. However, there were still some improvements that could be made. The ISA 2000 VPN server still required the firewall administrator to spend a significant amount of time fine-tuning the VPN server configuration via the Routing and Remote Access console.

ISA 2004 significantly enhanced the VPN components that were included with the Windows 2000 and Windows Server 2003 Routing and Remote Access Services (RRAS). An administrator could enable, configure, and manage the VPN server and gateway components directly from the ISA 2004 firewall management console, rather than having to go back and forth between the ISA MMC and the RRAS MMC. You rarely needed to use the Routing and Remote Access console to configure VPN components.

Other improvements to VPN functionality in ISA 2004 included:

- Firewall Policy Applied to VPN Client Connections
- Firewall Policy Applied to VPN Site-to-Site Connections
- VPN Quarantine
- User Mapping of VPN Clients
- SecureNAT Client Support for VPN Connections
- Site-to-Site VPN using Tunnel Mode IPSec
- Publishing PPTP VPN Servers
- Pre-shared Key Support for IPSec VPN Connections

- Advanced Name Server Assignment for VPN Clients
- Monitoring of VPN Client Connections

ISA 2000 had a comprehensive VPN site-to-site wizard. However this disappeared with ISA 2004. With ISA 2004, after running the site-to-site wizard, additional steps, like creating access rules and network rules were required. With ISA 2006 things have changed. While retaining the good things brought by ISA 2004, ISA 2006 includes new features like:

- An improved site-to-site wizard which simplify the creation of a site-to-site connection. We will discuss it later in this chapter.
- The Create Answer File Wizard
- The Branch Office Connectivity Wizard
- The site-to-site summary

One of the core deployment scenarios for ISA 2006 Firewall is the branch office security gateway. ISA 2006 includes along with the improved VPN site-to-site wizard and the especially designed wizards for the branch office, other technologies like BITS caching (available on ISA 2004 SP2 too), HTTP compression (available on ISA 2004 SP2 too), DiffServ (a method for packet prioritization, available on ISA 2004 SP2 too) and others. You can check all these at Microsoft site (http://www.microsoft.com/forefront/edgesecurity/bos.mspx).

SSL VPNs have gained increased popularity. The weaknesses of PPTP forced companies to migrate to other high security VPN remote access solutions. L2TP/IPSec represents such a solution. Properly designed SSL VPNs are an alternative to IPSec in terms of security and tend to offer better connectivity when you are behind restrictive firewalls (IPSec might be blocked) or behind poor NAT devices (which tend to break the NAT-T process). Unfortunately ISA 2006 does not include an SSL VPN component. However, IAG 2007, a new Microsoft product, offers a true SSL VPN solution. IAG 2007 integrated with ISA 2006, represents a single, powerful appliance for network perimeter defense, network separation, remote access and application-layer protection (for both SSL and IPSec connections), full control of inbound and outbound traffic. The two combined include technologies like advanced stateful packet inspection, circuit filtering, application-layer inspection and Web proxy. IAG 2007 also offers advanced VPN Quarantine options.

Another missed feature on ISA 2004 was support for AES (Advanced Encryption Standard). Things have not changed with ISA 2006 and AES is still not here.

With ISA 2006 Microsoft is pushing harder on L2TP/IPSec for both site-to-site connections and remote access. This protocol, for site-to-site connections, provides a "Highly Secure" connection method as compared to "IPSec tunnel mode" which offers "High Security and Interoperabilty with third party VPN vendors". We will discuss later in this chapter the two protocols.

Firewall Policy Applied to VPN Client Connections

When a VPN remote-access client establishes a connection with the VPN server, the VPN client acts like a machine that is directly connected to the corporate network. This virtual link to the corporate network enables the remote VPN user to access almost every resource on the corporate network, limited only by the access controls configured on the servers and workstations. However, this power to access virtually any resource on the corporate network can be a security risk. Generally, you should not allow users to have a full range of access to corporate resources when they connect over a remote access VPN connection. That's because these users might be connecting from computers that aren't within your control and don't conform to corporate software and security policies, or they may be connecting from computers that are on untrusted networks, such as hotel broadband networks. You have no way of knowing whether these machines pose a threat to your network.

Your VPN policy should stipulate that only highly-trusted users who are connecting from known trusted machines on known trusted networks are allowed unfettered access to the corporate network over a remote-access VPN link. Examples of users who might be granted such access include your network, security, and firewall administrators, and perhaps some highly-placed executives. All other users should be restricted to accessing only the subset of network resources that they need to do their jobs when connected via the VPN link.

For example, many firewall administrators allow users to connect over VPN so that they can use the full Outlook 2000/2002/2003/2007 MAPI client to access a Microsoft Exchange Server. Microsoft Exchange provides several different methods for remotely accessing Exchange Server resources. These include the SMTP, POP3, IMAP4, Outlook Web Access (OWA), Exchange ActiveSync and OMA services. However, users like to keep the broad range of options available to them when using the full Outlook MAPI client.

There are basically three ways to satisfy users' needs in this situation:

- Publish the Exchange Server using the ISA Server secure RPC Server Publishing Rule

- Have your users use the Outlook 2003/Exchange 2003 RPC over HTTP protocol

- Grant your users VPN access to the corporate network

The ISA firewall's secure RPC Server Publishing mechanism enables remote Outlook MAPI clients to connect to the full range of Microsoft Exchange Server services from any remote location. The only problem is that, for security reasons, many firewalls and ISPs have blocked access to the RPC port mapper port (TCP 135). This port is required to make the initial secure connection to the Exchange Server using a secure Exchange RPC publishing rule, but the Blaster worm, which exploited this port, caused most administrators to shut it down. Consequently, RPC publishing has lost much of its former utility.

RPC over HTTP(S) can solve this problem by encapsulating the RPC connection inside an HTTP header. This allows the Outlook MAPI client to send requests to the Exchange Server using HTTP. HTTPS is generally allowed by all corporate firewalls and ISPs, since it is used for Web communications. The problem with this solution is that not all organizations have upgraded to Outlook 2003/2007 and Exchange Server 2003 or 2007.

Granting users VPN access will circumvent the limitations of the other solutions, but providing such access can pose a security risk when all VPN clients can access the entire network. The ideal solution is to enforce Access Policy on VPN clients, based on user/group accounts. This way, users can access only the servers and protocols they require.

ISA 2004/2006 is the only VPN server solution that gives administrators this level of access control. When VPN clients connect to the VPN server, those clients are placed on a built-in network entity called the *VPN Clients Network*. The ISA 2004/2006 firewall treats this network like any other network, which means strong user- and group-based access controls can be placed on data that travels between the VPN Clients Network and the corporate network.

All you need to do is create the user accounts and create an access policy on the ISA 2004/2006 firewall/VPN server that limits what machines and protocols the users/groups can access and use, and all those network devices are protected from the VPN remote-access users.

This feature seems to eliminate the need for SSL VPNs (except in those circumstances where remote users are behind extremely restrictive firewalls that block all but HTTP and SSL connections outbound) and other proprietary remote-access solutions aimed at providing per protocol, per server, per user/group access to corporate network resources. Most commercial broadband networks at hotels and conference centers allow outbound PPTP and L2TP/IPSec via NAT Traversal. This way, you can provide remote access for your VPN users without the security threat that typically accompanies VPN client connections.

Firewall Policy Applied to VPN Site-to-Site Connections

A site-to-site VPN connection connects two or more networks (instead of an individual client and a network) over the Internet. Using a VPN site-to-site link can create substantial cost savings in comparison to dedicated WAN links that use dedicated circuits (for example, linking two sites via T-1).

To use a VPN site-to-site link, each site requires a VPN gateway and a relatively inexpensive Internet connection. When the VPN gateways establish connections with one another, the site-to-site VPN link is established. Then the users on each end can communicate with other networks over the VPN site-to-site link just as they would with a routed connection on their own network. The VPN gateways act as routers and route the packets to the appropriate network.

VPN site-to-site connections use the same technologies as do client-to-server (remote access) VPN connections – and traditionally suffered from the same security problem. That is, all users had access to the entire network to which their own network was connected. The only thing that kept users out of network resources for which they had no permission to access was local access controls on the servers.

Site-to-site VPN connections are typically set up between branch office and main office networks. Providing branch office users with access to the entire main office network can pose a major security threat.

The ISA 2004/2006 firewall/VPN server can solve this problem by controlling outbound data that travels through the site-to-site link. Users at the branch office can be limited to only the resources on the main office network required to do their jobs, and thus, prevented from accessing other computer resources on the main network. As with remote-access VPN clients, the users at the branch office should only be allowed to use the specific protocols they need on the servers they are allowed to access.

VPN site-to-site connections that take advantage of strong user and group-based access controls can save money without sacrificing security.

VPN Quarantine

VPN Quarantine (VPN-Q) was a new feature in ISA 2004 that allowed administrators to screen VPN client machines before allowing them access to the corporate network. The VPN Quarantine feature included with ISA 2004 was similar to the Network Quarantine feature found in Windows Server 2003 RRAS. On paper this feature looked great, but failed in real deployment scenario. It was only a basic framework. Frustration erupted through network administrators who were trying to deploy it on their networks. In the end VPN-Q turn into a big disappointment.

In order to use VPN-Q, you must create a CMAK (Connection Manager Administration Kit) package that includes a VPN-Q client and a VPN-Q client-side script. The client runs the script and reports the results to the VPN-Q server component on the ISA 2004/2006 firewall/VPN server. The VPN client is moved from the "VPN Quarantine" network to the "VPN Clients" network if the script reports that the client meets the software requirements for connecting to the network. You can set different access policies for hosts on the VPN Quarantine network versus the VPN Clients network.

The need of the script was a big issue. Microsoft provided some basic scripts (and an assistance quarantine tool), but to turn these scripts into a real checking system, hard and intense work was needed. Creating CMAC profiles requires additional work in order to make sure you have set everything properly. Also the user could release himself from the quarantine by running a command with some parameters and a shared secret (found in clear within the script) and he would have full access to the network without running any checks.

The ISA 2004 firewall extended the functionality of the Windows Server 2003 RRAS Quarantine controls because the Windows Server 2003 RRAS Quarantine feature did not let you set policy-based access controls. The RRAS Quarantine used simple "port-based" access controls, but it this didn't really provide any level of serious security. The ISA 2004 firewall aimed to apply strong firewall policy-based access controls over hosts on the VPN Quarantine network and exposes these connections to the ISA 2004 firewall's sophisticated application-layer filters.

Experienced programmers could turn the dream of the VPN-Q into reality. However not everybody is a programmer or has the resources to hire one. Another option, which is available for ISA 2006 too, is to use a commercial third party add-on solution that does not require any coding, scripting or similar activities.

VPN Quarantine is still available on ISA 2006. No improved wizard.

To enable Quarantine Control:

1. Open the **Microsoft Internet Security and Acceleration Server 2006** management console and expand the server name and Configuration. Click on the **Network** node.

2. Select the **Networks** tab, and then select the **Quarantined VPN Clients** network.

3. On the **Tasks** tab, click **Edit Selected Network**. On the **Quarantine** tab, **select Enable Quarantine Control**.

The same two options:

- **Enable quarantine according to RADIUS server policies**. The Routing and Remote Access policy determines whether the connection request is passed to ISA 2006. After the policy has been verified, the client can join the VPN Clients network. Windows 2003 VNP-Q is used.

- **Enable quarantine according to ISA Server policies**. In this scenario, ISA 2006 determines whether to quarantine the VPN user. The Quarantined VPN Clients network is used, for which you can set firewall policy. You can exempt the user you want from quarantine. Although ISA 2006 brings the VPN-Q, the minimum system requirements according to ISA's 2006 section from Microsoft site are set to Windows 2003 SP1 or Windows 2003 R2, so the old discussion of ISA 2004 installed Windows 2000 which can benefit from VPN-Q is of no use.

As said before, IAG 2007 comes by default with a great list of checking options that a VPN client must pass before it can join the network. The developers have done the work for you, delivering a final version and not a half done job, like the case of VPN-Q. ISA 2006 VPN-Q remains a promise that Microsoft never fulfilled.

User Mapping of VPN Clients

User mapping is a feature that allows you to map virtual private network (VPN) clients connecting to ISA Server using an authentication method that is not based on "Windows authentication" to the Windows Active Directory namespace (There are two general types of users in ISA. The first one is the Active Directory user or group, the second type is the non-Windows user. Non-Windows users are users who are authenticated using an authentication scheme other than that of Active Directory. Each non-Windows user is defined by a user name and a namespace that identifies the applicable authentication scheme (http://msdn2.microsoft.com/en-us/library/ms812609.aspx).

For example when EAP-TLS is used, and the ISA firewall is a domain member, no RADIUS server, the VPN client and ISA firewall authenticate themselves by presenting a user certificate (issued by an Enterprise CA) and respectively a server certificate. The client certificate contains a user name attribute. The ISA firewall can map this user name with the corresponding Windows User from Active Directory. Therefore with user mapping enabled and configured, Firewall policy access rules specifying user sets for Windows users and groups are also applied to authenticated users who use EAP-TLS authentication. We will discuss EAP-TLS later in this chapter. Default firewall policy access rules will not be applied to users from namespaces that are not based on Windows, unless you define user mapping for users.

The user mapping feature extends the strong user/group-based access controls you can apply to VPN clients that use an authentication method other than Windows (we understand by Windows authentication related to VPN clients, for example, protocols like ms-chapv2, which use explicit Windows User credentials (user name and password), and ISA, domain member, can validate these credentials against Active Directory).

This is important because Windows authentication of domain users is only available when the ISA 2006 firewall belongs to the domain that contains the users' accounts, or to a domain that is trusted by the user accounts' domain. If the ISA 2006 firewall does not belong to a domain, then Windows authentication is used only for user accounts stored on the ISA 2006 firewall machine itself.

With user mapping, you can use RADIUS authentication of domain users, and you can apply user/group-based access control over VPN clients who authenticate via RADIUS. Without user mapping, you would not have access to strong user/group-based access control, and Access Policies from the VPN Clients Network to the Internal network would be limited to controlling protocol and server access to all users connecting to the VPN.

SecureNAT Client Support for VPN Connections

When a VPN client connects to the VPN server, the routing table on the VPN client changes so that the default gateway is the IP address of the VPN server. This causes a potential problem for VPN clients in that, while they are connected to the VPN, they cannot access resources on the Internet at the same time.

A problem with the ISA 2000 firewall/VPN server was that, for VPN clients to access resources on the Internet, you had to choose from one of the three following options:

- Enabling split tunneling on the VPN client

- Installing the Firewall Client software on the VPN client machines

- Configuring the Dial-up and Virtual Private Network settings of the VPN connection with Proxy Server settings (this enables browsing with Internet Explorer only when the client is connected to the VPN).

Split tunneling refers to a configuration where the VPN client machine is *not* configured to use the default gateway on the remote network. The default setting for Microsoft VPN clients is to use the default gateway for the remote network. A VPN requires two connections: first, a connection is made to the Internet (with broadband or other always-on technology, this connection does not have to be manually established each time); second, the VPN connection is made *over* the Internet connection. When VPN clients are configured not to use the default gateway, they can access resources on the corporate network through the VPN connection, and they can also access resources on the Internet via the Internet connection that was established by the VPN client machine *before* the VPN connection took place.

There are some serious security threats that occur when the VPN client machine can access the Internet directly while at the same time being able to access the corporate network via the VPN link. This allows the VPN client computer to completely bypass all Internet access policies that were configured on the ISA 2000 firewall for the duration of the VPN connection. Split tunneling is like allowing users on the corporate network to have local modem connections along with their connections to the LAN. The modem connections would completely bypass the ISA 2000 firewall policy and allow the workstation access to the Internet that would not otherwise be allowed by the ISA 2000 firewall policies. This creates a potential for downloading worms, viruses, and other dangerous content. A malicious user on the Internet would even be able to route exploits from an outside computer through the machine that is performing split tunneling and into the corporate network.

Because of this risk, it was important to provide an alternate method of allowing VPN clients Internet access while connected to the ISA 2004/2006 firewall/VPN server. The preferred alternative with ISA 2000 is to install the firewall client software on the VPN client machine. The Firewall Client will forward requests directly to the ISA Server firewall's internal IP address and does not require split tunneling to allow the client computer to connect to the Internet. In addition, the Firewall Client exposes the VPN client machine to the ISA 2000 firewall access policies.

ISA 2004/2006 firewall/VPN servers solve the problem of split tunneling without requiring installation of the Firewall client by enabling Internet access for VPN SecureNAT clients. The VPN clients are SecureNAT clients of the ISA 2004/2006 firewall by default, because they use the firewall as their default gateway. The ISA 2004/2006 firewall/VPN server can use the log-on credentials of the VPN client to apply strong user- and group-based access controls in order to limit the sites, content, and protocols that the VPN client machines will be allowed to access on the Internet.

An alternative to using the Firewall client on the VPN client is to configure the Dial-up and Network settings of the VPN client connection object in Internet Explorer with Proxy Server settings. If you are using ISA 2000, you can configure the VPN connection object with the same Web Proxy settings that are used by internal clients. However, this approach allows VPN clients to use HTTP, HTTP(S) and FTP (download only) protocols for Internet access. This same feature is available when connecting to ISA 2004/2006 Firewall/VPN servers.

Site-to-Site VPN Using Tunnel Mode IPSec

With ISA 2000, VPN remote-access clients could use PPTP or L2TP/IPSec to connect to the ISA 2000 VPN server, and other VPN gateways could connect to the ISA 2000 VPN gateway and establish site-to-site VPN links between two geographically separate networks. However, most third-party VPN gateways (such as Cisco or other popular VPN gateway solutions) did not support PPTP or L2TP/IPSec for VPN site-to-site connections. Instead, they required IPSec tunnel mode VPN connections.

If you had an ISA 2000 firewall/VPN server on both sites, it was simple to create a highly secure L2TP/IPSec VPN connection between the two sites or a less secure PPTP VPN connection. However, if you had a third-party VPN gateway at the main office, and you wanted to install an ISA 2000 VPN gateway at a branch office, you couldn't establish a site-to-site VPN connection to the main office VPN gateway because the main office VPN gateway didn't support PPTP or L2TP/IPSec connections, and ISA 2000 didn't support IPSec tunnel mode connections for site-to-site links.

ISA 2004/2006 firewalls solve this problem because you can now use IPSec tunnel mode for site-to-site links between an ISA 2004/2006 VPN gateway and a third-party VPN gateway. You can still use PPTP or high security L2TP/IPSec to create site-to-site links between two ISA Server firewall/VPN gateways, but ISA 2004/2006 enables you to use a lower security IPSec tunnel mode connection to connect to third party VPN gateways.

Publishing PPTP VPN Servers

In ISA 2000, Server Publishing Rules limited you to publishing servers that required only TCP or UDP protocols. In other words, you could not publish servers that required non-TCP or UDP protocols, such as ICMP or GRE. This meant you could not publish a PPTP server because it uses the GRE protocol, which is a non-TCP or UDP protocol. The only alternative with ISA 2000 was to put these servers on a perimeter network segment and use packet filters to allow the required protocols to and from the Internet.

ISA 2004/2006 has solved this problem. You can create Server Publishing Rules for any IP protocol using ISA 2004/2006. This includes Server Publishing Rules for GRE. The ISA 2004/2006 Firewall's enhanced PPTP filter allows inbound and outbound access. The inbound access support meant you could publish a PPTP VPN server located behind an ISA 2004/2006 Firewall.

Pre-shared Key Support for IPSec VPN Connections

A Public Key Infrastructure (PKI) is necessary in high-security environments so that computer and user certificates can be issued to the computers that participate in an IPSec-based VPN connection.

Digital certificates are used for machine (computer) authentication for L2TP/IPSec remote access and gateway-to-gateway connections, and for IPSec tunnel mode connections. Certificates can also be used for user authentication for both PPTP and L2TP/IPSec connections.

Setting up a PKI is not a simple task, and many network administrators do not have the time or the expertise to implement one quickly. In that case, there is another way to benefit from the level of security provided by IPSec-protected VPN connections.

With ISA 2004/2006, you can use pre-shared keys instead of certificates when you create remote access and site-to-site VPN connections. All VPN client machines running the updated L2TP/IPSec VPN client software can use a pre-shared key to create an L2TP/IPSec remote-access VPN client connection with the ISA 2004/2006 firewall/VPN server. Windows 2000 and Windows Server 2003 VPN gateways can also be configured to use a pre-shared key to establish site-to-site links.

So be aware that a single remote-access server can use only one pre-shared key for all L2TP/IPSec connections that require a pre-shared key for authentication. You must issue the same pre-shared key to all L2TP/IPSec VPN clients connecting to the remote-access server using a pre-shared key. Unless you distribute the pre-shared key within a Connection Manager profile (CMAK), each user will have to manually enter the pre-shared key into the VPN client software settings. This reduces the security of the L2TP/IPSec VPN deployment and increases the probability of user error and increased number of support calls related to L2TP/IPSec connection failures.

Despite its security drawbacks, the ability to easily use pre-shared keys to create secure L2TP/IPSec connections to the ISA 2004/2006 firewall/VPN server is still popular among firewall administrators. Pre-shared keys are an ideal "stop gap" measure that you can put into place immediately and use while in the process of putting together a certificate-based Public Key Infrastructure. When the PKI is complete, you can then migrate the clients from pre-shared keys to high-security computer and user certificate authentication.

Advanced Name Server Assignment for VPN Clients

The ISA 2000 VPN server/gateway was based on the VPN components included with the Windows 2000 and Windows Server 2003 Routing and Remote Access Services. The RRAS VPN services allow you to assign name server addresses to VPN remote access clients. Proper name server assignment is very important to VPN clients because incorrect name server assignments can render the VPN client unable to connect to either Internal network resources or resources located on the Internet.

Alternatively, it is possible to configure the VPN client connectoid with the IP addresses of WINS and DNS server. You can automate this process by using the Connection Manager Administration Kit to distribute these settings. Client-side name server assignment requires that each connectoid object be manually configured or that you use CMAK to distribute these settings.

It is possible to distribute name resolution settings from the VPN server. However, if you wanted to distribute name server settings to a VPN client from the ISA 2000 VPN server, you had to use one of the following:

- Name server addresses that were bound to one of the network interfaces on the ISA Server 2000 firewall machine

- Name server addresses provided to the VPN client via DHCP options (this was available only if the DHCP Relay Agent was installed on the ISA 2000 firewall/VPN server)

You might sometimes want to assign VPN clients name server addresses that are not based on the network interface configuration on the firewall/VPN server, and you might not want to install the DHCP Relay Agent on the firewall. Unfortunately, if this was the case, you were out of luck with ISA 2000 because it did not support this scenario.

Good news: ISA 2004/2006 firewall/VPN servers do not have this problem because they allow you to override the name server settings on the ISA 2004/2006 firewall/VPN server and issue custom name server addresses to the VPN clients. This can be done within the ISA 2004/2006 management console; you don't have to enter the RRAS console to create the custom configuration.

Monitoring of VPN Client Connections

The ISA 2000 VPN server was limited by the logging and monitoring capabilities of the Windows 2000 and Windows Server 2003 RRAS VPN. Determining who connected to the network via a VPN connection required that you sift through text files or database entries. And that's not all; because the firewall did not manage the VPN remote-access client connections, there was no central mechanism in place at the firewall to allow you to determine which resources were being accessed by VPN remote-access clients.

ISA 2004/2006 solves this problem by applying firewall policy to *all* connections to the firewall, including VPN connections. You can use the real-time log viewer to look at ongoing VPN remote-access client connections and filter it to view only VPN client connections. If you log to an MSDE database, you can query the database to view an historical record of VPN connections. With ISA 2004/2006 firewall/VPN servers, you not only get complete information about who connected to the ISA 2004/2006 firewall/VPN, but you also get information about what resources those users connected to and what protocols they used to connect to those resources.

For example, you can filter VPN criteria in the log viewer if you are using live logging and are logging to a file. What you can't do with file-based logging is use the ISA firewall's log viewer to query the archived data. However, you can still filter and monitor real-time VPN connections in the log viewer. In addition, you can filter VPN connections in both the Sessions view and the Log view.

In the **Tasks** tab in the Task pane of the **Virtual Private Networks (VPN)** node in the **Microsoft Internet Security and Acceleration Server 2006** management console, you can click on a link that allows you to monitor the VPN client and gateway connections. If you choose this option, make sure you back up the default filter settings so that you can return to your baseline filtering configuration.

This ISA 2004/2006 logging and monitoring feature is a big improvement over the logging and monitoring features included with ISA 2000 and is also much better than the standalone Windows 2000 and Windows Server 2003 Routing and Remote Access Service VPN.

ISA 2004 SP3 brought to ISA 2004 the following capabilities: Improved Log Viewer, Enhanced Log Filtering, Improved Management of Log Filters and a new Diagnostic Logging. These features are currently unavailable on the ISA 2006 Firewall but are expected to be available with the soon to be released ISA 2006 SP1.

An Improved Site-to-Site Wizard (New ISA 2006 feature)

The improved site-to-site wizard simplifies the creation of a site-to-site connection. Now the creation of the site-to-site connection is almost completely automated. Within the wizard you can define the required network rule (or you can opt to define it later), the access rules (or you can opt to define it later) and for example if you use certificate authentication (machine, L2TP/IPSec or IPSec tunnel mode) ISA can enable for you the System Policy named "Allow HTTP from ISA Server to selected networks for downloading updated Certificate Revocation Lists (CRL)".

In the case of PPTP and L2TP/IPSec, new with ISA 2006, if this is the first VPN connection (no VPN client access configured or other site-to-site connections defined), the wizard allows you to specify the IP Address assignment (either static or dynamic) and the incoming authentication method for L2TP/IPSec (in case you select as the outgoing authentication method pre-shared keys, you can allow or not for incoming authentication pre-shared keys).

When ISA 2006 is the Answering Gateway for PPTP and L2TP/IPSec site-to-site connections, still the same policies (address assignment, the incoming authentication method for IKE, the user authentication method) that apply to VPN clients are applied to VPN gateways like in the case of ISA 2004.

In the case of IPSec tunnel mode, the remote VPN gateway IP address is automatically included in the remote site IP address range (the same thing must be done at the remote VPN server). The omission of this IP address from the definition of the remote site caused issues with IPSec tunnel mode site-to-site connections in the ISA 2004 days. If you tried to ping or access resources from the local ISA firewall located on the remote site you could not until you manually perform this step on both gateways. For example, in case of testing connectivity with ping, you only received a Negotiating IP Security reply.

We will discuss later in this chapter the improved site-to-site wizard from ISA 2006.

The Create Answer File Wizard (New ISA 2006 feature)

The Create Answer File Wizard creates an answer file at the main office ISA 2006 Enterprise Edition Firewall which will be used to setup the site-to-site VPN at the branch office. The wizard also gives you the option to make the branch office ISA Firewall a domain member. A simple and non-technical user can run the answer file to automatically connect the branch office ISA firewall to the main office network. The Create Answer File Wizard can only be used with IPSec tunnel mode and L2TP/IPSec site-to-site VPN connections.

The Branch Office Connectivity Wizard (New ISA 2006 feature)

Automated branch office ISA firewall deployment tool: The Branch Office Connectivity Wizard (the **appcfgwzd.exe** application) which is run at the branch office using the answer file created at the main office in order to setup the branch office ISA firewall. With ISA 2004, the branch office scenario represented a problem. It required an experienced ISA Firewall administrator to be available at the branch office to create the site-to-site connection, to bring up the tunnel and eventually to try and join the branch ISA Firewall to the domain, an ISA firewall best practice. When an answer file is available at the branch office the process is automated.

However the Branch Office Connectivity Wizard can be run without the answer file at the branch office by manually enter the configuration details.

The Branch Office Connectivity Wizard can only be used with IPSec tunnel mode and L2TP/IPSec site-to-site connections.

The Branch Office Connectivity Wizard represents a big improvement of ISA 2006 Enterprise Edition over ISA 2004.

The Site-to-Site Summary (New ISA 2006 feature)

While on ISA 2004 you had an IPSec policy summary for IPSec tunnel mode site-to-site, now with ISA 2006 all three types of VPN site-to-site connections benefit from a site-to-site summary which allows you to quickly view what you have configured. It is very useful since it describes the local settings and also it suggests you the required settings at the other end of the tunnel.

Creating a Remote Access PPTP VPN Server

A remote access VPN server accepts VPN calls from VPN client machines. A remote access VPN server allows *individual client machines and users* access to corporate network resources after the VPN connection is established. In contrast, a VPN gateway connects entire networks to each other and allows multiple hosts on each network to connect to other networks through a VPN site-to-site link.

You can use any VPN client software that supports PPTP or L2TP/IPSec to connect to a VPN server. The ideal VPN client software is the Microsoft VPN client, which is included with all versions of Windows. However, if you wish to use L2TP/IPSec with pre-shared keys and NAT traversal support, you should download and install the updated L2TP/IPSec client from the Microsoft download site for older Windows OSs. We'll go over the details on how to obtain this software later in the chapter.

In this section, we'll go over the procedures required to create a PPTP remote access VPN server on the ISA firewall. The specific steps we'll perform include:

- Enabling the ISA Firewall's VPN Server component
- Creating an Access Rule allowing VPN Clients access to the Internal network
- Enabling Dial-in Access for VPN User Accounts
- Testing a PPTP VPN Connection

Enable the VPN Server

You need to turn on the VPN server component, as it is disabled by default. The first step is to enable the VPN server feature and configure the VPN server components. You do this in the **Microsoft Internet Security and Acceleration Server 2006** management console and *not* in the RRAS console.

Most of the problems we've seen with the ISA firewall VPN configuration **were** related to fledgling ISA firewall administrators using the RRAS console to configure the VPN components. While there will be times when we want to use the RRAS console, the vast majority of the configuration for the ISA firewall's VPN server and VPN gateway is done in the **Microsoft Internet Security and Acceleration Server 2006** management console.

Perform the following steps to enable and configure the ISA 2006 VPN Server:

1. Open the **Microsoft Internet Security and Acceleration Server 2006** management console and expand the server name. Click on the **Virtual Private Networks (VPN)** node.

2. Click on the **Tasks** tab in the Task pane. Click the **Enable VPN Client Access** link (Figure 20.1). With ISA 2006 you cannot enable VPN Client access until you define the IP address assignment method. Scroll bellow into the **Configure Access Networks Options** and see how you can define Address Assignment (Figure 20.10). You will receive a warning when you click **Enable VPN Client Access** if **Address Assignment** was not configured (Figure 20.2).

Figure 20.1 The Enable VPN Client Access link

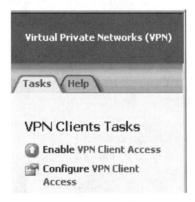

Figure 20.2 Warning About address assignment

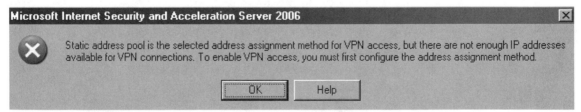

3. Click **Apply** to save the changes and update the firewall policy.

4. Click **OK** in the **Saving Configuration Changes** dialog box.

5. Click the Configure VPN Client Access link on the Tasks tab.

6. On the **General** tab in the **VPN Clients Properties** dialog box, change the value for the **Maximum number of VPN clients allowed** from **5** to **10**. The Standard Edition of the ISA firewall supports up to 1000 concurrent VPN connections. This is a hard-coded limit

and it is locked-in regardless of the number of VPN connections supported by the Windows operating system on which the ISA firewall is installed. In contrast, the Enterprise edition of the ISA firewall does not have a hard-coded limit and supports the number of VPN connections supported by the base operating system. The exact number is unclear, but we do know that when the ISA firewall is installed on the Enterprise version of Windows Server 2003, you can create over 16,000 PPTP connections and over 30,000 L2TP/IPSec VPN connections to the ISA firewall. The General tab is shown in Figure 20.3.

Figure 20.3 The General Tab

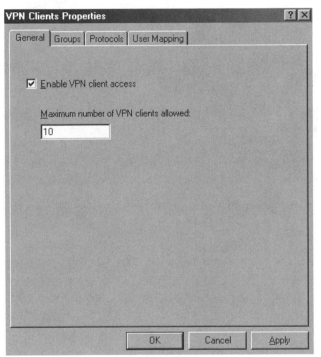

Make sure that you will have at least the number of IP addresses available to VPN clients as the number you list in the **Maximum number of VPN clients allowed** text box. Determine the number of VPN clients you want to connect to the ISA firewall, and then add one more for the ISA firewall itself. That's the number you want to enter into this text box.

1. Click on the **Groups** tab (Figure 20.4). On the **Groups** tab, click **Add**.

2. In the **Select Groups** dialog box, click the **Locations** button. In the **Locations** dialog box, click **msfirewall.org,** and click **OK**.

3. In the **Select Group** dialog box, enter **Domain Users** in the **Enter the object names to select** text box. Click **Check Names**. The group name will be underlined when it is found in the Active Directory. Click **OK**.

Figure 20.4 The Groups Tab

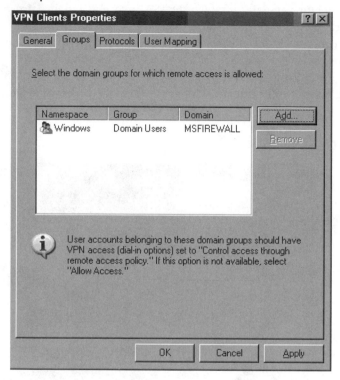

You can enter local groups that are configured on the ISA firewall machine itself, or you can use domain groups. The ISA firewall will use only domain Global Groups, it will not use Domain Local Groups. You configure domain Global Groups on the **Groups** tab *only* when the ISA firewall is a member of the domain. If the ISA firewall is not a member of the domain, then you can use RADIUS authentication to allow domain Global Groups access to the ISA firewall's VPN server. We will cover the details of configuring RADIUS authentication for VPN remote-access connections later in this chapter.

Another thing to keep in mind is that when you control access to the VPN server via a domain (or local) group, the users must have remote access permission. We'll discuss that issue later in this chapter.

1. Click the **Protocols** tab. On the **Protocols** tab, put a checkmark in the **Enable PPTP** check box only, as shown in Figure 20.5.

Figure 20.5 The Protocols Tab

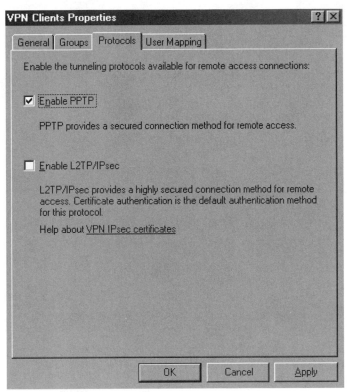

2. Click the **User Mapping** tab. Put a checkmark in the **Enable User Mapping** check box. Put a checkmark in the **When username does not contain a domain, use this domain** check box. Enter **msfirewall.org** in the **Domain Name** text box. Note that these settings will only apply when using RADIUS/EAP authentication. These settings are ignored when using Windows authentication (such as when the ISA 2006 firewall machine belongs to the domain and the user explicitly enters domain credentials). Click **Apply** and **OK.** You may see a **Microsoft Internet Security and Acceleration Server 2006** dialog box informing you that you need to restart the computer for the settings to take effect. If so, click **OK** in the dialog box. The User Mapping tab is shown in Figure 20.6.

Figure 20.6 The User Mapping tab

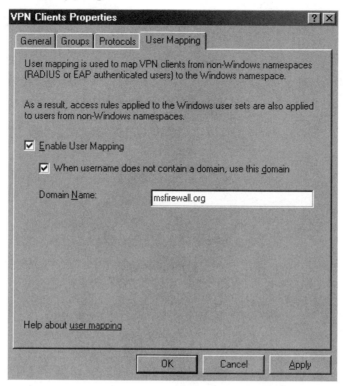

You can prevent all VPN connections to your ISA firewall if you enable user mapping and *do not* make the ISA firewall a member of the domain (Error 619). User mapping can be used when the ISA firewall is a member of your domain, and you use RADIUS authentication to support authentication for users that belong to multiple domains or if you use EAP-TLS authentication. You can enable user mapping to support creating user/group-based access control over users who log on via RADIUS and map those user accounts to accounts in the domain the ISA firewall belongs to, and then create Access Rules using those accounts by creating **User Sets** on the ISA firewall. In case of EAP-TLS (no RADIUS), when ISA is a domain member the user name from the certificate can be mapped to a Windows Active Directory account.

In case ISA does not belong to the domain (workgroup mode) you can use user mapping with RADIUS authentication (example IAS, Active Directory integrated) as long as you are using authentication protocols like PAP or SPAP (very weak protocols) enabled on ISA (if not you receive Error 919) and enabled on the RADIUS server and you specify a simple user name (just Administrator and not Administrator@msfirewall.org) when the client connects. Also you need to mirror the groups/accounts on ISA (if not you will not be able to connect) in order to apply group based firewall policy (i.e., use these local groups for the rules). You need user mapping only when you create group-based access rules. If you use user-based access rules then you can define **User Sets** with RADIUS namespace on ISA. Keep in mind that:

- In case of PPTP, PAP means that credentials will be sent in clear. When you configure the VPN client connection you receive a warning informing you that data encryption will not be used (keys used to encrypt data can only be obtain when MS-CHAP or MS-CHAPv2 is used, MMPE cannot be used with PAP and SPAP). So you need to tell the client to connect using no encryption. The RADIUS server must be configured to accept connections that use no encryption and to use PAP and/or SPAP. If not Error 742 will be received. PPTP is weak at its best, so using PAP and SPAP will make it useless (credentials sent in clear, no data encryption)

- In case of L2TP/IPSec keys used to encrypt data are obtained from IPSec, the PPP authentication is protected by IPSec ESP, so the RADIUS server does not need to be configured to use no encryption and you do not receive any warning when selecting PAP or SPAP at the client side. The second level of authentication, user authentication (PPP), provided by L2TP/IPSec must be as strong as possible and PAP and SPAP are as weak as possible. Again an unfeasible scenario.

In case of using EAP-TLS with a RADIUS server, ISA workgroup mode, once again you can use user mapping if you select "Use a different name for the connection" when configuring the client connection and you do not specify the domain name (the user/groups accounts need to be mirrored on ISA). See Figure 20.7 and Figure 20.8

Figure 20.7 Use a different name for the connection

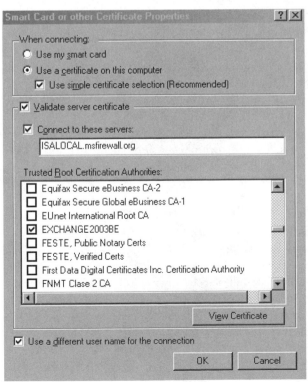

Figure 20.8 Enter a simple user name

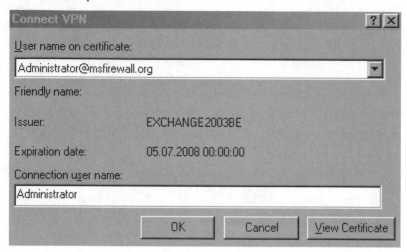

In ISA's help file there is a strong recommendation that PAP, SPAP and CHAP to remain disabled.

Therefore, we can conclude that if you want group-based firewall access policies you must make ISA a domain member and enable user mapping when EAP-TLS or RADIUS (IAS, Active Directory integrated) authentication is used. Since ISA is a domain member the RADIUS server is not needed. One remote access scenario when you would need a RADIUS server (and the ISA firewall is domain member) is when you might have a small group of users using PPTP and other group(s) using the stronger L2TP/IPSec and you want to explicitly specify who can use PPTP, due to security issues. You can create the required Remote Access Policies on the RADIUS server and create user/groups based firewall policies (access rules) on ISA with user mapping. Currently with ISA 2006 Firewall is not possible of doing that from the ISA's GUI.

We will discuss the user mapping subject in more detail later in this chapter and also discuss how to use apply user/group-based access control over VPN clients that log on via RADIUS.

We will go over the details of how User Mapping works with EAP user certificate authentication later in the chapter.

3. On the **Tasks** tab, click **Select Access Networks**.

4. In the **Virtual Private Networks (VPN) Properties** dialog box, click **Access Networks**. Note that the **External** checkbox is selected. This indicates that the external interface is listening for incoming VPN client connections. If you want internal users to connect to the ISA firewall, select **Internal**. You also have the options to allow VPN connections from All Networks (and Local Host) Network and All Protected Networks. The Virtual Private Networks Properties dialog box is shown in Figure 20.9, Select and Configure Access Networks Options.

Figure 20.9 Select and Configure Access Networks Options

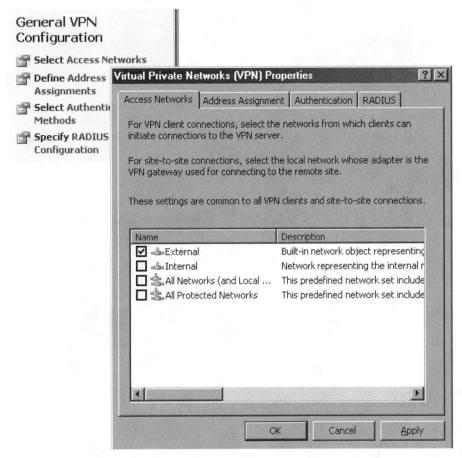

The ability to select VPN connections from multiple networks can be useful when you have unsecured networks located behind the ISA firewall. For example, suppose you have a trihomed ISA firewall that has an external interface, an Internal interface, and a WLAN interface. You use the WLAN for users who bring in laptops that are not managed by your organization. You also require users who have managed computers to use the WLAN segment as well when they bring laptops that are moved between the corporate network and untrusted networks.

You configure Access Rules on the ISA firewall to prevent connections from the WLAN segment. However, you configure Access Rules that allow VPN connections on the WLAN interface to connect to resources on the corporate Internal network. In this way, no users connected to the WLAN segment are able to access resources on the corporate Internal network segment except those corporate users who can VPN into the WLAN interface on the ISA firewall and present the proper credentials to complete a VPN link.

Another scenario where you might want to allow a VPN connection into the ISA firewall is when the ISA firewall is acting as a front-end firewall. In that case, you probably do not want to allow direct RDP or remote MMC connections to the ISA firewall. What you can do is allow RDP connections *only from VPN Clients* and then allow VPN clients RDP access to the Local Host Network. In this way, a user must establish a secure VPN connection to the front-end ISA firewall before an RDP connection can be established. Hosts connecting via any other means are denied access to the RDP protocols. Nice!

5. Click the **Address Assignment** tab (Figure 20.10). Select *Internal* from the **Use the following network to obtain DHCP, DNS and WINS services** drop down list box. This is a critical setting as it defines the network on which access to the DHCP is made.

Figure 20.10 The Address Assignment Tab

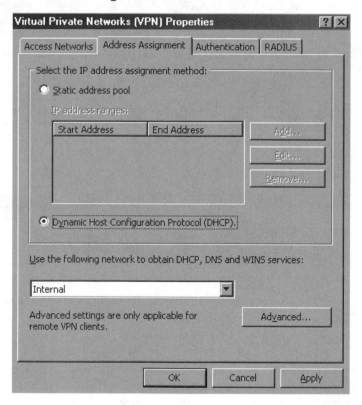

Note that this isn't your only option. You can select any of the adapters on the ISA firewall from **Use the following network to obtain DHCP, DNS and WINS services**. The key issue is that you select the adapter that has the correct name server information on it, and the most likely candidate is the Internal interface of the ISA firewall.

You also have the option to use a **Static address pool** to assign addresses to the VPN clients. The problem with using a static address pool is, if you assign *on subnet* addresses (addresses in the same network ID as one of the interfaces on the ISA firewall), you will need to remove those addresses from the definition of the Network to which the ISA firewall is connected.

For example, suppose the ISA firewall has two network interfaces: an external and an internal interface. The internal interface is connected to your default Internal Network and the Internal Network ID is 10.0.0.0/24. If you want to assign VPN clients addresses in the Internal Network address range using a static address pool, such as 10.0.0.200 to 10.0.0.211(total of 10 addresses), you will need to manually remove those addresses from the definition of the Internal Network before you can create a static address pool with these addresses. If you try to create a static address pool with these *on subnet* addresses, you'll see the following error (Figure 20.11).

Figure 20.11 A Network Warning Dialog Box

You can assign name server addresses to VPN clients that are independent of the name server configuration on any of the interfaces on the ISA firewall. Click the **Advanced** button, and you'll see the **Name Resolution** dialog box. The default settings are **Obtain DNS server addresses using DHCP configuration** and **Obtain WINS server addresses using DHCP configuration**. Of course, you cannot obtain DHCP options for VPN clients unless you install and configure a DHCP Relay Agent on the ISA firewall. The ISA firewall's RRAS service will only obtain blocks of IP addresses for the VPN clients, not DHCP options. We will discuss this issue in more detail later in this chapter.

If you want to avoid installing the DHCP Relay Agent, you can still deliver custom DNS and WINS server addresses to VPN clients by selecting **Use the following DNS server addresses** and **Use the following WINS server addresses**. See Figure 20.12.

Figure 20.12 The Name Resolution Dialog Box

6. Click on the **Authentication** tab. Note that the default setting enables only **Microsoft encrypted authentication version 2 (MS-CHAPv2)**. Note the **Allow custom IPSec policy for L2TP connection** checkbox. If you do not want to create a public key infrastructure (PKI), or, you are in the process of creating one but have not yet finished, you can enable this checkbox and enter a **pre-shared** key. You should also enable a custom IPSec policy pre-shared key if you want to create a site-to-site VPN connection with pre-shared keys. We'll discuss this issue in detail later in this chapter. For the highest level of authentication security, enable the **Extensible authentication protocol (EAP) with smart card or other certificate** option. We will discuss later in this chapter how to configure the ISA firewall and VPN clients to use User Certificates to authenticate to the ISA firewall. Figure 20.13 shows the Authentication tab options.

Figure 20.13 The Authentication Tab

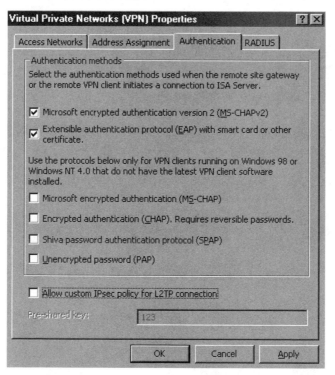

7. Click the **RADIUS** tab. Here you can configure the ISA 2006 firewall VPN server to use RADIUS to authenticate the VPN users. The advantage of RADIUS authentication is that you can leverage the Active Directory's (and other directories) user database to authenticate users without requiring the ISA firewall to be a member of a domain. See Figure 20.14. We'll go over the details of how to configure RADIUS support for VPN user authentication later in this chapter.

Figure 20.14 Virtual Private Networks Properties

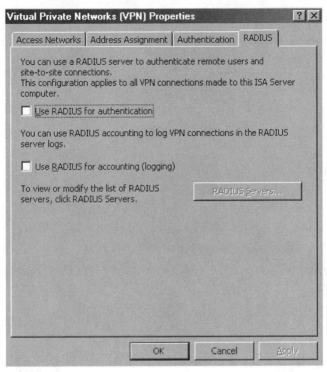

8. Click **Apply** in the **Virtual Private Networks (VPN) Properties** dialog box and then click **OK**.

9. Click **Apply** to save the changes and update the firewall policy.

10. Click **OK** in the **Saving Configuration Changes** dialog box.

11. Restart the ISA firewall machine.

The ISA firewall will obtain a block of IP addresses from the DHCP Server on the Internal network when it restarts. Note that on a production network where the DHCP server is located on a network segment remote from the ISA 2006 firewall, all interposed routers will need to have BOOTP or DHCP relay enabled so that DHCP requests from the firewall can reach the remote DHCP servers.

Create an Access Rule Allowing VPN Clients Access to Allowed Resources

The ISA firewall will be able to accept incoming VPN connections after the restart. However, VPN clients cannot access any resources because there are no Access Rules allowing the VPN clients to get to anything. You must create Access Rules allowing members of the VPN Clients network access to the resources you want them to access. This is a stark contrast to other combined firewall/VPN server solutions in that the ISA firewall VPN server applies stateful packet and application-layer inspection on all VPN client connections.

In the following example, you will create an Access Rule allowing all traffic to pass from the VPN Clients network to the Internal network. In a production environment, you would create more restrictive access rules so that users on the VPN Clients network have access only to resources they require. Later in this chapter, we will demonstrate how you can configure a more restrictive Access Policy using user/group-based access control on VPN clients.

Perform the following steps to create an unrestricted-access VPN client Access Rule:

1. In the **Microsoft Internet Security and Acceleration Server 2006** management console, expand the server name and click the **Firewall Policy** node. Right-click the **Firewall Policy** node, point to **New** and click **Access Rule**.

2. In the **Welcome to the New Access Rule Wizard** page, enter a name for the rule in the **Access Rule name** text box. In this example, enter **VPN Client to Internal**. Click **Next**.

3. On the **Rule Action** page, select **Allow** and click **Next**.

4. On the **Protocols** page, select **All outbound traffic** in the **Apply the rule to this protocols** list. Click **Next**.

5. On the **Access Rule Sources** page, click **Add**. In the **Add Network Entities** dialog box (Figure 20.15), click the **Networks** folder and double-click on **VPN Clients**. Click **Close**.

Figure 20.15 The Add Network Entities Dialog Box

6. Click **Next** on the **Access Rule Sources** page.

7. On the **Access Rule Destinations** page, click **Add**. In the **Add Network Entities** dialog box, click the **Networks** folder, and double-click **Internal**. Click **Close**.

8. On the **User Sets** page, accept the default setting, **All Users**, and click **Next**.

9. Click **Finish** on the **Completing the New Access Rule Wizard** page.

10. Click **Apply** to save the changes and update the firewall policy.

11. Click **OK** in the **Saving Configuration Changes** dialog box. The VPN client policy is now the top-listed Access Rule in the Access Policy list as shown in Figure 20.16.

Figure 20.16 VPN Client Policy

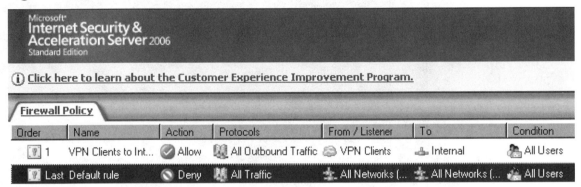

At this point VPN clients that successfully authenticate and have Dial-in permission will be able to access all resources, using any protocol, on the Internal network.

Enable Dial-in Access

In non-native mode Active Directory domains, all user accounts have dial-in access *disabled* by default. You must enable dial-in access on a *per account* basis for these non-native mode Active Directory domains. In contrast, native-mode Active Directory domains have dial-in access controlled by *Remote Access Policy* by default. Windows NT 4.0 domains always have dial-in access controlled on a per user account basis.

In the lab environment used in this section, Active Directory is in Windows Server 2003 mixed mode, so we will need to manually change the dial-in settings on each domain user account that requires access to the VPN server.

Perform the following steps on the domain controller to enable Dial-in access for the Administrator account:

1. Click Start and point to Administrative Tools. Click Active Directory Users and Computers.

2. In the Active Directory Users and Computers console, click on the Users node in the left pane. Double-click on the Administrator account in the right pane of the console.

3. Click on the Dial-in tab. In the Remote Access Permission (Dial-in or VPN) frame, select Allow access as shown in Figure 20.17. Click Apply and OK.

Figure 20.17 The account dial-in tab

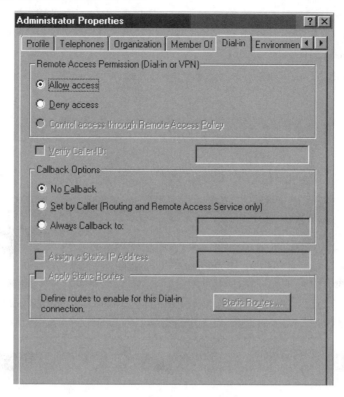

4.   Close the Active Directory Users and Computers console.

Another option is to create groups on the ISA firewall itself. You can create local users on the ISA firewall and then place those users into groups. This method allows you to use the default setting on the user accounts created on the ISA firewall, where the default dial-in setting is **control access via Remote Access Policy**.

While this option doesn't scale very well, it's a viable option for those organizations that have a limited number of VPN users and who don't want to use RADIUS or don't have a RADIUS server to use.

Perform the following steps to create a user group that has access to the ISA firewall's VPN server:

1.   On the ISA firewall, right-click **My Computer** on the desktop and click **Manage**.

2.   In the **Computer Management** console, expand **System Tools**, and expand the **Local Users and Groups** node. Right-click the **Groups** node, and click **New Group**.

3.   In the **New Group** dialog box, enter a name for the group in the **Group Name** text box. In this example, we'll name the group **VPN Users**. Click **Add**.

4.   In the **Select Users** dialog box, click **Advanced**.

5.   In the **Select Users** dialog box, select the users or groups you want to make part of the **VPN Users** group. In this example, we'll select **Authenticated Users**. Click **OK**.

6. Click **OK** in the **Select Users** dialog box.

7. Click **Create**, and then **Close**.

Now let's configure the ISA firewall's VPN server component to allow access to members of the **VPN Users** group:

1. In the **Microsoft Internet Security and Acceleration Server 2006** management console, expand the server name, and then click **Virtual Private Networking (VPN)**. Click **Configure VPN Client Access** on the **Tasks** tab in the Task pane.

2. In the **VPN Clients Properties Groups** tab, click **Add**.

3. In the **Select Groups** dialog box, enter **VPN Users** in the **Enter the object name to select** text box, and click **Check Names**. The group name will be underlined when it's found. Click **OK**.

We enter the local **VPN Users** group in the **Groups** tab in this example because VPN access can be controlled via the **Control access through Remote Access Policy** setting on the user accounts of users in the local SAM of the ISA firewall. You can also enter domain users and groups (when the ISA firewall is a member of the user domain) when the domain supports Dial-in access via Remote Access Policy. We will talk more about domain users and groups and Remote Access Policy later in this chapter. See Figure 20.18 for controlling permission via Remote Access Policy.

Figure 20.18 Controlling permission via Remote Access Policy

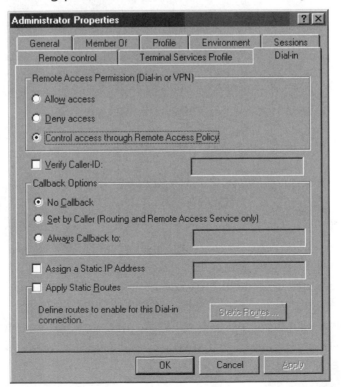

4. Click **Apply**, and then click **OK** in the **VPN Client Properties** dialog box (Figure 20.19).

Figure 20.19 The Groups Tab

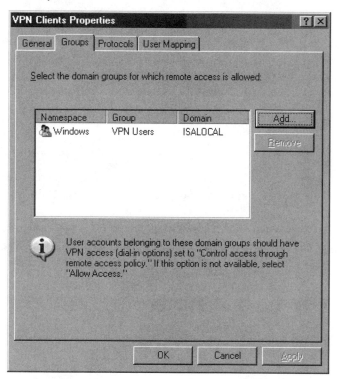

5. Click **Apply** to save the changes and update the firewall policy.

6. Click **OK** in the **Saving Configuration Changes** dialog box.

Test the PPTP VPN Connection

The ISA 2006 VPN server is now ready to accept VPN client connections. Set up the VPN connectoid on your VPN client, and then establish the VPN connection to the ISA firewall. In this book's test lab, we use a Windows XP client running Service Pack 2.

Perform the following steps to test the VPN Server:

1. On the Windows XP external client machine, right-click **My Network Places** on the desktop, and click **Properties**.

2. **Click Create a new connection wizard** in the **Network Connections** window, **Network Tasks panel**.

3. Click **Next** on the **Welcome to the New Connection Wizard** page.

4. On the **Network Connection Type** page, select **Connect to the network at my workplace**, and click **Next**.

5. On the **Network Connection** page, select the **Virtual Private Network connection**, and click **Next**.

6. On the **Connection Name** page, enter **VPN** in the **Company Name** text box, and click **Next**.

7. On the **VPN Server Selection** page, enter the IP address on the external interface of the ISA firewall (in this example, the external IP address is 192.168.1.70) in the **Host name or IP address** text box. Click **Next**.

8. On the **Connection Availability** select **Create this connection for My use only.** Click **Next.**

9. Click **Finish** on the **Completing the New Connection Wizard** page.

10. In the **Connect VPN** dialog box, enter the user name **Administrator** and the password for the administrator user account. (**NOTE:** If the ISA firewall is a member of a domain, enter the machine name or the domain name before the user name in the format NAMEusername, depending on whether the account is a local ISA firewall account or a domain account). Click **Connect**.

11. The VPN client establishes a connection with the ISA 2006 VPN server. Click **OK** in the **Connection Complete** dialog box informing that the connection is established.

12. Double-click the connection icon in the system tray, and click **Details**. You can see that **MPPE 128** encryption is used to protect the data and the IP address assigned to the VPN client (Figure 20.20). Click **Close**.

Figure 20.20 Details of PPTP connection

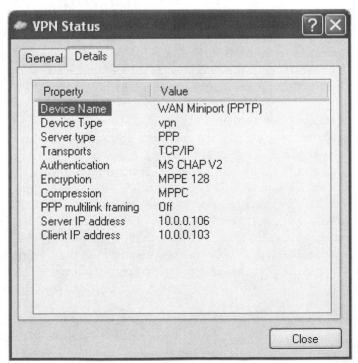

13.   If you're using the lab setup for this book, click **Start** and **Run**. In the **Run** dialog box, enter **EXCHANGE2003BE** in the **Open** textbox, and click **OK**. The shares on the domain controller computer appear. Close the windows displaying the domain controller's contents. Note that we were able to use a single label name to connect to the domain controller because the ISA firewall assigned the VPN client a WINS server address. A single label name would also work via a DNS query if the VPN client machine were configured to fully qualify single label names with the correct domain name.

14.   Right-click the connection icon in the system tray, and click **Disconnect**.

Creating a Remote Access L2TP/IPSec Server

In the last section, we discussed the procedures required to enable and configure the ISA firewall's VPN server component to allow remote access VPN client PPTP connections. In the following section, we'll build on the configuration we created in the last section and configure the ISA firewall to support a L2TP/IPSec remote access VPN client connection.

We'll perform the following procedures to allow L2TP/IPSec remote access VPN client connections to the ISA firewall:

■   Issue certificates to the ISA 2006 firewall and VPN clients

■   Test a L2TP/IPSec VPN connection

■   Monitor VPN Client Connections

Issue Certificates to the ISA Firewall and VPN Clients

You can significantly improve the level of security on your VPN connections by using the L2TP/IPSec VPN protocol. The IPSec encryption protocol provides a number of security advantages over the Microsoft Point-to-Point Encryption (MPPE) protocol used to secure PPTP connections. While the ISA firewall supports using a pre-shared key to support the IPSec encryption process, this should be considered a low-security option and should be avoided if possible.

However, if you just aren't in the position to roll out a PKI, then a pre-shared key for L2TP/IPSec is still a viable option. Just be aware that it lowers the level of security for your L2TP/IPSec connections compared to those created using machine certificates. The secure IPSec solution is to use computer certificates on the VPN server and VPN clients. We'll discuss using pre-shared keys after going through the procedures for using certificate authentication for the L2TP/IPSec connection.

The first step is to issue a computer certificate to the ISA firewall. There are a number of methods you can use to request a computer certificate. In the following example, we will use the **Certificates** stand-alone MMC snap-in. Note that you can only use the Certificate MMC snap-in when the ISA firewall is a member of the same domain where an enterprise CA is installed. If the ISA firewall is not a member of a domain where there is an enterprise CA, then you can use the Web enrollment site to obtain a machine certificate.

In order for the stand-alone MMC snap-in to communicate with the certificate authority, we will need to enable an "all open" rule that allows all traffic from the Local Host network to the Internet network. We will disable this rule after the certificate request is complete.

Perform the following steps on the ISA 2006 firewall to request a certificate from the enterprise CA on the Internal network:

1. In the **Microsoft Internet Security and Acceleration Server 2006** management console, expand the server name in the left pane, and then click the **Firewall Policy** node. Click the **Tasks** tab in the Task pane, and then click **Create Access Rule**.

2. On the **Welcome to the New Access Rule Wizard** page, enter a name for the rule in the **Access Rule name** text box. In this example, we will enter **All Open from Local Host to Internal**. Click **Next**.

3. On the **Rule Action** page, select **Allow**, and click **Next**.

4. On the **Protocols** page, accept the default selection, **All outbound traffic**, and click **Next**.

5. On the **Access Rule Sources** page, click **Add**. In the **Add Network Entities** dialog box, click the **Networks** folder. Double-click **Local Host**, and click **Close**.

6. On the **Access Rule Destinations** page, click **Add**. In the **Add Network Entities** dialog box, click the **Networks** folder. Double-click **Internal**, and click **Close**.

7. On the **User Sets** page, accept the default setting, **All Users**, and click **Next**.

8. Click **Finish** on the **Completing the Access Rule Wizard** page.

9. Right-click the **All Open from Local Host to Internal** Access Rule, and click the **Configure RPC Protocol** command.

10. In the **Configure RPC protocol policy** dialog box, remove the checkmark from the **Enforce strict RPC compliance** checkbox. Click **Apply**, and then click **OK**.

11. In the **Microsoft Internet Security and Acceleration Server 2006** management console, expand the **Configuration** node, and click on the **Add-ins** node. Right-click on the **RPC Filter** entry in the Details pane, and click **Disable**.

12. In the **ISA Server Warning** dialog box, select **Save the changes and restart the services**. Click **OK**.

13. Click **Apply** to save the changes and update the firewall policy.

14. Click **OK** in the **Saving Configuration Changes** dialog box.

15. Click **Start** and the **Run** command. Enter **mmc** in the **Open** text box, and click **OK**.

16. In **Console1**, click the **File** menu and the **Add/Remove Snap-in** command.

17. In the **Add/Remove Snap-in** dialog box, click **Add**.

18. In the **Add Standalone Snap-in** dialog box, select the **Certificates** entry from the **Available Standalone Snap-ins** list. Click **Add**.

19. On the **Certificates snap-in** page, select **Computer account**.

20. On the **Select Computer** page, select **Local computer**.

21. Click **Close** in the **Add Standalone Snap-in** dialog box.

22. Click **OK** in the **Add/Remove Snap-in** dialog box.

23. In the left pane of the console, expand **Certificates (Local Computer)** and click on **Personal**. Right-click on the **Personal** node. Point to **All Tasks**, and click **Request New Certificate**.

24. Click **Next** on the **Welcome to the Certificate Request Wizard** page.

25. On the **Certificate Types** page, select the **Computer** entry in the **Certificate types** lists, and click **Next**.

26. On the **Certificate Friendly Name and Description** page, enter a name in the **Friendly name** text box. In this example, enter **Firewall Computer Certificate**. Click **Next**.

27. Click **Finish** on the **Completing the Certificate Request Wizard** page.

28. Click **OK** in the dialog box informing you that the certificate request was successful.

29. Return to the **Microsoft Internet Security and Acceleration Server 2006** management console, and expand the computer name in the left pane. Click on the **Firewall Policy** node. Right-click on the **All Open from Local Host to Internal** Access Rule, and click **Disable**.

30. In the **Microsoft Internet Security and Acceleration Server 2006** management console, expand the **Configuration** node, and click on the **Add-ins** node. Right-click on the **RPC Filter** entry in the Details pane, and click **Enable**.

31. Click **Apply** to save the changes and update the firewall policy

32. In the **ISA Server Warning** dialog box, select **Save the changes and restart the services**. Click **OK**.

33. Click **OK** in the **Saving Configuration Changes** dialog box.

Note that you will not need to manually copy the enterprise CA certificate into the ISA firewall's **Trusted Root Certification Authorities** certificate store because CA certificate is automatically installed on domain members. If the firewall were not a member of the domain where an enterprise CA is installed, then you would need to manually place the CA certificate into the **Trusted Root Certification Authorities** certificate store.

The next step is to issue a computer certificate to the VPN client computer. In this example, the VPN client machine is not a member of the domain. You need to request a "computer" certificate using the enterprise CA's Web enrollment site and manually place the enterprise CA certificate into the client's **Trusted Root Certification Authorities** machine certificate store. The easiest way to accomplish this is to have the VPN client machine request the certificate when connected via a PPTP link.

Perform the following steps to request and install the CA certificate:

1. Establish a PPTP VPN connection to the ISA firewall.

2. Open **Internet Explorer**. In the **Address** bar, enter **http://10.0.0.2/certsrv** (where 10.0.0.2 is the IP address of the CA on the Internal Network), and click **OK**.

3. In the **Enter Network Password** dialog box, enter **Administrator** in the **User Name** text box and enter the Administrator's password in the **Password** text box. Click **OK**.

4. Click **Request a Certificate** on the **Welcome** page.

5. On the **Request a Certificate** page, click **advanced certificate request**.

6. On the **Advanced Certificate Request** page, click **Create and submit a request to this CA**.

7. On the **Advanced Certificate Request** page, select the **Administrator** certificate from the **Certificate Template** list. Place a checkmark in the **Store certificate in the local computer certificate store** checkbox. Click **Submit**.

8. Click **Yes** in the **Potential Scripting Violation** dialog box.

9. On the **Certificate Issued** page, click **Install this certificate**.

10. Click **Yes** on the **Potential Scripting Violation** page.

11. Close the browser after viewing the **Certificate Installed** page.

12. Click **Start,** and then click **Run**. Enter **mmc** in the **Open** text box, and click **OK**.

13. In **Console1**, click the **File** menu, and click the **Add/Remove Snap-in** command.

14. Click **Add** in the **Add/Remove Snap-in** dialog box.

15. In the **Add Standalone Snap-in** dialog box, select the **Certificates** entry from the **Available Standalone Snap-ins** list. Click **Add**.

16. Select **Computer account** on the **Certificates snap-in** page.

17. Select **Local computer** on the **Select Computer** page.

18. Click **Close** in the **Add Standalone Snap-in** dialog box.

19. Click **OK** in the **Add/Remove Snap-in** dialog box.

20. In the left pane of the console, expand **Certificates (Local Computer) Personal**. Click on **\Personal\Certificates**. Double-click on **Administrator** certificate in the right pane of the console.

21. In the **Certificate** dialog box, click **Certification Path**. At the top of the certificate hierarchy seen in the **Certification path** frame is the root CA certificate. Click the **EXCHANGE2003BE** certificate at the top of the list. Click **View Certificate**.

22. In the CA certificate's **Certificate** dialog box, click the **Details** tab. Click **Copy to File**.

23. Click **Next** on the **Welcome to the Certificate Export Wizard** page.

24. On the **Export File Format** page, select **Cryptographic Message Syntax Standard – PKCS #7 Certificates (.P7B)**, and click **Next**.

25. On the **File to Export** page, enter **c:\cacert** in the **File name** text box. Click **Next**.

26. Click **Finish** on the **Completing the Certificate Export Wizard** page.

27. Click **OK** in the **Certificate Export Wizard** dialog box.

28. Click **OK** in the **Certificate** dialog box. Click **OK** again in the **Certificate** dialog box.

29. In the left pane of the console, expand the **Trusted Root Certification Authorities** node, and click **Certificates**. Right-click **\Trusted Root Certification Authorities\Certificates**. Point to **All Tasks**, and click **Import**.

30. Click **Next** on the **Welcome to the Certificate Import Wizard** page.

31. On the **File to Import** page. Use the **Browse** button to locate the CA certificate you saved to the local hard disk, and click **Next**.

32. On the **Certificate Store** page, accept the default settings, and click **Next**.

33. On the **Completing the Certificate Import Wizard** page, click **Finish**.

34. In the **Certificate Import Wizard** dialog box informing you that the import was successful, click **OK**.

35. Disconnect from the VPN server. Right-click on the connection icon in the system tray, and click **Disconnect**.

Test the L2TP/IPSec VPN Connection

Now that both the ISA firewall and the VPN client machines have machine certificates, you can test a secure L2TP/IPSec remote-access client VPN connection to the firewall. The first step is to restart the Routing and Remote Access Service so that it registers the new certificate.

Perform the following steps to enable L2TP/IPSec support:

1. In the **Microsoft Internet Security and Acceleration Server 2006** management console, expand the server name, and click **Virtual Private Networking (VPN)**.

2. Click **Configure VPN Client Access** on the **Tasks** tab in the Task panel. Click the **Protocols** tab. On the **Protocols** tab, put a checkmark in the **Enable L2TP/IPSec** check box.

3. Click **Apply**, and then you will be prompted to enable the **System Policy** rule "**Allow all HTTP traffic from ISA server to all networks (for CRL downloads)**" (Figure 20.21). Click **Yes**. The click **OK**.

Figure 20.21 Enable the System Policy

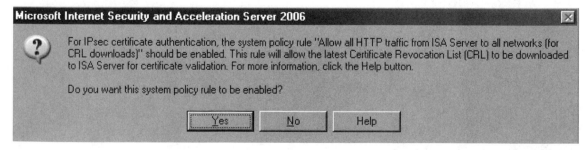

4. Click **Apply** to save the changes and update the firewall policy.

5. Click **OK** in the **Saving Configuration Changes** dialog box.

6. Restart the ISA firewall machine.

The next step is to start the VPN client connection:

1. From the VPN client computer, open the VPN client connectoid. Click **Properties**. In the **VPN Properties** dialog box, click **Networking**. On the **Networking** tab, change the **Type of VPN** to **L2TP/IPSec VPN**. Click **OK**.

2. Initiate the VPN connection to the ISA firewall.

3. Click **OK** in the **Connection Complete** dialog box informing you that the connection is established.

4. Double-click on the connection icon in the system tray.

5. In the **ISA VPN Status** dialog box (Figure 20.22), click the **Details** tab. You will see an entry for **IPSEC Encryption**, indicating that the L2TP/IPSec connection was successful.

Figure 20.22 L2TP/IPSec Connection Details

6. Click **Close** in the **ISA VPN Status** dialog box.

Monitor VPN Clients

The ISA firewall allows you to monitor the VPN client connections. Perform the following steps to see how you can view connections from VPN clients:

1. In the **Microsoft Internet Security and Acceleration Server 2006** management console, expand the server name, and click the **Virtual Private Networks (VPN)** node. Click the **Tasks** tab in the Task pane, and click **Monitor VPN Clients** (Figure 20.23). Note that this option will change the nature of the Sessions filter. You might want to back up your current sessions filter so that you can get back to it after the VPN filter is created.

Figure 20.23 The Monitor VPN Clients Link

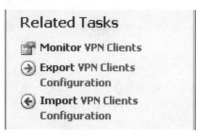

2. You are moved to the **Sessions** tab in the **Monitoring** node. Here you can see that the sessions have been filtered to show only the **VPN Client** connections.

3. Click on the **Dashboard** tab. Here you can see in the **Sessions** pane the **VPN Remote Client** connections (Figure 20.24).

Figure 20.24 The ISA Firewall Dashboard (New)

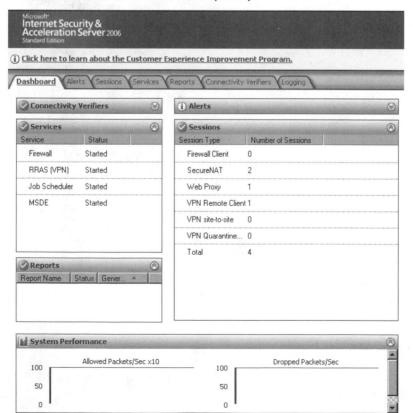

4. You can also use the real-time logging feature to see VPN client connections. Click on the **Logging** tab, and then click the **Tasks** tab in the Task pane. Click **Start Query**. You can use the filter capabilities to focus on specific VPN clients or only the VPN Clients network. Figure 20.25 shows the log file entries.

Figure 20.25 Log File Entries for the VPN Client Connection

9/7/2007 11:06:31 AM	255.255.255.255	138		NetBios Datagram	Denied Connection	Default rule	10.0.0.108		VPN Clients	Local Host
9/7/2007 11:06:31 AM	10.0.0.2	137		NetBios Name Ser...	Initiated Connection	VPN Client to Internal	10.0.0.108		VPN Clients	Internal
9/7/2007 11:06:31 AM	10.0.0.2	53		DNS	Closed Connection	VPN Client to Internal	10.0.0.108	Administrator	VPN Clients	Internal
9/7/2007 11:06:31 AM	10.0.0.2	0		Ping	Initiated Connection	VPN Client to Internal	10.0.0.108	Administrator	VPN Clients	Internal

As said before the new logging features brought by the ISA 2004 SP3 are not available on ISA 2006 Firewall.

Using a Pre-shared Key for VPN Client Remote Access Connections

As mentioned earlier in this chapter, you can use pre-shared keys for IPSec authentication if you don't have a PKI setup. The ISA firewall can be configured to support both pre-shared keys and certificates for VPN remote access client connections. The VPN client must support pre-shared keys for IPSec authentication. You can download the updated Windows L2TP/IPSec VPN client at http://download.microsoft.com/download/win98/Install/1.0/W9XNT4Me/EN-US/msl2tp.exe. This VPN client, a free download, allows Windows 9X, Windows Millennium and Windows 2000 client operating systems to use L2TP/IPSec with pre-shared keys.

The ISA firewall must be configured to support pre-shared keys. Perform the following steps to configure the ISA firewall to support pre-shared keys for IPSec authentication:

1. In the Microsoft Internet Security and Acceleration Server **2006** management console, expand the server name, and click the Virtual Private Networking (VPN) node.

2. Click the Select Authentication Methods link on the Tasks tab in the Task pane.

3. In the Virtual Private Networks (VPN) Properties dialog box, put a checkmark in the Allow **custom IPSec** policy for L2TP connection checkbox. Enter a pre-shared key in the Pre-shared key text box. Make sure that the key is complex and contains letters, numbers, and symbols (see Figure 20.26). Make the key at least 17 characters in length.

Figure 20.26 The Authentication Tab

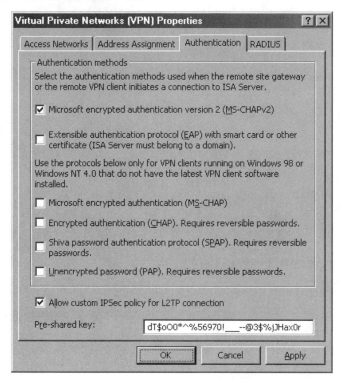

4. Click **Apply**, and then click **OK** in the **ISA** 2006 dialog box informing you that the Routing and Remote Access Service must be restarted. Click **OK** in the **Virtual Private Networking (VPN) Properties** dialog box.

5. Click **Apply** to save the changes and update the firewall policy.

6. Click **OK** in the **Saving Configuration Changes** dialog box.

You need to configure the VPN client to support a pre-shared key. The procedures will vary with the client you're using. The following describes how to configure the Windows XP VPN client to use a pre-shared key:

1. Open the VPN connectoid that you use to connect to the ISA firewall and click the **Properties** button.

2. In the connectoid's **Properties** dialog box, click the **Security** tab.

3. On the **Security** tab, click the **IPSec Settings** button.

4. In the **IPSec Settings** dialog box, put a checkmark in the **Use a pre-shared key for authentication** checkbox, and then enter the key in the **Key** text box as shown in Figure 20.27. Click **OK**.

Figure 20.27 Enter a pre-shared key on the L2TP/IPSec client

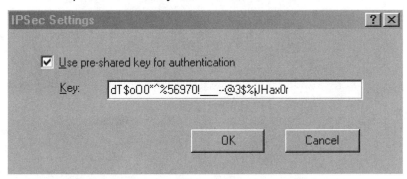

5. Click **OK** in the connectoid's **Properties** dialog box.

6. Connect to the ISA firewall. You can see that the pre-shared key is used for the IPSec connection by viewing the connection's characteristics in the **IPSec Security Monitor** MMC snap-in (Figure 20.28).

Figure 20.28 Viewing IPSec Information in the IPSec MMC

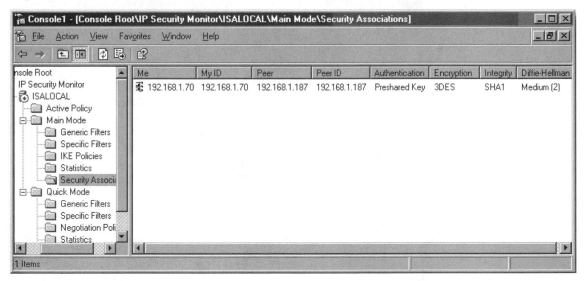

Creating a PPTP Site-to-Site VPN

Site-to-site VPNs allow you to connect entire networks to one another. This can lead to significant cost savings for organizations that are using dedicated frame relay links to connect branch offices to the main office, or branch offices to one another. The ISA firewall supports site-to-site VPN networking using the following VPN protocols:

- PPTP (Point-to-Point Tunneling Protocol)

- L2TP/IPSec (Layer Two Tunneling Protocol over IPSec)

- IPSec Tunnel Mode

The most secure VPN protocol for site-to-site VPNs is the L2TP/IPSec VPN protocol. L2TP/IPSec allows you to require both machine and user authentication. If you connect two ISA 2004/2006 Firewalls you should use LT2P/IPSec. IPSec tunnel mode should only be used when you need to connect to down-level VPN gateways. The major problem with IPSec tunnel mode *might be* that most down-level VPN gateway vendors require you to use a pre-shared key instead of certificate authentication, and there are a number of exploits that can take advantage of this situation (In the case of ISA 2004/2006 you must use a very long, complex and unguessable pre-shared key and you will stay out of trouble, ISA is using only IKE Main Mode and not IKE Aggressive Mode).

The use of PPTP should be avoided (it is the weakest VPN protocol available on ISA 2006).

Creating a site-to-site VPN used to be a complex process in ISA 2004 days, because of the number of steps involved. However, with the ISA 2006 new site-to-site wizard, you'll find that setting up a site-to-site VPN is a lot easier than you think. In this section we'll begin with creating a site-to-site VPN using the PPTP VPN protocol. After we establish the PPTP link, we'll use the link to connect to the Web enrollment site on the enterprise CA at the main office network and install a machine certificate on the branch office ISA firewall.

In the following exercise, the main office ISA firewall is named **ISALOCAL**, and the branch office ISA firewall is named **REMOTEISA**. We will be used the lab network setup described in Chapter 19, so if you don't recall the details of the lab setup, you should take a look at it now. Refreshing your knowledge of the lab setup will help you understand the site-to-site VPN procedures we'll be carrying out.

You'll need to perform the following steps to get the PPTP site-to-site VPN working (note that with the new ISA 2006 ISA Firewall, most of them are automatically done using the improved site-to-site VPN wizard):

- **Create the Remote Network at the Main Office** A Remote Site Network is what the ISA firewall uses for site-to-site VPN connections. Whenever you connect the ISA firewall to another network using a site-to-site VPN, you must first create the Remote Site Network. The Remote Site Network is then used in Access Rules to control access to and from that Network. The Remote Site Network we create at the main office will represent the IP addresses used at the branch office network.

- **Create the Network Rule at the Main Office** A Network Rule controls the route relationship between Networks. We will configure the site-to-site Network so that there is a Route relationship between the main office and the branch office. We prefer to use Route relationships because not all protocols work with NAT.

- **Create the Access Rules at the Main Office** The Access Rules at the main office will allow all traffic from the main office to reach the branch office and all the traffic from the branch office to reach the main office. On your production network, you will likely want to lock down your rules a bit so that branch office users can only access the information they require at the main office. For example, if branch office users only need to access the

OWA sites at the main office, then create Access Rules that only allow users access to the HTTPS protocol to the OWA server.

- **Create the VPN Gateway Dial-in Account at the Main Office** We must create a user account that the branch office ISA firewall can use to authenticate with the main office ISA firewall. This account is created on the main office ISA firewall. When the branch office ISA firewall calls the main office ISA firewall, the branch office will use this user name and password to authenticate with the main office. The branch office ISA firewall's demand-dial interface is configured to use this account.

- **Create the Remote Network at the Branch Office** Once the site-to-site VPN configuration is done at the main office, we move our attention to the branch office's ISA firewall. At the branch office ISA firewall, we begin by creating the Remote Site Network that represents the IP addresses in use at the main office. We'll use this Network Object to control traffic moving to and from the main office from the Branch office.

- **Create the Network Rule at the Branch Office** As we did at the main office, we need to create a Network Rule controlling the route relationship for communications between the branch office network and the main office network. We'll configure the Network Rule so that there is a Route relationship between the branch office and the main office.

- **Create the Access Rules at the Branch Office** We will create two Access Rules on the branch office ISA firewall. One allows all traffic to the branch office to reach the main office, and the second rule allows all traffic from the main office to reach the branch office. In a production environment you might wish to limit what traffic can leave the branch office to the main office. Note that you can set these access controls at either or both the branch office and the main office ISA firewall. We prefer to implement the access controls at both sites, but the access controls at the main office are more important because you often may not have change controls tightly regulated at the branch offices.

- **Create the VPN Gateway Dial-in Account at the Branch Office** We need to create a user account on the branch office ISA firewall that the main office ISA firewall can use to authenticate when it calls the branch office ISA firewall. The demand-dial interface on the main office ISA firewall uses this account to authenticate with the branch office ISA firewall.

- **Activate the Site-to-Site Links** We'll activate the site-to-site VPN connection by initiating a connection from a host on the branch office to a host on the main office network.

Create the Remote Site Network at the Main Office

We begin by configuring the ISA firewall at the main office. The first step is to configure the Remote Site Network in the **Microsoft Internet Security and Acceleration Server 2006** management console.

Perform the following steps to create the Remote Site Network at the main office ISA firewall:

1. Open the Microsoft Internet Security and Acceleration Server **2006** management console and expand the server name. Click Virtual Private Networks (VPN).

2. Click on the Remote Sites tab in the Details pane. Click on the Tasks tab in the Task pane. Click **Create VPN** Site**-to-Site Connection**.

3. On the Welcome to the **Create VPN Site-to-Site Connection** Wizard page, enter a name for the remote network in the *Site-to-Site network* name text box. In this example, we will name the remote network Branch. This name is very important because this will be the name of the demand-dial interface created on the ISA firewall at the main office, and it will be the name of the user account that the branch office ISA firewall will use to connect to the main office ISA firewall. Click Next.

On the VPN Protocol page, you have the choice of using IP Security protocol (IPSec tunnel mode, Layer Two Tunneling Protocol (L2TP) over IPSec and Point-to-Point Tunneling Protocol. If you have certificates installed on the main and branch office firewalls, or if you plan to install them in the future, choose the L2TP/IPSec option (you can use the pre-shared key until you get the certificates installed). Do *not* use the IPSec option unless you are connecting to a third-party VPN gateway (because of the low security conferred by IPSec tunnel mode site-to-site links which typically depend on pre-shared keys). In this example, we will configure a site-to-site VPN using PPTP, so select the **Point-to-Point Tunneling Protocol (PPTP)** (as shown in Figure 20.29). Click **Next**.

Figure 20.29 Selecting the VPN Protocol

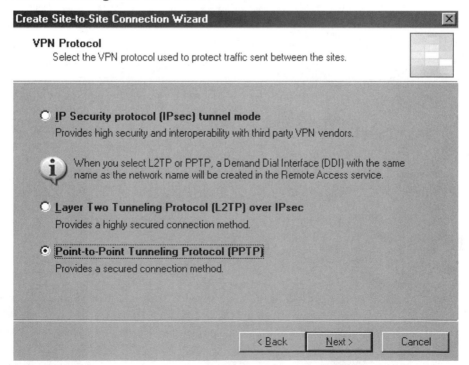

4.   A user warning will appear informing you that you must specify a user account at the remote site. The user name must match the name of this site-to-site connection (Branch), the same name as the demand dial interface on this machine. See Figure 20.30. This user account will be created on the main office, with the Dial-in permissions. Click **OK**.

Figure 20.30 PPTP User Warning

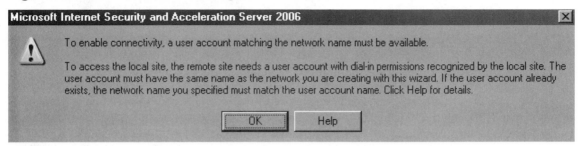

5.   With the new ISA 2006 wizard if you did not set the IP Address Assignment method you will be prompted to do it now within the **Local Network VPN Settings** page. If you have a DHCP server select the **Dynamic Host Configuration protocol** (recommended). See Figure 31. This will automatically set the Internal Network as the network from where it will be obtain DHCP, DNS and WINS services.

Figure 20.31 Set Address Assignment

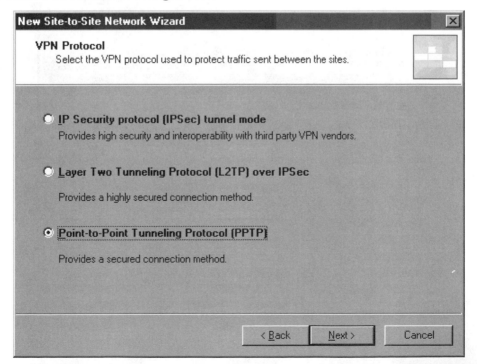

6. On the **Remote Site Gateway** page, enter the IP address on the external interface of the remote ISA firewall. In this example, the IP address is **192.168.1.71**, so we will enter this value into the text box.

Note that you can also use a fully-qualified domain name in this text box. This is helpful if the branch office uses a dynamic address on its external interface and you use a DDNS service like TZO (www.tzo.com). We have been using TZO for years and highly recommend their service. Click **Next**.

7. On the **Remote Authentication** page, put a checkmark in the **Allow Local site to initiate connections to remote site using this user account** checkbox. Enter the name of the account that you will create on the remote ISA firewall to allow the main office ISA firewall to authenticate to the branch office ISA firewall.

In this example, the user account will be named **Main** (the user account much match the name of the demand-dial interface created on the remote site; we haven't created that demand-dial interface yet, but we will when we configure the branch office ISA firewall). The **Domain** name is the computer name of the branch office ISA firewall, which in this example is **REMOTEISA** (if the remote ISA firewall were a domain controller, you would use the domain name instead of the computer name, since there are no local accounts stored on a domain controller). Enter a password for the account and confirm the password as shown in Figure 20.32. Make sure that you write down the password so you will remember it when you create the account later on the branch office ISA firewall. Click **Next**.

Figure 20.32 Setting Dial-in Credentials

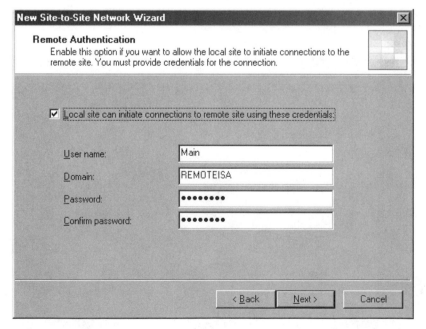

8. Read the information on the **Local Authentication** page, and click **Next**.

The information on this page reminds you that you must create a user account on this ISA firewall that the branch office ISA firewall can use to authenticate when it initiates a site-to-site VPN connection. If you forget to create the user account, the authenticate attempt will fail and the site-to-site VPN link will not establish.

9. Click **Add** on the **Network Addresses** page. In the **IP Address Range Properties** dialog box, enter **10.0.1.0** in the **Starting address** text box. Enter **10.0.1.255** in the **Ending address** text box. Click **OK**.

This is a critical step in your site-to-site VPN configuration. You should include all addresses on the Remote Site Network. While you might create Access Rules that allow access only to a subset of addresses on that network, you should still include all addresses in use on that network. Also, keep in mind any network IDs that are reachable from the branch office ISA firewall. For example, there may be multiple networks reachable from the LAN interface (any of the internal or DMZ interfaces of the branch office ISA firewall). Include all those addresses in this dialog box. See Figure 20.33.

Figure 20.33 Configuring the IP Address Range for the Remote Site Network

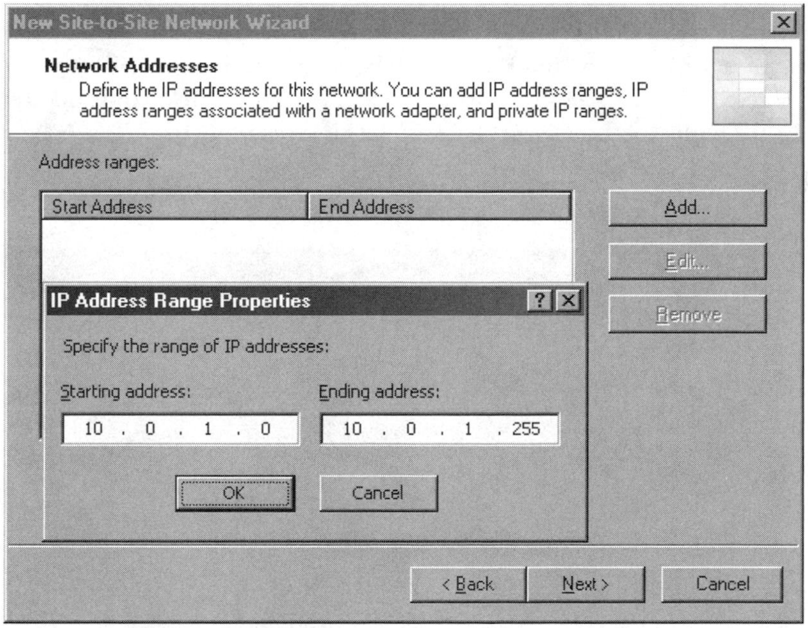

10. Click **Next** on the **Network Addresses** page.
11. With the new ISA 2006 wizard you can define the required network rule in the **Site-to-Site Network Rule** page. A route relationship will be defined between Branch and Internal. See Figure 34. Accept and click **Next**.

Figure 20.34 Site-to-site Wizard: Define the Network Rule

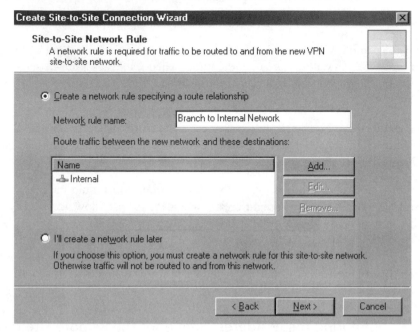

12. With the new ISA 2006 wizard you can define the required access rule for allowing communications between the Branch Network and the Internal Network in the **Site-to-Site Network Access Rule** page. See Figure 35. Select **All outbound traffic** in the **Apply the rule to these protocols** list. Click **Next**.

Figure 20.35 Site-to-site Wizard: Define the Access Rule

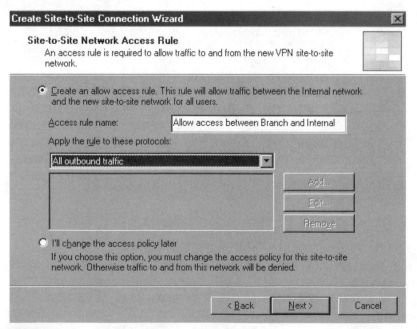

13. Click **Finish** on the **Completing the New VPN Site-to-Site Network Wizard** page.

14. A new window, **The Remaining VPN Site-to-Site Tasks** dialog box will appear. It tells us that we need to define a local account name Branch that will be used by the remote ISA Firewall to authenticate against the local ISA Firewall (in case the remote ISA is acting as the Calling Gateway and local ISA as the Answering Gateway). See Figure 36. Click **OK**.

Figure 20.36 The user account to be defined

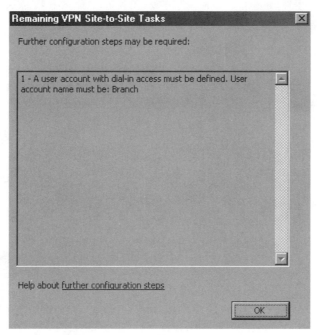

15. Click **Apply** to save the changes. As you have seen, with ISA 2006 you completed many tasks on the fly.

16. You can check the site-to-site summary by right-clicking on the new Branch remote site and click Summary. The site-to-site summary is shown in Figure 20.37.

Figure 20.37 The Site-to-Site Summary

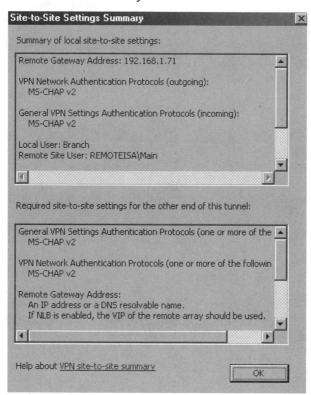

If you scroll **the Summary of local site-to-site settings** you will see a **Routable Local IP Addresses** field. This one comprises IP addresses from 10.0.0.0 to 10.0.0.255(the main office ISA Internal Network). It tells you that you have a network rule in place between the remote site and the Internal Network. Also you can check the incoming and outgoing authentication protocols, the local and remote users. So the small summary can be very useful.

One thing you must do at the main office ISA is to disable automatic DNS registration on the demand-dial interfaces for the ISA 2006 Firewall using the RRAS console. The changing of the DDNS registration for the demand-dial interface is not overwritten by the ISA Firewall VPN configuration. When the demand-dial interface registers with the DDNS, it can causes problems.

Perform the following steps at the main office ISA Firewall:

1. Click **Start**, point to **Administrative Tools** and click **Routing and Remote Access**.

2. In the **Routing and Remote Access** console, expand the server name.

3. Click on the **Network Interfaces** node in the left pane of the console. Right click on the **Branch** entry in the right pane of the console and click **Properties**.

4. In the **Branch Properties** dialog box, click the **Networking** tab and then click the **Properties** button.

5. On the **Internet Protocol (TCP/IP) Properties** dialog box, click the **Advanced** button.

6. In the **Advanced TCP/IP Settings** dialog box, click the **DNS** tab. On the **DNS** tab, remove the checkmark from the **Register this connection's addresses in DNS** checkbox. Click **OK**. See Figure 20.38.

7. Click **OK** in the **Internet Protocol (TCP/IP) Properties** dialog box. Click **OK** in the **Branch Properties** dialog box.

8. Close the **Routing and Remote Access** console.

Figure 20.38 Register this connection's addresses in DNS checkbox

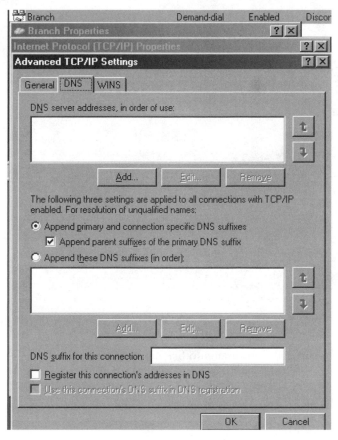

The Network Rule at the Main Office

The ISA firewall must know how to route packets to the branch office network. There are two options: **Route** and **NAT**. A Route relationship routes packets to the branch office and preserves the source IP address of the clients making a connection over the site-to-site link. A NAT relationship replaces the source IP address of the client making the connection. In general, the route relationship provides a higher level of protocol support, but the NAT relationship provides a higher level of security because it hides the original source IP address of the host on the NATed side.

One important reason for why you might want to use a Route relationship is if you plan to have domain members on the Remote Site Network. Kerberos authentication embeds the source IP address in the payload and has no NAT editor or application filter to make this work.

In Figure 20.39 you can see the network rule, with a route relationship, created by the site-to-site wizard.

Figure 20.39 The Network Relationship Page

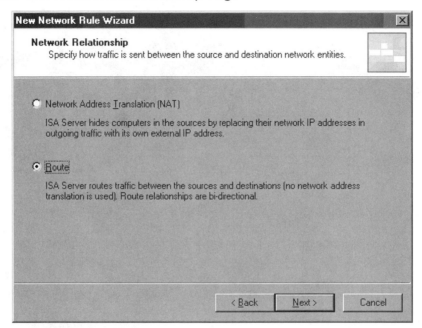

The Access Rules at the Main Office

We want hosts on both the main and branch office networks to have full access to all resources on each network. We must create Access Rules allowing traffic from the main office to the branch office and from the branch office to the main office.

Figure 20.40 shows the resulting firewall policy after we have run the site-to-site wizard were we created the access rule allowing communications between the branch office and the main office.

Figure 20.40 The Resulting Firewall Policy

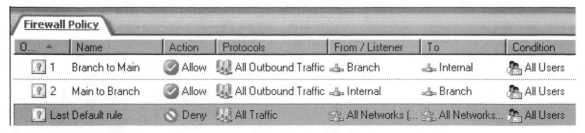

O...	Name	Action	Protocols	From / Listener	To	Condition
1	Branch to Main	Allow	All Outbound Traffic	Branch	Internal	All Users
2	Main to Branch	Allow	All Outbound Traffic	Internal	Branch	All Users
	Last Default rule	Deny	All Traffic	All Networks [...	All Networks...	All Users

Create the VPN Gateway Dial-in Account at the Main Office

You must create a user account on the main office firewall that the branch office firewall can use to authenticate the site-to-site VPN link. This user account *must have the same name* as the demand-dial interface on the main office computer. You will later configure the branch office ISA 2006 to use this account when it dials the VPN site-to-site link.

User accounts and demand-dial interface naming conventions are a common source of confusion for ISA firewall administrators. The key here is that the calling VPN gateway must present credentials with a user name *that is the same as the name of the demand-dial interface answering the call*. In Figure 20.31, you can see how this works when the main office calls the branch office and when the branch office calls the main office.

The name of the demand dial interface at the main office is **Branch**. When the branch office calls the main office, the user account the branch office uses to authenticate with the main office ISA firewall is **Branch**. Because the name of the user account is the same as the name of the demand-dial interface, the main office ISA firewall knows that it's a remote VPN gateway making the call, and the ISA firewall does *not* treat this as a remote access VPN client connection.

When the main office calls the branch office, it presents the user credentials of a user named **Main**, which is the same name as the demand-dial interface on the branch office ISA firewall. Because the name of the user account presented during authentication is the same as the name of the demand-dial interface, the branch office ISA firewall knows that this is a VPN gateway connection (VPN router) and not a remote access client VPN connection. Figure 20.41 shows the demand dial interface configuration.

Figure 20.41 Demand Dial Interface Configuration on Local and Remote Sites

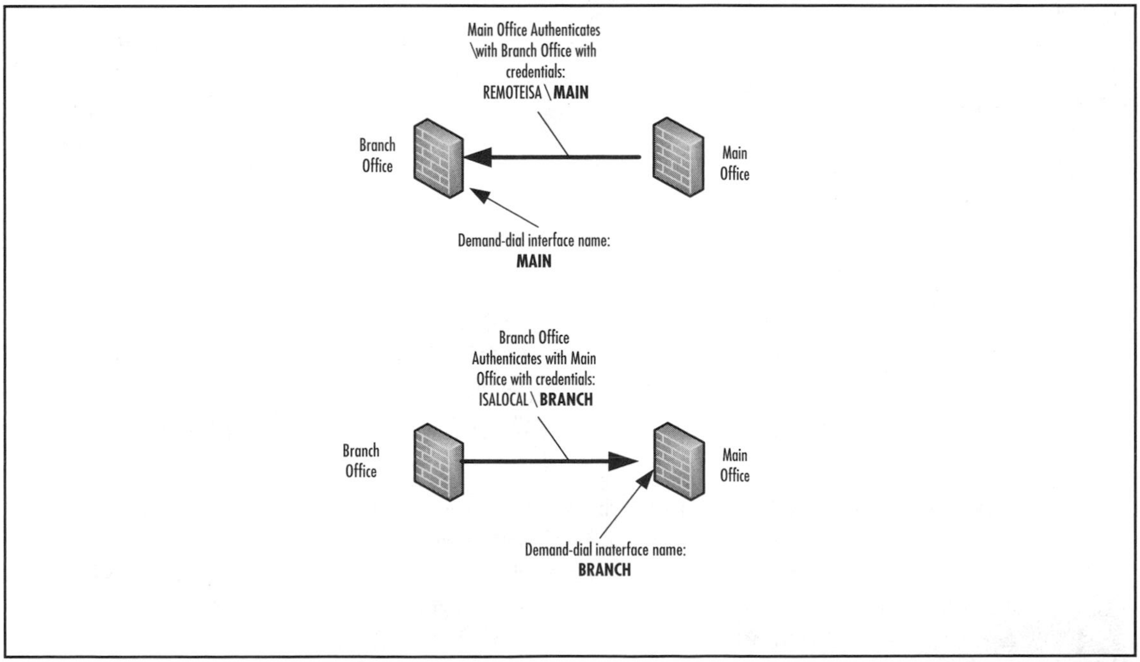

Perform the following steps to create the account the remote ISA 2006 firewall will use to connect to the main office VPN gateway:

1. Right-click **My Computer** on the desktop, and click **Manage**.

2. In the **Computer Management** console, expand the **Local Users and Groups** node. Right-click the **Users** node, and click **New User**.

3. In the **New User** dialog box, enter the name of the main office demand-dial interface. In our current example, the demand-dial interface is named **Branch**. Enter **Branch** into the text box. Enter a **Password** and confirm the **Password**. Write down this password because you'll need to use it when you configure the branch office ISA firewall. Remove the checkmark from the **User must change password at next logon** checkbox. Place checkmarks in the **User cannot change password** and **Password never expires** checkboxes. Click **Create**.

4. Click **Close** in the **New User** dialog box.

5. Double-click the **Branch** user in the right pane of the console.

6. In the **Branch Properties** dialog box, click the **Dial-in** tab. Select **Allow access**.

7. Click **Apply**, and then click **OK**.

8. Restart the ISA firewall computer.

Create the Remote Site Network at the Branch Office

We can now turn our attention to the branch office ISA firewall. We will repeat the same steps we performed on the main office ISA firewall, but this time we begin by creating a Remote Site Network on the branch office firewall that represents the IP addresses used on the main office network.

Perform the following steps to create the Remote Site Network at the branch office:

1. Open the Microsoft Internet Security and Acceleration Server **2006** management console and expand the server name. Click the Virtual Private Networks (VPN) node.

2. Click Remote Sites in the Details pane. Click Tasks in the Task pane. Click **Create VPN Site-to-Site VPN Connection**.

3. On the Welcome to the **Create VPN Site-to-Site VPN Connection** Wizard page, enter a name for the remote network in the **Site-to-Site** Network name text box. In this example, we will name the remote network Main. Click Next.

4. On the VPN Protocol page, select Point-to-Point Tunneling Protocol (PPTP), and click Next. Click **OK** on the warning box.

5. Select the IP address assignment method on the Local Network VPN Settings page. If you have a DHCP server on the branch office you can specify "**Dynamic Host Configuration Protocol**". If not you must use static, say 10.0.1.252 to 10.0.1.255. Attention, you must exclude this IP addresses from the Internal Network range. Therefore define the Internal Network range as 10.0.1.0 to 10.10.0.251.

6. On the Remote Site Gateway page, enter the IP address on the external interface of the main office ISA firewall. In this example, the IP address is 192.168.1.70, so we will enter this value into the text box. Click Next.

7. On the Remote Authentication page, put a checkmark by **Allow** Local site **to** initiate connections to remote site using **this user account**. Enter the name of the account that you created on the main office ISA firewall to allow the branch office VPN gateway access.

In this example, the user account is named **Branch** (the user account much match the name of the demand-dial interface created at the main office). The Domain name is the name of the remote ISA 2006 firewall computer, which, in this example, is **ISALOCAL** (if the remote ISA firewall was a domain member and the user was a domain user, you would use the *domain name* instead of the computer name). Enter the password for the account and confirm the password as shown in Figure 20.42. Click **Next**.

Figure 20.42 Configure Dial-in Credentials

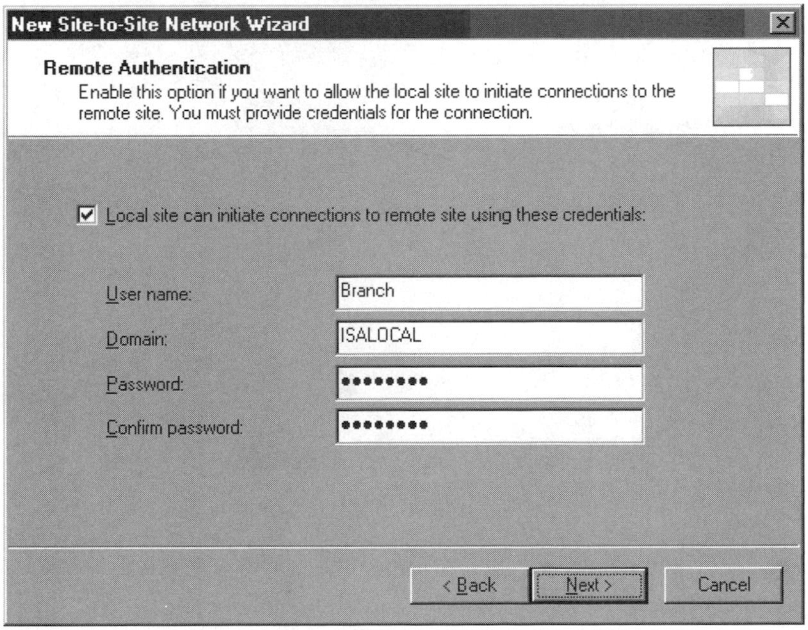

1. Click Add on the Network Addresses page. In the IP Address Range Properties dialog box, enter 10.0.0.0 in the Starting address text box. Enter 10.0.0.255 in the Ending address text box. Click OK.

2. Click Next on the Network Addresses page.

3. Create the Network Rule on the Site-to-Site Network Rule page between Internal and the remote site. Click Next.

4. Define the Access Rule on the Site-to-Site Network Access Rule between Main and Internal. Select All outbound traffic in the Apply the rule to this protocols list. Click Next.

5. Click Finish on the Completing the New VPN Site-to-Site Network Wizard page.

6. The new window, The Remaining VPN Site-to-Site Tasks dialog box will appear. It tells you that you need to define a local account name Main that will be used by the remote main office ISA Firewall to authenticate against the branch office ISA Firewall. Click OK.

7. Click Apply to save the changes.

8. Right-click on the new Main remote site and click **Summary** in order to quickly check the settings of the site-to-site connection. Figure 20.43 shows the **site-to-site summary**.

Figure 20.43 Site-to-Site Summary

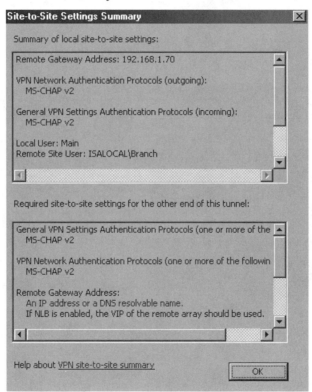

One thing you could do at the branch office ISA is to disable automatic DNS registration on the demand-dial interfaces for the ISA 2006 Firewall using the RRAS console. Just in case you later add the branch ISA 2006 Firewall to the domain.

The Network Rule at the Branch Office

The network rule was already created for you by the site-to-site wizard. Figure 20.44 shows the network rule.

Figure 20.44 The Network Rule

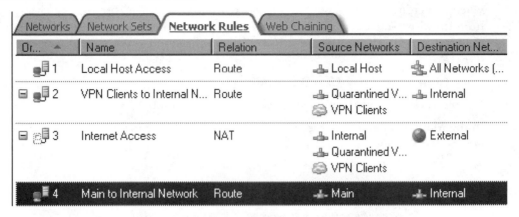

The Access Rules at the Branch Office

The access rule was already created for you by the site-to-site wizard. See Figure 20.45.

Figure 20.45 The Resulting Firewall Policy

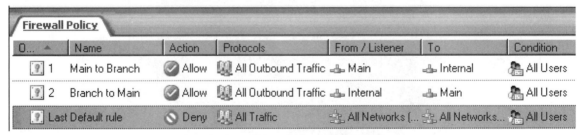

Create the VPN Gateway Dial-in Account at the Branch Office

We must create a user account the main office VPN gateway can use to authenticate when it initiates the VPN site-to-site connection to the branch office. The user account must have the same name as the demand-dial interface created on the branch office machine, which, in this example, is **Main**.

Perform the following steps to create the account the main ISA 2006 firewall will use to connect to the branch office VPN gateway:

1. Right-click **My Computer** on the desktop, and click **Manage**.

2. In the **Computer Management** console, expand the **Local Users and Groups** node. Right-click the **Users** node, and click **New User**.

3. In the **New User** dialog box, enter the name of the main office demand-dial interface. In our current example, the demand-dial interface is named **Main**. Enter **Main** into the

text box. Enter a **Password** and confirm the **Password**. This is the same password you used when you created the Remote Site Network at the Main office. Remove the checkmark from the **User must change password at next logon** checkbox. Place checkmarks in the **User cannot change password** and **Password never expires** checkboxes. Click **Create**.

4. Click **Close** in the **New User** dialog box.

5. Double-click the **Main** user in the right pane of the console.

6. In the **Main Properties** dialog box, click the **Dial-in** tab (Figure 20.46). Select **Allow access**. Click **Apply**, and then click **OK**.

Figure 20.46 The Dial-in Tab

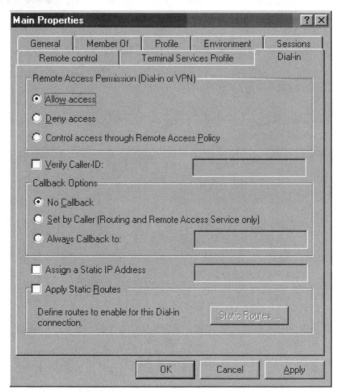

7. Restart the ISA firewall computer.

Activate the Site-to-Site Links

Now that both the main and branch office ISA firewalls are configured as VPN routers, you can test the site-to-site connection.

Perform the following steps to test the site-to-site link:

1. At the remote client computer behind the remote ISA 2006 firewall machine, click **Start**, and then click **Run**.

2. In the **Run** dialog box, enter **cmd** in the **Open** text box, and click **OK**.

3. In the command prompt window, enter **ping –t 10.0.0.2**, and press ENTER

4. You will see a few pings time out, and then the ping responses will be returned by the domain controller on the main office network.

5. Perform the same procedures at the domain controller at the main office network, but this time ping **10.0.1.2**.

TIP

If the site-to-site connection fails, check to make sure that you have defined valid IP address assignments to VPN clients and gateways. A common reason for failure of site-to-site VPN connections is that the ISA firewalls are not able to obtain an address from a DHCP server, and there are no addresses defined for a static address pool. When this happens, the ISA firewall assigns VPN clients and gateways IP addresses in the autonet range (169.254.0.0/16). When both gateways are assigned addresses in the autonet range, both machines' demand-dial interfaces are located on the same network ID and this causes the site-to-site link to fail.

Creating an L2TP/IPSec Site-to-Site VPN

We recommend that you use L2TP/IPSec as your VPN protocol for site-to-site VPN connections. L2TP/IPSec is more secure than PPTP and IPSec tunnel mode. However, to ensure that you have a secure site-to-site VPN connection using L2TP/IPSec, you must use machine certificates on all ISA firewall VPN gateways.

We can leverage the PPTP VPN site-to-site link we created in the previous section to allow the branch office ISA firewall access to the Web enrollment site of the enterprise CA located on the main office network.

We will perform the following procedures to enable the L2TP/IPSec site-to-site VPN link:

- **Enable the System Policy Rule on the Main office firewall to access the enterprise CA** We will enable a system policy rule that allows the ISA firewall to connect from the Local Host Network to all Networks. While, ostensibly, this rule is to allow for CRL checking, we can use it to allow the ISA firewall at the main office access to the Web enrollment site on the Internal network.

- **Request and install a Web site certificate for the Main office firewall** Once we connect to the Web enrollment site, we will request an Administrator certificate that we will install into the main office's local machine certificate store. We will also install the enterprise CA's certificate into the main office ISA firewall's Trusted Root Certification Authorities machine certificate store.

- **Configure the main office ISA firewall to use L2TP/IPSec for the site-to-site link** The Remote Site Network configuration that defines the branch office Network is set to use PPTP for the site-to-site link. We need to change this so that L2TP/IPSec is used instead of PPTP.

- **Enable the System Policy Rule on the Branch office firewall to access the enterprise CA** For the same reason we did so on the main office ISA firewall, we need to enable a System Policy rule that will allow the branch office's Local Host Network access to the Web enrollment site on the main office network.

- **Request and install a Web site certificate for the Branch office firewall** When the PPTP site-to-site link is established, the branch office ISA firewall will be able to connect to the Web enrollment site over that connection. We will install an Administrator certificate on the branch office firewall in its machine certificate store, and install the CA certificate for the main office enterprise CA in the branch office ISA firewall's Trusted Root Certification Authorities machine certificate store.

- **Configure the branch office ISA firewall to use L2TP/IPSec for the site-to-site link** The Remote Site Network representing the main office network must be configured to use L2TP/IPSec instead of PPTP for the site-to-site link.

- **Establish the IPSec Site-to-Site Connection** After we install the certificates and make the changes to the ISA firewall configurations, we'll trigger the site-to-site link and see the L2TP/IPSec connection in the ISA firewall's Monitoring node.

- **Configuring Pre-shared keys for Site-to-Site L2TP/IPSec VPN Links** This is an optional procedure. While we prefer that everyone use certificates for machine authentication, we realize that this is not always possible. We discuss the procedures you can use to support pre-shared key authentication for your L2TP/IPSec site-to-site VPN links.

Enable the System Policy Rule on the Main Office Firewall to Access the Enterprise CA

The ISA 2006 firewall is locked down by default and only a very limited set of protocols and sites are allowed outbound from the ISA firewall immediately after installation. As for any other communications moving through the ISA firewall, Access Rules are required to allow the firewall access to *any* network or network host. We will need to configure the ISA firewall at the main office with an Access Rule allowing it HTTP access to the Web enrollment site. We could create an Access Rule, or we could enable a System Policy rule. Creating an Access Rule allowing access from the Local Host Network to the enterprise CA using only the HTTP protocol would be more secure, but it's easier to enable the System Policy rule. In this example, we will enable a System Policy Rule that allows the firewall access to the Web enrollment site.

Perform the following steps to enable the System Policy rule on the Main Office firewall:

1. In the **Microsoft Internet Security and Acceleration Server 2006** management console, expand the server name, and click the **Firewall Policy** node.

2. Right-click **Firewall Policy**; point to **View**, and click **Show System Policy Rules**.

3. In the System Policy Rule list, double-click **Allow HTTP from ISA Server to all networks (for CRL downloads).** This is System Policy Rule #*18*.

4. In the **System Policy Editor** dialog box, check the **Enable** checkbox on the **General** tab as shown in Figure 20.47. Click **OK**.

Figure 20.47 Configuring System Policy

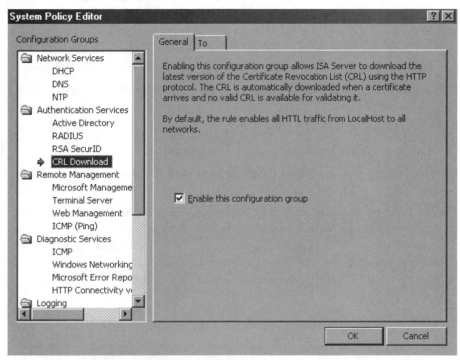

5. Click **Apply** to save the changes and update the firewall policy.

6. Click **OK** in the **Saving Configuration Changes** dialog box.

7. Click **Show/Hide System Policy Rules** (on the far right of the button bar in the MMC console) to hide System Policy.

Figure 20.48 and **Figure 20.49** The Show/Hide System Policy Rules Button

Request and Install a Certificate for the Main Office Firewall

The next step is to request a certificate from the enterprise CA's Web enrollment site. After obtaining the certificate, we will copy the CA certificate into the ISA firewall's **Trusted Root Certification Authorities** certificate store.

Perform the following steps on the main office ISA firewall to request and install the certificates:

1. Open **Internet Explorer**. In the **Address** bar, enter **http://10.0.0.2/certsrv** (where 10.0.0.2 is the IP address of the enterprise CA), and click **OK**.

2. In the **Enter Network Password** dialog box, enter **Administrator** in the **User Name** text box, and enter the **Administrator's** password in the **Password** text box. Click **OK**.

3. In the **Internet Explorer** security dialog box, click **Add**. In the **Trusted Sites** dialog box, click **Add** and **Close**.

4. Click **Request a Certificate** on the **Welcome** page.

5. On the **Request a Certificate** page, click **advanced certificate request**.

6. On the **Advanced Certificate Request** page, click **Create and submit a request to this CA**.

7. On the **Advanced Certificate Request** page, select the **Administrator** certificate from the **Certificate Template** list as shown in Figure 20.50. Remove the checkmark from the **Mark keys as exportable** checkbox. Place a checkmark in the **Store certificate in the local computer certificate store** checkbox as shown in Figure 20.51. It is recommended to use **Key Sizes** of 2048 bits. Click **Submit**.

Figure 20.50 The Advanced Certificate Request Page

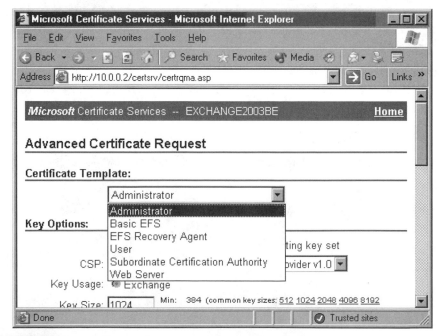

Figure 20.51 The Store Certificate in the Local Computer Certificate Store Option

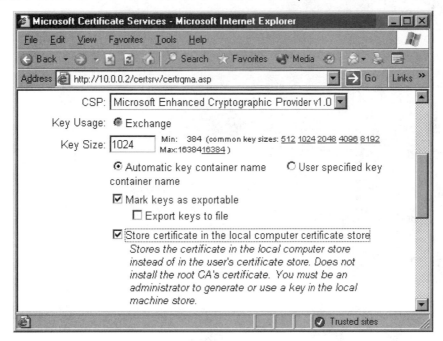

8.   Click Yes in the Potential Scripting Violation dialog box.

9.   On the Certificate Issued page, click Install this certificate.

10. Click Yes on the Potential Scripting Violation page.

11. Close the browser after viewing the Certificate Installed page.

12. Click Start, and then click Run. Enter mmc in the Open text box, and click OK.

13. In Console1, click the File menu, and then click Add/Remove Snap-in.

14. Click Add in the Add/Remove Snap-in dialog box.

15. Select the Certificates entry in the Available Standalone Snap-ins list in the Add Standalone Snap-in dialog box. Click Add.

16. Select Computer account on the Certificates snap-in page.

17. Select Local computer on the Select Computer page.

18. Click Close in the Add Standalone Snap-in dialog box.

19. Click OK in the Add/Remove Snap-in dialog box.

20. In the left pane of the console, expand Certificates (Local Computer), and then expand Personal. Click on \Personal\Certificates. Double-click on the Administrator certificate in the right pane of the console.

21. In the Certificate dialog box, click the Certification Path tab. The root CA certificate is at the top of the certificate hierarchy seen in the Certification path frame. Click the

EXCHANGE2003BE certificate (which is the CA that issued the Administrator certificate) at the top of the list. Click View Certificate (Figure 20.52).

Figure 20.52 The Certificate Path Tab

22. In the CA certificate's **Certificate** dialog box, click the **Details** tab. Click **Copy to File**.

23. Click **Next** in the **Welcome to the Certificate Export Wizard** page.

24. On the **Export File Format** page, select **Cryptographic Message Syntax Standard – PKCS #7 Certificates (.P7B)**, and click **Next**.

25. On the **File to Export** page, enter **c:\cacert** in the **File name** text box. Click **Next**.

26. Click **Finish** on the **Completing the Certificate Export Wizard** page.

27. Click **OK** in the **Certificate Export Wizard** dialog box.

28. Click **OK** in the **Certificate** dialog box. Click **OK** again in the **Certificate** dialog box.

29. In the left pane of the console, expand **Trusted Root Certification Authorities** and click the **Certificates** node. Right-click **Trusted Root Certification Authorities\Certificates**; point to **All Tasks**, and click **Import**.

30. Click **Next** on the **Welcome to the Certificate Import Wizard** page.

31. On the **File to Import** page, use **Browse** to locate the CA certificate you saved to the local hard disk, and click **Next**.

32. On the **Certificate Store** page, accept the default settings, and click **Next**.

33. Click **Finish** on the **Completing the Certificate Import Wizard** page.

34. Click **OK** in the **Certificate Import Wizard** dialog box informing you that the import was successful.

Configure the Main Office ISA Firewall to use L2TP/IPSec for the Site-to-Site Link

The Remote Site Network on the main office ISA firewall representing the branch office network is configured to use PPTP for the site-to-site connection. We need to change this to L2TP/IPSec. Perform the following steps to make the change:

1. In the **Microsoft Internet Security and Acceleration Server 2006** management console, expand the server name, and then click the **Virtual Private Networks (VPN)** node in the left pane of the console.

2. On the **Virtual Private Networks (VPN)** node, click the **Remote Sites** tab in the Details pane. Double-click the **Branch** Remote Site Network entry.

3. In the **Branch Properties** dialog box, **Protocol** tab, select the **L2TP/IPSec (provides a highly secure connection method)** option. Click **Apply** and then click **OK**.

4. Do *not* apply the new configuration to the Firewall Policy yet. This will break our PPTP site-to-site link, and we need this PPTP site-to-site link to stay up until we have installed a certificate on the branch office ISA firewall. After the branch office ISA firewall has been configured, and then you can apply the changes to the Firewall Policy at the main office.

5. Take a look at the **site-to-site summary** (Figure 20.53). It gives you information about the incoming and outgoing authentication methods (for both IKE and PPP), about the remote and local user, the remote IP address ranges and the routable local IP addresses (we have a network rule between Branch and Internal).

Figure 20.53 L2TP/IPSec site-to-site summary

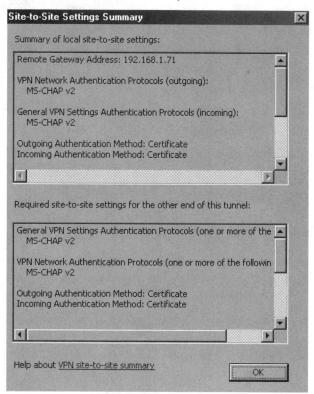

If this was the first site-to-site connection, because you do not want to use PPTP at all and you were using the new site-to-site wizard, then you would have the chance to specify the incoming L2TP/IPSec authentication method (in case you select as the outgoing authentication method the pre-shared key because you currently do not have certificates installed), either allowing or not the pre-shared key for incoming connections, within the site-to-site wizard (Figure 20.55). The same options, like in case of PPTP, specify address assignment, define the network rules and access rules are available for L2TP/IPSec VPN site-to-site connections. As you can see from Figure 20.54 the default outgoing method is certificate authentication.

Figure 20.54 The Outgoing L2TP/IPSec Authentication method

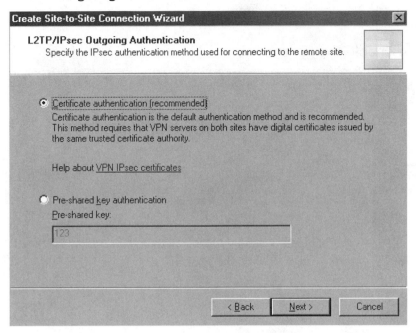

Figure 20.55 The Incoming L2TP/IPSec Authentication method

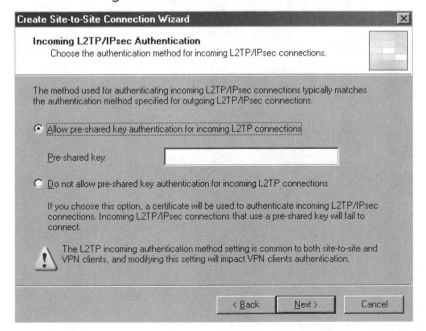

If you use certificates, ISA 2006 will also give you the option to enable System Policy #18 within the site-to-site wizard (Figure 20.56).

Figure 20.56 Enable the System Policy

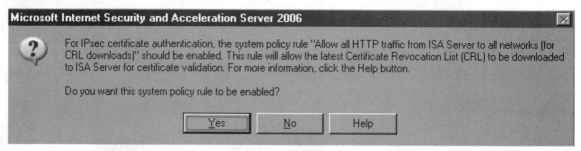

In case of certificate authentication ISA would inform you that you need to assign a proper certificate to ISA and to make available (publish) the CRL within the **Remaining VPN site-to-site Tasks** (Figure 20.57).

Figure 20.57 Remaining Tasks

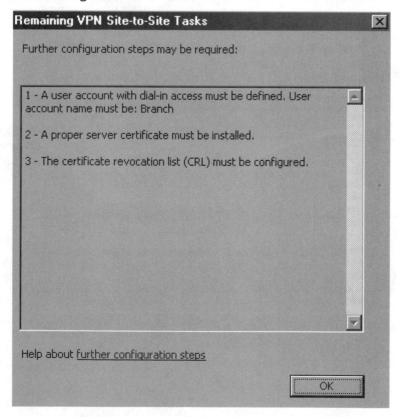

Enable the System Policy Rule on the Branch Office Firewall to Access the Enterprise CA

Now we'll switch our attention to the branch office ISA firewall. We need to enable the System Policy Rule allowing the branch office firewall to connect to the enterprise CA on the main office network.

Perform the following steps to enable the System Policy rule on the branch office firewall:

1. In the **Microsoft Internet Security and Acceleration Server 2006** management console, expand the server name, and click the **Firewall Policy** node.

2. Right-click **Firewall Policy**; point to **View**, and click **Show System Policy Rules**.

3. In the System Policy Rule list, double-click **Allow HTTP from ISA Server to all networks (for CRL downloads).** This is System Policy Rule #*18*.

4. In the **System Policy Editor** dialog box (Figure 20.58), put a checkmark in the **Enable** checkbox on the **General** tab. Click **OK**.

Figure 20.58 Configuring The System Policy

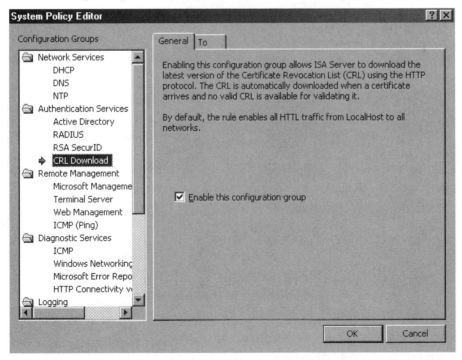

5. Click **Apply** to save the changes and update the firewall policy.

6. Click **OK** in the **Saving Configuration Changes** dialog box

Request and Install a Certificate for the Branch Office Firewall

Now we'll request a certificate for the branch office firewall. After we obtain the certificate, we will copy the CA certificate into the machine's **Trusted Root Certification Authorities** certificate store.

Perform the following steps on the branch office ISA firewall to request and install the certificates:

1. Open **Internet Explorer**. In the Address bar, enter **http://10.0.0.2/certsrv**, and click **OK**.

2. In the **Enter Network Password** dialog box, enter **Administrator** in the **User Name** text box, and enter the **Administrator's** password in the **Password** text box. Click **OK**.

3. In the **Internet Explorer** security dialog box, click **Add**. In the **Trusted Sites** dialog box, click **Add and Close**.

4. Click **Request a Certificate** on the **Welcome** page.

5. On the **Request a Certificate** page, click **advanced certificate request**.

6. On the **Advanced Certificate Request** page, click **Create and submit a request to this CA**.

7. On the **Advanced Certificate Request** page, select the **Administrator** certificate from the **Certificate Template** list. Remove the checkmark from the **Mark keys as exportable** checkbox. Place a checkmark in the **Store certificate in the local computer certificate store** checkbox. Click **Submit**.

8. Click **Yes** in the **Potential Scripting Violation** dialog box.

9. On the **Certificate Issued** page, click **Install this certificate**.

10. Click **Yes** on the **Potential Scripting Violation** page.

11. Close the browser after viewing the **Certificate Installed** page.

12. Click **Start** and **Run**. Enter **mmc** in the **Open** text box, and click **OK**.

13. In **Console1**, click the **File** menu, and then click **Add/Remove Snap-in**.

14. Click **Add** in the **Add/Remove Snap-in** dialog box.

15. Select the **Certificates** entry from the **Available Standalone Snap-ins** list in the **Add Standalone Snap-in** dialog box. Click **Add**.

16. Select **Computer account** on the **Certificates snap-in** page.

17. Select **Local computer** on the **Select Computer** page.

18. Click **Close** in the **Add Standalone Snap-in** dialog box.

19. Click **OK** in the **Add/Remove Snap-in** dialog box.

20. In the left pane of the console, expand **Certificates (Local Computer)**, then expand **Personal**. Click on **\Personal\Certificates**. Double-click on the **Administrator** certificate in the right pane of the console.

21. In the **Certificate** dialog box, click the **Certification Path** tab. The root CA certificate is at the top of the certificate hierarchy seen in the Certification path frame. Click the **EXCHANGE2003BE** certificate at the top of the list. Click **View Certificate**.

22. In the CA certificate's **Certificate** dialog box, click **Details**. Click **Copy to File**.

23. Click **Next** in the **Welcome to the Certificate Export Wizard** page.

24. On the **Export File Format** page, select **Cryptographic Message Syntax Standard – PKCS #7 Certificates (.P7B)**, and click **Next**.

25. On the **File to Export** page, enter **c:\cacert** in the **File name** text box. Click **Next**.

26. Click **Finish** on the **Completing the Certificate Export Wizard** page.

27. Click **OK** in the **Certificate Export Wizard** dialog box.

28. Click **OK** in the **Certificate** dialog box. Click **OK** again in the **Certificate** dialog box.

29. In the left pane of the console, expand the **Trusted Root Certification Authorities** node, and click **Certificates**. Right-click the **\Trusted Root Certification Authorities\Certificates** node; point to **All Tasks** and click **Import**.

30. Click **Next** on the **Welcome to the Certificate Import Wizard** page.

31. On the **File to Import** page, use **Browse** to locate the CA certificate you saved to the local hard disk, and click **Next**.

32. On the **Certificate Store** page, accept the default settings, and click **Next**.

33. Click **Finish** on the **Completing the Certificate Import Wizard** page.

34. Click **OK** on the **Certificate Import Wizard** dialog box informing you that the import was successful.

Configure the Branch Office ISA Firewall to use L2TP/IPSec for the Site-to-Site Link

The Remote Site Network at the branch office ISA firewall representing the main office network is configured to use PPTP for the site-to-site connection. We need to change this to L2TP/IPSec. Perform the following steps to make the change:

1. In the **Microsoft Internet Security and Acceleration Server 2006** management console, expand the server name, and then click the **Virtual Private Networks (VPN)** node in the left pane of the console.

2. On the **Virtual Private Networks (VPN)** node, click the **Remote Sites** tab in the Details pane. Double-click the **Main** Remote Site Network entry.

3. In the **Main Properties** dialog box, **Protocol** tab, select **L2TP/IPSec (provides a highly secure connection method)**. Click **Apply**, and then click **OK**.

4. Click **Apply** to save the changes and update the firewall policy.

5. Click **OK** in the **Saving Configuration Changes** dialog box.

6. Now you can save the changes to the Firewall Policy at the main office.

Activate the L2TP/IPSec Site-to-Site VPN Connection

Let's see if our L2TP/IPSec site-to-site VPN connection works:

1. First, you need to restart the **Routing and Remote Access Service** on both ISA firewalls so that the **Routing and Remote Access Service** recognizes the certificate.

2. In the **Microsoft Internet Security and Acceleration Server 2006** management console, expand the server name and click the **Monitoring** node.

3. On the **Monitoring** node, click the **Services** tab. Right-click the **Routing and Remote Access Service**, and click **Stop**.

4. When the service is stopped, right-click it again, and click **Start**.

5. From a host on the branch office network, ping the domain controller on the main office network.

6. When you receive ping responses, go to the branch office ISA firewall and open the **Microsoft Internet Security and Acceleration Server 2006** management console. Expand the server name, and then click the **Monitoring** node.

7. On the **Monitoring** node, click the **Sessions** tab. On the **Sessions** tab, right-click any of the column headers, and then click the **Application Name** entry (see Figure 20.59).

Figure 20.59 Adding the Application Name column

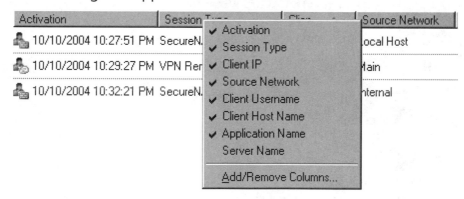

8. In the **Application Name** column you'll see that an L2TP/IPSec connection was established (see Figure 20.60).

Figure 20.60 Viewing the L2TP/IPSec

Activation	Session Type	Client IP	Source Network	Client Username	Client Host Name	Application Name
10/10/2004 10:27:51 PM	SecureNAT	192.168.1.71	Local Host		192.168.1.71	
10/10/2004 10:29:27 PM	VPN Remote Site	10.0.2.2	Main	Main	192.168.1.70	VPN (L2TP/IPSec)

Configuring Pre-shared Keys for Site-to-Site L2TP/IPSec VPN Links

In the previous example, we demonstrated the procedures required to create the site-to-site L2TP/IPSec connection using certificates for computer authentication. If you don't have a PKI in place yet, or if you do not plan on implementing a certificate infrastructure, you can use pre-shared keys for the computer authentication component of L2TP/IPSec connection establishment. This provides a more secure connection than you would see with IPSec tunnel mode and pre-shared keys, because you still have the user authentication requirement for the L2TP/IPSec connection.

Perform the following steps on both the main and branch office ISA firewalls to enable pre-shared keys for the site-to-site VPN connection:

1. In the **Microsoft Internet Security and Acceleration Server 2006** management console, expand the server name, and then click the **Virtual Private Networking (VPN)** node in the left pane of the console.

2. On the **Virtual Private Networking (VPN)** node, click the **VPN Clients** tab in the Details pane. Or you can click **Remote Sites** too. As said before the changes will reflect from **VPN Clients** to **Remote Sites** and vice-versa.

3. Click the **Tasks** tab in the Task pane. Click the **Select Authentication Methods** link.

4. In the **Virtual Private Networks (VPN) Properties** dialog box, put a checkmark in the **Allow custom IPSec policy for L2TP connection** checkbox and enter the pre-shared key (for incoming authentication).

5. Click **Apply** and then click **OK**.

6. Double-click the remote site. In the **remote site Properties**, **Protocols** tab, put a check into the "**Use pre-shared key IPSec authentication instead of certificate authentication**" check box and enter the pre-shared key (for outgoing authentication). If, for example the pre-shared key (for outgoing authentication) is 12345 on the main ISA Firewall, then on the branch ISA Firewall the pre-shared key for incoming authentication must be 12345 (make sure you use a very long, complex and unguessable pre-shared key).

7. Click **Apply** and then click **OK.**

8. Click **Apply** to save the changes and update the firewall policy.

9. Click **OK** in the **Saving Configuration Changes** dialog box.

IPSec Tunnel Mode Site-to-Site VPNs with Downlevel VPN Gateways

One of the major improvements that the ISA 2004/2006 firewall has over ISA Server 2000 is that it can be configured to use IPSec tunnel mode for site-to-site VPN connections. Most third-party VPN gateways require that you use IPSec tunnel mode for site-to-site VPN connections. It was very difficult to find a third-party VPN gateway that would work with ISA Server 2000. But with the ISA

2004/2006 firewall, you can establish an IPSec tunnel mode site-to-site link with just about any third-party VPN gateway.

Because of the number of third-party VPN gateways available on the market today, it's not possible for us to go into detail on how to configure the ISA firewall to connect to each of these devices. The good news is that Microsoft has published a comprehensive set of documents on how to connect the ISA firewall to a number of popular VPN gateways. At the time of this writing, there are documents on how to connect the ISA firewall to the following VPN gateways:

- Cisco PIX

- Astaro Linux

- SmoothWall Express

- Generic third-party gateways

You can find these documents and more on the Microsoft ISA 2004 VPN documentation site at http://www.microsoft.com/isaserver/techinfo/guidance/2004/vpn.asp

As said before the wizard for IPSec tunnel mode is also updated, so you can specify the network rule and access rules, enable the System Policy for CRL download(in case of authentication with certificates) and the wizard automatically adds for you the remote VPN server IP address into the remote site IP address ranges.

Using RADIUS for VPN Authentication and Remote Access Policy

We prefer to not join front-end ISA firewalls to the user domain. The reason for this is that the network segments between the front-end ISA firewall and back-end firewalls are unauthenticated DMZ segments, and we want to avoid passing domain information through those segments as much as possible.

When the ISA firewall is not a member of the user domain, we must use a mechanism other than Windows to authenticate and authorize domain users. The ISA firewall can authenticate VPN users with RADIUS (Remote Access Dial-In User Service). The RADIUS Protocol allows the ISA 2006 firewall to forward user credentials of a RADIUS server on the Internal network. The RADIUS server sends the authentication request to an authentication server, such as an Active Directory domain controller. The Microsoft implementation of RADIUS is the Internet Authentication Service (IAS).

In addition to authenticating users, the IAS server can be used to centralize Remote Access Policy. For example, if you have six ISA firewall/VPN servers under your administrative control, you can apply the same Remote Access Policy to all these machines by creating policy on an IAS server on your network.

The ISA firewall is not limited to working with just IAS, and it supports all types of RADIUS servers. However, the Microsoft IAS server is included with all Windows 2000 and Windows Server 2003 server family products, which makes it very convenient to use for any Microsoft shop.

In this section we will discuss procedures required to enable RADIUS authentication and RADIUS Remote Access Policy for VPN clients. We will carry out the following procedures:

- Configure the IAS Server

- Create a VPN Clients Remote Access Policy

- Enable the VPN Server on the ISA 2006 firewall and configure RADIUS Support

- Create a VPN Client Access Rule

- Make the connection from a PPTP VPN client

Configure the Internet Authentication Services (RADIUS) Server

If you have not installed the IAS server, you can install it now using the **Add/Remove Programs** Control Panel applet on your Windows 2000 or Windows Server 2003 machines on the Internal Network. You need to configure the IAS server to communicate with the Active Directory and then instruct the IAS server to work with the ISA 2006 firewall/VPN server machine. In our current example, the IAS server is installed on the domain controller on the Internal Network (EXCHANGE2003BE).

Perform the following steps to configure the IAS server:

1. Click Start; point to Administrative Tools, and click on Internet Authentication Services.

2. In the Internet Authentication Services console, right-click on the Internet Authentication Service (Local) node in the left pane of the console. Click the Register Server in Active Directory command.

3. This setting allows the IAS Server to authenticate users in the Active Directory domain. Click OK in the Register Internet Authentication Server in Active Directory dialog box.

4. Click OK in the Server registered dialog box. This dialog box informs you that the IAS Server was registered in a specific domain and if you want this IAS Server to read users' dial-in properties from other domains, you'll need to enter this server into the RAS/IAS Server Group in that domain. This automatically places the machine in the RAS and IAS Server Group in the Active Directory. If you want to register the server in another domain, you must place it in the RAS and IAS Servers group in that domain or use the command netsh ras add registeredserver *Domain IASServer* command.

5. Right-click on the RADIUS Clients node in the left pane of the console, and click the New RADIUS Client command.

6. In the New RADIUS Client dialog box, type in a Friendly name for the ISA firewall. You can use any name you like. In this example we'll use the DNS host name of the ISA firewall, which is ISALOCAL. Enter either the FQDN or the IP address of the ISA 2006 firewall/VPN server in the Client address (IP or DNS) dialog box. Do not enter a FQDN if your ISA firewall has not registered its internal interface IP address with your internal DNS server. You can use the Verify button to test whether the IAS Server can resolve the FQDN. Click Next.

7. On the Additional Information page, leave the RADIUS Standard entry in the Client-Vendor drop-down list box. Your ISA firewall will use this setting. Enter a complex shared secret in

the Shared secret text box, and confirm it in the Confirm shared secret text box. The shared secret should be a complex string consisting of upper and lower case letters, numbers, and symbols. Put a checkmark in the Request must contain the Message Authenticator attribute checkbox. This option enhances the security of the RADIUS messages passed between the ISA firewall and IAS servers. Click Finish. See Figure 20.61.

Figure 20.61 Configuring the Shared Secret

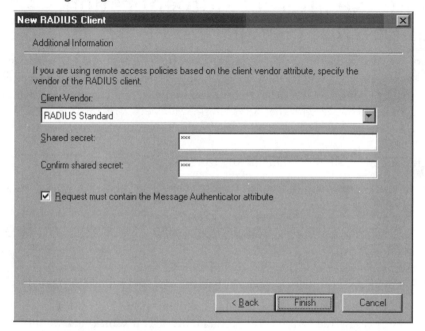

Create a VPN Clients Remote Access Policy

We're now ready to create a Remote Access Policy on the IAS Server. Remote Access Policies configured on the IAS Server are applied to VPN client connections made to the ISA firewall when the ISA firewall is configured to use RADIUS authentication and policy, and when the ISA firewall is configured as a RADIUS client. Fortunately for us, the Windows Server 2003 IAS server has a Remote Access Policy Wizard that makes it easy to create a secure VPN client Remote Access Policy.

Perform the following steps to create a VPN client Remote Access Policy on the IAS Server:

1. In the Internet Authentication Service console, right-click on the Remote Access Policies node, and click the New Remote Access Policy command.

2. Click Next on the Welcome to the New Remote Access Policy Wizard page.

3. On the Policy Configuration Method page, select Use the wizard to set up a typical policy for a common scenario. In the Policy name text box, type a name for the policy. In this example, we'll call it VPN Access Policy. Click Next.

4. Select the VPN option on the Access Method page. This policy is used for all VPN connections. You have the option to create separate policies for PPTP and L2TP/IPSec VPN links. However, to create separate policies for PPTP and L2TP/IPSec connections, you'll need to go back to the previous page in the Wizard and create two custom policies. In this example, we apply the same policy to all remote access VPN connections. Click Next.

5. You can grant access to the VPN server based on user or group. The best access control method is on a per-group basis because it entails less administrative overhead. You can create a group such as VPN Users and allow them access, or allow all your users access. In this example, we will select the Group option and click the Add button. This brings up the Select Groups dialog box. Enter the name of the group in for Enter the object name to select, and click Check names to confirm that you entered the name correctly. In this example, use the Domain Users group. Click OK in the Select Groups dialog box and Next in the User or Group Access dialog box.

6. Select user authentication methods you want to allow on the Authentication Methods page. You may wish to allow both Microsoft Encrypted Authentication version 2 and Extensible Authentication Protocol (EAP). Both EAP and MS-CHAP version 2 authentication are secure, so we'll select both the Extensible Authentication Protocol (EAP) and Microsoft Encrypted Authentication version 2 (MS-CHAPv2) checkboxes. Click the down arrow from the Type (based on method of access and network configuration) drop-down list and select the Smart Card or other certificate option, then click the Configure button (as shown in Figure 20.62). In the Smart Card or other Certificate Properties dialog box, select the certificate you want the server to use to identify itself to VPN clients. The self-signed certificate appears in the Certificate issued to drop-down list. This certificate is used to identify the server when VPN clients are configured to confirm the server's validity. Click OK in the Smart Card or other Certificate Properties dialog box (as shown in Figure 20.63), and then click Next.

Figure 20.62 The Authentication Method Page

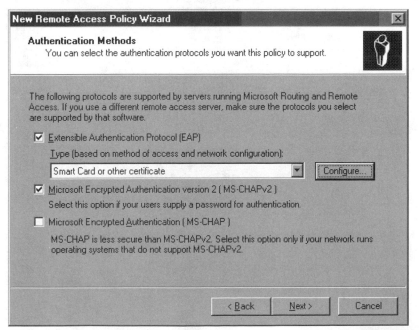

Figure 20.63 The Smart Card or other Certificate Properties Dialog Box

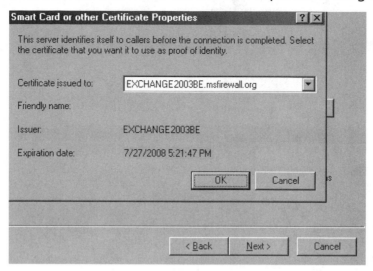

7. Select the level(s) of encryption you want to enforce on VPN connections. All Microsoft clients support the strongest level of encryption. If you have clients that don't support 128 bit encryption, select lower levels, but realize that you lower the level of security provided by the encryption method used by the VPN protocol. In this example, we'll select all three options (see Figure 20.64). In a high-security environment, you should select on the strongest encryption option. Just make sure all your VPN clients support this level of encryption. Click **Next**.

Figure 20.64 The Policy Encrypted Level

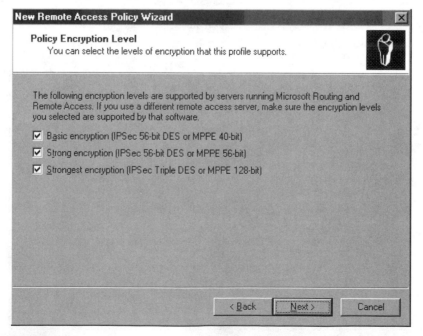

8. Review your settings on the Completing the New Remote Access Policy Wizard page and click Finish.

Remote Access Permissions and Domain Functional Level

The new Remote Access Policy requires the connection be a VPN connection. The VPN protocol can be either PPTP or L2TP/IPSec. The VPN client must use MS-CHAP v2 or EAP-TLS to authenticate, and the client must support the level of encryption set in the Remote Access Policy. The user must belong to the **Domain Users** group in the domain specified in the Remote Access Policy.

The next step is to configure Remote Access Permissions. Remote Access Permissions are different than Remote Access Policies.

When a VPN user calls the ISA firewall, the parameters of the connection are compared against Remote Access Policy (the remote access policy can be either on the ISA firewall itself or on a IAS server). Remote Access Policies are represented as a hierarchical list. The policy on top of the list is evaluated first, then the second-listed policy is evaluated, then the third, and so forth.

The VPN client's connection parameters are compared to the *conditions* in the policy. In the remote access policy we created above, there were two conditions:

- The connection type is a virtual connection, and
- The user is a member of the **Domain Users** group.

If the connection request matches both of those conditions, then Remote Access Permissions are determined. Remote access permissions are determined differently depending on the type of domain the user account belongs to.

Windows Server 2003 domains do not use the Mixed and Native Mode designations you might be familiar with in Windows 2000. Windows Server 2003 supports domains of varying *functional levels*. If all the domain controllers in your domain run Windows Server 2003, the default functional level is *Windows 2000 mixed*. All user accounts are denied VPN (Dial-up) access by default in Windows 2000 Mixed Mode functional level. In Windows 2000 Mixed Mode, *you must configure each user account* to have permission to log on to the VPN server. The reason is that user account permissions override Remote Access Policy permissions in Mixed Mode domains.

If you want to control Remote Access Permissions via Remote Access Policy, you must raise the domain functional level to Windows 2000 Native or Windows Server 2003. The default Remote Access Permission in Windows 2000 and Windows Server 2003 domains is **Control access through Remote Access Policy**. Once you are able to use Remote Access Policy to assign VPN access permission, you can take advantage of group membership to allow or deny VPN access to the VPN server.

When a VPN connection matches the *conditions* in the Remote Access Policy, and the user is granted access via either the user account Dial-in settings or Remote Access Policy, then the VPN connection parameters are compared to a number of settings defined by the *Remote Access Profile*. If the incoming connection does not comply with the settings in the Remote Access Profile, then the next Remote Access Policy is compared to the connection. If no policy matches the incoming connection's parameters, the VPN connection request to the ISA firewall is dropped.

The VPN Remote Access Policy you created earlier includes all the parameters required for a secure VPN connection. Your decision now centers on how you want to control Remote Access Permissions:

- **Enable Remote Access on a per group basis:** this requires that you run in Windows 2000 Native or Windows Server 2003 functional level

- **Enable Remote Access on a per user basis:** supported by Windows 2000 Native, Windows 2000 Mixed and Windows Server 2003 functional levels

- **Enable Remote Access on both a per user and per group basis:** this requires Windows 2000 Native or Windows Server 2003 functional level; granular user-based access control overriding group-based access control is done on a per user basis

Procedures required to allow *per user* and *per group* access include:

- Change the **Dial-in** permissions on the user account in the Active Directory to control Remote Access Permission on a per user basis.

- Change the domain functional level to support Dial-in permissions based on Remote Access Policy.

- Change the Permissions settings on the Remote Access Policy.

Changing the User Account Dial-in Permissions

You enable dial-in permissions on a per account basis, or create Remote Access Policies that can be configured to enable dial-in permissions to entire groups.

Perform the following steps if you want to control access on a per user basis, or if you have no other choice because of your domain's functional level:

1. Click Start; point to Administrative Tools, and click on Active Directory Users and Computers.

2. In the Active Directory Users and Computers console, expand your domain name and click on the User node.

3. Double-click on the Administrator account in the right pane of the console. In the user account Properties dialog box, click on the Dial-in tab. The default setting on the account is Deny access. You can allow VPN access for the account by selecting the Allow access option. Per user account settings override permissions set on the Remote Access Policy. Notice the Control access through Remote Access Policy option is disabled. This option is available only when the domain is at the Windows 2000 or Windows Server 2003 functional level. Make no changes to the account setting at this time. See Figure 20.65.

Figure 20.65 Changing the Dial-in Permissions

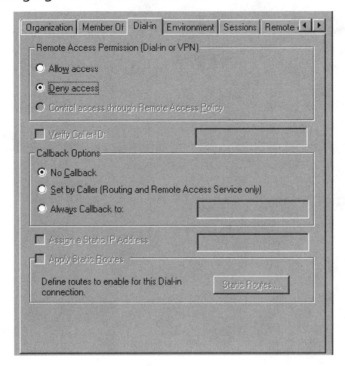

4. Click **Cancel** to escape this dialog box.

Changing the Domain Functional Level

If you want to control access on a per group basis, you will need to change the default domain functional level. Perform the following steps to change the domain functional level:

1. On a domain controller in your domain, open the Active Directory Domains and Trusts console. Click Start; point to Administrative Tools and click on Active Directory Domains and Trusts.

2. In the Active Directory Domains and Trusts console, right-click on your domain, and click on the Raise Domain Functional Level command.

3. In the Raise Domain Functional Level dialog box, click the down arrow in the Select an available domain functional level drop-down list and select either Windows 2000 native or Windows Server 2003, depending on the type of domain functional level your network can support. In this example, we will select the Windows Server 2003 option. Click the Raise button after making your selection (as shown in Figure 20.66).

Figure 20.66 The Raise Domain Functional Level

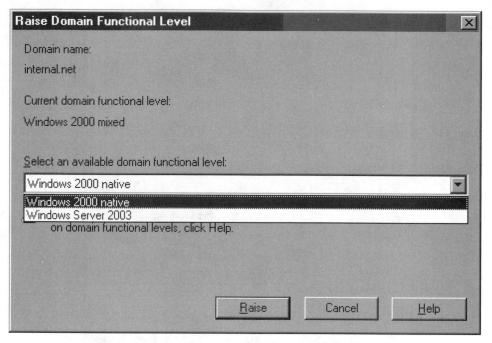

4. Click **OK** in the **Raise Domain Functional Level** dialog box. This dialog box explains that the change affects the entire domain and after the change is made, it cannot be reversed.

5. Click **OK** in the **Raise Domain Functional Level** dialog box informing you that the functional level was raised successfully. Note that you do not need to restart the computer for the changes to take effect. However, the default Remote Access Permission will not change for user accounts until Active Directory replication is completed. In this example, we will restart the computer. Restart the computer now and log in as Administrator.

6. Return to the **Active Directory Users and Computers** console and double-click on a user account. Click on the **Dial-in** tab in the user's **Properties** dialog box. Notice how the **Control access through Remote Access Policy** option is enabled and selected by default (Figure 20.67).

Figure 20.67 Controlling Access via Remote Access Policy

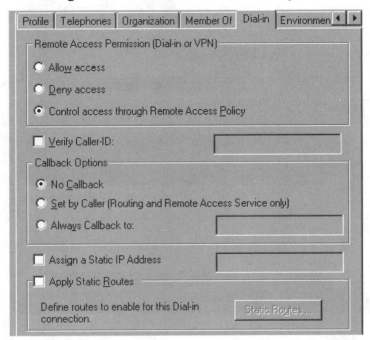

Controlling Remote Access Permission via Remote Access Policy

Now that we have the option to control access via Remote Access Policy (instead of a per user account basis), let's see how VPN access control via Remote Access Policy is performed:

1. Click Start; point to Administrative Tools, and click Internet Authentication Service.

2. Click Remote Access Policies in the left pane of the console. You will see the VPN Access Policy and two other built-in Remote Access Policies. You can delete the other policies if you require only VPN connections to your ISA firewall. Right-click on Connections to other access servers, and click Delete. Repeat with Connections to Microsoft Routing and Remote Access server.

3. Double-click on the VPN Access Policy in the right pane of the console. In the VPN Access Policy Properties dialog box there are two options that control access permissions based on Remote Access Policy:

- Deny remote access permission
- Grant remote access permission

Notice that this dialog box does inform you that the user account settings override the Remote Access Permission settings: **Unless individual access permissions are specified in the user**

profile, this policy controls access to the network. Select the **Grant remote access permission** to allow members of the **Domain Users** group access to the VPN server (Figure 20.68).

Figure 20.68 Remote Access Policy Properties

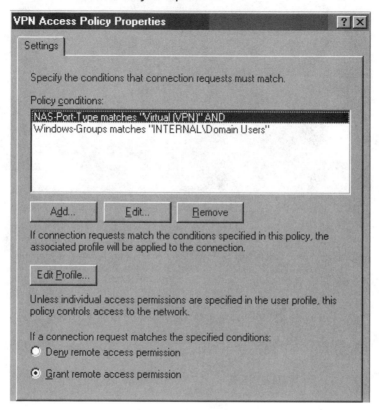

4. Click **Apply** and then click **OK** in the **VPN Access Policy Properties** dialog box to save the changes.

Enable the VPN Server on the ISA Firewall and Configure RADIUS Support

After the RADIUS server is installed and configured and Remote Access Policies are in place, we can start configuring the ISA firewall. First, we will first enable the VPN server component and then configure the VPN server to support RADIUS authentication.

Perform the following steps to enable the VPN server and configure it for RADIUS support:

1. In the Microsoft Internet Security and Acceleration Server **2006** management console, expand the server name, and click on Virtual Private Networks (VPN).

2. Click the Tasks tab in the Task pane. Click Enable VPN Client Access.

3. Click Configure VPN Client Access.

4. In the VPN Clients Properties dialog box, put a checkmark in the Enable VPN client access checkbox. Configure the number of VPN clients you want to allow in the Maximum number of VPN allowed text box.

5. Click the Protocols tab. Put checkmarks in the Enable PPTP and Enable L2TP/**IPSec** checkboxes. Click Apply and then click OK. (Figure 20.69)

Figure 20.69 Enabling the VPN Protocols (New)

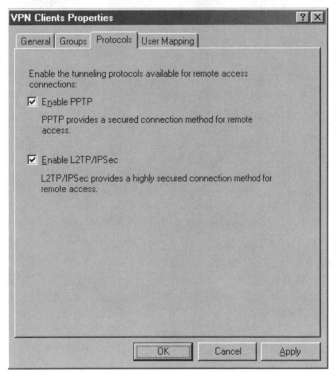

6. Click the Specify RADIUS Configuration link on the Tasks tab.

7. On the RADIUS tab in the Virtual Private Networks (VPN) Properties dialog box (Figure 20.70), put a checkmark in the Use RADIUS for authentication checkbox.

Figure 20.70 Configuring RADIUS Authentication

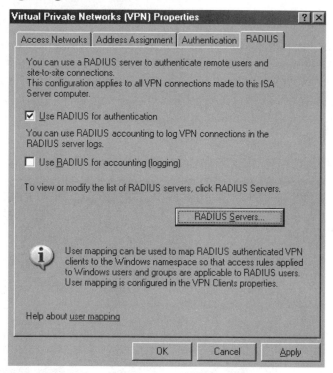

8. Click the **RADIUS Servers** button. In the **RADIUS** dialog box, click **Add**.

9. In the **Add RADIUS Server** dialog box, enter the name of the IAS server machine in the **Server name** text box. In this example, the name of the IAS server is **EXCHANGE2003BE.msfirewall.org**. Enter a description of the server in the **Server description** text box. In this example, enter the description **IAS Server**. Click the **Change** button (Figure 20.71).

Figure 20.71 The Add RADIUS Server Dialog Box

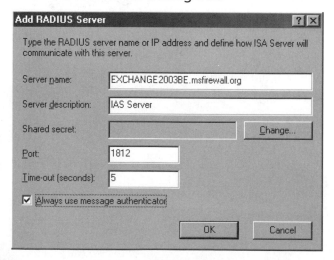

10. In the **Shared Secret** dialog box, enter a **New Secret** and then **Confirm new secret**. Make sure this is the *same secret* you entered in the RADIUS client configuration at the IAS server machine. Click **OK**.

11. Click **OK** in the **Add RADIUS Server** dialog box.

12. Click **OK** in the **RADIUS Servers** dialog box (Figure 20.72).

Figure 20.72 RADIUS Server Dialog Box

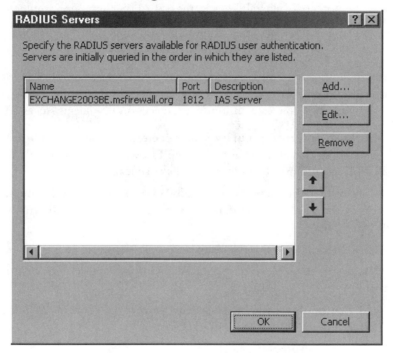

13. Click Apply in the Virtual Private Networks (VPN) Properties dialog box. Click OK in the ISA 2006 dialog box informing you that the Routing and Remote Access Service may restart. Click OK in the Virtual Private Networks (VPN) Properties dialog box.

14. Click Apply to save the changes and update the firewall policy.

15. Click OK in the **Saving** Configuration **Changes** dialog box.

16. Restart the ISA firewall, and log on as Administrator.

Create an Access Rule Allowing VPN Clients Access to Approved Resources

The ISA firewall can accept incoming VPN connections after the restart. However, the VPN clients cannot access any resources on the Internal network because there are no Access Rules enabling this access. You must create an Access Rule allowing machines belonging to the VPN clients network access to the Internal network. In contrast to other combined firewall VPN server solutions, the ISA firewall applies access controls for network access to VPN clients.

In this example, we will create an Access Rule allowing VPN clients access to the OWA server on the Internal network and no other servers. In addition, we'll limit the users to using only HTTP when making the connection.

This type of configuration would be attractive to organizations that want to allow secure remote access to their corporate OWA site, but that do not want to use SSL-to-SSL bridging because:

- There may be potential vulnerabilities in the SSL/TLS encryption implementations, and

- They want to allow non-encrypted communications through the corporate network to enable internal network IDS to evaluate the connections.

We will demonstrate other ways you can implement access control on VPN clients using user/group members later in this chapter.

Perform the following steps to create an unrestricted access VPN clients Access Rule:

1. In the **Microsoft Internet Security and Acceleration Server 2006** management console, expand the server name and click the **Firewall Policy** node. Right-click the **Firewall Policy** node, point to **New**, and click **Access Rule**.

2. In the **Welcome to the New Access Rule Wizard** page, enter a name for the rule in the **Access Rule name** text box. In this example, we will name the rule **OWA for VPN Clients**. Click **Next**.

3. On the **Rule Action** page, select **Allow**, and click **Next**.

4. On the **Protocols** page, select the **Selected protocols** option in the **Apply the rule to this protocols** list. Click **Add**.

5. In the **Add Protocols** dialog box, click the **Common Protocols** folder, and double-click the **HTTP** and **HTTPS** Protocols. Click **Close**.

6. Click **Next** on the **Protocols** page.

7. On the **Access Rule Sources** page, click **Add**. In the **Add Network Entities** dialog box, click the **Networks** folder, and double-click **VPN Clients**. Click **Close**.

8. Click **Next** on the **Access Rule Sources** page.

9. On the **Access Rule Destinations** page, click **Add**. In the **Add Network Entities** dialog box, click the **New** menu, and click **Computer**.

10. In the **New Computer Rule Element** dialog box, enter the name of the OWA server in the **Name** text box. In this example, we'll name it **OWA Server**. Enter the IP address of the OWA server in the **Computer IP Address** text box. Click **OK**.

11. Click the **Computers** folder and double-click the **OWA Server** entry. Click **Close**.

12. Click **Next** on the **Access Rule Destinations** page.

13. On the **User Sets** page, accept the default setting, **All Users**, and click **Next**.

14. Click Finish on the **Completing the New Access Rule Wizard** page.

15.   Click **Apply** to save the changes and update the firewall policy.

16.   Click **OK** in the **Saving Configuration Changes** dialog box. The **OWA for VPN Clients** policy is now the top-listed Access Rule in the Access Policy list (Figure 20.73).

Figure 20.73 The resulting firewall policy

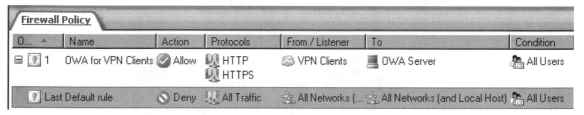

Make the Connection from a PPTP VPN Client

All the elements are in place to support RADIUS authentication for VPN clients. In the following exercise you will establish a PPTP VPN connection from an external network VPN client.

Perform the following steps to connect to the VPN server via RADIUS authentication:

1.   In the **Dial-up and Network Connections** window on the external network client, create a new VPN connectoid. Configure the connectoid to use the IP address **192.168.1.70** as the address of the VPN server. Log on with the user name **Administrator**.

2.   Click **OK** in the dialog box informing you that the VPN connection is established.

3.   At the domain controller machine, click **Start** and point to **Administrative Tools**. Click **Event Viewer**.

4.   In the **Event Viewer**, click on the **System** node in the left pane of the console. Double-click on the **Information** entry with the source as **IAS**. (See Figure 20.74)

Figure 20.74 Event Viewer Entry

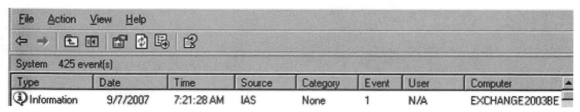

5.   In the **Event Properties** dialog box, you will see a **Description** of the log-on request. The information indicates that the RADIUS server authenticated the request and includes the RADIUS-specific information sent to the domain controller. Review this information and close the **Event Properties** dialog box (Figure 20.75).

Figure 20.75 Log-On Request Details

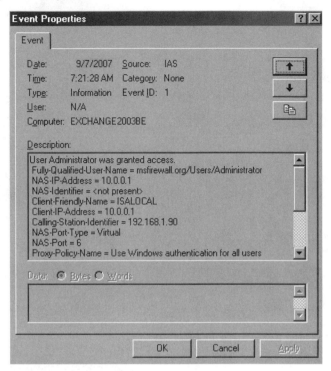

6. At the ISA firewall, you can see log file entries specific to this VPN request. Note the PPTP and the RADIUS connections (Figure 20.76).

Figure 20.76 Log File Entries for VPN RADIUS Authentication

192.168.1.90	192.168.1.70	1723	PPTP	Initiated Connection	Allow VPN client traffic to ISA Server	
192.168.1.90	192.168.1.70	0	PPTP	Initiated Connection	Allow VPN client traffic to ISA Server	
10.0.0.1	10.0.0.2	1812	RADIUS	Initiated Connection	Allow RADIUS authentication from ISA Server to trusted RADIUS servers	
10.0.0.108	10.0.0.109	0	WAN Miniport (PPTP)	Initiated VPN Connection		Administrator

7. At the ISA firewall server, you can see the VPN client session in the **Sessions** tab in the **Monitoring** node of the **Microsoft Internet Security and Acceleration Server 2006** management console (Figure 20.77).

Figure 20.77 VPN Session Appears in Sessions Section

Activation	Session Type	Client IP ▲	Source Network	Client Username	Client Host Name	Application Name
🦻 3/26/2004 7:41:34 AM	SecureNAT	10.0.0.1	Local Host		10.0.0.1	
🦻 3/26/2004 7:47:05 AM	SecureNAT	192.168.1.90	External		192.168.1.90	
🦻 3/26/2004 7:47:10 AM	VPN Client	10.0.0.106	VPN Clients	Administrator		VPN (PPTP)

8. At the VPN client computer, disconnect the VPN connection.

9. If you run a **Network Monitor** session on the RADIUS server, you can see that a single RADIUS **Access Request** is sent from the ISA firewall to the RADIUS server and a single **Access Accept** message is sent to the ISA firewall from the RADIUS server (Figure 20.78).

Figure 20.78 RADIUS Messages in Network Monitor Trace

Protocol	Description	Src Other Addr	Dst Other Addr
RADIUS	Message Type: Access Request(1)	ISALOCAL	EXCHANGE2003BE
RADIUS	Message Type: Access Accept(2)	EXCHANGE2003BE	ISALOCAL

If you want to create user-based firewall policies while ISA is not a domain member and you are authenticating against the RADIUS server you can create **User Sets** belonging to the RADIUS namespace on ISA. But you must use weak protocols like PAP and SPAP in order that users to be able to access resources.

Using EAP User Certificate Authentication for Remote Access VPNs

You can significantly enhance the security of your ISA firewall's VPN remote access client connections by using EAP user certificate authentication. User certificate authentication requires that the user possess a user certificate issued by a trusted certificate authority.

Both the ISA firewall and the remote access VPN client must have the appropriate certificates assignment to them. You must assign the ISA firewall a machine certificate that the firewall can use to identify itself. Users must be assigned user certificates from a certificate authority that the ISA firewall trusts. When both the remote access client machine presenting the user certificate and the ISA firewall contain a common CA certificate in their Trusted Root Certification Authorities certificate stores, the client and server trust the same certificate hierarchy.

The steps required to support user certificate authentication for remote access client VPN connections to the ISA firewall include:

- Issuing a machine certificate to the ISA firewall
- Configuring the ISA firewall software to support EAP authentication
- Enabling User Mapping for EAP authenticated users
- Configuring the Routing and Remote Access Service to support EAP authentication
- Issuing a user certificate to the remote access VPN client machine

We have discussed the procedures for issuing a machine certificate to the ISA firewall in other chapters in this book and in the ISA Deployment Kits at www.isaserver.org, so we will not reiterate that procedure here. Instead, we'll start with configuring the ISA firewall software to support EAP authentication, and then discuss how to configure the RRAS service and the clients.

Configuring the ISA Firewall Software to Support EAP Authentication

Perform the following steps to configure the ISA firewall to support EAP authentication:

1. In the **Microsoft Internet Security and Acceleration Server 2006** management console, expand the server name, and click **Virtual Private Networks (VPN)** in the left pane of the console.

2. While in **Virtual Private Networks (VPN)**, click the **Tasks** tab in the Task pane. On the **Tasks** tab, click **Authentication Methods**.

3. In the **Virtual Private Networks (VPN) Properties** dialog box, put a checkmark in the **Extensible authentication protocol (EAP) with smart card or other certificate (ISA Server must belong to a domain)** checkbox (Figure 20.79).

Figure 20.79 Setting EAP Authentication

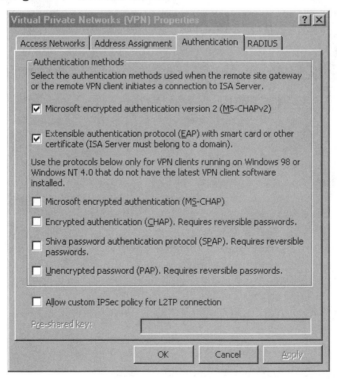

4. Read the information in the Microsoft Internet Security and Acceleration Server *2006* dialog box. The dialog box reports that EAP authenticated users belong to the RADIUS namespace and are not part of the Windows namespace. To apply user-based access rules to these users you can either define a RADIUS user set for them or you can use user mapping to map these users to the Windows namespace. If user mapping is enabled, access rules applied to the Windows users and group will be applicable to EAP authenticated users.

This is important information and describes the real utility of the User Mapping feature we discussed earlier in this chapter. Because EAP authentication doesn't use "Windows" authentication, you cannot by default apply user/group access policy on VPN clients authenticating with EAP user certificates. However, if we enable User Mapping for these users and map the user names of the EAP certificate authenticated users to domain users, then the same access rules that you apply to users who log on using Windows authentication will be applied to the EAP user certificate authenticated users. We'll go over the procedures of enabling and configuring User Mapping in the next procedures in this section.

5.   Click **OK** (as shown in Figure 20.80) to acknowledge that you read and understand this information.

Figure 20.80 Warning about User Mapping and EAP

6.   Click **Apply**, and then click **OK**.

Enabling User Mapping for EAP Authenticated Users

Perform the following steps to enable and configure User Mapping for EAP certificate authenticated users:

1.   In the **Microsoft Internet Security and Acceleration Server 2006** management console, expand the server name, and click **Virtual Private Networks (VPN)** in the left pane of the console.

2.   While in **Virtual Private Networks (VPN)**, click the **Tasks** tab in the Task pane. Click **Configure VPN Client Access** in the **Tasks** tab.

3.   In the **VPN Clients Properties** dialog box, click the **User Mapping** tab.

4.   On the **User Mapping** tab, put a checkmark in the **Enable User Mapping** checkbox. Put a checkmark in the **When username does not contain a domain, use this domain**. In the **Domain Name** text box, enter a domain name for the domain that the ISA firewall belongs to. This allows the ISA firewall to map the user name of the EAP certificate-authenticated user to accounts in that domain, and then rules applying to those users will apply to the EAP-authenticated users in the same way as they would if the users had authenticated using traditional "Windows" authentication.

5.   Click **Apply** and then click **OK** (Figure 20.81).

Figure 20.81 Enabling User Mapping for EAP Authentication

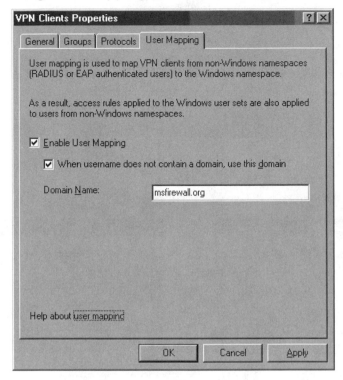

6. Click **Apply** to save the changes and update the firewall policy.

7. Click **OK** in the **Saving Configuration Changes** dialog box.

Issuing a User Certificate to the Remote Access VPN Client Machine

The VPN remote access client machines need to obtain user certificates and be configured to use the certificates to authenticate with the ISA firewall's remote access VPN server.

Perform the following steps to obtain a user certificate for the remote access VPN client:

1. Open **Internet Explorer**. In the **Address** bar, enter the URL for your certificate authority's Web enrollment site, and press **ENTER**.

2. Enter **Administrator** (or any name for which you want to obtain a user certificate) in the **User Name** text box. Enter the **Administrator's** password in the **Password** text box. Click **OK**.

3. On the **Welcome** page of the CA's Web enrollment site, click **Request a certificate**.

4. On the **Request a Certificate** page, click **User Certificate**.

5. Click **Submit** on the **User Certificate – Identifying Information** page.

6. Click **Yes** in the **Potential Scripting Violation** dialog box informing you that the Web site is requesting a new certificate on your behalf.

7. On the **Certificate Issued** page, click **Install this certificate**.

8. Click **Yes** in the **Potential Scripting Violation** dialog box informing you that the Web site is adding one or more certificates.

9. Close Internet Explorer.

We can configure the VPN connectoid to use user certificate authentication now that we have a user certificate installed on the remote access VPN client machine:

1. In the **Dial-up and Network Connections** window on the external network client, create a new VPN connectoid. Configure the connectoid to use the IP address **192.168.1.70** as the address of the VPN server.

2. When you complete the connection Wizard, you will see the **Connect** dialog box. Click **Properties**.

3. In the connectoid's **Properties** dialog box, click the **Security** tab. On the **Security** tab (Figure 20.82), select **Advanced (custom settings)**. Click **Settings**.

Figure 20.82 The Security Tab

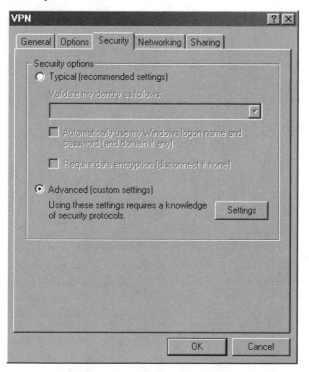

4. In the Advanced Security Settings dialog box (Figure 20.83), select Use Extensible Authentication Protocol (EAP). Click Properties.

Figure 20.83 Enabling EAP Authentication

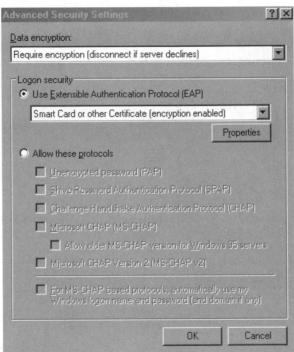

5. In the Smart Card or other Certificate Properties dialog box, select Use a certificate on this computer. Place a checkmark by Validate server certificate. Place a checkmark by Connect **to these servers**, and enter the server name of the authentication server. In this example, the server name is ISALOCAL.msfirewall.org (*the CN from the ISA certificate*), so enter that name in the text box. In the Trusted root certificate authority list, select the name of the CA that issued the certificates. In this example, the CA name is EXCHANGE2003BE, so select that option. Click OK in the Smart Card or other Certificate Properties dialog box (Figure 20.84).

Figure 20.84 The Smart Card or other Certificate Properties Dialog Box

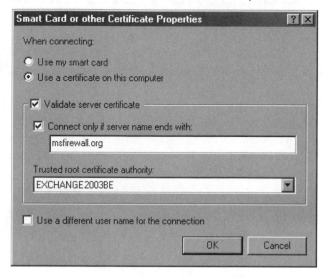

6. Click **OK** in the **Advanced Security Settings** dialog box.

7. Click **OK** in the connectoid's **Properties** dialog box.

8. A **Connect** dialog box appears which contains the name on the user certificate you obtained from the CA (Figure 20.85). Click **OK**.

Figure 20.85 Selecting the User Certificate for EAP User Authentication

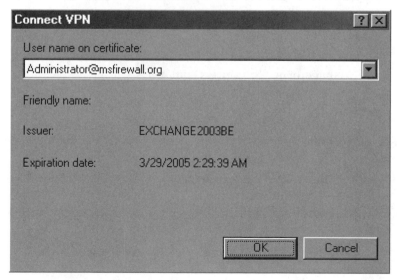

The VPN link will establish, and you'll be authenticated by the DC on the corporate network.

Supporting Outbound VPN Connections through the ISA Firewall

You can configure the ISA firewall to allow outbound access to VPN servers on the Internet. The ISA firewall supports all true VPN protocols, including PPTP, L2TP/IPSec, and IPSec NAT Traversal (NAT-T).

The ISA firewall can pass PPTP VPN connections from any Protected Network to the Internet with the help of its PPTP filter. The ISA firewall's PPTP filter intercepts the outbound PPTP connection from the Protected Network client and mediates the GRE (Generic Routing Encapsulation/IP Protocol 47) Protocol and the PPTP control channel (TCP 1723) communications. The only thing you need to do is create an Access Rule allowing outbound access to PPTP.

Perform the following steps to allow outbound PPTP access through the ISA firewall:

1. In the **Microsoft Internet Security and Acceleration Server 2006** management console, expand the server name, and click **Firewall Policy**.

2. In the **Firewall Policy** node, click **Create Access Rule** on the **Tasks** tab in the Task pane.

3. On the **Welcome to the New Access Rule Wizard** page, enter a name for the rule in the **Access Rule name** text box. In this example, enter **Outbound PPTP for Administrators**. Click **Next**.

4. On the **Rule Action** page, select **Allow**, and click **Next**.

5. On the **Protocols** page, select the **Selected protocols** option from the **Apply the rule to this protocols** list. Click **Add**.

6. In the **Add Network Entities** dialog box, click the **VPN and IPSec** folder and double-click the **PPTP** entry. Click **Close**.

7. Click **Next** on the **Protocols** page.

8. In the **Add Network Entities** dialog box, click the **Computer Sets** folder and double-click the **Remote Management Computers** entry. Click **Close**.

9. Click **Next** on the **Access Rule Sources** page.

10. On the **Access Rule Destinations** page, click **Add**.

11. In the **Add Network Entities** dialog box, click the **New** menu, and then click **Computer**.

12. In the **New Computer Rule Element** dialog box, enter a name for the external VPN server in the **Name** text box. Enter the IP address of the authorized VPN server in the **Computer IP Address** text box. In this example, enter **Authorized VPN Server**. Click **OK**.

13. Click the **Computers** folder and double-click the **Authorized VPN Server** entry. Click **Close**.

14. Click **Next** on the **Access Rule Destinations** page.

15. Click **Next** on the **User Sets** page.

16. Click **Finish** on the **Completing the New Access Rule Wizard** page.

All modern IPSec-based VPN clients support some type of NAT traversal. The Microsoft L2TP/IPSec client supports the IETF Internet draft (http://www.ietf.org/internet-drafts/draft-ietf-ipsec-nat-t-ike-08.txt) for supporting IPSec through NAT devices. While historically a number of non-Microsoft VPN vendors fragmented the IPSec NAT-T market by implementing proprietary NAT-T solutions for their VPN clients, most of them are following Microsoft's lead and are implementing the IETF draft recommendations for their VPN clients and servers.

Now NAT-T is standardized in RFC3947 (Negotiation of NAT-Traversal in the IKE) and RFC3948 (UDP Encapsulation of IPSec ESP Packets). ISA 2006, like ISA 2004 is based on the draft implementation and thus does not return the VID (Vendor ID) based on RFC3947 (the content of the payload is the MD5 hash of RFC 3947. The exact content in hex for the payload is 4a131c81070 358455c5728f20e95452f), just the VID for the draft. Windows Vista is the first Windows OS that is based on the new RFC. Vista will return both VIDs (for draft and RFC).

RFC-compliant NAT traversal requires that you allow outbound UDP 500 and UDP 4500 (the L2TP tunnel is protected(encapsulated) by IPSec ESP and thus it will never be seen by the intermediate device, UDP 1701 must be enabled at the VPN endpoint) through the ISA firewall. UDP port 500 is for the Internet Key Exchange (IKE) negotiation and UDP 4500 for UDP Encapsulation of IPSec ESP packets. For this reason, you might expect that using RFC-compliant IPSec NAT-T would allow you to control outbound VPN access on a user/group basis since most UDP and TCP protocols use Winsock.

Unfortunately, this is not the case for the Microsoft L2TP/IPSec NAT-T and most other IPSec NAT-T protocols because the NAT-T client is implemented as a *shim* in the Windows TCP/IP protocol stack and allows it to bypass the Winsock interface.

Perform the following steps to allow RFC-compliant IPSec NAT-T VPN connections (such as the Windows L2TP/IPSec client) through the ISA firewall:

1. In the **Microsoft Internet Security and Acceleration Server 2006** management console, expand the server name and click **Firewall Policy**.

2. In the **Firewall Policy** node, click **Create Access Rule** on the **Tasks** tab in the Task pane.

3. On the **Welcome to the New Access Rule Wizard** page, enter a name for the rule in the **Access Rule name** text box. In this example, we'll name it **Outbound L2TP/IPSec NAT-T for Administrators**. Click **Next**.

4. On the **Rule Action** page, select **Allow** and click **Next**.

5. On the **Protocols** page, select the **Selected protocols** option from the **Apply the rule to this protocols** list. Click **Add**.

6. In the **Add Network Entities** dialog box, click the **VPN and IPSec** folder and double-click the **IKE Client(for UDP 500)** and **IPSec NAT-T Client(for UDP 4500)** entries. Click **Close**.

7. Click **Next** on the **Protocols** page.

8. On the **Access Rule Sources** page, click **Add**.

9. In the **Add Network Entities** dialog box, click the **Computer Sets** folder and double-click the **Remote Management Computers** entry. Click **Close**.

10. Click **Next** on the **Access Rule Sources** page.

11. On the **Access Rule Destinations** page, click **Add**.

12. In the **Add Network Entities** dialog box, click **New** and **Computer**.

13. In the **New Computer Rule Element** dialog box, enter a name for the external VPN server in the **Name** text box. Enter the IP address of the authorized VPN server in the **Computer IP Address** text box. In this example, enter **Authorized VPN Server**. Click **OK**.

14. Click the **Computers** folder, and double-click **Authorized VPN Server**. Click **Close**.

15. Click **Next** on the **Access Rule Destinations** page.

16. Click **Next** on the **User Sets** page.

17. Click **Finish** on the **Completing the New Access Rule Wizard** page.

Installing and Configuring the DHCP Server and DHCP Relay Agent on the ISA Firewall

Many smaller organizations may wish to install a DHCP server on the ISA firewall itself (not recommended). This allows smaller companies the ability to automatically assign IP addressing information to hosts on the corporate network without requiring them to install the DHCP server on a separate server on the corporate network. Many of these companies may have only one other Windows Server on their network, and that server is often a Windows domain controller.

However there are potential negative security implications of putting a DHCP server on a Windows domain controller (http://support.microsoft.com/default.aspx?scid=kb;en-us;816592). You should not install any additional services on ISA 2006 Firewall (like DHCP server, DNS server) because this would increase the attack surface area.

The ISA firewall has a System Policy that enables the firewall itself to be a DHCP client. There are two System Policy Rules listed in Table 20.1.

Table 20.1 System Policy Rules Enabling the ISA Firewall to be a DHCP Client

Rule #	Rule Name	Action	Protocols	From/Listener	To	Condition
9	Allow DHCP requests from ISA Server to all networks	Allow	DHCP (request)	Local Host	Anywhere	All Users
10	Allow DHCP replies from DHCP servers to ISA Server	Allow	DHCP (reply)	Internal	Local Host	All Users

The DHCP System Policy Rules allow DHCP requests from the ISA firewall, and DHCP replies from the Internal Network to the ISA firewall. These rules won't help us when we want to run the DHCP server on the ISA firewall itself because we want to allow DHCP requests *from the Internal Network* to the ISA firewall. We also want to allow DHCP Replies *from the ISA firewall* to the Internal Network. We'll need to create Access Rules to allow the required DHCP communications to and from the ISA firewall.

Perform the following steps to create the Access Rules allowing DHCP Requests to the ISA firewall and DHCP Replies from the ISA firewall:

1. In the **Microsoft Internet Security and Acceleration Server 2006** management console, expand the server name, and click the **Firewall Policy** node.

2. In the **Firewall Policy** node, click **Create Access Rule** on the **Tasks** tab in the Task pane.

3. On the **Welcome to the New Access Rule Wizard** page, enter a name for the rule in the **Access Rule name** text box. In this example, enter **DHCP Request**. Click **Next**.

4. On the **Rule Action** page, select **Allow** and **Next**.

5. On the **Protocols** page, select the **Selected protocols** option from the **Apply the rule to this protocols** list. Click **Add**.

6. In the **Protocols** dialog box, click the **Infrastructure** folder and double-click the **DHCP (request)** entry. Click **Close**.

7. Click **Next** on the **Protocols** page.

8. On the **Access Rule Sources** page, click **Add**.

9. In the **Add Network Entities** dialog box, click the **Networks** folder and double-click the **Internal** entry. If you want clients from multiple Protected Networks to access the DHCP server on the ISA firewall, make sure to include those Networks, too. Click **Close**.

10. Click **Next** on the **Access Rule Sources** page.

11. On the **Access Rule Destinations** page, click **Add**.

12. In the **Add Network Entities** dialog box, click the **Networks** folder, and double-click the **Local Host** network.

13. Click **Next** on the **Access Rule Destinations** page.

14. Click **Next** on the **User Sets** page.

15. Click **Finish** on the **Completing the New Access Rule Wizard** page.

16. Next, we'll create the rule for the DHCP reply from the ISA firewall:

17. In the **Microsoft Internet Security and Acceleration Server 2006** management console, expand the server name, and click the **Firewall Policy** node.

18. In the **Firewall Policy** node, click **Create Access Rule** on the **Tasks** tab in the Task pane.

19. On the **Welcome to the New Access Rule Wizard** page, enter a name for the rule in the **Access Rule name** text box. In this example, we'll name it **DHCP Reply**. Click **Next**.

20. On the **Rule Action** page, select **Allow** and click **Next**.

21. On the **Protocols** page, select the **Selected protocols** option from the **Apply the rule to this protocols** list. Click **Add**.

22. In the **Protocols** dialog box, click the **Infrastructure** folder and double-click the **DHCP (reply)** entry. Click **Close**.

23. Click **Next** on the **Protocols** page.

24. On the **Access Rule Sources** page, click **Add**.

25. In the **Add Network Entities** dialog box, click the **Networks** folder and double-click the **Local Host** entry. Click **Close**.

26. Click **Next** on the **Access Rule Sources** page.

27. On the **Access Rule Destinations** page, click **Add**.

28. In the **Add Network Entities** dialog box, click the **Networks** folder and double-click the **Internal** network. If you want the ISA firewall to respond to clients from multiple Protected Networks to access the DHCP server on the ISA firewall, make sure to include those Networks, too. Click **Close**.

29. Click **Next** on the **Access Rule Destinations** page.

30. Click **Next** on the **User Sets** page.

31. Click **Finish** on the **Completing the New Access Rule Wizard** page.

Summary

In this chapter, we discussed the ISA 2006 firewall's VPN remote access server and VPN gateway features. The VPN remote access server supports both PPTP and L2TP/IPSec connections from remote access VPN clients. The ISA 2006 firewall's VPN gateway supports IPSec tunnel mode, PPTP and L2TP/IPSec connections from other VPN gateways. We also discussed other topics related to the ISA firewall's support for VPN clients and gateways, including EAP authentication and DHCP server configuration.

ISA 2006 Stateful Inspection and Application Layer Filtering

Solutions in this chapter:

- **Application Filters**
- **Web Filters**

☑ **Summary**

Introduction

The ISA firewall is able to perform both stateful filtering and stateful application layer inspection. Its stateful filtering feature set makes it a network layer stateful firewall in the same class as any hardware firewall that performs stateful filtering at the network and transport layers. Stateful filtering is often referred to as *stateful packet inspection*, which is a bit of a misnomer because packets are Layer 3 entities, and to assess connection state, Layer 4 information must be assessed.

However, in contrast to traditional packet filter-based stateful hardware firewalls, the ISA firewall is able to perform stateful application layer inspection, which enables it to fully inspect the communication streams passed by it from one network to another. In contrast to stateful filtering where only the network and transport layer information is filtered, true stateful inspection requires that the firewall be able to analyze and make decisions on all layers of the communication, including the most important layer, the application layer.

The Web filters perform stateful application layer inspection on communications handled by the ISA firewall's Web Proxy components. The Web Proxy handles connections for HTTP, HTTPS (SSL), and HTTP tunneled FTP connections. The Web filters take apart the HTTP communications and expose them to the ISA firewall's application layer inspection mechanisms, examples of which include the HTTP Security filter and the OWA forms-based authentication filter.

The Application filters are responsible for performing stateful application layer inspection on non-HTTP protocols, such as SMTP, POP3, and DNS. These application layer filters also take apart the communication and expose them to deep stateful inspection at the ISA firewall.

Web and Application filters can perform two duties:

- Protocol access
- Protocol security

Protocol access allows access to protocols that require secondary connections. Complex protocols may require more than one connection, either inbound or outbound through the ISA firewall. SecureNAT clients require these filters to use complex protocols because the SecureNAT client does not have the power of the Firewall client. In contrast to the Firewall client that can work together with the ISA firewall to negotiate complex protocols, the SecureNAT client is a simple NAT client of the ISA firewall and requires the aid of application filters to connect using these complex protocols (such as FTP or MMS).

Protocol security protects the connections moving through the ISA firewall. Protocol security filters such as the SMTP and DNS filters inspect the communications that apply to those filters and block connections that are deemed outside of secure parameters. Some of these filters block connections that may represent buffer overflows (such as the DNS and SMTP filters), and some of them perform much deeper inspection and block connections or content based on policy (such as the SMTP Message Screener).

Application Filters

The ISA firewall includes a number of Application filters. In this section, we discuss:

- SMTP filter
- DNS filter

- POP Intrusion Detection filter
- SOCKS V4 filter
- FTP Access filter
- H.323 filter
- MMS filter
- PNM filter
- PPTP filter
- RPC filter
- RTSP filter

The SMTP Filter

The ISA firewall's SMTP filter configuration interface can be accessed by opening the **Microsoft Internet Security and Acceleration Server 2006** management console, expand the server name, and then expand the **Configuration** node. Click the **Add-ins** node. In the Details Pane, double-click the **SMTP Filter**. Click the **SMTP Commands** tab. (See Figure 21.1.)

The settings on the **SMTP Commands** tab are mediated by the SMTP filter component. The SMTP Message Screener does not evaluate SMTP commands and does not protect against buffer overflow conditions. The commands in the list are limited to a predefined length. If an incoming SMTP connection sends a command that exceeds the length allowed, the connection is dropped. In addition, if a command that is sent over the SMTP channel is not on this list, it is dropped. (See Figure 21.1.)

Figure 21.1 The SMTP Commands Tab

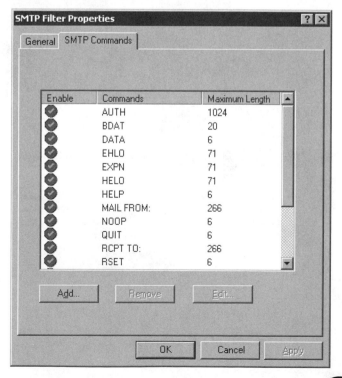

The DNS Filter

The ISA firewall's DNS filter protects the DNS server published by the ISA firewall using Server Publishing Rules. You can access the configuration interface for the DNS filter's attack prevention configuration page in the **Intrusion Detection** dialog box. Expand the server name and then expand the **Configuration** node. Click the **General** node.

In the Details Pane, click the **Enable Intrusion Detection and DNS Attack Detection** link. In the **Intrusion Detection** dialog box, click the **DNS Attacks** tab. On the **DNS Attacks** tab, put a checkmark in the **Enable detection and filtering of DNS attacks** checkbox. (See Figure 21.2.)

Figure 21.2 The DNS Attacks Tab

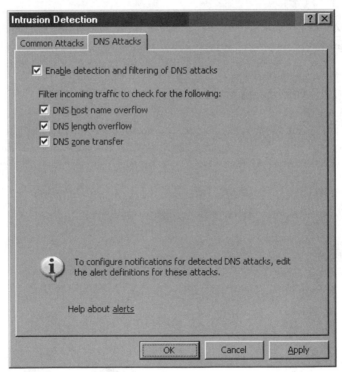

Once detection is enabled, you can then enable prevention. You can protect yourself from three attacks:

- DNS host name overflow
- DNS length overflow
- DNS zone transfer

The **DNS host name overflow** and **DNS length overflow** attacks are DNS denial-of-service (DoS) type attacks. The DNS DoS attack exploits the difference in size between a DNS query and a DNS response, in which all of the network's bandwidth is consumed by bogus DNS queries. The attacker uses the DNS servers as "amplifiers" to multiply the DNS traffic.

The attacker begins by sending small DNS queries to each DNS server that contains the spoofed IP address of the intended victim. The responses returned to the small queries are much larger, so if a large number of responses are returned at the same time, the link will become congested and denial of service will take place.

One solution to this problem is for administrators to configure DNS servers to respond with a "refused" response, which is much smaller than a name resolution response, when they receive DNS queries from suspicious or unexpected sources.

You can find detailed information for configuring DNS servers to prevent this problem in the U.S. Department of Energy's Computer Incident Advisory Capability information bulletin J-063, available at www.ciac.org/ciac/bulletins/j-063.shtml.

The POP Intrusion Detection Filter

The POP Intrusion Detection filter protects POP3 servers you publish via ISA firewall Server Publishing Rules from POP services buffer overflow attacks. There is no configuration interface for the POP Intrusion Detection filter.

The SOCKS V4 Filter

The SOCKS v4 filter is used to accept SOCKS version 4 connection requests from applications written to the SOCKS version 4 specification. Windows operating systems should never need to use the SOCKS filter because you can install the Firewall client on these machines to transparently authenticate to the ISA firewall and support complex protocol negotiation.

For hosts that cannot be configured as Firewall clients, such as Linux and Mac hosts, you can use the SOCKS v4 filter to support them. The SOCKS v4 filter is disabled by default. To enable the filter, open the **Microsoft Internet Security and Acceleration Server 2006** management console, expand the server name, and then expand the **Configuration** node. Click the **Add-ins** node. In the Details Pane, right-click the **SOCKS V4** filter and click **Enable**.

You will need to configure the SOCKS V4 filter to listen on the specific network(s) for which you want it to accept connections. Double-click the **SOCKS V4** filter. In the **SOCKS V4 Filter Properties** dialog box, click the **Networks** tab. On the **Networks** tab, you can configure the **Port** on which the SOCKS filter listens for SOCKS client connections. Next, put a checkmark in the checkbox next to the network for which you want the SOCKS filter to accept connections. Click **Apply** and then click **OK**. (See Figure 21.3.)

Figure 21.3 The SOCKS V4 Filter Properties Dialog Box

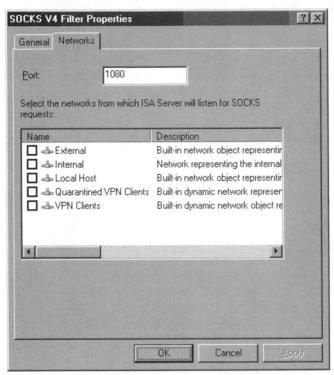

The SOCKS v4 filter supports SOCKS v4.3 client applications. The SOCKS filter is a generic sockets filter that supports all client applications that are designed to support the SOCKS v4.3 specification. The SOCKS filter performs duties similar to that performed by the Firewall client. However, there are some significant differences between how SOCKS and the Firewall client work:

- The Firewall client is a generic Winsock Proxy client application. All applications designed to the Windows Sockets specification will automatically use the Firewall client.

- The SOCKS filter supports applications written to the SOCKS v4.3 specification.

- When the Firewall client is installed on the client machine, all Winsock applications automatically use the Firewall client, and user credentials are automatically sent to the ISA firewall. In addition, the Firewall client will work with the ISA firewall service to manage complex protocols that require secondary connections (such as FTP, MMS, and many others).

- The SOCKS client must be configured on a per-application basis. Each application must be explicitly configured to use the ISA firewall as its SOCKS server. When the application is configured to use the ISA firewall as its SOCKS server, the SOCKS filter will manage complex protocols for the SOCKS client application.

- The SOCKS 4.3a filter included with the ISA firewall does not support authentication. SOCKS 5 introduced the capability to authenticate the client application that attempts to access content through the SOCKS proxy.

We always recommend that you use the Firewall client because of the impressive advantages it provides by allowing you the ability to authenticate all Winsock connections made through the ISA firewall. However, SOCKS is a good "second best" when you cannot install the Firewall client.

The FTP Access Filter

The FTP Access filter is used to mediate FTP connections between Protected Network clients and FTP servers on the Internet, and from external hosts and published FTP servers. The FTP Access filter supports both PASV and PORT (passive and standard) mode FTP connections.

The FTP Access filter is required for SecureNAT clients because FTP uses secondary connections for PORT-mode FTP connections. FTP is a complex protocol that requires outbound connections from the FTP PORT-mode client and new secondary inbound connections from the FTP server. While the Firewall client does not require application filter support for secondary connections, SecureNAT clients do require application layer filter support, which is why the ISA firewall dev team included the FTP Access application filter.

Stefaan Pouseele, an ISA Server MVP, has written an excellent article on the FTP protocol and how FTP challenges firewall security. Check out his article, *How the FTP Protocol Challenges Firewall Security* at http://isaserver.org/articles/How_the_FTP_protocol_Challenges_Firewall_Security.html.

There is no configuration interface for the FTP Access filter. However, if there is an Access Rule that applies to FTP connection, the right click menu on the Access Rule will allow you to **Configure FTP**. The **Configure FTP** option allows you to control whether or not FTP uploads are allowed.

The H.323 Filter

The H.323 filter is used to support H.323 connections through the ISA firewall. To configure the H.323 filter, open the **Microsoft Internet Security and Acceleration Server 2006** management console and expand the server name. Next, expand the **Configuration** node and click the **Add-ins** node. Double-click the **H.323 Filter** entry in the Details Pane.

In the **H.323 Filter Properties** dialog box, click the **Call Control** tab. You have the following options:

- Use this Gatekeeper
- Use DNS gateway lookup and LRQs for alias resolution
- Allow audio
- Allow video
- Allow T120 and application sharing

Click the **Networks** tab. On the **Networks** tab, put a checkmark in the checkbox to the left of the networks on which you want the H.323 filter to accept connections requests.

The MMS Filter

The MMS filter supports Microsoft Media Services connections through the ISA firewall for Access Rules and Server Publishing Rules. The MMS filter is an access filter that allows SecureNAT client access to the complex protocols and secondary connections required to connect to Microsoft Media Services hosted content. Firewall clients do not require the help of the MMS filter to connect to MMS servers. There is no configuration interface for the MMS filter.

The PNM Filter

The PNM filter supports connections for the Progressive Networks Media Protocol from Real Networks. The PNM filter is an access filter allowing SecureNAT client access to the complex protocols and secondary connection required to connect to Progressive Networks Media servers. There is no configuration interface for the PNM filter.

The PPTP Filter

The PPTP filter supports PPTP connections through the ISA firewall for outbound connections made through Access Rules and inbound connections made through Server Publishing Rules. The ISA firewall's PPTP filter differs from the ISA Server 2000 PPTP filter in that it supports both inbound and outbound PPTP connections. The ISA Server 2000 PPTP filter only supports outbound PPTP connections.

The PPTP filter is required by both SecureNAT and Firewall clients. In fact, a machine located on an ISA firewall protected network must be configured as a SecureNAT client to use the PPTP filter to connect to PPTP VPN servers through the ISA firewall. The reason for this is that the Firewall client does not mediate non-TCP/UDP protocols. The PPTP VPN protocol requires the use of the Generic Routing Encapsulation (GRE) protocol (IP Protocol 47) and TCP protocol 1723. The TCP session is used by PPTP for tunnel management.

When the outbound access to the PPTP protocol is enabled, the PPTP filter automatically intercepts the GRE and TCP connections made by the PPTP VPN client. You do not need to create an Access Rule allowing outbound access to TCP 1723 for VPN clients.

The RPC Filter

The RPC filter is used to mediate RPC connections to servers requiring Remote Procedure Calls (RPCs) for both outbound connections using Access Rules and inbound connections using Server Publishing Rules. This includes secure Exchange RPC publishing.

There is no configuration interface for the RPC filter.

The RTSP Filter

The RTSP filter supports Microsoft Real Time Streaming Protocol connections through the ISA firewall for Access Rules and Server Publishing Rules. The RTSP filter is an access filter that allows SecureNAT client access to the complex protocols and secondary connections required to connect to Microsoft Real Time Streaming Protocol hosted content (such as that on Windows Server 2003 Microsoft Media Servers). Firewall clients do not require the help of the MMS filter to connect to MMS servers.

There is no configuration interface for the RTSP filter.

Web Filters

ISA firewall Web filters are used to mediate HTTP, HTTPS, and FTP tunneled (Web proxied) connections through the ISA firewall. In this section, we discuss the following Web filters:

- HTTP Security filter
- ISA Server Link Translator
- Web Proxy filter
- SecurID filter
- OWA Forms–based Authentication filter

The HTTP Security Filter (HTTP Filter)

The ISA firewall's HTTP Security filter is one of the key application layer filtering and inspection mechanisms included with the ISA firewall. The HTTP Security filter allows the ISA firewall to perform application layer inspection on all HTTP communications moving through the ISA firewall and block connections that do not match your HTTP security requirements.

The HTTP Security filter is tightly tied to the Web Proxy filter. When the Web Proxy filter is bound to the HTTP protocol, all communications outbound through the ISA firewall with a destination port of TCP 80 are subjected to the HTTP Security filter's deep application layer inspection. We'll see later how to unbind the Web Proxy filter from the HTTP protocol if you do not want all communications to be scrubbed by the HTTP Security filter.

The HTTP Security filter is applied on a per–rule basis, and you can apply different HTTP filtering properties on each rule that allows outbound HTTP communications. This provides you very granular, fine-tuned control over what type of connections can move over the HTTP channel. In addition, you can bind the Web Proxy filter to other ports and enforce HTTP Security Filter policy over connections moving over alternate ports. This provides you another potent weapon against users and applications that try to subvert your network and Firewall Security policy by tunneling Web connections over alternate ports.

In this section, we discuss:

- Overview of HTTP Security Filter Settings
- HTTP Security Filter Logging
- Disabling the HTTP Security Filter for Web Requests
- Exporting and Importing HTTP Security Filter Settings
- Investigating HTTP Headers for Potentially Dangerous Applications
- Example HTTP Security Filter Policies
- Commonly Blocked Application Signatures
- The Dangers of SSL Tunneling

Overview of HTTP Security Filter Settings

The HTTP Security filter includes a number of tabs that allow you precise control over what HTTP communications are allowed through the ISA firewall on a per-rule basis. Configuration of the HTTP Security filter is done on the following tabs:

- General
- Methods
- Extensions
- Headers
- Signatures

The General Tab

On the **General** tab, you can configure the following options (see Figure 21.4):

- Maximum header length
- Payload length
- Maximum URL length
- Verify normalization
- Block high bit characters
- Block responses containing Windows executable content

Figure 21.4 The General Tab

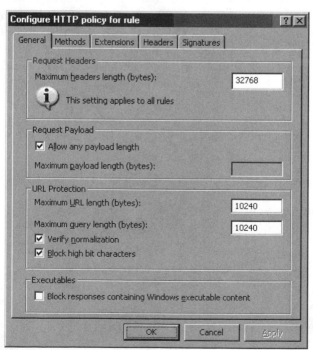

The **Maximum headers length (bytes)** option allows you to configure the maximum length of all headers included in a request HTTP communication. This setting applies to *all* rules that use the HTTP Security filter. This setting protects you from attacks that try to overflow Web site buffers by sending excessively long headers to the Web server. If you set the value too low, some applications on your site might not work correctly. If you set it too high, intruders may be able to construct a special HTTP request that could exploit known and unknown buffer overflow issues with your Web site or Web server. You might want to start with a value of 10,000 bytes and work upward from there. Your Web site administrator should be able to help you with the maximum header length required for sites your ISA firewall protects.

In the **Request Payload** frame, you have the option to **Allow any payload length** or to set a specific maximum payload length. The payload is the part of the HTTP communication that is not part of the HTTP header or command structure. For example, if you allow users to post content to your Web site (an ordering form or a discussion forum), you can set a limit on the length of their posts by unchecking the **Allow any payload length** checkbox and entering a custom value in the **Maximum payload length (bytes)** text box. Again, you may want to discuss your Web site's requirements with your Web site administrator or Web programmer to get specific details on maximum payload length requirements for your protected Web sites.

There are several options in the **URL Protection** frame. The **Maximum URL length (bytes)** option allows you to set the maximum URL that the user can send through the ISA firewall when making a request through the firewall for a Web site. Exploits can send excessively long URLs in an attempt to execute a buffer overflow or other attack against a Web server. The default value is **10240**, but you can increase or decrease this value based on your own site's custom requirements. The **Maximum query length (bytes)** value allows you to set the maximum length of the query portion of the URL. The query part of the URL appears after a question mark (?) in the request URL. The default value is **10240**, but you can make it longer or shorter, based on your requirements. Keep in mind that the **Maximum URL length** must be longer than the **Maximum query length** because the query is part of the URL.

The **Verify normalization** option is also included in the **URL Protection** frame. *Normalization* is the process of decoding so-called "escaped" characters. Web servers can receive requests that are encoded using escaped characters. One of the most common examples is when there is a space in the URL, as in the URL http://msfirewall.org/Dir%20One/default%20file.htm. The %20 is an "escape" character representing a "space." The problem is that bad guys can also encode the "%" character and perform what is called "double encoded" requests. Double encoding can be used to attack Web servers. When the **Verify Normalization** option is selected, the HTTP Security filter will normalize or decode the request twice. If the request of the first and second decodings is not the same, the HTTP Security filter will drop the request. This prevents "double encoding" attacks. You should enable this feature, but keep in mind that poorly designed Web sites and Web applications are not always security aware, and may actually accept and require double encoded requests. If that is the case for sites you want to access on the Internet or for sites you publish through the ISA firewall, you will need to disable this option.

The **Block high bit characters** option allows you to block HTTP requests that include URLs with high bit characters in them. High bit characters are used by many languages that use extended character sets, so if you find that you can't access Web sites that use these extended character sets in their URLs, you will need to disable this option.

The **Block responses containing Windows executable content** option allows you to prevent users from downloading files that are Windows executable files (such as .exe files, but any file extension can be used on a Windows executable). The HTTP Security filter is able to determine if the file is a Windows executable because the response will begin with an **MZ**. This can be very helpful when you need to prevent your users from downloading executables through the ISA firewall.

The Methods Tab

You can control what HTTP methods are used through an Access Rule or Web Publishing Rule using the settings on the **Methods** tab (see Figure 21.5). You have three options:

- Allow all methods

- Allow only specified methods

- Block specified methods (allow all others)

Figure 21.5 The Methods Tab

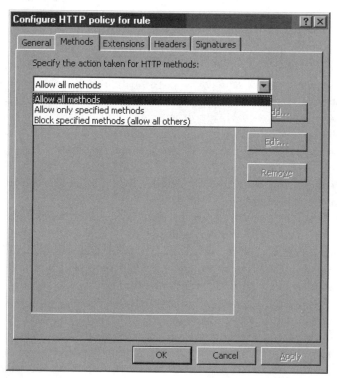

HTTP methods are HTTP commands that hosts can send to a Web server to perform specific actions; for example, GET, PUT, and POST. There are others that you, as a network and firewall administrator might not be familiar with, such as HEAD, SEARCH, and CHECKOUT. There are other methods that are proprietary and used by specific Web applications, such as Outlook Web Access.

The **Allow all methods** option allows you to allow HTTP methods used in an HTTP communication through the ISA firewall.

The **Allow only specified methods** option allows you to specify the exact methods you want to allow through the ISA firewall. If you can identify what methods are required by your Web site and Web application, then you can allow those only and block any other method. Other methods could be used to compromise your Web site, so if they're not needed, block them.

The **Block specified methods (allow all others)** option allows you to allow all methods except those specific methods you want to allow. This option provides you a bit more latitude in that even if you don't know all the methods your site might require, you might know some that are definitely not required. One example might be the POST method. If you don't allow users to post content to your Web site, then there's no reason to allow the POST method, and you can explicitly block it.

When you select either the **Allow only specified methods** or the **Block specified methods (allow all others)** option, you need to click the **Add** button to add the method you want to allow or block. The **Method** dialog box appears after clicking the **Add** button.

In the **Add** dialog box, you enter the method in the **Method** text box (Figure 21.6). You might also want to add a description of this method in the **Description** text box. This helps you remember what the method does and helps the next person who might need to manage your ISA firewall and isn't aware of the insides of the HTTP protocol command set.

Figure 21.6 The Methods Dialog Box

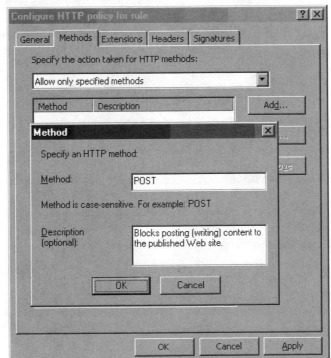

The Extensions Tab

On the **Extensions** tab, you have the following options (see Figure 21.7):

- Allow all extensions

- Allow only specified extensions

- Block specified extensions (allow all others)

- Block requests containing ambiguous extensions

Figure 21.7 The Extensions Tab

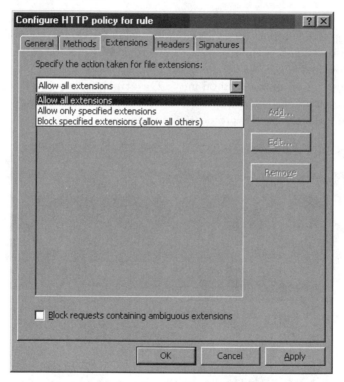

You can control what file extensions are allowed to be requested through the ISA firewall. This is extremely useful when you want to block users from requesting certain file types through the ISA firewall. For example, you can block users from accessing .exe, .com, .zip, and any other file extension through the ISA firewall.

The **Allow all extensions** option allows you to configure the Access Rule or Web Publishing Rule to allow users access to any type of file based on file extension through the ISA firewall. The **Allow only specified extensions** option allows you to specify the precise file extensions that users can access through the ISA firewall. The **Block specified extensions (allow all others)** option allows you to block specified file extensions that you deem dangerous.

If you select the **Allow only specified extensions** or **Block specified extensions (allow all others)** option, you need to click the **Add** button and add the extensions you want to allow or block.

The **Extension** dialog box appears after you click the **Add** button. Enter the name of the extension in the **Extension** text box. For example, if you want to block access to .exe files, enter **.exe**. Enter a description if you like in the **Description (optional)** text box. Click **OK** to save the new extension. (See Figure 21.8.)

Figure 21.8 The Extensions Dialog Box

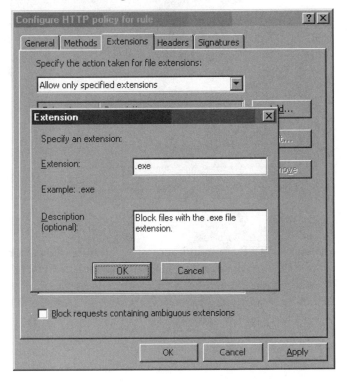

The Headers Tab

On the **Headers** tab, you have the following options (see Figure 21.9):

- Allow all headers except the following
- Server header
- Via header

Figure 21.9 The Headers Tab

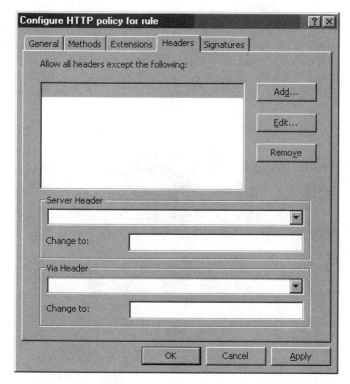

An HTTP header contains HTTP communication specific information that is included in HTTP requests made from a Web client (such as your Web browser) and HTTP responses sent back to the Web client from a Web server. These headers perform multiple functions that determine the status or state of the HTTP communications and other characteristics of the HTTP session.

Examples of common HTTP headers include:

- Content-length

- Pragma

- User-Agent

- Accept-Encoding

You can accept all HTTP headers or you can block certain specific HTTP headers. There are certain HTTP headers you might always want to block, such as the P2P-Agent header, which is used by many peer-to-peer applications. If you want to block a specific HTTP header, click the **Add** button.

In the **Header** dialog box, select either the **Request headers** or **Response headers** option from the **Search in** drop-down list. In the **HTTP header** text box, enter the HTTP header you want to block. Click **OK**. (See Figure 21.10.)

Figure 21.10 The Header Dialog Box

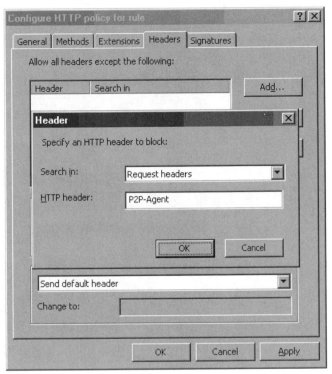

You can configure the Server Header returned in the HTTP responses by making a selection in the **Server Header** drop-down list. The Server Header is an HTTP header that the Web server sends back to the Web client informing the client of the type of Web server to which the client is connecting. Intruders can use this information to attack a Web server. You have the options to:

- Send original header
- Strip header from response
- Modify header in response

The **Send original header** option lets the header sent by the Web server go unchanged. The **Strip header from response** option allows the ISA firewall to remove the Server Header, and the **Modify header in response** allows you to change the header. You should change the header to confuse the attacker. Since this header isn't required by Web clients, you can change it to something like **Private** or **CompanyName** or anything else you like.

These options all help to prevent (or at least slow down) attackers. Attackers will have to expend more effort and use alternate methods to "fingerprint" your Web server. (See Figure 21.11.)

Figure 21.11 The Server Header Option

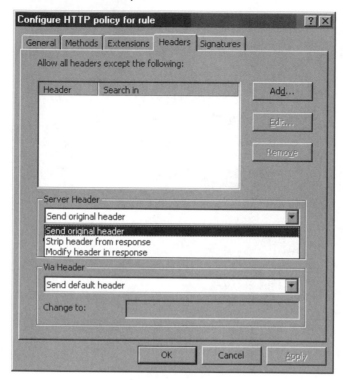

The **Via Header** option allows you to control the Via Header sent to the Web client. When Web Proxy servers are located between a client and Web server, the Web Proxy server will insert a Via Header in the HTTP communication informing the client that the request was handled by the Web Proxy server in transit. Each Web Proxy server in the request path can add its own Via Header, and each sender along the response path removes its own Via Header and forwards the response to the server specified in the next Via Header on the Via Header "stack." The **Via Header** settings allows you to change the name your ISA firewall includes in its own Via Header and enables you to hide the name of your ISA firewall. The default setting is for your ISA firewall to include its own Computer name in the Via Header.

You have two options:

- Send default header
- Modify header in request and response

The **Send default header** option leave the Via Header unchanged. The **Modify header in request and response** option allows you to change the name included in the Via Header inserted by your ISA firewall. We recommend that you change this to hide the actual name of your ISA firewall to prevent attackers from learning the actual name of your ISA firewall machine. (See Figure 21.12.)

Enter the alternate Via Header in the **Change To** text box.

Figure 21.12 The Via Header

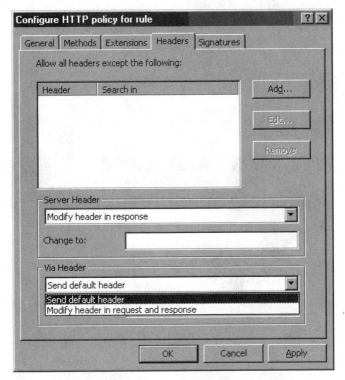

The Signatures Tab

The **Signatures** tab allows you to control access through the ISA firewall based on HTTP signatures you create. These signatures are based on strings contained in the following components of an HTTP communication:

- Request URL
- Request headers
- Request body
- Response headers
- Response body

You access the **Signature** dialog box by clicking the **Add** button. (See Figure 21.13.)

Figure 21.13 The Signatures Tab

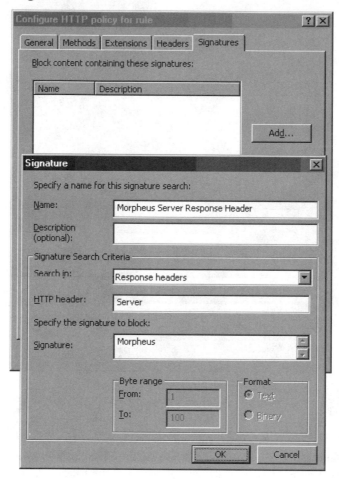

In the **Signature** dialog box, enter a name for the signature in the **Name** text box and a description of the signature in the **Description** text box. This is especially helpful so that you know the purpose and rationale for this signature.

In the **Search in** drop-down list, select where you want the ISA firewall to search for the specified string. You have the follow options:

- **Request URL**   When you select this option, you can enter a string that when found in the Web client's request URL, the connection is blocked. For example, if you wanted to prevent all requests to sites that have the string **Kazaa** in the URL included in the Web client's request, you enter **Kazaa** in the **Signature** text box.

- **Request headers**   When you select this option, you enter the specific HTTP header you want the ISA firewall to check in the **HTTP header** text box and then enter the string in the header you want the ISA firewall to block in the **Signature** text box. For example, if you want to block eDonkey P2P applications, you can select this option and then **User-Agent** in the **HTTP header** text box. In the **Signature** text box, you then enter **ed2k**. Note that this option gives you more granular control than you would have if you just blocked headers in the **Headers** tab. If you block a specific header in the **Headers** tab, you end up blocking all HTTP communications that use that specific header. By creating a signature that incorporates a specific header, you can allow that HTTP header for all communications that do not include the header value you enter for the signature.

- **Request body**   You can block HTTP communications based on the body of the Web request outside of that contained in the HTTP commands and headers. While this is a very powerful feature, it has the potential to consume a great deal of resources on the ISA firewall computer. For this reason, you need to configure the byte range you want the ISA firewall to inspect in the **Byte range From** and **To** text boxes. We don't have any explicit recommendations on specific entries you might want to include in this section, but will provide updates on www.isaserver.org when we do.

- **Response headers**   When you select this option, you enter the specific HTTP header you want to block based on the HTTP response returned by the Web server. You enter the specific HTTP header in the **HTTP header** text box and the HTTP header value in the **Signature** text box.

- **Response body**   The response body option works the same as the **Request body** option, except it applies to the content returned to the Web client from the Web server. For example, if you want to block Web pages that contain specific strings that are identified as dangerous or inappropriate, you can create a signature to block those strings. Keep this in mind when reading about the latest Web-based attack and create a signature that blocks connections that employ such an attack.

Figure 21.14 shows some example signatures blocking some commonly encountered applications that might be considered a major security risk for corporate networks.

Figure 21.14 Example Signatures

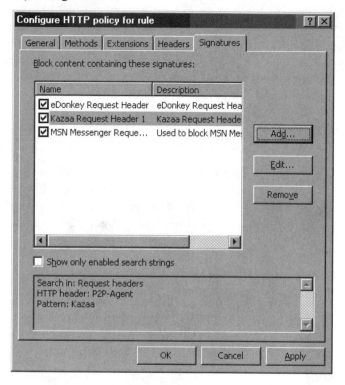

HTTP Security Filter Logging

How do you know if your security filters are working? One way to determine the effectiveness of the entries you've made in the HTTP Security filter is to use the ISA firewall's built-in log viewer. Perform the following steps to configure the ISA firewall's built-in log viewer to view HTTP Security Filter actions:

1. In the **Microsoft Internet Security and Acceleration Server 2006** management console, expand the server name and click the **Monitoring** node in the left pane of the console.

2. In the **Monitoring** node, click the **Logging** tab. In the **Tasks** tab of the Task Pane, click the **Start Query** link.

3. Right-click one of the column headers and click the **Add/Remove Columns** command.

4. In the **Add/Remove Columns** dialog box, click the **Filter Information** entry in the **Available Columns** list and click **Add**. The **Filter Information** entry now appears in the list of **Displayed columns**. Click **OK**.

5. Issue a request from a client behind the ISA firewall that would be blocked by your HTTP Security Filter settings. Figure 21.15 shows an example of a connection that was blocked because the URL contained a string that was disallowed by the HTTP Security filter.

Figure 21.15 Log File Entries Showing the HTTP Security Filter Blocking a Connection

Client IP	Destinatio...	Destination Port	Protocol	HTTP Method	URL	Filter Information
10.0.0.5	10.0.0.1	8080	http	GET	http://www.cisco.com/	Blocked by the HTTP Security filter: URL contains sequences which are disallowed
10.0.0.5	10.0.0.1	8080	Unidentifie...	-	-	-
10.0.0.1	10.0.0.2	53	DNS	-	-	-
192.168.1.70	192.168.1.34	53	DNS	-	-	-
10.0.0.5	10.0.0.1	8080	Unidentifie...	-	-	-
10.0.0.5	10.0.0.1	8080	http	GET	http://www.cisco.com/	Blocked by the HTTP Security filter: URL contains sequences which are disallowed

Exporting and Importing HTTP Security Filter Settings

An HTTP policy can be exported from or imported into an Access Rule that uses the HTTP protocol or a Web Publishing Rule. The **HttpFilterConfig.vbs** script in the SDK kit located at http://www.microsoft.com/downloads/details.aspx?familyid=16682C4F-7645-4279-97E4-9A0C73C5162E&displaylang=en can be used to export an existing HTTP policy that has already been configured in an Access Rule or Web Publishing Rule or an HTTP policy that has already been exported to a file can be imported into an existing Access Rule or Web Publishing Rule.

The **HttpFilterConfig.vbs** script greatly simplifies configuration of complex HTTP policies that include multiple entries for parameters such as signature, file extensions, and headers. We recommend that you export your HTTP policies after you create them in the **Microsoft Internet Security and Acceleration Server 2006** management console.

In this section, we discuss how you can export and import an HTTP policy from and to a Web Publishing Rule.

Exporting an HTTP Policy from a Web Publishing Rule

HTTP policies can be exported from an Access Rule or Web Publishing Rule using the **HttpFilterConfig.vbs** file located on the ISA 2006 CD-ROM. Follow these steps to export the HTTP policy from an existing Web Publishing Rule:

1. Copy the **HttpFilterConfig.vbs** file to the root of the C: drive.

2. Open a command prompt and change the focus to the root of the C: drive. Enter the following command and press **Enter** (notice that if the rule name has a space in it you must enclose the name in quotes):

   ```
   C:\Httpfilterconfig.vbs import "Publish OWA Site"
   c:\webpol.xml
   ```

3. You will see a dialog box confirming that the information was successfully imported into the rule (see Figure 21.16).

Figure 21.16 Successful Import Dialog Box

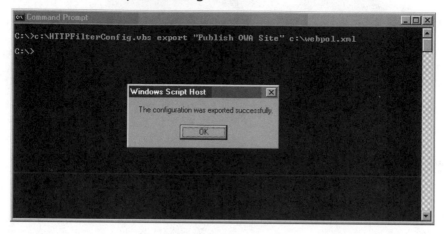

Importing an HTTP Policy into a Web Publishing Rule

HTTP policies can be imported into Access Rules that include the HTTP protocol and Web Publishing Rules. We use the same script we used when exporting an HTTP policy, the **HttpFilterConfig.vbs** file. To import an HTTP policy saved to an .xml file into a Web Publishing Rule named **Publish OWA Site**:

1. Copy both the .xml file and the **HttpFilterConfig.vbs** file from the ISA 2006 CD-ROM to the root of the C: drive. In this example, the .xml file is named **webpol.xml**.

2. Open a command prompt and change the focus to the root of the C: drive. Enter the following command and press **Enter** (notice that if the rule name has spaces in it, you must enclose the name in quotes):

   ```
   C:\Httpfilterconfig.vbs import "Publish OWA Site"
   c:\webpol.xml
   ```

3. You will see a dialog box confirming that the information was successfully imported into the rule (see Figure 21.17).

Figure 21.17 Successful Import Dialog Box

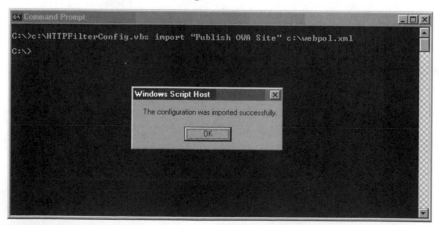

Investigating HTTP Headers for Potentially Dangerous Applications

One of your primary tasks as an ISA firewall administrator is to investigate characteristics of network traffic with the goal of blocking new and ever more dangerous network applications. These dangerous applications might be peer-to-peer applications, instant messaging applications, or other applications that hide by wrapping themselves in an HTTP header. Many vendors now wrap their applications in an HTTP header in an attempt to subvert your Firewall policy. Your goal as an ISA firewall administrator is to subvert the vendors' attempt to subvert your Network Usage policy.

As you can imagine, the vendors of these applications aren't very cooperative when it comes to getting information on how to prevent their applications from violating your firewall security. You'll often have to figure out this information for yourself, especially for new and obscure applications.

Your main tool in fighting the war against network scumware is a protocol analyzer. Two of the most popular protocol analyzers are Microsoft Network Monitor and the freeware tool Ethereal. Both are excellent, the only major downside of Ethereal being that you need to install a network driver to make it work correctly. Since the WinPcaP driver required by Ethereal hasn't been regression tested against the ISA firewall software, it's hard to know whether it may cause problems with firewall stability or performance. For this reason, we'll use the built-in version of Network Monitor included with Windows Server 2003 in the following examples.

Let's look at a couple of examples of how you can determine how to block some dangerous applications. One such application is eDonkey, a peer-to-peer file-sharing application. The first step is to start Network Monitor and run a network monitor trace while running the eDonkey application on a client that accesses the Internet through the ISA firewall. The best way to start is by configuring Network Monitor to listen on the Internal interface of the ISA firewall, or whatever interface eDonkey or other offending applications use to access the Internet through the ISA firewall.

Stop the trace after running the offending application for a while. Since we're only interested in Web connections moving through TCP port 80, we can filter out all other communications in the trace. We can do this with Display filters.

Click the **Display** menu and then click the **Filter** command. In the **Display Filter** dialog box, double-click the **Protocol == Any** entry. (See Figure 21.18.)

Figure 21.18 The Display Filter Dialog Box

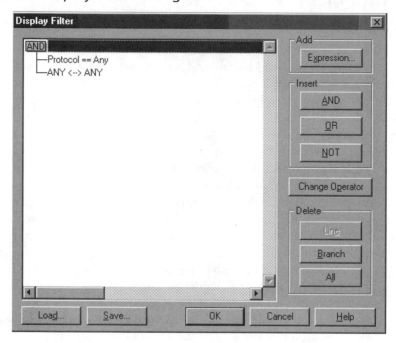

In the **Expression** dialog box, click the **Protocol** tab and then click the **Disable All** button. In the list of **Disabled Protocols**, click the **HTTP** protocol, click the **Enable** button, and then click **OK**. (See Figure 21.19.)

Figure 21.19 The Expression Dialog Box

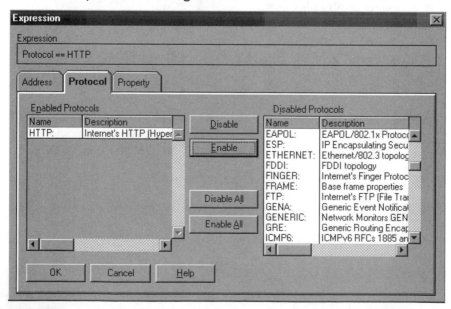

Click **OK** in the **Display Filter** dialog box. The top pane of the Network Monitor console now only displays HTTP connections. A good place to start is by looking at the **GET** requests, which appear as **GET Request from Client** in the **Description** column. Double-click on the GET requests and expand the **HTTP: Get Request from Client** entry in the middle form. This displays a list of request headers.

In Figure 21.20, you can see that one of the request headers appears to be unusual (only if you have experience looking at Network Monitor traces; don't worry, it won't take long before you get good at this). The **HTTP: User-Agent=ed2k** seems like it might be specific for eDonkey2000. We can use this information to create an HTTP Security Filter entry to block the **User-Agent** Request Header value **ed2k**.

Figure 21.20 The Network Monitor Display Window

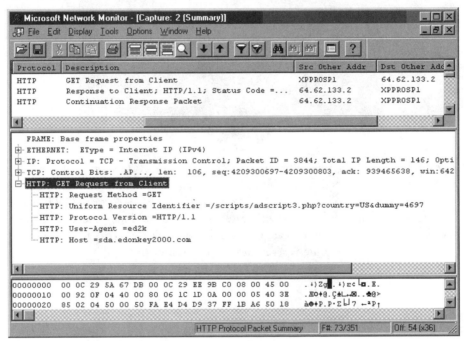

You can do this by creating an HTTP Security Filter signature using these values. Figure 21.21 shows what the HTTP Security Filter signature would look like to block the eDonkey application.

Figure 21.21 The Signature Dialog Box

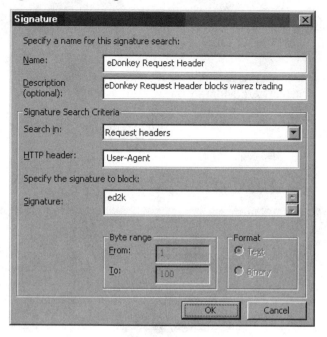

Another example of a dangerous application is Kazaa. Figure 21.22 shows a frame displaying the GET request the Kazaa client sends through the ISA firewall. In the list of HTTP headers, you can see one that can be used to help block the Kazaa client. The **P2P-Agent** HTTP request header can be blocked completely, or you can create a signature and block the **P2P-Agent** HTTP request header when it has the value **Kazaa**. You could also block the **Host** header in the HTTP request header when the value is set as **desktop.kazaa.com**.

Figure 21.22 Network Monitor Display Showing Kazaa Request Headers

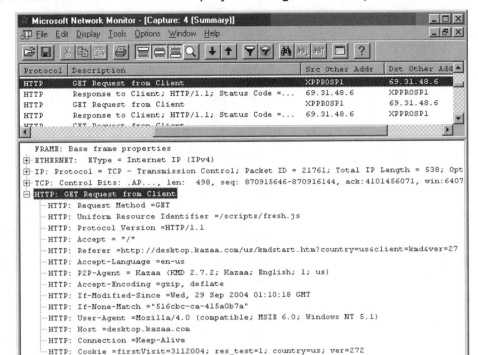

Example HTTP Security Filter Policies

Creating HTTP Security Filter policies can take some time. You need to run the required applications and then determine the required methods, extensions, headers, and other signatures that are specific for your application. While the effort is well spent, sometimes you need to get critical applications up and running quickly.

For this reason, we include a couple of example HTTP Security Filter policies you can use right away to protect IIS Web sites and Outlook Web Access sites.

Table 21.1 provides the defaults of a good default Web site HTTP Security Filter policy you can use. This policy allows the most common methods required for simple Web sites and restricts extensions that might allow an attacker to compromise your site. There are also several HTTP signatures included that block common strings that Internet criminals might use to compromise your Web site or server.

Table 21.1 Example HTTP Security Filter for Generic Web Sites

Tab	Parameter
General	Maximum header length is 32768.
	Allow any payload length is selected.
	Maximum URL length is 260.
	Maximum query length is 4096.
	Verify normalization is selected.
	Block high bit characters is not selected.
Methods	Allow only specified methods:
	GET
	HEAD
	POST
Extensions	Block specified extensions (allow all others):
	.exe
	.bat
	.cmd
	.com
	.htw
	.ida
	.idq
	.htr
	.idc
	.shtm
	.shtml
	.stm
	.printer
	.ini
	.log
	.pol
	.dat
Headers	No changes from the default.
Signatures (Request URL)	Block content containing these signatures
	..
	./
	\

Table 21.1 Continued

Tab	Parameter
	:
	%
	&
Tab	Parameter

Table 21.2 provides settings you can use to configure an HTTP Security Filter policy for OWA publishing. Notice the methods required by OWA. You can see these in action by using the ISA firewall's built-in log filter and watching the HTTP Methods column.

Table 21.2 HTTP Security Filter Settings for OWA Web Publishing Rules

Tab	Parameter
General	Maximum header length is 32768.
	Allow any payload length is selected.
	Maximum URL length is 260.
	Maximum query length is 4096.
	Verify normalization is selected.
	Block high bit characters is not selected.
Methods	Allow only specified methods:
	GET
	POST
	PROPFIND
	PROPPATCH
	BPROPPATCH
	MKCOL
	DELETE
	BDELETE
	BCOPY
	MOVE
	SUBSCRIBE
	BMOVE
	POLL
	SEARCH

Continued

Table 21.2 Continued

Tab	Parameter
Extensions	Block specified extensions (allow all others):
	.exe
	.bat
	.cmd
	.com
	.htw
	.ida
	.idq
	.htr
	.idc
	.shtm
	.shtml
	.stm
	.printer
	.ini
	.log
	.pol
	.dat
Headers	No changes from the default.
Signatures (Request URL)	Block content containing these signatures
	./
	\
	:
	%
	&

Table 21.3 shows entries for an HTTP Security Filter policy you can use for an RPC-over-HTTP Web Publishing Rule. Notice the unusual HTTP methods used by the Outlook 2003 RPC-over-HTTP protocol.

Table 21.3 HTTP Security Filter Policy Settings for RPC-over-HTTP
Web Publishing Rule

Tab	Parameter
General	Maximum headers length is 32768.
	Maximum Payload Length: 2000000000.
	Maximum URL length is 16384.
	Maximum query length is 4096.
	Verify normalization is selected.
	Block high bit characters is not selected.
Methods	Allow only specified methods:
	RPC_IN_DATA
	RPC_OUT_DATA
Extensions	No changes from the default.
Headers	No changes from the default.
Signatures (Request URL)	No changes from the default.

Commonly Blocked Headers and Application Signatures

While we consider it an entertaining pastime spending long evenings with Network Monitor and discovering how to block dangerous applications, not all ISA firewall administrators share this predilection. For those of you who need to configure your ISA firewall to protect your network from dangerous applications as soon as possible, we provide the information in Tables 7.4 and 7.5.

Table 21.4 lists the information you need to include in signatures to block commonly encountered dangerous applications. You use the information in this table to create a signature entry in the HTTP Security filter.

Table 21.4 Sample Signatures for Blocking Commonly Encountered
Dangerous Applications

Application	Location	HTTP Header	Signature
MSN Messenger	Request headers	User-Agent:	MSN Messenger
Windows Messenger	Request headers	User-Agent:	MSMSGS
Netscape 7	Request headers	User-Agent:	Netscape/7
Netscape 6	Request headers	User-Agent:	Netscape/6
AOL Messenger (and all Gecko browsers)	Request headers	User-Agent:	Gecko/

Continued

Table 21.4 Continued

Application	Location	HTTP Header	Signature
Yahoo Messenger	Request headers	Host	msg.yahoo.com
Kazaa	Request headers	P2P-Agent	Kazaa Kazaaclient:
Kazaa	Request headers	User-Agent:	KazaaClient
Kazaa	Request headers	X-Kazaa-Network:	KaZaA
Gnutella	Request headers	User-Agent:	Gnutella Gnucleus
eDonkey	Request headers	User-Agent:	e2dk
Internet Explorer 6.0	Request headers	User-Agent:	MSIE 6.0
Morpheus	Response header	Server	Morpheus
Bearshare	Response header	Server	Bearshare
BitTorrent	Request headers	User-Agent:	BitTorrent
SOAP over HTTP	Request headers Response headers	User-Agent:	SOAPAction

Table 21.5 contains some HTTP header values you can use to block dangerous applications. In contrast to signatures that require the HTTP header name and value, the entries in Table 21.5 can be configured in the **Headers** tab of the HTTP Security filter. These headers are specific for the listed dangerous applications and are not used for legitimate HTTP communications, so you do not need to specify a specific value for the HTTP headers blocked here.

Table 21.5 HTTP Headers Used to Bock Dangerous Applications

Application	Location	Type	Value
Kazaa	Headers	Request Header	X-Kazaa-Username: X-Kazaa-IP: X-Kazaa-SupernodeIP:
BitTorrent	Extensions	None	.torrent
Many peer-to-peer clients	Headers	Request Header	P2P-Agent

The ISA Server Link Translator

Link Translation solves a number of issues that may arise for external users connecting through the ISA firewall to an internal Web site.

The ISA firewall Link Translator is implemented as an ISA firewall Web filter. Because of the Link Translator's built-in functionality, and because it comes with a built-in default dictionary, you can use it right out of the box to solve many common problems encountered with proxy-based Web publishing scenarios.

For example, when pages on the internal Web site contain absolute URLs pointing to itself, the Link Translator will return the appropriate links to the external user, even when those URLs contain http:// prefixes and the external user connects to the Web site using https://.

The default Link Translator dictionary can also appropriately translate requests made to nonstandard ports. For example, if users connect to a Web site that is published on a nonstandard port, such as http://www.msfirewall.org:8181, link translation will include the port number in the URLs sent back to the external client.

When you enable link translation for a Web Publishing Rule, a Link Translation dictionary is automatically created. In most cases, you won't have to add to the default dictionary.

The default dictionary includes the following entries:

- Any occurrence on the Web site of the computer name specified on the **To** tab of the Web Publishing Rule Properties is replaced with the Web site name (or IP address). For example, if a rule redirects all requests for http://www.microsoft.com to an internal computer called SERVER1 (or 192.168.1.1), all occurrences of http://SERVER1 in the response page returned to the client are replaced with http://www.microsoft.com.

- If a nondefault port is specified on the Web listener, that port is used when replacing links on the response page. If a default port is specified, the port is removed when replacing links on the response page. For example, if the Web listener is listening on TCP port 88, the responses returned to the Web client will include links to TCP port 88.

- If the client specifies HTTPS in the request to the ISA firewall, the firewall will replace all occurrences of HTTP with HTTPS.

For example, suppose the ISA firewall publishes a site located on a machine with the internal name SERVER1. The ISA firewall publishes the site using the public name www.msfirewall.orgdocs. An external Web client then makes the following request:

```
GET /docs HTTP/1.1
Host: www.msfirewall.org
```

Note that the directory name in the request is not terminated by a slash (/). When the server running Internet Information Services (IIS) receives this request, it automatically returns a 302 response with the location header set to http://SERVER1/docs/, which is the internal name of the server followed by the directory name and terminated by a slash.

The ISA firewall's Link Translator then translates the response header value to http://www.msfirewall.org/docs/.

In this example, the following entries are automatically added to the Link Translation dictionary:

- http://SERVER1 is mapped to http://www.msfirewall.org

- http://SERVER1:80 is mapped to http://www.msfirewall.org

- https://SERVER1 is mapped to https://www.msfirewall.org

- https://SERVER1:443 is mapped to https://www.msfirewall.org

For security reasons, if an initial client request was sent via SSL, all links to the same Web server are translated to SSL. The following entries are automatically included in the Link Translation dictionary:

- http://SERVER1 is mapped to https://www.msfirewall.org

- http://SERVER1:80 is mapped to https://www.msfirewall.org

- https://SERVER1 is mapped to https://www.msfirewall.org

- https://SERVER1:443 is mapped to https://www.msfirewall.org

If the published Web site uses ports other than the default HTTP and SSL ports (for example, 88 for HTTP and 488 for SSL), links containing that port number will also be translated. For example:

- http://SERVER1:88 is mapped to http://www.msfirewall.org

- https://SERVER1:488 is mapped to https://www.msfirewall.org

In the same way, if the ISA firewall publishes the site using a Web listener on nondefault ports (for example, 85 for HTTP and 885 for SSL), links will be translated to the published ports:

- http://SERVER1 is mapped to http://www.msfirewall.org:85

- http://SERVER1:80 is mapped to http://www.msfirewall.org:85

- https://SERVER1 is mapped to https://www.msfirewall.org:885

- https://SERVER1:443 is mapped to https://www.msfirewall.org:885

While the default dictionary is effective for most simple Web publishing scenario, things get a bit stickier when you publish more complex Web sites. For more complex Web publishing scenarios, or when complex ASP code is involved (for example, with SharePoint services), it's necessary to configure dictionary entries that map to names returned by the internal Web site.

The Link Translator checks the Content-type header of the response to determine whether link translation should be applied to the body of the message. The default settings allow for link translation only MIME types belonging to the HTML document's content group. The ISA firewall's Link Translator works by first looking for a Content-type header to determine if it needs to perform translation. If no Content-type header is present, the filter will look for a Content-location header to perform translation. If neither header is present, the filter will look at the file extension.

The Link Translator maps text strings according to the following rules:

- The Link Translator searches for the longest strings, then shorter strings, and finally the default strings.

- If the Link Translator finds a matching text string, it will then look at the next character to the right to see if it is a *terminating* character. The following are considered terminating characters:

  \t \r \n ; ~ < ! " & ') $) *
  + , – / > = ? [\ ] ^ { | }

- If the Link Translator finds a terminating character immediately to the right of the string, it will perform translation on that string.

For example, consider a scenario where the Link Translation dictionary is configured to replace "sps" with "extranet.external.net" and a response page returned by the Web server includes a hard-coded link to http://Sps/SpsDocs/. The Link Translator translates the string to http://extranet.external.net/ SpsDocs/. However, if the response page includes a link to http://sps/sps-isa/, *both* instances of "sps" would be translated because they are both followed by a terminating character, resulting in http:// extranet.external.net/extranet.external.net-isa/ being sent to the external client.

Because of these potential translation issues, it's critical that you understand the behavior of link translation mapping to prevent problems with your custom Link Translator dictionaries.

Determining Custom Dictionary Entries

You must test the behavior of the Link Translator to see if any custom dictionary entries are required. SharePoint Portal Services provides a fertile test bed for testing the Link Translator. Begin your test by connecting to a published SharePoint site using an external client and testing the functionality of the published site. You should look for links pointing to internal server names and links that use the wrong prefix (for example, http instead of https).

Be aware that some links will be included in client-side scripts returned to the browser for processing. You should therefore also view the HTML source code that is returned, not just the rendered HTML in the browser.

In the case of a published SharePoint site, it may be necessary to add custom dictionary entries. For example, even though the Link Translator is enabled, the search function on the SharePoint site may return results with both the wrong prefix (http instead of https) and internal server names.

In addition, after adding custom dictionary entries to fix these problems, the source code of the search results page contains JavaScript that includes references to the wrong prefix, causing errors to be returned to the browser when trying to perform an additional search from the search results page.

For example, after adding two dictionary entries to replace "http://" with "https://" and to replace "sps" with "extranet.external.net," the returned source code included the following strings in the client-side JavaScript code:

```
f.action='http:\/\/extranet.external.net\/Search.aspx', and
http:\\\/\\\/extranet.external.net\\\/Search.aspx
```

To fix this problem, it is necessary to explicitly map the shorter string "http:" to "https:". Importantly, it is necessary to include the colon (:) in the dictionary entry. Simply mapping "http" to "https" (without the colon) causes the entire site to be inaccessible.

It should be clear to you at this point that finding the correct custom dictionary entries can involve extensive and repetitive testing. Incorrect link translation mappings can break the Web site for external clients, so we highly recommend that you test configurations in your test lab before deploying link translation in a production environment.

Configuring Custom Link Translation Dictionary Entries

Custom Link Translation dictionaries are configured on a per-rule basis. Remember, link translation is only performed on links returned by Web servers published by Web Publishing Rules; you do not configure Link Translation for outgoing requests to Internet Web servers.

To configure Link Translation:

1. Right-click the Web Publishing Rule and click **Properties**.

2. In the Web Publishing Rule's **Properties** dialog box, click the **Link Translation** tab.

3. On the **Link Translation** tab, put a checkmark in the **Replace absolute links in Web pages** checkbox. Click the **Add** button.

4. In the **Add/Edit Dictionary Item** dialog box, enter the name of the string you want replaced in returned links in the **Replace this text** text box. Enter the value you want to replace the string in the **With this text** text box. Click **OK**. (See Figure 21.23.)

Figure 21.23 Add/Edit Dictionary Text Box

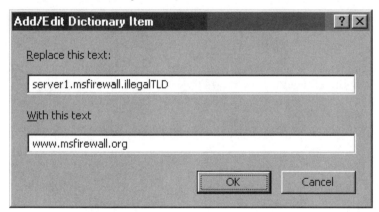

5. The dictionary entry appears in the list of dictionary entries. Click the **Content Types** button. (See Figure 21.24.)

Figure 21.24 Link Translation Tab in Web Publishing Rule Properties

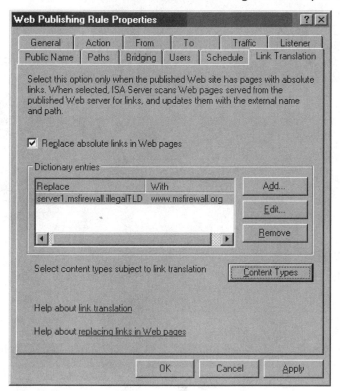

6. In the **Link Translation** dialog box, select the content types to which you want to apply Link Translation. By default, only the **HTML Documents** content type is selected. Your selection here is global and applies to all Web Publishing Rules. Even though you can create custom dictionaries for each Web Publishing Rule, the content types are the same for all dictionaries.

The Web Proxy Filter

The Web Proxy filter allows connections from hosts not configured as Web Proxy clients to be forwarded to the ISA firewall's Cache and Web Proxy components. If you want only hosts that are explicitly configured as Web Proxy clients to use the ISA firewall's Web Proxy feature set, you can unbind the Web Proxy filter by removing the checkmark from the **Web Proxy Filter** checkbox.

Figure 21.25 The HTTP Properties Dialog Box

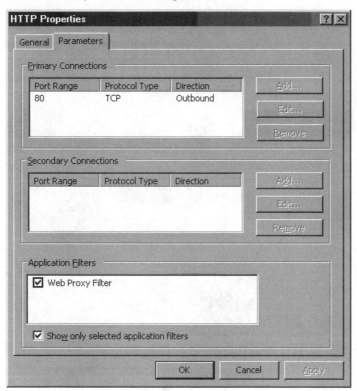

The OWA Forms-Based Authentication Filter

The OWA Forms-Based Authentication filter is used to mediate Forms-based authentication to OWA Web sites that are made accessible via ISA firewall Web Publishing Rules. Figure 21.26 shows the configuration interface for the OWA Forms-Based Authentication filter, which is accessible from the Authentication dialog box for the Web listener.

Figure 21.26 The OWA Forms-Based Authentication Dialog Box

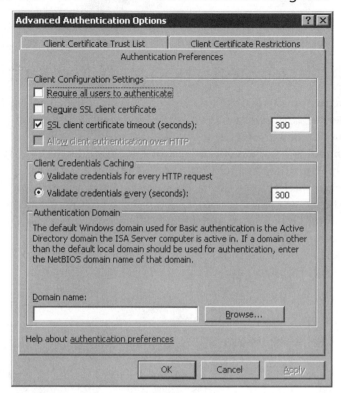

The RADIUS Authentication Filter

The RADIUS Authentication filter is used to mediate RADIUS authentication for Web Proxy clients and external hosts connecting to published Web sites via Web Publishing Rules.

The RADIUS filter is used by Web listeners when the listeners are configured to use RADIUS authentication. While the RADIUS filter provides you the ability to authenticate against any RADIUS-compliant directory (including the Active Directory), it does limit you to use only RADIUS authentication on the listener configured to use RADIUS. In contrast, when using other authentication methods, such as basic or integrated authentication, you can support multiple authentication protocols on a single Web listener.

IP Filtering and Intrusion Detection/ Intrusion Prevention

The ISA firewall performs intrusion detection and intrusion prevention. In this section, we discuss the following intrusion detection and intrusion prevention features:

- Common Attacks Detection and Prevention
- DNS Attacks Detection and Prevention
- IP Options and IP Fragment Filtering

Common Attacks Detection and Prevention

You can access the **Intrusion Detection** dialog box by opening the **Microsoft Internet Security and Acceleration Server 2006** management console, expanding the server name, and then expanding the **Configuration** node. Click the **General** node.

In the **General** node, click the **Enable Intrusion Detection and DNS Attack Detection** link. This brings up the **Common Attacks** tab.

On the **Common Attacks** tab, put a checkmark in the **Enable intrusion detection** checkbox. Put a checkmark to the left of each of the attacks you want to prevent. If you enable the **Port scan** attack, enter values for the **Detect after attacks … well-known ports** and **Detect after attacks on … ports**. (See Figure 21.27.)

You can disable logging for packets dropped by the Intrusion Detection filter by removing the checkmark from the **Log dropped packets** checkbox.

Figure 21.27 The Common Attacks Tab

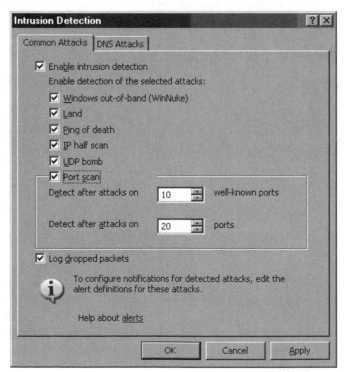

DNS Attacks Detection and Prevention

The ISA firewall's DNS filter protects DNS servers published by the ISA firewall using Server Publishing Rules. You can access the configuration interface for the DNS filter's attack prevention configuration page in the **Intrusion Detection** dialog box. Expand the server name and then expand the **Configuration** node. Click the **General** node.

In the Details Pane, click the **Enable Intrusion Detection and DNS Attack Detection** link. In the **Intrusion Detection** dialog box, click the **DNS Attacks** tab. On the **DNS Attacks** tab, put a checkmark in the **Enable detection and filtering of DNS attacks** checkbox. (See Figure 21.28.)

Once detection is enabled, you can enable prevention, and protect yourself from three attacks:

- DNS host name overflow
- DNS length overflow
- DNS zone transfer

Figure 21.28 The DNS Attacks Tab

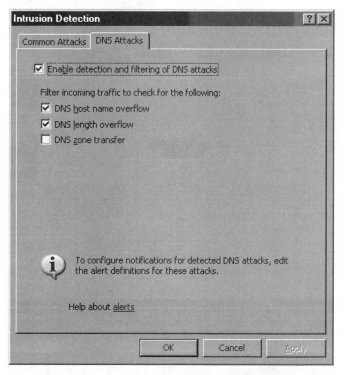

The *DNS host name overflow* and *DNS length overflow* attacks are DNS DoS type attacks. The DNS DoS attack exploits the difference in size between a DNS query and a DNS response, in which all of the network's bandwidth is tied up by bogus DNS queries. The attacker uses the DNS servers as "amplifiers" to multiply the DNS traffic.

The attacker begins by sending small DNS queries to each DNS server that contain the spoofed IP address of the intended victim. The responses returned to the small queries are much larger, so that if there are a large number of responses returned at the same time, the link will become congested and denial of service will take place.

One solution to this problem is for administrators to configure DNS servers to respond with a "refused" response, which is much smaller than a name resolution response, when they receive DNS queries from suspicious or unexpected sources.

Detailed information for configuring DNS servers to prevent this problem is contained in the U.S. Department of Energy's Computer Incident Advisory Capability information bulletin J-063, available at http://www.ciac.org/ciac/bulletins/j-063.shtml.

IP Options and IP Fragment Filtering

You can configure what IP Options are allowed through the ISA firewall and whether IP Fragments are allowed through. Figures 21.29 and 21.30 show the configuration interfaces for IP Options filtering and IP Fragment filtering. Figure 21.31 shows a dialog box warning that enabling Fragment filtering may interfere with L2TP/IPSec and streaming media services.

Figure 21.29 The IP Options Tab

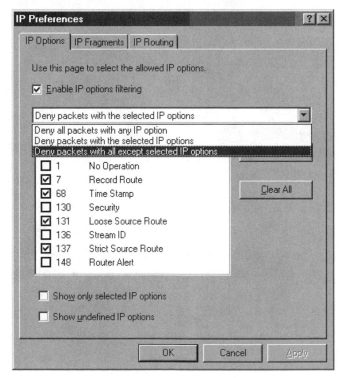

Figure 21.30 The IP Fragments Tab

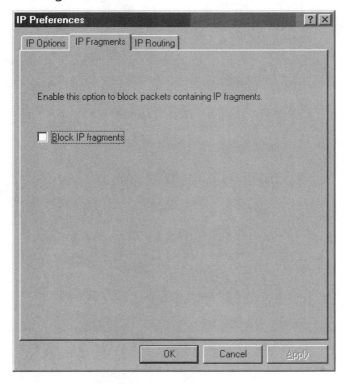

Figure 21.31 The IP Fragment Filter Warning Dialog Box

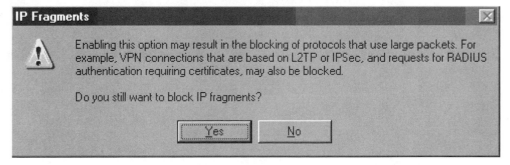

Source Routing Attack

TCP/IP supports *source routing*, which is a means to permit the sender of network data to route the packets through a specific point on the network. There are two types of source routing:

- **Strict source routing**   The sender of the data can specify the exact route (rarely used).
- **Loose source record route (LSRR)**   The sender can specify certain routers (hops) through which the packet must pass.

The source route is an option in the IP header that allows the sender to override routing decisions that are normally made by the routers between the source and destination machines. Source routing is used by network administrators to map the network, or for troubleshooting routing and communications problems. It can also be used to force traffic through a route that will provide the best performance. Unfortunately, source routing can be exploited by hackers.

If the system allows source routing, an intruder can use it to reach private internal addresses on the LAN that normally would not be reachable from the Internet, by routing the traffic through another machine that is reachable from both the Internet and the internal machine.

Source routing can be disabled on most routers to prevent this type of attack. The ISA firewall also blocks source routing by default.

Summary

In this chapter, we discussed the ISA firewall's application layer filtering feature set. We discussed the two main types of application filters employed by the ISA firewall: access filters and security filters. While we broke down the ISA firewall's filters into these two main categories, this is not to say that access filters are unsecure. Both the access filters and the security filters impose requirements that the connections meet specifications of legitimate communications using those protocols.

We finished the chapter with a discussion of the ISA firewall's intrusion detection and prevention mechanisms. You learned about common network layer attacks that can be launched against the ISA firewall and how the ISA firewall protects you against them.

Deploying NetScreen Firewalls

Solutions in this chapter:

- **Managing the NetScreen Firewall**
- **Configuring NetScreen**
- **Configuring Your NetScreen for the Network**
- **Configuring System Services**

☑ **Summary**

Introduction

In this chapter we will look at the basics of deploying a NetScreen firewall. The "basics" covers a great deal of information. The NetScreen firewall has a large number of configuration options. Before you can deploy a device, you must first understand how to manage it, so in the first section of this chapter we will look at the various methods of managing your NetScreen firewall. Each option and best-known procedure is discussed. Strong system management is important, but no more so than preventing intruder attacks.

There are many management options available on the NetScreen firewall. Of these options, there are effectively two ways to manage the device directly. The first is from the *command line interface* (CLI). Many people still prefer this method of device management. Fully comprehending the command line interface allows you to understand the NetScreen firewall device better. There are specific functions that can only be done from the command line interface, such as setting the flow options. The flow options are specific to the internals of how the firewall works with packets. You most likely will not have to use these commands.

The second firewall management option is the *Web User Interface* (WebUI). This streamlined interface is user-friendly and intuitive, allowing anyone to jump in and manage your firewall with ease. Even command line junkies will use the WebUI to reference the configuration or to see a configuration more clearly.

Since a firewall is a core network component of the network, we will focus heavily on how to configure your device to interact with the network. This covers *zone configuration* and *IP address assignment*. Properly configuring the network is crucial to the functionality of your network entity. Each type of zone and interface is documented to explain the different configuration options to you.

Finally, we will configure various system services. These services empower your firewall and stretch its possibilities.

Managing the NetScreen Firewall

The first step in NetScreen firewall execution is learning how to effectively manage them. In this section we will look at all of the various management options. Each option brings certain strengths and weaknesses to the table, so you should never rely on just one method. Instead, take advantage of the range of security options NetScreen offers, and use multiple configurations.

All management access requires authentication, and it's critical that only authorized administrators are permitted to change your firewall's configuration. The last thing that you want to happen is to lose control of your firewall.

There may be times when you mistakenly erase parts of your configuration or lose your configuration altogether. We will review how to recover from these mistakes. Losing access to your device can be devastating. With so many different passwords to remember, you can easily forget how to gain access to your NetScreen firewall. Even the most experienced administrators can find themselves in this scenario, and several methods of recovery have been documented.

Finally, we will look at how to update the operating system on your NetScreen device. Staying current with software revisions is very important. It provides you with security-related fixes as well as new software enhancements. For each type of management option there is a different way to update ScreenOS. Some options may be more effective then others, depending on your needs. At the completion of this section you should be familiar with WebUI and CLI. Knowing this is a requirement for managing your NetScreen firewall.

NetScreen Management Options

Every NetScreen management option centers around two forms of management: the WebUI and the CLI. There is a third type of management, an enterprise class of security, called the NetScreen-Security Manager (NSM).

Serial Console

The *Serial Console* is a 9-pin female serial connection. This option gives you CLI access to the firewall. Serial Console is used to initially connect to your device and to conduct *out-of-band management*. Out-of-band management is management that is not network-based, such as access via a modem. There are certain benefits to using a serial console that you do not get from using any other type of connection. The console provides a secure, physical and dedicated access. Network connectivity issues cannot interrupt this type of connection, and no one can intercept your management traffic. It is completely secured because of its direct connection.

When configuring over a serial port, you are not using any sort of network connectivity. In the case when you need to change Internet Protocol (IP) addressing on the firewall and guarantee connectivity, using the serial console is an excellent option. With, and only with serial console can you view and interact with the booting process. This cannot be accomplished remotely because the OS has not started and it is unable to provide management services. Many devices from UNIX-type servers, as well as other embedded devices, use serial consoles to provide serial console management. On the NetScreen 5XP/5GT/5XP and NetScreen-500, use a DB9 female to DB9 male straight through serial cable to connect for console management. On the NetScreen 25/50/204/208/ISG 2000/5200/5400, use an RJ-45 serial cable with a DB9 female connector. Table 22.1 outlines the proper connection settings when connecting with a serial terminal or serial terminal emulator.

Table 22.1 The Serial Terminal Settings

Setting	Value
Speed	9600 bps
Character Size	8 Bit
Parity	None
Stop Bit	1
Flow Control	None

Telnet

A second form of CLI management is *Telnet*. Telnet is a protocol that has been used for years and is like a network-based version of a serial console. However, it lacks many of the advantages of a serial console. First of all, it is a very unstable connection. The connection is made over the network in clear text. This means that the transmitted data is not encrypted in any way, allowing easy access to your login and password. Most client operating systems provide an easy-to-use Telnet client. A Telnet connection is not an ideal configuration for managing your device from a remote location. You can have a maximum of two Telnet sessions active concurrently.

Secure Shell

The third form of command line management is called *secure shell*, or SSH. Like Telnet, SSH is a remote command line session. Telnet's security concerns are removed when using SSH. Secure Shell provides an encrypted command line session to the NetScreen firewall. It also provides protection from IP spoofing and DNS (Domain Name Service) spoofing attacks. SSH has two different versions: v1 and v2. The versions are not backward-compatible. Version two is considered more popular because of its higher level of security. You are required to have a client that is compatible with the version of SSH you are using. Many UNIX-based operating systems include clients, but Windows based operating systems do not. You can use a client named *putty* for Windows. It is free and easy to use. The putty client can be found at: www.chiark.greenend.org.uk/~sgtatham/putty/download.html.

WebUI

The web user interface is the easiest type of management to use. Because of its simple point-and-click nature, it gives the end user a great jumpstart into the management of the NetScreen firewall. You can see in Figure 22.1 that the interface is very straight-forward. On the left hand side of the browser you have the menu column. From here you can choose from the different configuration options. This menu can be either Dynamic HyperText Markup Language (DHTML)-based, the default, or java-based. The functionality is the same, but the look and feel is slightly different. By default the WebUI is configured to work over just the Hyper Text Transfer Protocol (HTTP). It can, however, be configured to work over Hyper Text Transfer Protocol Secure (HTTPS). This provides a mechanism to secure your web management traffic.

Figure 22.1 Web User Interface

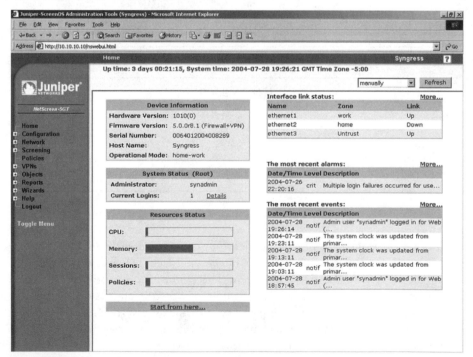

The NetScreen-Security Manager

The NetScreen-Security Manager is a separate tool that can be used to manage a NetScreen firewall device. The NSM is an application that runs on either a Solaris server or a Red Hat Linux server. It requires a separate license, and it is licensed based on how many devices you want to manage. This product is used most effectively if you want to manage several devices at the same time.

Administrative Users

When connecting to a NetScreen firewall for management, you must always authenticate to the firewall. There are several types of users you can employ to connect a NetScreen firewall. The first user is the *root user*. This user is the principal user of the NetScreen firewall device. The root user has the most power of any user on a NetScreen firewall. There is only one root user per device. By default, the root user's name is *netscreen* and the default password is *netscreen*. It is highly recommended that you change the login name and password immediately. The root user has the most administrative privilege of any device. The *root user administrative privileges* are listed below:

- Add, remove, and manage all other administrators
- Create and manage virtual systems
- Create, delete, and manage virtual routers
- Add, delete, and manage security zones
- Assign security zones to interfaces
- Perform asset recovery
- Set the device to FIPS mode
- Reset the device to default settings
- Manage the devices firmware
- Load configuration files
- Perform management on the root system

The next level administrator is *read/write*. Read/write is very similar to the root user, however, read/write users cannot create other administrators. This type of access is most useful when you want to distribute administrative privileges to other people. The NetScreen firewall provides a very detailed audit log of what each administrator does. You should capitalize on this by creating administrative users for each person that administers your firewall. This way you can identify which users make which modifications. The read/write administrative privileges include:

- Create and manage virtual systems
- Create, delete, and manage virtual routers
- Add, delete, and manage security zones
- Assign security zones to interfaces
- Perform asset recovery

- Set the device to FIPS mode
- Reset the device to default settings
- Manage the devices firmware
- Load configuration files
- Perform management on the root system

The next type of user is the *read-only* administrator. This user has limited access to the system. As the name suggests, the user can only view the configuration and they are unable to modify the system in any way. This is useful if you want to have someone document your configurations, or if you want to give someone limited access to the device to perform troubleshooting on the network. The following list includes the limited privileges of the read-only administrator.

- Read-only privileges in the root system
- Read-only privileges in all virtual systems

On some devices you can have *virtual systems*. A virtual system acts as its own separate security domain. Virtual system administrators only have permission on a specific system. The following lists the virtual system administrator privileges:

- Create and manage auth, IKE, L2TP, XAuth, and Manual Key users
- Create and manage services
- Create and manage policies
- Create and manage addresses
- Create and manage VPNs (virtual private networks)
- Modify the virtual system administrator login password
- Create and remove virtual system read-only administrators

The last type of user is the *virtual system read-only administrator*. They have almost the same privileges as a read-only administrator, but they can only see the configuration of a single specified virtual system. The only privileges that the virtual system read-only administrator has are read-only privileges on the specified virtual system.

Knowing the different types of administrators can give you the options to create an efficient strategy for delegating authority on your system. Don't be afraid to create many different administrative users for your NetScreen device. This will provide you with granular access to your system. Again, all users' actions are logged, providing a detailed list of access for each different user. This can be helpful when determining issues caused by a particular administrator, or in determining if an administrator account has been compromised.

The Local File System and the Configuration File

Each NetScreen firewall device has a similar design for its internal system components. Long-term storage on the device is stored into *flash memory*. Flash memory is a non-volatile type of memory that retains information after the system is turned off. Some devices have a Personal Computer Memory Card International Association (PCMCIA) card slot for external storage. This card is still just flash memory, but it is removable; the internal flash is not. All of the component information that NetScreen needs to store is in flash memory, including ScreenOS log files, license keys, attack databases, and virus definitions.

Each NetScreen device also contains Random Access Memory (RAM). This is a volatile type of memory that is lost whenever the system is powered off or reset. When the NetScreen device powers on, and after the *power on self test* (POST) is completed, the ScreenOS image is loaded into RAM. After ScreenOS is up and functional, it loads the saved configuration file from flash memory. The configuration that is stored in RAM is called the *running configuration*.

Whenever you make a change to the configuration, it is always saved to the running configuration. If you did not save your configuration, whenever you reset or rebooted your device, you would lose all of your changes. In those cases you can simply have someone remove power to the device, and then restore power. This will bring you back to the previously saved configuration. When using the CLI, your configuration must be manually saved. This can be done by using the save command. The save command is simple: **save**. By typing that command, your running configuration is saved into the *saved configuration*, which is stored in flash memory. The file system components are shown in Figure 22.2.

Figure 22.2 File System Components

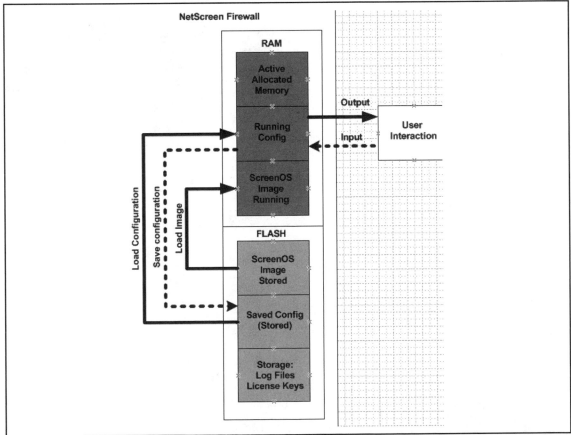

Using the WebUI is even easier. The WebUI automatically saves your configuration after every change. However, when using the CLI, if you exit your session or attempt to reset the device, you are notified that your configuration has changed. At that point you are given the option of saving the configuration. The NetScreen device is much more user-friendly then other devices when it comes to notifying you that your configuration has changed.

There are times when the flash may not provide you with the kind of storage that you need. You may require long-term storage of the log files, or perhaps a backup of your configuration file. There are a couple ways to accomplish this:

- When using the command line you can apply the command **get config** to look at your configuration, then copy and paste it into a simple text document.

- From the command line you can copy the configuration to a TFTP (Trivial File Transfer Protocol) server. TFTP is a simple type of FTP (File Transfer Protocol) server. It requires no authentication, just specification of the filename you are placing on the server. To save your configuration to a TFTP server use the command **save config to tftp** *<a.b.c.d> <file>* where *<a.b.c.d>* is the IP address of the TFTP server and *<file>* is the filename you want to save to.

Depending on the data that is being transferred from the file system, you may want a more secure option than TFTP. You can use *secure copy* (SCP) to transfer files as well. Secure copy is similar to the secure shell. It requires a special client to interact with it. This is included on many UNIX systems. Windows has many clients. I like to use the PSCP software, which is part of the Putty freeware secure shell clients. In the following example we will turn on SCP and copy a file from the NetScreen firewall to our UNIX system.

```
From the CLI:
Syngress-> set scp enable
Syngress-> get scp
SCP is enabled
SCP is ready
Syngress-> get file
  flash:/envar.rec          98
  flash:/golerd.rec         1220
  flash:/burnin_log1        10240
  flash:/burnin_log0        10240
  flash:/dhcpservl.txt      52
  flash:/ns_sys_config      1092
  flash:/dnstb.rec          1
  flash:/license.key        395
  flash:/$lkg$.cfg          922
  flash:/expire.rec         23
  flash:/attacks.sig        198833
Syngress->
From the UNIX Host:
UNIX-Host:~ syngress$ scp synadmin@10.6.0.1:license.key license.txt
```

```
The authenticity of host '10.6.0.1 (10.6.0.1)' can't be established.
DSA key fingerprint is f9:a7:4c:53:4c:0a:cc:5a:50:6b:eb:df:42:42:63:c0.
Are you sure you want to continue connecting (yes/no)? yes
Warning: Permanently added '10.6.0.1' (DSA) to the list of known hosts.
synadmin@10.6.0.1's password:
license.key 100% 395      4.8KB/s 00:00
UNIX-Host:~ syngress$ cat license.txt
1k=d2f5fb8aa5b9a000&n=capacity_key
k=2JQcSPh1ogana6h82NJeAfDwgb3aiOXT2UFcm9OFQDkuK4iT6YfKefMZjTODboIN2JQ0oWnWWX+nKkYSM
ytB8gF1ID7tWXI9lvZ11JURDENckexZ7IwtmRmDEh+YT3dJvDSOAYeGuuWFtGYE5tVnPfZq6cnlO254GPPm
5HJ3qTG4sRBSRR/QFqL6WAnfnoSpByJu/Xr9vxx9GSU4fTMGLFkWsbRP5cVpTGWmyOBapFfn1qWzu/bMLzD
kox8zUHFZ2NcNCOSGOk5PvCMcZwOaADRIFqJj1oh4u7+toY37gdrEM5sQqmELemAlUi90dhLPl7jsTy1R/
V0/ourYn00XcMw==&n=di_db_key
UNIX-Host:~ Syngress$
```

As you can see, we enabled SCP, allowing us to view all of the files stored in flash memory. Next we went over to the UNIX host and copied the file from the NetScreen device to the local UNIX system. Finally, we used the **cat** command to concatenate the contents of the file so you can see them. SCP can be effective and easy to use for removing files from NetScreen devices.

If you're using WebUI, you can access (**Configuration | Update | Config File**) and then click the button that says **Save To File**. This will allow you to save the configuration to your local PC (Figure 22.3). Alternatively, from this same screen you can select the text in the text window, then copy and paste the configuration to a text file.

Figure 22.3 WebUI Save Screen

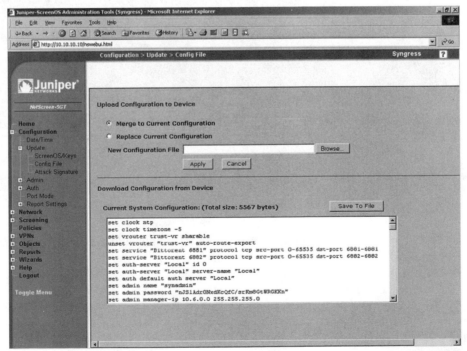

As you have seen from these files, the config files are a bunch of commands. The configuration file operates similarly to manually typing these commands in line-by-line. This is great because it gives you one format to understand. It also allows you to easily modify the configuration files you have saved to reflect new changes you may want to implement. This is one of the reasons I will continue to stress that you understand the CLI. In the next section, "Using the Command Line Interface," we will look at the configuration of the device and what all of these commands mean.

Using the Command Line Interface

The command line interface is essentially the core of configuring your NetScreen firewall device. No matter what method you use to manage your firewall, the CLI commands control the device, and a strong understanding the CLI is crucial. Even the NSM still generates the same CLI commands that you would apply if you were to modify the configuration manually. The CLI commands are straightforward and are easy to learn. Some other devices use very cryptic commands, or commands that seem to do one thing, but actually do something else. When this firewall was designed, the engineers took the need for simplicity into consideration. In Figure 22.4, an example of the help screen is shown. This gives you an idea of the information provided by the help command.

Figure 22.4 Command Line Session Using Help

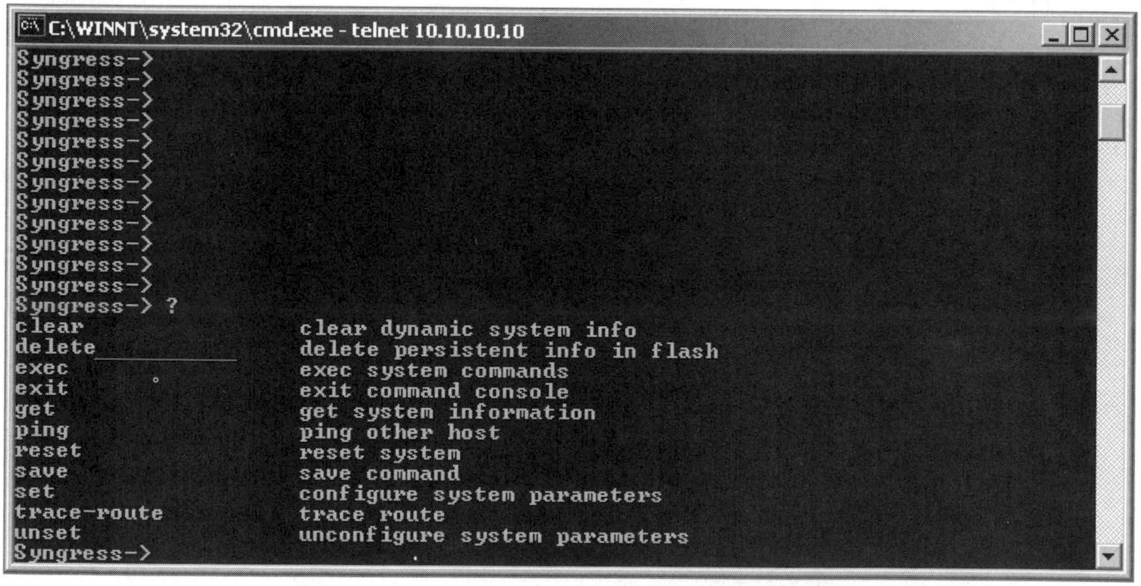

```
C:\WINNT\system32\cmd.exe - telnet 10.10.10.10
Syngress->
Syngress->
Syngress->
Syngress->
Syngress->
Syngress->
Syngress->
Syngress->
Syngress->
Syngress->
Syngress->
Syngress->
Syngress-> ?
clear              clear dynamic system info
delete             delete persistent info in flash
exec               exec system commands
exit               exit command console
get                get system information
ping               ping other host
reset              reset system
save               save command
set                configure system parameters
trace-route        trace route
unset              unconfigure system parameters
Syngress->
```

If you look at Figure 22.4 you can see an example of the command line. The prompt shows the device's current host name. This is very useful if you have several different devices that look very much the same from the command line. Starting from the root of these commands, there are literally thousands of command options. This can be confusing because there are a great number of commands to memorize. Thankfully, there is an easy-to-use built-in help system. From anywhere in the command line simply type **?** to access the help system. This will list most of the available commands. Some commands are not listed; these specific commands will be discussed in later sections.

From here there are several *base commands*, including **clear, exec, exit, get, ping, reset, save, set, trace-route,** and **unset.** Under each one of these commands are sub-commands.

Let's look at a quick example before continuing. We will first look at the **get** command. This command is used to retrieve information from the device. If we wanted to look at system information from the device such as uptime, serial number, and some configuration information, we would use the **get system** command. At the end of any get command you can do one of three things:

- You can press **Enter** and have the information displayed in your terminal window.

- You can redirect the output to a TFTP server much like we did earlier when we saved the configuration. You would use this command **get system > tftp <a.b.c.d> <string>** to send the output to a TFTP server, where *<a.b.c.d>* is the IP address of the TFTP server and *<string>* is the filename of the file you want to save to.

- You can also use the pipe (|) to match output. If you were going to use the **get system** command to look for just the serial number of your device you would use the following command: **get system | include "Serial Num".** This would then display only the serial number and omit the rest of the data. You can also exclude specific information if you wanted to. You would use the same procedure as above but use the term **exclude** instead of **include.** This helps sort though all of the information that can be provided from a get command.

The next command we'll examine is the **set** command. This command is used to set a configuration in the current running configuration. Suppose you wanted to set the hostname to *Syngress*. You would use the following command to set the hostname of your NetScreen device: **set hostname Syngress.** Now your prompt should look like this: **Syngress->.** This again is only in the running configuration, so if you wanted to save this configuration, you would simply use the command **save** to commit the running configuration to the saved configuration. The set command will be used throughout the book, so you will get plenty of exposure to it.

You should familiarize yourself with the *five system-controlling commands*: **save, exec, exit, delete,** and **reset.** Each one of these commands directly performs a system task. The **save** command can be used to perform several other functions. The **save** command is used to save files to and from the local system. The **reset** command is used to reboot the NetScreen device. There are several sub-options that allow you to reboot without prompting you to confirm the configuration. You can also force a reboot, saving the running configuration, or discarding it. This way, when you want to reboot the system you do not have to answer to prompts before doing so. This is very helpful to place inside of a configuration script.

We will now look at the **exec** command. This command is powerful and is multi-purposeful. The **exec** command essentially is like running a command on the system. For example the command **exec save software from flash to tftp 1.2.3.4 CurrentOS.bin** would save the current version of ScreenOS to a TFTP server. So it would be much like copying a file in DOS or UNIX shell from one location to another. This is an example of the type of functions that the `exec` command can provide.

The command **delete** allows you to manage your local system by deleting several types of stored information. This can range from you local stored SSH information to files on the local flash file system. For example, if you wanted to delete a file named *old_data* that was stored in flash memory, you would use the following command: **delete file flash:old_data.** This would delete that file permanently from flash.

The **exit** command serves only one function: to exit your current session. When you use this command your current CLI session is terminated. If you have made unsaved configuration changes, you will be prompted to save them before you exit.

The **clear** command allows you to clear current data out of memory. This can include dozens of options anywhere from the current local DNS cache to the current sessions that are passing though the firewall. This is useful if you want to remote this information and then you want that data to accumulate again. Sessions are a great example of something that you may need to clear. You would want to clear you session table if you were perhaps troubleshooting a connectivity problem and you wanted to see the session be recreated in your debugging logs. This is as easy as typing **clear session** at the command line and pressing **Enter** to clear out all of the sessions. You could also selectively delete all of your sessions depending upon your situation.

There are two commands that you can use to for troubleshooting purposes. These commands are **ping** and **trace-route**. I am sure you have used these before on other operating systems. Ping is a tool to test connectivity between two systems. You would use ping, for example, if you wanted to verify that your firewall could see a specific host. The **ping** command can be used with other options besides just a host. You can also specify how many ping packets you want to send, as well as the size and the timeout for each packet. To use the ping command, just type **ping** and then the hostname or IP address of device you are trying to contact. The other command is **trace-route**. Trace route is similar to a ping, but it is designed to determine all of the routers' IP addresses and the path across the network you need to take to get to a specified remote host.

When using the command line there are a few special commands that you can use to get around to make things easier for the end user. We already covered the **?** command for getting help. This can be used for every sub-command as well as partial commands to tell you what the rest of the available commands are. The help command is very helpful and should be used liberally when you need it. Next is the **TAB** key to provide command completion. For example, you can type **set add** and then press **TAB** to have the command completed for you, resulting in the command **set address**. If there is more then one match to the command, both will be listed. You must type out the command until it is unique for command completion to work. This is universal for the CLI on the NetScreen device, it is the same functionality provided by the UNIX bash shell. If you look at Table 22.2 you can see the rest of the special key combinations that you can use.

Table 22.2 Special Key Combinations for the CLI

Special Key	Action
Up Arrow	Recalls previous command
Down Arrow	Recalls next command
Control-A	Brings cursor to beginning of the current line
Control-E	Brings the cursor to the end of the current line
Control-C	This is the escape sequence
Left Arrow	Move cursor back one position
Right Arrow	Move cursor forward one position
TAB	Completes partially typed command
Question Mark (?)	Displays Help and command options

As you can see, the command line has many different options. Once you begin to use these options you can quickly get used to the CLI environment. Many people begin to use the WebUI and then abandon the CLI. At first you may find the WebUI easier to use, but more advanced options can only be carried out from the CLI (such as debugging).

Using the Web User Interface

The Web User Interface is a simple tool to use for managing your NetScreen firewall. It is very intuitive and allows even those with little firewall experience to easily control a NetScreen device. As we continue through the book we will use both the WebUI and the CLI for examples. In Figure 22.1 above, we looked at the main WebUI page following authentication. On the left side is the menu bar, where you can select the different configuration options. On the right-hand side of the screen is the current status of the device. On this screen there are six different boxes: **Device Information**, **System Status**, **Resource Status**, **Interface Link Status**, **The most recent alarms**, and **The most recent events**.

Each of these boxes shows you the current events. The current uptime and the current system time are also displayed (at the top of the screen). The **Device Information** box shows you several different bits of information, including the hardware version, current firmware version, Serial Number, Host name, and its current operational mode. The **System Status** box shows the status for the various systems. It shows the current number of logins to the device and who you are logged in as. The **Resources Status** box shows four different device resources in a bar graph format. If you hover over any of the bar graphs, you will see specific numbers for each graph. The stats that are profiled are CPU, memory, sessions, and policies. These are the core performance metrics of the NetScreen device. As we discussed earlier, the memory bar graph will read higher then you would expect. This is again because ScreenOS pre-allocates memory for performance.

If you look at the box titled **Interface Link Status** you will see all of the interfaces and their link statuses. This is handy for determining which interfaces are up or down. **The most recent alarms** lists the most recent alarms that have occurred. Finally, just as its name implies, **The most recent events** box lists the most recent events. Some boxes in the upper right-hand corner have a **more** hyperlink. This brings you directly to the detail page for each one of those items.

Securing the Management Interface

Now that you are beginning to understand the management of the NetScreen firewall device, it is time to secure the management access to your device. The last thing you want to do is leave the doors wide open for another individual to take over your device. There are some easy things that you can do to prevent this. First, as we mentioned earlier, you should change the root username and password. Everyone who owns a NetScreen firewall is well aware of the default login and password to the device.

Use the following steps to change the root username and password via the WebUI:

1. Select **Configuration | Admin | Administrators**. A screen similar to Figure 22.5 will be displayed.

Figure 22.5 WebUI Administrators Screen

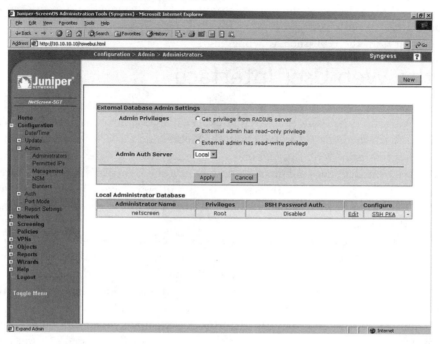

2. Click the **Edit** link for the user with *root* privileges (in our example, the *root* user is the only username entry). A screen similar to that in Figure 22.6 will be displayed.

Figure 22.6 Edit Administrator

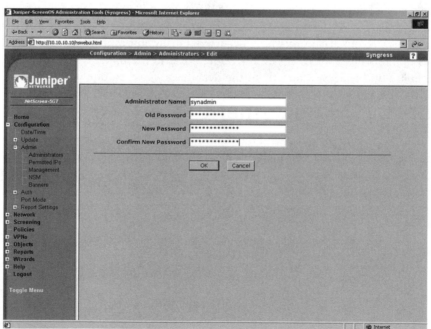

3. Change the **Administrator Name** from **netscreen** to **synadmin**.

4. Enter **netscreen** in the **Old Password** field.

5. Enter the new password in the **New Password** and **Confirm New Password** fields.

6. Click **OK**.

Use the following steps to change the root username and password via the CLI:

1. Enter the following command to change the admin name:

```
Syngress-> set admin name synadmin
```

You will see the following message:

```
Password has been restored to default "netscreen". For security reasons,
please change password immediately.
```

2. Enter the following command to change the password:

```
Syngress-> set admin password password
```

3. Use the following command to verify the changes:

```
Syngress-> get admin user
```

You will see an output similar to the following:

```
Name                              Privilege
----------------------------      ----------------------------
synadmin                          Root
Syngress->
```

The device now has its root users name set to **synadmin** and its password has been changed. It is suggested that you make the password a minimum of eight characters. The maximum allowed number of characters in the password is thirty-one.

It is also suggested that you make a read-write administrator to use for regular maintenance. If that administrator is compromised, there is no direct root access to the device. Use the following steps to create a read-write administrator via the WebUI:

1. Select **Configuration | Admin | Administrators | New**. The screen shown in Figure 22.7 will appear.

Figure 22.7 Administrator Configuration

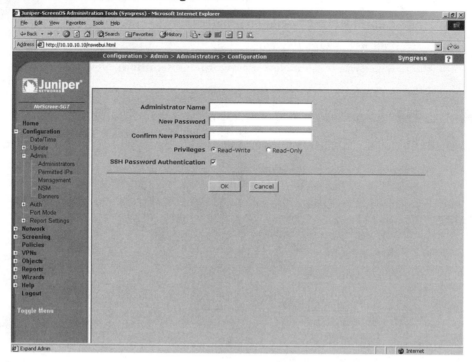

2. Use the **Administrator Name** field to enter the new name (in this example, **backupadmin**).

3 Enter this user's password in the **New Password** and **Confirm New Password** fields.

4. Enable the **Read-Write** option.

5. Click **OK**.

Use the following to create a read-only administrator via the WebUI:

1. Select **Configuration | Admin | Administrators | New**.

2. Use the **Administrator Name** field to enter the new name (in this example, **roadmin**).

3. Enter this user's password in the **New Password** and **Confirm New Password** fields.

4. Enable the **Read-Only** option.

5. Click **OK**.

Enter the following command to create a read-write administrator via the CLI:

```
Syngress-> set admin user backupadmin password %so%back privilege all
```

Verify the entry by using the **get admin user** command. The output will look like the following:

```
Name                                 Privilege
-------------------------------      ------------------------------
synadmin                             Root
backupadmin                          Read-Write
```

Enter the following command to create a read-only administrator via the CLI:

```
Syngress-> set admin user roadmin password n0tru$t privilege read-only
```

Verify the entry by using the **get admin user** command. The output will look like the following:

```
Name                                    Privilege
-------------------------------         --------------------------------
synadmin                                Root
backupadmin                             Read-Write
roadmin                                 Read-Only
```

Another option that you should configure is the idle timeout. I have been to many locations where you would simply connect to the console and have a privileged account ready and waiting for you because the previous user had left and not logged out, or not yet returned. This is a bad situation. Anyone with a little know-how can cause trouble on your network this way. Set the idle timeout to something reasonable (the default is ten minutes for the console, Telnet, SSH, and WebUI sessions). Use the following steps to set the console, Telnet, and WebUI sessions to timeout after five minutes via the WebUI:

1. Select **Configuration | Admin | Management**. A screen similar to the one shown in Figure 22.8 will appear.

Figure 22.8 Admin Management

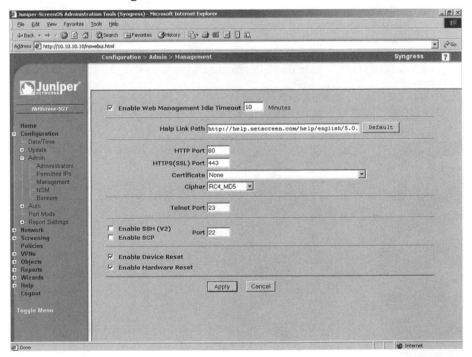

2.   Ensure the **Enable Web Management Idle Timeout** option is enabled and enter **5**
     in the corresponding text field.

3.   Click **Apply**.

You can also modify the console timeout option via the CLI by entering **set console timeout 5**.
Note that a timeout value of **0** will disable the timeout feature. Use the **get console** command to
verify the change. The output will resemble the following:

```
Console timeout: 5(minute), Page size: 22/22, debug: buffer
privilege 250, config was changed and not saved!
ID StateDuration Task Type                 Host
 0 Login    660 13433716 Telnet 10.254.5.32:49401
 1 Logout   0 13435768 Local
 2 Logout   0 13424824 Local
 3 Logout   0 13410460 Local
```

To set the admin authentication timeout, enter **set admin auth timeout 5**. Use the **get admin
auth** command to verify the setting. The output will resemble the following:

```
Admin user authentication timeout: 5 minutes
Admin user authentication type: Local
```

The next step is to limit the systems that can access your firewall. for management purposes.
By specifying *permitted* IP addresses, you can limit which IP addresses are accepted for management
services. You are limited to six total entries. This can be for either networks or host entries. Once you
enable this setting, it immediately takes effect, so if you are setting this up remotely, ensure that you
add your own IP address and/or source network. Use the following steps to create a permitted IP
address entry via the WebUI:

1.   Select **Configuration | Admin | Permitted IPs**. A screen similar to that shown
     in Figure 22.9 will be displayed.

Figure 22.9 Permitted IPs

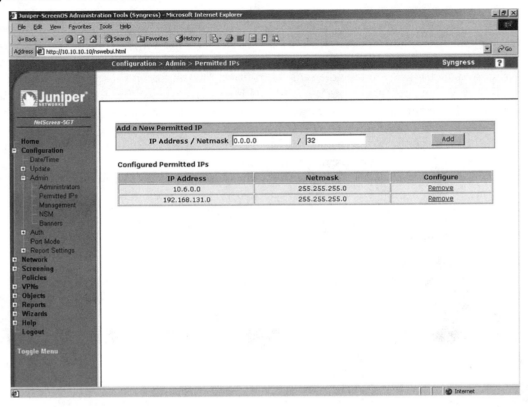

2. Use the available text fields to enter the IP address and netmask, then click **Add**. You can remove an IP address from the list by clicking its **Remove** link. Note that if the list contains no IP addresses, any IP address will be able to access the firewall.

To add a permitted IP address via the CLI, enter the command **set admin manager-ip** *ipaddress*, where *ipaddress* is the full IP address using dotted quad (###.###.###.###) notation. You can verify the setting by entering **get admin manager-ip**. To remove an IP address entry via the CLI, enter the command **unset admin manager-ip** *ipaddress*.

Secure Shell is highly suggested over Telnet, as we discussed earlier when we were looking at our different management options. However, it must be enabled before you can use it. Again earlier we looked at using SSH version two. In the following code snippet we enable SSH version two in both the WebUI and the CLI. After enabling SSH it may take several minutes for the SSH servers to be enabled. This is because the SSH keys are generating during this time.

Use the following steps to enable SSH via the WebUI:

1. Select **Configuration | Admin | Management**.

2. Enable the **Enable SSH (v2)** option.

3. Click **Apply**.

To enable SSH via the CLI, enter the command **set ssh version v2**. To set version 1 instead of version 2, simply replace **v2** in the command with **v1**.

It is strongly recommended that you use SSL only when using the WebUI. In general, it is very easy to set up and configure. However, there is one task that may prove to be a challenge. You must generate a certificate-signing request (CSR) and submit it back to a certificate authority (CA) to get the certificate signed. Once you have the signed certificate, you can load it back onto your NetScreen device. We will review how to generate the CSR and how to load the certificate. However, signing a certificate varies based upon which certificate authority you use. If you are using your device on your company's network, you should use a certificate purchased from a reputable website such as www.verisign.com or www.godaddy.com. Either site can provide you with a certificate. However if you want to just get a signed certificate for testing purposes go to www.cacert.org to get one for free.

Use the following steps to generate a certificate request. Note that this example includes company-specific information that you should substitute with your own information.

1. Access **Objects | Certificates**. The screen will display the existing certificates (Figure 22.10).

Figure 22.10 Certificates

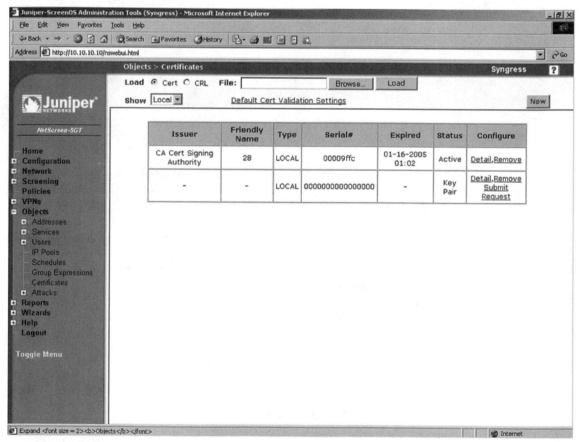

2. Click **New**. The New Request screen will be displayed (Figure 22.11).

Figure 22.11 New Certificate Request

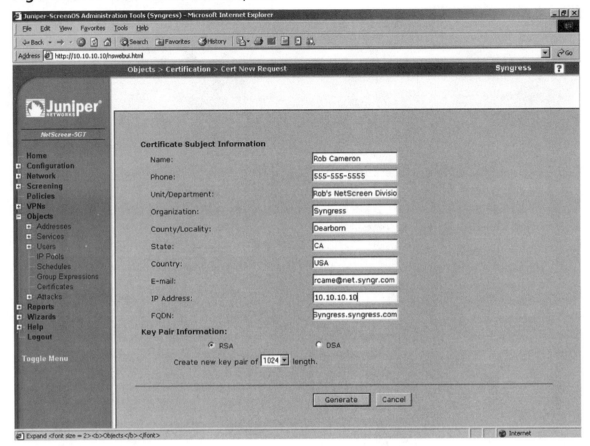

3. Enter your **Name**, **Phone**, **Unit/Department**, **Organization**, **County/Locality**, **State**, **Country**, **E-mail**, **IP Address**, and **FQDN** (Fully Qualified Domain Name).

4. Select the **RSA** option.

5. Select **1024** or **2048** from the **Create new key pair** drop-down list (the higher the number, the more secure the certificate).

6. Click **Generate**. In several minutes a new page will displayed containing a section of text.

7. Copy the text contents from "-----BEGIN CERTIFICATE REQUEST-----" to "-----END CERTIFICATE REQUEST-----".

8. Supply this to your certificate authority. They will supply you with a certificate file.

9. Access **Objects | Certificates** and click **Browse**. Choose the certificate file the CA sent you and click **Load**. The certificate is now active and loaded.

10. Now access **Configuration | Admin | Management**. Select the certificate from the **Certificate** field.

Use the following steps to request and set up a certificate via the CLI (use your own personal and company information):

1. Enter the following commands to request a certificate:

```
Syngress-> set admin mail server-name 123.123.123.100
Syngress-> set pki x509 dn country-name US
Syngress-> set pki x509 dn email rob@netscreen.com
Syngress-> set pki x509 dn ip 123.123.123.123
Syngress-> set pki x509 dn local-name "Dearborn"
Syngress-> set pki x509 dn name "Rob Cameron"
Syngress-> set pki x509 dn org-name "Rob's NetScreen division"
Syngress-> set pki x509 dn org-unit-name Books
Syngress-> set pki x509 dn phone 555-555-5555
Syngress-> set pki x509 dn state-name CA
Syngress-> set pki x509 cert-fqdn manage.netscreen.com
Syngress-> set pki x509 dn default send-to rob@netscreen.com
Syngress-> exec pki rsa new-key 1024
```

2. The certificate will be e-mailed to the address you specified. Copy the contents starting with "-----BEGIN CERTIFICATE REQUEST----" and ending with "-----END CERTIFICATE REQUEST----".

3. Supply this information to your certificate authority. They will supply you with a certificate file. The CA may also supply you with a local certificate and a certificate revocation list (CRL). A CRL contains a list of all of the revoked certificates that the CA has signed that are no longer valid.

4. To import these files, use the following commands:

```
Syngress-> exec tftp 123.123.123.100 cert-name newcer.cer
Syngress-> exec tftp 123.123.123.100 cert-name localpro.cer
Syngress-> exec tftp 123.123.123.100 crl-name notrust.crl
Syngress-> set ssl encrypt 3des sha-1
Syngress-> set ssl cert 1
Syngress-> set ssl enable
```

Now that we have the access restricted to specific hosts there are yet several more options we can do to enhance the security. The first option is to disable unnecessary management services. Management services are bound to individual interfaces. It is important to restrict them to the bare minimum. This can be done easily from both the WebUI and the CLI. In this case, we are using a NetScreen-5GT so we will be modifying the *untrust* interface. We are going to enable the WebUI, SSL for the WebUI, and SSH. We will only use the WebUI with SSL and SSH because they are secured.

Use the following steps to disable unnecessary management services via the WebUI:

1. Access **Network | Interfaces**. Click the **Edit** link for the entry title **untrust** A screen similar to Figure 22.12 will be displayed.

Figure 22.12 Editing Network Interfaces

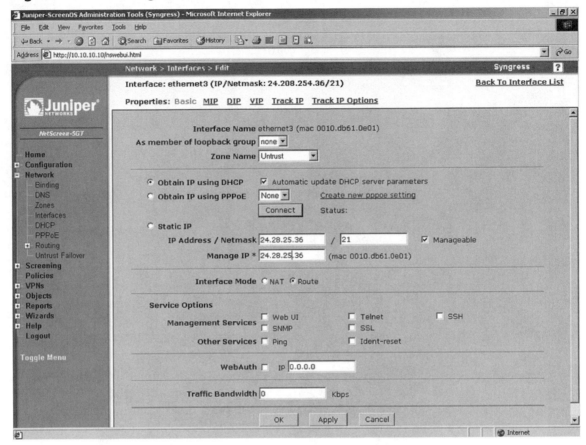

2. Ensure that **WebUI**, **SSH**, and **SSL** are all enabled, and ensure the remaining option are disabled.

3. Click **Apply**.

To disable unnecessary management services via the CLI, enter the following commands:

```
Syngress-> unset interface untrust manage ping
Syngress-> unset interface untrust manage snmp
Syngress-> unset interface untrust manage telnet
Syngress-> set interface untrust manage ssh
Syngress-> set interface untrust manage web
Syngress-> set interface untrust manage ssl
```

Use the **get interface trust** command to verify the settings. The output should resemble the following:

```
Interface untrust:
  number 1, if_info 88, if_index 0, mode route
  link up, phy-link up/full-duplex
  vsys Root, zone Untrust, vr trust-vr
  dhcp client enabled
  PPPoE disabled
  *ip 123.208.123.254/24 mac 0010.db61.1231
  gateway 123.208.123.1
  *manage ip 123.208.123.254, mac 0010.db61.1231
  route-deny disable
  ping disabled, telnet disabled, SSH enabled, SNMP disabled
  web enabled, ident-reset disabled, SSL enabled
  webauth disabled, webauth-ip 0.0.0.0
  OSPF disabled BGP disabled RIP disabled
  bandwidth: physical 100000kbps, configured 0kbps, current 0kbps
    total configured gbw 0kbps, total allocated gbw 0kbps
  DHCP-Relay disabled
  DHCP-server disabled
```

Next, you can change the local port that your management services listen on. This can help prevent your services from being detected if someone was to do a scan looking for open services. Telnet (TCP 23), SSH (TCP 22), WebUI (TCP 80), and WebUI SSL (TCP 443) can all be changed to different ports. Use the following steps to change the ports via the WebUI:

1   Access **Configuration | Admin | Administrators**.

2.   Specify new port numbers for Telnet, SSH, WebUI and WebUI SSL (port numbers must be in the range 1024–32767).

3.   Click **Apply**.

Enter the following commands to set the port numbers via the CLI:

```
Syngress-> set admin ssh port 1024
Syngress-> set admin port 32000
Syngress-> set admin telnet port 4000
Syngress-> set ssl port 5000
```

All of the management we have been doing has been to the IP address of the interface. It will be easy for people to determine what the IP address is of the firewall. This can lead them to attempt to connect to it and try and mange your device. You can, however, set up what is called a management IP. This IP address is used only for management. This is configured directly on the interface. For this example we will be using a NetScreen-5GT and we will be modifying the *untrust* interface.

Use the following steps to set up a management IP via the WebUI:

1. Access **Network | Interfaces (List)**. The screen shown in Figure 22.13 will be displayed.

Figure 22.13 Network Interfaces List

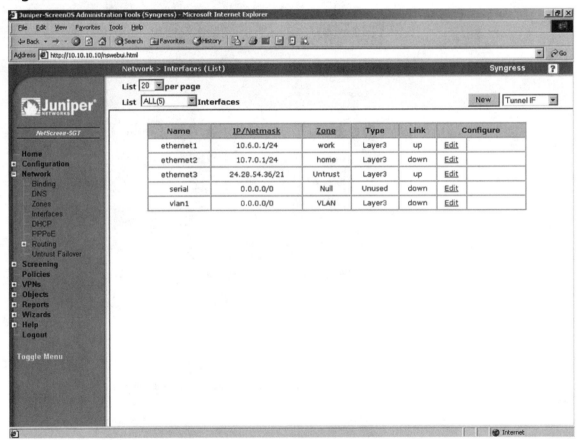

2. Click the **Edit** link for the *untrust* entry. A screen similar to the one shown in Figure 22.14 will be displayed.

Figure 22.14 Edit Network Interface

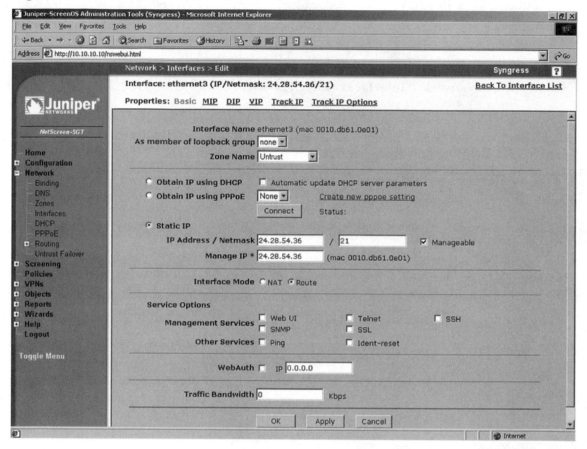

3. Use the **Manage IP*** field to enter the new IP address.

4. Click **Apply**.

To set up a management IP via the CLI, enter the command **set interface untrust manage-ip** *ipaddress*.

For remote command line access you can set up custom login banners. This is useful to give a legal statement or perhaps a help message. This can also identify specific repercussions if someone connects without permission. There are two limitations on using banners, however. First, you are limited to a single line. Second, you are limited to 127 characters. A banner can be configured for both the console and for remote Telnet sessions. This option can be configured from both the WebUI and the CLI.

From the WebUI:

1. Access **Configuration** | **Admin** | **Banners**. A screen similar to Figure 22.15 will be displayed.

Figure 22.15 Banners

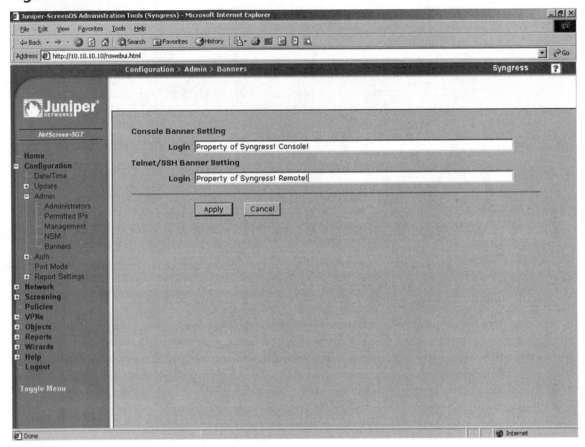

2. Use the **Console Banner Setting Login** field to enter the login banner text that will be displayed for users using the console.

3. Use the **Telnet/SSH Banner Setting Login** field to enter the login banner text that will be displayed for users using Telnet or SSH.

4. Click **Apply**.

Use the following CLI command to set the banner for console users.

```
Syngress-> set admin auth banner console login "Only permitted individuals are
allowed to use this access. If you are not permitted please disconnect!"
```

Use the following CLI command to set the banner for Telnet users.

```
Syngress-> set admin auth banner telnet login "Authorized users only!!!
All actions are logged!!!"
```

Finally, there are three options that can be configured from the command line only that can enhance your security. Two of these options are not going to save your system, but since they are new to the 5.0 ScreenOS release, they are worth mentioning. First, you can enforce a minimum length for administrative user passwords. Second, you can restrict how many unsuccessful login attempts that a user can have before they are kicked out of the system. The default is three and it does not lock out the user; that same person could attempt to Telnet back in and do it again. Finally, you can restrict the root user to gain access from the console only. This can prevent anyone from gaining root access to the device unless they had physical access to the device.

Use the following CLI commands to set a minimum password length, limit access attempts, and restrict root user access to the console, respectively.

```
Syngress-> set admin password restrict length 8
Syngress-> set admin access attempts 2
Syngress-> set admin root access console
```

The ideas in this section will definitely help you secure your device. Security is all about mitigating risk. With these management security procedures in place you significantly lower the chances of encountering a security problem. You can mix and match the configurations that work best in your environment.

Updating ScreenOS

Juniper Networks is committed to providing a secure and robust operating system for the NetScreen firewall product line. From time to time Juniper will publish new version of ScreenOS. These may include security updates, feature enhancements, or both. It is very important that you maintain the software on your firewall. It is a core component of your network security and it has to be secure. There are several methods that you can use to upgrade ScreenOS. First we will focus on the command line methods. From the command line you can not only update your OS, but you can also back up your operating system. When using the command line you are required to use a TFTP server. Use the following command to back up your software:

```
Syngress-> save software from flash to tftp ipaddress 5.0.0r8.1-5GT.bin
```

Use the following command to update the software:

```
Syngress-> save software from tftp 1.2.3.4 5.0.0r8.1-5GT.bin to flash
```

You can also use the WebUI to update the firmware. However, as we mentioned before, you cannot download the current software from the WebUI.

1. Access **Configuration | Update | ScreenOS/Keys**. A screen similar to Figure 22.16 will be displayed.

Figure 22.16 ScreenOS/Keys

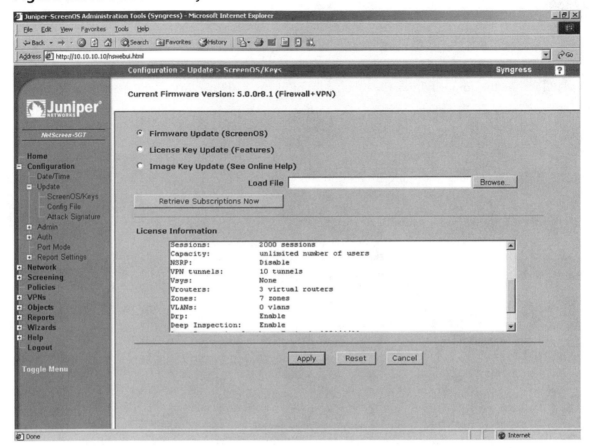

2. Enable the **Firmware Update (ScreenOS)** option.

3. Click **Browse** and locate and select the previously downloaded firmware file (stored on the local system).

4. Click **Apply**. It may take several minutes to update the system with the new OS.

System Recovery

There may be times when your NetScreen firewall runs into problems from which you cannot recover. There are three situations that we will go over in this section. One of the major issues that people run into is configuration management. There may be scenarios that you run into where you are about to make changes that you are unsure of. You may be adding a new route or a new policy that could create havoc on your network, but currently you are running on a successful configuration. In cases where you need a backup copy of a correctly functioning configuration file, you can use the configuration rollback feature.

The configuration rollback feature allows you maintain a backup configuration file that you can use in case your primary configuration file, saved or running, runs into problems. This is a great feature that can get you out of tight squeezes if you run into issues. The configuration rollback cannot be performed from the WebUI. Use the following steps to save your system configuration.

1. Use the command **get file** to get a list of files in flash memory.

2. Enter the command **save config to last-known good**. A new file called lkg.cfg will be created. This file is your rollback configuration file. It is a saved copy of the running configuration at the time you executed the command. That file stays on the system unless you use the **delete** command to remove it. This means that even if you reset the configuration to the defaults, you still will keep this configuration.

To restore a previously saved system configuration, enter the command **exec config rollback**. Note that this process forces your device to reboot.

You can use this restoration process at any time as long as the file exists. There is one additional way to use the configuration rollback. If you are working on a new configuration that could possibly cause you to lose access to your system for whatever reason, configuration rollback can be put into a *watching* mode. In this mode, if the device is reset, it will automatically reset the configuration back to the stored rollback configuration. This is excellent in cases where you need to ensure the safe restoration of your devices provided networking services.

To put the rollback in watching mode, enter the command **exec config rollback enable**. The command prompt will include the text "(rollback enabled)". To turn this mode off, enter **exec config rollback disable**.

Now that we have discussed how to recover your configuration, we now need to look at another scenario. What if you lose your root password? This is a tough scenario to recover from, because you have lost access to the system. There are two methods to recover from this error. Both methods require you to have console access to the device. In the first scenario, you would log into the serial console using the serial number of the device as the username and password. Once you do this, you will be notified that you will lose your configuration and all of your settings. If you have processed proper configuration management, you will be fine. Just as a note; even the configuration rollback file is deleted. So you must have saved your configuration somewhere off of the system if you want to restore it.

The following shows a typical serial number login and the resulting messages.

```
login: 00642120012308289
password:
!!! Lost Password Reset !!! You have initiated a command to reset the device to
factory defaults, clearing all current configuration and settings. Would you like
to continue? y/[n] y

!! Reconfirm Lost Password Reset !! If you continue, the entire configuration of the
device will be erased. In addition, a permanent counter will be incremented to
signify that this device has been reset. This is your last chance to cancel this
command. If you proceed, the device will return to factory default configuration,
which is: System IP: 192.168.1.1; username: netscreen, password: netscreen. Would
you like to continue? y/[n] y
```

Another way to access a system when you have forgotten the root password is to use the reset button located on the exterior if the system. To use this type of configuration use the following procedure:

1. Locate the reset button on the system. The button is recessed and you would need to use a paper clip or pin to use it

2. Press and hold the button down until the flashing green status light turns red then turns back to flashing green.

3. Release the button and then press it again.

Doing this will reset the system and you will lose all of your configurations. This is done for security reasons. These are both powerful methods to recover your device, however you may want to disable these options. You may not want someone to simply be able to walk up to your device and reset your configuration. You are in luck because both methods can be disabled. However, if you do this the device will be unrecoverable if you lose the root password! So do not lose your root password unless you want to return the device back to Juniper Networks.

To disable the ability to log in using the serial number, enter **unset admin device-reset**. To re-enable this feature, enter **set admin device-reset**. To disable the device's reset button, enter **unset admin hw-reset**. To re-enable this feature, enter **set admin hw-reset**.

In the previous section we looked at ways to upgrade ScreenOS. However, there are many ways in which the image can be corrupted when you upload the file. More then likely your file was previously damaged before you uploaded it. However, there is no reason to worry if your system cannot boot. To restore your system to a functional configuration you need to have serial console access to the system and a TFTP server on the local network to the device. During the boot process a prompt will be displayed four times. The prompt will say, "Hit any key to run loader". Press any key and you will be asked for the file you want to load, the IP address you want to assign to your device, and the IP address of the TFTP server. The interface that gets the IP address you assign is one of the following depending on what type of device you have: Trust, E1, or E1/1. If the file can be found on the TFTP server it will be loaded into flash and then your device will reboot. When the device reboots it will load the new OS image.

```
NetScreen NS-5GT Boot Loader Version 2.1.0 (Checksum: 61D07DA5)
Copyright (c) 1997-2003 NetScreen Technologies, Inc.
Total physical memory: 128MB
  Test - Pass
  Initialization.… Done
Hit any key to run loader
Hit any key to run loader
Hit any key to run loader
Serial Number [0123012123008289]: READ ONLY
HW Version Number [1010]: READ ONLY
Self MAC Address [0010-db61-1230]: READ ONLY
Boot File Name [ns5gt.5.0.0r8.1]:
Self IP Address [192.168.1.1]:
TFTP IP Address [192.168.1.31]:
Save loader config (56 bytes)… Done
```

Configuring NetScreen

Now that you are familiar with the basics of managing your NetScreen firewall, it is now time to configure your firewall for the first time. In this section we will look at configuring basic requirements to make your system functional on your network. There are three basics for getting your device running on the network. The first thing you need is a zone. In this section we will look at how to use existing zones, create new zones, and binding zones to interfaces. The primary type of zone that exists is the *security zone*, but there are several other types of zones that can be used. It is important to know each type of zone, as they determine how an interface will function. Some zones you many never use, but knowing is half the battle.

There are several types of interfaces on a NetScreen firewall device. You will always have physical interfaces, of course, as they are required to connect to the network. NetScreen also offers several other types of interfaces that you can use. These interfaces provide different functions and are not all actual physical devices. These types of interfaces include subinterfaces, management interfaces, high availability interfaces, and tunnel interfaces. Each type of interface was designed to provide a specific function on the NetScreen device. We will look at each interface type, its function, and how you can leverage their special abilities on your network.

Your newly configured interface will require an IP address if you want it to interact with your network. I am sure that you are fairly familiar with IP addressing and you have used it on at least one type of system. This process is similar for every device, as each system is implementing the IP standard. A NetScreen firewall is no exception when using IP addressing.

Some SOHO class devices have a configuration mode called *port mode*. The SOHO devices have five physical interfaces. By default, there is one external untrust interface and four trust interfaces. However, you can change the port mode to modify the distribution of ports. This is a great feature that you can use to extend the value of the SOHO class devices. In this section we will also look at the various options you can use when configuring a network interface and using the built in PPPoE client.

Types of Zones

There are three types of zones on a NetScreen firewall. Each zone provides its own specific function and is used for a specific purpose. The security zone is the most commonly used type of zone. The other two zone types are used much less commonly. One of these types is the tunnel zone. This type of zone is used for creating route-based VPNs. The other type of zone is the function zone. This zone is used for special purposes in high availability. Each type of zone is used to bind to an interface. One exception to this rule will be defined below.

Security Zones

A security zone is used to break your network into logical segments. At a minimum, you need to define two security zones. Most NetScreen firewall devices come with predefined zones that you can use. These zones are usually trust, untrust, and DMZ (de-militarized zone). This varies from device to device. You need to use two zones because this will allow you to separate your network into two parts, usually the two areas you want to separate from each other. Each NetScreen firewall can use only a limited amount of zones. On some devices you can only have a few, while on the higher end firewalls you could have several hundred zones. There is another type of security zone called a layer two zone.

Tunnel Zones

Tunnel zones are used with tunnel interfaces. Tunnel interfaces are a special type of virtual interface that can terminate VPN traffic. Tunnel interfaces are first bound to the tunnel zone. Then the tunnel zone is bound to a security zone, which is in turn bound to a physical interface. Tunnel zones are covered in depth the chapters working with VPNs.

Function Zones

Function zones are used to provide a single type of unique function. There are five types of function zones. The first type is the null zone. The null zone is used as a placeholder for interfaces that are not bound to a zone. The next type of function zone is the MGT zone. This zone is used on out-of-band management interfaces. The HA function zone is used for high availability interfaces. There are no configurable options for the HA zone. The self zone is used to host management connections. When using the remote management protocols to connect to your NetScreen device for management you are connecting to the self zone. The last type of zone is the VLAN zone. It is used to host the VLAN1 interface. The VLAN1 interface is used to manage a NetScreen firewall that is running in transparent mode.

Virtual Routers

As we have discussed, any device that uses the IP protocol must have a routing table that determines how to send information from one place to another. The NetScreen takes this idea to a whole new level by allowing you to have multiple routing tables called virtual routers. Each virtual router has its own routing table that is a complete separate routing domain from other virtual routers. In this chapter we will only be looking at the trust virtual router and configuring routes in it. A full explanation of routing is covered in Chapter 25.

Types of Interfaces

A NetScreen firewall can contain several types of interfaces. An interface allows traffic to enter a zone and leave a zone. If you want an interface to pass traffic, you need to bind it to a zone. Once you bind an interface to a zone, you can apply an IP address to it. There are four types of interfaces: security zone interfaces, function zone interfaces, tunnel interfaces and loopback interfaces. As you can see, each type of interface has a corresponding zone type, except for the loopback interface, which is a special type of interface.

Security Zone Interfaces

Security zone interfaces are used primarily for the passing of traffic from one zone to another. In this category is any type of interface related to physical interfaces or virtual interfaces that are a collection of multiple physical interfaces. This is the most common type interface you will work with on a NetScreen firewall.

Physical Interfaces

Every NetScreen firewall has some sort of physical interface. These interfaces are used to connect the firewall to the network. The naming convention of the physical interfaces varies based upon the platform.

On the SOHO class of the NetScreen appliances, the interface names are based upon the zones. For example, the internal interface is named trust and the external interface is named untrust. On the NetScreen-25 up to the NetScreen-208 products, the interfaces are named beginning with the media type *Ethernet* and then specified by the port number, such as "ethernet1". NetScreen firewalls that are systems, including the NetScreen-500, ISG-2000, NetScreen-5200, and NetScreen-5400, are named with the media type, slot number, and then the port number. For example, ethernet2/1 would be an Ethernet interface in slot number two and port number one. Physical interfaces can be assigned a single primary IP address.

There are some situations where you may need to have multiple IP address on an interface. You can add multiple secondary IP addresses on each physical interface. When a secondary IP address is added, the NetScreen firewall automatically adds a route between the two IP address segments. This way you can connect between the two segments. This will automatically remove the route if you delete the secondary IP address. If you want to segment these two networks, you can disable routing between the two. This will just drop packets between the two, but the routing table will not be modified.

Secondary IP addresses have some restrictions as well. First, subnets between the multiple secondary interfaces cannot overlap. Second, interfaces in the untrust zone are unable to use multiple secondary IP addresses. If you choose to manage your firewall with the secondary IP address, it inherits the management properties of the primary interface. The secondary interface is unable to have a gateway, which means anything connecting to that interface must be on that local network.

Subinterfaces

Subinterfaces are used primarily with VLANs. If, for example, you had a network that contained several VLANs, a NetScreen firewall could act as a central point to connect between the separate VLANs. Each subinterface acts just like a physical interface. All of the subinterfaces that are bound to a physical interface can only use the bandwidth that is provided by that interface. So if you have a single 100Mbps interface and several subinterfaces, they can only use the maximum bandwidth of that 100Mbps interface shared amongst them. The properties of a subinterface are otherwise identical to that of a physical interface. However, each subinterface *must* be assigned to a different VLAN and they *must* have a different IP subnet than all of physical interfaces and the other subinterfaces defined on the firewall.

Aggregate Interfaces

When you create an aggregate interface you are binding multiple physical interfaces together to create one super interface. This interface acts as if it was a single physical interface. It provides cumulative bandwidth. So if you bound two 1 gigabit interfaces together, you would have a combined throughput of 2Gbps for that interface. If one of the interfaces was to fail, the remaining interface would continue to carry the traffic. However, that remaining interface can only carry as much traffic as the interface is rated for. So if you had two gigabit interfaces bound together and lost one, you would lower your maximum throughput to 1Gbps. This is a great feature, but is only available on the NetScreen-5200 and the NetScreen-5400 systems.

Redundant Interfaces

The redundant interface is much like the aggregate interface, but only has one of the two benefits of the aggregate interface. Redundant interfaces are unable to combine their bandwidth, and only provide redundancy in case of a failure. This is still a great option to use when redundancy is a requirement.

VLAN1 Interface

The VLAN1 interface is used for one purpose. When you configure a NetScreen firewall to operate in transparent mode, the physical interfaces do not have IP addresses. You will need a way still to manage the firewall and to terminate VPNs. The VLAN1 interface is a virtual security interface that can have an IP address assigned to it. This allows you to remotely manage your firewall and, if need be, have an IP address to terminate VPNs to.

Virtual Security Interfaces

The last type of security interface is the virtual security interface (VSI). This type of interface is used when two NetScreen devices are used in a high availability configuration. The two firewalls are combined to create a single entity called a virtual security device (VSD). Each device in the cluster defines a physical interface to create a VSI. This VSI has its own MAC address and IP address and operates just like a physical interface.

Function Zone Interfaces

Function zone interfaces are special interfaces that are used for a single purpose or task. These interfaces are dedicated to that task and cannot be used to do anything else.

Management Interfaces

Some NetScreen firewalls contain an interface dedicated for management of the device. This interface is called the MGT interface. It allows you to separate the management of the device from rest of the network by using this special interface. It is ensures that you will have bandwidth for management applications. Because the interface does not pass general-purpose traffic, it provides additional security by being dedicated to management.

HA Interfaces

On NetScreen systems (NetScreen-500 and later), each device contains two HA interfaces, HA1, and HA2. These interfaces are used exclusively for high availability. One interface passes control messages to each device. The second HA interface is used for traffic synchronization. If one of the interfaces fails, the remaining HA interface would provide both services. You must use a minimum of 100Mbps interfaces for high availability interfaces.

Some devices that can function in a HA cluster do not have dedicated interfaces for high availability. You can use a virtual HA interface, which is bound to a physical interface. This allows you to use the high availability configurations even though you do not have a dedicated interface to do this.

Tunnel Interfaces

A tunnel interface is used as a gateway to a VPN. This allows you to create a VPN configuration and then bind that VPN to the tunnel interface. If you wanted to pass traffic to the VPN, you would simply create a route on your firewall to point to the tunnel interface for the remote network. The VPN will be automatically established and traffic will be encrypted and sent to the remote gateway.

Loopback Interfaces

The last type of interface we are going to discuss is the loopback interface. The loopback interface is a special interface. It is a virtual interface that does not exist except logically inside of the firewall. A loopback interface is assigned to a zone and it is not accessible from other zones unless you specify a policy to permit the traffic. A loopback interface can be used to manage your firewall as well as to manage it.

Configuring Security Zones

The security zones are the core part for creating policies in the NetScreen firewall. Policies are not discussed in this chapter, but are discussed in the next chapter, "Basic Policy Configuration". Here, though, it is important that you become an expert on managing security zones. Once you have the security zones created and configured, it will be much easier for you to effectively create policies. As mentioned before, there will be several predefined security zones on your firewall. These are typically trust, untrust, and DMZ. The trust zone is designed for the internal protected network. The untrust zone is designed typically for the Internet or other undesirable places. The DMZ zone is to be used for your DMZ network. The trust zone and untrust zone have some unique properties that will be discussed later in the chapter. The predefined zones cannot be deleted, but they can be modified.

First, let's look at the zones we have configured on our device. This can be done from both the command line as well as the WebUI. To view the zones using the WebUI, access **Network | Zones**. A screen similar to the one shown in Figure 22.17 will be displayed.

Figure 22.17 Network Zones

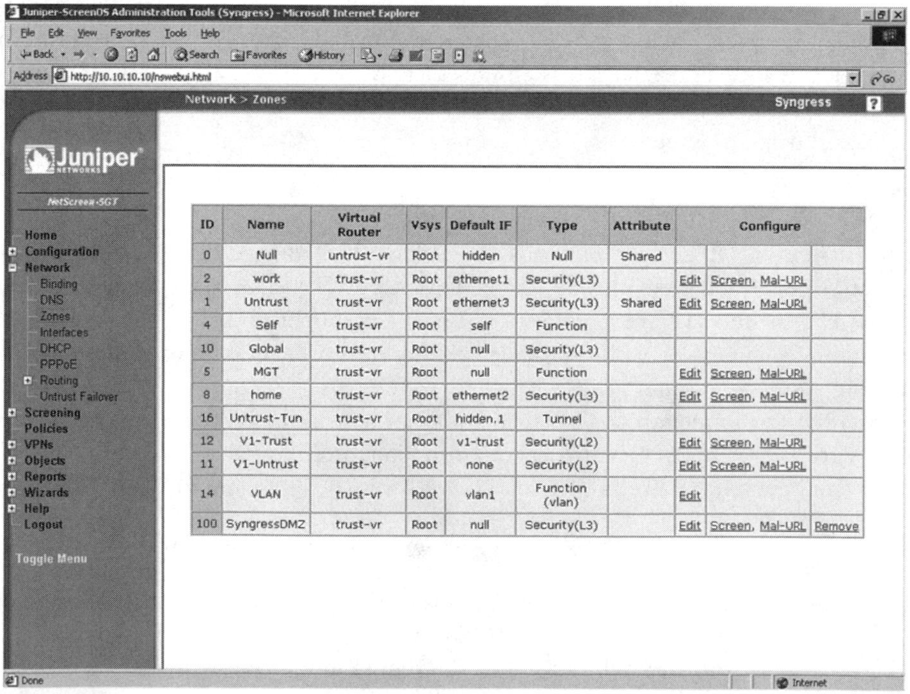

To view the zones using the CLI, enter the command **get zone**. You will see each zone listed in an output similar to the following:

```
Total 10 zones created in vsys Root - 5 are policy configurable.
Total policy configurable zones for Root is 5.
-----------------------------------------------------------------------
 ID  Name            Type        Attr      VR           Default-IF  VSYS
  0  Null            Null        Shared    untrust-vr   hidden      Root
  1  Untrust         Sec(L3)     Shared    trust-vr     untrust     Root
  2  Trust           Sec(L3)               trust-vr     trust       Root
  4  Self            Func                  trust-vr     self        Root
  5  MGT             Func                  trust-vr     null        Root
 10  Global          Sec(L3)               trust-vr     null        Root
 11  V1-Untrust      Sec(L2)               trust-vr     None        Root
 12  V1-Trust        Sec(L2)               trust-vr     v1-trust    Root
 14  VLAN            Func                  trust-vr     vlan1       Root
 16  Untrust-Tun     Tun                   trust-vr     hidden.1    Root
-----------------------------------------------------------------------
```

Both the WebUI and the CLI look very similar as far as the way that zones are displayed. Both show the following information:

- **ID**   The ID is used when doing debugging. It is important to understand where to locate the zone ID.

- **Name**   The name is used as a label for the zone.

- **Type**   This tells you what type of zone this is. As you can see, there are several of the zone types we have mentioned.

- **Attr**   This specifies any additional attributes for the zone. *Shared* means that the zone is shared among all local VSYS. By default, untrust and null are shared.

- **VR**   This specifies which virtual router that the zone is operating in.

- **Default-IF**   This identifies which interface is bound to the zone by default.

- **VSYS**   This lists which VSYS or virtual system the zone is bound to.

It is a simple task to create a new zone. However, before doing so, you should know the following information:

- **Name**   What you want to name your zone. It helps to be descriptive. If you have a DMZ for web servers, naming it WebDMZ is more helpful than if you were to just choose DMZ02. This is really a personal preference. If you are creating a layer two security zone, the zone must be prefixed with "L2-"

- **Type of zone**   You can create three types of zones; security layer three zones, security layer two zones, and tunnel zones.

This is the minimum information you would need to configure a zone. There are some additional options that can be configured on a zone:

- **SCREEN**   SCREEN options are defense options that protect against specific attacks and malicious traffic.

- **Malicious URL protection**   This feature provides pattern matching for HTTP traffic. It allows you to identify malicious URLs and block those requests.

- **Block Intra-Zone Traffic**   If this option is selected, it will allow you to block traffic between two interfaces bound to the same zone. This would be called intrazone traffic.

- **If TCP non SYN, send RESET back**   This option is only valid for layer three security zones and tunnel zones. If this option is enabled, the NetScreen firewall will send a RESET TCP packet to any host that sends a TCP segment with a TCP flag set other than SYN and that does not belong to an existing session. If you have SYN checking enabled (this is done from the CLI using the command **set flow tcp-syn-check**) the unsolicited SYN packet is dropped and the session initiator is notified to reset the TCP connection without initializing a new session in the session table. If the NetScreen firewall was to skip sending the RESET notice, the system that was attempting to initiate the session would continually send SYN packets until its connection attempt timed out. If SYN checking is disabled, the NetScreen firewall passes the SYN packet to the end system if a policy permits it. This is useful for blocking packets that can be used in different types of network scans. If you are unsure if this will help you, it is best to leave this at the default setting.

- **IP/TCP Reassembly for ALG**   (Application Layer Gateway) If this option is selected, the NetScreen firewall will reassemble fragmented HTTP and FTP packets before they are inspected. This will allow for more efficient enforcement for the Mal-URL engine to inspect the traffic. If you are not using the Mal-URL feature, leave this option off.

- **Shared Zone**   This option is only available if you have a NetScreen device that supports virtual systems. This option enables the zone to be shared among all of the virtual systems. Once you enable this option, you are unable to disable it. You must either delete the zone or disable all virtual systems first.

- **IP Classification**   This option is used with virtual systems only. If this option is selected, the firewall will associate all traffic with this zone to a particular virtual system.

- **WebUI**   (layer two zones only) Selecting this option enables management for the WebUI on this zone.

- **SNMP**   (layer two zones only) Select this option to enable SNMP (Simple Network Management Protocol) services on this zone.

- **Telnet**   (layer two zones only) Select this option to enable Telnet management on this zone.

- **SSL**   (layer two zones only) Selecting this option enables SSL WebUI management on this zone.

- **SSH**   (layer two zones only) Selecting this option enables SSH management on this zone.

- **NSM**   (layer two zones only) Selecting this option enables NSM management on this zone.

- **Ping**   (layer two zones only) Selecting this option enables ping from the firewall in this zone.

- **Ident-reset**   (layer two zones only) – Some services such as SMTP and FTP send an ident, or identification request. If you have Ident-reset enabled, it will reset this ident request and allow you access to that service.

- **WebAuth**   (layer two zones only) Selecting this option enables web authentication when passing through the interface that this zone is bound to.

Most of the time you would just define the name for the new zone and what type of zone it is. However, it is always a good idea to know all of the options when creating your new zone. Some of the above options are seldom used, but may serve as a good reference to use in the future.

Next we will go through the actual zone creation process. We will again focus on layer three zones, as the other zone types will be covered in later chapters. Use the following steps to create a zone using the WebUI:

1. Access **Network | Zones** and click **New**. A screen similar to Figure 22.18 will be displayed.

Figure 22.18 Create a New Zone

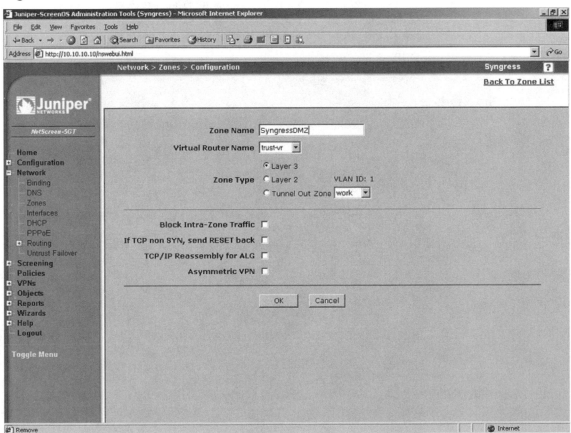

2. Enter the **Zone Name**.

3. Ensure **trust-vr** is selected in the **Virtual Router Name** drop-down list.

4. In the **Zone Type** section, select the **Layer 3** option.

5. Click **OK**.

```
To create a zone using the CLI, enter the command set zone name name, where name
is the name for the zone.
```

Once a zone is created, you can modify all of its properties except for its name. To change the name, you must delete the zone, then re-create it using the desired name. Use the following steps to delete a zone using the WebUI:

1. Access **Network | Zones** and click the **Remove** link of the zone you wish to delete.

2. Click **OK** to confirm.

To remove a zone using the CLI, enter the command **unset zone *name***, where *name* is the name of the zone you wish to remove.

Use the following steps to modify an existing zone via the WebUI:

1. Access **Network | Zones** and click the **Edit** link of the zone you wish to modify. A screen similar to the one shown in Figure 22.19 will be displayed.

Figure 22.19 Edit a Zone

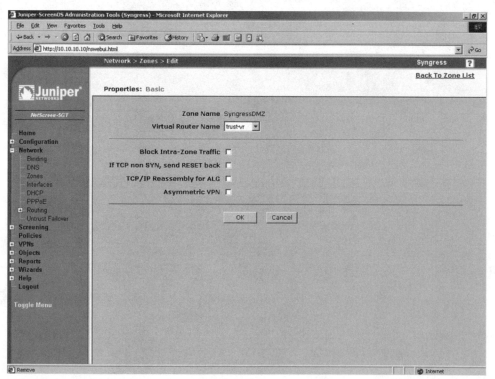

2. Change the desired fields and click **OK**.

Configuring Your NetScreen for the Network

When configuring a NetScreen device, there are several steps you need to perform before it can interact with the network. A physical interface must be first bound to a zone before it can be assigned an IP address. Figure 22.20 depicts the relationship between a zone and an interface. A zone is a parent to a physical interface and the IP address is a child to the physical interface.

Figure 22.20 Zone Interface/IP Relationship

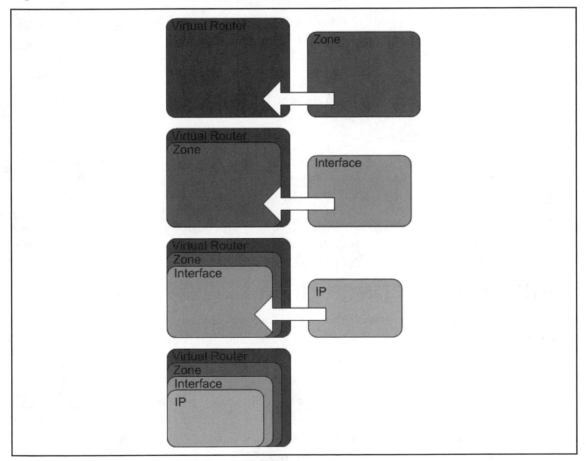

Binding an Interface to a Zone

First let's bind an interface to a zone. In this case we will be using a NetScreen-5GT and we will bind the trust zone to the trust interface. This can be done in both the WebUI and the CLI. However, to change the zone you must first remove the IP address by setting it to **0.0.0.0/0**. Then you can select a new Zone.

From the WebUI:

1. Access **Network | Interfaces**.

2. Click the **Edit** link for the **trust** interface.

3. Select **Trust** from the **Zone Name** drop-down list.

4. Click **OK**.

To bind an interface to a zone using the CLI, enter the command **set interface *interfacename* zone *zonename***, where *interfacename* is the name of the interface you wish to bind and *zonename* is the name of the zone you wish to bind the specified interface to.

Setting up IP Addressing

We will now assign an IP address of 192.168.0.1 with a twenty-four-bit subnet mask to the interface. This can be done in both the WebUI and the CLI. If you wanted to modify the IP address of an interface, it is the same as if you were setting it up for the first time.

From the WebUI:

1. Access **Network | Interfaces** and click the **Edit** link for the **trust** interface (or whichever interface you are binding to).

2. Select the **Static IP** option.

3. Enter **192.168.0.1** (or whatever IP address you want to assign) in the IP address text field, and enter **24** (or another value) in the netmask text field.

4. Click **OK**.

To assign an IP address to an interface using the CLI, enter the command **set interface *interfacename* ip *ipaddress netmask***, where *interfacename* is the name of the interface, *ipaddress* is the IP address you want to assign, and *netmask* is the netmask.

Configuring the DHCP Client

Now let's take our NetScreen-5GT and set the untrust interface to receive an IP address from DHCP. This will allow the NetScreen to be plugged into any cable modem, DSL, or internal network and seamlessly get an IP address.

From the WebUI:

1. Access **Network | Interfaces** and click the **Edit** link for the **untrust** interface (or whichever interface you are configuring).

2. Select the **Obtain IP using DHCP** option.

3. Enable the **Automatic update of DHCP server parameters** option.

4. Click **OK**.

To set this configuration using the CLI, enter the command **set interface *interfacename* dhcp client enable**, where *interfacename* is the name of the interface you wish to configure.

Using PPPoE

Some DSL service providers require the use of a protocol called PPPoE, or Point-to-Point Protocol over Ethernet. This requires an additional configuration. You must configure a PPPoE instance and bind to an interface, then configure the interface to use PPPoE to negotiate the connection. You will then get an IP address from PPPoE, just as you would with DHCP.

From the WebUI:

1. Access **Network | PPPoE**. A screen similar to Figure 22.21 will be displayed.

Figure 22.21 Network PPPoE

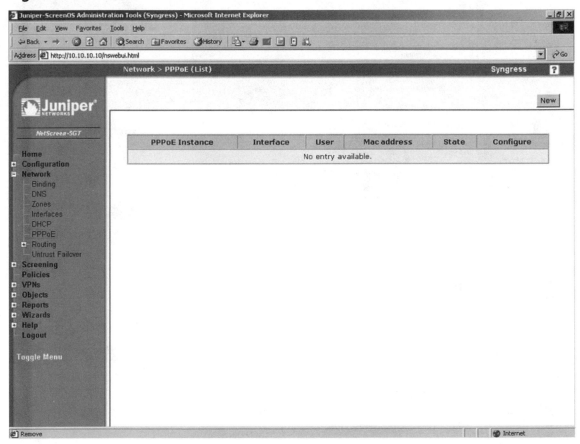

2. Click **New**. A screen similar to the one shown in Figure 22.22 will be displayed.

Figure 22.22 Network | PPPoE | Edit

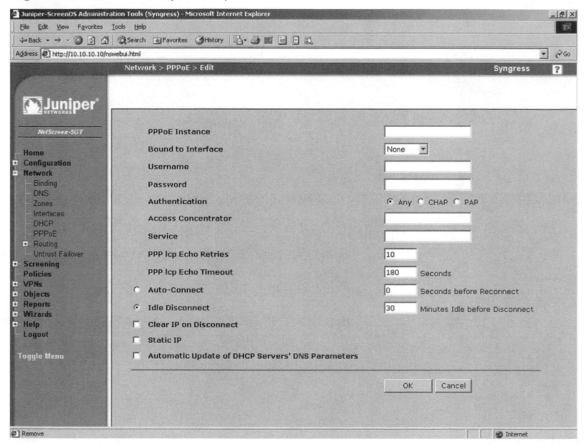

3. Use the PPPoE Instance field to enter the name.

4. Choose **untrust** from the **Bound to Interface** drop-down list (or whichever interface you are binding to).

5. Enter your ISP-provided username and password in the **Username** and **Password** fields, respectively.

6. Select the **Any Authentication** option.

7. Enable the **Automatic Update of DHCP Servers' DNS Parameters** option.

8. Click **OK**.

To create a PPPoE connection via the CLI, enter the command **set pppoe name "*name*" username "*username*" password "*password*"**, ensuring you include the quotes, and where *name* is the name of the interface, *username* is your ISP-provided username, and *password* is your ISP-provided password.

Interface Speed Modes

By default, all of the ports on your NetScreen firewall are auto-sensing. This means they negotiate the Ethernet settings such as speed and duplex. This is great most of the time, but in an ideal world you may want to hard code these settings to ensure that you are getting the proper performance out of your network. This configuration can only be done from the CLI. In the following example, we will hardcode the trust interface port four interface to 100Mbps full duplex.

```
Syngress-> get interface trust port phy
Port 1: link is down, 10Mbps, forced to half duplex
Port 2: link is down, 10Mbps, forced to half duplex
Port 3: link is down, 10Mbps, forced to half duplex
Port 4: link is up, 100Mbps, auto negotiated to full duplex
Syngress-> set int trust port 4 phy full 100mb
Syngress-> get interface trust port phy
Port 1: link is down, 10Mbps, forced to half duplex
Port 2: link is down, 10Mbps, forced to half duplex
Port 3: link is down, 10Mbps, forced to half duplex
Port 4: link is up, 100Mbps, forced to full duplex
```

Port Mode Configuration

Some devices in the SOHO product line support something called port mode. These devices contain one untrust or external port and four internal ports. By default, the four internal ports are called trust and are bound to the trust zone. However, there are four other modes you can use as well. The *extended* mode requires an additional license. When you change between port modes, this removes your existing configuration. If you clear your configuration by using the **unset all** command, the port mode setting will be unaffected. In Table 22.3 you can see the differences between the different modes.

Table 22.3 Port Modes

Port	Trust-Untrust		Home-Work		Dual Untrust		Combined		Extended	
	Int	Zone	Int	Zone	Int	Zone	Int	Zone	Int	Zone
Untrusted	Untrust	Untrust	Eth3	Untrust	Eth3	Untrust	Eth4	Untrust	Eth3	Untrust
1	Trust	Trust	Eth1	Work	Eth1	Trust	Eth1	Work	Eth1	Trust
2	Trust	Trust	Eth1	Work	Eth1	Trust	Eth2	Home	Eth1	Trust
3	Trust	Trust	Eth2	Home	Eth1	Trust	Eth2	Home	Eth2	DMZ
4	Trust	Trust	Eth2	Home	Eth2	Untrust	Eth3	Untrust	Eth2	DMZ
Modem	Serial	Null	Serial	Null	Serial	N/A	N/A	N/A	Serial	Untrust

You can change the port mode settings from both the WebUI. You can see the port mode WebUI configuration in Figure 22.23.

Figure 22.23 Port Mode Configuration

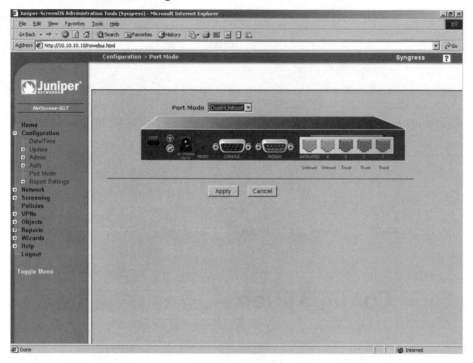

Use the following steps to change the port mode settings via the WebUI:

1. Access **Configuration | Port Mode**.

2. Select the desired mode from the **Port Mode** drop-down list.

3. Click **Apply**, then click **OK** to confirm. Your current configuration will be erased and the device will reboot.

To change modes using the CLI, enter the command **exec port-mode combined** and press **y** to confirm. Your current configuration will be erased and the device will reboot.

Configuring Basic Network Routing

When you want to connect to a remote network, you need to inform your firewall of its location. You would do this by adding network routes on your firewall. These routes tell the firewall where the remote network can be found. In this section we will look at adding a static route to access a remote network. We will also be adding a default route. A default route is also known as the route of last resort. So if a packet on a device needs to get to a location and no other routes on the device are able to identify the next gateway for it to go to, it will use the default gateway. When a system is determining what route to use, it will always use the most specific route first.

In this example we will add a static route on our NetScreen firewall to determine the next hop for the 192.168.1.0/24 network. In this chapter we will only be using the trust-vr. Routing with multiple virtual routers will fully be explained in Chapter 24. Adding routes can be done from both the WebUI and the CLI. When adding a route there are several pieces of information you need to know beforehand:

- **Remote network**   you need to identify what the remote network you will be adding the route for is. In our example we will be using 192.168.1.0/24. You can also add routes for single hosts if you like such as 192.168.1.20/32.

- **Interface or virtual router**   For our purposes here we will only be looking at interfaces. The interface will be on what physical interface that gateway is located.

- **Next hop gateway**   You need to know which system can take your packets to the specified remote network. This device must be capable of connecting to the remote network, or if not, it must know where the remote network can be located.

- **Metric**   The metric is a preference number, with the lowest number having the highest priority. All directly connected networks have a metric of zero. All static routes have a default metric of one. There may be cases in which you need to add the same route twice, the preferred route with the lower metric and the less preferred route with the higher metric. If the first route is unavailable, the firewall will use the next route.

Let's begin with our first example of adding our static route in the WebUI.

1. Access **Network | Routing | Routing Entries**. A screen similar to the one shown in Figure 22.24 will be displayed.

Figure 22.24 Routing Entries

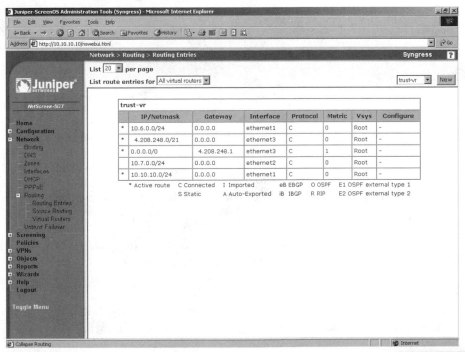

2. Use the drop-down list in the upper right-hand corner to select the virtual router and click **New**. In our example, we will select **trust-vr**. A screen similar to the one shown in Figure 22.25 will be displayed.

Figure 22.25 Configure a Routing Entry

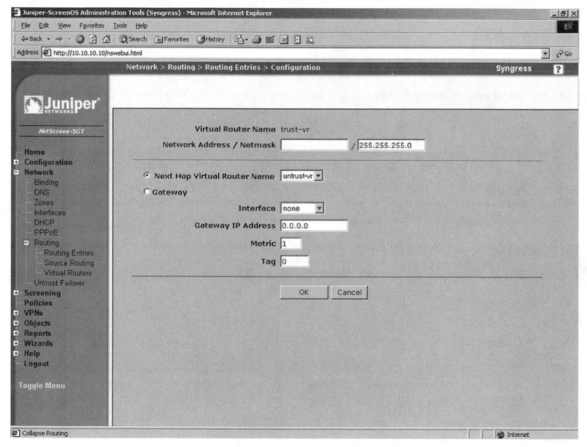

3. Enter the **Network Address / Netmask**.

4. Select the **Gateway** option.

5. Use the **Interface** drop-down list to select the interface (gateway) that is the next hop and use the **Gateway IP Address** field to enter the gateway's IP address.

6. Click **OK**.

To add a static route using the CLI, enter the command **set route *ipaddress/netmask* interface *interfacename* gateway *gatewayip***, where *ipaddress* is the virtual router's IP address, *netmask* is the cirtual router's netmask, *interfacename* is the next hop gateway, and *gatewayip* is the IP address of the next hop gateway.

To remove a static route via the WebUI, access **Network | Routing | Routing Entries** and click the **Remove** link of the route you wish to delete. Click **OK** to confirm.

The most important and often most used route on a firewall is the default route, or route of last resort. This route is used when no other route matches the traffic. Typically this route will point to your Internet router. If you are running either DHCP or PPPoE, your default route will likely come from that source. However, there may be times when you need to add your own default route. This can be done from both the WebUI and the CLI. It is much like adding a static route, as we did above.

From the WebUI:

1. Access **Network | Routing | Routing Entries**.

2. Select your virtual router from the drop-down list in the upper right-hand corner and click **New**.

3. Enter **0.0.0.0** in the **Network Address** field and enter 0 in the **Netmask** field.

4. Select the **Gateway** option.

5. Use the **Interface** drop-down list to select the interface that acts as the next hop gateway and enter the **Gateway IP Address**.

6. Click **OK**.

To remove the static route using the CLI, enter the command **set route 0.0.0.0/0 interface** *interfacename* **gateway** *gatewayip*, where *interfacename* is the next hop gateway and *gatewayip* is the gateway's IP address.

Configuring System Services

On your NetScreen firewall there are some other notable things to configure. These are important options that you will want to know about. We will first look at configuring the local clock on the device. Configuring the time is very important for being able to correlate information in the logs to a specific time. Also, the firewall executes certain events at given times. If the time is configured improperly, this can cause events to not occur at the correct times.

Most NetScreen firewalls contain a built in DHCP server. Typically, you can have a server on each interface. This allows you to manage your internal IP addressing in a single location. All NetScreen firewalls are able to query DNS servers. This allows them to resolve hostnames to IP addresses just as normal systems do. It is important to have working DNS servers configured on your firewall in case you would use the network to synchronize time to an NTP server.

There is a great deal of information generated by your firewall in the form of logs. Because all NetScreen firewalls have very limited space for storing the logs, you may want to be able to send this logging information to a remote system. We will look at how to configure and use two different remote log repositories. Finally we will look at license keys. These keys unlock the features of your firewall device. We will investigate how license keys work and how to update your license key.

Setting The Time

Every NetScreen device contains an internal clock. This clock continually runs while the device is turned on. You can manually set the clock from both the WebUI and the CLI. Ideally, you want to configure your firewall to contact a timeserver using the Network Time Protocol (NTP). This way the firewall can periodically query the timeserver to ensure that it has the proper time. First we will look at how to manually set the time on your firewall. Figure 22.26 shows the time configuration page from the WebUI.

Figure 22.26 Date/Time Configuration

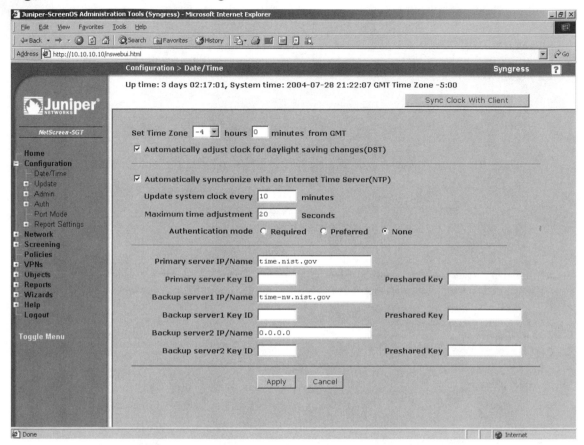

From the WebUI:

1. Access **Configuration | Date/Time**.

2. Use the **Set Time Zone** fields to specify the difference between your time zone and GMT (Greenwich Mean Time).

3. Enable the **Automatically adjust clock for daylight saving changes (DST)** option.

4. Click **Apply**.

5. Click the **Sync Clock With Client** button and click **Yes** to confirm.

To set the timezone and date/time using CLI, enter the following commands:

```
Syngress-> set clock timezone vv
Syngress-> set clock MM/DD/YYYY hh:mm:ss
```

where vv in the first command is the difference between local time and GMT (expressed as + or −, for example, +3 or −5), and where MM/DD/YYYY is the month, date, and year, and where hh:mm: ss is the hour, minute, and second.

Now we will look at setting up timeservers to sync with the NTP protocol. This protocol allows up to sub-second accuracy for time synchronization. NTP is a free service and every system should use it. The only time you shouldn't use it is when you want your firewall to generate no traffic. NTP can be configured from both the CLI and the WebUI. However, you can only force NTP synchronization from the CLI. Figure 22.25 above shows the time screen, which contains the NTP settings.

From the WebUI:

1   Access **Configuration | Date/Time**.
2. Enable the **Automatically synchronize with an Internet Time Server(NTP)** option.
3. Enter **time.nist.gov** in the **Primary server IP/Name** field.
4. Enter **time-nw.nist.gov** in the **Backup server1 IP/Name** field.
5. Click **Apply**.

To synchronize the time via the CLI, enter the following commands:

```
Syngress-> set ntp timezone -5
Syngress-> set ntp server time.nist.gov
Syngress-> set ntp server backup1 time-nw.nist.gov
Syngress-> set clock ntp
Syngress-> exec ntp update
```

When asked if you want to update the system clock, press **y** for yes.

Finally, you can use something called secure network time protocol (SNTP). This provides MD5-based authentication of each packet to ensure that the packet is from the specified server. If you want to use authentication, you are required to assign a key ID and a preshared key for every timeserver you configure. Additionally, you must configure whether authenticaton is required or simply preferred.

DHCP Server

NetScreen firewall devices can act as a DHCP server. This allows your firewall to control IP address allocation on your network. Any NetScreen device is capable of hosting up to eight DHCP servers. The server can give out IP addresses from a pool or from a reserved list based on MAC address. Another great feature of the DHCP server on the NetScreen firewall is that you can have it determine if another DHCP server is running on the network. This can prevent a conflict between two servers handing out IP addresses. In our example we will set up a DHCP server on the eth2 interface of a NetScreen-5GT. We will assign a pool of IP addresses (as shown in Figure 22.27) and create one reservation based upon MAC address. DHCP servers can be configured from both the WebUI and the CLI.

Figure 22.27 DHCP List

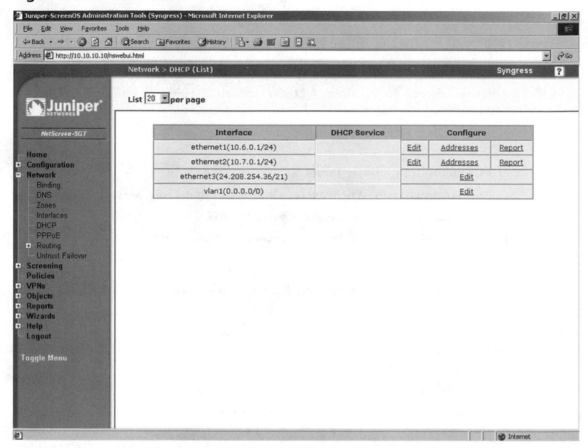

From the WebUI:

1. Access **Network | DHCP**.

2. Locate the ethernet2 interface and click its **Edit** link. A screen similar to the one shown in Figure 22.28 will be displayed.

Figure 22.28 Edit a DHCP Entry

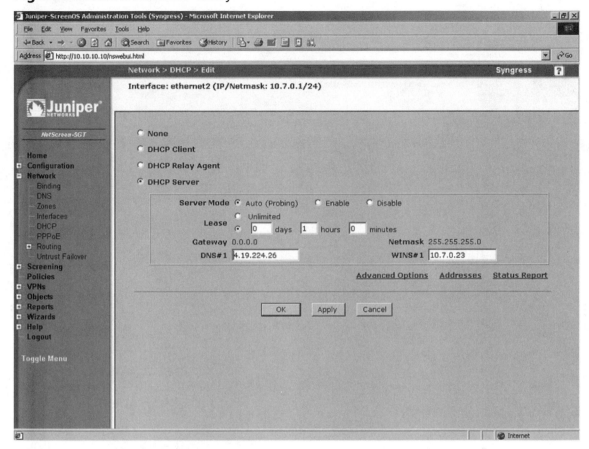

3. Enable the **DHCP Server** option.

4. For **Server Mode**, enable the **Auto (Probing)** option.

5. In the **Lease** section, click the option button that allows you to enter a specific time period, then enter the desired **days**, **hours**, and **minutes**.

6. Use the **DNS#1** field to enter the IP address of the primary DNS server.

7. Use the **WINS#1** field to enter the IP address of the primary WINS server.

8. Click **OK**. The DHCP list will be displayed.

9. Locate the ethernet2 interface in the list and click its **Addresses** link. A screen similar to the one shown in Figure 22.29 will be displayed.

Figure 22.29 DHCP Server Address List

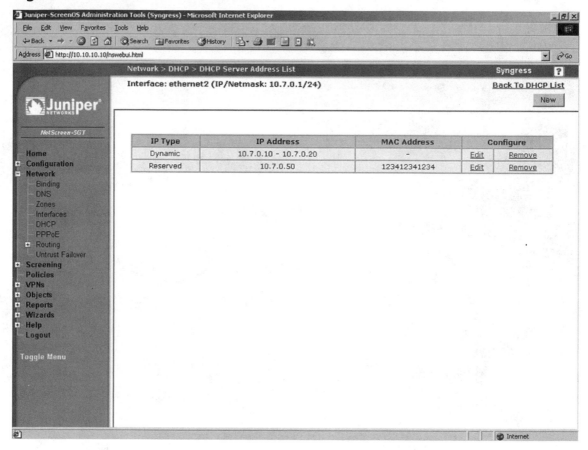

10. Click **New**.

11. Ensure the **Dynamic** option is selected.

12. Use the **IP Address Start** field to enter the first IP address in the address pool.

13. Use the **IP Address End** field to enter the last IP address in the address pool.

14. Click **OK**. The DHCP Server Address List screen will be displayed.

15. Click **New**.

16. Select the **Reserved** option.

17. Use the **IP Address** field to enter the IP address that you wish to reserve.

18. Use the **Ethernet Address** field to enter the MAC address of the device for which you wish to reserve the specified IP address.

19. Click **OK**.

Use the following commands to configure the DHCP server via the CLI:

```
Syngress-> set interface ethernet2 dhcp server auto
Syngress-> set interface ethernet2 dhcp server enable
Syngress-> set interface ethernet2 dhcp server option lease 60
Syngress-> set interface ethernet2 dhcp server option dns1 10.7.0.23
Syngress-> set interface ethernet2 dhcp server option wins1 10.7.0.23
Syngress-> set interface ethernet2 dhcp server option netmask 255.255.255.0
Syngress-> set interface ethernet2 dhcp server ip 10.7.0.10 to 10.7.0.20
Syngress-> set interface ethernet2 dhcp server ip 10.7.0.50 mac 123412341234
```

DNS

Setting up your NetScreen firewall as a DNS client is fairly simple. The firewall keeps a local cache of DNS entries, and you must decide when you want the cache to be cleared. DNS can be configured from both the WebUI and the CLI. Figure 22.30 shows the WebUI screen for configuring DNS. The hostname and domain name are also set on this page. If you are using a DHCP or PPPoE client on your firewall, the DNS server settings and domain name may be passed down and configured for you.

Figure 22.30 DNS Configuration

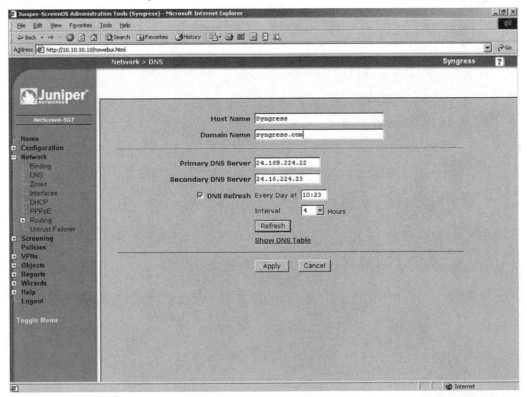

From the WebUI:

1. Access **Network | DNS**.
2. Enter a **Host Name** and a **Domain Name**.
3. Enter the IP address of the **Primary DNS Server** and the **Secondary DNS Server**.
4. Enable the **DNS Refresh** option and enter the refresh time and frequency.
5. Click **Apply**.

Enter the following commands to configure the DNS server via the CLI:

```
Syngress-> set hostname Syngress
Syngress-> set domain syngress.com
Syngress-> set dns host dns1 2.32.23.23
Syngress-> set dns host dns2 2.32.23.24
Syngress-> set dns host schedule 10:23 interval 4
```

SNMP

Simple Network Management Protocol allowsremote administrators to view data statistics on a NetScreen device. It also allows a NetScreen device to send information to a central server. NetScreen firewalls support SNMPv1 and SNMPv2c. It also supports the MIB II, or Management Information Base two standard groups. The SNMP agent supports sending the following traps:

- Cold Start Trap
- Trap for SNMP Authentication Failure
- Traps for System Alarms
- Traps for Traffic Alarms

By default, the SNMP manager has no configuration. This prevents unauthorized viewing of the system based upon default parameters. To configure your NetScreen device for SNMP you must configure community strings, SNMP host addresses, and permissions. In our configuration example we will first set up the basic system information, then we will create a new community. This can be done from both the WebUI and the CLI. You can create up to three communities with up to eight IP ranges in each. An IP range can consist of a single host or a network. If you configure a network those defined IP addresses can only poll the device and not.

Use the following steps to configure SNMP via the WebUI:

1. Access **Configuration | Report Settings | SNMP**. A screen similar to the one shown in Figure 22.31 will be displayed.

Figure 22.31 SNMP Report Settings

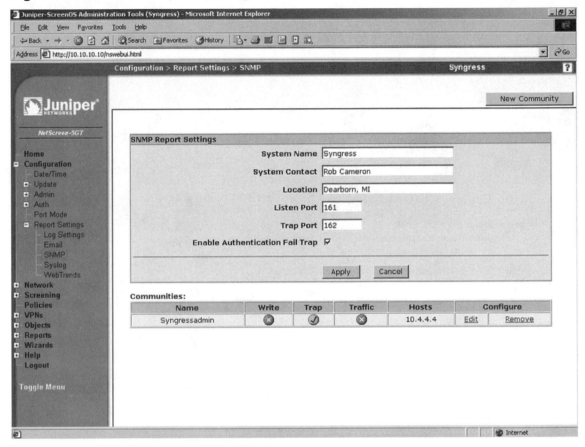

2. Enter the desired **System Name**, **System Contact**, and **Location**.

3. Enter the port numbers of the **Listen Port** and the **Trap Port**.

4. Ensure that the **Enable Authentication Fail Trap** option is enabled.

5. Click **Apply**.

6. Click **New Community**. A screen similar to the one shown in Figure 22.32 will be displayed.

Figure 22.32 New Community

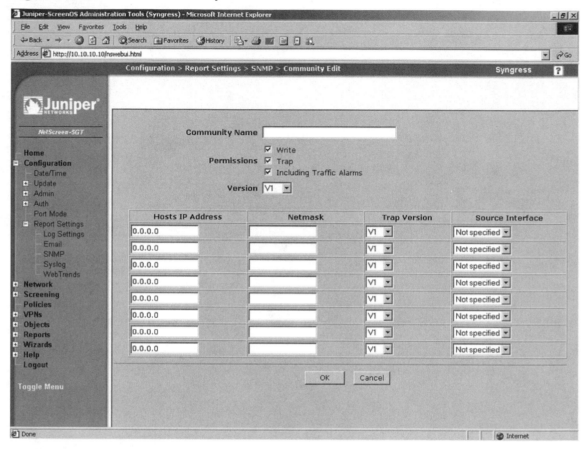

7. Enter a **Community Name**.

8. Enable the **Write** option if you want to allow the remote SNMP user to modify this configuration.

9. Enable the **Trap** option to allow the SNMP agent to send traps to the defined hosts.

10. Enable the **Including Traffic Alarms** option if you wish to force the local SNMP agent to send traffic alarms to the defined hosts.

11. Use the **Version** drop-down list to select the SNMP version that this community will support. The **Any** option will cause the community to support both the v1 and v2c versions.

12. You must define at lease one host or network in the lower portion of the screen. To do so, enter the **Host's IP Address** and **Netmask**. Next, select the **Trap Version** and use the **Source Interface** drop-down list to select the SNMP interface.

13. Click **OK**.

To remove a community, locate it in the community list and click its **Remove** link. Click **OK** to confirm.

To configure SNMP via the CLI, enter the following commands:

```
Syngress-> set snmp name Syngress
Syngress-> set snmp location "Dearborn, MI"
Syngress-> set snmp community Syngressadmin Read-Only version v2c
Syngress-> set snmp host Syngressadmin 10.4.4.4
```

Syslog

NetScreen firewalls generate a great deal of logging. Logged information is contained on the local flash file system using a first-in-first-out method. The first log in will be the first log removed when logging space fills up. If you want to keep your logs for an extended period of time, you must archive them to an external log server. A NetScreen firewall can send information to up to four syslog hosts at a time. Syslog can be configured from both the WebUI and the CLI. Logging will be discussed in depth in the next chapter.

Use the following steps to configure the syslog server via the WebUI:

1. **Configuration | Report Settings | Syslog**. A screen similar to the one shown in Figure 22.33 will be displayed.

Figure 22.33 Syslog Configuration

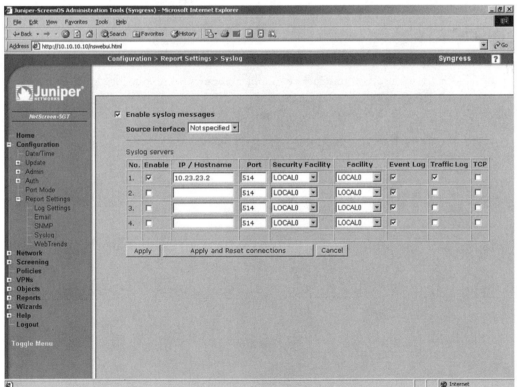

2. Enable the **Enable syslog messages** option.

3. Use the **Source interface** drop-down list to specify the interface from which messages will be sent. If you do not specify an interface here, messages will be sent from the interface closest to the syslog host.

4. In the row labeled **No. 1**, enable the **Enable** checkbox and enter the **IP / Hostname** and **Port** of the remote syslog server.

5. Use the **Security Facility** drop-down list to select the syslog facility to which emergency and critical messages will be sent.

6. Use the **Facility** drop-down list to select the syslog facility to which all other messages will be sent.

7. Enable the **Event Log**, **Traffic Log**, and **TCP** options.

8. Click **Apply**. If you are updating an existing syslog configuration, click **Apply and Reset connections**.

Enter the following commands to configure syslog via the CLI:

```
Syngress-> set syslog config 10.23.23.2 facilities local0 local0
Syngress-> set syslog config 10.23.23.2 port 514
Syngress-> set syslog config 10.23.23.2 log all
Syngress-> set syslog enable
```

WebTrends

WebTrends firewall suite is a product from the company NetIQ. It is a syslog server that collects all of your logs and it allows also you to generate graphical reports from your logs. You can configure a remote WebTrends server from both the CLI and the WebUI.

Use the following steps to configure WebTrends via the WebUI:

1. Access **Configuration | Report Settings | WebTrends**. A screen similar to the one shown in Figure 22.34 will be displayed.

Figure 22.34 WebTrends Configuration

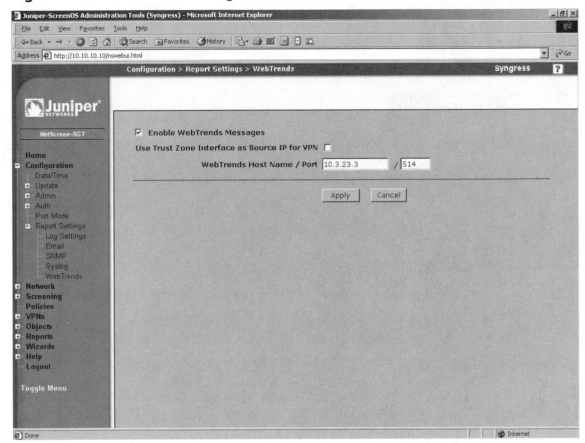

2. Enable the **Enable WebTrends Messages** option.

3. Enter the IP address and port number in the **WebTrends Host Name / Port** fields.

4. Click **Apply**.

Enter the following commands to configure WebTrends via the CLI:

```
Syngress-> set webtrends host-name 10.3.23.3
Syngress-> set webtrends port 514
Syngress-> set webtrends enable
```

Resources

Windows SSH client putty: www.chiark.greenend.org.uk/~sgtatham/putty/
Windows TFTP server Pumpkin: http://kin.klever.net/pumpkin/binaries
Windows Serial/telnet Client Tera Term: http://hp.vector.co.jp/authors/VA002416/teraterm.html

Summary

In this chapter we covered a great deal of information. The purpose of this chapter was to get you familiar with the initial configuration of your NetScreen firewall. Before you begin using your firewall you must understand how to manage it. We looked at various methods you can use to manage your firewall. It is important to understand each individual option to you. Each option is a different tool you can use to control your firewall.

There are two core types of remote management, the WebUI and the CLI. If you are using the serial console, Telnet, or secure shell, you are using the CLI. It is important to be proficient in both management tools. The WebUI is initially easier to use. However, in the later chapters you will see that advanced troubleshooting techniques can only be carried out from the command line interface. These techniques are invaluable if you intend to do more advanced configuration. We also mentioned a third type of management called the NetScreen-Security Manager.

This chapter also discussed configuring your NetScreen firewall to run on the network. Zones are a core part of the NetScreen security infrastructure. The security zone is the most commonly used zone. It is used on every interface and in every policy. Each interface must be bound to a zone. In the next chapter we will focus on basic policy creation and policy theory. In that chapter you will see the application of security zones. We looked at all of the various types of interfaces that the firewall supports. The physical interface will be used on each type of NetScreen device to interact with the network. The firewall can operate in two modes, layer three and layer two. In this chapter we focused on the layer three configuration of the device.

In the last section of the chapter we looked configuring various system components. Configuring the time on your device is critical. Time is the central reference point used to correlate all events on your firewall. If someone was to break in your network and your logs were off by several hours or days, this could hinder your investigation of the break-in. Configuring your logs to be sent to a separate location is also important if you intend to keep your logs long-term. The syslog server and WebTrends server are both great options. If you use the NetScreen-Security Manager, it also can be used as a central log repository.

Policy Configuration

Solutions in this chapter:

- NetScreen Policies
- Policy Components
- Creating Policies

☑ Summary

Introduction

In a NetScreen firewall, a policy is the fundamental core of access control. In this section we will explore the basic principles of a policy and how to create them. All firewall devices uses some sort of statement that provides access control between two segments of a network. Each product implements access control differently. If you have experience with any firewall product, then NetScreen policies should come easy for you. If you have never had the opportunity to create a network access control policy before, this section will help you understand the principles of access control as well as the methodology of creating a policy.

First we will look at the definition of a policy and what creating one really means. We will also look into the theory of access control and specific methodologies behind allowing or denying access to network resources. In the second part of this section we will review what makes up a policy on a NetScreen firewall. Every policy must have several basic components before it can be created. We will look at each component and how to create them on your firewall.

Much like building a house, NetScreen firewalls use different components to build policies. There are several required components for a policy. In this chapter we will look at these components and how to create them for use in a policy. Components can be created via the Web user interface (WebUI) or the command line interface (CLI). Each method generates the same result, but the process is different. As discussed throughout this book, becoming familiar with both methods will help you better understand the NetScreen firewall platform.

In the final section of this chapter we will take the components we created and use them to form policies. For the first time in this book, we will look at the WebUI and CLI separately, because the methods differ enough that each requires separate attention.

NetScreen Policies

A policy permits, denies, or tunnels specified types of traffic between two points. That is the official definition of a firewall policy according to Juniper Networks. Let's look deeper into that definition. A policy is a single statement defining whether a resource can be accessed and by whom. On a Cisco PIX or router, a policy is the equivalent to a conduit or access list. On a Check Point firewall, a policy is the equivalent of a firewall rule.

A policy does not reference a complete list of rules or the entire embodiment of the access control statements. Nor is a policy referenced as any sort of written statement in this case. A policy is a single access control statement. There are five basic elements of any policy. Any policy you create must contain all five of these following elements.

- **Direction**   The first element is direction. The direction is based upon security zones. You must define two security zones in each policy. The first security zone must be the source of the traffic that you want to access a specific resource. The second zone is the destination zone. The destination zone is where the destination system or network is located.

- **Source Address**   The next component of a policy is the source addresses. This component defines the source Internet Protocol (IP) address of the source hosts. These hosts must be in the source zone as well. These source IP addresses can access the destination hosts in the destination zone. At a maximum you may use **Any** as the source; this specifies any IP address in the source zone.

- **Destination Address**   The destination hosts are the hosts that the source addresses will attempt to access. The destination hosts must be in the destination zone. Destination addresses must have a minimum of a single host. At a maximum, you may use **Any** as the destination; this specifies any IP address in the destination zone.

- **Service**   When you define a service, you define which application you want the source address to access. Defining this is based upon both port and protocol. You can allow ICMP (Internet Control Message Protocol), TCP (Transmission Control Protocol), IP, and UDP (User Datagram Protocol) protocols. Each predefined service has these protocols specified. Much like the source and destination address, you can also specify **Any** for the service; this will allow any protocol using any port from the source address to access the destination address through the firewall.

- **Action**   The specified action is what you want to happen to the traffic that matches the specified policy. There are three actions that you can impose on traffic that matches the policy. The first action is *permit*. When specifying permit as your action, you are allowing the matching traffic to pass through the firewall. The second action you can select is *deny*. This action denies and drops the traffic if it matches the defined policy. The last action that you can specify is *tunnel*. Tunnel first inherently permits the traffic that is specified by the policy. However, this traffic is only permitted to pass through the specified VPN (virtual private network) tunnel. If you use the action of tunnel then you must specify a VPN tunnel as well.

There are additional items that can be defined for each policy. These additional items include logging, network address translation (NAT), traffic shaping, counting, traffic alarms, antivirus scanning, scheduling, URL (Uniform Resource Locator) filtering, and user authentication.

- **Logging**   Logging is an essential tool for both troubleshooting and recording who has accessed your network. We will look at logging in more detail later in this chapter.

- **NAT**   NAT allows you to hide your internal IP addresses. It is used in almost every internal network. There are many intricacies of NAT on the NetScreen platform so NAT has its own dedicated chapter in this book.

- **Traffic Shaping**   Traffic shaping allows you to control the amount of bandwidth certain traffic can consume.

- **Counting**   When you turn on counting for a policy, the NetScreen firewall creates graphs for the traffic that has passed through the policy. These graphs are displayed in bytes and are useful in determining how much traffic has passed through an interface.

- **Traffic Alarms**   Traffic alarms allow you to generate an alert when a specific number of bytes per second or bytes per minute are exceeded. To use traffic alarms you must enable counting.

- **Antivirus Scanning**   Using antivirus scanning on your firewall allows you to scan traffic for viruses as the traffic passes through your firewall

- **Scheduling**   Configuring scheduling for a policy allows you to create a policy that is in effect only at specific times. This allows you to create a policy that allows your users to browse the Internet only during specified hours. Scheduling is a powerful tool that keeps you from having to enable and disable access at specific times.

- **URL Filtering** There are times that you may want to allow a user to access the Internet, but require some method of limiting access to appropriate websites. URL filtering allows you to allow or deny access to websites based upon their content. NetScreen has teamed up with the Websense Enterprise Engine product to allow you to do just that.

- **User Authentication** User authentication allows you to require authentication to the NetScreen firewall before accessing specified resources in a policy. User authentication and using authentication servers is a large subject, requiring its own chapter. The chapter titled "User Authentication" covers this subject in its entirety.

Theory Of Access Control

The theory of access control is quite simple; allow access to the required resources and deny everything else. On a NetScreen firewall, everything is denied by default unless specifically allowed. This makes creating your access control policies a straightforward process. If you want a resource to be accessed by another system, create a policy to allow access to it. If you do not want access allowed to a system, do not create a policy.

Now that you understand the beginnings of access control on a NetScreen firewall, there are a couple different ideas to add into this mix when creating a policy. When traffic passes through the firewall, policies are checked in a top-down order, so the policy at the top will be checked first and then the second policy in order will be checked and so on. The best thing you can do is to create more specific policies at the top of your policy list and less specific policies as you go down the list.

Let's look at an example. Figure 23.1 shows an example of policy ordering. This is a screenshot of a NetScreen policy. There are three policies in this example. In the first policy you see the source is very specific with only one host (WebMaster) connecting to a single destination (WebServer). This is the most specific policy in this example. The first policy only allows one single system to connect to another single system. In the second policy, any host can connect to the destination WebServer with only HTTP (Hypertext Transfer Protocol). This is a less specific policy as it allows literally any host to connect to WebServer, as long as it uses the proper protocol. In the last policy, any host can connect to the destination "FTP Servers" with the File Transfer Protocol (FTP). This is the least specific policy as it allows any host to connect to the group of FTP servers.

Figure 23.1 Policy Ordering

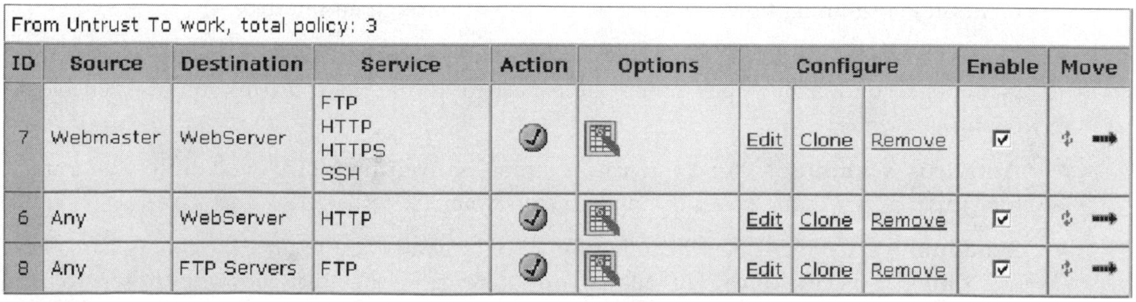

From Untrust To work, total policy: 3											
ID	Source	Destination	Service	Action	Options		Configure			Enable	Move
7	Webmaster	WebServer	FTP HTTP HTTPS SSH	✓	▦	Edit	Clone	Remove		☑	⇕ ➡
6	Any	WebServer	HTTP	✓	▦	Edit	Clone	Remove		☑	⇕ ➡
8	Any	FTP Servers	FTP	✓	▦	Edit	Clone	Remove		☑	⇕ ➡

Why does the idea of most specific to least specific matter so much? Let's switch around policy number 6 and number 7 in the example above. 6 is now the top-most policy and 7 is the second policy down. If we were to do this, all connections from "WebMaster" with the HTTP protocol would be logged to policy number 6. This could create havoc when attempting to troubleshoot or for long term purposes of logging. The ID or identification for a policy is automatically generated when you create a policy from the WebUI. When creating a policy from the CLI you get the option of setting the ID if you want or allow the firewall to choose the next available number.

The last component of access control we need to look at is zones. Zones identify the direction a policy works in. Every policy requires a source zone and a destination zone. The source zone is the location from which the source traffic is originating. The destination zone is where the destination traffic is going. When creating a policy you must choose both a source and destination zone. The "Creating Policies" section later in this chapter discusses how to determine which components you need to create a policy.

Types of NetScreen Policies

On a NetScreen firewall, there are three different types of policies. The policies all contain the same five core components. The only difference is the zones that the policy contains. A policy is classified by which source and destination zones are used in the policy. If you look at Figure 23.2, you will see a diagram representing the policy checking order. Before we look at the diagram we will briefly define the three types of policies:

- **Intrazone Policies**   An intrazone policy is a policy in which the source and destination zones are the same.

- **Interzone Policies**   An intrazone policy is a policy in which the source and destination zones are different.

- **Global Policies**   A global policy is a policy in which the source and destination zones are both in the global zone.

Figure 23.2 Policy Checking Order

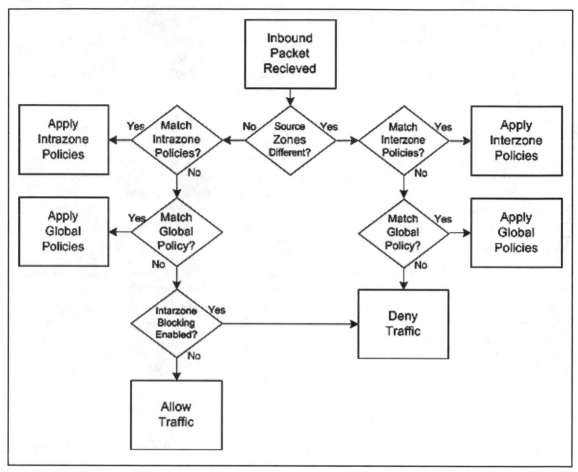

Intrazone Policies

There will be times on your NetScreen firewall when you have multiple interfaces bound to the same zone. By default, traffic within the same zone is not blocked. You have the option of blocking intrazone traffic just as if the traffic was interzone traffic. If you do not enable intrazone blocking, all intrazone traffic is allowed. Use the following command to determine the current zone blocking state, where *zonename* is the name of the zone:

```
zone zonename
```

The status will be listed on the "Intra-zone block" line. For example, the following output indicates that intrazone blocking is *not* enabled:

```
Intra-zone block: Off, attrib: Non-shared, flag:0x0008
```

To enable intrazone blocking, use the following command, where *zonename* is the name of the desired zone:

```
set zone zonename block
```

To disable intrazone blocking, use the following command, where *zonename* is the name of the desired zone:

```
unset zone home block
```

Interzone Policies

An interzone policy (in which the source and destination are in different zones) is the most common type of policy you are going to encounter. There are no configuration changes that you can make to change the behavior of interzone policies.

Global Policies

A global policy is a policy in which the source and destination zone are in the global zone. In Figure 23.2 above, you can see where global policies fall in the policy checking order. Global policies are very useful when you want to allow or deny a specific type of traffic regardless of the type of zone. For example, if you want to allow all zones to be able to get out to browse the Internet with HTTP traffic, but you only want to make one policy, you can do so using a global policy.

Default Policy

NetScreen firewalls have a default out of the box policy that will drop any traffic that does not match any other policies. This default policy is a hidden global policy. Juniper offers this as a security feature to ensure any traffic that you do not want to allow through is automatically dropped. This mitigates the risk of the firewall on the network by dropping any unmatched traffic. It is possible to change the behavior of this traffic from the CLI.

To override the default behavior (and therefore allow all traffic), enter the following command:

```
set policy default-permit-all
```

To change the firewall to deny all traffic by default, enter the following command:

```
unset policy default-permit-all
```

Policy Checking

When a connection is attempted, the NetScreen firewall will receive the source packet on an interface in the source zone. To determine the destination zone, the NetScreen firewall will perform either a route check or an Address Resolution Protocol (ARP) check to determine where the destination zone is. Once the destination zone is determined, the firewall will perform a check against the list of policies that match that zone configuration.

For example, if the source zone is determined as the trust zone and the destination zone is determined as the untrust zone, the firewall will check that list of policies. It will check the matching policy list starting from the first policy at the top of the list down to the bottom policy in that list. The first policy that matches the source IP address, destination IP address, and the service will be applied to that connection. The action of the first matching policy is then applied to that connection. If the connection is permitted, then the connection creates a session in the firewall's internal session table. The allowed session is granted access to pass through the firewall. If the action of the connection is to deny the connection, then the connection is dropped. Finally, if the action on the connection is to tunnel, then the connection is permitted, and a session is created and passed into the applicable VPN connection.

The session table is a table that is stored in memory on the NetScreen firewall. It contains a list of all of the allowed connections that have already passed through the policy and have been allowed. Before a connection is compared against the policy, it is compared against the session table to see if an active session has already been started. If the firewall sees that an existing session matches a session in the session table, then that traffic is allowed through the firewall. For example, if you open your browser and access a website, that entire connection will be stored in one session in the session table. Figure 23.3 shows a condensed version of how a NetScreen firewall determines what to do with network traffic as it passes though the firewall.

Figure 23.3 NetScreen Packet Logic

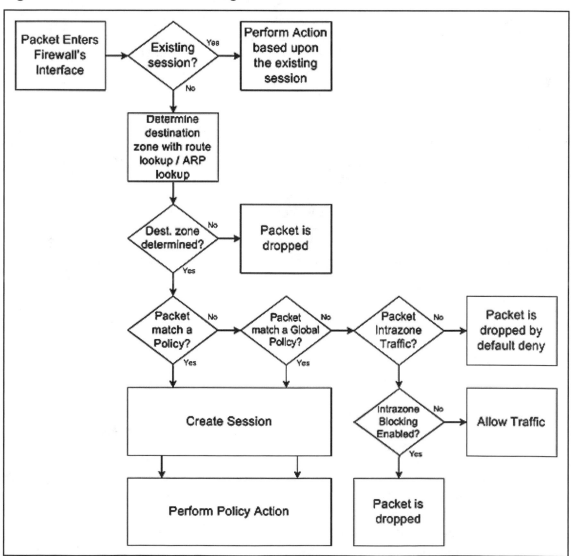

Getting Ready to Make a Policy

Creating policies is actually a very easy process once you have all of your components in place. Much like building a house, you cannot build if you do not have all of the materials. Let's review our steps in creating a policy.

- **Have you determined your source and destination zones?** The source zone is going to be where the originating traffic for your connection is coming from. This is tied into your interfaces. If you can determine which interface the traffic is going to come in, then you can determine which zone the traffic will come in as the interface is tied to the zone. The destination zone is the zone that the traffic will use to exit the NetScreen firewall. You can determine this by identifying which interface the traffic will come out with routing. Look at the configuration of your network and see where the packet will route as it exits your firewall. The interface it exits is bound to a zone, and that zone is your destination zone.

- **Have you determined your source and destination IP addresses?** The source IP address can be a single IP address, multiple IP addresses, or every available IP address. In the interest of security, you should limit the IP addresses to as few as possible. If you are unsure which IP address you want to use, open the source up to a larger pool of IP addresses, then log the traffic as it is goes through the firewall. Over time you can specify a smaller group of IP addresses for the source IP address. When determining your destination, you can use the same procedure by using logging to determine which IP addresses you can limit your traffic to. Ensure that the source and destination addresses have been created as address book entries. If the address book entries have not been created, now is the time to create them.

- **Have you determined which services you are going to allow in your policy?** Determining the services that you want to use in your policy is a key factor in creating your policies. It is very important that you limit the amount of allowed services to the bare minimum, even if this means you will have 500 services allowed in your policy. This amount of services is much better then allowing all 65535 possible ports. Even policies that are outbound from your internal network should be limited. The more ports you have open, the more risk there is. An example of this would be if a virus was to infect a desktop and then that desktop began sending SMTP (Simple Mail Transfer Protocol) mail out directly to the Internet. Should all desktops be allowed to access the Internet directly with SMTP? These are the questions you should ask yourself as you create your policy.

- **Which action do you want to perform on matching traffic?** Now that you have narrowed down your traffic to exactly what you want to match, it is now time to determine what you want to do with this traffic. There are three options: permit, deny, or tunnel. When you select to permit traffic, you are allowing the traffic to pass between the two security zones on the firewall. The second option is to deny, or drop the traffic before it passes through your firewall. By default, the firewall blocks all traffic as it attempts to pass through, so creating a policy to deny traffic allows you to apply special properties to the traffic such as logging. The last option is to tunnel the traffic. When you choose to tunnel the traffic, first you are explicitly permitting the traffic, but only to pass into a VPN tunnel. Choosing the tunnel option also forces you to choose a VPN that the traffic must pass into.

■ **Where are you going to position your policy?** The position of your policy determines when your policy will take effect. Policies are checked in a top-down order based upon your source and destination zones. Once the source and destination zones are determined, the list of policies that matched the source and destination zone are checked starting from the top policy going to the bottom of the policy list. Once all of the policies in the matching source and destination zone are checked, the global policies are applied to your traffic.

■ **Are there any additional options that you want to apply to the traffic?** As we mentioned earlier in the chapter, there are many different options you can apply to your policy beyond the required components. In this chapter we will look at the logging option only. When you turn on logging for a policy, each connection that passes through the firewall is written into the traffic log.

Policy Components

When you create a policy, you must define five separate components

Zones

When creating a policy, you must first determine the source and destination zones. The source zone will be where the source traffic is going to come from. The destination zone is the location where the destination traffic is going. Because zones are bound to interfaces, you are also inherently choosing which interface the traffic will be using. This may help you when creating a policy, as the concept of zones is different from many other firewall products.

Address Book Entries

The next component that you need to determine when creating a policy is which source systems should be able to access which destination systems – essentially, the source IP addresses and the destination IP addresses for your policy. This is a common firewall concept that you may have come across before. When using the command line interface, you must create all of your address book entries before you make your policies. However, when using the WebUI to create policies, you can create new address book entries as you create the policy. If you choose this latter method of creating address book entries while creating a policy in the WebUI, you can only specify the IP address and netmask for the entry. You will have to go back at a later time and edit the address book entry if you want to associate a name with the address book entry. This idea will become clearer below as we look at some examples of address book entry creation.

Creating Address Book Entries

Figure 23.4 shows the WebUI address entry creation screen. Use the steps below to create an address book entry via the WebUI:

Figure 23.4 Address Book Entry Creation (WebUI)

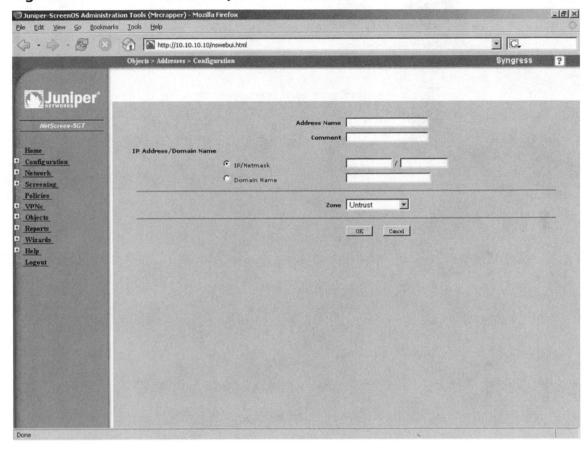

1. Select **Objects** | **Addresses** | **List**.

2. Click the **New** button in the upper right-hand corner of the page.

3. Enter the **Address Name**. Refer to the "Naming Convention Errors" sidebar in this chapter to avoid naming errors.

4. If desired, use the **Comment** field to enter additional information about the address book entry.

5. If you wish to identify the address book entry by IP address, select and use the **IP/Netmask** fields to enter the desired IP Address or IP Subnet.

6. If you wish to identify the entry by domain name, rather than by IP address, select the Domain Name option and enter the DNS-resolvable name. Note that your system must have DNS enabled for this feature to work properly.

7. Use the **Zone** drop-down list to specify the zone with which the entry will belong.

8. Click **OK**. The new entry will be displayed in the address book list (Figure 23.5).

Figure 23.5 Address Book List (WebUI)

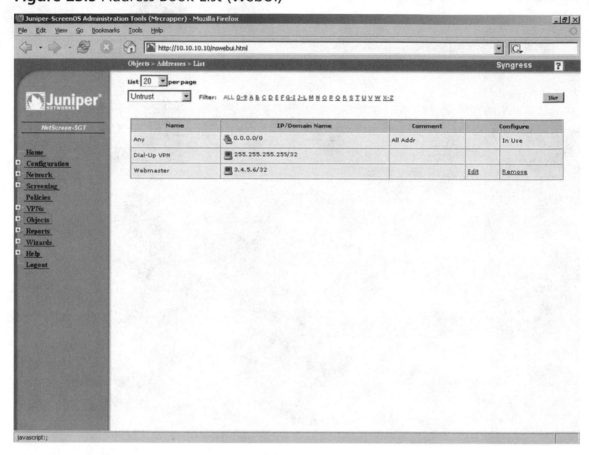

You can also create an address book entry via the CLI. To do so, enter the following command:

```
set address zone name IPaddress "comment"
```

In the command above, *zone* is the zone to which this entry will belong, *name* is the name of the entry, *IPaddress* is the IPaddress/subnet that specifies the range, and *"comment"* is a text string (in quotes) that serves as an optional comment about the entry. For example, the following command specifies that the WebServer entry (at 10.2.2.2/32) belongs to the untrust zone and includes the comment, "This is Darren's Web Server"

```
set address untrust WebServer 10.2.2.2/32 "This is Darren's Web Server"
```

Modifying and Deleting Address Book Entries

You can update existing address book entries via the WebUI. You may wish to do so as servers change IP addresses, or you may want to update the comments about an address object. You can modify everything about an address book entry except its zone. Note that you cannot modify an address object from the CLI; if you wish to change an address object's properties via the CLI, you must first delete it and then recreate it.

Use the following steps to modify an existing address book entry via the WebUI:

1. Access **Objects** | **Addresses** | **List**.

2. Click the **Edit** link of the address entry you wish to modify.

3. Update the desired fields and click **OK**.

Use the following steps to delete an existing address book entry via the WebUI:

1. Access **Objects** | **Addresses** | **List**.

2. Click the **Remove** link of the address entry you wish to delete.

3. Click **OK** to confirm.

Use the following commands to delete and re-create an address book entry (in lieu of being able to modify it directly).

```
unset address domain "name"
set address domain name IPaddress "comment"
```

Address Groups

As you begin to amass many address objects, you will want a method to bring all of these address objects together into logical containers. This is accomplished with the use of address groups. An address group is a logical container that literally groups together address objects. Address groups are very handy when creating policies. Use the following steps to create an address group via the WebUI:

1. Access **Objects** | **Addresses** | **Groups**.

2. Click **New**. A screen similar to the one shown in Figure 23.6 will be displayed.

Figure 23.6 Address Group Creation (WebUI)

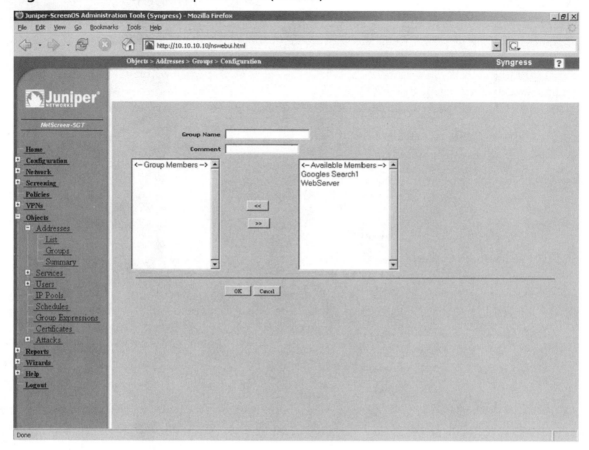

3. Enter the **Group Name** and, if desired, a **Comment**.

4. To place hosts in this group, select them from the list of **Available Members** on the right and click the << button. The host(s) will be placed in the **Group Members** list. To remove a member from the group, click it and click the >> button. Continue this process until the **Group Members** list contains all of the desired hosts.

5. Click **OK**.

To modify a group, access the group list and click its **Edit** button. To delete a group, access the group list and click its **Remove** button, then click **OK** to confirm.

To create an address group using the CLI, enter the following command:

```
Set group address zone groupname comment "commenttext"
```

In the command above, *zone* is the zone to which the group will be placed, *groupname* is the name you wish to give the new group, and *commenttext* is the text you wish to place in the comment field (must be in quotes).

Use the following command to add an address to the group:

```
Set group address zone groupname add addressname
```

In the command above, *zone* is the zone that contains the desired address and group, *groupname* is the name of the group, and *addressname* is the name of the address you wish to place in the specified group.

Services

The next component in creating your policy is using *services*. Services are the protocols that you would use to access a system over the network. Services on a NetScreen firewall are represented by service objects. A service object is used to specify which applications can be used in a policy. Every NetScreen firewall comes with a predefined set of services. The set of services that comes on your firewall varies per version of ScreenOS you are running on your firewall.

Currently, ScreenOS contains about eighty predefined services. These services are some of the more commonly used services that you will use when defining your policies. Some protocols are also predefined because they function in a non-standard way. One example is the FTP protocol. Because FTP sends special port redirects during its communication, Juniper has created a special mechanism to read inside the FTP connection to determine which ports to open up during the communication. Even though the predefined service only allows TCP port 21, the firewall is still able to dynamically allow ports based upon the FTP communication.

It would be impractical for Juniper to create every service that exists. Juniper allows you to create your own custom service objects. These custom service objects can be used just like a predefined service object in your policy.

Creating Custom Services

A service object has several defining properties that tell the firewall how to identify traffic. These properties are specified when defining a new service object. The options that you use when creating a new policy depend on the type of protocol you are creating. Use the following steps to create a custom service via the WebUI:

1. Access **Objects | Services | Custom**.
2. Click **New**. A screen similar to the one shown in Figure 23.7 will be displayed.

Figure 23.7 Service Object Configuration (WebUI)

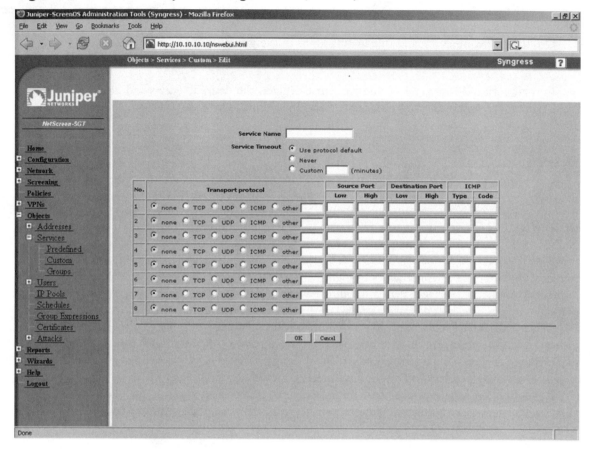

3. Enter the **Service Name**.

4. Use the **Service Timeout** options to specify how long the service session should stay open. The protocol default is thirty minutes for TCP and one minute for UDP. Select **Never** if you do not want to impose a timeout value. To specify your own timeout value, select the **Custom** option and enter the desired number of minutes (up to a maximum of forty minutes).

5. You can define up to eight protocols for this service object. This can be useful in creating a service that uses multiple ports. To define a protocol, select its type from the **Transport Protocol** field. Next, enter the **Low** and **High Source Ports** and the **Low** and **High Destination Ports**. To specify a single port, enter the same number in the **High** and **Low** fields.

6. Click **OK**.

To create a custom service via the CLI, enter the following command:

```
set service servicename protocol protocol src-port srclow-high dst-port
dstlow-high
```

In the command above, *servicename* is the name of the service, *protocol* is the protocol type (TCP, UDP, or ICMP), *srclow-high* is the low and high source port range, and *dstlow-high* is the low and high destination port range.

Modifying and Deleting Services

After creating your service, there may be times when you will want to modify that service or perhaps delete it. Modifying a service is much like creating it. The only difference is that when you come to the editing screen, the portions of the service you have created are already defined for you. From the CLI if you want to add additional protocols to a service you can. However, if you need to edit existing parts of the service, you must delete the service then recreate it.

Use the following steps to modify an existing service via the WebUI:

1.   Access **Objects | Services | Custom**.

2.   Click the **Edit** link of the service you wish to edit.

3.   Make the desired changes to the **Service Name** and/or **Service Timeout** fields.

4.   Modify the values for any of the existing protocols. You can add new protocols to this service simply by entering the appropriate data, and you can remove protocols by selecting the **none** option of the protocol you wish to remove.

5.   Click **OK**.

To delete a service via the WebUI, access the services list and click the **Remove** link of the service you wish to delete. Click **OK** to confirm. To delete a service via the CLI, enter the following command:

```
unset service "servicename"
```

Service Groups

Even though each individual service can contain up to eight service definitions, you will still want to group services together into logical containers. You can do this through the use of service groups. A service group functions just like an address group, and its creation is nearly identical. Use the following steps to create a service group via the WebUI:

1.   Access **Objects | Services | Groups**.

2.   Click **New**. A screen similar to the one shown in Figure 23.8 will be displayed.

Figure 23.8 Service Group Creation (WebUI)

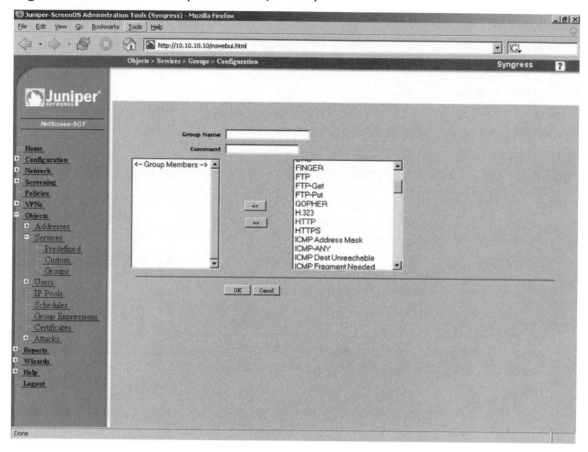

3. Enter the **Group Name** and, if desired, enter a **Comment**.

4. To place hosts in this group, select them from the list of **Available Members** on the right and click the << button. The host(s) will be placed in the **Group Members** list. To remove a member from the group, click it and click the >> button. Continue this process until the **Group Members** list contains all of the desired hosts.

5. Click **OK**.

To modify an existing service group, access the service group list and click the **Edit** link of the group you wish to modify. To delete a service group, access the service group list and click the **Remove** link of the group you wish to delete. Click **OK** to confirm.

Use the following command to create a service group via the CLI, where *groupname* is the name of the new group:

```
set group service "groupname"
```

To add items to the group, enter the following command:

```
set group service "groupname" add item
```

In the command above, *groupname* is the name of the service group and *item* is the name of the service that will be added to the specified group. To delete a service group via the CLI, enter the following command:

```
unset group service "groupname"
```

Creating Policies

Now that you are familiar with the components of creating policies, you can begin actually creating them. Polices are the main reason why you are implementing your firewall in the first place; to control network traffic. In this section we will begin to look at putting together policy components into a policy.

Creating a Policy

In this section we will begin to work with policies. In all of the previous sections of the book we have worked with both the CLI and the WebUI in the same section. However, in this section we will look at the WebUI and the CLI in separate sections. This will bring better clarity to the two different methods of creating a policy. Even though the CLI is not as easy to use as the WebUI, knowing how to use the CLI is crucial. The configuration is always stored as CLI commands, so knowing what each command does will empower your use of the platform.

Creating a Policy via the WebUI

The WebUI is easier to interpret, it allows for easier modification of the policy, and at times can be faster to use. When you start to have over twenty policies on your firewall, the CLI will seem as if all the policies run together, whereas on the WebUI, the icons and coloration of the policies will seem to flow. This is all a matter of preference, but I suggest using whatever tool makes the most sense to you. There is no reason to make the administration of the NetScreen firewall harder on yourself than it has to be. In Figure 23.9, you will see what the main policy page looks like. This page is the root of all policy creation in the WebUI.

Figure 23.9 The Root Of Policy Creation

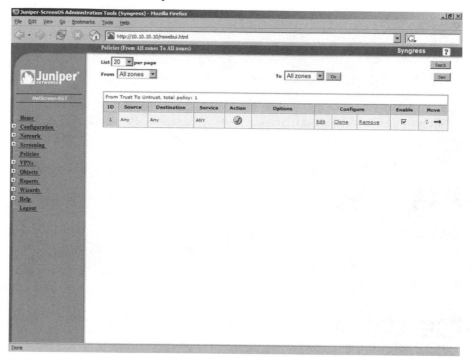

From here we can do everything we need to do with policies. We can create, remove, reorder, search, enable, disable, and clone policies. To access this screen, simply select the **Policies** link from the menu on the left side of the screen. As you can see in Figure 23.9, currently we only have one policy. This policy allows any source to go to any destination via any protocol. The action (indicated by the checkmark in the green circle) is permit. Table 23.1 lists the different icons that may be displayed on this screen, as well as their descriptions.

Table 23.1 Policy Action Icons

Action	Icon	Description
Permit		Permits the traffic specified in the policy.
Deny		Denies the traffic specified in the policy.
Tunnel		The policy permits and then tunnels the matching traffic into a VPN.
Bi-Directional Tunnel		The policy permits and then tunnels the matching traffic. It also has a matching policy that has the source and destination reversed.
Policy Based NAT		This policy permits the traffic matching the policy, but it also performs NAT on the traffic.

These various policy icons are very informative and simple to understand. When defining a new policy from the WebUI, you begin by selecting the source and the destination zones. Once you select the zones and create the new policy, there is no way to change the source and destination zones. If you wish to change the source and destination zones you must delete the undesired policy and then create a new one with the correct zones.

Use the following steps to create a policy via the WebUI:

1. Access the Juniper screen administration tools page and click **Policies** in the menu.

2. Click **New**. A screen similar to the one shown in Figure 23.10 will be displayed.

Figure 23.10 Policy Definition Screen

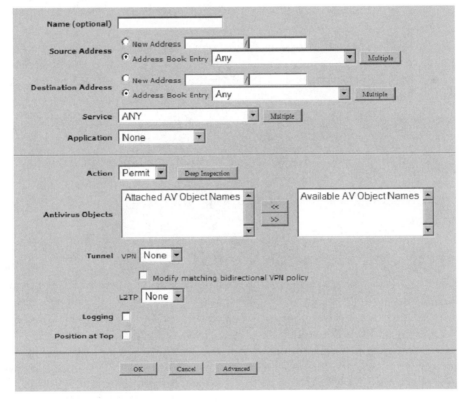

3. Enter the policy **Name**. This should be a descriptive name that will allow you to identify what the policy does.

4. Use the **Source Address** options to specify the source address for the policy. If it is a new address, select the **New Address** option and enter the IP address range. If the address already exists in the address book, select the **Address Book Entry** option and enter the name of the entry. You can select multiple address book entries by clicking the **Multiple** button.

5. Use the **Destination Address** options to specify the source address for the policy. If it is a new address, select the **New Address** option and enter the IP address range. If the address

already exists in the address book, select the **Address Book Entry** option and enter the name of the entry. You can select multiple address book entries by clicking the **Multiple** button

6. Use the **Service** drop-down list to specify the services that you want to use in this policy. Select a single service or group of services, or select **ANY**, or click **Multiple** if you wish to specify multiple (but not all) services.

7. Use the **Application** drop-down list to map a custom-defined service to a specific application layer.

8. Use the **Action** drop-down list to specify whether matching traffic will be permitted, denied, or tunneled. If you select **Tunnel**, you must also select an option from the **Tunnel** drop-down list. To apply deep inspection groups to the policy, click the **Deep Inspection** button

9. The **Antivirus Objects** section allows you to specify which antivirus scanners will be applied to the policy. To select an antivirus object, select it from the **Available AV Object Names** list on the right, then click the << button to place it in the **Attached AV Object Names** list on the left.

10. If you selected **Tunnel** in the **Action** drop-down list, use the **Tunnel VPN** drop-down list to specify the appropriate VPN tunnel.

11. If you wish to turn on logging for this policy, enable the **Logging** checkbox.

12. If you wish to place this policy at the top of the list of policies with matching source and destination zones, enable the **Position at Top** checkbox.

13. Click **OK**.

Reordering Policies in the WebUI

Once you have all of your policies created in the WebUI, there will be many times that you will need to reorder them. Every newly created policy is placed at the bottom of the policies that have the same source and destination zones unless you enabled the **Position at Top** option when creating the policy. Once the policy is created you can modify the policy placement on the Policies list page. Table 23.2 shows the different icons you can use to reorder policies.

Table 23.2 Policy Action Icons

Icon	Description
	Selecting this option allows you to choose the placement of your policy, by policy number. A pop-up window will be displayed, asking you where you want to place your policy based up upon the number of your policy. See Figure 23.11 for an example.
	This option allows you to specify where you want to place your policy based upon a selection screen. At the selection screen you can click on a similar arrow to choose where you want to place your policy. See Figure 23.12 for an example.

Figure 23.11 Order Policies by Number

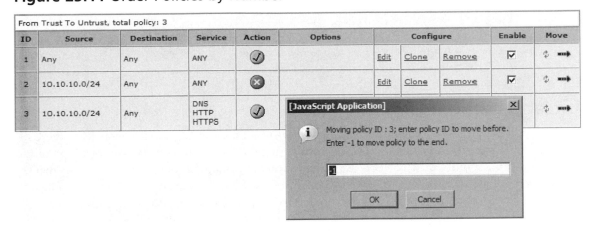

Figure 23.12 Choose Policy Placement

	ID	Source	Destination	Service	Action
Policy to move :	2	Trust/10.10.10.0/24	Untrust/Any	ANY	Deny

Move location	ID	Source	Destination	Service	Action
➡	1	Any	Any	ANY	✓
➡	3	10.10.10.0/24	Any	DNS HTTP HTTPS	✓
➡					

Other Policy Options in the WebUI

There are some additional WebUI options that may be helpful as you begin to create policies. These options are available from the root policies page in the WebUI. These options are displayed in Figure 23.13.

- **Edit**   Use a policy's **Edit** link to modify its configuration.
- **Clone**   Use this option to create a copy of the policy. The policy's original information will be displayed, but can be edited for your needs. This can save time when creating multiple policies that have only slight differences.
- **Remove**   Click a policy's **Remove** link to delete it. The policy will immediately be removed from the firewall.
- **Enable**   Use this option to enable or disable the policy.

Figure 23.13 Additional Policy Options

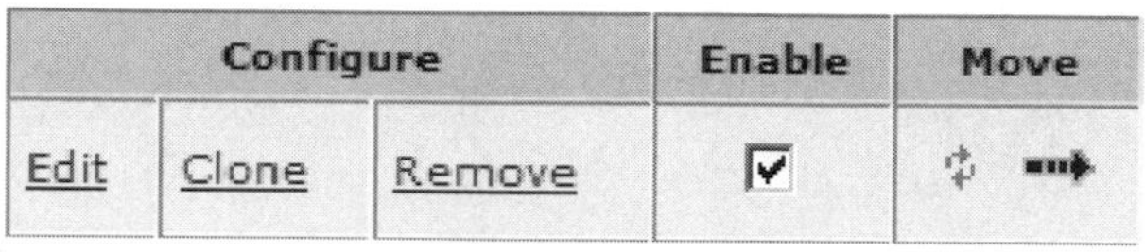

Creating a Policy via the CLI

Even though the point-and-click nature of the WebUI may make policy management easier, the CLI provides the fastest methods of policy management. Using the CLI requires more memorization of the commands and the order in which you use them. Once you get a grasp of CLI policy management, it will become an effective management tool. There are three basic commands for managing policies. The first command is **set policy** , which is the root of all policy creation. All commands that involve creating and manipulating policies begin here. The second command is **get policy**, which displays information about all or specified policies. Finally, the **unset policy** command is used for removing policies.

```
Syngress-> set policy ?
before                        insert a policy
default-permit-all            permit if no policy match
from                          from zone
global                        set global policy
id                            specify policy id
move                          move a policy
name                          specify policy name
top                           put this policy as the first one in the list
Syngress-> get policy ?
>                             redirect output
|                             match output
<return>
id                            show one policy
all                           show all policies(including global policy)
from                          from zone
global                        show global policies
Syngress-> unset policy ?
<number>                      policy id
default-permit-all            permit if no policy match
id                            policy id
Syngress->
```

To view a list of all existing policies, enter the command **get policy**. You can also list policies by specifying the source and destination zones. This is done with the command **get policy from**

<Src-Zone> to <Dst-Zone>. A list of all policies matching the specified parameters will be displayed. Use the command **get policy global** to view all of the global policies. Finally, use the command **get policy all** to view all of the policies, including the global policies. The **get policy** command supports the following parameter:

- **ID** This is the ID number of the policy. It is a unique number that is used to identify the policy.

- **From** The source zone.

- **To** The destination zone.

- **Src-address** The source address objects.

- **Dst-address** The destination address objects.

- **Service** The service specified for the policy.

- **Action** The action to apply to the traffic that matches the policy.

- **State** Whether the policy is enabled or disabled.

- **ASTLCB** This represents which special properties are turned on in the policy. A = Authentication, S = Scheduling, T = Traffic Shaping, L = Logging, C = Counting, B = HA Backup.

```
Syngress-> get policy
Total regular policies 4, Default deny.
ID   From    To        Src-address    Dst-address   Service   Action    State      ASTLCB
1    Trust   Untrust   Any            Any           ANY       Permit    enabled    -----X
2    Trust   Untrust   10.10.10.0/    Any           ANY       Deny      enabled    -----X
3    Trust   Untrust   10.10.10.0/    Any           DNS       Permit    enabled    -----X
                                                    HTTP
                                                    HTTPS
4    Trust   Untrust   Any            Any           ANY       Permit    enabled    -----X
Syngress->
```

You can even look at the configuration of a policy by using the **get policy id <number>** command, where <number> is the policy ID.

```
Syngress-> get policy id 1
name:"none" (id 1), zone Trust -> Untrust,action Permit, status "enabled"
src "Any", dst "Any", serv "ANY"
Policies on this vpn tunnel: 0
nat off, url filtering OFF
vpn unknown vpn, policy flag 0000, session backup: on
traffic shaping off, scheduler n/a, serv flag 00
log no, log count 0, alert no, counter no(0) byte rate(sec/min) 0/0
```

```
total octets 1301676800, counter(session/packet/octet) 0/0/0
priority 7, diffserv marking Off
tadapter: state off, gbw/mbw 0/-1
No Authentication
No User, User Group or Group expression set
```

Creating a policy via the CLI requires the same components as if you were using the WebUI. The full command for creating a policy via the CLI is:

```
set policy from <Src-Zone> to <Dst-Zone> <Src-Address> <Dst-Address> <Service>
<Action>
```

There are five areas in the above example command that you must fill in to complete the policy. The *<Src-Zone>* or source zone, *<Dst-Zone>* or destination zone, *<Src-Address>* or source address book entry, *<Dst-Address>* or destination address book entry, *service*, and *action*. These are the same five minimum options you would use when creating a policy from the WebUI. Once you create the policy, it is give a policy ID or unique identifier. This identifier is used to reference the policy throughout the system. The firewall will return **policy ID = <Identifier>** once the policy has been created.

Notice that this command only allows you to specify one source address, one destination address, and one service. You can add more once the policy has been created by using the **set policy id <ID Number>** to enter the sub-shell that allows you to modify the policy. The sub-shell for policies is the only sub-command shell in the entire firewall.

Once in the policy sub-shell, you have the same options as in the regular shell: set, get, and unset. Using the **set** command, you can add additional source addresses, destination addresses, and services, as well as other policy options. The **unset** command is used to remove parts from the policy, and the **get** command is used to obtain information about the policy. When creating policies from the CLI, you can place a policy in a specific position as it is created by entering the following command:

```
set policy before <ID> from <Src-Zone> to <Dst-Zone> <Src-Address> <Dst-Address>
<Service> <Action>
```

Specify the <ID> as the ID number of the policy you want to place the policy before. If you want to create a policy and place it at the top of the list of policies with the same source and destination zone, you would use the following command:

```
set policy top <Src-Zone> to <Dst-Zone> <Src-Address> <Dst-Address> <Service>
<Action>
```

Below is a snippet of code that shows an example of creating a policy and manipulating it in the sub-shell.

```
Syngress-> set policy from trust to untrust 10.10.10.0/24 any FTP permit
policy id = 6
Syngress-> get policy id 6
name:"none" (id 6), zone Trust -> Untrust,action Permit, status "enabled"
```

```
src "10.10.10.0/24", dst "Any", serv "FTP"
Policies on this vpn tunnel: 0
nat off, url filtering OFF
vpn unknown vpn, policy flag 0000, session backup: on
traffic shapping off, scheduler n/a, scrv flag 00
log no, log count 0, alert no, counter no(0) byte rate(sec/min) 0/0
total octets 0, counter(session/packet/octet) 0/0/0
priority 7, diffserv marking Off
tadapter: state off, gbw/mbw 0/-1
No Authentication
No User, User Group or Group expression set
Syngress-> set policy id 6
Syngress(policy:6)-> set service DNS
Syngress(policy:6)-> set src-address 10.10.9.0/24
Syngress(policy:6)-> set name "Allow FTP"
Syngress(policy:6)-> set log
Syngress(policy:6)-> exit
Syngress-> get policy id 6
name:"Allow FTP" (id 6), zone Trust -> Untrust,action Permit, status "enabled"
2 sources: "10.10.10.0/24", "10.10.9.0/24"
1 destination: "Any"
2 services: "DNS", "FTP"
Policies on this vpn tunnel: 0
nat off, url filtering OFF
vpn unknown vpn, policy flag 0000, session backup: on
traffic shapping off, scheduler n/a, serv flag 00
log yes, log count 0, alert no, counter no(0) byte rate(sec/min) 0/0
total octets 0, counter(session/packet/octet) 0/0/0
priority 7, diffserv marking Off
tadapter: state off, gbw/mbw 0/-1
No Authentication
No User, User Group or Group expression set
Syngress->
```

Other Policy Options Available in the CLI

Once you have all of your policies defined, you can use the CLI to reorder the policies. To move an existing policy above another, use the following command:

```
set policy move <ID1> before <ID2>
```

Specify the policy you want to move with its policy ID as <ID1> and the policy you want to move it before as its policy ID as <ID2>. To move an existing policy after another, use the following command:

```
set policy move <ID1> after <ID2>
```

Specify the policy you want to move with its policy ID as <ID1> and the policy you want to move it after as its policy ID as <ID2>. This may seem like an insignificant option, but if you have ever used a Cisco IOS or Cisco PIX access list you will appreciate this option. Neither Cisco OS allows you to manipulate the policies or access lists this way. Instead, you must first remove all of the applied policies and then add them all back to the firewall. Finally, you can delete policies via the CLI. To delete a policy from the CLI you must know the policy ID of the policy you want to remove, then use either the **unset policy id <ID>** or **unset policy <ID>** command.

Summary

In this chapter we focused on the basics of policy creation. The basics that we looked at are the foundation for much more to come in the way of policies. We looked at policies in this chapter as a primary tool of access control. When creating a policy on a NetScreen firewall, you must have a minimum of five components. This idea is continually stressed, as it will help you ease into policy creation on a NetScreen firewall.

The first section of the chapter NetScreen Policies took us through the main ideas of policies on a NetScreen firewall. When creating your list of policies you must create policies from least specific to most specific. This will apply the specific policies first to your traffic as the least specific policies may unintendedly match your traffic. Also in the first section, we looked at the three types of polices and how and where they take effect. All three policies are very similar, but they are classified based upon the combination of zones in the policy.

When creating policies on a NetScreen firewall, you build them out of components. These components must be created before you make a policy. Each one of the components for a NetScreen firewall is treated as an object. The components that we looked at in this chapter are the main components for a policy. Address objects represent hosts or subnets of IP addresses. Service objects can be a strange concept. Many competitive firewall products create services as a single protocol. If you want to create several services and represent them as a compilation you must make a group. On a NetScreen firewall, a service object can contain up to eight protocols. This allows you to take an entire suite of protocols and make them into one logical object.

Policy creation is common task for an administrator of a NetScreen firewall. In this chapter we looked at the two methods of policy creation: the WebUI and the CLI. Each has its own merits. The WebUI may be easier to use for looking at policies, while the CLI may be faster for creating policies. The choice is yours, but never limit yourself to a single option. It always pays to be familiar with both options because in the end all policies are stored as CLI commands. If you want to use the CLI to do something, but are unsure of the command, it is most likely possible to do what you need to do from the WebUI. Then look at the configuration from the CLI to see what the commands are to use the CLI in the future.

User Authentication

Solutions in this chapter:

- Types of users
- User databases
- External Auth Servers

Introduction

User authentication is probably one of the two most important aspects of the Netscreen firewall. Without a method of providing for the authentication of users, the firewall would lack the ability to limit who has access to administrative features or virtual private networks (VPNs). By providing a set of strong user authentication capabilities, the Netscreen firewall helps secure your network. The Netscreen firewall also provides a balance between security and ease-of-use via the many features supported in its authentication mechanisms.

User authentication on the Netscreen firewall can at first seem like a daunting task. With five types of supported users, four ways to store the users—one internal, and three external—and limitations that exist only for some of the users, it's no wonder it seems confusing.

In this chapter, we will discuss the types of users and how they should be used. We will discuss the types of authentication servers, the features that each authentication user has and what limitations you should be aware of. Finally, we will show you how to set up users, authentication servers, and more by using both Netscreen's WebUI and the CLI (command line interface).

Types of Users

The Netscreen authentication system has the following different types of users:

- IKE (Internet Key Exchange)
- Auth
- XAUTH
- L2TP
- Admin

Each different type of user has specific capabilities associated with its use. In the next section, we will discuss the types of users further and what their uses can or should be.

Uses of Each Type

The uses of each type of user are varied and each has its own advantages and disadvantages. The biggest difference between the users lies in the capabilities each has with regard to features and the network layer in which the authentication happens. For example, only Auth users can perform IKE authentication. Furthermore, IKE users authenticate before both XAuth and L2TP users, XAuth users authenticate after IKE, but before the VPN tunnel is established, and L2TP authenticates only after the IPSec (Internet Protocol Security) VPN has been established.

Auth Users

Auth users are users that must authenticate to the firewall before being given authorization to access either the firewall or systems behind the firewall. Authentication users may use any supported authentication server for storage of authentication credentials, whether they are the local database, LDAP (Lightweight Directory Access Protocol) directory, SecurID server, or RADIUS (Remote Access Dial-In User Service) server.

There are two different types of authentication that Auth users are capable of utilizing. Run-time, a setting in which the user is queried for authentication credentials after an attempt to contact a protected host, and WebAuth, a setting where users pre-authenticates themselves to the firewall before attempting to access protected resources.

The authentication steps for **Run-time** are as follows:

1. An unauthenticated user attempts to connect to a server behind the firewall.

2. The Netscreen firewall intercepts the packet, looks at the payload, and because the session is unauthenticated, places the packet in a buffer while sending back a Username/Password prompt to the user.

3. The unauthenticated user enters the appropriate login credentials.

4. Based on whether the authentication server is local or external, the firewall either compares the authentication credentials with those in the local database or sends the credentials to an external authentication server for comparison.

5. If the comparison is successful, the Netscreen firewall announces the completion of authentication, sets an internal policy allowing future access through the firewall, and forwards the buffered packet to the host being contacted.

The authentication steps for **WebAuth** are as follows:

1. An unauthenticated user accesses the WebAuth address and enters the appropriate authentication credentials.

2. Based on whether the authentication server is local or external, the firewall either compares the authentication credentials with those in the local database or sends the credentials to an external authentication server for comparison.

3. If the comparison is successful, the Netscreen firewall sets an internal policy allowing future access through the firewall.

4. The currently authenticated user is now able to access computers behind the firewall.

IKE Users

IKE is a key management protocol designed for secure exchange of encryption keys used by other encryption and authentication schemes. IKE is the key exchange used by the IPSEC protocol and therefore IKE is directly related to VPN technologies used by the Netscreen firewall.

IPSEC has two negotiation phases, the first of which is the IKE key negotiation phase. Authentication happens during the first phase of IKE negotiation. IKE users may be authenticated either by pre-shared key or digital certificate. If using pre-shared keys, the Netscreen firewall stores the keys within its internal database; however, if using digital certificates, the Netscreen must get the IKE ID portion of the authentication credentials from the DN (distinguished name) record within the certificate. In either case, the IKE records may only be stored within the internal Local database.

L2TP Users

L2TP is a data link layer VPN tunneling protocol published and proposed as a standard in 1999. L2TP originated as an extension to the PPP protocol—L2TP was meant to act as a tunnel through which PPP and other protocols could travel. Unlike IPSEC, because L2TP functions at such a low layer in the OSI model it is ideal for tunneling other protocols through as well as IP (Internet Protocol).

L2TP is not a secure VPN technology because it only supports tunneling and does not provide for privacy via encryption. L2TP should be combined with an IPSEC VPN for complete security. The biggest reason that L2TP is still in active use is because it supports addressing of IP, DNS (Domain Name Service), and WINS (Windows Internet Naming Service) as well as tunneling of many other protocols such as Appletalk, IPX, SNA, and more.

Unlike IKE, Netscreen firewalls are capable of performing L2TP authentication from not just the local database but also SecurID, RADIUS, LDAP, or a combination thereof. Although L2TP authentication may be done by one or a combination of authentication sources, it's important to recognize that it cannot perform addressing of IP, DNS, and WINS without using RADIUS and the Netscreen dictionary file for RADIUS, nor can it perform encryption of the data.

XAuth Users

XAuth is a VPN tunneling protocol that allows for a greater level of assurance that the data being transmitted is coming from the correct user. Unlike IKE, XAuth authenticates via a username and password instead of a pre-shared key. Also unlike IKE, XAuth is capable of tunneling more than the IP protocol and is also capable of performing addressing functions for IP, DNS, and WINS by assigning a virtual adapter and tunneling all traffic via the network adapter.

Admin Users

Admin users are users capable of viewing or modifying the Netscreen device either via the WebUI or via the CLI. Admin users may be stored on the internal local database or on external authentication servers. Admin users stored on external SecurID or LDAP devices must have privileges assigned on the Netscreen firewall. The only exception to his is admin users stored in RADIUS. If the Netscreen dictionary file is loaded on the RADIUS server, then the admin user can use the RADIUS server for both authentication and authorization.

Vsys admin users have the same capabilities as the Admin users mentioned above.

User Databases

In the next section, we discuss the five different types of user authentication and authorization databases, and the appropriate use of each. This section has been divided into two subsections, local database and external Auth servers for ease of understanding.

Local Database

The local database is the default database used by the Netscreen firewall appliance. The local database is the only database that supports all user and authentication types except for group expressions.

Types of Users

Users supported by the Local database include:

- Admin
- Auth
- IKE
- L2TP
- XAuth

Features

Features supported by the Local database include:

- Admin privileges
- User groups
- WebAuth

External Auth Servers

Netscreen devices support a variety of external authentication servers. These authentication servers—including RADIUS, SecurID, and LDAP—allow a properly configured Netscreen firewall to perform authentication and authorization against an externally maintained and configured database of users.

When set to use an external authentication server, upon receipt of an event requiring authentication, the Netscreen device first requests the username/password combination, then forwards the user-supplied credentials to the authentication server. The authentication server verifies the credentials and sends the appropriate response to the Netscreen firewall. The Netscreen firewall then sends a message of success or failure back to the client and finishes establishing the connection with the server.

Object Properties

When created, each authentication server becomes an object on the Netscreen firewall. In order to reference the object when used in rules and VPN endpoints, each object has a set of properties that define pieces of info used when communicating with the external authentication server.

A list of common object properties is as follows:

- **Name** The name of the object.
- **IP/Domain Name** IP or domain name address of the external authentication server.
- **Backup1** IP or domain name address of the backup external authentication server.
- **Backup2** IP or domain name address of the second backup external authentication server.
- **Timeout** An integer value for the number of seconds until timeout during authentication.
- **Account Type** Will be one of either Auth, L2TP, Admin, or Xauth.

In addition to the above object properties, you may also see these additional object properties:

- **Radius Port**   The port number used by the RADIUS server.

- **Retry Timeout**   Number of seconds until timeout for the RADIUS server.

- **Shared Secret**   Visibility protected shared secret used for securing the connection between the Netscreen firewall and the RADIUS server.

- **Client Retries**   Number of client retries to attempt.

- **Client Timeout**   Time in seconds before timeout and retry.

- **Authentication Port**   The port that the external SecurID server listens for connections on.

- **Encryption Type**   The type of encryption used for communication between the Netscreen firewall and the SecurID server.

- **LDAP Port**   The port the LDAP server listens on for connections.

- **Common Name Identifier**   The record name for common names within the LDAP directory.

- **Distinguished Name**   The distinguished name—also known as root DN of the server—comes immediately after the cn.

Auth Server Types

In the following sections you will find descriptions of the three different external authentication servers supported by Netscreen. In addition, you will find both WebUI and CLI directions for configuring a Netscreen firewall to use an external authentication server. Finally, directions to make an external authentication device the default device for authentication are provided.

RADIUS

RADIUS is a protocol developed by Livingston—now Lucent Technologies—that provides for user authentication, authorization, and accountability from a centralized server. Originally developed based on an RFI from Merit, RADIUS quickly grew into the de-facto standard for user authentication of dial-in systems. Being an easily extensible standard, RADIUS lent itself to modification and over time emerged as a robust authentication, authorization, and accountability solution.

Types of Users

Netscreen's RADIUS implementation supports the following types of users:

- Auth

- XAuth

- L2TR

- Admin

Features

Netscreen's RADIUS implementation supports the following features:

- Auth
- L2TP – Auth & Remote
- Admin – Auth & Privileges
- XAuth – Auth & Remote
- User Groups
- Group Expressions

How to Configure

To configure RADIUS under Netscreen's WebUI:

1. From the WebUI, select **Configuration | Auth | AuthServers**, then click the **New** button.
2. Enter the following fields:

   - **Name**   radiusserver1
   - **IP/Domain Name**   radius1.example.com
   - **Backup1**   radius2.example.com
   - **Backup2**   radius3.example.com
   - **Timeout**   10
   - **Account Type**   **Any combination of Auth, L2TP, Admin, XAuth**
   - **Radius Port**   1645
   - **Retry Timeout**   3
   - **Shared Secret**   secret

3. Click on the **OK** button.

To configure RADIUS under Netscreen's CLI:

```
set auth-server radiusserver1 account-type auth xauth
set auth-server radiusserver1 server-name radius1.example.com
set auth-server radiusserver1 backup1 radius2.example.com
set auth-server radiusserver1 backup2 radius3.example.com
set auth-server radiusserver1 radius secret MySecret
set auth-server radiusserver1 timeout 10
set auth-server radiusserver1 radius port 1645
set auth-server radiusserver1 radius timeout 3
```

SecurID

RSA SecurID is a two-factor dynamic token authentication and authorization system. SecurID utilizes a hardware token—slightly larger than a credit card—to generate a password token that changes every 60 seconds. The second factor in the SecurID authentication is a PIN number. The PIN number and generated token are entered together to complete the authentication process. Once entered, the values are looked up in the SecurID server and compared to the stored values. If successful, the SecurID server transmits a success message back to the Netscreen firewall. In real world use, SecureID is more secure than RADIUS due to its inability to be compromised without access to both the PIN and hardware token.

Types of Users

Netscreen's SecurID implementation supports the following types of users:

- Auth
- L2TP
- XAuth
- Admin

Features

Netscreen's SecurID implementation supports the following features:

- Auth
- L2TP – Auth
- XAuth – Auth
- Admin – Auth

How to Configure

To configure a SecurID server under Netscreen's WebUI:

1. From the WebUI, select **Configuration | Auth | AuthServers** and then select **New**.
2. Enter the following fields:

   - **Name**   aceserver1
   - **IP/Domain Name**   ace1.example.com
   - **Backup1**   ace2.example.com
   - **Backup2**
   - **Timeout**   10
   - **Account Type**   **Any combination of Auth, L2TP, Admin, XAuth**

- **Client Retries**   3
- **Client Timeout**   5
- **Authentication Port**   5500
- **Encryption Type**   DES or SDI
- **Use Duress**   No

3. Click the **OK** button.

To configure a SecurID server under Netscreen's CLI:

```
set auth-server aceserver1 type securid
set auth-server aceserver1 server-name ace1.example.com
set auth-server aceserver1 backup1 ace2.example.com
set auth-server aceserver1 timeout 10
set auth-server aceserver1 account-type admin
set auth-server aceserver1 securid retries 3
set auth-server aceserver1 securid timeout 5
set auth-server aceserver1 securid encr 1
set auth-server aceserver1 securid duress 0
set auth-server aceserver1 securid auth-port 5500
save
```

LDAP

LDAP is a protocol developed in 1996 by the University of Michigan for accessing information directories. Based on x.500, LDAP was created because the need existed to have a Directory Access Protocol capable of utilizing TCP (Transmission Control Protocol)/IP as the transport mechanism. A directory is structured much like a tree, branching for every different level of the DIT (Directory Information Tree).

The DIT allows us to follow the DN (distinguished name) with the following branches:

- DN: c=US : c (country) is the first suffix of this DIT.
- DN: o=Sygress, c=US : o (organization) is the name of the organization
- DN: ou=Authors, o=Syngress, c=US : ou (organizational unit) is the name of the group or organization with the organization
- DN: cn=Kevin Lynn2, ou=Authors, o=Syngress, c=US : cn (common name) is the name of a person under the DIT.

Notice that each branch of the tree builds on those above it. By specifying a DN with a base of ou=Authors,o=Syngress,c=US, the LDAP directory has a much smaller space to look for the user with the common name of Kevin Lynn2.

Types of Users

Netscreen's LDAP implementation supports the following types of users:

- Auth
- L2TP
- XAuth
- Admin

Features

Netscreen's LDAP implementation supports the following features:

- Auth
- L2TP – Auth
- XAuth – Auth
- Admin – Auth

How to Configure

To configure LDAP under Netscreen's WebUI:

1. From the WebUI, select **Configuration | Auth | AuthServers** and then select **New**.
2. Enter the following fields:

   - **Name**   ldapserver1
   - **IP/Domain Name**   ldap1.example.com
   - **Backup1**   ldap2.example.com
   - **Backup2**   ldap3.example.com
   - **Timeout**   10
   - **Account Type**   **Any combination of Auth, L2TP, Admin, XAuth**
   - **LDAP Port**   389
   - **Common Name Identifier**   **cn**
   - **Distinguished Name**   **ou=someorgunit,dc=example,dc=com**

3. Click the OK button.

To configure LDAP under Netscreen's CLI:

```
set auth-server ldapserver1 type ldap
set auth-server ldapserver1 account-type auth
set auth-server ldapserver1 server-name ldap1.example.com
set auth-server ldapserver1 backup1 ldap2.example.com
```

```
set auth-server ldapserver1 backup2 ldap3.example.com
set auth-server ldapserver1 timeout 10
set auth-server ldapserver1 ldap port 389
set auth-server ldapserver1 ldap cn cn
set auth-server ldapserver1 ldap dn c=us;o=Syngress;ou=Authors
save
```

Default Auth Servers

The default authentication server for any Netscreen firewall is the internal Local database. The following is a list of features and types of users the Local database is capable of utilizing:

- Admin
- Auth
- IKE
- L2TP
- XAuth
- Admin privileges
- WebAuth
- User groups
- Group expressions

How to Change

To change the default auth server under Netscreen's WebUI:

Local:

1. Select **VPNs | AutoKey Advanced | XAuth Settings**.
2. Select **Default Authentication Server: Local**, then click **Apply**.

RADIUS:

1. Select **VPNs | L2TP | Default Settings**.
2. Select **Default authentication server: radiusserver1**, then click **Apply**.

SecurID:

1. Select **Configuration | Admin | Administrator**.
2. Select **Admin Auth Server: aceserver1**, then click **Apply**.

LDAP:

1. Select **Configuration | Auth | Firewall**.
2. Select **Default Auth Server: ldapserver1**, then click **Apply**.

To change the default auth server under Netscreen's CLI:

```
set xauth default auth server Local
set l2tp default auth server radiusserver1
set admin auth server aceserver1
set auth default auth server ldapserver1
```

When to Use

Deciding on which to authentication server to use depends on your specific needs. If you have few users, don't see yourself making a lot of modifications to the internal Local file, and have only the one Netscreen firewall, then the Local database is probably a good choice. If you have a lot of users, make sure that you are using a more scaleable solution such as RADIUS or LDAP. If security is what you really need then you can't go wrong with the RSA SecurID server.

You should also consider whether you need to use any of the authorization and addressing features of the firewall or just need the authentication features. All of the external authentication servers support the authentication of user credentials; however, only RADIUS supports the loading of a Netscreen dictionary file and the use of RADIUS as a source for external authorization and addressing.

Authentication Types

In the coming sections, we step through the configuration of users in both WebUI and CLI modes. Then, we assign an authentication type to the user. Finally, we set policies to force users to authenticate themselves when accessing the Netscreen device or protected network addresses.

Auth Users and User Groups

In the following example, we first define an Auth user, and then set policies that allow an authenticated user to access hosts inside the firewall.

To set Auth users under Netscreen's WebUI:

1. Select **Objects | Users | Local** then select **New**.
2. Enable the **Authentication User** option.
3. Enter the user password in the **User Password** and **Confirm Password** text fields, then select **OK**.
4. Select **Policies** and set **From: Trust** and **To: Untrust** then select **New**.
5. Enter the following fields:

   - **Name:**   testpolicy
   - **Source Address:**   10.4.4.1/32
   - **Destination Address:**   10.50.0.0/16

6. Select **Advanced** and enable the **Authentication** option.
7. Enable the **Auth Server** and **Use Default** options.
8. Select the **User** option and then **Local Auth User – klynn**.

To set Auth users under Netscreen's CLI:

```
set user klynn password "password"
set user "klynn" ike-id fqdn "klynn" share-limit 1
set user "klynn" type auth
set policy id 1 from "Trust" to "Untrust" "Any" "Any" "ANY" permit
set policy id 2 name "testpolicy" from "Trust" to "Untrust" "10.4.4.1/32"
"10.50.0.0/16" ANY permit auth user klynn
```

Next, create a new address assigned to the Local group, then assign it to a policy. To create a new address and assign it to a policy under WebUI:

1. Select **Objects | Addresses | List** and then click the **New** button.

2. Enter the following text fields:

   - **Address Name:**   1_address
   - **IP/Netmask:**   10.4.4.1/24

To set a user group and then assign it to a policy under Netscreen's CLI:

```
set user-group group1 location local
set user-group group1 user klynn
set address trust 1_address "10.4.4.1/24"
set policy top from trust to untrust 1_address Any permit auth
user-group group1
```

IKE Users and User Groups

In the next configuration, we create an IKE user, then set policies that allow authenticated users to access hosts inside the firewall.

To create an IKE user under Netscreen's WebUI:

1. Select **Objects | Users | Local** then select **New**.

2. Fill out the text field **User Name: klynn**, enable the **IKE User** option, and click the **Simple Identity** button.

3. Fill out the following fields:

   - **IKE ID Type:**   Auto
   - **IKE Identity:**   klynn

4. Enable the **Authentication User** option.

5. Enter the user password under the **User Password**: and **Confirm Password** text fields the select **OK**.

6. Select **Policies** and set **From: Trust** and To: **Untrust** then select **New**.

7. Enter the following fields:

- **Name:**   **testpolicy**
- **Source Address:**   **10.4.4.1/32**
- **Destination Address:**   **10.50.0.0/16**

8. Select **Advanced** and then enable the **Authentication** option.

9. Enable the **Auth Server** and **Use Default** options.

10. Enable the **User** option and then **Local Auth User – klynn**.

To create an IKE user under Netscreen's CLI:

```
set user klynn password "password"
set user "klynn" ike-id fqdn "klynn" share-limit 1
set user "klynn" ike-id ip 10.4.4.201
set user "klynn" type ike
```

Create a new address assigned to the Local group, and then assign it to a policy. The group automatically becomes an IKE group after an IKE user is added to it.

To create a new address under the local group and assign it to a policy under Netscreen's WebUI:

1. Select **Objects | Users | Local Groups** and then select **New**.
   Group Name: **1_address**

2. Select the user you want to assign and then select the << button to assign the user to the **Group Members** column.

CLI:

```
set user-group group1 location local
set user-group group1 user klynn
set address trust 1_address "10.4.4.1/24"
set policy top from trust to untrust 1_address Any permit auth
user-group group1
```

XAuth Users and User Groups

When we're creating XAuth users, first we create an IKE user, and then we create a VPN by creating a new AutoKey Gateway and finally by creating a New AutoKey IKE.

To create an IKE user under Netscreen's WebUI:

1. Select **Objects | Users | Local** then select **New**.

2. Fill out the text field **User Name: klynn**, enable the **IKE User** option, and click the **Simple Identity** button.

3. Fill out the following fields:

- **IKE ID Type:**   **Auto**
- **IKE Identity:**   **klynn**

4. Enable the **Authentication User** option.

5. Enter the user password under the **User Password**: and **Confirm Password** text fields the select **OK**.

6. Enable the **XAuth User** option and enter the following fields:

   - **IP Pool:**   **10.4.4**
   - **Primary DNS IP:**   **10.4.4.1**
   - **Secondary DNS IP:**   **10.4.4.1**
   - **Primary WINS IP:**   **10.4.4.1**
   - **Secondary WINS IP:**   **10.4.4.1**

Create an AutoKey Gateway with Netscreen's WebUI:

1. Select **VPNs | AutoKey Advanced | Gateway** and then select **New**.

   - **Gateway Name:**   **gateway1**
   - **Security Level:**   **Custom**
   - **Remote Gateway Type:**   **Static IP Address**
   - **IP Address/Hostname:**   **192.168.0.1**
   - **Preshared Key:**   **secret**
   - **Outgoing Interface:**   **untrust**

Create an AutoKey Gateway with Netscreen's CLI:

```
set user klynn password "password"
set user "klynn" ike-id fqdn "klynn" share-limit 1
set user "klynn" ike-id ip 10.4.4.201
set user "klynn" type ike xauth
set user "klynn" remote ippool "10.4.4"
set user "klynn" remote dns1 "10.4.4.1"
set user "klynn" remote dns2 "10.4.4.1"
set user "klynn" remote wins1 "10.4.4.1"
set user "klynn" remote wins2 "10.4.4.1"
set ike gateway "gateway1" address 192.168.0.4 Main outgoing-interface "untrust"
preshare secret sec-level standard
set ike gateway "gateway1" xauth server Local user-group xauthgroup1
set vpn "ike1" gateway "gateway1" no-replay tunnel idletime 0 proposal
"nopfs-esp-aes128-md5"
```

Create a new address assigned to the Local group, and then assign it to a policy. The group automatically becomes an IKE group after an IKE user is added to it.

To create a new address under Netscreen's WebUI:

1. Select **Objects | Addresses | List** and then select the **New** button.

Address Name:	1_address
IP/Netmask:	10.4.4.1/24

To create a new address under Netscreen's CLI:

```
set user-group group1 location local
set user-group group1 user klynn
save
```

L2TP Users and User Groups

When we're creating L2TP users, first we create an IKE user, and then we create a VPN by creating a new AutoKey Gateway and finally by creating a New AutoKey IKE.

To create an IKE user under Netscreen's WebUI:

1. Select **Objects | Users | Local** then select **New**.
2. Fill out the text field **User Name: klynn**, enable the **IKE User** option, and click the **Simple Identity** button.
3. Fill out the following fields:

    - **IKE ID Type:**   Auto
    - **IKE Identity:**   klynn

4. Enable the **Authentication User** option.
5. Enter the user password under the **User Password**: and **Confirm Password** text fields the select **OK**.
6. Select the L2TP User checkbox and enter in the following fields:

    - **IP Pool:**   10.4.4
    - **Primary DNS IP:**   10.4.4.1
    - **Secondary DNS IP:**   10.4.4.1
    - **Primary WINS IP:**   10.4.4.1
    - **Secondary WINS IP:** 10.4.4.1

Create an AutoKey Gateway with Netscreen's WebUI:

1. Select **VPNs | AutoKey Advanced | Gateway** and then select **New**.

    - **Gateway Name:**   gateway1
    - **Security Level:**   Custom

- **Remote Gateway Type:** **Static IP Address**
- **IP Address/Hostname:** **192.168.0.1**
- **Preshared Key:** **secret**
- **Outgoing Interface:** **untrust**

Create an AutoKey Gateway with Netscreen's CLI:

```
set user klynn password "password"
set user "klynn" ike-id fqdn "klynn" share-limit 1
set user "klynn" ike-id ip 10.4.4.201
set user "klynn" type ike l2tp
set user "klynn" remote ippool "10.4.4"
set user "klynn" remote dns1 "10.4.4.1"
set user "klynn" remote dns2 "10.4.4.1"
set user "klynn" remote wins1 "10.4.4.1"
set user "klynn" remote wins2 "10.4.4.1"
set ike gateway "gateway1" address 192.168.0.4 Main outgoing-interface "untrust"
preshare secret sec-level standard
set ike gateway "gateway1" xauth server Local user-group xauthgroup1
set vpn "ike1" gateway "gateway1" no-replay tunnel idletime 0 proposal
"nopfs-esp-aes128-md5"
```

Create a new address assigned to the Local group, and then assign it to a policy. The group automatically becomes an IKE group after an IKE user is added to it.

To create a new address under Netscreen's WebUI:

1. Select **Objects | Addresses | List** and then select the **New** button.

    Address Name: **1_address**

    IP/Netmask: **10.4.4.1/24**

To create a new address under Netscreen's CLI:

```
set user-group group1 location local
set user-group group1 user klynn
save
```

Admin Users and User Groups

Administrative users at a minimum have the ability to view everything; however, if created with read-write access, the administrator has full administrative privileges. Administrator privileges may be read from a RADIUS database if an external authentication server has been set already.

Add an external authentication server to the Netscreen's configuration and configure the firewall to read admin authentication and authorization credentials from the RADIUS server.

To create an admin user under Netscreen's WebUI:

1. First, Configure a new RADIUS server to hold the Admin credentials:
2. Select **Configuration | Auth | Auth Servers** and then select the **New** button.
3. Enter in the following text fields:

   - **Name:** radiusserver1
   - **IP/Domain Name:** radius1.example.com
   - **Backup1:** radius2.example.com
   - **Backup2:** radius3.example.com
   - **Timeout:** 10
   - **Account Type:** Any combination of Auth, L2TP, Admin, XAuth
   - **Radius Port:** 1645
   - **Retry Timeout:** 3
   - **Shared Secret:** secret

4. Click the **OK** button.

Next, Configure the Administrators to get the Admin credentials from RADIUS server:

1. Select Configuration|Admin|Administrators
2. Select **Admin Privileges: Get privilege from RADIUS server**.
3. Select **Admin Auth Server: radiusserver1**.

Finally, Create a new Administrator:

1. Select **Configuration | Admin | Administrators** and click the **New** button.
2. Enter in the following text fields:

   - **Administrator Name:** admin2
   - **New Password:** secret
   - **Confirm New Password:** secret
   - **Privileges:** Read-Write

   SSH Password Authentication
To create an admin user under Netscreen's CLI:

```
set admin user "admin2" password "nPbcE7r4IayFcqDPis8KX2Mt2BEX4n" privilege "all"
```

Multi-type Users

Users may be assigned one or more user types during or after creation. Any user may be assigned any user type; however, as a practical rule it's usually better to assign IKE to groups instead of users. The local database has a finite amount of users it is capable of storing. When you assign IKE to groups you use less of the user records the local database is capable of storing. This enables the Netscreen administrators to scale the firewalls.

User Groups and Group expressions

Group expressions are Boolean—AND, OR, NOT—expressions that allow a Netscreen administrator to select more than one user, group, or previous group expression. The use of group expressions allows an administrator to select or not select users or groups by following these rules:

The following are some examples of how to create a group expression under Netscreen's WebUI:

1. Select **Objects | Group Expressions** and then click the **New** button.

2. Enter in the following text fields:

- **Group Expression:**   **Males_and_Females**
- **Males AND Females :**   **True if the current user/group exists in both Males and Females.**
- **Males OR Females :**   **True if the current user/group is either Males or Females.**
- **NOT Females:**   **True if the current user/group is not Females.**

CLI:

```
set group-expression males_and_females males and females
set group-expression males_or_females males or females
set group-expression only_males not females
```

Routing

Solutions in this chapter:

- Virtual Routers
- Routing Information Protocol
- Open Shortest Path First (OSPF)
- Border Gateway Protocol

☑ **Summary**

Introduction

Routing is a fundamental part of any IP (Internet Protocol)-based infrastructure. Every device on an IP-based network uses routes to determine the next hop or location it needs to access the desired host. In many cases, firewalls are just glorified routers. They provide firewall features, but are still a core routing component in many organizations' networks. Routers themselves are usually capable of providing a stateful firewall.

Juniper's NetScreen firewalls are capable of providing routing services above and beyond the average router. NetScreen firewalls can provide the capability to split a normal single routing table into multiple virtual routers. A virtual router is a logical router that can perform all of the tasks a normal routing engine can do. It can contain all of the static routes including the default route. Virtual routers are also capable of supporting dynamic routing protocols.

Most firewall products are very limited in supporting dynamic routing. It is often argued that firewalls should not be integrated into a dynamic routing environment. However, this is often difficult, as firewalls are at the core of most networks. Juniper helps mitigate this risk with virtual routers by allowing you to split your routing domain into multiple virtual routers.

One virtual router can contain all of your outward routes toward the Internet or other untrusted area. A second virtual router can contain all of your internal routes. These routes are contained separate from each other and by default are unknown between each virtual router.

There are three routing protocols that can be used with a NetScreen firewall. The first protocol, Routing Information Protocol (RIP), is an older protocol, but it is the most commonly supported protocol. Open Shortest Path First (OSPF) is an extremely robust protocol. OSPF is an open standard protocol and is used by many organizations for their internal networks. Last, but certainly not least, is Border Gateway Protocol (BGP). BGP is used to run the routing architecture of the Internet. It is often the most misunderstood protocol due to its complexity.

Virtual Routers

Virtual routers provide the capability to split their routing tables into multiple routing tables. A traditional IP routing device contains a single routing table. This routing table contains all routes known to the device. This routing table is known as a *routing domain*. By default, the NetScreen firewall operates as a traditional routing device by using a single virtual router.

A NetScreen firewall, by default, contains two virtual routers. These routers cannot be removed from the firewall. These routers are named *trust-vr* and *untrust-vr*. The trust-vr is the default virtual router. Depending on the device you are using, you may create additional virtual routers.

Using Virtual Routers

Using a virtual router may seem like a complex process at first. However, it is just like using a traditional routing device. Think about having multiple virtual routers in your firewall as having multiple real routers. The virtual routers will function the same way. If you remember from Chapter 22 that zones are bound to virtual routers. This determines which routers are used on your firewall. If your firewall supports it, you can create additional virtual routers.

Creating Virtual Routers

To create a new virtual router, you must be able to provide it with a name. You can choose to name it anything you want; there are no requirements for a prefix or suffix when naming the virtual router. A virtual router's name can contain up to 32 characters, and you can create new virtual routers using both the CLI (command line interface) and the WebUI. Figure 25.1 shows the WebUI virtual router creation screen.

Figure 25.1 Virtual Router Creation (WebUI)

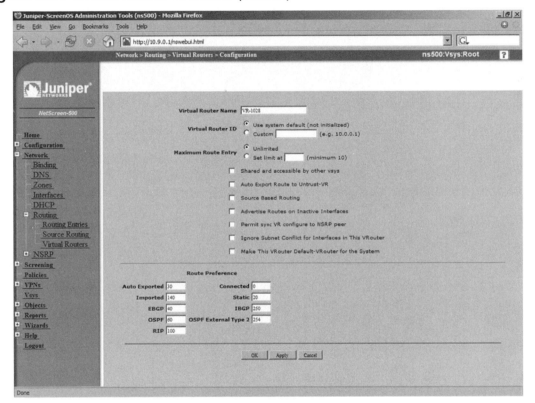

Use the following steps to create a virtual router via the WebUI:

1. Access **Network | Routing | Virtual Routers**.
2. On the top right-hand side of the page, click the button labeled **New**.
3. A default name (**VR-<number>**) will be generated for you. You can keep this name, or use a different name simply by entering it in the **Virtual Router Name** field.
4. Click **OK**.

Use the following to create a virtual router via the CLI:

```
ns500-> get vrouter
* indicates default vrouter for the current vsys
A - AutoExport, R - RIP, O - OSPF, B - BGP
    ID Name                Vsys       Owner      Routes          Flags
     1 untrust-vr          Root       shared     0/max
*    2 trust-vr            Root       shared     1/max

total 2 vrouters shown and 0 of them defined by user
ns500-> set vrouter name Syngress-WAN
ns500-> get vrouter
* indicates default vrouter for the current vsys
A - AutoExport, R - RIP, O - OSPF, B - BGP

    ID Name                Vsys       Owner      Routes          Flags
     1 untrust-vr          Root       shared     0/max
*    2 trust-vr            Root       shared     1/max
  1025 Syngress-WAN        Root       user       0/max

total 3 vrouters shown and 1 of them defined by user
ns500->
```

Route Selection

If your routing table contains a single route to a destination, it will have little difficulty on deciding what route to select. However, with the use of dynamic routing protocols your firewall may be in the position of having to decide the appropriate route. Your NetScreen firewall uses a three-step method to determine which route to select:

- **Most Specific** First, the firewall identifies the most specific route for the host. The most specific route is the route with the smallest possible subnet. The firewall would prefer the route with the most bits in its netmask.

- **Route Preference** The route preference is a table internal to the firewall. The firewall will define a preference based upon the source of the route. The firewall keeps an internal table that defines the preference set for each route. The preference can be modified for all of the route types if so desired. Table 25.1 lists the default route preferences.

- **Route Metric** The metric is the last component checked if there are still two matching routes. The metric is set to zero for all directly connected routes. Static routes receive a metric of one. When adding a route to a NetScreen firewall, you can set the metric manually.

Table 25.1 Route Preferences

Protocol	Default Preference
Connected	0
Static	20
Auto-Exported	30
EBGP	40
OSPF	60
RIP	100
Imported	140
OSPF External Type 2	200
IBGP	250

Set Route Preference

The route preference can be modified for each of the route types. This is configured for each virtual router separately. This task can be accomplished from both the CLI and the WebUI. Figure 25.2 shows an example of setting the route preference from the WebUI. If you change the route preference on an already learned route, you must wait until the route is relearned until the new preference takes effect.

Figure 25.2 Route Preference Configuration (WebUI)

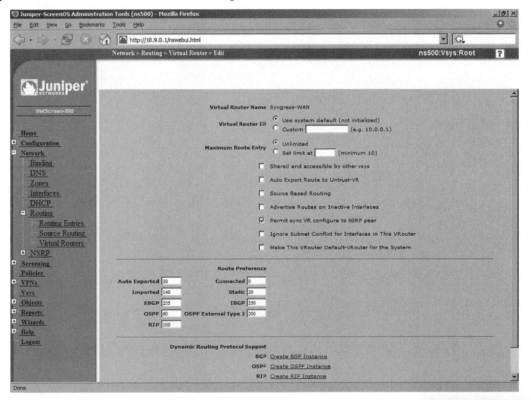

Use the following steps to configure route preference via the WebUI:

1. Access **Network | Routing | Virtual Routers**.
2. Click the **Edit** link of the virtual router you wish to configure.
3. Use the Route Type field to enter the number of the desired route preference.
4. Click **OK**.

Use the following to configure route preference via the CLI:

```
ns500-> get vrouter Syngress-WAN preference
vrouter Syngress-WAN route preference table
---------------------------------------------
Connected Routes:               0
Static Routes:                  20
Auto-exported Routes:           30
Imported Routes:                140
RIP Routes:                     100
EBGP Routes:                    40
IBGP Routes:                    250
OSPF Routes:                    60
OSPF External Type-2 Routes:    200
ns500->
ns500-> set vrouter Syngress-WAN preference ebgp 255
ns500-> get vrouter Syngress-WAN preference
vrouter Syngress-WAN route preference table
---------------------------------------------
Connected Routes:               0
Static Routes:                  20
Auto-exported Routes:           30
Imported Routes:                140
RIP Routes:                     100
EBGP Routes:                    255
IBGP Routes:                    250
OSPF Routes:                    60
OSPF External Type-2 Routes:    200
ns500->
```

Set Route Metric

The route metric is configured when a static route is added into your firewall. This can be done from both the CLI and the WebUI. Figure 25.3 shows an example of the WebUI configuration of a route metric.

Figure 25.3 Route Metric Configuration (WebUI)

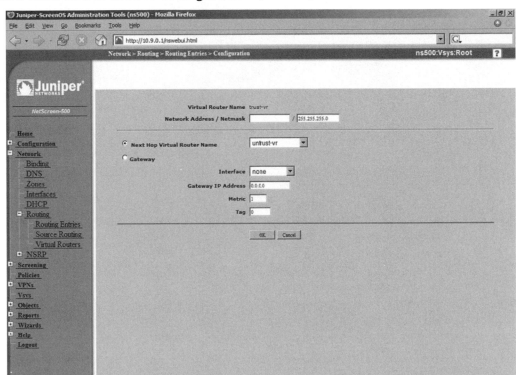

Use the following steps to configure a route metric via the WebUI:

1. Access **Network | Routing | Routing Entries**.

2. Use the available drop-down list in the upper right-hand corner to select the virtual router to which you will add a route. 3. Click **New**.

4. Configure the properties for the new route.

5. In the text box labeled **Metric**, enter the metric you want to apply to the route.

6. Click **OK**.

Use the following to configure a route metric via the CLI:

```
ns500-> get route
untrust-vr (0 entries)
--------------------------------------------------------------------------------
-------
C - Connected, S - Static, A - Auto-Exported, I - Imported, R - RIP
iB - IBGP, eB - EBGP, O - OSPF, E1 - OSPF external type 1
E2 - OSPF external type 2
trust-vr (2 entries)
```

```
--------------------------------------------------------------------------
-------
    ID       IP-Prefix       Interface    Gateway       P    Pref    Mtr    Vsys
--------------------------------------------------------------------------
-------
*    2       10.9.0.0/24     mgt          0.0.0.0       C    0       0      Root
*    3       1.2.3.0/24      mgt          10.9.0.10     S    20      1      Root
Syngress-WAN (0 entries)
--------------------------------------------------------------------------
-------
1099 (0 entries)
--------------------------------------------------------------------------
-------
ns500-> set route 10.123.0.0/24 interface ethernet3/2 metric 20
ns500-> get route
untrust-vr (0 entries)
--------------------------------------------------------------------------
-------
C - Connected, S - Static, A - Auto-Exported, I - Imported, R - RIP
iB - IBGP, eB - EBGP, O - OSPF, E1 - OSPF external type 1
E2 - OSPF external type 2
trust-vr (3 entries)
--------------------------------------------------------------------------
-------
    ID       IP-Prefix       Interface    Gateway       P    Pref    Mtr    Vsys
--------------------------------------------------------------------------
-------
     4       10.123.0.0/24   eth3/2       0.0.0.0       S    20      20     Root
*    2       10.9.0.0/24     mgt          0.0.0.0       C    0       0      Root
*    3       1.2.3.0/24      mgt          10.9.0.10     S    20      1      Root
Syngress-WAN (0 entries)
--------------------------------------------------------------------------
-------
1099 (0 entries)
--------------------------------------------------------------------------
-------
ns500->
```

Route Redistribution

Your NetScreen firewall is capable of passing known routes to other devices using routing protocols. Routes will automatically be distributed if the route was learned from that same protocol and the route is currently active in the routing table. You have the option of redistributing learned routes from routing protocol to another routing protocol. To do this you must configure two components.

- **Access List** A route access list specifies a set of matching IP addresses. IP addresses are specified with network prefixes.

- **Route Map** Route maps are a list of conditions listed in a sequential order, much like policies. If a route matches a condition, the action for the route map is then applied to the matching route.

Configuring a Route Access List

Route access lists are configured on specific virtual routers. Each access list contains several configuration components when it is created. Figure 25.4 shows how an access list is configured from the WebUI. An access list can be configured from both the WebUI and the CLI.

- **Access List ID** An access list ID is a unique identifier that is used to reference the access list.

- **Action** The configured action is applied to the routes that match the access list entry. You can choose **Permit** or **Deny** as the action.

- **IP Address/Netmask** The IP address and netmask are used to specify a matching route.

- **Sequence Number** This number is used to determine the sequence in which the access list is checked.

Figure 25.4 Route Access List Configuration (WebUI)

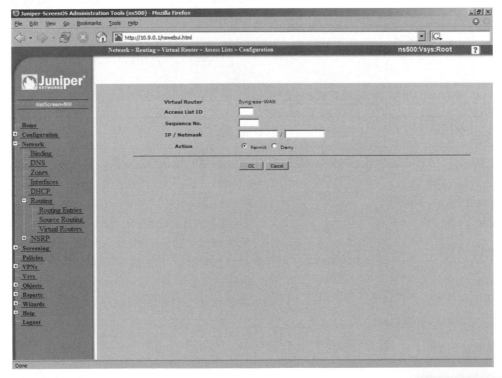

Use the following steps to configure a route access list via the WebUI:

1. Access **Network | Routing | Virtual Routers**.
2. Click the **Access List** link of the router to which you will add the new route access list.
3. Click **New**.
4. Enter the information for the access list in the provided text boxes.
5. Select the action by clicking on the radio button labeled with desired action.
6. Click **OK**.

Use the following to configure a route access list via the CLI:

```
ns500-> set vrouter Syngress-WAN access-list 10 permit ip 10.2.3.0/24 100
ns500-> get vrouter Syngress-WAN access-list
Access list (10)
----------------
Sequence 100: 10.2.3.0/24    -> Permit
ns500-> get vrouter trust-vr access-list
```

Configuring A Route Map

When configuring a route map, you must choose two components, the match condition and the set attributes.

- **Match Condition**   Match conditions are conditions on the route that are matched against. Table 25.2 shows the list of match conditions.

- **Set Attributes**   Set attributes are attributes that are set on matched routers. Set attributes are an optional component of route maps. Table 25.3 shows a listing of possible set conditions.

Table 25.2 Match Conditions for Route Maps

Match Condition	Description
BGP AS Path	Matches an AS path access list
BGP Community	Matches a BGP community list
OSPF route type	Matches a type of OSPF route
Interface	Matches a specific interface
IP Address	Matches a specific route access list
Metric	Matches a specific route metric
Next-hop	Matches a specific route access list
Tag	Matches a route tag value or IP address

Table 25.3 Set Conditions for Route Maps

Set Condition	Description
BGP AS Path	Prepends a BGP AS path to the route
BGP Community	Sets the BGP community attribute
BGP Local Preference	Sets the local preference value of the matching route
BGP Weight	Sets the weight of the matching route
OSPF metric	Sets the OSPF metric type of the matching route
RIP offset metric	Sets the offset of the matching route
Metric	Sets the route metric
Next-hop	Sets the next hop of the route
Tag	Sets the tag of the matching route

Routing Information Protocol

The Routing Information Protocol is one of the oldest routing protocols available today. It is highly inefficient, but this of course is made up for with its simple configuration. Almost all routing devices typically support the RIP protocol, even home user Cable/DSL routers. There are two versions of RIP: RIP version one and RIP version two. NetScreen firewalls support RIP version two. Even though the RIP protocol is old, it is mature and functions well in small networks.

RIP Concepts

The RIP protocol sends update messages at regular intervals and when the network changes. This makes RIP a "chatty" routing protocol because it constantly sends information out to the network. RIP uses only one single mechanism to determine the best route. RIP counts a hop or how many hops away a network is. RIP has a limitation of using up to 15 hops of distance. If a route's metric reaches 16 hops, the destination is considered unreachable.

Basic RIP Configuration

RIP is created on a per virtual router basis. To use RIP there are four simple steps you need to configure on your firewall:

- Configure a virtual router ID.
- On the virtual router create a RIP routing instance.
- Activate the new RIP instance.
- Configure the network interfaces to have RIP enabled.

Configuring RIP

In this section we will look at the steps for configuring RIP on your firewall. We will do all steps together for both the WebUI and the CLI.

Use the following steps to configure RIP via the WebUI:

1. Access **Network | Routing | Virtual Router**.
2. Click the **Edit** link of the virtual router you wish to modify.
3. Enable the **Virtual Router ID** option.
4. Use the **Custom** field to enter an ID for the RIP.
5. Click **Apply**.
6. Click **Create RIP Instance**.
7. Enable the **Enable RIP** option.
8. Click **OK**.
9. Access **Network | Interface**.
10. Click the **Edit** link of the interface that you want to enable RIP on.
11. Click the **RIP** link at the top of the page.
12. Enable the **Enable** option.
13. Click **OK**.

Use the following to configure RIP via the CLI:

```
ns500-> get vrouter trust-vr
Routing Table
--------------------------------------------------------------------------------
-------
C - Connected, S - Static, A - Auto-Exported, I - Imported, R - RIP
iB - IBGP, eB - EBGP, O - OSPF, E1 - OSPF external type 1
E2 - OSPF external type 2
Total 4/max entries
    ID       IP-Prefix      Interface    Gateway       P    Pref    Mtr    Vsys
--------------------------------------------------------------------------------
-------
     5       1.2.3.4/32     eth3/2       0.0.0.0       C    0       0      Root
     4       10.123.0.0/24  eth3/2       0.0.0.0       S    20      20     Root
*    2       10.9.0.0/24    mgt          0.0.0.0       C    0       0      Root
*    3       1.2.3.0/24     mgt          10.9.0.10     S    20      1      Root
Interfaces
--------------------------------------------------------------------------------
-------
tunnel, hidden.1, self, mgt, ha1, ha2
```

```
v1-trust, v1-untrust, v1-dmz, ethernet3/2, ethernet1/2, ethernet2/2
vlan1, ethernet4/1
```

Auto-exporting:	Disabled
Default-vrouter:	For vsys (Root)
Shared-vrouter:	Yes

```
---more---
```

nsrp-config-sync:	Yes
System-Default-route:	Not present
Advertise-Inactive-Interface:	Disabled
Source-Based-Routing:	Disabled
SNMP Trap:	Public
Ignore-Subnet-Conflict:	Disabled

```
ns500-> set vrouter trust-vr router-id 255
ns500-> get vrouter trust-vr
Routing Table
--------------------------------------------------------------------------------
-------
C - Connected, S - Static, A - Auto-Exported, I - Imported, R - RIP
iB - IBGP, eB - EBGP, O - OSPF, E1 - OSPF external type 1
E2 - OSPF external type 2
Total 4/max entries
```

	ID	IP-Prefix	Interface	Gateway	P	Pref	Mtr	Vsys
	5	1.2.3.4/32	eth3/2	0.0.0.0	C	0	0	Root
	4	10.123.0.0/24	eth3/2	0.0.0.0	S	20	20	Root
*	2	10.9.0.0/24	mgt	0.0.0.0	C	0	0	Root
*	3	1.2.3.0/24	mgt	10.9.0.10	S	20	1	Root

```
Interfaces
--------------------------------------------------------------------------------
-------
tunnel, hidden.1, self, mgt, ha1, ha2
v1-trust, v1-untrust, v1-dmz, ethernet3/2, ethernet1/2, ethernet2/2
vlan1, ethernet4/1
```

Auto-exporting:	Disabled
Default-vrouter:	For vsys (Root)
Shared-vrouter:	Yes

```
--- more ---
```

nsrp-config-sync:	Yes
System-Default-route:	Not present
Advertise-Inactive-Interface:	Disabled

```
Source-Based-Routing:          Disabled
SNMP Trap:                     Public
Ignore-Subnet-Conflict:        Disabled
ns500-> set vrouter trust-vr protocol rip
ns500-> set vrouter trust-vr protocol rip enable
ns500-> get vrouter trust-vr
Routing Table
---------------------------------------------------------------------------
-------
C - Connected, S - Static, A - Auto-Exported, I - Imported, R - RIP
iB - IBGP, eB - EBGP, O - OSPF, E1 - OSPF external type 1
E2 - OSPF external type 2
Total 4/max entries
    ID      IP-Prefix     Interface     Gateway       P     Pref    Mtr    Vsys
---------------------------------------------------------------------------
-------
    5       1.2.3.4/32    eth3/2        0.0.0.0       C     0       0      Root
    4       10.123.0.0/24 eth3/2        0.0.0.0       S     20      20     Root
*   2       10.9.0.0/24   mgt           0.0.0.0       C     0       0      Root
*   3       1.2.3.0/24    mgt           10.9.0.10     S     20      1      Root
Interfaces
---------------------------------------------------------------------------
-------
tunnel, hidden.1, self, mgt, ha1, ha2
v1-trust, v1-untrust, v1-dmz, ethernet3/2, ethernet1/2, ethernet2/2
vlan1, ethernet4/1

Auto-exporting:                Disabled
Default-vrouter:               For vsys (Root)
Shared-vrouter:                Yes
--- more ---
nsrp-config-sync:              Yes
System-Default-route:          Not present
Advertise-Inactive-Interface:  Disabled
Source-Based-Routing:          Disabled
SNMP Trap:                     Public
Ignore-Subnet-Conflict:        Disabled
ns500-> get interface ethernet3/2
Interface ethernet3/2:
  number 10, if_info 82000, if_index 0, mode nat
  link down, phy-link down
```

```
  vsys Root, zone Trust, vr trust-vr
  *ip 1.2.3.4/32 mac 0010.db0b.494a
  *manage ip 1.2.3.4, mac 0010.db0b.494a
  route-deny disable
  ping enabled, telnet enabled, SSH enabled, SNMP enabled
  web enabled, ident-reset disabled, SSL enabled
  webauth disabled, webauth-ip 0.0.0.0
  OSPF disabled BGP disabled RIP disabled
  bandwidth: physical 0kbps, configured 0kbps, current 0kbps
            total configured gbw 0kbps, total allocated gbw 0kbps
  DHCP-Relay disabled
ns500-> set interface ethernet3/2 protocol rip enable
ns500-> get interface ethernet3/2
Interface ethernet3/2:
  number 10, if_info 82000, if_index 0, mode nat
  link down, phy-link down
  vsys Root, zone Trust, vr trust-vr
  *ip 1.2.3.4/32     mac 0010.db0b.494a
  *manage ip 1.2.3.4, mac 0010.db0b.494a
  route-deny disable
  ping enabled, telnet enabled, SSH enabled, SNMP enabled
  web enabled, ident-reset disabled, SSL enabled
  webauth disabled, webauth-ip 0.0.0.0
  OSPF disabled BGP disabled RIP enabled
  bandwidth: physical 0kbps, configured 0kbps, current 0kbps
            total configured gbw 0kbps, total allocated gbw 0kbps
  DHCP-Relay disabled
ns500->
```

Open Shortest Path First (OSPF)

OSPF is a link state protocol and is considered one of the best protocols to run for your internal network. The open in OSPF represents that it is an open standard protocol. OSPF will only send out periodic updates and is not considered to be a chatty protocol. It is extremely efficient and is supported by most modern routing equipment.

OSPF Concepts

Before we look into the configuration of OSPF on your NetScreen firewall, we will first review a few OSPF concepts. These concepts are common throughout the configuration of OSPF and also across various vendors' devices. Routers are grouped into *areas*. By default, all routers participating in

OSPF are grouped in to area **0**, also known as area **0.0.0.0**. There will be occasions when you will want to want to divide your network into multiple areas. This is typically done in large networks.

Each router that participates in an OSPF network is classified as one of four types of routers:

- **Internal Router**   A router with all interfaces belonging to the same area.

- **Backbone Router**   A router that has an interface in the backbone area. The backbone area is also known as area **0**.

- **Area Border Router**   A router that connects to multiple areas.

- **AS Boundary Router**   A router that borders another autonomous systems (AS).

Basic OSPF Configuration

Configuring OSPF is similar to configuring RIP, as it is enabled on a per virtual router basis. Each virtual router is capable of supporting one instance of OSPF at a time.

- Configure a virtual router ID.

- On the virtual router, create a OSPF instance.

- Activate the new OSPF instance.

- Configure the network interfaces to have OSPF enabled.

Use the following steps to configure OSPF via the WebUI:

1. Access **Network | Routing | Virtual Router**.
2. Click the **Edit** link of the virtual router for which you will configure OSPF.
3. Enable the **Virtual Router ID** option.
4. Enter an ID in the text box labeled **Custom**, next to the raido button you selected.
5. Click **Apply**.
6. Click **Create OSPF Instance**.
7. Enable the **OSPF Enabled** option.
8. Click **OK**.
9. Access **Network | Interface**.
10. Click the **Edit** link of the interface you want to enable OSPF on.
11. Click the link labeled **OSPF**.
12. Enable the **Enable Protocol OSPF** option.
13. Click OK.

Use the following to configure OSPF via the CLI:

```
ns500-> get vrouter trust-vr
Routing Table
```

```
--------------------------------------------------------------------------------
-------
C - Connected, S - Static, A - Auto-Exported, I - Imported, R - RIP
iB - IBGP, eB - EBGP, O - OSPF, E1 - OSPF external type 1
E2 - OSPF external type 2
Total 4/max entries
    ID     IP-Prefix        Interface    Gateway        P      Pref     Mtr    Vsys
--------------------------------------------------------------------------------
-------
     5     1.2.3.4/32       eth3/2       0.0.0.0        C      0        0      Root
     4     10.123.0.0/24    eth3/2       0.0.0.0        S      20       20     Root
*    2     10.9.0.0/24      mgt          0.0.0.0        C      0        0      Root
*    3     1.2.3.0/24       mgt          10.9.0.10      S      20       1      Root
Interfaces
--------------------------------------------------------------------------------
-------
tunnel, hidden.1, self, mgt, ha1, ha2
v1-trust, v1-untrust, v1-dmz, ethernet3/2, ethernet1/2, ethernet2/2
vlan1, ethernet4/1

Auto-exporting:               Disabled
Default-vrouter:              For vsys (Root)
Shared-vrouter:               Yes
nsrp-config-sync:             Yes
System-Default-route:         Not present
Advertise-Inactive-Interface: Disabled
Source-Based-Routing:         Disabled
SNMP Trap:                    Public
Ignore-Subnet-Conflict:       Disabled
ns500-> set vrouter trust-vr router-id 255
ns500-> get vrouter trust-vr
Routing Table
--------------------------------------------------------------------------------
-------
C - Connected, S - Static, A - Auto-Exported, I - Imported, R - RIP
iB - IBGP, eB - EBGP, O - OSPF, E1 - OSPF external type 1
E2 - OSPF external type 2
Total 4/max entries
    ID     IP-Prefix        Interface    Gateway        P      Pref     Mtr    Vsys
--------------------------------------------------------------------------------
-------
     5     1.2.3.4/32       eth3/2       0.0.0.0        C      0        0      Root
```

```
      4      10.123.0.0/24      eth3/2      0.0.0.0      S     20      20     Root
*     2      10.9.0.0/24        mgt         0.0.0.0      C     0       0      Root
*     3      1.2.3.0/24         mgt         10.9.0.10    S     20      1      Root
Interfaces
--------------------------------------------------------------------------------
-------
tunnel, hidden.1, self, mgt, ha1, ha2
v1-trust, v1-untrust, v1-dmz, ethernet3/2, ethernet1/2, ethernet2/2
vlan1, ethernet4/1

Auto-exporting:                 Disabled
Default-vrouter:                For vsys (Root)
Shared-vrouter:                 Yes
nsrp-config-sync:               Yes
System-Default-route:           Not present
Advertise-Inactive-Interface:   Disabled
Source-Based-Routing:           Disabled
SNMP Trap:                      Public
Ignore-Subnet-Conflict:         Disabled
ns500-> set vrouter trust-vr protocol ospf
ns500-> set vrouter trust-vr protocol ospf enable
ns500-> get vrouter trust-vr
Routing Table
--------------------------------------------------------------------------------
-------
C - Connected, S - Static, A - Auto-Exported, I - Imported, R - RIP
iB - IBGP, eB - EBGP, O - OSPF, E1 - OSPF external type 1
E2 - OSPF external type 2
Total 4/max entries
      ID     IP-Prefix          Interface   Gateway      P     Pref    Mtr    Vsys
--------------------------------------------------------------------------------
-------
      5      1.2.3.4/32         eth3/2      0.0.0.0      C     0       0      Root
      4      10.123.0.0/24      eth3/2      0.0.0.0      S     20      20     Root
*     2      10.9.0.0/24        mgt         0.0.0.0      C     0       0      Root
*     3      1.2.3.0/24         mgt         10.9.0.10    S     20      1      Root
Interfaces
--------------------------------------------------------------------------------
-------
tunnel, hidden.1, self, mgt, ha1, ha2
v1-trust, v1-untrust, v1-dmz, ethernet3/2, ethernet1/2, ethernet2/2
vlan1, ethernet4/1
```

```
  Auto-exporting:              Disabled
  Default-vrouter:             For vsys (Root)
  Shared-vrouter:              Yes
  nsrp-config-sync:            Yes
  System-Default-route:        Not present
  Advertise-Inactive-Interface: Disabled
  Source-Based-Routing:        Disabled
  SNMP Trap:                   Public
  Ignore-Subnet-Conflict:      Disabled
ns500-> get interface ethernet3/2
Interface ethernet3/2:
  number 10, if_info 82000, if_index 0, mode nat
  link down, phy-link down
  vsys Root, zone Trust, vr trust-vr
  *ip 1.2.3.4/32 mac 0010.db0b.494a
  *manage ip 1.2.3.4, mac 0010.db0b.494a
  route-deny disable
  ping enabled, telnet enabled, SSH enabled, SNMP enabled
  web enabled, ident-reset disabled, SSL enabled
  webauth disabled, webauth-ip 0.0.0.0
  OSPF disabled BGP disabled RIP disabled
  bandwidth: physical 0kbps, configured 0kbps, current 0kbps
            total configured gbw 0kbps, total allocated gbw 0kbps
  DHCP-Relay disabled
ns500-> set interface ethernet3/2 protocol ospf enable
ns500-> get interface ethernet3/2
Interface ethernet3/2:
  number 10, if_info 82000, if_index 0, mode nat
  link down, phy-link down
  vsys Root, zone Trust, vr trust-vr
  *ip 1.2.3.4/32 mac 0010.db0b.494a
  *manage ip 1.2.3.4, mac 0010.db0b.494a
  route-deny disable
  ping enabled, telnet enabled, SSH enabled, SNMP enabled
  web enabled, ident-reset disabled, SSL enabled
  webauth disabled, webauth-ip 0.0.0.0
  OSPF enabled BGP disabled RIP disabled
  bandwidth: physical 0kbps, configured 0kbps, current 0kbps
            total configured gbw 0kbps, total allocated gbw 0kbps
  DHCP-Relay disabled
ns500->
```

Border Gateway Protocol

Border Gateway Protocol is the core routing protocol used on the Internet. BGP routing information is not broadcast like RIP or OSPF. Two BGP peers connect to each other and form a TCP (Transmission Control Protocol) session. This session is then used to transmit all of the routing data. BGP is a very complex protocol and in this book we are only focusing on the basic BGP configuration on a NetScreen firewall.

Basic BGP Configuration

Use the following steps to configure BGP via the WebUI:

1. Access **Network | Routing | Virtual Router**.
2. Click the **Edit** link of the virtual router on which you will create a BGP instance.
3. Enable the **Virtual Router ID** option.
4. Enter an ID in the **Custom** field next to the radio button you selected.
5. Click **Apply**.
6. At the bottom of the page, click the **Create BGP Instance** link.
7. Enter the number of your autonomous system in the **AS Number** field.
8. Enable the **BGP Enabled** option.
9. Click **OK**.
10. Access **Network | Interface**.
11. Click the **Edit** link of the interface that you want to enable BGP on.
12. Click the **BGP** link.
13. Enable the **Enable Protocol BGP** option.
14. Click **OK**.

Use the following to configure BGP via the CLI:

```
ns500-> get vrouter trust-vr
Routing Table
--------------------------------------------------------------------------------
-------
C - Connected, S - Static, A - Auto-Exported, I - Imported, R - RIP
iB - IBGP, eB - EBGP, O - OSPF, E1 - OSPF external type 1
E2 - OSPF external type 2
Total 4/max entries
    ID      IP-Prefix       Interface      Gateway       P     Pref    Mtr     Vsys
--------------------------------------------------------------------------------
-------
     5      1.2.3.4/32      eth3/2         0.0.0.0       C     0       0       Root
```

	ID	IP-Prefix	Interface	Gateway	P	Pref	Mtr	Vsys
	4	10.123.0.0/24	eth3/2	0.0.0.0	S	20	20	Root
*	2	10.9.0.0/24	mgt	0.0.0.0	C	0	0	Root
*	3	1.2.3.0/24	mgt	10.9.0.10	S	20	1	Root

Interfaces

----
tunnel, hidden.1, self, mgt, ha1, ha2
v1-trust, v1-untrust, v1-dmz, ethernet3/2, ethernet1/2, ethernet2/2
vlan1, ethernet4/1

Auto-exporting:	Disabled
Default-vrouter:	For vsys (Root)
Shared-vrouter:	Yes
nsrp-config-sync:	Yes
System-Default-route:	Not present
Advertise-Inactive-Interface:	Disabled
Source-Based-Routing:	Disabled
SNMP Trap:	Public
Ignore-Subnet-Conflict:	Disabled

ns500-> set vrouter trust-vr router-id 255
ns500-> get vrouter trust-vr
Routing Table

C - Connected, S - Static, A - Auto-Exported, I - Imported, R - RIP
iB - IBGP, eB - EBGP, O - OSPF, E1 - OSPF external type 1
E2 - OSPF external type 2
Total 4/max entries

	ID	IP-Prefix	Interface	Gateway	P	Pref	Mtr	Vsys
	5	1.2.3.4/32	eth3/2	0.0.0.0	C	0	0	Root
	4	10.123.0.0/24	eth3/2	0.0.0.0	S	20	20	Root
*	2	10.9.0.0/24	mgt	0.0.0.0	C	0	0	Root
*	3	1.2.3.0/24	mgt	10.9.0.10	S	20	1	Root

Interfaces

----
tunnel, hidden.1, self, mgt, ha1, ha2
v1-trust, v1-untrust, v1-dmz, ethernet3/2, ethernet1/2, ethernet2/2
vlan1, ethernet4/1

```
Auto-exporting:                 Disabled
Default-vrouter:                For vsys (Root)
Shared-vrouter:                 Yes
nsrp-config-sync:               Yes
System-Default-route:           Not present
Advertise-Inactive-Interface:   Disabled
Source-Based-Routing:           Disabled
SNMP Trap:                      Public
Ignore-Subnet-Conflict:         Disabled
ns500-> set vrouter trust-vr protocol bgp 10245
ns500-> set vrouter trust-vr protocol bgp enable
ns500-> get vrouter trust-vr
Routing Table
--------------------------------------------------------------------------------
-------
C - Connected, S - Static, A - Auto-Exported, I - Imported, R - RIP
iB - IBGP, eB - EBGP, O - OSPF, E1 - OSPF external type 1
E2 - OSPF external type 2
Total 4/max entries
    ID      IP-Prefix       Interface   Gateway        P    Pref    Mtr   Vsys
--------------------------------------------------------------------------------
-------
     5      1.2.3.4/32      eth3/2      0.0.0.0        C    0       0     Root
     4      10.123.0.0/24   eth3/2      0.0.0.0        S    20      20    Root
*    2      10.9.0.0/24     mgt         0.0.0.0        C    0       0     Root
*    3      1.2.3.0/24      mgt         10.9.0.10      S    20      1     Root
Interfaces
--------------------------------------------------------------------------------
-------
tunnel, hidden.1, self, mgt, ha1, ha2
v1-trust, v1-untrust, v1-dmz, ethernet3/2, ethernet1/2, ethernet2/2
vlan1, ethernet4/1
Auto-exporting:                 Disabled
Default-vrouter:                For vsys (Root)
Shared-vrouter:                 Yes
nsrp-config-sync:               Yes
System-Default-route:           Not present
Advertise-Inactive-Interface:   Disabled
Source-Based-Routing:           Disabled
SNMP Trap:                      Public
Ignore-Subnet-Conflict:         Disabled
```

```
ns500-> get interface ethernet3/2
Interface ethernet3/2:
  number 10, if_info 82000, if_index 0, mode nat
  link down, phy-link down
  vsys Root, zone Trust, vr trust-vr
  *ip 1.2.3.4/32 mac 0010.db0b.494a
  *manage ip 1.2.3.4, mac 0010.db0b.494a
  route-deny disable
  ping enabled, telnet enabled, SSH enabled, SNMP enabled
  web enabled, ident-reset disabled, SSL enabled
  webauth disabled, webauth-ip 0.0.0.0
  OSPF disabled BGP disabled RIP disabled
  bandwidth: physical 0kbps, configured 0kbps, current 0kbps
            total configured gbw 0kbps, total allocated gbw 0kbps
  DHCP-Relay disabled
ns500-> set interface ethernet3/2 protocol BGP enable
ns500-> get interface ethernet3/2
Interface ethernet3/2:
  number 10, if_info 82000, if_index 0, mode nat
  link down, phy-link down
  vsys Root, zone Trust, vr trust-vr
  *ip 1.2.3.4/32 mac 0010.db0b.494a
  *manage ip 1.2.3.4, mac 0010.db0b.494a
  route-deny disable
  ping enabled, telnet enabled, SSH enabled, SNMP enabled
  web enabled, ident-reset disabled, SSL enabled
  webauth disabled, webauth-ip 0.0.0.0
  OSPF disabled BGP enabled RIP disabled
  bandwidth: physical 0kbps, configured 0kbps, current 0kbps
            total configured gbw 0kbps, total allocated gbw 0kbps
  DHCP-Relay disabled
ns500->
```

Summary

Routing is a powerful tool for any network. In this chapter we presented an overview of routing on a NetScreen firewall. NetScreen firewalls have a very unique implementation of routing with the use of virtual routers. As we discussed earlier, a virtual router is capable of splitting your routing domain into multiple virtual domains. This allows you to securely use routing protocols in your network. Because a typical firewall only contains one routing table, it may be possible to send poisoned or illegitimate routes into your firewall possible creating outages.

However, with the ability to use multiple virtual routers on your firewall you can mitigate this risk. NetScreen firewalls are capable of supporting three different routing protocols. Depending on the model of your firewall, it may not support all three of these protocols. The first protocol is RIP version 2. RIP is supported on many routing devices for a few reasons. First, it is easy to configure; just turning it on enables you to have a RIP infrastructure. Second, it is reliable and contains tried and true algorithms. Finally, because it is not an intensive protocol it does not require a great deal of processing power.

OSPF is an excellent protocol for you to use inside of your network. It is extremely efficient and provides a very robust routing infrastructure. Unfortunately, it has a few downsides. First, it requires additional processing power and additional memory to compute its complex algorithms, and second, it is complex to configure. The third supported protocol is BGP. BGP is typically used on the Internet to provide dynamic routing. BGP can be extremely complex to use. Many firewalls do not support this protocol because of its complexities. Juniper is dedicated to providing top-notch products and the proof of that can be found in the fact that its products support the BGP protocol.

Address Translation

Solutions in this chapter:

- **Purpose of Address Translation**
- **NetScreen NAT Overview**
- **NetScreen Packet Flow**
- **Source NAT**
- **Destination NAT**

☑ **Summary**

Introduction

NetScreen is well known for its firewall and virtual private network (VPN) technologies primarily due to the Application-Specific Integrated Circuit (ASIC)-based design of most of their core features, including address translation. This chapter focuses on how the address translation features of NetScreen products have evolved from a simple physical interface translation (Screen OS 2.5 and below) to a solution capable of handling complex address translation design requirements.

Throughout this chapter are several NetScreen scenarios with different example configurations. The assumption for all of the examples within this chapter assumes the following:

- **Security Zones:** Ethernet3 (Untrust) and Ethernet1 (Trust)

Both security zones are within the Trust virtual router (Trust-VR). The example configurations highlight the key areas that relate to that specific scenario.

Purpose of Address Translation

High-level network address translation (NAT) is the ability to masquerade one Internet Protocol (IP) address from another. This functionality is completely transparent to the users. For example, Figure 26.1 shows a host on network 10.1.1.x/24 traversing through a NAT device. The NAT device then translates the source packet coming from host 10.1.1.100 and going to address 172.16.1.1, which then communicates with host 172.16.1.50. This method is called *source NAT*.

Figure 26.1 All Egress Traffic from 10.1.1.x Network will NAT from Source 172.16.1.1

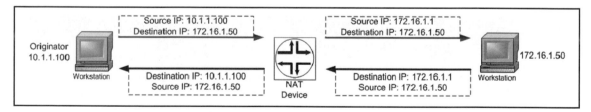

Advantages of Address Translation

Because of the tremendous growth of the Internet in the past decade, there were not enough IP v.4 addresses. NAT was developed to provide an immediate solution to this depletion. Request for Comment (RFC) 1631 was written in 1994 as the short-term solution to address the problem—the long-term solution was IP v.6.

Other ways that NAT is useful is:

- **Security** NAT can provide a hidden identity for host(s).

- **Addresses RFC 1918 Private Address Usage on a Routable Network** A NAT device can translate an existing non-public routable subnet to a public routable address(s).

Most companies use RFC 1918 addresses for their corporate networks because it helps conserve their routable Internet Assigned Numbers Authority (IANA) public addresses. RFC 1918 addresses are:

```
10.0.0.0 to 10.255.255.255 (10/8 prefix)
172.16.0.0 to 172.31.255.255 (172.16/12 prefix)
192.168.0.0 to 192.168.255.255 (192.168/16 prefix)
```

- **Addresses Overlapping Networks** NAT can provide a masquerade of different networks when two duplicate networks must be merged

- **Helps Maintain a Cohesive Network** Provides a method of maintaining one cohesive network when needed to communicate with different extranets.

Both the source and destination packets can be translated using NetScreen's NAT functionality. NetScreen also provides the ability to translate ports from protocols such as Transmission Control Protocol (TCP) and User Datagram Protocol (UDP). Port Address Translation (PAT) provides the translation for the source port and/or the destination port just as a NAT function translates for a source IP and/or destination IP. The ability to utilize source port PAT allows a company with hundreds of computers to access the Internet using only one public IP address. PAT can run over 64,000 sessions off of one NAT IP using source PAT. Like NetScreen, source PAT usually starts at port 1024 and above; therefore, it is possible to scale up to 64,512 ports (65,535 max number that a TCP/UDP port can reach − 1023 = 64,512) that can be allocated for one NAT IP. The reason that PAT ports start at 1024 and above is because ports 0 through 1023 are reserved and primarily used for well-known services (e.g., TCP port 23 is for Telnet, TCP port 22 is for Secure Shell [SSH], and TCP port 80 is for Hypertext Transfer Protocol [HTTP]). (See RFC 3022 for more information on PAT.)

An example of source PAT is illustrated in Figure 26.2. The image shows the NAT device performing a source NAT and a source PAT from the originator (10.1.1.100). Besides translating the source IP, such as shown in Figure 26.1, the NAT device will also translate the original source port to a random source port, which usually starts at 1024 and above. Notice that the return packet response from 172.16.1.50 is translated back to port 3001.

Figure 26.2 All Egress Traffic from the 10.1.1.x Network will NAT from 172.16.1.1 and PAT with a Random Source Port

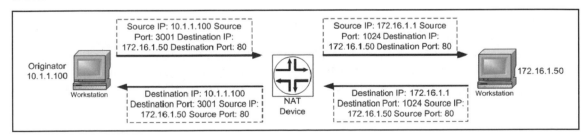

Figure 26.3 shows an example of a destination PAT function. Traffic destined for port 80 from the originator would be translated to a different port. Notice that the return packet response from 172.16.1.50 is translated back to port 80.

Figure 26.3 All Egress Traffic from 10.1.1.*x* Network will NAT from 172.16.1.1 and Destination PAT from Port 80 to Port 8080

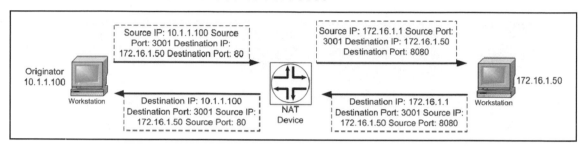

Disadvantages of Address Translation

When using address translation, certain scenarios come with certain concerns. The following is a list of the most common issues found when using NAPT:

- **Secure Internet Protocol (IPSec) usage through a NAT device.** There are two workarounds to this:

    - Create a one-to-one NAT and disable PAT

    - Use NAT Traversal

- **Protocol that requires dynamic port allocation.** For example: passive File Transfer Protocol (FTP), Sun Remote Procedure Call (RPC), MS-RPC, Domain Name System (DNS), Voice over Internet Protocol (VOIP), Serial Interface Protocol (SIP), and so on. There are workarounds available. Most firewalls implement a feature called Application Level Gateway (ALG) to address applications that require dynamic port opening.

- **Legacy application or custom application requires that the original packet information be maintained.** This varies from requiring the network address to the port to remain the same. In some cases, disabling NAT, PAT, or both will address this issue. It is generally recommended to disable PAT first, because the majority of these applications relate to restrictive ports.

NetScreen NAT Overview

The NetScreen firewall solution always incorporates NAT functionality; there is always some NAT enhancement with each major ScreenOS release. This section highlights the key NAT features from early ScreenOS to ScreenOS 5.0. It is important to note that some of the older features such as

Mapped IP (MIP) and Virtual IP (VIP) can also be performed in the newer ScreenOS releases. These NAT features are covered in detail in the following sections.

- **Source NAT** provides address translation on the source IP address. Source PAT is another functionality that may be performed along with source NAT. Source PAT provides address translation on the source port. There are several methods of Source NAT:

    - **Interface-based Source NAT** was the first method of NAT functionality included within NetScreen firewall solutions. It is a typical feature that is normally found with most NAT vendors. This feature provides the ability to NAT ingress traffic received in the defined interface, with NAT enabled with the last known egress interface. Source NAT is also performed by default. (If it cannot be disabled, use an alternative method such as policy-based NAT to over-source PAT, if needed.)

    - **MIP** provides a static NAT functionality for one-to-one address translation. This feature can be used for either source or destination NAT capabilities.

    - **Policy-based Source NAT** is similar in functionality to Interface-based Source NAT; the configuration is done on a firewall rule rather then a global interface setting. Based on the firewall rule, you can specify certain traffic up to a Layer 4 definition on whether or not to perform address translation on the source IP address.

- **Destination NAT** provides address translation on the destination IP address. Destination PAT is another feature set that can be enabled at the same time, which provides address translation for the destination port. There are several methods of destination NAT:

    - **VIP** provides one-to-many address translation functionality. This feature can be used to translate the destination IP and the destination port at the same time.

    - **MIP** can also be used in a destination one-to-one address translation and can be used for either source or destination NAT capabilities.

    - **Policy-based Destination NAT** is similar in functionality to Policy-based Source NAT except that it performs address translation on the destination IP or destination port on a per-firewall rule definition.

NetScreen Packet Flow

This section highlights the address translation portion of the NetScreen packet flow. Understanding how NetScreen handles a packet flow provides a good base to understanding how address translations are triggered and also makes troubleshooting and debugging a problem much easier. Figure 26.4 shows a high-level overview of how a NetScreen firewall handles packets flowing into their devices.

Figure 26.4 NetScreen Packet Flow

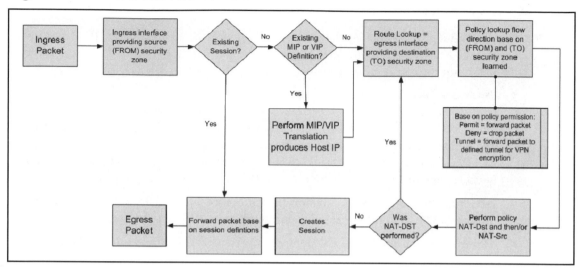

The process steps are as follows:

1. Based on the arriving ingress packet, the NetScreen device notes the incoming interface and the bonded security zone to that interface. (For the purposes of this book, the ingress security zone is considered the FROM zone.) The interface can be a physical Ethernet interface, a sub-interface, a VPN tunnel interface, or a VPN tunnel zone. At this point, the NetScreen screening functions are performed. The screening function detects any anomalous traffic behavior such as denial of service (DOS) attacks. The screen options are configurable at the security zone level.

2. Check to see if the session exists. If it does, forward the packet based on the session definition. If the session does not exist, check to see whether a MIP or VIP entry exists. If one does exist, perform a MIP or VIP translation.

3. Next, the route lookup is performed. Based on the destination packet IP address, the route lookup determines which egress interface the packet will eventually leave from. When you know the egress interface you will also know the egress security zone (remember, the security zones are bonded to an interface). (For the purposes of this book, the egress security zone is considered the TO zone.)

4. Now that you know the FROM and TO security zones, you can apply them to a policy lookup. At a minimum, a policy performs a permit or deny or pushes the packet through a VPN tunnel. Other miscellaneous operations can also be performed such as traffic shaping, deep inspection, authentication, logging, counters, anti-virus, and threshold alarms. If address translations are defined for either the source (NAT-Src) or the destination (NAT-Dst), those functions are also performed. If NAT-Dst is performed, another route lookup is required.

5. A session is created and the packet is forwarded to the egress interface as defined.

Source NAT

Source NAT is the most widely deployed method of address translation provided by vendors. It provides the ability to translate a source IP address to another IP address (as illustrated in Figure 26.1). By default (NetScreen solution), source NAT is enabled on the interfaces using the Trust security zone (see Figure 26.5).

Figure 26.5 Web UI Screen Shot of Interface-based Source NAT

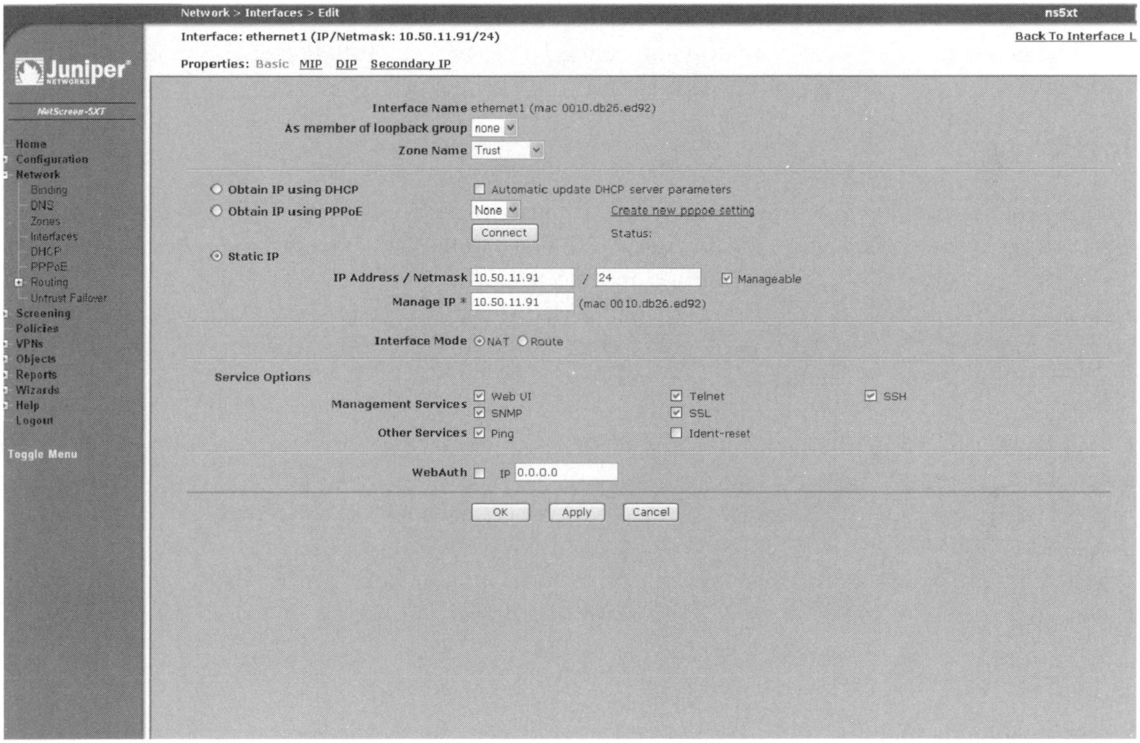

Interface-based Source Translation

Interface-based source translation provides the ability to launch NAT off of a physical interface or a logical interface (e.g., a sub-interface). The interface with NAT mode enabled will perform NAPT by default for the ingress traffic. The source IP address used for translation will be the egress interface. In other words, whichever interface the packet exits from is the interface IP address that will be used as the translated source IP address. Figure 26.6 shows what address translation looks like for a packet sourcing from a host behind Ethernet1 on the Trust zone with NAT enabled.

Figure 26.6 Source 10.1.1.100 will Source NAT from the Egress Interface Untrust

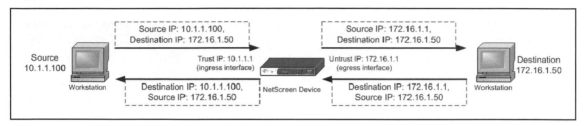

The egress interface used is determined via the NetScreen packet flow (see Figure 26.4). The key area is the route table lookup for the destination.

MIP

MIP provides the ability to perform a one-to-one mapping translation, which is referred to as *Static NAT*. This setting ensures that a host gets the same NAT every time traffic traverses the firewall, whether it's ingress or egress traffic. A MIP definition only performs NAT (no PAT), thus the IP address changes but the protocol ports remain the same. MIP(s) are defined on an interface that can be the physical Ethernet interface, a sub-interface, a tunnel interface, or a loop-back interface. Once a MIP is defined, a firewall rule is needed to allow access to the MIP.

Besides one-to-one mapping, a MIP can also be created to a subnet. In a MIP-to-subnet definition, it is important to define the subnet mask properly. The host range used for the MIP should not be used elsewhere on the NetScreen device.

All MIP definitions are placed within a global zone no matter which security zone originally defined the MIP. Once a MIP has been defined, a firewall rule must be set up to allow for traffic destined for the MIP address. Within the firewall rule creation, the destination MIP selection can be from a global zone or the zone the MIP address was originally defined in.

MIP Limitations

There are a limited number of MIPs that can be performed on a NetScreen firewall. The following matrix shows the MIP capacity as of ScreenOS 5.0. These numbers are the same for both basic and advanced license models:

Table 26.1 MIP Capacity Matrix

Product Name	MIP Capacity
NetScreen HSC	5
NetScreen 5XT	100
NetScreen 5GT	100
NetScreen 25	500

Table 26.1 Continued

Product Name	MIP Capacity
NetScreen 50	1,000
NetScreen 204/208	4,096
NetScreen 500	4,096
NetScreen ISG 2000	8,192
NetScreen 5200/5400	10,000

Policy-based NAT can perform the same functions as a MIP; however, there are a couple of advantages to using a policy-based NAT for one-to-one mapping. Using one form of translation such as policy-based translation over older features such as interface-based translation, MIP, and VIP provides a more unified way of managing your NAT functions. Another advantage of using policy-based NAT is that the only limitation is the number of policies you can create, which far exceeds any MIP capacity. The following matrix shows the policy capacity for each firewall platform:

Table 26.2 Policy Capacity Matrix

Product Name	Policy Capacity
NetScreen HSC	50
NetScreen 5XT	100
NetScreen 5GT	100
NetScreen 25	500
NetScreen 50	1,000
NetScreen 204	4,000
NetScreen 208	4,000
NetScreen 500	20,000
NetScreen ISG 2000	20,000 base/30,000 adv
NetScreen 5200/5400	40,000

MIP Scenarios

This section covers some real-world scenarios where MIP is useful. Each scenario provides a figure showing a visualization of the general concept and Web UI example steps for configuring the scenario. It is assumed that you have the necessary basic settings pre-defined on your firewall such as security zone definitions on interfaces, IP address definitions on interfaces, route definitions, and so on.

Scenario 1

This example shows a typical MIP scenario. MIP is defined for you to access a Web server located on your private network from the Internet.

The following Web UI configuration example is illustrated in Figure 26.7:

1. To define the MIP on the Untrust interface (Ethernet3), go to **Network | Interface | Ethernet3 | MIP | New**.

2. Fill in the following:

   Mapped IP: 2.2.2.10

   Netmask: 255.255.255.255

   Host IP Address: 10.1.1.10

   Host Virtual Router Name: Trust-VR

3. Define the firewall rule to permit traffic to the MIP. Go to **Policies | FROM | Untrust | TO | Trust | New**.

4. Fill in the following:

   Source Address: Any

   Destination Address: MIP (2.2.2.10)

   Services: HTTP

   Action: Permit

Figure 26.7 NetScreen with MIP Definition to a Host on the RFC 1918 Network

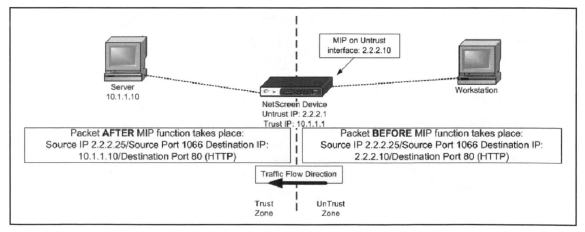

Scenario 2

The following example shows how a host defined within a MIP definition always uses the translated MIP address when originating traffic.

The configuration for this example is not very complicated. In fact, it can be as simple as defining an outgoing "permit all" rule. Note that there is no incoming rule (Untrust to Trust) because the 10.1.1.10 server is *initiating* the traffic. Because NetScreen is a stateful firewall, the response packet back is handled based on the session that was originally created from this server (see Figure 26.4, Step 2).

The following Web UI configuration example is illustrated Figure 26.8:

1. To define the MIP on the Untrust interface (Ethernet3) Go to **Network | Interface | Ethernet3 | MIP | New**.

2. Fill in the following:

   Mapped IP: 2.2.2.10

   Netmask: 255.255.255.255

   Host IP Address: 10.1.1.10

   Host Virtual Router Name: Trust-VR

3. Define the firewall rule to permit traffic to the MIP. Go to **Policies | FROM | Trust | TO | Untrust | New**.

4. Fill in the following:

   Source Address: Any

   Destination Address: Any

   Services: Any

   Action: Permit

Figure 26.8 MIP Outbound Traffic from Internal Host

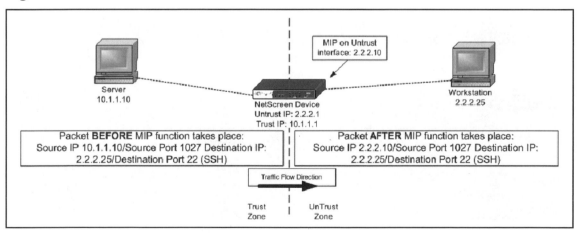

Again, you can always create a more granular rule for this scenario. Change the source address to 10.1.1.10/32 and the destination address to 2.2.2.25/32, and change the servers to SSH. Notice that there is no need to choose the MIP (2.2.2.10) for either the source or destination, because the translation occurs automatically (see Figure 26.4, Step 2).

Scenario 3

There may be certain scenarios where you have to create a route to reach the original host once a MIP translation occurs. Going back to NetScreen packet flow, a MIP translation occurs before a route lookup and a policy lookup. If the MIP translation to the original host route is not defined within the routing table(s), the packet either gets dropped or is sent to a default route, assuming one exists.

The following example scenario shows the need to create a route in order for the MIP translation to work. Figure 26.9 shows a diagram of MIP host 172.16.1.10 behind a different segment from the Trust side of the NetScreen firewall.

To reach the server on the 172.16.1.*x* network segment after MIP translation occurs, a static route is needed on the NetScreen device. This route would consist of the following:

Destination: 172.16.1.0/24

Interface: Trust (Ethernet1)

Gateway: 10.1.1.254

1. To define the static route, go to **Network | Routing | Routing Entries | Trust-VR | New**.

2. Fill in the following:

    Network Address/Network: 172.16.1.0/255.255.255.0

    Select Gateway

    Select Interface: Ethernet1

    Gateway IP Address: 10.1.1.254

    Metric: 1

Figure 26.9 MIP Host Behind Another Network Segment

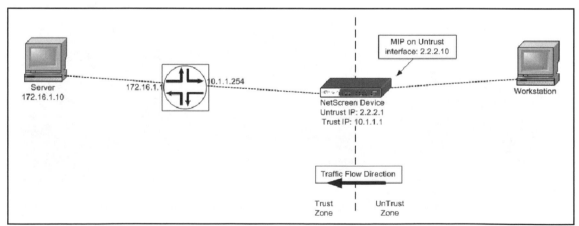

Policy-based Source NAT

Policy-based source translations are accomplished by creating a firewall rule with source NAT enabled. By default, the outbound interfaces' or egress interfaces' IP address in the destination zone is used as the newly translated source address. PAT is also enabled by default. Figure 26.10 shows a host behind the NetScreen Trust zone (10.1.1.15) sending a packet out to the Internet via the NetScreen device that is acting as the default gateway. The NetScreen policy is to use source NAT for traffic sourcing from the Trust side to the Untrust side. The source NAT address will be the egress interface IP, in this case the Untrust Ethernet interface. The figure shows the packet before and after translation using the IP address of the egress interface on the Untrust side of 2.2.2.1.

Address objects must be defined before any firewall rule is created. Two address objects are created for this example, one for the Trust zone and one for the Untrust zone.

1. For the Trust zone address definition go to **Objects | Addresses | List | New**.

2. Fill in the following:

    Address Name: 10.1.1.15

    Select IP/Netmask: 10.1.1.15/32

    Zone: Trust

3. For the Untrust zone address definition go to **Objects | Addresses | List | New**.

4. Fill in the following:

    Address Name: 2.2.2.25

    Select IP/Netmask: 2.2.2.25/32

    Zone: Untrust

4   Create the firewall rule to perform the Source NAT using the egress interface. Go to **Policies | FROM | Trust | TO | Untrust | New**.

5. Fill in the following:

    Source Address: 10.1.1.15

    Destination Address: 2.2.2.25

    Services: SSH

    Action: Permit

    Select: Advance

6. Select **Source Translation | None (Use Egress Interface IP)**.

Figure 26.10 Example of Policy-based Source NAT

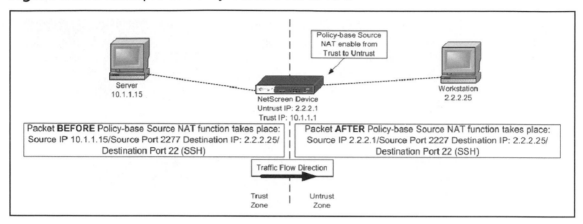

DIP

There are several other methods that can be used to translate the source address via the policy. These methods are primarily due to the functionality of dynamic IP pool definitions (DIP pool). DIP pool definitions are created on interfaces, which can be a physical interface, a sub-interface, a VPN tunnel interface, or a loop-back interface. A DIP can be either a host range definition or a pool of address definitions. If it is a pool of address definitions, the pool must be in consecutive order. Therefore, it is important to note that no other IP(s) within that pool can be used anywhere else (e.g., a MIP definition).

DIP pool definition also offers the option to disable or enable PAT . Since the DIP pool is only used in source NAT scenarios, PAT on the source ports can be utilized to increase the amount of usage for each address within the pool.

Figure 26.11 Policy-based Source NAT Using a DIP Pool

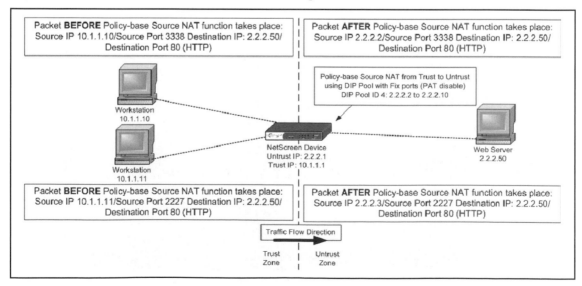

The following Web UI configuration example shows policy-based source NAT using a DIP pool with PAT disabled and traffic flow from Trust to Untrust. Address objects must be defined before a firewall can be created.

1. For the Trust zone address definition, go to **Objects | Addresses | List | New**.

2. Fill in the following:

   Address Name: 10.1.1.0/24

   Select IP/Netmask: 10.1.1.0/24

   Zone: Trust

3. For the Untrust zone address definition, go to **Objects | Addresses | List | New**.

4. Fill in the following:

   Address Name: 2.2.2.50

   Select IP/Netmask: 2.2.2.50/32

   Zone: Untrust

5. Create the DIP pool on the egress interface, which in this example is the Untrust (Ethernet3) interface. Go to **Network | Interfaces | Untrust | DIP | New**.

6. Fill in the following:

   ID: 4

   Select IP Address Range: 2.2.2.2 ~ 2.2.2.10

   Uncheck Port Translation

   Select: "In the same subnet as the interface IP or its secondary IPs."

7. Create the firewall rule to perform the Source NAT from a DIP pool. Go to **Policies | FROM | Trust | TO | Untrust | New**.

8. Fill in the following:

   Source Address: 10.1.1.0/24

   Destination Address: 2.2.2.50

   Services: HTTP

   Action: Permit

9. Select **Advance | NAT | Source Translation | DIP ON | 4(2.2.2.2-2.2.2.10)/fix-port**.

A DIP pool can also contain one IP range. For example, when defining the single IP address 2.2.2.2 within a DIP pool, the IP address range would be 2.2.2.2 ~ 2.2.2.2. This is an alternative way of using a different IP address than what is currently defined on the egress interface. It is recommended that you enable PAT within the DIP pool definition when creating for a one IP range.

Sticky DIP

Sticky DIP provides the ability for the translated host to maintain its IP pool assignment. By default, the IP addresses within the DIP pool are rotated in a round-robin fashion for each new session. For example, when there exist a DIP pool of 2.2.2.2 to 2.2.2.10, the host (10.1.1.10) utilizing the DIP pool will have a new NAT IP pool assignment starting at 2.2.2.10 for each new session. Figure 26.11 illustrates the default scenario without Sticky DIP enabled and Figure 26.12 shows the scenario with Sticky DIP enabled. Note that the Sticky DIP setting is a command line only setting.

Figure 26.12 Policy-based Source NAT DIP Pool Usages without Sticky DIP

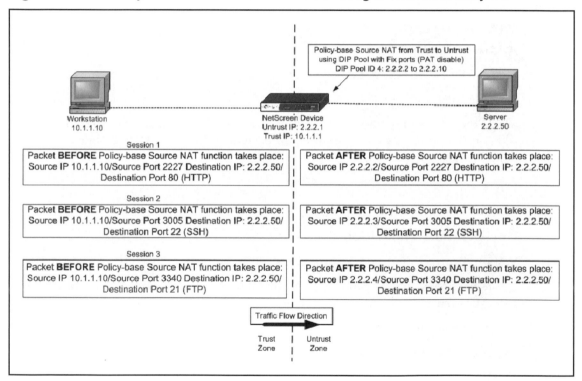

The example in Figure 26.12 shows that the NetScreen device assigns a different IP address from the pool for each new session originated from workstation 10.1.1.10. This pool assignment is done via round-robin fashion.

Figure 26.13 Policy-based Source NAT DIP Pool Usage with Sticky DIP

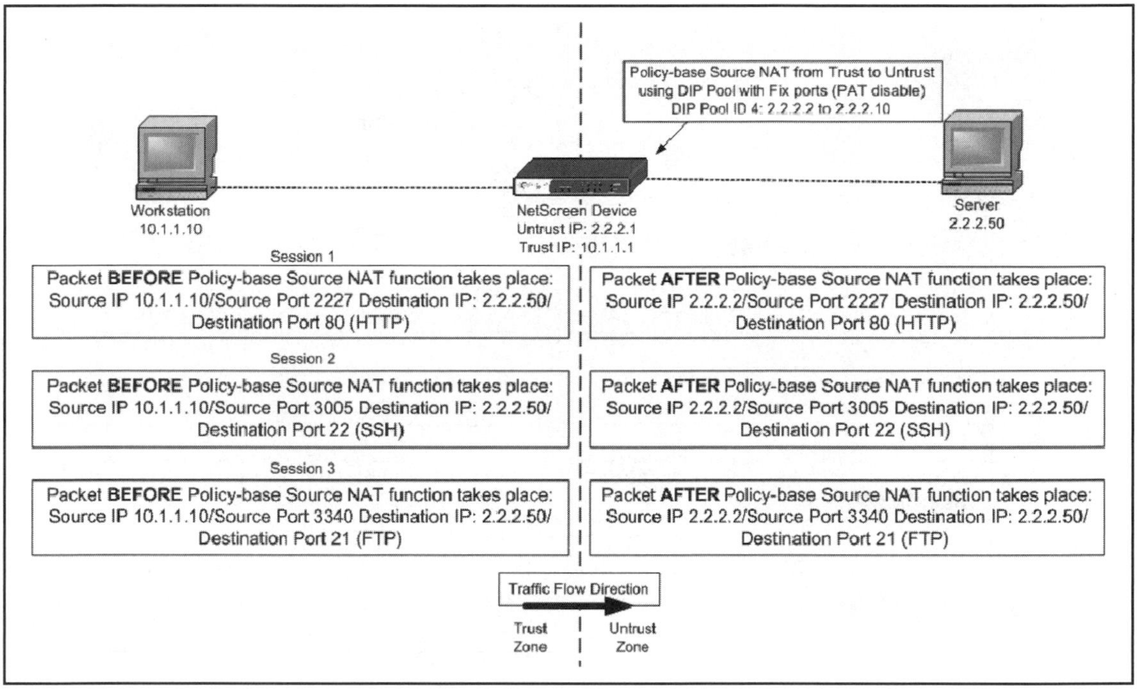

The example in Figure 26.13 shows the same DIP pool usage as shown in Figure 26.12, but with the Sticky DIP feature enabled. The NetScreen device now maintains the same IP address (2.2.2.2) assignment for all sessions generated from 10.1.1.10.

As of this writing, enabling Sticky DIP must be done via the Command Line Interface (CLI). The command to enable Sticky DIP is:

```
set dip sticky
```

DIP Shift

DIP Shift ensures that the translated IP pool assignment ranges are one-to-one mapping with the original host IP ranges requesting the translation. The advantage of this feature is that it provides a predictable translation. For example, if communication takes place to a remote end with another firewall, the administrator can define a more granular source IP access rather than allow a range of addresses to come in. The following example shows a range of hosts from 10.1.1.10 to 10.1.1.12 using a DIP Shift definition to map its one-to-one mapping translations. The DIP shift pool will always be assigned in order from the first mapping original IP. Figure 26.14 shows the one-to-one mapping translation for all traffic generated from the original host IP.

Figure 26.14 Policy-based Source NAT using DIP Shift

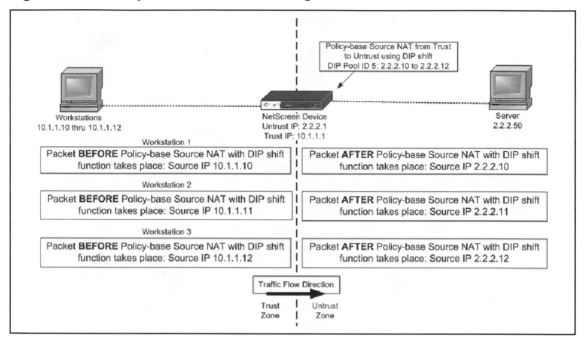

1. Create the DIP pool on the egress interface as defined in Figure 26.14. Go to **Network | Interfaces | Untrust |DIP | New**.

2. Fill in the following:

   ID: 5

   Select IP Shift

   From: 10.1.1.10

   To: 2.2.2.10 ~ 2.2.2.12

3. Select the same subnet as the interface IP or its secondary IP.

4. Create the firewall rule to perform the Source NAT from the DIP Shift pool defined in the previous step. Go to **Policies | FROM | Trust | TO | Untrust | New**.

5. Fill in the following:

   Source Address: 10.1.1.0/24

   Destination Address: 2.2.2.50

   Services: Any

   Action: Permit

6. Select **Advance | NAT | Source Translation | DIP ON | 5(2.2.2.10–2.2.2.12)/ip-shift**.

Destination NAT

The following section illustrates how the NetScreen firewall solution handles destination address translations.

VIP

A VIP provides a one-to-many mapping scenario, whereas a MIP provides a one-to-one mapping. The one-to-many mappings a VIP performs are more related to a combination of destination NAPTs.

VIP definitions are placed into the global zone no matter which interface/security zone it was originally defined in. Once a VIP is defined, a firewall rule must be set up to allow for traffic destined for the MIP address. Within the firewall rule creation, the VIP can be selected from a global zone or the zone that the VIP address was originally defined in (see Figure 26.15).

Figure 26.15 VIP Example

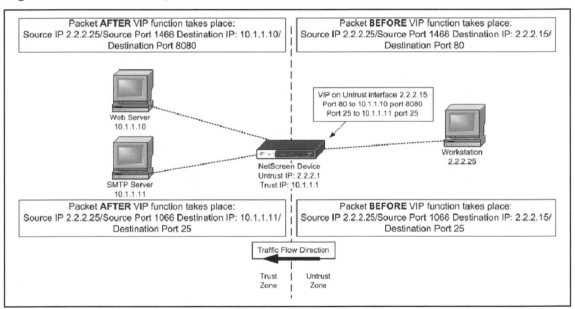

1. To define the VIP go to **Network | Interfaces | Ethernet3 | VIP**.

2. Select **Virtual IP Address**, enter **2.2.2.15**, and click on **Add**.

3. Add the VIP mapping for host 10.1.1.10 by selecting **New VIP Services** on the top left portion of the Web UI.

4. Fill in the following:

   Virtual IP: 2.2.2.15

   Virtual Port: 80

   Map to Service: 8080

   Map to IP: 10.1.1.10

   Server Auto Detection: Enable

5. Add the VIP mapping for host 10.1.1.11 by selecting **New VIP Service**.

6. Fill in the following:

   Virtual IP: 2.2.2.15

   Virtual Port: 25

   Map to Service: 25

   Map to IP: 10.1.1.11

   Server Auto Detection: Enable

7. Define the firewall rule to permit traffic to the VIP definitions. Go to **Policies** | **FROM** | **Untrust** | **TO** | **Trust** | **New**.

8. Fill in the following:

   Source Address: Any

   Destination Address: VIP::1

   Services: Select **Multiple** and move HTTP, SMTP to **Selected Members**

   Action: Permit

Policy-based Destination NAT

Policy-based destination NAT is also a subset setting within a firewall rule. Just like the source-based NAT configuration, there is a separate definition in place to define a destination NAT. Unlike source NAT, there are no requirements to predefine settings on the interfaces. For example, you do not need to create a DIP pool before actually creating a destination NAT firewall rule. The address schemes for the newly translated destination are all defined within the firewall rule. Besides destination NAT, a destination PAT can also be defined. The options available to perform destination NAT are as follows:

- Destination NAT to another IP

- Destination NAT to another IP with PAT to a different port

- Destination NAT to an IP range

Destination NAT Scenarios

The following are some possible scenarios that destination NAT can accomplish.

One-to-One Mapping

A one-to-one mapping scenario illustrates a translation from one host to another host. One-to-one mapping is equivalent to a static NAT or the MIP feature.

The following is a Web UI configuration example for a one-to-one mapping as defined in Figure 26.16.

1.   Create the firewall rule to perform the destination NAT. Go to **Policies | FROM | Trust | TO | Untrust | New**.

2.   Fill in the following:

     Source Address: 2.2.2.25

     Destination Address: 2.2.2.10

     Services: HTTP

     Action: Permit

3.   Select **Advance | NAT | Destination Translation | Translate to IP' | 10.1.1.10**.

Figure 26.16 One-to-one Policy-based Destination NAT

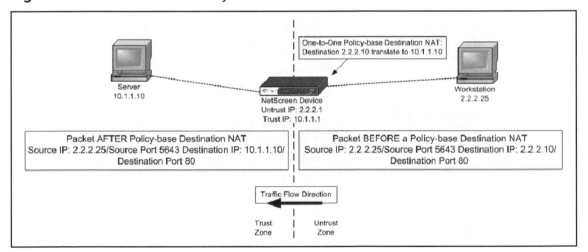

Many-to-one Mapping

A many-to-one mapping scenario illustrates that traffic sent to several different destination can be translated to a single host.

The following Web UI configuration example for a many-to-one mapping is defined in Figure 26.17.

1.   Create the address objects of the destination hosts and put them into an address group to be used in the policy-based rule definition. For this example, two address host objects (2.2.2.10/32 and 2.2.2.11/32) are created within the Untrust zone.

2. To create address objects go to **Objects** | **Addresses** | **List** | **New**. (Perform this function twice for each host address.)

3. For 2.2.2.10, fill in the following:

   Address Name: 2.2.2.10/32

   Select IP/Netmask: 2.2.2.10/32

   Zone: Untrust

4. For 2.2.2.11, fill in the following:

   Address Name: 2.2.2.11/32

   Select IP/Netmask: 2.2.2.11/32

   Zone: Untrust

5. Move the two host address objects into an address group. To create an address group go to **Objects** | **Addresses** | **Groups** | **New**.

6. Fill in the following for the address group:

   Group Name: Web_Servers

   Move **2.2.2.10/32** and **2.2.2.11/32** over to **Group Members**.

7. Create the policy-based NAT rule to perform the many-to-one destination NAT. Go to **Policies** | **FROM** | **Trust** | **TO** | **Untrust** | **New**.

8. Fill in the following:

   Source Address: 2.2.2.25

   Destination Address: Web_Servers

   Services: HTTP

   Action: Permit

9. Select **Advance** | **NAT** | **Destination Translation** | **Translate to IP** | **10.1.1.10**.

Figure 26.17 Many-to-one Policy-based Destination NAT

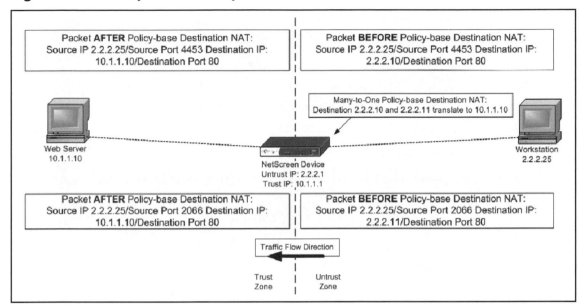

Many-to-Many Mapping

The many-to-many mapping scenario illustrates that traffic sent to several different destinations can be translated to several other destinations.

The following Web UI configuration example is defined in Figure 26.18.

1. Create the address objects of the destination hosts and put them into an address group to be used in the policy-based destination rule definition. For this example, three address host objects (2.2.2.10/32, 2.2.2.11/32, and 2.2.2.12/32) must be created within the Untrust zone.

2. To create address objects go to **Objects | Addresses | List | New**. (Perform this function twice for each host address.)

3. For 2.2.2.10, fill in the following:

   Address Name: 2.2.2.10/32

   Select IP/Netmask: 2.2.2.10/32

   Zone: Untrust

4. For 2.2.2.11, fill in the following:

   Address Name: 2.2.2.11/32

   Select IP/Netmask: 2.2.2.11/32

   Zone: Untrust

5. For 2.2.2.12, fill in the following:

    Address Name: 2.2.2.12/32

    Select IP/Netmask: 2.2.2.12/32

    Zone: Untrust

6. Move the two host address objects into an address group. To create an address group go to **Objects** | **Addresses** | **Groups** | **New**.

7. Fill in the following:

    Group Name: Servers

8. Move **2.2.2.10/32, 2.2.2.11/32, 2.2.2.12/32** to **Group Members**.

9. Create the policy-based NAT rule to perform the many-to-many destination NAT. Go to **Policies** | **FROM** | **Trust** | **TO** | **Untrust** | **New**.

10. Fill in the following:

    Source Address: 2.2.2.50

    Destination Address: Servers

    Services: Any

    Action: Permit

11. Select **Advance** | **NAT** | **Destination Translation** | **Translate to IP Range** | **10.1.1.10 − 10.1.1.12**.

Figure 26.18 Many-to-many Policy-based Destination NAT

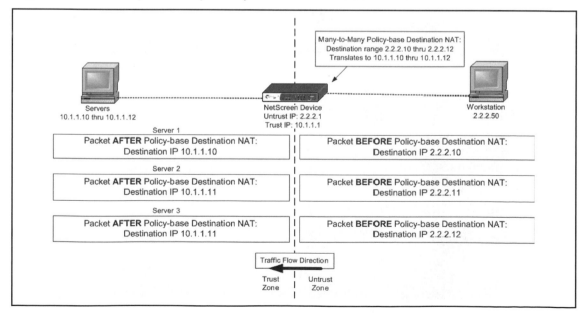

Destination PAT Scenario

Destination PAT provides an alternative destination port from what the original packet is sent to. It can also provide an extra security measure for hiding the original destination port.

The following Web UI configuration example is defined in Figure 26.19.

1. Create the firewall rule to perform the destination NAPT. Go to **Policies** | **FROM** | **Trust** | **TO** | **Untrust** | **New**.

2. Fill in the following:

   Source Address: 2.2.2.25

   Destination Address: 2.2.2.10

   Services: HTTP

   Action: Permit

3. Select **Advance** | **NAT** | **Destination Translation** | **Translate to IP** | **10.1.1.10** | **Map to Port** | **8080**.

Figure 26.19 One-to-one Policy-based Destination NAT with Destination PAT

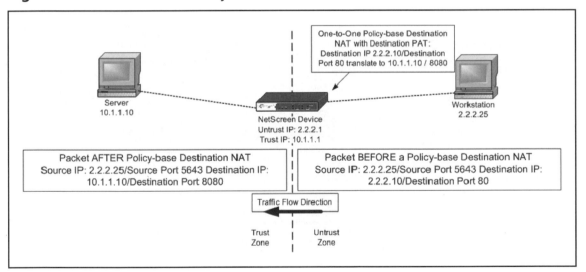

Source and Destination NAT Combined

Source and destination address translation can be combined together in a single firewall rule. The following example shows a source and destination NAT.

The following Web UI configuration example is defined in Figure 26.20.

1. Create the firewall rule to perform the source and destination NAT. Go to **Policies | FROM | Trust | TO | Untrust | New**.

2. Fill in the following:

   Source Address: 2.2.2.25

   Destination Address: 2.2.2.10

   Services: HTTP

   Action: Permit

3. Select **Advance | NAT | Source Translation | DIP ON | None (Use Egress Interface IP) | Destination Translation | Translate to IP | 10.1.1.10**.

Figure 26.20 Policy-based Source and Destination NAT

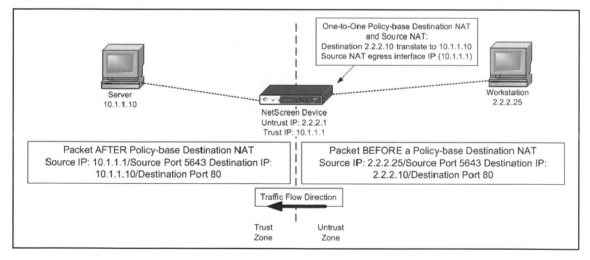

Summary

NAT has always been an essential part of network design. Whether for security reasons or to conserve IP addresses, it is a useful method. NAT provides the ability to hide the originating IP address thus providing an extra layer of security to protect the host's identity. NAT provides a short-term solution to the depleting IP v.4 addresses on the Internet. NAT provides the ability to utilize one IP for several thousand devices thus conserving non-RFC 1918 IP addresses. With the cost of NAT devices going down each year and the increase in Internet usage, it is not surprising that NAT is a widely used feature.

The NAPT features of the Juniper NetScreen products are covered in detail with example scenarios and their respective configurations steps.

One of the original methods used for NAT was the interface-based NAT mode, which is enabled by default on the Ethernet interface bonded to the Trust security zone. It is recommended that the interface-based NAT mode setting be disabled and set to Route mode all the time, thus using policy-based NAT instead. Policy-based NAT provides a more efficient and scalable method than interface-based NAT. As seen with MIP and VIP, there are capacity limitations that restrict the use of these NAPT methods. Policy-based translation can perform the same functions as a MIP or a VIP and also has a much larger capacity support.

It is good to note the tips provided throughout this chapter. The goal of these tips is to provide an understanding of the limitations and capabilities of the Juniper NetScreen firewall address translation features. Knowing how the firewall handles a packet is a key essential for troubleshooting NAT issues.

Index